Legal Aspects of Business

FIFTH EDITION

Dr Ravinder Kumar

Professor and Head, Dept of Commerce and Business Studies
Dean, Faculty of Social Sciences
Honorary Director, Dr. K.R. Narayanan Centre for Dalit and Minorities Studies
Officiating Director, Centre for Jawaharlal Nehru Studies
Officiating Director, Centre for Comparative Religions and Civilizations

***Jamia Millia Islamia**—a Central University*
New Delhi, India

CENGAGE

Australia • Brazil • India • Mexico • Singapore • United Kingdom • United States

CENGAGE

Legal Aspects of Business, 5e

Ravinder Kumar

ISBN-13: 978-93-5350-621-6
ISBN-10: 93-5350-621-2

Cengage Learning India Private Limited
T-303, 3rd Floor
DAV Complex, Plot 3
Mayur Vihar Phase 1
Delhi 110091

Cengage Learning is a leading provider of customized learning solutions with office locations around the globe, including Australia, Brazil, India, Mexico, Singapore, United Kingdom, and United States. Locate your local office at: **www.cengage.com/global**

Cengage Learning products are represented in Canada by Nelson Education, Ltd.

For product information, visit **www.cengage.co.in**

Fifth Impression 2022

To Anuradha, Shantanu, and Visheshta

Foreword

The legal aspects of business form a major part of the business environment as they reflect the policy structure and guidelines of the government. The legal regime seeks to ensure that every business concern functions in accordance with the statutory framework of the country. Every enterprise, big or small, must conform to the legal standards set up for its undisputable functioning. This is imperative to ensure good corporate governance too.

In India, there is a long list of regulatory mechanisms relating to the legal aspects of business. All these enactments play an important role in the country's economic development. An entrepreneur must take into account the regulatory structure of the country to ensure the sustainability of the business as well as smooth and efficient performance of the firm. Moreover, in recent times, a need has been felt to prohibit anticompetitive business practices and to regulate legal issues such as mergers and acquisitions. In fact, the list of legislations in the business domain is so long that it seems almost impossible to cover them under one landscape.

Legal Aspects of Business by Ravinder Kumar concentrates on the major business and corporate legislations such as The Indian Contract Act, 1872, The Negotiable Instruments Act, 1881, The Sale of Goods Act, 1930, The Partnership Act, 1932, The Consumer Protection Act, 2019, The Information Technology Act, 2000, The Right to Information Act, 2005, The Limited Liability Partnership Act, 2008, The SEBI Act, 1992, The Companies Act, 2013, The GST Act, 2017, and the laws relating to environment and intellectual property. These legislations are central to any business.

On the whole, the book is a genuinely good attempt and I am sure that its lucidity will hold the interest of management students and other professionals who are interested in understanding the legal aspects of business.

Prof. (Dr) Ranbir Singh
National Law University, Delhi

Preface to the Fifth Edition

Legal aspects of business imply interface of law with business. As every business is mandated to comply with the relevant regulations in force to create wealth, it is imperative on the part of those who run it to appreciate the issues pertaining to legality for both kinds of activities; run-of-the-mill and out-of-the-box. Needless to mention, knowledge of legal aspects of business is crucial for all stakeholders of business, including people working in different functional areas of management. Keeping this in mind, the present book, in its fifth edition now, has been designed to empower budding business managers to deal with legal issues, confronting their decisions.

The author expresses his gratitude to the readers for their awe-inspiring reaction to the preceding volume, *Legal Aspects of Business* 4e. Their overwhelming response has encouraged both, the author and the publisher, to bring out a revised and modified edition, keeping in view the recent, significant and noteworthy developments in the sphere of corporate law. It gives me immense pleasure and satisfaction to introduce to you the fifth edition of the book.

This revised and updated edition has been rationalized by incorporation of some of the major developments in the sphere of legal aspects of business while maintaining the hallmark features of the existing edition, which has been refined adequately with the aim to explain the core legal aspects of business in a logical, concise, and yet lucid manner by using a fresh and novel approach to present the various provisions of business law in a 'Teach Yourself' style; disproving the myth that business law is a complex and unexciting subject.

The present edition of the book has the following distinctive features:

1. The content has been organised in two column layout to make the presentation of the text more optimal, i.e., user-friendly. This is because, presentation in two columns makes text reading more comfortable as the shorter lines (fewer characters per line) are easier to read, the eye does not have to move as far horizontally from the end of one line back to the start of the next as in case of single-column text printing.
2. The contents have been modified at appropriate places to make the text more lucid and comprehensible.
3. Part V of the book that deals with the 'Company Law' has been thoroughly revised and updated in the the light of the recent amendments brought out by the Companies (Amendment) Bill, 2019.
4. Under Part VI – Other Business Legislations, Chapter 21, has been written afresh as the Consumer Protection Act, 1986 (erstwhile title of the chapter), has been repealed and replaced by the new consumer protection legislation—The Consumer Protection Act, 2019. In addition, a new chapter, 'The Goods and Services Tax Act, 2017' has been added under this part of the volume.
5. A compilation of 10 landmark judgements pronounced recently by the top courts of the country adding new dimensions to what are regarded as established constitutional principles concerning numerous important topics and issues covered by the volume.

Key Features of the Book

6. Each chapter begins with the learning objectives that enable the focus areas of the chapter; this certainly improves readability.
7. In every chapter, sidebars have been inserted adequately to facilitate the reader to understand the concepts covered in the chapter.
8. Every chapter ends with 'Chapter in Review' card which provides a bird's eye-view of the subject matter of the chapter vis-à-vis learning objectives covered in the chapter in addition to the glossary of key terms discussed therein.
9. For testing a student's understanding of the concepts discussed in the chapter, there are end-of-chapter exercises along with a comprehensive set of objective-type questions, case-lets, and review questions. Answers to the objective-type questions and 'hints' to the case-lets have been provided along with the exercise set.
10. A guide to case citations and list of references are provided at the end of the book so as to enable the reader to understand the cases cited in the book and to facilitate further study of legal cases, if one is interested.
11. A comprehensive set of case studies, appended to the book to help the readers judge their overall understanding of legal aspects of business they would have gained by reading this volume, are present.

Readers are the ultimate judge of a book and, hence, they are welcome to send in their comments and suggestions for further improvement of the content at *drkumar2005@gmail.com*.

Ravinder Kumar

Preface to the First Edition

Law is an integral part of any business. Every major area of business has a legal dimension—sales and advertisement, price and distribution, production and operations, finance and investment, personnel and industrial relations, export and import, and setting up and winding up of a business. With the increasing complexities of business, law is assuming added importance in business management. For the successful management of an organization, it is important that the managers have a fairly good knowledge of the legal provisions impinging upon the business. It is not possible for anyone to manage a business without adequate knowledge of business laws. This is why curricula of business programmes, such as MBA, MCom, BBA/BBS, BIBF/BFIA, and BCom, include at least one course on business law or legal aspects/legal environment of business.

About the Book

Legal Aspects of Business is intended to serve as a textbook for students of business schools and universities across India. The book is primarily designed to meet the needs of postgraduate students of business administration. It will also prove useful to the students of BCom, BBA/BBS, BFIA/BIBF, etc., and to the other readers who are interested in understanding the nuances of business law. It can also be used by students of law while dealing with courses on business and commercial laws, company law, and consumer protection law.

The book is written primarily from an Indian perspective with the aim to explain the core legal aspects of business in a systematic, concise, and illustrative manner. Landmark legal cases have been used as examples to illustrate the technical aspects of the subject matter. An effort has been made in this book to follow a fresh and novel approach to present the basic principles of business law in an interesting manner and to belie the myth that law is a complex and dull subject.

Content and Structure

The book is divided into six parts, which include 33 chapters.

Part I deals with the Indian Contract Act, 1872, a legislation that regulates various transactions of a business undertaking. It lays down the general principles relating to the formation and enforceability of contracts; rules governing the provisions of an agreement and offer; the various types of contracts including those of indemnity and guarantee, bailment and pledge, and agency. It also contains provisions pertaining to breach of contract. This part is divided into the following 13 chapters:

Chapter 1 provides introduction to the nature and kinds of contracts. After reading this chapter, the reader will be able to understand how a contract is formally established. This chapter describes the essentials of a valid contract and presents the classification of contracts on the basis of formation, execution, and enforceability.

Chapter 2 provides an introduction to offer and acceptance, two key elements required to make a contract. In this chapter, the legal rules are governing a valid offer and valid acceptance, including revocation thereof explained.

Chapter 3 deals with consideration, another basic requirement for establishing a contract. It spells out the essential elements of valid consideration and throws light on the legality of contracts without consideration.

Chapter 4 describes the competency of parties. This chapter elucidates the position of agreements with a minor, with a person of unsound mind, and with persons otherwise disqualified by law, viz., alien enemies, convicts, insolvents, and foreign sovereigns.

Chapter 5 covers the free consent of the parties to a contract. All the five key elements—coercion, undue influence, misrepresentation, fraud, and mistake—that may impair a free consent, are explained in the best possible manner.

Chapter 6 discusses the legality of the object behind a contract and describes on the agreements opposed to public policy.

Chapter 7 deals with void agreements and describes the remedies against a void agreement.

Chapter 8 introduces contingent contracts and discusses the rules governing their enforcement. The differences between a contingent contract and a wagering contract are also discussed here.

Chapter 9 is devoted to performance and discharge of a contract. This is one of the most important chapters on the law of contract, in which performance is considered to be the most obvious means of discharging a contract. The chapter also highlights other modes of discharge, including mutual agreement, operation of law, impossibility of performance lapse of time, and breach of contract.

Chapter 10 elucidates the meaning of breach of contract—anticipatory and actual. It also discusses the various remedies available to an aggrieved party in case of breach. These remedies are discussed under five specific heads—rescission, damages, specific performance, injunction, and quantum meruit.

Chapter 11 introduces indemnity and guarantee, two special types of contracts. Besides explaining the scope and essentials of a valid contract of indemnity, this chapter explains the rights of the indemnity holder, contracts of guarantee including the extent of surety's liability, revocation of continuing guarantee, and rights and discharge of surety.

Chapter 12 deals with contracts of bailment and pledge. This chapter also describes the rights and duties of bailor, bailee, pledger, and pledgee.

Chapter 13 discusses the contract of agency. Besides explaining the test of determining the existence of an agency, this chapter explains the rights and duties of agent, liability of the principal, and modes of creating and terminating an agency.

Part II deals with the Sale of Goods Act, 1930, and explains the issues concerning the sale of goods, in the following four chapters.

Chapter 14 deals with the nature of contracts of sale. This chapter compares sale and agreement to sell and discusses goods and modes of fixation of price.

Chapter 15 deals with conditions and warranties. This chapter also analyses two important doctrines arising out of a contract of sale—doctrine of *caveat emptor* and doctrine of *caveat venditor*.

Chapter 16 describes transfer of property in goods and performance of a contract of sale. Rules regarding transfer of property, sale by non-owners, modes of delivery of goods, and acceptance of delivery by buyer are explained.

Chapter 17 outlines the rights of an unpaid seller against the goods as well as against the buyer personally. This chapter also elucidates the buyers rights against the seller-in-default.

Part III examines the Indian Partnership Act, 1932, which contains the provisions relating to the nature and formation of partnership, the rights, duties, and liabilities of partners, and the procedure for dissolution of partnerships. This part of the book includes the following four chapters:

Chapter 18 deals with the nature of partnership. It also throws light on the mode of determining existence of partnership, partnership at will, and distinguishes partnership from co-ownership, HUF, and joint stock company.

Chapter 19 is devoted to formation of partnership. It explains partnership deed, duration of partnership, types of partners, position of a minor as a partner, and registration of partnership firms.

Chapter 20 is dedicated to the rights, duties, and liabilities of partners. This chapter also describes grounds of reconstitution of the firm, property of the firm, and rules relating to transfer of partnership interest.

Chapter 21 deals with the dissolution of partnership firms. It discusses at length the modes of dissolution of partnership firms, consequences of dissolution, settlement of accounts between partners, and sale of goodwill after dissolution.

Part IV is about the Negotiable Instruments Act, 1881. This part elaborates the provisions relating to negotiable instruments through the following six chapters:

Chapter 22 deals with the nature and kinds of negotiable instruments. This introductory chapter on negotiable instruments, besides highlighting characteristic features, classifications, and kinds of negotiable instruments, defends the provisions of the Negotiable Instruments Act regarding crossing of cheques, payment-in-due-course, and maturity of and interest on negotiable instruments.

Chapter 23 describes the competency and liabilities of parties to negotiable instruments. Position and privileges of holder-in-due-course are also discussed in this chapter.

Chapter 24 is devoted to negotiation and assignment of negotiable instruments, which are the two basic modes of transfer of property or ownership in a negotiable instrument.

Chapter 25 describes presentment of negotiable instruments for acceptance and/or payment, as the case may be, before the party is liable thereto.

Chapter 26 discusses the dishonour and discharge of negotiable instruments. In this chapter, grounds of dishonour, the consequences thereof, and modes of discharge of a negotiable instrument have been explained.

Chapter 27 deals with miscellaneous provisions concerning the banker and his clients, including special rules of evidence, liability of the banker, protection to the paying banker, and protection to the collecting banker.

Part V is about corporate legal framework. In India, the most important law that regulates all aspects relating to a company is the Companies Act, 1956. This part elaborates the provisions relating to formation of a company, powers and responsibilities of the directors and managers, raising of capital, holding company meetings, and winding up of a company.

Chapter 28 deals with the nature and kinds of companies. This introductory chapter on corporate legal framework also explains provisions of the Companies Act governing conversion of a private company to a public company and vice versa, and the lifting of the corporate veil.

Chapter 29 discusses the formation of a company. This chapter details the four major stages involved in the formation of a company—promotion, incorporation, raising of capital, and certificate of commencement of business.

Chapter 30 describes company management. This chapter explains the provisions of the Companies Act, 1956, concerning the qualifications and disqualifications, appointment, remuneration, removal, duties, powers and liabilities of directors, and the appointment and role of the managing director in company management.

Chapter 31 explains the provisions relating to meetings of a company. Requisites of a valid meeting, rules governing proxy, quorum, agenda, voting, motion, resolutions, and minutes are discussed at length.

Chapter 32 is about winding up of a company. This is the concluding chapter on the Companies Act, which details the different modes of winding up of a company and discusses the consequences of the winding up order. Differences between winding up and dissolution have also been delineated in this chapter.

Part VI details other business legislations, such as the Consumer Protection Act, the Securities and Exchange Board of India Act, the Information Technology Act, and the Right to Information Act.

Pedagogy

The contents of this book have been designed to appeal to first-time students of business law. The book is written in a lucid manner with a large number of examples that illustrate core concepts of the business legal framework. Each chapter begins with a set of Chapter Objectives that enable readers to view the list of inclusions within that chapter. Every chapter includes a summary that provides a birds-eye view of the concepts discussed. The students understanding of the concepts can be tested through the end-of-chapter exercises which include a comprehensive set of objective-type questions, problems, and review questions. Answers to objective-type questions and hints to problems have been included with the exercise set. A guide to cases has been provided at the end of the book to enable understanding of the cases cited in the book and to facilitate further study of legal cases.

Acknowledgement

I express my sincere gratitude to Prof. D.P.S. Verma, who despite his busy schedule reviewed certain parts of the manuscript and offered valuable comments for improvement of the text. I acknowledge the support of Anuradha, my better half. Without her support and co-operation, it would have been near impossible to translate the dream of writing this book into reality.

I would like to acknowledge the contribution of the editorial team at Cengage Learning, particularly Swati Meherishi, Surabhi Khare, and Debarati Roy.

I hope the book will be of help to teachers as well as students. The readers suggestions about further improvement of the book may be sent to drkumar2005@gmail.com or drkumar_ravi@rediffmail.com. Such feedback will be highly appreciated.

Ravinder Kumar

Acknowledgements

I would like to express my sincerest thanks to the following eminent academicians and academic administrators who extended their invaluable comments, compliments, and suggestions during the development of this edition:

Prof. D.P.S. Verma, Former Professor, Department of Commerce, Delhi School of Economics, University of Delhi, Delhi.

Prof. Ranbir Singh, Vice Chancellor, National Law University of Delhi, Delhi.

Mr. A.P. Siddiqui, IPS, Registrar, Jamia Millia Islamia—a Central University, New Delhi.

Prof. Shahid Akhtar, Centre for Management Studies, Jamia Millia Islamia—a Central University, New Delhi.

Prof. Attam Parkash, Formerly Professor at Indian Institute of Foreign Trade (IIFT), New Delhi.

Prof. R.K. Singh, Head, Department of Commerce, Dean, Faculty of Commerce and Business, Delhi School of Economics, University of Delhi, Delhi.

Dr S. Veeramani, Centre for Management Studies, Jamia Millia Islamia—a Central University, New Delhi.

Prof. Kaushik Rawal, Director, University School of Law, Gujarat University, Ahmedabad.

Finally, I would like to appreciate the uninterrupted support and dedication of the editorial team of Cengage Learning, the Publishers, to bring out this thoroughly revised, refined, and modified volume without impediment.

I hope the readers of this book will find the present edition even more interesting and useful. As no academic exercise is perfect, the author and the publisher, therefore, shall look forward to the views and comments of the readers for further improvement of the book.

Prof. Ravinder Kumar

Brief Contents

Detailed Contents

Introduction

Law affects almost every aspect of our life. It not only governs our conduct from the cradle to the grave, but its influence on our lives starts from our birth and continues even after our death. However, one finds it difficult to give a single and precise definition of law which may hold good for all times to come. This is so because, keeping in view the nature, object, need, function, legal development and sources of law, the subject has been viewed and dealt with differently by different legal theorists around the globe. Nonetheless, from a common person's perspective, it may be defined as a regulating mechanism enforced by the State to control and police human conduct so as to maintain peace and order in the society.

Need, Purpose, and Significance of Law

Law is a social institution. No civilised society can survive without law in force. As a social being, a person comes into contact with fellow humans in the society. If their conduct towards each other is hurtful, then equity, justice, and good conscience will not prevail in the society. For example, if a motorist hits a pedestrian and runs away, the State shall protect the pedestrian's life and prosecute the offender through a court of law. And if the offender is held guilty, he/she could be punished with an imprisonment and may also be liable to a fine. This punishment is imposed by the State by making laws and enforcing them. In the absence of law, nobody will care for others and their dealings may not materialise. With the development of the society and the concept of welfare state, law plays a pivotal role in achieving various socio-economic goals. It regulates the conduct of people and protects their property and contractual rights.

Thus, the basic aim of law is the attainment of justice in the society. It is required for the preservation of peace and orderliness in the society, besides removing any imbalance in the socio-economic structure.

Knowledge of law is imperative for every person. There is a well-known maxim, *ignorantia juris non-excusat*, which means, ignorance of law is no excuse. Accordingly, a person cannot escape liability on the ground of unawareness of law. For example, if somebody is caught smoking in a non-smoking zone, he/she cannot plead that he/she was not aware of the directive and, therefore, he/she may be excused. Hence, it is in our own interest that we should be well acquainted with the law to which we are subject. With the growth of materialism and individualism, which are prevailing in all spheres of life, civilization has demanded a reformed set of rules of conduct. Accordingly, law has undergone a vast transformation, both conceptually and structurally. Given that law is a social institution and it presupposes a society, the laws must also keep changing along with the changing value systems of the dynamic society.

From the foregoing discussion, it must be clear that the need of law is inevitable and its knowledge imperative to preserve peace and order in the society. The government has recognised and enacted various rules of conduct in the form of law to control and regulate peopleś behaviour with the ultimate objective to achieve justice, peaceful living, and social security.

Classification of Law

There are several branches of law; the most important among them are as follows:

1. Constitutional Law
2. International Law
3. Administration Law
4. Criminal Law
5. Civil Law
6. Business Law

Business Law: Meaning and Purpose

Legal rules in the domain of business are designed to fulfil certain purposes. These include the redressal of personal grievances, the control of anti-social activities, and the regulation of harmful activities. Business law, also known as 'mercantile law', 'commercial law', 'law merchant' or *Lex Mercatoria*, deals with the rights and obligations of persons arising out of commercial transactions. It comprises laws applicable to commerce and industry and includes laws relating to contracts, sale of goods, partnership, negotiable instruments, insurance, arbitration, etc. Business law, as such, is not a separate branch of law; it is a part of Civil Law which regulates various kinds of business transactions.

Sources of business law

There are four major sources of business law in India:

1. English Mercantile Law;
2. Judicial Decisions or Law by Precedents;
3. Indian Statute Law (Acts Enacted by Indian legislature); and
4. Customs and Trade Usage.

English mercantile law The Indian business law is primarily an adaptation of the English Mercantile Law. However, certain reservations and modifications have been made to provide for local customs and usage of trade in order to suit Indian conditions. Its dependence on English Mercantile Law is so much that in the absence of any specific law or customs or usage on a particular point, recourse is taken to the English Mercantile Law even now. Therefore, while studying the real sources of the Indian Mercantile Law, it would be necessary to understand the main sources of the English Mercantile Law, namely, the Law Merchant, Common Law, British Statute Law, and Principles of Equity.

The law merchant The Law Merchant or *Lex Mercatoria* is the basic source of the English Mercantile Law. Law Merchant refers to the branch of law that was based on customs and usages predominant among traders and merchants in their dealings with each other. Although it developed in the 14th and 15th centuries and was a separate law regulating the commercial transactions, it secured recognition of the common Law courts in the beginning of the 17th century. The legislation concerning negotiable instruments, carriage of goods by sea (i.e., contract of affreightment), insurance, and partnerships originate from Law Merchant.

Common law The term 'Common Law' is used to denote that body of legal rules, the primary sources of which were the general age-old customs, crucial decisions, and textbooks on jurisprudence. Common Law is unwritten law that has been followed for many years by the English Courts. The most important part of Mercantile Law, i.e., the Law of Contract, is still a part of the Common Law in Britain.

British statute law British statute law is that portion of the law which is laid down in the Acts passed by the Legislature or enactment of Parliament. Being a written law, it has been an important source of English Mercantile Law.

Principle of equity Principle of equity is also an unwritten law and developed separately from the Common Law in the Court of Chancery. It is that branch of English Law, the primary source of which was neither customs nor written law, but it dictates of common sense, natural justice, and good conscience. When people were not satisfied or aggrieved with the decision of the Common Law Court, they could file a mercy petition with the King in Council, who was considered as the fountainhead of justice. Originally, the King heard these petitions, but later on the King would refer these petitions to the Chancellor, the foremost officer of King's Council. The Chancellor, who was usually a Bishop, would organise Courts, known as Chancery Courts or Courts of Equity, and the matters were disposed of not according to the rigid letter of the law but on the principles of 'justice, equity, and good conscience'.

The Equity Courts had a separate existence distinct from the Common Law Courts in England until the enactment of the Judiciary Act of 1873. Thereupon, the separate existence of such courts was put to an end and all High Courts were empowered to grant either or both the remedies (Common Law as well as Equity) according to the circumstances of each case.

Judicial decisions or law by precedents The past judicial decisions of Courts are another important source of business law. The courts in deciding similar cases before them generally follow them.

Judges interpret and explain the statutes. Wherever the law is silent on a point, the judge has to decide the case according to the principles of equity, natural justice, and good conscience. Such decisions are called precedents that eventually become an important source of law.

Indian statute law (Acts enacted by indian legislature) The Acts passed by the Indian Legislature (Parliament) are another major source of the Indian Mercantile Law. Some important Acts passed by the Indian Legislature include, among others, the Indian Contract Act, 1872; the Sale of Goods Act, 1930; the Indian Partnership Act, 1932; the Negotiable Instruments Act, 1881; the Companies Act, 1956; the Insurance Act, 1938; the Arbitration Act, 1940; the Carriers Act, 1865; the Consumer Protection Act, 1986; the Securities and Exchange Board of India Act, 1992; the Information Technology Act, 2000; and the Right to Information Act, 2005. Thus, the bulk of the Indian Mercantile Law is the Statute Law.

Customs and trade usage Despite the fact that most of the Indian law has been codified, it has not altogether done away with local customs and usage of trade. They guide the courts in deciding disputes arising out of mercantile transactions. But to be a binding force on parties, such custom or usage must be uniformly accepted in the ordinary course of business—certain, reasonable, and consistent with the law, i.e., it must not be opposed to any legislative element. Many Indian Statutes make specific provisions to the effect that the rules of law laid down in a particular act are subject to any special custom or usage of trade. For example, Section 1 of the Indian Contract Act, 1872, recognises this fact by providing that 'nothing herein contained shall affect any usage or custom of trade'. The Negotiable Instruments Act, 1881, also makes a similar provision. It says 'nothing contained herein shall affect any local usage relating to instruments in an oriental language'. A custom may be defined as those rules of human action established by usage and regarded as legally binding by those to whom the rules are applicable. So, they are usually adopted and applied by the courts of law to be followed by society. In order to be binding, a custom must be ancient, reasonable, certain, definite, consistent with other customs in place and uniformly recognised in the ordinary course of business [*C.I. & B Syndicate vs Ramachandra*[1]]

The Importance of Legal Aspects of Business

The legal system affects businesses and individuals alike. Every aspect of business right from formation and operation to its dissolution occurs within a legal environment. Legal aspects of business provide a practical and comprehensive framework of legal rules and principles to assist an organization or people associated with it better deal with its commercial affairs. At the same time, they ensure a sufficient level of protection for the legitimate interests of those who come into direct contact with it. This includes not only members of the public in their capacity as consumers but also creditors and employees as well as owners of business enterprise. If a business firm fails to comply with the law of the land, it can cost it money, either directly or indirectly. A business which is in breach of law, whether the civil law or criminal law, will in most cases suffer from the breach. Moreover, legal proceedings often attract public attention and result in adverse publicity to the organisation involved. This further highlights the relevance of knowledge of business laws and the applications thereof for the business owners or managers to defend them should any dispute arises in connection with their commercial dealings with someones.

Test Questions

1. Explain the nature and meaning of law. Also discuss in brief the need, object and significance of law.
2. Define the term 'Business Law'. What are the sources of Indian Mercantile Law? Discuss in brief the importance of law to a business firm.

[1] 1968, AIR Mys. 133

Part I The Indian Contract Act, 1872

CHAPTER 1 Establishing Contractual Relationships

Learning Objectives

- **LO 1** Defining a contract
- **LO 2** Contract distinguished from agreement
- **LO 3** Agreements and contracts distinguished from MoU
- **LO 4** Contracts classified
- **LO 5** E-contracts
- **LO 6** Illegal and unenforceable agreements distinguished
- **LO 7** Defining an offer
- **LO 8** Essentials of a valid offer
- **LO 9** Acceptance; legal rules governing a valid acceptance
- **LO 10** Communication of offer, acceptance, and their revocation

We enter into contractual relationships so frequently in our day-to-day life that the term 'contract' has become an inseparable part of our lives. For instance, we incur a contractual obligation each time we purchase groceries, board a train or bus, get a television set repaired, hire a cab, or even consult a doctor or an advocate. A vast majority of contracts are entered into informally. It is quite possible that many a time the contracting parties are entirely unaware of the legal implications of their actions. In business, the most common relationship is that of contract because business basically comprises buying and selling of goods or services, and the sale or purchase of anything constitutes an important contract. Traders enter into countless number of contracts in the usual course of their business. The law of contract regulates all commercial activities by sorting out the promise that are enforceable, and how they can be enforced.

The law relating to contracts in India is contained in The Indian Contract Act, 1872[1]. The Act is mainly based on the English Common Law and came into force on the first day of September 1872. It extends to the whole of India except the State of Jammu and Kashmir[2].

Contract Defined

Contract: An agreement that legally binds the parties.

An agreement enforceable by law is a contract [Section 2(h)].

The above definition resolves that a contract is fundamentally an agreement that legally binds the parties. Thus,

Contract = Agreement + Legal Obligation

Let us now examine these two crucial elements of a contract.

[1] Throughout our discussion on the law of contract in this book (i.e., Chapters 1 to 8) the word 'Act' refers to The Indian Contract Act, 1872. Similarly, the references to sections in these chapters, unless otherwise specifically mentioned, pertain to the Indian Contract Act, 1872.

[2] The State of Jammu and Kashmir enjoys a special status under Article 370 of the Constitution of India.

Agreement

Agreement: Every promise or set of promises forming consideration for each other.

Section 2(c) of the Indian Contract Act defines the term 'agreement' as: 'Every promise and every set of promises, forming the consideration for each other'.

Thus, mutuality is the base of an agreement.

What is a Promise

Promise: A commitment given by one party to another.

The term 'promise' is defined in Section 2(b), which says, 'A proposal (offer), when accepted, becomes a promise'. Thus, a promise implies an accepted offer.

The term 'agreement' presumes the presence of at least two persons; as one person cannot enter into an agreement with one's ownself. Besides, identity of minds in respect to the subject matter of the agreement is a must to form an agreement. The parties entering into an agreement must agree upon a common purpose, i.e., they must mean the same thing, in the same sense, and at the same time. This meeting or identity of mind is called *consensus ad idem*, i.e., consent to the matter.

Thus, the formation of an agreement is a two-step process where one party makes a proposal and the other responds to that proposal. The examples in Box 1.1 would help achieve a better understanding of the concept.

Legal Obligation

The law of contract seeks to determine and define the promises to which legal effect is accorded, whether by enforceability or by way of recognition of a duty of performance. Thus, to become a contract, an agreement must have an accompanying legal obligation, i.e., it must be enforceable by law. That is why all contracts are agreements originally, but all agreements may not necessarily turn out to be contracts. In this context, the term 'agreement' has a wider scope than the term 'contract'. Only those agreements in respect of which a legal action can be brought in can be regarded as contracts. The courts have recognised that some agreements, by their very nature, are not intended to be legally binding. Agreements of domestic, social, moral, or religious nature cannot be

Box 1.1 **An Agreement in the Eyes of the Law**

Example 1

A offers to sell his car to *B* for a price. *B* accepts the offer. It has become a promise and can be treated as an agreement between *A* and *B*.

Example 2

A has two Maruti-800 cars, one being a 2005 model and the other a 2006 model. *A* offers to sell his 2005 model to *B* for ₹50,000 while *B* is under the impression that he is being offered the 2006 model. This deal lacks identity of minds. The buyer and the seller are thinking about different cars. Hence, there is no agreement, and therefore no consequent contract.

regarded as contracts, because they do not produce or are not intended to produce any legal binding between the concerned parties. For instance, where a father promises to buy his son an expensive watch if the latter secures a distinction in the university examination; but eventually fails to fulfil his promise. In such a case, he cannot be sued by the son. This is because at the time of making such an offer, it was not intended to create a legal obligation.

Contrary to this, in the case of a business agreement, the usual presumption or basic premise is that the parties intend to create a legal obligation. Thus, an agreement to sell certain goods at an agreed price constitutes a contract, as it gives rise to a legally enforceable obligation. In the event of default on the part of either party, an action for breach of contract can be enforced through a court of law, provided all other essentials of a valid contract are present in the agreement.

Contract, Agreement, Promise, and Offer

On the basis of the above discussion, the following relationship can be drawn between contract, agreement, promise, and an offer or proposal.

1. A contract, essentially, is an agreement.
2. An agreement is a set of two promises, one flowing from the offeror and the other from the acceptor.
3. A promise is an accepted offer or proposal.
4. An offer or proposal is a promise of performance, which is, however, conditional upon a return promise or an act or forbearance received in exchange for it.

The process of making a contract is shown in Figure 1.1.

Contract Distinguished from Agreement

The following are the main points of difference between an agreement and a contract:

Elements An agreement consists of an offer and its subsequent acceptance, whereas a contract is composed of an agreement and its legal enforceability.

Essence of a legal relationship An agreement may not create a legal relationship. Parties entering into a contract essentially have a common intention of entering into a legal obligation.

Scope Every agreement does not give rise to a contract, but a contract is a kind of an agreement. Simply stated, all agreements may not be contracts but all contracts are primarily agreements.

Enforceability by law A contract is legally enforceable, whereas an agreement is not necessarily so.

Figure 1.1 The process of making of a contract

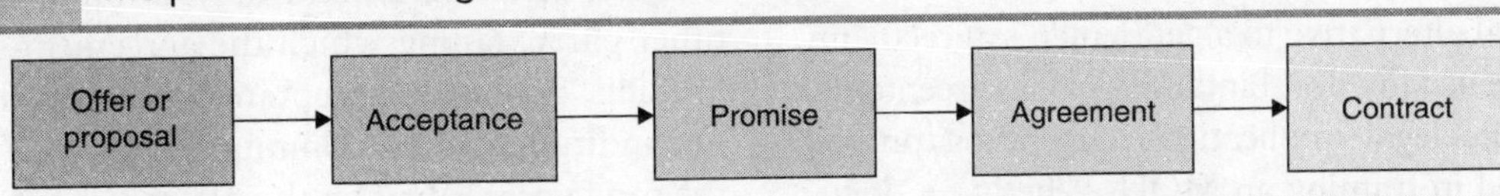

Box 1.2 Is Husband's Promise to Wife a Legally Binding Agreement?

A husband, native of England, was a Civil servant and posted in Ceylon. His wife could not accompany him on his posting to Ceylon because of ill health. The husband had promised her to pay £30 per month as maintenance during the time they were forced to live apart. However, he failed to keep his promise. The wife filed a suit against her husband for breach of agreement. Her petition was dismissed on the ground that it was an agreement of domestic nature and the parties never contemplated to give rise to legal obligations [*Balfaur vs Balfaur*[3]].

Agreements and Contracts Distinguished from Memorandum of Understanding

MoU: A document that describes the broad outlines of an agreement that two or more parties have reached. While not necessarily legally binding, an MoU signals that a binding contract is imminent.

Many a times students of business (corporate) law and even executives across the managerial hierarchy confuse the terms 'Contract' and 'Agreement' with 'Memorandum of Understanding' (MoU), probably due to lack of clarity about these terms. So, it is imperative to compare and contrast these terms against each other. An agreement, in its formal sense, is a set of promises, done usually voluntarily, forming consideration for each other whereas a contract is a legally enforceable agreement between the parties that creates an obligation to do or not do (i.e. abstinence) a particular thing. A 'Memorandum of Understanding' (MoU), on other hand, is (also) an agreement between two or more parties, except unlike a contract, it needs not contain legally enforceable promises. An MoU literally expresses a convergence of will between the parties, indicating an intended common line of action. It is often used either in cases where parties do not imply a legal commitment or in situations where the parties cannot create a legally enforceable agreement. In case of MoU, both the parties proposed their intention and a commitment to follow the intention in future. It does not create a valid contract. Notwithstanding, if one party does anything on the reliance of the MoU and sustains any loss, he can recover back the loss from the other party or parties but cannot enforce the same (i.e. MoU). It is a more formal alternative to a gentlemen's agreement.

MOUs are usually non-binding formal agreements, yet they invite legal implications depending on the language used in framing an MOU. Whether a document constitutes a binding contract depends only on the presence or absence of well-defined legal elements in the text proper of the document (the so-called "four corners"). The required elements are: offer and acceptance, consideration, and the intention to be legally bound (*Animus contrahendi*). However, to avoid such a conflicting situation, MoUs contain disclaimers stating that it shall not be enforceable in the court of law. Notwithstanding, in the event of infringement of the privacy policy mentioned in the MOU, legal action can be taken against the defaulting party.

Essential Elements of Establishing a Valid Contract

According to Section 10 of the Act, 'All agreements are contracts if they are made by the free consent of parties competent to contract for a lawful consideration and with a lawful object, and are not hereby expressly declared to be void.'

Thus, to become a valid contract, an agreement has to meet certain requirements. These are briefly discussed below.

Agreement

In order to ascertain whether a contract has come into being, it is necessary to establish that there has been an agreement between the parties. An agreement comes into existence when one party makes an offer and the other accepts it. The Act has laid down certain rules for making the offer and its acceptance, which must be adhered to while entering into an agreement. For instance, in order to be lawful, an offer must be definite, meaningful, and duly communicated to the other party, failing which the agreement shall not be binding. Similarly, acceptance must be absolute and unconditional, duly communicated, and must be in the mode prescribed by the offeror, if any.

Intention to Create Legal Relation

Intention to create legal relation is a necessary and independent element in the making of a contract. As far as the common law is concerned, the very presence of consideration often leads to the inference that an intention to create legal relations exists. However, in some cases, a mere presence of consideration does not automatically give rise to the presence of intention to create legal obligations. For example, suppose in an agreement between a husband and a wife, the husband agrees to buy his wife a bracelet if she types a manuscript for him, probably represents consideration in the literal sense but is lacking an intention to create legal obligations. Therefore, evidence should establish clearly that the intention of the parties is to enter into contract. Thus, purely domestic or social arrangements do not contemplate to give rise to legal consequences. For instance, an invitation to a feast is not intended to create legal obligations and, therefore, does not result in a contract if the invitation is accepted. Box 1.2 clearly explains this aspect of the law of contract in *Balfaur vs Balfaur*.

Legitimate Consideration

An agreement to be enforceable as a contract inter alia must be supported by consideration unless the agreement is by means of written deed. However, the consideration need not always be in terms of money. It may be an act (doing something) or forbearance (not doing something) or a promise to do or not to do something. However, an act, forbearance, or promise will amount to consideration only if the law recognises that it has some economic value. It must have such value even though the value cannot be precisely quantified, and may be past, present or future. But in order to be valid, a consideration must be lawful. As per Section 23, the consideration is lawful unless it is forbidden by law or is of such a nature that, if permitted, it would defeat the provisions of any law, or is fraudulent or is regarded as immoral by the court, or involves or implies injury to the person or to the property of another person, or courts regards as immoral, or opposed to public policy. In short, an illegal consideration renders the whole contract invalid.

[3] 1919, K.B. 571

Capacity of Parties

The parties must be legally capable of entering into a contract. But how can the competency of contracting parties be determined? In this regard, Section 11 specifies that every person is competent to contract who has attained the age of majority as per the law of his country, who is of sound mind, and who is not disqualified from contracting by any of his domestic laws. Simply put, a minor; a mentally unsound, or mentally challenged person; and a person otherwise disqualified from contracting by any law, for example, an alien enemy, insolvent, and convicts are not competent to contract.

Free Consent

The basis of a contract is an agreement, which presupposes manifestation of mutual consent between the contracting parties. The term 'consent' implies that the parties in a contract should mean the same thing, in the same sense, and voluntarily agree to the same thing. When there is such an evident meeting of minds, the law says that there is *consensus ad idem* between the parties [*Noorbhai vs Karuppan Chetty*[4]], or in short, that the parties are '*ad idem*' [*British Ceylon Corporation Ltd vs The United Shipping Board*[5]].

Consent is not free if (i) coercion, (ii) undue influence, (iii) fraud, (iv) misrepresentation, or (v) mistake vitiates it. In the first four cases, the contract becomes voidable at the option of the aggrieved party. But where an agreement is induced by mutual mistake, which is material to the agreement, it would be void [Section 20].

Lawful Object

As per Section 23, the object of an agreement must not be forbidden by law, fraudulent, immoral, opposed to public policy, or must not involve or imply injury to the person or to the property of another person. If the object is unlawful for any of the above reasons, the agreement shall be void. Thus, if a person at the behest of another person threatens to kill someone for a ransom, he cannot recover the sum through a court of law.

[4] 1925, 27 N.L.R. 325

[5] 1934, 36 N.L.R. 225, at 234

Form

The Indian Contract Act does not insist upon a written contract. For day-to-day transactions which are in bulk, written agreements would be burdensome and time-consuming and simply redundant. However, in some cases, certain formalities (writing, registration, etc.) must be observed. For instance, an agreement to make a gift for natural love and affection must be contained in the form of a deed, or else the agreement will be unenforceable. The obvious reason why some contracts should be in writing is that writing will not only stand as evidence of the transaction should anyone question its existence or validity, but it is likely to help the parties focus more precisely on what each promised to the other and avoid a 'he said, she said' dispute. Thus, good intentions do not always make a good contract. Proper documentation helps.

Contracts Where Writing Is Necessary

The types of agreements that require formal record and/or registration for making the transaction binding include the following:

1. An agreement to pay a time-barred debt;
2. Transfer of share certificate;
3. Hire–purchase agreement;
4. An assignment of assignment of copyright;
5. Cheques, bills of exchange, and promissory notes under the Negotiable Instruments Act, 1881; and
6. An agreement to sell land, building, etc.

Failure to comply with any of the statutory requirements (including writing and registration) would render these contracts invalid and unenforceable.

Certainty

The terms of a contract must be reasonably certain. Section 29 provides 'agreements, the meaning of which is not certain or capable of being made certain, are void'. Thus, in order to give rise to a valid contract, the terms of agreement must be clear and not vague or uncertain. A contract may also be declared void on the ground of uncertainty or ambiguity. For example, *A* agreed to sell 10 metres of cloth to *B*. Here, it is not clear what kind of fabric was intended to be sold. Hence, the agreement is void for lack of certainty of the subject-matter.

Possibility of Performance

The agreement should be capable of being performed. As per section 56, 'an agreement to do an act impossible in itself is void'. The agreement in question must be performable not only physically but also legally, failing which it will not result in a contract. Impossibility of performance may arise from the very nature of contract or due to change of the law subsequently. For example, a promise to double a given amount of money by magic is unenforceable due to the sheer impossibility of performing such an act.

Agreement not Expressly Declared Void

Certain types of agreements have been expressly declared void under the Act. These are: agreements in restraint of marriage, trade, or legal proceedings, and agreements by way of wager [Sections 26–28 and 30]. These are discussed at length in Chapter 5.

Types of Contracts

All contracts may broadly be classified into the following categories:

1. Valid contracts, void contracts, and voidable contracts;
2. Unenforceable contracts and Illegal contracts;
3. Executed contracts and executory contracts;
4. Express contracts and implied contracts;
5. Unilateral contracts and bilateral contracts; and
6. Quasi contracts.
7. E-contracts

Valid Contracts, Void Contracts, and Voidable Contracts

Depending on their enforceability and the extent to which they can be enforced, contracts can be classified as valid, void, or voidable.

Valid contract

A contract that fulfils all the legal requirements, such as the existence of agreement, intention for creating legal relations, certainty, etc., is said to be a valid contract. The absence of an essential element will render the contract void, voidable, illegal, or unenforceable.

Valid contract: A contract that fulfils all legal requirements.

Box 1.3 When Does a Valid Contract Become Void?

Example 1

A promises to sell his luxury car to *B*. If *B* dies or goes mad before the money changes hands, the contract would become void.

Example 2

A, a rice merchant based in Delhi, agreed to sell to *B*, residing in Agra, 100 bags of Basmati rice at the rate of ₹1500 per bag. But before the delivery could take place, the government imposed a ban on inter-state trading in rice. The contract becomes void.

The above instances make it clear that both the contracts were valid at the time of their inception but became unenforceable subsequently. Thus, they became void from the time they became unenforceable.

Void contract

Void contract: A contract that has no binding influence on any party.

A void contract has no binding effect in any party. According to Section 2(j), 'a contract which ceases to be enforceable by law becomes void, when it ceases to be enforceable.'

A close examination of the above definition reveals that a contract may not be void from its inception. It might be valid and binding on the parties when originally made, but subsequent to its creation it may become legally unenforceable (and so treated as void) for certain reasons. A valid contract may become void due to subsequent impossibility of performance, change of law, repudiation of a voidable contract, etc. The conditions when a valid contract becomes void are given in Box 1.3.

A void contract carries no contract ual rights or obligations. If, for instance, goods have been transferred under a void contract, ownership of goods will not pass and they can be recovered from the person in possession of them at any time before being consumed. However, if somebody has rendered his services under a void contract, he/she is entitled to reasonable remuneration, what is known as the quantum meruit[6] [*Craven-Ellis vs Canons Ltd*[7]].

Void contract vs void agreement

A void contract is different from a void agreement. Section 2(g) says, 'An agreement not enforceable by law is void'. Thus, in case of a void agreement, no contract comes into being. Such an agreement does not give rise to any legal consequences. It is void *ab-initio*, i.e., unenforceable from its very inception.

A void contract, on the other hand, is one which was valid when entered into, but subsequently, because of some reasons ceases to be enforceable. It is not void from the very beginning. We shall learn about void agreements in detail in Chapter 5. The following are some instances of void agreements:

1. Where both the parties to an agreement are under a mistake of fact [Section 20].
2. Where the object or consideration of an agreement is unlawful [Section 23].
3. Where the agreement is made without consideration [Section 25].
4. Where the agreement is regarding restraint of marriage [Section 26].
5. Where an agreement is pertaining to restraint of trade [Section 27].
6. Where an agreement relates to restraint of legal proceedings [Section 28].
7. Where an agreement is by way of wager [Section 30].
8. Where an agreement is made with a minor [Section 11].

Voidable contract

As per Section 2(i), an agreement, which is enforceable by law at the option of one or more of the parties thereto, but not at the option of other or others is a voidable contract. Accordingly, a voidable contract is one, which is legally enforceable unless avoided, i.e., a party to the contract refuses to abide by it. Contracts brought about as a result of coercion,

[6] *Quantum meruit* is an equitable remedy, which literally means 'as much as is deserved.' See Chapter 7.

[7] 1939, 2 K.B. 403

Box 1.4 **Voidable Contracts**

Example 1

A agreed to sell his horse to *B* for ₹5000. The consent of *A* was obtained by the use of force. The contract is voidable at the option of *A*.

Example 2

A threatens to shoot *B* if he does not sell his car worth ₹2,00,000 to *A* for ₹1,00,000. *B* agrees. The contract is voidable at the option of *B*, as his consent has been obtained by coercion, provided *B* exercises his option to set aside the contract within a reasonable period of time. However, if in the meantime, *A* sells the car to *C* who acquires it after paying the price and in good faith, the contract cannot be avoided or become voidable even at the behest of *B*.

undue influence, fraud, or misrepresentation, or agreements made by minors fall into this category. These contracts are voidable at the instance or behest of the aggrieved party [Sections 19 and 19A]. It is important to note that the option to repudiate the contract on this ground is not available to the party who has induced the contract. However, unless the aggrieved party takes steps to avoid the contract, it may operate in every respect as a valid contract. Furthermore, if the party having the right to repudiate the contract does not exercise the right within a reasonable time, and before the rights of third parties get involved, the contract will be binding and enforceable. Thus, a voidable transaction is valid for all purposes until steps are taken to avoid it.

A contract is also voidable under the following two situations:

1. When a contract contains reciprocal promises, and one party to the contract prevents the other from performing his promise, the contract becomes voidable at the option of the latter [Section 53]; and
2. When a party to a contract promises to perform an obligation within a specified time but fails to do so within the fixed time, the contract becomes voidable at the option of the promisee [Section 55].

Examples of voidable contracts are given in Box 1.4.

Difference between void contract and voidable contract

The major difference between void contract and voidable contract is summarised in Table 1.1.

Unenforceable and Illegal Contracts

At times, some contracts may suffer from some technical flaws that may render them unenforceable by law. There could also be some contracts that are not permissible under the law of the land. Such contracts are termed as unenforceable and illegal.

Unenforceable contract

> **Unenforceable contract:** A contract which may be valid otherwise but cannot be enforced by one or both the parties because of some technical flaw.

When a contract may be valid otherwise but cannot be enforced (i.e., in a court of law) by one or both the parties because of some technical flaw, it is described as an unenforceable contract. Literally and in a wider sense, this term would include voidable, void, and illegal contracts, but in a legal sense, it means a contract which is good in substance but which fails to satisfy some technical requirement, such as the need for registration, attestation, and payment of stamp fee. Similarly, sometimes the law may require that a particular agreement must be in writing or executed within a fixed period under the (Indian) Limitation Act, 1963. If these formalities are not properly observed, the contract becomes unenforceable. For instance, a contract of insurance is unenforceable unless evidenced in writing.

Illegal or unlawful contracts

Technically, a contract cannot be illegal because the term 'illegal' indicates 'contrary to law' and a contract implies 'an agreement enforceable by law'. As such, the former contradicts the latter and vice

Table 1.1 Difference between Void and Voidable Contracts

S. No.	Point of difference	Void contract	Voidable contract
1.	Definition	A contract, which ceases to be enforceable by law, becomes void when it ceases to be enforceable.	A voidable contract is an agreement which is enforceable by law at the option of one or more of the parties there to, but not at the option of the other(s).
2.	Nature and validity	A void contract is valid and binding upon the parties when entered into, but subsequent to its formation, it becomes unenforceable due to certain reasons.	Avoidable contract is repudiatable at the option of the aggrieved party. It remains a valid contract until it is set aside or rescinded by the party entitled to do so.
3.	Factors responsible	A valid contract may become void due to any supervening impossibility, change of law, a contingent contract due to emergence of an uncertain event, etc.	Coercion, undue influence, error, fraud, and misrepresentation are the main factors responsible for rendering a contract voidable.
4.	Enforceability	It cannot be enforced by either party.	It can be enforced or set aside at the option of the aggrieved party.
5.	Relationship	A void contract under no circumstances results in a voidable contract.	When a voidable contract is repudiated by the aggrieved party, it results in a void contract.
6.	Rights of third party	A void contract confers no rights or legal remedies to the third party.	Rights acquired under voidable contract by an innocent third party are not wiped out by such subsequent avoidance of the contract.
7.	Compensation	In case of void contract, question of compensation or damages does not arise on the non-performance of such contract.	In case of voidable contract, the party rescinding the contract can also claim damages.
8.	Effect of lapse of time	Lapse of reasonable time does not render a void contract enforceable. It always remains void and unenforceable.	If a voidable contract is not rescinded by the aggrieved, it would become enforceable at the option of the other party.

versa, because once the agreement is illegal how can it be enforceable at law and if the agreement is enforceable by law how can it be termed as illegal or unlawful. Therefore, it sounds illogical to speak of an 'illegal contract'. An agreement, of course, may be illegal or unlawful. Hence, it will be more appropriate if we use the term 'illegal agreement' in place of 'illegal contract'.

An illegal agreement is one which the law specifically forbids. An illegal agreement is void *ab initio*. In the eyes of law, not only illegal agreements are unenforceable as such, but any other agreement collateral to or arising from such agreements is also unforceable. For example, *A* agrees to pay *B* ₹1,00,000 for killing C. A managed the amount by taking a loan from *X* to pay *B*. *X* was aware of the purpose of the loan. In this case, the main agreement between *A* and *B* is illegal and void *ab initio* because its object is unlawful. Even if *B* kills *C*, he/she cannot recover the agreed amount from *A* through a legal action. Besides the main agreement between *A* and *B*, the collateral transaction between *A* and *X* is also void in the eyes of law.

Illegal agreement and void agreement distinguished

The term 'illegal agreement' has a wider connotation than the term 'void agreement'. All illegal agreements are void but all void agreements are not necessarily illegal. For example, an agreement to marry a minor girl though is void but not illegal because the object of this agreement is not unlawful. However, an agreement to commit robbery or have an intercourse with a minor below 16 years of age in consideration of a gift would not only be illegal but also void *ab initio*. Apart from the similarity between an illegal agreement and a void agreement that in both the cases the agreements are void and unenforceable at law, the two differ from each other in the following ways.

Scope An illegal agreement is narrower in scope than a void agreement. All illegal agreements are always void, but all void agreements are not necessarily illegal. A legal agreement may become void due to some other reasons. For example, an agreement whose object is uncertain is void but not illegal.

Effect on collateral transactions Collateral transactions to a void agreement may be enforced for execution, i.e., they do not become void. Contrarily, collateral transactions to an illegal agreement become illegal and thus cannot be enforced in a court of law as we saw in the example on ransom killing earlier. The collateral transaction of *A* taking loan from *X* to give to *B* for killing *C* is also illegal and cannot be enforced under law.

Restitution of benefit received If a valid contract becomes void subsequently because of certain reasons, then the party who has received benefit under such contract is bound to restore it to the party from whom he has received it. But this is not so in case of an illegal agreement. The benefit reached or money advanced in respect of an illegal agreement cannot be restored or claimed back. Thus, in the example on ransom killing agreement, *X* cannot recover the loan advanced to *A* by the count of law.

Void ab initio An illegal agreement is void since its inception, but under certain circumstances a valid agreement may subsequently become void.

Executed and Executory Contracts

Depending on whether all the obligations of a contract have been fulfilled or have remained to be accomplished, contracts can be either 'executed' or 'executory' in nature.

Executed contracts

A contract is said to be executed, where both the parties have done all that the contract required of them. A cash sale is an example of an executed contract.

Executory contracts

An 'executory contract' is one in which the reciprocal promises or obligations, which serve as consideration, are yet to be carried out. In other words, contract in which one or both the contracting parties have still to carry out their respective obligations is termed as an executory contract. For example, *A* agrees to sell his scooter to *B*. The latter has paid the price but *A* has yet to deliver the scooter. The contract is, thus, executory as the right to the goods is transferred but not the possession.

Thus, an executed contract conveys a chose in possession, whereas an executory contract conveys a chose in action.

Express and Implied Contracts

A contract may be express or implied depending on how it is established.

Express contracts

An express contract is the one that very lucidly conveys the purpose of the agreement. An express contract exists when parties state the terms and show their intentions in words. An express contract can be either oral or written. The majority of real estate contracts are express contracts since they are reduced to writing.

Executory contract: A contract in which the reciprocal promises or obligations, which serve as consideration, are yet to be carried out.

Implied contracts

Contrary to express contracts, an implied contract is based on an agreement, arises from some non-verbal conduct or assumed intentions, or relationship among the immediate parties, or the application of the legal principle of equity. In an implied contract, the agreement of the parties is demonstrated by their actions and roles. Such contracts are formed when one party accepts something of value knowing that the other party expects compensation. A contract is implied when a party knowingly accepts a benefit from another party in circumstances where the benefit cannot be considered a gift. Therefore, the party accepting the benefit is under a legal obligation to fair value for the benefit received. For example, while visiting a doctor, a patient agrees to pay a fair price for the service availed. If he/she refuses to pay after being examined, he/she has breached a contract implied in fact. Generally, an implied contract has the same legal force as an

Implied contract: A legally enforceable agreement arises from some non-verbal conduct, or assumed intentions, or relationship between the immediate parties, or the application of the legal principle of equity.

express contract. Denial of an implied contract would be unfair and/or result in unjust enrichment to one of the parties. However, it may be more difficult to prove the existence and terms of an implied contract, should a dispute arise.

Unilateral and Bilateral Contracts

Unilateral and bilateral contracts are the terms used to describe the way in which contracts arise. These terms are important because the unilateral or bilateral status of a contract may affect whether or not, and how, the contract is enforced. It is sometimes difficult to distinguish between unilateral and bilateral contracts.

Unilateral contracts

Unilateral contract: A contract in which one of the parties performs its promises at the time of making the contract and the other party promises to perform in the future.

A unilateral contract is one in which one of the parties performs its promises at the time of making the contract and the other party promises to perform in the future. Unilateral contracts often arise in an offer to sell an item to another person. If *A* tells *B*, 'I'll sell you my car if you give me ₹50,000'. *A* is unilaterally offering the car if *B* gives him that amount. The contract can be accepted only by the payment of the money, not by a promise to pay the money. Ordinarily, *A* is not bound to sell the car unless *B* hands him ₹50,000, and *A* can withdraw the offer to sell it at any time before *B* performs, i.e, pays the money in this case. It is thus, the party to a unilateral contract whose performance sought is not obligated to act, but if he or she does, the party that has made the promise is bound to comply with the terms of the agreement.

Bilateral contracts

Bilateral contract: A contract in which both the parties are to perform their respective promises or obligations at some future time but not necessarily concurrently.

A bilateral contract is one in which both the parties are to perform their respective promises or obligations at some future time but not necessarily at the same time. This is sometimes referred to as 'mutuality of undertaking'. If *A* tells *B*, 'I'll sell you my car if you promise to pay me ₹50,000, and *B* agrees by saying OK, I promise to give you the ₹50,000 next Tuesday, and *A* agrees saying OK,' then it is a bilateral contract. Ordinarily, under these circumstances, *A* has bound himself to sell the car at that price. Unlike a unilateral contract, in which only one party promises, bilateral contracts are more common in modern commerce. In these, both parties promise to do something for the other and are bound together from a precise moment.

Quasi Contract

Quasi contract: The act of a person, permitted by law, by which he/she obligates himself/herself towards another or binds himself/herself to him/her, without any agreement between them.

A 'quasi contract' is the act of a person, permitted by law, by which he/she obligates himself/herself towards another or by which another binds himself/herself to him/her, without any agreement between them. Thus, a quasi contract is not a 'contract' but an obligation created by law (in the absence of any agreement) for certain relations resembling those that are created by contract. It is based on the concept of equity.

An example of a quasi contract is the case of a delivery boy who, by mistake, delivers grocery to a wrong address. The owner of the house consumes the supply. The question arises if the owner will be held liable for payment. Surely, the man will be held liable for payment, as the law aims to create an obligation upon a non-contracting party to avoid injustice.

Other examples of quasi contracts are (a) supply of necessaries [Section 68], (b) payment of lawful dues by interested person [Section 69], (c) person enjoying benefit of a gratuitous act [Section 70], and (d) finder of lost goods [Section 71].

E-contracts

E-commerce (also written as e-commerce or eCommerce)—the practice of buying and selling goods, services and information online i.e. by Internet applications—has undisputedly become a part of our everyday life over the past few years. One good reason for the popularization of the same would be immoderate technological advancement and the increased awareness about the use of computer and communication technologies to simplify business procedures and enhance efficiency. The effectiveness of E-Commerce is predominantly based on electronically made contract known as e-contract. E-contract, also known as electronic contract or digital contract,

E-commerce: The practice of buying and selling goods, services and information online i.e. by Internet applications.

E-contract: Any kind of contract formed in the course of e-commerce by the interaction of two or more individuals using electronic means, such as e-mail, the interaction of an individual with an electronic agent, such as a computer program; or the interaction of at least two electronic agents that are programmed to recognize the existence of a contract.

is any kind of contract formed in the course of e-commerce by the interaction of two or more individuals using electronic means, such as e-mail, the interaction of an individual with an electronic agent, such as a computer program, or the interaction of at least two electronic agents that are programmed to recognize the existence of a contract. The Uniform Computer Information Transactions Act(UCITA) provides rules regarding the formation, governance, and basic terms of an e-contract. Traditional contract principles and remedies also apply to e-contracts. Though E-contracts are legalized by the Information Technology Act, still mainstream feels insecure while dealing online. This is probably due to lack of transparency in the terms and conditions attached to the contract and the jurisdiction incase of a dispute that may arise during the pendency of a transaction with an offshore site or store. The above reservation on part of masses poses a number of challenges before the businesses.

Understanding E-contracts

Acontract is a legally binding agreement between two or more persons by which rights are acquired by one or more to acts or forbearance on the part of the other or others[8].

Correspondingly, an electronic or digital contract (E-contract) is an agreement 'drafted' and 'signed' in electronic or digital form.

E-contract is an important aid to drafting and negotiating successful contracts for consumers and businesses for their online transactions. It is designed to assist people in formulating and implementing commercial contracts policies within e-businesses. It contains model contracts for the sale of products and supply of digital products and services to both consumers and businesses.

An e-contract is a contract modeled, executed and enacted by a software system. Computer programs are used to automate business processes that govern e-contracts. E-contracts can be mapped to inter-related programs, which have to be specified carefully to satisfy the contract requirements. These programs do not have the capabilities to handle complex relationships between parties to an e-contract.

An electronic agreement can be drafted in the similar manner in which a normal hard copy agreement is drafted. For example, an agreement is drafted on a computer and then sent to a business associate via e-mail. The business associate, in turn, e-mails it back to the sender with an electronic signature indicating acceptance. An e-contract can also be in the form of a 'Click to Agree' contract, commonly used with downloaded software: The user clicks an 'I Agree' button on a page containing the terms of the software license before the transaction can be completed. For a traditional ink signature isn't possible on an electronic contract, people use several different ways to indicate their electronic signatures, like typing the signer's name into the signature area, pasting in a scanned version of the signer's signature or clicking an 'I Accept' button and many more.

E-contracts can be categorized into two types i.e. web-wrap agreements and shrink-wrap agreements. A person witnesses these e-contracts everyday albeit unaware of the legal intricacies connected to it.

Web-wrap agreements are basically web based agreements which require assent of the party by way of clicking the 'I agree' or 'I accept' button e.g. E-bay user agreement, Citibank terms and conditions, etc.

Shrink-wrap agreements, on the other hand, are those agreements, which are accepted by a user when a software is installed from a CD-ROM e.g., Nokia pc-suite software.

Evidentiary value under Indian Evidence Act

It is pertinent to contextualize at this juncture that evidence recorded or stored by availing the electronic gadgets is given the evidentiary status. For instance: the voice recorded with the help of a tape recorder. Now-a-days, the digital voice recorder, digital cameras, digital video cameras, video conferencing are adding a new dimension to the evidentiary regime. Justice Gururajan, the Karnataka High Court judge, has held in a civil suit that video conferencing evidence is valid. The emergence of information and

[8] William Anson

communication witnessed sea change by elevating the status of the evidence recorded, generated or stored electronically from the secondary to primary evidential status. The shift in the paradigm owes to the efforts of the working group of the UNCITRAL Model law on electronic commerce and assigning of the legal recognition to e-record or data message.

The evidentiary value of e-contracts can be well understood in the light of the following sections of Indian Evidence Act. Sections 85A, 85B, 88A, 90A and 85C deals with the presumptions as to electronic records whereas Section 65B relates to the admissibility of electronic record. The above mentioned sections can be explained as follows:

Section 85a As regards presumption to electronic agreements, this section is incorporated. It says that every electronic record of the nature of an agreement is concluded as soon as a digital signature is affixed to the record. Section 85A has been added in order to ensure the validity of e-contracts. But there are some restrictions as regards the presumptive value. The presumption is only valid to electronic records, electronic records that are five years old and electronic messages that fall within the ambit of Section 85B, Section 88A and Section 90A of Indian Evidence Act.

Section 85b Section 85B provides that the court shall presume the fact that the record in question has not been put to any kind of alteration, in case contrary has not been proved. The secure status of the record may be demanded till a specific time. The digital signature should also be presumed to have been affixed with an intention of signing and approving the electronic record. Further it has been provided that the section should not be misread so as to create any presumption relating to the integrity or authenticity of the electronic record or digital signature in question.

Section 88a The court may presume that an electronic message forwarded by the originator through an electronic mail server to the addressee to whom the message purports to be addressed corresponds with the message as fed into his computer for transmission, but the court shall not make any presumption as to the person by whom such message was sent.

This section is self-explanatory as it purports to follow the basic rules of a valid hard-copy agreement. The words 'may presume' authorize the court to use its discretionary power as regards presumption. Sections 85A and 85B contained the words 'shall presume' which expressly excluded this discretionary power of the court.

Section 90a In case of an electronic record being five years old, if proved to be in proper custody, the court may presume that the digital signature was affixed so as to authenticate the validity of that agreement. The digital signature can also be affixed by any person authorized to do so. For the purpose of this section, electronic records are said to be in proper custody if they are in the custody of the person with whom they naturally be. An exception can be effected in case circumstances of a particular case render its origin probable.

Section 85c As far as a digital signature certificate is concerned, the court shall presume that the information listed in the certificate is true and correct. Inclusion of the words 'shall presume' again relates to the expressed exclusion of the discretionary power of the court.

Section 65b Section 65B talks about admissibility of electronic records. It says that any information contained in an electronic record which is printed on a paper or stored/recorded/copied on optical/magnetic media produced by a computer shall be deemed to be a document and is admissible as evidence in any proceeding without further proof of the original, in case the following conditions are satisfied:

- A certificate issued is also admissible if it contains a statement which identifies the electronic record containing the statement and gives information about the particulars of the computer involved in the production of record.
- The certificate issued should be signed by a person officially responsible for the use of that device in relation to the relevant activity. The information fed into the computer should be in appropriate form as well as by appropriate device.

To sum up, it can be said that all electronic contracts are valid contracts as they are legalized by the Information Technology Act and one could be made liable if there is any infringement with the terms and conditions involved therein. They carry the same credence as other hard copy contracts as far as its evidentiary value is concerned and in case of any discrepancy there are certain prerequisites that fill the lacunae.

Offer and Acceptance

We have learnt that a contract is an agreement which is reducible to an offer by one party and its acceptance by the other. An offer when accepted in its entirety and without any qualification results in *consensus ad idem* or meeting of the minds of the concerned parties. This is termed as agreement and a contract comes into being assuming that it would give rise to a legal commitment. Thus, for a contract to conclude, it is necessary to establish that there has been an agreement between the parties, which is possible through a definite offer and its unconditional acceptance. A proposal or an offer and its subsequent acceptance is the universally acknowledged two-step process to form a contract.

Defining an Offer

> **Offer:** A medium through which a person expresses his intention to enter into a contractual obligation against a promise or an act or forbearance.

An offer is a medium through which a person expresses his intention to enter into a contractual obligation against a promise or an act or forbearance. Section 2(a) defines the term offer or proposal[9] as: 'When one person signifies to another person his willingness to do or to abstain from doing anything, with a view to obtaining the assent of that other to such an act or abstinence, he is said to have made a proposal'. This definition reflects three properties of an offer, namely, expression of readiness, presence of second party, and intention of obtaining a response. Let us examine them one by one.

First, an offer is an expression of readiness 'to do' or 'not to do' something. That is, it may involve a positive act or abstinence. For example, *A* offers to sell his bike to *B* for ₹10,000. *A* is making an offer to do something, i.e., sell his bike. This is a positive act on the part of *A*. On the other hand, *Y* who is a victim of a road accident caused by *X*'s car, offers to *X* not to file an F.I.R. with the police if the latter pays him ₹5,000 as compensation. Here the act of *Y* is abstinence because he is offering not to resort to filing of the F.I.R.

Second, an offer is made to another person or party. An offer by a person made to himself is meaningless.

[9] The terms 'offer' and 'proposal' are often used interchangeably.

Third, it is made with the intention that the other person accepts it. Mere expression of willingness will not constitute an offer. For example, if *A* offers to sell a book to *B* for ₹100, and *B* accepts the offer, *then A* cannot refuse to deliver the book merely by saying that his actual intention was to offer the book for ₹200, or that he intended to sell a book at a price different from that stipulated in the offer earlier.

The person making the proposal or offer is referred to as the 'proposer' or 'offeror', and the person to whom it is addressed is called the 'proposee' or 'offeree'. When the offeree accepts the offer, he becomes the 'acceptor' or 'promisee'. For example, *A* offers to sell his car to *B* for ₹50,000. This is a proposal or offer made by *A*. He is the 'offeror' or 'proposer'. *B*, to whom the offer has been made, is the 'proposee' or 'offeree' and if he accepts the offer, he will become the 'acceptor' or 'promisee' and *A* will subseqently become the 'promisor'.

Characteristics of a Valid Offer

In order to be legally enforceable, an offer must satisfy the following requirements.

It must intend to create, and be capable of creating, a legal obligation The foremost requisite of a valid offer is that it must contemplate to give rise to legal consequences and at the same time be capable of creating legal obligations. The underlying reason is that the very purpose of entering into an agreement (i.e., accepting the offer) is to make it legally enforceable. Therefore, a domestic or social invitation cannot constitute a valid offer in the eye of the law, because if such an invitation is accepted, it will not create any legal binding on the part of offeror or offeree. For example, if someone invites his friend to dine with him or offers to take him to a movie, it cannot be regarded as an offer even though it was accepted and there was consideration, as the parties never intended to create legal obligations. The *Balfaur vs Balfaur* case, which was discussed earlier in this chapter, illustrated this point very well.

Its terms must be certain An offer must be clear, definite, absolute, and final. An offer with vague or loose terms does not convey what it exactly means. In such a case, a court will presume that there was no serious intention to establish a bond and, therefore, there is no contract. For example, if *A* enters into an agreement with *B* to agree in future to sell to the latter his car, it cannot result into a contract because the terms of agreement are not certain. They are yet to be settled. Similarly, a promise to pay a further sum for a horse if it proved to be a harbinger of good luck for the purchaser [*Gunthing vs Lynn*[10]], or an agreement that the plaintiff is to receive 'a reasonable share of the profits' [*Way vs Latilla*[11]] are all too vague to create a binding obligation in respect of the matters they cover.

It must be made to obtain the consent of the offeree The proposal or offer must be made with the intention that the offeree accepts it. For example, if *A* tells *B* that he desires to marry her by the end of December 2008, it does not amount to an offer of marriage by *A* to *B*. Instead if *A* says, 'I offer to marry you' or 'will you marry me?', then it constitutes an offer. Thus, for an offer to be enforceable in a court of law, expression of willingness must be made to obtain the assent of the other party.

It must be communicated An offer becomes effective only when it has been communicated to the person to whom it was made (i.e., offeree) so as to give him an opportunity to accept or reject it. The first part of the definition of proposal given in the Act emphasises upon the fact that the willingness to make a proposal should be 'signified'. Communication of offer is imperative to conclude an agreement because acceptance can be given only after one gets to know about the offer. Moreover, acceptance in the ignorance of the offer is no acceptance and confers no legal right on the acceptor.

It may be conditional An offer may be subject to any reasonable terms and conditions, and if a person accepts the offer, he/she is bound by the terms and conditions attached to it. The question of special terms and conditions arises in case of standard form contracts such as contracts made with banks, hotels, railways, shipping, or insurance companies. Such contracts are entered into by the delivery of a printed form agreement by one party to another party who is supposed to accept.

[10] 1831, 2 B & A 232
[11] 1937, 81 S.J. 786

In order to hold the offeree liable, with regard to the special terms and conditions, if any, the offeror should fulfil the following requirements:

1. Special terms or conditions must be clearly written, expressed, or communicated to the offeree. If these are brought to the notice of the offeree, they will bind him/her even if he/she is an illiterate or has not read them [Box 1.5 (Example 1)].
2. The special terms should be presented in such a manner as to make certain that a reasonable person can become aware of their existence before accepting the proposal [Box 1.5 (Example 2)].
3. The notice of special terms should be contemporaneous with the contract, i.e., the terms, if any, should be brought to the notice of the offeree before the contract is entered into. Subsequent communication of special terms or conditions will be of no use unless the acceptor himself agrees thereto [Box 1.5 (Example 3)].
4. The terms and conditions must be reasonable. A term or condition is considered to be unreasonable if it defeats the very purpose of the contract or if it is repugnant to public policy [Box 1.5 (Example 4)].
5. The terms should not be such that the non-compliance of them would amount to acceptance. The offer should not cause on the offeree an obligation to reply. Thus, a person cannot claim that if an acceptance is not communicated by a certain date or time, the offer would be considered as accepted.

An Offer Distinct from a Query

In the process of negotiating an agreement, many preliminary communications may be exchanged between the parties before a definite offer is made. One party may simply respond to a request for information (for example, by stating the price at which it might be prepared to sell a house [*Gibson vs Manchester C.C.*[16]] or may make a similar request, such as, asking a prospective supplier whether he can supply goods suitable for his purpose [*Interfoto Picture Library Ltd vs Stiletto Visual Programmes*

[12] 1930, 1 K.B. 41
[13] 1875, 32 L.T. 709
[14] 1949, 1 K.B. 532
[15] 1966, AIR Mad. 13
[16] 1979, 1 W.L.R. 294

Box 1.5 **Presentation of Terms and Conditions of an Offer**

Example 1

In *Thomson vs L.M. & S. Railway*[12], the plaintiff who was an illiterate took a railway excursion ticket. The face of the ticket specifically mentioned, 'For conditions see back'. One of the conditions printed on the reverse of the ticket was that the Railway Company would not be liable for personal injuries caused to passengers. The court held that the plaintiff was bound by the conditions and could not recover any damages.

Example 2

In *Handerson vs Stevenson*[13], the plaintiff bought a steamer ticket for travelling from Dublin to Whitehaven. The face of the ticket read, 'Dublin to Whitehaven' only, and on the reverse were printed certain conditions, one of which excluded the liability of the company for loss, injury, or delay of the passenger or his/her luggage. The plaintiff did not read the reverse side of the ticket nor was there any indication on the face of the ticket to draw his attention to the conditions printed on the backside. His luggage got lost in the shipwreck due to negligence on the part of the crew. The court held that the plaintiff was entitled to compensation for the loss of his luggage despite the exemption clause.

Example 3

In *Olley vs Marlborough Court Ltd*[14], O and her husband hired a room at a hotel for a week. When they entered the room they found a notice on one of the walls, which contained the clause: 'The proprietors will not hold themselves responsible for articles lost or stolen, unless handed over to the managers for safe custody'. Some of their items were stolen owing to negligence of the hotel staff. The owner of the hotel was held liable because the notice was not a part of the contract as it was brought to the notice of the plaintiff after the contract had been etered into.

Example 4

In *Lilly White vs Mannuswami*[15], a laundry receipt contained a condition that the customers would be entitled to claim only 15 per cent of the market price of the value of their article(s) in case of loss. The plaintiff's new sari was lost. The court held that a term which is not in the interest of public, and which is opposed to the fundamental principles of contracts, could not be enforced. It was observed that this (enforcement of the condition) might well be putting a premium upon dishonesty of the cleaner since it would enable him to buy a new sari at 15 per cent of their market price. The court in its decision held the condition unreasonable and ordered the laundry to pay full value of the article.

Ltd[17]]. An offer thus, must be distinguished from all such queries or supply of information.

Firm Offer vs Invitation to Treat

Invitation to treat: An invitation to another person to make an offer.

An offer must be distinguished from an invitation to treat, which is an invitation to another person to make an offer. An offer is different from an invitation to treat in that the former can be converted into a contract by acceptance, provided the other requirements of a valid contract are present. However, an invitation to treat cannot be 'accepted' as offer. The question whether a statement is an offer or an invitation to treat depends primarily on the intention with which it was made. In case of an invitation to treat, the person sending out the invitation does not intend to obtain the assent of the other party but merely aims at circulating information about his/her willingness to open negotiation with anybody, who on obtaining the same comes to the invitor. An offer, on the other hand, is a definite promise to enter into a contractual obligation in return for a promise, act, or forbearance. The following are some of the examples of invitations to treat.

Auction sale An advertisement of an auction sale, a request for bids, is an invitation to treat and not an offer to hold it or sell to the highest bidder. At an auction, the general rule is that the offer is made by the bidder and accepted by the auctioneer when he/she

[17] 1989, Q.B. 433 AT 436

signifies his/her acceptance in the customary manner, e.g., by the fall of the hammer. Before this happens, the bidder can withdraw his/her bid, and the auctioneer his goods. An auctioneer is not liable to the people travelling up to the venue of the auction, if the former changes his/her mind and does not hold the auction at all [*Harris vs Nickerson*[18]].

Display of goods for sale in a showroom The display of goods with a price tag in a shop window is not an offer to sell, but an invitation to customers to make an offer to buy [*Timothy vs Simpson*[19]]. Similarly, the display of goods on the shelves of a self-service store is merely an invitation to treat. The customer makes an offer to buy when he presents the goods for payment, which the retailer may accept or reject [*Pharmaceutical Society of Great Britain vs Boots Chemists Ltd*[20]]. The rationale behind such cases is that a shop is a place for bargaining, not for compulsory trading. An invitation to treat is merely a statement of price and not an offer to sell.

An invitation for tenders A tender is an estimate submitted in response to a prior request. An invitation for tenders does not generally amount to an offer in as much as the tenderer is not bound to sell to the person quoting the lowest price [*Spencer vs Harding*[21]]. The offer comes from the persons who submit the tender and there is no contract until the tenderer accepts any one of them.

Company prospectus A prospectus or advertisement inviting the public to subscribe for shares or debentures is an invitation to treat and not an offer to sell the securities. Members of the public make the offer by completing and sending in application forms. The company reserves the right to decide about the number of shares or debentures to be allotted to each applicant [*National Westminster Bank Plc vs I.R.C.*[22]], in case of over-subscription. The position is, however, different in case of 'rights issue', where a company offers its IPO to its existing shareholders, entitling each shareholder to subscribe a certain number of new shares in proportion to the shares he/she already holds. Here the letter informing the shareholder of his/her right is regarded as an offer.

General advertisement of goods An advertisement appearing in the print or electronic media that goods are for sale is not an offer. Also in *Grainger vs Gough*, it was held that the circulation of a price list by a wine merchant was only an invitation to treat. However, advertisements for rewards for return of lost or stolen items or promise to pay money in return for an act have been held by courts as offers, for they clearly show an intention to be bound by without any further negotiation.

Types of Offers

Depending on the manner in which they are made, or the kind of promises made, offers are of various kinds. There could be express or implied offers, specific or general offers, or standing offers, etc. The following are the different kinds of offers.

Express offer vs implied offer

An express offer is made by words—oral or written. Section 9 of the Indian Contract Act reads, 'Insofar as the proposal or acceptance of any promise is made in words, the promise is said to be express.'

An implied offer is the one that the law infers from the conduct of the parties or the circumstances of the particular case. Section 9 of the Contract Act reads, 'Insofar as such proposal or acceptance is made otherwise than in words, the promise is said to be implied'.

Examples of express and implied offers are cited in Box 1.6.

Specific offer vs general offer

An offer is called specific or particular when it is made to a specific person or a group of persons. Such an offer can be accepted only by that person or a member of the group, and by no one else, for it to turn into a contract [*Boulton vs Jones*[23]]. For instance, *A* offers to sell his dog to *B* for ₹5000. This is a specific offer as *B* alone can accept or reject it.

On the other hand, a general or public offer is one that is made to the world at large. Any person (i.e., competent to contract) with the notice of the offer may validly accept such an offer by complying with

[18] 1873, LR 8 Q.B. 286
[19] 1834, 6 C. & P. 499
[20] 1952, 2 Q.B. 795
[21] 1870, L.R. 5 C. P. 561
[22] 1995, 1 A.C. 119 at 126

[23] 1857, 2 H. & N. 564

Box 1.6 **Express and Implied Offers**

1. *A* says to *B* that he wants to sell his old computer for ₹5000. This is an express offer.
2. *A* writes to *B* that he offers to sell his computer for ₹10,000. This is also an express offer.
3. *X* steps into a restaurant and consumes some food. This act creates an implied promise to pay.
4. A porter picks up someone's luggage and carries it from the railway platform to a taxi without being asked to do so. It implies that he is offering his services for which he expects to be paid.
5. As soon as a shoeshiner starts cleaning someone's shoes, without being asked to do so, he is considered to have made an implied offer.

Box 1.7 **General Offer**

In *Harbhajan Lal vs Harcharan Lal*[24], a young boy ran away from his home. The father of the missing boy, by issuing a handbill, offered a reward of ₹500 to anyone who would bring the boy home. The plaintiff spotted the boy at Dharamsala railway station and took him to the police station. He then informed the boy's father through a telegram. It was held that the handbill was an offer open to the world at large and the plaintiff, by tracing the missing boy, had substantially performed the conditions of the offer and was thus entitled to the reward.

the terms of the offer. An advertisement addressed to the public at large is a common example of a general offer. Box 1.7 provides a case study making the understanding of a general offer very clear.

Cross-offers

Cross-offers: Identical offers made by two parties to each other in ignorance of each other's offer.

'Cross-offers' refer to identical offers made by two parties to each other, neither side knowing of the other's offer when they make their own. Cross-offers do not constitute acceptance of each other because they tend to promote uncertainty and as such no contract is concluded. For example, *A* writes to *B* offering to sell his bike for ₹5000 and *B* simultaneously writes to *A* offering to buy his bike for the same price. The two mails cross each other. If no further communication takes place in such a case, no contract can be concluded between *A* and *B*, as both sides have made offers without knowing about the offer made by the other. Also, this does not amount to acceptance of each other's offer.

Standing offer

Standing offer: An offer that is kept open for acceptance over a period of time.

An offer that is kept open for acceptance over a period of time is termed as 'standing', 'open', or 'continuing' offer. Thus, a tender to supply goods at specified prices as and when required are of the nature of standing offer. The tenderer must supply whenever an order is placed, but he cannot insist on any order being made at all. The quantity to be supplied may or may not be specified. For example, in the *Secretary of State vs Madho Ram*, military authorities accepted *M*'s tender for the supply of certain goods at a specified price. But no requisition was issued during the period of the tender. *M* sued for breach of the contract. It was held that, 'The military authorities were not bound, by their acceptance of the tender, to purchase any or all of the said goods needed by them, from the plaintiff in the absence of a covenant to that effect. If they would think fit and could buy the goods from any other source without any reference to him'.

Counter-offer

Counter-offer: An alternative offer or proposal made by the offeree in substitution for the original one.

Counter-offer refers to an offer to contract on terms materially different from the terms of the offer. It is, thus, an alternative proposal made by the offeree in substitution for the original offer. When the purported acceptance of an offer contains a counter-offer, it is no acceptance at all and is corresponding to rejection of the original offer. Such a counter-offer may, however, be accepted by the original offeror and can thus give rise to legal obligations. It is important to note that a simple request as to whether or not other terms

[24] 1925, AIR All 539

would be acceptable does not amount to a counter-offer, since such a request does not, by itself, reject an offer.

Revocation or Termination of Offer

Revocation of offer/acceptance: Taking back, withdrawing, or cancelling an offer/acceptance.

Revocation of offer implies taking back, withdrawing, or cancelling an offer. As a general rule, an offer can be withdrawn at any time before the offeree has accepted it.

Section 5 states, 'a proposal may be revoked at any time before the communication of its acceptance is complete as against the proposer, but not afterwards.'

Thus, revocation of offer is possible only up to a certain stage. An offeror can revoke his/her offer at any time before the offeree has signified his/her acceptance or before he/she has posted the letter of acceptance. For example, *A* offers, by a letter sent by post, to sell his house to *B*. *A* may revoke his offer at any time before *B* posts his letter of acceptance, but not afterwards. Once the letter of acceptance is posted, the revocation will not be effective. Hence, where the offeror wants to withdraw his/her offer, he/she should do so with a quicker means of communication, which will reach before the acceptor posts his/her acceptance. The notice of revocation must be delivered through the same channel by which the original offer was made.

According to Section 6, an offer stands lapsed in any of the following circumstances:

1. Communication of notice of revocation
2. Lapse of time
3. Failure to fulfil a condition precedent to acceptance
4. Death or insanity of either party
5. Refusal or counter-offer
6. Acceptance differs from the prescribed one
7. Subsequent illegality or destruction of subject matter.

Communication of notice of revocation Revocation is ineffective until communicated to the offeree. Section 6(1) says, 'a proposal or an offer may come to an end by the communication of notice of revocation by the proposer to the other party.' Therefore, revocation by post is ineffective until it reaches the offeree.

An offeror is free to withdraw his/her offer at any time before the offeree communicates his/her acceptance. Here it is important to note that in order to be effective, notice of revocation must move from the offeror personally or a duly authorised agent and not from a third person. For instance, at an auction of a real estate plot, *A* makes a bid and is the highest bidder. But before the fall of hammer, *A* comes to know of some defect in the title of the property in question, and he retracts his bid. The offer (bid) made by *A* lapses as soon as it is retracted by him. Here no contract is concluded as the offer has been revoked before acceptance of the auctioneer.

Lapse of time An offer comes to an end with the lapse of the time for acceptance, if any, prescribed in the offer. If no time is prescribed, the offer would come to an end by the lapse of a reasonable time [Section 6(2)]. Thus, an offer, which was expressly stated to last for a definite period of time, terminates on the expiry of the stipulated time or if there was no such time limit, after a reasonable time. What is a reasonable time would depend on the circumstances of each case. The case study in Box 1.8 explains what the courts could interpret as 'reasonable time'.

Failure to fulfil a condition precedent to acceptance Where the offer is subject to some condition precedent to acceptance, the offer stands terminated if it is accepted without fulfilling the condition. For

Box 1.8 What is Reasonable Time?

In *Ramsgate Victoria Hotel Co. Ltd vs Montefiore*, the defendant offered to subscribe for the shares in the plaintiff's company on 8 June 1866 and was allotted the shares on 23 November. The court held that the defendant was entitled to refuse the shares because the plaintiff's failure to accept his offer within a reasonable time caused it to lapse. Clearly, the market value of the shares can fluctuate widely over a period of six months. In India, this case was followed in *India Co-operative Navigation and Trading Co. Ltd vs Padamsey Premji.*

example, *A* proposed to let out his house to *B* for a monthly rent of ₹5000 subject to the condition that *B* should deposit with him ₹50,000 as security before a certain date. *B* accepted the proposal but failed to provide the security money. In this case, the acceptance has no validity and the offer stands revoked. Thus, if the offeror has imposed any condition, the acceptor's failure to satisfy the same shall lead to the lapse of the offer.

Death or insanity of either party automatically terminates an offer without notice if the offeree knows this at the time of his/her purported acceptance. If the offeree has accepted the offer in ignorance of the information about the death or insanity of the offeror, the latter's legal representatives will be bound by the contract to the extent of deceased's or insane person's estate.

Ironically, the Indian Contract Act is silent about the effect of the death or insanity of the offeree. But under the English Law, an offer made to a living person who ceases to be alive before the offer is accepted is no longer an offer at law [*Reynolds vs Atherton*[25]].

Therefore, as a general rule, death or insanity of either party before accepting the offer shall put an end to the offer, for a meeting of minds is obviously impossible when one of the parties has died or become insane.

Refusal or counter-offer An offer also comes to an end upon being rejected by the offeror. An offeree may expressly reject an offer by indicating that he/she is unwilling to accept it. He/she may also impliedly reject it by making a counter-offer. For instance, *A* says to *B*, 'I can sell my house to you for ₹10,000.' If *B* replies 'I am not interested to buy your house at all', it is an express rejection of the offer made by *A*. However, instead of rejecting the offer outrightly if *B* replies, 'I can purchase it for ₹9,000,' *A*'s offer has been met with a counter-offer that terminates the original offer. Once an offer is rejected, it cannot be revived later. Suppose *B* subsequently changes his mind and wants to pay ₹10,000, no contract would come into being since it would be a case of a fresh offer and not an acceptance of the original offer. The original offer will be deemed to have lapsed.

[25] 1921, 125 L.T. 690

Acceptance differs from the prescribed one The offer must be accepted in the very manner prescribed by the offeror, if any, failing which it would deem to have lapsed. For instance, *A* offers to sell his car to *B* and asks him to send his acceptance only by speed post. If *B* notifies *A* about his willingness to buy the car by some other mode, i.e., telephone, etc., *A* is not bound by his acceptance.

Subsequent illegality or destruction of subject matter An offer is also terminated if the performance of the contract it proposes has subsequently become illegal or unenforceable before the offer is accepted. For example, a firearms manufacturer offered to sell sophisticated weapons to another country. But two days later, before the offer was accepted, the government placed a ban on all such sales in the country of the purchaser. The offer thus stood terminated by the ban, as the offer subsequently became illegal. Similarly, an offer may also lapse on account of destruction of the subject matter of the offer before the acceptance. In some cases, subsequent illegality or destruction of subject matter can also serve as a legal excuse for a party's failure to perform his obligations under an existing contract.

Acceptance

Acceptance: Manifestation of assent to the terms of the offer.

Once the presence of a valid offer has been acknowledged, the next stage in the formation of an agreement is to find an acceptance of that offer. The acceptance must be made while the offer is in force, i.e., still open. An acceptance is a manifestation of assent to the terms of the offer. An offer *per se* cannot create legal relations between the parties unless accepted by the person to whom it was made.

Section 2(b) defines acceptance as, 'When the person to whom the proposal is made signifies his assent thereto, the proposal is said to be accepted. A proposal, when accepted, becomes a promise.'

Thus, an offer becomes irrevocable upon its acceptance. *Anson*[26] emphasizing the significance of acceptance observed, 'Acceptance to an offer is what

[26] Anson, William Reynell (1939), *Principles of the Law of Contracts*, 19th ed., Chicago

a lighted match is to a train of gunpowder.' Simply put, an acceptance brings the offer to an end because it then merges into the contract.

For instance, *A* offers to sell some goods to *B* for ₹500. *B* agrees to the price demanded by *A* and conveys the same to *A*. This is an acceptance of *A*'s offer by *B*. Now *A* is bound to sell the goods to *B* for the agreed price.

Acceptance of an offer may take place by express words—oral or written, or by conduct. For instance, *A* offers to sell his scooty to *B* for ₹5000. *B* may communicate his acceptance of this offer orally or by writing a letter to *A* (the offeror). In some cases, an acceptance may also be implied from conduct. For instance, when a passenger boards a bus there is an implied acceptance on his/her part to avail the service and is thus bound to pay the requisite fare.

Legal Rules Governing a Valid Acceptance

In order to be binding, an acceptance must fulfil the following conditions:

1. It should be made by the offeree.
2. It should be unconditional.
3. It should be communicated to the offeror.
4. It may be in any form, oral or written.
5. It should be in the mode prescribed by the offeror.
6. It should be given within a reasonable time, if no time limit is set.
7. It should be given while the offer is in force.

We shall study the significance and fall-out of each of these conditions that render an acceptance legally binding.

Acceptance by Offeree

An offer made to a particular person (specific offer) can be validly accepted either by him or by someone acting with his authority, and no one else. Likewise, an offer made to a group of persons (general offer) can be accepted by any member who belongs to that group provided he/she has the knowledge of the offer. The general rule is that if *X* wants to enter into a contract with *Y*, then a third person cannot substitute *Y* unless he/she has been so authorised. Thus, if an acceptance is communicated by a third party, it will not give rise to legal relations.

Acceptance Should Be Unconditional

In order to convert a proposal into promise, the acceptance must be absolute and unqualified, i.e., it must correspond directly with the terms of the offer [Section 7(1)]. Any alteration to the terms of offer constitutes a counter-offer, which will reject and extinguish an original offer. That is, the same cannot be revived by subsequent acceptance. Thus, to give a legal effect, an acceptance must conform to all the terms of the offer. An acceptance with a slightest variation from the terms of the offer may result in no acceptance at all. Besides, an acceptance must be in toto, i.e., for the whole of the offer. If only part of the offer is accepted, then the acceptance will not be binding and enforceable at law.

Acceptance to Be Communicated

The definition of acceptance given under section 2(b) emphasises that it should be signified. To become a promise, the acceptance must be communicated to the offeror or to his/her authorised agent. Mere mental assent to an offer, not expressed by words or conduct, does not lead to a binding contract. The case of *Brogden vs Metropolitan Railway Co*[27] is relevant at this point. In the above case, *B*, who had been supplying coal to a railway company without any formal agreement, suggested that a formal agreement be drawn up. The agents of both the parties met and a draft agreement was drawn. The agreement was approved by *B*, and then sent to the railway company for acceptance. The agent of the railway company, however, put the draft in his drawer and forgot. It was held that no contract had been concluded as the acceptance was never communicated to the offeror.

Acceptance May Take Any Form

An acceptance may take any form. It can be given either orally or in writing. Acceptance may also be inferred from the conduct, for example, despatching goods in response to an offer to buy. Thus, when a person performs the act intended by the proposer as the consideration for the promise offered by him/her, the performance of the act operates as an accep-

[27] 1877, 2 App. Cas. 666

tance, and no separate communication is required. Similarly, if somebody makes an offer by supplying the goods or rendering service and the other party chooses to consume them straight away, this also amounts to acceptance by conduct [*Weatherby vs Banham*[28]].

Acceptance to Be in the Prescribed Mode

The offeror, as the master of the offer, has the power to specify the precise time, place, and manner in which acceptance must be communicated. The offeree, in order to form a valid acceptance, must respond in the prescribed mode. Thus, the offeror asks for the acceptance to be sent to a particular place, an acceptance sent elsewhere will not bind him/her [*Frank vs Knight*[29]] nor, if he/she asks for an acceptance in writing, will he/she be bound by one that is oral [*Financings Ltd vs Stimson*[30]]. If the offeree conveys his/her acceptance in a manner different from the prescribed mode, it is up to the offeror whether to waive the stipulated mode or reject such an acceptance. However, if the offeror fails to inform the offeree within a reasonable time that he/she is not bound by his/her acceptance since it is not in the prescribed mode, he/she will be deemed to have accepted the acceptance and the same will result in a contract. Where the offeror does not prescribe any mode, the acceptance must be expressed in some usual and reasonable manner.

Acceptance to Be Given Within a Reasonable Time

If the offeror has fixed some time within which the offer should be accepted, the acceptance should be given within the stipulated time. On this account, the Calcutta High Court suggested that in such a situation it is enough if the acceptor has 'posted the acceptance before the stated time', even if it reaches the offeror after the fixed date. If no time has been stipulated, then the acceptance must be communicated within a reasonable timeframe. What is reasonable time, however, is a matter of fact for the judge to decide keeping in view the facts and circumstances of the case. In *Ramsgate Victoria Hotel Co. vs Montefiore*[31], an offer to buy shares in June accepted in November was held 'too late'.

The Offer Must Be in Force

An acceptance must succeed the offer, but it should be given before the offer ceases to exist. Once the offer stands lapsed or has been withdrawn in some way before the offeree accepts it, the acceptance is ineffective for there is no longer an offer to accept.

Mere Silence Is Not Acceptance

Since the law of contract usually requires some objective indication that an offeree intends to contract, the general rule is that an offeree's silence, vis-à-vis the offer made, cannot amount to an acceptance. In addition, an offeree who simply does nothing on receipt of an offer is not bound by the same. The underlying reason is that it is detrimental to impose on a person, who does not wish to accept the offer, the trouble and expense of rejecting it, i.e., the duty to respond. Thus, the offeror cannot unilaterally impose the term that silence shall be deemed to be assent. The offeror can prescribe the manner of acceptance but not the manner of rejection.

The following case provides an interesting illustration in this regard. In *Felthouse vs Bindley*, *A* offered to buy his nephew's horse for $33.5 by a letter in which he said, 'If I hear no more about the horse, I shall consider the horse is mine at $33.5'. The nephew did not reply, but he told the defendant, his auctioneer, not to sell that particular horse because it had already been sold to his uncle. The auctioneer, by mistake, sold the horse by including it in an auction sale of the nephew's property. A sued the auctioneer for damages. The court held that the plaintiff had no claim against the auctioneer as the nephew did not communicate his intention to his uncle.

However, the general rule that, 'offeree's silence not amounting to acceptance' is subject to certain exceptions. The circumstances of a case sometimes impose a duty on the offeree to reject the offer firmly, or else be bound by its terms. Customary trade practice or prior dealings between the parties may indicate that silence objectively signals acceptance.

[28] 1832, 5 C. & P. 228
[29] 1962, 1 W.L.R. 1184
[30] 1866, L.R. 1 Ex 109
[31] 1862, 11 C.B.N.S. 869

Communication of Offer, Acceptance, and Their Revocation

In order to be effective, offer and acceptance must be communicated, either orally or in writing or by conduct. An offer cannot take effect until it is received, for unless the offeree knows about it he/she cannot take any action. Similarly, an acceptance is ineffectual to conclude a contract until it is communicated to the offeror or his authorised agent. In other words, lack of communication of offer to the offeree and its acceptance to the offeror does not create any legal relations between the parties.

Where both the parties transact face to face, either in person or over telephone or through Internet, there is instantaneous communication of offer and its acceptance. The problem arises when the parties are at a distance and the conventional mail is the proper method of communication between them. In such a situation the moot question is whether the contract concludes when the acceptance is posted (by the offeree), or when it is received (by the offeror). This is because the moment the communication is complete, the parties lose the right of withdrawal or revocation.

Communication of Offer

The communication of an offer is complete when it comes to the knowledge of the person to whom it was made [Section 4].

Thus, when the letter containing the offer reaches the offeree, the communication of offer is complete. For example, *A* proposes, by a letter, to sell a house to *B* at a certain price. The letter is posted on 1st May and reaches *B* on 3rd May. The communication of the proposal is complete when *B*, the offeree, receives the letter, i.e., on 3rd May. Suppose the letter containing the offer was lost in transit, and *B* after knowing about the offer from some other source, mails his acceptance to *A*. This will not amount to proper communication of offer and hence no contract will result in.

Communication of Acceptance

Section 4 also provides that, the communication of an acceptance is complete, as against/for

1. the proposer, when it is put in a course of transmission to him, so as to be out of the power of the acceptor.
2. the acceptor, when it comes to the knowledge of the proposer.

Thus, the offeror is bound by the acceptance as soon as the letter of acceptance is properly mailed or despatched to him/her by the acceptor. However, the acceptor (i.e., offeree) shall be bound by his/her acceptance only upon its reaching the offeror. The consequences of the post rules can thus be remarkable (see Box 1.9).

But the acceptor will not be bound by his/her acceptance until it is received by the offeror. For example, *B* accepts *A*'s proposal through a letter sent by post. The communication of the acceptance is complete as against

1. *A*, when the letter is posted
2. *B*, when *A* receives the letter

It is important to note that where acceptance is by word of mouth it is not enough that it be spoken; it must actually be heard by the offeror.

Thus, if an acceptance is not received because of disturbance in a telephone line, or because the offeree's words are too indistinct to be heard by the offeror, there is no contract.

Box 1.9 When Post-malfunction Affects the Course of a Contract

In *Household Fire Insurance Co. vs Grant*, 1879, the defendant applied for 100 shares in the plaintiff company. The company received his application form, and its secretary consequently completed and posted a letter of allotment to the defendant and entered the name of the defendant in the register of shareholders.

The letter, however, never arrived. Sometime later, the company went into liquidation, and the liquidator claimed the payment outstanding on the shares from the defendant. It was held that the defendant was liable for this sum. The shares became his property as soon as the letter of allotment was posted, even though he never received it, and was thereby unaware that he had becomea shareholder.

Communication of Revocation of Offer or Acceptance

The communication of revocation is complete as against the person who makes it, when it is put into a course of transmission to the person to whom it is made, so as to be put out of the power of the person who makes it; as against the person to whom it is made, when it comes to his knowledge [Section 4].

This means that the communication of revocation of offer is complete for the person revoking it when the letter of revocation is posted, and for the person to whom it is made when the letter of revocation reaches him.

For instance, *A* of Delhi offers by post to sell his car to *B* of Mumbai for ₹2 lakh. The letter is posted on November 1 and it reaches *B* on November 3. *B* accepts the offer with a letter sent by post on November 3, which is received by *A* on November 5. However, *A* revokes his offer with a telegram sent on November 2. The telegram reaches *B* on November 3 after *B* has already mailed his acceptance. The revocation of the offer is complete as against *A*, as the telegram had already been despatched on November 2. It is complete as against *B* the moment the telegram reached him, i.e., on November 3. *B* revokes his acceptance with a telegram sent on November 4. The telegram containing *B*'s revocation reaches *A* on November 5. *B*'s revocation of acceptance is complete as against *B* the moment he despatched the telegram on November 4, and as against *A* when it reaches him, i.e., on November 5.

Thus, the law has given a chance both to the offeror and to the acceptor to withdraw their proposal and acceptance, respectively, in due course of time. In this regard, Section 5 clearly provides that, 'a proposal may be revoked at any time before the communication of its acceptance is complete as against the proposer, but not afterwards. An acceptance may be revoked at any time before the communication of the acceptance is complete as against the acceptor, but not afterwards'.

In Bhagwandas Goverdhandas kedia v. Girdharilal Parshottamdas & Co. (see Box 1.10), Supreme Court held that in the case of telephonic conversation, the position is the same as in the case where the parties are in the presence of each other, and the rule of a contract through post does not apply to such contracts. In case of acceptance sent by post, the contract is concluded when the letter of acceptance is posted, whereas in the case of acceptance by phone, the contract is deemed to be complete when the offeror hears the acceptance at his end rather than when the acceptor speaks the words of acceptance.

Consequence of Unlawfully Repudiating a Contract[33]

In a reminiscence of law of land's strong disapproval of illegitimate breach of a contract, an international arbitration court has recently directed Antrix, the marketing arm of Indian Space Research Organization (ISRO), for promotion and commercialization of space products, technical consultancy services, and transfer of technologies developed by the latter to pay $672 million or ₹4,435.20 crore, in damages to Devas Multimedia, a Bengaluru-based Satellite Communications and Technology Company, for "unlawfully" cancelling a contract. The International Court of Arbitration (ICA) of the International Chamber of Commerce (ICC) had unanimously ruled in favour of Devas Multimedia and found that Antrix is liable for unlawfully terminating the Devas-Antrix agreement in 2011. Besides damages and pre-award interest totaling $672 million, the ICC Tribunal also awarded to the plaintiff post-award interest accruing at 18% per annum on that sum until the award is fully paid.

According to the contract signed in January 2005, Devas was to lease 70MHz of S-band spectrum from two satellites that were to be launched by ISRO. Devas was to pay $300 million for the right to use the airwaves for 12 years, which could be further extended by another corresponding period. The company intended to use the airwaves to provide communication services, using a combination of satellite and terrestrial technology. However, the Central Government (Antrix being a PSU) in 2011 cancelled the contract assigning lack of technical feasibility for delivering the deal.

---

32 1966 AIR 543

33 Adapted from, "Court Orders Antrix to Pay $672 m to Devas", *The Economic Times*, New Delhi, 30 Sep'15, pp 1,12.

Box 1.10 **Bhagwandas Goverdhandas Kedia v. M/s. Girdharilal Parshottamdas & Co.**[32]

Facts: Plaintiff offered to get certain goods supplied at Ahmedabad to defendants who accepted the offer at Khamgaon and that payment was also to be made at Khamgaon. On defendants' failure to supply requisite goods, plaintiff sued them at Ahmedabad. Dispute arose as to where was contract formed-at Khamgaon where acceptance was given by defendants or at Ahmedabad where acceptance was received by plaintiffs.

Contentions(s): Defendants contended that according to the section 2, 3 and 4 of ICA, the place where the offer is accepted is the place where the contract is made and therefore, Ahmedabad trial court did not have the jurisdiction to try the suit.

Held: When a **contract** is made by conversation on telephone, the place where acceptance of offer is intimated to the offeror, is the place where the **contract** is made, and therefore the Civil Court at Ahmedabad had jurisdiction to try the suit.

Court's Observations:

- The contract act does not expressly deal with the place where a contract is made. The conversation over telephone is analogous to the conversation when the parties are in presence of each other, wherein, the negotiations are concluded by **instantaneous speech** and therefore, **communication of the acceptance becomes a necessary part of the contract** and the exception to the rule on grounds of commercial inexpediency is inapplicable.
- Further, in case of correspondence by post or telegram, a third agency intervenes which is responsible for effective transmission of letters at every instance, however, in case of telephonic conversation, once the connection has been established, there is no need of any third agency to transmit the correspondence between the parties.

But the Court held that when a **contract** is made by conversation on telephone, the place where acceptance of offer is intimated to the offeror, is the place where the **contract** is made, and therefore the Civil Court at Ahmedabad had jurisdiction to try the suit. Hence, as against cases of correspondence by post or telegram, in present case where there was correspondence by telephone, contract was formed when acceptance was duly communicated to the offeror and hence, at Ahmedabad.

According to the Tribunal, the defendant had no legal justification for terminating the agreement and, thus, unlawfully repudiated the pact. In its ruling, the tribunal noted that the agreement between Devas and Antrix concluded after several rounds of discussion and scrutiny, and that for five years, the two parties had cooperated in executing the deal, with Antrix/ISRO building the satellites and Devas obtaining licences and capital necessary to deliver the planned services in India. However, after five years of cooperation, Antrix moved to terminate the pact in February 2011, arguing that it was entitled to do so as it had not been able to obtain the necessary frequency and orbital slot coordination necessary to launch and operate satellites. Devas disagreed with Antrix's reasons for cancelling the deal and sought negotiations but Antrix refused to engage, which forced the company to start arbitration proceedings in June 2011.

Case Highlights

Jan 2005: ISRO arm Antrix signs deal with Devas, which involves building, launching, and operating two satellites and leasing spectrum capacity on those satellites to Devas.

Feb 2011: Antrix decides to terminate the pact as it had not been able to obtain frequency and orbital slot coordination necessary to launch and operate the satellites. Devas, however, rejects Antrix's assertions and seeks talks but the latter refuses.

Jun 2011: Devas along with US investment firms Columbia Capital LLC and Telecom Ventures LLC – all investors in Devas– moves ICC Tribunal, and seeks damages.

Sep 2015: Tribunal directs Antrix to pay $672 m to Devas; also sets simple interest @ 18% p.a. until Antrix pays the full amount, which is about $336,000 per day.

Exercises

I. Objective-type Questions

1. State whether each of the following statements is True or False:
   (i) The law of contract is concerned with only those obligations that arise out of an agreement.
   (ii) All contracts are agreements.
   (iii) Agreement and its enforceability constitute a contract.
   (iv) The terms 'executory contract' and 'bilateral contract' convey the same meaning.
   (v) In commercial and business agreements, the presumption is that the parties intend to create legal obligations.
   (vi) Cross-offer and counter-offer convey the same meaning.
   (vii) An implied offer is inferred from the conduct of the parties or the circumstances of the particular case.
   (viii) A mere mental acceptance not evidenced by words or conduct, in the eye of law, is no acceptance.
   (ix) Anyone on behalf of the offeree may communicate acceptance.
   (x) Death or insanity of the offeror causes the offer to terminate automatically.

2. Fill in the blanks:
   (i) Offer and its acceptance constitute ________.
   (ii) ________ is concluded and binding on the concerned parties.
   (iii) A contract that is made by words either spoken or written is said to be ________.
   (iv) A contract is ________, if the consent of a party is not free.
   (v) In the case of ________ agreements, even the collateral agreements become void.
   (vi) ________ is a medium through which a person signifies to another his willingness to do or to abstain from doing anything.
   (vii) The offer must be distingushed from ________.
   (viii) Once an offer is accepted it becomes a ________ and cannot be ________.
   (ix) An offer lapses if it becomes illegal ________ it is accepted.
   (x) The communication of ________ is complete when it comes to the knowledge of the person to whom it is made.

3. Indicate the correct answer:
   (i) Which of the following is not an essential element of a valid contract?
      (a) Offer and acceptance
      (b) Free consent and consideration
      (c) Lawful object
      (d) Performance
   (ii) Which of the following contracts is based on execution?
      (a) Express contract
      (b) Implied contract
      (c) Unilatéral contract
      (d) Unenforceable contract
   (iii) Which of the following is not a void agreement?
      (a) Agreement in restraint of marriage
      (b) Agreement in restraint of trade
      (c) Agreement in restraint of legal proceeding
      (d) Service rendered without mandate
   (iv) A void contract is
      (a) Not enforceable at all
      (b) Enforceable at the option of either party
      (c) Enforceable at the option of the aggrieved party only
      (d) Enforceable at the option of the party who is not aggrieved

(v) A valid contract becomes a void contract due to
- (a) Supervening impossibility
- (b) Change of law
- (c) Repudiation of a voidable contract
- (d) All of the above

(vi) Identical offers made by two parties to each other, in ignorance of each other's offer are known as
- (a) Counter offer
- (b) Cross-offers
- (c) Standing offer
- (d) None of the above

(vii) An offer comes to an end
- (a) By lapse of stipulated or reasonable time
- (b) By death or insanity of the offeror or the offeree before acceptance
- (c) By revocation by the offeror or rejection by the offeree
- (d) In all the above cases

(viii) To make an effective acceptance, which of the following requirements must be fulfilled?
- (a) Acceptance must be absolute and unqualified
- (b) Acceptance must be communicated to the offeror
- (c) Acceptance must be in the prescribed manner
- (d) All of the above

(ix) An offer which is allowed to remain open for acceptance over a period of time is known as
- (a) General offer
- (b) Specific offer
- (c) Standing offer
- (d) Counter-offer

(x) Which of the following rule does not apply to a valid offer?
- (a) The offer must be capable of creating legal relations
- (b) The offer must be certain, definite, and not vague
- (c) The offer must be communicated
- (d) The offer must be unconditional

II. Review Questions

1. 'An agreement enforceable by law is a contract.' Comment. Also enumerate the essentials of a valid contract.

   OR

   'All contracts are agreements but all agreements are not contracts.' Comment. Also explain the essential elements of a valid contract.
2. 'All illegal agreements are void but all void agreements are not necessarily illegal'. Comment. Bring out the differences between an illegal agreement and void agreement. Give examples.
3. Distinguish between the following:
   (a) Void contract and voidable contract
   (b) Contract and agreement
   (c) Executed contract and executory contract
   (d) Illegal contract and unenforceable contract
   (e) Unilateral contract and bilateral contract
4. Write short notes on the following:
   (a) Voidable contract
   (b) Intention to create legal relationship
   (c) Executory contract
5. What is an offer? When does an offer become a promise? Explain the rules governing a valid offer.
6. When does an offer cease to exist?
7. Distinguish the following with suitable examples

(a) Offer and an invitation to offer
(b) General offer and specific offer
(c) Cross-offers and counter-offer
(d) Express offer and implied offer
(e) Revocation of offer and rejection of offer
(f) Contract and MoU

8. Define acceptance. Discuss the rules governing a valid acceptance.
9. Comment on the following
(a) Contracts over telephone (b) Standing offer
(c) Revocation of acceptance (d) Communication of offer
10. If the offeror does not fix any time for acceptance, when can the offer deem to have been revoked? What happens if an offer is not accepted in the prescribed mode?

III. Caselets

1. *A* invited *B* and his family to dine with him on a special occasion. *B* accepted the invitation but failed to turn up. Can *A* sue *B* for the damages?
[**Hint:** No, the agreement being of social nature does not create a duty enforceable by law]

2. *A* has two PCs—P III and P IV. He offers to sell his P III machine to *B*, while *B* is under the impression that he is buying P IV. How would you deal with this communication gap in the context of the Indian Contract Act.
[**Hint:** There is no agreement for lack of *consensus ad idem*]

3. X, a trader, delivered certain goods at Y's house by mistake. *Y* treated the goods as his own and consumed them. Discuss the remedy available to *X*.
[**Hint:** Quasi contract, '*B*' is bound to pay for the goods]

4. *A* engages *B* to assault *C*. *B* does so. To pay *B*, *A* borrows ₹5000 from *D* who is aware of the purpose of the loan. Can *B* recover the amount from *A*? What is the nature of agreement between *A* and *D*?
[**Hint:** Transactions and collateral transactions flowing from illegal agreements are also illegal]

5. *A* agreed to pay *B* ₹1,00,000 if *B* shifted his real estate business from the area where the former was doing the same business. *B* promised but later refused to do so. Discuss the validity of the agreement.
[**Hint:** Agreement in restraint of trade is void under Section 27]

6. *A* offers to sell *B* 100 litres of oil. Does it constitute a valid offer?
[**Hint:** No, the offer is not capable of being accepted for want of certainty]

7. *A* offered to sell his diamond ring to *B* for £280. *B* replied purporting to accept and enclosed £80, promising to pay the balance of £200 by monthly instalments of £50 each. Is *B's* acceptance enforceable?
[**Hint:** No. *B's* acceptance is no acceptance but a counter-offer (*Refer Neale vs Merret*[34])]

8. X makes an offer by a letter to Y on a particular day. Two days later, X revokes his offer by a telegram. The telegram reaches the offeree *Y* after the letter. Will the offer be deemed to have been revoked?
[**Hint:** Yes, provided the letter of acceptance has not been posted]

9. *A* gives an advertisement in the newspaper that he would auction his household furniture on 15 July 2008 at his residence at Ghaziabad. *B* from New Delhi reaches *A's* residence on the appointed date and time to find that *A* had subsequently cancelled the auction. What is the remedy available to *B* against *A*?
[**Hint:** Auctions are invitations to treat and not offers]

10. *X* offered a reward to anyone who would restore him his lost dog. *Y* brought the dog to *X* without any knowledge of the offer of reward. Can *Y* claim the reward?

[33] 1930, W.N. 189

Answers to Objective-type Questions

1.	(i) True	(ii) True	(iii) True	(iv) True	(v) True
	(vi) False	(vii) True	(viii) True	(ix) False	(x) False
2.	(i) agreement	(ii) contract	(iii) express	(iv) voidable	(v) illegal
	(vi) Offer	(vii) invitation to treat	(viii) promise, revoked		
	(ix) before	(x) offer			
3.	(i) (d)	(ii) (c)	(iii) (d)	(iv) (a)	(v) (d)
	(vi) (b)	(vii) (d)	(viii) (d)	(ix) (c)	(x) (d)

1 Chapter in Review

LEARNING OUTCOMES

LO 1 Defining a contract
LO 2 Contract distinguished from agreement
LO 3 Agreements and contracts distinguished from MoU
LO 4 Contracts classified
LO 5 E-contracts
LO 6 Illegal and unenforceable agreements distinguished
LO 7 Defining an offer
LO 8 Essentials of a valid offer
LO 9 Acceptance; legal rules governing a valid acceptance
LO 10 Communication of offer, acceptance, and their revocation

KEY TERMS

Contract: An agreement that legally binds the parties.

Agreement: Every promise or set of promises forming consideration for each other.

Promise: A commitment given by one party (promisor) to another (promisee).

Valid contract: A contract that fulfils all legal requirements.

Void contract: A contract that has no binding influence on any party.

Unenforceable contract: A contract which may be valid otherwise, but cannot be enforced by one or both the parties because of some technical flaw.

Executory contract: A contract in which the reciprocal promises or obligations, which serve as consideration, are yet to be carried out.

Implied contract: A legally enforceable agreement arises from some non-verbal conduct, or assumed intentions, or relationship between the immediate parties, or the application of the legal principle of equity.

LO1 A contract is fundamentally an agreement that legally binds the parties. The formation of a contract is generally a two-step process in which one party makes a proposal and the other responds to that proposal. Agreements of domestic, social, moral, or religious agreements cannot be regarded as contracts because they do not produce, or are not intended to produce any legal binding between the parties.

LO2 All agreements are contracts if they are made by the free consent of parties competent to contract for a lawful consideration and with a lawful object and are not hereby expressly declared to be void.

LO3 An agreement, in its formal sense, is a set of promises, done usually voluntarily, forming consideration for each other whereas a contract is a legally enforceable agreement between the parties that creates an obligation to do or not do (i.e. abstinence) a particular thing. A 'Memorandum of Understanding' (MoU), on other hand, is (also) an agreement between two or more parties, except unlike a contract, it needs not contain legally enforceable promises.

LO4 Contracts may broadly be classified as Valid contracts, Void contracts, and Voidable contracts; Unenforceable contracts and Illegal contracts; Executed contracts and Executory contracts; Express contracts and Implied contracts; Unilateral contracts and Bilateral contracts; and Quasi contracts.

LO5 A contract over telephone, and presumably, by fax and e-mail operate on the same footing as an oral agreement negotiated by the parties in the actual presence of each other.

LO6 An illegal agreement is void *ab initio*. In the eye of the law not only illegal agreements are unenforceable as such but any other agreement collateral to or arising from such agreements are also unenforceable.

LO7 An offer is a medium through which a person expresses his intention to enter into a contractual obligation in return for a promise or an act or forbearance.

LO8 In order to be legally winning, an offer should be capable of creating legal obligations, its terms must be certain, it must be made to obtain the consent of the offeree, it must be communicated.

Unilateral contract: A contract in which one of the parties performs its promises at the time of making the contract and the other party promises to perform in the future.

Bilateral contract: A contract in which both the parties are to perform their respective promises or obligations at some future time but not necessarily concurrently.

Quasi contract: The act of a person, permitted by law, by which he/she obligates himself/herself towards another or binds himself/herself to him/her, without any agreement between them.

E-commerce: The practice of buying and selling goods, services and information online i.e. by Internet applications.

E-contract: Any kind of contract formed in the course of e-commerce by the interaction of two or more individuals using electronic means, such as e-mail; the interaction of an individual with an electronic agent, such as a computer program; or the interaction of at least two electronic agents that are programmed to recognize the existence of a contract.

Offer: A medium through which a person expresses his intention to enter into a contractual obligation against a promise or an act or forbearance.

Invitation to treat: An invitation to another person to make an offer.

MoU: A document that describes the broad outlines of an agreement that two or more parties have reached. While not necessarily legally binding, an MoU signals that a binding contract is imminent.

Cross-offers: Identical offers made by two parties to each other, in ignorance of each other's offer.

Standing offer: An offer that is kept open for acceptance over a period of time.

Counter-offer: An alternative offer or proposal made by the offeree in substitution for the original one.

Revocation of offer/acceptance: Taking back, withdrawing, or cancelling an offer/acceptance.

Acceptance: Manifestation of assent to the terms of the offer.

LO9 An acceptance is a manifestation of assent to the terms of the offer. An offer *per se* cannot create legal relations between the parties unless accepted by the person or group of persons to whom it is made. An offer becomes irrevocable upon its acceptance.

LO10 In order to be effective, offer and acceptance must be communicated, either orally or in writing or by conduct. The law has given a chance to both the offeror and the acceptor to withdraw their proposal and acceptance respectively. Accordingly, an offer may be revoked at any time before the communication of its acceptance is complete as against the proposer but not afterwards. An acceptance may be revoked at any time before the communication of the acceptance is complete as against the acceptor but not afterwards.

CHAPTER

2 Consideration and Legality of Object

Learning Objectives

LO 1 Consideration defined
LO 2 Rules governing valid consideration
LO 3 Validity of agreement without consideration
LO 4 Bearing of lawful object on the validity of contract
LO 5 When the object or consideration is deemed to be unlawful
LO 6 Effect of partial illegality

If the parties to a contract intend to show that their agreement is part of a bargain, each side must promise to give or do something for the other. This is simply because a promise is not binding unless it is made for something in return. The requirement of something in return is referred to as 'consideration'. For instance, the seller of goods undertakes to transfer ownership in the goods and specifies the price to be paid by the buyer for acquiring the ownership. Similarly, an employer indicates the type of work the employee will be required to perform and promises remuneration for doing it. Thus, consideration is fundamental to the formation of any contract unless not made by deed.

Besides, to be enforceable, a contract must be made for a lawful object or purpose. Courts will not enforce a contract the object of which is illegal or will violate public policy. Such contracts are considered void. For example, a gambling contract would be illegal in many states.

Consideration Defined

Consideration: Something in return; a positive act or some forbearance.

Consideration implies that both the contracting parties undertake to give something 'of value' to each other.

Section 2(d) says, 'When at the desire of the promisor, the promisee or any other person has done or abstained from doing, or does or abstains from doing, or promises to do or to abstain from doing something, such an act or abstinence or promise is called a consideration for the promise.'

The above definition shows that the term 'consideration' is used in the sense of *quid pro quo*, meaning, thereby, something in return. It may involve a positive act (i.e., doing something), or abstinence (i.e., giving up something). Thus, consideration may be in the form of some right, interest, profit, or benefit accruing to one party, or some forbearance, detriment, loss, or responsibility given, suffered or undertaken by the other. Nevertheless paying or promising to pay money in return for the supply of goods or services happens to be the most common form of consideration. A few examples of what is considered as consideration in the eyes of the law are given in Box 2.1.

Rules Governing Consideration

The rules governing consideration in the context of the contract are as follows:

1. A contract must be supported by consideration
2. Consideration must move at the desire of the promisor (promissory estoppels)
3. Consideration may move from the promisee or any other person
4. Consideration must have some value
5. Consideration must be defined as benefit or detriment
6. Consideration must be defined as past, present, or future consideration

Box 2.1 What is Consideration?

Example 1

A offers to sell his plasma TV set to *B* for ₹50,000. *B* accepts the offer. Here, *B*'s promise to pay ₹50,000 is the consideration for *A*'s promise to sell the TV and *A*'s promise to sell the TV is the consideration for *B*'s promise to pay ₹50,000.

Example 2

A promises *Y*, his debtor, not to file a recovery suit against him on *B*'s agreeing to repay the amount of loan along with a compound interest at the rate of 12 per cent, per annum within a year. Here, abstinence on the part of *A* to file a suit is the consideration for *Y* based on *B*'s promise to pay.

Example 3

A promises to maintain *B*'s child, and *B* promises to pay *A* ₹1000 annually for the purpose. Here, the promise of each party is the consideration for the promise of the other party [*Illustration appended to Section 23*].

Box 2.2 Consideration at Desire of Third Person Not Valid

In *Durga Prasad vs Baldeo, D* the plaintiff had constructed, at his own expense, a market at the instance of the Collector of the District. The occupants of the shops, i.e., shopkeepers in the market promised to pay the plaintiff a commission on the articles sold through their shops. Subsequently, the shopkeepers refused to pay any commission. *D* sued the shopkeepers against their alleged default. It was held that there was no consideration because the plaintiff (the promisee) had constructed market not at the desire or request of the defendants (the promisors), but at the desire of a third person (i.e., the Collector) to oblige him, and thus the contract between *D* and the shopkeepers was void.

7. Consideration need not be adequate, but it must be sufficient
8. Consideration must be legal.

These rules are eloborated in the following subsections.

Contract Must Be Supported by Consideration

In the absence of a valid consideration passing between the parties, the contract will be of no legal effect. Section 25 provides that, subject to certain exceptions (which have been dealt with later in the chapter), an agreement made without consideration is void. The purpose of the requirement of consideration is to put some legal limits on the enforceability of agreements even when they are intended to be legally binding otherwise and are not vitiated by factors, such as mistake, misrepresentation, and illegality. Consideration acts as an aid in determining whether promises are worth enforcing. The existence of a consideration implies that the parties have devoted some reflection to the matter, and seriously desire their promises to have legal consequences. In English Law also, no single promise is enforceable unless it is either made in a *deed*[1] or supported by some consideration.

Consideration Must Move at the Desire of the Promisor

Section 2(d) of the Act provides that consideration must move at the desire of the promisor. Accordingly, for a promise to be binding as a contract, it is not sufficient that it is supported by some consideration but also that the consideration has been supplied at the desire of the promisor. This follows that if an *act*[2] is committed at the desire or request of a third person and not the promisor, that act does not amount to a valid consideration. In other words, whatever is done must be done at the desire or request of the promisor and not voluntarily or at the desire of a third party. For instance, if *A* rushes to the rescue of *B* whose house has been trapped in fire, it is not a consideration but a voluntary act on the part of *A*. *A* cannot ask *B* to compensate him for the services rendered by him as *B* had never requested him to help. However, if *A* goes to *B*'s rescue at the latter's express request, this will be regarded as consideration as *A* did not wish to do the act voluntarily. The case law illustration in Box 2.2 will help us understand the point better.

Consideration May Move from the Promisee

The second rule as to consideration as contained in the definition of Section 2(d) is that the act, which is to constitute a consideration, may be done by 'the promisee or any other person'. This means that as long as there is a consideration for the promise, it is immaterial who has furnished it. This is sometimes referred to as *Doctrine of Constructive Consideration*. It may proceed from the promisee, or if the promisor has no objection, from any other person who is not a party to the contract. But the English Law on this point is different. In the United Kingdom,

[1] As per Section 9 of English Common Law, consideration is not necessary for the validity of a promise in a deed. The binding force of such a promise does not depend on contract at all. Thus, it can take effect, although the person in whose favour it was made did not know of it.

[2] The word 'act' for the purpose of this discussion, includes 'abstinence'.

Box 2.3 Consideration from a Third Party: Chinnayya vs Ramaya

In this case, *A*, by a deed of gift, handed over certain property to her daughter with a direction that the daughter should pay an annuity to *A*'s brother. On the same day the daughter executed a document in favour of *A*'s brother agreeing to pay the annuity. But subsequently, the daughter declined to fulfil her promise. *A*'s brother sued the daughter. The daughter's defence was thus: As the promisee (*A*'s brother) had not furnished the consideration, she was not bound by her promise. The court, however, held that the words 'the promisee or any other person' in Section 2(d) clearly show that the consideration need not necessarily move from the promisee, it may move from a third party. Hence, *A*'s brother, though a stranger to the consideration, was entitled to maintain the suit.

In the United Kingdom, this suit would have been dismissed for want of consideration, as according to the British Law, consideration must move from the promisee.

the consideration for the promise moved from third party is not recognised by British law and is, thus, unenforceable there. The famous case of *Chinnayya vs Ramaya* clarifies how a consideration can move from a third party. Box 2.3 will illustrate the case as follows.

Consideration Must Have Some Value

Another notable feature of valid consideration is the idea of reciprocity. 'Something of value' must be given for a promise in order to make it enforceable as a contract. An informal gratuitous promise, therefore, does not amount to a contract[3]. A person or body to whom a promise of gift is made from purely charitable or sentimental motive gives nothing for the promise. Justice Patterson observed in *Thomas vs Thomas*[4] that consideration means something which is of some value in the eyes of the law. It may be some benefit to the plaintiff or some detriment to the defendant.

Benefit and Detriment

Lush J. in *Currie vs Misa* concentrated on the requirement that 'something of value' must be given, and accordingly stated that consideration is either some detriment to the promisee (in that he may give value) or some benefit to the promisor (in that he may receive value). Thus, payment by a buyer is consideration for the seller's promise to deliver and can be described as a detriment to the buyer, or as a benefit to the seller. Conversely, delivery by a seller is consideration for the buyer's promise to pay and can be described either as a detriment to the seller or as a benefit to the buyer.

Past, Present, or Future Consideration

Depending on the circumstances and facts of each case, consideration may be either past, present, or future.

Past consideration In Section 2(d), the expression, 'has done or abstained from doing' is recognition of the doctrine of past consideration. Past consideration means a past act or forbearance that took place and is complete (wholly executed) before the agreement is made. Past consideration may consist of services rendered at request but without any promise at the time, or it may consist of voluntary services. Box 2.4 presents some examples of past consideration.

Present or executed consideration The expression in Section 2(d) 'does or abstains from doing' refers to present or executed consideration. It is an act or forbearance, which moves simultaneously with the promise. In other words, a consideration, which consists in the performance of an act or forbearance, is said to be executed at present.[5]

For instance, *A* pays ₹1000 to *B*, and *B* promises to deliver a certain quantity of wheat the following day. In this case, *A* pays the amount but *B* has merely made a promise. Therefore, the consideration paid by *B* is executed, whereas the consideration promised by *B* is executory. If *A* pays the price and *B* delivers the goods at the same time, consideration is said to be executed by both the parties.

[3] *Re Hudson* (1885), 54. L.J. Ch. 811
[4] 1842, 2 Q.B. 851
[5] 1896, ILR 20 Bom. 755

Box 2.4 Strangers to Contracts

Example 1

In *Sindha vs Abraham*[5], the plaintiff rendered services to *A*, the defendant, at his desire when he was a minor. These services were continued even after *A* attained the age of majority at his request. *A* subsequently promised to pay an annuity to the plaintiff. The Bombay High Court held that services rendered to a minor at his request and which were continued after attaining majority at the same request were good consideration for his promise to pay.

Example 2

A finds *B*'s purse and gives it to him. *B* sent promises to pay *A*'s expenses in doing so. This is a contract [Illustration appended to Section 25].

Future or executory consideration The expression 'promises to do or to abstain from doing' in Section 2(d) refers to future. Here the bargain consists of mutual promises. An example is an agreement in which the seller promises to deliver goods next week, and the buyer agrees to pay for them on delivery. However, consideration on part of one party may be executed, and on part of the other executory. Consider the following illustration in this behalf.

In a contract of general insurance, the policy holder pays the premium, and the insurance company, in return, promises to make good the value of the insured property, if it is damaged or lost. Here the promise made by the insurance company is a kind of executory consideration and insurance premium paid by the policy holder is a sort of executed or present consideration.

Consideration Need Not Be Adequate, But It Must Be Sufficient

Sufficiency of consideration is not the same thing as adequacy of consideration, at least in law. The word *adequate* in this context refers to fairly equal to the promise given. On the contrary, sufficiency is used here as a legal term, and it means that what is promised must be real, tangible, and have some actual value. The courts do not exist to repair bad bargains [*Haigh vs Brooks*[6]]. Adequacy will be decided by the parties themselves. Explanation 2, added to Section 25 states, 'An agreement to which the consent of the promisor is freely given is not void merely because the consideration is inadequate...' Thus, if *A* promises to sell his car worth ₹2,00,000 for ₹50,000 only, transaction shall not be invalid merely because it is not supported by adequate consideration. It is up to the parties to fix their own prices. Justice Blackburn in *Belton vs Madden*[7] observed that the adequacy of the consideration is for the parties to consider at the time of making the agreement, not for the court when it is sought to be enforced. Similarly, in case of a gratuitous bailment of goods, the fact that the owner has parted with the possession of the goods is sufficient consideration for a promise by the bailee to take reasonable care of the goods. However, the fact that the consideration is inadequate may be taken into account by the court in determining whether the consent of the promisor was freely given (Explanation 2 attached to Section 25). For example, *A* agrees to sell a house worth ₹5,00,000 for ₹50,000 only. *A* subsequently denies that his consent to the agreement was freely given. In this case, the fact that the consideration is inadequate may be taken into account by the court in deciding whether or not *A*'s consent was freely given.

Consideration Must Be Legal and Genuine

Consideration may not be adequate but must invariably be legal, i.e., it must not involve an illegal act. For example, promising to pay money to a witness to turn hostile. An illegal consideration makes the

[6] 1840, 10 A & E 309

[7] 1995, S.E. 299, 21 Ga

Box 2.5 **Strangers to Contracts**

Example 1

A is indebted to *B*. *A* sells his property to *C* who undertakes to discharge his debt vis-à-vis *B*. In case *C* fails to keep his promise, *B* has no right to sue *C* because privity of contract exists between *B* and *C*. *C* is a stranger to the contract (between *A* and *B*). The example is based on *Jamna Das vs Ram Autar*[8].

Example 2

In the famous English case of *Tweedle vs Atkinson*[9], *A* promised *B* to pay a certain amount to *B*'s son *C* on *C*'s marriage to *A*'s daughter, as the young man was to take up the new responsibilities of marital life. After the demise of both the contracting parties, *C* sued the executors of *A* (his father-in-law) upon the agreement between *A* and his father. It was held that *C* could not maintain the suit against the defendant, being stranger to the contract.

whole contract invalid. It should be noted that attempting to enter into an illegal contract might itself give rise to criminal liability.

Furthermore, consideration should not be physically impossible or illusory. For example, promise to double the money by magic or to make a dead man alive, are impossible acts, and, therefore, such promises constitute no consideration. Similarly, a son's promise to his father 'stop being a nuisance', or an agreement to 'perform an existing obligation' made with the promisor being illusory with no considerations.

'Stranger to a Contract' and 'Stranger to Consideration'

Stranger to a contract: One who is not party to the contract.

A stranger to a contract is one who is not a party to the contract. The rule that consideration 'may move from the promisee or any other person' implies that the consideration is permitted to be supplied by a third person (i.e., stranger) as well, thereby need not necessarily be supplied by the promisee himself. In other words, as long as there is a consideration in exchange of a promise, it is immaterial who has furnished it. Thus, a stranger to the consideration may maintain a suit. But the English Law on this point is different. In the United Kingdom, the rule is that consideration must 'move from the promisee', which means a person to whom a promise was made can enforce it only if he himself provided the consideration for it. Nonetheless, a stranger to a contract cannot sue upon a contract under both the British Law and the Indian Law. From this arises the *Doctrine of privity of contract*, discussed ahead.

Privity of Contract

'Doctrine of Privity': A person who has no personal interest in a contract can neither sue nor be sued on the contract.

The 'Doctrine of Privity' implies that, in general, a person who is not privy (i.e., having no personal interest or part in) to a contract, that is a third party, can neither sue nor be sued on the contract. The rule prevents the burden of a contract being imposed on a third party. Therefore, a stranger to the consideration must be distinguished from a stranger to a contract. The instances in Box 2.5 will help understand the concept better.

To sum up, in the eyes of the law, there can be a stranger to a consideration but not stranger to a contract.

Exceptions to the Doctrine of Privity of Contract

The rule that a stranger to a contract cannot sue on the contract is, however, subject to certain statutory exceptions under both the Indian Law and the English Law. Thus, a person who is not a party to a contract can sue upon it in the following cases:

1. Trust or charge
2. Assignment
3. Marriage settlements

[8] 1911, ILR 34 All 63
[9] 1861, 1 B & S 393

4. Family settlements
5. Agency
6. Acknowledgement of liability.

Trust or charge In the case of trust or charge, the beneficiary can enforce an agreement, even though he/she is not a party to it. For example, in *Khwaja Muhammad vs Hussaini Begum*[10], *K*, the father-in-law of *H*, executed an agreement with *H*'s father to pay ₹500 a month in perpetuity to the bride (*H*) in the name of *Kharchi-I-Pandan* (betel-leaf expenses) which is equivalent of pin money, in consideration of her marriage to his son. *K* also gave the charge of certain properties with payment to *H* and vested her (*H*) with the power to enforce it. However, *H* separated from her husband following a quarrel. This resulted in stoppage of allowance by *H*'s father-in-law, *K*. *H*, the plaintiff brought a suit against her father-in-law for the recovery of the arrears of the said annuity. The Privy Council held that although *H* was not a party to the agreement (as the agreement was between *K* and *H*'s father), yet, she was entitled, in equity, to enforce her claim.

Assignment In the case of assignment of a contract, when the benefit under a contract has been assigned, the assignee can sue upon the contract for the enforcement of his rights, title, and interest. [*Kishan Lal Sadhu vs Pramila Bala Dasi*[11]]. However, a mere nominee cannot sue on the policy as the nominee is not an assignee.

Marriage settlement In the case of certain marriage contracts, provision of marriage expenses to female members of Hindu Undivided Family entitles a female member to sue for such expenses on a partition of the family [*Sunder Raja vs Lakshm*[12]].

Family settlements In the case of a family settlement, if the terms of the settlement are reduced to writing, the members of the family, who originally had not been parties to the settlement, may enforce the agreement [*Shuppu vs Subramanium*[13]].

Agency Agency is a major common law exception to the doctrine of privity. A contract of agency arises when one person (the principal) appoints an agent to make a contract on his or her behalf with third parties. As a general rule, the principal, even if undisclosed, may sue the third party. We will learn about this aspect in details in Chapter 13.

Acknowledgement of liability In case someone acknowledges liability to a third person, a binding obligation is thereby incurred towards the former. This exception covers cases where the promisor by his conduct, acknowledgement, or otherwise, constitutes himself as an agent of the third party. For example, *A* receives money from *B* for paying it to *C*, the creditor of *B*. *A* subsequently makes part payment to *C* informing him that this was out of the money held for him. But *A* afterwards refuses to remit the balance. In this case, *C* will be entitled to recover the same from *A* [based on *Devaraja vs Ram Krishniah*[14]].

Contracts Without Consideration

As a general rule, an agreement made without consideration is void [Section 25]. Consideration is one of the essential elements to render a contract valid and enforceable. However, the Indian Contract Act contains certain exceptions that make a promise without consideration valid and binding, stated as under.

An agreement without consideration is valid if it is made out of natural love and affection, and if

1. made in writing
2. registered
3. promise to pay a debt barred by limitation law [Section 25(1)]

The case of *Venkataswamy vs Rangaswamy*[15] is illustrative on this count. In this case, an elder brother, on account of natural love and affection, promised to pay off the debts of his younger brother. The agreement was put into writing and was registered. The court held the agreement as valid and binding.

It should be noted that for an agreement to be enforceable under this clause, it is imperative that it be made out of natural love and affection. Mere existence of near relation between the parties does not necessarily import natural love and affection. For example, in *Rajlukhy Daber vs Bhootnath Mook-*

10 1910, 37 I. A. 152 12 Bom. L.R. 638
11 1928, Cal. 1315
12 1915, 38 Mad. 788
13 1964, 1 MLJ 121 (Mad.)
14 1952, AIR Mys. 109
15 1943, 2 MLJ 41 (Mad.)

Box 2.6 Compensation for Past Voluntary Services

Example 1

A finds B's missing purse and gives it back to B. B promises to give A ₹50. This is a valid contract.

Example 2

A supports B's infant son. B promises to pay A's expenses in doing so. This is a valid contract.

erjee[16], *B* the husband of *R* by a registered document, after referring to quarrels and disagreements between them, promised to pay his wife a sum of money for her maintenance and separate residence. It was held that the promise was unenforceable, as it was not made out of love and affection.

Promise to compensate for past voluntary services As per Section 25(2), a promise to compensate, wholly or in part, to a person who has already done something voluntarily for the promisor, or something that the promisor was legally compellable to do, is enforceable. Box 2.6 presents some illustrations appended to Section 25 on this count.

Promise to pay time-barred debt A promise made in writing and signed by the person to be charged therewith, or by his/her agent to pay a debt (wholly or in part) barred by the law of limitation, is valid without consideration [Section 25(3)]. For example, loan agreements and insurance contracts in which the promisor agrees to repay a debt or premium, respectively, fall in this category.

Completed gift Explanation 1 to Section 25 states that 'Nothing in this section shall affect the validity, as between the donor and donee, of any gift actually made.' Thus, in case of completed gifts (i.e., gifts actually made), the rule 'no consideration no contract' does not apply. Here nearness of relation between the parties is immaterial even if there may not be any natural love and affection between them.

Agency No consideration is mandatory to create an agency [Section 185].

Guarantee In a contract of guarantee, there is no consideration between the creditor and the surety [Section 127].

[16] 1900, 4 Cal WN 488

Legality of Object

Bearing a lawful object or aim is one of the essentials of a valid contract. As a general rule, even if all other requirements for the formation of a contract are complied with, but the object of the contract is illegal, the contract will not be enforceable. Section 10 of the Contract Act says, 'All agreements are contracts if they are made by the free consent of the parties competent to contract, for a lawful consideration and with a lawful object, and are not expressly declared to be void'. In the absence of a lawful object, an agreement is void and cannot become a contract. In this regard Section 23 specifically states, 'Every agreement of which the object or consideration is unlawful is void'. Thus, an unlawful object renders an agreement void *ab initio*.

What is a Lawful Object?

The consideration, or object of an agreement, is lawful unless it

1. is forbidden by law, or
2. is of such a nature that, if permitted, it would defeat the provisions of any law, or
3. is fraudulent, or
4. involves or implies injury to the person or property of another, or
5. is regarded as immoral by a court, or is opposed to public policy.

In each of these cases, the consideration or object of an agreement is said to be unlawful. Every agreement of which the object or consideration is unlawful is void. Box 2.7 presents some illustrations of agreements with unlawful objects which are appended to Section 23.

Box 2.7 **Agreements with Unlawful Objects**

Example 1

A, *B*, and *C* enter into an agreement for the division of gains acquired or to be acquired by them by fraud. The agreement is void as its object is unlawful.

Example 2

A, an agent of a land proprietor, agrees to obtain for *B* a lease of land belonging to his principal, without the knowledge of his principal. *A* also agrees on the money to be paid. The agreement between *A* and *B* is void, as it implies a fraud by concealment, by *A*, on his principal.

Example 3

A agrees to live with *B* as a concubine. The agreement is void, because it is immoral, though the act may not be punishable under the Indian Penal Code.

When the Object or Consideration is Deemed to be Unlawful?

In the light of the above provision, the circumstances which would make a consideration as well as object of an agreement unlawful, are discussed as under.

Forbidden by Law

Where the object or the consideration of an agreement is the performance of an act which is forbidden by law, the agreement is void. Acts or undertakings forbidden by law are those punishable under any statute as well as those prohibited (expressly or implicitly) by special legislations of Parliament and state legislatures. For example, the Excise Act prohibits the production or sale of excisable articles except upon a licence from the government. For this very reason, the sale of liquor without licence is prohibited (under the Excise Act) and is, therefore, illegal. A contract entered into in contravention of a statutory prohibition will be null and void whether such prohibition is express or implied. To sum up, all agreements involving breach of laws enacted for the protection or promotion of public interest are void. Box 2.8 provides examples of some void agreements.

Defeat the Purpose of Provisions of Any Law

Sometimes the object of, or the consideration for, an agreement is of such a nature that, though not directly forbidden by law, it would, if permitted, defeat the purpose of the provisions of the law. An agreement having such an object or consideration is void. Where a legislative enactment provides penalty

Box 2.8 **Void Agreements Forbidden by Law**

Example 1

A promises *B* to drop a prosecution which he instituted against *B* for robbery, while *B* promises to restore the value of the things taken. The agreement is void, as its object is unlawful [Illustration (h) appended to Section 23].

Example 2

Where a loan was granted to the guardian of a minor to arrange the minor's marriage has been held to be contrary to the enactment (Child Marriage Restraint Act) and, therefore, void. Therefore, the money advanced cannot be recovered [*Srinivas vs Raja Ram Mohan*].

Box 2.9 Agreements Based on Immorality Are Also Void

Example 1

A, a landlord, let his house on rent to B, a commercial sex worker, knowing that it would be used for immoral trafficking. The landlord cannot recover the rent. Here, the object being immoral, the agreement to pay rent is void [*Pearce vs Brookes*[18]].

Example 2

A agrees to let her daughter to B as a concubine. The agreement is void, because it is immoral, though the letting may not be punishable under the Indian Penal Code (45 of 1860) [Illustration (k) appended to Section 23].

for an act or promise, the performance of such an act or promise would amount to the defeat of that enactment, as it is implicit that the statute intends to forbid that act. For instance, *A*'s estate is sold for arrears of revenue under the provisions of an Act of the Legislature, by which the defaulter is prohibited from purchasing the estate. *B*, on an understanding with *A*, becomes the purchaser and agrees to convey the estate to *A* on receiving from him the price, which *B* has paid. The agreement is void, as it renders the transaction, in effect, a purchase by the defaulter and would so defeat the object of the law [Illustration appended to Section 23].

Fraudulent

An agreement the object of which is to defraud others is void. Where the parties agree to practice a fraud on a third person, not a party to the contract, their agreement is unlawful and void. The first two examples in Box 2.7 fall under this category.

To render an agreement unlawful and void on the basis of fraudulent object or consideration, the fraud must, however, be established beyond reasonable doubt and cannot be based on mere suspicion and conjecture.

Injurious to Person or Property

If the object of an agreement involves or implies injury to the person or property of another, the agreement is unlawful and void. For example, in *Ram Saroop vs Bansi*[17], a person borrowed ₹100, and in consideration, executed a bond in favour of the lender, also the plaintiff in this case. The person, in the bond, promised to work for him for two years failing which he agreed to pay a very exorbitant rate of interest and the principal amount at once. It was held that the contract was void since the promise contained in the bond was tantamount to slavery on part of the defendant, which is both injurious to a person and illegal.

Immoral

If the object or consideration of an agreement is opposed to morality, it is void. The following examples in Box 2.9 would help understand the point better.

Agreements Opposed to Public Policy

The term public policy in a wider sense means restriction of freedom of persons from doing something in the larger interest or for the good of the community. In the context of the Indian Contract Act, it restricts the freedom of persons to contract in certain areas which are detrimental to public interest. An agreement is void if the law regards it as opposed to public policy. In law, the doctrine of public policy covers many heads such as the following:

1. Trading with an alien enemy
2. Interference with administration of justice
3. Marriage brokerage agreements
4. Trafficking in public offices
5. Unfair or unreasonable dealings.

The ordinary function of the courts is to rely on the well-settled heads of public policy and to

[17] 1915, 42 Cal. 742

[18] 1866, L.R. 1, Ex 213

Box 2.10 What the Law Says on Partially Legal Agreements

Example 1

A promises to superintend on behalf of *B*, a legal manufacture of indigo, and an illegal trafficker in other articles. *B* promises to pay *A* a salary of ₹10,000 rupees per month. The agreement is void, as the object of *A*'s promise, and the consideration for *B*'s promise, is in part unlawful [Illustration appended to Section 24].

Example 2

A acquired a licence to sell opium and marijuana with the restriction that he would not take any partner in his ganja business without permission from the collector. He, however, admitted *B* into the whole business on receiving from him a fixed sum of money as his share of capital, without seeking the collector's permission. Later on because of some disagreement between the two, *B* sought a dissolution and refund of his capital.

It was held that the contract as to partnership was void and *B*'s claim was dismissed. The court in its verdict observed, 'it is impossible to separate the contract or to say how much capital was advanced for the opium and how much for the marijuana' [*Gopal Rao vs Kallappa*[19]].

apply them to varying situations. For example, *A*, the manager of a firm, agrees to pass a contract to *B* if the latter pays a sum of ₹5000 to the former privately. The agreement tends to create an interest against obligation and is void on the ground of trafficking in public offices.

Effect of Partial Illegality

If any part of a single consideration for one or more objects, or any one, or any part of any one of several considerations for a single object is unlawful, the agreement is void [Section 24]. Box 2.10 provides some examples in this regard.

The working rule behind the enforceability of such agreements was explained by Justice Wiles in *Pickering vs Illfracombe*[20] as, 'Where you cannot sever the illegal element from the legal part of a promise, the contract is altogether void, but where you can sever them whether the illegality be created by statute or by common law, you may reject the bad part and retain the good'.

In other words, where the illegal part can be severed or separated from the legal part (and, of course, effect can be given to the legal part), the contract is not altogether void but is valid in regard to that part of it which is legal. If, on the other hand, the different parts of the contract are so closely interknit that it is not possible to separate the legal from the illegal parts without destroying the whole, the contract is altogether void.

Where persons reciprocally promise, first to do certain things which are legal, and then, under specified circumstances, to do certain other things, which are illegal, the first set of promises is a contract, but the second part is a void agreement [Section 57]. For example, *A* and *B* agree that *A* shall sell *B* a house for ₹10,000, but if *B* were to use it as a gambling den, he would pay *A* ₹50,000. The first set of reciprocal promises is legal and, therefore, valid. However, the second set is for an unlawful object—that *B* may use the house as a gambling house—and is thus a void agreement.

Similarly, in the case of an alternative promise, one branch of which is legal and the other illegal, the legal branch alone can be enforced [Section 58]. For example, *A* and *B* agree that *A* shall pay *B* ₹1000 for which *B* shall afterwards deliver to *A* either rice or smuggled opium. This is a valid contract as far as delivery of rice is concerned, and a void agreement as to the supply of opium.

[19] 1901, 3 Bom. L.R. 164
[20] 1868, L.R. 3 C.P. 235, 250

Exercises

I. Objective-type Questions

1. State whether each of the following statements is True or False:
   (i) Consideration must move at the desire of the promisor.
   (ii) No agreement made without consideration is valid.
   (iii) A stranger to consideration may enforce a contract.
   (iv) Inadequacy of consideration will render the contract void.
   (v) Consideration may be past, present, or future.
   (vi) An agreement to procure the marriage of a person in consideration of a sum of money is voidable.
   (vii) An agreement for a 'fraudulent' purpose is void.
   (viii) Interference with marital relations being an immoral act is unlawful.
   (ix) An agreement, the object of which is opposed to the law of land, is void.
   (x) During the war an Indian citizen cannot enter into contract with an alien enemy.

2. Fill in the blanks:
   (i) There can be a stranger to ________ but not stranger to a ________.
   (ii) Consideration may move from the ________ or any third party.
   (iii) A contract without consideration is ________.
   (iv) For creation of an agency ________ is required.
   (v) Consideration to be valid must not only be supplied at the desire of the ________ but it also should be ________.
   (vi) In the name of public policy, freedom of contract is ________ by law in the interest of the community.
   (vii) An agreement to commit fraud is ________.
   (viii) An act intended to induce a public officer to act corruptly is opposed to ________.
   (ix) Sale of liquor without license is ________ and the price ________.
   (x) An agreement by a client to pay his lawyer according to the result of the case is ________.

3. Indicate the correct answer:
   (i) The expression 'quid pro quo' means adequacy of
   (a) Consideration (b) Something in return
   (c) Damage or injury to one's interest (d) None of the above
   (ii) Which of the following clauses is not mandatory as regards consideration?
   (a) Consideration must move at the desire of the promisor
   (b) Consideration may be past, present, or future
   (c) Consideration must be legal
   (d) Consideration must be adequate
   (iii) In which of the following cases the rule 'no consideration no contract' does not apply?
   (a) Agreements in writing (b) Promise to compensate
   (c) Creation of an agency (d) In all of the above cases
   (iv) The doctrine of 'Constructive consideration' implies:
   (a) As long as there is a consideration for a promise, it is immaterial who has furnished it.
   (b) Consideration must be real and not illusory.
   (c) Consideration must be legal.
   (d) Consideration must move at the desire of the promisor.
   (v) The term *nudum pactum* implies:
   (a) Something of value (b) Bare promise
   (c) Inadequacy of consideration (d) Stranger to consideration
   (vi) An act or a promise is forbidden by law when
   (a) It is punishable under the criminal law of the country or is prohibited by special legislation derived from the legislature
   (b) It defeats the provision of any law
   (c) It is fraudulent
   (d) It involves or implies injury to person or property of another

(vii) Consideration and object of an agreement are unlawful if
(a) It is forbidden by law
(b) It defeats the provisions of any law or it is fraudulent
(c) It involves or implies injury to the person or property of another or the court regards it as immoral or opposed to public policy
(d) In all the above cases

(viii) Dealings with commercial sex workers have already been regarded as
(a) Immoral (b) Opposed to public policy
(c) Forbidden by law (d) Fraudulent

(ix) Which of the following does not fall under the 'heads of public policy'?
(a) Trading with enemy (b) Illegal cohabitation
(c) Marriage breakage agreements (d) Trafficking in public offices

(x) What is the general rule to decide upon a partially illegal agreement/contract?
(a) If any part of a single consideration for one or more objects, or any one, or any part of any one of several considerations for a single object is unlawful, the agreement is void
(b) Where one cannot sever the illegal from the legal part of a covenant, the contract is altogether void; but where one can sever them, the bad part can be rejected and the good can be enforced provided the illegality is created by common law and not by statute
(c) Where one cannot sever the illegal from the legal part of a covenant, the contract is altogether void; but where one can sever them, the bad part can be rejected and the good can be enforced provided the illegality be created by statute and not by common law
(d) Where one cannot sever the illegal from the legal part of a covenant, the contract is altogether void; but where one can sever them, the bad part can be rejected and the good can be enforced whether the illegality be created by statute or common law

II. Review Questions

1. Define the term 'consideration'. Discuss in brief the legal rules governing valid consideration.
2. 'No consideration, no contract'. Do you agree? Explain.
3. 'Consideration need not be adequate but it must be certain, real, and lawful'. Explain.
4. 'A stranger to contract cannot sue, but a stranger to consideration can'. Elaborate.
5. Discuss the rule that a stranger to a contract cannot sue. Are there any exceptions to this rule?
6. State the exceptions to the rule, 'No consideration, no contract'.
7. Comment on the following:
   (a) Consideration may be past, present, or future
   (b) Consideration may move from the promisee or any other person on the latter's behalf
   (c) Stranger to consideration and stranger to contract
   (d) Legality of agreements without consideration
   (e) Consideration must be 'something of value'
8. Under what circumstances is the object of a contract deemed unlawful? Explain giving suitable examples.
9. Explain the doctrine of public policy. Give instances of agreements that are considered contrary to public policy. Discuss also the heads of public policy in brief.
10. Discuss and illustrate the enforceability of a partially illegal agreement.

III. Caselets

1. *A* promises in writing to give *B* ₹500 for no consideration. Is *A* liable to pay?
   [Hint: No, *A* is not liable to pay for the promise is not supported by consideration from *B*. Refer Sections 10 and 25]

2. *A* owes *B* ₹5000 but the Limitation Act bars the debt. *A* orally promises to pay the debt. Can *B* recover the money from *A*?
[Hint: No, as the promise to pay is not in writing. Refer Section 25(2)]

3. *X* contracts with *Y* to give his minor son in adoption to *Y* and takes ₹50,000 towards the consideration for the promise. *X* later on refuses to fulfil the contract. Can *Y* be successful if he tries to enforce the contract or brings an action for damages against *X*?
[Hint: No. The agreement is void as the consideration is forbidden by law]

4. *X* promises to obtain for *Y* an employment in the public services and *Y* promises to pay *X* ₹50,000. Decide the validity of the agreement.
[Hint: The contract is void as the consideration is unlawful vide Section 23. *X*'s promise to procure an employment in the public services is opposed to public policy and hence unlawful]

5. *B* agrees to illicit cohabitation with *A*. *A* agrees to pay ₹5000 per month in consideration of her services. Can *B* lawfully recover the promised amount from *A*, if the latter refuses to pay her?
[Hint: No, for the consideration involves an unlawful act]

6. A promises to pay ₹5000 per month to *B*, a married woman, for extra-marital cohabitation but later refuses to pay. Can *B* lawfully recover the amount?
[Hint: No, the object being unlawful, the contract is void. Refer Section 23]

Answers to Objective-type Questions

1. (i) True (ii) False (iii) True (iv) False (v) True
(vi) False (vii) True (viii) True (ix) True (x) True

2. (i) consideration, contract (ii) promisee (iii) void *ab initio*
(iv) no consideration (v) promisor, real and legal (vi) restricted
(vii) void (viii) public policy (ix) void, irrecoverable (x) unenforceable

3. (i) (b) (ii) (d) (iii) (d) (iv) (a) (v) (b)
(vi) (a) (vii) (d) (viii) (a) (ix) (b) (x) (d)

2 Chapter in Review

LEARNING OUTCOMES

LO1 Consideration defined

LO2 Rules governing valid consideration

LO3 Validity of agreement without consideration

LO4 Bearing of lawful object on the validity of contract

LO5 When the object or consideration is deemed to be unlawful

LO6 Effect of partial illegality

KEY TERMS

Consideration: Something in return; a positive act or some forbearance.

Stranger to a contract: One who is not party to the contract.

'Doctrine of Privity': A person who has no personal interest in a contract can neither sue nor be sued on the contract.

LO1 The term 'consideration' is used in the sense of *quid pro quo*, meaning, thereby, something in return. It may involve a positive act (i.e., doing something) or some forbearance (i.e., something given up).

LO2 There are certain rules governing consideration in terms of the formation of the contract, foremost among them being the existence of a consideration in simple contracts. Second, consideration moves as per the desire of the promisor, although it may be moved by the promisee or any other person. The next rule is that it must have some value and prove to bring some benefit to the promisor or detriment to the promise. A bare promise (*nudum pactum*) is not binding. Consideration can be past, present, or future. It may not be adequate but must invariably be legal, i.e., it must not involve an illegal act.

LO3 The cases wherein agreements made without consideration may be valid and enforceable are those related to natural love and affection, promise to compensate for past voluntary services, promise to pay time-barred debt, completed gift, agency, and guarantee.

LO4 Illegality of object also renders an agreement in valid and therefore unenforceable.

LO5 The consideration or object of an agreement is deemed to be unlawful if prohibited by law, defeats the purpose of any provisions of the law, fraudulent, immoral, involves or implies injury to another person, and is opposed to public policy.

LO6 The case of a partially illegal contract is different. Wherever illegal part can be disengaged from the legal part (and, of course, effect can be given to the legal part), the contract is not altogether void but is valid and enforceable in regard to such part of it as is legal. Conversely, if the different parts of the contract are so closely interknit that it is not possible to sever the legal from the rest of the contract without destroying the whole, then the contract is altogether null and void.

CHAPTER

3 Competency of Parties

Learning Objectives

LO 1 Competency to contract
LO 2 Who is incompetent to contract?
LO 3 Position of an agreement with a minor
LO 4 Minor can be a promise
LO 5 Contract on behalf of minor
LO 6 Agreements made by a person of unsound mind

Competency: One's ability to enter into a contractual relationship.

Competency or capacity is an expression that describes a person's aptness to do something. In the context of the Indian Contract Act, it refers to the ability to enter into contractual relationships. Contractual incompetence or disability on the part of either party may render an agreement void and unenforceable. Therefore, both the parties, the promisor and the promisee, must be legally capable of entering into a contract so as to translate the agreement between them into a legally binding contract.

Competency to Contract

Every person who has attained the age of majority who is of sound mind, and who is not disqualified from contracting by any law to which he is subject is competent to contract [Section 11].

In the light of above provision, the following persons can be deemed to be incompetent to enter into a contract:

1. Minor,
2. Persons of unsound mind and
3. Persons disqualified by law.

Minor

Minor: A person, domiciled in India, who has not attained the age of 18 years.

As per Section 3 of the Indian Majority Act, 1875, a minor is a person, domiciled in India, who has not attained the age of 18 years. Accordingly, every person, male or female, who is under 18 years of age is a minor. However, in the following two cases, a person continues to be a minor until he/she completes 21 years of age:

1. Where a guardian of a minor or his/her property or both has been appointed by a court of law under the Guardian and Wards Act, 1890, and
2. Where his/her property has passed under the superintendence of the court of wards.

Thus, a person normally attains majority upon completing his/her 18 years of age. But in case a person or his/her property is under the guardianship of someone, the former shall remain minor unless he/she attains 21 years of age. Also, a person whose property has been under a court-appointed custodian cannot enjoy his independent rights as an adult unless he/she attains 21 years of age.

Position of Agreements with a Minor

A valid agreement requires that both the contracting parties must be able to understand the legal implications of their conduct, i.e., they must have a mature mind. The legal yardstick to measure maturity, according to the law of contract, is that both the parties must have attained majority. Otherwise, the law would presume that they do not possess the capacity to judge what is good and what is bad for them, hence, a bar on minors' competency to contract.

The legal position of minor's agreements In the eyes of the law, an agreement with a minor is held void altogether. Besides, a minor can always plead minority despite entering into a contract by falsely representing himself as a major. There could be many other cases related to the involvement of minors in contractual obligations. The legal position of minor's agreements may be studied under the following heads.

An Agreement by a Minor is Void Altogether

The law has always sought to protect minors from the consequences of making transactions detrimental to themselves. For example, if a minor agrees to buy something that he cannot afford, cannot be compelled to pay for that. Thus, contracts with or by a minor are held void altogether. The Act makes it essential that all contracting parties should be competent to contract and expressly provides that no person is competent to contract who has not attained majority. Hence, a minor is not bound by the promise made by him under an agreement. The case of *Mohori Bibi vs Dharmodas Ghose*[1] (Box 3.1) is a case in point.

Minor Can Always Plead Minority

Estoppel is an important principle of the Law of Evidence. In the words of Lord Halsbury, 'Estoppel arises when you are precluded from denying the truth of anything, which you have represented as a

[1] 1903, ILR 30 Cal. 539

Box 3.1 Minor Not Bound by Promise Made

In the *Mohori Bibi vs Dharmodas Ghose* case, the plaintiff, a minor, executed a mortgage in favour of the defendant, a moneylender, to secure a loan of ₹20,000. A part of this amount was actually advanced to him. Subsequently, the minor sued for setting the mortgage aside. The Privy Council held that a minor had no capacity to contract and, therefore, the mortgage was not valid. Then, the moneylender requested to refund a sum of ₹10,500 advanced as part of the consideration for the mortgage. The Privy Council further held that the contract by the minor was void and he cannot be compelled to repay the amount advanced to him.

fact, although it is not a fact'. But there is one exception to this general rule. A minor can always plead minority and is not stopped from doing so even when he/she has procured a loan or entered into some other contract by falsely representing himself/herself as a major, when in reality he/she was a minor. The reason behind this is quite apparent. The policy of the law of contract is to protect minors from contractual liability, and if such a thing is permitted, it would defeat that very policy.

But where the loan was obtained by fraudulent representation by the minor or some property was sold by him/her, and those transactions were set aside as being void, then the court might direct the minor, on equitable grounds, to restore the money or property to the other party [*Khan Gul vs Lakha Singh*[2]].

No Ratification on Attaining the Age of Majority

Since the contract with a minor is void *ab initio*, the minor on attaining majority cannot ratify the same. In *Indran Rama Swami vs Anthoapa*[3], a promise made by a minor that the money advanced during his minority will be repaid by him/her after attaining majority has been held invalid. However, when a person on attaining majority actually repays the debt incurred by him/her during his/her minority is regarded as a valid transaction. The reason for the same is that an agreement with a minor is merely void and not unlawful and, therefore, the sum paid cannot be sued for subsequently.

Contract for the Minor's Benefits

Despite the fact that a minor is incompetent to contract, nothing in the law prevents him/her from becoming a promisee, transferee, payee, endorsee, and receiver of a benefit arising under a contract. Accordingly, a minor is allowed to enforce a contract, which is of some benefit to him and under which he/she is required to bear no obligation. Thus, a promissory note duly executed in favour of a minor is not void because although he/she is incapable of contracting, yet he/she can receive a benefit. On the same footing, it has been held that a minor is capable of purchasing immovable property, and he/she may sue to recover the possession of the property purchased upon tender of the purchase money [*Thakur Dar vs Mt. Putli*[4]].

According to Transfer of Property Act, 1882, also, a minor cannot transfer property but he/she can be a transferee (person accepting a transfer). Similarly, if a minor sells goods to an adult on credit, he/she shall be entitled to recover its price from the buyer [*Abdul Ghaffar vs Prem Pyarelal*[5]]. Common examples of contracts for the minor's benefit include contracts of service, apprenticeship, and education.

Contract by a Parent or Guardian

A contract entered into by a parent or guardian on behalf of the minor is binding on the minor provided that the contract

1. is within the scope of the authority of the parent or guardian, and
2. is for his/her benefit or is for legal necessity [*Subramanyam vs Subba Rao*[6]].

It should, however, be noted that all contracts made by guardian on behalf of a minor are not enforceable. For example, an agreement for service,

[2] AIR 1928 Lah. 609
[3] 1906, 16 Mad. L.J. 422
[4] 1924, AIR Lah. 611.
[5] 1934, AIR Lah. 480.
[6] 1948, AIRP C 25.

entered into by a father on behalf of his daughter who is a minor is not enforceable at law [*Raj Rani vs Prem Adib*[7]]. Similarly, the guardian of a minor has no power to bind the minor by a contract for the purchase of immovable property [*Mir Sarwarjan vs Fakhruddin Mohd Chowdhury*[8]].

Contract by Minor and Adult Jointly

When a minor and an adult jointly enter into a contract with another person, the contract would be void vis-à-vis the minor. But the contract (as a whole) can be enforced against the adult [*Jamna Bai vs Vasanta Rao*[9]].

Minor As a Partner

A minor cannot become a partner in a partnership firm. However, he/she may, with the consent of all the partners, be admitted to the benefits of partnership (Section 30 of the Indian Partnership Act). This implies that he/she can share the profits without incurring any personal liability for losses.

Minor As an Agent

A minor can act as an agent and bind his/her principal by his/her acts done in the course of such an agency. But he/she does not incur any personal liability towards the principal for his/her wrong actions, negligence, or breach of duty, whatsoever.

Minor As a Shareholder

A minor can become a shareholder, or a member in a company in respect of fully paid shares (e.g., in case of transfer or transmission of shares), if the articles of the company so permit. However, if a minor is allotted partly paid shares, he/she being incompetent to contract, incurs no liability. Thus, a company will not be able to recover the uncalled amount from the minor in future. In a Chennai case [*Palaniapa vs Pasupati Bank*[10]], shares were allotted to a minor under an application signed by his guardian. Neither the minor nor the guardian was held liable when the company was wound up subsequently. Hence, the bar on minor to become a shareholder.

Minor and Insolvency

A minor cannot be adjudicated insolvent simply because he/she is incompetent to contract.

Contract of Apprenticeship by the Guardian of a Minor

A contract of apprenticeship entered into on behalf of the minor by his/her parent or guardian is valid and is binding upon a minor, as such a contract is protected by the Apprentices Act, 1961, provided that the minor is not less than 14 years of age at the time of making the contract.

Minor's Liability for Supply of Necessaries

Any person would be entitled to be reimbursed from the property of the minor for necessaries supplied to him or to anyone whom the minor is bound to support, i.e., his family [Section 60].

Thus, for the supply of necessaries, a minor is not personally liable; it is only his property which shall be liable. If a minor owns no property, the supplier cannot recover the price of the necessaries.

Necessaries: Basic requirements of one's life.

Necessaries defined The term ' necessaries' refers to basic requirements of one's life. Necessary goods or services are those without which an individual cannot reasonably exist [*Chappel vs Cooper*[11]]. Accordingly, necessaries supplied must be according to economic and social status of the minor in question and must be the goods or services, the minor actually needs to support himself/herself. Necessaries as defined by Section 2 of English Sale of Goods Act refer to the goods suitable to the condition in life of a minor and to his actual requirements at the time of sale and delivery. This follows that an item will not come under the purview of necessaries if a minor is already sufficiently supplied with things of that kind. Necessaries include not only goods—food, shelter, clothing, etc. but also necessary services—education

[7] 1948, 51 Bom. LR 256.
[8] 1912, 29 Cal. 232.
[9] 1916, 39 Mad. 409.
[10] 1942, A I R Mad. 47.
[11] 1844, 13 M and W 252, 258.

and instruction. In India besides the above things, the costs incurred in successfully defending a suit on behalf of a minor in which his/her property was in jeopardy, and expenditure incurred in defending him/her in a prosecution, and amount advanced to a Hindu minor girl to meet her marriage expenses have also been held to be necessaries. Thus, necessaries are not confined to basic necessities—things that one must have and cannot manage without, i.e., important to all, such as food and clothings.

If the goods are deemed necessaries, the minor may be compelled to pay a reasonable price, and not the contract price. However, a minor is not liable if the goods, though necessaries, have not been delivered, or the service has not yet been rendered, i.e., there is no claim for breach of contract.

The burden of proving that the goods are necessaries lies on the seller. Therefore, the seller must show that the goods are, in fact, necessary for the particular minor in question. For instance, a tailor sued a minor for the price of clothes, including eleven waistcoats. His action failed because he could not show that the minor was not already adequately supplied with the required articles. A minor is not liable if he has an adequate supply, even if the supplier did not know this. His properties, thus, could not be attached for the recovery of the price [*Nash vs Inman*[12]].

A Minor's Liability in Tort

Tort: A civil wrong or breach of duty (other than under the contract) leading to incurring liability for damages.

A tort implies a civil wrong or a breach of duty (other than under the contract) leading to incurring liability for damages. That is, torts are civil wrongs recognized by law as grounds for a lawsuit. Under the law of torts the injured party may seek damages against loss of earnings capacity, pain and suffering, reasonable medical expenses, present and future expected losses etc. A minor is liable in tort unless his/her act is directly connected with the contract and is the means of producing it. In *Burnard vs Haggis*[13], the defendant, a minor, hired a horse subject to the condition that he would not use it for jumping or playing any other stunt. The minor lent the horse to a friend, who used it for jumping, with the result that the horse was injured and ultimately died. The minor was held liable on the ground that he had done an act not contemplated by the contract and had thus taken himself out of scope of the law of contract, and the protection it affords to juveniles.

However, where the wrongful action is contemplated by the contract, the minor cannot be held liable. Hence in *Jennings vs Rundall*[14], where the defendant, a minor, had hired a horse for 'riding' and rode it so hard that it was injured, the defendant was not held liable. The court observed, 'If a minor in the course of doing what he is entitled to do under the contract is guilty of negligence, he cannot be made liable in tort if he is not liable on the contract'.

Persons of Unsound Mind

Sound mind: Having the capacity to think, reason and understanding for oneself.

Sound mind, in legal parlance, implies having the capacity to think, reason, and understand for oneself. Adults by nature are considered in general to be in sound mind, but through certain circumstances can be rendered as being not in sound mind, due to intensive brain damage or other major incapacities. Sound mind is considered a legal requirement for entering into a contract.

A person is said to be of sound mind for the purpose of making a contract if at the time, when he/she makes it, he/she is capable of understanding it and forming a rational judgment as to its effect upon his/her interests [Section 12].

Now on the basis of the above provision it can be interpreted that for the purpose of making a contract, a person is deemed to be of unsound mind if at the time of entering into an agreement he/she is

1. incapable of understanding its terms and
2. unable to form a rational judgment as to its effect or implications upon his/her interests.

Unsoundness of mind may be caused by various factors, viz., idiocy, lunacy or insanity, intoxication (either from alcohol or the use of narcotic drugs), mental festering due to old age, etc.

[12] 1908, 2 K.B. 1.

[13] 1863, 14 C.B. 45.

[14] 1799, 8 T. R. 335.

Box 3.2 **When Is a Person Capable of Making a Contract?**

Example 1

A patient in a lunatic asylum, who is, at intervals, of sound mind, may contract during those intervals.

Example 2

A sane person, who is delirious from fever, or who is so drunk that he/she cannot understand the terms of a contract, or form a rational judgment as to its effect on his/her interest, cannot contract whilst such delirium or drunkenness lasts.

Agreement with a Person of Unsound Mind

A person of unsound mind, under the Indian Contract Act, is incapable of entering into a contract. In *Machaiman vs Usman Boari*[15], it has been held that, in India, a contract with or by a person of unsound mind is, like that of minor, absolutely void. Section 12 further clarifies:

1. A person, who is usually of unsound mind, but occasionally of sound mind, may make a contract when he is of sound mind.
2. A person, who is usually of sound mind, but occasionally of unsound mind, may not make a contract when he is of unsound mind.

The circumstances where a person can make a contract are given in Box 3.2.

Effect of Agreements Made by Persons of Unsound Mind

The law recognises different levels of mental instability or unsoundness of minds, such as lunacy, idiocy, and intoxicated persons. Accordingly, agreements with such persons have been dealt with differently. The position of contracts and agreements with such people is discussed separately as follows.

Idiot: A mentally deficient person who is permanently incapable of rational conduct.

Agreements by idiots Idiocy, in the eyes of the law, implies extreme mental imbecility with no interval of saneness called lucid intervals. Accordingly, an idiot is a mentally deficient person who is permanently incapable of rational conduct. He/she has no lucid intervals (of saneness), so he/she cannot make a valid contract. A case in point is the decision of the Patna High Court in *Inder Singh vs Parmeshwardhari Singh*[16]. A property worth about ₹25,000 was agreed to be sold by a person for ₹7000 only. His mother proved that he was a congenital idiot, incapable of understanding the transaction. Holding the sale to be void, Sinha J. stated 'It does not necessarily mean that a man must be suffering from lunacy to disable him from entering into a contract. A person may to all appearances behave in a normal fashion but at the same time he may be incapable of forming a judgment of his own, as to whether the act he is about to do is in his interest or not. In the present case, he was incapable of exercising his own judgment'.

Agreements by lunatics As against idiocy, lunacy is not God-given. Hence, a person can become a lunatic at any stage of his life. He/she is a person who is mentally disturbed on account of mental strain or other personal experiences and, of course, he/she may have some lucid intervals of sanity. Accordingly, he/she is bound for contracts entered into during lucid intervals of sanity. But he/she shall not be liable as regards contracts entered into during bouts of lunacy, i.e., while he/she was of unsound mind.

Agreements by intoxicated persons An intoxicated person is placed in the same category as a lunatic. Therefore, a contract by such persons is altogether void. However, merely partial or ordinary intoxication cannot deprive a person of capacity to contract. In order to avoid a contract on this ground it must be shown that the person was so intoxicated that he/she

[15] 1907, 17 Mad. L. J. 78.

[16] 1957, AIR Pat 491.

was unable to understand the terms of the contract, or form a rational judgment, as to its effects on his/her interests.

Exceptions If a contract, entered into by a person of unsound mind, is for his/her benefit, it can be enforced (for his/her benefit) at law against the other party [*Jugal Kishor vs Chedelu*[17]]. A person of unsound mind usually incurs no liability. But for necessaries supplied to such a person or to any member of his/her family, from his/her estate, if any, he/she will be liable [Section 68].

Burden of proof The presence or absence of mental soundness at the time of making the contract in all cases is a question of fact to be decided by the court of law. Where a person is usually of sound mind, the burden of proving that he/she was of unsound mind at the time of the execution of a document lies on him/her who challenges the validity of the contract.

Persons Disqualified by Law

Apart from minors and persons of unsound mind or lunatics, there are certain other catagories persons who are disqualified from contracting under some statutes so that the contracts by such persons are void. For example, the Indian Penal Code debars convicts from entering into contracts while they are serving their sentence of imprisonment. Such persons are called 'legally disqualified persons'. Besides convicts, the term includes alien enemies, insolvents, foreign sovereigns and ambassadors, corporations, etc. A brief account of these persons is summarised as under.

> **Alien:** A person who is not a citizen of the country in which they live or work or enter into a contract with any of its residents, i.e. a foreign national in Indian context.

Alien enemies An alien refers to a person who is not a citizen of the country in which they live or work or enter into a contract with any of its residents. That is, in Indian context, an alien is one who is the citizen of a foreign country. An alien may be either a friend or an enemy. An alien friend or a foreigner, whose country is at peace with the Republic of India, can enter into a contract with an Indian citizen subject to the provisions of the International Law. But in case of contracts with an alien enemy, i.e., a foreign national, whose country is at war with India, the position is different. Contracts, except by licence from the Central Government, entered into during the outbreak of war become unenforceable and cannot be sued in Indian Courts.

As regards contracts entered into before the declaration of war, they stand suspended for the duration of the war and can be revived after the war is over, provided they have not already become time-barred under the law of limitations. However, the contracts (i.e., entered before the war breaks out) that are against the public policy can never be revived and, hence, stand dissolved.

Convicts All convicts are legally disqualified from being entered into the contract from the date of imprisonment till the date of their release from the jail. They may, however, contract

1. on the expiration of the period of sentence,
2. during their parole, or
3. on remission of the legal consequences of their crime.

Undischarged insolvents If a person's debts exceed his property, he/she is adjudicated as insolvent. An adjudged insolvent's property stands vested in the official receiver or official assignee appointed by the court. He/she cannot enter into contracts relating to his/her property and sue and be sued until he/she obtains a certificate of discharge from the court.

Foreign sovereigns and ambassadors Foreign sovereigns and accredited representatives of a foreign nation, i.e., Ambassadors and High Commissioners, enjoy special privilege in that they cannot be legally proceeded against in Indian Courts. However, they can, in their personal capacity, enter into contracts that may be enforceable in Indian Courts.

Joint stock companies and statutory corporations A joint stock company and a statutory corporation created by a special Act exist only in contemplation of law. They are artificial persons and have no physical shape or form. The contractual capacity of a company is determined by its charter, i.e., Memorandum of Association. Similarly, the statute creating a statutory corporation expressly

[17] 1903, 1 All L.J. 43.

defines its contractual capacity. Any act by a company or a corporation, which is outside the limits of contractual capacity is *ultra vires* (beyond the powers) and void. Moreover, no company or corporation is allowed to enter into the contracts of personal nature such as contracts of marriage and divorce.

Exercises

I. Objective-type Questions

1. State whether each of the following statements is True or False:
   - (i) A minor is not bound by any promises made by him/her under an agreement.
   - (ii) A contract with a minor is voidable at the option of the minor.
   - (iii) A person, who is usually of unsound mind but occasionally of sound mind, cannot make a contract during his lucid intervals.
   - (iv) A minor can act as an agent and can bind his principal by his acts.
   - (v) An idiot cannot conclude a valid contract but a lunatic can.

2. Fill in the blanks:
   - (i) A person, who is usually of sound mind, but occasionally of unsound mind, ________ make a contract when he is of sound mind.
   - (ii) A contract by an intoxicated person is ________.
   - (iii) A person who is permanently of unsound mind is called ________.
   - (iv) A person can become ________ at any stage of his life.
   - (v) A person domiciled in India normally attains majority on the completion of ________ years of age. (18/21)

3. Indicate the correct answer:
   - (i) Which among the following persons are not competent to contract?
     (a) Minors (b) Persons of an unsound mind
     (c) Persons disqualified from contracting (d) All of the above.
   - (ii) Who among the following are usually regarded as persons of unsound mind?
     (a) Lunatics (b) Idiots
     (c) Intoxicated persons (d) All of the above
   - (iii) Which of the following contracts can be enforced against a minor?
     (a) Contract for the benefit of a minor (b) Contract for supply of necessaries
     (c) Both (a) and (b) (d) None of the above
   - (iv) A minor was facing a criminal prosecution for smuggling drugs. He borrowed ₹5000 to hire an advocate to defend him in the court of law. What is the remedy available to the creditor if the minor does not return the money on his own?
     (a) The creditor cannot recover the amount from the minor since a contract with a minor is void *ab initio*.
     (b) The amount of loan can be recovered from minor's property since it is a loan for necessaries.
     (c) The creditor can recover his amount of loan from the minor on his (minor's) attaining the age of majority.
     (d) The creditor can recover his amount from the parent or guardian of the minor.
   - (v) A minor can be
     (a) A promisor (b) A promisee
     (c) Both (a) or (b) (d) None of the above

II. Review Questions

1. What do you mean by contractual disability? State and illustrate the law relating to minor's agreements.
2. Can a minor, though incompetent to contract, receive a benefit arising there under?
3. 'A minor's estate is liable for the necessaries supplied'. Comment.
4. Can a person who is usually of unsound mind, but occasionally of sound mind, make a contract?

5. Enumerate persons who are treated as persons of unsound mind. State the legal position of agreements with such persons.

6. Name the persons disqualified of contracting under other laws for the time being in force. State and illustrate the legal position of contracts made with them.

III. Caselets

1. A minor, by misrepresenting himself to be of 21 years, obtained a loan of ₹5000 from a bank stating that the amount was needed by him to complete his higher education. The Bank, without making any further inquiry, lent the amount to the minor. Can bank recover the amount from him?
[Hint: No, vide Section 11, a minor is not capable of entering into a contract. A minor can always plead his/her minority]

2. A minor purchased on credit half a dozen woollen suit length pieces from a cloth merchant. Later on, he refused to make the payment. Can the supplier recover the money from him? Give reasons.
[Hint: No, vide Section 11, an agreement by or with the minor is absolutely void. This agreement cannot be covered under the supply of necessaries supplied to him/her]

3. A minor sold some goods on credit to an adult. The buyer on due date refuses to pay the price. Can the minor recover the amount?
[Hint: Yes, a minor can be a promisee]

4. A grocer supplies monthly rations for five months to *B*, who was aged 17 years and 5 months. *B* having failed to pay the bills for the supplies, the grocer decided to sue him for the realization of his dues. Could he succeed had he done so?
[Hint: Yes, he could recover the amount from *B*'s property (Section 68)]

5. A film producer engaged a minor girl to act in his film, and for this he entered into an agreement with her father. The producer fails to pay salary of the actress under the agreement. The girl in turn sues the producer through her father for the arrears of the salary. Will she succeed?
[Hint: No. A guardian/parent of a minor cannot enter into a valid contract of service on his/her behalf]

Answers to Objective-type Questions

1.	(i) True	(ii) False	(iii) True	(iv) True	(v) False
2.	(i) cannot	(ii) void ab initio	(iii) idiot	(iv) lunatic	(v) 18
3.	(i) (d)	(ii) (d)	(iii) (c)	(iv) (b)	(v) (b)

3 Chapter in Review

LEARNING OUTCOMES

LO[1] Competency to contract
LO[2] Who is incompetent to contract?
LO[3] Position of an agreement with a minor
LO[4] Minor can be a promise
LO[5] Contract on behalf of minor
LO[6] Agreements made by a person of unsound mind

KEY TERMS

Competency: One's ability to enter into a contractual relationship.

Minor: A person, domiciled in India, who has not attained the age of 18 years.

Necessaries: Basic requirements of one's life.

Tort: A civil wrong or breach of duty (other than under the contract) leading to incurring liability for damages.

Sound mind: Having the capacity to think, reason, and understand for oneself.

Idiot: A mentally deficient person who is permanently incapable of a rational conduct.

Alien: A person who is not a citizen of the country in which they live or work or enter into a contract with any of its residents, i.e. a foreign national in Indian context.

LO[1] Every person who has attained the age of majority, who is of sound mind, and who is not disqualified from contracting by any law to which he/she is subject is competent to contract.

LO[2] Minors, persons of unsound mind (lunatics), and persons disqualified (from contracting) by law to which they are subject are barred from making contracts.

LO[3] An agreement with a minor is void *ab initio*. i.e. a nullity, which cannot be enforced in any circumstances, whatsoever.

LO[4] Despite the fact that a minor is incompetent to contract, nothing in the law prevents him/her from becoming a promisee, transferee, payee, endorsee, and receiver of a benefit arising under a contract.

LO[5] A contract entered into by a parent or guardian on behalf of the minor is binding on him/her provided that the contract is within the scope of the authority of the parent or guardian, is for his/her benefit, or is for legal necessity.

LO[6] A person of unsound mind, under the Indian Contract Act, is incapable of entering into a contract. However, if a contract, entered into by a person of unsound mind, is for his/her benefit, it can be enforced (for his/her benefit) at law against the other party. A person of unsound mind usually incurs no liability. But for necessaries supplied to such a person or to any member of his/her family, from his/her estate, if any, he/she will be liable.

CHAPTER

4 Free Consent

Learning Objectives

LO1 Free consent: significance and subject matter
LO2 Coercion: definition; effect, acts that amount to inducing coercion
LO3 Undue influence; presumption of domination of will
LO4 Misrepresentation: definition, classification, consequences
LO5 Fraud: definition, essentials, consequences
LO6 Mistake: definition, types, consequences
LO7 Contracts induced by flaw in consent

The most basic requirement to reach a contract is the presence of an agreement. The agreement must have been entered into voluntarily and involved a 'genuine consent'. Consent stands 'not genuine' or disputable if caused by mistake, misrepresentation, undue influence, fraud, or coercion. The presence of these elements may vitiate an otherwise enforceable contract. A person who has concluded a contract under these conditions would be at liberty to rescind it.

Consent Defined

The term 'consent' indicates meeting of minds, i.e., contracting parties understanding the same thing in the same sense. According to Section 13, 'Two or more persons are said to have consented when they agree upon the same thing in the same sense.' Consequently, if there is any misunderstanding between the parties about the subject matter of the contract, they cannot be said to have agreed upon the same thing in the same sense. And, if they do not agree in the same sense there can be no consent. As a general rule also, no contract arises in the absence of consent. In English Law, this is known as *consensus ad idem,* i.e., meeting of minds of the parties to a contract. For example, *A* has two horses, one is black and the other red. He offers to sell his black horse to *B* for ₹5000. *B* who is aware of only *A's* red horse, accepts the offer made by the latter thinking it to be an offer for the red horse. The so-called agreement between *A* and *B* is invalid on the ground that there is no consent. The two parties are not thinking in terms of the same subject matter.

Free Consent

Free consent: A consent that is not caused by coercion, undue influence, fraud, misrepresentation, or mistake.

According to Section 14, consent is said to be free when it is not caused by coercion, undue influence, fraud, misrepresentation, mistake. Thus, consent is not said to be genuine when it would have been given due to any of the above-mentioned reasons.

For maintaining the validity of a contract, not only consent is necessary, but it must also be a free consent altogether. If the consent is not free, a contract is voidable at the option of the party whose consent was not free. But where both the parties to an agreement are under a mistake as to a matter of fact essential to the contract in question, the agreement is void. This is so because in case of a 'bilateral mistake', there is virtually no consent. A void agreement is not enforceable at the option of either party. Figure 4.1 shows the various flaws in consent and their legal effect.

Coercion

The term 'coercion' simply means forcing or compelling (physically or mentally) a person to enter into a contract. The consent to an agreement is said to be caused by coercion when it is obtained by use of force or under a threat.

Coercion: Forcing or compelling (physically or mentally) a person to enter into a contract.

Section 15 says, 'Coercion' is the committing, or threatening to commit, any act forbidden by the Indian Penal Code (45 of 1860) or the unlawful detaining, or threatening to detain, any property, to the prejudice

Figure 4.1 Flaws in consent and their effect on contract validity

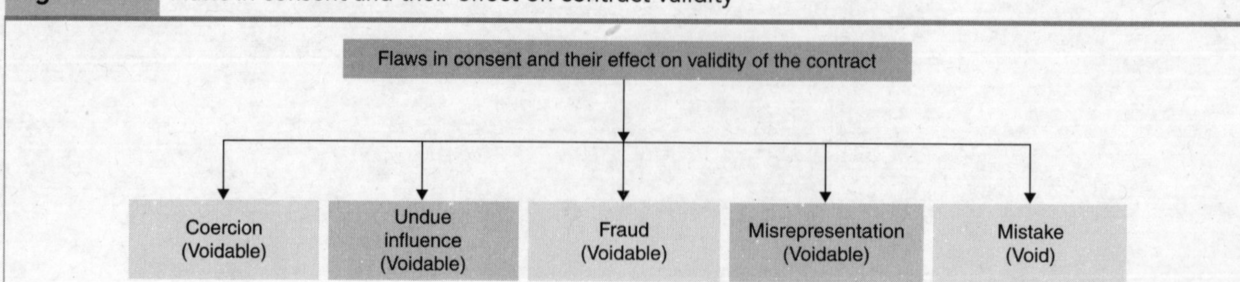

Box 4.1 **Coercion in Ranganaya Kamma vs Alwar Sette Case**

A Tamil man died leaving behind a young widow, aged 13 years. The relatives of the deceased forced the widow to adopt a boy or they would not allow her to have her husband's body cremated. The widow was forced to adopt the boy. Subsequently, she applied for cancellation of the adoption. It was held that the adoption was voidable at her option as her consent was not free but induced by coercion because obstructing a dead body from being removed for cremation is an offence under Section 297 of the IPC.

of any person whatever, with the intention of causing any person to enter into any agreement'.

The explanation to the section adds – 'it is immaterial whether the Indian Penal Code [Section 45 of 1860] is or is not in force in the place where the coercion is employed.'

Simply put, doing anything that is contrary to law or forbidden by the Indian Penal Code (IPC) is coercion, even though such an act is done in a place where the Code may not be in force. The fundamental object of causing coercion is to induce or compel a person to enter into a contract. For example, *A*, on board in an English ship on the high seas, induces *B* to enter into an agreement by an act that amounts to criminal intimidation under the IPC. *A* afterwards sues *B* for breach of contract at Kolkata. *A* has employed coercion, although his act is not an offence by the law of England, and although Section 506 of the IPC is or is not in force in place where the coercion was employed by *A*, i.e., the ship.

What Amounts to Inducing Coercion?

The analysis of the definition of 'coercion' given under Section 15 shows that the following four actions would amount to inducing coercion in the eyes of the law:

1. Committing any act forbidden by the Indian Penal Code
2. Threatening to commit any act forbidden by the IPC
3. Unlawful detaining of any property
4. Threatening to detain any property.

Committing Any Forbidden Act

Indian Penal Code [Section 45 of 1860] has forbidden certain acts. Committing a murder, kidnapping, causing hurt, rape, defamation, theft, giving wrong evidence are some of the examples of such acts. If a party to a contract procures the consent of another contracting party by committing any such act, the consent is said to have been gained through coercion. For example, *A* kidnaps *B's* son to induce *B* to sell his house worth ₹5 lakh for ₹2 lakh in return of release of his son. *B* agrees to do so. The consent of *B* is deemed an act of coercion forbidden by the IPC. The case of *Ranganaya Kamma vs Alwar Sette*[1] shown in Box 4.1 is illustrative on this point.

Threatening to Commit Any Act Forbidden by IPC

Coercion as defined under Section 15 implies not only committing an act, which is contrary to law, but even threatening to commit such an act amounts to coercion. Thus, obtaining consent at gunpoint, or by threatening to cause hurt, intimidation, and by threatening to kidnap will amount to coercion. The leading case of *Ammiraju vs Seshamma*[2] is a case in point.

In the above case, a husband, by threatening to commit suicide, induced his wife and son to execute a release in favour of his brother in respect of certain properties, which they claimed as their own. The Madras High Court in its decision held that, 'the threat of suicide amounted to coercion within Section 15 and the release deed was, therefore, voidable.'

It is worthwhile to note that even a threat to third party, for example, *A* pressurizing *B* to sign a document threatening to harm *C* (who is a relative of *B*) if *B* refuses to sign, would also amount to coercion.

Unlawful Detaining of Any Property

If a person induces someone to enter into a contract with him/her by detaining his property, the former

[1] 1889, AIR 13 Mad. 214
[2] 1917, AIR 41 Mad. 33

is said to have employed coercion. He cannot, therefore, enforce the contract. In the English case of *Astley vs Reynolds*[3], the plaintiff had pledged his silver plate with the defendant for £20. When he went to redeem it, the creditor insisted that an additional £10 interest was also owed. The plaintiff had to pay this to redeem his plate. He subsequently sued the creditor to recover it back. Holding that money, which had actually been paid for such a purpose, could be recovered back.

Threatening to Detain Any Property

If a person threatens someone to detain any of his property with the intention of compelling him to enter into a contract, such an act also constitutes a clear case of coercion. In *Bansraj vs The Secretary of State*[4], the government gave a threat of attachment against the property of *B*, the plaintiff for the recovery of a fine due from his son. *B* paid the fine and subsequently sued the government against this recovery. The court held that the payment of fine was induced by coercion and, therefore, *B* was entitled to recover the amount he had paid under coercion.

Acts Outside the Purview of Coercion

Often a doubt arises on the types of actions that would amount to coercion. Does mere warning or threat to filing suits also come under the ambit of forcing a person into a contract? Absolutely no. Following are the actions that are not deemed as coercion in their legal interpretation.

Threat to file a suit

A doubt often arises whether a threat to file suit amounts to coercion. In this relation it must be noted that a threat of civil or criminal prosecution does not constitute coercion, since the same is not an act forbidden by the Indian Penal Code. However, a threat to file a suit on false charge is forbidden by the Indian Penal Code and, therefore, amounts to coercion. The case of *Askari Mirza vs Bibi Jai Kishori*[5] is relevant to this discussion.

[3] 1731, 2 STR 915

[4] 1939, A. W. R. 247

[5] 1912, AIR 16 I.C. 344

In the above-referred case, a minor, the plaintiff, having borrowed on mortgage deed, agreed to a compromise decree though the mortgages were void. He compromised because he was under the threat of being prosecuted for falsely misrepresenting his age and that this amounted to coercion. The Privy Council observed, 'The law as contained in Section 15 is much wider than anything found in the English authorities (read law) and in India it is not correct to say that a contract is vitiated merely by proof of a threat to bring a criminal charge. Of course, if the charge of cheating was a true one, there is an end to the plaintiff's case, for a threat to bring such a charge would not be an act forbidden by the Indian Penal Code.'

Threat to commit suicide

A 'suicide' and a 'threat to commit suicide' are not punishable under the IPC. An attempt and abetment to suicide are, however, offenses under IPC and, therefore, punishable under it. Now the question arises if a person obtains the consent of the other by threatening to commit suicide, would it amount to coercion? Such consent is also said to be caused by coercion. In *Ammiraju vs Seshamma*[6], the Madras High Court observed, 'The term "any act forbidden by the Indian Penal Code" is wider than the term "punishable by the Indian Penal Code"'. Simply because a man escapes punishment, it does not follow that the act is not forbidden by Indian Penal Code. For example, if a lunatic or a minor may not be punished, it does not show that the Indian Penal Code does not forbid their criminal acts. In the same case it was held by a majority (of judges) 'that the threat to commit suicide amounted to coercion within the meaning of Section 15 ... the man who commits suicide goes unpunished, not because the act is not forbidden, but because there is nobody left to be punished.' It may, thus, be concluded that although a threat to commit suicide is not punishable under the Indian Penal Code, it is deemed to be forbidden by that code.

Effect of Coercion

The ultimate effect of coercion is that it renders the contract voidable at the option of the party whose

[6] 1917, 41 Mad. 33

consent was obtained by coercion, called aggrieved party. The reference of Sections 19, 64, and 72 is explanatory here.

According to Section 19, 'When the consent to an agreement is caused by coercion, the agreement is a contract voidable at the option of the party whose consent was so caused.'

In other words, the party whose consent is obtained by coercion can put an end to the contract, if it so chooses. Thus, it is up to the aggrieved party whether to rescind the contract or perform it. However, as per Section 64, if the aggrieved party decides to avoid the contract, it has to restore any benefit received by it under the contract to the other party from whom it had been received.

Section 72 further provides, 'A person to whom money has been paid, or anything delivered under coercion, must repay or return it.' For example, a railway company refuses to deliver certain goods to the consignee except upon the payment of an illegal charge for carriage. The consignee pays the sum charged in order to obtain the goods. He is entitled to recover so much of the charge as was illegally excessive [Illustration (b) appended to Section 72].

Burden of Proof

The onus of proof that the consent was caused by coercion indeed lies on the party who wants to rescind the contract on the ground of coercion. Thus, it is for the aggrieved party to prove that its consent was not free. Moreover, such a party has to prove that it would not have entered into this contract had the coercion not been employed.

Undue Influence

Undue influence: Unreasonable use of power/supremacy by a person over another person to win latter's will.

The term 'undue' implies excessive or beyond what is expected or required, whereas the term 'influence' refers a person's indirect power over other people, events or things. Hence, when a person makes excessive or improper use of his/her power over another person and obtains the latter's consent, the former is said to have used undue influence.

Undue influence, in effect, wipes out the intellect of a person and induces him/her to do something, which is against his/her will. For example if *A* by virtue of his wisdom, wealth, force of character, or just his superior position obtains the consent of someone who is in a weaker position, such consent is said to be caused by undue influence.

Section 16(i) defines undue influence as follows:

'A contract is said to be induced by "undue influence" where the relations subsisting between the parties are such that one of the parties was in a position to dominate the will of the other and used that position to obtain an unfair advantage over the other.'

Prerequisites of Undue Influence

The above definition highlights the following two essential elements of 'undue influence':

1. The relationship between the parties is such that one of them is in a dominant position, and
2. The dominant party uses his/her position to obtain an unfair advantage over the weaker party.

For an undue influence to occur, both the above-mentioned factors should be concurrently present. The presence of one without the other will not invalidate consent on the ground of undue influence. Box 4.2 presents some examples of consent induced by undue influence.

Presumption of Domination of Will

From the definition given under Section 16(1), it is clear that to exercise undue influence it is necessary to prove that one of the contracting parties was in a position to dominate the will of the other. This gives birth to a fundamental question as to when can a person be said to be in a position to dominate the will of the other. The answer to this is provided in Section 16(2). According to the section, a person is deemed to be in a position to dominate the will of another in the following circumstances.

Where he holds a real or apparent authority over the other Instances of such relations are relations between father and son, master and servant, police officer and culprit, etc.

Box 4.2 **Illustrations of Consent Obtained by Undue Influence**

Example 1

A advanced money to his son, *B*, during his minority. Upon *B*'s coming of age, he obtained, by misuse of parental influence, a bond from *B* of a greater amount than the sum due in respect of the advance. *A* thus employed undue influence [Illustrations appended to Section 16].

Example 2

A, a devotee induced by her spiritual advisor (guru), gifted her entire property to him to secure benefits to her soul in next world. It was held that the consent of *A* had been obtained by undue influence [*Based on Mannu Sing vs Umadatt Pande*[7]].

Where he stands in a fiduciary relationship to the other Fiduciary relationship refers to relationship based on trust and confidence. Bond of trust and confidence presents a very good opportunity to the person in whom confidence is placed to exploit it for his own benefits. Instances of this category of affairs are relations between

1. Doctor and patient[8]
2. Trustee and beneficiary[9]
3. Solicitor and client[10]
4. Spiritual advisor (guru) and his devotee[11]
5. Woman and her confidential managing agent[12]
6. Parent or guardian and child[13].

Where he makes a contract with a person whose mental capacity is temporarily or permanently affected by reason of age, illness, mental, or physical distress. It is a common observation that a 'person in mental distress' can be easily persuaded to give consent to a contract, which may be unfavourable to him. Accordingly, if a contract is made with someone by taking advantage of his/her distress, it is voidable on the ground of undue influence.

Effect of Undue Influence

The effect of undue influence is that it renders a contract voidable at the option of the aggrieved party. Thus, if the consent of a party is induced by undue influence, the party can put an end to the contract if it so chooses. Section 19(A) substantiates the above effect of undue influence as under.

'When consent to an agreement is caused by undue influence, the agreement is a contract voidable at the option of the party whose consent was so caused.'

Any such contract may be set aside either absolutely, or if the party who was entitled to avoid it has received any benefits there under, upon such terms and conditions as the court may seem just. Some examples of undue influence are given in Box 4.3.

Burden of Proof

When the aggrieved party chooses to rescind the contract on the ground of undue influence, it will have to prove the following two points:

- The other party was in a position to dominate its will and
- By the use of such dominant position, the other party actually obtained an unfair advantage over it.

Thus, it is not enough for a person to avoid the contract by showing that the other person was his/her father who could have influenced him/her. He/she must go further and show that his/her father actually did influence him/her.

Transactions with *Pardanashin* Woman

The expression *pardanashin* (veiled) implies complete seclusion; the state of being private and away from other people. Thus, a *pardanashin* woman is one who

[7] 1890, 12 All. 523
[8] Mitcnell V. Humfray, 1881, 8 QBD. 587
[9] Raghunath V. Varjivanda, 1906, 30 Bom. 579
[10] Pushong V. Mania Halwani, 1860, BLR. AC 95
[11] Mannu Singh V. Umadatt Pande, 1890, 12 All, 523
[12] Subbamma V. Mohd. Abdul, AIR, 1950, Hyd. 55
[13] Lakshmi Doss V. Rooplal, 1907, 30 Mad. 169

Box 4.3 **Illustrations of Effect of Undue Influence**

Case 1

A's son has forged *B*'s name to a promissory note. *B* threatens to prosecute the son and obtains a bond from *A* for the amount of the forged note. If *B* sues on this bond, the court may set the bond aside if *A* approaches the court for the same [Illustration (a) appended to Section 19(A)].

Case 2

A, a moneylender, advances ₹100 to *B*, an agriculturist, and, by undue influence, induces *B* to execute a bond for ₹200 with an interest rate of 6 per cent per month. The court may set the bond aside, ordering *B* to repay ₹100 with such interest as may seem just [Illustration (b) appended to Section 19(A)].

observes complete isolation from people other than her family members due to custom of her community. It may, however, be noted that a woman does not become *pardanashin* simply because 'she lives in some degree of seclusion' [*Shaik Ismail vs Amir Bibi*[14]]. The concept legally means a woman who is totally 'secluded from ordinary social intercourse'.

Accordingly, a woman who goes to a court and gives evidence, who fixes rents with tenants and collects rents, who communicates when necessary in matters of business, with men other than members of her own family would not be regarded as *pardanashin* woman [*Ismail Mustafa vs Hafiz Boo*[15]].

The law grants a special protection to such *pardanashin* women on the ground of their being ignorant insofar as the worldly knowledge goes [*Kalibaksh Singh vs Ram Gopal Singh*[16]]. A contract with a *pardanashin* woman is presumed to have been induced by undue influence. She can avoid the contract unless the other party can prove that she freely consented to the contract. The principles to be applied to transactions with *pardanashin* woman are founded on equity and good conscience and, accordingly, a person who contracts with a *pardanashin* woman has to prove the following points:

1. The terms of the contract were fully explained to her,
2. She understood the implications of the contract,
3. She had free and independent advice, and
4. It was a deliberate and voluntary act based on her intelligence.

[14] 1902, 4 Bom LR 146
[15] 1906, 33 Cal. LR 773
[16] 1913, L. R. 41 I.A. 23, 28–29

Undue Influence Distinguished from Coercion

Both coercion and undue influence invalidate consent and cause the contract voidable at the option of the aggrieved party. Yet, there are some basic points of difference between the two, as explained in Table 4.1.

Misrepresentation

Misrepresentation: A misstatement of fact made by one party to the other, which, while not being a term of contract, induces the other party to enter into the contract.

Misrepresentation refers to a misstatement of fact made by one party to the other, which, whilst not being a term of contract, induces the other party to enter into the contract. Misrepresentation may be innocent, negligent, or willful. In law, when a wrong representation is made intentionally or deliberately with the intention to deceive the other party, the term 'fraud' is used. But, when it is made innocently or negligently, it is termed as 'misrepresentation'. Thus, when a person asserts something, which is not true, though he/she believes it to be true, that assertion amounts to misrepresentation. A contract, the consent to which is induced by misrepresentation, is voidable, i.e., valid and enforceable until avoided or protested.

According to Section 18, 'misrepresentation' means and includes the following:

1. The positive assertion, in a manner not warranted by the information of the person making it, of that which is not true, though he believes it to be true.

Table 4.1 Difference Between Coercion and Undue Influence

S. no.	Point of difference	Coercion	Undue influence
1.	Mode of operation	It involves the physical force or threat.	It involves moral or mental pressure.
2.	Relationship between the parties	Existence of relationship between the parties is immaterial.	Some kind of relationship between the parties is absolutely necessary.
3.	Nature of act	Coercion encompasses committing or threatening to commit an act forbidden by Indian Panel Code, or detaining or threatening to detaining any property of another person.	Committing or threatning to commit any illegal act is not the subject matter of undue influence.
4.	Third party	Coercion may proceed from even a stranger, i.e, third party and need not be directed against the promisor. It can be directed against a third party in whose welfare the promisor was interested.	Undue influence is always employed by one contracting party upon the other party.
5.	Presumption by law	The law under no circumstances presumes the use of coercion.	Law in certain types of relationships can presume undue influence, e.g,. in case of a contract with a *pardanashin* woman.
6.	Rights available	The contract is voidable at the option of the party whose consent has been obtained by coercion. But any benefit received by the aggrieved party has to be restored to the other party.	In case of undue influence, the court has the discretion to direct the aggrieved party to return the benefit in whole or in part, or rescined the contract withoutany such direction.
7.	Nature of liability	In case of coercion, not only is the contract voidable at the opion of the aggrieved party, but the party exercising it also exposes itself to criminal liabilities.	Undue influence involves no criminal liability except an action on the contract.

2. Any breach of duty that without an intent to deceive, gains an advantage of the person committing it, or anyone claiming under him, by misleading another to his prejudice, or to the prejudice of anyone claiming under him.
3. Causing, however innocently, a party to an agreement to make a mistake as to the substance of the thing, which is subject of the agreement.

Essentials of Misrepresentation

1. There should be a representation or assertion, made innocently, believing it to be true and without an intent to deceive the other party.
2. The representation or assertion should be, of facts, material to the agreement. A mere expression of opinion or hearsay or commendation (reasonable praise) cannot be regarded as misstatement of facts even if the same turn out to be untrue.
3. The statement must be untrue or turned out to be untrue but was made with an honest belief in its truth.
4. The person to whom the misrepresentation was made must have relied on it in the sense that it must have induced him to enter into the contract [as per explanation to Section 19].

5. A party cannot complain of misrepresentation if it had the means of discovering the truth with ordinary diligence [see Exception to Section 19].

Classification of Misrepresentations

The above provisions classifiy acts of misrepresentation into the following three groups:

1. Unwarranted statement of material facts
2. Breach of duty that brings advantage to the person committing it
3. Inducing mistake about subject matter.

Unwarranted statement of material facts

'Where a person makes a positive statement of material facts not warranted by his information, say, without any reasonable ground, believing it to be true though it is not true; such act amounts to misrepresentation' [Section 18(1)]. For example, *A*, while selling his scooter to *B* tells him that the scooter runs 40 kilometres per litre (kmpl). *B* honestly believes the statement to be true, although *A* did not have any basis for his claim. Later it is found that the mileage is just 30 kmpl. The statement made by *A* is misrepresentation.

A statement is said to be warranted by the information of the person making it when he/she gathers the information from a reliable source. It should not be a mere opinion or hearsay or commendation. For example, *A* made a positive statement to *B* that *C* was to become the director of a company. *A* made the statement on information obtained, not directly from *C* but from another person, called *M*. *B*, relying on the statement, applied for shares of the company. The fact stated proved untrue. The statement amounts to misrepresentation for a piece of information received secondhand and did not warrant *A* to make the positive assertion to *B* about *C* [*Mohanlal vs Sri Gungaji Cotton Mills Co.*].

Breach of duty

When a person commits a breach of duty that without an intent to deceive, brings an advantage to him or anyone under him by misleading another to his prejudice or to the prejudice of anyone claiming under him, it amounts to misrepresentation [Section18(2)].

The above provision presupposes that

1. the representor owes a duty to the representee in respect of the statement,
2. the representor makes a statement innocent or negligent,
3. the representee is misled to his prejudice, and
4. the representor derives some benefit and causes loss to the other party.

Breach of duty is also there where a party legally bound to disclose certain information does not do so. Misrepresentation may arise from concealment or suppression of such information.

This type of misrepresentation is intended to meet all those cases which are called, in the 'Courts of Equity' cases of constructive fraud, in which there is no intention to deceive, but where the circumstances are such as to make the party who derives a benefit from the transaction equally answerable in effect, as if he had been actuated by motives of fraud or deceit [*Oriental Banking Corporation vs John Fleming*]. Box 4.4 presents some instances of such misrepresentation.

Inducing mistake about subject matter

Inducing mistake about the subject matter of the agreement innocently constitutes yet another form of misrepresentation. If one of the contracting parties leads the other, however innocently, to commit a mistake as to the nature or quality of the subject matter, there is misrepresentation. The cases of concealment or suppression of vital information

Box 4.4 Suppressing or Hiding Facts is Misrepresentation

A while entering into an agreement with *B* for the sale of his car correctly stated that the car runs 15 kmpl on petrol. Negotiations lasted for one month, when the delivery of the car was affected. During this period the mileage of the car dropped to 10 kmpl. *A* unintentionally failed to inform *B* about this degeneracy. *A* had made the misrepresentation, and *B* was entitled to rescind the contract [Based on *With vs O'Flanagan*].

Box 4.5 **Illustrations of Misrepresentation**

Example 1

The directors of a company, while acting within their authority, discounted on the company's behalf a bill of exchange with a bank. On due date the bank failed to realise the amount of the bill. The company denied liability on the bill. It was held that the bank was entitled to recover the amount of the bill from the company.

Example 2

In the negotiations for a marriage contract, the relatives speaking for the girl failed to disclose that she was suffering from epilepsy. The engagement was held to be voidable on the ground of misrepresentation of a very material fact having been concealed [*Haji Ahmad Yar Khan vs Abdul Gani Khan*[17]].

may also fall under this group. This is so because the concealment or suppression of material facts by one party may induce other party to commit a mistake about the subject matter of the agreement. The examples in Box 4.5 would help understand the point.

Effect of Misrepresentation

The effect of misrepresentation is that the party misled by it can avoid the contract. Section 19 says, 'when consent to an agreement is caused by misrepresentation, the agreement is a contract voidable at the option of the party whose consent was so caused'.

A party to contract whose consent was caused by misrepresentation, may, if it deems fit, insist that the contract be performed, and that it be put in the position in which it would have been, if the representations made had been true.

Thus, the aggrieved party has the following two alternate rights:

- It may rescind the contract, or
- It may continue with the contract.

The discussion ahead makes the repercussions of both the options clear.

When party rescinds the contract

The aggrieved party can avoid a contract on the ground of misrepresentation. However, this right is not available to it in the following two cases.

1. Where it (aggrieved party) had the means of discovering the truth with ordinary diligence [as per Exception to Section 19].

   For example, *A*, by misrepresentation, leads *B* erroneously to believe that 500 tons of sugar is produced annually at *A's* factory. *B* examines the accounts of the factory, which should have disclosed, if ordinary diligence had been exercised by *B*, that only 300 tons of sugar had been produced. After this *B* buys the factory. The contract cannot be repudiated on account of *A's* misrepresentation.
2. Where it is not, in fact, misled by the misrepresentation [as per Explanation to Section 19]. For example, a person bought shares in a company on the faith of its prospectus, which contained an untrue statement that one Grieve was a director of the company. The representee's claim to set aside the contract and for damages was dismissed on the ground that the statement was 'immaterial', as the representee had never heard of Grieve. It is more appropriate to say that for this reason the representee did not rely on the statement, which was clearly material in the sense that it could influence a reasonable person. That is, the consent by the representee was given independently despite the misrepresentation [*Smith vs Chadwick*[18]].

Party may act upon the contract

The aggrieved party, if it deems fit, may choose to act upon the contract and may insist that it be put in the same position in which it would have been, if the representation made had been true. For example, *A*, while selling his Cyber cafe that contains 20 PCs to *B*, describes that all the machines are in working

[17] 1937, AIR Nag. 270

[18] 1884, 9 App. Cas. 187

condition. *A* personally thinks so. Later on, *B* finds that two of the computers are not functional. In the circumstance, *B* may either avoid the contract or may insist on its being carried out after *A* agrees to get the non-functional computers repaired.

Damages for Misrepresentation

Misrepresentation generally does not entitle the aggrieved party to claim damages. However, damages can be claimed in case of misrepresentation in the following exception cases:

1. Where the prospectus of a company inviting the public to subscribe for shares in the company contains a misstatement about a material fact, and someone relying on the prospectus subscribes shares and thereby suffers losses, he/she (the injured party) can claim damages from the promoters or directors of the company.
2. Where an agent commits a breach of warranty of authority, he/she exposes himself/herself to pay damages to the injured party.
3. Where the relationship between the parties is that of a confidential nature (e.g., relationship between a doctor and patient) and one party suffers loss due to misrepresentation made by another party, the former can claim damages from the latter caused by such misrepresentation.

Burden of Proof

To avoid a contract on the ground of misrepresentation, the representee needs only to explain that the misrepresentation was made, and that it was capable of inducing the contract. The burden then passes to the representor to prove that the representee would have entered into the contract anyway, even if the misrepresentation had not been made.

Fraud

Fraud: Wilful misrepresentation of material facts with intent to deceive someone.

Fraud indicates wilful misrepresentation. Section 17 defines the term as: 'Fraud' means and includes any of the following acts committed by a party to a contract, or with his connivance, or by his agent, with intent to deceive another party thereto or his agent, or to induce him to enter into the contract.

1. The suggestion, as a fact, of that which is not true, by one who does not believe it to be true,
2. The active concealment of a fact by one having knowledge or belief of the fact,
3. A promise made without any intention of performing it,
4. Any other act fitted to deceive, and
5. Any such act or omission as the law specially declares to be fraudulent.

Essential Elements of Fraud

The analysis of the above section makes it evident that the following elements must be present in the act in order to constitute it fraud.

False and willful representation or assertion

To constitute fraud there must be some representation or assertion that is untrue. In the absence of representation or assertion, except in the following two cases, there can be no fraud.

1. Where silence may itself amount to fraud, and
2. Where there is active concealment of facts.

Furthermore, such representation must have been made either with the knowledge that it was false or without belief in its truth or recklessly without caring whether it was true or false. In *Derry vs Peck*[19], Lord Herschell said, 'Fraud is proved when it is shown that a false representation has been made knowingly, or without belief in its truth, or recklessly whether it is true or false'. Thus, the person making the representation should not believe it to be true, otherwise he/she will not be guilty of fraud. Moreover, to constitute fraud, the false representation must have been made wilfully or intentionally. For example, *A*, intending to deceive *B*, informs him that his estate is free from encumbrance. *B* thereupon buys the estate. The estate is, however, subject to mortgage. The contract is induced by fraud.

Perpetrator of representation

The false representation or misstatement must have been made by a party to the contract or by anyone

[19] 1889, 14 App Cas 337

with its connivance, or by its agent. If a stranger makes the misstatement to the contract, it cannot result in fraud. For instance, *A* suggests *B* to buy *C's* car, which according to *A* runs 15 kmpl. Later on, *B* finds that the car runs only 8 kmpl. *A* was, however, acting neither on instance of *C* nor was his agent; he was a stranger. The contract that took place between *B* and *C* cannot be stated to be induced by fraud.

Intention to deceive

Intention to deceive the other party is the essence of fraud. In order to commit a fraud, a person asserts or misstates the fact with the intention that it should be acted upon. As a matter of fact, misrepresentation elevates to fraud when it is prefixed by the element of intention to deceive the other party. For example, *A*, intending to deceive *B*, falsely represents that 1000 tons of sugar is produced annually at his factory, although *A* is fully aware that only 600 tons of sugar can be produced annually. *B* thereby agrees to buy the factory. *A* has resorted to fraud to obtain the consent of *B*.

Representation must relate to a fact

The representation made by the party must relate to a fact, which is material to the formation of the contract. A mere statement of opinion, belief, or commendation cannot be treated as fraud.

For instance, *A* states that the detergent produced at his factory washes whiter than whitest. The statement made by *A* is merely a commendation of the product and not a fact. But if *A* describes the ingredients, which the detergent contains, it becomes a statement of fact. And if that is found incorrect it amounts to fraud, provided *A* does not believe it to be true.

Active concealment of facts

'Active concealment' must be distinguished from 'passive concealment'. Passive concealment implies mere silence as to material facts, which barring a few cases, does not amount to fraud. Whereas, active concealment results in when the party takes positive or deliberate steps to prevent information from reaching the other party and this is treated as fraud. For example, *A* sells a horse to *B* in an auction despite knowing that the horse is unsound. *A* says nothing to *B* about the horse's soundness. This is a case of passive concealment of fact and cannot tantamount to fraud.

In another example, *A*, a horse dealer, sells a horse to *B* by inspection. *A* knows that the horse has a cracked hoof, which he fills up in such a way as to defy detection. *B* subsequently discovers the defect. There is a 'fraud' on the part of *A* on account of active concealment of material fact. *B* can avoid the contract as his consent has been induced by fraudulently.

Promise made without intention of performing it

If a person while entering into a contract has no intention to perform his/her promise, there is a fraud on his/her part, for the intention to deceive the other party is there from the very beginning. For example, an English merchant appointed an Indian woman as his personal secretary and promised that he would marry her. Later she came to know that he was already married and had made the promise without any intention to perform it. It was held that she could avoid the contract on the ground of fraud [*Shireen Mal vs J.J. Taylor*[20]].

On similar count, a purchase of goods without any intention of paying the price is a fraud and the contract can be avoided on this ground.

Representation must have actually deceived the other party

The representation made with the intention to deceive must actually deceive. The party, induced by fraudulent statement, must have relied on it to accord its consent. According to explanation appended to Section 19 of the Contract Act, 'A fraud which did not cause the consent to a contract of the party on whom such fraud was practiced does not render a contract voidable'. Thus, an attempt to deceive does not amount to fraud until the other party is deceived thereby. A case in point is the following example based on *Horse Fall vs Thomas*[21]. *A* had a defective cannon. With a view to conceal the defect, he put a metal plug on it. *B* without examining it bought it. The cannon burst when used by *B*. *B* refused to pay

[20] 1952, AIR Punj. 277

[21] 1862, AR 1 H & C 90

the price and accused *A* of fraud. It was held that *B* was bound to pay because he was not actually deceived, as he would have bought the cannon even if the deceptive plug had not been inserted.

Any other act fitted to deceive

The expression 'any other act fitted to deceive' obviously means any act that is done with the intention of committing fraud. This category includes all tricks, dissembling, and other unfair ways, which are used by cunning and clever people to cheat others. For example, in *Ningawwa vs B.S. Hirekurabar*[22] case, a husband persuaded his illiterate wife to sign certain documents telling her that by the papers he was going to mortgage her two plots of land to secure his indebtedness. But, in fact, he mortgaged four plots of land belonging to her. This was held as an act done with the intention of deceiving the wife.

Other acts or omissions specially declared void

This category includes the acts or omission that the law specially declares to be fraudulent. For example, the Insolvency Act and the Companies Act declare certain kinds of transfers to be fraudulent. Similarly, under the Transfer of Property Act, the transferor of real estate is bound to disclose to the transferee the following details:

- Material defects, if any, in the property such as cracks in the wall or in beams, and/or
- Any defect or dispute as regards transferor's title, such as property is subject to encumbrance, i.e., mortgaged or is subject to some dispute pending in a court of law. An omission to make such disclosure on the part of transferor amounts to fraud.

The Party Misled Must Have Suffered Some Loss

The party deceived must have suffered some loss because as a general rule there can be no fraud without damage and there can be no damages without an injury. The damage or injury may be some loss in terms of money or money's worth or some other detriment, which can be assessed with ease.

[22] 1960, 2 SCR 797

Does Silence Amount to Fraud?

A person normally cannot be held liable for fraud when he/she simply observes silence over certain material facts relating to the subject matter of the contract.

The explanation to Section 17 provides: 'Mere silence as to facts likely to affect the willingness of a person to enter in to a contract is not fraud, unless

1. The circumstances of the case are such that, it is the duty of the person keeping silence to speak, or
2. Silence, is, in itself, equivalent to speech'.

Hence, ordinarily, mere silence is no fraud, even if its result in to conceal facts likely to affect the willingness of a person to enter a contract. The analysis of the Explanation to Section 17 (mentioned above) shows that silence amounts to fraud in the following two cases:

1. Where it is the duty of the person keeping quiet to speak, and
2. Where the silence is equivalent to speech.

Where 'it is the duty of the person keeping silence to speak'

Duty to speak arises in contracts of *uberrimae fidei*, i.e., utmost good faith. These are the contracts in which the law imposes a special duty to disclose all material facts. Failure to disclose such facts will amount to fraud and render the contract voidable at the option of the aggrieved party. Examples of contracts *uberrimae fidei* are as follows.

Contracts of insurance In all contracts of insurance, it is the duty of the assured to disclose to the insurer all material facts concerning the risks to be undertaken. And whatever he/she states must be correct and truthful. If an assured misstates or conceals material facts (e.g., chronic illness, etc.), it will render the contract voidable at the option of the insurer.

Contracts of family settlements Where members of a joint family make agreements for the settlement of family property, each member of the family must make full disclosure of every material fact within his/her knowledge.

Fiduciary relationship Duty to reveal truth also arises where one contracting party reposes trust and confidence in the other. A father, for example, while selling a horse to his son, who has just come of age, must tell him if the horse is unsound, for the son is likely to rely upon his father. The relationships between a guardian and ward, trustee and beneficiary, and solicitor and client, etc., fall under this category.

Contract of share allotment Where a company invites the public to subscribe to its shares, the promoters and directors are under statutory obligation to disclose all material information regarding the company.

Others Full disclosure of material facts must also be made in contracts of marriage, engagement, sale of immovable property, guarantee, etc.

Where silence is equivalent to speech

The silence of a person is equivalent to speech when he keeps silent irrespective of an enquiry made by the other person in a positive manner. The person so maintaining silence is no less guilty of fraud. For example, *A* sells a TV set to *B* for a price. The set apparently seems to be faultless. Even then *B* says to *A*, 'If you don't deny it, I shall assume that the TV set is not defective'. *A* keeps mum. Here *A's* silence is equivalent to speech. And if *B* subsequently discovers any latent defect in the set, it will amount to fraud.

Consequences of Fraud

When consent to a contract is induced by fraud, the aggrieved party usually has the following remedies:

- He/she can rescind the contract by filing a suit in a court of law and prove the fraud [Section 19].
- He may, if he thinks fit, insist that the contract be performed, and that he be put in the position in which they would have been if the representation made had been true [Section 19]. For example, *A* fraudulently informs *B* that *A's* estate is free from encumbrance. *B* thereupon buys the estate. The estate is subject to a mortgage. *B* may either avoid the contract or may insist on it being carried out and the mortgage debt redeemed [Illustration (c) to Section 19].
- The party defrauded can also claim damages for the loss sustained by him if it is capable of assessment. Fraud is a civil wrong, hence compensation is payable.

Fraud Distinguished from Misrepresentation

Fraud and misrepresentation have many points in common. For instance in both the cases,

Table 4.2 Differences Between Fraud and Misrepresentation

S. no.	Point of difference	Fraud	Misrepresentation
1.	Nature of act	Fraud is an intentional wrong. The person making the false representation does not believe it to be true.	Misrepresentation is an innocent wrong. The person behind the false representation believes it to be true.
2.	Intention to deceive	There is intention to deceive the other (contracting) party.	There is no such intention.
3.	Silence	In some cases silence may amount to fraud, e.g., in the cases of contracts requiring utmost good faith.	Silence can never be construed as an act of misrepresentation.
4.	Remedies available	The party defrauded can rescind (i.e., cancel) the contract. A person who suffers loss as a result of acting in reliance on a fraudulent statement can recover damages in an action of deceit.	Misrepresentation merely entitles the aggrieved party to rescind the contract. Damages can not be claimed under misrepresentation.
5.	Defence	Excepting fraud by silence, the defendant cannot take the plea that the aggrieved party had the means of discovering the truth with ordinary diligence.	A person accused of misrepresentation can be met with the defence that the misrepresentee had the means of discovering the truth with ordinary diligence.

1. consent of one of the parties is not free,
2. there is a false representation of facts,
3. contract is voidable at the option of the aggrieved party, etc.

Yet the two differ in a number of respects. The major differences between fraud and misrepresentation are summarised in Table 4.2.

Loss of Right to Rescind a Contract

We have seen that a contract induced by coercion, undue influence, misrepresentation, or fraud is voidable at the option of the party whose consent was so caused. However, an aggrieved party loses this right in the following circumstances:

1. Where the aggrieved party after becoming aware of its right of rescission
   (a) Expressly affirms the contract, or
   (b) Acts in such a manner which shows that it has accepted the contract, or
   (c) Takes a benefit under the said contract.
2. Where the parties cannot be restored to their original position, e.g., where the subject matter of the contract has been destroyed or consumed.
3. Where the aggrieved party fails to exercise its right to rescind the contract promptly, i.e., within a reasonable time.
4. Where before the contract is rescinded, the third party acquires some right in the subject matter of the contract of *bona fide* value.

Mistake

Mistake: A wrong idea or opinion about something caused by lack of attention, skill, or knowledge etc.

The term 'mistake' literally means incorrect, or wrong idea or opinion about something caused by lack of attention, skill, or knowledge etc. In the context of the law of contracts, it may be defined as the erroneous belief or misunderstanding in the minds of the contracting parties concerning the law or facts about the contract. It usually takes place when the concerned parties are not well acquainted with the terms or subject matter of the agreement and they take the terms in a different sense.

An agreement made under a mistake is not valid for there is no consent.

Types of Mistake

The mistakes in relation to contracts are of two types:

1. Mistake of Law
2. Mistake of Fact
   The mistake of law can be classified into the following:
   (a) Mistake of Law of the Country, and
   (b) Mistake of the Foreign Law
   Similarly, the mistake of fact may be classified as follows:
   (a) Bilateral Mistake, and
   (b) Unilateral Mistake

Mistake of law

One of the essential elements of a valid contract is that the parties must contemplate to give rise to legal consequences and intend to create legal relations. Therefore, a person while entering into a contract must have the knowledge of regulatory framework, i.e., law concerning the contract so that he can bind himself and the other party legally.

Section 21 provides, 'A contract is not voidable because it was caused by a mistake as to any law in force in India; but a mistake as to a law not in force in India has the same effect as a mistake of fact'. Accordingly, mistake of law as stated earlier, may be (a) mistake of law of country or (b) mistake of foreign law.

Mistake of law of the country As per Section 21, 'if there is a mistake of law of the country, the contract is binding'. It is because everyone is deemed to have knowledge of law of the country and there will be no excuse if he ignores the national law (*Ignorantia juris non-excusat*). Thus, a mistake of Indian law will not invalidate the contract.

For example, *A* and *B* make a contract grounded on the erroneous belief that a particular debt is time-barred by the Indian Law of limitation. The contract is valid and not voidable.

Mistake of foreign law A person while entering into a contract with a foreigner should refer to the law of that country. However, in this case the maxim 'ignorance of law is no excuse' does not apply; the mistake of foreign law is treated as a mistake of fact. Accordingly, mistake of foreign law renders the contract void.

Mistake of fact

Mistake of fact arises when the parties enter into a contract without understanding the terms and conditions of the contract properly. It may occur on the part of either party or both the parties. Accordingly, mistake of facts may be classified further as (a) bilateral mistake, or (b) unilateral mistake.

Bilateral mistake Where both the contracting parties are under a mistake of fact material to the formation of the contract, it is called a bilateral mistake of fact. In such a situation there is no agreement at all, for there being complete absence of consent. Bilateral mistake of material facts renders an agreement void *ab initio*.

Section 20 provides, 'Where both the parties to an agreement are under a mistake as to a matter of fact essential to the agreement, the agreement is void.' Thus, for declaring an agreement void under this section, the following three conditions must be satisfied:

Both the parties must be mistaken Here parties to the agreement assume that a certain state of things exist which does not actually exist, or in their utter ignorance, the agreement means one thing to one and a different to the other, and they enter into the contract subject to the assumption or under that ignorance. For example, *A* who is having two sets of air conditioners, one imported and another domestic, offers to sell the domestic one to *B*. *B* not knowing that *A* has two air conditioners, thinks of the imported one and agrees to buy it. In this case, there is no consent whatsoever, and hence, the agreement is void.

Mistake must be of fact As per explanation to Section 20, 'An erroneous opinion as to the value of the thing which forms the subject matter of the agreement is not deemed to be a mistake as to a matter of fact'. For example, *A* buys a secondhand TV set from *B* believing it to be worth ₹5000 and pays ₹5000 for it. While, in fact, it was only worth ₹2000. The contract remains valid. *A* cannot blame *B* for charging exorbitant price for the goods. In fact, he himself is responsible for ignoring the true value of the TV set and the contract cannot be avoided on the ground of mistake.

The fact about which the parties are mistaken must be essential to the agreement The fact to which mistake relates must be essential for the formation of the contract. In express words, mistake of only such facts renders the agreement void that goes to the very root of the agreement. For example, *A* agrees to buy from *B* a certain horse. It turns out that the horse was dead at the time of the bargain, though neither party was aware of the fact. The agreement is void [Illustration (b) to Section 20].

Types of bilateral mistakes A bilateral mistake of facts may be of two kinds.

- Mistake as to subject matter or
- Mistake as to the possibility of performance.

Bilateral mistake of facts as to subject matter In such mistakes, both the parties to an agreement are mistaken about the subject matter of the contract, and the agreement is void. A mistake as to the subject matter may take various forms. This may relate to existence, identity, title, quantity, quality, or price of the subject matter. A brief account of all these is given below.

Mistake as to existence of subject matter Where both the parties at the time of making the contract believe that subject matter of the contract existences, but in reality it does not, there is a mistake and the agreement is void. For example, *A* agrees to sell to *B* a specific cargo of goods supposed to be on its way from England to Bombay. It turns out that, before the day of the bargain the ship conveying the cargo had been cast away and the goods lost. Neither party was aware of the fact. The agreement is void.

Mistake as to identity Where the parties to a contract have different subject matter in their minds, i.e., one party intends to deal with one thing and the other with another; contract is void there being lack of consensus *ad idem*. For example, *A* agreed to buy from *B* a cargo of 125 bales of Surat cotton to arrive from Bombay. There were two ships called 'Peerless' sailing from Bombay, one arriving in October and the other in December. *A* meant the earlier ship and *B* the latter. It was held there was no agreement between the parties [*Raffles vs Wichelhaus*[23]].

Mistake as to quantity Where both the seller and the buyer have a misunderstanding about the quantity or extent of the subject matter, this will render

[23] 1864, 2 H & C 906

the contract void. For example, *P* inquired about the price of rifles from *H* suggesting that he might buy as many as fifty. On receipt of the quotation he wired, 'Send three rifles'. But because of the mistake of the telegraph clerk, the message transmitted to *H* was 'send the rifles'. *H* dispatched fifty rifles. *P* accepted three rifles and returned the remaining forty seven. It was held that there was no contract between the parties. However, *P* was liable to pay for the three rifles, there being an implied contract entered into.

Mistake as to quality If there is a mistake as to quality of subject matter on the part of both the parties, the contract is void. For example, *A* offers to buy a race horse from *B*, a horse dealer. *B* accepts the offer believing it to be for a cart horse. The agreement is void.

Mistake as to title Sometimes, the buyer already owns the property, which a person wants to sell to him. But the concerned parties are not aware of the fact. In such cases the agreement is void. For example, *A* agreed to take a lease of a fishery from *B*. *A* was already entitled to the fishery. But neither party at the time of the transaction was aware of the true state of the title. The agreement was held to be void [*Cooper vs Phibbs*[24]].

Mistake as to price The agreement is also void where both the parties are mistaken about the price of the subject matter. For example, *A* agreed to lease out his quarry to *B* at the rate of ₹1 per cubic feet of stone extracted, subject to a minimum rent of ₹5000 per month. But in agreement, the figure of rent was written as ₹50,000 by mistake. The agreement is void *ab initio*.

Bilateral mistake as to the possibility of performance When parties to a contract enter into it believing that it is capable of performance, while in fact it is not so, there is a mistake of facts as to the possibility of performance, and the contract is void on this ground, i.e., impossibility. The impossibility to perform may arise due to physical reasons or legal reasons. For example, *D* entered into a contract with *R* to play in a concert, on a particular day, to be organised by the latter. But *D* could not participate in the programme due to illness on that day. The court of law held that the contract became void on account of impossibility to perform [*Robinson vs Davison*[25]].

Unilateral mistake When only one party to an agreement is under a mistake of facts, it is termed as a unilateral mistake. A unilateral mistake is generally of no effect unless

1. it concerns some fundamental fact and
2. the other party has the knowledge of the mistake.

For this reason, error of judgment on the part of one of the parties generally does not make the agreement void. As per Section 22, 'a contract is not voidable merely because it was caused by one of the parties to it being under a mistake as to a matter of fact'. The rationale behind enforceability of a contract caused by a unilateral mistake is a person, who, due to his own misapprehension or lack of reasonable care does not ascertain what he is contracting about, must bear the consequences.

In contracts of sale of goods, this rule is summed up in the maxim *caveat emptor* (let the buyer beware). The seller is under no duty to reveal the defects of his goods to the buyer. For example, *A*, a farmer exhibits oats in his farm for sale. *B* buys oats from *A*, a sample of which had been shown to him. *B* buys the oats erroneously thinking that they were old oats. In fact they were new ones. *B* wants to return the oats and refuses to pay the price. *B* cannot do so, their being an error of judgment on his part, which has no effect, and the contract will remain valid.

However, in some cases, a unilateral mistake may be fundamental and may affect the validity of the contract. The courts in India have established two judicial precedents, wherein even though the mistake is unilateral, the agreements are void. They are as under.

Unilateral mistake as to the nature of the contract As a general rule, a person who signs an instrument is bound by its terms, no matter whether he/she has not gone through its contents. But a person, who without any fault of his/her own, signs a document under a fundamental mistake as to its very nature, may avoid it provided the mistake was due to either

1. the blindness, illiteracy, or senility of the person signing or

[24] 1877, L. R. 2 HL 149

[25] 1871, L. R. 6 Ex. 269

Box 4.6 When Mistaken Identity Renders the Contract Void

A woman told a jeweller that she was married to one Vander Borgh, a millionaire (with whom she was in fact living as his mistress), and that he wanted to give her a necklace, which he wished to buy on approval. The jeweller let her have possession of the necklace and entered in his book as being out on approval to Vander Borgh. She pledged the necklace with a broker, who in good faith paid her some amount of money. It was held that there was no contract between the jeweller and the woman, since there was no consensus. And even the innocent buyer or a broker did not get a better title. Accordingly, the broker had to return the necklace to the jeweller. The jeweller thought that he was dealing with a different person, the wife of Vander Borgh ... he never intended to contract with the woman in question as such [*Lake vs Simmons*[27]].

2. a trick or fraudulent misrepresentation as to the nature of the document.

For example, *B*, an illiterate old lady with poor eyesight appointed *M*, one of her close relatives to manage her property. *M* prepared a sale deed of all her property in his own name and obtained her signature thereon, on the pretext that it was needed so as to legally authorise him to manage the property. It was held that she can avoid the agreement on the basis of unilateral mistake of fact as to the very nature of the transaction [*Bala Devi vs Sante Mazumdar*[26]].

Unilateral mistake as to the identity of the person contracted with A mistake of facts as to the identity of the person with whom the contract is made will vitiate the contract, there being no *consensus ad idem*. For example, where *M* intends to contract only with *A* but enters into contract with *B* believing him to be *A*, the contract is void. It should, however, be noted that a mistake about the identity of the contracting party will render the contract void only if

1. the identity of the party is of material importance to the contracts and
2. the other party knows that it is not intended that it should become a party to the contract.

The matter is best brought out in the case law illustration in Box 4.6.

[26] 1956, AIR, Cal. 575
[27] 1927, AIR A. C. 487

Effect of Mistake

A mistake as to error of judgment or omission on the part of any one or both the parties generally has no effect on the validity of the contract. For example, if a seller charges excessive price for an article under a mistake as to its true value, it does not render the contract void on the part of the buyer.

To be operative, a mistake must be, as to a matter of fact, essential to the agreement. The effect of various types of mistakes can be summarised as under.

1. A bilateral mistake of fact, which is fundamental to the agreement, prevents the formation of any contract at all and it will be declared void [Section 20].
2. A unilateral mistake usually does not vitiate the agreement in question. However, in case of unilateral mistake of fact, as to the identity of the person contracted with or as to the nature of the contract, the agreement is treated as void, there being absence of true consent of the parties.
3. A mistake as to any law in force in India does not affect the validity of the contract. However, where both the parties are under a mistake as to a foreign law, the contract is void. This is so because a mistake of foreign law is treated as a mistake of fact [Section 21].
4. A person of whom money has been paid or anything delivered under mistake is bound to return it, or to make compensation for the same, to the person from whom hehad received it.

Exercises

I. Objective-type Questions

1. State whether each of the following statements is True or False:
   (i) Consent indicates identity of minds in respect of the subject matter of the contract.
   (ii) For a contract to be valid, it is enough that the parties have agreed upon the same thing in the same sense.
   (iii) A mere silence as to facts is not fraud.
   (iv) Doing of anything, which is contrary to law or forbidden by Indian Penal Code, amounts to coercion.
   (v) In case of misrepresentation, the maker does not believe it to be true.

2. Fill in the blanks:
   (i) ____________ involves use of moral pressure.
   (ii) A threat to commit suicide amounts to ____________.
   (iii) A contract is ____________ if one of the parties to the contract is under a mistake of fact.
   (iv) Wilful wrong representation of material facts with the intention to deceive the other party is ____________.
   (v) Ignorance of ____________ is no excuse.
3. Indicate the correct answer:
   (i) Undue influence cannot be presumed between
      (a) Guardian and ward
      (b) Mother and daughter
      (c) Both (a) and (b)
      (d) Doctor and patient
   (ii) In which of the following cases, the agreement is void ab initio?
      (a) Coercion
      (b) Fraud
      (c) Bilateral mistake
      (d) Misrepresentation
   (iii) 'Misrepresentation', means and includes
      (a) The positive assertion, in a manner not warranted by the information of the person making it, of that which is not true, though he believes it to be true.
      (b) Any breach of duty which, without intent to deceive, gains an advantage of the person committing it, or any one claiming under him, by misleading another to his prejudice, or to the prejudice of any one claiming under him.
      (c) Causing, however innocently, a party to an agreement to make a mistake as to the substance of the thing which is the subject of the agreement
      (d) All of the above
   (iv) The party whose consent was caused by misrepresentation looses the right to rescind the contract
      (a) If he could discover the truth with ordinary diligence
      (b) If his consent is not induced by misrepresentation
      (c) In both (a) and (b) cases
      (d) In none of the above cases
   (v) A person is deemed to be in a position to dominate the will of another where
      (a) He holds a real or apparent authority over the other
      (b) He stands in a fiduciary position to the other
      (c) He makes a contract with a person whose mental capacity is temporarily or permanently affected by reason of age, illness, or mental or physical distress
      (d) In all the above circumstances

II. Review Questions

1. Define consent. When is consent said to be free?

   Or

   'It is not only the consent but free consent of the parties which is necessary for making the contract binding.' Elaborate.

2. What do you mean by the term coercion? Describe the effect of coercion on the validity of the contact.
3. Explain and illustrate the effect of undue influence on contracts. On whom lies the burden of proving that the contract (i) was and (ii) was not induced by undue influence?
4. Comment on the following:
   (i) 'Mere silence as to facts is not fraud.'
   (ii) 'An attempt to deceive which does not deceive is no fraud.'
5. State the position of a contract made with a *Pardanashin* woman.
6. What is fraud? Point out its effects on the validity of the contract.
7. Distinguish between:
   (i) Coercion and undue influence
   (ii) Fraud and misrepresentation
8. Define 'mistake'. Explain and illustrate the consequences of a mistake on contracts.

III. Caselets

1. *X* sold a horse to *Y*, his son-in-law, knowing well that the horse was vicious. *X* did not disclose the nature of the horse. *Y* injured while riding the horse. Is *X* guilty of fraud?
   [**Hint:** Yes, *X*'s silence in this case amounts to a fraud. Duty to speak arises in contracts of *uberrimae fidei*. Refer explanation to Section 17]
2. *A* applies to a banker for a loan at a time when there is stringency in the money market. The banker declines to make the loan except at an unusually high rate of interest. *A* accepts the loan on these terms. Is the contract induced by undue influence?
   [**Hint:** No. The transaction is enforceable for it is not a case of undue influence but one of normal operations of market forces]
3. Romesh threatens to shoot Shyam if he does not sell his BMW car to him for ₹1,00,000. Shyam signs the necessary documents to effect the sale of the car. Advise Shyam.
   [**Hint:** Shyam can rescind the contract on the ground of coercion]
4. *X* and *Y* are traders and enter into some contract. *X* has private information of a change in price, which would affect *Y*'s willingness to proceed with the contract. Is *X* bound to inform *Y*?
   [**Hint:** No. Refer Section 17]
5. *A* agrees to buy a car from *B* for ₹15,000 and pays half of the purchase price in advance. Unknown to both the parties at the time of making the contract, the car had been destroyed by an accident. Advise *A*.
   [**Hint:** Bilateral mistake, *A* can treat the contract void and can ask for refund of the money already paid. Refer Section 20]

Answers to Objective-type Questions

1.	(i) True	(ii) False	(iii) True	(iv) True	(v) False
2.	(i) Undue influence	(ii) coercion	(iii) voidable	(iv) fraud	(v) law
3.	(i) (b)	(ii) (c)	(iii) (d)	(iv) (c)	(v) (d)

4 Chapter in Review

LEARNING OUTCOMES

LO 1 Free consent: significance and subject matter

LO 2 Coercion: definition; effect, acts that amount to inducing coercion

LO 3 Undue influence; presumption of domination of will

LO 4 Misrepresentation: definition, classification, consequences

LO 5 Fraud: definition, essentials, consequences

LO 6 Mistake: definition, types, consequences

LO 7 Contracts induced by flaw in consent

KEY TERMS

Free consent: A consent that is not caused by coercion, undue influence, fraud, misrepresentation, or mistake.

Coercion: Forcing or compelling (physically or mentally) a person to enter into a contract.

Undue influence: Unreasonable use of power/supremacy by a person over another person to win latter's will.

Misrepresentation: A misstatement of fact made by one party to the other, which, while not being a term of contract, induces the other party to enter the contract.

Fraud: Wilful misrepresentation of material facts with intent to deceive someone.

Mistake: A wrong idea or opinion about something caused by lack of attention, skill, or knowledge, etc.

LO1 To be legally enforceable, a contract should be based on free consent. Consent is said to be free when it is not caused by coercion, undue influence, fraud, misrepresentation, and mistake.

LO2 The consent to an agreement is said to be caused by coercion when it is obtained by use of force or under a threat. Committing or threatening to commit an unlawful act is coercion. Consent induced by coercion renders a contract voidable at the option of the party whose consent was so obtained.

LO3 A contract is said to be induced by 'undue influence' where the relations subsisting between the parties are such that one of the parties is in a position to dominate the will of the other and uses that position to obtain an unfair advantage over the other.

LO4 Misrepresentation refers to a misstatement of facts. Misrepresentation may be innocent, negligent, or wilful. A contract, the consent to which is induced by misrepresentation, is voidable, i.e., valid until avoided.

LO5 When a wrong representation is made intentionally or deliberately with the intention to deceive the other party, the term 'fraud' is used.

LO6 In the context of the law of contracts, mistake may be defined as some erroneous belief or misunderstanding in the minds of the contracting parties concerning the law or facts about the contract.

LO7 In cases of coercion, undue influence, misrepresentation, and fraud, an aggrieved party loses its right to rescind the contract, if despite becoming aware of its right of rescission, it expressly affirms the contract, or takes a benefit under the said contract. A bilateral mistake of fact, however, can render a contract void.

CHAPTER

5 Void Agreements and Contingent Contracts

Learning Objectives

LO[1] Void agreement versus void contract
LO[2] Void agreement versus illegal agreement
LO[3] Agreements expressly declared void
LO[4] Restitution of benefits received under void agreements
LO[5] Essentials of a contingent contract
LO[6] Enforcement of contingent contracts
LO[7] Contingent contracts distinguished from wagering contracts

Void agreement: Agreement (legally) unenforceable from its very inception.

An agreement enforceable by law is a *contract*[1], but when it is not enforceable it is said to be *void*[2]. Thus, the real test of voidness of an agreement lies in its enforceability at law. A void agreement never matures into a contract. It is unenforceable from the very beginning and devoid of any legal effect for being a nullity.

Void Agreement Versus Void Contract

Void contract: A contract not enforceable by law.

A void agreement should be distinguished from a void contract. Some agreements are (legally) unenforceable from their very inception. These agreements are called void *ab initio*. They have no legal effect at all. A void agreement is a nullity and cannot be ratified even at the pleasure of the aggrieved party. For example, an agreement with a minor is void *ab initio*. The minor on attaining the age of majority cannot ratify it. On the other hand, there are some agreements, which may be enforceable at the time of their formation but at a later stage, due to certain reasons, may become unenforceable. Since such agreements are enforceable initially, they assume the character of a contract but their subsequent unenforceability renders them to be treated as 'void contracts' [Section 2(j)]. According to this section, 'A contract, which ceases to be enforceable by law, becomes void when it ceases to be enforceable'. For instance, suppose a contract between a foreign national and an Indian citizen is enforceable in the ordinary course. But the same contract would cease to be enforceable in the event of an outbreak of war between India and the country, the foreign national belongs to, and be treated as void. Therefore, a contract may become void for one reason or the other. But it cannot be void *ab initio*; it is only an agreement that can be void *ab initio*.

Void Agreement Versus Illegal Agreement

A void agreement and an illegal agreement have several things in common in terms of legal effects. For instance, both are unenforceable and, in general, incapable of specific performance. However, the two differ in a number of ways. A void agreement is different from an illegal one inasmuch as the former is simply unenforceable but may not necessarily be forbidden by law. For instance, marrying a minor girl is void but not forbidden by law as the object behind the same is not unlawful. An illegal agreement, on the other hand, is one in which the consideration or object is also unlawful. Accordingly, an illegal agreement is not only void and unenforceable but also unlawful (under the Contract Act) and, therefore, taints and renders all the agreements collateral to it, or springing from it, as void and unenforceable. But in case of a merely void agreement, a transaction collateral or ancillary to the main transaction is not itself void. In short, every illegal agreement is void, but a void agreement is not necessarily illegal.

Illegal agreement: An agreement supported by unlawful consideration and/or object which renders it not only void and unenforceable but unlawful too over and above.

Agreements Expressly Declared Void

The following types of agreements are expressly declared void under the Indian Contract Act:

1. Agreements by or with person(s) incapable of contract [Sections 10 & 11]
2. Agreements entered into under a mutual mistake of fact [Section 20]
3. Agreements of which considerations and objects are unlawful in full or in part [Sections 23–24]
4. Agreements without consideration [Section 25]
5. Agreements in restraint of marriage [Section 26]
6. Agreements in restraint of trade [Section 27]
7. Agreements in restraint of legal proceedings [Section 28]
8. Agreements—the meaning of which is uncertain [Section 29]
9. Agreements by way of wager [Section 30]
10. Agreements to do an impossible act [Section 56].

The first five types of agreements have already been discussed in the previous chapters. This chapter, therefore, is devoted to the discussion of the remaining kinds of void agreements.

[1] Section 2(h) of the Indian Contract Act
[2] Section 2(g) of the Indian Contract Act

Box 5.1 Agreements in Restraint of Trade

Example 1

X, a trader operating in a particular locality, agrees to pay *Y*, his competitor, in the business, a fixed amount as compensation so that *Y* shuts down his business in that locality. The agreement is void. If *X* subsequently refuses to pay *Y* the agreed compensation, the law will not safeguard *Y*'s interest.

Similarly, if *X* files a suit seeking closure of *Y*'s business, the suit will be dismissed no matter whether the former has already paid the said compensation to the latter.

Example 2

J, the defendant, at the time of taking employment with a company, promised his previous employer, the plaintiff, that he would not carry on the same business within 800 miles from Chennai after leaving the company. It was held that the agreement was void [*Oakes and Co. vs Jackson*[6]].

Agreements in Restraint of Marriage

A marriage contract flows from free consent, therefore, restrictions on marriage are regarded as *contra bonos mores*, i.e., opposed to public policy.

Section 26 states 'Every agreement in restraint of the marriage of any person, other than a minor, is void.' An agreement in restraint of marriage is unenforceable on the ground of public policy, whether it contains an express undertaking that the subject will not marry, or whether on financial or other grounds it tends to discourage a subject to marry [*Re Michelhoms Will Trust*[3]].

The Restraint May Be General or Partial

If a person, being a major, agrees for good consideration not to marry at all, or not to marry for a fixed period, or not to marry a particular person or a class of persons, the promise is not binding.

However, a penalty imposed on remarriage does not amount to restraint of marriage. Thus, an agreement between two co-widows that if one of them remarried, she should forfeit her right to her share in the deceased husband's property has been upheld, the court pointing out that no restraint was imposed upon either of the two widows for remarriage [*Rao Rani vs Gulab Rani*[4]]. Similarly, an agreement that upon the husband marrying a second woman, if the first elects to divorce him, the divorce shall be valid and she will not be deprived of her right to maintenance from him.

[3] 1963, 2 W.L.R. 1238, 1244.
[4] 1942, I. L. R.

Agreements in Restraint of Trade

Certain agreements that seek to impose a restriction on a person's right to carry on a trade or profession fall within the restraint of trade doctrine.

In view of their tendency to create monopolies, all restraints of trade are contrary to public policy and *prima facie* void, unless they can be regarded as reasonable between the contracting parties, and as regards the public policy. Freedom of trade and commerce is a fundamental right protected by the Constitution of India under Article 19(g). Just as the legislature cannot take away individual freedom of trade, so also the individual cannot barter it away by an agreement. Justice James V.C. in *Leather Cloth Co. vs Lovsont*[6] observed, 'The principle of law is this: Public policy requires that every man shall be at liberty to work for himself, and shall not be at liberty to deprive himself of the state of his labour, skill of talent, by any contract that he enters into'.

Section 27 declares in express terms that 'Every agreement by which any one is restrained from exercising a lawful profession, trade, or business of any kind is to that extent void'. Some examples of agreements in restraint of trade are presented in Box 5.1.

In Section 27, the expression 'to that extent' suggests that if in an agreement there are some covenants which are prohibited whereas others are not, and if the latter can be severed from the former, then only the former (i.e., covenants that operate as restraint of trade) would be void and not the

[6] 1876, 1 Mad. 134
[5] 1869, LR 9 Eq 345, 354: 39 LJ (Ch) 86:21 LT 661

whole of the agreement. However, the elimination of objectionable phrases should not alter the entire scope and intention of the agreement. For example, in *Brahmputra Tea Co. Ltd vs Scarth*[7], *A* upon being employed by *B*, agreed first, not to compete with *B* (his employer) after leaving the job and, second, not to injure his employer's interest during employment. It was held that the first condition is a restraint of trade but the second is binding.

But where the agreement is not so divisible, it is wholly void [*Parasullah Malik vs Chandrakanta Das*[8]].

Exceptions

Section 27 is general in its terms and declares all agreements in restraint of trade void. But certain exceptions to this general rule are recognised. These exceptions can broadly be classified in the following two categories:

1. Statutory exceptions
2. Judicially interpretative exceptions.

Statutory exceptions These are the ones created by the statutes and include the following:

Sale of goodwill 'One who sells the goodwill of a business may agree with the buyer to refrain from carrying on a similar business, within specified local limits, so long as the buyer, or any person deriving title to the goodwill from him, carries on a like business therein, provided that such limits appear to the court reasonable, regard being had to the nature of the business' [proviso to Section 27].

Putting the above proviso simply, if the seller of the goodwill of a business promises not to compete with the purchaser of the goodwill, the contract is not void and is enforceable, provided the restraint appears to be reasonable as to territorial limits and the length of time. In case of dispute, the court keeping in view the nature of business will decide whether the limits are reasonable. For instance, *A* and *B* are involved in boat manufacturing business at the banks of river Hooghly in Howrah. Suppose *A* sells off his business to *B* for a specified amount and agrees to abstain from carrying on the same business for a period of three years (i) in Howrah and (ii) in certain other parts of India. There is a sale of goodwill but with regard to first promise only. The second promise being unreasonable in terms of territorial limits is void.

[7] 1885, I.L.R. Cal. 545
[8] 1917, 21 C.W.N. 979

Partnership Act The Partnership Act, 1932 validates restraint of trade in the following four cases:

1. A partner shall not carry on any business other than that of the firm while he is a partner [Section 11(2)].
2. A partner may make an agreement with his/her partners that on ceasing to be a partner he/she will not carry on any business similar to that of the firm within a specified period or within specified local limits. Such an agreement shall be valid if the restrictions imposed are reasonable [Section 36(2)].
3. Partners may, upon or in anticipation of the dissolution of the firm, make an agreement that some or all of them will not carry on a business similar to that of the firm within a specified period or within specified local limits. Such an agreement shall be valid provided the restrictions imposed are reasonable [Section 54].
4. Any partner may, upon the sale of the goodwill of a firm, make an agreement with the buyer that he will not carry on any business similar to that of the firm within a specified period or within specified local limits. Such an agreement shall be valid only if the restrictions imposed are reasonable [Section 55(3)].

From the above, it is clear that to recognise any agreement in restraint of trade to be valid under Sections 36(2), 54, or 55(3) of the Partnership Act, the following two conditions must be satisfied:

1. The agreement specifies the local limits or the period of restraint and
2. The restrictions imposed are reasonable.

Judicially interpretative exceptions These are the exceptions arising from judicial interpretations of Section 27. A brief description of such exceptions is given ahead.

Trade combinations Trade combinations are voluntary agreements among traders or manufacturers in the same line of business to carry on their business in an organised way. Sugar syndicates, Association of Cement Companies (ACC), General Insurance Corporation of India (GIC), Federation of Indian Chambers of Commerce and Industry (FICCI) are some of the examples of trade or business associations in India. Since all these bodies are aimed at regulating their area of business, besides value addition to the goods they manufacture or the services they provide, and not restraining the same, formation of such associations are often desirable not only in the interest of trade itself but also in public interest in general. Restrictions imposed on the activities of their group members are, therefore, not to be considered void on the ground of restraints of trade. For example, In *Haribhai vs Sharef Ali*[9], four ginning factories entered into an agreement of fixing uniform rate for ginning production and pooling their earnings to be divided among them in certain proportions. It was held that the agreement among them was valid and enforceable.

The courts, however, would not allow a restraint to be imposed under the guise or pretext of trade regulations. Thus, an agreement among some persons to carry on business with the members of their caste only [*Vaithelinga vs Saminanda*[10]] and an agreement to confine the business of a sugar mill within a zone allotted to it [*Carew & Co. Ltd. vs North Bengal Sugar Mills*[11]] were held void and unenforceable.

Exclusive dealings agreements An agreement by a manufacturer to sell during a certain period his entire production to a wholesale merchant or distributor, and the latter in turn agrees to not to deal with the products of any other manufacturer is valid and not a restraint of trade. Similarly, an agreement among the sellers of a particular commodity not to sell the commodity for less than a fixed price has been held as enforceable. To enforce any exclusive dealing agreement, it is, however, necessary that their terms be reasonable, i.e., they do not unreasonably check competition.

In the light of the above doctrine, the following agreements have been held to be outside the scope of Section 27 and, therefore, valid and enforceable:

1. An agreement by a manufacturer of dhotis to supply 1,36,000 pairs of certain description to the defendant and not to sell goods of that kind to anybody else for a fixed period [*Carlies Nephews & Co. vs Ricknauth Bucktermull*[12]].
2. An agreement by a person to send all the mica (a mineral found as tiny shiny scales in rocks) produced by him to the plaintiffs, and not to any other firm nor keep any in stock [*Subha Naidu vs Haji Badsha Sahib*[13]].
3. An agreement by a person to sell all the salt manufactured by him to a firm for five years and further agreed not to sell salt to third parties [*Mackenzie vs Sriramiah*[14]].

However, the above exception does not apply in the following cases:

1. Where a manufacturer or supplier, after meeting all the requirements of a sole buyer, has surplus to sell to others, cannot be restrained from doing so [*Har Bilas vs Mahadeo Pandit*[15]].
2. Where a seller of combs entered into an agreement with all the manufacturers of combs in Patna city in which the latter undertook during their life time to sell all their products to *R* and to his heirs and not to sell the same to any one else. Holding the agreement void under Section 27, the court observed, 'It bound the manufacturers from generation to generation; it was unrestricted both as to time and place; it was oppressive; it was intended to create monopolies' [*Shaikh Kalu vs Ram Saran Bhagat*[16]].

Restraints upon employees An agreement of service by which an employee binds himself/herself during the term of his/her agreement, not to compete with employer, is not a restraint of trade and therefore valid [*Charlesworth vs Macdonald*[17]].

However, an agreement to restrain an employee from competing with his/her employer after the termination of employment would not be allowed by the courts [*Brahmputra Tea Co. vs E. Scarth*[18]]. A contract of employment, as a matter of fact, by

[9] 1897, 22 ILR Bom. 861
[10] 1872, ILR 2 Mad 44
[11] 1951, ILR 2 Cal 386
[12] 1882, ILR 8 Cal 809
[13] 1902, ILR 26 Mad 168
[14] 1890, ILR 8 Mad 472
[15] 1931, AIR All 539
[16] 1908, AIR 8 CWN 388
[17] 1898, ILR 23 Bom 103
[18] 1885, ILR, 11 Cal 545

its very nature ties the employee to his/her master only so long as the employment lasts. Public policy requires that neither the worker nor the master should be deprived of the benefits of the former's labour, skill, or talent by imposing restrictions upon his/her future activities. An agreement imposing a restriction on the employee after leaving an employer will only be reasonable between the parties if there is some proprietary interest of the employer meriting protection, i.e., trade secrets or business connection. The restriction must not be wider than reasonably necessary to protect such interests. Such restrictions must be expressed and will not be implied by the court [*Faccenda Chicken Ltd vs Fowler*[19]].

From the above discussion, it becomes clear that every restraint of trade is *prima facie* void, but certain exceptions to this general rule are recognised. Accordingly, each case must be examined with regard to its special circumstances so as to consider whether the restraint is reasonable and justified or not. The philosophy to test the justification of every such agreement is that the restraint is reasonable with respect to both the interests of contracting parties and the interests of the public at large. The burden of establishing that, as between the parties, the restraint is reasonable lies on the promisee; the burden of proving that, as far as the public interest is concerned, the restraint is unreasonable lies on the promisor.

Agreements in Restraint of Legal Proceedings

According to Section 28, every such agreement

1. by which any party thereto is restricted absolutely from enforcing its rights under or in respect of any contract, by the usual legal proceedings in the ordinary tribunals, or which limits the time within which he may, thus, enforce his rights, or
2. which extinguishes the rights of any party thereto, or discharges any party thereto from any liability, under or in respect of any contract on the expiry of a specified period so as to restrict any party from enforcing his rights, is void to that extent.

[19] 1987, C.A.

Exceptions

The above provision is, however, subject to the following exceptions:

Referring a dispute to arbitration This section (i.e., 28) shall not render a contract illegal by which two or more persons agree that any dispute that may arise between them in respect of any subject or class of subjects shall be referred to arbitration, and that only the amount awarded in such arbitration shall be recoverable in respect of the dispute so referred.

Referring questions that have already arisen to arbitration Section 28 shall also not render illegal any contract in writing by which two or more persons agree to refer to arbitration any question between them which has already arisen, or affect any provision of any law in force for the time being as to references to arbitration.

Agreements with Uncertain Meaning

Agreements the meaning of which is not certain or capable of being made certain are void [Section 29].

Some illustrations [appended to Section 29], in which agreements have been declared void for uncertainty are provided in Box 5.2.

It is a necessary requirement that an agreement, in order to be binding, must be sufficiently definite to enable the court to give it a practical meaning. Its terms must be so definite, or capable of being made definite without further agreement of the parties, that promises and performances to be rendered by each party are reasonably certain [*Scammell vs Ousten*[20]].

However, an agreement cannot be declared void for uncertainty if it is totally silent as to price, because in such a situation, reasonable price can be determined in accordance with Section 2 of the Sale of Goods Act and the agreement will be valid.

Moreover, an agreement to agree in future for want of certainty whether the parties will be able to agree is void. For example, where *A* agrees to supply to *B* 100 tons of Basmati rice at terms and conditions to be finalised, the agreement is unenforceable [*Punit Beriwala vs Suva Sanyal*]. A contract to negotiate has also been held void for uncertainty [*Courtney and Fairbaion Ltd vs Tolani Bros. Hotels Ltd*].

[20] 1941, AC 251

Box 5.2 Uncertain Agreements Are Void

Example 1

A agrees to sell to *B* 100 tons of oil of a specified description, known as an article of commerce. There is no certainty here to make the agreement void.

Example 2

A, who exclusively deals in coconut oil, agrees to sell to *B* '100 tons of oil.' The nature of *A*'s trade affords an indication of the meaning of the words, and *A* has entered into a contract for the sale of 100 tons of coconut oil.

Example 3

A agrees to sell *B* his white horse for ₹500 or ₹1000. There is nothing to show which of the two amounts was to be given. The agreement is void.

Example 4

A agrees to sell to *B* all the grain in his granary at Ramnagar. There is no uncertainty here to make the agreement void.

Example 5

A agrees to sell to *B* 1000 tons of rice at a price to be fixed by *C*. As the price is capable of being made certain, there is no uncertainty here to make the agreement void.

Agreements by Way of Wager

Wagering agreement: A promise to give money or money's worth upon the determination or ascertainment of an uncertain event.

The term 'wager' literally means 'a bet'. It implies an arrangement to risk money on the result of an (uncertain) event. Therefore, wagering agreements are ordinarily betting agreements.

For example, *A* and *B*, who are neighbours, bet as to whether a tremor would rock their city on a particular day or not. *A* promises to pay *B* ₹5000 if the city experiences a tremor, and *B* promises an equal amount to *A*, if it does not. This is an arrangement by way of wager.

The Indian Contract Act has, however, nowhere defined a wager or an agreement by way of wager. Let us now, examine the following two definitions of a wagering contract given by two law experts to understand the true nature of ' wager'.

'A wagering contract may be defined as a promise by *A* to pay money to *B* on the happening of a given uncertain event, in consideration of *B* paying money to *A* on the event not happening'. [Cockburn C.J.]

'A wagering contract is one by which two persons, professing to hold opposite views touching the issue of a future uncertain event, mutually agree that, depending on the determination of that event, one shall win from the other, and that other shall pay or handover to him a sum of money or other stake; neither of the contracting parties having any other interest in that contract than the sum or stake he will win or lose, there being no other real consideration for the making of such contract by either of the parties. It is essential to a wagering contract that each party under it may either win or lose, his win or lose being dependent on the issue of the event, and therefore remaining uncertain until that issue is known. If either of the parties may win but cannot lose, or may lose but cannot win, it is not a wagering contract.' [Hawkins J.]

An agreement by way of wager, therefore, implies nothing but a promise to give money or money's worth upon the determination of an uncertain event. The following are the common examples of agreements by way of wager:

1. Lottery
2. Gambling
3. Competitions in which prizes depend on chance.

Wagering Agreements are void and unenforceable but these agreements can also be made illegal by enactment.

Essentials of a Wagering Agreement

Analysis of the above definitions makes it clear that to make a transaction wager the following features must be present:

Uncertain event A wagering transaction in fact is a game of chance. The essence of a wager is the uncertainty of the event. To constitute a wager, the performance of the bargain must depend on the ascertainment of an uncertain event.

Mutuality There must be mutual chances of gain and loss (i.e., each party should stand to win or lose), according to the result of the uncertain event. If either of the parties may win but cannot lose or may lose but cannot win, it is not a wagering agreement.

Neither party to have control over the event In order to effect an agreement by way of wager, neither party should have control over the happening of the event one way or the other.

No proprietary interest in the event There being no other real consideration for the making of such contract, neither party should have any other interest in that contract other than the sum or stake he will win or lose.

Consequences of Wagering Agreements

Agreements by way of wager are unenforceable as well as null and void, as they are considered being opposed to public policy. Section 30 says:

'Agreements by way of wager are void, and no suit shall be brought for recovering anything alleged to be won on any wager, or entrusted to any person to abide the result of any game or other uncertain event on which any wager is made.'

In India, wagering agreements are simply void but not illegal. However, the States of Maharastra and Gujarat have, also, declared them as illegal. Therefore, particularly in these two states, a wagering agreement being illegal is not only void between the immediate parties but also taints and renders all the collateral agreements to it void.

Exceptions to Wagering Agreements

Horse race A subscription, contribution, or agreement to subscribe or contribute, made or entered into for or towards any prize or sum of money of the value or amount of ₹500 or upwards, to be rewarded to the winner or winners of any horse race shall not be void [See proviso to Section 30]. Put simply, contributions, or betting money in horse races, in which there are cash rewards for the winner or winners are not deemed illegal in the eyes of the law, provided the sum is ₹500 or more.

Prize competitions Prize competitions, which involve skill and intelligence (i.e., where prizes do not depend on chance), for example, picture puzzles, literary competitions, and athletic event are not wagers, provided the amount of prize does not exceed ₹1000. Lord Heward C.J. observed in *Cole vs Odhams Press*[21], 'If skill plays a substantial part in the result, and prizes are awarded according to the merits of the solution, the competition is not a lottery. Otherwise it is'. An agreement to subscribe or contribute towards a prize to be awarded to the winner of a lawful game would be perfectly lawful and enforceable under the law, although depends on the outcome of an uncertain event. Thus, in an agreement to enter into a wrestling match wherein the winner was to be rewarded out of the gate money, it was held that the agreement could not be looked upon as one of wagering in law [*Babasaheb vs Rajaram*[22]].

Contracts of insurance Despite bearing a resemblance to wagering contracts, contracts of insurance cannot be recognised as wagers. The law distinguishes between the two, for the simple reason that in a contract of insurance the insurer's object is to preserve himself/herself from financial loss, called insurable interest, and not to arrange that he/she should gain, or someone else should lose, if an uncertain event turns out in a particular way. Contracts of insurance have in fact become a necessity with the development of trade and are recognised as contracts that the law would enforce. An insurance contract could sometimes turn out to be a wager if the party insuring has no insurable interest.

Agreements to Do Impossible Acts

An agreement to do an act impossible in itself is void [Section 56].

[21] 1936, 1 KB 416
[22] 1931, AIR Bom. 264

For example, *A* agrees with *B* to double treasure by magic. The agreement is void [Illustration (a) to Section 56].

The law disregards all the agreements to do impossible acts, mainly because of the following two reasons:

1. First, the persons who purport to agree to do such obviously impossible acts are deemed to be either non-serious as to performing such acts or unable to understand what they are doing.
2. Second, a promise to do an act impossible in itself cannot be of any value to the other party and, therefore, such agreements lack consideration.

Restitution of Benefits Received Under a Void Agreement

Restitution: Giving back or restoration of the money or benefit received from the plaintiff under the agreement.

The term 'restitution' legally implies giving back or restoration of the money or benefit received from the plaintiff under the agreement. Section 65, which provides for restitution, says thus:

'When an agreement is discovered to be void, or when a contract becomes void, any person who has received any advantage under such an agreement or contract is bound to restore it, or to make compensation for it, to the person from whom he received it.'

This provision is based on the simple logic that when a contract is no more enforceable, the party who has received any benefit under such a contract from the other party must return it or make compensation for the same to the other party. Box 5.3 presents some examples of restitution of benefit in the event of non-performance of a contract.

It is important to note that the restitution of benefit received is not allowed in case of expressly declared void agreements with the exception where the minor has entered into an agreement by misrepresenting his/her age or otherwise. The doctrine of restitution is applicable to only those agreements discovered to be void (later on) in addition to contracts, which subsequently become unenforceable for one reason or the other provided the said reason(s) was/were beyond the control of the promisor.

For example, *A* agrees to deliver to *B* after one month 100 quintals of wheat at the rate of ₹500 per quintal and receives ₹10,000 as advance. However, soon after the agreement, the government by passing a special Act prohibit private sale of wheat. The contract becomes void, but *A* must return the advance money received from *B*.

Contingent Contracts

Contingent contract: A contract to do or not to do something, if some event collateral to the contract does or does not happen.

A contingent contract implies a contract, the performance of which depends on the happening or non-happening of an uncertain event, incidental to such contract. Section 31 defines a contingent contract as follows:

A 'contingent contract' is a contract to do or not to do something, if some event, collateral to such contract does or does not happen.

For example, *A* contracts to pay to *B* ₹10,000 if *B*'s house gets burnt down, or *X* contracts to pay *Y* ₹5000 if his scooter is destroyed.

The nature of both the above-mentioned contracts is contingent. Contracts of insurance, indemnity,

Box 5.3 Illustrations of Restitution [Appended to Section 65]

Example 1

A pays *B* ₹1000 in consideration of *B* promising to marry *C*, *A*'s daughter. *C* dies by the time of execution of the promise. The agreement is void, but *B* must return *A* the sum of ₹1000.

Example 2

A make a contract with *B* to deliver him 250 bags of rice before the first of May. *A* delivers only 130 bags by the specified date, and none after. *B* retains these 130 bags after the first of May. He is bound to pay *A* for the bags that he has kept.

and guarantee are common instances of contingent contracts.

Essentials of a Contingent Contract

A contingent contract has some essential elements such as it is subject to the occurrence or non-occurrence of an uncertain event, the event is incidental to the contract, and the contingency should not be merely a will of the promisor. Let us examine these key elements of a contingent contract.

1. A contingent contract is subject to happening or non-happening of an uncertain event, collateral to it. In other words, performance of such a contract becomes due only upon occurrence or non-occurrence of some future uncertain event.
2. The contingent event is of uncertain nature. A contract that is subject to a certain or an absolute type of condition cannot be regarded as a contingent contract. For example, a contract in which *A* agrees to sell 10 bags of cement to *B* and *B* agrees to pay the price at delivery of goods or afterwards is not a contingent contract because these conditions are of a certain nature. The delivery would take place and the price will become payable. Similarly, a contract in which *A* promises to pay *B* a fixed sum of money on the death of *C* is not a contingent contract for the certainty of event. The person in question will definitely expire one day and an obligation to perform the contract (i.e., to pay the money to *B*) will arise on part of *A* eventually. But where *A* agrees to deliver to *B* a certain quantity of cement should the government lift the ban on free trading of cement is a contingent contract, for the event, i.e, lifting of the ban in this case, may or may not occur.
3. The uncertain event on which the performance of a contingent contract depends is collateral or incidental to the contract, i.e., it does not form part of the consideration of the contract and is independent of it. For example where *A*, a contractor, agrees to construct a shop for *B* and the latter agrees to pay the former ₹10,000 upon the completion of construction, the contract is merely a conditional one and not contingent because the event (*A*'s completing the construction) on which *B*'s obligation to pay arises is a part of the reciprocal promises which constitute the contract and not a collateral event. If, however, in the above case, *B* promises to pay *A* the said amount, provided the latter could complete the construction within a week, the deal in question turns out to be a contingent contract because now the event, namely, completion of construction work within a week, is a collateral event, upon the happening of which the contract would be enforced. Thus, to constitute a contingent contract, it is essential that the future uncertain event be collateral to the bargain in question.
4. The contingency should depend on the will of the promisor or the promisee; it (contingency) should not be the mere will of the promisor. For instance, where *A* agrees to construct a swimming pool for *B* and *B* agrees to pay *A* ₹20,000 upon completion of construction work, provided his architect approves the construction, is a contingent contract. But in the above case, if *B* simply promises to pay to *A* the stated sum if he so chooses, it cannot be a contingent contract.

Enforcement of a Contingent Contract

The rules regarding enforcement of contingent contracts, as contained in sections 32 to 36 of the Act, are summarised as under.

1. Contingent contracts about doing or not doing anything if an uncertain future event happens, cannot be enforced by law unless and until that event has happened.

   If the event becomes impossible, such contracts become void [Section 32]. Box 5.4 explains the point with some examples.
2. Contingent contracts to do or not to do anything if an uncertain future event does not happen, can be enforced when the happening of that event becomes impossible, and not before [Section 33]. For example, *A* agrees to pay *B* a sum of money if a certain ship does not return to a particular port. The ship, however, sinks. The contract can be enforced after the ship sinks, as after the tragedy the ship's return will not be possible.
3. If the future event in which a contract is contingent is the way in which a person will act at an unspecified time, the event shall be considered

Box 5.4 **Illustrations [Appended to Section 32]**

Example 1

A makes a contract with *B* to buy *B*'s house if *A* survives *C*. This contract cannot be enforced by law unless and until *C* dies during *A*'s lifetime.

Example 2

A makes a contract with *B* to sell a horse to *B* at a specified price, if *C*, to whom the horse has been offered, refuses to buy it. The contract between *A* and *B* cannot be enforced by law unless and until *C* refuses to buy the horse.

Example 3

A contracts to pay *B* a sum of money when *B* marries *C*. *C* dies without being married to *B*. The contract is contingent at the time of inception but has become void subsequently.

to become impossible when such person does anything which renders it impossible that he should so act within any definite time, or otherwise than under futher contingencies [Section 34]. For example, *A* agrees to give *B* a sum of money if *B* marries C. However, C marries *D*. The marriage of *B* to C must now be considered impossible although it is possible that *D* may die one day and that C may afterwards marry *B* [Illustration appended to Section 34].

4. Contingent contracts to do or not to do anything if a specified uncertain event happens within a fixed time become void if, at the expiration of the time fixed, such event has not occurred, or if, before the time fixed, such event becomes impossible [Section 35]. For example, *A* promises to pay *B* a fixed sum of money if a certain ship returns within the year. The contract may be enforced if the ship returns within the year and becomes void if the ship is destroyed during the year [Illustration (a) appended to Section 35].
5. Contingent contracts to do or not to do anything, if a specified uncertain event does not happen within a fixed time, may be enforced by law when the time fixed has expired, and such event has not happened or, before the time fixed has expired if it becomes certain that such event will not happen. For example, *A* promises to pay *B* a fixed sum of money if a certain ship does not return within the year. The contract may be enforced if the ship does not return within a year, or is destroyed within the year [Illustration (b) appended to Section 35].
6. Contingent agreements to do or not to do anything, if an impossible event happens, are void, whether the impossibility of the event is known or not to the parties to agreement when it is made [Section 36]. For example, *A* agrees to pay *B* ₹1000 if two straight lines should enclose a space. The agreement is void due to sheer impossibility of the agreement [Illustration (a) appended to Section 36].

   or
7. *A* agrees to pay *B* ₹1000 if *B* will marry *A*'s daughter C. *C* was dead at the time of agreement. The agreement is void [Illustration (b) appended to Section 36].

Contingent Contract Versus Wagering Agreement

Wagering agreement: An agreement which entails an arrangement to risk money on the result of a particular event.

Although the occurrence of a specified uncertain event is essential to both a contingent contract and a wagering or betting agreement, there are some fundamental points of difference between the two, discussed as under:

1. A contingent contract is a valid contract, whereas a wagering agreement is void.
2. A contingent contract may not consist of reciprocal promises, whereas an agreement by way of wager is composed of reciprocal promises.
3. In a contingent contract, the future uncertain event is merely collateral, whereas in a wagering

agreement, the future uncertain event is the sole determining factor.

4. The parties to a contingent contract have real interest in the occurrence or non-occurrence of the contingency, whereas it is not so in a wagering agreement. In a wager, the parties have no other interest in the occurrence or non-occurrence of event except winning the bet amount.

Exercises

I. Objective-type Questions

1. State whether each of the following statements is True or False:
   (i) A void agreement is one that is not enforceable by law.
   (ii) Every illegal contract is also void but a void contract need not necessarily be illegal.
   (iii) Penalty upon remarriage is tantamount to a restraint of marriage.
   (iv) A wager is nothing but a bet.
   (v) An agreement 'to enter into an agreement in future' is void for uncertainty.
   (vi) Contingent contracts are a class of conditional contracts except that the condition collateral to such contracts is of uncertain nature.
   (vii) A contingent contract consists of reciprocal promises.
   (viii) The performance of a contingent contract depends on the happening or non-happening of the future uncertain event.
   (ix) In a contingent contract the parties have real interest in the occurrence or non-occurrence of the event.
   (x) A contract that is subject to a certain or an absolute event cannot be regarded as a contingent contract.

2. Fill in the blanks:
   (i) An agreement to buy a lottery ticket authorized by the government is ________.
   (ii) When a transaction is simply void but not illegal, the collateral transaction would be ________.
   (ii) The essence of a wager is the ________ of the event.
   (iv) When the seller of the goodwill of a business undertakes not to compete with the purchaser of the goodwill, the contract is ________.
   (v) A winner of a bet ________ bring a suit to recover the amount he wins.
   (vi) A contingent contract is ________.
   (vii) In a contingent contract, future event is ________.
   (viii) If the happening of the future uncertain event becomes impossible, it renders a contingent contract ________.
   (ix) The contingent event should not be mere will of the ________.
   (x) A contract for the sale of goods prescribing the condition that the goods would be inspected before dispatch is a ________ contract.

3. Indicate the correct answer:
   (i) An agreement that provides for release or forfeiture of rights if no suit is brought within the time stipulated in the agreement is
   (a) Valid (b) Void
   (c) Void and illegal (d) Enforceable
   (ii) When a transaction is simply void but not illegal, the collateral transaction would be
   (a) Void (b) Illegal
   (c) Void and illegal (d) Valid
   (iii) An illegal agreement taints and renders all the incidental transactions
   (a) Void (b) Illegal
   (c) Void ab initio (d) Enforceable

(iv) The exceptions arising under judicial interpretation of Section 27 do not include
(a) Trade combinations (b) Exclusive dealing agreements
(c) Sale of goodwill (d) Service agreements

(v) Which of the following is one of the exceptions to wagering agreements
(a) Lottery (b) Crossword puzzle
(c) Athletic competitions (d) Competitive event where prize depends upon chance

II. Review Questions

1. Discuss in brief the law relating to agreements, expressly declared void under the Indian Contract Act.
2. 'An agreement in restraint of trade is void'. Elaborate mentioning exceptions to it, if any.
3. What is a wager? Discuss the law relating to wagering agreements.
4. 'An agreement by way of wager is simply void and not illegal'. Examine the truth in the statement.
5. 'Contingent contracts are a class of conditional contracts and the condition is of uncertain nature.' Comment.
6. What do you mean by contingent contracts? Give examples. Differentiate a contingent contract from a wagering agreement.
7. What are the essential features of contingent contracts? State the rules regarding enforcement of such contracts.

III. Caselets

1. *A* agrees to sell to *B* all the wheat in his warehouse. Comment on the validity of the agreement.
[Hint: Agreement is valid as there is no uncertainty involved, Section 29]
2. *A* lends ₹500 to *B* to enable him purchase a Manipur State Lottery ticket. *B* upon losing in the lottery refuses to repay *A*'s money. Can *A* recover his money from *B*?
[Hint: Yes, lottery being a wager is a void agreement (except in Maharastra and Gujarat where wagering agreements have been declared illegal), and transaction collateral to a void agreement remains valid]
3. *A* agreed to sell to *B* all the salt he manufactured and *B* agreed to buy such salt. *A* further agreed not to sell the salt to any third parties. Decide.
[Hint: The agreement is valid as it does not restrain business, refer *Mackenzie vs Sitaramiah*[23]]
4. *A* agrees to pay ₹1000 to *B* if it rains, and *B* promises to pay a like amount to *A*, if it does not rain. Comment on the nature and enforceability of this agreement?
[Hint: The agreement in question is by way of wager, and such agreement being expressly declared void (except in Maharashtra and Gujarat States where a wagering agreement is not only void but illegal too) is unenforceable, refer Section 30]
5. *A* promises to marry *B* and in case of default agrees to pay her ₹50,000 as compensation. *A* subsequently ties the knot with *C* and even refuses to pay *B* the agreed compensation. Decide.
[Hint: The agreement between *A* and *B* being restraint of marriage is void, therefore *B* cannot claim the said compensation from *A*]
6. *A* entered into a contract with *B* that he would sell certain shares belonging to *A* within a year failing which he would buy them himself at a stipulated price. Is it a contingent contract?
[Hint: No, the contingent liability would ripen into a perfect obligation at the end of the year. Refer *Jethalal vs R.N. Kapur*[24]]

[23] 15 Mad. 79
[24] 1956, A.B. 74

7. *A* contracts to pay *B* ₹50,000 on the destruction of the latter's premises in the event of a fire. Comment on the nature of contract]
[**Hint:** It is a contingent contract for the contingency may or may not happen]

8. *A* promises to pay *B* ₹5000 if he so chooses. Is it a contingent contract?
[**Hint:** No, the event collateral to the contract cannot be the mere will of the promisor]

9. *A* promises to pay *B* a sum of money if a certain ship returns safely within six months. The ship sinks into the deep seas before the stipulated time. Decide.
[**Hint:** The contract becomes void as the event has become impossible. Refer Section 35]

10. *A* contracts to pay *B* ₹50,000 if a certain ship does not return. The ship sinks. Decide.
[**Hint:** The contingent contract is valid and can be enforced after the ship has sunk]

Answers to Objective-type Questions

1. (i) True (ii) True (iii) False (iv) True (v) True
(vi) True (vii) False (viii) True (ix) True (x) True

2. (i) void (ii) valid (iii) uncertainty (iv) enforceable (v) cannot
(vi) valid (vii) only collateral (viii) void (ix) promisor (x) firm

3. (i) (b) (ii) (d) (iii) (b) (iv) (c) (v) (c)

5 Chapter in Review

LEARNING OUTCOMES

LO[1] Void agreement versus void contract

LO[2] Void agreement versus illegal agreement

LO[3] Agreements expressly declared void

LO[4] Restitution of benefits received under void agreements

LO[5] Essentials of a contingent contract

LO[6] Enforcement of contingent contracts

LO[7] Contingent contracts distinguished from wagering contracts

KEY TERMS

Void agreement: Agreement (legally) unenforceable from its very inception.

Void contract: A contract not enforceable by law.

Illegal agreement: An agreement supported by unlawful consideration and/or object which renders it not only void and unenforceable but unlawful too over and above.

Wagering agreement: A promise to give money or money's worth upon the determination or ascertainment of an uncertain event.

Restitution: Giving back or restoration of the money or benefit received from the plaintiff under the agreement.

Contingent contract: A contract to do or not to do something, if some event collateral to the contract, does or does not happen.

Wagering agreement: An agreement which entails an arrangement to risk money on the result of a particular event.

LO[1] A void agreement implies a set of promises which is unenforceable since its inception; a *nullity*. Whereas a void contract is an agreement, enforceable in the ordinary course but ceases to be enforceable by law under compelling or extraordinary circumstances. For instance, an agreement with a minor is void but a contract between a foreign national and an Indian citizen is enforceable in the ordinary course. But the same contract would cease to be enforceable in the event of an outbreak of war between India and the country, the foreign national belongs to, and be treated as void. Therefore, a contract may become void for one reason or the other. But it cannot be void *ab initio*; it is only an agreement that can be void *ab initio*.

LO[2] A void agreement is different from an illegal one for the former is merely unenforceable but may not be forbidden by law. For instance, marrying a minor girl is void but not forbidden by law as the object behind the same is not unlawful. An illegal agreement, on the other hand, is one in which the consideration or object is also unlawful and therefore, it is not only void and unenforceable but unlawful too and thus devoid of any legal effect.

LO[3] The Contract Act has declared some agreements as expressly void. They include agreements by or with parties incompetent to contract; persons incapable of contracting; agreements of which considerations and objects are unlawful; agreements without consideration; agreements in restraint of marriage; agreements in restraint of trade; agreements in restraint of legal proceedings; agreements with an element of uncertainty; agreements by way of wager; and agreements to perform an impossible act.

LO[4] Damages cannot be claimed by a party injured by attempting to comply with a void contract. When a contract is exposed to be void, any person who has received any benefit under such contract is bound to restore it, or to make compensation for it, to the person from whom he received it.

LO[5] A 'contingent contract' is one to do or not to do something, if some event, collateral to such contract, does or does not happen. Contingent contracts to do or not to do anything if an uncertain future event happens cannot be enforced by law unless that event has happened. If the event becomes impossible, such contracts become void.

LO6 Contingent contracts to do or not to do anything if an uncertain future event does not happen can be enforced when the happening of that event becomes impossible and not before.

LO7 Although the occurrence of a specified uncertain event is essential to both contingent and wagering contracts, there are some fundamental points of difference between the two. The former is valid, but a wagering contract is void, and even illegal in the states of Gujarat and Maharashtra. Contingent contracts do not contain reciprocal promises like wagering contracts. Parties to a contingent contract have real interest in the occurrence or non-occurrence of the contingency, whereas in a wagering agreement there is no other interest in the incident except winning or losing the bet amount.

CHAPTER

6 Performance and Discharge of Contract

Learning Objectives

LO[1] Performance of a contract

LO[2] Discharge of a contract

LO[3] Modes of discharging a contract

A contract places a legal obligation upon the contracting parties to perform their mutual promises, and it carries on until the discharge or termination of the contract. The most natural and usual mode of discharging a contract is to perform it. A person who performs a contract in accordance with its terms stands discharged from any further obligations. As a rule, such performance entitles him to receive the other party's performance. Exact and complete performance by both the parties puts an end to the contract. In expecting exact performance, the law looks forward that performance must match contractual obligations. A contract should be performed at the time specified and at the place agreed upon. When this has been accomplished, the parties are discharged automatically and the contract is discharged eventually. There are, however, many other ways in which a discharge may be brought about. For example, it may result from an excuse for non-performance. In certain cases, attempted performance may also operate as a substitute for actual performance and can result in complete discharge of the contract.

Performance of a Contract Defined

Performance of contract: Fulfilling respective contractual obligations by both the parties.

The term 'performance of contract' means that both the promisor and the promisee have fulfilled their respective obligations, which the contract placed upon them. For instance, *A* visits a stationery shop to buy a calculator. The shopkeeper delivers the calculator and *A* pays the price. The contract is said to have been discharged by mutual performance.

According to Section 37, 'The parties to a contract must either perform or offer to perform their respective promises, unless such performance is dispensed with or excused under the provisions of this Act, or any other law'.

Promises bind the representatives of the promisor in case of the death of the latter before performance, unless a contrary intention appears in the contract.

Thus, it is the primary duty of each contracting party to either perform or offer to perform their respective promises. For performance to be effective, the courts expect it to be exact and complete, i.e., the same must match the contractual obligations. However, where under the provisions of the Contract Act or any other law, the performance can be dispensed with or excused, a party is absolved from such a responsibility.

Types of Performance

Performance, as an action of the performing, may be actual or attempted.

Actual performance: Fulfilment of contractual obligation(s) by the promisor in accordance with the terms of contract.

Actual Performance

When a promisor to a contract has fulfilled his obligation in accordance with the terms of the contract, the promise is said to have been actually performed. Actual performance gives a discharge to the contract and the liability of the promisor ceases to exist. For example, *A* agrees to deliver 10 bags of cement at *B*'s factory and *B* promises to pay the price on delivery. *A* delivers the cement on the due date and *B* makes the payment. This is actual performance.

Actual performance can further be subdivided into substantial performance and partial performance.

Substantial performance

Substantial performance: Fulfilment of the obligations agreed to in a contract, with only slight variances from the exact terms and/or unimportant omissions or minor defects.

In the law of contracts, 'substantial performance' implies fulfilment of the obligations agreed to in a contract, with only slight variances from the exact terms and/or unimportant omissions or minor defects. That is, where the work agreed upon is almost finished. The court then may order that the money must be paid, but deducts the amount needed to correct minor existing defect. Substantial performance is applicable only if the contract is not an entire contract and is severable. The rationale behind creating the doctrine of substantial performance is to avoid the possibility of one party evading his liabilities by claiming that the contract has not been completely performed. However, what is deemed to be substantial performance is a question of fact to be decided in each case. It will largely depend on what remains undone and its value in comparison to the contract as a whole.

Partial performance

Partial performance: Execution of a part of a divisible contract by one party acceptable by the other party.

This is where one of the parties has performed the contract, but not completely, and the other side has shown willingness to accept the part performed. Partial performance may occur where there is shortfall on delivery of goods or where a service is not fully carried out.

There is a thin line of difference between substantial and partial performance. The two following points would help in distinguishing the two types of performance.

Partial performance must be accepted by the other party In other words, the party who is at the receiving end of the partial performance has a genuine choice whether to accept or reject. Substantial performance, on the other hand, is legally enforceable against the other party.

Payment is made on a different basis from that for substantial performance It is made on *quantum meruit*, which literally means as much as is deserved. So, for example, if half of the work has been completed, half of the negotiated money would be payable. In case of substantial performance, the party that has performed can recover the amount appropriate to what has been done under the contract, provided that the contract is not an entire contract, i.e., severable with ease. The price is, thus, often payable in such circumstances, and the sum deducted represents the cost of repairing defective workmanship.

Attempted Performance

Attempted performance/ Tender: An offer to perform the obligation under the contract in accordance with the terms of the contract.

When the performance has become due, it is sometimes sufficient if the promisor offers to perform his obligation under the contract. This offer is known as attempted performance or more commonly as tender. Thus, attempted performance or tender may be defined as an offer to perform the obligation under the contract in accordance with the terms of the contract. It is not actual performance. If goods are tendered by the seller but refused by the buyer, the seller is discharged from further liability, given that the goods are in accordance with the contract as to quantity and quality, and he may sue the buyer for breach of contract if he so desires. The rationale being that when a person offers to perform, he is ready, willing, and capable to perform. Accordingly, a tender of performance may operate as a substitute for actual performance and can effect a complete discharge.

In this regard, Section 38 says:

'Where a promisor has made an offer of performance to the promisee, and the offer has not been accepted, the promisor is not responsible for non-performance nor does he thereby lose his rights under the contract. For example, *A* contracts to deliver to *B* 100 tons of basmati rice at his warehouse on 6 March 2004. *A* takes the goods to *B*'s place on the due date during business hours, but *B*, without assigning any good reason, refuses to take the delivery. Here, *A* has performed what he was required to perform under the contract. It is a case of attemped performance and *A* is not responsible for non-performance of *B* nor does he thereby lose his rights under the contract.'

Essentials of a Valid Tender

In order to be a valid tender or offer of performance, it must fulfil the following conditions:

1. It must be unconditional [Section 38(1)]. In order to be legally enforceable, a tender should not only be in accordance with the contractual terms, the promisor should also not attach any condition to it, because it is not reasonable to compel the other party to accept a changed or otherwise modified performance, whatsoever.
2. It must be made at a proper time and place [Section 38(2)]. If a person's obligation is to deliver goods or render services, they must be tendered at a reasonable hour, for example, not in the middle of the night. If such a tender is refused, it will not release the tendering party from further obligation.
3. It must be made under such circumstances that the person to whom it is made may have a reasonable opportunity of ascertaining that the person by whom it is made is able and willing, and then do what he is bound by his promise to do [Section 38(2)]. For instance, if a debtor sends money by

post and it is lost, he will have to pay again, unless the mode of delivery was requested by the creditor and the debtor took reasonable care.

4. If the offer is to deliver a particular thing to the promisee, the promisee must have a reasonable opportunity of seeing that the thing offered is the same that the promisor is bound by his promise to deliver [Section 38(3)]. For example, if a seller tenders too few goods, too many goods, or the right amount of goods mixed with other goods, the buyer may reject all of them because the performance is not exact. The buyer can also reject the tender where the goods are not packed in accordance with the contract.

   As regards payment of money, it must comply with the following rules:

   (a) It must be in accordance with the rules relating to 'legal tender'. For instance, a tender of notes of any bank other than the Reserve Bank of India is not legal tender, even though the creditor may waive his objection to the tender, if he wishes. If a debtor offers 100 US Dollars towards the payment of ₹3000, it will not be a legal tender although it is worth much more than collector's amount.
   (b) There must be no request for change. In other words, exactly the right amount of cash must be tendered. For example, if someone offers a ₹1000 note for the settlement of ₹600 debt, the same will not release the debtor from his obligation to pay, since it is not reasonable to compel the creditor to provide change.
   (c) Tender by cheque or any other negotiable instrument such as a debit card or credit card is not a good tender, unless the creditor does not object. It should be noted that if a proper tender of money is refused, the debt is not discharged, but if the money is paid into court, the debtor has a good defence to an action by his creditor, and the debt does not bear interest.

5. An offer to one of the several joint promises has the same legal consequences as an offer to all of them. For instance, *A* contracts to deliver at *B*'s warehouse, which is jointly owned by *B*, *C*, and *D* on March 1, 100 bales of cotton of a particular quality. In order to make an offer of performance with the effect stated in this section, *A* must bring the cotton to *B*'s warehouse, on the appointed day, under such circumstances that *B* or even *C* or *D* on *B*'s behalf may have a reasonable opportunity of satisfying himself that the commodity offered (brought in this case) is cotton of the quality contracted for, and that there are 100 bales.

By Whom Can a Contract Be Performed?

The following are the entities that are competent to perform a contract.

Promisor If it appears from the nature of any case that it was the intention of the contracting parties that any promise contained in the contract should be performed by the promisor himself, such a promise must be performed by the promisor himself [Section 40].

Agent Where personal consideration is not the subject matter of the contract, the promisor or his representatives may employ a competent person to perform it [Section 40]. For example, *A* promises to pay *B* a sum of money. *A* may perform this promise, either by personally paying the money to *B* or by causing it to be paid to *B* by someone else; if *A* dies before the time appointed for payment, his representatives must perform the promise, or they may employ some able person to do so.

Or,

A promises to paint a picture for *B*. He must perform this promise personally. In other words, he cannot have the picture painted by any agent or representative.

Legal representative Promises bind the representatives of the promisors. This will hold good even in case of death of the promisors before performance, unless an exemption to that effect is stated in the contract itself [Section 37]. However, in contracts of personal nature or where personal consideration is the subject matter of the contract, such promises come to an end should the promisor die, and therefore, such contracts cannot be performed by the representatives. This has been illustrated in Box 6.1.

Box 6.1 **Performance of Contract—Examples [Appended to Section 37]**

Example 1

A promises to deliver goods to *B* on a certain day on payment of ₹1000. *A* expires before the contracted date. *A*'s representatives are bound to deliver the goods to *B*, and *B* is bound to pay ₹1000 to *A*'s representatives.

Example 2

A promises to paint a picture for *B* by a certain day for an agreed price. *A* dies before the day. The contract cannot be enforced either by *A*'s representatives or by *B*.

Third person When a promisee accepts performance of a promise from a third person, he cannot afterwards enforce it against the promisor [Section 41].

Joint promisors When two or more persons have made a joint promise, then, unless a contrary intention appears by the contract, all such persons must perform the promise during their lifetime. In case of death of any of them, his representative jointly with the survivor or survivors must perform the promise, and, after the death of the last survivor, the representatives of all the promisors, must fulfil the promise jointly [Section 42].

Simply put, it means that if two or more persons jointly make a promise, then unless stated otherwise in the contract, the promise should be jointly fulfilled by all the promisors, and in the event of the death of any promisor/s, the representatives of the deceased promisor would be liable to perform the promise, jointly with the surviving promisors. After the death of the last survivor, the promise would be fulfilled by the representatives of the promisors jointly.

Who Can Demand Performance?

Ordinarily, it is only the promisee who can demand performance of the promise under a contract. This is simply because a stranger to the contract cannot sue, and the person who can demand performance is the party to whom the promise is made. In other words, a third party cannot demand performance of the contract even if it was made for his benefit due to privity of contract. For example, *A* promises *B* to carve the statute of *C*, father of *B*. The person who can demand performance is *B* and not *C*. However, depending on the circumstances, persons other than the promisee can also demand performance. In accordance with Section 37, in the event of the death of the promisee, his legal representative can demand performance unless a contrary intention appears in the contract. However, this is not possible if the contract is of personal nature. Moreover, in case of a joint promise, the promisee may, in the absence of express agreement to the contrary, compel any one or more of the joint promisors to perform the entire promise [Section 43].

Time and Place for Performance

The time and place of performance are the matters to be determined by agreement between the parties to the contact. Certain general rules have been laid down regarding the same by the Contract Act under Sections 46–50. They are summarised as follows.

Where no time is specified A contract is not bad for want of certainty if time for performance is not stated. Where the time for performance is not specified in the contract, the promise must be performed within a reasonable time. The question 'What is a reasonable time' is a question of fact in each particular case. Reasonable time is a relative term that is considered on a case-to-case basis [explanation added to Section 46].

Where time is specified When a contract specifies the time and place for its performance, the parties must perform accordingly. But, when the contract is to be performed on a certain day, and the promisor has undertaken to perform without a request from the promisee, he may perform it at any time during the usual business hours on that day at the specified place. For example, *A* promises to deliver goods at

Box 6.2 **Performance at the Desire of Promisee [Appended to Section 50]**

Example 1

A and *B* are mutually indebted. They settle an account by setting off one item against another, and *B* pays *A* the balance found to be due from him upon such settlement. This amounts to a payment by *A* and *B*, respectively, of the sums they owed to each other.

Example 2

A owes *B* ₹2000. *B* accepts some of *A*'s goods in reduction of the debt. The delivery of goods operates as a part payment.

B's warehouse on the January 1. On that day *A* brings the goods to *B's* warehouse, but after the usual hours for closing, and they are not received. It is deemed that *A* has not performed his promise [Section 47].

On application by promisee for performance When a promise is to be performed on a certain day, and the promisor has not undertaken to perform it without application by the promisee, it is the duty of the promisee to apply for performance at a proper place and within the usual hours of business. The question 'What is a proper time and place' is, in each particular case, a question of fact [Section 48].

Without application by the promisee When a promise is to be performed without a request by the promisee, and no place is fixed for its performance, the promisor must request the promisee to fix a reasonable place for the performance and perform the promise at such place. For example, *A* undertakes to deliver a thousand sacks of jute to *B* on a specific date. *A* must apply to *B* to appoint a suitable place for the delivery and must deliver it to *B* there [Section 49].

Performance in manner or at time prescribed or sanctioned by promisee Sometimes the promisee himself prescribes or states the manner and the time of performance. If it is so, the promisor must perform accordingly. Box 6.2 presents some examples to help understand the point better [Section 50].

Performance of Reciprocal Promises

The legal rules governing reciprocal promises are contained in Sections 51–54 of the Contract Act. They can be summarised as follows.

Promisor is not bound to perform unless promisee is ready and willing A promisor is not bound to perform, unless the promisee reciprocates and is ready and willing to perform his part of the contract. When a contract consists of reciprocal promises to be simultaneously performed, no promisor need to perform his promise unless the promisee is ready and willing to perform his reciprocal promise [Section 51]. Refer to Box 6.3 for examples explaining Section 51.

Box 6.3 **Promisor Not Bound to Perform Unless Promisee Is Ready to Perform**

Example 1

A and *B* entered into a contract that *A* shall deliver goods to *B* and *B* will pay for the good to *A* on the delivery of the goods. *A* need not deliver the goods, unless *B* expresses readiness and willing to pay for the goods on delivery. *B* need not pay for the goods, unless *A* is ready and willing to deliver them on payment.

Example 2

A and *B* entered into a contract that *A* shall deliver goods to *B* at a price to be paid in installments, the first installment to be paid on delivery. *A* need not deliver, unless *B* is ready and willing to pay the first installment on delivery. Likewise, *B* need not pay the first installment, unless *A* is ready and willing to deliver the goods on payment of the first installment.

Box 6.4 **Order of Performance of a Contract**

Example 1

A and *B* contract that *A* shall build a house for *B* at a fixed price. *A*'s promise to build the house must be performed before *B*'s promise to pay for it.

Example 2

A and *B* contract that *A* shall make over his stock-in-trade to *B* at a fixed price, and *B* promises to give security for the payment of the money. *A*'s promise need not be performed until the security is given, for the nature of the transaction requires that *A* should have the security before he delivers his stock.

Order of performance of reciprocal promises Where the order in which reciprocal promises are to be performed is expressly fixed by the contract, they shall be performed in that order; where the order is not expressly fixed by the contract, they shall be performed in that order which the nature of the transaction requires [Section 52]. The following examples in Box 6.4 drive home the point.

Liability of party preventing event on which the contract is to take effect When a contract contains reciprocal promises, and one party to the contract prevents the other from performing his promise, the contract becomes voidable at the option of the party so prevented, and it is entitled to compensation from the other party for any loss which it may sustain in consequence of the non-performance of the contract [Section 53]. For instance, *A* and *B* contract that *B* shall execute certain work for *A* for ₹1000. *B* is ready and willing to execute the work accordingly, but *A* prevents him from doing so. The contract is voidable at the option of *B*, and if he elects to rescind it, he is entitled to recover compensation from *A* for any loss which he has incurred due to the non-performance of the contract.

Effect of default as to that promise which should be first performed When a contract consists of reciprocal promises, such that one of them cannot be performed, or that its performance cannot be claimed till the other has been performed, and the promisor of the promise fails to perform it, such promisor cannot claim the performance of the reciprocal promise and must make compensation to the other party to the contract for any loss which it may sustain by the non-performance of the contract [Section 54].

In other words, in a contract involving reciprocal promises, wherein the performance of one depend on the other and cannot precede the other, then the promisor of the first promise cannot claim the performance of the reciprocal promise without fulfilling his obligation and is bound to compensate the other party for any loss it may incur on account of non-performance of the contract. Some examples to this effect are provided in Box 6.5.

Box 6.5 **Defaulting Promisor Must Compensate the Other Party**

Example 1

A hires *B*'s ship to dispatch a cargo from Kolkata to Mauritius. The cargo is to be provided by *A*, while *B* is to receive a certain freight for its conveyance. *A* does not provide any cargo for the ship. *A* cannot claim the performance of *B*'s promise and must make compensation to *B* for the loss which *B* sustains by the non-performance of the contract on the part of *A*.

Example 2

A promises *B* to sell him 100 bales of merchandise to be delivered next day, and *B* promises *A* to pay for them within a month. *A* does not deliver the bales as per the promise. *B*'s reciprocal promise to pay need not be performed, and *A* must make compensation.

Discharge of a Contract

Discharge of a contract: Termination of contractual obligations by performance or otherwise.

Discharge of a contract implies termination of contractual obligations. This is because when the parties originally entered into the contract, the rights and duties in terms of contractual obligations were set up. Consequently when those rights and duties are put out then the contract is said to have been discharged. Once a contract stands discharged, parties to it are no more liable even though the obligations under the contract remain incomplete.

A contract is deemed to be discharged, that is, concluded, and no longer binding, in the following circumstances.

1. Performance
2. Agreement
3. Lapse of time
4. Impossibility of performance
5. Operation of law
6. Accord and satisfaction
7. Breach

We shall examine each of them as follows.

Discharge by Performance

Where both the parties have either carried out or tendered (attempted) to carry out their obligations under the contract, it is referred to as discharge of the contract by performance. Because performance by one party constitutes the occurrence of a constructive condition, the other party's duty to perform is also triggered, and the person who has performed has the right to receive the other party's performance. The overwhelming majority of contracts are discharged in this way. We have already learnt about it earlier in the chapter.

Discharge by Substituted Agreement

A contract emanates from an agreement between the parties. It thus follows that, the contract must also be discharged by agreement. Therefore, what is required, inevitably, is mutuality. Discharge by substituted agreement arises when a contract is abandoned, or the terms within it are altered, and both the parties are in conformity over it. For instance, *A* and *B* enter into some agreement, and *A* wants to change his mind and not to carry out his terms of the contract. If he does this unilaterally, then he will be in breach of contract to *B*. However, if he approaches *B* and states that he would like to be released from his liabilities under the contract, then the latter might agree. In that case, the contract is said to be discharged by (bilateral) agreement. In effect *B* has promised not to sue *A* if he does not perform his part of the contract and the consideration for his promise is *A*'s promise not to sue *B*. Discharge by agreement may arise in the following ways.

Novation: Substitution of a new contract for the original one.

Novation The term novation implies the substitution of a new contract for the original one. This arrangement may be either between the same parties or between different parties. For a novation to be valid and effective, the consent of all the parties, including the new one(s), if any, is essential. Moreover, the subsequent or second agreement must be one capable of enforcement in law, the consideration for which is the exchange of promises not to enforce the original contract.

Rescission: Cancellation of all or some of the material terms of the contract.

Rescission This refers to cancellation of all or some of the material terms of the contract. If the contracting parties mutually decide to do so, the respective contractual obligations of the parties stand terminated.

Alteration This refers to a change in one or more of the terms of a contract with the consent of all the contracting parties. Alteration results in a new contract but parties to it remain the same. Here the assumption is that both the parties are to gain a fresh but different benefit from the new agreement.

Remission: Acceptance of a lesser sum than what was contracted for, or a lesser fulfilment of the promise made.

Remission This means the acceptance (by the promisee) of a lesser sum than what was contracted for, or a lesser fulfilment of the promise made. As per Section 63, 'every promisee may (a) remit or dispense with it, wholly or in part, or (b) extend the time of performance, or (c) accept any other satisfaction instead of performance'.

Waiver The term waiver implies abandonment or relinquishment of a right. Where a party deliberately

Waiver: Abandonment or relinquishment of a right under a contract.

abandons its rights under the contract, the other party is released of its obligations, otherwise binding upon it.

Discharge by Lapse of Time

A contract stands discharged if not enforced within a specified time called the 'period of limitation'. The Limitation Act, 1963, prescribes the period of limitation for various contracts. For instance, period of limitation for exercising right to recover an immovable property is 12 years, and right to recover a debt is 3 years. Contractual rights become time barred after the expiry of this limitation period. Accordingly, if a debt is not recovered within three years of its payment becoming due, the debt ceases to be payable and is discharged by lapse of time.

Discharge by Impossibility of Performance

The performance of a contractual obligation may become subsequently impossible[1] on a number of grounds. They include the following.

Objective impossibility of performance A contract may be discharged if, after it is made, performance becomes objectively impossible, as in the following cases:

1. Death or incapacity of one of the parties,
2. Specific subject matter of the contract is destroyed, or
3. Change in the law that renders performance illegal. A contract that was lawful at the time of making it but later on becomes unlawful because of new legislation, the performance becomes impossible, and the contract stands discharged.

Commercial impracticability A contract is discharged when performance may be excused if it becomes much more difficult or expensive than contemplated when the contract was formed.

Frustration of purpose A contract will be discharged if supervening circumstances make it impossible to attain the purpose the parties had in mind.

Temporary impossibility An event that makes it temporarily impossible to perform will suspend performance until the impossibility ceases. This too might lead to discharge of a contract on ground of impossibility.

Discharge by Operation of Law

A contract stands discharged by operation of law in the following circumstances.

Unauthorised material alteration of a written document A party can treat a contract discharged (i.e., from his side) if the other party alters a term (such as quantity or price) of the contract without seeking the consent of the former.

Statutes of limitations A contract stands discharged if not enforced within a specified period called the 'period of limitation'. The Limitation Act, 1963, prescribes the period of limitation for various contracts. For instance, period of limitation for exercising right to recover an immovable property is 12 years and right to recover a debt is 3 years. Contractual rights become time barred after the expiry of this limitation period. Accordingly, if a debt is not recovered within three years of its payment becoming due, the debt ceases to be payable and is discharged by lapse of time.

Insolvency A discharge in insolvency or bankruptcy will ordinarily bar enforcement of most of a debtor's contracts.

Merger A contract also stands discharged through a merger that occurs when an inferior right accruing to party in a contract amalgamates into the superior right ensuing to the same party. For instance, *A* hires a factory premises from *B* for some manufacturing activity for a year, but 3 months ahead of the expiry of lease purchases that very premises. Now since *A* has become the owner of the building, his rights associated with the lease (inferior rights) subsequently merge into the rights of ownership (superior rights). The previous rental contract ceases to exist.

Discharge by Accord and Satisfaction

To discharge a contract by accord and satisfaction, the parties must agree to accept performance that is

[1] This subsequent or supervening impossibility is known as 'Doctrine of Frustration' under the English Law.

different from the performance originally promised. It may be studied under the following sub-heads.

Accord An accord is an executory contract to perform an act that will satisfy an existing duty. An accord suspends, but does not discharge, the original contract.

Satisfaction Satisfaction is the performance of the accord, which discharges the original contractual obligation.

If the obligor refuses to perform The obligee can sue on the original obligation or seek a decree for specific performance on the accord.

Discharge by Breach

Breach occurs where a party to a contract fails to perform its contractual obligations, or the performance is defective. A breach of contract does not *per se* bring a contract to an end. The breach may give to the aggrieved party the right to terminate the contract, but it is for the non-breaching side to decide whether or not to exercise that option. The aggrieved party has a right of election; that is to say, it can choose either to affirm the contract or to terminate it. However, once that decision has been taken, it is, in principle, irrevocable.

A Breach may be anticipatory or actual.

Anticipatory breach

Also known as 'breach by repudiation', anticipatory breach occurs when one party states, before the arrival of the date fixed for performance, without justification that it cannot or will not carry out the material part of the contractual obligations on the agreed date or that it intends to perform in a way that is inconsistent with the terms of the contract. This may also occur where one party by some action makes performance impossible. For instance, *A*, after agreeing to sell his car to *B* on a fixed date, sells it to *C*. This is anticipatory breach.

Effect of anticipatory breach Where there is an anticipatory breach, the non-breaching party may either (i) rescind the contract or (ii) treat the contract in force and wait for the time of performance. In the first case, it can immediately sue for damages, i.e., it is not required to wait for the time for performance to expire. If the non-breaching party elects to treat the contract operative, it could wait until the time of performance and then hold the other party liable for the non-performance. Thus, by doing so the non-breaching party is giving an opportunity to the breaching party to still perform, if it can, in order to get a valid discharge.

Actual breach

Actual breach refers to the failure to perform contractual obligations when performance is due. Failure to perform obligations is the most common form of breach, wherein a seller fails to deliver the goods by the appointed time, or where, although delivered, the goods are not up to the mark in respect of quality or quantity specified in the contract.

Effect of actual breach Breach is described as a method of discharge, although it may not automatically discharge the contract. Breach of contract leads to two main remedies, namely, breach of condition and breach of warranty.

Breach of a condition This is a major term, known as material breach, which entitles the injured party to damages and gives it an option to treat the contract as subsisting or discharged.

Breach of a warranty This is a minor term, known as non-material breach, which entitles the non-breaching party to damages. It does not have the right to repudiate the contract, although a non-material breach can give it the right to defer performance until the breach is made good. However, once the breach is remedied, the non-breaching party must go ahead and render its performance, minus any damages caused by the breach.

Thus, it is clear from the above that not every breach entitles the injured party to treat the contract as discharged. It must be shown that the breach has affected a vital part of the contract, and that it is a breach of condition rather than breach of warranty. We will study remedies against breach in the next chapter.

Assignment of a Contract

Assignment: Transfer of contractual rights and benefits by a party to a contract to a third party.

Assignment is a method by which a party to a contract transfers the rights and benefits accruing to it out of the contract to a third party, so as to enable it to enforce the performance of the contract. The party that transfers its contractual rights is called 'assignor' and the third party so appointed is known as 'assignee.' Unlike a novation where consent of both the promissor and the promisee is required for the third party to assume all obligations and liabilities of the original promisee, an assignment does not always need the consent of all parties. If the contract terms state specifically that the promisor's consent is not needed to assign the contract, then the promisee can assign the contract to whomever he wants to.

For example, If party *A* contracts with party *B* to sell *A*'s car to *B* for ₹50,000, *A* can later assign the benefits of the contract—the right to be paid ₹50,000—to party *C*. In this scenario, party *A* is the obligee/assignor, party *B* is an obligor, and party *C* is the assignee.

An assignment may be donative (essentially given as a gift), or it may be contractually exchanged for consideration. However, contract of personal nature cannot be assigned under the Act.

It may be noted that there is no question of this situation breaking the privity of contract, since a party is actually assigning its position to enforce the contract to the third party; the contract, thus, remaining essentially bilateral in character.

Section 37 of the Contracts Act enables parties to assign their contractual obligations, although there is no explicit provision regarding assignment. The section relates to the obligation of parties to contract and the relevant portion states that, '...promises bind the representatives of the promisor in case of the death of such promisor before performance; unless such a contrary intention appears from the contract'.

Exercises

I. Objective-type Questions

1. State whether each of the following statements is True or False:
   (i) Assignment is the obvious mode of discharge of a contract.
   (ii) Novation means substitution of a new contract for the original one.
   (iii) Where a party waives its rights under the contract, the other party is released of its obligations under the contract.
   (iv) Where the subject matter of a contract is destroyed for no fault of the promisor, the contract does not become void by impossibility of performance.
   (v) The term 'tender' refers to 'attempted performance'.

2. Fill in the blanks:
   (i) ________ means cancellation of all or some of the terms of the original contract.
   (ii) ________ implies the acceptance of a lesser sum than what was contracted for or a lesser fulfilment of the promise made.
   (iii) A contract is said to be discharged by way of ________ when an inferior right possessed by a party coincides with a superior right of the same party.
   (iv) When a party repudiates a contract before the time fixed for performance has arrived, it is known as ________.
   (v) In case of ________ assignment, the assignor merely transfers the rights and benefits (accruing to him) to a third party and not the liabilities or obligations.

3. Indicate the correct answer:
   (i) A contract stands discharged by
      (a) Performance
      (b) Substituted agreement
      (c) Impossibility of performance
      (d) All of the above
   (ii) A substituted agreement embraces
      (a) Novation and rescission only
      (b) Alteration and remission only
      (c) Waiver alone
      (d) All of the above
   (iii) Discharge of a contract due to material alteration falls under
      (a) Novation
      (b) Operation of law

(c) Substituted agreement (d) Remission

(iv) Objective impossibility renders a contract terminated in which of the following situations?
(a) Death or incapacity of one of the parties
(b) Specific subject matter of the contract is destroyed
(c) Change in the law that renders performance illegal
(d) All the above

(v) Who among the following can demand performance?
(a) Promisee (b) Legal representative
(c) Joint promisee (d) All of the above

II. Review Questions

1. What do you mean by performance of a contract? Discuss in detail.
2. Define 'Tender'. Outline the essentials of a valid tender.
3. What are the different modes of discharging a contract? Discuss in brief.
4. State the rules regarding discharge of contract by
   (a) Substituted agreement (b) Operation of law
   (c) Impossibility of performance
5. Distinguish between actual breach and anticipatory breach. Describe the effect of breach.
6. Discuss the legal rules governing time and place of performance.

III. Caselets

1. *A* agreed to advertise *B*'s business for three years on plates attached to litter bins. *B* repudiated the contract on the same day that it was made. *A* nevertheless manufactured and displayed the plates as originally agreed and claimed the full amount due under the contract. Decide.
[**Hint:** *A's* claim is genuine. Repudiation does not *per se* bring the contract to an end]

2. On 14 May 2007, *P* entered into a contract to purchase a motor vehicle from *D*, an auto dealer, and paid ₹10,000 as down payment. *P* informed *D* that he intended to use the vehicle for camping during the summer. The vehicle was supposed to be delivered during June, but no delivery was made through August. *P* seeks to cancel the contract and to obtain a refund of the ₹10,000. Will he succeed?
[**Hint:** Yes, failure to make delivery in time constitutes a material breach of contract]

3. A flat was to be decorated and furnished for ₹50,000. When the work was over, the customer only paid ₹26,000 by installments. Then, because of defects to a bookcase and a wardrobe that would cost about ₹15,000 to put right, he refused to pay the remaining sum of ₹24,000. Decide.
[**Hint:** Decorator can claim the balance less the amount representing the defects on the basis of substantial performance]

4. *A* and *B* contract to marry each other. Before the marriage could take place *B* turns lunatic. Decide.
[**Hint:** Contract stands discharged and has become void due to objective impossibility of performance]

5. A, a refrigeration contractor, had agreed to fix a central cooling system in the defendant's premises for ₹50,000. On completion of the work, the system proved to be so defective that it would cost the client ₹10,000 to repair. The defendant refused to pay any of the cost of the work and the plaintiff sued. Comment.
[**Hint:** Plaintiff can claim his bill on the basis of substantial performance]

Answers to Objective-type Questions

1.	(i) False	(ii) True	(iii) True	(iv) True	(v) True
2.	(i) Rescission	(ii) Remission	(iii) merger	(iv) anticipatory breach	(v) deliberate
3.	(i) (d)	(ii) (d).	(iii) (b)	(iv) (d)	(v) (d)

6 Chapter in Review

LEARNING OUTCOMES

LO[1] Performance of a contract
LO[2] Discharge of a contract
LO[3] Modes of discharging a contract

KEY TERMS

Performance of contract: Fulfilling respective contractual obligations by both the parties.

Actual performance: Fulfilment of contractual obligation(s) by the promisor in accordance with the terms of contract.

Substantial performance: Fulfilment of the obligations agreed to in a contract, with only slight variances from the exact terms and/or unimportant omissions or minor defects.

Partial performance: Execution of a part of a divisible contract by one party acceptable by the other party.

Attempted performance/Tender: An offer to perform the obligation under the contract in accordance with the terms of the contract.

Discharge of a contract: Termination of contractual obligations by performance or otherwise.

Novation: Substitution of a new contract for the original one.

Rescission: Cancellation of all or some of the material terms of the contract.

Remission: Acceptance of a lesser sum than what was contracted for, or a lesser fulfilment of the promise made.

Waiver: Abandonment or relinquishment of a right under a contract.

Breach (of contract): Failure to perform contractual obligations by either party or a defective performance at their end.

Assignment: Transfer of contractual rights and benefits by a party to a contract to a third party.

LO[1] Carrying out respective obligations by the respective parties.

LO[2] Discharge refers to the termination of a party's obligations arising under a contract by performance or otherwise.

LO[3] A contract stands discharged by the following modes:

1. Performance
2. Mutual agreement: by novation; or rescission; or alteration; remission; or waiver
3. Lapse of time
4. Operation of law: due to material alteration; or statutes of limitations; or insolvency; or merger
5. Impossibility of performance
6. Accord and satisfaction
7. Breach: actual or anticipatory.

The most natural way of discharging the contract, however, is to perform it.

CHAPTER

7 Remedies for Breach of Contract

Learning Objectives

LO 1 What is breach of contract?
LO 2 Remedies against breach of contract
LO 3 Damages
LO 4 Rescission
LO 5 Specific performance
LO 6 Injunction
LO 7 *Quantum meruit*

Anticipatory breach: An action that demonstrates a party's intention to repudiate (break) a contract.

Actual breach: Failure to perform contractual obligations upon performance becoming due.

A breach of contract implies refusal by one party to abide by its terms without any lawful excuse. Even defective performance or late performance are tantamount to breach. Many commercial agreements contain express provisions for remedies available to the aggrieved party in the event of breach. For example, in a contract of sale of goods, the buyer may be entitled to ask the seller to make good or replace defective items. The contract may contain a clause that all the terms, which are to govern their contractual relationship, have been included by the parties in written form in the contract itself. By incorporating such a clause, the contracting parties, perhaps, intended to displace any rights and remedies provided by law (such as the buyer's right to seek damages for fundamental breach by the seller), which are not specified in the contract. A breach of contract does not *per se* bring a contract to an end. The breach in fact may give to the aggrieved party the right to terminate the contract. However, it is for the aggrieved or distressed party to decide whether or not to exercise that right. If it elects to terminate the contract, it need not perform its part of the promise and will also be entitled to compensation for the loss incurred by it, if any.

Remedies Available to an Aggrieved Party

Remedy: A relief provided to the injured party should the other side commit a breach.

A remedy is a relief provided to an aggrieved party should the other side commit a breach. It is the means, employed to enforce a right, or redress an injury. Once a party fails to perform or performs inadequately, the other party—the non-breaching party—can choose one or more of several remedies. The most common remedies available to an aggrieved party are rescission, damages, specific performance, injunction, and quantum meruit. All these will be examined in turn.

Rescission

Rescission: The act of terminating contractual obligation(s).

Rescission is the revocation of a contract. Section 39 of the Contract Act provides that when a party to a contract has refused to perform, or disabled itself from performing in its entirety, the promisee may put an end to the contract. In such a case, the other (aggrieved) party can refuse further performance and is absolved of all of its obligations under the contract.

For example, *A* promises to supply a PC for *B*'s office on a certain date on cash-on-delivery (COD) basis. However, *A* fails to deliver the computer on the agreed date. *B* is absolved of the liability of paying the price and entitled to rescind the contract.

Rescission is done to bring the parties, as far as possible, back to the position in which they were before they entered into the contract. This is known as *status quo ante*. It is an equitable remedy and is discretionary. The court may decline to rescind a contract if one party has affirmed the contract by its action [*Long vs Lloyd*[1]], or a third party has acquired some rights, or there has been substantial performance in implementing the contract.

Damages

Damages: Compensation payable to injured party by the breaching party under a decree.

A breach of contract also entitles the non-breaching or injured party to sue for monetary damages besides rescinding the contract. Damages are designed to compensate the aggrieved party for the loss sustained in the bargain. Often, courts rule that aggrieved parties are to be placed in the position they would have occupied had the contract been performed fully. Section 73 of the Contract Act, which deals with compensation for loss or damage caused by breach of contract, states that when a contract has been broken, the aggrieved party is entitled to receive, from the breaching party such damages which

[1] 1958, 1 WLR 753

1. arose naturally in the usual course of things from such breach. This relates to ordinary damages, and
2. the parties knew, when they made the contract, to be likely to result from the breach of it. This relates to special damages.

A claim for damages raises the following issues.

Remoteness of damage It means for what kind of damage should the plaintiff be compensated? That is, whether the court will take the step of recognizing that a breach of contract can, in principle, give rise to a claim for damages to the injured party.

Assessment of damages It means what monetary compensation or damages should the plaintiff receive in respect of the damage, which is not too remote or indirect?

Note The distinction between damage and damages ought to be noted carefully. Damage is the loss suffered by the plaintiff, whereas damages are the financial compensation awarded to him. It is very important to use the correct word, for instance, 'Remoteness of damages' will be a meaningless expression.

Remoteness of damage

The injured party may only recover damages for the loss suffered as a result of the breach, provided it is not too remote, i.e., far-flung or indirect. The aim of awarding damages is to put the aggrieved party in the position it would have been had the contract been properly and fully performed. It has been perceptively observed by *Farnsworth*[2] that in comparison to the bargaining power which the parties enjoy in negotiating their substantive contractual rights and duties, their power to bargain over their remedial rights is limited. They are not at liberty to name an extravagant sum having no relation to the breach, for fear of it being construed as a penalty. It is interesting to contrast this with the law relating to consideration. A man may sell his car for a handful of marbles, and the law cares not as long as he is satisfied. Yet the law would extend no remedy to a man who claims ₹10,000 for someone's failure to deliver a handful of marbles, branding such a clause penalty. The principles of remoteness are described lucidly in the *Hadley vs Baxendale*[3] case. According to it the following losses are recoverable:

- All loses that may fairly and reasonably be considered as arising naturally, i.e., according to the usual course of things from the breach itself.
- All loses that may reasonably be supposed to have been in the contemplation of both parties at the time they made the contract, as a probable result of the breach.

The rule in *Hadley v Baxendale* in the Indian context has been interpreted to mean that only loss that is within the reasonable contemplation of the parties may be recovered [*The Heron II*[4]].

Assessment of damages

This is the method for measuring the damages to which the aggrieved or non-breaching party is entitled. It covers loss incurred in bargain or loss that was due, or expected by way of contract. The basic aim of the court is to put the claimant in the position he/she would have been had the contract been properly performed [*Robinson vs Harman*[5]]. The two general methods of assessing damages are difference in value or cost of cure. Thus, in an action wherein an employee has been wrongfully dismissed, the court will base its award on 'net' wages, i.e., after deduction of income tax and notional group insurance contribution, if any. In assessing the award of damages, the court may also take into account inconvenience and annoyance caused to the aggrieved or non-breaching party.

Types of damages

Depending on the nature of the awards in compensating the injured or aggrieved party, damages have been classified as follows:

1. Compensatory damages
2. Nominal damages
3. Consequential damages
4. Punitive damages

[2] Farnsworth Allan. E., 2008, *Farnsworth on Contracts*, Third Edition, (New York: Wolters Kluwer), pp 748

[3] 1854, 9 Exch. 341

[4] 1969, 1 AC 350

[5] 1848, 18 LJ Ex 202

5. Incidental damages
6. Liquidated or agreed damages and penalty.

All these damages shall be examined in turn.

Compensatory damages Damages making up for the non-breaching party's loss in the bargain are known as compensatory damages. These are also called ordinary damages. Since these damages compensate the aggrieved party for the injuries actually sustained and proved to have arisen directly from the loss in the bargain due to the breach, the measure of ordinary damages is the difference between the contract price and the market price on the date of the breach. Accordingly, they simply replace the loss caused by the wrong or injury. The aim of awarding compensatory damages is, thus, to protect the claimant's 'expectation of interest' or his 'performance interest'.

Compensatory damages: Damages making up for the non-breaching party's loss in the bargain.

Nominal damages Nominal damages are a 'damage award' issued by a court when a legal wrong occurred, but where there was no actual financial loss as a result of that legal wrong. Nominal damages are very small damages awarded to show that the loss or harm suffered was technical rather than actual. They are awarded to show the court's disapproval of the legal wrong. For example, when a seller fails to deliver the goods, but the buyer is able to purchase from elsewhere at no extra cost. An award of a small sum such as ₹100 is granted to the non-breaching party to reflect the view that any loss or damage is purely technical.

Nominal damages: 'Damage award' issued by a court when a legal wrong occurred, but where there was no actual financial loss as a result of that legal wrong.

Consequential damages Consequential damages are also called special damages. These are awarded as monetary compensation for loss suffered as a consequence of the other party's breach. Consequential damage occurs because of some special or unusual circumstances of the particular contractual relationship of the parties. However, an aggrieved party cannot recover special damages for loss that he could have avoided by taking reasonable steps. This is sometimes expressed as the duty to mitigate (or minimise) these damages. For an injured party to obtain consequential damages, it must show that it has suffered loss as a result of the breach. It is up to the party in breach to argue that the injured party failed to mitigate its loss.

Consequential/Special damages: Monetary compensation award for the loss suffered as a consequence of the breach.

Punitive damages Also known as exemplary or vindictive damages, punitive damages are available in a breach of contract not often. These are imposed not with an idea to compensate the injured party but to punish the wrongdoer so as to deter such conduct in future. They reflect the court's strong disapproval of a defendant's predominantly reprehensible behaviour.

Punitive/Vindictive/Exemplary damages: Damages awarded not with an idea to compensate the injured party but to punish the wrongdoer so as to deter such conduct in future; reflecting the court's strong disapproval of a defendant's predominantly reprehensible behaviour.

Box 7.1 Examples of Compensatory or Ordinary Damages

Example 1

A contracts to sell and deliver 50 kg of saltpetre to *B*, at a certain price to be paid on delivery. *A* breaks his promise. *B* is entitled to receive from *A*, by way of compensation, the sum, if any, by which the contract price falls short of the price for which *B* might have obtained 50 kg of saltpetre of the same quality at the time when the saltpetre ought to have been delivered.

Example 2

A contracts to buy from *B*, 50 tons of rice at a stated price. No time is fixed for delivery. Subsequently *A* informs *B* that he will not accept the rice if tendered to him. *B* is entitled to receive from *A*, by way of compensation, the amount, if any, by which the contract price exceeds that which *B* can obtain for the rice at the time when *A* informs him that he will not accept it [Illustrations appended to Section 74].

Box 7.2 Examples of Consequential Damages

Example 1

A, having contracted with *B* to supply *B* with 1000 tons of iron at ₹100 per ton, to be delivered at a stated time, contracts with *C* for the purchase of 1000 tons of iron at ₹80 per ton, telling *C* that he does so for the purpose of performing his contract with *B*. *C* fails to perform his contract with *A*, and *B*, in turn, rescinds the contract. *C* will have to pay ₹20,000 to *A*, that being the profit which *A* would have made by fulfilling his contract with *B*.

Example 2

A, a builder, contracts to erect and finish a house by January 1, so that *B* may give possession of it at that time to *C*, with whom *B* has contracted to let it. *A* is informed of the contract between *B* and *C*. *A* builds the house so badly that, before January 1, it crumbles down and has to be re-built by *B*, who, in consequence, loses the rent that he was to have received from *C* and is obliged to make compensation to *C* for the breach of his contract. *A* is liable to compensate to *B* for the cost of rebuilding the house, for the rent loss he has incurred, as well as for the compensation made to *C* [Illustrations appended to Section 74].

However, the mere fact that the defendant has broken the contract with the claimant in order to pursue a more profitable relationship with another party does not suffice to entitle the claimant to punitive damages. Much more is required before a conclusion is drawn that a defendant has behaved in an outrageous manner. Oppressive, arbitrary, or unconstitutional action by the servants of the insurance and healthcare undertakings are usually the most frequent targets to recover punitive damages, followed by employers and bankers who are often subjected to punitive damages. In case of wrongful dishonour of a cheque (due to the negligence or mistake on part of the banker), the governing rule is—smaller the amount of the cheque, larger will be the amount of damages awarded, and vice versa.

Incidental damages Incidental damages are awarded to compensate for the reasonable cost that the injured party incurs after the breach in an effort to avoid further loss. For example, if an employer breaches an employment contract with one of his employees, the latter could recover as incidental damages those reasonable expenses he would incur in attempting to procure substitute employment, such as long-distance telephone calls or the cost of printing new resumes, etc.

> **Incidental damages:** Damages to compensate for the reasonable cost that the injured party incurs after the breach in an effort to avoid further loss.

Liquidated and penalty Liquidated damages implies sum of money (agreed-to and written into a contract) specified as the total amount of compensation an aggrieved party should get, if the other party breaches certain part(s) of the contract. It is common for the contracting parties to expressly state in the contract that a certain sum of money will be paid to the injured party or that goods will be forfeited (the latter being known as retention clause) should a breach of contract occur. Clauses covering these areas are known as liquidated or agreed damages clauses. These are self-help remedies and generally appear in commercial contracts, most commonly so, in relation to late rather than defective performance, especially in the fields of construction and engineering, and supply or sale of goods. Such clauses do not usually appear in contracts of employment.

> **Liquidated damages:** Sum of money (agreed-to and written into a contract) specified as the total amount of compensation an aggrieved party should get, if the other party breaches certain part(s) of the contract.

The purpose of such clauses is to make the recovery of damages easier, avoiding the problems of proving actual loss; to avoid arguments as to the remoteness of certain types of consequential or indirect losses; and to assure the other party of their intention to be bound by the contract.

On the other hand, a clause will be construed as a penalty clause, if the sum specified is extravagant and disproportionate to the damage likely to occur. Penalty clauses are generally not enforceable whereas liquidated damages clauses are.

Whether a particular sum is liquidated damages or a penalty depends on the intentions of the parties. And the mere use of the words 'penalty' or 'liquidated damages' are not conclusive evidence of intentions. It is necessary to examine whether the amount specified is befitting penalty or liquidated damages.

Specific Performance

Specific performance: Decree issued by a court ordering the party (accused of breaching the contract) to perform its obligations under the contract.

Specific performance is a decree issued by the court, which orders the defendant (party accused of breaching a contract) to perform its obligations under the contract. Where damages represent inadequate or unjust remedy, for example, where the subject matter of the contract is unique or where there are no standards to ascertain the quantum of loss, the non-breaching party may approach the court for the grant of an order for specific performance of the contract. The courts have broad discretion to award specific performance and in exercising this discretion take into account factors such as

1. whether the person seeking performance is prepared to perform his/her side of the contract [*Chappell vs Times Newspapers Ltd*[6]].
2. whether the person against whom the order is sought would suffer hardship in performing it [*Patel vs Ali*[7]].
3. The difference between the benefits that the court order would give to one party and the cost of performance to the other [*Tito vs Waddell*[8]]

However, an order of specific performance would not be granted in the following circumstances:

1. Monetary compensation is an adequate remedy.
2. It will be inequitable to either party. Thus, it is not available to an infant in respect of a contract not enforceable against him/her.
3. The performance consists of a personal service such as employment contracts because such an order would restrict an individual's freedom [*Chappell vs Times Newspapers Ltd*[9]].
4. The contracts require constant supervision, for example, building contracts.
5. The defendant cannot perform exactly in accordance with the original contractual obligation. That is, specific performance is impossible.
6. Specific performance would cause severe hardship to the defendant.
7. Contract made for no conideration.

On the basis of above-mentioned constraints, it can be argued that specific performance is a *substitutionary* and not a specific remedy.

Injunction

Injunction: A court order directing a person (accused of breaching the contract) to do or refrain from doing some specified act.

An injunction is a court order directing a person to do or refrain from doing some specified act, which, obviously, has been the subject matter of a contract. Like specific performance, an injunction is an equitable remedy and, therefore, only granted at the discretion of the court. It is awarded in circumstances in which damages would not be an adequate remedy to compensate the claimant.

Injunction orders are of two types—prohibitory and mandatory.

Prohibitory injunction: Court order restraining breach of a negative contractual obligation by the defendant.

Prohibitory injunction This orders the defendant to restrain from committing a breach of a negative contractual obligation, i.e., where he/she does something, which he/she had promised not to do. Such an injunction may be granted to prevent the breach of a reasonable restraint of trade clause. For instance, *G* agreed to source all the electric power required for his house from *M* but started buying part of his requirement from some other company. He was restrained by an injunction order from buying electricity from the other source [Based on *Metropolitan Electric Supply Company vs Ginder*[10]].

Mandatory injunction: Court order compelling the performance of a positive act by the breaching party.

Mandatory injunction This, on the other hand, compels the performance of a positive contractual obligation, for example, compelling an employee to do any work or attend at any place in order to do any work.

[6] 1975, 1 WLR 482
[7] 1984, 1 All ER 978
[8] 1977, No. 2 ch 106
[9] 1975, 1 WLR 482
[10] 1901, 2 Ch. D 799

Thus, mandatory injunction shall have a similar effect to specific performance, whereas prohibitory injunction is usually the opposite of specific performance.

The main use of injunction in the contractual situation has been as an indirect means of enforcing a contract involving *personal services*. In exercising its discretion (of injunction), the court will use the balance of convenience test—weighing the benefit to the injured party and the detriment to the other party. For example, a factory begins to allow noxious fumes to escape from a chimney, affecting the health of neighbouring residents. Damages here would be inadequate, as the residents would want to stop the fumes being emitted. This can only be remedied by an injunction order. An injunction will not be granted if its effect would be to compel a party to do something, which he could not have been ordered to do by a decree of specific performance [*Lumley vs Wagner*[11]].

An injunction order may be granted for an indefinite period or temporarily (an interlocutory injunction) until a case goes to trial.

Quantum Meruit

Quantum meruit: Allowing reasonable remuneration (by the court) to a party for the work done to avoid unjust enrichment of one party at the expense of another.

Quantum meruit is a Latin term meaning, 'as much as is merited' or 'as much as earned'. In the context of contract law, it means something along the lines of 'reasonable value of services rendered'.

The normal rule of law is that unless a party has performed its promise in its entirety, it cannot claim performance from the other party. Contrary to it, in certain cases, when a person has done some work under a contract, and the other party repudiates the contract or some such event occurs that renders the rest of the performance unworkable, then the court may allow remuneration to the party, which has performed for the work he has done. Thus, *quantum meruit* is imposed to avoid the unjust enrichment of one party at the expense of another. The action of *quantum meruit* is allowed in Indian courts under Section 70 of the Contract Act.

The concept of *quantum meruit* applies to the following situations:

1. When a person employs (impliedly or expressly) another person to do work for him, without any agreement as to his compensation, the law implies a promise from the employer to the workman that he will pay for the services, as much as the workman may deserve or merit.
2. When there is an express contract for a stipulated amount and mode of compensation for services, the plaintiff cannot abandon the contract and resort to an action for a *quantum meruit*. However, if there is a total failure of consideration, the plaintiff has a right to elect to repudiate the contract and then seek compensation on a *quantum meruit* basis.
3. If a contract is divisible and a party to a contract is prevented from fulfilling its contractual obligations by the other party, then obviously he will not be in default. For example, in a building contract, if the owner should prevent the builder from completing, such as not allowing him to enter the construction site, the builder can recover a reasonable price for the work done on a *quantum meruit* basis.
4. If an indivisible contract is completely executed, but badly, the person who has performed will be entitled to a lump sum less deduction to overcome the defect in the perormance.

In all the above cases, the claim is not based on the original contract but on the implied promise by the other party arising from the acceptance of an executed contract. For example, *A*, a contractor, is contracted to work on a school. He does some work but quits (breach of contract) midway. The contractor is entitled to be paid for the services he has already rendered for the school on the basis of *quantum meruit*. However, the school would also be entitled to damages arising out of the need to look for a new contractor.

Quasi-contractual Relationships: Other Remedies

Quasi-contract: An obligation that the law creates in the absence of an agreement between the parties.

Quasi-contractual obligations are the obligations that the common law implies in circumstances distinct from obligations under a contract. It is an area of law in its own right.

[11] 1852, 1 DM & G 604

Quasi-contractual remedies are sometimes available either as an alternative to a remedy for breach of contract or where there is no remedy for breach of contract, for example, a claim for *quantum meruit* (a reasonable remuneration for work done, or for goods supplied under a contract which is later discovered to be void). Chapter V of the Indian Contract Act deals with the quasi-contractual relationships under Sections 68–72. These can be summarised as under.

Claim for necessaries supplied to person incapable of contracting, or on his account If a person incapable of entering into a contract, or anyone whom he is legally bound to support, is supplied by another person with necessaries suited to his condition in life, the person who has furnished such supplies is entitled to be reimbursed from the property of such incapable person [Section 68].

Reimbursement of person paying money due by another, in payment of which he is interested A person who is interested in the payment of money that another is bound by law to pay, and who therefore pays it, is entitled to be reimbursed by the other [Section 69]. For example, *B* holds land in West Bengal, on a lease granted by *A*, the *zamindar*. The revenue payable by *A* to the government being in arrears, his land is advertised for sale by the government. Under the revenue law, the consequence of such a sale will be the annulment of *B*'s lease. *B*, to prevent the sale and the consequent annulment of his own lease, pays to the government the sum due from *A*. *A* is bound to make good to *B* the amount so paid.

Obligation of person enjoying benefit of non-gratuitous act Where a person lawfully does anything for another person, or delivers anything to him, not intending to do so gratuitously, and such other person enjoys the benefit thereof, the latter is bound to make compensation to the former in respect of, or to restore, the thing so done or delivered [Section 70]. For example, *A*, a tradesman, leaves goods at *B*'s house by mistake. *B* treats the goods as his own. He is bound to pay *A* for them. Or, *A* saves *B*'s property from fire. *A* is not entitled to compensation from *B*, if the circumstances show that he intended to deliver the said goods gratuitously.

Responsibility of finder of lost goods A person who finds goods belonging to another and takes them into his custody is subject to the same responsibility as a bailee [Section 71].

Liability of person to whom money is paid, or thing delivered, by mistake or under coercion A person to whom money has been paid or anything delivered by mistake or under coercion must repay for or return it [Section 72].

Exercises

I. Objective-type Questions

1. State whether each of the following statements is True or False:
   (i) Rescission is the right not to perform a contractual obligation.
   (ii) Special damages are awarded to create an example.
   (iii) Penalty corresponds to fair and genuine estimate of the damage or injury likely to arise should the breach of contract occur.
   (iv) The measure of exemplary damages is the difference between contract price and the market price on the date of the breach.
   (v) Specific performance is a substitutionary and not a specific remedy.

2. Fill in the blanks:
   (i) In case of divisible contract, if the party not in default has enjoyed the benefits of the part performance, the party in default may sue on __________.

(ii) __________ contracts are in the nature of contracts or similar to contracts.
(iii) __________ is a remedy that orders the defendant party to perform his obligations under the contract.
(iv) An order of the court compelling or prohibiting a person to do a particular act is commonly known as __________.
(v) __________ of damages refers to for what kind of loss an injured party should be compensated.

3. Indicate the correct answer:
   (i) The right not to perform a contractual obligation is known as
      (a) Injunction (b) Rescission
      (c) Specific performance (d) *Quantum meruit*
   (ii) The amount of compensation payable in case of breach and stated in the contract is a case of
      (a) Liquidated damages (b) Penalty
      (c) Special damages (d) Punitive damages
   (iii) Which of the following is irrelevant in case of a contract of personal nature?
      (a) Damages (b) Rescission
      (c) Injunction (d) Specific performance
   (iv) Where a party is restrained from breach of a negative term of a contract, this refers to
      (a) Rescission (b) Injunction
      (c) *Quantum meruit* (d) Ordinary damages
   (v) Specific performance is *not* granted when
      (a) Monetary compensation is an adequate remedy
      (b) It will be inequitable to either party
      (c) The court cannot supervise its execution
      (d) In all the above cases

II. Review Questions

1. What is breach of contract? What remedies are available to the non-breaching party in the event of breach of contract?
2. What are the different types of damages available to an aggrieved party? Discuss in detail.
3. Distinguish between the following:
   (a) Penalty and liquidated damages (b) Rescission and Injunction
4. Write short notes on the following:
   (a) Quantum meruit (b) Specific performance
5. In what circumstances will a court grant or order
   (a) An injunction to restrain a breach of contract
   (b) Specific performance of a contract?
6. In the law of contract describe the rules relating to
   (a) Remoteness of damage (b) The measure of damages

III. Caselets

1. John agrees to sell a painting to Dave for $200. The painting needs a new frame. John tells Dave that the painting will be ready for him to collect in a fortnight. However, when Dave came to collect and pay for the painting, John refuses to give it to him. Advise Dave.
   [Hint: Dave can approach the court for the grant of specific performance]
2. While negotiating to sell his business to Ivan, Henry made a true statement that gave total figures for turnover and profits for the previous five years. This created an impression that the business was in a healthy state. Henry did not disclose nor did Ivan request, a breakdown of figures, which would have

revealed a steady decline in profitability over this period. Ivan, having purchased the business, discovered the true state of affairs. What remedies, if any, does Ivan have?
[Hint: Ivan cannot claim special or consequential damages as he did not fail to mitigate his loss]

3. *A* purchased a sports car from *B*, who deals in sports cars and bikes, but later refused to accept the delivery of it. *B's* profit on the sale would have been $500, but *A* argued that he was not liable for this amount, since the profit would still be made when the car was sold to another customer. Advise.
[Hint: *A* is liable to pay damages]

4. An actor entered into a contract with a theatre to perform a daily show for a week for a daily fee of $50. The contract provided that if either he or the theatre management broke their contract then the party in breach must pay the other $1000 as liquidated damages. The actor didn't turn up after performing for three days and refused to pay $1000 as damages. Decide.
[Hint: The claimant cannot recover $1000 as the clause is tantamount to penalty for being disproportionate both to the actor's daily fee of $50, and to the greatest possible loss that would result from the breach]

5. *D*, an actress, agreed to act for *P*'s movies and undertook that she would not act for any one else during the period of the agreement without *P*'s written consent. She later on broke the promise. Decide.
[Hint: She could be restrained by an injunction from breaking her undertaking]

Answers to Objective-type Questions

1. (i) True (ii) False (iii) False (iv) False (v) True
2. (i) quantum meruit (ii) Quasi (iii) Specific performance (iv) injunction (v) Remoteness
3. (i) (b) (ii) (a) (iii) (d) (iv) (b) (v) (d)

7 Chapter in Review

LEARNING OUTCOMES

LO 1 What is breach of contract?
LO 2 Remedies against breach of contract
LO 3 Damages
LO 4 Rescission
LO 5 Specific performance
LO 6 Injunction
LO 7 *Quantum meruit*

KEY TERMS

Anticipatory breach: An action that demonstrates a party's intention to repudiate (break) a contract.

Actual breach: Failure to perform contractual obligations on performance becoming due.

Remedy: A relief provided to the injured party should the other side commit a breach.

Rescission: The act of terminating contractual obligation(s).

Damages: Compensation payable to injured party by the breaching party under a decree.

Compensatory damages: Damages making up the non-breaching party for the loss in the bargain.

Nominal damages: 'Damage award' issued by a court when a legal wrong occurred, but where there was no actual financial loss as a result of that legal wrong.

Consequential/Special damages: Monetary compensation award for the loss suffered as a consequence of the breach.

Punitive/Vindictive/Exemplarydamages: Damages awarded not with an idea to compensate the injured party but to punish the wrongdoer so as to deter such conduct in future; reflecting the court's strong disapproval of a defendant's predominantly reprehensible behaviour.

LO1 Breach of contract implies non-fulfilment of a promise under the contract by either party.

LO2 Where the failure to perform cannot be adequately redressed by money, the common remedies available to an aggrieved party are damages,rescission, specific performance, injunction, and *quantum meruit*.

LO3 Damages refers monetary compensation that a court decides should be paid to the injured party by the party responsible for the breach of a contract.

LO4 Rescission is resorted to bring the parties, as far as possible, back to the position in which they were before they entered into a contract. However, the court may decline to rescind a contract if one party has affirmed the contract by its action, or a third party has acquired some rights, or there has been substantial performance in implementing the contract.

LO5 Specific performance is a remedy that requires the defendant to perform his contractual obligations. Where damages represent inadequate or unjust remedy, the non-breaching party may approach the court for the grant of a decree for specific performance of the contract.

LO6 An injunction is a court order directing a person to do or refrain from doing some specified act, and it is awarded in circumstances in which damages would not be an adequate remedy to compensate the claimant.

LO7 In *quantum meruit*, the injured party, instead of claiming damages, may claim payment for what has been done under the contract on proportional basis.

Incidental damages: Damages to compensate for the reasonable costs that the injured party incurs after the breach in an effort to avoid further loss.

Liquidated damages: Sum of money (agreed-to and written into a contract) specified as the total amount of compensation an aggrieved party should get, if the other party breaches certain part(s) of the contract..

Specific performance: Decree issued by a court ordering the party (accused of breaching the contract) to perform its obligations under the contract.

Injunction: A court order directing a person (accused of breaching the contract) to do or refrain from doing some specified act.

Prohibitory injunction: Court order restraining breach of a negative contractual obligation by the defendant.

Mandatory injunction: Court order compelling the performance of a positive act by the breaching party.

Quantum meruit: Allowing reasonable remuneration (by the court) to a party for the work done to avoid unjust enrichment of one party at the expense of another.

Quasi-contract: An obligation that the law creates in the absence of an agreement between the parties.

CHAPTER

8 Special Contracts

Learning Objectives

LO 1 Contract of indemnity: meaning; definition; scope

LO 2 Contract of guarantee: meaning; definition

LO 3 Discharge of surety

LO 4 Contract of bailment: definition; essentials; kinds

LO 5 Contract of pledge: definition; who can pledge

LO 6 Contract of agency: general rules; essentials

LO 7 Agency: modes of creation; scope and extent of authority

LO 8 Termination of agency; irrevocable agency

Part II (Sections 144–238) of the Indian Contract Act, 1872, spreads over Chapters VIII – X, deals with special types of contractual relationships, namely, Contracts of Indemnity and Guarantee; Contracts of Bailment and Pledge; and Contracts of Agency. These are termed as special types of contacts as many of the general principles of law of contract, contained in Part I of the Act (Sections 1–75), do not apply to them. These kinds of contractual relationships, for instance, may not be supported by consideration. Similarly, an indemnity-holder in case of a contract of indemnity; principal debtor in case of contract of guarantee; bailor in case of a bailment contract; and an agent in case of a contract of agency can be a minor who is otherwise incompetent to contract under the Contract Act. Present chapter discusses these species of contracts in turn.

Contracts of Indemnity and Guarantee

One often comes across the terms 'guarantee' and 'indemnity' in hire-purchase and loan agreements, and many other commercial transactions in his or her life. While seeking a bank loan, a person is often asked to provide a guarantee. Sometimes with a view to provide protection against some loss or damage, the term 'indemnity' is also supplemented in the document. If someone tends to think that it probably has something to do with the guarantee, he/she is wrong. A contract of indemnity is fundamentally different from a contract of guarantee. However, both are special types of contracts. Chapter VIII of the Indian Contract Act deals exclusively and extensively with these kinds of contracts under Sections 124 to 147. Let us now discuss these species of contracts and the issues related to them.

Contract of Indemnity

Indemnity: Protection against some loss or damage to goods or property.

A contract of indemnity is a type of contingent contract. The term 'indemnity' indicates protection against some loss or damage. When a person undertakes to make good the loss or to compensate the party which has suffered some loss, a contract of indemnity results in between the two. Section 124 defines the term 'contract of indemnity' as follows:

'A contract, by which one party promises to save the other from loss caused to him by the conduct of the promisor himself, or by the conduct of any other person, is called a contract of indemnity'. The person who promises to save the other from a loss is called the indemnifier and the person to whom this promise is made, or is going to be protected from the loss, is known as indemnified or indemnity holder. For example, *A* contracts to indemnify *B* against the consequences of any proceedings that *C* may take against *B* in respect of a sum of ₹2000. This is a contract of indemnity, wherein *A* is the 'indemnifier' and *B* the indemnified. This example is an illustration appended to Section 124.

Scope of Contracts of Indemnity

The definition given in Section 124 restricts the scope of contracts of indemnity to only such cases where the loss, promised to be reimbursed, is caused by the conduct of the promisor or of any other person. The definition does not cover the cases of loss arising from events or accidents such as fire, or perils of the seas. In that sense contracts of insurance should not fall within the ambit of contracts of indemnity. But the fact is that the contracts of fire insurance and marine insurance are regarded as contracts of indemnity. In India, the law experts or the jurists have taken the view that the definition of contract of indemnity, as given in Section 124, is not exhaustive and the courts will follow the English law in this regard [*Gajanan Moreshwar vs Moreshwar Madan*]. The English law defines a contract of indemnity as 'a promise to save another harmless from loss caused as a result of a transaction entered into at the instance of the promisor'. Therefore, the losses arising from accidents or events, which do not depend on the conduct of human agency, are also covered under the contracts of indemnity.

Essentials of a Valid Contract of Indemnity

Apart from the regular features of a valid contract, such as offer, acceptance, and free consent, a contract of indemnity has some additional essential elements that are discussed as follows:

1. Under a contract of indemnity, the indemnifier promises to make good the loss or to compensate the party (indemnified) who has suffered some loss due to the conduct of the promisor or any other person acting on its behalf, or specified by it. In its wider sense, a contract of indemnity also includes a promise of indemnity against loss arising from any cause whatsoever, for example, fire, accident, or natural calamity.
2. A contract of indemnity is primarily a contingent contract. The liability of the indemnifier arises only at the occurrence of the contingency, i.e., when the indemnity-holder suffers a loss.
3. The liability of an indemnifier commences as soon as the liability of the indemnity holder to pay becomes clear and certain, although he has himself not paid anything [*Osman Jamal & Sons Ltd vs Gopal Purshottam*[1]].

Rights of an Indemnity Holder

The indemnity holder, acting within the scope of his authority, is entitled to recover from the indemnifier the following amounts:

1. All damages which he/she may be compelled to pay in any suit in respect of any matter to which the promise to indemnify applies.
2. All costs which he/she may be compelled to pay in any such suit if, in bringing or defending it, he/she did not contravene the orders of the promisor and acted as it would have been prudent for him/her to act in the absence of any contract of indemnity, or if the promisor authorised him/her to bring or defend the suit.
3. All sums which he/she may have paid under the terms of any compromise of any such suit, if the compromise was not contrary to the orders of the promisor and was one that was prudent for the promisee to make in the absence of any contract of indemnity, or if the promisor authorised him/her to compromise the suit.

In a nutshell, the indemnity holder is entitled to all damages plus all costs of the suit and promised money provided he/she has acted *intra-vires* (within powers). Besides, if he (indemnity holder) has incurred a liability and that liability is absolute, he has the right to require the indemnifier to put him/her in a position to meet the claim [Section 125].

[1] 1928, ILR 56 Cal. 262

Contract of Guarantee

Guarantee: A contract to perform the promise, or discharge the liability of a third party in the event of his default.

The term guarantee implies a formal promise or assurance made by one person to another person to be responsible, if a third person fails to perform a certain duty, for example, repay a debt. Therefore, a 'contract of guarantee' takes shape when a person comes forward and undertakes to discharge the debt or obligation of a third person in case of his/her default. Section 126 of the Indian Contract Act defines a contract of guarantee as follows:

'A contract of guarantee is a contract to perform the promise, or discharge the liability, of a third person in case of his default.'

Thus, a contract of guarantee is entered into with an objective to enable a person to get a loan, or goods on credit, and even an employment.

The person who gives the guarantee is called the surety[2], the person in respect of whose default the guarantee is given is called the principal debtor, and the person to whom the guarantee is given is called the creditor. A guarantee may be either oral or written [Section 126]. For instance, *A* applies for shares in a public limited company and *B* assures the company that if *A* does not pay the calls, *B* will. This is a contract of guarantee. The primary liability to pay the calls made by the company is that of *A*, but if he fails to pay, *B* will become liable to pay. In this example, *B* is the surety, *A* is the principal debtor, and the company is the creditor.

Thus, a contract of guarantee is a collateral engagement in which the surety undertakes to be liable to the creditor for the debt of another (i.e., the principal debtor) in case of his default. There must

[2] Guarantor is a person who agrees to be responsible for somebody or makes sure that something happens or is done, and

- Surety is a person who accepts responsibility if somebody else does not pay a debt, apper in a court of law, etc.

Therefore the term surety has been used deliberately and appropriately.

Box 8.1 Consideration for Guarantee

Example 1

B requests *A* to sell and deliver to him goods on credit. *A* agrees to do so, provided *C* will guarantee the payment of the price of the goods. *C* promises to guarantee the payment in consideration of *A*'s promise to deliver the goods. This is a sufficient consideration for *C*'s promise.

Example 2

A sells and delivers goods to *B*. Subsequently, *C* requests *A* to forbear to sue *B* for the debt for a year and promises that, if *A* does so, he (*C*) will pay for them in default of payment by *B*. *A* agrees to forbear as requested. This is a sufficient consideration for *C*'s promise.

be a conditional promise to pay if the principal debtor fails to pay. A liability that is incurred independently of a 'default', is not within the definition of guarantee [*Punjab National Bank vs Sri Vikram Cotton Mills*[3]].

Consideration for Guarantee

Like every other contract, a contract of guarantee must have all the essential elements of a valid contract, such as, competence of parties, free consent, legality of object, and consideration. There is, however, a special feature with regard to consideration in contract of guarantee. There need not be any direct consideration between the surety and the creditor. Consideration received by the principal debtor is sufficient for the surety. Section 127 expressly provides to this effect, saying, 'anything done or any promise made, for the benefit of the principal debtor, may be a sufficient consideration to the surety for giving the guarantee. Box 8.1 presents some examples in this regard.

Incapacity of the Principal Debtor

It is true that the parties to a contract of guarantee should be competent to contract. However, the incapacity of the principal debtor does not impair the validity of a contract of guarantee. A principal debtor may be a minor; in such a situation, the surety would be regarded as the principal debtor and he/she will personally become liable to pay. In that case, the contract between the creditor and the surety is treated as a primary and independent one, and not collateral. Therefore, the requirement is that the creditor and the surety must be competent to contract.

Contract of Indemnity and Contract of Guarantee Distinguished

The distinction between an indemnity and guarantee can be explained with the help of an example. Suppose *A* and *B* go to an electronic items shop, and *B* tells the seller, 'Supply the TV set required by *A*, and should he fail to pay you the price, I will'. This is a contract of guarantee. The primary liability to pay is that of *A*, but if he fails to do so, *B* would be required to pay. On the other hand, if *B* asks the showroom owner, 'Let him have the TV set and I will see that you are paid', then the contract is one of indemnity and not of guarantee. The main points of difference between a contract of indemnity and a contract of guarantee are summarised in Table 8.1 as follows.

Extent of Surety's Liability

The liability of the surety is co-extensive with that of the principal debtor unless it is otherwise provided by the contract [Section 128].

The above provision implies that the surety is liable to the same extent to which the principal debtor is liable. However, if at the time of giving the guarantee, the surety has undertaken to be liable for a fixed sum, the surety shall be liable to the extent of the specified sum only.

[3] 1970, 1 SCC6

Table 8.1 Difference Between Contract of Guarantee and Contract of Indemnity

S. No.	Point of difference	Contract of indemnity	Contract of guarantee
1.	Parties	A contract of indemnity requires the concurrence of only two parties, viz., the indemnifier and the indemnity holder or the indemnified.	A contract of guarantee is a tripartite agreement, which contemplates three persons: the principal debtor, the creditor, and the surety.
2.	Object	The object of a contract of indemnity is to make good the loss or to compensate the party that has suffered some loss.	The object of a contract of guarantee is to enable a person to obtain a loan, or goods on credit, or even employment.
3.	Nature of contract	The contract of indemnity is for the re-imbursement of the loss. The indemnifier promises to save the indemnity holder from a contingent risk, i.e., when he suffers some loss.	The contract of guarantee is for the security of the creditor. The surety undertakes to discharge the liability of the principal debtor, which is not contingent but is subsisting. In a contract of guarantee, there is an existing debt or duty,the performance of which is guaranteed by the surety.
4.	Nature of liability	The promisor (i.e., the indemnifier) undertakes an independent liability. In other words, the liability of the indemnifier is primary.	The promisor (i.e., the surety) undertakes to be liable when the principal debtor fails to pay, i.e., the liability of the surety is collateral.
5.	Independence of the promisor	Indemnifier acts independently without any request of the debtor or the third party.	The surety gives guarantee only at the request of the principal debtor.
6.	Right to sue third parties	The indemnifier cannot sue third parties in his own name unless there be an assignment in there be an assignment in the name of the indemnified.	If the principal debtor fails to pay, the surety, after he has discharged the debt, can proceed against the principal debtor in his own right.

For instance, *A* guarantees to *B* the payment of a bill of exchange by C, the acceptor. C dishonours the bill. *A* is liable not only for the amount of the bill, but also for any interest and charges that may have become due on it.

However, if *A* gives the guarantee for the principal amount of the bill, and if *B* makes a default, *A* shall be liable only for the principal amount, as the bill bears.

Kinds of Guarantee

The contracts of guarantee may be classified into two types, namely, specific guarantee and continuing guarantee.

Specific Guarantee

Specific guarantee: A guarantee applicable in respect of a single debt or a specific transaction.

When a guarantee is given only for a single debt or a specific transaction only, it is called specific guarantee. The responsibility of the surety ceases as soon as the guaranteed debt is paid or the promise is duly performed. In other words, specific guarantee will not extend to other contracts, if any, between the creditor and the principal debtor. For example, *A*, a money lender, agrees to give a loan of ₹10,000 to *B*, under the contract that if *B* does not repay the loan, his friend C would repay the same. This is a contract of specific guarantee and C's liability would come to an end as soon as *B* repays the debt that he had guaranteed.

Continuing Guarantee

Continuing guarantee: A guarantee that extends to a series of transactions.

A guarantee that extends to a series of transactions is called a continuing guarantee [Section 129]. Under this kind of guarantee, the surety undertakes responsibility for a series of separable and distinct transactions over a period of time. For instance, a fidelity guarantee, in which the insurer provides cover for a business against theft by an employee, is a continuing guarantee, as it remains in force for a period of time. Some illustrations of continuing guarantee are given in Box 8.2.

Revocation of continuing guarantee

A continuing guarantee may be revoked in respect of future transaction in any of the following ways.

By notice of revocation The surety, as to future transactions, may at any time revoke a continuing guarantee by serving a notice to the creditor [Section 130].

For instance, *A* guarantees to *B*, to the extent of ₹10,000, that *C* shall pay all the bills that *B* shall draw upon him (*C*). *B* draws upon *C*, who accepts the bill. Later on, *A* serves a notice of revocation. *C* dishonours the bill on maturity. *A* is liable upon his guarantee.

By death of surety The death of the surety, in the absence of any contract to the contrary, operates as a revocation of a continuing guarantee, as regards future transactions [Section 131].

The termination of a continuing guarantee by death of the surety, however, becomes effective only for the future transactions.

In the same manner as the surety is discharged A continuing guarantee is also annulled (i.e., no longer legally valid) under all the circumstances under which a surety is discharged from the liability. In other words, a continuing guarantee stands as along as the surety is not discharged and the same rules that apply for the discharge of a surety are applicable to a continuing guarantee, such as

1. Novation [Section 62]
2. Variance in terms of contract [Section 133]
3. Release or discharge of principal debtor [Section 134]
4. Arrangement with the principal debtor [Section 135]
5. Creditor's act or omission impairing surety's eventual remedy [Section 139]
6. Loss of security [Section 141]

We shall study these points in detail later in this chapter under the heading 'Discharge of Surety'.

Rights of Surety

The rights of a surety can be studied under the following three heads:

1. Rights against the principal debtor
2. Rights against the creditor
3. Rights against the co-sureties.

Box 8.2 Examples of Continuing Guarantee

Example 1

A guarantees payment to *B*, a tea-dealer, to the amount of 100 pounds, for any tea he may supply from time to time to *C*. *B* supplies *C* with tea to the value of 100 pounds, and *C* pays *B* for it. Afterwards, *B* supplies *C* with tea to the value of 200 pounds. *C* fails to pay. The guarantee given by *A* was a continuing guarantee, and he is accordingly liable to *B* to the extent of 100 pounds.

Example 2

A guarantees payment to *B* of the price of five sacks of flour to be delivered by *B* to *C* and to be paid for in a month. *B* delivers five sacks to *C*. *C* pays for them. Afterwards *B* delivers four sacks to *C*, which *C* does not pay for. The guarantee given by *A* was not a continuing guarantee, and accordingly, he is not liable for the price of the four sacks.

Rights Against the Principal Debtor

The surety has the following two rights against the principal debtor.

Right of subrogation After discharging the debt, the surety steps into the shoes of the creditor, i.e., subrogated to all the rights of the creditor against the principal debtor. Section 140 provides, 'Where a guaranteed debt has become due, or default of the principal debtor to perform guaranteed duty has taken place, the surety upon payment or performance of all that he is liable for is invested with all the rights which the creditor had against the principal debtor'.

Right of indemnity A surety is entitled to be indemnified by the principal debtor for whatever sum he has rightfully paid under the guarantee. Section 145 provides that 'In every contract of guarantee there is an implied promise by the principal debtor to indemnify the surety, and the surety is entitled to recover from the principal debtor whatever sum he has rightfully paid under the guarantee, but no sums, which he has paid wrongfully'.

Rights Against the Creditor

The surety enjoys the following two rights against the creditor.

Right to security A surety is entitled to the benefit of every security which the creditor has against the principal debtor at the time when the contract of surety is entered into, even if the surety is unaware of the existence of the security, and if the creditor loses, or without the consent of the surety parts with such security, the surety is discharged to the extent of the value of the security [Section 141]. Examples in Box 8.3 help understand the law in this regard.

Right of set-off When the creditor calls upon the surety to pay the guaranteed amount, the surety is entitled to plead any set-off which the principal debtor may have against the creditor. He can claim such a right not only against the creditor but also against third parties who have derived their title from the creditor.

Rights against the co-sureties Where more than one person has guaranteed a single debt, they are called co-sureties. In such cases, the liability of co-sureties becomes joint and several. They are liable to contribute, as agreed, towards the payment of guaranteed debt. But in the absence of any agreement, if one of the sureties has paid the entire debt to the creditor, he has a right to have contribution from the co-sureties who are equally bound to pay. The rules relating to contribution can be studied under Sections 146 and 147.

Where sureties become liable to contribute equally Where two or more persons are co-sureties for a contract of guarantee, they in the absence of any contract to the contrary become liable, as between themselves, to pay an equal share of the whole debt, or of that part of it which remains unpaid by the principal debtor [Section 146]. The examples in Box 8.4 derive home the point.

Where sureties become liable to contribute subject to the maximum amounts guaranteed by each one Co-sureties who are bound in different sums are liable to pay equally as far as the limits of their respective obligations permit [Section 147]. The two instances in Box 8.5 help explain the point better.

Box 8.3 A Surety's Right to Securities [Section 141]

Example 1

C advances to *B*, his tenant, ₹2000 on the guarantee of *A*. *C* also has a further security for ₹2000 by way of a mortgage of *B*'s furniture. *C* cancels the mortgage. *B* becomes insolvent and *C* sues *A* on his guarantee. *A* is discharged from the liability to the amount of the value of the furniture.

Example 2

C, a creditor, whose advance to *B* is secured by a decree, also receives a guarantee for that advance from *A*. *C* afterwards takes *B*'s goods in execution of the decree, and then, without the knowledge of *A*, withdraws the execution. *A* is discharged.

Box 8.4 **Co-sureties Liable to Pay Equally [Section 146]**

Example 1

A, *B*, and *C* are sureties to *D* for a sum of ₹3000 lent to *E*. *E* defaults in payment. *A*, *B*, and *C* are liable, as between themselves, to pay ₹1000 each.

Example 2

A, *B*, and *C* are sureties to *D* for a sum of ₹1000 lent to *E*, and there is a contract between *A*, *B*, and *C* that *A* is to be responsible to the extent of one-quarter, *B* to the extent of one-quarter, and *C* to the extent of one-half. *E* defaults in payment. Between the sureties, *A* and *B* are liable to pay ₹250 each, and *C* is liable for ₹500.

Box 8.5 **Co-sureties Liable to Contribute Maximum Sums Guaranteed [Section 147]**

Example 1

A, *B*, and *C*, as sureties for *D*, enter into three separate bonds, each in a different penalty, namely, *A* in the penalty of ₹10,000, *B* in that of ₹20,000, *C* in that of ₹40,000, conditioned for *D*'s duly accounting to *E*. *D* defaults in payment to the extent of ₹30,000. *A*, *B*, and *C*, are liable to pay ₹10,000 each.

Example 2

A, *B*, and *C*, as sureties for *D*, enter into three separate bonds, each in a different penalty, namely, *A* in the penalty of ₹10,000 , *B* in that of ₹20,000, *C* in that of ₹40,000, conditioned for *D*'s duly accounting to *E*. *D* defaults to the extent of ₹40,000. *A* is liable to pay ₹10,000, and *B* and *C* ₹15,000 each.

Discharge of Surety

A surety's liability comes to an end under any of the following circumstances:

1. By notice of revocation
2. By death of surety
3. By novation
4. By variance in terms of contract
5. By release or discharge of principal debtor
6. By arrangement between the principal debtor and the creditor
7. By impairing surety's remedy
8. By loss of security
9. By invalidation of the contract.

Notice of Revocation

Ordinarily a guarantee cannot be revoked if the liability has already been accrued. But Section 130 provides for revocation of continuing guarantee. For example, if *A* has stood surety for a ₹5,00,000 home loan of *B* from a bank and the money has been disbursed, then *A* cannot revoke the guarantee, as the liability has accrued. Accordingly, where a guarantee is a continuing one and extends to a series of transactions, the surety as to future transactions may revoke it, by giving notice to the creditor. However, the surety shall remain liable for the acts already acted upon, i.e., prior to the notice of revocation.

Death of Surety

In case of a continuing guarantee, the death of the surety, in the absence of any contract to the contrary, discharges him from liability as regards future transactions (i.e., transactions after his death). In other words, the surety's survivors or legal representatives would not be liable unless expressly mentioned in the contract [Section 131].

Novation

Novation, i.e., replacing an existing contract (of guarantee) by a fresh one, with or without changing the composition of the parties, consti-

Novation: Voluntarily substituting an original contract (of guarantee) by a fresh one by the parties.

tutes another mode of discharging a surety from the liability. If the parties to a contract (of guarantee) agree to substitute it with a new contract, the original contract need not be performed and so the surety stands discharged with regard to the old contract. For the surety, too, a fresh contract would have to be drafted [Section 62].

Variance in Terms of Contract

Any variance or alteration in the terms of the contract made between the principal debtor and the creditor, without the surety's consent, discharges the surety as to the transactions taking place subsequent to the variance [Section 133].

Box 8.6 provides a couple of examples in this regard.

Release or Discharge of Principal Debtor

The surety is discharged by any contract between the creditor and the principal debtor, by which the principal debtor is released, or by any act or omission of the creditor, the legal consequence of which is the discharge of the principal debtor [Section 134]. Box 8.7 presents some examples to explain the point.

Arrangement Between Principal Debtor and Creditor

Where the creditor, without the consent of the surety, arrives at a settlement with the principal debtor, or promises to give him more time, or promises not to sue him by a contract between the creditor and the principal debtor, the surety is absolved from the liability, unless the surety assents to such contract [Section 135].

Where, however, a contract to give time to the principal debtor is made by the creditor with a third person and not with the principal debtor, the surety is not discharged [Section 136]. For instance, *C*, the holder of an overdue bill of exchange drawn by *A* as surety for *B*, and accepted by *B*, contracts with *M* to give time to *B*. *A* is not discharged.

Box 8.6 **Altering Contract Terms Discharge Surety [Section 133]**

Example 1

A becomes surety to *C* for payment of rent by *B* under a lease. Afterwards *B* and *C* contract to hike the rent, without informing *A*. *A* would hence be discharged from his liability as a surety for the rent accruing subsequent to the variance in terms of the contract without his consent.

Example 2

C contracts to lend *B* ₹5000 on March 1. *A* guarantees repayment. *C* pays ₹5000 to *B* on January 1, *A* is discharged from his liability, as the contract has been varied for early release of loan by the creditor [illustration (e) appended to Section 133].

Box 8.7 **Creditor's Omission May Discharge Surety [Section 134] [Appended to Section 134]**

Example 1

A gives a guarantee to *C* for goods to be supplied by *C* to *B*. *C* supplies the goods to *B* but afterwards *B* is embarrassed and contracts with his creditors (including *C*) to assign to them his property in consideration of their releasing him from their demands. Here *B* is released from his debt by the contracts with *C*, and *A* is discharged from his surety.

Example 2

A contracts with *B* to grow a crop of indigo on *A*'s land and deliver it to *B* at a fixed rate. *C* guarantees *A*'s performance of this contract. *B*, however, diverts stream of water, which is necessary for the irrigation of *A*'s land, and thereby prevents him from raising the indigo. *C* is no longer liable on his guarantee.

Box 8.8 **Surety Discharged if creditor Impairs Remedy for Him [Appended to Section 139]**

Example 1

B contracts to build a ship for *C* for a given sum to be paid in installments as the work reaches certain stages. *A* becomes surety to *C* for *B*'s due performance of the contract. *C*, without the knowledge of *A*, prepays the last two installments to *B*. *A* is discharged by the prepayment.

Example 2

C lends money to *B* on the security of a joint and several promissory note made in *C*'s favour by *B*, and by *A* as surety for *B*, together with a bill of sale of *B*'s furniture, which gives power to *C* to sell the furniture. Owing to his (*C*'s) misconduct and wilful negligence, only a small price is realised. *A* is discharged from liability on the note.

Impairing Surety's Remedy

If the creditor commits any act, which is inconsistent with the rights of the surety, or fails to perform any act that his duty to the surety requires him to do, such that the eventual remedy of the surety himself against the principal debtor is impaired; the surety is discharged [Section 139]. Box 8.8 provides illustrations in this regard.

Loss of Security

If the creditor loses, or without the consent of the surety, parts with such security, the surety is discharged to the extent of the value of the security. It is immaterial whether the surety was or is aware of such security or not [Section 141]. For instance, *C* advances to *B* his tenant, ₹2000 on the guarantee of *A*. *C* has also a further security for ₹2000 by a mortgage of *B*'s furniture. *C*, however cancels the mortgage. *B* becomes insolvent and *C* sues *A* on his guarantee. *A* is discharged from liability to the amount of the value of the furniture.

Invalidation of Contract

A surety is also discharged upon invalidation of the contract (i.e., between the creditor and the surety). A contract of guarantee is invalid in the following circumstances.

Guarantee obtained by misrepresentation Any guarantee that has been obtained by means of misrepresentation made by the creditor, or with his knowledge or assent, concerning a material part of the transaction is invalid [Section 142].

Guarantee obtained by concealment Any guarantee that the creditor has obtained by means of keeping silence as to the material circumstances is invalid [Section 143].

Default on part of co-surety Where a person gives a guarantee upon a contract that the creditor shall not act upon it until another person has joined in it as co-surety, the guarantee is not valid if that other person does not join [Section 144].

Contracts of Bailment and Pledge

Contracts of bailment and pledge are specific types of contracts, as the Contract Act has laid down special rules for such types of contracts. Sections 148–181, contained in Chapter IX of the Indian Contract Act of 1872, govern these types of contracts. Present part of the chapter describes the meaning and kinds of bailment, duties, and rights of bailee as well as of bailor, finder of lost goods—his rights and duties, termination of bailment, pledge, differences between pledge and bailment, rights and duties of pawnor and pawnee, and pledge by persons, other than owners.

Bailment

A bailment is a situation wherein the owner of goods entrusts their possession into the care of another person for some purpose briefly. Section 148 defines the term 'bailment' as under:

Bailment: Entrusting possession of movable goods by the owner thereof into the care of another person for some purpose briefly.

'A bailment is the delivery of goods by one person to another for some purpose, upon a contract that they shall, when the purpose is accomplished, be returned

Box 8.9 Common Examples of Contracts of Bailment

1. Giving watch, TV or a radio set, computers, etc. for repair or servicing.
2. Leaving car or scooter for service/repairs or at a parking lot.
3. Delivering cloth to tailor for stitching a suit.
4. Hiring car, AC, tent, etc.
5. Delivering goods to transporter for despatching and delivering them to the consignee.
6. Leaving diamonds with goldsmith for being studded in gold jewellery.
7. Handing over valuables or pets to the safe custody of a friend or neighbour while leaving station.
8. Leaving luggage at cloakrooms.
9. Depositing 'documents of title' with the banker as a security (mortage) against a loan.

or otherwise disposed of according to the directions of the person delivering them'. The person delivering the goods is called the bailor. The person to whom they are delivered is called the bailee.

For instance, *A* delivers his car to *B* for repair. Here a relationship of bailment is created between *A* and *B*, where *A* is the bailor and *B* is the bailee. Some common examples of bailment that we frequently enter into our day-to-day lives are provided in Box 8.9.

Essentials of Bailment

Bailment, as we have learnt, is a special contract in which the possession of goods changes in order to achieve a specific purpose. It essentially involves change in possession and not change in ownership. Delivery of goods or return of goods by the bailee also constitutes an essential feature of a bailment. Following are the key elements that make up a valid bailment.

Contract

Bailment is based on a contract between two persons, namely, the bailor and the bailee. The contract, may, however, be implied in some cases such as finder of lost goods and seizing of someone's goods by the State in the exercise of its powers under various Acts.

Subject matter

Goods form the subject matter of the bailment. As per section 2(7) of the Sale of Goods Act, 'goods' means every kind of movable property other than money and actionable claim. Thus, depositing money in a bank account does not constitute bailment. Similarly, a contract of bailment cannot be entered into with regard to immovable property.

Delivery of goods

Delivery of goods is the essence of bailment. The term bailment though literally means to handover, it technically signifies change of possession in law. In bailment, therefore, possession of goods must change. Placing of ornaments or other valuables in a bank locker on this account does not create a bailment, as ornaments are never delivered to the banker. It is further necessary that the goods change hands temporarily, voluntarily, and in accordance with the contract. For example, if somebody obtains the possession of someone's goods under undue influence, threat, or fraud, it does not amount to bailment of goods for the lack of agreement and voluntary transfer. Similarly, a servant or a guest having access to or use of goods is not a bailee.

Delivery may be actual or constructive

Delivery of goods may be actual or constructive. Actual delivery implies physical transfer of goods from one person to another. For instance, when a student borrows a book from a library, there is actual delivery. When possession of goods changes by doing anything, which has the effect of putting the goods in the possession of the bailee, or of any person, authorised to hold them on behalf of the bailor, or the owner, it amounts to constructive delivery. For example, where the key of a warehouse is handed over to another person, it amounts to delivery of goods in the store. Here it is important to note that the constructive delivery is as good and effective for all practical purposes as actual delivery.

No change in ownership

Ownership is not transferred. Bailment signifies change of possession of goods from one person to another. But there is no change in the ownership. The bailor continues to be the owner of the goods.

Purpose

The bailor delivers his goods to the bailee for some definite purpose. The purpose for which the goods are delivered is usually in the contemplation of both the parties.

Return of goods

Every bailment pre-supposes a condition that the goods bailed would be returned to the bailor, or otherwise be disposed of according to the directions of the bailor, on the accomplishment of the purpose, or after the expiry of period of bailment. On this account, it is important to note that in order to discharge his duty, a bailee is supposed to return the goods bailed out, and not any other goods although of an equal or even higher value.

Kinds of Bailment

Bailment may broadly be classified into the following two categories:

1. Gratuitous bailment and
2. Non-gratuitous bailment.

Gratuitous bailment

Gratuitous bailment: A bailment without any consideration.

A bailment with no consideration is called a gratuitous bailment. In this kind of bailment, neither the bailor nor the bailee is entitled to any remuneration or reward. Such a bailment may be for the exclusive benefit of either party, i.e., the bailor or the bailee, discussed as follows.

Bailment for the exclusive benefit of the bailor In this case, the bailor delivers the goods for his exclusive benefits and the bailee does not derive any benefit out of it. For example, *A* leaves his pets with *B*, his neighbour, to be looked after during *A*'s physical absence. In this case, *A* alone is being benefited by the bailment. Or, if you park your car in your neighbour's premises to be taken care in your absence, you as a bailor derive the exclusive benefit from the bailment.

Bailment for the exclusive benefit of the bailee This is the case in which a bailor delivers the goods to the bailee for the exclusive benefits of the bailee and does not gain anything from the contract himself. For example, you lend your book to a friend of yours for a week without any charge or favour. In this case, the recipient of the book as the bailee is the sole beneficiary of this transaction of bailment.

Non-gratuitous bailment

Non-gratuitous bailment: Bailment for the mutual benefit, involving some consideration passing between the parties.

Contrary to gratuitous bailment, a non-gratuitous bailment or bailment for reward is one that involves some consideration passing between the bailor and the bailee. Obviously in this case, the delivery of goods takes place for the mutual benefit of both the parties. For example, *A* hires *B*'s car. Here *B* is the bailor and receives the hire charges, and *A* is the bailee and enjoys the use of the car. Similarly, when you give your *PC* or laptop for repair to some techie, both you and the computer techie are going to be benefited by this contract—while you get your computer repaired, he gets his fees or charges.

Duties and Rights of the Bailor

Duties of the bailor

The bailor owes the following duties to bailee in respect of the goods bailed out by him.

Duty to disclose faults According to Section 150, the bailor is bound to disclose to the bailee faults in the goods bailed, of which he is aware, and which materially interfere with the use of them, or could expose the bailee to extraordinary risks. If he does not make such a disclosure, he is responsible for the damage arising to the bailee directly from such faults. If the goods are bailed for hire, the bailor is responsible for such damage, whether he was or was not aware of the existence of such faults in the goods.

Duty to repay bailee's expenses A bailor is duty bound to repay to the bailee expenses incurred by him for work done on the goods received under conditions of bailment, and for which he is not receiving any remuneration or deriving any benefit. In this regard, Section 158 states, 'Where, by the conditions of the bailment, the goods are to be kept or to be carried, or to have work done upon them by the bailee for the bailor, and the bailee is to receive no remuneration, the bailor shall repay to the bailee the necessary expenses incurred by him for the purpose of the bailment'.

Duty to indemnify the bailee The bailor is bound to make good the loss suffered by the bailee that is in excess of the benefit actually derived, where he had delivered the goods gratuitously and compelled the bailee to return them before the expiry of the period of bailment [Section 159].

Duty to compensate bailee for breach of warranty Every contract of bailment warrants the bailee about the bailor's title being defect free. Thus, if bailee subsequently suffers any loss by the reason of the bailor's title being defective, it is the duty of the bailor to compensate the bailee for breach of warranty [Section 164].

Duty to claim back the goods The bailor is bound to accept the goods upon being returned by the bailee in accordance with the terms of bailment. If he refuses or fails to accept back the goods, if offered at a proper time and at a proper place, without any reasonable ground, he shall be responsible for any loss or damage to the goods and not the bailee. Moreover, the bailee, in such a case, can also claim from the bailor all necessary and incidental expenses that he might have incurred to keep and protect the goods.

Rights of the bailor

A bailor has the following rights.

Right to enforce bailee's performance Since the bailor delivers goods to the bailee for some specific purpose, the former, especially in case of non-gratuitous bailment, has an elemental right to achieve that purpose or obtain the benefit (i.e., performance) through the latter. For example, if *X* delivers a suit length to *Y*, his tailor, to stitch a suit for him, *X* (bailor) will see that the tailor does the needful in the desired manner.

Right to claim damages In all cases of bailment, the bailee is bound to take as much care of the goods bailed to him as a man of ordinary prudence would, under similar circumstances, take of his own goods of the same bulk, quality, and value as the goods bailed [Section 151]. This gives bailor a right to claim for damages against the loss, if any, caused to the goods bailed due to the bailee's negligence or misconduct.

Right to claim compensation against unauthorised use of goods If the bailee makes any use of the goods bailed, which is not according to the conditions of the bailment, the bailor has a right to claim compensation from the bailee in respect of any damage arising to the goods from or during such use of them [Sections 154–56]. For example, *A* lets *B* use his car but with a condition that only *B* shall drive. *B* allows *C*, a member of his family, to drive the car. *C* rides with care, but the car meets with some accident. *B* is liable to make compensation to *A* for the damage done to the car.

Right to terminate the contract Bailor has a right to terminate the contract if the bailee does any act with regard to the goods bailed, inconsistent with the conditions of the bailment [Section 153]. For example, *A* lets his horse to *B*, on hire, for his own riding. *B* drives the horse in his carriage. *A* can terminate the contract immediately.

Right to demand return of goods along with accretion to, if any The bailor enjoys the exclusive right to have the goods bailed delivered back to him in safe and sound condition after the time of bailment has expired or the purpose behind the bailment has been achieved. Moreover, in the absence of any contrary term in the contract, the bailor is also entitled to any accretion to the goods bailed if it occurred while the goods were in the study of bailee. For example, *A* leaves his hen in the custody of *B* to be taken care of for a week. The hen has laid eggs and thereby hatched the chicks. *A* is entitled not only to the hen but also to the chicks.

Duties and Rights of Bailee

The rights and duties of bailee are discussed as under.

Duties of the bailee

The bailor and the bailee are reciprocally related to one another. Hence rights of the bailor are the duties of the bailee and vice versa. Accordingly, the bailee owes the following duties in respect of goods bailed to him.

Duty to take reasonable care of the goods whilst they are in his possession In all cases of bailment, the bailee is bound to take as much care of the goods bailed to him as a man of ordinary prudence, under similar circumstances, would take of his own goods of the same bulk, quality, and value [Section 151]. The degree of care required from the bailee is the same whether the bailment is for reward, or gratuitous.

Duty not to make any unauthorised use of the goods bailed The bailee is under an obligation not to resort to unauthorised use of the goods bailed to him. In this regard, an unauthorised use refers to any act in relation to goods bailed, inconsistent with the condition of bailment. As per Section 153, a contract of bailment is voidable at the option of the bailor, if the bailee does any act with regard to goods bailed, inconsistent with the conditions of the bailment. Section 154 further provides that if the bailee makes any unauthorised use of the goods bailed, he is liable to make compensation to the bailor for any damage arising to the goods from or during such use of them.

Duty not to set up *jus tertii* The bailee should not set up *jus tertii,* i.e., adverse title (his own title or the title of a third party) to the bailed goods, as the same will be inconsistent with the conditions of bailment. Even if a third person claims a better title to the goods other than that of the bailor, the bailee is duty bound to return the goods to the bailor only.

Duty not to mix the goods bailed with his own goods A bailee is duty bound not to mix the bailed goods with his own goods, without the consent of the bailor. In other words, he must keep the goods bailed to him separate from his own goods. If the bailee, with the consent of the bailor, mixes the goods of the bailor with his own, the bailor and the bailee shall have an interest, in proportion to their respective shares, in the mixture thus produced.

Duty to return the goods in accordance with the contract It is the duty of the bailee to return, or deliver the goods bailed, according to the bailor's directions, without any demand, as soon as the time for which they were bailed has expired, or the purpose for which they were bailed has been accomplished [Section 160].

If by the default of the bailee, the goods are not returned, delivered or tendered at the proper time, he will be liable to the bailor for any loss, destruction, or deterioration of the goods from that time.

Duty to return any accretion to the goods In the absence of any contract to the contrary, the bailee is bound to deliver to the bailor, or according to his directions, any increase or profit, which may have accrued from the goods bailed [Section 163]. For example, *A* leaves a pregnant cow in the custody of *B* to be taken care of. The cow gives birth to a calf. *B* is bound to deliver the calf as well the cow to *A*.

Rights of the bailee

Because of the reciprocity of relationships, most of the duties of the bailor are the rights of the bailee. Accordingly, a bailee enjoys the following rights.

Right to enforce bailor's duties The bailee has a right

1. to claim damages from the bailor if he has suffered some loss due to non-disclosure of defects in the goods on the bailor's part. If the goods were bailed for hire, the bailee would be entitled to recover damages from the bailor even if the latter was not aware of the existence of such faults in the goods bailed [Section 150].
2. to claim from the bailor all necessary expenses incurred by him for the purpose of the bailment if the bailment was non-gratuitous [Section 158].
3. to be indemnified against any loss or damage sustained by him by reason of defective title of the bailor [Section 164].

Similarly, in case of bailment for reward, the bailee will be entitled to recover from the bailor, all extraordinary expenses, borne by the bailor for the purpose of bailment.

Right of Lien

Where the bailee has, in accordance with the purpose of the bailment, rendered any service involving the exercise of labour or skill in respect of the goods bailed, he has, in the absence of a contract to the contrary, a right to retain such goods until he receives due remuneration for the services he has rendered in respect of them [Section 170]. Examples to this effect are presented in Box 8.10.

Bankers, factors (merchants buying and selling on commission basis), wharfingers (ship loaders),

Box 8.10 **Right of Lien; When Bailee Can Retain Goods [Section 170]**

Example 1

A delivers a rough diamond to *B*, a jeweller, to be cut and polished, which is accordingly done. *B* is entitled to retain the stone till he is paid for the services he has rendered.

Example 2

A gives a piece of cloth to *B*, a tailor, to make into a coat. *B* promises *A* to deliver the coat as soon as it is finished, and to give a three months' credit to *A* for the price. *B* is entitled to retain the coat until he is paid the stitching charges.

attorneys of a High Court, and policy-brokers may, in the absence of a contract to the contrary, retain as a security for general balance of account, any goods bailed to them, but no other persons have a right to retain as a security for such balance, goods bailed to them, unless there is an express contract to the effect [Section 171].

Right to sell the goods If the bailor fails to take delivery of the goods and to pay the bailee's charges, the bailee has a right to sell the goods after giving a notice to the bailor of his intention. After the sale, the bailee must account to the bailor for the proceeds of sale less the costs of sale and the amount owed to the bailee in respect of the goods [Section 169].

Right to return the goods to any of the joint-bailors If several joint owners of goods bail them, the bailee may deliver them back to, or according to the directions of, one joint-owner without the consent of all in the absence of any agreement to the contrary [Section 165].

Right to deliver goods to the bailor without title If the bailor has no title to the goods, and the bailee, in good faith, delivers them back to, or according to the directions of, the bailor, the bailee is not responsible to the owner of the goods in respect of such delivery [Section 166].

From the foregone discussion it is clear that the duties of the bailor are the rights of bailee, and the rights of bailor are the duties of bailee. This is simply because bailor and bailee sit in reciprocal relationship to each other.

Termination of a Bailment

The following circumstances render a contract of bailment terminated.

Unauthorised use of goods bailed A bailor may terminate the bailment where the bailee does any act with regard to goods bailed, inconsistent with the conditions of bailment [Section 153]. Simply put, it means that a bailor can terminate a bailment before its term runs out, in case he finds the bailee's conduct, with respect to the bailed goods, contrary to the agreed terms. In such a case, a bailment can be terminated even before the expiry of the term of the bailment.

Expiry of term of bailment A contract of bailment automatically comes to an end upon the expiry of the period for which the goods were bailed.

A gratuitous bailment may, however, be terminated at any time, even before the agreed time, except where the termination before the fixed period causes loss to the bailee exceeding the benefit actually derived by him from the bailment. In that case the bailor must compensate him [Section 159].

Accomplishment of purpose If the goods were bailed for a specific object, the bailment comes to an end upon achievement of the said object or purpose.

Death of either party A gratuitous bailment terminates by the death of either the bailor or the bailee.

Destruction of subject matter A contract of bailment also comes to an end if the goods that are the subject matter of the bailment get destroyed or otherwise become incapable of being used for bailment any more.

Lien

Lien refers to the bailee's right to retain the possession of the bailed goods lest he is not paid his dues. Liens are of two kinds, namely, particular lien and general lien.

Lien: The bailee's right to retain the possession of the bailed goods until his/her dues are cleared.

Particular Lien

Particular lien: Lien available only against the goods in respect of which the bailee has rendered some service.

A particular lien is one that is available only against the goods in respect of which the bailee has rendered any service. Section 170 says, 'Where the bailee has, in accordance with the purpose of the bailment, rendered any service involving the exercise of labour or skill in respect of the goods bailed, he has in absence of a contract to the contrary, a right to retain such goods until he receives due remuneration for the services he has rendered in respect of them'.

Thus, in the exercise of particular lien, only such goods can be retained on which the bailee has exercised labour and skill. He cannot retain any other goods belonging to the bailor, which are in his possession otherwise [*Chase vs Wetmore*]. As a general rule, only a bailee is entitled to particular lien. We have studied the examples to this effect in Box 8.10.

General Lien

General lien: The bailee's right to retain the bailed goods for any of his/her lawful dues.

A general lien, on the other hand, is the right to hold the bailed goods for any lawful dues. Section 171 provides, 'Bankers, factors, wharfingers, attorneys of a high court, and policy-brokers, in the absence of a contract to the contrary, retain as a security for a general balance of account, any goods bailed to them; but no other persons have a right to retain, as a security for such balance, goods bailed to them, unless there is an express contract to that effect'.

Thus, a general lien is the extension of particular lien, which entitles the bailee to retain any goods bailed to him for any amount due to him whether in respect of those goods or any other goods.

Parties entitled to general lien

Being a privilege, the right of general lien has been specifically conferred by Section 171 of the Indian Contract Act on bankers, factors, wharfingers, attorneys of a high court, and policy-brokers. Box 8.11 presents examples on this count.

Finder of Lost Goods

Finder of lost goods: A person who finds an article belonging to another person.

A person who finds an article belonging to another person is called the finder of lost goods. In the eyes of the law, the position of a finder of lost goods is exactly that of a bailee. Section 71 says, 'A person who finds goods belonging to another, and takes them into his custody, is subject to the same responsibility as a bailee'. It should be noted that the finder of goods occupies the position of bailee only against the true owner, since he keeps the goods found in trust only for the real owner. As against everyone else, the property as regards the goods found vests in the finder on his taking possession of it.

Duties and Rights of Finder of Lost Goods

A finder of goods has the following duties:

1. To exercise reasonable care in preserving the goods found
2. To find the actual owner and restore the goods to him

Box 8.11 General Lien: When Bailee Can Retain Any Goods

Example 1

A obtains a personal loan amounting ₹5000 from a bank without any security. He later borrows a further sum of ₹10,000 from the same bank but provides some gold jewellery as security this time. Even after *A* has discharged the second debt of ₹10,000, the banker can retain the jewellery as security in respect of the sum of ₹5000, initially advanced without any security.

Example 2

In *Jowitt & Sons vs Union Cold Storage Co.*[4], a quantity of imported meat was stored with a warehouse keeper who by a general term of the trade had a general lien. It was held that he could retain the meat for his charges due in respect of other goods.

3. Not to make any personal use of the goods found
4. Not to mix the goods found with his own goods
5. Not to set up any adverse title to the goods found

The law confers the following rights on a finder of goods.

Retain the goods A finder of goods can retain them against the owner until he (the finder) receives compensation for expenses and trouble voluntarily incurred by him in finding out the true owner, and in preserving the goods he has found. He, however, has no right to sue the owner for such compensation [Section 168].

Sue the owner for reward Where the owner has offered a specific reward for the return of the goods lost, he (finder) may sue the owner for such reward and may retain the goods until he receives it [Section 168].

Sell the found articles When an article found is commonly the subject of sale and the owner cannot with reasonable diligence be found, or if he refuses, upon demand, to pay the lawful charges of the finder, the finder may sell it

1. when the thing is in danger of perishing or of losing the greater part of its value, or
2. when the lawful charges of the finder, in respect of the thing found, amounts to two-thirds of its value [Section 169].

Pledge

Pledge: Bailment of goods as security for the repayment of a debt or performance of a promise.

A pledge or pawn is a kind of bailment. It is the bailment of a movable thing as security for the repayment of a debt or performance of a promise. The bailor in this case is called the Pawnor or Pledgor, whereas the bailee is called the Pawnee or Pledgee [Section 172].

In order to enforce a contract of pledge, the property pledged should be actually or constructively delivered to the pawnee. Ownership of the pledged goods does not pass to the pledgee. A pawnee has only a special property in the pledge, the general property remains in the pawnor and wholly reverts to him on discharge of the debt [*Lallan Prasad vs Rahmat Ali*[4]]. Any kinds of movable goods or property, valuables, documents, or securities may be pledged. The government securities should, however, be pledged by endorsement and delivery.

Pledge and Bailment Compared

The contracts of pledge and bailment are similar in two of the following respects

1. In both the cases, there is a delivery of movable goods or property;
2. The goods are delivered back to the bailor or pawnor after accomplishment of purpose or expiry of stipulated time.

The two, however, differ in a number of ways such as the following.

Purpose Pledge has a specific purpose, i.e., repayment of a debt or performance of a promise, whereas bailment has a general purpose.

Use of goods The pawnee has no right to make any use of the goods pledged. On the other hand, in bailment the bailee uses the goods if the terms of bailment so provide.

Rights and Duties of the Pawnee

Pledge being a species of bailment, the rights and duties of the pawnor and pawnee are almost similar to those of the bailor and bailee.

Rights of pawnee

The Law confers the following rights to the pawnee.

Right of retaining goods The pawnee has a right to retain the goods pledged for

1. payment of the debt
2. performance of the promise, and
3. all expenses incurred by him in respect of the possession or for the preservation of the goods pledged [Section 173].

However, the pawnee shall not, in the absence of a contract to that effect, retain the goods pledged for any debt or promise other than the debt or promise for which they are pledged. Still, such a contract, in the absence of anything to the contrary, shall be

[4] 1967, A.S.C. 1322; 1967, 2 S.C.R.233

presumed in regard to subsequent advances made by the pawnee (i.e., without fresh security) [Section 174].

Right as to extraordinary expenses The pawnee is entitled to receive from the pawnor extraordinary expenses incurred by him for the preservation of the goods pledged [Section 175].

Right to sue when pawnor makes default Should the pawnor default in payment of the debt, or performance of the promise, at the stipulated time, the pawnee may bring a suit against the pawnor upon the debt or promise while retaining the goods pledged as collateral security [Section 176].

Right to sale Upon pawnor's default as regards payment of debt or performance of the promise, the pawnee may sell the goods pledged, on giving the pawnor reasonable notice of the sale. If the proceeds of such sale are less than the amount due in respect of the debt or promise, the pawnor is still liable to pay the balance. If the proceeds of the sale are greater than the amount so due, the pawnee shall pay over the surplus to the pawnor [Section 176].

Right to have good title to the goods Where the pawnor's title with regard to the goods pledged by him is defective, the pawnee acquires a good title to the goods, provided he acted in good faith and without notice of the pawnor's defect in title [Section 178A].

Duties of pawnee

A pawnee has the following duties:

1. Duty to take reasonable care of the goods pledged
2. Duty not to make personal use of the goods pledged
3. Duty not to mix goods pledged with his own goods
4. Duty to return the goods pledged after the debt has been paid or the promise has been performed
5. Duty not to commit any act that is inconsistent with the terms of pledge
6. Duty to deliver accretion, if any, to the goods pledged.

Rights and Duties of the Pawnor

Rights of pawnor

Foremost of all his rights, the pawnor has a right to get back the goods pledged plus increase thereon, if any, by him, after paying off the amount of debt in full and other charges (if applicable), or performing the promise.

Moreover, if a time is stipulated for the payment of the debt, or the performance of the promise, for which the pledge is made, and the pawnor defaults on that count, i.e, repaying the debt or performing the promise, he may redeem the goods pledged at any subsequent time before the actual sale of them. However, he must, in that case, pay, in addition, any expenses that have arisen from his default [Section 177].

Duties of pawnor

The pawnor has the following duties.

Duty to repay the debt or perform the promise The pawnee is bound to comply with the terms of pledge. Accordingly, he must repay the debt in full along with interest and other charges, if any, or perform the promise at the stipulated date or time.

Duty to disclose defects in the goods pledged The pawnor should disclose to the pawnee defects in the goods pledged, if any, of which he is aware, failing which he will be liable for any loss to the pawnee due to such defect.

Duty to meet extraordinary expenses If the pawnee has incurred any extraordinary expenses for preserving the goods pledged, it is the duty of the pawnor to compensate him for the same.

Pledge by Non-owners

Generally, only the owner or co-owner of the goods can pledge them. But to facilitate mercantile transactions, the law, under certain circumstances, permits a pledge by a person who is not the owner but is in the possession of the goods. Accordingly, the following non-owners too can make a valid pledge of the goods.

1. A mercantile agent
2. Person in possession under voidable contract
3. Seller or buyer in possession after sale
4. Person having limited interest.

Mercantile agent Where a mercantile agent is, with the consent of the owner, in possession of goods or the document of title to goods, any pledge made by him, when acting in the ordinary course of business of a mercantile agent, shall be as valid as if he were expressly authorised by the owner of the goods to make the same, provided that the pawnee acts in good faith and has, at the time of pledge, no notice of the fact that the agent has no authority to pledge [Section 178].

Person in possession under voidable contract A person who is in possession of goods under a voidable contract can make a valid pledge provided the pawnee has acted in good faith and without any knowledge of the defect in pawnor's title [See Section 178 A].

Seller or buyer in possession A seller left in possession of goods sold or documents of title thereof is no more the owner. But the pledge made by him will be valid provided the pawnee acted in good faith and had no knowledge of the defect in the pawnor's title. On the same footing, a buyer, who with the consent of the seller, obtains possession of goods before sale can make a valid contract [See Section 30 of Sale of Goods Act].

Person having limited interest Where a person who pledges goods in which he has only a limited interest, for example, he is a mortgagee or has a lien over these goods, the pledge will be valid to the extent of that interest [See Section 179].

Contract of Agency

Agency: The legal relationship in which the agent deals with a third party on behalf of the principal.

If a person asks someone else to purchase or sell certain goods, or provide a service on his/her behalf, and the latter promises to do the needful, a contract of agency comes into being. Agency is basically a relationship that arises when one person, called the principal, authorises another, called the agent, to act on his/her behalf, and the other person agrees to do so. Hence, the agency implies legal relationship in which the agent deals with a third party on behalf of the principal. The law of agency is based on the principle 'what a person does by another, he/she does by himself/herself'. Accordingly, the most important effect of establishing an agency relationship is that it enables the agent to make a contract between his/her principal and a third party. In case of large businesses, it is not possible for a single person to transact all the business personally; hence the emergence, growth, and importance of the agency. This last part of the present chapter discusses various aspects of the contractual obligations related to agency relationship, such as essentials of agency, modes of creation of an agency; scope and extent of an agent's authority; rights, duties and personal liability of an agent; termination of agency etc.

Agency Defined

Agent: A person employed to do any act for another person, or to represent another in his dealings with the third party.

The Act attempts to define agency in terms of agent and principal relationship. According to Section 182 of the Contract Act, 'an agent is a person employed to do any act for another person, or to represent another in his dealings with third persons. The person for whom such an act is done or who is so represented is called the principal'.

As the definition indicates, an agent acts as a connecting link between the principal and the third parties. After enforcing the contract on behalf of the principal (i.e., the promisor) with a third party (i.e., the promisee), he/she ceases to be a party to the contract, and the contract comes into existence only between the principal and the third party. In this way, the role of an agent is essentially to bring the principal into contractual relations with a third party.

General Rules Governing an Agency

Following are the two important general rules regarding agency:

1. Whatever a man *sui juris* (i.e., a person competent to contract) may lawfully do by himself, he may do the same through an agent. This means that any person possessing the capacity to contract may act through a representative, i.e., an agent. However, the process cannot be adopted in the transactions or acts requiring personal skills and abilities. For example, a person cannot enter into a contract of marriage through an agent. Similarly, no one can make a painting or carve a statue through an agent.
2. *Maxim qui facit per alium facit per se*, i.e., he who acts through an agent is himself/herself acting. In other words, for legal purposes, the acts of an agent are the acts of his principal. In this regard,

Section 226 says, 'Contracts entered into through an agent, and obligations arising from acts done by an agent, may be enforced in the same manner and will have the same legal consequences as if the contracts had been entered into and the acts done by the principal in person'. For example, *A* buys goods from *B* knowing that he is an agent for their sale but not knowing who is the principal. *B*'s principal is the person entitled to claim from *A* the price of the goods, and *A* cannot, in a suit by the principal, set off against that claim a debt due to himself from *B* [illustration (a) appended to Section 226].

Essentials of Agency

An agency has three distinct characteristics, which are as follows.

Intention and power to act on behalf of the principal

The mere fact that a person says he/she is an agent does not make them one if they intend to act on their own behalf and not on behalf of their supposed principal. Therefore, to become an agent of another, a person must be intended and adequately authorised to represent another so that he/she can render the person so represented answerable to a third person. Thus, a person who agrees in friendship to ferry another's car from one place to another can be regarded as the owner's agent, such that his negligent driving may make the owner liable in tort; but a person who borrows another's car for his own purposes would not be so regarded.

Capacity of the parties

The first rule makes it clear that since an agent brings about a contractual relationship between his/her principal (i.e., the promisor) and a third party (i.e., the promisee), it is essential that both the principal and the third party should be competent to contract. As per Section 183, 'Any person who is of the age of majority according to the law to which he is subject and who is of sound mind may employ an agent'.

However, the second rule of agency shows that the agent need not have the capacity to contract, since his/her act is deemed to be the act of the principal. According to Section 184, 'As between the principal and third persons, any person may become an agent, but no person who is not of the age of majority and of sound mind can become an agent, so as to be responsible to his principal according to the provisions in that behalf herein contained'.

Thus, a person may contract through a minor agent, but the minor will not be responsible to his principal [*Foreman vs Great Western Rly. Co.*[5]].

Consideration not necessary

Unlike other forms of contract, a valid agency can be created without consideration. The principal may agree to pay consideration to the agent in the form of commission or salary, but it is not a deciding factor for the validity of their agency relationship. Section 105 clearly provides, 'No consideration is necessary to create an agency'. A contract of agency, therefore, constitutes an exception to the general rule contained in Section 25 that no contract will be valid unless it is supported by consideration.

Factors Determining Existence of Agency Relationship

The use of the words 'agency agreement' and 'agent' by the parties in a contract does not necessarily establish a relationship of agency in the legal sense. The true test of determining whether a relationship is that of principal and agent is if the agent can make the principal answerable to a third person. In other words, an agency exists whenever a person has the authority to represent the other and create a contractual relationship between the latter (principal) and the third parties. An agency relationship does not exist if a person is only acting at the advice or direction of the other but not on his/her behalf. Thus, a 'procurement agent' has been held 'to be not an agent' [*State of Madras vs Jaya Lakshmi Rice Mills*[6]], as he/she is only a person directed to do an act on commission and not to represent anyone. Similarly, a person is not an agent merely because he/she gives advice to others in matters of business [*Mahesh Chandra Basu vs Ratha Kishore Bhattacharjee*[7]]. The agent's representative capacity

[5] 1878, 38 LT 851
[6] 1958, ILR AP 671
[7] 1908, 12 Cal. W. N. 28

along with a derivative authority to effect legal relationship between the principal and third persons is the distinctive feature of a contract of agency.

Agent Distinguished from Servant

A servant occupies a position that sounds parallel to that occupied by an agent. For instance, both are employed to act for and on behalf of the master. Similarly, an agent and a servant transact business (to a greater or less extent) under the control and supervision of their respective employers. Yet, there is a material difference between the two, which can be summed up as follows[8]:

1. Apart from acting on behalf of his/her principal, an agent has the authority to create contractual relationship between the principal and a third party. A servant ordinarily has no such authority.
2. A servant acts under the direct control and supervision of his employer and is bound to conform to all reasonable orders given to him during the course of his work. An agent although bound to exercise his/her authority in accordance with all lawful instructions, it is not subject in its exercise to the direct control of the supervision of the principal [*Qamar Shaffi vs Commr*[9]]. In other words, a 'principal' directs the agent as to what is to be done, but a master or employer of a servant not only has that right, but also the right to direct how it is to be done.
3. A servant usually serves only one master, but an agent may work for several principals at the same time [*Shedut Sahakari Ginning and Pressing Society vs State of Gurajat*[10]].
4. The mode of remuneration is usually different. A servant is paid his remuneration by way of salary or wages, whereas an agent generally gets his remuneration in terms of commission calculated on the basis of the amount of business transacted.
5. A servant in certain cases to some extent may be assigned the duties of an agent and may act as one. For example, the secretary of a company is regarded as the servant of the company, but in respect of the matters that come under his/her domain he/she becomes an agent in their dealings with third persons [*Chandi Pd. Singh vs State of UP*[11]].
6. A principal is liable on contracts made by his agent within scope of authority. But a master is answerable for any wrongful act of his servant if it is committed in the course of the servant's employment.

Agent Distinguished from Independent Contractor

An independent contractor is one who undertakes to perform some specified work. But in actual execution he/she is not under the control and supervision of the employer. The contractor may use his/her own discretion to produce a given result. Independent contractors do not represent their employers and, therefore, cannot bind the employers by their acts. Agents, on the other hand, perform their duties on behalf of their principals and legally bind them to contracts entered into by them, acting within the scope of their authority.

Creation of Agency

The law recognises various modes to create a contract of agency, namely,

1. Agency by express agreement
2. Agency by implied agreement
3. Agency by ratification
4. Agency by operation of law.

Agency by express agreement

A contract of agency may be made through an express agreement between a principal and his/her alleged agent. The said agreement may be oral or in writing. The agency so created is called 'express agency'. As per Section 187, the authority of an agent is said to be express when it is given by words, spoken or written. The usual form of a written contract of agency is the 'Power of Attorney', which gives the agent the authority to act on behalf of the principal in accordance with the terms and condi-

[8] Based on Powell's Law of Agency and Halsbury's Laws of England
[9] 1960, AIR SC 1269
[10] 1971, 3 S C C 480
[11] 1956, AIR SC 149

Box 8.12 Driving for Friend is an Implied Contract of Agency

X has a car but he does not know how to drive. He usually takes the services of *Y*, his neighbour, in this regard, whenever he goes outside. *Y* while driving the car meets with an accident and injures *Z*, a passerby. *X* will be liable to *Z* for damages, since *Y* is the implied agent of *X*.

tions therein. An oral appointment is also valid even though the contract that the agent is authorised to make has to be in writing [*Heard vs Pilley*[12]].

Agency by implied agreement

A contract of agency may be implied from the circumstances of the case, things spoken or written, or the ordinary course of dealing [Section 187]. For example, a solicitor or a counsel engaged to conduct litigation may have the implied authority to compromise the suit. Similarly, it has been held that a husband who lives with his wife impliedly authorises her to pledge his credit for necessary household expenses. An implied agency also results in the circumstances described in Box 8.12.

An implied agency may take the following three distinct forms:

1. Agency by estoppel
2. Agency by holding out
3. Agency by Necessity.

Agency by estoppel *Estoppel* arises when someone is stopped or precluded from denying the truth of anything that he/she has represented by his/her words or conduct as a fact, although such a state of thing did not exist at all. Section 237, which deals with agency by estoppel, states, 'When an agent has, without authority, done acts or incurred obligations to third persons on behalf of his principal, the principal is bound by such acts or obligations, if he has by his words or conduct induced such third persons to believe that such acts and obligations were within the scope of the agent's authority'.

> **Estoppel:** A legal principle that bars a party from denying or alleging a certain fact owing to that party's previous conduct, allegation, or denial.

A practical situation will help understand the point better. *A* tells *B* in presence and within hearing distance of *P* that he is *P*'s agent. *P* does not contradict the statement. Later on *B* enters into a contract with *A*, honestly presuming that *A* is *P*'s agent. *P* will be bound by this contract for there is an agency by *estoppel* between him and *A*.

Agency by holding out The doctrine of 'holding out' is also based on the principle of *estoppel*. Here, the alleged principal by his/her words or conduct wilfully leads another person to believe that the alleged agent is representing him/her. If someone enters into a contract with the person so representing on that belief, then the person so represented (i.e., the alleged principal) is stopped from denying the truth of such statements subsequently. In this way, agency, by holding out is a type of agency by *estoppel*, where the agency by *estoppel* is created by the actions of the agent, the agency by holding out comes into existence by the actions of the principal. For example, *P* allows his servant to purchase certain goods from *B*'s shop on credit and later on he pays for the goods. It is repeated many times. Later on, when the servant was not in *P*'s employment, he purchased goods on *P*'s credit from the same shop and disappeared. *B* can recover the price from *P* on the basis of the doctrine of holding out.

Agency by necessity Sometimes, owing to the exigencies of circumstances, a person may be compelled to act as an agent to the other without requiring or seeking the consent of the latter. Such an agency is called the agency by necessity. For example, a shipmaster can borrow money at a port where the shipping company has no agent, to get the ship repaired or fuelled so as to complete the voyage. In this case, the shipmaster becomes an agent by necessity.

Agency by ratification

Where a person without being authorised, purports to act as agent, or a duly authorised agent acts beyond his/her authority, the principal may elect to ratify or

[12] 1869, LR 4 Ch. 548

disown such acts. If he chooses to ratify the agent's transactions supposedly based on his behalf, an agency by ratification arises. The effect of ratification is that it renders the ratifier (i.e., the principal) bound to the contract as if he had expressly authorised the person to transact the business on his behalf.

An agency by ratification is also known as *ex post facto* agency, i.e., agency arising after the event. The Contract Act recognises the creation of agency by ratification.

Rules governing agency by ratification Although the law provides for an agent, exceeding his brief at times, and has given the principal the power to ratify or disclaim such acts, it has also spelt out the circumstances and rules under which such an act can or cannot be considered as agency by ratification. The following are the rules governing the agency by ratification:

1. An act will be regarded as a ratification only if the principal had a free choice whether to do it or not.
2. The agent must purport (intend to seem) to act as an agent [Section 196]. A principal can only ratify acts that the agent purported to do on his behalf. This rule follows that if the agent purports to act on his own behalf, the principal cannot ratify.
3. The person ratifying must have contractual capacity [Section 196]. This implies that the principal must be competent to contract not only at the time when the agent exceeded his authority but also when he ratified such act of the agent.
4. Ratification may be express or it may be implied in the conduct of the person on whose behalf the acts are done [Section 196]. For instance, without *A*'s authority, his brother *B* lends his house to *C*. Later on *C* pays the rent for the house and *A* accepts the same. By this conduct *B* shall be deemed to have ratified the act of *A*.
5. The principal must exist when the act is done [Section 196]. Hence, a company cannot ratify pre-incorporation agreements.
6. The principal at the time of ratification must have the full knowledge of the material facts [Section 198].
7. The principal must ratify the whole of the transaction [Section 199]. This implies that he cannot ratify at his will a part of the transaction and repudiate the rest.
8. The act must be ratified in time. A contract cannot be ratified after the time fixed for its performance. If no such time is fixed, it must be ratified within a reasonable period of time, from the principal's acquiring notice of the unauthorised act.
9. Ratification cannot be made so as to subject a third party to damage [Section 196], or terminate any right or interest of a third person [Section 200]. For example, *A*, not being authorised thereto by *B*, demands, on behalf of *B*, the delivery of a chattel, which is the property of *B*, from C who is in the possession of it. This demand cannot be ratified by *B* so as to make C liable for his refusal to deliver [Illustration (a) appended to Section 200].
10. The ratification should relate back to the actual date of the formation of the contract between the agent and the third party. In other words, it should have retrospective effect and not prospective. For example, if *A* without being authorised thereto lends *B*'s money to *C* and afterwards *B* ratifies the transaction. The contract will be deemed to have been ratified by *B* on the date on which *A* lent *B*'s money to *C*.
11. Although ratification is not confined to lawful acts, an act, which is simply void in law, cannot be validated by ratification. In other words, only lawful acts can be ratified [Section 196].

Effect of ratification The effect of ratification is to put the principal, agent, and the third party into the position that they would have been if the agent's acts had been authorised from the beginning. Ratification, in fact, relates back to the time of the unauthorised act and not to the date when the principal ratified the said act.

Agency by operation of law

An agency, under certain circumstances, also comes into existence by operation of law. Such an agency comes into existence neither by an express agreement nor by estoppel and ratification, but by the provisions of the law of land. Partnership firm is an universal example of this type of agency. When a partnership is formed, every partner, by operation of law, automatically becomes the agent of other partners and the firm. Similarly, the promoters become agents of the company they promote, MPs and MLAs become agents of their respective constituencies, ministers become agents of governments, and so on.

Scope and Extent of an Agent's Authority

All that a person can do as an agent, on behalf of his principal, depends on the terms expressed in his appointment, or is implied by the circumstances of the particular case. People dealing with an agent are entitled to presume that he has the authority to do all such acts as are necessary or incidental to such business. The scope and extent of an agent's authority is determined by the following two principles:

1. Agent's authority in normal circumstances [Section 188].
2. Agent's authority in an emergency [Section 189].

Agent's Authority in Normal Circumstances

An agent, having an authority to do an act, has the authority to do every lawful thing, which is necessary in order to do such an act.

An agent having an authority to carry on a business has the authority to do every lawful thing necessary for the purpose, or to do what is generally done in the course of conducting such business [Section 188].

However, the custom or usage must not be unreasonable or unlawful. Whether a custom or usage is unreasonable or unlawful is a question of law. Any custom that changes the very nature of the agency, as for example, which converts the agent into principal, is unreasonable [*Dr Avtar Singh*[13]].

For example, *B*, who is based in London, employs *A* to recover a debt in Mumbai due to him. *A* may adopt any legal process necessary for the purpose and may give a valid discharge for the same.

In another instance, *A* appoints *B* as his agent to carry on his business of a ship builder. *B* may purchase timber and other materials and hire workmen for the purpose of carrying on the business.

However, the above principle is subject to an agreement to the contrary between a principal and his agent. In *Ferguson vs Um Chand Boid*[14], the power of attorney categorically did not authorise his agent to borrow money. The agent, however, borrowed money on behalf of the principal. It was held that the principal was not liable for the same.

Agent's Authority in an Emergency

In an emergency, an agent has the authority to do all such acts for the purpose of protecting his/her principal from incurring loss as would be done by a person of ordinary prudence, in his/her own case, under similar circumstances [Section 189]. For example, *A* consigns provisions to *B* at Kolkata, with directions to send them immediately to *C* at Cuttack. *B* may sell the provisions at Kolkata, if they will not bear the journey to Cuttack without perishing. Similarly, an agent for the purpose of sale may buy goods if it were necessary.

Delegation of Authority by an Agent

Incidentally, the agent himself is a delegate of his/her principal. He/she, therefore, cannot further delegate except with the permission of the principal. Section 190 provides that 'an agent cannot lawfully employ another to perform an act which he has expressly or impliedly undertaken to perform personally, unless by the ordinary custom of trade a sub-agent may or from the nature of the agency, a sub-agent must be employed'.

The above provision is based on the Latin Maxim, '*delegates non protest delegare*' that is, a delegate cannot further delegate. An agent occupies a fiduciary position, which means the principal has got the full confidence in his integrity and competence. Accordingly, he is not supposed to delegate further or involve someone else (i.e., appoint a sub-agent) while acting on behalf of his principal without obtaining his permission. This general rule is, however, subject to the following exceptions:

1. Where the principal knows that the agent intends to appoint a sub-agent but does not object to it.
2. Where by the ordinary custom of trade, a sub-agent may be employed.
3. Where the duties of the agent do not involve any skill or exercise of discretion, e.g., clerical or routine task.
4. Where the very nature of agency requires delegation. For instance, a managing director may appoint someone as his personal secretary.

[13] Singh, Dr Avtar, 2008, Law of Contract 10th ed. pp 568.
[14] 1905, 33 Cal 343

5. When an emergency makes it necessary to appoint some sub-agent(s).

Sub-agent

Sub-agent: Person employed by and acting under the control of the original agent.

Where an agent having authority to delegate further appoints another person to act in the matter of the agency, the person so appointed is called a 'sub-agent', provided he/she acts under the control and supervision of the former (i.e., original agent). As per Section 191, 'a sub-agent is a person employed by, and acting under the control of, the original agent in the business of the agency'. Thus, in a way, the sub-agent is the agent of the original agent.

Impact of the appointment of a sub-agent The impact or legal effect related to sub-agents depends on whether their appointment is proper or improper. Sections 192 and 193 of the Contract Act have defined the legal course in both the circumstances, which have been discussed subsequently.

In case of proper appointment In such a case, as per Section 192, the following consequences arise:

1. So far as regards third persons, the principal is bound to and responsible for the acts of the sub-agent, as if he were an agent originally appointed by the principal.
2. The agent is responsible to the principal for the acts of the sub-agent. In *Calico Printers' Association vs Barclay's Bank*[15], a sub-agent failed to insure the principal's goods, which were destroyed in fire. But the principal could not recover against the sub-agent.
3. The sub-agent is responsible for his acts to the [original] agent, but not to the principal, except in case of fraud or wilful misconduct. Thus, this provision gives the principal, in case of fraud or wilful wrong, the right of recourse to the sub-agent. But in such a case the principal has the choice to sue either the agent or the sub-agent [*Nensukhdas vs Birdichand*[16]]. This is so because the provision does not in any way exclude the principal's normal right of recourse to his agent [Section 192].

[15] 1931, 145 LT 51 CA

[16] 1917, 19 Bom. L.R. 948

In case of improper appointment In terms of Section 193, improper appointment of a sub-agent results in the following consequences:

1. The principal is not responsible for the acts of the person so employed (i.e., sub-agent).
2. The agent is liable for the acts of the sub-agent both to the principal and to third party. In other words, the agent is the principal of the sub-agent, both to the principal and the third party.
3. The sub-agent is not at all responsible to the principal.

Substituted Agent

Substituted agent: A person appointed by the original agent to act for the principal in the business of agency with the consent of the principal.

A substituted agent is defined by Section 194 thus: 'Where an agent, holding an express or implied authority to name another person to act for the principal in the business of the agency, has named another person accordingly, such person is not a sub-agent, but an agent of the principal for such part of the business of the agency as is entrusted to him'.

The analysis of this section shows that a substituted agent, also called co-agent at times, is different from a sub-agent. A sub-agent cannot replace a substituted agent. A substituted agent, in fact, is the agent of the principal. The reason behind the same is quite obvious. The moment the substituted agent is appointed, privity of contract is established between him and the principal, and the original agent ceases to remain in the picture.

In selecting a 'substituted agent' for his principal, the agent ought to exercise as much care as a man of ordinary prudence would exercise in his own case. Examples to this effect are presented in Box 8.13.

Rights of Agent

An agent enjoys the following rights against the principal:

1. Right to remuneration
2. Right of retainer
3. Right of lien

Box 8.13 **Who Is a Substituted Agent [Section 194]**

Example 1

A directs *B*, his solicitor, to sell his estate by auction and to employ an auctioneer for the purpose. *B* names *C*, an auctioneer, to conduct the sale. *C* is not a sub-agent, but is *A*'s substituted agent for the conduct of the sale.

Example 2

A authorises *B*, a merchant in Kolkata, to recover the money due to him from *C* & Co. *B* instructs *D*, a solicitor, to take legal proceedings against *C* & Co. for the recovery of the money. *D* is not a sub-agent, but a substituted agent of *A*.

4. Right to be indemnified against consequences of lawful acts
5. Right to be indemnified against consequences of acts done in good faith
6. Right to compensation.

Right to Remuneration

An agent is a person employed or engaged to perform for another. Therefore, as a general rule, he/she is entitled to receive remuneration for the performance of any act in the business of the agency. An agent's right to remuneration is subject to the following four rules:

1. Unless the services rendered by the agent are gratuitous or voluntary, the agent is entitled to receive agreed remuneration (usually in the form of commission).
2. Where no specific remuneration was fixed, then the agent is entitled to be paid a reasonable remuneration, i.e., what is usual and customary in the business in which he/she has been employed.
3. In the absence of any special contract, payment for the performance of any act is not due to the agent until the completion of such act [Section 219]. In simple words, an agent becomes entitled to receive remuneration as soon as he/she has performed what he/she had promised to perform. For example, the owner of a house employed an agent to find a tenant. The agent found a tenant who later bought the house. His/her claim for commission on the sale failed, since he/she was only employed to let the house [*Toulmin vs Millar*[17]].
4. An agent who is guilty of misconduct in the business of the agency is not entitled to any remuneration in respect of that part of the business that he/she has not conducted appropriately [Section 220].

Right of Retainer

An agent may retain out of any sum received on account of the principal in the business of the agency the following:

1. all moneys due to him/her in respect of advances made,
2. expenses properly incurred by him/her in conducting such business, and
3. such remuneration as may be payable to him/her for acting as an agent [Section 217].

Right of Lien

An agent is (unless otherwise agreed) entitled to a lien on all property (including papers) of the principal, which has come into his/her possession in the course of the agency [Section 221].

Right To Be Indemnified Against Consequences of Lawful Acts

The employer of an agent is bound to indemnify him/her against the consequences of all lawful acts done by such agent in the exercise of the authority conferred upon him/her [Section 222]. Some case studies in Box 8.14 drive home the point.

Right To Be Indemnified Against Consequences of Acts Done in Good Faith

An agent's right to be indemnified also extends for the consequences of the acts done in good faith even

[17] 1887, 12 App. Cas. 746

Box 8.14 **Agent's Right to Be Indemnified Against Fallout of Lawful Acts [Section 222]**

Example 1

B, at Singapore, under instructions from *A* of Delhi, contracts with *C* to deliver certain goods to *C*. *A* does not send the goods to *B* for breach of contract. *C* files a suit in the court. *B* informs *A* of the suit, and *A* authorises him to defend the suit. *B* defends the suit and is compelled to pay damages, costs, and incurs expenses. *A* is liable to *B* for such damages, costs, and expenses.

Example 2

B, a broker at Kolkata, by the orders of *A*, a merchant, contracts with *C* for the purchase of 10 casks of oil for *A*. Afterwards *A* refuses to receive the oil, and *C* sues *B*. *B* informs *A*, who in turn repudiates the contract altogether. *B* defends but becomes unsuccessful and has to pay damages and costs and incurs expenses. *A* is liable to *B* for such damages, costs, and expenses.

though they turn out to be injurious to the rights of third persons [Section 223]. Examples explaining the point are presented in Box 8.15.

Right to Compensation

An agent is also entitled to compensation in respect of injury or loss suffered by him/her due to the principal's neglect or want of skill [Section 225]. For example, *A* employs *B* as a bricklayer in building a house and puts up the scaffolding himself. The scaffolding is put up unskillfully and *B* is hurt. *A* must make compensation to *B*.

Duties of an Agent

Having known the rights of the agents, we should know their corresponding duties. An agent owes the following obligations or duties to the principal:

1. Duty to act within the scope of the authority
2. Duty to follow instructions or customs
3. Duty to act with due care and skill
4. Duty to render accounts
5. Duty to communicate
6. Duty to remit sums
7. Fiduciary duty.

Duty to Act Within the Scope of the Authority

The first and foremost duty of every agent is to act within the scope of the authority conferred upon him/her. He/she will be liable for breach of contract, if he/she acts in a way not authorised by the terms of his/her appointment. An agent who acts gratuitously or under a unilateral contract is not bound to do anything but may be liable if he/she begins to perform and then leaves the task unfinished.

Box 8.15 **Agent Has Right to Be Indemnified for Acts Done in Good Faith [Section 223]**

Example 1

A, a decree-holder and entitled to execution of *B*'s goods, requires the officer of the court to seize certain goods, presenting them to be the goods of *B*. The officer seizes the goods, and is sued by *C*, the true owner of the goods. *A* is liable to indemnify the officer for the sum, which he is compelled to pay to *C*, as a consequence of obeying *A*'s directions.

Example 2

B, at the request of *A*, sells goods in the possession of *A*, but which *A* had no right to dispose of. *B* does not know this, and hands over the proceeds of the sale to *A*. Afterwards *C*, the true owner of the goods, sues *B* and recovers the value of the goods and costs. *A* is liable to indemnify *B* for what he has been compelled to pay to *C*, and for *B*'s own expenses.

Box 8.16 Agent is Duty Bound to Follow Instructions or Custom

Example 1

X instructs his agent *Y*, employed for the trans-shipment of *X*'s goods, to get the goods insured, but *Y* fails to do so and later the goods are destroyed on the way. *Y* is liable to compensate *X* [*Pannalal Jankidas vs Mohanlal*[18]].

Example 2

A, an auctioneer, contrary to the usual custom of the business, accepts a bill of exchange from *B* in payment of the price of goods sold. The bill when presented is dishonoured. *A* must make good the loss to his principal [*Ferrer vs Robbins*[19]].

Duty to Follow Instructions or Customs

An agent is bound to carry out strictly the instructions of the principal. In the absence of express instructions, he/she must follow the prevailing custom in the same kind of business at the place where the agent conducts the business. When an agent acts otherwise, he/she would be liable to make good any loss if sustained, and if any profit accrues, he/she must account for it [Section 211]. The following two examples in Box 8.16 are cases in point.

Duty to Act with Due Care and Skill

The criteria of care and skill expected from an agent are laid down in Section 212.

According to it, an agent is bound to conduct the business of the agency with as much skill as is generally possessed by persons engaged in similar business unless the principal is aware of his/her lack of skill. The agent is always bound to act with reasonable diligence and use his/her skill and make compensation to the principal in respect of the direct consequences of his/her own neglect, lack of skill, or misconduct but not in respect of loss or damage that are indirectly or remotely caused by such neglect, lack of skill, or misconduct.

Thus, an agent must conduct the business of the agency with reasonable skill and diligence.

Duty to Render Accounts

An agent is bound to render proper accounts to his/her principal on demand [Section 213].

Duty to Communicate

In case of difficulty, an agent must use reasonable diligence in communicating with his principal and to obtain instructions from him [Section 214].

Duty to Remit Sums

The agent is bound to pay to the principal all sums received on the latter's account [Section 218].

Fiduciary Duty

Since a principal places confidence in an agent, the latter owes a fiduciary duty to the former in some respects. Its most important consequences are the following:

1. An agent must not allow his/her interest to conflict with his/her duty. He/she must not, for instance, sell his/her own goods to the principal when he/she is employed, since his/her interest as a seller would be to get the highest possible price, whereas his/her duty as an agent is to buy at the lowest possible price [Section 215].
2. He/she must not make any secret profits in the business of the agency, i.e., he/she must not obtain any advantage over and above the agreed remuneration, which he/she would not have been able to make, but for his/her position as an agent.
3. An agent must perform the acts personally that he/she has expressly or impliedly undertaken to perform personally [Section 190].
4. He/she must not disclose confidential information to anyone, entrusted to him/her by the principal.
5. Lastly, when an agency is terminated due to the death of the principal or if the principal

[18] 1951, A.I.R. S.C. 144, 147

[19] 1835, 2 CM & R 152

becomes unsound, the agent is bound to take, on behalf of the representatives of the principal, all reasonable steps for the protection and reservation of the interests entrusted to him/her.

Rights and Duties of Principal Towards Agent

Because of the element of reciprocal relationship between an agent and the principal, all the duties of the agent become the rights of the principal and all the rights of the agent become the duties of the principal.

Personal Liability of Agent to Third Party

An agent is merely a connecting link between the principal and the third parties. After creating a contractual relationship between the principal and a third party, he/she drops out and ceases to be a party to the contract. As a principle, therefore, the agent can neither enforce the contract personally nor is he/she personally liable on the contract unless provided in it. This is known as the principle of the agent's immunity from personal liability. This rule applies even where the agent has contracted beyond his/her authority.

However, there are circumstances when the agent becomes personally liable. These are as follows:

1. Where the contract expressly provides for the personal liability of the agent.
2. Where an agent acts for a principal residing abroad [Section 230].
3. Where he/she does not disclose the name of the principal, he/she is treated as a party to the contract, hence personally liable to third party [Section 230].
4. Where the principal, though disclosed, cannot be sued on account of his/her being a minor, a foreign sovereign, or an ambassador, etc [Section 230].
5. When an agent enters into a contract with the third party in his/her own name, concealing not only the name of the principal but also the fact that there is a principal.
6. An agent is liable for breach of warranty of authority. As per Section 235, when a person untruly represents himself/herself to be the authorised agent of another and, thereby, induces a third party to deal with him/her as agent, or the agent exceeds his/her authority, and the alleged employer does not ratify his/her act, the alleged agent is personally liable for any loss sustained by a third party who relies upon the representation.
7. Where the custom or usage of a trade makes the agent personally liable, he/she will be liable to the third party.
8. An agent's authority is said to be coupled with interest when the agent has a personal interest in the subject matter of the contract. For example, *A* appoints *B* to dispose of his/her land and authorises to pay *B* a commission at the rate of 5 per cent out of the sale proceeds. *B*'s authority is coupled with interest.

Principal's Liability for Agent's Acts

When an agent makes a contract on behalf of his/her principal with a third party, the transaction gives rise to legal effect between the principal and third party, i.e., the principal is liable to third parties for the acts of the agent. However, the effect of a contract made by an agent varies according to the circumstances under which the agent contracted. Accordingly, the extent of the principal's liability to third parties for the acts of the agent may be discussed under the following heads:

1. When agent acts within the scope of his authority
2. When agent exceeds his authority
3. Principal is bound by notice given to agent
4. Liability of principal under doctrine of estoppel
5. Liability for agent's torts or other wrongs
6. Liability of unnamed principal
7. Liability of undisclosed principal

When Agent Acts Within the Scope of His Authority

The principal is bound by all acts of the agent done within the scope of his/her actual or orostensible (apparent) authority. Such acts of the agent may be enforced in the same manner and will have the same legal consequences as if the contracts had been entered into and the acts done by the principal in person [Section 226].

When Agent Exceeds His Authority

When an agent exceeds his/her authority, actual or apparent, and the excess work can be separated from the authorised work, the principal is bound to the extent of authorised work [Section 227]. But where the excess cannot be separated from the authorised work, the principal is not bound by the transaction, i.e., he/she may repudiate the whole of the transaction [Section 228]. The examples in Box 8.17 drive home the point.

Principal Bound by Notice Given to Agent

The principal is bound by any notice given to, or information obtained by the agent, provided it be given or obtained in the course of the business transacted by him/her for the principal [Section 229]. Any information, which is material for the business of the agency if brought to the notice of the agent, is deemed to have been brought to the notice of the principal. But, if the agent in the course of his/her employment does not acquire the notice or information, he/she (agent) cannot be imputed to the principal [Section 229]. The examples in Box 8.18 explain the point.

Liability for Agent's Torts or Other Wrongs

Where an agent commits a tort or other wrongful act (for example, misrepresentation or fraud) during his/her agency, the principal is liable. The principal is liable even if the tort or wrongful act is committed exclusively for the benefit of the agent and against the interest of the principal [Section 230]. Examples to this effect are presented in Box 8.19.

Liability of Principal Under Doctrine of Estoppel

When an agent has, without authority, done acts or incurred obligations to third persons on behalf of his/

Box 8.17 Principal's Liability Where Agent Exceeds Authority [Sections 227 and 228]

Example 1

A, an owner of a ship and cargo, authorises *B* to procure insurance for ₹4000 on the ship. *B* procures a policy for the said amount on the ship, and another for the like sum on the cargo. *A* is bound to pay the premium for the policy on the ship but not the premium of the policy on the cargo.

Example 2

A authorises *B* to buy 500 sheep for him. *B* buys 500 sheep and 200 lambs for a sum of ₹6000 . *A* may repudiate the whole transaction.

Box 8.18 Principal Bound by Notice Served on Agent [Section 229]

Example 1

A is employed by *B* to buy from *C* certain goods, of which *C* is the apparent owner. In the course of the treaty for the sale, *A* learns that the goods actually belonged to *D*, but *B* is ignorant of that fact. *B* is not entitled to set-off a debt owing to him from *C* against the price of the goods.

Example 2

A is employed by *B* to buy goods from *C*, of which *C* is the apparent owner. *A*, before his employment with *B*, was a servant of *C* and had then learnt that the goods really belonged to *D*, but *B* is ignorant of that fact. Despite the knowledge of his agent, *B* may set off against the price of the goods a debt owing to him from *C*.

Box 8.19 **Principal Liable for Agent's Torts [Section 230]**

Example 1

An agent, employed to collect evidence for his principal in a pending law suit, offered to bribe a witness. It was held that the act was within the course of the employment of the agent and that the principal was bound by it [*Chicago City Rly. Co. vs McMohan*[20]].

Example 2

A, being *B*'s agent for the sale of goods, induces *C* to buy them by a misrepresentation, which he was not authorised by *B* to make. The contract is voidable, as between *B* and *C*, at the option of *C* [illustration (a) appended to Section 230].

her principal, the principal is bound by such acts or obligations, if he/she has by his words or conduct induced such third persons to believe that such acts and obligations were within the scope of the agent's authority [Section 237]. In this case, the principal incurs his/her liability to third persons by estoppel.

Liability of Unnamed Principal

If the agent while contracting with third parties discloses the existence of the principal but does not disclose the name of the principal, the principal is bound by the contract. If however, the agent refuses to disclose the identity of his principal upon being asked by third parties, the agent becomes personally liable on the contract.

Liability of Undisclosed Principal

When an agent who has the authority to contract on behalf of another enters into a contract in his/her own name (i.e., he/she discloses neither the name of the principal nor his/her existence), the principal is called 'undisclosed principal'. In such a case the agent becomes personally liable to third party. However, if the third party discovers that there is a principal, then as per Section 233, the third party has the option to sue the agent or the principal or both.

Termination of Agency

Agency, as a species of contract, gets terminated by any event that terminates a contract, such as by performance, revocation, or destruction of subject matter, and also in certain special ways. Accordingly, the various modes of terminating an agency can broadly be classified into the following two categories:

1. By act of the party
2. By operation of law.

Termination by Act of the Parties

The termination of agency may be caused by an act of the principal or the agent, or by an agreement between the two. A brief description of putting an end to agency relationship by act of the parties is given below.

Revocation of authority by the principal

The rules governing revocation of authority by the principal may be summarised as under.

When can the principal revoke the agent's authority The principal can revoke the authority given to his agent at any time before the authority has been exercised so as to bind the principal provided the agency is not irrevocable [Section 203].

Revocation cannot be exercised in respect of partly exercised authority The principal cannot revoke the authority given to his agent after the authority has been partly exercised, as regards such acts and obligations that arise from acts already done in the agency. In other words, where the agent has partly exercised his authority, the principal may revoke agency for future acts only [Section 204]. Examples to this effect are presented in Box 8.20.

Compensation for revocation Where there is an express or implied contract that the agency should be continued for any period of time, the principal must

[20] 1882, 103 ILJ 485

Box 8.20 **Revocation of Authority for Future Acts of Agent [Section 204]**

Example 1

A authorises *B* to buy 1000 bales of cotton on account of *A* and to pay for it out of *A*'s money, which remains in *B*'s hands. *B* buys 1000 bales of cotton in his own name, so as to make himself personally liable for the price. *A* cannot revoke *B*'s authority so far as payment for the cotton is concerned.

Example 2

A authorises *B* to buy 1000 bales of cotton on account of *A*, and to pay for it out of *A*'s money remaining in *B*'s hands. *B* buys 1000 bales of cotton in *A*'s name, so as not to render himself personally liable for the price. *A* can revoke *B*'s authority to pay for the cotton.

make compensation to the agent for any previous revocation of the agency without sufficient cause [Section 205].

Notice of revocation Reasonable notice must be given of revocation or renunciation, otherwise, the damage thereby resulting to the agent must be made good to by the principal [Section 206].

Revocation may be expressed or implied Revocation may be expressed or may be implied in the conduct of the principal or agent, respectively [Section 207]. For example, *A* empowers *B* to let *A*'s house. Afterwards *A* lets it himself. This is an implied revocation of *B*'s authority.

Renunciation of authority by the agent

An agency also comes to an end if the agent himself/herself renounces his/her authority to contract on behalf of the principal. Section 206 says that reasonable notice must be given of renunciation, otherwise, the damage thereby resulting to the principal must be made good by the agent. Like, revocation, renunciation may also be expressed or implied in the conduct of that agent. For example, *A* employs *B* to sell his car within a week. *B* fails to sell the car within the stipulated time. There is an implied renunciation of authority on part of *B*.

By mutual agreement An agency, like any other agreement, can be terminated, at any time by mutual agreement between the principal and the agent.

Termination of Agency by Operation of Law

The relationship of principal and agent comes to an end automatically under any of the following circumstances.

Completion of business

An agency automatically comes to an end when its business is completed [Section 201]. For example, *A* employs *B* to sell his goods. The authority of *B* to sell goods ceases to be exercisable as soon as the sale is complete.

Death or insanity of the principal or agent

An agency is terminated automatically in the event of the death of the principal or the agent, or if either becomes insane [Section 201]. The principal's insanity puts an end to the agency even though the agent has no notice of it [*Yonge vs Toynbee*[21]].

Insolvency of the principal

The principal's insolvency does terminate the agent's authority. Besides, the insolvency of the agent also terminates his authority if it makes him unfit to perform his duties [Section 201].

Expiry of time

Where the agent is appointed for a fixed term, the agency comes to an end by the expiration of the stipulated time (unless the term of agency has been extended), whether the purpose of the agency has been accomplished or not [*Lalljee vs Dadabhai*[22]].

Destruction of the subject matter

Destruction of the subject matter of the agency automatically puts an end to it. For example, *A* employs someone to let his house. The house collapses in an earthquake, the agency ceases to exist.

[21] 1910, 1 K.B. 215

[22] 1915, 23 cal. 190

Dissolution of company

Where the principal or the agent is an incorporated body (i.e, company), the agency comes to an end on dissolution of the company.

Upon principal or agent becoming an alien enemy

Where the principal and agent are the citizens of two different countries, their agency relationship comes to an end in the event of an outbreak of war between the two nations. The reason behind the same is simple. As a consequence of war, the principal and the agent become alien enemies to each other and the existing contract of the agency becomes unlawful.

Termination of Sub-agent's Authority

The termination of the authority of an agent causes the termination (subject to the rules herein contained regarding the termination of an agent's authority) of the authority of all sub-agents appointed by him [Section 210].

Termination of Agency: When Does It Take Effect?

The termination of agency as regards the agent and as regards the third parties takes effect at different points of time. Section 208 is very clear in this regard. It states as follows:

1. The termination of the authority of an agent takes effect when the agent is apprised or informed about it. Thus, where the principal revokes agent's authority, the revocation will take effect when the agent comes to know that the principal has revoked his authority.
2. As regards third parties, the termination takes effect when it comes to their knowledge. So, where an agent whose authority has been revoked to his knowledge makes a contract with a third party who deals with him *bona fide*, the contract will be binding on the principal as against the third party. Hence, third parties may deal with the agent, as such, till they come to know of the termination of the agent's authority. Examples in Box 8.21 will help understand the point better.

Irrevocable Agency

Irrevocable agency: An agency wherein agent's authority cannot be revoked or recalled by the principal.

When the principal cannot revoke the authority given to an agent, the agency is termed as an 'irrevocable' one. An agency is irrevocable in the following cases in the sense that any attempt to revoke it is not merely a breach of contract but also ineffective. The agent's authority continues despite the attempt to revoke it.

Where Agency is Coupled with Interest

An agency coupled with interest is irrevocable. Even the death or insanity of the principal does not terminate such an agency [Section 202]. The following examples in Box 8.22 drive home the point.

Box 8.21 Termination of Agency with Respect to Agent, Third Parties

Example 1

A directs *B* to sell goods for him and agrees to give *B* 5 per cent commission on the price fetched by the goods. Afterwards *A* revokes *B*'s authority by a letter. *B*, after the letter is sent, but before he receives it, sells the goods for ₹100. The sale is binding on *A*, and *B* is entitled to ₹5 as his commission.

Example 2

A, at Chennai, by letter, directs *B* to sell for him some cotton lying in a warehouse in Mumbai, and afterwards, by letter revokes his authority to sell, and directs *B* to send the cotton to Madras. *B* after receiving the second letter enters into a contract with *C*, who knows of the first letter, but not of the second for the sale to him of the cotton. *C* pays *B* the money, with which *B* absconds. *C*'s payment is good as against *A*.

Box 8.22 **When Agency Cannot be Revoked Due to Death or Insanity of Principal [Section 202]**

Example 1

A gives authority to *B* to sell *A*'s land and to pay himself out of the proceeds the debts due to him from *A*. *A* cannot revoke this authority nor can it be terminated by his insanity or death.

Example 2

A consigns 1000 bales of cotton to *B*, who has made advances to him on such cotton, and desires *B* to sell the cotton and repay himself out of the price the amount of his own advances. *A* cannot revoke this authority nor it is terminated by his insanity or death.

Where Authority Has Been Partly Exercised

The principal cannot revoke the authority given to his/her agent after the authority has been partly exercised, so far as such acts and obligations arise from acts already done in the agency [Section 204].

Moreover, an agency also becomes irrevocable where the agent has incurred a personal liaility.

Exercises

I. Objective-type Questions

1. State whether each of the following statements is True or False:
   (i) The term 'indemnity' implies protection against loss or damage.
   (ii) In the absence of any contract to the contrary, the liability of surety is co-extensive with that of the liability of the principal debtor.
   (iii) A contract of guarantee pre-supposes the existence of a liability enforceable by law.
   (iv) Specific guarantee extends to a series of transactions.
   (v) Guarantee for a specific transaction can be revoked at any time.
   (vi) Pledge is a species of bailment.
   (vii) In bailment, possession of goods must change.
   (viii) Placing of ornaments in a bank locker is a contract of bailment.
   (ix) If the owner refuses to pay compensation, the finder of lost goods can bring a legal suit against him for compensation.
   (x) As a general rule, a bailee is entitled only to a particular lien.
   (xi) There can be an agency without agreement.
   (xii) The acts of the agent are the acts of the principal.
   (xiii) A sub-agent does his work under the control of the agent in the business of the agency.
   (xiv) An agency comes to an end by the destruction of the subject matter.
   (xv) There is no privity of contract between a substituted agent and the principal.
2. Fill in the blanks:
   (i) The contract of __________ is a contract of *uberrimae fidei*.
   (ii) The person who promises to make good the loss is called __________.
   (iii) The object of a contract of __________ is to enable a person to obtain a loan, goods on credit, or an employment.

(iv) In the absence of a contract to the contrary, the liability of surety is co-extensive with that of the ________.

(v) The liability of ________ is primary and independent.

(vi) The goods, which form the subject matter of the bailment, must be ________.

(vii) Transfer of railway receipt being document of title to goods, effects a/n ________ delivery of the goods.

(viii) Pledge made by a seller, left in possession of goods sold, will be ________.

(ix) The bailment in which neither the bailor nor the bailee is entitled to any remuneration is called ________ bailment.

(x) In a contract of pledge, ________ remains with the pledger but a ________ passes to the pledgee.

(xi) A ________ acts under the control and supervision of principal.

(xii) Consideration is ________ to create an agency.

(xiii) The principal is ________ for all the acts of his agent.

(xiv) The doctrine of 'holding out' is based on the principle of ________.

(xv) A minor ________ an agent.

3. Indicate the correct answer:

(i) A continuing guarantee may be revoked
   (a) By a notice of revocation by the surety
   (b) By death of the surety
   (c) In the same manner in which the surety is discharged
   (d) By any of the above-mentioned ways

(ii) Against the principal debtor, the surety has
   (a) Right of subrogation
   (b) Right of indemnity
   (c) Both (a) and (b) above
   (d) None of the above

(iii) A contract of guarantee is invalid
   (a) When the guarantee has been obtained by misrepresentation
   (b) When guarantee has been obtained by concealment of material facts
   (c) When co-surety (if any) fails to join the surety
   (d) In all the above cases

(iv) The indemnity holder is entitled to
   (a) All damages that he may be compelled to pay in any suit in respect of any matter to which the promise to indemnity applies
   (b) All costs that he may be compelled to bear in bringing or defending any such suit
   (c) All sums that he may have paid under the terms of any compromise of such suit
   (d) All of the above

(v) The liability of a surety comes to an end by
   (a) Novation
   (b) Variance in terms of contract
   (c) Invalidation of the contract
   (d) All the above

(vi) Who among the following can make a valid pledge?
   (a) The owner or his authorized agent
   (b) A mercantile agent who with the consent of the owner is in possession of goods or documents of title to goods
   (c) A person having limited interest
   (d) All of the above

(vii) The bailor is duty bound to compensate bailee for necessary expenses incurred by the latter in preserving the goods bailed in case of
   (a) Gratuitous bailment
   (b) Non-gratuitous bailment
   (c) Both
   (d) None of the above

(viii) A finder of lost goods has a right to sell the goods found by him
   (a) Where the owner cannot, with reasonable diligence, be found and if found, refuses to pay the lawful charges of finder of goods
   (b) The goods are in danger of perishing or of losing the greater part of their value
   (c) When the lawful charges of the finder for preservation and finding out the owner amounts to two-thirds of the value of the goods
   (d) In all the above cases

(ix) Which of the following transactions does not fall in the ambit of bailment?
   (a) Delivering goods for carriage
   (b) Delivering goods for repair with or without remuneration
   (c) Placing of ornaments in a bank locker
   (d) Delivering goods to a creditor to serve as security of loan

(x) The pawnee can retain the goods pledged for
   (a) Payment of the debt or performance of the promise
   (b) Interest on the debt
   (c) All necessary expenses incurred by him in respect of the possession or for preservation of the pledged goods
   (d) All of the above

(xi) The relationship of principal and agent may be created by
   (a) Express or implied offer   (b) Ratification
   (c) Operation   (d) Any of the above

(xii) Implied agency includes
   (a) Agency by estoppel   (b) Agency by holding out
   (c) Agency by necessity   (d) All of the above

(xiii) The crucial test of agency is that
   (a) A person possessing capacity to contract may lawfully do by himself or he may get it done by another
   (b) He who acts through an agent is himself acting
   (c) Acts of the agent bind the principal
   (d) The principal is not responsible if the agent exceeds his authority

(xiv) Agency is irrevocable
   (a) Where the agent has an interest in the property that forms the subject matter of the agency
   (b) Where the agent has partly exercised his authority
   (c) Where the agent has incurred a personal liability
   (d) In all the above cases

(xv) An agent can retain from any sums received on account of the principal for the following payments:
   (a) All moneys due to himself in respect of advance made
   (b) In respect of expenses properly incurred by him in conducting such business
   (c) Such remuneration as may be payable to him for acting as agent
   (d) All of the above

II. Review Questions

1. What is a 'contract of indemnity'? Bring out difference between a contract of indemnity and a contract of guarantee.

2. Explain the ways in which a continuing guarantee may be revoked.

3. State the rights of surety against
   (i) The principal debtor
   (ii) The creditor, and
   (iii) Co-sureties

4. 'The liability of surety is co-extensive with that of the liability of the principal debtor.' Elucidate.
5. 'Between co-sureties there is equality of burden and the benefits.' Elaborate.
6. Explain the circumstances under which a surety is discharged from his liability.
7. Write short notes on the following:
   (i) Rights of an indemnity holder
   (ii) Commencement of 'indemnifier's liability
   (iii) Invalidation of contract of guarantee
8. What are the essentials of a contract of bailment? Distinguish between bailment and pledge.
9. 'Pledge is a special kind of bailment'. Explain. Enumerate the circumstances under which a person other than the owner can make a valid pledge.
10. State the respective rights and duties of a bailee and a bailor.
11. Examine the duties and rights of a pawnee and pawnor.
12. Distinguish between particular lien and general lien. Who are entitled to general lien?
13. Discuss the rights and duties of a finder of lost goods.
14. What are the different kinds of bailment? When a contract of bailment comes to an end?
15. What do you understand by the term agency? How is an agency created?

    Or

    Define agent and principal relationship. What are the various modes of creating such a relationship?
16. What do you mean by agency by ratification? Discuss the essentials of a valid ratification.
17. Examine the obligations cast upon an agent. Also bring out the legal rights of an agent.

    Or

    Examine the rights and duties of an agent.
18. 'Delegatus non-protest delegare'. Examine this principle in relation to an agency. State the exceptions to the rule.
19. 'A principal is empowered to revoke the authority of the agent, but he cannot do so in certain circumstances'. Explain and illustrate the truth of the statement.
20. Explain in brief the various modes by which an agency may be terminated.
21. When is an agent personally liable for the contracts made by him on behalf of his principal? Discuss in detail.
22. Discuss in detail the extent of principal's liability to third parties for the acts of the agent.
23. Write short notes on the following:
   (a) Irrevocable agency
   (b) Sub-agent and substituted agent
   (c) Test of agency
   (d) Agency by necessity
   (e) Agency coupled with interest
24. Distinguish between
   (a) Agent and servant
   (b) Agent and independent contractor
   (c) Agency by estoppel and agency by holding out
   (d) Unnamed principal and undisclosed principal

III. Caselets

1. *A* guarantees to *B* the payment of a bill of exchange by *C*, the acceptor. *C* dishonours the bill. Is *A* liable for the interest on the bill due?

   [**Hint:** Yes, the liability of surety is co-extensive with that of the principal debtor (Section 128)]

2. *X* agrees with *Y* to stand as a surety for *Z* for a loan of ₹2000, provided *A* also joins him as surety. *A* refuses to join. Is *X* liable as a surety?

   [**Hint:** No, *X* is not liable as a surety (Section 144)]

3. *B* owes to *C* a debt guaranteed by *A*. The debt becomes payable. *C* does not sue *B* for a year after the debt has become payable. Is *A* discharged from his surety?

   [**Hint:** No, creditor's forbearance to sue the principal debtor does not discharge surety unless there is a provision in the guarantee to the contrary]

4. A becomes a surety to C for payment of rent by B under a lease. Thereafter, B and C contract, without A's consent, that B will pay rent at higher rate. State whether A is discharged.

   [**Hint:** Yes. A would be discharged from his liability as a surety for rent accruing subsequent to the variance (Section 133)]

5. A, B, and C, as sureties for 'D' enter into three separate bonds, each in a different penalty, namely, A in the penalty of `10,000, B in that of `20,000, C in that of `40,000, conditioned for D's duly accounting to E. D defaults to the extent of `70,000. How much A, B, and C are liable to pay?

   [**Hint:** A, B, and C are liable to pay, each, the full penalty of their respective bonds, i.e., `10,000, `20,000, and `40,000, respectively (Section 147)]

6. A hires a car from B. The car on the way broke down and A had to spend `1000 on its repair. Can A claim `1000 from B?

   [**Hint:** Yes, being extraordinary expenses]

7. A while proceeding on tour leaves his mare in the custody of B to be taken care of. The mare delivers a calf. Decide.

   [**Hint:** B is bound to return the calf along with the mare]

8. A found a mobile phone lying on the road. He picked it up and since the mobile was not working, he spent `1000 on its repair. Later on pledged the article for `500. Discuss the remedy available to the true owner.

   [**Hint:** The true owner can recover the mobile only on paying `500 to the pledgee, Refer Section 179]

9. A purchases a gold necklace from B's shop, but leaves the necklace with the seller. B then pledges the necklace with C who is ignorant about the sale to A and acted in good faith. Is this a valid pledge?

   [**Hint:** Yes, this pledge is valid. Refer Section 30 of Sale of Goods Act]

10. A hires B's car for personal use. Instead A starts using the car as a taxi. Can B avoid the contract?

    [**Hint:** Yes, any act inconsistent with the terms of contract may render the contract of bailment voidable on part of the bailor]

11. A delivers his two suits to B to be dry-cleaned. B keeps both the suits duly dry-cleaned. A is ready to take back one of the suits on payment of the charges for dry-cleaning it. But B refuses to deliver any one at a time and asks the charges for both the suits. Is B justified?

    [**Hint:** No, B has a particular lien only in respect of one suit that A is unable to take back due to non-payment of its dry-cleaning charges. Refer Section 170]

12. A, without B's authority, lends B's money to C. Afterwards B accepts interest on the money from C. Does B's conduct imply a ratification of the loan?

    [**Hint:** Yes. See Section 197]

13. X forged Y's signature and withdrew some money from bank. Y, subsequently ratified X's act of withdrawing money. Does it convey good title to X?

    [**Hint:** No. The ratification is invalid as forgery is an offence]

14. *A* gives authority to *B* to sell *A*'s land and to pay himself out of the proceeds the debts due to him. Can *A* revoke this authority?

    [**Hint:** No. An agency coupled with interest cannot be revoked (Section 202)]

15. X directs Y, who is a solicitor, to sell his estate by auction and to employ an auctioneer for the purpose. Y names Z, an auctioneer, to conduct the sale. Is Z a sub-agent?

    [**Hint:** No. Z is not a sub-agent, but a substituted agent for X]

16. An agent is authorized to buy 10 buffaloes. He buys 10 buffaloes and 5 cows for `50,000. Can the principal repudiate the whole transaction?

    [**Hint:** No. Refer Section 228]

Answers to Objective-type Questions

1.	(i) True	(ii) True	(iii) True	(iv) False	(v) False
	(vi) True	(vii) True	(viii) False	(ix) False	(x) True
	(xi) True	(xii) True	(xiii) True	(xiv) True	(xv) False
2.	(i) indemnity	(ii) indemnifier	(iii) guarantee	(iv) guarantee	
	(v) principal debtor	(vi) movable	(vii) constructive	(viii) valid	
	(ix) gratuitous	(x) general property/special property		(xi) substituted agent	
	(xii) immaterial	(xiii) not liable	(xiv) estoppel	(xv) may be	
3.	(i) (d)	(ii) (c)	(iii) (d)	(iv) (d)	(v) (d)
	(vi) (d)	(vii) (a)	(viii) (d)	(ix) (c)	(x) (d)
	(xi) (d)	(xii) (d)	(xiii) (c)	(xiv) (d)	(xv) (d)

8 Chapter in Review

LEARNING OUTCOMES

LO1 Contract of indemnity: meaning; definition; scope

LO2 Contract of guarantee: meaning; definition

LO3 Discharge of surety

LO4 Contract of bailment: definition; essentials; kinds

LO5 Contract of pledge: definition; who can pledge

LO6 Contract of agency: general rules; essentials

LO7 Agency: modes of creation; scope and extent of authority

LO8 Termination of agency; irrevocable agency

KEY TERMS

Indemnity: Protection against some loss or damage to goods or property.

Guarantee: A contract to perform the promise, or discharge the liability of a third person in the event of his default.

Specific guarantee: A guarantee applicable in respect of a single debt or a specific transaction.

Continuing guarantee: A guarantee that extends to a series of transactions.

Novation: Voluntarily substituting an original contract (of guarantee) by a fresh one by the parties.

Bailment: Entrusting possession of movable goods (by the owner thereof) into the care of another person for some purpose briefly.

Gratuitous bailment: A bailment without any consideration.

Non-gratuitous bailment: Bailment for the mutual benefit involving some consideration passing between the parties.

LO1 A contract of indemnity is one whereby a person promises to save the other from loss caused to him by the conduct of the promisor himself or of any third person.

LO2 A contract of 'guarantee', is a contract, whether oral or written, to perform the promise or discharge the liability of a third person in case of his default. A contract of guarantee involves three parties, viz., a person who gives the guarantee is called the 'surety', the person in respect of whose default the guarantee is given is called the 'principal debtor', and the person to whom the guarantee is given is called the 'creditor'.

LO3 The discharge or release of the principal debtor is sufficient enough to give a valid discharge to the surety. Besides the surety is discharged from liability by (i) notice of revocation, (ii) death of surety, (iii) novation, (iv) alteration in terms of contract, (v) arrangement between the principal debtor and the creditor, (vi) impairing surety's remedy, (vii) loss of security, and (viii) invalidation of the contract. The first two modes of discharge apply exclusively to continuing guarantee, whereas the remaining ones are applicable in respect of both specific and continuing guarantees.

LO4 Bailment is an act of delivering goods for a specified purpose on faith. The goods are to be returned after the purpose is over. Bailment can be only of 'goods' which means every kind of movable property other than money and actionable claim. Thus, keeping money in bank account is not bailment.

LO5 A pledge, is a bailment of goods wherein the goods are delivered as a security for payment of a debt or performance of a promise. Pledge can be made only of movable properties. In order to make the pledge legally valid, it is essential that the pledgor has the legal right or title to retain the goods.

LO6 The relationship between an agent and his/her principal is called 'Agency'. The essence of a contract of agency is the agent's representative capacity coupled with a power to effect legal relations between the principal and the third parties.

LO7 The law recognises the following modes to form an agency:

Lien: The bailee's right to retain the possession of the bailed goods until his/her dues are cleared.

Particular lien: Lien available only against the goods in respect of which the bailee has rendered some service.

General lien: The bailee's right to retain the bailed goods for any of his/her lawful dues.

Finder of lost goods: A person who finds an article belonging to another.

Pledge: A kind of bailment of a moving thing as security for the repayment of a debt or performance of a promise.

Agency: The legal relationship in which the agent deals with a third party on behalf of the principal.

Agent: A person employed to do any act for another person, or to represent another in his dealings with the third party.

Sub-agent: Person employed by and acting under the control of the original agent.

Substituted agent: A person appointed by the original agent to act for the principal in the business of agency with the consent of the principal.

Estoppel: A legal principle that bars a party from denying or alleging a certain fact owing to that party's previous conduct, allegation, or denial.

Irrevocable agency: An agency wherein agent's authority cannot be revoked or recalled by the principal.

- **By agreement:** When agency is formed through express consent (oral or written) or implied conduct.
- **By ratification:** In this case, the principal either by act or by agreement approves the conduct of an agent who acted outside the given scope of authority or the conduct of a person who in fact is not an agent.
- **By estoppel:** When the principal reasons a third person to believe that another person is his agent.
- **By operation of law:** This arises in emergency situations, for instance, when the agent or someone is unable to contact the principal.

LO8 An agency can be terminated by the principal revoking his authority, by the agent renouncing the business of the agency, by the business of the agency being completed, by lapse of time, by the death or insanity of the principal or agent, or by the principal being adjudicated an insolvent for the relief of insolvent debtors.

Part II The Sale of Goods Act, 1930

CHAPTER 9 Contract of Sale of Goods

Learning Objectives

LO1 Contract of sale: definition, essentials
LO2 Sale distinguished from agreement to sell
LO3 Goods: meaning; classification
LO4 Price: meaning, modes of fixation
LO5 Conditions and Warranties
LO6 Doctrine of caveat emptor
LO7 Delivery of goods; modes of delivery; actual, symbolic, and constructive delivery
LO8 Rights of an unpaid seller

Contract of Sale of Goods

The most common deal in business world is about sale of goods. The law relating to sale of goods is contained in The Sale of Goods Act, 1930[1]. It came into force on 1 July 1930 and extends to the whole of India except the State of Jammu and Kashmir[2]. Prior to that the legal provisions relating to the contract of sale were contained in the Indian Contract Act, 1872, under Sections 76 to 123. In view of the importance, and intricacies of such (sales) contracts, and as a result of multifarious developments in modern commerce, certain amendments were needed in these provisions. In order to fulfil these requirements, Sections 76 to 123 of the Indian Contract Act, 1872, were revoked and a separate Act called 'The Sale of Goods Act' was enacted in 1930. Nevertheless, the unrepealed or general provisions of the Indian Contract Act, 1872, still apply to the contract of sale of goods insofar as they are not inconsistent with the express provisions of the Sale of Goods Act.

Contract of Sale Defined

Contract of sale: A contract whereby a seller transfers or agrees to transfer the property in goods to the buyer for a price.

Section 4(1) of the Sale of Goods Act defines a contract of sale of goods as 'a contract, whereby, the seller transfers or agrees to transfer the property in goods to the buyer for a price'. There can be a contract of sale between one part-owner and another. In other words, under a contract of sale, a seller (or vendor) in the capacity of the owner, or part-owner of the goods, transfers or agrees to transfer the ownership in goods to the buyer (or purchaser) for an agreed upon value in money (or money equivalent), called the price, paid or the promise to pay same.

A contract of sale may be absolute or conditional depending upon the desire of the contracting parties [Section 4(2)].

[1] Throughout our discussion on the law of sale of goods in this chapter, unless otherwise specifically stated, the sections mentioned are those of the Sale of Goods Act, 1930. The word 'Act' wherever used in the chapter refers to the Sale of Goods Act, 1930.

[2] The state of Jammu and Kashmir enjoys a special status under Article 356 of Indian constitution.

Making Contract of Sale

A contract of sale is made by an offer to buy or sell goods for a price and the acceptance of such an offer. The contract may provide for the immediate delivery of the goods or immediate payment of the price or both, or for the delivery or payment by installments, or that the delivery or payment or both shall be postponed [Section 5(1)].

Subject to the provisions of any law for the time being in force, a contract of sale may be made in writing, or by word of mouth, or partly in writing and partly by word of mouth, or may be implied from the conduct of the parties [Section 5(2)].

Essentials of Contract of Sale

A close examination of Sections 4 and 5 shows that the following six features are the essential elements of any contract of sale of goods:

1. Two parties
2. Goods
3. Transfer of ownership
4. Price
5. All essentials of a valid contract of sale
6. Includes both a 'sale' and 'an agreement to sell'

Two parties

A contract of sale of goods is bilateral in nature wherein property in goods has to pass from one party to another. One cannot buy one's own goods. For example, *A* is the owner of a grocery shop. If he supplies the goods (from the stock meant for sale) to his family, it does not amount to a sale and there is no contract of sale. However, there may be a contract of sale between one part-owner and another part-owner [Section 4(1)]. Suppose *A* and *B* jointly own a television set, *A* may transfer his ownership in the television set to anyone including *B*, thereby making latter the sole owner of the goods. In the same way, a partner may buy goods from the firm in which he is a partner and vice-versa.

However, there is an exception against the general rule that no person can buy his own goods. Where a pawnee sells the goods pledged with him/her on non-payment of his/her money, the pawnor (i.e. actual owner of the goods) may buy them in execution of a decree [*Moore vs. Singer Manufacturing Company*[3]].

Goods

Goods: Every kind of movable property other than actionable claims and money.

The subject matter of a contract of sale must be goods. According to Section 2(7) of 'The Sale of Goods Act, 1881' the term 'goods' has been defined thus: 'Goods' means every kind of movable property other than actionable claims[4] and money, and includes stock and shares, growing crops, grass, and things attached to or forming part of the land which are agreed to be severed before sale or under the contract of sale. It means that every kind of movable property except actionable claims and money is regarded as 'goods'. Contracts relating to services are not considered as contract of sale.

The Act also does not cover the sale and purchase of 'immovable property', which is governed by a separate statute, 'The Transfer of Property Act, 1882'.

Transfer of ownership

Transfer of property in goods is also integral to a contract of sale. The term 'property in goods' means the ownership of the goods. According to Section 2(11), property means the general property in goods and not merely a special property. Thus, it is the general property, which is transferred under a contract of sale as distinguished from special property, which is transferred in case of pledge of goods, i.e., possession of goods is transferred to the pledgee or pawnee while the ownership rights remain with the pledger. Thus, in a contract of sale there must be an absolute transfer of the ownership. It must be noted that the physical delivery of goods is not essential for transferring the ownership.

Price

Price: Money consideration for a sale of goods.

The buyer must pay some price for the goods. Section 2(10) of the Sale of Goods Act defines the term 'price' as 'the money consideration for a sale of goods'. Accordingly, consideration in a contract of sale has necessarily to be in money. Where goods are offered as consideration for goods, it will not amount to sale, but it will be called barter or exchange, which was prevalent in ancient times. Similarly, if a person offers the goods to somebody else without consideration, it amounts to a gift or charity and not sale. In explicit terms, goods must be sold for a definite amount of money, called the price. However, the consideration can be partly in money and partly in valued up[5] goods [*Aldridge vs Johnson*[6]]. Furthermore, payment is not necessary at the time of making the contract of sale.

Essentials of a valid contract

A contract of sale is a species of contract, therefore, to be valid, it must have all the essential elements of a valid contract, viz., free consent, consideration, competency of contracting parties, lawful object, legal formalities to be completed, etc. If any of the essential elements of a valid contract is missing, then the contract of sale will not be valid. For instance, if *A* agreed to sell his car to *B* because *B* forced him to do so by means of undue influence, this contract of sale is not valid, since there is no free consent on the part of the transferor.

Contract to include both a 'sale' and 'an agreement to sell'

Sale: Instant transfer of property (in goods) from seller to buyer.

The 'contract of sale' is a generic term and includes both sale and an agreement to sell [Section 4(1)]. According to Section 4(3), 'Where under a contract of sale the property in the goods is transferred from the seller to the buyer, the contract is called a sale, but where the transfer of the property in the goods is to take place at a future time or subject to some condition thereafter to be fulfilled, the contract is called an agreement to sell'. The sale is an executed or absolute contract, whereas 'an agreement to sell' is an executory contract and implies a conditional sale.

---

[3] 1904, 1KB 820 CA

[4] The term 'actionable claims' refers to a claim, which can be enforced through a court of law, e.g., a book debt.

[5] Valued up goods means the goods, the price of which can definitely be measured in terms of money.

[6] 1857, 7E & B. 885

Formalities to Be Fulfilled

Agreement to sell: Transfer of property (in goods) from seller to buyer in future; usually subject to fulfilment of some condition(s).

The Act does not prescribe any particular form of a valid contract of sale. A contract of sale can be made merely by an offer, to buy or sell goods for a price, followed by acceptance of such an offer [Section 5(1)]. Interestingly, neither the payment of price nor the delivery of goods is essential at the time of making the contract of sale unless otherwise agreed. That is, the contract may provide for the immediate delivery of the goods or immediate payment of the price or both, or for the delivery or payment by installments, or delivery or payment or both can be postponed subject to convenience of the parties.

Section 5(2) further provides that a contract of sale may be made either orally or in writing, or partly orally and partly in writing, or may even be implied from the conduct of the parties.

Sale and agreement to sell distinguished

As pointed out earlier in this chapter, a contract of sale includes both sale and an agreement to sell. These two, however, are legally different in terms of their subject matter. And the fact whether the transaction is a sale or an agreement to sell determines the rights and obligations of the parties to a contract of sale. The distinction between the two is, therefore, of principal significance.

There are eight main points of distinction between a sale and an agreement to sell, which are listed as follows:

1. Transfer of ownership
2. Nature of contract
3. Nature of rights of buyer
4. Consequence of breach by buyer
5. Risk of Loss
6. Insolvency of the seller
7. Insolvency of the buyer
8. Consequences in case of resale

Transfer of Ownership

Transfer of ownership (property in goods) is the most significant point of distinction betwen sale and agreement to sell. All other points of differentiation arise from this basic difference. In the case of sale, the title (ownership) in the goods passes to the buyer immediately at the time of making the contract, but in the case of an agreement to sell, the title passes at a future time subject to the conditions to be fulfilled thereafter. Therefore, in a sale the buyer becomes the proprietor of the goods no sooner as the contract is made, whereas in an agreement to sell, the seller continues to be the proprietor of the goods agreed to be sold until it becomes a sale.

Nature of Contract

A sale is an executed contract because through this all the formalities of the contract are said to have been completed, and the ownership of the goods is said to have passed to the buyer. An agreement to sell, on the other hand, is an executory contract, as all the formalities of the contract are not completed but something vital remains to be done, i.e., ownership will pass on some future date. An agreement to sell becomes a sale on the expiry of the stipulated time or on the fulfilment of the conditions subject to which the property in goods is to be transferred.

Nature of Rights of Buyer

A sale creates *jus in rem,* i.e., gives the right to the buyers to claim the goods as against anybody who disturbs their right to use the goods, including the seller. As against this, an agreement to sell creates merely *jus in personam,* i.e., the right to either party (buyer or seller) against each other for any default in fulfilling its part of agreement. This means that the buyer gets the rights against the seller and vice-versa. In other words, an agreement to sell is a contract, pure and simple, but a sale is a contract plus conveyance, or a fulfilled contract.

Consequence of Breach by Buyer

In case of a sale, if the buyer wrongly refuses to accept (the goods) and pay the price, the seller may sue him/her for the price, even though the goods are still in his/her (seller) possession and have never been delivered to the buyer. But in case of an agreement to sell, if the buyer refuses to accept the goods or pay for them, the only remedy available to the seller is to sue for damages. He cannot sue for price, even though the goods are in the possession of buyer.

Risk of Loss

In case of sale, if there is any loss or damage to the goods, it falls on the buyer even if the goods are with the seller. The general rule is that unless otherwise agreed, risk follows ownership, which implies whosoever is the owner of the goods at the time of loss, will bear the loss. Accordingly, in an agreement to sell, if the goods are lost or destroyed by accident, the loss falls on the seller even if the goods are in the possession of the buyer. This is because till delivery, the agreement to sell becomes a sale, the ownership of the goods remains with the seller.

Insolvency of the Seller

In a sale, if the seller becomes insolvent while the goods are with him/her, the buyer is entitled to recover the goods from the assignee or the official receiver as the property in the goods has already passed on to the buyer. However, in case of an agreement to sell, if the seller goes bankrupt, the buyer cannot claim the goods even if he/she has paid the price. The buyer can only claim ratable dividend for the money paid from the estate of the insolvent seller.

Insolvency of the Buyer

In case of a sale, if the buyer is adjudicated insolvent before paying the price, the seller must deliver the goods to the official receiver or assignee as the ownership has already passed on to the buyer. The seller (as an unsecured creditor) is entitled only to a ratable dividend for the unpaid price. But in an agreement to sell, where the ownership in respect of goods continues to vest in the seller, the seller may refuse to deliver the goods to the official receiver or assignee unless he has paid the full price of the goods.

Consequences in Case of Resale

In a sale, the seller, if still in the possession of goods after sale, cannot resell the goods because the ownership of goods has already passed on to the buyer. If that is done, the original buyer shall have a double remedy—a suit for damages against the seller and the right to recover the goods from the subsequent purchaser. However, it is important to note that the right to recover the goods from the subsequent buyer ceases to exist, if the third person had purchased them in good faith and without notice of previous sale or any lien in respect of the goods [Section 30]. In an agreement to sell, the seller (still being the owner) can dispose of the goods as he/she likes, and the buyer's (original one) remedy against the seller's breach of contract is only a suit for damages. He/she has no right to follow property in the hands of the subsequent buyer.

Goods: Meaning and Classification

The subject matter of a contract of sale is essentially movable property, i.e., goods. Let us, therefore, elaborate the meaning of the term 'goods' and also understand its various types that form the subject matter of a contract of sale.

'Goods' means every kind of movable property other than actionable claims and money. It includes stock and shares, growing crops, grass, and things attached to, or forming part of the land, which are agreed to be severed before sale or under the contract of sale [Section 2(7)].

As per the above definition, goods includes every kind of transportable property, i.e., the things, which can be carried from one place to another. But money and actionable claims, although movable, have been expressly excluded from the scope of goods. Money means legal tender, i.e., the currency that cannot legally be refused in payment of a debt. Currency includes coins and bank notes as a medium of exchange. However, it excludes old coinage (that has gone out of circulation) and foreign currency. Exchange (i.e., sale and purchase) of foreign currency is nevertheless governed by the Foreign Exchange Management Act (FEMA) and thus cannot be included in goods even if it is not includible as money in the legal terms. But old and ancient coins are regarded as antiques and may be treated as goods. Actionable claims have also been excluded from goods for they cannot be sold or purchased and like goods they can only be assigned. For instance, a debt due from one person to another is an actionable claim that can be enforced by means of a legal action and cannot be the subject matter of a sale. On the other hand, the things attached to a land or which form part of land itself (e.g., crops, trees, minerals, and metals) can be the subject matter of sale provided they are agreed to be severed from the land under the contract of sale. It is interesting to note that in order to be included as goods, the goods-in-question need not necessarily be tangible or visible. Goodwill, patents, copyrights, trademarks, gas, water, etc., are all goods and can be the subject matter of a contract of sale.

Classification of Goods

The various kinds of goods relevant to the contract of sale may broadly be classified into the following three categories:

1. Existing goods,
2. Future goods, and
3. Contingent goods

Existing goods

Existing goods: Goods physically in existence, owned and/or possessed by the seller at the time entering into contract of sale by the latter.

These are the goods that are physically in existence at the time of entering the contract of sale. As per Section 6 of the Sale of Goods Act, existing goods are those goods, that are owned and/or possessed by the seller at the time of the contract of sale. Where seller is the owner, he has the general property in them. On the other hand, where the seller is merely in the possession of the goods, e.g., as an agent, he has a right to sell them (on behalf of his principal), even though the goods are not owned by him.

The existing goods may be further sub-divided as

1. specific goods,
2. ascertained goods, and
3. unascertained goods.

Specific goods: Goods identified and agreed upon at the time of making the contract of sale.

Specific goods Goods identified and agreed upon at the time of making the contract of sale are specific goods [Section 2(14)]. It is important to note that the goods are not considered to be specific merely because they are identifiable, rather they must be actually identified. For example, if *A* agrees to sell his car or watch to *B*, it shall be a sale of specific goods if *A* has only one car or only one watch.

Ascertained goods: Goods identified subsequent to the formation of the contract of sale.

Ascertainedgoods These are the goods that have been ascertained or identified subsequent to the formation of the contract of sale. Ascertainment basically involves unconditional appropriation of the goods as the subject matter of a particular contract. For example, *A*, who deals in Enfield Motor Bikes, has 100 bikes in his showroom and agrees to sell 40 bikes to Delhi Police under an agreement to sell. Suppose the buyer selects and sets aside 40 bikes (i.e., quantity agreed) out of the mass of 100 for the given contract, the contract is for ascertained goods because the quantity contracted has been identified and appropriated towards the contract.

Unascertained goods: Goods not specifically identified or ascertained at the time of entering the contract of sale.

Unascertained goods Contrary to ascertained goods, these are the goods that are not specifically identified or ascertained at the time of entering the contract of sale. They are identified or defined only by description. For example, Mohan, a timber merchant, agrees to supply 50 chairs to a school out of the lot of 200 chairs lying in his godown. It is a sale of unascertained goods because which of the chairs shall be delivered to the buyer have not been identified at the time of the contract of sale. As soon as 50 particular chairs are identified and set aside for the delivery from the mass, they become ascertained or specific goods. Unascertained goods are sometimes termed as 'generic goods.'

Future goods

Future goods: Goods that are yet to be manufactured, produced, or acquired by the seller after making the contract of sale.

As per Section 2(6), future goods refers to goods that have to be manufactured, produced, or acquired by the seller after making of the contract of sale. Thus, future goods are goods that either may not exist at the time of the contract or they exist but have to be acquired by the seller at the time of the contract. For example, *A* enters into a contract with *B* to buy all the apples that would be produced in *B*'s orchard over the next year. This is a contract for the sale of future goods amounting to an agreement to sell.

From the above example, it can be realised that there cannot be a sale of future goods because ownership cannot be transferred before the goods comes into existence. Since future goods are not in the possession of the seller at the time of contract, they can become the subject matter of an agreement to sell and not the sale.

Contingent goods

Contingent goods: Goods whose acquisition by the seller depends on a contingency, which may or may not happen.

Contingent goods are those whose acquisition by the seller depends on a contingency, which may or may not happen [Section 6(2)].

The above definition indicates that contingent goods are a type of future goods with a minor difference that the future goods are more certain to come into existence, whereas contingent goods are less certain to come into existence. Hence, a contract of sale of contingent goods also operates as 'an agreement to sell' and not a sale, as regards transfer of ownership from the seller to buyer. Such a contract is enforceable only at the occurrence of the contingency, otherwise the contract becomes void.

For example, *A* agrees to sell to *B* a vintage car only if *C*, its present owner, sells it to him. This is a contract for the sale of contingent goods as the availability of the car to *A* depends on its sale by *C* to *A*.

Effect of Perishing of Goods

The subject matter of a contract of sale is goods; therefore, the contract becomes void if they get perished. The effect of perishing of subject matter (i.e., the goods) may be discussed under the following two heads:

1. Perishing of goods before making of the contract
2. Perishing of goods after agreement to sell but before sale

Perishing of goods before making of the contract

Sometimes, the goods might have perished before the making of the contract of sale. In such circumstances, the contract of sale is void. Section 7 of the Sale of Goods Act provides that a contract for the sale of specific goods is void, if the goods without the knowledge of the seller have, at the time when the contract was made, perished or become so damaged as to no longer answer their description in the contract. This provision is rooted in the principle of impossibility of performance of the contract, or the rule that mutual mistake of fact essential to the contract renders it void.

For a contract to be rendered void on the ground of perishing of goods, the under-mentioned conditions must be satisfied in the contract of sale.

1. The contract must be for the sale of specific or ascertained goods. This follows that if the subject matter of the sale was unascertained goods, the perishing of such goods would not affect the contract. For instance, *A* agreed to sell to *B*, 50 bags of cement from his stock of 200 bags in his godown. The entire stock of cement perished in rainwater. *A* is bound to deliver 50 bags of cement to *B*. Otherwise, he will be liable for damages.
2. The goods must have perished at the time or before the making of the contract. If the goods perish subsequent to the agreement to sell, it does not come under the purview of Section 7, but Section 8. The effect of the same will be distinct as will be discussed later.
3. The seller must not have the knowledge of the destruction of goods. If the seller was aware of the destruction and still entered into the contract, he is stopped from disputing the contract.

It should be noted that 'perishing of goods' not only includes physical destruction and loss by theft but also includes the cases where the goods have lost their commercial value or merchantable character, e.g., where sugar becomes sticky by soaking moisture and is rendered unsaleable as sugar. Box 9.1 provides some more examples for better understanding of the issue.

At times, only a part of the goods may get destroyed or damaged. In such a situation, the effect of perishing will depend on whether the contract is divisible. If the contract is entire, i.e., indivisible, and only a part of the goods have perished, it will still render the contract void as the same makes the rest of the goods useless for the buyer. On the other hand, if the contract is divisible and only a part of the goods are perished or lost, then the contract remains valid for that part which is available in good condition.

Perishing of goods before sale but after 'agreement to sell'

It is also possible that the goods might perish after an agreement to sell has been made but before the risk passes on to the buyer, i.e., before it becomes a

[7] 1853, 5HL, Cas 673

Box 9.1 **Effect of Perishing of Goods**

Example 1

A agrees to sell a dog to *B*. Unknown to both the parties, the dog was dead at the time of making the contract. This contract of sale is void.

Example 2

A sold to *B* a specific cargo of goods, which was on its way to Mumbai from England. The ship conveying the cargo sunk along with the goods before the day of the bargain. Neither party was aware of this fact. In this case, the contract of sale was held to be void [*Hastie vs Conturier*[7]].

sale. Section 8 provides, 'Where there is an agreement to sell specific goods, and subsequently the goods without any fault on the part of the seller or buyer perish or become so damaged as no longer to answer their description in the agreement before the risk passes to the buyer, the agreement is thereby avoided'. That is, an agreement to sell becomes void if the agreement is for the sale of specific goods and the goods are destroyed without any fault of either the seller or the buyer. Thus, under this provision a contract of sale can be avoided and both the parties are excused from the performance of the contract if the following conditions are satisfied:

1. The contract in question is an agreement to sell, and not actual sale.
2. The agreement is for the sale of specific goods.
3. The goods perished or got damaged before the buyer became the owner of the goods, i.e., before the risk or property passed on to the buyer.
4. The goods have been damaged or perished with no fault on the part of either the buyer or the seller.

Of the above, condition no. 3 is most decisive to make a contract of sale void, as it constitutes the ground of supervening impossibility of the performance of the contract. The rule to render a contract of sale void on perishing of goods, before sale but after agreement to sell, is based on the fact that it was only an agreement to sell and the goods were lost before the passing of the risk.

The difference between Sections 7 and 8 is that a contract is void *ab initio* under Section 7, whereas a contract becomes void later under Section 8. However, in line with Section 7, Section 8 is also applicable only in case of specific or ascertained goods. Therefore, even if the entire stock of unascertained goods perishes either before or after making the agreement, the contract shall not become void. Similarly, if the goods are destroyed partly, the contract of sale becomes void if it is indivisible. Conversely, if the contract is divisible, the contract remains valid as regards the part available in good condition. For instance, *A* delivered a horse to *B* on a trial for 8 days on condition that if found suitable by the buyer for his purpose, the bargain would become absolute. The horse, however, died on the third day without any fault on part of either party. It was held that this agreement is void and the seller should bear the loss [*Elphic vs Barnes*[8]].

Price

Price: Money consideration for the sale of goods.

'Price' means the money consideration for the sale of goods [Section 2(10)].

Price is a prerequisite to constitute a valid contract of sale. No sale of goods can take place without a price. The price should be paid or promised to be paid in money, unless otherwise agreed. The money here implies the legal tender, i.e., the coins and bank notes in circulation (currency of the country). Further the price may also be paid by means of a negotiable instrument, e.g., cheque, bill of exchange, pro-note, and *hundi*, for it is not the mode of payment of a price that is prerequisite for a sale of goods, but the money consideration that constitutes the essence for a valid contract of sale.

[8] 1880, 5C. P.D. 321

Modes of Fixing the Price

Sections 9 and 10 contain the different modes of fixing the price, which may be discussed under the following heads.

Price expressly fixed in the contract itself

The price in a contract of sale may be expressly fixed by the parties themselves. The parties are free to fix any price they negotiate and in such case the adequacy of the price cannot be questioned [Section 9(1)].

Price fixed in manner provided in the contract

Where the price is not determined in accordance with the foregoing provisions, the buyer shall pay the seller a reasonable price. What is a reasonable price is a question of fact dependent on the circumstances of each particular case [Section 9(2)].

Price fixed by the valuation of a third party

Where there is an agreement to sell goods on the terms that the price is to be fixed by the valuation of a third party and such third party cannot or does not make such valuation, the agreement is thereby avoided.

Section 10 lays down that if the goods or any part thereof have been delivered to and appropriated by the buyer, he shall pay a reasonable price. If, however, such third party is prevented from making the valuation by the fault of the seller or buyer, the party not in fault may maintain a suit for damages against the party in default.

What is reasonable price will vary from case to case. The market price may, however, represent the reasonable price, if possible to obtain.

Conditions and Warranties

As a measure of consumer protection, the Sale of Goods Act assumes that every contract of sale of goods (unless otherwise agreed to between the parties) is subject to certain terms. These terms may relate to the quality, use, utility, suitability, price (and the mode of its payment), delivery (including time and place thereof) of the goods. Conditions are those terms, which form the very basis of a contract of sale. Warranties, on the other hand, are those obligations that are collateral to the main purpose of the contract. Warranties, thus, as a matter of fact, are of lesser significance as compared to conditions.

Conditions

A condition is a stipulation essential to the main purpose of the contract, breach of which gives rise to a right to treat the contract as repudiated [Section 12(2)]. Thus, a condition in a contract of sale is that stipulation which constitutes the hardcore of the contract and is essential to the main purpose of the contract. The failure to fulfil the condition gives the aggrieved party a right to repudiate the contract. Therefore, if the seller fails to fulfil a condition, the buyer has a right to put an end to the contract, refuse the goods and, if he has already paid for them, recover the price and also maintain an action for damages for the breach of contract.

Condition: A stipulation essential to the main purpose of the contract, the breach of which gives rise to a right to treat the contract as repudiated.

The concept of condition is better understood by the following examples in Box 9.2.

Kinds of Conditions

Conditions may be either express or implied.

Express conditions

A condition that has been expressly provided for or agreed upon by both the parties at the time of the contract of sale is called an express condition. For example, if a buyer desires to buy a black horse, the colour of the horse intended to be bought becomes an express condition. The parties are at liberty to include any number of express conditions by an express stipulation in a contract of sale.

Express conditions: Conditions expressly provided or agreed upon by both the parties at the time of entering contract of sale.

Implied conditions

Conditions are said to be implied when the law incorporates their existence as implicit to a contract of

Implied conditions: Conditions which the law incorporates as implicit to a contract of sale unless otherwise agreed upon between the parties.

[9] 1925, 1 KB 260

Box 9.2 Condition in Contract of Sale

Example 1

A consulted *B*, a motorcar dealer, for buying a car suitable for touring purposes. *B* suggested that a Bugatti car would be appropriate. *A* purchased the same car relying upon his recommendation. The car turned out to be unfit for the purpose bought for. *A*, the buyer, wished to repudiate the contract by rejecting the car and demanded the refund of the price paid.

In this case, it was held that the term that the car should be suitable for touring purposes was a condition of the contract, and thereby essential to be fulfilled. It was so vital that its non-fulfilment defeated the very purpose for which *A* had bought the car. He was, therefore, entitled to reject the car and have the refund of the price. In this case, the suitability of the car for touring purpose was held to be a condition of the contract [*Baldry vs Marshall*[9]].

Example 2

X goes to *Y*, a horse dealer, and tells him that he wants a horse that can run 35 km/hour. *Y* points to a particular horse and says that this will suit the purpose. *X* buys the horse relying on his representation. Subsequently, *X* finds that the horse can run only at a speed of 25 km in an hour. There is a breach of condition. *X* may reject the horse and get back the price paid by him.

sale unless otherwise agreed upon between the parties. It may be noted that an express condition does not negate an implied condition unless inconsistent therewith. Moreover, in the event of any inconsistency or conflict between express and implied conditions, the express terms shall prevail over the implied ones. Sections 14 to 17 relate to implied conditions which are of the following seven types:

1. Condition as to title
2. Condition as to description
3. Condition as to sample
4. Condition as to sample as well as description
5. Condition as to quality or fitness
6. Condition as to merchantability
7. Condition as to wholesomeness.

Condition as to title This condition applies when the sale involves transfer of property in goods and possession thereof. In this regard, Section 14(a) clearly provides that in a contract of sale, unless the circumstances of the contract are such as to show a different intention, there is an implied condition that the seller in an actual sale has the right to sell the goods, and in an agreement to sell, he/she will have it (the right to sell) when the property (title or ownership) is to pass.

The rule *Nemo dat quod non-habet,* i.e., 'one cannot give what one does not have' strengthens this condition. As a result of this condition, if the seller's title turns out to be defective, the buyer is entitled to reject the goods and have the price back. It should be noted that in such a case the buyer must restore the goods to the true owner, but he/she can of course recover the price paid by him/her from the seller for a total failure of consideration.

The condition as to title may, however, be disproved by an express stipulation. For instance, if the custom authorities dispose of any confiscated items, they are absolved of any responsibility as regard owner's title. The person who buys such goods gets good title thereupon.

Condition as to description At times the goods are sold by description. In such cases, Section 15 provides that 'where there is a contract for the sale of goods by description, there is an implied condition that the goods shall correspond with the description'. The term 'correspond with description' means that the goods supplied by the seller must be the same as described by him. If subsequently, it is found that the goods supplied do not match the description, the buyer has a right to reject the goods and claim the refund of the price, if already paid. He/she can also sue the seller for damages.

Interestingly, even if the buyer has seen the goods but he/she purchases them relying on the description given by the seller and not on what he/she has seen, it may be treated a sale by description. That is, in such cases also the goods must be in accordance with the description given by the seller [*Beale vs Taylor*[10]].

10. 1967, ANER 253

Sometimes, the method of packing may also form part of the description. For example, *A* sold to *B* 4000 tins of Australian fruits, which were agreed to be packed in cases each containing 40 tins. But a substantial portion of these cases contained only 25 tins. Held, the method of packing was a part of the description, and although the total number of tins was the same, *B* was entitled to reject the goods [*Moore & Co. vs Landaure & Co.*[11]].

Condition as to sample Many a time, the seller shows a sample of the goods to the buyer and agrees to supply the goods according to the sample. In such a case since the buyer buys the goods relying upon the quality of the goods from the sample, there is an implied condition that the goods supplied will be in accordance with the sample in quality.

Condition as to sample as well as description If the seller shows sample of the goods to the buyer and also provides him the description, the goods must correspond with both the sample and the description [Section 15]. If the goods do not correspond either with the sample or the description, the buyer can terminate the contract.

Condition as to quality or fitness Ordinarily, in a contract of sale, there is no implied condition as to the quality of fitness for any particular purpose of the goods supplied. The buyer is supposed to satisfy himself/herself about the quality as well as the suitability of the goods. Thus, subsequently if the goods delivered turn out to be unfit or unsuitable for the buyer's purpose, he/she cannot terminate the contract and return or exchange the goods, or sue the seller for damages.

But there are certain exceptions to the aforesaid rule. In this regard, Section 16(1) provides thus: 'where the buyer, expressly or by implication, makes known to the seller the particular purpose for which the goods are required so as to show that the buyer relies on the seller's skill or judgment, and the goods are of a description which it is in the course of the seller's business to supply (whether he is the manufacturer or producer or not), there is an implied condition that the goods shall be reasonably fit for such purpose'.

In order to avail the implied condition that the goods are reasonably suitable or fit for the purpose for which they are required, the following requirements must be satisfied:

1. The buyer requires the goods for a particular purpose.
2. The buyer expressly or impliedly makes known to the seller the intended purpose.
3. The buyer relies upon the seller's skill and judgment with respect to the fitness of the goods for the intended purpose.
4. The seller's business is to supply such goods whether or not he/she is the manufacturer or producer thereof.

The case studies provided in Box 9.3 drive home the point.

[11] 1921, 2 K.B. 519

[12] 1903, 2 K.B. 148

[13] 1904, 1 K.B. 725

Box 9.3 **Condition As to Quality or Fitness of Goods [Section 16(1)]**

Example 1

In *Priest vs Last*[12], *P*, a draper, bought a hot water bottle from *L*, a chemist. The buyer, *P, could not be expected to have special skill or knowledge with regard to hot water* bottles, and the chemist, *L*, while delivering him the bottle stated that it was meant for hot water. While being used by plaintiff's wife, the bottle burst and injured her. It was found that the bottle was not fit for use as a hot water bottle. It was held that the seller, *L*, was responsible for damages since the purpose was clear from the nature of goods.

Example 2

In *Evens vs Stelle Benjamin*[13], the plaintiff purchased a refrigerator from a seller dealing in electrical appliances without asking the dealer whether it is fit to make ice. The refrigerator failed to make ice. It was held that the buyer was entitled to reject the refrigerator and get the refund of the price paid as the very purpose of buying the article could not be fulfilled.

Box 9.4 **Implied Condition with Respect to Defects [Section 16(2)]**

Example 1

A bought black yarn from *D* and, when delivered, found it damaged by white ants. The condition as to merchantability was breached.

Example 2

A purchased a bottle of wine from *B*. While opening its cork in a normal manner, the neck of the bottle broke off and *A*'s hand was injured in the process. Held, the goods were not of merchantable quality and *A* could recover damages from *B* [*Morelli vs Fitch & Gibbons*[15]].

Here, it is important to note that the implied condition as to fitness is applicable only in case of a sale under normal circumstances. Sometimes, there may be abnormal or special circumstances affecting the use of the goods for a particular purpose. In such cases, the aforesaid condition shall not work. For instance, if someone buys an article for a particular usage, the implied condition as regards fitness does not apply if the usage is not made known to the seller at the time of purchase. For example, in *Griffith vs Peter Conway Ltd*[14], a woman bought a tweed coat from a retailer whose business was to sell goods of that description. After wearing the jacket sometime, she developed dermatitis due to her abnormally sensitive skin—a fact which was not disclosed to the seller at the time of sale. It was held that the seller was not liable because the implied condition with respect to fitness as the buyer's purpose was not broken and the coat was fit for anyone with a normal skin. Her claim for return of price and damages was struck down.

Condition to merchantable quality 'Where the goods are bought by description from a seller who deals in goods of that description (whether he is the manufacture or producer or not), there is an implied condition that the goods shall be of merchantable quality' [Section 16(2)].

Thus, in order to avail the relief under this condition, the following two requirements must be fulfilled:

1. The goods should be bought by description.
2. The seller should be dealing in goods of that description.

The expression 'merchantable quality' means two things. First, where the goods are purchased for self-use, they should be capable of being used as the goods of that description, and second, where the goods are purchased for resale, they should be resalable in the market under their description, i.e., the goods should be such as would be acceptable to a reasonable person.

But, if the buyer has examined the goods, there shall be no implied condition as regards defects, which such examination ought to have revealed [Proviso to Section 16(2)]. Examples in this regard are presented in Box 9.4.

Condition as to wholesomeness This condition is a part of the condition as to merchantability and is applicable only in a contract of sale of provisions and food stuffs, i.e., the items, which are supposed to be physically consumed. Such items must not only answer their description but they must also be wholesome or sound, i.e., they should be fit for human consumption. In simple words, any provision or food item should not be stale, contaminated or otherwise unfit for human consumption. The following case study is a case in point.

C bought a bun from *M*'s bakery and confectionery shop. The bun contained a stone, which broke *C*'s tooth. It was held that *M* was liable for damages for violating the condition of wholesomeness [*Chaproneere vs Mason*[16]].

Warranties

A warranty is a stipulation collateral to the main purpose of the contract, the breach of which gives rise to a claim for damages but not to a right to

[14] 1939, 1 ALL E.R. 685

[15] 1928, 2 KB 636

[16] 1905, 21 T.L.R. 633

Box 9.5 What is a Warranty?

Example 1

A buyer goes to a car dealer and asks for a good car. While selling the car, the dealer claims that the mileage of the car is 16 km per litre. But subsequently the buyer discovers that the car gives a mileage of only 12 km per litre. Here the buyer cannot repudiate the contract but can only claim damages from the seller because the statement made by the seller amounts to a warranty.

Example 2

H bought two small ships from *K* relying upon the latter's statement that the Dead Weight Tonnage (DWT) of each ship was 460 tons, whereas the actual DWT of each ship was just 360 tons. The buyer wanted to reject the ships. It was held that the representation made by the seller about the capacity was not a condition but merely a warranty and, thus, *H*, could not reject the ships but could only sue *K* for damages [*Harrison vs Knowles & Foster*[17]].

> **Warranty:** A stipulation collateral to the main purpose of the contract, the breach of which gives rise to a claim for damages but not to a right to reject the goods and treat the contract as repudiated.

reject the goods and treat the contract as repudiated [Section 12(3)].

Thus, a warranty is a stipulation, which is not essential to the main purpose of the contract, it is only of a subsidiary and collateral nature. Its non-fulfilment does not defeat the very purpose of the buyer. The effect of a breach of a warranty is that the aggrieved party cannot terminate the contract but can only claim damages. That is, if the seller fails to fulfil a warranty, the buyer is not entitled to reject the goods, he/she can only claim damages from the seller for breach of warranty.

According to Section 12(4), 'whether a stipulation in a contract of sale is a condition or warranty will depend, in each case, on the construction of the contract'. It means that the terms used in the contract do not matter much. Sometimes, a stipulation, referred as a warranty in a contract of sale, may be a condition, if it is of great significance. Box 9.5 presents examples of warranty.

Kinds of Warranties

As in the case of conditions, warranties may also be either express or implied.

Express warranties

A warranty is said to be express when the term of the contract expressly provides for it. That is, express warranties are those which are openly and clearly provided by the seller in the contract and the buyer find them easy to understand. At the time of contract of sale, both the parties may agree upon any number of express warranties.

> **Express warranty:** Warranty provided explicitly by the term of the contract of sale.

Implied warranties

An implied warranty is one which the law incorporates into a contract of sale. Unless otherwise agreed, the Sale of Goods Act incorporates into every contract of sale of goods, the following three implied warranties.

> **Implied warranty:** Warranty which the law incorporates into a contract of sale.

1. Warranty as to quiet possession
2. Warranty against encumbrances
3. Warranty to disclose the dangerous nature of goods

Warranty as to quiet possession In every contract of sale, unless different intention appears from the circumstances of the contract, there is an implied warranty that the buyer shall have the freedom to a possessed property without interference, i.e., he is entitled to use the goods in the way he likes. This follows that if the right of possession and enjoyment of the buyer is disturbed by the seller or any other person (having a superior title to the goods), the buyer shall

[17] 1917, 2 K.B. 606

be in any way entitled to sue the seller for damages. Breach of this warranty is likely to occur where the seller's title is defective or he has not been conferred a clear right to effect the sale [Section 14(b)]. For example, *A* purchased a secondhand typewriter from *B*. *A* thereafter spent some money on its repair and service and used it for sometime. Unknown to both the parties the typewriter subsequently turned out to be a stolen one and as such *A* was compelled to restore it to the true owner. *A* was held entitled to recover damages from *B* amounting to not merely the price paid but also the cost of repair for the breach of this warranty [*Mason vs Burningham*[18]].

Warranty against encumbrances There is a further warranty that the goods are not subject to any charge or encumbrance in favour of a third party. If the buyer's possession is disturbed by the reason of the existence of encumbrances, he can claim damages from the seller. For example, *A* sold his scooter to *B* for ₹5000. The scooter was already hypothecated as security against a loan of ₹3000. *B* was not aware about this charge on the goods. Consequently *B* had to pay ₹3000 to *X* in order to enjoy the goods. Now *B* is entitled to claim this amount from the seller, *A*.

Warranty to disclose the dangerous nature of goods There is third implied warranty applicable in case of dangerous goods. If the goods sold are inherently dangerous or likely to cause a mishap, the seller must warn the innocent buyer of the probable danger. If there is breach of this warranty, the buyer shall be entitled to claim compensation from the seller for any injury suffered by him on this count.

When Condition Sinks to Level of Warranty

In some cases, a condition sinks or descends to the level of a warranty and, thereby, breach of condition is treated as the breach of a warranty. As a result of it, the buyer loses his right to reject the goods and treating the contract as repudiated. However, his remedy to claim damages continues. Section 13 of the Sale of Goods Act deals with the circumstances, wherein, a condition may be reduced to the status of a warranty. A condition may slip to a warranty under the following two circumstances.

[18] 1949, 2 K.B. 545

Voluntary waiver by the buyer

A condition becomes a warranty when the buyer waives the condition on its non-fulfilment or treats its breach as a breach of warranty. If a buyer elects to waive the breach of condition, he/she remains liable for the price if not already paid and cannot reject the goods [Section 13(1)]. But in such a case, however, he/she can sue the seller for damages for breach of warranty. The waiver, by the buyer, may be express or implied. Once the buyer exercises her/his option, i.e., waives the condition or elects to treat the breach of condition as a breach of warranty, he/she cannot later compel the seller for its fulfilment.

Compulsory treatment of breach of condition as breach of warranty

In certain circumstances, the buyer is bound to treat the breach of condition as a breach of warranty. Section 13(2) provides that where a contract of sale is not divisible and the buyer has accepted the goods or part thereof, the breach of condition can only be treated as a breach of warranty. The buyer in such a case cannot reject the goods and treat the contract as repudiated on the ground that certain condition was not fulfilled. He/she can only maintain an action against the seller for damages. But where the contract is separable, and the buyer has accepted part of the goods, he/she can still exercise his/her right to reject the remaining goods.

What Is Acceptance of Goods?

It is important to note that mere possession or taking delivery of the goods does not amount to acceptance. As per Section 42, the buyer is deemed to have accepted the goods in any of the following circumstances:

1. When he/she intimates to the seller that he/she has accepted them, or
2. When the goods have been delivered to him/her and he/she does any act in relation to them which is not inconsistent with the ownership, e.g., he/she pledges the same, or
3. When after the lapse of reasonable time, he/she retains the goods without intimating to the seller that he/she has rejected them.

Table 9.1 Difference Between Condition and Warranty

S. No.	Point of difference	Condition	Warranty
1.	Nature	It is a stipulation that is essential to the main purpose of the contract.	It is a stipulation, which is only collateral or subsidiary to the main purpose of the contract.
2.	Effect of breach	If there is breach of condition, the aggrieved party can repudiate the contract itself and sue the seller for damage.	In case of breach of warranty, since it is affecting only the collateral or auxiliary part of the contract, the aggrieved party can claim only damages.
3.	Importance	It is of vital importance for completion of the contract.	It is not of vital importance. The main contract can be completed even if the warranty is not fulfilled.
4.	Treatment	A breach of condition may be treated as breach of warranties if the aggrieved party chooses to be satisfied only with claiming damages or when the contract is not divisible and the buyer has accepted the goods or part thereof.	A breach of warranty under no circumstances can be treated as breach of condition.

Condition and Warranty Distinguished

As a matter of fact, the difference between the two terms, viz., 'condition' and 'warranty' is that of a degree and not that of kind. The distinction between the two stipulations has been summarised in Table 9.1.

Doctrine of *Caveat Emptor*

Doctrine of *caveat emptor*: A principle that often places on buyers the burden to reasonably examine goods before purchase, and take responsibility for its condition post purchase.

The term *caveat emptor* is a Latin expression that means caution buyer, i.e., 'let the buyer beware'. Doctrine of *caveat emptor* in this behalf is a principle that often places on buyers the burden to reasonably examine goods before purchase and take responsibility for its condition post purchase. This is a cardinal principle of the law relating to sale of goods, which states that it is for the buyer to satisfy himself/herself about the quality of the goods while entering into a deal with the seller. If the buyer buys the goods for a particular purpose, he/she must satisfy that they are fit for the purpose. It is no part of seller's duty to point out defects of the goods that he/she is offering for sale. Under the doctrine of *caveat emptor*, the buyer cannot recover from the seller for defects on the property that rendered it unfit for ordinary purposes. Thus, the buyer must take care of his/her own interest while purchasing goods. Doctrine of *Caveat Emptor* is an ancient principle that is intended to resolve disputes arising from information asymmetry, the pervasive situation in which the seller knows more than the buyer about the quality of a good or service. The same principle is contained in Section 16, which reads as follows.

'Subject to the provisions of this Act and of any other law for the time being in force, there is no implied warranty or condition as to the quality or fitness for any particular purpose of goods supplied under a contract of sale'. Box 9.6 presents some examples with respect to the doctrine of *caveat emptor*.

Exceptions to the Doctrine of *Caveat Emptor*

The rule of *caveat emptor* is not applicable in the following six cases:

[19] 1878, 4 AHP. Cas. 13

Box 9.6 Doctrine of Caveat Emptor

Example 1

A person bought some pigs in an auction. The pigs were sold 'subject to faults', i.e., no warranty was given by the seller in respect of any fault or error of description. The buyer, however, paid the price for healthy pigs. As they were infected all but one died of swine fever. The infected pigs also spread disease to other healthy pigs of the buyer. It was held that the seller was not bound to disclose the fact of ill health of the pigs. It was the buyer's duty to satisfy himself as regards the health of the pigs [*Ward vs Goddard Hobbs*[19]].

Example 2

A purchases a trouser for his son from *B*, a merchant dealing in ready-made garments. But the trouser does not fit his son exactly. It's too loose. Here the doctrine of *caveat emptor* operates, and hence the buyer will not have a right to return or exchange the goods.

1. Where the seller makes a misrepresentation and the buyer relies on it, the doctrine of caveat emptor does not apply and the contract entered between the parties would be a contract voidable at the option of the buyer.
2. Where the seller actively conceals a defect in the goods which is not visible on reasonable examination of the same, or where the seller makes a false representation amounting to fraud, and the buyer, relying upon it, enters into a contract with the seller, the doctrine of *caveat emptor* does not apply. The buyer is entitled to terminate such a contract and also claim damages from the seller for fraud.
3. Where the buyer, relying upon the skill and judgment of the seller, has expressly or impliedly communicated to him the purpose for which the goods are required, and the goods do not reasonably fit such purpose [Section 16(1)].
4. Where goods are bought by description from a seller who deals in goods of that description (whether or not he is the manufacture or producer), there is an implied condition that the goods purchased shall be of merchantable quality. If the goods are not found of merchantable quality, the seller cannot take the defence of the doctrine of *caveat emptor*. But the doctrine applies, if the buyer has examined the goods, as regards defects, in which such examination ought to have discovered [Section 16(2)].
5. Where the goods are sold by sample and the bulk of the goods supplied do not correspond with the sample in quality, the doctrine of *caveat emptor* would not apply [Section 17].
6. The doctrine of *caveat emptor* also does not apply in case of sale by sample as well as description, if the bulk of goods supplied do not correspond with the sample as well as with the description [Section 15].

Doctrine of *Caveat Venditor*

Caveat venditor is the Latin for 'let the seller beware'. It is counter to *caveat emptor*, and suggests that sellers too can deceive innocent buyers in a market transaction. This encourages the seller to take responsibility for the product and discourages them from selling products of unreasonable quality. The seller shall be under an obligation to inform the buyer of any defect in the goods sold at the time of the contract, except in a case where the defect was obviously known to the buyer.

> *Caveat venditor*: Let the seller beware.

Transfer of Ownership and Delivery

Every contract of sale of goods aims at transferring the ownership, i.e., passing of property in goods from the seller to the buyer, whereby the seller ceases to be the owner of the goods. It is important to note that in order to conclude the transfer of ownership,

> Doctrine of *caveat venditor*: The seller shall be under an obligation to inform the buyer of any latent defect in the goods sold at the time of the contract.

Box 9.7 **Risk Follows Ownership [Section 26]**

Example 1

A purchased a suit length from *B*'s shop. But he left the cloth in *B*'s shop to be collected by him later on. Incidentally, fire broke out in the shop as a result of which the suit length was gutted. The loss would fall on *A* because at the time of loss of cloth he had become its (good) owner.

Example 2

A hired a van from *B*. As a result of an accidental fire, the van was totally damaged while it was in the custody of *A*. The loss would be borne by *B* because at the time of loss he was the owner of the van.

the seller sometimes may not be the owner of the goods. Under certain circumstances even a non-owner can pass on a better title to the buyer. Apart from transferring the ownership to the buyer, it is the duty of the seller to deliver the goods. Correspondingly, besides accepting the delivery of the goods, it is the duty of the buyer to pay for the goods as per the terms of the contract of sale.

Significance of Transfer of Ownership

In a contract of sale, the precise moment at which property or ownership in goods passes from the seller to the buyer is of great importance because it has multiple legal ramifications. This is so because it is the ownership or title in goods that dictates the legal course in several extra-ordinary circumstances. The significance of transfer of ownership in goods can broadly be studied under the following four heads.

1. Risk '*Prima facie*' passes with property
2. Action against third party
3. Suit for price
4. Insolvency of the buyer or seller.

Risk '*Prima Facie*' Passes with Property

The general rule of law is that the 'risk' *prima facie* follows ownership. According to Section 26 of the Sale of Goods Act, 'Unless otherwise agreed, the goods remain at the seller's risk until the property therein is transferred to the buyer. But when the property therein is transferred to the buyer, the goods are at the buyer's risk whether the delivery has been made or not'. Thus, if the goods are lost or damaged by some accident or otherwise, then, subject to certain exceptions, whosoever is the owner of the goods at the time of loss or damage, shall bear the loss.

However, the parties to a contract of sale may agree that the risk will pass at the time different from the time of passing of property in the goods. The case studies in Box 9.8 drive home the point.

Box 9.8 **Passing of Risk Can Be Different from Passing of Property**

Example 1

In *Consolidated Coffee Ltd vs Coffee Board*[20], one of the terms adopted by the coffee board for auction of coffee was that property in coffee knocked down to a bidder would remain with the seller but at the buyer's risk. In such cases, the property and risk pass on at two different stages.

Example 2

In *Multanmal Chempalal vs Shah & Co.*[21], certain goods were delivered by the seller from Bombay to Bellary through a public carrier. One of the terms of the contract was that the goods were to remain the property of the seller until the price was paid, although the risk was to pass to the buyer immediately after they were conveyed to the public carrier for dispatch. However, the goods were subsequently lost before the payment of the price. It was held that since the goods were lost consequent to the passing of property therein to the buyer, the loss was to be borne by the buyer.

The guiding rule is *resperit demino,* which means the loss falls on the buyer. Thus, it is immaterial whether the price has been paid by the buyer and the goods have been delivered to him.

Exception to the rule

The proviso to Section 26, however, lays down an exception to the 'risk follows ownership' rule. It states, 'where the delivery has been delayed through the fault of either the buyer or the seller, the goods are at the risk of the party in fault as regards any loss which might not have occurred but for such fault'.

However, nothing in this section shall affect the duties or liabilities of either the seller or the buyer as a bailee of the goods of the other party [Second Proviso to Section 26].

Action Against Third Party

If after the contract of sale, there is a risk of the goods being damaged by the action of third parties, it is generally the owner who can take action and not the person who is merely in possession of the goods.

Suit for Price

Price being an integral part of a contract of sale, the seller can sue the buyer for the price when the property in goods has passed to the latter. Here it is important to note that the seller is not bound to accept the price in any form or mode except in legal tender money unless there is an agreement, express or implied, to the contrary. Hence, he cannot be compelled to accept by cheque.

Insolvency of the Buyer or Seller

If the buyer or seller becomes insolvent, it is necessary to ascertain whether the goods can be taken over by the 'official receiver' or 'official assignee'. This depends on whether the property in the goods was with the party adjudged insolvent. If the buyer is adjudged insolvent, the buyer's official receiver or official assignee shall be entitled to take the possession of the goods even though the goods have not been delivered by the seller. On the other hand, if the seller becomes insolvent before effecting delivery of the goods but the property in goods has already passed to the buyer who has paid the price, the seller's official receiver shall have no claim against the goods.

Rules Regarding Transfer of Property

The rules regarding transfer of property or ownership are contained in Sections 18 to 24. These rules can be better understood by classifying them under the following heads:

1. Transfer of property in specific or ascertained goods
2. Transfer of property in generic or unascertained goods
3. Transfer of property in goods sent 'on approval' or 'on sale or return' basis.

Transfer of Property in Specific or Ascertained Goods

Specific goods refer to goods identified and agreed upon at the time a contract of sale of goods is made. As per Section 19(1), 'where there is a contract for the sale of specific or ascertained goods, the property in them is transferred to the buyer at such time as the parties to the contract intend or want it to be transferred'.

Unless a contrary intention appears, the following rules are applicable for ascertaining the intention of the parties.

Specific goods in deliverable state

Where there is an unconditional contract for the sale of specific goods in a deliverable state, the property in the goods passes to the buyer when the contract is made. It is immaterial whether the time of payment of the price or the time of delivery of the goods, or both, is postponed [Section 20].

The analysis of this section clearly shows that the ownership of goods shall pass at the time of making the contract if the under-mentioned conditions are satisfied.

- The goods are specific
- The contract is an unconditional one, i.e., not subject to any condition regarding the transfer of ownership of goods, and
- The goods are in a deliverable state.

For example, *A* buys a TV set for ₹5000 on one month credit and asks the shopkeeper to deliver it

[20] 1980, 3 SCC 358
[21] 1970, AIR, Mysore 106

at his house. The shopkeeper agrees to do so. The TV set immediately becomes the property of *A*. Furthermore, suppose, before the delivery of the same is effected by the shopkeeper, a fire breaks out accidentally in the showroom and the TV set is destroyed. In that situation also, *A* shall remain liable to pay the price as the property in goods has already passed to him. It is interesting to note that in this case neither the price has been paid nor the goods have been delivered, even then the ownership has passed on from the seller to the buyer.

The goods are said to be in a 'deliverable state' when they are in a condition that the buyer would under the contract be bound to take delivery of them.

Specific goods not in deliverable state

According to Section 21, when there is a contract for the sale of specific goods (not in a deliverable state) and the seller has to work on them so as to make them deliverable, the property does not pass until such work has been done and the buyer has notice thereof. Simply put, it means the property in goods that are not in a deliverable state will not pass to the buyer unless 'something' is done in order to put them in a deliverable state.

Specific goods in a deliverable state but seller has to do something to ascertain the price

Where there is a contract for the sale of specific goods in a deliverable state, but the seller is bound to weigh, measure, test, or do some other act or thing with reference to the goods for the purpose of ascertaining the price, the property does not pass until such act or thing is done and the buyer has notice thereof [Section 22]. For example, *A* purchases a heap of fodder at the rate of ₹100 per quintal from *B*. However, *B*, the seller, has to weigh the fodder in order to ascertain the price of the entire quantity of fodder sold to *A*. The property in goods will pass to *A* when *B* has weighed the fodder and a notice thereof is given to *A*.

Transfer of Property in Generic and Future Goods

The property in generic or unascertained goods and future goods does not pass until the goods are ascertained. According to Section 18, 'where there is a contract for the sale of unascertained goods, no property in the goods is transferred to the buyer unless and until the goods are ascertained'.

Generic goods: Unascertained goods, having no brand name and, therefore, defined by description only.

Generic or unascertained goods are goods having no brand name and therefore defined by description only, for example, 100 quintals of wheat. These are the goods not being identified and agreed upon when the contract is made.

Transfer of Ownership When Goods Are Delivered on Approval

When goods are delivered to the buyer on approval or 'on sale or return' basis, or other similar terms, the property therein passes to the buyer

1. when the buyer signifies his/her approval or acceptance to the seller or does any other act adopting the transaction
2. if the buyer does not signify his/her approval or acceptance to the seller but retains the goods without giving notice of rejection, then on the expiration of a reasonable time if no time has been fixed for the return of the goods by the seller [Section 24].

For example, *E* delivered a horse to *B* on the terms of 'sale or return' within eight days. The horse died on the third day from the date of delivery for no fault of *B*. It was held that *E* (i.e., seller) was to bear the loss as the ownership of horse was still with him when it expired [*Elphick vs Barnes*[22]].

Rule Regarding Transfer of Title on Sale

The general rule as to transfer of property is that only the owner of goods can validly transfer the ownership in the goods to the buyer. In other words, a non-owner cannot sell the goods and transfer the ownership therein to the buyer even if the buyer has purchased them *bona fide* and for value. This general rule is expressed by the maxim '*Nemo dat quod non-*

[22] 1880, 5 C.P.D. 321

habet', which means that 'no one can pass a better title than what he himself has'. When applied to the sale of goods, this rule provides that if a person deals with the goods of another person, and without the owner's authority, such a transaction is a nullity, i.e., of no value in the eyes of the law. Thus, even a *bona fide* buyer, who buys stolen goods from a thief or from a transferee from such a thief will get no valid title to them for the thief has no title nor could he give one to any transferee. In simple words, if the seller's title is defective, the buyer's title will also be defective.

Section 27 contains the above rule, according to which, 'subject to the provisions of this Act and of any other law for the time being in force, where goods are sold by a person who is not the owner thereof and who does not sell them under the authority or with the consent of the owner, the buyer acquires no better title to the goods than what the seller had'. This simply follows that a person who does not possess the ownership of the goods cannot make a third person owner thereof.

Exceptions to the Rule

Under some exceptional circumstances the buyer gets a better title to the goods than the transferor himself has. These exceptions are as follows:

1. Sale by a mercantile agent
2. Transfer of title by estoppel
3. Sale by one of the joint owners
4. Sale by a person in possession under a voidable contract
5. Sale by seller in possession after sale
6. Sale by a buyer in possession after agreement to buy
7. Sale by an unpaid seller
8. Sale by a finder of lost goods
9. Sale by pledgee
10. Sale by official assignee or official receiver.

Sale by a mercantile agent

A buyer will get a good title from a mercantile agent who is in the possession either of the goods or documents of title of goods with the consent of the owner, and who sells the goods in the ordinary course of his business, provided the buyer buys them in good faith and for value. In a sale by mercantile agent, the buyer will acquire a good title to the goods only if the following conditions are satisfied:

1. The mercantile agent should be in the possession of the goods to sell the goods with the consent of the owner,
2. The agent should sell the goods while acting in the ordinary course of business as a mercantile agent, and
3. The buyer must act in good faith, i.e., at the time of the contract he must have no knowledge that the agent had no authority to sell. The following case law is an illustration in point. In *Folks vs King*[23], *F*, the owner of the car, instructed a mercantile agent to sell the car at a stipulated price and not below that. But the agent sold the car to *A*, a *bona fide* buyer, below the stipulated price and misappropriated the proceeds. The buyer (*A*) resold the car to *K*, the defendant. It was held that *A* had obtained a good title to the car from the mercantile agent and conveyed a good title to *K*, the ultimate buyer, and therefore *F*, the real owner cannot recover the car from *K*.

Transfer of title by estoppel

As we have learnt earlier, *estoppel* arises when a person by his/her words or conduct makes another person believe that certain state of affairs existed. He/she is later on not allowed to deny that such a state of affairs did not exist. Applying this rule to a contract of sale of goods, where the true owner of the goods by his act or omission leads an innocent buyer to believe that the seller has the authority to sell, later on he may be prevented from denying the seller's authority to sell.

Sale by one of the joint owners

Section 28 provides, if one of several joint owners of goods has the sole possession thereof, with the permission of the others, the property in the goods is transferred to any person who buys them from such joint owner for value and without being aware of the fact that the seller has no authority to sell, the buyer will acquire a good title thereto. Ordinarily, a co-owner can only transfer his/her share, i.e., the buyer would obtain only the title of the co-owner. But this section enables a co-owner to sell not only his/her share but also of other co-owners (provided the co-owner was in possession with the consent of

[23] 1923, 1 K.B. 282

Box 9.9 **Transfer of Title by Estoppel**

Example 1

A sells the goods of *B* to *C* in his presence. *B* does not raise any objections to it. Here, *C* will get a good title. In this case, if *B*, the real owner subsequently decides to deny *A* the authority to sell the goods, he (*B*) may be estoppel from doing so and the sale will be binding on *B*.

the other co-owners) and, thereby, constitutes an exception to the rule that 'no one can give what he has not got'. For instance, *A*, *B*, and *C* are the joint-owners of a car. With the consent of *B* and *C*, the car was in the custody of *A*. *A* sells the car to *P* who purchases it for value. Without notice of the fact that *A* had no authority to sell, *P* gets a good title to the goods as he acted *bona fide* and for value.

Sale by a person in possession under a voidable contract

As per Section 29, if a person has obtained possession of goods under a contract that is voidable on the ground of fraud, misrepresentation, coercion, or undue influence, and he sells those goods to a *bona fide* buyer before the contract has been rescinded, the buyer of such goods acquires a good title thereto. This exception is limited to contract of sale of goods obtained under a contract voidable under Sections 19 or 19 A of the Indian Contract Act[24]. For the application of this exception, the following conditions must be satisfied:

1. the seller is in possession of goods under a voidable contract,
2. the goods are sold before the contract has been rescinded, and
3. the buyer procures the goods in good faith and for value.

For example, *A* by misrepresentation induces *B*, a jeweller, to sell and deliver to him a diamond ring. This contract is voidable at the option of *B* under Section 19 or 19A of the Indian Contract Act. But before *B* could rescind the contract, *A* resells the ring to *C* who buys it for value in good faith. Thus, without notice of *A's* defective title C acquires a good title.

[24] A contract is voidable under Section 19 or 19A of the Indian Contract Act on the ground of coercion, undue influence, misrepresentation, or fraud.

Sale by a seller in possession of goods after sale

Section 30(1) provides, 'where a seller, after having sold the goods, continues in possession of goods or of the document of title to the goods, and again sells them himself or through his mercantile agent to a person who buys for value and without notice of the previous sale, such a buyer gets a good title to the goods'. For example, *A* buys a TV set from *B*. Although the TV set was in a deliverable state at the time of purchase, yet *A* leaves it with *B* for the time being. In the mean time, *B* sells the same TV set to *C* who buys the same *bona fide* and without knowledge about the previous sale. *C* acquires a good title to the goods.

Sale by a buyer in possession after 'agreement to buy'

If a person who has bought or agreed to buy goods, obtains with the seller's consent, possession of the goods or of the document of title to them, any sale by him/her or his/her mercantile agent to a second buyer who takes in good faith without notice of any lien or other claim of the original seller against the goods, will give a good title to the second buyer. For example, *A* sells his car for a certain price to *B* on installment basis with a condition that *A* will remain the owner of the car till the last installment is paid. After paying few installments, *B* disposed of the car for an agreed price to *C* who bought the same in good faith and without knowledge about any amount due to *A* (the real owner). *C* acquires a good title to the goods.

Sale by an unpaid seller

As per Section 54(3), where an unpaid seller has exercised his right of lien or stoppage in transit and is in possession of the goods, he may resell them and the second buyer will get a good title to the goods as against the original buyer even if no notice of the resale has been given to the original buyer. We shall learn about this topic in greater detail in the next chapter.

Sale by a finder of the lost goods

Section 169 of the Indian Contract Act, 1872, provides that a finder of lost goods has the power to sell them under certain circumstances and the buyer will acquire an absolute title thereto. Accordingly, a finder of lost goods can sell such goods under the following conditions:

1. The real owner cannot be found with reasonable search and diligence;
2. If found, he/she refuses to reimburse the lawful charges incurred by the finder in respect of the goods found;
3. If the goods found are highly perishable or likely to lose the substantial part of its mercantile value; or
4. If the lawful charges of the finder, in respect of the thing found, amount to two-thirds or more of its value.

Sale by a pledgee

On default of the pawnor or pledger to repay a loan, or on the failure of the performance of the promise at the stipulated time, the pawnee or pledgee has a right to sell the goods pledged with him/her after giving a reasonable notice to the pawner. In such a case, the pawnee, even though not being the owner of the goods, can sell the goods and convey a good title to the buyer.

Sale by official assignee or official receiver, liquidator

The official assignee or official receiver under the Presidency Towns Insolvency Act or Provincial Towns Insolvency Act and the liquidator, under the Companies Act, although not the owners of a property (or goods), can convey better title than they have under certain circumstances.

Delivery of Goods

Delivery in the Sale of Goods Act is defined as a voluntary transfer of possession from one person to another [Section 2(2)]. Thus, to effect a valid delivery, goods from one person to another must be transferred willingly and not by means of fraud, theft, or force, etc. Mere possession of goods does not amount to delivery of goods.

Delivery: Voluntary transfer of possession of goods from one person to another.

Modes of Delivery

Delivery of goods sold may be made by doing anything that the parties agree, shall be treated as delivery or which has the effect of putting the goods in the possession of the buyer or of any person authorised to hold them on his/her behalf [Section 33].

Accordingly, delivery of goods may be made in any of the following three ways:

Actual delivery

Also known as 'physical delivery', 'actual delivery' takes place when the goods are physically handed over by the seller or his/her authorised agent to the buyer or his/her agent authorised to take possession of the goods. For example, *A*, the seller of a car, hands the car over to *B*, the buyer; it is a case of actual delivery of the goods.

Actual delivery: Goods physically handed over by the seller or his/her authorised agent to the buyer or his/her authorised agent.

Symbolic delivery

Where the goods are bulky and heavy and it is not possible to physically hand them over to the buyer, delivery thereof may be made by indicating or giving a symbol. Here the goods itself are not delivered, but the 'means of obtaining possession' of goods are delivered. For example, delivering the keys of the warehouse where the goods are stored, or the keys of a purchased car to its buyer, bill of lading which will entitle the holder to receive the goods on arrival of the ship.

Symbolic delivery: Delivery of means of obtaining possession of goods.

Constructive delivery

In this case neither physical nor symbolic delivery is made. In constructive delivery, the person in possession of the goods acknowledges that he holds the goods on behalf of and at the disposal

Box 9.10 **Effect of Part-delivery [Section 34]**

Example 1

A sold certain goods to *B* lying at a wharf. The seller directed the wharfingers to deliver the goods to *B*. *B* weighed all the goods and took away a part of them. It was held that the delivery amounted to a delivery of whole of the goods [*Hammond vs Anderson*[25]].

Example 2

A sold a stake of hay, grown on his field to *B*. The buyer was permitted to remove only a part of it and *B* acted accordingly. It was held that this did not amount to delivery of the whole, as the intentions of the parties were to separate the part delivered from the rest of hay [*Bunnery vs Poyntz*[26]].

Constructive delivery: Acknowledgment by the person, in possession of goods, that he/she holds the goods on behalf of and at the disposal of the buyer.

of the buyer. Constructive delivery is also called attornment. This type of delivery may be effected in the following three ways:

1. Where the seller, after having sold the goods, agrees to hold them as bailee for the buyer;
2. Where the buyer, who is already in possession of the goods as bailee of the seller, holds them as his own, after the sale; and
3. Where a third party, for example, a carrier/transporter, who holds the goods, as bailee for the seller, agrees and acknowledges holding them for the buyer.

Rules Regarding Delivery of Goods

The following rules apply with respect to delivery of goods.

Effect of delivery

Whether the delivery is actual, symbolic, or constructive, it should have the effect of putting the goods in the possession of the buyer or his/her authorised agent. Thus, an effective delivery is one that enables the buyer to exercise his/her contract over the goods [Section 33].

Delivery and payment are concurrent conditions

Unless otherwise agreed, the delivery of goods and payment of price are concurrent conditions, i.e., the seller should be ready and willing to give possession of the goods to the buyer, who in turn should be ready and willing to pay the price in exchange for possession of goods simultaneously [Section 32].

Effect of part-delivery

A delivery of part of the goods in progress of the delivery of the whole has the same effect for the purpose of passing the property in such goods, as a delivery of the whole. But where part delivery is made with the intention of severing it from the whole lot, then it does not operate as a delivery of the whole of the goods [Section 34]. The case illustrations in Box 9.10 would help understand the point better.

Buyer to apply for delivery

In the absence of any express term to do so, the seller is not bound to deliver the goods unless the buyer applies for delivery [Section 35]. Even where the goods to be delivered are to be acquired or procured by the seller, the duty of the seller ends with intimating the buyer that the goods have been procured and are ready for delivery. In such cases also, it is the duty of the buyer to demand delivery, and if he/she fails to do so, he/she can have no cause of action against the seller. The parties to the contract of sale may, however, agree otherwise.

Place of delivery

The place of delivery is usually stated in the contract. Where it is so stated, the goods must be delivered at the stipulated place during business hours on a working day. But where no place is mentioned, then

[25] 1803, 13 & P.N.R. 69; RR 763
[26] 1833, 4 B & Ad. 568; R.R. 309

in accordance with Section 36(1) the following rules shall apply:

1. In case of actual sale, the goods sold are to be delivered at the place at which they are at the time of sale.
2. In case of an agreement to sell, the goods agreed to be sold are to be delivered at the place decided at the time of the agreement.

In case, at the time of agreement to sell, the goods are not in existence, they are to be delivered at the place at which they are manufactured or produced.

Time of delivery

The contract may expressly specify the time for delivery of goods. When it is so specified, the seller is bound to deliver the goods to the buyer within the specified time. But where no time for sending them is fixed, then the delivery must be made within a reasonable time [Section 36(2)]. What is 'reasonable time' is a question of fact. It varies from case to case depending on the facts and circumstances of each particular case.

Delivery when goods are in possession of third party

Where the goods at the time of sale are in the possession of a third person, there is no delivery by the seller unless and until such third person acknowledges to the buyer that he holds the goods on his behalf. As already commented, such a delivery is termed as 'constructive delivery' or 'attornment' and requires the consent of all the three parties, i.e., the seller, the buyer, and the person having possession of the goods. Thus, in such a case the 'delivery order' will not do anything unless the seller's agent who is in the possession of goods has consented thereto [Section 36(3)].

Expenses of delivery

Unless otherwise agreed, the expenses of and incidental to putting the goods into a deliverable state shall be borne by the seller. Similarly, the expenses of and incidental to receiving delivery must be borne by the buyer [Section 36(5)].

Delivery of wrong quantity

The seller is bound to deliver the goods according to the contract. The delivery of goods should be in the quantity contracted for. Any delivery less or more than the contracted quantity is treated as defective delivery or delivery of wrong quantity. Section 37 recognises three cases of wrong delivery, viz., short delivery, excess delivery, or mixed delivery. The rules vis-à-vis delivery of wrong quantity in each of the three types is as follows.

Short delivery Where the seller delivers to the buyer a quantity of goods less than what he contracted to sell, the buyer may reject them. But if he (buyer) accepts the goods so delivered, he shall pay for them at the contract rate [Section 37(1)]. However, by accepting the delivery of lesser quantity, the buyer is not debarred from suing the seller for damages for short delivery of the goods. For example, a seller agreed to sell and supply to a buyer 10 bags of basmati rice at an agreed price of ₹1000 per bag. The seller could, however, deliver only six bags to the buyer. The buyer is entitled to reject the goods on account of short delivery. But if he accepts these six bags, he will have to pay for them at the rate of ₹1000 per bag. He may, nevertheless, claim damages from the seller for short delivery of the goods.

Excess delivery Where the seller delivers to the buyer a quantity of goods larger than he contracted to sell, the buyer has the option

1. to accept the contracted quantity and reject the rest, or
2. to reject the whole quantity, or
3. to accept the whole quantity [Section 37(2)].

If the buyer accepts the whole of the goods so delivered, he shall become liable to pay for all the goods at the contract rate. For example, *A* agrees to sell and delivers to *B* 50 quintal of wheat at an agreed rate of ₹5000 per quintal. Instead *A* delivers 55 quintals. Now it is up to the buyer, *B*, to reject the whole lot, or accept only 50 quintals and reject the excess, or accept the whole lot and pay for them at the contract rate.

Mixed delivery Where the seller delivers to the buyer the goods he contracted to sell, mixed with goods of a different description not included in the contract, the buyer may accept the goods, which are in accordance with the contract and reject the rest, or may reject the whole lot [Section 37(3)]. For example, *A* agrees to sell and deliver 100 bags of 'Aahar' flour, each of 5 kg to *B* at the rate of ₹65 per bag. But *A* delivers 90 bags of 'Aahar' flour brand and 10 bags of 'Rose' brand. In this case, the buyer *B* can either reject the whole quantity of flour or may accept 90 bags of 'Aahar' brand and reject 10 bags of 'Rose' brand. In case of the latter, he will have to pay only for 90 bags of 'Aahar' brand at the rate of ₹65 per bag.

It should be noted that, if the buyer rejects the whole lot on ground of delivery of wrong quantity, it does not result in cancellation of the contract. The seller still has the right to deliver the goods contracted for again and the buyer shall be bound to accept the same [*Vilas Udyog Ltd vs Prag Vanaspati*[27]].

Moreover, the above provisions are subject to any usage of trade, special agreement of dealing between the parties [Section 37(4)].

Installment deliveries

Unless otherwise agreed, the buyer of goods is not bound to accept delivery thereof by installments [Section 38(1)]. It means that if the parties so agree, the delivery of the goods can be made by installments. In other words, the delivery of goods by installments may be made and demanded only if the contract of sale provides for the same either expressly or impliedly.

For example, in *Richardson vs Dunn*[28], *A*, a coal merchant, agreed to sell to *B* 200 tons of coal. But *A* shipped only 152 tons and intimated about the same. But the buyer didn't reply. It was held, that the buyer (*B*) impliedly assented to the delivery of coal in installments.

Sometimes, there may be a contract for delivering the goods by installments and each installment of goods is to be separately paid for. In such a case, the problem arises when there is a breach either by the seller or the buyer, i.e.,

- The seller makes no delivery or defective delivery in respect of one or more installments or
- The buyer neglects or refuses to take delivery of or pay for one or more installments.

In such a situation, the issue is whether the whole contract is to be treated as repudiated or only one installment is repudiated for which the party may claim damages and the rest of the installments are to be duly delivered and accepted [Section 38(2)].

[27] 1803, 13 & P.N.R. 69; RR 763
[28] 1841, 2 Q.B. 218

In *Maple Flock Co Ltd vs Universal Furniture Products (Wembley) Ltd*[29], *M* agreed to supply to *U* 10 tons of flock in 20 installments. The first 15 installments were delivered as per the terms of the contract but the 16th installment was defective. However, the subsequent deliveries were again satisfactory. The buyer wanted to repudiate the whole contract. It was held that the buyer could not treat the whole contract as repudiated because the circumstances of the case showed that there was no possibility of the default being repeated.

Deterioration of goods in transit [Section 40]

If the goods are to be delivered at a place other than that where they are when sold at the risk of the seller, the risk of deterioration of goods in transit will, unless otherwise agreed, be borne by the buyer. [Section 40]

Acceptance of Delivery by Buyer

As described at the beginning of this chapter, for the performance of a contract of sale, it is necessary that when the seller delivers the goods according to the contract, the buyer accepts them and pays the price, if not already paid for. In other words, a contract of sale of goods is said to be duly performed when the goods are accepted and duly paid for by the buyer. Here, it is important to note that the mere fact that the buyer has accepted the goods and taken possession thereof does not amount to acceptance of goods. In the eyes of the law, 'acceptance' is something more than this. Section 42 provides that a buyer is considered to have accepted the goods in any of the following circumstances:

1. When he/she intimates to the seller that he/she has accepted the goods.
2. When he/she does any act in relation to the goods which is inconsistent with the ownership of the seller. For example, when the buyer uses, consumes, pledges, resells, etc., in the capacity of an owner.

   Dealing with the document of title, however, does not amount to acceptance [*Chao vs British Traders & Shippers Ltd*[30]]. In *Hardy & Co vs Hillens & Fowlers*[31], *A* sold a certain quantity

[29] 1943, 1 K.B. 148
[30] ALLER 779
[31] 1923, 2 K.B. 409, C.A.

of wheat to *B* and conveyed the same by ship. On the arrival of the ship, *B* took the delivery of the wheat and subsequently sold a part of it, and afterwards found that the wheat was not in accordance with the contract in terms of quality and, therefore, sought to reject it by giving a notice to the seller. It was held that the buyer had lost the right of rejection as he had accepted the wheat by a dealing, inconsistent with the right of the seller, insofar as he sold out a portion of it, and the notice of rejection was ineffective.

3. When after the lapse of a reasonable time, he retains the goods without intimating to the seller that he has rejected them.

Buyer's right of examining the goods

Before intimating to the seller about his acceptance, the buyer has a right to examine and test the goods with a view to ascertaining and satisfying himself whether the goods are in accordance with the contract in terms of quality as well as quantity. In this regard, Section 41 provides as under.

- 'Where goods are delivered to the buyer, which he has not previously examined, he is not deemed to have accepted them unless and until he has had a reasonable opportunity of examining them for the purpose of ascertaining whether they are in conformity with the contract' [Section 41(1)].
- 'Unless otherwise agreed, when the seller tenders delivery of goods to the buyer, he is bound, on request, to afford the buyer a reasonable opportunity of examining the goods for the purpose of ascertaining whether they are in conformity with the contract' [Section 41(2)].

Buyer not bound to return rejected goods

Unless otherwise agreed, where goods are delivered to the buyer and he refuses to accept them, having the right to do so, he is not bound to return them to the seller. It is sufficient, if he intimates to the seller that he has refused to accept them [Section 43].

Liability of the buyer for neglecting or refusing to take delivery

When the seller is ready and willing to deliver the goods and requests the buyer to take delivery, and the buyer does not within a reasonable time after such request take delivery of the goods, he is liable to the seller for

1. any loss occasioned by his neglect or refusal to take delivery and also
2. a reasonable charge for the care and custody of the goods.

Furthermore, nothing in this section shall affect the rights of the seller where the neglect or refusal of the buyer to take delivery amounts to a repudiation of the contract [Proviso to Section 44]. To put in simple words, the seller in such a case may sue for the price for damages.

Rights of Unpaid Seller and Rights of Buyer

Who is an Unpaid Seller?

An unpaid seller is one who has not received the full price of the goods sold by him. Section 45 of the Sale of Goods Act defines an unpaid seller as under.

Unpaid seller: The seller who has not received the full price of the goods sold by him.

'The seller of goods is deemed to be an unpaid seller

1. When whole of the price has not been paid or tendered, or
2. When a bill of exchange or other negotiable instrument has been received as conditional payment and the condition on which it has been received has not been fulfilled by reason of the dishonour of the instrument or otherwise'.

A closer look of this section makes it clear that a seller is considered to be an unpaid seller when

1. The goods have been sold and the price is overdue.
2. The full price has not been paid or tendered to the seller.
3. A bill of exchange or other negotiable instrument made a conditional payment, and the instrument has been dishonoured.

Thus, where a major part of the price has been paid and only a small portion remains unpaid, the seller is still deemed as unpaid. However, the seller ceases to be unpaid where the buyer has tendered whole of the price but the seller has refused to accept it.

Similarly, a seller in respect of credit sales cannot be termed as unpaid unless the credit period has expired and the buyer has not paid the price in full. Yet, if during the credit period, the buyer becomes insolvent, the seller becomes an unpaid seller even before the expiry of the credit period. Finally, it should be taken into account that it is only non-payment of price that may render a seller an unpaid one. If the price has been paid but some other expenses incidental to delivery, such as, cartage, loading, and unloading expenses, toll tax, etc., remain unpaid, the seller cannot be termed as an unpaid one.

The term 'seller' in this chapter includes any person who is in the position to sell, as, for instance, an agent of the seller to whom the bill of lading has been endorsed, or a consignor who himself/herself has paid, or is directly responsible for the recovery of price. Thus, the protection has been extended by the Act to the seller's agent, consignor, etc., as well. Box 9.11 presents various instances when a seller can be rendered as an unpaid one.

Rights of an Unpaid Seller

The rights of an unpaid seller can be classified under two heads:

1. Rights against the goods
2. Rights against the buyer.

Rights Against Goods

The Act confers the following four rights to an unpaid seller against the goods:

- Right of lien or retention
- Right of stoppage of goods in transit
- Right of resale
- Right to withhold delivery.

Right of lien or retention

The term 'lien' implies retaining the possession of the goods until the price due in respect of the same is paid or tendered. As per Section 47, an unpaid seller of goods who is in possession of them is entitled to retain possession of them until payment or tender of the price under the following conditions:

- Where the goods have been sold without any stipulation as to credit.
- Where the goods have been sold on credit, but the term of credit has expired.
- Where the buyer becomes insolvent (even though the credit period has not expired).

The term insolvent should not be confused with a person who has been adjudged insolvent under the Insolvency Law. In Sale of Goods Act, an insolvent person is one who has ceased to pay his debts in the ordinary course of business or is unable to pay his debts when they become due, whether he has committed an act of insolvency or not [Section 2(8)].

The seller may exercise his right of lien no matter whether he is in possession of the goods, merely as an agent or bailee for the buyer.

The real test of exercising the right of lien subsists in the fact whether the property in goods has passed

Box 9.11 The Unpaid Seller [Section 45]

Example 1

A sold certain goods to *B* for ₹5000. *B* cleared the payment by cheque. On presentment, the cheque was dishonoured. *A* is unpaid seller.

Example 2

A purchased a music system from *B*'s showroom for ₹20,000. *A* paid ₹10,000 instantly and agreed to pay the balance one month later. *B* is not an unpaid seller during this credit period. But, *B* shall become an unpaid seller, if *A* does not discharge his liability on expiry of the credit period of one month.

In the above case, *B* may become an unpaid seller before the expiry of one month (i.e., credit period) in case of *A*'s insolvency.

Lien: Retention of possession of goods until the price thereof is paid or duly tendered.

to the buyer. If the seller still retains the title, then it will be anomalous or incorrect to state that the seller has a lien against his own goods. Technically, this should be termed as 'a right of withholding delivery' and not 'a right to retain possession of goods (lien)'.

Moreover, the seller can exercise the right of lien exclusively for non-payment of the price. He cannot retain the goods for any other charges, such as maintenance charges and storage cost borne by him during the possession of the goods on behalf of the buyer. Box 9.12 presents examples that make clear the circumstances when an unpaid seller can exercise his right to lien.

Rules regarding the right of lien The following legal provisions are relevant to an unpaid seller's right of lien and guide the course of action in various situations. They may be studied under the following 10 heads.

The seller must possess the goods The seller's possession over the goods is the first prerequisite to exercise a right of lien. In other words, the right of lien is lost along with the possession of goods.

In case of cash sale Where the goods have been sold without any stipulation as to credit, the unpaid seller may retain the goods if the buyer fails to pay or tender the whole price upon delivery [Section 47(1)(a)].

In case of credit sale Where the goods have been sold on credit, the seller may retain the goods if the buyer fails to pay the whole price after the expiry of credit period [Section 47(1)(b)]. This implies, in case of credit sales, the right of lien cannot be exercised during the period of credit.

In case of buyer insolvency Where the buyer becomes insolvent, the unpaid seller can retain the possession of the goods [Section 47(1)(c)]. In the case of buyer's insolvency, the unpaid seller can exercise his right of lien even before the expiry of the credit period.

In case of part delivery Where an unpaid seller has made part delivery of the goods, he may exercise his right of lien on the remainder, unless such part delivery has been made under such circumstances, as to show an agreement, to waive the lien [Section 48]. In other words, the right of lien is lost where part delivery is intended as delivery of the whole.

Subject matter-price As a matter of fact, the right of lien can only be exercised against non-payment of price and not for incidental charges such as freight, godown rent, and interest.

Where documents of title have already been delivered Mere delivery of document(s) of title to the goods cannot prevent an unpaid seller exercise his right of lien if he is in actual possession of the goods.

The right of lien is absolute The right of lien being absolute, the unpaid seller is entitled to refuse to deliver a part of the goods against payment of a proportionate price by the buyer.

When the seller possesses the goods otherwise The right of lien can be exercised even if the unpaid seller

Box 9.12 Right to Lien: When Can It Be Exercised?

Example 1

A sold certain goods to *B* for ₹10,000 and allowed him to pay the price within a month. *B*, the buyer, becomes insolvent during the period of credit. *A* being the unpaid seller can retain the possession of the goods for non-payment of the price by *B*.

Example 2

A sells his car to *B*. The price is to be paid within a month of the sale. While the vehicle is still in the possession of *A*, he issues the sale letter in favour of *B* and hands over other documents of title to him. *B*, however, does not pay the price within the stipulated period. *A* being an unpaid seller is entitled to refuse to deliver the car until the price is paid. Transfer of documents of title to the goods does not impede the right of lien. The right of lien, as a matter of fact, is linked with the possession of goods and not with the property therein.

is in possession of the goods in any other capacity, such as an agent or a bailee.

Where the seller has obtained a decree for the price of the goods The unpaid seller of goods, having a lien thereon, does not lose his lien by reason only that he has obtained a decree (i.e, court order) for the recovery of the price of the goods [Section 49(2)].

Termination of lien The lien depends on physical possession. This means an unpaid seller can exercise his right of lien on the goods for non-payment of the price in full so long as he is in actual possession of the goods. The moment possession is lost, the lien is also lost. The unpaid seller of goods loses his lien thereon in the following five cases:

1. When he delivers the goods to a carrier or other bailee for subsequent transmission of the same without reserving the right of disposal of the goods [Section 49(1)(a)]. The reason for the same is that, delivery to the carrier amounts to delivery to the buyer and, therefore, right of lien is lost.
2. An unpaid seller also loses his right of lien, when the buyer or his/her agent lawfully obtains possession of the goods [Section 49(1)(b)]. Furthermore, where goods are delivered back (i.e., after obtaining the lawful possession) to the seller for some specific purpose, e.g., repair, lien does not revive [*Eduljee vs John Bros*[32]].
3. The lien is lost by waiver thereof [Section 49(1)(c)]. The seller is free to waive his right of lien expressly or impliedly. An express waiver takes place where the contract of sale provides in express terms that the seller shall not be entitled to retain the possession of the goods, even if the price is not paid, whereas an implied waiver occurs when the contract of sale implies that the seller will not exercise his right of lien. For example, where the seller grants fresh terms of credit or allows the buyer to accept a bill of exchange payable at a future date or agrees to a sub-sale, which the buyer may have made, there is an implied waiver.
4. By tender of the price by the buyer. When the buyer tenders the price but the seller refuses to accept the same, the right of lien is lost as he ceases to be an unpaid seller.
5. By subsequent sale by the buyer where property in the goods has been lawfully passed to the buyer and, thereby, it transfers the same to someone else who obtains it for a consideration and in good faith and the seller has assented to it, the unpaid seller's right of lien is defeated [Proviso to Section 53(1)].

Right of stoppage in transit

The right of stoppage of goods in transit implies preventing the goods from being delivered to the buyer, resuming possession, thereof, while in transit and retaining them until payment or tender of the price. This right is earned only when the lien is lost. In one sense, the right of stoppage in transit is an extension of right of lien as by exercising this right, the unpaid seller regains possession of the goods.

When can this right be exercised? According to Section 50, 'subject to the provisions of this Act, when the buyer of the goods becomes insolvent, the unpaid seller who has parted with the possession of the goods has the right of stopping them in transit, that is to say, he may resume possession of the goods as long as they are in the course of transit, and may retain them until payment or tender of the price'.

The analysis of this Section shows that in order to exercise the right of stoppage in transit, the following conditions must be fulfilled:

1. The seller is unpaid;
2. The property has passed to the buyer;
3. The buyer has become insolvent; and
4. The goods are in transit, i.e., neither with the seller nor with the buyer or his agent.

The right of lien can be exercised only for non-payment of price. That is, the right of stoppage in transit shall be available to an unpaid seller until payment or tender of price, i.e., seller will lose this right, the moment the price is paid or tendered by the buyer.

The right of stopping the goods in transit can be exercised only when the goods are in the course of transit.

Stoppage in transit: How is it effected?

The unpaid seller may exercise his right of stoppage in transit either

- by taking actual possession of the goods or
- by giving notice of his claim to the carrier or other bailee in whose possession the goods are.

[32] 1943, AIR Nag 249

Such notice may be given either to the person in actual possession of the goods or to his/her agent. In case the notice is given to the principal, to be effectual, it must be given at such a time and under such circumstances that the principal, by exercise of reasonable diligence, may communicate it to his servant or agent in time, so as to prevent a delivery to the buyer [Section 52(1)].

Right of resale

As per Section 54, a seller who is in possession of self-sold goods that have not been paid for by the buyer is entitled to resell them in the following circumstances.

Where the goods are of perishable nature In case goods sold are perishable, the unpaid seller can resell them after the expiry of reasonable time. He does not need to serve any notice to the original buyer in such a case. Significantly, perishability of the goods is not restricted only to their physical deterioration but also implies commercial atrophy of the same.

Where the seller expressly reserves such right Where the seller expressly reserves a right of re-sale, in case the buyer defaults in payment, the unpaid seller may resell the goods when the buyer defaults. In such a case the original contract of sale will of course be rescinded but without prejudice to any claim which the seller may have for damages.

Where the unpaid seller gives notice to buyer of his intention to resell Having exercised the right of lien or stoppage in transit, the unpaid seller should give notice to the buyer of his/her intention to resell. If the buyer does not, within a reasonable time, pay or tender the price, the unpaid seller may re-sell the goods within a reasonable time. In such a case the unpaid seller will also be entitled to recover from the original buyer damages for any loss occasioned by his/her breach of contract.

Right to withhold delivery

Where the property in goods has not passed to the buyer, the unpaid seller, in addition to the remedies discussed hitherto, has a right to withhold delivery, similar to and co-extensive with his rights of lien and stoppage-in-transit, where the property has passed to the buyer [Section 46(2)].

Rights of Unpaid Seller Against Buyer

In addition to the rights against the goods, an unpaid seller has certain remedies against the buyer personally. These rights are as follows:

1. Suit for Price
2. Suit for damages for non-acceptance
3. Suit for damages for repudiating contract before due date
4. Suit for interest and special damages.

Suit for price

The buyer is legally bound to pay the price for the goods he/she has purchased. Where under a contract of sale the property in the goods has passed to the buyer and he/she wrongfully neglects or refuses to pay for the goods as per the terms of the contract, the seller may sue him/her for the price of the goods [Section 55(1)].

On the other hand, if the property in goods has not passed to the buyer, as a general rule, the seller can only sue for damages; he cannot file a suit for the price. However, as per Section 55(2), 'where under a contract of sale the price is payable on a certain day irrespective of delivery and the buyer wrongfully neglects or refuses to pay such price, the seller may sue him for the price, although the property in goods has not passed and the goods have not been appropriated to the contract'.

Suit for damages for non-acceptance

'Where the buyer wrongfully neglects or refuses to accept and pay for the goods, the seller may sue him for the damages for non-acceptance' [Section 56].

What should be the amount of damages, however, is to be calculated in accordance with the rules contained in Sections 73 and 74 of the Indian Contract Act, 1972, which may briefly be summarised as follows:

1. Where the goods in question have a ready market, the conventional rule is that the seller may recover from the buyer damages equal to the difference between the contract price and the market price on the date of the breach of the contract, if the market price exceeds the contract price.

2. Where the goods do not have a ready market, the measure of damages will depend on the facts of each case. As a general rule, the damages in such a case will be equal to the estimated loss arising directly and naturally in the ordinary course of events, from the buyer's breach of contract. For instance, where the goods have been manufactured on some special order, and the buyer wrongfully neglects or refuses to accept the delivery and pay for the same, then the seller will be entitled to full price of the goods as damages, for the simple reason that such goods may not be saleable or may have no commercial value for other buyers.

Suit for damages for repudiating contract before due date

If the buyer repudiates the contract before the due date of delivery of goods, the seller may either treat the contract as subsisting or wait till the due date of delivery, or he may treat the contract as rescinded and sue for damages for the breach. In the latter case, amount of damages will be determined according to the price prevailing on the date of breach and the contract price. But where the seller treats the contract subsisting (i.e., operative) and waits till the due date of delivery, then the buyer may demand the goods when the date of delivery arrives and the seller will be bound to deliver the goods. In such a situation, the unpaid seller can claim damages only if the buyer repudiates the contract on the due date of delivery of the goods.

Suit for interest and special damages

Section 61 entitles an unpaid seller to recover interest or special damages in any case where by law, interest or special damages may be recoverable. This section also acknowledges that in the absence of a contract to the contrary, the court may award interest at a reasonable rate to the seller on the amount he is entitled to recover from the buyer. The interest may be calculated from the date of the tender of the goods or from the date on which the price was payable. It is important to note that the seller can claim interest only when he is entitled to recover the price. If the unpaid seller has the only remedy to claim damages, then he will not be entitled to any interest.

Buyer's Rights Against a Seller

There are certain rights that can be exercised by the buyer against the seller if the latter is in default. These rights can be discussed under the following heads:

1. Suit for damages for non-delivery
2. Suit for specific performance
3. Suit for damages for breach of warranty
4. Suit for damages for rescission of contract before due date
5. Suit for recovery of price along with interest.

Suit for Damages for Non-Delivery

Where the seller wrongfully neglects or refuses to deliver the goods to the buyer, the latter can sue the seller for damages for non-delivery. What shall be the amount of damages, however, will be determined in accordance with the rules contained in Section 73 of the Indian Contract Act. The prevailing principle in this regard is that the amount of damages shall be equal to the estimated loss resulting directly and spontaneously in the ordinary course of events due to the seller's breach of contract. In case of non-delivery of goods, the buyer shall, of course, be entitled to the price, if paid already.

Suit for Specific Performance

Where the seller rescinds a contract of sale of specific or ascertained goods, the buyer may file a suit for the specific performance of the contract. The court may then, if it deems fit, on the application of the plaintiff, pass the order for specific performance, i.e., compel the seller to deliver the goods he/she has agreed to sell notwithstanding that he/she is ready to pay compensation for breach of contract. However, this remedy is available to the buyer only if

1. The goods are of unique nature and
2. The damages or compensation is not an equitable remedy.

For instance, *A* agreed to sell a rare painting of Mughal period to *B* for ₹10,000. Later on, *A* refused to deliver the same to the buyer on due date. *B* may approach the court for granting him an order compelling *A* to specifically perform his promise. That is, *A* is bound to deliver the painting to *B* at the price as agreed between the two.

Suit for Damages for Breach of Warranty

Where there is a breach of warranty by the seller, or where breach of condition on the part of the seller is to be treated as a breach of warranty, the buyer can claim damages from the seller if the price has already been paid. But if the buyer has not yet paid the price, he may deduct from the price, the loss suffered by him and tender the balance.

Suit for Damages for Rescission of Contract Before Due Date

Where the seller rescinds the contract before due date of delivery, the buyer may either treat the contract as subsisting (i.e., existing and operative) and wait until the expiry of due date of delivery or treat the contract repudiated and bring an action against the seller for the recovery of the damages. In the latter case, the buyer need not wait till the date of delivery to sue the seller for the breach.

Suit for Recovery of the Price Along with Interest

Where the price has already been paid by the buyer and the seller fails to deliver the goods on due date, or the title of the goods supplied is defective, e.g., goods supplied are stolen ones, the buyer can sue the seller for not only the refund of the price but also for interest thereon. The interest will be calculated at a reasonable rate from the date of payment of the price up to the date of refund [Section 61].

Auction Sale

Auction sale: A public event at which things are sold to the person who offers the highest price for them.

The term auction refers to a public event at which things are sold to the person who offers the highest price for them. An auction sale, in fact, is one of the modes of disposing the goods. In an auction sale, intended buyers, called bidders, assemble at one place and offer the price (known as bid) at which they are ready to buy the goods. The goods are ultimately sold to the highest bidder. The owner of the goods may organise an auction sale directly or he may appoint an auctioneer on this behalf. The relationship between the owner of the goods and the auctioneer, as we learnt earlier, is that of a principal and an agent.

Rules Regarding Sale by Auction

The various seven rules regarding sale by auction are as follows:

1. Where goods are put up for an auction sale in lots, each lot is *prima facie* deemed to be the subject of a separate contract of sale [Section 64(1)].
2. The sale is complete when the auctioneer announces its completion by the fall of hammer or in any other customary manner, and, until such announcement is made, any bidder may retract or withdraw his bid [Section 64(2)]. On the completion of the sale, the property in the goods immediately passes to the buyer if the goods are specific or ascertained and are in a deliverable state.
3. A right to bid may be reserved expressly by or on behalf of the seller and, where such right is expressly so reserved, but not otherwise, the seller or any one person on his behalf, may bid at the auction [Section 64(3)]. This right is granted to the seller so as to enable him to safeguard his interests in case the bidders agree not to outbid each other.
4. If the seller makes use of pretended bidding to raise the price, the sale is voidable at the option of the buyer [Section 64(6)]. Sellers sometimes employ some persons, called puffers, to raise the price of goods or to counter any negative impact of knockout agreements on the business of auction sale. Puffers have no intention to buy the goods but to raise the price through fictitious bids. Puffers are also termed as 'by bidders or 'decoy ducks'. The seller or auctioneer can, however, legally employ only one puffer.
5. Where the sale is not notified to be subject to a right to bid on behalf of the seller, it shall not be lawful for the seller to bid himself at such sale, or to employ any such person, on his behalf to bid at such sale, or for the auctioneer knowingly to accept any bid from such person. The buyer may treat any sale contravening this rule as fraudulent [Section 64(4)].

6. The sale may be notified to be subject to a reserved or upset price [Section 64(5)]. It is customary on the part of the auctioneer to fix and announce a 'reserve price', below which no bid would be accepted. By fixing such a reserve price, the seller protects his interest against selling the goods at a very low price.

7. An auctioneer warrants
   - that he has authority to sell on behalf of the seller,
   - that he has no knowledge of any defect in the title of his principal, and
   - to give quiet possession of the goods against payment of the price.

Exercises

I. Objective-type Questions

1. State whether each of the following statements is True or False:
   (i) A contract of sale includes both a sale and an agreement to sell.
   (ii) Delivery of goods and payment of price are prerequisites to form a valid contract of sale.
   (iii) In a sale property, goods immediately passes to the buyer irrespective of payment of price or delivery of goods.
   (iv) In an agreement of sale, if the goods are destroyed, the loss falls on the buyer.
   (v) Consideration may be partly in money and partly in goods.
   (vi) Breach of a condition may render a contract repudiated.
   (vii) Warranty is a stipulation, which is collateral to the main purpose of the contract.
   (viii) The term 'right to pass ownership' is wider than the term 'right to sell'.
   (ix) Condition as to merchantable quality amounts to conditions as to quality or fitness of goods purchased.
   (x) When the goods are purchased under a patent or trademark, there is no implied condition as to their fitness.
   (xi) Property in goods can pass only in case of ascertained goods.
   (xii) Physical possession of goods results in transfer of ownership therein.
   (xiii) The property in goods does not pass if the seller has reserved the right of disposal.
   (xiv) Delivery may be made by doing anything, which has the effect of putting the goods in possession of the buyer.
   (xv) Delivery of goods and payment of price are concurrent conditions.
   (xvi) An unpaid seller is one who has not received the full price of the goods sold by him.
   (xvii) The right of lien cannot be exercised when goods have been sold on credit and the period of credit has not yet expired.
   (xviii) The seller can sue for the price, unless otherwise agreed, only if the goods have become property of the buyer.
   (xix) Puffers are the persons employed by the auctioneer to raise the price.
   (xx) A contract of sale is rescinded immediately after the seller has exercised his rights of lien or stoppage in transit.

2. Fill in the blanks:
   (i) The breach of warranty gives the buyer the right to ________.
   (ii) A breach of warranty ________ treated as breach of condition.
   (iii) Stipulation as to disclose the dangerous nature of goods is an implied ________.
   (iv) Breach of warranty entitles the buyer to claim ________.
   (v) Doctrine of '*caveat emptor*' provides protection to the ________.
   (vi) Property in goods means ________ of goods and not the ________ of goods.
   (vii) Risk *prima facie* passes with the ________.

(viii) If the seller is in possession of goods under a contract that is ________, even an innocent buyer will not acquire an absolute title to the goods.

(ix) Where the buyer rejects the whole lot for delivery of wrong quantity, it ________ cancellation of the contract.

(x) The buyer is ________ to accept delivery by installments, if agreed already.

(xi) The right of lien of an unpaid seller depends solely on the ________ of goods.

(xii) An agreement between the bidders not to bid against each other is called ________ agreement.

(xiii) The right of ________ arises only when the lien is lost.

(xiv) The right of stoppage in transit is a right to ________ possession of the goods.

(xv) Right to withhold delivery of goods is available where the property in goods ________.

3. Indicate the correct answer:

(i) Which of the following is not a basic requirement to form a valid contract of sale?
(a) Two parties (b) Transfer of property in goods
(c) Consideration in price (d) Delivery of goods

(ii) Which of the following is mistaken in respect of a contract of sale?
(a) There may be immediate delivery of goods
(b) The delivery of goods or payment of price or both may be made at some future date
(c) There may be immediate delivery of goods but price to be paid at some future date
(d) None of the above

(iii) Which of the following creates *jus in rem* (i.e., gives the right to the buyers to enjoy the goods as against the whole world including the seller)?
(a) Sale (b) Agreement to sell
(c) Hire–purchase agreement (d) Contract for work and labour

(iv) Which is the odd one out?
(a) Specific goods
(b) Future goods
(c) Ascertained goods
(d) Unascertained goods

(v) For a contract of sale to be void on the ground of destruction of subject matter, which of the following conditions must be satisfied:
(a) It must be a contract of sale for specific goods
(b) The goods must have perished before making the contract
(c) The seller must not be aware about the destruction of goods
(d) All of the above

(vi) The term 'wholesomeness' in relation to sale of goods means
(a) that the goods are fit for human consumption
(b) that the goods are of merchantable quality
(c) that the goods are suitable for a particular purpose
(d) that the goods are of merchantable quality as well as suitable for a particular purpose

(vii) To avail relief under condition as to fitness, the condition(s) to be satisfied is/are
(a) the exact purpose must have disclosed
(b) the seller must be a dealer in such goods
(c) the buyer must have relied upon the seller's skill or judgment
(d) all of the above

(viii) The expression 'Nemo dat quod non-habet' means
(a) let the buyer beware
(b) only the owner of the goods can transfer a title thereto
(c) one cannot give what one does not have
(d) condition as to little may be negative by express terms

(ix) The doctrine of *caveat emptor* does not apply
  (a) where the seller makes a false or mis-representation, or fraud
  (b) where the seller conceals a defect in the goods, which cannot be found out on reasonable examination
  (c) in case of implied conditions and warranties
  (d) in all the above situations

(x) Which of the following is not an implied condition in a contract of sale?
  (a) Condition as to quality or fitness
  (b) Condition as to merchantable quality
  (c) Condition as to wholesomeness
  (d) Condition as to free from encumbrances

(xi) When goods are sent on 'approval' or 'sale or return' basis, the property therein passes to the buyer
  (a) When he signifies his approval or acceptance
  (b) When he adopts the transaction
  (c) When he fails to return the goods
  (d) In all the above cases

(xii) Who among the following can convey a good title to the buyer?
  (a) An unpaid seller
  (b) A mercantile agent
  (c) One of the joint owners
  (d) All of the above

(xiii) The term 'resperit demino' means
  (a) Risk follows ownership
  (b) No one can give better title than what he himself has
  (c) Loss falls on the buyer
  (d) None of the above

(xiv) A finder of lost goods can sell such goods:
  (a) If the owner cannot be found with reasonable diligence, or if found, he refuses to pay lawful charges of the finder
  (b) If the goods are in danger of perishing or losing the greater part of its value
  (c) If the lawful charges of the finder, in respect of the goods found, amount to two-thirds of its value
  (d) In all the above cases

(xv) Which of the following is not the case of 'Delivery of wrong quantity'?
  (a) Short delivery
  (b) Excess delivery
  (c) Part delivery
  (d) Mixed delivery

(xvi) To be called an 'unpaid seller', the condition(s) to be satisfied is/are
  (a) The goods have been sold and the price is due
  (b) The buyer has not yet paid or tendered the full price
  (c) A bill of exchange or other negotiable instrument, such as cheque, was received as payment of the price but the same has dishonoured on presentation
  (d) All of the above

(xvii) Where the property in goods has passed to the buyer, which of the following is immaterial for an unpaid seller?
  (a) Lien
  (b) Stoppage in transit
  (c) Resale
  (d) Withholding delivery

(xviii) In which of the following circumstances, an unpaid seller cannot resell the goods?
  (a) Where the goods are perishable
  (b) Where the seller expressly reserves a right of resale
  (c) Where the buyer transfers the document of title of goods to a person who buys them in good faith and for consideration
  (d) Where the unpaid seller has given a notice to the buyer about his intention to resell and the buyer does not pay or tender the price within a reasonable time

(xix) Which of the following rights is/are available to the unpaid seller against the buyer personally?
  (a) Suit for the price
  (b) Suit for damages
  (c) Suit for interest and special damages
  (d) All of the above

(xx) In case of breach of contract by the seller, where the damages are not a suitable remedy or the goods are of a unique nature then which of the following rights is available to the buyer?
  (a) Suit for specific performance
  (b) Suit for breach of warranty
  (c) Suit for interest
  (d) Suit for repudiation of contract

II. Review Questions

1. What is a contract of sale? Distinguish between a sale and an agreement to sell.
2. Outline the characteristic features of a contract of sale.
3. Define goods. What is the effect of destruction of specific goods on a contract of sale?
4. Discuss briefly the formalities to be fulfilled to make a contract of sale.
5. What do you mean by price? What are the methods of determining the price of goods?
6. Define and distinguish between 'condition' and 'warranty'.
7. State the implied conditions in a contract of sale of goods.
8. Explain the doctrine of *caveat emptor*. What are the exceptions to this doctrine?
9. Under what circumstances does a 'condition' descend to the level of a 'warranty'?
10. Describe the provisions of the Sale of Goods Act relating to the implied conditions in a contract of-
    (i) 'Sale of sample' and
    (ii) 'Sale by sample as well as by description'
11. Define the term 'property' as used in the Sale of Goods Act. What are the rules relating to transfer of property of specific goods from seller to the buyer?
12. 'Nemo dat quod non-habet'. Explain the maxim and discuss the exceptions to the rule.
13. When goods are delivered on 'approval' or 'sale or return basis', when does ownership therein pass to the buyer?
14. State the circumstances in which the following persons can sell goods
    (a) A mercantile agent
    (b) One of joint owners
    (c) A finder of lost goods
    (d) A pawnee or pledgee
15. (i) 'Risk prima facie passes with ownership'. Comment.
    (ii) State the rules with respect to passing of property from seller to buyer in respect of unascertained goods.
16. What do you mean by the term 'delivery of goods' in a contract of sale? Explain in brief the rules relating to the delivery of goods.
17. What are the remedies available to the buyer if the seller makes (a) part delivery, (b) short delivery, (c) excess delivery, and (d) mixed delivery of goods?
18. State the legal provisions relating to delivery of goods to the carrier or wharfingers.
19. 'Delivery does not amount to acceptance of goods'. Comment. Also discuss the liability of the buyer.
20. Who is an unpaid seller? What are his rights?
21. Explain the rights of an unpaid seller against the goods.
22. Explain fully the right of lien. When is this right said to have lost?

23. When can an unpaid seller resell the goods? Is it necessary to give a notice of resale to the buyer? If yes what are the reasons behind it?
24. 'Right of stoppage in transit is an extension of the right of lien.' Elucidate.
25. Explain in brief the rules applicable to an auction sale.
26. Discuss in brief the rights of unpaid seller and the buyer against each other.

III. Caselets

1. *X* agreed to sell to *Y* 100 bags of cement from his stock of 1000 bags in his warehouse. The entire stock was reduced to concrete due to rainwater inundating the warehouse. Decide
[**Hint:** The contract is void for the destruction of subject matter]
2. *A* sells a rare painting to *B* on cash-on-delivery basis. *B* subsequently refuses to accept the delivery. Decide.
[**Hint:** *A* can sue *B* for the price. Besides he can exercise right of lien, stoppage-in-transit, and resale]
3. *X* agrees to supply 10 bags of sugar to *Y*. *Y* refuses to accept the consignment. Decide.
[**Hint:** *Y* is liable to pay for the damages to *X*]
4. *A* agrees to sell to *B* an antique statue and *B* pays the price in advance. *A* later became insolvent while the statue is still in his possession. Decide.
[**Hint:** *B* can claim a ratable dividend for the advance money paid from the official receiver or assignee of *A* out of the estate of *A*]
5. X sold his car to Y to be delivered to the latter on a future date upon payment of price. While the car was still in possession of X, buyer proved insolvent. Decide.
[**Hint:** X shall be entitled to ratable dividend out of the estate of Y]
6. *A*, a farmer, exhibits oats in his farm for sale. *B* buys oats from *A*, a sample of which had been shown to him. *B* buys the oats erroneously thinking that they were old ones. *B* wants to return the oats and refuses to pay the price. Decide.
[**Hint:** *B* is bound by the contract. Refer Doctrine of *Caveat Emptor*]
7. *A* told a car dealer *B* that he wanted a comfortable car suitable for touring purposes. The dealer recommended him a car, which was being sold under the trade name *Onida*. The car was found unsuitable. Discuss the rights of *A*.
[**Hint:** *A* can terminate the contract and can claim for damages as the condition as to fitness had been broken (Section 16(1))]
8. X purchases a TV set from Y, who deals in electronic goods, on Y's plea that though it is old, yet it is in an excellent set. *A* finds later that the TV set does not work at all. Can he reject the set and recover the price paid by him?
[**Hint:** Yes. Failure of condition as to sale of goods by description. Refer Section 15]
9. Certain goods were sold by sample by *A* to *B*, who in turn sold them by sample to C. The goods were not according to the sample. Therefore, C rejected the goods and gave notice to *B*. *B* sued *A*. Advise *B*.
[**Hint:** *B* can repudiate the contract and refuse the goods and if he has already paid for them, he can even recover the price (failure of implied condition as to 'sale by sample')]
10. *A* agreed to sell to *B* 20 kg of rice described as 'Dehradun Basmati' as per the sample shown. Although the rice supplied was in accordance with the sample but the sample itself was of 'Punjab sela' an inferior quality. The buyer refuses to make payment. What remedies are available to the seller?
[**Hint:** Buyer has got the right to set aside the contract for breach of implied condition of 'Sale by sample as well as description']

11. *A* delivers a horse to *B* on trial for a week. The horse dies on the fourth day without any negligence on part of *B*. Is *B* liable to pay the price?
[**Hint:** No, '*B*' is not liable to pay the price because the ownership has not yet passed to him]

12. *A*, by fraud, obtains a necklace from *B*, a jeweller. But before *B* could rescind the contract, *A* sells the necklace to *C* who purchases it in good faith and for value. Does *C* get the good title?
[**Hint:** Yes. Sale by person in possession under voidable contract. Refer Section 29]

13. *A*, *B*, and *C* are three brothers who own a cow in common. The cow is left with *A* with the consent of *B* and *C*. *A* sells the cow to *P* who buys it in good faith for value and without notice that *A* had no authority to sell. Does '*P*' become the owner?
[**Hint:** Yes. Refer Section 29]

14. *A* found a diamond ring. When he could not trace the true owner with reasonable efforts, he sold it to *B* who bought the same without knowledge that *A* was merely the finder. Can the true owner recover the ring from *B*?
[**Hint:** Yes, Section 169 of the Indian Contract Act]

15. Raja buys a sofa-set from a furniture dealer. He neither makes the payment nor takes the delivery of the sofa-set. He asks the dealer to deliver the sofa-set at his residence the next day and collect the payment. As a result of accidental fire, the sofa-set is destroyed. Can the dealer recover the price from the buyer?
[**Hint:** Yes. Risk passes with the ownership. Refer Section 26]

16. *A* purchased certain specified goods from *B* & Co. *B* & Co. delivered the goods to *A* along with some other goods. What course of action is open to *A*?
[**Hint:** Mixed delivery. *A* may reject the whole or accept the whole or accept the goods ordered by him and reject the rest]

17. Amit of Mumbai writes to M/s Surjeet & Co. Nai Sarak, New Delhi, to supply him Singhania's Income Tax Ready Reckoner by parcel post. The seller acts accordingly but the parcel is lost on the way. Can Amit deny paying the price?
[**Hint:** No, delivery to the carrier (i.e., the post-office) is delivery to buyer. Refer Section 39]

18. *A* agrees to deliver to *B* 50 quintals of wheat in May. But *A* delivers only 40 quintals in May and the remaining 10 quintals in the second week of June. What is the position of *B*.
[**Hint:** Installment delivery. *B* is entitled to reject the whole 50 quintals of wheat]

19. *A* agreed to sell to *B* 150 cotton shirts of a particular brand at the rate of ₹300 per shirt. But *A* delivered 160 shirts. Although all the shirts were of uniform quality as agreed upon, yet *B* rejected the whole lot. Was *B* right in his action?
[**Hint:** Yes. Mixed delivery Section 37(3)]

20. *A* sells to *B* 200 bags of J.K. cement, which is locked up in a godown. *A* hands over the keys of the godown to *B*. Does it constitute a valid delivery of the goods to *B*?
[**Hint:** Yes. The goods have been delivered to *B* by way of symbolic delivery]

21. *A* delivers some jewellery to *B*, a regular customer at his shop, on approval basis without stipulating any time for its return in case of non-acceptance on her (*B*'s) part. *B* keeps the jewellery without signifying her approval or refusal. In the meantime, burglary takes place in her house and the jewellery is stolen. Can *A* sue *B* for the price of the goods?
[**Hint:** Yes, because the property in goods has already passed to the buyer (Section 24)]

22. *A* advertised to sell his car. *B* reached *A*'s place and agreed to pay the price quoted by *A* for the vehicle. When the latter took out the chequebook, the former refused to accept the cheque and demanded the price in cash only. *B* anyhow persuaded *A* to allow him to take the delivery of the car against the cheque. *B* pledged the car with C. In the meantime the bank returned the cheque to *B* being dishonoured as bogus one. Can *A* recover the car from *B*?

[Hint: Yes, because *B*'s cheque was forged one and a forged negotiable instrument is inoperative. In this case, *A* cannot be described as an 'unpaid seller', as it is not a case of simple dishonour of a cheque received as payment of price of the goods sold]

23. *A* sold some goods to *B* for ₹5000 and promised to deliver them within 15 days. The price was paid by a cheque, which was subsequently dishonored by the bank on its presentment before delivery of the goods. What is the remedy available to *A*?
[Hint: *A* is unpaid seller and so can retain the goods until *B* pays the full price]

24. *A* of Delhi sold certain goods to *B* of Indore and sent the R/R to him. *B*, without paying for the goods, pledged the railway receipt with C as a sacristy for a loan of ₹5000. Thereafter, *B* becomes insolvent. Discuss the right of the seller.
[Hint: *A* can get back the railway receipt to regain the possession over the goods but only after paying off C ₹5000 (i.e., amount of loan). Refer Section 53(2)]

25. *B* of Mumbai sold 1000 bags of white cement to *K* of Kanpur and dispatched the same through railway. The goods reached Kanpur and the buyer after taking the delivery of the goods started loading the same in his truck. When the goods were in the process of being loaded on the truck, the seller came to know that the buyer became insolvent. He therefore pleaded to stop the loading and wished to take the delivery back in the exercise of his right of stoppage in transit arguing that the truck is still in the premises of railway station. Would *B* succeed?
[Hint: The seller cannot stop the goods legally because the transit came to an end when the buyer had taken the delivery]

Answers to Objective-type Questions

1. (i) True (ii) False (iii) True (iv) False (v) True
(vi) True (vii) True (viii) False (ix) False (x) True
(xi) True (xii) False (xiii) True (xiv) True (xv) True
(xvi) True (xvii) True (xviii) True (xix) True (xx) False

2. (i) (d) (ii) (d) (iii) (a) (iv) (b) (v) (d)
(vi) (a) (vii) (d) (viii) (c) (ix) (d) (x) (d)
(xi) (d) (xii) (d) (xiii) (c) (xiv) (d) (xv) (c)
(xvi) (d) (xvii) (c) (xviii) (c) (xix) (d) (xx) (a)

3. (i) claim damages only (ii) cannot (iii) warranty (iv) damages
(v) seller (vi) ownership of goods, possession of goods (vii) property (viii) void
(ix) does not tanta amount to (x) bound (xi) actual possession
(xii) knock-out (xiii) stoppage in transit (xiv) regain (xv) has passed

9 Chapter in Review

LEARNING OUTCOMES

LO1 Contract of sale: definition, essentials

LO2 Sale distinguished from agreement to sell

LO3 Goods: meaning; classification

LO4 Price: meaning, modes of fixation

LO5 Conditions and Warranties

LO6 Doctrine of caveat emptor

LO7 Delivery of goods; modes of delivery; actual, symbolic, and constructive delivery

LO8 Rights of an unpaid seller

KEY TERMS

Contract of sale: A contract whereby a seller transfers or agrees to transfer the property in goods to the buyer for a price.

Goods: Every kind of movable property other than actionable claims and money.

Price: Money consideration for a sale of goods.

Sale: Instant transfer of property (in goods) from seller to buyer.

Agreement to sell: Transfer of property (in goods) from seller to buyer in future; usually subject to fulfilment of some condition(s).

Existing goods: Goods physically in existence, owned and/or possessed by the seller at the time entering into contract of sale by the latter.

Specific goods: Goods identified and agreed upon at the time of making the contract of sale.

Ascertained goods: Goods identified subsequent to the formation of the contract of sale.

Unascertained goods: Goods not specifically identified or ascertained at the time of entering the contract of sale.

Future goods: Goods that are yet to be manufactured, produced, or acquired by the seller after making the contract of sale.

LO1 A contract of sale of goods is a contract, whereby, the seller transfers or agrees to transfer the property in goods to the buyer for a price. There can be a contract of sale between one co-owner and another co-owner.

LO2 A sale consists in the passing of title from the seller to the buyer for a price but in an agreement to sell, the transfer of property in the goods is to take place at a future time or subject to some condition thereafter to be fulfilled.

LO3 The goods, which form the subject matter of a contract of sale, may be either existing goods, owned or possessed by the seller, or future goods. When a seller, by a contract of sale, purports to effect a sale of future goods or contingent goods, the contract operates as an agreement to sell.

LO4 *Price* represents the money consideration for a sale of goods. The price in a contract of sale may be fixed by the contract, or may be left to be fixed in a manner thereby agreed, or may be determined by the course of dealing between the parties. Where the price is not determined in accordance with the foregoing provisions, the buyer shall pay the seller a reasonable price. What is a reasonable price is a question of fact dependent on the circumstances of each particular case.

LO5 A condition is a stipulation essential to the main purpose of the contract, the breach of which gives rise to a right to treat the contract as repudiated besides seeking for damages. A warranty, on the other hand, is a stipulation collateral to the main purpose of the contract, the breach of which gives rise to claim for damages but not a right to reject the goods and treat the contract as repudiated.

LO6 Under the doctrine of 'caveat emptor', the buyer alone is responsible for checking the quality and suitability of goods before a purchase is made. This doctrine is subject to certain exceptions such as where the seller actively conceals latent defects; where the seller misrepresents or commits a fraud; where goods are bought by description from a seller who deals in goods of that description and the goods supplied by the seller do not correspond with the description; etc.

Contingent goods: Goods whose acquisition by the seller depends on a contingency, which may or may not happen.

Condition: A stipulation essential to the main purpose of the contract, the breach of which gives rise to a right to treat the contract as repudiated.

Express conditions: Conditions expressly provided or agreed upon by both the parties at the time of entering contract of sale.

Implied conditions: Conditions which the law incorporates as implicit to a contract of sale unless otherwise agreed upon between the parties..

Warranty: A stipulation collateral to the main purpose of the contract, the breach of which gives rise to a claim for damages but not to a right to reject the goods and treat the contract as repudiated.

Express warranty: Warranty provided explicitly by the term of the contract of sale.

Implied warranty: Warranty which the law incorporates into a contract of sale.

***Caveat emptor*:** Let the buyer beware.

Doctrine of caveat emptor: A principle that often places on buyers the burden to reasonably examine goods before purchase and take responsibility for its condition post purchase.

***Caveat venditor*:** Let the seller beware.

Doctrine of *caveat venditor*: The seller shall be under an obligation to inform the buyer of any latent defect in the goods sold at the time of the contract.

Generic goods: Unascertained goods, having no brand name and therefore defined by description only.

Delivery: Voluntary transfer of possession of goods from one person to another.

Actual delivery: Goods physically handed over by the seller or his/her authorised agent to the buyer or his/her authorised agent.

Symbolic delivery: Delivery of means of obtaining possession of goods.

Constructive delivery: Acknowledgment by the person, in possession of goods, that he/she holds the goods on behalf of and at the disposal of the buyer.

Unpaid seller: The seller who has not received the full price of the goods sold by him.

Lien: Retention of possession of goods until the price thereof is paid or duly tendered.

Auction sale: A public event at which things are sold to the person who offers the highest price for them.

LO7 It is the duty of the seller to deliver the goods sold and of the buyer to accept and pay for them, in accordance with the terms of the contract of sale. Whether the delivery is actual, symbolic, or constructive, it should have the effect of putting the goods in the possession of the buyer or his/her authorised agent.

LO8 The seller of goods is deemed to be an 'unpaid seller' when the whole of the price has not been paid or tendered. The rights of an unpaid seller may be classified as against the goods and against the buyer personally.

Part III The Indian Partnership Act, 1932

CHAPTER 10 Partnership: Nature and Formation

Learning Objectives

LO 1 Essential characteristics of partnership
LO 2 Mutual agency
LO 3 Sharing of profits
LO 4 Statutory limit of number of partners
LO 5 Partnership versus HUF
LO 6 Partnership versus company
LO 7 Formation of partnership
LO 8 Partnership deed
LO 9 Types of partners
LO 10 Minor as a partner
LO 11 Registration of partnership firm

The law relating to partnership is contained in the Indian Partnership Act, 1932. Initially, this act was part of the Indian Contract Act, 1872 (Chapter IX-Sections 239–266), but was converted into a separate Act in 1932. It contains 74 sections and extends to the whole of India except the State of Jammu and Kashmir[1]. Although Partnership Act is a Central Act, it is administered by state governments, i.e., work of registration of firms and related matters are looked after by the government of the state, where the firm is located and registered. Since partnership comes into being only as a result of an agreement between the parties, general principles of law of contracts and agency (as contained in the Contract Act) are also relevant to partnership insofar as they are not inconsistent with the express provisions of this Act. In this behalf basic requirements of contract, i.e., legally enforceable agreement, mutual consent, competency of parties, free consent, lawful object, consideration, etc., do apply to partnership contract.

Partnership: Definition and Essentials

Partnership: Association of persons to carry on a business jointly and share the profits thereof.

A partnership is simply an association of persons who have agreed to carry on a joint business and share the profits thereof.

Section 4 of the Partnership Act, 1932, defines partnership in the following terms:

'Partnership is the relation between persons who have agreed to share the profits of a business carried on by all or any one of them acting for all. The people who have entered into partnership with one another are individually called "partners" and collectively "firm", and the name under which their business is carried on is called the "firm name".'

Analysis of this definition shows that the following features are essential to the formation of a partnership:

1. Association of two or more persons
2. Result of an agreement
3. Agreement to carry on some business
4. Sharing of profits
5. Mutual agency

[1] The state of Jammu and Kashmir enjoys a special status under Article 370 of Indian Constitution.

Association of Two or More Persons

It is one of the most basic elements of a valid partnership. To form a partnership there should be at least two persons. A partnership cannot survive if the number of partners gets reduced to one for whatever reasons—death, insolvency, lunacy, etc.,—it may be. This is so because, one cannot be one's own partner. Although the Partnership Act is silent over the maximum number of partners in a firm, the Companies Act, 2013, puts a ceiling on the number of partners in a partnership firm as under.

As per Rule 10 of Companies (Miscellaneous) Rules, 2014, if a partnership firm consists more than 50 persons, it will be illegal. Thus, the current limit is 50.

However, Section 464(1) of 2013 Act states, 'Provided that the number of persons which may be prescribed under this sub-section shall not exceed one hundred'. This means, by rules limit (ceiling) can be prescribed, but whatever limit is prescribed it must not be greater than 100 (i.e. up to 100).

Notwithstanding, the above maximum ceiling of 100 partners does not apply to a partnership firm, formed by professionals who are governed by special Acts [Section 464(2)]. Accordingly, a firm of chartered accountants, for instance, can have maximum 50 partners (i.e. at par with a business firm), all being chartered accountants of-course, but by amendment of Companies Rules, the said limit may go even beyond 100.

Accordingly, as per Section 464, Chartered Accountants' firms are now allowed to be registered/reconstituted with more than 20 partners w.e.f. 01.04.2014 under the Indian Partnership Act as in the case of a firm under the Limited Liability Partnership Act.

If the number of partners exceeds this statutory limit, the partnership is rendered an illegal association.

In order to enter into a partnership, the persons must be competent to contract. It is, however, immaterial whether the persons so entered into a partnership contract are natural or artificial. A company may, if so authorised by its charter (Memorandum of Association), become a partner in a firm, as it is a person in legal terms, though artificial one [*MM Pulimoad vs Registrar of Firms*[2]]. There could be a

[2] 1987, 61 Comp. Cas. 209 (Kerala)

Box 10.1 **Sharing of Profits Does Not Make One a Partner**

Example 1

A and *B*, who jointly own a house, let it out on a rent of ₹5000 per month. They share the rental income equally. Yet *A* and *B* cannot be regarded as partners. They are simply co-owners of the property.

Example 2

X and *Y* buy 100 bales of cotton, which they agree to sell for their joint account, each party sharing profits equally. Here, *X* and *Y* are partners in respect of such an account.

partnership even between two or more companies [*Steel Bros. & Co. Ltd vs Commissioner of Income Tax*[3]]. But a partnership firm not being a person in legal terms cannot enter into partnership [*Dule Chand vs Commissioner of Income Tax*[4]].

Result of an Agreement

Partnership is formed as a result of an agreement between two parties. It does not arise out of status or inheritance as in the case of Hindu Undivided Family (HUF). It even does not arise by operation of law as in the case of co-ownership or Joint Stock Company. Thus, creation of an agreement [whether express (written or oral) or implied] between two or more people is the very foundation of partnership. Besides, the contract must contain all essential elements of a valid contract.

Agreement to Carry on Some Business

Another essential element of a partnership is that it is formed for the purpose of carrying on some (but lawful) business. An association or society formed primarily to carry on some charitable, religious, or social works cannot be regarded as partnership. Even a co-ownership does not amount to partnership. The term 'business' includes every trade, occupation, and profession [Section 2(b) of the Partnership Act]. Thus, business is used in its widest sense as it does not refer merely to trade or industry but also includes occupations and professions such as chartered accountancy, legal practice, and placement services.

Sharing of Profits

Sharing the profits of business amongst all the partners is the core of partnership. There will be no partnership where only one of the partners is entitled to the whole of the profits of the business. Unless otherwise agreed, sharing of profits implies sharing of losses as well. However, all the partners may not concur to share losses. It is open to one or more partners to agree to bear all the losses of the business. Thus, one can become a partner on the term that he will not share the losses. Section 13(b), however, provides that the partners are entitled to share equally in the profits earned and shall contribute equally to the losses sustained by the firm. The ratio in which the profits and losses will be shared need not be equal. But merely sharing of profits does not necessarily entitle someone to be treated as partner. For instance, a manager, who besides his fixed salary gets a share in the profits of a firm's business, can only claim to be an employee of the firm and not a partner.

Sharing of profits not a conclusive test The division of profits amongst the partners is an essential condition to sustain a partnership. But merely sharing profits does not automatically make someone a partner.

It is also true that there can be no partnership without sharing of profits of the business, but sharing of profits *per se* does not constitute partnership. A person may have a share in the partnership profits, but still may not be a partner. Examples in Box 10.1 drive home the point.

Mutual Agency

Mutual agency is the conclusive test of a partnership. Business of the firm may be carried on by all or any of the partners acting

Mutual agency: A partner is both an agent and a principal in a partnership firm.

[3] A.I.R. 1958, S.C. 315
[4] A.I.R. 1956, S.C. 354

for all. This means that a partner is both an agent and a principal in a partnership firm. He is an agent because he can bind other partners, who are his principals, by his acts and he is again a principal, who in turn is bound by the acts of other partners. Thus, the partner who conducts the business of the firm not only acts for himself but for the other partners as well. Section 18 of the Partnership Act emphasises the element of mutual agency, thus:

'Subject to the provisions of this Act, a partner is the agent of the firm for the purpose of the business of the firm.'

The true test, therefore, to determine whether a person is a partner or not is to see *interalia*, whether the relationship of principal and agent exists between the parties. In fact, existence of the element of agency is the foundation of partnership, which is regarded as an extension of the general law of agency.

It is, however, not necessary that all partners should actively participate in business. The partners may authorise any one or more amongst themselves to manage the business of the firm. Under such an arrangement, the remaining partners will be bound by their acts, subject to the understanding that such acts relate to carrying on the business of the firm and have been carried out in the name of the firm. Also, participation in management by all partners is not compulsory.

Partners, Firm, and Firm's Name

Persons who have entered into partnership with one another are individually called 'partners' and collectively 'firm', and the name under which their business is carried on is called the 'firm name' [Section 4].

A firm has no legal existence independent of its partners. In law, it is only a convenient phrase for describing the partners bracketed together under one name. It is neither a legal entity nor an artificial person as a company. In the eyes of the law, it cannot possess property; it cannot sue or be sued by others. Similarly, it can neither be a debtor nor a creditor. It is only for the sake of commercial usage, a firm comprises all those elements. It is, however, worth noting that from the taxation point of view, a partnership firm is identifiable from the partners comprising it and, therefore, assessable separately.

As regards the 'firm name', partners have a right to carry on business under any name and style, which they would like to adopt. However, while choosing the name of their firm, the partners are supposed to observe the restriction contained in Section 58(3) of the Indian Partnership Act, which reads as follows:

'A firm name shall not contain any of the following words: "Crown", "Emperor", "Empress", "Empire", "Imperial", "King", "Queen", "Royal", or words expressing or implying the sanction, approval or patronage of government except when the State Government signifies its consent to the use of such words as part of the firm name by order in writing'.

The partners must also not adopt a name calculated to mislead the public or confuse them with a firm of repute already in existence with a similar name. The court has the power to contain the use of such names, which are alike or similar to the name of an existing firm and used with deceitful intention. Moreover, a partnership firm cannot use the word 'Limited' as a part of its name.

Partnership and Co-ownership Distinguished

Co-ownership: A relationship whereby two or more persons jointly employ their property in a business to share its income.

Explanation I to Section 6 reads, 'The sharing of profits or of gross returns arising from property by persons holding a joint or common interest in that property does not itself make such persons partners'.

Thus, the mere fact that two or more persons jointly employ their property in a business and share its income does not mean that there exists a partnership between them. They are rather co-owners. For instance, sons who inherit some property from their father are not partners even though the property was to be managed jointly and its income were to be shared. Such type of relationship is regarded as co-ownership.

A partnership comes into existence only when there is an agreement between the persons to carry on some lawful business and share the profits arising from there. For example, if the sons of a father enter into an agreement to run a café in the building, inherited from their father and share the income thereof, they will be regarded as partners immediately on starting the café.

Difference between partnership and co-ownership can be summed up in the following seven points:

1. Co-ownership is not necessarily the result of an agreement, but a partnership is.
2. Co-ownership may not involve profit or loss, but partnership does, as the former does not necessarily involve carrying on of a business, whereas a partnership does.
3. One co-owner can, without the consent of the others, transfer his interest to a stranger. A partner cannot do this without the consent of all the other partners.
4. A co-owner is not an agent of the other co-owner, but a partner is.
5. A co-owner has no lien on the property co-owned, neither for expenses nor for what may be due from the others as their share of a common debt, but a partner has.
6. In co-ownership there is no maximum limit of co-owners. In partnership, the maximum limit of partners has been fixed at 10 for a banking business and 20 for other businesses.
7. A co-owner has the right to claim partition of property owned with other co-owners. A partner has no such exclusive right. He can sue the other partners for his share in the property of the firm only in the event of the dissolution of firm.

Partnership and Joint Hindu Family Distinguished

The relation of partnership arises from contract and not from status, and, in particular, the members of a joint Hindu family carrying on a family business as such are not partners in such business [Section 5].

The analysis of above section shows that a partnership comes into existence by means of a contract between partners, whereas a joint Hindu family (hereinafter referred to as HUF) arises as a result of status, i.e., by birth in the family. Accordingly, if two or more members of an HUF carry on an inherited business, it is not a partnership because it has been created by status or obtained by birth and not by an agreement.

HUF is a unique form of business existing only in India and is governed by the provisions of the Hindu Law. It comes into existence by operation of Hindu Law and not out of contract. The firm is owned by the members of undivided Hindu family, called co-parceners. The business of an HUF is managed by the senior-most male member, also known as *Karta* or Manager. There are two schools of Hindu Law, namely, Dayabhaga and Mitakshara.

Dayabhaga It is applicable only to the states of West Bengal and Assam. According to this school, only the male members become heirs on the death of their father. Technically, HUF business is not possible under this system.

> **Dayabhaga:** Applicable only to the states of West Bengal and Assam; only the male members become heirs on the death of their father.

Mitakshara It is applicable to the rest of India. According to this school, a joint Hindu family consists of all persons including the wives and unmarried daughters lineally descended from a common ancestor. But only those persons constitute the firm who acquire by birth a co-parcenary interest in the joint ancestral property. Such interest belongs to three successive generations in the male line (son, grandson, and great grandson) who inherit the ancestral property immediately on their birth in the family. Thus, the property inherited by a Hindu from his father, grandfather, and great grandfather is regarded as his ancestral property. The Hindu Law Succession Act, 1956, has extended the line of co-parcenary interest to female relatives of the deceased co-parceners and male relative claiming through such female relatives.

> **Mitakshara:** Applicable to the rest of India; a joint Hindu family consists of all persons including the wives and unmarried daughters.

The main points of distinction between a partnership and HUF business are as follows.

Basis of formation A partnership arises out of a contract between partners, whereas an HUF arises by the operation of Hindu Law. It is created by status or birth in the family, no agreement is needed for it.

Regulating law A partnership is governed by the provisions of the Indian Partnership Act, 1932. An HUF business is governed by Hindu Law Succession Act.

Number of members In a partnership business, the number of members cannot exceed 20 in case of non-banking business and 10 in case of banking business. But there is no such ceiling on the number of members (co-parceners) in HUF.

Admission of new members No new partner can be admitted to the existing partnership without the consent of all the other partners. In case of HUF firm, a person becomes a member (co-parcener) merely by his birth.

Minor member A minor cannot become a full-fledged partner in a firm; he can be admitted only to the benefits of partnership. In an HUF, a male child becomes a full-fledged member by birth.

Rights of females In a partnership, women can become partners and they enjoy the same rights and privileges as do male partners. In case of an HUF business, on the other hand, the membership is restricted to male members only. However, as per Hindu Law Succession Act, 1956, a female relative of a deceased male member gets a co-parcenery interest in the event of his death.

Implied agency In a partnership, every partner has implied authority to represent the firm and bind the other partners by his acts. In HUF this right rests with the *Karta* only, other members may be allowed by Karta expressly or impliedly to contract debts on behalf of the firm [*Lal Chand vs Ghanaya lal*[5]].

Liability of members In a partnership, the liability of all the partners is unlimited. Every partner is jointly and severally liable to third parties for the full debts of the firm. However, in case of HUF, liability of each member, except that of the *Karta*, is limited to the extent of his share in the property of the family.

Right to accounts Each partner not only enjoys a right to inspect the books of account of the firm and demand a copy thereof, he can even demand the accounts of the past dealings. But a co-parcener has no right to ask for the accounts of past dealings. He can ask for the position of the existing assets only.

Mode of dissolution A partnership firm is dissolved on the insolvency or death of a partner. But the death, lunacy, or insolvency of a co-parcener does not affect an HUF. It continues to operate even after the death of a co-parcener [*Baji Nath vs Ram Gopal*[6]].

[5] 1887, 12 AC 284
[6] 1854, 158 E.R. 426

Partnership and Company Distinguished

A company as well as a partnership are an association of persons but two differ widely in material respect. Following are the 10 points of distinction between the two entities.

Formation, registration, and the regulating act A partnership comes into existence by an agreement between the partners. The formation of partnership involves no legal formalities. Even registration of a partnership firm is not compulsory. In contrast, a company can only be formed after fulfilling certain legal formalities. Its registration under the Companies Act is essential. A partnership firm is governed by the provisions of the Indian Partnership Act, 1932, whereas a company is governed by the provisions of the Companies Act, 2013.

Legal status A partnership firm has no legal existence independent of its members. The firm and partners are one and the same in the eyes of the law except for the purposes of taxation. But a company enjoys a legal existence separate from and independent of its members.

Number of members The minimum number of partners in a partnership firm is 2 and the maximum is 50 which can be further extended up to 100 in case of a business firm and even beyond 100 in case of a firm of professionals. There is difference between a public and private company regarding number of members. In a private company, the minimum number of members is 2 and the maximum is 200. In a public company, the minimum number of members is 7 and there is no limit as to the maximum number of members. Notwithstanding, one person company (OPC) can be managed only one individual.

Liability of associates The liability of partners is unlimited. They are jointly and severally liable to pay the firm's debts to an unlimited extent. But the liability of shareholders is invariably limited to the unpaid amount on the shares held or the amount of guarantee undertaken by them.

Relationship of agency Partnership is based on the relationship of mutual agency between the partners, i.e., every partner is an agent of the rest of the partners. But a member of a company is the agent of neither the company nor the other members.

Transferability of share A partner cannot transfer his share and interest in the firm so as to substitute the transferee in his place as the partner without the unanimous consent of all the other partners. But a member of a public company can transfer his share to anyone he likes without the consent of other members.

Management In a partnership, every partner is at liberty to take part in the management of the firm's business. In case of a company, the right to control and manage the affairs of business is vested in directors elected by the shareholders.

Change of objects Partners by mutual agreement can change the objects of their firm as and when they like. On the contrary, the objects of a company, as laid down in its Memorandum, can be altered only by fulfilling certain legal formalities.

Audit If the turnover or gross receipts of a partnership firm does not exceed ₹40 lakh in a year, audit of its accounts is not mandatory. But the audit of financial statements of a company is a statutory requirement, irrespective of turnover or gross receipts, the company has had in a given financial year.

Winding up A partnership firm may be dissolved following the death or insolvency of a partner. It can also be wound up any time by any partner, if it is 'at will'. But a company is not affected by the death or insolvency of a shareholder and no sole member can call for its liquidation voluntarily. Besides, winding up of a company involves many legal formalities prescribed in this regard in the Companies Act.

Formation of Partnership

As per the statutory definition of partnership, the relation of partnership arises from the agreement and not from status. Accordingly, a partnership firm comes into being only by an agreement between all the prospective partners and not by operation of law. The agreement may, however, be express or implied. An express agreement is one that is made by words, spoken or written, whereas an implied agreement infers from the conduct of the parties.

The partnership agreement should, however, fulfil all the essential requirements of a valid contract. That is, there should be free consent of the parties who must be competent to contract, and the object of partnership should not be forbidden by law or otherwise immoral or opposed to public policy. Furthermore, mutual rights and obligations of the partners must be discussed in detail and should preferably be put into writing in the form of a 'Partnership Deed'.

Partnership Deed

Partnership deed: An agreement-in-writing that contains terms and conditions of a partnership.

Although a partnership agreement may be oral, yet it is always healthier to have it in writing. Such an agreement-in-writing is called a 'Partnership Deed'. This document contains terms and conditions of the partnership and sets forth the rights and obligations of the partners. A partnership deed should be carefully drafted and stamped according to the provisions of the Indian Stamp Act. Each partner should be given a copy of the deed and if the firm is registered, a copy should be filed with the Registrar of Firms at the time of such registration.

A partnership deed typically contains the following information:

1. Name of the firm;
2. Names and addresses of the partners;
3. Nature and scope of business and place(s) of business of the firm;
4. Date of commencement and duration of partnership;
5. The amount of capital to be initially contributed by each partner;
6. Provision for future capital and loans by partners to the firm;
7. Ratio in which profits and losses are to be shared amongst the partners;
8. Rules regarding operation of accounts, and arrangement for audit and safe custody of funds;
9. Interest on partners' capital, partners' loans, and interest, if any, to be charged on drawings made by the partners;
10. Salaries, commission, and remuneration, if any, payable to partners;
11. Accounting period and the date on which final accounts are to be prepared;
12. Rights, powers, and duties of the partners;
13. Rules relating to the admission, retirement, or expulsion of partners;
14. Valuation of goodwill on admission, retirement, and death of a partner;

15. Mode of dissolution of the firm;
16. Settlement of accounts on the dissolution of the, firm, etc.; and
17. The arbitration clause for the amicable settlement of disputes among the partners.

According to Section 11(1) of the Partnership Act, 1932, the terms contained in the partnership deed can be altered by the consent of all the partners, and such consent may be expressed or implied by a course of dealing. However, the deed should not contain any terms that flout the provisions of the Partnership Act.

Duration of Partnership

From the duration point of view, a partnership may be classified into two categories, namely, partnership at will and particular partnership.

Partnership at Will

Partnership at will: A partnership for indefinite period.

Where no provision is made by the partners for the duration of their partnership, or for the determination of their partnership, the partnership is 'partnership at will'. In other words, a partnership is deemed to be a partnership at will where

1. no fixed period has been agreed upon for the duration of partnership and
2. no provision is made as to the determination of partnership in any other way [Section 7].

Thus, it is a partnership for an indefinite period. The death or retirement of a partner does not affect the existence of such a partnership.

Section 43(1) provides 'where the partnership is at will, the firm may be dissolved by any partner giving notice in writing to all the other partners of his intention to dissolve the firm. The firm is dissolved from the date mentioned in the notice as the date of dissolution. And where no such date is mentioned, the firm is dissolved from the date of communication of the notice'.

However, if the agreement provides that the partnership can be dissolved by 'a mutual agreement only', it will not be a partnership at will. This is so because such a firm cannot be dissolved by only giving a notice [*Iqbalnath Premnath vs Rameshwarnath*[7]].

[7] 1976, AIR, Bombay 405

Particular Partnership

Particular partnership: A partnership formed for a specific venture, or for a particular period.

When a partnership is formed for a specific venture, or for a particular period, it is called particular partnership. Such a partnership is automatically dissolved on the completion of the venture, or on the expiry of the period [Section 8]. However, if the partners want to dissolve the firm before the fixed period, it may be dissolved with the consent of all the partners [Section 40]. Similarly, if the partners decide to continue such a partnership after the expiry of the fixed term or completion of the venture, it shall be deemed to be a partnership at will.

Types of Partners

The following types of partners generally exist in a partnership:

1. Active or ostensible partner
2. Dormant or sleeping partner
3. Nominal partner
4. Partner-in-profits only
5. Sub-partner
6. Partner by estoppel or holding out.

Active or Ostensible Partner

Active/Ostensible partner: One who enters into partnership by agreement and actively participates in the firm's business so as to produce in third parties a reasonable belief that he is a partner.

A person who enters into partnership by agreement and takes active part in the conduct of the partnership business so as to produce in third parties a reasonable belief that he is a partner is called an active or ostensible partner. He/she is an ordinary partner who invests money into the business of the firm, acts as an agent of other partners for all acts done in the ordinary course of business, and shares its profits (and losses). As he/she actively participates in the functioning and management of the firm, he/she has the capacity of binding himself/herself and other partners vis-à-vis third parties for all acts committed in the firm's name and in the usual course of business.

Such a partner must give a public notice of his/her retirement from the firm in order to absolve himself/herself of the liability for the acts done by other partners after his/her retirement.

Dormant or Sleeping Partner

ant partner: A partner nvests in a firm's business ares its profits but does tively participate in the oning of firm's business.

A dormant or sleeping partner is one who invests funds in the firm's business and has a share in the profits of the firm but does not actively participate in the functioning and management of the business. However, he is equally liable to third parties for all the debts of the firm such as an undisclosed principal in case of agency. Thus, the liability of a sleeping partner is also unlimited notwithstanding the fact that other parties are unaware of his existence as partner. The Partnership Act specifically provides that if an act is binding on the firm, every partner is liable for it.

At the time of his retirement or otherwise expulsion from partnership, a sleeping partner need not give a public notice to that effect. His liability for the acts of the firm ceases soon after his retirement/expulsion. Although such a partner has no duty to perform, yet he is entitled to inspect the books of account of the firm. He can also demand a copy of them.

Nominal Partner

Nominal partner: One who just lends his name to a partnership firm but neither contributes to the capital nor shares its profits.

A nominal partner is one who just lends his name to the firm without any material interest in the firm's business. A nominal partner neither contributes to the capital of the firm nor shares the profits (or losses) nor takes part in the management of the firm. He along with other partners is liable to third parties dealing with the firm for all the acts of the firm.

Partner-in-Profits Only

A partner-in-profits as the term indicates is one who is entitled to a share in the profits of a partnership without being liable for losses, if any. A person who has sufficient funds to introduce towards the capital of the firm but is not inclined to take risk may be admitted to the partnership firm by mutual agreement amongst other partners. Despite his specific position, he continues to be liable towards the third parties for all the acts of the firm, just like other partners. In the event of over-debtness of the firm due to heavy losses, such a partner may also be required to contribute the major share if other partners are not in a position to pay off the debts of the firm. The reason behind the same is that the liability of partners is joint and several.

Sub-partner

Where a partner agrees to share his profits in the firm with a third person, that third person is known as a 'sub-partner'. A sub-partner, however, is in no way connected with the firm, for lack of privity of contract between the two and, hence, has no rights or duties towards the firm and does not carry any liability for the debts of the firm as well. For the same reason, he cannot bind the firm or other partners by his acts.

Partner by Estoppel or 'Holding Out'

Normally, a person becomes a partner by a deal. But if the conduct of a person causes an impression to the outsiders that he is a partner in a firm (where in reality he is not), he can also be treated as a partner. This occurs by way of estoppel or holding out. Such a person is stopped (i.e., prevented) later on from denying the liabilities for the acts of the firm. According to Section 28(1), which contains the law relating to partners by holding out, 'Anyone who by words, spoken or written, or by conduct represents himself or knowingly permits himself to be represented as a partner in a firm is liable as a partner in that firm to anyone who has on the faith of any such representation extended credit to the firm'. The person so representing himself is called a partner by estoppel or holding out. A retiring partner, who has not given a public notice of his retirement, can also be held liable on grounds of holding out if his name is still being used by the firm. The reason for the same is that the third parties may continue to regard him as a partner. The rule to holding out is based on the 'Doctrine of Estoppel' as contained in Section 115 of the Indian Evidence Act, 1872.

Effect of holding out

Although the holding-out partner does not become a partner in the firm and is not entitled to any rights or claim upon the firm, yet he is personally and individually liable for the debts undertaken by the firm. An outsider, who has given credit to the firm presuming him to be a partner (i.e., by virtue of his conduct), can hold him liable as if he is a partner in that firm. Such a partner may alone be required to pay the whole debts, as the liability of the partners is joint and several. But he can recover the amount so paid from all the solvent partners of the firm under the 'Doctrine of Subrogation' as well as on the basis of 'Quasi-contract'.

Exceptions to holding out

According to Section 28(2), 'Where after a partner's death the business is continued in the old firm name, the unrelenting use of that name or of the deceased partner's name as a part thereof shall not itself make his legal representative or his estate liable for any act of the firm done after his death'. Put differently, the 'doctrine of holding out' does not extend to bind the estate of a deceased partner, where after the death of a partner the business of the firm is continued in the old firm name. Moreover, the principle of holding out does not apply in the case of a partner who has been adjudicated insolvent [see Section 45].

Position of Minor As Partner

A partnership is created by an agreement not by status, and an agreement by, or with, a minor is void ab *initio*[8]. It follows that a minor cannot enter into partnership. Section 5 of the Partnership Act clearly states, 'The relation of partnership arises from a contract...'. A minor is incompetent to contract. Therefore, a partnership cannot come into existence if the parties to a contract of partnership consist of one major and a minor. A minor can, however, be admitted to the benefits of partnership with the consent of all the partners by an agreement executed through his/her guardian with the other partners [Section 30].

The above provision implies that a minor cannot be a full-fledged partner. He can at the most be admitted into the benefits of the firm. In this regard consent of all the existing partners is must. Consent only of the majority of partners will not suffice.

It must be noted that a partnership firm cannot be formed with only minors as partners[9]. There must be at least two major partners before a minor is admitted to a partnership firm to derive benefits under it.

Rights of Minor in Partnership

Section 30 grants the following rights to a minor:

1. He/she is entitled to share the profits and the property of the firm in accordance with the agreement. But he/she cannot participate in the functioning and management of the firm's business, as he/she has no representative capacity to bind the firm.
2. He/she has the right to have access to and inspect and copy any of the accounts of the firm. He/she has, however, no such right in respect of books other than books of account as they may contain secrets, which may be restricted to real partners only.
3. He/she has a right to bring a suit for his/her share of profits or the property of the firm when he/she is not given his/her due share of profits. However, he/she can exercise this right when he/she intends to sever his/her connections with the firm and not otherwise.
4. He/she can become a partner in the firm on attaining majority but shall be entitled to the same share of profits, which he/she was getting as a minor.

Liability of Minor

A minor partner's liability is confined only to the extent of his share in the profits and the property in the firm. As per Section 30(3), a minor's share is liable for the acts of the firm. But a minor is not personally liable for any such act and so his/her private estate cannot be attached towards the payment of the firm's debts incurred during his/her minority.

On attaining majority, however, if he/she elects to become a partner, he/she becomes personally liable to third parties for all the acts of the firm done, since he/she was admitted to the benefits of partnership.

Position of a Minor on Attaining Majority

Within six months of attaining majority or obtaining knowledge that he/she had been admitted to the benefits of partnership, whichever date is later, the

---

[8] In view of Section 11 of the Indian Contract Act, 1872, and the decision of the Privy Council in *Mohri Bibi vs Dharmodas Ghose* (1930) 30 I.A. 14, a minor's agreement is altogether void and unenforceable.

[9] 1961, A.I.R. Mumbai, 136

minor partner has to elect whether he/she wants to continue or sever his/her connections with the firm. If he/she decides to leave the firm, he/she must give a public notice of his/her intention. If he/she fails to give any public notice within period stated above, it will be presumed that he/she has opted to become a partner in the firm [Section 35(5)].

When minor elects to become partner

If the minor elects to become a partner or becomes a partner by his/her failure to give public notice within the stipulated time, his/her position will be as follows:

1. His/her rights and liabilities will be similar to those of a full-fledged partner.
2. He/she will be personally liable to third parties for all acts of the firm, done since he/she was admitted to the benefits of the partnership.
3. His/her share in the property and profits of the firm remains the same, as he/she was entitled as a minor, unless altered by agreement [Section 30(7)].

When minor elects not to become a partner

If the minor decides to sever his/her connection with the firm, his/her position with regard to rights and liabilities will be as follows:

1. His/her rights and liabilities shall continue to be those of a minor up to the date of giving public notice.
2. His/her share shall not be liable for any acts of the firm done after the date of the public notice.
3. He/she shall be entitled to sue the partners for his/her share of the property and profits in the firm [Section 30(8)].

Registration of a Firm

The registration of a firm means getting the firm's name recorded along with necessary particulars in the 'Register of Firms' kept in the office of the Registrar of Firms. Prior to the enactment of the Indian Partnership Act, 1932, there was no provision for the registration of partnership firms in India. And as a matter of fact, it is still not compulsory for a partnership firm to get it registered. The Act has made the registration optional, solely at the discretion of the partners. However, by creating certain disabilities, an unregistered firm suffers from, the Indian Partnership Act has made the registration of firms sought-after.

Time of Registration

Since registration of a firm is not compulsory, it can be effected at any stage. A firm may get itself registered at any time during the continuance of its business. Getting a firm registered has its own advantages, which are as follows:

Registration is compulsory for filing a suit

If the firm contemplates to file a suit in a court of law for any tort, it must be registered before the suit is filed failing which the court shall dismiss the suit. Section 69(2) clearly states, 'No suit to enforce a right arising from a contract shall be instituted in any court of law by or on behalf of a firm against any third party unless the firm is registered and the persons suing are or have been shown in the Register of Firms as partners in the firm' [Section 69(2)].

Thus, registration must be affected before the suit is instituted. Registration of the firm subsequent to the institution of the suit cannot by itself cure the defect. This does not mean that a firm cannot be registered after filing a suit. It can be. But in that case it is necessary to withdraw the suit, get the firm registered, and then file a fresh suit (i.e., after registration).

Procedure for Registration

The procedure of registration is very simple. The partners may get their firm registered at any time or stage during the continuance of the partnership by filing a statement in the prescribed form and sending the same along with the prescribed fee by post or delivering it to the Registrar of Firms of the area in which any place of business of the firm is situated or is proposed to be situated. The statement must be signed by all the partners or by their agents specifically authorised in this regard. It shall state the followings:

1. the firm's name;
2. the place of business of the firm or if there is more than one place of its business, the principal place of business;
3. the names of any other places where the firm carries on business;
4. the date when each partner joined the firm;

5. the names in full and permanent addresses of the partners; and
6. the duration of the firm [Section 58 & 59].

Section 58(2) requires that the contents of the statement should be duly verified by the persons signing it. Furthermore, as per Section 58(3), a firm name shall not contain any of the following words: 'Crown', 'Emperor', 'Empress', 'Empire', 'Imperial', 'King', 'Queen', 'Royal', or words expressing or implying the sanction, approval or patronage of the government. Once the Registrar is satisfied that the provisions of Section 58 have been duly complied with, he/she shall record an entry of the statement in a register called the Register of Firms and shall file the statement. He/she shall then issue a 'Certificate of Registration' to the firm concerned.

Change of particulars

If any alteration is made in the name of the firm or in the location of the principal place of business, or in any other particulars given after registration of the firm, the same should be duly notified to the Registrar of Firms so that the changes can be incorporated in the register of firms [Section 60].

Penalty for furnishing false particulars

If any person knowingly, or without belief in its truth, furnishes false or incomplete information, he/she shall be punishable with imprisonment, which may extend to three months, or with fine, or with both [Section 70].

Consequences of Non-registration

As stated earlier, although registration of firms is not mandatory under the Partnership Act in India, yet it is considered desirable. An unregistered firm suffers from several disabilities. Registration is the only evidence of the existence of a partnership, and the facts entered in the records of the Registrar of Firms are treated as conclusive proof by the courts of law.

In accordance with Section 69, an unregistered firm and its partners suffer from the following disabilities.

No suit can be filed in a civil court by a partner against the firm or other co-partners If any dispute arises among the partners or between a partner and the firm, or between a partner and his co-partner, and the dispute is based on the rights arising from the partnership agreement (i.e., partnership deed) or related to the rights conferred by the Partnership Act, then a partner of an unregistered firm cannot institute a suit (in any court of law) against the firm or the ex-partners(s). Only a partner of a registered firm whose name appears on the register of firms as a partner can sue for enforcement of such rights and to settle the disputes [Section 69(1)].

However, criminal proceedings can be brought by one partner against the other(s). For example, if a partner steals the property of the firm or sets fire to the premises of the firm, any partner(s) can prosecute him for the same. In such a case, registration of firm is immaterial.

No suit can be filed in a civil court by the firm against third party An unregistered firm cannot institute a case against a third party in a civil court to enforce any right arising out of the contract with the latter, such as for the recovery of the price of goods supplied [Section 69(2)]. But, of course, criminal proceedings can be brought against the wrong doers by an unregistered firm also.

No right of set off

The above two disabilities also apply to a claim of set-off or other proceedings to enforce a right arising from a contract. Accordingly, if any suit is filed by a third party against an unregistered firm to recover a sum of money, the firm is not allowed to claim a set-off, i.e., the firm cannot say that since the third party also owes some money to it, the same should be adjusted against the claim in question [Section 69(3)].

Exceptions

Non-registration of a firm, however, does not affect the following rights of a partnership firm:

1. The right of third parties to sue the firm or any partner(s).
2. The right of the firm to institute a suit or claim a set-off if the value of suit does not exceed ₹100.
3. The right of partners to sue for the dissolution of the firm or for the accounts of a dissolved firm, or any right or power to realise the property of a dissolved firm.

4. The powers of an official assignee, or official receiver or court to realise the property of an insolvent partner.
5. The rights of firms or partners of the firm having no place of business in India.

It should be clear from the above that though there is no legal compulsion for a firm to get it registered but, by creating (indirectly) certain disabilities, an unregistered firm suffers from, the law has made it advisable for a partnership firm to get itself registered. These disabilities are such that sooner or later, every firm would have to get itself registered for its smooth operation or runing.

Exercises

I. Objective-type Questions

1. State whether each of the following statements is True or False:
   (i) The relation of partnership arises from contract and not from status.
   (ii) There can be a partnership agreement between two or more independent partnership firms.
   (iii) Sharing of profits is an essential element of partnership.
   (iv) Co-ownership does not necessarily involve carrying on of a business.
   (v) A partnership firm has a separate legal existence apart from its members.
   (vi) 'Partnership Deed' sets forth the terms of partnership as agreed by the partners.
   (vii) Partnership is created neither by status nor by operation of law.
   (viii) Registration of partnership firm provides protection to the outsiders dealing with the firm.
   (ix) Where no provision is made in partnership agreement for duration of the partnership, it is termed as particular partnership.
   (x) A sub-partner can represent himself to the outsiders as a partner.

2. Fill in the blanks:
   (i) It is open to one or more partners to bear all the ____________ of the business.
   (ii) The law of partnership is regarded as an extension of the ____________.
   (iii) Carrying on of a business is the necessary characteristic of ____________.
   (iv) ____________ school of Hindu Law prevails in Bengal and Assam.
   (v) In a partnership, the liability of all the partners is ____________.
   (vi) Registration of firm is ____________ under the Indian Partnership Act.
   (vii) If the partnership is continued after the expiry of term or completion of the adventure, it is deemed to be a ____________.
   (viii) A ____________ partner is one who has no real interest in the business.
   (ix) ____________ provides a proof of the existence of the partnership.

3. Indicate the correct answer:
   (i) Which of the following is considered 'exact test' of partnership?
   (a) Sharing of profits (b) Agreement
   (c) Mutual agency (d) Carrying on business
   (ii) The maximum number of partners in a partnership firm, carrying on an ordinary business, may be
   (a) 10 (b) 20
   (c) 50 (d) None of the above
   (iii) Who among the following has no right to claim partition of property?
   (a) A co-owner (b) A co-parcener
   (c) A partner (d) None of the above

(iv) Which of the following is not an essential element of partnership?
(a) Association of two or more persons (b) Mutual agency
(c) Result of an agreement (d) Separate legal entity

(v) *Cox vs Hickman* supports which of the following element(s) of partnership?
(a) Agency relationship—a conclusive test of partnership
(b) Sharing of profits—a *prima facie* evidence of existence of partnership
(c) Both (a) and (b)
(d) None of the above

(vi) Who among the following is not entitled to have an access to books of account maintained by a partnership firm?
(a) Ostensible partner (b) Partner in profits only
(c) Minor (d) Sub-partner

(vii) Which of the statements given below is correct in respect of a minor partner who on attaining majority elects not to become a partner?
(a) His rights and liabilities continue to be those of a minor upto the date of giving public notice
(b) His share is not liable for any acts of the firm done after the date of the public notice
(c) He is entitled to sue the partners for his share of the property and profits in the firm
(d) All of the above

(viii) If a person knowingly or without belief in its truth furnishes false particulars to the Registrar of Firms, he shall be punishable
(a) With imprisonment which may extend upto three months
(b) With fine
(c) With both (a) and (b)
(d) None of the above

(ix) Which of the following is not the disability of any unregistered firm and its partners?
(a) No suit can be filed by a partner against the firm or other co-partners
(b) No suit can be filed by the firm against third parties
(c) The firm or its partners cannot make a claim of set-off exceeding ₹100
(d) The firm cannot be sued by third parties

(x) Which of the following statements is not true about the registration of a firm?
(a) It may take place any time during the continuance of the partnership
(b) It must be effected before the suit is instituted otherwise the court of law shall not entertain the contract
(c) It must be done at the time of its formation
(d) Registration of the firm subsequent to the institution of the suit cannot by itself cure the defect

II. Review Questions

1. Define partnership. What are the essential features of a partnership?
2. 'The sharing of profits is only a *prima facie* evidence of partnership'. Comment.
3. Discuss how you would determine whether a group of persons is a partnership or not?
4. 'A partnership comes into existence by virtue of an agreement and not by status.' Explain.
5. Distinguish partnership from
   (i) Co-ownership
   (ii) Joint Hindu family business
   (iii) Joint stock company
6. What is partnership deed? State its main contents.

7. Enumerate the various types of partners. Briefly explain the extent of their liabilities.

8. Can a minor be admitted to a partnership? If so what are the rules governing his/her rights and liabilities during minority and after he/she has attained majority?

9. Explain briefly the procedure for registration of firms. Is such registration compulsory in respect of every partnership firm? What is the time of registration?

10. What is the procedure for the registration of a firm? What are the consequences of non-registration?

11. Explain the circumstances under which a person can be made liable as a partner even if he/she is not a partner.

12. 'The Indian Partnership Act has effectively ensured the registration of firms without making it compulsory'. Comment.

13. Write short notes on the following:
    (i) Partnership at will
    (ii) Exceptions to non-registration
    (iii) Penalty for giving false particulars about registration

III. Caselets

1. *X* and *Y* agree to work together as electricians. According to the terms, *X* shall receive all the profits and he will pay wages to *Y*. Are *X* and *Y* partners?
   [**Hint:** No. The element of sharing of profits is missing, which is the *prima facie* evidence of partnership]

2. *A* and *B* buy 100 bales of cotton, which they agree to sell for their joint account, each party sharing profits and bearing losses equally. Are *A* and *B* partners?
   [**Hint:** Yes. Refer Section 4]

3. *X* and *Y* jointly own a ship, which is entirely operated by *X*. *X* alone does its expenses and *Y* contributes nothing. One-thirds of the annual net earning is passed over by *X* to *Y*. Is it a relationship of partnership between *X* and *Y*?
   [**Hint:** No. Principal and agent relationship missing]

4. *A* and *B* acquire a tea shop and incur additional expense for purchasing utensils, renovating, etc., each contributing half of the total expense and the shop is leased out on a daily rent, which is divided between both of them. Does this arrangement constitute a partnership between *A* and *B*?
   [**Hint:** No. Lack of mutual agency; *A* and *B* are simply co-owners]

5. *X*, *Y*, and *Z* separately tender for a contract to pick up stray cows from Delhi cantonment area and restore them to a cowpen managed by MCD. However, by mutual agreement they decide to share the income arising from such activity, lest one of them is granted the contract. They also agree to share the total expense in this regard equally. Is this partnership?
   [**Hint:** No. Element of business is missing for they have sent only tenders, which may or may not be accepted]

6. *X* carried on business as Ram Dayal & Co. and employed a person named Ram Dayal as manager of the business. Examine his position.
   [**Hint:** Ram Dayal is a partner by estoppel. Refer Section 28(1)]

7. *X* enters into a partnership agreement with *Y*, who is a minor, for the benefits of *Y*. Is the partnership valid?
   [**Hint:** No. Partnership must be in existence before a minor is admitted to its benefits]

8. *X* & Co., an unregistered firm, was doing business of readymade garments. It purchased some exported stuff on credit from *Y*. But, the firm refused to pay the price, and *Y* filed a suit against it for the recovery of the price. Will Y succeed in his suit against the firm?
[**Hint:** Yes. The firm cannot take the plea of its non-registration, and the suit is not liable to be dismissed on this ground]

9. *A* & Co., an unregistered firm, applied for registration on 15 July 2000. On 20 July 2000 before the registration could be effected, the firm filed a suit against *B*, a customer for the recovery of ₹1000. Certificate of Registration was issued by the Registrar on 31 July 2000. Is the suit maintainable?
[**Hint:** The suit is not maintainable for want of registration of the firm on the date of institution of the suit. Refer Section 69(2)]

Answers to Objective-type Questions

1. (i) True (ii) False (iii) True (iv) True (v) False
(vi) True (vii) True (viii) True (ix) False (x) False

2. (i) bear, losses (ii) general law of agency (iii) partnership (iv) Dayabhaga
(v) Unlimited (vi) optional (vii) partnership at will (viii) nominal
(ix) Registration (x) firm

3. (i) (c) (ii) (b) (iii) (c) (iv) (d) (v) (a)
(vi) (d) (vii) (d) (viii) (c) (ix) (d) (x) (c)

10 Chapter in Review

LEARNING OUTCOMES

LO 1 Essential characteristics of partnership
LO 2 Mutual agency
LO 3 Sharing of profits
LO 4 Statutory limit of number of partners
LO 5 Partnership versus HUF
LO 6 Partnership versus company
LO 7 Formation of partnership
LO 8 Partnership deed
LO 9 Types of partners
LO 10 Minor as a partner
LO 11 Registration of partnership firm

KEY TERMS

Partnership: Association of persons to carry on a business jointly and share the profits thereof.

Mutual agency: A partner is both an agent and a principal in a partnership firm.

Co-ownership: A relationship whereby two or more persons jointly employ their property in a business to share its income.

Dayabhaga: Applicable only to the states of West Bengal and Assam; only the male members become heirs on the death of their father.

Mitakshara: Applicable to the rest of India; a joint Hindu family consists of all persons including the wives and unmarried daughters.

Partnership deed: An agreement-in-writing that contains terms and conditions of a partnership.

Partnership at will: A partnership for indefinite period.

Particular partnership: A partnership formed for a specific venture, or for a particular period.

LO1 Essential characteristics of a partnership include association of two or more persons; agreement to carry on some business, sharing of profits, and mutual agency.

LO2 A partner is both an agent and a principal in a partnership firm. Mutual agency is the convincing test of a partnership.

LO3 Sharing of profits, though is the *prima facie* evidence of partnership, is not the conclusive test of partnership.

LO4 In partnership, the maximum limit of partners has been fixed at 50, which can be extended up to 100 in case of a business firm and even beyond 100 in case of a professional firm.

LO5 Partnership and joint Hindu family are distinct in more ways than one. A partnership comes into existence by means of a contract between the partners, whereas a joint Hindu family arises as a result of status. HUF is a unique form of business existing only in India and is governed by the provisions of the Hindu Law Succession Act.

LO6 Partnership is different from a company in that a partnership comes into existence by an agreement between the partners, whereas a company can be formed only after fulfilling certain legal formalities and its registration under the Companies Act.

LO7 A partnership firm comes into existence only by an agreement between all the prospective partners and not by operation of law.

LO8 'Partnership deed' is a partnership agreement-in-writing that contains terms and conditions of the partnership and outlines the rights and obligations of all the partners.

LO9 Depending on their nature of role in the affairs of a partnership firm, the partners can be classified as active or ostensible, dormant or sleeping, nominal partner, partner-in-profits only, sub-partner, and partner by estoppels or holding out.

Active/Ostensible partner: One who enters into partnership by agreement and actively participates in the firm's business so as to produce in third parties a reasonable belief that he is a partner.

Dormant partner: A partner who invests in a firm's business and shares its profits but does not actively participate in the functioning of firm's business.

Nominal partner: One who just lends his name to a partnership firm but neither contributes to the capital nor shares its profits.

Partner by estoppel or holding out: A person liable as a partner to outsiders whose conduct causes an impression to the latter that he is partner in the firm.

LO[10] A minor being incompetent to contract cannot enter into partnership. He/she can, however, be admitted to the benefits of partnership with the consent of all the (major) partners.

LO[11] Although, it is not mandatory for a partnership firm to get it registered under the Partnership Act, but by creating certain disabilities from which an unregistered firm and its partners suffer, the Act has made the registration of firms desirable.

CHAPTER

11 Rights, Duties, and Liabilities of Partners

Learning Objectives

LO 1 Partnership deed vis-à-vis mutual relations of partners
LO 2 Rights of partners
LO 3 Duties of partners
LO 4 Liability of partners
LO 5 Reconstitution of partnership firm

A partnership comes into being through an agreement between two or more parties and such an agreement normally provides for mutual rights and obligations or duties of the partners. However, all agreements may not provide for all the rights and duties of partners. In such a situation, the provisions of the Partnership Act become automatically applicable. The provisions of the Act are also attracted by default in cases where the partnership arises by implication, or where the partnership deed is silent, or where the deed does not exist. Thus, the mutual relations between partners are governed by the partnership agreement as well as by the Act.

Partners: Mutual Relations

The mutual rights and duties between partners are spelt out in Section 11(1) of the Partnership Act, 1932. It states that, 'the mutual rights and duties of the partners of a firm may be determined by contract between the partners, and such contract may be expressed or may be implied by a course of dealing. Such contract may be varied by the consent of all the partners, and such consent may be expressed or may be implied by a course of dealing'. Thus, the mutual rights and duties of partners will be determined only by the provisions made in the agreement, apart from the cases where the Act contains mandatory provisions that are binding on all the partners. These are contained in Sections 9 and 10 and cannot be altered by individual agreements.

Rights of Partners

Unless agreed otherwise, the Act confers the following rights upon the partners of a firm.

Right to take part in the conduct of business Every partner has an inherent right to take part in the conduct and management of the affairs of the business of the firm [Section 12(a)].

Right to be consulted Every partner has a right to be consulted and heard in all the matters affecting the business of the firm. Any divergence arising as to ordinary matters connected with the business may be decided by a majority of the partners. But no change may be made in the nature of the business or constitution of the partnership without the consent of all the partners [Section 12(c)].

Right of access to books Every partner, whether active or dormant, has a right of access to all the records, books, and accounts of the business and also to inspect and copy them [Section 12(c)].

Right to share profits equally Every partner, irrespective of the amount of capital contribution or business expertise, is entitled to a share in the profits of the business equally [Section 13(b)].

Right to claim interest on capital Usually no interest is allowed on the capital contributed by the partners. But where a partner is entitled through the partnership deed, such interest shall be payable out of profits. If there are losses, the interest on capital will not be allowed [Section 13(c)].

Right to interest on advances Where a partner has made, for the purpose of the business, any payment or advanced some amount as loan to the firm, he will be entitled to interest at a rate agreed upon, and where no rate is stipulated, at 6 per cent per annum. Interest on loan will be payable despite the losses being suffered by the firm [Section 13(9d)].

Right to be indemnified Every partner has a right to be indemnified by the firm in respect of payments made or liabilities incurred by him under the following circumstances:

1. in the ordinary and proper conduct of the business and
2. in doing such act, in an emergency, for the purpose of protecting the firm from loss, as would be done by a person of ordinary prudence in his/her own case under similar circumstances [Section 13(e)].

Right to use partnership property Every partner is, as a rule, a joint owner of the partnership property and is entitled to have held and applied exclusively for the purposes of partnership business [Section 15].

Right in emergency A partner has the power in an emergency to do all such acts as are reasonably necessary for protecting the firm from losses [Section 21].

Right to prevent admission of a new partner Every partner is entitled to prevent the admission of a new partner into the firm without his/her consent [Section 21].

Right to retire Every partner has a right to retire by giving notice where the partnership is at will, or with the consent of all the partners in case of a particular partnership [Section 32(1)(c)].

Right not to be expelled Every partner has a right to continue in the partnership and not to be expelled from it. But the power to expel may be conferred by express agreement. In such a case, the power should, however, be exercised in good faith [Section 33(1)].

Right to carry on competing business An outgoing partner may carry on a business competing with that of the firm and he may advertise such business. But he cannot seek to do the following:

- using the firm's name,
- representing himself as carrying on the business of the firm, or
- soliciting the firm's customers [Section 36].

Right to share profits subsequent to retirement Unless otherwise agreed, an outgoing partner is entitled to share profits of the firm or claim interest at the rate of 6 per cent per annum on the amount of his share in the property of the firm if the other partners continue the business of the firm without any final settlement of accounts with the outgoing partner. This rule is also applicable in the case of death of a partner [Section 37].

Right to dissolve the firm A partner has the right to dissolve the partnership with the consent of all the partners. But where the partnership is at will the firm may be dissolved by any partner giving notice in writing to all other partners of his intention to dissolve the firm [Section 40].

Duties of Partners

The duties of partners' *inter-se* may broadly be classified into two heads.

1. Absolute duties and
2. Duties subject to agreement by partners.

Absolute duties

Absolute duties: Duties mandatory in nature and binding on all the partners as per the Partnership Act.

These duties are mandatory in nature and are binding on all the partners. These are imposed by the law and cannot be varied by individual agreements on partnership. Following are the absolute or mandatory duties of the partners.

Duty to carry on firm business to the greatest common advantage [Section 9] Any partnership is based on the doctrine of mutuality. Hence, each partner must act in good faith and carry on the business of the firm for mutual benefit and not for solely personal gain. Every partner must make the best use of his/her knowledge and skill while conducting business so as to secure maximum benefit for the firm. A partner should not make any personal or private profits through his dealings on behalf of the firm.

For example, *A* and *B* were partners in a firm of sugar refiners. *A*, who had greater skill and experience of buying sugarcane, was entrusted with the job of buying the same for the firm. He supplied the sugarcane from his personal stock, which he had bought earlier when the prices were low. He, however, charged the prevailing market price and made secret profits for himself. It was held that the firm was entitled to those profits and *A* must account to the firm for these private profits. *A* was negligent in his duty to carry on the firm business to the greatest common advantage [*Bentley vs Craven*[1]].

Duty to act in good faith [Section 9] An ideal partnership is based on mutual trust and confidence among the partners. Every partner should act in good faith and should be just and faithful to other partners. He/she should not deceive the co-partners by concealment of material facts.

Duty to render true accounts [Section 9] A partner is bound to keep and render true, fair, and correct accounts of the firm to other partners. Each partner should explain all the accounts kept by him to other co-partners and give true and correct picture of the same. He/she should not attempt to make private and secret profits at the expense of the firm.

Duty to provide full information [Section 9] This duty is also based on the fundamental principle of utmost good faith. As an agent of other partners, every partner is bound to communicate full information of all things affecting the business of the firm to co-partners. Thus, if a partner is in the possession of

[1] 1853, 104 RR 373

material facts related to the partnership affairs, he/she should not conceal that.

Duty to indemnify for loss caused by fraud [Section 10] Every partner is bound to make good or compensate the loss suffered by the firm due to his/her fraud in the conduct of the business of the firm. The object of this provision is to discourage partners to deal fraudulently in the conduct of the business. It may, however, be noted that the firm and other innocent partners shall remain liable to third parties for the fraud of any one of them. But they can proceed to claim damages against the partner who has committed fraud.

Duties subject to agreement: Duties as laid down by the 'Partnership Deed' or Agreement on the partners.

Duty not to transfer one's rights and interests [Section 29] It is the duty of every partner not to assign or transfer his/her rights and partnership interests to an outsider so as to make that person a partner in the firm.

Duties subject to agreement by partners

Subject to agreement among the partners, the Act lays down the following duties of partners *Inter-se*.

Duty to attend diligently [Section 12(b)] Every partner is obligated to attend diligently to his/her duties in the conduct of the business of the firm.

Duty to work without remuneration [Section 13(a)] A partner is not entitled to receive remuneration for taking part in the conduct of the business.

Duty to share losses [Section 13(b)] In the absence of an agreement to the contrary, every partner is bound to contribute to the losses equally. An agreement to share profits implies an agreement to bear the losses as well.

Duty to indemnify for wilful neglect [Section 12(f)] A partner, who is guilty of wilful neglect in the conduct of the business and if the firm suffers loss in consequence, is bound to indemnify (make compensation to) the firm and other partners. However, no partner will be liable for mere error of judgment or for the acts, resulting in loss, done in good faith without any *mala fide* or ill intention.

Duty to hold and use property of the firm exclusively for the firm [Section 15] Subject to contrary contract between the partners, every partner must hold and use the partnership property exclusively for the purpose of the business of the firm.

Duty to account for personal profits [Section 16(a)] Every partner must account for and pay back to the firm any profits derived by him/her for himself/herself from any transaction of the firm, or from use of the firm's property or through business connections of the firm or firm name.

Duty to account for profits of a competing business [Section 16(b)] Normally, there is no restriction on a partner as to carry on any competing business. But if the partners have agreed that no partner shall do any business, which is similar to or likely to compete with the business of the firm, he/she should not carry on such business without the consent of other partners. If he/she does that, then he/she shall be bound to account for and pay to the firm all profits made by him/her in that business.

Duty to act within authority [Section 19(1)] Every partner is bound to act within the scope of his/her actual or apparent authority. If he/she exceeds that authority and other partners do not ratify it, he/she shall compensate the co-partners for the loss suffered on account of such acts.

Relations of Partners with Third Parties

'Third Party' used in relation to a firm or a partner means any person who is not a partner in the firm. So far we have discussed the relationships between partners *inter se,* i.e., the rights and duties of partners towards one another. The business of the firm, of course, is conducted by its partners and during their usual course of transactions they have to deal with third parties on behalf of the firm. Such dealings of a partner give rise to legal relationship, which obviously binds the firm to third parties. Section 18 of the Partnership Act clearly states that, from the point of view of the third parties, a partner is an agent of the firm for the purpose of the business of the firm. Accordingly, all partners are liable to third parties for their acts, done on behalf of the firm,

Box 11.1 Acts of Partners Deemed As Implied Authority

Example 1

A and *B* are in a partnership business of exporting footwears. *B*, who is the managing partner, places an order for a huge quantity of cotton bales in the name of the firm. As this act does not relate to the norm of the business of the firm, it will not fall within the scope of implied authority. The firm, therefore, will not be liable for it.

Example 2

A, *B*, and *C* are in partnership. Their firm deals in readymade garments. *X*, a retailer, purchased goods worth ₹1000 on credit. Later on, *A* collected the amount due from *X* on behalf of the firm and utilised the sum for his personal use. *B* and *C* are not aware of this receipt. Here the firm cannot claim the amount from *X* on the plea that *A* had no authority to collect the amount. Collecting and receiving money from debtors is an act done in the usual course of business.

provided these are done in the ordinary course of business and in the name of the firm.

Authority of a Partner

The authority of a partner to bind the firm in the context of third parties may be express or implied.

Express authority

Express authority: Authority conferred on a partner by mutual agreement.

Authority is said to be express when it is given by words, spoken or written. Thus, the authority conferred on a partner by mutual agreement is called an express authority. The firm is bound by all acts of a partner done within the scope of his express authority, notwithstanding that the acts are beyond the scope of the partnership business.

Implied authority

Apparent/implied/ostensible authority: Authority arises by implication of law and not conferred by express agreement among the partners.

Also known as ostensible or apparent authority, implied authority is derived from either usage of trade, conduct of parties, or statute. It arises by implication of law and is not conferred by express agreement among the partners.

Doctrine and scope of implied authority Section 19 provides, 'Subject to the provisions of Section 22, the act of a partner which is done to carry on, in the usual way, business of the kind carried on by the firm, binds the firm'. However, Section 22 reads, 'In order to bind a firm, an act or instrument done or executed in the firm name, or on any other manner expressing or implying an intention to bind the firm'. Accordingly, for an act to be deemed as one with implied authority it is necessary that

- the act done by the partners must relate to the normal business of the firm [Box 11.1 (Example 1)].
- the act must have been done in the usual way of carrying on the firm's business [Box 11.1 (Example 2)], and
- the act must be done in the name of the firm and in some manner indicating an intention to bind the firm [Box 11.1 (Example 3)].

Acts within the implied authority of partner Subject to the limitations mentioned above, every partner has an implied authority to bind the firm by the following acts, i.e., the implied authority of a partner shall normally include

1. Selling firm's goods;
2. Buying, on behalf of the firm, goods in which the firm deals or which are used in the firm's business;
3. Receiving payments of the debts due to the firm and giving valid receipts for them;
4. Engaging and discharging employees;
5. Pledging movable property or goods of the firm as security for the purpose of getting loans;
6. Drawing, accepting, and endorsing negotiable instruments in the name of the firm; and
7. Employing solicitor or attorney on behalf of the firm to defend action against it [*Bank of Australia vs Beriliat*[2]] [Section 19(1) of the Indian Partnership Act].

[2] 1847, 6 Moor, P.C. 152

Acts outside the implied authority of partner Certain acts have been statutorily excluded from the scope of implied authority of a partner. A partner, therefore, cannot bind the firm by such acts unless the usage or custom of trade permits him/her. According to Section 19(2), which has restricted the scope of implied authority of a partner, in the absence of any usage or custom of trade to the contrary, the implied authority of a partner does not empower him/her to do the following:

1. Submit a dispute relating to the business of the firm to arbitration,
2. Open a bank account on behalf of the firm in his own name,
3. Compromise or relinquish any claim or portion of a claim by the firm,
4. Withdraw a suit or proceeding filed on behalf of the firm,
5. Admit any liability in a suit or proceeding against the firm,
6. Acquire immovable property on behalf of the firm,
7. Transfer immovable property belonging to the firm, or
8. Enter into partnership on behalf of the firm [Section 19(2)].

However, the partners by mutual agreement can extend or limit the implied authority of any partner [Section 20].

Partners' authority in emergency

Section 21 extends the scope of implied authority of a partner in an emergency and prescribes that 'a partner has authority, in an emergency, to do all such acts for the purpose of protecting the firm from loss as would be done by a person of ordinary prudence, in his own case, acting under similar circumstances, and such acts bind the firm'.

Thus, to enforce a partner's authority in an emergency, the following three requirements must be fulfilled:

1. there should be an emergency, i.e., a situation that requires urgent action,
2. the act should be done to protect the firm from loss or damage likely to be caused by such emergency, and
3. the nature of act should be such as would have been undertaken by a prudent person in his/her own case under similar circumstances.

Despite the fact that these acts do not form part of the implied authority of the partner, they would bind the firm [Section 21].

For example, Ram and Shyam are in partnership business of cement. They have decided by an express agreement that no partner would have the authority to sell the goods of the firm by allowing a cash discount of more than 10 per cent without consulting the co-partner. Owing to sudden slump in the market, the prices crashed. Ram, in order to save the firm from loss, sold all the stock of cement at 20 per cent discount without consulting his counterpart, Shyam. The firm is bound by such act undertaken by Ram.

Liabilities of Partners

The liability of partners may be classified as follows:

1. Liability of partners for acts of the firm
2. Liability of the firm for wrongful acts of a partner
3. Liability of the firm for misapplication by partners.

Liability of Partners for Acts of the Firm

Every partner is liable, jointly with all the partners and individually for all acts of the firm done while he/she was a partner. This is known as liability of partners for the acts of the firm. Furthermore, the liability of all the partners is unlimited. By virtue of joint and several or separate liabilities for every act of the firm, the third party can sue each partner individually and also jointly with other partners [Section 25]. Moreover, the act must have been undertaken in the ordinary course of the business of the firm [Sections 19(1) and 22].

Liability of the Firm for Wrongful Acts of a Partner

Where a partner, in the ordinary course of business, commits a wrongful act and some loss or injury is caused to any third party, the firm is liable for such an act. The wrongful act may be tort, fraud, or negligence [Section 26]. Section 10, however, provides protection to the firm in this regard stating that 'every partner shall indemnify the firm for any loss caused to it by his fraud in the conduct of the business of the firm'. This implies that such loss will be borne ultimately by the partner committing the fraud and cannot be shared amongst all the partners.

But in case loss is caused to third party by tort (i.e., breach of duty) or due to negligence on the part of any partner, all the partners shall be liable thereto. For instance, *X*, *Y*, and *Z* are partners. The business of the firm is to publish magazines. *X*, who is the editor of the magazine, allows the publication of a defamatory article about an eminent person *K*, without confirming its validity. *K* in turn sues the firm. The firm will be liable for this act of the editor partner as it was committed in the ordinary course of business.

Liability of the Firm by Misapplication by Partners

'Where a partner acting within the scope of his apparent authority receives money or property from a third party and misapplies it, or a firm in the course of its business receives money or property from a third party, and that money or property is misapplied by any of the partners while it is in the custody of the firm, the partner or the firm, as the case may be, is liable to make good the loss [Section 27]. For example, *A*, *B*, and *C* are partners in a business of financing real estate. *X*, a client of the firm, repays his loans of ₹50,000 to *A* who does not intimate his co-partners about the recovery of the loan and misuses the money. In this case, *X* would be discharged of the debts on account of payment made to *A*. It is up to the firm whether it initiates any suit against *A* to recover the amount held by him.

Reconstitution of a Partnership Firm

Reconstitution of a partnership firm: Any change in the composition or relations of partners.

Any change in the composition or relations of partners has the effect of 'reconstitution of the partnership firm'. Reconstitution takes place in the following circumstances:

1. A new partner is admitted
2. A partner retires
3. A partner is expelled
4. A partner is declared insolvent
5. A partner dies
6. A partner transfers his share in the firm to another person.

Admission of a New Partner or Incoming Partner

Subject to the contract between the partners and to the provisions of Section 31, 'no person shall be introduced as a partner into a firm without the consent of all the existing partners' [Section 31(1)]. Thus, a person cannot be admitted as a partner in an existing firm without the consent of all the partners. The reason behind this is quite obvious. Mutual trust and confidence among the partners being an essential ingredient of an ideal partnership, only such persons can be admitted in whom all the existing partners place their trust and confidence. This rule is, however, subject to any provision to the contrary in the partnership agreement. For instance, the partnership agreement between *A* and *B* provides that either partner could introduce into partnership any one of their sons on attaining the age of 18 years. In such a situation, there is no need for the consent of *B* if *A* decides to admit his son (who has attained majority) as a partner.

Liability of an incoming partner

Subject to the provisions of Section 30, a person who is introduced as a partner into a firm does not thereby become liable for any act of the firm done before he became a partner [Section 31(2)].

The above provision indicates that the liability of an incoming partner is limited only to those acts of the firm, which are committed after his/her becoming a partner. Thus, the liability of a new partner commences from the date of his/her admission. However, this general rule has two exceptions, which are as follows.

1. By mutual agreement, he/she may undertake to share the liabilities existing prior to his admission. But such an agreement is binding only among partners and does not entitle the creditors to proceed against the new partner for the recovery of old debts for the 'absence of privity of contract'. In order to make the new partner liable to creditor for past debts, the following two conditions should be satisfied.
   - The new partner or the reconstituted firm has assumed the liabilities for the past debts expressly or impliedly and
   - The creditors have accepted the new firm as their debtor.

2. Where a minor partner elects to become a full-fledged one on attaining majority, he/she shall be personally liable to third parties for all acts of the firm done, since he/she was admitted to the benefits of the firm.

Outgoing Partner

Outgoing partner: One who discontinues or ceases to be a partner in a firm for whatever reasons.

An outgoing partner is one who discontinues being a partner in the firm. Normally, a person discontinues or ceases to be a partner in a firm in any of the following five ways:

1. When he retires
2. When he is expelled
3. When he is adjudicated as insolvent
4. When he dies, and
5. When he transfers his interest in the firm

Retirement of a partner

According to Section 32(1), a partner may retire from the firm

- With the consent of all the other partners,
- In accordance with an express agreement by the partners, or
- Where the partnership is at will, by giving notice in writing to all the other partners of his intention to retire.

Liability of retiring partner A retiring partner remains liable for all the acts of the firm that had been done while he/she was a partner or acts pending at the time of his retirement. But as per Section 32(2), a retiring partner may be discharged from any liability to any third party for acts of the firm done before his retirement by novation, i.e., by an agreement made by him with such third party and the partners of the reconstituted firm. Such an agreement may be express or implied. He may also continue to be liable after retirement if he allows himself to be held out as a partner, e.g., by allowing his name to remain the firm name. Section 32(3) specially provides that 'until public notice of the retirement of a partner is given, the retiring partner and other partners continue to be liable as partners to third parties for any act done by any of them which would have been an act of the firm if done before his retirement'.

Expulsion of a partner

Expulsion of a partner: Removal or dismissal of a partner from the firm on certain grounds.

Expulsion of a partner means removal or dismissal of a partner from the partnership of the firm. In the normal course, a partner cannot be expelled from the firm. As per Section 33(1), 'a partner may not be expelled from a firm by any majority of the partners, save in the exercise in good faith of power conferred by contract between the partners'.

It means that a partner can be expelled from the firm only when the following three conditions are satisfied:

1. The power to expel a partner is available to firm, i.e., partners, by an express agreement between them;
2. The power of expulsion has been exercised by a majority of partners; and
3. The power has been exercised in good faith and for the benefit of the firm.

A partner who is otherwise expelled is entitled to be re-instated in the partnership. However, he/she is not entitled to damages for improper expulsion unless the expulsion was *mala fide*.

The partner who is being expelled must be given reasonable notice and opportunity to defend his/her position and to remove the cause of his/her expulsion [*Nemi Dass vs Kunj Behari*[3]]. A partner who is expelled from the firm is subject to the same rights and liabilities for acts done before or after his expulsion as those of a retired partner.

Insolvency of a partner

A person also ceases to be a partner if a court of competent jurisdiction declares him insolvent. Section 34(1) provides that 'where a partner in a firm is adjudicated an insolvent, he ceases to be a partner on the date on which the order of adjudication is made, whether or not the firm is thereby dissolved'. Thus, if a partner is declared insolvent, he/she thereby ceases to be a partner in the firm from the date on which the order of adjudication is made. It is not necessary that the firm be dissolved when a partner is declared insolvent.

[3] 1928, AIR, Oudh 424

Where under a contract between the partners, the firm is not dissolved by the adjudication of a partner as an insolvent, the estate of a partner so adjudicated is not liable for any act of the firm and the firm is not liable for any act of the insolvent, done after the date on which the order of adjudication[4] is made [Section 34(2)]. That is, if a firm is not dissolved, the estate of a partner, who becomes insolvent, is not liable for partnership debts contracted after the date of insolvency. It will, however, be liable for debts incurred before insolvency. In similar way, the firm is not liable for any act of the insolvent, done after the date on which the order of adjudication is passed. Nevertheless, the insolvent partner's share in the firm's assets may, of course, be utilised for firm's debts.

Furthermore, unlike a retiring partner, an insolvent partner is not required to give a public notice of his being adjudicated insolvent in order to terminate his liability for future acts of the firm. The adjudication of insolvency of an individual is by itself a public notice.

Death of a partner

Normally, the death of a partner results in the dissolution of the firm. If the partners agree that the death of any one of them will not have the effect of dissolution of the partnership as regards the surviving partners, the firm may not be dissolved unless it consists of only two partners [*Commissioner of Income-tax vs G.S. Mill*[5]]. As per Section 35, where under a contract between the partners, the firm is not dissolved by the death of a partner, the estate of a deceased partner is not liable for any act of the firm done after his/her death. It, thus, implies that the estate of a deceased partner will be liable only for the debts incurred before his/her death.

No public notice is needed in respect of a deceased partner to discharge his/her estate from liability for future acts of the firm. Death is a notice by itself. In *Bagel vs Wilter*[6], *X* who was a partner in *X* & Co. placed an order with the supplier of the firm to supply goods in his lifetime. But when the goods were delivered, *X* was no more. It was held that the estate of *X* (the deceased partner) was not liable for the debt. This is because there was no debt due in respect of the goods in *X's* lifetime.

Transfer of partner's interest in the firm

A partner can transfer his interest in the firm in full or partially to third party with or without any consideration. In certain cases, the transfer of a partner's interest in the firm may take place due to operation of law. For example, in the event of death of a partner, his interest in the firm may pass on to his/her legal heirs. But such persons (the transferee) are not treated as partners. Section 29 clearly states that 'a transfer by a partner of his interest in the firm, either absolute or by mortgage, or by the creation by him of a charge on such interest, does not entitle the transferee, during the continuance of the firm, to interfere in the conduct of the business, or to require accounts, or to inspect the books of the firm, but entitles the transferee only to receive the share of profits of the transferring partner, and the transferee shall accept the account of profits agreed to by partners'. The Supreme Court has also held that the assignee will enjoy only the rights to receive the share of the profits of the assignor and account of profits agreed to by other partners [*Narayanappa vs Krishanappa*[7]]. Thus, the transferee can neither participate in the conduct of the business of the reconstituted firm nor inspect the books of account. He/she can simply claim the transferring partner's share in the profits of the firm.

If the firm is dissolved or if the transferring partner ceases to be partner, the transferee will be entitled as against the remaining partners to receive the share of the assets of the firm to which the transferring partner is entitled and for the purpose of ascertaining that share, he can ask for an account as from the date of the dissolution [Section 29(2)].

It must, however, be noted that as a matter of fact, no partner can transfer his partnership interest with the intention of making the transferee a partner in the firm without the consent of all the other partners.

Rights of an outgoing partner

The rights of an outgoing partner include the following.

Right to carry on competing business An outgoing partner may carry on a business competing with that

[4] Order of Adjudication refers to judicial order declaring a person insolvent.

[5] 1966, AIR. S.C. 24

[6] 1903, 2 K.B. 212

[7] 1966 , 2 M.L.J. S.C. 6

of the firm, and he may advertise such business, but, subject to the contract to the contrary, he may not

1. Use the firm's name,
2. Represent himself as carrying on the business of the firm, or
3. Solicit the customers of persons who were dealing with the firm before he ceased to be a partner [Section 36(1)].

Furthermore, if the partners think that the above statutory restrictions are not sufficient to protect the interest of the firm, then as per Section 36, they may enter into an agreement that on ceasing to be a partner, any partner shall not carry on any business similar to that of the firm for a specified period or within a specified local limit. Such an agreement shall be valid if the restrictions imposed are reasonable.

Right to share subsequent profits in certain cases Where any member of a firm has died or otherwise ceased to be a partner, and the surviving or continuing partners carry on the business of the firm with the property of the firm without any final settlement of accounts as between them and the outgoing partner or his estate, then, in the absence of a contract to the contrary, the outgoing partner or his/her estate is entitled at the option of himself/herself or their representatives to such share of the profits made since he/she ceased to be a partner as may be attributable to the use of his/her share of the property of the firm or to interest at the rate of 6 per cent per annum on the amount of his/her share in the property of the firm [Section 37].

Where by contract between the partners an option is given to the surviving or continuing partners to purchase the interest of a deceased or outgoing partner, and that option is duly exercised, the estate of the deceased partner, or the outgoing partner or his/her estate, as the case may be, is not entitled to any further share of profits. But if the purchasing partner does not in all material respects comply with the terms of purchase, the right to share profits is revived [Proviso to Section 37].

Revocation of continuing guarantee by change in firm A continuing guarantee given to a firm, or to a third party in respect of the transactions of a firm, is, in the absence of agreement to the contrary, revoked as to future transactions from the date of any change in the constitution of the firm [Section 38].

Property of Firm

Subject to contract between the partners, the property of the firm includes all property and rights and interests in property originally brought into the stock of the firm, or acquired by purchase or otherwise or for the firm, or for the purposes and in the course of business of the firm, and also includes the goodwill of the business. Where a partner who does not contribute in cash towards the capital of the firm instead brings in immovable property as his share of capital, the same becomes the property of the firm. Here it is immaterial whether a formal document of transfer bas been executed in the name of the firm. Similarly, property acquired with money belonging to the firm is deemed to be the property of the firm, regardless of the fact that the partner has acquired that property in his own name, unless a contrary intention appears from his conduct [Section 14].

Exercises

I. Objective-type Questions

1. State whether each of the following statements is True or False:
   - (i) Partners are not bound to carry on the business of the firm to the greatest common advantage.
   - (ii) Where a partner is entitled to interest on the capital subscribed by him, such interest shall be payable whether or not there are profits.
   - (iii) An outgoing partner has a right to claim a share in the profits of the firm till his account is finally settled.
   - (iv) To attend diligently to his duties in the conduct of the business of the firm is the statutory duty of every partner.
   - (v) A partner may be expelled from the firm only with the consent of all other partners.

2. Fill in the blanks:
   (i) When there is any change in the composition of partners, it is called ________.
   (ii) The rights, duties, and liabilities of partners are usually determined by the ________.
   (iii) A new partner can be admitted with the consent of ________.
   (iv) Pledging goods of the firm as security for the purpose of getting loans is an act ________ implied authority of a partner.
   (v) An insolvent partner ________ required to give a public notice of his being adjudicated insolvent in order to absolve himself from any future liability.

3. Indicate the correct answer:
   (i) The 'reconstitution of the partnership firm' takes place
      (a) When a new partner is admitted or any partner retires
      (b) When a partner is expelled or is declared insolvent
      (c) When a partner dies or he transfers his interest to another person
      (d) In any of the above cases
   (ii) Any partner may retire from the firm
      (a) With the consent of all the other partners
      (b) In accordance with an express agreement among the partners
      (c) Where the partnership is at will, by giving a notice in writing to all other partners of his intention to retire
      (d) In any of the above ways
   (iii) To render the expulsion of a partner from the firm, which of the following conditions must by satisfied?
      (a) The power to expel a partner is available through an express agreement among the partners
      (b) The power has been exercised by majority of the partners and in good faith and for the benefit of the firm
      (c) Both (a) and (b)
      (d) The power has been exercised unanimously, i.e., by all the partners
   (iv) A partner ceases to be a partner in a firm
      (a) When he retires or is expelled
      (b) When he dies or is adjudicated as insolvent
      (c) When he transfers his interest in the partnership to another person
      (d) In any of the above ways
   (v) 'Order of Adjudication' is concerned with
      (a) Statutory duties of partners
      (b) Rights of partners
      (c) Insolvency of a partner
      (d) Expulsion of a partner

II. Review Questions

1. Explain in brief mutual rights and duties of partners in the absence of any express agreement between them.
2. Who is an outgoing partner? Explain his rights and liabilities.
3. What are the provisions of the Indian Partnership Act with regard to the expulsion of a partner from the partnership?
4. What do you understand by an implied authority of a partner? Describe the restrictions on the implied authority of a partner.
5. State the liabilities
   (a) Of a partner for the acts of the firm
   (b) Of the firm for torts (i.e., wrongful acts) of a partner
   (c) Of the firm for misapplication of money or property by a partner

6. Write short notes on
   (a) Insolvency of a partner
   (b) Incoming partner
   (c) Transfer of partner's interest in the firm
   (d) Reconstitution of a firm
   (e) Partnership Property

III. Caselets

1. *A*, being a partner in a firm of solicitors, committed a wrongful act, though he acted in the ordinary course of business. State whether the firm (i.e., partners) is liable for the tort.
   [**Hint:** Yes. Refer Section 26]

2. *A*, *B*, and *C* are partners in a business. The firm deals in sugar on wholesale basis. *C* was appointed to buy sugar for the firm. Without the knowledge of other partners, he supplied his own sugar to the firm at market price and made huge profits. Is he accountable to firm?
   [**Hint:** Yes. *C* will have to surrender the whole of the profit from the transaction. Refer Section 16(9)]

3. *X*, *Y*, and *Z* were three partners in a firm. *X* and *Z* by a resolution expelled *Y* from the firm, for *Y* by his willful neglect had caused much damage to the firm. By the same resolution, they admitted *P* into partnership in place of *Y*. *Y* objected to this arrangement. Decide.
   [**Hint:** Assuming the absence of an express agreement conferring the power to expel a partner by majority and permitting introduction of a new partner (as the problem is silent), *Y* is entitled to object his expulsion and also to the admission of *P*. Refer Sections 33 and 31(1)]

4. *A* was a partner in a firm. *A* ordered goods in his life time, but delivery was made after his (*A's*) death. The supplier of the goods claims to be paid off out of *A's* estate. Decide whether the creditor will succeed.
   [**Hint:** No. The estate of a deceased partner is not liable for any act of the firm done after his death. Refer Section 35]

5. *A* and *B* are partners in a retail business of readymade garments. Goods were sold on credit to *X*. Later on, *A* received the amount from *X* on behalf of the firm. But *B* did not know of this receipt. *A* used the money for his domestic purposes. Can the firm claim the amount from *X* on the plea that *A* had no authority to receive the amount?
   [**Hint:** No. Act is within the implied authority. Refer Section 19(2)]

6. *A*, *B*, and *C* are partners in *ABC* & Co. *A* without the authority of *B* and *C*, purchases 500 shares of Tata Iron & Steel Co. Ltd with the firm's money in his own name. Discuss if the shares are partnership property.
   [**Hint:** Yes. Refer Section 14]

Answers to Objective-type Questions

1. (i) False (ii) False (iii) True (iv) False (v) False
2. (i) reconstitution of partnership firm (ii) terms specified in the agreement (iii) all the partners (iv) within (v) is not
3. (i) (d) (ii) (d) (iii) (c) (iv) (d) (v) (c)

11 Chapter in Review

LEARNING OUTCOMES

LO1 Partnership deed vis-à-vis mutual relations of partners

LO2 Rights of partners

LO3 Duties of partners

LO4 Liability of partners

LO5 Reconstitution of partnership firm

KEY TERMS

Absolute duties: Duties mandatory in nature and binding on all the partners as per the Partnership Act.

Duties subject to agreement: Duties as laid down by the 'Partnership Deed' or Agreement on the partners.

Express authority: Authority conferred on a partner by mutual agreement.

Apparent/implied/ostensible authority: Authority arises by implication of law and not conferred by express agreement among the partners.

Reconstitution of a partnership firm: Any change in the composition or relations of partners.

Outgoing partner: One who discontinues or ceases to be a partner in a firm for whatever reasons.

Expulsion of a partner: Removal or dismissal of a partner from the firm on certain grounds.

LO1 Partnership deed usually provides for mutual rights and duties of partners. But if the agreement is silent about them, or where a partnership arises by implication, they will be automatically settled by the provisions of the Partnership Act.

LO2 Except otherwise agreed, the Act confers upon the partners of a firm to take part in the conduct of business, to be consulted and heard in all matters affecting the business of the firm, to have access to books of account and copy them, to have equal share in the profits, to have interest on loan to firm, to be indemnified by the firm in respect of payments made or liabilities incurred by them in the ordinary and proper conduct of the business.

LO3 Duties of partners may be classified as absolute or mandatory duties, and duties subject to agreement among partners. Absolute or mandatory duties of partners include acting in good faith and carrying on the firm's business to the greatest common advantage; rendering true, proper, and correct accounts of the firm; indemnifying the firm for loss suffered by it by their fraud; and not transferring their rights and interests to others.

LO4 Where a partner acting within the scope of his/her authority receives money or property from a third party and misapplies it, he/she is liable to the third party to make good the loss.

LO5 Reconstitution of a partnership firm implies any change in the composition or relations of partners that takes place when a new partner is admitted; or when a partner retires, or is expelled, or is declared insolvent; or dies, or transfers his/her share in the firm to another person.

CHAPTER

12 Dissolution of a Partnership Firm

Learning Objectives

LO 1 Dissolution of partnership
LO 2 Dissolution of partnership firm
LO 3 Modes of dissolution of a partnership firm without the order of court
LO 4 Dissolution of a partnership firm by the order of court

The term 'dissolution' implies breaking up of any constituted body of persons. The dissolution of a firm refers to discontinuation of the mutual relations existing between all the partners of the firm. The Partnership Act makes a distinction between the 'dissolution of partnership' and 'dissolution of firm'.

Dissolution of Partnership

Dissolution of partnership: End the relation between some of the partners.

Where there is an end to relation between some of the partners only, it is called dissolution of the partnership. When any one of the partners retires or becomes incapacitated from continuing as a partner due to death, insolvency, transfer of partnership interest, or insanity, the relationship between such a partner and others comes to an end, but the rest of the partners may resolve to continue with the partnership. If they do not do so then the dissolution of the firm may take place automatically. Thus, the dissolution of partnership may or may not involve the dissolution of a firm. A firm, after a change in the composition of partners may decide to continue as a reconstituted firm.

It must be noted that although the dissolution of partnership usually takes place when a firm is reconstituted, yet the terms dissolution and reconstitution cannot be used interchangeably. These are two distinctly legal concepts. While dissolution brings the partnership to an end, a reconstitution means the continuation of the partnership under altered circumstances. In law, there would be no difficulty if the dissolution of a firm is followed by the constitution of a new firm by some of the erstwhile partners who may take over the assets and liabilities of the dissolved firm [*I.T. Commissioner, W.B. vs M/S Pigot Chapman* & *Co.*[1]].

Dissolution of a Firm

Dissolution of a firm: Termination of partnership between all the partners of a firm.

Dissolution of a firm implies termination of partnership as between each and every partner of the firm. As per Section 9 of the Partnership Act, 'the dissolution of partnership between all the partners of a firm is called the dissolution of the firm'. Accordingly, the dissolution of a firm is a situation wherein the firm is dissolved as a whole. The following acts are done when the dissolution of a firm takes place:

1. The business of the firm is completely stopped;
2. Its assets are realised;
3. The liabilities are paid off; and
4. The surplus, if any, is distributed amongst the partners as per their share in the property of the firm.

As a result, the partnership is given a complete end.

Firm: Modes of Dissolution

Dissolution of a firm may take place with or without the order of court.

Dissolution Without Order of Court

Dissolution of a partnership firm without the order of court may take place in the following four modes.

Dissolution by mutual agreement

A firm may be dissolved with the consent of all the partners or in accordance with a contract between the partners. A partnership is the result of an agreement therefore, it can be put to an end by agreement between all the partners [Section 40].

Dissolution by notice

Where the partnership is at will, the firm may be dissolved any time, and by any partner giving a written notice of his intention to dissolve the firm to all the other partners. Such a dissolution will take effect from the date mentioned in the notice as the date of dissolution, or if no date is mentioned, as from the date of the communication of the notice [Section 43].

Compulsory dissolution

A firm is compulsorily dissolved

1. by the adjudication of all the partners or of all the partners but one as insolvent, or
2. by the happening of any event which makes it unlawful for the business of the firm to be carried on, or for the partners to carry it on in partnership [Section 44].

Thus, where all the partners or all except one become insolvent, or where the business of the firm

[1] A.I.R. 1982, S.C. 1085

Box 12.1 Circumstances of Compulsory Dissolution of Firm

Example 1

There were two partners in a firm. One of them was adjudicated as insolvent by a court of law. The firm must come to an end, as the partnership with one partner cannot continue.

Example 2

A firm is doing the business of trading in free sale cement. After sometime a law is passed, by which the business of free sale cement is prohibited. In this case the business of the firm becomes illegal, and so the firm will have to be compulsorily dissolved.

becomes unlawful because of some subsequent events, for instance, due to change of law a firm is automatically or compulsorily dissolved by the operation of law. Box 12.1 presents two examples to drive home the point.

Dissolution due to certain contingencies

In the absence of a contract to the contrary, a firm stands dissolved on the occurrence of any of the following contingencies:

1. Where the firm is constituted for a fixed term, it is dissolved at the expiry of that time;
2. Where the firm is constituted to carry out one or more ventures or undertakings, the firm is dissolved by the completion thereof;
3. On the death of a partner; and
4. On the adjudication of a partner as an insolvent [Section 42].

However, the above section does not apply to a partnership between two partners. The pact between the partners that on the death or insolvency of one of them, the partnership will not be dissolved may be made only if their number exceeds two. If there are only two partners, the only consequence of either's death or insolvency will necessarily mean the dissolution of the firm. This was made clear by the Supreme Court of India in *Commissioner of Income Tax vs Seth Govindram Sugar Mills*[2].

Dissolution of the Firm by Order of Court

On the receipt of a petition by a partner, the court may order the dissolution of the firm under any of the following circumstances.

When a partner becomes of unsound mind

When a partner becomes of unsound mind, he/she is incapable of forming a rational judgment. On this ground, a lunatic partner through his representative, or other partners may file a suit seeking the dissolution of the firm. In either case the court may order dissolution of the firm which will take effect from the date of the order [Section 44(a)].

Permanent incapacity of a partner

When a partner is in any way rendered permanently incapable of performing his duties, for example, he/she turns blind, or paralytic, etc., the court may at the instance of any other partner, order the dissolution of the firm. However, the incapacity of the partner must be of permanent nature [Section 44(b)]. The court may not pass an order for dissolution if the incapacity or disability is of a temporary and recoverable nature. For example, in *Whitewell vs Arthur*[3], a partner suffered a paralytic stroke. On this ground one of his co-partners filed a suit in the court seeking dissolution of the firm. The court deputed a doctor to examine the paralytic partner. The doctor diagnosed that the paralysis was of a temporary nature and the patient was improving. Accordingly, the court refused to pass on order of dissolution of the firm.

Misconduct of a partner

Where a partner is guilty of misconduct, the court may, at the instance of other co-partners, dissolve the firm if the misconduct is likely to be detrimental (i.e. damaging) to the business of the firm. In determining the effect of misconduct on the partnership business,

[2] AIR, 1966, S.C. 24

[3] 1804, 5 Esp 160

the nature of business should be kept in view [Section 44(c)]. Gambling by a partner, conviction of a partner for travelling without ticket, adultery by one partner with the wife of another partner etc., have been held to be sufficient ground for dissolution.

Persistent breach of agreement

Where a partner wilfully or persistently commits a breach of agreement related to the management of the affairs of the firm or the conduct of partnership business in such a way that the other partners find it impossible to carry on the partnership business with him, the court may order dissolution at the instance of the other partners [Section 44(d)]. Thus, embezzlement, keeping erroneous accounts, and not entering receipts, continuing to quarrel with other partners, fraudulent breach of trust, refusal to meet on matters of business, etc., may be sufficient ground for the court to order dissolution of the firm.

Transfer of interest

A partner is not entitled to assign away his/her partnership interest or share to a person so as to introduce him/her as a new partner to a firm. The court shall order dissolution of the firm at the behest of other co-partners if the partner-in-question transfers his/her partnership interest or share in any of the following ways [Section 44(e)]:

1. Transfers the whole of his/her interest in the firm to a third person;
2. Allows his/her share to be charged against a decree passed by a court towards payment of liabilities of that partner; or
3. Allowed his/her share to be sold in the recovery of arrears of land revenue, or of any dues recoverable as arrears of land revenue due by the partner [Section 44(e)].

Perpetual losses in business

The main object of a partnership is to earn profits. If this object cannot be achieved, there is no use of carrying on partnership business [Section 44(f)]. Thus, where the firm is continuously suffering losses and it is apparent that in future also the business cannot be carried on except at a loss, the court may allow the dissolution of the firm. The petition for dissolution may be filed by any one of the partners. It is to be noted that under this clause, a firm can also be dissolved before the expiry of the fixed period.

Any other just and equitable ground

As the grounds enumerated above are not exhaustive, the court may dissolve a firm on any other ground if it is satisfied that it would be just and equitable to dissolve the firm [Section 44(g)]. For example, the partners are not on speaking terms. A just and equitable ground is one, which is fair and reasonable as per the discretion of the court. The court may order the dissolution of a firm where the sub-stratum of the partnership has gone or where there is a complete deadlock and destruction of confidence among the partners [*Re: Yenidjee Tobacco Co. Ltd*[4]].

Consequences of Dissolution of a Firm

The dissolution of a firm has the following consequences on the partnership business.

Continuing Liability of Partners

Notwithstanding the dissolution of a firm, the partners continue to be liable to third parties for any act done by any of them which would have been deemed a general act of the firm done before the dissolution, until public notice is given of the dissolution [Section 45]. The notice of dissolution may be given by any partner. As per Section 72, the notice must be given to the Registrar of Firms and published in the official gazette and in at least one local newspaper circulating in the district where the firm to which it relates has its place or principal place of business. Here, it is to be noted that the notice of dissolution to the Registrar of Firms is required only in case of a registered firm. For third parties, partnership continues until a public notice is given of its dissolution. For example, *A* and *B* after carrying on business in partnership for several years, resolved on 31 March to dissolve the firm from the date. But they failed to give a public notice of the dissolution. On 1 July, *A* borrowed certain sum of money from *X* who was ignorant of the dissolution. In such a case *B* would also be liable for the amount individually as well as jointly with *A*.

[4] 1916, 2 Ch. 426

However, the above rule does not apply to the following:

1. the estate of deceased partner,
2. the estate of insolvent partner, and
3. a dormant (sleeping) partner who has retired from the firm.

These partners shall not be liable for acts done after the dissolution of the firm even though no public notice had been given by the dissolving firm.

Continuing Authority of Partners for Winding Up

After the dissolution of a firm, the authority of each partner to bind the firm, and the other mutual rights and obligations of the partners continue, so far as may be necessary. For example,

1. to wind up the affairs of the firm such as, realizing assets, discharging liabilities, etc., or
2. to complete transactions begun but unfinished at the time of the dissolution such as, effecting the delivery of the goods for order received by the firm before dissolution, and realizing sale proceeds, etc [Section 47].

It must, however, be noted that the firm is in no case bound by the acts of a partner who has been adjudged an insolvent except on the principle of holding out.

Right to Enforce Winding Up

On the dissolution of a firm every partner or his representative is entitled as against the others to have the property of the firm applied in payment of the debts of the firm, and to have the surplus distributed amongst the partners or their representatives according to their respective rights [Section 46].

Liability to Account for Personal Profits Earned After Dissolution

Where a firm is dissolved by the death of a partner and before its affairs are completely wound up, if the surviving partners along with the representatives of the deceased partner carry on business of the firm, any personal profits earned by them at the expense of the firm, i.e., by using firm's name or firm's property, must be accounted for by them to other co-partners [Section 50].

Right to Earn Personal Profits by Using Firm's Name

Where on dissolution of the firm, any partner or his/her representative has bought the goodwill of the firm, he/she will have the right to use the firm's name and earn personal profits [Section 50].

Right to Return of Premium on Premature Winding Up

Where a partner has paid a premium (goodwill) on entering into partnership of a fixed term, and the firm is dissolved before the expiration of that term, he/she shall be entitled to repayment of the premium, or of such part thereof as may be reasonable, keeping in view the terms of agreement and the duration of time during which he/she was a partner, except when

1. The dissolution is caused by the death of a partner, or
2. The dissolution is mainly due to the misconduct of the partner paying the premium, or
3. The dissolution is in pursuance of an agreement containing no provision for the return of the premium or any part thereof [Section 51].

For example, *A*, *B*, and *C* were partners in a firm. *C*, a new partner was admitted to the firm. *C* paid a premium of ₹10,000 and was told by *A* and *B* that the firm will last for next 5 years. At the end of 3rd year of his admission quarrels arose between *B* and *C* leading to dissolution of the firm by court order. In such a case *C* would be entitled to the refund of such amount of the premium from *A* and *B* as may be deemed reasonable. What is reasonable will depend upon the circumstances of each case.

Right in Case of Rescission of Partnership for Fraud or Misrepresentation

Where a partnership contract is rescinded on the ground of fraud or misrepresentation by any of the partners thereto, the aggrieved partner, besides other rights, is entitled to

1. a lien on the surplus, after payment of firm's debts, for any sum paid by him/her for purchase of a share in the firm and for any capital contributed by him/her,

2. To rank as a creditor of the firm in respect of any payment made by him/her towards the firm's debts, and
3. To an indemnity from the partners guilty of fraud or misrepresentation against all the debts of the firm [Section 52].

Right to Impose Restrictions

In the absence of a contract between the partners to the contrary, every partner or his/her representative has the right to restrain any other partner or his/her representative from carrying on a similar business in the name of the firm or from using any of the property of the firm for his own benefit, until the affairs of the firm have been completely wound up [Section 53].

Further as per Section 54, partners, upon or in anticipation of the dissolution of the firm, may agree that some or all of them will not carry on a business similar to that of the firm within a specified period or within specified local limits and such agreement shall be valid, if the restrictions imposed are reasonable.

Settlement of Accounts Between Partners

In settling the accounts between the partners of a firm after dissolution, the following rule shall be observed, subject to agreement by partners.

- Losses, including deficiencies of capital, are to be paid first out of undistributed profits, then out of capital, and lastly if necessary, by the partners individually in the proportions in which they were entitled to share profits [Section 48(a)].

For instance, *A* and *B* were partners sharing profits and losses equally. *B* died and the accounts of the firm transpired that he had contributed ₹5000 towards the capital of the firm and *A* has contributed ₹10,000. The net realizable value of the assets was ₹7000, and the firm had retained profits amounting to ₹5000. The deficiency [(₹10,000 + ₹5000) – (₹5000 + ₹7000), i.e., ₹3,000] would have to be borne equally by *A* and *B's* estate.

It must, however, be noted that the above-mentioned rules apply subject to agreement by the partners. The rules laid down in Section 48 are modal rules, i.e., they just specify, as to what will be the mode of settlement of accounts in the normal course of business. The partners are free to express any different intention as to the mode in which losses will have to be borne eventually. Such an intention must be given effect to. But no such agreement can affect the rights of the creditors of the firm.

- The assets of the firm, including any sums contributed by the partners to make up deficiencies of capital, shall be applied in the following manner and order
  - In paying off the debts of the firm to third parties,
  - In paying to each partner ratably what is due to him from the firm for advances as distinguished from capital,
  - In paying to each partner ratably what is due to him on account of capital, and
  - The surplus, if any, shall be divided among the partners in the proportions in which they were entitled to share profits [Section 48(b)].

Where the assets of the firm are not sufficient to pay off the liabilities of the firm including the amount due to each partner on account of capital, the partners have to contribute towards the losses, including deficiencies of capital in the proportion in which they are entitled to share profits. After they have contributed their share of deficiency they will be paid ratably the amount due to them by way of return of their capital [*The Rule Followed in the English Case of Garner vs Murray*[5]].

Furthermore, under the Rule in *Garner vs Murray* the deficiency of capital of an insolvent partner is to be borne by the solvent partners in their capital ratio. Box 12.2 would help us understand the point.

Payment of Firm's Debts and Private Debts of Partners

Where there are joint debts due from the firm, and also separate debts due from any partner, then for the settlement of such debts the following rules apply.

1. The property of the firm that shall be applied for the payment of the firm's debts first and if there is any surplus, then the share of each partner shall be applied in payment of his/her debts or paid to him/her.
2. The separate property of any partner shall be applied first in the payment of his separate debts, and the surplus (if any) in the payment of the debts of the firm [Section 49].

[5] 1904, 73 L.J. Ch. 66

Box 12.2 Settling Accounts Among Partners After Dissolution

X, *Y*, and *Z* are equal partners in a partnership business. The firm was dissolved on the expiry of the term it was constituted for. Partnership accounts maintained by the firm disclosed that contributions of *X*, *Y*, and *Z* to the capital of the firm were ₹20,000, ₹10,000 and ₹2000 respectively. The assets realised of the firm after paying off all the external liabilities were ₹14,000. The deficiency of capital being ₹18,000 (i.e., ₹20,000 + ₹10,000 + ₹2000 – ₹14,000) will be borne equally by all the partners, i.e., each partner would contribute ₹6000 towards the deficiency. After this is done, the assets then available, ₹14,000 + ₹18,000, i.e., ₹32,000/- will be distributed amongst the partners with the result that each partner will have suffered a loss of ₹6000. In actual practice, *X* and *Y* need not contribute ₹6000 each, but the matter will be settled on the basis of notional contributions. Accordingly their capital balances reduce to *X* (₹14,000), *Y* (₹4000), and *Z* (₹–4000). There is no problem if *Z* can bring in ₹4000 due from him. But if he becomes insolvent and only ₹1000 can be realised from him, then there will be a deficiency of ₹3000 which will be shared by *X* and *Y* in the ratio of their capitals, i.e., 2:1 (as per Garner vs Murray rule). Thus, their capitals will stand reduced to *X* [₹12,000, i.e., (₹14,000–₹2000)], and *Y* [₹3000, i.e., (₹4000–₹1000)] which can now be paid to them out of the amount (₹14,000) left after paying outside debts plus ₹1000 realised from Z's estate.

Sale of Goodwill After Dissolution

Section 55 provides the following rules relating to the sale of goodwill upon dissolution of a firm:

1. Goodwill to be included in the assets of the firm
2. Rights of buyer and seller of goodwill
3. Agreement in restraint of trade.

Goodwill to Be Included in the Assets of the Firm

While settling the accounts of a firm after dissolution, the goodwill shall, subject to contract between the partners to the contrary, be included in the assets, and it may be sold either separately or along with other property of the firm.

Rights of the Buyer and Seller of Goodwill

Where the goodwill of a firm is sold after dissolution, any partner of the dissolved firm may carry on a business competing with that of the buyer of goodwill. He/she may advertise such business, but, subject to agreement between him and buyer, he may not

1. use the dissolved firm's name,
2. represent himself as carrying on the business of the dissolved firm, or
3. solicit the customers or persons who were dealing with the firm before its dissolution.

Agreement in Restraint of Trade

Any partner of the dissolved firm may, upon the sale of the goodwill, enter into an agreement with the buyer of goodwill that he/she will not carry on any business similar to that of the dissolved firm within a specified period or within the specified local limits. Such agreement shall be valid if the restrictions imposed are reasonable, as it would not be prevented by Section 27 of the Indian Contract Act, 1872, which deals with the agreements in restraint of trade.

Exercises

I. Objective-type Questions

1. State whether each of the following statements is True or False:
   (i) Dissolution of partnership refers to a change in relation of partners caused by events like admission, insolvency, death of a partner, etc.

(ii) The expressions 'dissolution of firm' and 'dissolution of partnership' have the same meaning and can be used interchangeably.
(iii) As per Garner vs Murray Rule, any deficiency of capital arising from the insolvency of a partner is to be shared by other solvent partners in the ratio of their respective capitals.
(iv) The dormant partner is jointly liable for the acts of the other partners done after the dissolution of the firm if the firm fails to give a public notice of its dissolution.
(v) A partnership-at-will can be dissolved by a notice to all the partners.

2. Fill in the blanks:
(i) The dissolution of ______________ may or may not involve the dissolution of ______________ .
(ii) Insolvency of all partners except one can be a ground for ______________ dissolution.
(iii) In the event of continued losses, the court may dissolve even a partnership ______________ .
(iv) A partner has a right to return ______________ on premature winding-up.
(v) Any surplus left after payment of firm's debts is divided among the partners in a manner that is ______________ .

3. Indicate the correct answer:
(i) Which of the following cannot be a valid ground for a compulsory dissolution of a partnership firm?
(a) Death of a partner
(b) Insolvency of a partner
(c) Expiry of the fixed term for which the firm was constituted
(d) Persistent breach of agreement
(ii) On which of the following grounds, a partner may apply to the court for dissolution of the firm?
(a) Permanent incapacity of a partner to perform his duties as a partner
(b) Misconduct of a partner
(c) Transfer of interest (in firm) by a partner to a third party
(d) All of the above
(iii) In case of sale of goodwill in the event of dissolution of a firm, subject to agreement between a partner of the dissolved firm and the buyer of goodwill, he (i.e., partner) may not
(a) use the firm's name
(b) represent himself as carrying on the business of the old firm
(c) solicit the business from the customers of dissolved firm
(d) All of the above
(iv) The assets of the firm, including any sums contributed by the partners to make up deficiencies of capital, shall be applied
(1) in paying advances made by partner (distinct from investment of capital)
(2) in paying outside creditors
(3) in paying to each partner ratably what is due to him on account of capital
(4) the residue, if any among the partners in the proportions in which profits are divisible

What is correct manner and order of the above distribution of assets?
(a) 1,2,3,4 (b) 2,1,3,4
(c) 1,3,2,4 (d) 2,3,1,4
(v) Which of the following rights is usually not available to a partner consequent to the dissolution of a firm?
(a) Right of equitable distribution of firm's property
(b) Right to return of premium on premature winding up
(c) Right to be consulted
(d) Right to restrain any partner or his representatives from the use of firm name or firm property

II. Review Questions

1. Explain clearly 'dissolution of partnership' and 'dissolution of a firm'. Enumerate the various modes of dissolution of a partnership firm.
2. Discuss the circumstances under which the court can order dissolution of a partnership the firm on a petition filed by a partner.
3. What are the consequences of the dissolution of a partnership firm? Explain in brief rights and liabilities of partners.

   Or

   Describe the rights and liabilities of partners' consequent to dissolution of a firm.
4. Explain fully the rules relating to settlement of accounts of a partnership firm after dissolution.
5. Write short notes on
   (a) Compulsory dissolution of partnership firm
   (b) Sale of goodwill upon dissolution of a firm
   (c) Loss arising from insolvency of a partner
   (d) Dissolution of a partnership firm on happening of certain contingencies

III. Caselets

1. *A* and *B* form a trading partnership firm for ten years. After five years, *B* is convicted of travelling in train without ticket with intent to commit a fraud. Will the court dissolve the firm on the petition filed by *A* before expiry of the term?
   [**Hint:** Yes. The court may order for the dissolution if *A* could prove that the effect of *B's* misconduct will be detrimental to the partnership business. Refer Section 4(c)]
2. *A, B, C,* and *D* are partners. *C* is a sleeping partner who has not been known to creditors to be partner of *A, B,* and *D*. *C* retires from the firm. The firm is subsequently dissolved by mutual agreement among the remaining partners without giving public notice of dissolution. Is *C* liable for subsequent debts incurred by *A* and *B*?
   [**Hint:** No. Refer Section 5]
3. *P* and *Q* are equal partners in a business. On dissolution, it is transpired through the books of account that *P* has advanced more capital than *Q* to the tune of ₹20,000. The net assets were realized only ₹15,000. There is, thus, a deficiency of capital to the extent of ₹5000. In the circumstances, how much should *Q* pay to *P*?
   [**Hint:** ₹2500. Refer Section 48(a)]
4. *X, Y,* and *Z* are partners in a trading business who share profits and bear losses equally. *X* dies and the firm is dissolved subsequently. On the date of dissolution it was found that the capitals of *X* and *Y* were ₹25,000 each and that of *Z* ₹10,000. The external liabilities stood at ₹15,000 and the net realizable value of assets is ₹60,000. Workout the deficiency of capital, if any. State also how the partners will share the same?
   [**Hint:** The deficiency comes to ₹15,000 [(25000 × 2) + 10,000 + 15,000 – 60,000]. *Y, Z* and the legal heirs of *X* would share this equally. Refer Section 48]
5. *X, Y,* and *Z* are equal partners in a firm. The firm is dissolved by mutual agreement among the partners. The accounts show that on the date of dissolution the capitals of *X, Y* and *Z* were ₹10,000, ₹5000, and ₹3000, respectively. *Z* has advanced ₹5000 as loan to the firm and the creditors were ₹15,000. The assets realized ₹32,000. How would you settle the accounts?
   [**Hint:** Deficiency of capital comes to ₹6000 [₹10,000 + ₹5000 + ₹3000 + ₹5000 + ₹15,000 – ₹32,000]. *X, Y,* and *Z* shall share this loss equally reducing their capital balances to ₹8000, ₹3000, and ₹1000, respectively. Amount of ₹32,000 shall be utilized in the following manner and order.
   (i) ₹15,000 to pay creditors

(ii) ₹5000 to pay *Z's* loan
(iii) Balance of ₹12,000 to pay the capital balances of *X*—₹8000; *Y*—₹3000; and *Z*—₹1000]

Answers to Objective-type Questions

1. (i) True (ii) False (iii) True (iv) False (v) True
2. (i) partnership, firm (ii) Compulsory dissolution (iii) for fixed term
   (iv) premium (v) in the proportion in which they were entitled to share profits
3. (i) (d) (ii) (d) (iii) (d) (iv) (b) (v) (c)

12 Chapter in Review

LEARNING OUTCOMES

LO 1 Dissolution of partnership

LO 2 Dissolution of partnership firm

LO 3 Modes of dissolution of a partnership firm without the order of court

LO 4 Dissolution of a partnership firm by the order of court

KEY TERMS

Dissolution of partnership: End to relation between some of the partners.

Dissolution of a firm: Termination of partnership between all the partners of a firm.

LO1 Termination of relationship between some of the partners only. Due to expulsion of one of the partners, the relationship between such a partner and others comes to an end, but the rest may resolve to continue.

LO2 An extreme state wherein the business of a firm is completely closed, its assets are realized, the liabilities are paid off, the surplus is distributed amongst the partners as per their share in the property of the firm, and as a result, the partnership is given an absolute end.

LO3 By mutual agreement; by any partner giving notice in writing of his intention to dissolve the firm to all the other partners; by compulsory dissolution; on the occurrence of certain contingencies; on the expiry of term for which the firm was formed; on accomplishment of the purpose for which it was established; on the death of a partner; and on the adjudication of a partner as an insolvent.

LO4 The court may order the dissolution of a firm on any such ground as a partner becoming of unsound mind; permanent incapacity of a partner; misconduct on part of any partner; persistent breach of agreements; transfer of interest by a partner; perpetual losses in business; and any other ground that the court deems 'just and equitable'.

Part IV The Negotiable Instruments Act, 1881

CHAPTER

13 Negotiable Instruments: An Introduction

Learning Objectives

LO 1 Negotiable Instrument: Meaning and definition
LO 2 Kinds of negotiable instruments
LO 3 Payment-in-due-course
LO 4 Payment of interest
LO 5 Negotiable instruments: Special rules of evidence
LO 6 Negotiable instruments: Rules of international law
LO 7 Holder and holder-in-due-course

The law regulating promissory notes, bills of exchange, and cheques is contained in The Negotiable Instruments Act, 1881[1]. Though the Act was enacted with an object to define and amend the then existing law relating to promissory notes, bills of exchange and cheques, yet other instruments which satisfy the conditions of negotiability by usage or custom of trade, namely, share warrants and bearer debentures, also come under its purview. This Act is based on the English Common Law related to promissory notes, bills of exchange and cheques. The Act came into force on 1 March 1881. It extends to the whole of India.

The Act is divided into 147 sections, spread over 17 chapters. Section 1 of the Act deals with short title of the Act and its commencement; Section 2 addresses repeal of enactments; Section 3 contains interpretation clause of 'banker'; Sections 4–25 deal with the key terms used in the Act; Sections 26–45 describe the parties to negotiable instruments and outline their rights and liabilities; Section 46–60 deal with the intricacies involved in the act of negotiation; Sections 61–76 discuss presentment of an instrument for acceptance/payment; Section 77 describes liability of banker for negligently dealing with bill presented for payment; Sections 78–81 deal with payment of an instrument and interest applicable thereon, if any; Sections 82–90 elaborate the mode of getting parties discharged from liabilities; Sections 91–98 dishonour of negotiable instruments and notice served in relation thereto; Sections 99–104A deal with noting and protest in relation to dishonour of an instrument whereas Sections 105–106 discuss the reasonable time of giving and serving notice of dishonour; Sections 108–116 of the Act deal with acceptance and payment of an instrument for honour and reference in case of need; Section 117 exclusively deal with rules as to compensation in case of dishonour of an instrument; Sections 118–122 discuss special rules of evidence; Sections 123–131 deal with special provisions pertaining to crossed cheques; Sections 138–147 of the Act prescribe penalties in case of dishonour of certain cheques for insufficiency of funds in the accounts. The present chapter, however, unveils provisions of the Act as regards the nature and kinds of negotiable instruments; parties to an instrument; special rules of evidence; holder and holder-in-due-course, etc.

[1] Throughout our discussion on law of negotiable instruments in this book (i.e. Chapters 13 to 16) the word 'Act' refers to The Negotiable instruments Act, 1881. Similarly, the references to sections in these chapters, unless otherwise mentioned, pertain to The Negotiable Instruments Act, 1881

Negotiable Instrument: Meaning and Definition

A negotiable instrument is essentially an instrument of credit, readily convertible into money and easily deliverable from one person to another. The word 'negotiable' means 'passable by delivery', and 'instrument' means 'a written document which creates a right in favour of some person'. Thus, the expression 'negotiable instrument' implies a written document transferable by delivery from one person to another. The unique advantage associated with a negotiable instrument is its easy negotiability. It is transferable with a simple procedure requiring a signature and delivery (in case of order instruments) or just delivery (in case of bearer instruments). The law endorses such a way of transfer of a negotiable instrument and protects the interest of the parties involved therein. As per Section 13 of the Act, 'a negotiable instrument' means a promissory note, bill of exchange, or cheque payable either to order or to bearer. Accordingly, an account payee cheque fails the test of a negotiable instrument. However, it is important to note that once an account payee cheque stands dishonoured (for insufficiency of funds in the drawer's account), it assumes the character of a negotiable instrument, hence governed by Section 138 of the Act. Thus, instruments marked as 'not negotiable' may be legally binding and governed by the provisions of the Act.

Major Drawback of Statutory Definition

A major drawback of the definition of negotiable instrument as given in Section 13, is that it hardly defines a negotiable instrument. It does not explain any of its salient features, rather it provides an idea of the types of negotiable instruments. Moreover, this definition narrows down the meaning of a negotiable instrument and deals with only three most common types of negotiable instruments: promissory notes, bills of exchange, and cheques.

The Act does not even cover all kinds of instruments, which have an element of negotiability in them, such as banker's cheques, dividend warrants, bills of lading, and railway receipts. Therefore, an instrument may not come under the purview of this Act, although the same may be negotiable due to its unique features. Thus, this definition does not befit the term in the complete sense of its usage and coverage. Let us examine some more comprehensive expressions that seek to define negotiable instruments in explicit term.

Negotiable instrument: An instrument of credit wherein the transferee gets the better title than that of the transferor.

'A negotiable instrument is one, the property in which is acquired by any one who takes it bona fide and for the value, notwithstanding any defect of title in the person from whom he took it.'
[Justice K.C. Wills, *The Law of Negotiable Securities*]

'An instrument is negotiable when it is, by a legally recognised custom of trade or by law, transferable by delivery or by endorsement and delivery without notice to the party liable in such a way that (a) the holder of it for the time being may sue upon it in his own name, and (b) the property in it passes to a bona fide transferee for value free from any defect in the title of the person from whom he obtained it.'
[Thomas, *Commerce: Its Theory and Practice*]

The above definitions not only attempt to highlight the salient features of a negotiable instrument but also signify the real test of a negotiable instrument that the person who takes it for value and in good faith is not affected by the defect in the title of the transferor. Thus, the transferee of a negotiable instrument gets the better title than that of transferor provided that he (transferee) acquires it in good faith and for valuable consideration. For instance, *X* steals a signed cheque (bearer one) from the drawer of *Y* and transfers it to *Z* who takes it for value and *bona fide*. In this case, the title of the transferee (*Z*) will be good, even though the title of the transferor (i.e., *X*) is defective as the cheque is stolen one.

Salient Features of Negotiable Instruments

A thorough examination of the above-mentioned definitions, including the statutory one, shows the following eight salient features (or essential elements) of a negotiable instrument.

1. Freely transferable
2. Defect-free title to the transferee
3. Recovering
4. Ceiling on transfers
5. Payable to order
6. Payable to bearer
7. Payment
8. Presumptions

These are briefly discussed here.

Freely transferable

Hassle-free transferability is the indispensable feature of a negotiable instrument. A negotiable instrument is movable from one person to another without any legal or documentary procedure. The property in a negotiable instrument passes by mere delivery if the instrument is payable to bearer, and by endorsement and delivery if it is payable to order.

Defect-free title to the transferee

The real test of a negotiable instrument is whether the transferee gets the instrument free of all defects. The general rule is that no one can transfer a better title to a property than that he himself has. For example, if a person steals a car and sells it to someone, the buyer does not get any legal title to the car, as the transferor himself had no title to the car. The real owner of car can anytime obtain possession from the buyer, even if the buyer had purchased the car in good faith and had no idea that the seller had no title to the car. This provision, no doubt, sounds healthy, but would make free negotiability of instruments difficult, if it extends to negotiable instruments, as it would be difficult to verify title of transferor in every case. Hence, it is provided that if a person acquires a negotiable instrument in good faith and without knowledge of defect in title of the transferor, the transferee can enjoy better title to the instrument, even if the title of transferor was defective. Thus, a negotiable instrument constitutes an exception to the general rule of the law of transfer of title that '*nemo dat quod non-habet*'—no one can transfer a better title than that he himself has.

Recovery

The holder-in-due-course is presumed to be the owner of the property contained in the negotiable instrument and is entitled to sue the instrument in his own name (in case of dishonour) for the recovery of the amount. Also, it is not required on his part to give notice to the debtor of the fact that he has become the holder.

Ceiling on transfers

There is no definite upper limit on the number of transfers in case of a negotiable instrument. It can be transferred any number of times till its maturity. But a cheque, whether by order or bearer, can be transferred any number of times till it becomes stale, i.e., within three months from the date of its issue.

Payable to order

It should be noted that where the instrument prohibits its transferability or indicates that it shall not be transferable but remains valid as between the parties thereto, it is not a negotiable instrument, as it cannot be negotiated further. Thus, for an instrument to be negotiable, it should be made payable to order. The various forms in which an instrument can be made payable are as follows.

1. Pay Ram
2. Pay Ram or Order
3. Pay to the Order of A
4. Pay Ram and Shyam, and
5. Pay Ram or Shyam, etc.

A promissory note, bill of exchange, or a cheque payable to order, which is expressed to be so payable, or which is expressed to be payable to a particular person, and does not contain words prohibiting transfer or indicating that it shall not be transferable, are all good examples of a negotiable instrument.

But a negotiable instrument may contain any words restricting its transferability, expressly or impliedly, e.g., 'Pay to Ram only' or 'Pay to Ram and none else'. If it is made so, it will not be treated as 'payable to order' and thereby shall not be a negotiable one.

Payable to bearer

The 'bearer' refers to the person who is in the possession of an instrument. Therefore, 'payable to bearer' means payable to any person who possesses it. A promissory note, bill of exchange, or cheque is payable to bearer which is expressed to be so payable, or on which the only or last endorsement is an endorsement in blank. The most common forms of a bearer instrument are as follows.

1. Pay Ram or bearer
2. Pay Ram, Shyam, or bearer
3. Pay self or bearer
4. Pay self

In all the above cases, the sum of money contained in a negotiable instrument would be payable to the bearer. It should also be noted that if an instrument is originally made payable to order, it may become payable to bearer, if it is endorsed in blank by the payee. For example, a cheque is made 'payable to Kumar'. Kumar endorses it merely by signing on the back (without making it payable to Verma or Verma's order) and delivers it to Verma. The cheque subsequently becomes a bearer instrument in the hands of Verma.

Payment

A negotiable instrument may be made payable to two or more payees jointly, or it may be made payable in the alternative to one or two, or one or several payees [Section 13(2)].

Presumptions

Sections 118–119 of the Act lay down certain presumptions that generally apply to negotiable instruments. These eight presumptions are said to prevail, unless the contrary is proved.

Consideration It is presumed that every negotiable instrument was made, drawn, accepted, endorsed, negotiated or transferred for negotiation [Section 118(a)].

Date It is presumed that every negotiable instrument bearing a date was made or drawn on the due date [Section 118(b)]. An instrument could also be post-dated and even be issued on a public holiday. But a post-dated instrument can be sued on only after the passing of the due date.

Time of acceptance It is presumed that every accepted bill of exchange was accepted within a reasonable time after its date and before its maturity [Section 118(c)].

Time of transfer It is presumed that every transfer of a negotiable instrument was made before its maturity [Section 118(d)].

Order of endorsement It is presumed that the endorsements appearing up on a negotiable instrument were made in the order in which they appear thereon [Section 118(e)].

Stamp It is presumed that a negotiable instrument, except a cheque (as no stamp duty is prescribed for cheques under the Indian Stamp Act) was duly stamped. This proves helpful in case the instrument is destroyed or lost.

Holder-in-due-course It is presumed that the holder of a negotiable instrument is also a holder-in-due-course unless it is proved that the holder has obtained the instrument from its lawful owner or from any person in lawful possession thereof, by committing an offence, fraud, or for unlawful consideration. Thus, a holder-in-due-course is one who has obtained the instrument in good faith and for value.

Proof of protest In a suit upon an instrument, which has been dishonoured, the court shall, on proof of the protest, presume the fact of dishonour unless such fact is disproved. In the event of dishonour of a negotiable instrument, the holder can file a suit for recovery of the amount contained in the instrument but before doing so, he/she should obtain a certificate from a notary about the fact of dishonour. This certificate is called protest. The 'protest' must be properly drawn up in conformity with the provisions of Section 101 of the Act. The court shall, on proof of protest, presume that the instrument was presented for payment or acceptance and that it was dishonoured by non-acceptance or non-payment, as the case may be. Protest acts as a *prima facie* evidence of dishonour.

All the above presumptions can, however, be refuted by the defendant by means of evidence to the contrary.

Kinds of Negotiable Instruments

The Negotiable Instruments Act, under Section 13, recognises only three kinds of instruments, i.e., promissory notes, bills of exchange, and cheques. The Act, however, does not exclude any other instrument if it entitles a person a sum of money and is transferable by delivery, and the transferee can acquire a better title. Accordingly, shares/dividend warrants, bearer debentures, government bonds payable to bearer, treasury bills, port trust or improvement trust debentures and instruments written in local languages, i.e., *hundis*, etc., have also been included in the category of negotiable instruments. Promissory notes, bills of exchange, and cheques, being prominent negotiable instruments, have been discussed at length in this chapter.

Promissory Note

According to Section 4 of the Act, 'A "promissory note" is an instrument in writing (not being a bank note or currency note) containing an unconditional undertaking, signed by the maker to pay a certain sum of money only to, or the order of a certain person, or only to bearer of the instrument'.

The person making the promise to pay is called the 'maker' and the person who is to receive the money stated in the instrument is called the 'payee'.

Parties to a promissory note

A promissory note, also called 'pro-note', may have the following parties.

Maker A person who issues or executes the note promising to pay the amount stated therein is called the maker.

Payee This is the person who is to receive the money stated in the pro-note.

Holder This is the person who is entitled in his own name to the possession of a pro-note, and to receive or recover the amount thereon. He/She may be either the payee or some other person to whom he may have endorsed the note.

Endorser This is the maker or payee who may endorse an instrument.

Endorsee The endorsee is the transferee or the person in whose favour the pro-note has been endorsed.

Essentials of valid promissory note

The definition given in the Act sets out the essentials of a promissory note. It also makes it clear that although banknotes (i.e., promissory notes issued by a banker payable to bearer on demand) and currency notes (i.e., promissory notes issued by RBI or the Central Government payable to bearer on demand) bear almost all the characteristics of a promissory note, yet they should not be treated as a promissory note. The following are the essential characteristics of a promissory note.

1. It must be in writing.
2. It must contain an express undertaking to pay.
3. The promise or undertaking to pay must be unconditional.
4. The promise must be for paying certain sum of money.
5. It must be signed by the maker.
6. The maker must be a certain person.
7. The payee must be certain.
8. Payment must be in legal tender money of India.
9. It must be properly stamped.
10. It must contain number, place and date of signature.

These features are described below.

It must be in writing A promissory note must be in writing. An oral promise to pay is not enforceable. It may be written in ink or with pencil and includes printing or typing also. No particular format of words is necessary. But, of course, the words used must indicate a clear undertaking to pay. It is even not necessary that the word 'promise' be used as held in *Balmukund vs Munnalal*.

The specimens of a typical promissory note are given in Box 13.1.

It must contain an express undertaking to pay. A promissory note must contain an express undertaking or promise to pay. Though the use of word 'promise' or 'undertaking' is not necessary, there must be a clear and fair intention to show an express undertaking to pay. A promissory note, which contains 'I am indebted to *X* for ₹1000', is not a promissory note since there is no express promise to pay. This implies a mere acknowledgement of indebtedness but is not a promissory note (although it may be valid as an agreement and may be binding upon the parties involved). Let us consider the following expressions:

(a) 'I promise to pay *X* or order ₹50,000.'
(b) 'Mr *B*, I.O.U. (I owe you) ₹50,000.'

Box 13.1 Specimens of a Typical Promissory Note

Specimen 1

₹5000 /-

New Delhi,
2 June 2013

Sixty days after date I promise to pay Mr *Y* the sum of rupees fifty thousand only, with interest thereon at 12% per annum, for value received.

To,
Mr *Y*
New Delhi

Revenue Stamp

Mr *X* (Sd/- on stamp)

Specimen 2

₹5000 /-

New Delhi,
2 June 2013

Ninety days after date, I promise to pay Mr *Y* or order the sum of rupees fifty thousand only.

To,
Mr *Y*
New Delhi

Revenue Stamp

Mr *X* (Sd/- on stamp)

(c) 'I am liable to pay *X* ₹50,000.'
(d) 'I have borrowed from *X* ₹50,000 and I shall be accountable to him for the same with interest thereon.'

Of the above, only (a) truly represents a promissory note. The rest are not promissory notes, as they do not contain an express and clear promise or undertaking to shell out.

The promise or undertaking to pay must be unconditional A promissory note, in order to be valid, should contain an unconditional promise to pay. The promise to pay should not be dependent upon the happening of some uncertain and contingent event. An uncertain and conditional promise may render it invalid. It should, however, be noted that if a promise is conditional or contingent on the happening of an event which is certain to occur, the promise shall not be held conditional within the meaning of Section 4. Thus, an instrument, which bears such type of undertaking or promise, will be valid and become negotiable after the happening of such event or fulfilment of such condition.

For instance, let us consider the following examples:

(a) 'I promise to pay Mr *Y* ₹5000 when I am able to pay.'
(b) 'I promise to pay Mr *Y* ₹5000 on my marriage with *Z*.'
(c) 'I promise to pay Mr *Y* ₹5000 seven days after the death of *Z*.'

Of the above cited examples (a) and (b) do not represent a valid promissory note as the promise in both the cases is conditional and uncertain. Example (c), however, truly characterises a promissory note as the promise is based on a condition or event which is certain to happen. Such a promise is not considered to be conditional within the meaning of Section 4.

The promise must be for paying certain sum of money. The amount of a promissory must be definite and certain so as to deliver the validity of the instrument.

For example, *X*, being maker of a promissory note, signs the instrument in the following terms:

(a) 'I promise to pay *A* ₹1000 and all other sums which become due.'
(b) 'I promise to pay *Y* ₹1000 with interest thereon.'
(c) 'I promise to pay *Z* ₹1000 and all fines according to rules.'

The above-mentioned terms in all instruments are invalid as promissory notes since the exact sum of money payable by *X* is not certain. Hence these instruments are not negotiable.

It must be signed by the maker A pro-note will not be authentic unless the maker or promisor signs it, even if the promisor writes it in his/her own handwriting. Place and form of signature are, however, immaterial. If the maker is illiterate, his/her thumb impression is sufficient.

The maker must be a certain person The maker, i.e., the person by whom the payment is to be made must be certain. If a person signs under a fictitious or an assumed name, he/she shall be liable as a maker, since a maker is presumed certain if his/her for identity depicts from his description. In case there are two or more makers, they will bind themselves jointly or jointly and severally but not alternatively as the general rule implies 'Where liability lies no ambiguity must lie'.

The payee must be a certain person Like the maker, the payee of a promissory note must also be a certain and definite person on the face of the instrument. A promissory note in favour of a fictitious person is illegal and void. Nonetheless, it is immaterial whether the payee is named properly or misnamed. A payee may even be indicated by his official designation provided he can be identified by evidence. A promissory note may be made payable to two or more people jointly or alternatively. But if it is payable to alternative payees, it must be made payable originally to order. A promissory note made payable to bearer originally is illegal and void as per the RBI Act, 1934. Finally, a promissory note made payable to the maker himself shall not render any validity because of the fact a promisor cannot be promisee for the same instrument.

The payment must be in legal tender The amount payable must be in legal tender of money of India, i.e., rupees only. If an instrument is payable in foreign currency or in kind (goods, etc.), it shall not be valid as a promissory note. For example, consider the following expressions of promissory notes:

(a) 'I promise to pay *B* ₹50,000/- on demand.'
(b) 'I promise to pay *B* \$ 20,000 at New Delhi.'

(c) 'I promise to pay *B* ₹50,000 and to deliver him my black horse.'

(d) 'I promise to pay Peter ₹1,00,000 in cash and a suit length worth ₹5,000.'

Of the above-cited illustrations all, except (a), are invalid promissory notes.

It must be properly stamped A promissory note must be duly stamped as per the requirements of the Indian Stamps Act, 1899, and the maker's signature, or initials, or thumb impression on it must duly cancel it. A pro-note can be stamped either with adhesive stamps or engrossed on a stamp paper of proper value. An unstamped or improperly or inadequately stamped pro-note is not admissible in evidence and suit cannot be maintained upon it. It should, however, be noted that an unstamped or improperly or insufficiently stamped pro-note is though invalid but it does not hamper the recovery of loan if proved otherwise.

It must contain the number, date, and place of signature A pro-note must contain the number, name of place and the date on which it was made. Their omission, however, will not cause the instrument to be invalid. If it is undated, it shall be deemed to be dated on the date of delivery. Beside date, it is usual to provide for the place of signature and signature of two witnesses, though the law does not insist upon them for ensuring the validity of the note.

Bill of Exchange

A 'bill of exchange' is an instrument in writing, containing an unconditional order, signed by the maker, directing a certain person to pay a sum of money only to, or to the order of, a certain person, or to the bearer of the instrument [Section 5].

The bill of exchange is used primarily in international trade, and is a written order by one person to pay another a specific sum on a specific date, sometime in the future. It is known as 'draft' in the US. If the bill of exchange is drawn on a bank, it is called a bank draft.

Parties to bills of exchange

A bill of exchange may involve the following parties:

Drawer This is the person who writes and signs the bill.

Drawee This is the person on whom the bill is drawn.

Acceptor This is the person who accepts the bill. In practice, the drawee is the acceptor but a third person may accept a bill on behalf of the drawee.

Payee This is the person to whom the money stated in the bill is payable. He may be the drawer or any other person to whom the bill has been endorsed.

Holder This is the person who is in the possession of the bill, after being drawn. He/She may be the original payee, endorsee and bearer in case of a bearer bill.

Endorser The person, either the drawer or holder, who endorses the bill to any one by signing on the back of it is called an endorser.

Endorsee He/she is the person in whose favour the bill is endorsed.

'Drawee in case of need' This is a person who is introduced at the option of the drawer. Any endorser may insert the name of such person, and the effect of it is that a resort may be had to him in case the bill is dishonoured for non-acceptance or non-payment or in any other need.

'Acceptor for honour' The person who voluntarily becomes a party to a bill as acceptor in the event of the refusal by original drawee to accept the bill if demanded by the notary, is known as 'acceptor for honor. The acceptor for honour offers to accept the bill *supra protest*[2] with a view to safeguard the honour or prestige of the original drawer or any other endorser, as the case may be. This happens when the bill gets dishonoured and a formal certificate of dishonour, known as protest, is issued by the Notary Public to the holder of a bill in question. Hence the term supra protest.

It is not necessary that all the above-mentioned parties are involved in one bill of exchange. Usually there are three parties to a bill of exchange — drawer, drawee, and payee. It is also not necessary that three separate persons should answer to the description

[2] This happens when the bill gets dishonoured and a formal certificate of dishonour, known as protest, is issued by the Notary Public to the holder of a bill in question. Hence the term supra protest.

Specimen of a bill of exchange

₹1,00,000 /-		New Delhi, 1st June 2018
Sixty days after date pay Bhushan or order the sum of rupees one lakh only, for value received.		
To, Ashok Kumar Jamia Nagar,		Revenue Stamp
New Delhi-110025	Accepted Sd/- Ashok kumar	Mr Ajay (Sd/- on stamp)

of drawer, drawee, and payee. Depending upon the situation one person may fill any two of three positions. Accordingly, drawer and payee may be the same person. For instance, when the bill is drawn as 'pay to me or my order', drawer and drawee may be the same person. Similarly, when a principal draws a bill on his agent or upon himself, drawee and payee may be the same person.

In the above specimen bill of exchange Ajay is the drawer, Ashok Kumar is drawee and Bhushan is the payee (original).

Essentials of bill of exchange

The definition of a bill of exchange is very close to that of a promissory note. Therefore, a bill of exchange has more or less the same essential characteristics as a promissory note. The following are the essential elements of a bill of exchange.

1. It must be in writing.
2. It must contain an express order directing a certain person to pay.
3. The order to pay must be unconditional.
4. There are parties to a bill of exchange, viz., drawer, drawee, and payee.
5. It must be signed by the drawer.
6. The drawer must be a certain person.
7. The drawee must be a certain person.
8. The payee must be a certain person.
9. The sum payable must be certain.
10. The order must be to pay money only.
11. A bill of exchange can be drawn payable to bearer but cannot originally be drawn payable to bearer on demand.
12. It must be duly stamped according to the Indian Stamps Act.
13. Other formalities, like date, place and the words 'For value received', etc., are usually found in a bill of exchange though they are not necessary a legal requirement.

Distinction between promissory note and bill of exchange

Although the fundamentals of a bill of exchange are very close to that of a promissory note, yet there are several points of distinction between the two, which are given as follows.

1. Number of parties
2. Promise and order
3. Maker as a payee
4. Nature of liability
5. Acceptance
6. Maker's position
7. Payable to bearer
8. Notice of dishonour
9. Protest
10. Exemption

Number of parties A promissory note is a two-party instrument with a maker and the payee, both being distinct and different persons. In a bill of exchange there are three parties—drawer, drawee and payee. It is possible that any two out of three positions may be filled up by the same person, i.e., drawer and drawee may be the same person, drawee and payee may be the same person, and drawer and payee may be the same person.

Promise and order A promissory note contains an unconditional undertaking to pay the drawee, whereas a bill contains an unconditional order to pay.

Maker as a payee In case of a promissory note the maker cannot be the payee. That is, a pro-note cannot be made payable to the maker. But in a bill of exchange, the drawee and the payee may be one and the same person when a bill is drawn as 'pay to me or my order'.

Nature of liability The liability of the maker of a pro-note is primary and absolute since the maker himself promises to pay. But the liability of the drawer of a bill is secondary and conditional. He becomes liable to pay only when the drawee or acceptor refuses to honour the bill or fails to pay.

Acceptance A pro-note does not require any acceptance before it is presented for payment as it is payable by a person who makes it. A bill of exchange, on the other hand, generally requires acceptance of the drawee before it is presented for payment since it is payable by the other person directed by the drawer. The acceptance, however, may be conditional.

Maker's position In a pro-note, the maker stands in immediate relationship with the payee, but the drawer of a bill stands in immediate relation with the acceptor and not the payee.

Payable to bearer A pro-note cannot be made payable to bearer, even if it is made payable otherwise than on demand [Section 31(2) of the RBI Act, 1934]. A bill can be made payable to bearer provided it is not made payable to bearer on demand [Section 31(1) of the RBI Act, 1934].

Notice of dishonour In case of dishonour of a pro-note, no notice (of dishonour) is needed to be given to maker. But when a bill is dishonoured, due notice must be given by the holder to all the parties who are liable under the bill, particularly the drawer and the immediate endorsee. If notice of dishonour is not given, such parties will not be liable to pay.

Protest No protest is necessary in case of a promissory note. But foreign bills must be protested for dishonour, if the law of the land, where they are drawn, so requires. The term 'protest' refers to a formal certificate of dishonour issued by the Notary Public to the holder of a bill in question.

Exemption The provisions relating to presentment for acceptance, acceptance supra protest, drawing of bills-in-sets, especially foreign bills, do not apply in case of promissory notes. All these provisions are applicable to a bill of exchange only.

Forms of bills of exchange

The various bills of exchange can be classified as follows:

1. Inland bill
3. Trade bill
5. Documentary bill
7. Fictitious bill
9. Escrow
2. Foreign bill
4. Accommodation bill
6. Clean bill
8. Bill-in-sets
10. Bank draft

Inland bill A bill of exchange is an inland bill if it is (i) drawn or made payable in India even though it has been drawn on a foreign resident, or (ii) drawn in India upon any person who is a resident in India even though it is made payable in a foreign country. Thus, to be an inland instrument, it must satisfy either of the two conditions:

Inland bill: A bill drawn or made payable in India although it has been drawn on a foreign resident, or drawn in India upon an Indian resident even though it is made payable in a foreign country.

- The instrument must have been drawn or made payable in India or
- The drawee must be in India.

For example, a bill drawn in India and payable in India but drawn upon a person in Canada, i.e., resident thereof is an inland bill. Similarly, a bill drawn in India made payable in Canada upon a person in India is also an inland bill.

Foreign bill Any bill other than an inland bill is deemed to be a foreign bill. Normally, a foreign bill is drawn in a set of three copies.

Foreign bill: A bill (of exchange) other than an inland bill.

Trade bill When a bill is drawn, accepted or endorsed for a genuine trade transaction, it is a trade bill. A trader usually makes use of a trade bill when he sells goods on credit. A trade bill is invariably backed by consideration and based on a genuine trade transaction. Box 13.2 gives an illustration of a genuine trade bill.

Trade bill: A bill drawn, accepted, or endorsed for a genuine trade transaction.

Accommodation bill An accommodation bill is one, which is made to provide financial help to some party. It is a bill in which a person lends or gives his name to oblige a friend or

Accommodation bill: A bill drew, accepted or endorsed without consideration to provide financial aid to someone.

Box 13.2 A Typical Trade Bill and the Parties Involved

A sells goods worth ₹40,000 to *B* on credit and gives him 60 days to pay the price. *A* owes the same amount of money to *C* who supplies goods to *A*. To conclude the transaction, *A* may draw a bill on *B* directing him to pay the money after 60 days of the date of bill to *C*. *A* will sign the bill and present it to *B* for acceptance. Acceptance is necessary in order to create right and obligation. If *B* agrees to obey the order of *A* he will accept the bill by writing across its face the word 'accepted' and signing his name underneath and then delivering the bill to the holder. By doing so *B*, the drawee, now becomes the acceptor of the bill and shall be liable to its holder, such a bill is termed as a genuine trade bill.

some person to whom he is known or otherwise. An accommodation bill is drawn, accepted, or endorsed without consideration. The party lending his name to oblige the other party is known as the accommodating party and the party so obliged is called the accommodated party. It must be noted that the accommodating party will no longer be liable on the instrument to the party accommodated for lack of consideration between them, and the instrument is merely to help. But the accommodating party is liable to the holder for value. The following example will help understand the point better. *A*, who is in need of ₹10,000, approaches his friend *B*, who instead of lending the money directly suggests that *A* should draw a bill in his favour, which he would accept. Accordingly, *A* draws the bill and *B* accepts it. *A* in turn gets the bill discounted with his banker at the commercial rate of discount. On due date, *A* would pay ₹10,000 to *B* to enable him to meet the bill. The real creditor in this case is the banker and not *B*. *B* is mere surety and *A* is the real debtor.

Documentary bill: A bill where the relative shipping documents such as bill of lading, insurance policy, invoice etc. are sent along with the bill.

Documentary bill When documents of title to the goods or other documents, such as bill of lading, invoice, railway receipt, insurance policy, etc., are attached to the bill of exchange, it is called documentary bill. Such documents are delivered to the buyer only on acceptance or payment of the bill. Such bills are usually used in connection with foreign trade.

Clean bill: A bill with which no documents related to the goods represented by the bill are attached.

Clean bill Contrary to a documentary bill, a clean bill is one, with which no documents related to the goods represented by the bill are attached. In inland trade, normally clean bills are used.

Fictitious bill: A bill wherein name of the drawer or the payee or both is fictitious.

Fictitious bill When the name of the drawer or the payee or both is fictitious in a bill, the bill is termed as fictitious bill. Such type of bill is drawn in a fictitious name and is made payable to the drawer's order and as such both the drawer and the payee are said to be fictitious persons. A fictitious person is one who is non-existing or a pretended one. As per Section 42, if a fictitious bill is accepted by a genuine person, it becomes a good bill in the hands of a holder-in-due-course and acceptor is liable to him if he can show that the signature of the supposed drawer and that of the first endorser (payee) are in the same handwriting.

Bill-in-sets: A bill drawn in sets of three.

Bill-in-sets A bill-in-sets is one, which is drawn in sets of three. A bill is sometimes drawn in more than one original copy, especially when such copies are required by various parties as in case of a foreign trade transaction. The three copies (called parts) of a bill-in-set are sent by different mail routes in order to avoid delay or inconvenience, likely to arise due to loss or miscarriage of the bill and to ensure safe transmission of at least one part of the bill to the drawee and his acceptance thereon as early as possible.

This bill is drawn by the London Trading Company Ltd (Drawer or maker), directing Hindustan Machinery Company Ltd, of Mumbai (drawee or acceptor) to pay five thousand Sterling pounds to Messer Mumbai Export Company Ltd, Mumbai (payee).

Like wise second and third parts of the bill are drawn. The second part contains a reference to the

Specimen of a bill-in-sets

First part

£ 50,000/-	London, 10th June 2019
Three months after sight of this first bill of exchange (second and third of the same tenor and date being unpaid) pay to Messers Mumbai Export Company Ltd, Mumbai or order the sum of Sterling Pounds five thousand only for value received.	
To Messers Hindustan Machinery Company Ltd, Mumbai	Revenue Stamp London Trading Co.Ltd

first, and the third part contains a reference to the first and second parts.

Escrow: An instrument delivered conditionally, or for a special purpose such as a collateral security, or for safe custody only and not for the negotiation.

Escrow When an instrument is delivered conditionally, or for a special purpose such as a collateral security, or for safe custody only, and not for the purpose of transferring property absolutely therein, i.e., negotiation, it is termed as escrow. As between the immediate parties, when an instrument is delivered, conditions agreed upon are fulfilled. Such an instrument does not create any liability to pay until and unless conditions agreed upon are fulfilled or the purpose for which the said instrument was delivered is satisfied. This, however, in compliance of Section 46, does not affect the rights of a holder-in-due-course and the defence of conditional delivery cannot be set up against a holder-in-due-course.

Bank draft: An order to pay money drawn by a bank upon another branch or bank instructing the latter to pay a certain sum of money to a specified person or his order.

Bank draft Also known as demand draft, a bank draft is an order to pay money drawn by one office or branch of a bank upon another office or branch of the same bank or on a different bank instructing the latter to pay a certain sum of money to a specified person or his order. When the order is on another branch of the same bank, it is actually a cheque but the same is still termed as a draft. When a draft is issued on another bank, it has all the features of a bill of exchange except that it is not stamped and accepted. Even if it is drawn upon another branch of the same bank, it can be treated as a bill of exchange as it satisfies all the conditions of Section 5.

Cheque

Cheque: A bill of exchange drawn on a specified banker and not expressed to be payable otherwise than on demand.

A cheque is a bill of exchange drawn on a specified banker, and not expressed to be payable otherwise than on demand, and it includes the electronic image of a truncated cheque and a cheque in the electronic form [Section 6].

Explanation I For the purposes of this section:

'A cheque in the electronic form' means a cheque which contains the exact mirror image of a paper cheque, and is generated, written, and is signed in a secure system ensuring the minimum safety standards with the use of digital signature (with or without biometrics signature) and asymmetric crypto system.

'A truncated cheque' means a cheque which is truncated, (i.e., shortened or reduced in size) during the course of a clearing cycle, either by the clearing house or by the bank whether paying or receiving payment, immediately on generation of an electronic image for transmission, substituting the further physical movement of the cheque in writing.

Explanation II For the purposes of this section, the expression clearing house means the clearing house managed by the Reserve Bank of India (RBI) or a clearing house recognized as such by the RBI [Section 6].

Thus, a cheque is a species of bill of exchange with two added qualifications, namely, (i) it is always drawn on a specified banker, and (ii) it is always payable on demand. Besides, unlike a bill, it does not require any acceptance and bears no stamp. Consequently, all cheques are bill of exchange, but all bills are not cheque.

A cheque must satisfy all the requirements of a bill of exchange; that is, it must be signed by the drawer, and must contain an unconditional order on a specified banker to pay a certain sum of money to or to the order of a certain person or to the bearer of the cheque.

Parties to a cheque

A cheque generally involves the following parties.

Drawer The person who makes the cheque

Drawee The banker of the drawer on whom the cheque is drawn

Payee The person who is to receive the money stated in the cheque

Holder A person who is in the possession of a cheque and is entitled to receive or recover the amount thereon.

Endorser The maker, drawee, payee or endorsee can endorse a cheque by signing on the back of it. The endorser of a cheque has the status of a new drawer.

Endorsee The transferee or the person in whose favour the instrument has been endorsed.

Essentials of a cheque

The statutory definition of the cheque and the explanation followed reveal the following essential elements of the instrument.

It must be in writing A cheque must be in writing. An oral order to pay does not constitute a cheque.

It should be drawn on a banker It is always drawn on a specified banker. A cheque can be drawn on a bank where the drawer has an account, saving bank account, or current one.

It contains an unconditional order to pay A cheque cannot be drawn so as to be payable conditionally. The drawer's order to the drawee bank must be unconditional and should not make the cheque payable dependent on a contingency. A conditional cheque shall be invalid.

The cheque must have an order to pay a certain sum The cheque should contain an order to pay a certain sum of money only. If a cheque is drawn to do something in addition to, or other than to pay money, it cannot be a cheque. For example, if a cheque contains 'Pay ₹5,000 and a TV worth ₹10,000 to *A*' it is not a cheque.

It must be signed by the drawer and must be dated A cheque does not have any validity unless signed by the original drawer. It should be dated as well.

It is payable on demand A cheque is always payable on demand.

Validity A cheque is normally valid for three months from the date it bears. Thereafter it is termed as stale cheque. A post-dated or antedated cheque will not be invalid. In both cases, the validity of the cheque is presumed to commence from the date mentioned on it.

It may be payable to the drawer himself Cheques may be payable to the drawer himself/herself. It may be drawn payable to bearer on demand unlike a bill or a pro-note.

Banker is liable only to the drawer The banker on whom the cheque is drawn shall be liable only to the drawer. A holder or bearer has no remedy against the banker if a cheque is dishonoured.

It does not require acceptance and stamp Unlike a bill of exchange, a cheque does not require any acceptance of the drawee. It is, however, customary for the banks to mark a cheque as 'good' for the purpose of clearance. But this marking does not amount to acceptance. Similarly, no revenue stamp is required to be affixed on a cheque.

Distinction Between Bill of Exchange and Cheque

Although by definition, and even otherwise, a cheque is similar to a bill of exchange and the provisions of the Negotiable Instruments Act applicable to bills of exchange do apply to cheques too, yet there are certain differences between the two. The major differences between a Bill of Exchange and a cheque are summarised in Table 13.1.

Table 13.1 Difference Between Bill of Exchange and Cheque

S. no.	Point of difference	Bill of exchange	Cheque
1.	Drawee	A bill can be drawn on any person (i.e., upon an individual as well as a banker).	A cheque is always drawn on a banker.
2.	Payable	It may be drawn payable on demand or on the expiry of a certain period or days after sight or date.	It can only be drawn payable on demand, and within three months of the date mentioned on the cheque.
3.	Grace period	A grace of 3 days is allowed in the case of payment of bill payable after sight or date.	No grace is given in case of a cheque for payment for the sole reason that a cheque is payable on demand.
4.	Acceptance	Acceptance by the drawee is must before payment can be demanded in respect of a bill.	It does not require any acceptance and is intended for immediate payment.
5.	Payable to bearer	A bill cannot be made payable to bearer on demand.	A cheque can be made payable to the bearer on demand.
6.	Estoppel of payment	The drawer cannot stop payment of a bill, that is, a bill of exchange cannot be countermanded.	Countermanding of payment can revoke a cheque being a revocable mandate. Banker or the drawee is empowered to stop payment of a cheque if all the required formalities are not adhered to.
7.	Presentment for payment	The drawer of a bill is discharged (i.e., not liable to pay), if it is not presented for payment.	The drawer of a cheque is discharged only if he suffers any loss or damage due to delay in its presentment for payment and he shall be discharged to the extent of such damage. He is not discharged from liability if the cheque is not presented for payment.
8.	Notice of dishonour	Notice of dishonour of a bill is necessary in order to charge its drawer.	If a cheque is dishonoured, notice of dishonour need not be given to the drawer. Insufficiency of funds in his (drawer) account is sufficient and appropriate evidence to charge him.
9.	Crossing	The Act contains no provision for crossing of a bill.	A cheque may be crossed, i.e., made 'account payee'.
10.	Stamp duty	It should be adequately stamped.	It does not require any stamp duty.
11.	Noting and Protesting	A dishonoured bill should be 'noted' (i.e., with the notary) and 'protested' for payment.	It neither requires 'noting' nor 'protest' in the event of dishonour.
12.	Statutory protection to the drawee	No statutory protection is available to the drawee or acceptor of a bill of exchange.	Privilege of certain statutory protection is granted to the drawee bank with regard to payment of cheques in specific circumstances.

[*Note*: Section 85 discharges a drawee bank, from the liability, making payment in due course of a cheque payable to order. Similarly, Section 128 discharges a drawee bank making payment in due course of a crossed cheque even if the money does not reach the true owner.]

Crossing of a cheque

A cheque can be either open or crossed. An open cheque is one, which can be paid over the counter of the bank. A crossed cheque cannot be cashed across the counter but must be collected through a banker.

When two parallel lines are drawn, usually on the left hand top corner of the cheque, it is called crossing. By doing so, a cheque becomes 'account payee'. A crossing acts as a direction to the drawee or paying banker to pay the money to a specified banker as desired by the payee or credit the amount stated on the cheque in the account of the payee if he has an account with the drawee bank and not to pay otherwise. The primary objective of crossing is to secure payment to a holder so that it could be traced to the person collecting the amount of cheque. To restrain negotiability, words such as, 'Account payee only' or 'Not Negotiable' can be inserted on the free space between the two parallel lines. Crossing, in fact, provides protection and security to the holder or beneficiary.

Modes of crossing There are three types of crossing of a cheque:

1. General crossing,
2. Special crossing, and
3. Account payee's crossing.

General crossing According to Section 123, 'where a cheque bears across its face an addition of the words "and company" or any abbreviation thereof, between two parallel transverse lines, or of two parallel transverse lines only, either with or without the words "not negotiable" that addition shall be deemed to be a crossing and cheque shall be deemed to be crossed generally'.

The above definition illustrates that two transverse parallel lines are a must for a general crossing. Where a cheque is crossed generally, the banker on whom it is drawn shall not pay it to anyone other than to a banker [Section 126]. Therefore, the holder may get the cheque collected through his banker only and not cashed over the counter of a bank. The addition of the words 'and company' do not have any significance but the addition of the words 'not negotiable' restrict the negotiability of the cheque and in case of transfer, the transferee will not get a better title than that of a transferor.

Special crossing When the name of a banker is written across the face of a cheque with or without the words 'not negotiable', it is a special crossing. The transverse parallel lines may or may not be used in this kind of crossing. Thus, where the cheque is crossed specially, the paying banker will pay only to the banker whose name appears across the cheque, or to his collecting agent. Thus, in case of special crossing, the paying banker is to honour the cheque only when it is presented through bank mentioned in the crossing, or an agent of such bank, i.e., another banker acting as agent.

'Account payee' crossing It is the most prevalent one which restricts the negotiability of a cheque. It may be made both under general crossing as well as special crossing. Such crossing warns the collecting banker that the proceeds are to be credited only to the account of the payee. If the collecting banker allows the proceeds of a cheque bearing such a crossing to be credited to any other account, it would be guilty of negligence and will not be entitled to the protection given to collecting bankers under Section 131.

A cheque crossed specially or generally bearing the words 'not negotiable', lacks negotiability and, therefore, is not a negotiable instrument in the true sense. This means, in case of transfer, the transferee will not get a better title than that of the transferor. It does not restrict transferability but restricts negotiability only. The fundamental object of 'not negotiable' crossing is to provide protection to the drawer or holder of a cheque. Even if such a cheque

Figure 13.1(b) Specimen of Special Crossing

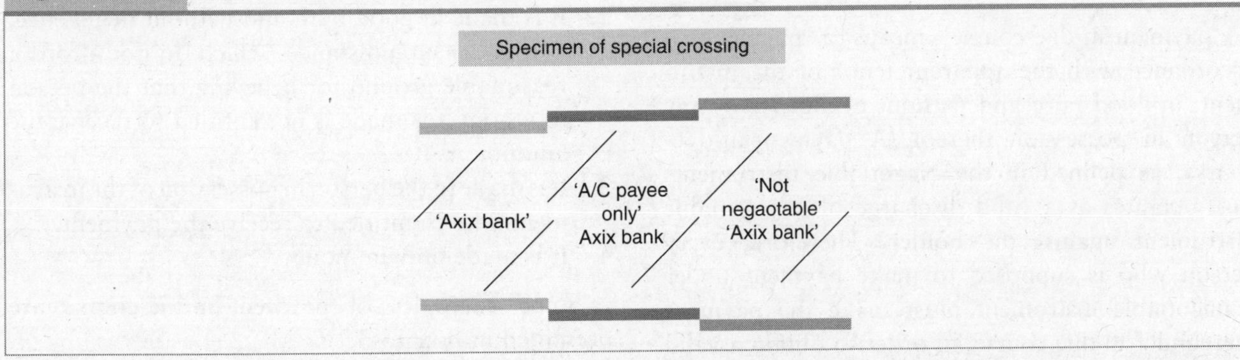

Figure 13.1(a) Specimen of General Crossing

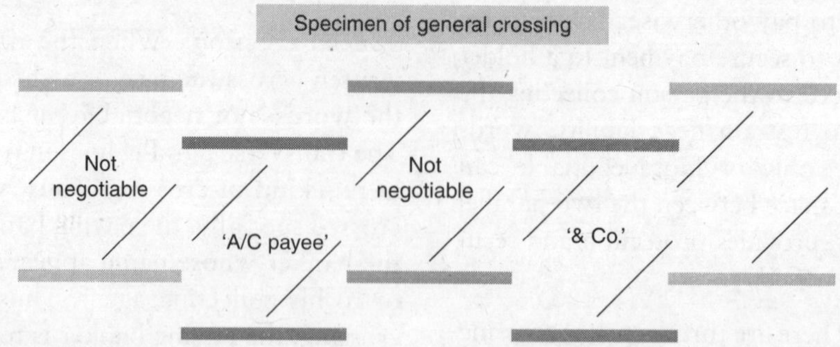

Box 13.3 **Payment-in-due-course**

Example 1

A executes a promissory note in favour of *B* and the amount is payable to *B* or his order. *C*, who is the son of *B*, approaches *A* who is not in possession of the pro-note and demands payment. However, *A* believing in C makes the payment to *C*. The above payment is not a payment-in-due-course for the sole reason that *C* was not in the possession of the instrument.

Example 2

A presents a bearer cheque to a banker, which bears the account number of the drawer, i.e., account holder (*A*) correctly. Also, the amount is properly written on it in figures as well as in words. It bears the signature of the drawer and date. Since there is sufficient fund in the account of the drawer, the banker after completing the necessary formalities makes the payment to the holder. Later on it is discovered that the cheque was a forged one. On this ground it is not a payment in due course.

gets into the hands of a wrong person it would have to be transferred to a holder-in-due-course, the true owner will not lose his claim against such an endorsement. Hence, an endorsee of such a crossed cheque must take special care while accepting the same. He should not accept the cheque unless he knows the endorser and his ownership, i.e., title very well.

Payment-in-Due-Course

A 'payment-in-due-course' means a payment in accordance with the apparent tenor of the instrument, in good faith and without negligence of any person in possession thereof. A payment-in-due-course, as defined in the Negotiable Instruments Act, operates as a valid discharge of a negotiable instrument against the holder. Therefore, every person who is supposed to make payment under a negotiable instrument must make the payment thereunder in due course, in order to obtain a valid discharge against the holder. If he/she fails to do so, he/she will be liable for it.

According to Section 10 of the Act, a payment will be a payment-in-due-course under the following circumstances:

1. It is in accordance with the apparent tenor of the instrument, i.e., according to what appears on the face of the instrument to be the intention of the parties.
2. It is made in good faith and without negligence, and under circumstances which do not afford a reasonable ground for believing that the person to whom it is made is not entitled to receive the amount.
3. It is made to the person in possession of the instrument who is entitled to receive the payment.
4. It is made only in money.

Some examples of payment-in-due-course are presented in Box 13.3.

In *Allahabad Bank Ltd vs Kul Bhushan*[3], it was held that if a cheque bears a forged signature of the drawer, the payment would not be a payment-in-due-course; the banker failed to exercise reasonable care and caution since the drawer had never intended that the payment should be made.

Payment of Interest

The rules relating to the payment of interest are given below.

If the Rate of Interest Is Specified

In some cases, the rate of interest payable on a bill or note is specified in the instrument itself. In such cases, the interest shall be payable at the rate specified on the principal amount due on the instrument. The interest will be calculated from the date of the instrument to the date of realization or tender of such amount. And, if a suit is instituted to recover such amount (i.e., due on the instrument), the interest shall be payable upto the date as the court directs. The court is empowered to reduce the specified rate of interest in such a case and can grant relief to the payer against the excessive rate of interest [Section 79]. The court may not allow the payment of interest at the rate specified in the instrument in the following three cases:

1. Where the negotiable instrument has been acquired by means of coercion, undue influence, fraud, or misrepresentation.
   [Section 19A of the Indian Contract Act]
2. Where the provision for the payment of interest is in the nature of a penalty.
   [Section 74 of the Indian Contract Act]
3. Where the specified rate of interest is excessively high and the transaction between the parties is substantially unfair.
   [The Usurious Loans Act, 1918[4]]

If the Rate of Interest Is Not Specified

Where no rate of interest is specified in the instrument, interest is payable at the rate of 18 per cent per annum on the principal amount due thereon. The interest shall be calculated from the date at which the principal amount (due on the instrument) ought to have been paid to the date of tender or realization of such amount. And, if a suit is filed for the recovery of the amount due on the instrument, the interest shall be payable up to the date as the court directs.

Furthermore, it is important to note that if the instrument-in-question has been dishonoured due to non-payment and the party charged is an endorser of the same, it is liable to pay the interest only from the time when it receives notice of dishonour [Explanation added to Section 80].

Negotiable Instruments: Special Rules of Evidence

Under the Act, there are certain special rules of evidence, applicable to all types of negotiable instruments. A summary of the same is as follows.

Presumptions

Sections 118 and 119 deal with certain assumptions as to negotiable instruments. These assumptions basically imply certain facts that are presumed in case of every negotiable instrument, which have already been discussed at length earlier in the Chapter.

Estoppel

Estoppel simply implies prevention of disclaim by a party liable on the instrument, if any.

Estoppel: Prevention of disclaim by the party liable on a negotiable instrument, if any.

Sections 120–122 of the Negotiable Instruments Act deal with the following three estoppels, which are considered to be there against the parties to the negotiable instruments. In other words, the Act binds the parties liable upon an instrument by the following three estoppels.

Estoppel against denying the original validity of the instrument

No maker of a promissory note, and no drawer of a bill of exchange or cheque, and no acceptor of a bill for the honour of the drawer shall be permitted to deny the validity of the instrument as originally

[3] 1961, AIR, Punjab, 571

[4] The term 'usurious' means lending money at very high rates of interest. The Usurious Loans Act, 1918, is an Act that gives additional powers to courts to deal in certain cases with usurious loans of money or in kind (i.e., harsh and unconscionable loans carrying interest at usurious rates).

made or drawn in a suit thereon by a holder-in-due-course [Section 120].

Estoppel against denying the capacity of the payee to endorse the instrument

No maker of a promissory note, and no acceptor of a bill of exchange payable to order shall, in a suit thereon by a holder-in-due-course, be permitted to deny the payee's capacity to endorse the instrument at the date of the note [Section 121].

Estoppel against denying the signature or capacity of prior parties

No endorser of a negotiable instrument shall, in a suit thereon by a subsequent holder, be permitted to deny the signature or capacity to contract of any prior party to the instrument [Section 122].

Negotiable Instruments: Rules of International Law

A negotiable instrument may be drawn in one country and be payable in another. That is, drawer or maker, drawee and payee in relation to a negotiable instrument may not belong to or be located in one country. In such cases, different laws of the land will govern the liability of the parties. Sections 134 to 137 deal with the rules of International Law related to foreign instruments, which may be discussed under the following heads.

Law Governing the Liability of Parties to Foreign Instruments

The liability of the maker or drawer of a foreign promissory note, bill of exchange, or cheque is governed in all essential matters by the law of the place where he/she made the instrument. Similarly, respective liabilities of the acceptor and endorser of a foreign instrument are also regulated by the law of the place where the instrument is made payable. The above rule is, however, subject to a contrary contract between the parties. The parties to a foreign negotiable instrument may provide by an agreement which country's law shall determine their liability [Section 134].

For example, a bill of exchange was drawn by *A* in California where the rate of interest is 25 per cent, and accepted by *B*, payable in Washington where the rate of interest is 6 per cent. The bill is endorsed in India, and dishonoured subsequently. An action on the bill is brought against *B* in India. He is liable to pay interest at the rate of 6 per cent, only, but if *A* is charged as drawer, *A* is liable to pay interest at the rate of 25 per cent.

Law Governing the Dishonour of Foreign Instruments

Section 135 provides that 'where a promissory note, bill of exchange, or cheque is made payable in a country different from that in which it is made or endorsed, the law of the country where it is made payable determines what constitutes dishonour and what notice of dishonour is sufficient'. That is, dishonour of a foreign negotiable instrument and the notice in connection with the dishonour shall be governed by the law of the country where the instrument was made payable.

For example, a bill of exchange drawn and endorsed in India but accepted and payable in France is dishonoured. The endorsee causes it to be protested for such dishonour and gives notice thereof in accordance with the law of France, though not in accordance with the rules contained in the Negotiable Instruments Act (of India). The notice is sufficient.

Instruments Made Out of India But in Accordance with Indian Law

According to Section 136, 'where a negotiable instrument is made, drawn, accepted, or endorsed outside India but in accordance with the law of India (i.e., the Negotiable Instruments Act, 1881), the fact that the instrument is invalid according to the law of the country where it is made, does not invalidate any subsequent acceptance or endorsement made thereon within India'. Thus, where the making or drawing of an instrument is invalidated in a foreign country for want of stamp or similar other reason, the subsequent acceptance or endorsement, being an independent contract will be valid provided that it was valid according to the Indian law.

The law of any foreign country regarding promissory notes, bills of exchange, and cheques shall be presumed to be the same as that of India unless and until the contrary is proved [Section 17].

Holder and Holder-in-Due-Course

Holder: Person entitled in his own name to the possession of a negotiable instrument and to recover the amount due thereon.

The real test of a negotiable instrument lies in the fact that the transferee must get the title of it free from all defects. However, this transfer of ownership depends on whether the transferee is a 'holder-in-due-course' or just a 'holder'.

Holder

Holder of a negotiable instrument means a person who is entitled in his own name to the possession of the instrument and to receive or recover the amount due thereon, from the parties thereto [Section 8]. This definition implies that mere possession of a negotiable instrument does not entitle a person to be its holder. In order to be a holder, the person should be named in the instrument as the payee, or the endorsee, or the bearer thereof. Section 8 further provides that in case a note, bill, or cheque is lost or destroyed, its holder is the person, who was entitled to be so at the time of such loss or destruction. A person who has obtained the possession of an instrument by theft or under forged endorsement is not a holder, as he is not entitled to recover the instrument. Similarly, a finder of a lost negotiable instrument does not become its holder on his own.

The term 'holder', thus, does not include a person who, though is in possession of the instrument, does not have the right to claim the amount due thereon from the parties concerned. The holder implies *de jure holder* (holder-in-law) and *not de facto holder* (holder-in-fact). For the same reason, an agent holding an instrument for his principal is not a holder, although he can collect the payment. The holder of a negotiable instrument can give or transfer its title to any person honestly acquiring it. The very essence of a negotiable instrument is that the person in possession of it gets the authority to deal with it, unless something is known to the contrary. Furthermore, a person who has lent his name in the place of a real owner, i.e., *benamidar*, can also become the holder. This is so because of the fact that the Act does not recognise such a practice and the person whose name appears on the face of the instrument, whether real or *benami*, is to be held as the holder.

Section 78 further provides that the significance of the holder also lies in the fact that the negotiable instrument must, in order to discharge the maker or acceptor, be paid to the holder of the instrument. The holder, therefore, is the only person who can sue upon the instrument, and can give a valid discharge for it.

Holder-in-Due-Course

A holder-in-due-course is the true and lawful owner of a negotiable instrument. According to Section 9, holder-in-due-course is

1. a person who for consideration becomes the possessor of a promissory note, bill of exchange, or cheque, if payable to bearer, or
2. the payee or endorsee thereof (negotiable instrument), if payable to order, before its maturity, and without having sufficient cause to believe that any defect existed in the title of the person from whom he derived his title.

Thus, a person who takes an instrument 'in good faith' and 'for value' becomes the true owner of the instrument and is known as holder-in-due-course. Accordingly, in order to be a holder-in-due-course, a person must satisfy the following qualifications:

1. He must be the holder of the instrument if payable to bearer, i.e., first of all he must be entitled in his own name to the possession of that instrument and he should have the right to receive or recover the amount due thereon from the parties thereto.
2. The holder should have acquired the instrument for valuable consideration and the same should be lawful. A person, who obtains a note, bill, cheque, etc., without consideration cannot enforce it and thereby cannot become holder-in-due-course in respect of the same.
3. The person should have obtained the instrument before maturity. Once a negotiable instrument reaches its maturity, it is no more negotiable. Accordingly, if a person takes a note or bill, or a cheque after it has become due, he will have no better title to it than the party from whom he has taken it. An instrument payable on demand such as a demand note, demand bill, or a cheque is current as long as no demand for payment is

made. The law of limitation, however, is applicable in case of a cheque. The banks insist that a cheque should be encashed within three months of the date of its issue.

4. The instrument should be complete and regular on the face of it. It is the duty of every person who accepts or obtains a negotiable instrument to examine its form, for if it contains any material defect, he/she will not become a holder-in-due-course. An instrument may be defective in several ways—it may be incomplete as it does not contain drawer's signature or name, or because it is not duly stamped or dated. Similarly, if an instrument has been improperly endorsed, the same renders the whole of the instrument irregular.
5. The holder should have received the instrument in good faith. Possibly there are two methods to ascertain whether a person has obtained an instrument in good faith. One method is to check whether he took due care and caution. Section 9, however, states in this regard that, a person will be treated as a holder-in-due-course if he became the payee or endorsee of the promissory note, bill of exchange, or cheque without having sufficient cause to believe that any defect existed in the title of the person from whom he derived his title. Thus, mere good faith on the part of the holder will not suffice. Due care and caution is more important. Any gross negligence on the part of a holder while taking a negotiable instrument which itself indicates lack of due care and caution, will debar him from acquiring the rights of a holder-in-due-course.

To sum up, if a holder is to be called or treated as a holder-in-due-course, he must satisfy the abovementioned qualifications. Furthermore, if a holder derives his title from a holder-in-due-course, he shall obviously have the right of a holder-in-due-course.

Rights and privileges of a holder-in-due-course

A holder-in-due-course enjoys special rights and privileges. He/she not only protects himself/herself against all defects of title of his/her immediate predecessor but also safeguards the interest of all subsequent holders. A holder who derives his title from a holder-in-course has the rights of a holder-in-due-course. It is thus—once an instrument passes through the hands of a holder-in-due-course, it is cleansed of all defects, In particular, the holder-in-due-course enjoys the following privileges under the Negotiable Instruments Act:

1. Derivation of better title than that of the transferor [Section 58]
2. Rights in case of inchoate stamped instruments [Section 20]
3. Liability of prior parties to a holder-in-due-course [Section 36]
4. Privilege in case of fictitious bills [Section 42]
5. Privilege in case of conditionally delivered instrument [Section 46]
6. Instrument is absolved from all prior defects once it passes through a holder-in-due-course [Section 53]
7. Estoppel against denying original validity of instrument [Section 120]
8. Presumptions as to title [Section 118]
9. Estoppel against denying capacity of the payee to endorsee [Section 121]
10. Estoppel against denying the signature of prior party [Section 122]
11. Right to recover amount from all previous parties.

Let us examine these privileges one by one.

Derivation of better title As against a holder, the holder-in-due-course is a privileged person in the sense that no holder gets a better title than that of the transferor, but a holder-in-due-course does. Moreover, the party liable to pay an instrument cannot plead against a holder-in-due-course that the instrument had been stolen or was obtained by means of fraud or theft or for unlawful consideration. Box 13.4 presents a couple of examples in this regard.

> **Inchoate instrument:** A bill or note duly signed and stamped but left incomplete in some respect.

Right in case of inchoate stamped instrument In an inchoate stamped instrument wherein, for instance, if the drawee or the holder or the original payee fraudulently fills up a higher amount than what was authorised (but adequately covered by stamp duty), he cannot enforce the instrument for the whole amount. Only actual authorised amount

Box 13.4 **Holder-in-due-course Gets Better Title Than Transferor**

Example 1

A draws a cheque payable to *B*, the bearer. *C* steals the cheque and transfers it to *D* who accepts the same in good faith and for value. In this case, since *D* has obtained the instrument for value and in good faith, it renders him a holder-in-due-course. Hence, his title will be defect free notwithstanding the fact that the cheque is a stolen one. *D* can sue on the instrument. The party liable (*A*) can take, as against *C*, the defence of theft or fraud, but as against *D* it will not be allowed to take such recourse.

Example 2

A, the holder of a bearer bill, endorses it to *B*, who is a minor. The bill is stolen from the drawer of *B* by *C* who forges *B*'s endorsement and transfers it to *D* for consideration. Since *D* accepts the bill for value in good faith, he is a holder-in-due-course and entitled to sue *A* and all parties prior to *A*, viz., drawer, the acceptor, and all prior endorsees, if any. He can also sue *C* but not *B*. This means *D* holds the bill free from defect in title caused by *C*'s theft and forgery.

can be recovered. But if such an instrument is transferred for value lacking of anyone suspecting the fraud, the holder-in-due-course is protected. Accordingly, he can claim whole of the amount so entered. The defence that the amount filled by the holder was in excess of the authority given cannot be taken against a holder-in-due-course.

Liability of prior parties to a holder-in-due-course Section 36 states that every prior party to a negotiable instrument (i.e., its maker or drawer, acceptor, and intervening endorsers) is liable to a holder-in-due-course, both collectively and separately, i.e., he can hold any or all prior parties liable until the instrument is duly satisfied. For example, *A* draws a bill on *B* payable to *C*. The bill is duly accepted by *B* and *C* endorses it to *D* who later endorses it to *E* who receives the same for value in good faith. In this case, *E* being the holder-in-due-course can recover the amount of the bill either from *B* (i.e., acceptor) and on *B*'s failure he can recover it from *A*, *C*, and *D*.

Privilege in case of fictitious bills A fictitious bill is not enforceable by law. Nevertheless, an acceptor of a bill drawn in a fictitious name and made payable to drawer's order cannot be relieved from his liability to a holder-in-due-course on the ground that both the drawer, and the payee are fictitious persons. Thus, the acceptor of a bill of exchange as against the holder-in-due-course cannot say that the other parties to the bill were fictitious. However, the holder-in-due-course must prove that the first endorsement on the bill and the signature of the supposed drawer are in the same handwriting. For example, *A* draws a bill on *B* for ₹1,000 which was made payable to *R* who is a fictitious person. The bill was duly accepted by *B* and returned to *A*. Subsequently, *A* endorsed the bill in favour of *S* by signing as *R* (i.e., the endorser). Later on, during the course of negotiation, the bill reached *P* who obtained the same for value and in good faith. *P*, a holder-in-due-course, can realise the amount of the bill from *B* by showing the signature of the drawer (*A*) and the first endorser (*R*) are in the same handwriting.

Privilege in case of conditionally delivered instrument Conditional delivery of a negotiable instrument means the instrument has been delivered or endorsed for a special or express purpose, such as safe custody or as collateral security and not with the idea of transferring the property therein absolutely. In such a situation, the property in the instrument does not pass to the endorsee and he merely acts as a bailee with limited power of negotiation. A holder-in-due-course, however, is not affected by such a restriction. If a bill is delivered conditionally or for a special purpose and subsequently negotiated to a holder-in-due-course, a valid delivery of it is presumed conclusively, and he acquires the good title to it. The parties liable on the instrument cannot escape liability by taking the plea of conditional delivery of the instrument. For example, *A*, the owner of a grocery shop, issues a cheque to his supplier, *B*, with the condition that he should not encash the cheque till the goods are delivered to *A*. The cheque so issued is a conditionally delivered instrument. Suppose the same cheque is endorsed by *B* in favour of *C* who obtains the same in good faith and for value. *C* being the holder-in-due-course can get the cheque encashed before fulfilling the condition as he is not affected by the restriction. However, any one else encashing the cheque before fulfilling the condition shall be liable to return the money to *A*.

Instrument is absolved from all prior defects once passes through holder-in-due-course Section 53 implies that once an instrument passes through the hands of a holder-in-due-course, it is purged of (i.e., freed from) all defects. It is treated like a legal tender. Whoever takes it can recover the amount from all the parties prior to such holder. Thus, a holder who receives an instrument from the holder-in-due-course gets the rights of the latter, even if he was not a party to it. A holder-in-due-course, therefore, not only protects himself against all defects of title of the transferor but also serves as a channel to safeguard the interests of all subsequent holders.

Estoppel against denying original validity of instrument The validity of an instrument as originally drawn or made cannot be denied against the holder-in-due-course by the drawer of a bill of exchange, or cheque, or by the maker of a promissory note, or by the acceptor of a bill for the honour of the drawer. The drawer and the maker are the parties directly accountable for bringing the negotiable instruments into existence. They cannot take the plea of original invalidity of the instrument, i.e., no considerations actually exchanged between the maker and the payee. In the same way, an acceptor for honour of the drawer is bound by all estoppels, which bind the drawer, and, therefore, supposed cannot deny the original validity of the bill. It should, however, be noticed that either of the above parties shall not be liable if at the time of executing the instrument, it was a minor or their signatures had been fabricated, or the instrument was unenforceable.

Presumption as to title Every holder is deemed *prima facie* to be a holder-in-due-course. Thus, the burden of proving his title does not lie on him. It is for the defendant to prove it. However, if it is proved that a negotiable instrument has been obtained from any of its lawful owners or acceptor or drawer by means of fraud, offence, theft or, for unlawful consideration, the underlying responsibility to prove the title is shifted to the holder and he has to establish that he is a holder-in-due-course.

Estoppel against denying capacity of payee to endorse According to Section 121, no maker of promissory note and no acceptor of a bill of exchange payable to order shall, in a suit thereon by a holder-in-due-course, be permitted to deny the payee's capacity at the date of note or bill, to endorse the same. As a general rule, the holder will not be entitled to claim the payment of a negotiable instrument in his own name until it is endorsed by a competent person, i.e., payee (in case he receives the same by means of endorsement). It follows that the payee must be competent to endorse an instrument. Section 26 declares that a minor is competent to endorse. An insolvent, however, is not competent to endorse. However, by virtue of Section 121, a holder-in-due-course can enforce payment in his own name despite the fact that the payee (being an insolvent) was incompetent to endorse the instrument. Similarly, the maker of a note or bill or the acceptor of the bill cannot take the plea that the payee was a minor or an insane person, in case a suit is filed by a holder-in-due-course. For example, *A* draws a bill on *B* payable to *C*, a minor. The bill is duly accepted by *B* and returned to *A*. Later on, *C* being payee, endorses the same to *D*, a holder-in-due-course. As against *D*, *A*, and *B* are stopped from denying the capacity of *C* to endorse. They are liable to *C* on the bill.

Estoppel against denying the signature or capacity of prior party Section 122 provides that no endorser shall be permitted as against the holder-in-due-course to deny the signature or capacity to contract of any prior party to the instrument, in case of a suit thereon by a subsequent holder. However, in no case he can be stopped from denying the validity or genuineness of the instrument. For instance, *X* draws a bill on *Y* payable to *Z*, a minor, who subsequently endorses the same in favour of *A*. Later on, the bill is endorsed by *A* to *B* who is a holder-in-due-course. The bill gets dishonoured on its maturity. *B* has the right to file a suit against all or any of the parties to the bill except *Z*, being minor. *A*, the ultimate endorser, cannot contend that, since *Z* was a minor and therefore not competent to endorse the bill. He (*A*) shall also remain liable to *B*.

Right to recover amount from all previous parties Once a bill, or pro-note, or a cheque gets into the hands of a holder-in-due-course, he/she can enforce the payment on it in his/her name from any of the prior parties thereof, irrespective of the fact that the negotiable instrument in question was made without consideration or there was a defect in the title of the party from whom he took it. For example, *A* gifts a cheque for a certain amount to *B* on his marriage anniversary. *B* endorses it to *C* who in turn endorses the same to *D*, a holder-in-due-course. On the due date the cheque bounces. Here *D* can recover the amount from *C*, *B*, or *A*. None of them can plead that the cheque was drawn without consideration and hence, *D* cannot hold them liable. They will remain liable to *D* jointly as well as severally.

Holder and Holder-In-Due-Course Distinguished

The distinction between a holder and a holder-in-due-course can be made on the basis of the following points:

1. Entitlement
2. Consideration
3. Maturity
4. Title
5. Right to recover amount
6. Notice of defect in the title
7. Privileges

Entitlement Holder is a person who is entitled in his own name to the possession of a negotiable instrument, and to receive or recover the amount due thereon. Holder-in-due-course, on the other hand, is a person who has obtained the instrument for consideration and in good faith and before maturity.

Consideration Consideration is not necessary to become a holder. The instrument may also be given by way of a donation or gift and thus, the donee of an instrument can also become a holder of it. However, consideration is a must to become a holder-in-due-course and thereby the donee of a negotiable instrument can be a holder but not holder-in-due-course.

Maturity A holder may acquire the instrument even after its maturity. But a holder-in-due-course must acquire the instrument before its maturity failing which he will not enjoy the rights of a holder-in-due-course.

Title A holder does not acquire a better title than that of transferor. In simple words, if the title of any of the prior party is defective, his title will not be defect free. However, a holder-in-due-course derives a good title freed from all defects. His title is better than that of the transferor.

Right to recover amount A holder has a right to recover the amount due on the instrument from the transferor (i.e., just preceding party) only from whom he has obtained the instrument. Holder-in-due-course, on the other hand, can recover the amount due on the instrument from any of the prior parties till the instrument is duly discharged. Thus, all prior parties shall remain liable towards the holder-in-due-course, jointly as well as severally, till the instrument is duly discharged.

Notice of defect in the title A holder-in-due-course is not only supposed to have acquired the instrument without any notice of the defect of the title of the person from whom he obtained it, but also there should be no cause on his part to believe that any defect sustains in the transferor's title. But a holder is exempt from this condition. He may have notice of defect in the title but he shall not be liable for it unless he is a party to that defect, fraud, or forgery.

Privileges A holder-in-due-course enjoys certain privileges under the Negotiable Instruments Act (as discussed earlier), which are not available to a holder.

Exercises

I. Objective-type Questions

1. State whether each of the following statements is True or False:
   (i) Negotiable instrument implies a written document which creates a right in favour of some person and which is freely transferable.
   (ii) The transferee of a negotiable instrument cannot get a better title than that of the transferor.
   (iii) A promissory note can be in the form of an oral undertaking.
   (iv) Crossing is mandatory for a cheque.
   (v) All types of bills of exchange are entitled for three days of grace.
   (vi) The contractual capacity of a person enables him to become a party to a negotiable instrument.
   (vii) A minor can be a promisee in respect to a negotiable instrument.
   (viii) An insolvent does not have the contractual capacity to draw, accept, or endorse any negotiable instrument.
   (ix) A bill of exchange drawn to or endorsed by an alien enemy can be enforced after peace is restored.
   (x) Every holder is deemed *prima facie* to be a holder-in-due-course.

2. Fill in the blanks:
   (i) A negotiable instrument properly stamped and signed but blank or incomplete in some respect is called an ________ instrument.
   (ii) Stamp is not essential for a valid ________.
   (iii) In special crossing, the name of ________ is written.
   (iv) A banker is liable only to the ________.
   (v) Bills-in-sets are used in ________ trade transactions.
   (vi) The ________ of a negotiable instrument means a person entitled in his own name to the possession of a negotiable instrument and to recover the amount due thereon.
   (vii) The donee of a negotiable instrument cannot become its ________.
   (viii) The liability of a drawer of a bill of exchange is ________.
   (ix) The drawee of a ________ must always be a banker.
   (x) The ________ stands in a position of a drawer to all subsequent holders.

3. Indicate the correct answer:
   (i) Which of the following is not a presumption about negotiable instruments?
      (a) Consideration (b) Date
      (c) Absolute and good title to the transferee (d) Stamp
   (ii) Which of the following is a negotiable instrument by custom and usage among the businessmen?
      (a) Deposit receipt (b) Dividend warrant
      (c) Share certificate (d) Demand draft
   (iii) An instrument drawn incompletely in such a way that it can either be treated as a bill of exchange or promissory note is known as
      (a) Inchoate or incomplete instrument (b) Ambiguous instrument
      (c) demand instrument (d) Fictitious bill
   (iv) When a negotiable instrument is delivered conditionally or for a special purpose as a collateral security or for safe custody only, it is called
      (a) Accommodation bill ' (b) Genuine trade bill
      (c) Escrow (d) Documentary bill
   (v) When the interest rate is not specified in a negotiable instrument, the interest as permitted by the Negotiable Instrument Act will be
      (a) 6% per annum (b) 10% per annum
      (c) 12% per annum (d) 18% per annum
   (vi) Who among the following is not competent to endorse a negotiable instrument?
      (a) A minor
      (b) An insane
      (c) An insolvent who is not a payee to subsequent holder-in-due-course
      (d) All of the above

(vii) In a bill, when the name of another drawee is mentioned in addition to the original drawee, such a person is known as
(a) Benamidar (b) Drawee in case of need
(c) Acceptor for honour (d) None of the above

(viii) Which among the following conditions is not applicable to a holder-in-due-course?
(a) He must be the holder of the instrument
(b) He should have obtained the instrument bona fide and for value.
(c) He must be entitled in his own name to the possession of the instrument.
(d) He must have obtained the instrument before maturity

(ix) Which among the following is not a privilege or right of a holder-in-due-course?
(a) Estoppel against denying signature or capacity of prior party
(b) Estoppel against denying original validity of the instrument
(c) Estoppel against denying capacity of the payee to endorse
(d) Estoppel against denying the genuineness or validity of the payee's endorsement

(x) Acceptor for honour can be a party to
(a) A cheque (b) A bill of exchange
(c) A promissory note (d) A hundi

II. Review Questions

1. Describe the basic features of negotiable instruments. Also explain the presumptions, legally permitted in respect of a negotiable instrument.
2. Explain the law relating to ambiguous and inchoate instruments.
3. 'A cheque is a bill of exchange'. Comment. Also distinguish between a bill of exchange and a cheque.
4. Explain 'payment-in-due-course'. Discuss 'maturity' of negotiable instruments and payment of interest thereon.
5. What is crossing of a cheque? Explain various types of crossing.
6. Describe the provisions related to the payment of interest due on a bill or pro-note contained in the Negotiable Instruments Act, 1881.
7. Summarise 'special rules of evidence' governing negotiable instruments.
8. Briefly discuss the rules of International Law related to negotiable instruments.
9. Discuss in brief the capacity of various parties to a negotiable instrument.
10. Discuss the nature of liabilities of drawer and drawee of a bill and a cheque.
11. Discuss the liability of 'maker' and 'endorser' of a cheque and promissory note.
12. Who is a holder-in-due-course? Explain his privileges.
13. Distinguish between a holder and a holder-in-due-course.
14. Discuss the liability of prior parties to a negotiable instrument to a subsequent holder and among themselves in case of its dishonour.
15. Write short notes on the following
    (i) Drawee in case of need (ii) Acceptor for honour
    (iii) Holder-in-due-course (iv) Holder and his rights

III. Caselets

1. *A* signs a pro-note in this form: 'I promise to pay *B* ₹5,000 fifteen days after my marriage with C.' Can it be called a valid promissory note?
   [Hint: No, a pro-note cannot be contingent]

2. In a cheque the amount in figures is written as ₹5,000 but in words it is written as ₹5,000. What amount is considered as the amount payable or ordered to be paid?
   [Hint: The cheque will be dishonoured]

3. A promissory note is stamped and signed with the words, 'I promise to pay *A* a sum of Rupees Five thousand only with interest thereon.' Is this note valid?
[**Hint:** No, the amount payable is not certain]

4. The drawee's name mentioned in a bill of exchange is that of a non-existent person. How would you treat this instrument?
[**Hint:** Ambiguous Instrument (Section 17)]

5. *A* signed a duly stamped pro-note and gave it to *B* and authorised him to fill ₹500 which *A* owed to *B*. *B* filled ₹700 in the space provided for payment and endorsed it to *C* who is a holder in due course. (i) Can *C* recover ₹700 from *A*. (ii) If the pro-note was not endorsed by *B* in favour of *C*, could *B* recover ₹700 from *A*.
[**Hint:** (i) Yes. *C*, being a holder-in-due-course derived a better title than that of transferor. (ii) No. *B*, being a holder of the instrument has committed a breach of trust and voilated the presumption as regards considertion. Refer Section 118(a)]

6. A bill dated 30 June 2013, is made payable one month after date. When would this bill mature?
[**Hint:** 3 August 2013]

7. *A* the holder of a bearer cheque endorses it to *B*, a minor. *C* steals the cheque from *B* and forges *B*'s endorsement and transfers the bill to *D* for consideration. Discuss the rights of *D*.
[**Hint:** *D* being a holder-in-due-course is entitled to sue *A*, *C*, and all parties prior to *A* except *B*]

8. *A* draws a bill on *B*, payable to *C*, 90 days after sight. It passes through *X*, *Y*, and *Z* by endorsement even before acceptance. On presentment by *Z* who is a holder-in-due-course, *B* refuses to accept. Now, who are liable to *Z*?
[**Hint:** *A*, *C*, *X*, and *Y* are liable to *Z*]

9. A cheque drawn by *X* payable to *Y* and endorsed to *Z* has been dishonoured by the bank for insufficiency of funds in *X*'s account. What is the remedy to the holder?
[**Hint:** *Z* can sue *X* only]

10. *A* draws a cheque payable to *B*, the bearer. *C* steals the cheque. Can *C* demand the payment from the bank or from *A* or *B*?
[**Hint:** No, *C* is not the holder (Section 8)]

11. *A* draws a bill on *B* payable to *C*. The bill is duly accepted by *B* and returned to *A*. *D* obtains the bill through fraud and endorses the same to *E* who obtains the same in good faith for value. *E* subsequently endorses the bill to *F* by way of gift. Discuss the right of *F*.
[**Hint:** *F* can sue *B*, the acceptor, as he stands on *E*'s title]

12. A bill is drawn on *A* payable to '*B* or order'. It is stolen by *C* from *B* and *C* forges *A*'s signature and endorses it to *D* who takes the same as a holder-in-due-course. Discuss the entitlement of *D*.
[**Hint:** *A*'s, forged endorsement conveys no title and therefore *D* cannot claim to be a holder-in-due-course]

Answers to Objective-type Questions

1. (i) True (ii) False (iii) False (iv) False (v) False
(vi) True (vii) True (viii) True (ix) False (x) True

2. (i) inchoate (ii) cheque (iii) a banker (iv) *drawer* (v) foreign
(vi) holder (vii) holder-in-due-course (viii) secondary (ix) cheque (x) acceptor

3. (i) (c) (ii) (d) (iii) (b) (iv) (c) (v) (d)
(vi) (c) (vii) (b) (viii) (c) (ix) (d) (x) (b)

13 Chapter in Review

LEARNING OUTCOMES

LO1 Negotiable Instrument: Meaning and definition

LO2 Kinds of negotiable instruments

LO3 Payment-in-due-course

LO4 Payment of interest

LO5 Negotiable instruments: Special rules of evidence

LO6 Negotiable instruments: Rules of international law

LO7 Holder and holder-in-due-course

KEY TERMS

Negotiable instrument: An instrument of credit wherein the transferee gets the better title than that of the transferor.

Inchoate instrument: A bill or note duly signed and stamped but left incomplete in some respect.

Inland bill: A bill drawn or made payable in India although it has been drawn on a foreign resident, or drawn in India upon an Indian resident even though it is made payable in a foreign country.

Foreign bill: A bill (of exchange) other than an inland bill.

Trade bill: A bill drawn, accepted, or endorsed for a genuine trade transaction.

Accommodation bill: A bill drew, accepted or endorsed without consideration to provide financial aid to someone.

Documentary bill: A bill where the relative shipping documents such as bill of lading, insurance policy, invoice etc. are sent along with (the bill).

Clean bill: A bill with which no documents related to the goods represented by the bill are attached.

Fictitious bill: A bill wherein name of the drawer or the payee or both is fictitious.

Bill-in-sets: A bill drawn in sets of three.

Escrow: An instrument delivered conditionally, or for a special purpose such as a collateral security, or for safe custody only and not for the negotiation.

LO1 A written document that requires a party to pay a certain sum of money on specified terms.

It is freely passable from one person to another, wherein the transferee enjoys a better title than that of the transferor.

LO2 There are three types of negotiable instruments, namely, Promissory note; bill of exchange; and cheques, payable either to order or to bearer.

LO3 Payment-in-due course implies a payment in accordance with the apparent tenor of the instrument; in good faith; and without negligence at the end of any person in possession thereof. It operates as a valid discharge of a negotiable instrument against the holder.

LO4 If the rate of interest payable on a bill or note, is specified in the instrument, it will be payable accordingly.The interest will be calculated from the date of the instrument to the date of realisation or tender of such amount. However, court of law is empowered to reduce the specified rate of interest to grant relief to the payer against the excessive rate of interest. Where, no rate of interest is specified in the instrument, interest is payable at the rate of 18 percent per annum on the principal amount due thereon.

LO5 There are special rules of evidence, applicable to all types of negotiable instruments. Besides certain presumptions, these rules comprise estoppel against denying the original validity of the instrument; and estoppel against denying the capacity of the payee to endorse the instrument; and estoppel against denying the signature or capacity of prior parties.

LO6 As a negotiable instrument may be drawn in one country and payable on another, different laws of the land will govern the liabilities of the parties. Sections 134 - 137 deal with the rules of International Law related to foreign instruments.

LO7 Holder is the person entitled in his own name to the possession of a negotiable instrument and recover the amount due thereon. Whereas, a holder-in-due-course is true and lawful owner of a negotiable instrument. Accordingly, unlike holder, a holder-in-due-course derives a better title than that of the tarnsferor.

Bank draft: An order to pay money drawn by a bank upon another branch or bank instructing the latter to pay a certain sum of money to a specified person or his order.

Cheque: A bill of exchange drawn on a specified banker and not expressed to be payable otherwise than on demand.

Estoppel: Prevention of disclaim by the party liable on a negotiable instrument, if any.

Holder: Person entitled in his own name to the possession of a negotiable instrument and to recover the amount due thereon.

Holder-in-due-course: True and lawful owner of a negotiable instrument.

CHAPTER

14 Negotiation and Assignment

Learning Objectives

LO 1 Negotiation

LO 2 Assignment

LO 3 Difference between negotiation and assignment

LO 4 Negotiation back

Since negotiable instruments are used as substitute for money, easy exchangeability is one of their distinctive features. In this behalf, negotiation simply refers to transfer of an instrument so as to invest its ownership in the holder. The ownership right, called 'title' or 'property', in a negotiable instrument can be passed from one person to another in one of the following two ways:

- By negotiation under The Negotiable Instruments Act, 1881 or
- By assignment under The Transfer of Property Act, 1882.

Negotiation

Negotiation: Process by which property in a negotiable instrument passes from one person to another by delivery alone or endorsement coupled with delivery of the instrument.

Negotiation enables the transferee to become a party to the contract, and to enforce the contract in his own name. Negotiation can be effected by endorsement and delivery in respect of order instruments, or by delivery alone in respect of bearer instruments.

Section 14 of the Negotiable Instruments Act lays down that when a promissory note, bill of exchange, or cheque is transferred to any person so as to render that person the holder thereof, the instrument is said to be negotiated.

The above definition makes it clear that for negotiation to take place, the following two conditions must be satisfied:

- The negotiable instrument is passed from one person to another and
- The transfer is made in such a manner that it renders the transferee the holder of the instrument.

Thus, merely transfer of a negotiable instrument does not automatically result in negotiation. The substance of negotiation lies in the fact that it is made with the intention of passing the ownership or title of the instrument. For example, if *A* delivers a cheque amounting ₹5000 to *B* and requests him to keep it in his safe custody, such a transfer of cheque is not a negotiation of the cheque to *B*. In this case, the transfer of (possession) of the cheque to *B* will make him a bailee only and not the holder (title) of the cheque.

Assignment

Assignment: Process of transferring the ownership right in a negotiable instrument by written and registered document under the provisions of the Transfer of Property Act.

Unlike negotiation, assignment refers to transfer of title or ownership of a negotiable instrument by means of a written and registered document under the provisions of The Transfer of Property Act, 1882. The Negotiable Instruments Act does not deal with the transfer of negotiable instruments by means of assignment. As we know, in order to be validly negotiable, an instrument must be transferable by custom of trade, besides being recognised by law for being sued upon by the holder. Negotiation, therefore, is not the exclusive means by which an instrument can be transferred. A bill of exchange, cheque, or a promissory note can be transferred by assignment as well. The law recognises the transfer of negotiable instruments by a written and registered sale deed i.e. by way of assignment. It must, however, be remembered that when the transfer is made by assignment, unlike negotiation, the assignee has only those rights which the assignor possessed. It follows that the assignee must take the instrument subject to all equities, which arise between the party liable and the assignor.

Negotiation and Assignment Distinguished

The points of difference between negotiation and assignment are summarised in Table 14.1.

Modes of Negotiation

Negotiation by Mere Delivery

Negotiation by delivery: The act of physically passing a negotiable instrument to its holder.

A negotiable instrument payable to bearer can be negotiated by plain delivery of the instrument. Section 47 lays down, 'subject to the provisions of Section 58[1], a promissory note, bill of exchange

[1] Section 58 lays down the circumstances under which a holder becomes disentitled to recover on negotiable instrument or negotiate it. Sometimes a person may obtain an

Table 14.1 Difference between Negotiation and Assignment

S. No.	Point of difference	Negotiation	Assignment
1.	Mode of transfer	Negotiation can be effected by mere delivery or endorsement followed by delivery.	Mode of transfer is not so undemanding. Assignment is always done by writing, usually by executing a separate document signed by the transferor.
2.	Consideration	Consideration is normally presumed in case of negotiation. The endorsee is not required to prove that he has obtained the instrument for consideration. The burden of proof, in fact, lies on the opposite party.	Consideration is not presumed in case of assignment. The assignee has to prove that he has obtained the instrument for consideration.
3.	Title	In case of negotiation the transferee, as a holder-in-due-course, takes the instrument free from defect in the title of the transferor, if any and acquires the better title than his transferor.	Assignee of an actionable claim takes it subject to the defect(s) that may exist in the title of the transferor.
4.	Notice of transfer	Notice of transfer by the transferee to the debtor is not necessary. In case of transfer by endorsement, if the debtor, e.g., maker, payee, etc., is not given any notice, he will still be liable to pay the amount on maturity.	In case of transfer by assignment, notice of transfer must be given to the debtor by the transferee.
5.	Relevancy	Negotiation is relevant chiefly in case of negotiable instruments.	Assignment is usually done in case of other documents but may be done in respect of negotiable instrument as well.
6.	Suit against party in his own name.	A transferee can sue the third party in his own name.	An assignee cannot do so.
7.	Governing Act	Transfer by negotiation is regulated by the Negotiable Instruments Act, 1881.	Transfer of negotiable instruments by means of assignment is regulated by the Transfer of the Property Act.

Figure 14.1 Modes of negotiation

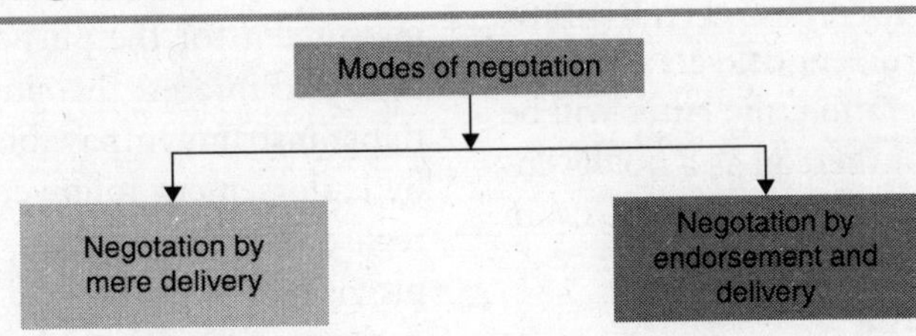

payable to bearer is negotiable by delivery thereof'. An instrument is payable to bearer if

- it is made so payable, or
- it was originally made payable to order but the only or ultimate endorsement is in blank, or
- if the payee is a fictitious or non-existing person.

The analysis of above points shows that the expression 'instrument payable to bearer' includes not only

instrument through fraud, theft, or for an unlawful consideration. In such cases, any possessor or endorsee of the instrument in question is not entitled to recover the amount of the instrument unless he is a holder-in-due-course.

Box 14.1 Instruments Payable to Bearer

Example 1

A, the holder of a cheque for ₹5000 payable to bearer, delivers it to *B*'s agent to keep it on behalf of his principal, i.e., *B*. The instrument has been negotiated to *B* so as to make him the holder. This amounts to the negotiation of the cheque by simple delivery.

Example 2

C steals a bearer cheque for ₹2000 from the table drawer of *A*. In this case, although *C* is currently in the possession of the cheque made payable to bearer, yet he is not entitled to the instrument as a holder as there is no negotiation of cheque from *A* to *C* for want of voluntary delivery. If *C*, however, delivers the cheque to any third person for consideration, the subsequent holder will be entitled to recover the amount due thereon provided he obtains the same in good faith and before maturity. Therefore, in the latter case, though the instrument so negotiated, is stolen one, the person who has obtained the instrument from *C* in this manner can sue in his own name against *A* and *C* in the capacity of a holder-in-due-course.

an instrument that is expressed to be so payable, but also one that is endorsed in blank, though originally payable to order, or for which the payee is a fictitious person. Even if a blank endorsement is followed by an endorsement in full, the instrument continues to be payable to bearer, as regards all parties prior to the endorsement in full.

Thus, an instrument payable to bearer may be negotiated by mere delivery without the formality of an endorsement, i.e., signature of the transferor and the person to whom such instrument is delivered becomes the holder and entitled to sue in his own name. It may, however, be noted that the delivery of the instrument must not only be actual but also voluntary. Thus, a person who finds or obtains a bearer instrument through theft, fraud, or offence is not the holder of the same for the sole reason that the instrument has not been delivered to him voluntarily. However, if a thief or finder of a lost bearer instrument delivers the same to another person for consideration, the latter will be entitled to recover the amount thereon as a holder-in-due-course if he/she receives the same bona fide (i.e. in good faith) and before maturity.

Exception

There is an exception to the rule that bearer negotiable instruments are negotiable by mere delivery. Section 47 provides that 'a promissory note, bill of exchange, or cheque delivered on condition that it is not to take effect in a certain event, is not negotiable (except in the hands of a holder for value without notice of the condition) unless such event happens'. Thus, only a holder for value can negotiate a conditional instrument, i.e., without notice of such condition. He acquires a good title to the instrument and can enforce payment due on it.

Negotiation by Endorsement and Delivery

Endorsement implies backing an instrument by signing it by a person to whose order the instrument runs. According to Section 15, 'when the maker or the holder of a negotiable instrument signs it, for the purpose of negotiation, on the back or face thereof, he is said to have endorsed the same and is called the endorser'. Thus, endorsement means and involves the signing of a negotiable instrument for the purpose of transferring the right, title, and interest therein to another person. A negotiable instrument payable to order can be negotiated by endorsement followed by delivery thereof. In this regard Section 48 lays down that, 'subject to the provisions of Section 58[2], a promissory note, bill of exchange, or cheque payable to order is negotiable by the holder by endorsement and delivery thereof'. Thus, negotiation through endorsement encompasses two elements. First, the holder should put his signa-

Endorsement: Backing an instrument by signing the same by the maker or holder thereof.

[2] Section 58 provides that negotiation of instrument by 'endorsement and delivery' is effective only when the instrument in question is not obtained by unlawful means, i.e., theft, fraud, etc., and for unlawful consideration.

ture (usually) on the back of the instrument. Second, after being signed by the holder, the instrument must be delivered to the transferee. Where an instrument payable to order is delivered without endorsement, it is merely assigned and not negotiated and the holder thereof is not entitled to the rights of a holder-in-due-course and he cannot negotiate it to a third party. Similarly, a mere endorsement on the instrument does not amount to negotiation, unless there is a delivery of the same. For example, *X* drew a cheque for ₹5000 payable to *Y* or order and delivered the same to him. *Y* later on endorsed the cheque in favour of *Z* but kept it in his table drawer. Subsequently *Y* died, and *Z* discovered the cheque in *Y*'s table drawer. In this case, *Z* does not become the holder of that cheque, as the negotiation was incomplete for lack of delivery of the cheque to him.

Kinds of endorsement

Normally signing one's name on the back of an instrument makes an endorsement. But it may also be made on the face (on the space available) of the instrument. If the back of the instrument is already full of endorsements, further endorsement may be signed on a slip of paper attached thereto. Such a slip is called 'Allonge' and becomes part of the instrument. However, no particular form of words/language is necessary for an endorsement. The word 'endorsement' should desirably be written on the back of the instrument and must be signed by the endorser. However, a simple signature of the endorser without the additional word—endorsement—is enough and alone constitutes a valid endorsement of the instrument. An endorsement involves two parties, viz., endorser—the person, i.e., the payee, holder, etc., who signs the instrument for the purpose of its negotiation, and endorsee—the person, to whom the instrument is transferred as a result of endorsement.

Depending on the way the endorsements are made on the instruments, they are classified as follows:

1. Blank or general endorsement
2. Full or special endorsement
3. Restrictive endorsement
4. Partial endorsement
5. Conditional endorsement
6. Facultative endorsement

This classification is also shown in Fig. 14.2.

Blank or general endorsement An endorsement is said to be blank or general when the endorser merely puts his signature on the back of the instrument, and the instrument so endorsed becomes payable to bearer, even though originally it was made payable to order. That is, blank endorsement is when someone signs the back of a check that does not indicate a particular payee. The effect of a blank endorsement is that the instrument can be further negotiated by its simple delivery, as long as the endorsement continues to be in blank. A holder of an instrument endorsed in blank, may, however, convert the same into an endorsement in full, by simply writing above the endorser's signature a direction to pay the instrument to another person or his order. For instance, a cheque was originally made payable to Shyam. Shyam just put his signature at the back of the cheque and delivered it to Mohan. This is an endorsement in blank and the cheque becomes a bearer one and can be further transferred by mere delivery.

Blank/general endorsement: An endorsement when someone signs the back of a check that does not indicate a particular payee.

Special or full endorsement An endorsement is said to be special or in full where the endorser

Special/full endorsement: An endorsement that names the endorsee to whose order a negotiable instrument is payable.

Figure 14.2 Kinds of endorsement

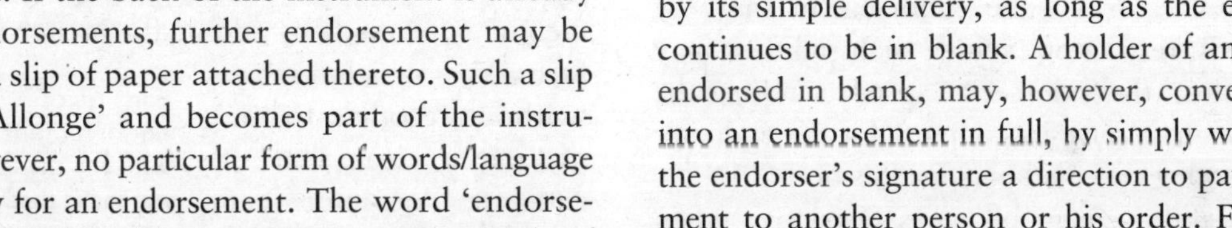

signs his name and adds a direction to pay the instrument to, or to the order of a specified person. That is, special endorsement is one that names the endorsee to whose order a negotiable instrument is payable. Such an endorsement is generally made in the form of 'Pay to *X* or order' or 'Pay to *X*' followed by the signature of the endorser. Section 16, which deals with 'endorsement in full', however, does not insist on any specific form of words for this purpose. It would be enough if the words used could be properly interpreted as a direction of such endorsement. As mentioned earlier, a blank endorsement can also be turned into a special one by the addition of an order making the bill payable to the transferee or his order. For example, a bill made payable to *A* or '*A* or order', and endorsed by *A* as 'pay to the order of *B*' would be considered specially endorsed and *B* may endorse it further.

Restrictive endorsement The endorsement of a negotiable instrument followed by delivery, transfers to the endorsee the property therein with the right of further negotiation but the endorsement may, by express words, restrict or exclude such right, or may merely constitute the endorsee an agent to endorse the instrument or to receive its contents for the endorser or for some other specified persons [Section 50].

> **Restrictive endorsement:** Endorsement that prohibits further negotiation of an instrument.

Thus, an endorsement becomes restrictive when it prohibits or restricts the further negotiation of an instrument.

Examples of restrictive endorsements

1. 'Pay *A* only'
2. 'Pay the contents to *A* only'
3. 'Pay *A* for my use'
4. 'Pay *A* or order for the account of *A*'. Here *B* is the endorser.

Partial endorsement A partial endorsement is one whereby the endorser is willing to transfer to the endorsee only a part of the amount of the instrument. According to Section 50, a partial endorsement is invalid and therefore does not operate as a negotiation of the instrument. For example, *X* holds a bill for ₹5000 and endorses the same as 'Pay *Y* or order ₹2500'. The endorsement is partial and invalid. However, there is an exception to this general rule. Where an instrument has been paid in part, the fact of the part payment may be endorsed on the instrument and it may then be negotiated for the residue. For example, a bill may be endorsed validly by writing 'Pay *Y* or order, being the unpaid residue of the bill'.

> **Partial endorsement:** An endorsement whereby the endorser is willing to transfer to the endorsee only a part of the amount of the instrument.

Conditional or qualified endorsement An endorsement, which limits or excludes the liability of the endorser, is called conditional or qualified endorsements. It is different from restrictive endorsement. The restrictive endorsement prohibits further negotiability whereas conditional endorsement simply limits or negates the liability of the endorser. It does not prohibit future negotiability. It only qualifies the liabilities of the endorser. An endorser may qualify or limit his liability in one of the following two ways:

> **Conditional/qualified endorsement:** An endorsement that limits or excludes the liability of the endorser.

By sans recours endorsement A qualified endorsement may be made by adding the French words '*sans recours*', which means 'without recourse to me', making it clear that the endorser does not incur the liability of an endorser to the endorsee or subsequent holders and they should not look to him in case of dishonour of instrument.

> **Sans recours endorsement:** Endorsement whereby the endorser does not incur the liability of an endorser to the endorsee or any subsequent holders.

For example, *B*, the holder of a bill, endorses it in favour of *A* by writing 'Pay *A* or order sans recours' or 'Pay *A* or order without recourse to me'. In this case, *B* has disowned his liability. If the instrument is dishonoured, *A* or any subsequent holder cannot ask *B* for payment of the same.

Contingent endorsement If the holder while endorsing a negotiable instrument makes his liability dependent upon the occurrence of a specified event, the endorsee acquires no right to maintain an action for the recovery of the amount until the condition is satisfied. If the condition

> **Contingent endorsement:** Endorsement wherein liability of the holder (endorser) is dependent upon the occurrence of a specified event.

becomes impossible to perform or the conditions specified are not fulfilled, the endorsee gets no title to the instrument and cannot sue the endorser or any prior party thereto.

For example, it is mentioned in a bill, 'Pay *B* or order, if a certain ship arrives within six months'. In this case, the right to receive payment is absolute and irrevocable if the ship arrives within the stipulated time. Or, another bill mentions 'Pay *B* or order on his marrying *C*'. In such a case, the endorser shall not be liable until *B* marries *C*.

Facultative endorsement: Endorsement whereby the endorser by express words abandons some of his rights or increases his liability under the negotiable instrument.

Facultative endorsement

Contrary to 'sans recours' endorsement, when the endorser, by express words, abandons some of his rights or increases his liability under the negotiable instrument, the endorsement is said to be 'facultative'. He may do so by giving up some of his rights, he is entitled to under the instrument.

For example, *X* is the holder of a bill of exchange for ₹5000. He makes an endorsement on it reading as 'Pay to *Y* or order, notice of dishonour waived'. This is a facultative endorsement as in this case *X* has given up his right to receive the notice in case of dishonour of bill but will remain liable to the endorsee for non-payment of the instrument.

Negotiation Back

Negotiation back: The process under which an endorser of a negotiable becomes its holder before maturity.

In some cases, the drawer or endorser, after they have negotiated the instrument, again become its holder before maturity. On such occasions, the instrument is said to be negotiated back to the holder.

Consequences of Negotiation Back

Where a cheque is transferred by negotiation back to the drawer, the drawer

- may strike out the endorsements (if any) on the cheque, and
- may, whether the endorsements have been struck out, reissue the cheque, but is not entitled to enforce payment against any person to whom the drawer was previously liable.

Where a cheque is transferred by negotiation back to an endorser, the endorser

- may strike out the endorser's own endorsement and subsequent endorsements (if any), and
- may, whether the endorser's own endorsement and subsequent endorsements have been struck out, further transfer the cheque by negotiation, but is not entitled to enforce payment against any person to whom the endorser was previously liable.

Exercises

I. Objective-type Questions

1. State whether each of the following statements is True or False:
   (i) Negotiation implies settlement of a negotiable instrument.
   (ii) The transferee of a negotiable instrument cannot get a better title than that of transferor.
   (iii) Transfer of a negotiable instrument automatically results in negotiation.
   (iv) The assignee has to prove that he has obtained the instrument for consideration.
   (v) A holder of an instrument endorsed in blank may convert the same into full.

2. Fill in the blanks:
   (i) __________ means transfer of ownership of a negotiable instrument by writing a separate deed.
   (ii) An endorsement in blank is also know as __________ endorsement.
   (ii) __________ is the process of negotiation in which an endorser, after one or more endorsements have taken place, becomes an endorsee.

(iv) An order cheque can be transferred by __________.
(v) A __________ endorsement has no effect upon the negotiability of the instrument.

3. Indicate the correct answer:
   (i) Transferee can get a better title than that of transferor under:
   (a) Negotiation (b) Assignment
   (c) Under both (a) and (b) above (d) Under none
   (ii) Which of the following can be transferred by assignment?
   (a) Bill of exchange (b) Cheque
   (c) Promissory note (d) All of the above
   (iii) When the endorser, by express words, abandons some of his rights or increases his liability under the negotiable instrument, the endorsement is said to be
   (a) *sans recours* (b) Contingent
   (c) Qualified (d) Facultative
   (iv) An instrument is payable to bearer in which of the following case?
   (a) If it is made so payable
   (b) If it was originally made payable to order but the only or ultimate endorsement is in blank
   (c) If the payee is a fictitious or non-existing person
   (d) In all of the above
   (v) Consideration is normally presumed in
   (a) Assignment (b) Negotiation
   (c) Under both assignment and negotiation (d) Under none

II. Review Questions

1. Compare and contrast 'negotiation' and 'assignment'.
2. What are the two principal modes of negotiating a negotiable instrument?
3. Discuss the essentials of a valid endorsement of a negotiable instrument. Discuss fully.
4. What do you mean by negotiation back? Discuss its consequences.
5. What are the different types of negotiation?

III. Problems

1. *X*, the holder of a negotiable instrument payable to bearer, delivers it to *Y*'s agent to keep it for *Y*. Comment on the validity of the instrument.
   [**Hint:** The instrument has been validly negotiated]

2. An instrument is drawn payable to 'Mr *A* or order'. *A* upon receiving it endorses it in blank. Discuss.
   [**Hint:** The instrument becomes payable to bearer]

3. A cheque is endorsed as 'Pay *X* only'. *X* signs the instrument and delivers it to *Y* as a part of discharge of debt the former owes to latter. Can *Y* collect the amount due on the instrument from *A*'s banker?
   [**Hint:** No. A restrictive endorsement prohibits further negotiation]

4. *A* endorses a cheque as 'Pay *B* or order *Sans Recours*'. The cheque subsequently gets dishonoured. Whether *A* is liable?
   [**Hint:** No. *A* has already excluded his liability]

5. A cheque is endorsed in blank by *X* to *Y*. *Y* further endorses the instrument as 'Pay *Z* or order', above *X*'s signature. Comment whether this is a valid endorsement.
   [**Hint:** Yes. 'Blank endorsement' can be converted into 'endorsement in full']

Answers to Objective-type Questions

1. (i) True (ii) False (iii) False (iv) True (v) True
2. (i) Assignment (ii) general (iii) Negotiation back (iv) endorsement and delivery (v) conditional
3. (i) (a) (ii) (d) (iii) (d) (iv) (d) (v) (b)

14 Chapter in Review

LEARNING OUTCOMES

LO1 Negotiation
LO2 Assignment
LO3 Difference between negotiation and assignment
LO4 Negotiation back

LO1 Negotiation enables the holder to enforce the instrument in his own name. It can be done by endorsement and delivery in case of order instruments, or by mere delivery in case of bearer instruments.

LO2 Negotiation is not the only way by which an instrument can be transferred. A bill of exchange, cheque, or a promissory note can be transferred by assignment as well. It takes place by means of a written and registered deed under the provisions of the Transfer of Property Act, 1882.

LO3 The material difference between negotiation and assignment is that in case of the former, the transferee can get better title than transferor, which can never happen in the latter. Moreover, unlike negotiation, consideration is not presumed in case of assignment. The assignee has to prove that he has obtained the instrument for consideration in the event of any dispute.

LO4 Where an instrument is negotiated back to a prior party, such party may reissue and further negotiate the same, but he is not entitled to enforce payment thereof against any intervening party to whom he/she was personally liable earlier.

KEY TERMS

Negotiation: Process by which property in a negotiable instrument passes from one person to another by delivery alone or endorsement coupled with delivery of the instrument.

Assignment: Process of transferring the ownership right in a negotiable instrument by written and registered document under the provisions of the Transfer of Property Act.

Negotiation by delivery: The act of physically passing a negotiable instrument to its holder.

Endorsement: Backing an instrument by signing the same by the maker or holder thereof.

Blank/general endorsement: An endorsement when someone signs the back of a check that does not indicate a particular payee.

Special/full endorsement: An endorsement that names the endorsee to whose order a negotiable instrument is payable.

Restrictive endorsement: Endorsement that prohibits further negotiation of an instrument.

Partial endorsement: An endorsement whereby the endorser is willing to transfer to the endorsee only a part of the amount of the instrument.

Conditional/qualified endorsement: An endorsement that limits or excludes the liability of the endorser.

Sans recours endorsement: Endorsement whereby the endorser does not incur the liability of an endorser to the endorsee or any subsequent holders.

Contingent endorsement: Endorsement wherein liability of the holder (endorser) is dependent upon the occurrence of a specified event.

Facultative endorsement: Endorsement whereby the endorser by express words abandons some of his rights or increases his liability under the negotiable instrument.

Negotiation back: The process under which an endorser of a negotiable becomes its holder before maturity.

CHAPTER

15 Presentment of Negotiable Instruments

Learning Objectives

LO 1 Presentment of a negotiable instrument

LO 2 Presentment (of a bill) for acceptance—When necessary

LO 3 Essentials of valid acceptance

LO 4 Presentment (of a negotiable instrument) for payment

LO 5 Consequence of non-presentment

LO 6 Presentment for payment—When excused

Presentment implies placing or exhibiting a negotiable instrument for acceptance, sight, or payment to the acceptor, maker, drawee, or any other party liable thereto by or on behalf of the holder thereof. This entails that presentment is done for any of the following three purposes:

Presentment: Placing a negotiable instrument, before the party liable thereto, for acceptance, sight, or payment, as the case may be.

1. Presentment for Acceptance,
2. Presentment for Sight, and
3. Presentment for Payment.

Presentment for Acceptance

Out of three principal negotiable instruments—bill of exchange, promissory note, and cheque, it is only the bill of exchange that is required to be presented for acceptance. However, it is not necessary to present every bill for acceptance, before presenting it for payment. A bill 'payable on demand', 'or payable on a certain day', or 'payable on the expiry of fixed period after date' (say payable 60 days after due date), or 'payable on happening of a certain event' need not be presented for acceptance. The holder in the above cases may, if he/she deems fit, present the bill for acceptance but the bill in question will become due for payment, even otherwise, i.e., without being presented for acceptance.

Negligence to present the bill in such cases, however, will not affect the liability of the parties liable to the holder, in case the bill is dishonoured by non-payment.

Presentment for acceptance is, nevertheless, essential in the following cases in order to render the parties liable under the bill:

1. Where a bill is payable at a specified period after acceptance or after sight. The expression 'after sight' in a bill of exchange means after acceptance. Such a bill must be presented to the drawee for sight or acceptance in order to ensure the responsibility for payment on maturity of the instrument [Section 61].
2. Where a bill expressly stipulates that before it is paid it shall be presented for acceptance.

In other cases, presentment is optional and depends on the discretion of the payee. It is, however, advisable that the bill be presented to the drawer for his/her acceptance in any case so that the holder obtains an additional security of the acceptor as well as the immediate right of recourse against the drawer and the endorser, if any, in the event of dishonour of a bill by non-acceptance, and he/she needs not wait till the maturity date of the bill. Presentment for acceptance is advantageous from the drawer's point of view too because if acceptance is refused, he/she may on receiving early notice of dishonour will be better equipped to get his property out of the hands of the drawee.

Bill: Mode of Acceptance

The acceptance of a bill is the indication of courtesy extended by the drawee or his/her agent towards the order of the drawer. A bill is said to have been accepted when its drawee signs across the face of the bill with or without writing the word 'accepted' and delivers it back to the holder or separately gives him a note of his acceptance. The drawee of a bill incurs no liability on any bill addressed to him for payment until gives his/her acceptance and thereby becomes the acceptor thereof. A refusal to accept gives the holder (payee) no right against the drawee. However, the holder in such a situation can give notice of dishonour and sue the drawer or endorser straight away, i.e., without waiting for the date of maturity of the bill.

Requisites of Valid Acceptance

In order to be valid, an acceptance must fulfil the following conditions. It must

1. be in writing,
2. be duly signed by the acceptor,
3. be apparent on the instrument,
4. after signing (the instrument) be delivered back to the holder,
5. be absolute and unconditional, and
6. be made by drawee only.

Must be in writing The drawee of a bill should give his assent by putting his signature on the bill. An oral promise will not do. However, writing the word 'accepted' is not essential and thus mere acceptor's signatures shall be enough to indicate the acceptance.

Duly signed by the acceptor Signature of the acceptor is necessary not only to constitute a valid acceptance but also to make the acceptor or drawee liable on the bill. If the acceptor does not sign, the acceptance will be rendered invalid even though he/she writes the word 'accepted' in his own handwriting.

Apparent on the instrument Acceptance must be made on the face or back of the instrument either by writing the word 'accepted' followed by acceptor's signature or by merely signing. Acceptance should not be given on its (instrument's) replica, copy, or any attached slip of paper, called Allonge.

Instrument must be delivered back The drawee/acceptor after giving their assent to pay the amount as mentioned in the bill must return the instrument back to the drawer/endorser.

Absolute and unconditional The acceptor must agree to pay the amount as mentioned in the instrument in full without any condition or limitation. In case of conditional acceptance, the holder may treat the negotiable instrument dishonoured.

Made by drawee only A bill of exchange is accepted by the drawee only. In case of more than one drawee, acceptance made by one or more drawees, but not by all, is also a qualified acceptance. In such a case the holder may treat the bill dishonoured for non-acceptance. However, in case of partnership, due to agency relationship, acceptance by one partner amounts to acceptance by all or the firm.

Types of Acceptance

An acceptance on the bill may be classified into general acceptance and qualified acceptance.

General or unqualified acceptance

General/unqualified acceptance: An acceptance wherein the drawee accepts a bill without any condition or qualification.

A general acceptance is absolute. An acceptance which gives assent without qualification to the order of the drawer, is termed as a 'general acceptance'. In general or unqualified acceptance, the drawee accepts the order of the drawer to pay the amount as specified in a bill in full, without any condition or qualification. As a rule, an acceptance has to be general in order to be valid.

Qualified acceptance

Qualified acceptance: Acceptance wherein the drawee accepts a bill subject to some conditions.

A qualified acceptance is one wherein the drawee accepts a bill subject to conditions or qualifications as to time, place, event, amount, etc. According to Section 86, 'If the holder of a bill of exchange acquiesces (agrees) in a qualification acceptance, or one limited to part of the sum mentioned in bill, or which substitutes a different place or time for payment, or which, where the drawees are not partners, is not signed by all the drawees, all previous parties whose consent is not obtained to such acceptance are discharged as against the holder and those claiming under him, unless on notice given by holder they assent to such acceptance'. The above section makes it clear that the holder of a bill is not bound to take a qualified acceptance. If, however, he accepts a conditionally accepted bill, he must be careful to secure the assent (if possible) of all the prior parties, because they are discharged unless they give their consent to such qualified acceptance. Simply put, if the holder takes a conditionally accepted bill, no other party prior to him would be liable to pay the bill in the absence of their consent to the qualified acceptance. Also, a conditional or qualified acceptance may render a bill invalid.

Classification of qualified acceptance An acceptance is deemed to be qualified where

1. it is conditional; declaring the payment to be dependent on the happening of an event therein stated.
2. it undertakes the payment of part only of the sum ordered to be paid.
3. no place of payment being specified on the order, it undertakes the payment at a specified place, and not otherwise or elsewhere, or where a place of payment being specified in the order it undertakes the payment at some other place and not otherwise or elsewhere.
4. it undertakes the payment at a time other than that at which under the order or would be legally due.

Thus, a qualified acceptance can be classified as follows:

1. Qualified as to place
2. Qualified as to amount

3. Qualified as to time
4. Made by some of the drawees only, and
5. Made for payment in installments.

Qualified as to place An acceptance qualified as to place is one by which the drawee undertakes to pay a bill only at a specified place and not elsewhere. For example, an acceptance reading as 'Accepted payable at Canara Bank only', or 'Accepted payable at Canara bank and not elsewhere'. It must be noted that the usage of the words 'only' or 'not elsewhere', is important to render an acceptance qualified otherwise it will be treated as general acceptance. For example, if a bill is accepted reading as 'Accepted payable at Canara bank', then it will be a general acceptance and not a qualified one for the fact it does not explicitly state that the bill is nowhere payable except at Canara bank.

Qualified as to amount If the drawee while accepting a bill of exchange undertakes the payment of part only of the sum ordered to be paid, the acceptance is said to be qualified as to amount.

Qualified as to time An acceptance can be made qualified as to time. If the drawee while accepting a bill of exchange undertakes to pay the bill at a time different from that mentioned in the instrument itself, whether sooner or later. For instance, a bill drawn payable 60 days after date and accepted in words reading as 'Accepted payable 75 days after date'. Or, 'Accepted payable 30 days after date', the acceptance is qualified as to time.

Made by some of the drawees only An acceptance made by one or more of the several drawees but not by all is also a qualified acceptance. As a rule, however, if a bill is drawn on several persons (not being partners), acceptance must be made by all. If only some of the drawees accept the bill and even one of them refuses to accept, the holder has a right to treat the bill dishonoured. The case of a partnership firm is, however, different wherein due to agency relationship, acceptance by any one or more drawees (partners) is considered acceptance by all and therefore, will be binding on the firm.

Made for payment in instalments It is the acceptance by which the drawee agrees to discharge the bill in instalments.

Condition or qualification of acceptance must be stated very clearly. It should appear on the face of the instrument in clear and unambiguous language. If the drawee wishes to make any qualification while giving acceptance, he/she must do so on the face of the instrument in such a manner that the holder of it does not fall short to understand that it was accepted subject to certain qualifications.

Presentment of Bill of Exchange

The rules for the presentment of a bill of exchange for acceptance are discussed under the following heads.

Presentment for acceptance by whom?

A bill of exchange should be presented for acceptance by the person entitled to demand the acceptance thereof [Section 61]. Thus, the holder of the bill or his/her duly authorised agent can present the bill for acceptance. If, however, somebody else on behalf of the holder who is not entitled to demand acceptance, presents a bill and the bill is accepted by the drawee, such acceptance would be deemed to have been made for the benefit of the person entitled to the bill and shall be valid.

Presentment for acceptance to whom?

A bill of exchange should be presented for acceptance to the person who can give his acceptance thereto. In this regard Section 33 reads:

'No person except the drawee of a bill of exchange, or all or some of several drawees, or a person named therein as a 'drawee in case of need' or an 'acceptor for honour', can bind himself by an acceptance.'

Section 34 however states, 'where there are several drawees of a bill of exchange who are not partners, each of them can accept it for another without his authority'. Section 75 conversely provides that 'Presentment for acceptance or payment may be made to the duly authorised agent of the drawee, maker, or acceptor, as the case may be, or where the drawee, maker, or acceptor has died, to his legal representative, or where he has been declared an insolvent, to his assignee'.

A close examination of the above-mentioned sections suggests that a bill of exchange can be presented for acceptance to the following persons:

1. Drawee or his/her duly authorised agent
2. If there are many drawees, the bill must be presented to all of them
3. Legal representatives of the drawee, if the drawee is dead

4. Official receiver or assignee of the insolvent drawee
5. 'Drawee in case of need', if any, if the original drawee refuses to accept the bill
6. 'Acceptor for honour' may also accept the bill in case the bill is not accepted and is noted or protested for non-acceptance. An acceptor for honour is a person who comes forward to accept the bill dishonoured by non-acceptance.

Time for presentment

1. If no time is specified in the bill for presentment, it must be made before maturity or within a reasonable time after it is drawn.
2. If the bill itself specifies a period for presentment, it must be presented within the stipulated period.
3. In the case of the bill in which presentment for acceptance is optional, presentment must be made at any time before payment.

It is important to note that the presentment in all the above cases must be made on a business day within usual business hours.

Place of presentment

If the place of presentment for acceptance is specified in the instrument, it must be presented at that place. On the other hand, if no place for presentment is mentioned, the bill should be presented at the place of business or residence of the drawee.

Effect of non-presentment

In cases where presentment for acceptance is essential, a default of such presentment will discharge the party liable to the holder [Section 61]. Thus, if the holder fails to present the bill before the drawee or the party liable to give his acceptance therein, the drawer and all the endorsers prior to the defaulting holder shall not be liable to such order. In such a case no action is maintainable in respect of consideration.

Presentment for acceptance: When excused

The bill in question should not be treated as dishonoured by non-acceptance in the following cases:

1. Where the drawee cannot be found even after a reasonable search [Section 61]
2. Where the drawee is a fictitious person or one incapable of contracting [Section 91]
3. Where although presentment has been irregular, acceptance has been refused on some other ground

Proof of presentment

In case of compulsory presentment, presentment must be proved in order to enable a party to recover its claim thereon.

Presentment of promissory note made after sight

If a promissory note is made payable after sight, it implies that payment cannot be demanded till the instrument is exhibited to the maker thereof. In this regard Section 62 states, 'A promissory note payable at a certain period after sight must be presented to the maker thereof for sight (if can after reasonable search be found) by a person entitled to demand payment, within a reasonable time after it is made and in business hours on a business day. In default of such presentment, no party thereto is liable therein to the person making such default'. This implies that where a promissory note is made payable after sight, presentment of it for sight is necessary in order to fix the maturity of the instrument. If the holder commit default in such presentment, all the antecedent parties are discharged from their liability to the holder making such default.

Drawee's time for deliberation

According to Section 63, 'the holder must, if so required by the drawee of a bill of exchange, allow the drawee forty-eight hours (exclusive of public holidays) to consider whether he will accept it'. This suggests that after 48 hours, the drawee should return the bill to the holder or else the holder thereof can treat the bill dishonoured.

Delay on part of drawee may, however, be excused, if it has been caused by circumstances over which the holder of the bill had absolutely no control, e.g., declaration of war or a moratorium, illness of holder, etc.

It is relevant to note that the holder, as soon as the bill is dishonoured for non-acceptance, becomes entitled to maintain a legal action against the parties liable to him.

Acceptance for honour

Acceptance for honour: When a third party agrees to pay a bill on behalf of the drawee.

Acceptance for honour occurs when a third party agrees to pay a bill on behalf of the drawee. Generally, a bill of exchange can be accepted only by the drawee. But Section 108 provides, 'When a bill of exchange has been noted or protested for non-acceptance or for better security, any person, not being a party already liable thereon, may with the consent of the holder by writing on the bill accept the same for the honour of any party thereto'. This is called the acceptance for honour. The question of acceptance for honour does not arise in case of promissory notes or cheques. Moreover, a bill can be accepted for honour only in the following cases:

1. When it has been noted or protested for non-acceptance or
2. For better security otherwise.

Any person who is not otherwise liable on the bill can accept it for honour. Even the drawee, despite having refused to accept the bill originally, may accept it for the honour of any party thereto. However, a bill can be accepted for honour only with the consent of the holder. The holder at his option may take or refuse such acceptance. But, if he chooses to give his consent, he waives his right of action against the prior parties liable to him on the bill.

There is no prescribed form of acceptance for honour. If the requirements stated above are fulfilled, the acceptance is valid. An acceptor for honour may give his acceptance by writing across the bill—'Accepted *supra protest*' or 'Accepted S.P'.

Liabilities and rights of acceptor for honour

An acceptor for honour is liable to pay only when the instrument has been duly presented at maturity to the drawee for payment and the bill been noted or protested for non-payment. Furthermore, if a bill has been protested for non-payment after having been accepted, any person may intervene and pay it *supra protest* on behalf of any party liable thereon. A person accepting for honour is entitled to recover the amount paid by him to the holder from the person for whose honour he has accepted the bill notwithstanding that the acceptance had been given without his order or knowledge.

Presentment for sight

Presentment for sight: Showing or exhibiting the instrument (promissory note) to the maker for his knowledge.

Presentment for sight is required only in respect of a promissory note payable after sight, which means showing or exhibiting the instrument to the maker for his knowledge. According to Section 62, 'A promissory note, payable at a certain period after sight must be presented to the maker thereof for sight (if he can after reasonable search be found) by a person entitled to demand payment, within a reasonable time after it is made and business hours on a business day. In default of such presentment, no party thereto is liable therein to the person making such default'. It is thus clear that the payment on promissory note which is made payable after sight cannot be demanded till the note has been exhibited to the maker and if the holder fails to present the note, the effect is the same as in case of non-presentment of a bill of exchange for acceptance and thereby no party on the note shall be liable to the holder making such default.

A promissory note made payable at a certain period after sight, must be presented for the acknowledgement of the maker in order to fix the maturity of the instrument. All the subsequent parties shall be discharged from their liability to the holder, if he commits default in such presentment. Significantly, it is not necessary to present every pro-note for sight. No presentment for sight is needed in respect of the following pro-notes:

1. Note payable 'at sight'
2. Note payable 'on demand'
3. Note payable 'on a fixed day/date', e.g., 15 July 2008 or last working day of month
4. Note payable 'on the expiry of a fixed period', e.g., 60 days after date.

Conversely, the following types of promissory notes should invariably be presented for sight:

1. Payable at a specified period 'after sight' and
2. The one that stipulates that it shall be presented for sight before it is presented for payment.

As started earlier, if the holder fails to present the above promissory notes for sight, no party shall be liable to him.

Presentment for Payment

> **Presentment for payment:** Placing the instrument before the maker, acceptor, or drawee thereof, as the case may be, to demand the payment due on the instrument.

Presentment (of an instrument) for payment implies placing the instrument before the maker, acceptor, or drawee thereof, as the case may be, to demand the payment due on the same. Every negotiable instrument must be properly presented for payment. Section 64 says: 'Promissory notes, bills of exchange, and cheques must be presented for payment to the maker, acceptor, or drawee thereof respectively, by or on behalf of the holder'.

The fundamental object of presenting an instrument is to give the maker an opportunity to honour the instrument. No right to sue arises in the absence of such presentment. The Exception to Section 64 provides, 'where a promissory note is payable on demand and is not payable at a specified place, no presentment is necessary in order to charge the maker thereof'. It is clear now that all notes (except those payable on demand and those not payable at a specified place), bills and cheques must be presented for payment to the maker, acceptor, or drawee thereof, by or on behalf of the holder during the usual hours of business, and if drawn at bankers, within banking hours [See Section 65]. Any default in presenting the instrument for payment would discharge the parties other than the maker, acceptor, or drawee as against the holder of the instrument.

Rules Regarding Presentment for Payment

The rules regarding presentment for payment may be studied under the following heads.

Presentment to whom? All negotiable instruments, which are subject to presentment for payment, must be so presented to the maker, acceptor, or drawee thereof, as the case may be or to his/her duly authorised agent, or where the drawee, maker, or acceptor has died to his/her legal representative, or where he/she has been declared an insolvent, to his/her assignee [Section 64 read with Section 75]. If there are more than one makers, drawees, or acceptors (not being partners) and no place of payment is specified, presentment must be made to all of them.

Presentment by whom? The person presenting a negotiable instrument for payment must be capable of giving a valid discharge to the debtor. Hence, either the endorsee or the payee can present a negotiable instrument for payment.

Time for presentment A promissory note or bill of exchange, made payable after a specified period at a specified date or sight thereof must be presented for payment at maturity [Section 66].

A premature presentment, and even one-day delay would render the presentment ineffectual and discharge the parties liable on the instrument (except maker or acceptor) as against the holder.

Presentment for payment of promissory note payable by installments A promissory note payable by installments must be presented for payment on the third day after the date fixed for payment of each installment. Non-payment on such presentment has the same effect as non-payment of a note at maturity [Section 67]. It means in such a case, three days of grace for such installment after the date when it falls due (for payment) are allowed.

Presentment of cheque to charge drawer A cheque , in order to charge the drawer, must be presented at the bank upon which it is drawn before the relation between the drawer and his banker has been altered to the prejudice of the drawer [Section 72 read with Section 84]. Simply put, it implies that a cheque may be presented for payment at the bank on which it is drawn without delay, and before the relations between the drawer and banker undergo a change against the drawer.

Presentment of instrument payable at demand Subject to the provisions of Section 31, a negotiable instrument payable on demand must be presented for payment within a reasonable time after it is received by the holder [Section 74]. Accordingly, every bill, promissory note, and cheque needs to be presented within a reasonable time after being received by the holder in order to make drawer of the instrument liable thereto.

Presentment of cheque to charge any other person A cheque , in order to charge any other person except the drawer, must be presented within a reasonable time after delivery thereof by such person [Section 73]. Any other person here predominantly refers to the endorsers. In order to hold the endorser liable, it is necessary that the cheque be presented for payment within a reasonable time after delivery of the cheque. If an endorsee keeps a cheque for an unreasonable length of time before he endorses it, he will be held liable for the subsequent dishonour of the cheque provided that the holder (endorsee) presents the cheque for payment to the drawee bank within a reasonable time after tracking it.

Hours for presentment Presentment for payment must be made during the usual hours of business, and if at banker, within banking hours.

However, delay in presentment [for acceptance or payment] is excused if the delay is caused by circumstances beyond the control of the holder, and not imputable to his default, misconduct, or negligence. When the cause of the delay ceases to operate, presentment must be made within a reasonable time [Section 75A].

Place of presentment for payment Sections 68 to 71 lay down the provisions as regards the proper place at which presentment for payment must be made. A brief account of the same is given below.

Where instrument is made payable at a specified place and not elsewhere A promissory note, bill of exchange, or cheque made, drawn, or accepted payable at a specified place and not elsewhere must, in order to charge any party thereto, be presented for payment at that place [Section 68]. Thus, if in such cases the instrument is not presented at that place, no party thereto will be liable thereon to the holder of the instrument.

Where no exclusive place of payment has been specified A promissory note or bill of exchange, wherein no place of payment has been indicated, must be presented for payment at the place of business (if any), or at the usual residence of the maker, drawee, or acceptor thereof, as the case may be [Section 70].

Where maker, drawee, or acceptor has no known place of business or fixed residence If the maker, drawee, or acceptor of a negotiable instrument has no known place of business or fixed residence and no place is specified in the instrument for presentment for acceptance or payment, such presentment may be made to him in person wherever he can be found [Section 71].

Payee must be able to find the addressee by the exercise of reasonable diligence.

Presentment of Cheque

Subject to the provision of Section 84, in order to charge the drawer of a cheque, it must be noticed that a crossed or account payee cheque can be presented to any bank in which the holder operates his/her account. It is the uncrossed or bearer cheque which must be presented at the bank upon which it has been drawn for cash payment. Moreover, a cheque must be presented at the bank upon which it is drawn before the relation between the drawer and his banker has been altered to the prejudice of the drawer [Section 72].

To sum up, the holder should exercise reasonable diligence to find the maker or acceptor or drawee, as the case may be, whether or not his place of business or residence has been specified or even there is no known place of business or fixed residence. Section 64 also states that where authorised by agreement or usage, presentment through the post office by means of a registered letter is sufficient. In the event of failure or undue delay or default in making the instrument available for payment (in compliance with the above mentioned rules), the parties there to (except the maker, drawee, or acceptor thereof) are not liable thereupon to the holder.

Effect of Non-Presentment for Payment

Non-presentment of bills of exchange and cheques for payment discharges the drawer and endorsers thereof. But in case of a promissory note, non-presentment for payment discharges only the endorsers, if any, not the other parties, if presentment is necessary thereof [Sections 68–69 read with section 64]. This is due to the fact that their liability is conditional, and if the condition is not fulfilled, the liability stands discharged.

Presentment for Payment: When Excused?

After maturity no presentment for payment is necessary against any party if, after maturity, with knowledge that the instrument has not been presented, it makes a part payment on account of the amount due on the instrument, or promises to pay the amount due thereon, whole or in part, or otherwise waives its right to take advantage of any default in presentment for payment [Clause (c) to Section 76]. Proof of such a payment or promise to pay is, of course, necessary.

Moreover, presentment of a bill or cheque for payment is excused.

Where drawer does not suffer damage Presentment for payment is excused against the drawer, if he/she could not suffer damage for want of such presentment [Clause (d) to Section 76]. When the drawer has no funds, belonging to him/her in the hands of the drawee or when drawee is a fictitious person or incompetent to contract or where drawer and drawee is the same person, the holder can make the drawer liable without presentation. In such cases, neither notice of dishonour nor presentment for payment shall be required within a reasonable time.

Delay in making presentation Delay in making presentation for payment is excused, when delay is caused by circumstances beyond the control of the holder and not due to any lapse or negligence on the latter's part. For example, if due to declaration of war between country of the holder and that of the drawee, the holder could not present the bill at maturity, delay in presentment is excusable. But when the impossibility of presentment ceases to operate, the instrument must be presented with reasonable diligence and within a reasonable time.

Exercises

I. Objective-type Questions

1. State whether each of the following statements are True or False:
   (i) Presentment for acceptance is necessary in respect of all bills, pro-notes as well as cheques.
   (ii) Where presentment is essential, in the absence of proof of presentment, no claim can succeed.
   (iii) Presentation is optional in case of a bill of exchange being payable on demand or on a fixed date.
   (iv) If presentment for acceptance, wherever required, is not established, the plaintiff suit is liable to dismissal.
   (v) Presentation of a bill for payment cannot be waived by express stipulation inserted in the bill.

2. Fill in the blanks:
   (i) Presentment means placing the negotiable instrument before the __________.
   (ii) An acceptance without qualification to the order is called __________ acceptance.
   (iii) Non-presentment of a bill for payment discharges __________.
   (iv) The person who can be approached in case of dishonour of a bill by the acceptor/drawee is called __________.
   (v) As against the __________ presentment is not necessary, if he cannot suffer any damage for lack of presentation (drawee/drawer).

3. Indicate the correct answer:
   (i) Presentment for sight is necessary in case of
      (a) All promissory notes
      (b) Promissory note being made payable at a certain period after sight
      (c) All promissory notes and bills of exchange
      (d) Bill of exchange being payable after sight

(ii) Presentation is required for
   (a) Acceptance
   (b) Sight
   (c) Payment
   (d) Any of the above three purposes

(iii) Presentment for acceptance is excused and consequently bill in question may be treated as dishonoured by non-acceptance in which of the following cases?
   (a) Where the drawee is a fictitious person, or is a person incapable of contracting
   (b) When the drawee could not be found even after a reasonable search by the holder
   (c) Where although presentment has been irregular, acceptance has been refused on some other ground.
   (d) In all the above cases

(iv) How much time a holder must, if so required by the drawee of a bill of exchange presented to him for acceptance, allow the drawee to consider whether he will accept it?
   (a) 48 hours (inclusive of public holidays)
   (b) 48 hours (exclusive of public holidays)
   (c) 24 hours (inclusive of public holidays)
   (d) 24 hours (exclusive of public holidays)

(v) In which of the following cases presentation of a negotiable instrument for payment is necessary on the part of the holder?
   (a) Where the maker, drawee, or acceptor, i.e., the payer does something intentionally which prevents the presentment of instrument
   (b) When the payer closes the place of business during business hours on a working day (if the instrument is payable at his place of business)
   (c) When the payer cannot be found even after reasonable search (if the instrument is not payable at any specified place)
   (d) In all the above cases

II. Review Questions

1. What do you mean by 'presentment for acceptance'? Discuss the rules regarding presentment for acceptance in brief.
2. Define the term acceptance? What are the different types of acceptance? Discuss in detail.
3. Explain 'presentment for payment'. What are the rules to be followed in order to constitute a valid presentment of negotiable instruments for payment?
4. When is the presentment for acceptance excused and the bill treated as dishonoured?
5. What is acceptance for honour? Explain fully.
6. When does presentment for payment become unnecessary? Elaborate.
7. Explain 'presentment for sight'. Also discuss effect of non-presentment for acceptance.

III. Problems

1. *A* draws a bill on *B* payable 10 days after the date of the bill. *B* accepts the same stating that it is payable 60 days after acceptance. Discuss nature and validity of the acceptance.
   [**Hint:** Qualified acceptance as to time, invalid]
2. A drawer gives his acceptance to a bill of exchange in the form 'Acceptance payable at ABC & Co'. Is this a valid acceptance? Does it make any difference if he gives his acceptance in the form 'Acceptance payable at ABC & Co., and not elsewhere'. If yes, discuss its validity.

[**Hint:** Being a general acceptance in the first case, it is valid. In the second case, it is a qualified acceptance (as to place); thus invalid]

3. A promissory note is made payable '75 days after sight'. Is presentation for acceptance thereof necessary? If yes, why?
[**Hint:** Yes. In case of a promissory note being payable at a certain period after sight', its presentment for sight is a must in order to fix the maturity of the instrument (see Section 62)]

4. *A* draws a bill of exchange on *B* for ₹1,000. *C* writes an acceptance on it. Is this acceptance valid?
[**Hint:** No It is not a valid acceptance as *C* is a stranger]

5. A promissory note is presented for payment by its holder 4 days after its maturity. State whether both the maker and endorser are discharged by such delay.
[**Hint:** No. Only the endorser is discharged by the delay whereas the maker continues to be liable as he is primarily liable on the instrument]

Answers to Objective-type Questions

1. (i) False (ii) True (iii) True (iv) True (v) False
2. (i) drawee (ii) conditional (iii) drawer and endorsee
(iv) Drawee in case of need (v) drawer
3. (i) (b) (ii) (d) (iii) (d) (iv) (b) (v) (d)

15 Chapter in Review

LEARNING OUTCOMES

LO 1 Presentment of a negotiable instrument

LO 2 Presentment (of a bill) for acceptance—When necessary

LO 3 Essentials of valid acceptance

LO 4 Presentment (of a negotiable instrument) for acceptance

LO 5 Consequence of non-presentment

LO 6 Presentment for payment—When excused

KEY TERMS

Presentment: Placing a negotiable instrument for, before the party liable thereto, acceptance, sight, or payment, as the case may be.

General/unqualified acceptance: An acceptance wherein the drawee accepts a bill without any condition or qualification.

Qualified acceptance: Acceptance wherein the drawee accepts a bill subject to some conditions.

Acceptance for honour: When a third party agrees to pay a bill on behalf of the drawee.

Presentment for sight: Showing or exhibiting the instrument (promissory note) to the maker for his knowledge.

Presentment for payment: Placing the instrument before the maker, acceptor, or drawee thereof, as the case may be, to demand the payment due on the instrument.

LO1 A negotiable instrument is presented for three purposes: presentment for acceptance, presentment for sight, and presentment for payment. However, it is only a bill of exchange, which may require presentment thereof for acceptance.

LO2 Presentment of a bill for acceptance is essential in the following cases:

1. Where a bill is payable at a specified period after acceptance or after sight. The expression 'after sight' in a bill of exchange means after acceptance.
2. Where a bill expressly stipulates that before it is paid it shall be presented for acceptance.

In other cases, presentment depends on the discretion of the payee.

LO3 In order to be valid, an acceptance must be in writing, duly signed by the acceptor, apparent on the instrument, instrument must be delivered back, absolute and unconditional, and made by drawee only.

LO4 Every negotiable instrument must be properly presented for payment.

LO5 Any default in presenting the instrument for payment would discharge the parties other than the maker, acceptor, or drawee (primary liable) as against the holder of the instrument. But in case of a promissory note, non-presentment for payment discharges only the endorsers, if any, not the other parties, if presentment is necessary thereof.

LO6 However, no presentment for payment is necessary against any party if, after maturity, with the knowledge that the instrument has not been presented, it makes a part payment on account of the amount due on the instrument, or promises to pay the amount due therein, whole or in part, or otherwise waives its right to take advantage of any default in presentment for payment.

Moreover, delay dedelay in making presentation for payment is excused, when delay is caused by circumstances beyond the control of the holder and not due to any lapse or negligence on the latter's part.

CHAPTER

16 Dishonour and Discharge of Negotiable Instruments

Learning Objectives

- **LO 1** Dishonour of a negotiable instrument
- **LO 2** Modes of dishonour
- **LO 3** Consequence of dishonour
- **LO 4** Notice of dishonour
- **LO 5** Notice of dishonour—When excused
- **LO 6** Noting and protest of a dishonoured instrument
- **LO 7** Discharge of a negotiable instrument
- **LO 8** Modes of discharge
- **LO 9** Material alteration

Dishonour of negotiable instrument: Loss of honour for an instrument at the end of the party liable thereto resulting in non-realization of payment due on the same.

Dishonour in relation to a negotiable instrument means loss of honour or respect for the instrument in question on the part of the maker, drawee, or acceptor, as the case may be, which eventually results in non-realisation of payment due on the instrument. Any type of negotiable instrument, i.e., bill of exchange, promissory note, or cheque (including an account payee one) may get dishonoured by non-payment by the drawee/acceptor thereof. But a bill stands dishonoured by non-acceptance because bill of exchange is the only negotiable instrument that requires its presentment for acceptance and non-acceptance thereof can amount to dishonour. A cheque being drawn on a specified bank and not expressed to be payable otherwise than on demand is never presented to the drawee bank for acceptance and same is the case of a promissory note. However, as discussed in the previous chapter, a pro-note made payable at a certain period after sight is required to be presented for sight, but it is never subject to presentment for acceptance. If a cheque gets dishonoured due to insufficiency of funds in the account, it may attract civil as well as criminal liability against the drawer.

Dishonour by Non-acceptance

A bill is said to be dishonoured by non-acceptance in the following circumstances:

1. When the drawee or one of the several drawees (not being partners) does not accept the bill within 48 hours (exclusive of public holidays) from the time of presentment of the instrument for the acceptance [Section 63].
2. Where presentment is required and the bill remains unpresented.
3. Where the drawee is incompetent to enter into a valid contract.
4. Where the bill is given a qualified acceptance.
5. If the drawee is a fictitious person.
6. If the drawee cannot be found even after reasonable search [Section 61].
7. Where the drawee has either become insolvent or is dead and the holder does not present the bill to the assignee or legal representative of the insolvent or deceased drawee.

It is relevant to note that where a drawee-in-case-of-need is named in a bill of exchange or in any endorsement thereon, the bill is not dishonoured until it has been dishonoured by such drawee [Section 115].

Dishonour by Non-payment

A promissory note, bill of exchange, or cheque is said to be dishonoured by non-payment when the maker of the note, acceptor of the bill, or drawee of the cheque commit default in payment upon being duly required to pay the same. Also, the holder of a bill or pro-note may treat it as dishonoured, without placing for payment when presentment for payment is excused expressly by the maker of the pro-note, or acceptor of the bill and the note or bill when overdue remains unpaid [Section 92 read with Section 76].

If a bill is dishonoured either by non-acceptance or by non-payment, the drawer and all the endorsers of the bill are liable to the holder, provided notice of such dishonour is given to them. The drawee, on the other hand, shall be liable to the holder only in the event of dishonour by non-payment.

Dishonour of Cheque for Insufficiency of Funds in the Account

A cheque (bearer, order or even account payee) drawn by a person on an account maintained by him with a bank for payment of any amount of money to another person can be returned unpaid for lack of enough funds in the said account. This is called dishonour of cheques for insufficiency of funds (in the drawer's account). In such cases, the drawer is also criminally liable for this offence and may be punished with imprisonment for a term, which may extend to one year, or with fine that may extend to twice the amount of the cheque, or with both [Section 138]. The most remarkable feature of Section 138 is that it treats even an account payee cheque as negotiable instrument if it gets dishonoured due to insufficiency of funds in drawer's account.

Notice of Dishonour

Notice of dishonour: A formal communication, oral or written, of the fact of dishonour.

Notice of dishonour refers to formal communication, oral or written, of the fact of dishonour. When a negotiable instrument is dishonoured either by non-acceptance or non-payment, the holder should give notice of the dishonour to all the parties, he seeks to hold liable. A notice of dishonour has its own significance. If it is not given to the drawer and endorsers, it will discharge them all from liability not only on the bill or pro-note but also with regard to the original consideration. Such notice also enables a person (drawer) so notified to protect himself/herself as against the drawee or acceptor who has illegitimately dishonoured the instrument issued by him/her.

Rules Regarding Notice of Dishonour

The rules regarding notice of dishonour can be discussed under the following heads.

Notice of dishonour in case of non-acceptance

If the drawee refuses to accept the bill duly presented to him/her for acceptance, the bill stands dishonoured, and the notice of dishonour must be given in accordance with the Act. However, it must be remembered that in the event of dishonour by non-acceptance, the rights of a person, who becomes a holder-in-due-course subsequent to the omission to give notice, are not perjured by the omission.

Notice of dishonour in case of non-payment

Where an instrument has been dishonoured due to non-payment, and proper notice of dishonour has been served, notice of a subsequent dishonour on account of non-payment is no more required unless the instrument in the meantime has been accepted. Conversely, where a bill has been duly accepted by its drawer but the holder fails to get the payment, notice of dishonour by non-payment must be given to the drawee.

Notice by whom?

According to Section 93, notice of dishonour must be given by the holder or by some party liable on the instrument. 'A notice given by a stranger stands invalid and inoperative. Moreover, any party receiving notice of dishonour must, in order to render any prior party liable to him, give notice of dishonour to such party within a reasonable time unless such party otherwise receives due notice from the holder or some other party liable to the instrument dishonoured' [Section 95]. It means, where the holder has given a notice of dishonour to any party liable on the instrument and that party, in turn, has given notice of dishonour to all prior parties, the holder can treat that notice as one given by him.

Notice to whom?

Notice of dishonour must be given to all the parties (other than the maker of the dishonoured promissory note or the drawer or acceptor of the dishonoured cheque or bill) or their duly authorised agents who are sought to be made liable. Where there are two or more persons, jointly liable as drawers or endorsers, notice to any one of them is enough if the holder seeks to make them jointly liable on the instrument. If the holder seeks to make all the drawers and endorsers individually liable, he should give the notice of dishonour separately to all of them [Section 93]. In case the party entitled to notice has expired, the notice of dishonour may be given to his/her legal representative, or where, he/she has been declared an insolvent, notice may be given to his/her official assignee or receiver [Section 94]. But if the party to whom notice of dishonour is dispatched is dead and the party dispatching the notice is ignorant of the fact, a fresh notice must be given to his legal representative [Section 97].

It is important to note that the notice of dishonour is not necessary to the maker of a pro-note, or acceptor of a bill or drawer of a cheque because of the underlying fact that they are primarily liable on the instrument. As principal debtors, this is their duty to pay the instrument on due date.

Form and mode of giving notice

There is no prescribed mode or format for giving a notice of dishonour. It may be given in any form satisfying the requirements of law. According to Section 94, the notice of dishonour may be oral or written; may, if written, be sent by post; it may be in any form; but it must inform the party to whom it is given, either in express terms or reasonable intendment (sense) that the instrument has been dishonoured, and in what way, and that he/she will be held liable thereon, and it must be given within a reasonable time after dishonour, at the place of business or (in case such party has no place of business) at the residence of the party for whom it is intended. Thus, a notice of dishonour may be oral or in writing, but it must be an actual formal notice and the language used must indicate that the instrument has been dishonoured due to non-acceptance or non-payment, as the case may be, and that the recipient of the notice will be held liable.

Reasonable time of giving notice

The determination of 'reasonable time' for giving notice of dishonour depends on the nature of the instrument. While calculating reasonable time, public holidays must be excluded [Section 105].

Furthermore, Section 106 lays down the following rules for determining reasonable time for giving a notice of dishonour:

1. If the holder and the party to whom notice of dishonour is to be given carry on business or live (as the case may be) at different places, it is deemed to be reasonable time if the notice is dispatched by the next post or on the next day, after the day of dishonour.
2. If the said parties carry on business or live in the same place, such notice is considered, given within a reasonable time, if it is dispatched to reach its destination on the day, after the day of dishonour.

Reasonable time for transmitting such notice

A party receiving notice of dishonour, who seeks to enforce its rights against a prior party, is said to have transmitted the notice within a reasonable time if it transmits the notice within the same time after its receipt as it would have had to give notice if it had been the holder [Section 107].

Cases in which notice of dishonour is excused

As per Section 98, notice of dishonour is excused in the following cases:

1. When it is dispensed by the party entitled thereto.
2. When the drawer has countermanded payment, i.e., issued stop payment instructions to the drawee, no notice of dishonour is necessary to charge him/her.
3. When the party charged could not suffer damage for want of notice.
4. When the party entitled to notice cannot be found after due search.
5. When the party bound to give notice is unable to give it for any other reason but without any fault of its own.
6. When the acceptor is also a drawer (i.e., when drawer and acceptor are the same person) no notice of dishonour is necessary to charge the drawer, for instance, when a firm draws a bill on its branch.
7. When the party entitled to notice, knowing the fact of dishonour, promises unconditionally to pay the amount due on the instrument.

Dishonoured Instrument: Noting and Protest

Noting

Noting: Act of recording the fact of dishonour of an instrument by the notary public.

The term 'noting' refers to the recording of the fact of dishonour of a negotiable instrument by the notary public[1]. When a promissory note or bill of exchange is dishonoured by non-acceptance or non-payment, the holder may cause such dishonour to be noted by a public notary upon the instrument, or upon a piece of paper attached thereto, or partly upon each [Section 99].

Noting serves as the authentic and legal proof of presentment and acceptance. Section 99 in this regard further provides that noting must be made within a reasonable time after dishonour, and must specify the date of dishonour, the reason why the holder treats it as dishonoured, and the notary charges.

[1] Notary public is a person who is officially designated for this purpose and is appointed under The Notaries Act, 1952 to attest certain documents.

Protest

Protest: Formal certificate of dishonour of an instrument by the notary public.

The term 'protest', that follows noting, implies the formal certificate of dishonour of the instrument by the notary public. According to Section 100, where a promissory note or bill of exchange has been dishonoured by non-acceptance or non-payment, the holder may, within a reasonable time, reason such dishonour to be noted and certified by a notary public, such certificate is called a protest. Noting does not afford any evidence of presentment for dishonour unless it is followed by protest notwithstanding that the former contains the full name of the notary public.

Contents of protest

According to Section 101, a protest under Section 100 must contain

1. The instrument itself or a literal transcript (i.e., a copy) of the instrument and of everything written or printed there upon.
2. The name of the person for whom and against whom the instrument has been protested.
3. Fact of the presentment of the instrument and its subsequent dishonour and the reason given by the drawee or acceptor for non-acceptance, or non-payment, or refusal to give better security[2].
4. The place and time of dishonour, when note or bill has been dishonoured, and the place and time of refusal, when better security has been refused.
5. The signature of the notary public making the protest.
6. The name of the person by whom and of the person for whom, in case of an acceptance for honour or payment for honour, and the manner in which such acceptance or payment was offered and affected.

In accordance with Section 138, if a cheque drawn by a person against an account maintained by him with a banker for payment of any amount of money to another person from out of that account for the discharge, in whole or in part, of any debt or other liability, is returned by the bank unpaid, either because of the amount of money standing to the credit of that account is insufficient to honour the cheque or that it exceeds the amount arranged to be paid from that account by an agreement made with that bank, such person shall be punishable with imprisonment for a term which may be extended to two years, or with fine which may extend to twice the amount of the cheque, or with both.

In this behalf the following points are worth noting; non-observance thereof may absolve the drawer from being criminally liable on account of bouncing of cheque.

1. The cheque must have been dishonoured for want of amount of money standing to the credit of the account on which the cheque was drawn, or for the reason that the amount payable on the cheque drawn exceeds the sanctioned limit of overdraft facility, if any.
2. The cheque must have been issued by the drawer for the payment of any legally enforceable debt or other liability, in whole or in part. This follows that where any cheque is drawn in favour of the payee by way of a gift, present, charity, or on account of any other social obligation and the said cheque is dishonoured subsequently for insufficiency of funds, no offence would be deemed to have been committed on the part of the drawer.
3. The cheque must have been presented to the bank within a period of three months from the date on which it was drawn or within the period of its validity, whichever is earlier.

Here it is pertinent to note that in the case of non-payment of a post-dated cheque, the aforesaid period of three months shall be counted from the date stated on the cheque, since a post-dated cheque becomes a regular cheque only after it becomes payable on demand [*Anil Kumar Sawhney vs Gulshan Rai*[3]]. Moreover,

---

[2] When the acceptor of a bill of exchange has become insolvent, or his credit has been publicly impeached, before the maturity of the bill, the holder may, within a reasonable time, cause a notary public to demand better security of the acceptor, and on its being refused may, within a reasonable time, cause such facts to be noted and certified as aforesaid. Such certificate is called a protest for better security.

[3] JT 1993 (6) SC 280

in respect of a post-dated cheque, Section 138 can indeed be attracted when a cheque is dishonoured on account of 'stop payment' instructions sent by the accused to his bank irrespective of insufficiency of funds in the account (*Rangappa vs Sri Mohan*[4]).

4. The payee or the holder-in-due-course must have made a demand for the payment of the said amount of money by giving a notice, in writing, to the drawer of the cheque, within 30 days of the receipt of information about the return of the cheque as unpaid.
5. The drawer of such a cheque must have failed to make the payment of the said amount of money to the payee or the holder-in-due-course within 15 days of the receipt of the said notice. That is cause of action commences from the 16th day onward.

Further, Section 139 provides that it shall be presumed that the holder received the cheque in the discharge of a debt or liability unless the contrary is proved.

Furthermore, it has also been provided under Section 140 that the drawer shall not be allowed the defence that he had no reason to believe while issuing cheque that it would be dishonoured subsequently.

It is also worth noting that unless the dishonoured cheque is returned by the banker as unpaid, no offence can be enforced against the drawer under Section 138 [*Anil Kumar Sawhney vs Gulshan Rai*]. Furthermore, the dishonour of a cheque by itself does not hold the drawer criminally liable. It is only the subsequent failure on part of the drawer to pay the amount due on the dishonoured cheque within 15 days of the receipt of demand notice, which renders a cause of action against the drawer [*M/S Anand Engg. Co. vs Amitava Goswami*[5]].

Moreover, the payee cannot lodge a complaint after the expiry of one month from the date on which cause of action arose under the said provisions [*V.N. Samant vs M/S KGN Traders*[6]].

In case an offence under the aforesaid provisions is committed by a company, it shall be liable to be punished accordingly. In this regard Section 141(1) provides that if the person committing an offence under Section 138 is a company, every person, who, at the time the offence was committed, was in charge, and is responsible to the company for the conduct of the business of the company, as well as the company, shall be deemed to be guilty of offence and shall be liable to be proceeded against and punished accordingly. But this section does not render any person liable to the punishment if he could prove that

1. the offence was committed without his knowledge or
2. that he had exercised all due diligence to deter the commission of such offence.

Moreover, the director, manager, secretary, or other officers of the company shall also be deemed to be guilty of that offence and shall be liable to be proceeded against and punished accordingly, if it can be shown that the offence was committed.

Discharge of a Negotiable Instrument

When the liability of the party, primarily and ultimately liable on the instrument, comes to an end, the instrument is said to be discharged. The discharge of the instrument results in extinguishments of all rights of action under it and the instrument ceases to be negotiable. After discharge of a negotiable instrument, even a holder-in-due-course acquires no right under it and he cannot bring a suit on the face of it. A negotiable instrument may be discharged in any one of the following ways:

1. By payment in due course
2. By the principal debtor becoming the holder
3. By renunciation of the rights by the holder
4. By cancellation of the instrument
5. By an act that would discharge an ordinary contract.

Discharge by Payment in Due Course

Payment-in-due-course, as per Section 10, is the payment made in good faith and in accordance with the apparent tenor of the instrument to the rightful holder thereof. Accordingly, it is the payment made

[4] AIR 2010 SC 1898
[5] AIR 1978 Ker 201
[6] (1994) 3 Crimes 725 (Karn)

in money only on maturity of the instrument and of the entire amount due on it and the person to whom it is made should be in possession of the instrument. It may be noted that a payment of a post-dated cheque before maturity is not according to the apparent tenor of the instrument and, hence, does not discharge the instrument unless the instrument is cancelled or the fact of payment is duly recorded on the instrument to prevent its further negotiation.

Section 81 further lays down that the person making the payment is entitled to have the instrument delivered back to him upon payment or if the instrument is lost or cannot be produced, to be indemnified against any further claim thereon against him. Moreover, in order to discharge a negotiable instrument by payment-in-due-course, the payment should be made by the party who is primarily liable on the instrument. So if a party, who is not primarily liable, makes payment, the instrument is not discharged. The payment-in-due-course discharges not only the negotiable instrument in question but also the parties who are primarily and ultimately liable on the instrument as well.

Discharge by the Acceptor Becoming the Holder

According to Section 90, when the acceptor of a bill of exchange becomes its holder on or after maturity thereof, all rights of actions thereon are extinguished. As a result, the instrument is discharged. An acceptor may become the holder of a bill by the process of negotiation back. But in order to discharge the bill it is essential that this happens after maturity because if he becomes holder of the bill before maturity, he may again endorse the same. Thus, a negotiable instrument stands discharged if the acceptor has become the holder of the instrument at or after maturity in his own rights, i.e., not in any other capacity such as agent, executor, trustee, etc. For instance, *A* accepts a bill drawn on him by *B*. *B* later on transfers the instrument to *C*, and *C* indorses it to *D*, who indorses it to *A*. The instrument-in-question stands discharged by acceptor (*A*) becoming holder of it. This rule is based on the principle that a present right and liability united in the same person cancel each other [*Chalmer's Bill of Exchange Act, 1882*[7]].

[7] 1967, M. D. Chalmers 18th ed. Waterlow [London]

Discharge by Renunciation of the Rights by the Holder

If the holder of a negotiable instrument expressly gives up or renounces his rights against all the parties, the instrument stands discharged. The renunciation can be made by surrendering or delivering the instrument to the party who is primarily liable thereon or declaring in writing the fact of renunciation. Such renunciation discharges the instrument as well as all the parties thereto.

Discharge by Cancellation of the Instrument

If the holder intentionally cancels the name of the drawer or acceptor of a promissory note or bill of exchange, the instrument gets discharged auttomatically. It is important to note that the cancellation should be made with an intention to release the party primarily liable on it, which in turn would discharge the other parties thereto. Cancellation of the instrument can be executed either by physical destruction or by crossing out signatures of drawer, acceptor, etc., on the instrument.

Discharge by an Act That Would Discharge a Simple Contract

A negotiable instrument can also be discharged by an act that would discharge a simple contract for payment of money. This is called 'discharge of negotiable instrument by operation of law'. Such a discharge may occur due to the expiry of period prescribed for recovery of sum of money due on the instrument, or by substitution of another negotiable instrument for the original instrument or by an agreement between the parties in the form of novation. It may also take place by way of merger of one or more debt into another or by the debtor being adjudicated insolvent.

Discharge of Parties to an Instrument

A party to a negotiable instrument is said to be discharged from its liability when its liability on the instrument comes to an end. Where only one or more but not all the parties are discharged, the instrument continues to be negotiable and the undischarged parties remain liable on it. For example, if a bill is not placed for payment on due date, it will discharge the endorsers from their liability, but the acceptor will still remain liable to it and the instrument-in-question, negotiable. Discharge of a party who is primarily and ultimately liable, i.e., principal debtor or acceptor, drawer, amounts to discharge of all parties and consequently the discharge of the instrument.

A party to a negotiable instrument is discharged in the following ways:

1. By cancellation of the name of a party to the instrument
2. By release of any party to the instrument
3. By payment
4. By allowing drawee more than forty-eight hours to accept
5. By delay in presenting a cheque for payment
6. By payment in due course of a cheque (payable to order) or a draft
7. By taking qualified acceptance
8. By non-presentment for acceptance of a bill of exchange
9. By operation of law
10. By material alteration.

Discharge by Cancellation

The holder of a negotiable instrument may deliberately cancel the name of any of the parties liable on the instrument with the intention of discharging him from his liability thereon. The party whose name is so cancelled, all the endorsers subsequent to him are discharged from their liability to the holder and to any person who gets the instrument from such a holder [Section 82(A)]. Thus, such a cancellation disentitles a holder to recover the amount due on the instrument from that party, whose name has been so cancelled. Here it must be remembered that the cancellation of one or more names of endorsers does not result in cancellation of the instrument. This is so because the parties prior to the endorser(s) whose name(s) have been cancelled will remain liable under that instrument. But, if the holder cancels the name of the maker or acceptor then the liability of all other parties to the instrument comes to an end which in turn discharges the instrument itself.

Discharge by Release

Sometimes the holder of a negotiable instrument may release any party to the instrument by any method other than cancellation [Section 82(B)]. For example, by means of a separate agreement of waiver, renunciation, or remissions, etc. In such cases the party so released and all other parties who have a right of action against the party so released are discharged from their liability to the holder and to all parties deriving title from such holder after notice of such discharge.

Discharge by Payment

If the instrument is payable to the bearer, or has been endorsed in blank, and the maker, acceptor, or endorser (i.e., party primarily liable on the instrument) makes payment in due course, he/she (payer) is discharged from the liability on the instrument to all parties thereto. And all the parties in turn, stand discharged, the reason being that the instrument as such is discharged by such payment [Section 82(C)].

Discharge by Allowing Drawee More Than 48 Hours to Accept

Where the holder of a bill of exchange allows the drawee more than 48 hours, excluding public holidays, to consider whether he will accept the same, all previous parties not consenting to such allocation are thereby discharged from their liability to such holder [Section 83].

Discharge by Delay in Presenting Cheque for Payment

If the holder of a cheque does not present the instrument within reasonable time[8] of its issue, and the drawer suffers some damage through such delay, he is discharged from the liability to the extent of actual damage suffered by him. Such delay may cause a loss to the drawer because the drawee bank may become insolvent in the meantime, i.e., before the cheque is presented [Section 84]. Thus, if the amount payable under a cheque exceeds the sum of money the drawer has in his account (with the banker), he suffers damage only in the event of failure of the bank and due to this fact

[8] In determining reasonable time, regard shall be had to the nature of the instrument, the usage of trade and of bankers, and the facts of the particular case.

Box 16.1 Discharge by Delay in Presenting Cheque for Payment

Example 1

Jeeva drew a cheque for ₹5000 on New Bank of India in favour of Sadhana and delivered the same to her. When the cheque was to be presented, Jeeva had only ₹3000 in his account with the bank. Sadhana did not present the cheque to the drawee bank within a reasonable time. Meanwhile, the bank failed. In this case, Jeeva, i.e., the drawer is discharged from his liability to the extent of ₹3000 only. Thus, Sadhana, the holder, can recover the remaining ₹2000 from the drawer (Jeeva), and can prove his claim in the insolvency proceedings of the bank in respect of the balance of ₹2000.

Example 2

A draws a cheque for ₹1000. He had sufficient funds in his bank account. The bank fails before the cheque was presented. The drawer is discharged (in full), but the holder can prove against the bank for the amount of the cheque [Illustration (a) appended to Section 84].

Example 3

A draws a cheque for ₹1000 in favour of *B* on his bank in Mumbai. Before the cheque could be presented for payment in ordinary course, the bank fails (i.e., becomes insolvent). *A* is not discharged for the reason he has not suffered actual damage through the delay in presenting the cheque before the banker for the payment.

is discharged from his liability to that extent. But if the drawer had sufficient funds with the bank to meet the cheque at the time when bank failed, he will be discharged in full. It is important to note that in such a situation, though the drawer is discharged from the liability, the holder becomes a creditor of the bank in respect of the amount of the cheque and a set off is equitable in respect of such amount against the insolvent banker [Section 84(3)]. Examples in Box 16.1 will help understand the point better.

Discharge by Payment in Due Course of Cheque (Payable to Order) or Draft

Under Section 85, a banker who pays a cheque payable to order in due course, drawn upon him is discharged. Similarly, in compliance with Section 85(A), a bank is also protected by payment-in-due-course of drafts drawn by one branch of a bank on another branch payable to order.

Discharge by Taking Qualified Acceptance

If the holder of a bill of exchange acquiesces in a qualified acceptance, then all the parties prior to him whose consent is not obtained to such acceptance are discharged from their liability as against the holder and those claiming under him [Section 86].

Discharge by Non-presentment for Acceptance of Bill

The holder of a bill of exchange, which is stipulated to be payable after certain period or on sight, must present the bill for acceptance to the drawee within a reasonable time after it is drawn. If he fails to do so, the drawer and all intervening endorsers shall stand discharged [Section 61].

Discharge by Operation of Law

In certain cases, the parties are also discharged from their liability by operation of law. For example, where the debtor is declared an insolvent, he is discharged from his liability. Similarly, when the remedy against a party becomes time barred by the expiry of limitation period[9], the party who was otherwise liable, stands discharged.

[9] The term limitation period refers to the time prescribed by law for the recovery of debt, which is three years in normal course from the date of default.

Discharge by Material Alteration

Section 87 provides that any material alteration of a negotiable instrument renders it void, i.e., discharges the instrument itself against the parties thereto at the time of making such alteration unless they have consented to the alteration. But an acceptor or endorser who accepts or endorses a materially altered instrument are bound, i.e., liable under the altered instrument [Section 87]. This point has been elaborated in the succeeding section.

Material Alteration

Material alteration: Any change that alters the very nature of the instrument.

The term 'material alteration' indicates alteration or change in any material part of the instrument. It may be defined as any change, which alters the very nature of the instrument. Thus, it is the alteration, which changes and destroys the legal identity of the original instrument and causes it to speak a different language in legal effect from that which it originally included. A material alteration makes the instrument void, i.e., inoperative and affects the rights and obligations of the parties to the instrument. It, however, does not affect one who becomes a party to an instrument subsequent to its material alteration, if any.

Material Alteration—What Constitutes

Every alteration or change on a negotiable instrument cannot be established as material alteration and would not necessarily vitiate the instrument or affect the rights and obligations of the parties thereto. The Negotiable Instruments Act is silent on the subject as to what constitutes a material alteration. Courts of Law in India in this regard have followed the English Common Law, which held that anything, which has the effect of altering the legal relations between the parties, the character of the instrument, or the sum payable, amounts to a material alteration. Accordingly, an alteration can be termed as material alteration if it is such that it alters or attempts to alter the character of the instrument and affects or attempts to affect the contract, which the instrument contains. It may arise not only by means of altering, changing, or erasing a certain thing already written on the instrument but also by a new insertion.

Instances of material alteration

The following are considered as material alterations:

1. Alteration of the date of the instrument[10]
2. Alteration of the amount payable[11]
3. Alteration in time of payment
4. Alteration of the place of payment[12]
5. Alteration of rate of interest or any change of party thereto, if any[13]
6. Tearing of the material part of the instrument
7. Where a bill is accepted generally, the insertion of a place of payment
8. Addition of a new party to the instrument
9. Addition of words to a bill of exchange endorsed in blank so as to convert the same into special endorsement.

The above list of material alterations is not conclusive or exhaustive. There may be other alteration or changes that may be regarded as material alterations depending on the facts and nature of each particular case.

Instances that are not material alteration or immaterial alteration

The following are, however, not taken as material alterations.

1. Filling up an inchoate (incomplete) instrument [Section 20].
2. Converting a blank endorsement into a full one [Section 49].
3. Converting a bearer cheque into an order cheque or even account payee.
4. Crossing of an uncrossed cheque.

[10] Banking Laws Committee Report on Negotiable Instruments Law-1975, p. 48
[11] Banking Laws Committee Report on Negotiable Instruments Law-1975, p. 48
[12] Section 62(2) of the English Bill of Exchange Act, 1882
[13] Verso Pvt. Ltd vs. Newandram, AIR (1974), Madras

5. The addition of the words 'on demand' to a promissory note wherein no time of payment is expressed [*Gardener vs Walsh*[14]].
6. Making qualified acceptance [Section 86].

In these cases, the document in terms of its value remains valid and enforceable and the parties thereto cannot be discharged from their liabilities on such grounds.

Effect of Material Alteration

According to Section 87, 'any material alteration of a negotiable instrument renders the same void as against anyone who is a party thereto at the time of making such alteration and does not consent thereto, unless it was made in order to carry out the common intention of the original parties'.

Thus, the main effect of a material alteration is that it makes the instrument void, i.e., it discharges the instrument itself as against any person who was a party to such instrument at the time of material alteration and did not give his approval to it. All the prior parties to a negotiable instrument, which was altered subsequently without their consent thereto, shall not be liable even to holder-in-due-course, having no notice or knowledge of the alteration. It makes no discrimination whether the alteration was for the benefit or detrimental to any party to the instrument [*Rampadarth vs Hari Narain*[15]]. Moreover, it is also immaterial whether the holder himself altered the instrument or any stranger altered it while the instrument was in the custody of the holder because a party, who is in custody of an instrument, is bound to preserve it in its original state [*Davidson vs Cooper*[16]].

It is, however, worth noting that a materially altered instrument is not absolutely void, i.e., not unenforceable against all the parties thereto. It is void only against those who did not give their approval to the alteration, and can be enforced against those who consented to the alteration or effected the alteration. Such an instrument is also operative against those who become parties to the instrument subsequent to the alteration. There is, however, an exception to this rule. An acceptor or endorser of a negotiable instrument is bound by his acceptance or endorsement notwithstanding any previous alterations of the instrument [Section 88]. On the other hand, Section 89 provides protection to a party who pays a materially altered bill of exchange or promissory note or cheque provided that the alteration does not appear on the face of the instrument in-question and pays so in good faith and without negligence on its part. Such a party shall stand discharged if it makes payment to a person in the possession of the instrument under the circumstances, which do not afford a reasonable ground for believing that it is disentitled to such payment. Besides, the payer under the above circumstances is also entitled to debit the party on whose account the payment was made with the amount paid. For instance, *A* drew a cheque for ₹500 in favour of *B*, who altered the figure 500 into 5000 without taking the consent of the maker. The instrument appeared to be drawn for ₹5000 on the face of it. The drawee banker paid ₹5000 to *B* on the presentment of cheque for payment. The banker did so according to the apparent tenor of the instrument and in good faith. In this case, since the banker acted *bona fide* and without negligence, it is entitled to debit *A* with ₹5000.

However, where the cheque is an electronic image of a truncated cheque, any difference in apparent tenor of such electronic image and the truncated cheque shall be a material alteration and it shall be the duty of the bank or the clearing house, as the case may be, to ensure the exactness of the apparent tenor of electronic image of the truncated cheque while truncating and transmitting the image [Section 89(2)].

Moreover, it shall be the duty of the banker who receives payment based on an electronic image of a truncated cheque held with him, to verify the *prima facie* genuineness of the cheque to be truncated and any fraud, forgery, or tampering apparent on the face of the instrument that can be verified with due diligence and ordinary care [explanation added to Section 131].

[14] 1885, A.I.R. 5E and B-83
[15] 1965, A.I.R. Patna 2241
[16] 1844, 13 M. & W. 343

Exercises

I. Objective-type Questions

1. State whether each of the following statements is True or False:
   (i) A bill is presumed dishonoured for non-acceptance if the drawee is a fictitious person.
   (ii) Notice means the actual notification of the dishonour of instrument by non-acceptance or non-payment.
   (iii) A notice of dishonour given by a stranger is valid.
   (iv) The discharge of a negotiable instrument results in extinguishments of all rights of action under it and puts an end to its further negotiability.
   (v) Material alteration need not necessarily affect the validity of the instrument.

2. Fill in the blanks:
   (i) The addition of a new party to an instrument ________ to a material alteration.
   (ii) A material alteration in a negotiable instrument can render it ________.
   (iii) Notice of dishonour by ________ is necessary in all cases.
   (iv) Noting must be done within reasonable time ________ dishonour.
   (v) If the holder of a cheque presents the cheque (for payment) after a reasonable time, the liability of the ________ stands discharged.

3. Indicate the correct answer:
   (i) Both noting and protest are compulsory in case of
   (a) Foreign bills (b) Inland bills
   (c) Foreign as well as inland bills (d) None of them
   (ii) Which among the following is not an instance of material alteration?
   (a) Addition of a new party to the instrument
   (b) Addition of words to a bill, which was endorsed in blank so as to convert the same into special endorsement
   (c) Affixing stamps on a bill of exchange besides signature and cancellation by two parallel lines
   (d) Addition of a new party to the instrument
   (iii) The maker, acceptor, or endorser may be discharged from their liability to the holder by means of
   (a) Cancellation only (b) Release only
   (c) Payment only (d) Any of them
   (iv) Notice of dishonour must be given
   (a) To the drawer and drawee only
   (b) To the drawer, acceptor, and endorser(s) only
   (c) To all the parties liable on the instrument or to their duly authorized agent
   (d) To all the parties who are secondarily liable on the instrument or to their duly authorized agent
   (v) Notice of dishonour is excused
   (a) When the party charged could not suffer damage for want of notice
   (b) When the party entitled to notice cannot be found after reasonable search
   (c) When the drawer has countermanded payment
   (d) In all the above cases

II. Review Questions

1. What is meant by dishonour of a negotiable instrument? In what different ways may an instrument be dishonoured? State the instruments, which can be dishonoured by non-acceptance, and those by non-payment.

2. Under what circumstances presentment for payment is unnecessary and the instrument will be taken as dishonoured?

3. Discuss the rules regarding notice of dishonour. What is the effect when the notice of dishonour is not given?

4. What are the various modes through which one or more parties to a negotiable instrument is/are discharged?

5. What do you mean by discharge of a negotiable instrument? Discuss the ways through which an instrument may be discharged.

6. 'Material alteration renders the instrument void'. Elaborate. Give instances of material alterations. What alterations are permissible under the Negotiable Instruments Act?

7. Discuss 'noting' and 'protest'. Are 'noting' and 'protest' obligatory under the Negotiable Instruments Act? Explain 'protest for better security'.

8. Discuss the rules relating to payment for honour. What are the rights of payer for honour?

9. Discuss the consequence of dishonour of a cheque for insufficiency of funds in the drawer's account.

III. Problems

1. *A* drew a bill on *B* for ₹500 and endorsed it in favor of *C*. The bill was duly accepted by *B* but it was dishonoured on due date for non-payment. *C* failed to give notice of dishonour to *A*. Is A discharged from liability? If yes, who will be liable against *C*?
[**Hint:** Yes. Being drawer, *A* is discharged. *B* being acceptor is principal debtor and hence liable against C]

2. *P* drew a cheque for ₹1000 in favour of *Q* and delivered the same to him. When the cheque ought to be presented, *P* had sufficient funds with the banker to meet it. *Q*, however, did not present the cheque for an unreasonably long time and in the meantime the bank went bankrupt. Discuss the remedy *Q* has against the drawer and the banker.
[**Hint:** The drawer *P* is fully discharged but *Q* can prove against the banker for the amount of cheque]

3. *A* draws a cheque of ₹5000 but when the cheque ought to be presented, *A* has only ₹2,500 in his bank account and has no authority to overdraw. The cheque gets dishonoured (on presentment) for insufficiency of funds in the drawer's account. Is *A* entitled to notice of dishonour?
[**Hint:** No. Notice of dishonour is excused when the party charged could not suffer damage (Section 90)]

4. A bill was drawn as 'payable to order or bearer'. The holder struck out the words 'or bearer'. The acceptor refused to make payment. Can the holder enforce its payment against the acceptor or drawer?
[**Hint:** No, Material alteration renders the instrument void (Section 87)]

5. The drawer of a bill intimates its holder before maturity of the instrument that he has no fixed place of residence and that he will call in a few days to see if, the bill has been discharged by the acceptor. The bill got dishonoured by non-payment. Is the drawer entitled to notice of dishonour?
[**Hint:** No. Notice of dishonour is unnecessary when it is dispensed with by the party entitled thereto (Section 98, clause a)]

Answers to Objective-type Questions

1.	(i) True	(ii) True	(iii) False	(iv) True	(v) False
2.	(i) amounts to	(ii) void	(iii) by non-acceptance		(iv) after
	(v) drawer				
3.	(i) (a)	(ii) (c)	(iii) (d)	(iv) (d)	(v) (d)

16 Chapter in Review

LEARNING OUTCOMES

- **LO1** Dishonour of a negotiable instrument
- **LO2** Modes of dishonour
- **LO3** Consequence of dishonour
- **LO4** Notice of dishonour
- **LO5** Notice of dishonour—When excused
- **LO6** Noting and protest of a dishonoured instrument
- **LO7** Discharge of a negotiable instrument
- **LO8** Modes of discharge
- **LO9** Material alteration

KEY TERMS

Dishonour of negotiable instrument: Loss of honour for an instrument at the end of the party liable thereto resulting in non-realization of payment due on the same.

Material alteration: Any change that alters the very nature of the instrument.

Notice of dishonour: A formal communication, oral or written, of the fact of dishonour.

Noting: Act of recording the fact of dishonour of an instrument by the notary public.

Protest: Formal certificate of dishonour of an instrument by the notary public.

LO1 Dishonour in relation to a negotiable instrument is denial to maintain a promise by the party liable thereon which eventually results in non-realization of amount due on the instrument.

LO2 Any type of negotiable instrument may be dishonoured by non-payment by the drawee or acceptor thereof. But a bill may be dishonoured by non-acceptance as well as by non-payment since it requires placement for acceptance before it can be presented for payment.

LO4 If a bill is dishonoured either by non-acceptance or by non-payment, the drawee and all the endorsers of the bill are liable to the holder, provided a notice of such dishonour is given to them. The drawee, on the other hand, shall be liable only in the event of dishonour by non-payment. The drawer of a cheque is also criminally liable if his banker returns his cheque for insufficiency of funds in his account.

LO5 When a negotiable instrument is dishonoured either by non-acceptance or non-payment, the holder or his/her duly authorised agent must give notice of dishonour to all other parties whom he/she seeks to hold liable.

LO6 Notice of dishonour is excused when it is dispensed by the party entitled thereto; when the drawer has countermanded payment; when the party charged could not suffer damage for want for notice; when the party entitled to notice cannot be found after due search; when the party bound to give notice is unable to give it for any other reason but, of course, without any fault of his own; and when the drawer and acceptor is the same person.

LO7 When a promissory note or bill of exchange has been dishonoured by non-acceptance or non-payment, the holder may cause such dishonour to be noted by a notary public upon the instrument, or upon a paper attached thereto, or partly upon each. Noting serves as the authentic and legal proof of presentment for acceptance or payment. Noting must be followed by protest notwithstanding the fact that the former contains the full name of the notary public. Protest is based upon the noting and acts as a legal proof of dishonour.

LO8 The discharge with respect to negotiable instrument may either discharge the instrument or discharge one or more parties to the instrument from the liabilities. The instrument stands discharged when the liability of the party, primarily and ultimately liable on the instrument, comes to an end.

LO9 A negotiable instrument may be discharged in any of the following ways: by payment-in-due-course, by the principal debtor becoming the holder, by renunciation of the rights by the holder, by cancellation of the instrument, by an act that would discharge a simple contract.

LO10 Material alteration is one which alters or destroys the legal identity of the original instrument and renders the instrument ineffective.

Part V The Companies Act, 2013

CHAPTER 17 Nature and Kinds of Companies, Company Formation and Prospectus

Learning Objectives

- LO[1] Company: meaning and defining characteristics
- LO[2] Kinds of companies
- LO[3] Lifting the corporate veil
- LO[4] Formation of company
- LO[5] Prospectus
- LO[6] Online incorporation of company

The Companies Act, 2013: An Overview

The laws governing companies in India have been compiled and contained in the Companies Act, 2013, which through its various provisions seeks to protect the interest of various stakeholders dealing with the company. The new Act consists of 469 sections, spread over 29 chapters and seven schedules appended to it. Thus, as many as 188 sections of the preceding legislation (The Companies Act, 1956) have been scrapped in the new Act so as to make it a more compact and effective legislation. The new company law adopts forward looking approach, which empowers Central Government to frame rules governing companies and makes contravention of any of the rules punishable with fine. As many as 16 amendments have been made to the law, correcting issues with provisions relating to winding up, board resolutions, bail provisions and utilisation of unclaimed dividends to bring the law in tune with the global standards. This is a landmark legislation that will have far-reaching implications, set to significantly change the manner in which corporates operate in India as it *inter alia* introduces higher standards of corporate governance and makes spending on corporate social responsibility (CSR) mandatory; promotes gender equality on corporate boards; allows for class action suits; and looks forward to overhaul the way companies function and are regulated in the country. The main amendments brought about by the new legislation (Companies Act, 2013), in a nut shell, are given in the box below.

The Companies Act, 2013: Major Provisions at a Glance

- Provision for a uniform financial year i.e. from 1st April to 31st March for all the companies subject to certain exceptions [Section 2(41)].
- Provision made for 'One Person Company' (OPC), which means a private limited company having only one person as a member – a new vehicle for individuals for carrying on business with limited liability [Section 2(62)].
- Maximum number of members in a 'private limited company' increased from 50 to 200 to expand the scope of operations of private limited companies [Section 2(68)].
- The concept of 'small company' has been introduced for the first time by the new Act, which means a private company, the paid up share capital of which does not exceeds fifty lakh rupees and turnover of which as per its last profit and loss account does not exceeds two crore rupees [Section 2(85)].
- The organization of 'object clause' of the memorandum into three distinct sub-clauses i.e., the main, ancillary and other objects has been done away with. Now the memorandum should contain only the object(s) for which the company is proposed to be incorporated and any matter considered necessary for furtherance thereof [Section 4(c)].
- Entrenchment provisions in respect of 'articles of association' of a company introduced; requiring a company to follow a more restrictive procedure than merely passing a special resolution for altering its articles [Section 5].
- Tribunal has been empowered to direct removal of a company's name from the register of companies, if the company got incorporated by furnishing false or incorrect information or by suppressing material facts [Section 7(7)].
- A company incorporated after the commencement of the Companies (Amendment) Ordinance, 2019 and having a share capital shall not commence any business or exercise any borrowing powers unless—(a) a declaration is filed by a director within a period of one hundred and eighty days of the date of incorporation of the company in such form and verified in such manner as may be prescribed, with the Registrar that every subscriber to the memorandum has paid the value of the shares agreed to be taken by him on the date of making of such declaration; and (b) The company has filed with the Registrar a verification of its registered office as provided in sub-section (2) of section 12 [Section 10A].
- A new provision to enable a company issue depository receipts in any foreign country (GDRs) subject to prescribed conditions introduced [Section 41].
- Private limited companies now can issue equity shares with differential voting rights without complying with the requirement of Rule 4 of Companies (Share Capital and Debentures) Rules, 2014 which otherwise requires a track record of distributable profit for last three years, authority in AOA, ordinary resolutions, etc. [Sections 43 & 47].
- Companies would no longer be permitted to issue shares at a discount. The only shares that could be issued at a discount are the shares issued by a company to its creditors when its debt is converted into shares in pursuance of any statutory resolution plan or debt restructuring scheme as per RBI Regulations, and sweat equity shares wherein shares are issued to employees in lieu of their services [Sections 53 & 54].

- Buy-back of shares by the companies has been liberalized by relaxing certain conditions. Companies now can buy-back their shares and other securities even the company has defaulted in repayment of deposits or interest payable thereon, redemption of debentures, or payment of dividends provided the default is remedied and a period of three years has lapsed from the date of closing of the first financial year of the company after such default ceases to subsist [Section 70].
- The time limit of 18 months for holding first AGM by a company (other than 'OPC') from the date of its incorporation has been curtailed to 9 months. Every subsequent AGM must be held within six months from the date of closing of the relevant financial year [Section 96(1)].
- To call an AGM at shorter notice the consent of 95% of the members will suffice as against the erstwhile provision (in the 1956 Act) that required consent of all the members [Section 101(1)].
- Every listed company or one having 1000 or more shareholders will have to mandatorily provide an e-voting facility to its members to vote at general meetings after 31 December 2014. However, all listed companies shall have to provide the e-voting facility to its members for all resolutions in general meetings with immediate effect [Section 108 read with Companies (M & A) Rules, 2014].
- Some specified business by any company other than 'OPC' or a private limited company can be transacted only by means of postal ballot, which means voting (for passing resolutions) by post or any electronic mode [Section 110].
- A company will be under legal obligation to transfer the unpaid or unclaimed dividend to a special account opened in any scheduled bank, called the 'Unpaid Dividend Account' [Section 124].
- 'Consolidated Financial Statements' shall be mandatory if a company has one or more subsidiaries or associate companies, which shall include its balance sheet, profit and loss account and cash flow statement. Earlier (under the Companies Act, 1956) these documents were required to be filed separately [Section 129].
- Provision made for constitution of the National Financial Reporting Authority (NFRA) by the Central Government to provide for matters related to accounting and auditing standards under the Act. NFRA shall be a quasi-judicial body, empowered to exercise disciplinary control over the chartered accountants [Section 132].
- Every company having a net worth of ₹500 crore or more, or a turnover of ₹1000 crore or more, or a net profit of ₹5 crore or more, during the immediately preceding financial year shall constitute the Corporate Social Responsibility Committee of the Board for the social and economic welfare of the neglected or deprived class of the society [Section 135].
- Internal audit by CAs/CWAs/such other professionals as may be decided by the Board shall be mandatory for prescribed classes of companies [Section 138].
- Unlike the appointment process at each annual general meeting (AGM) under the 1956 Act, the auditor will now be appointed for a period of five years [Section 139(1)].
- Maximum tenure of 'Auditors' and 'Independent Directors' specified [Sections 139(2) & 149(11)].
- Compliance with the auditing standards by the company auditor shall be mandatory [Section 143(9)].
- Frauds beyond a certain threshold would need to be mandatorily reported by the auditors to the Central Government [Section 143(12)].
- Any service to be rendered by the auditor needs to be approved by the board of directors or the audit committee. Additionally, the auditor is restricted from providing specific non-audit services to the audit client [Section 144].
- Every listed public company and other prescribed classes of companies shall have at least one-third of the total number of directors as 'Independent Directors' [Section 149].
- Every company shall have at least one 'Resident Director' who has stayed in India for not less than 182 days during the financial year [Section 149(3)].
- One 'woman director' shall be mandatory for prescribed classes of companies [Section 149(1)].
- The limit for number of directorships that can be held by an individual increased from 12 to 15 [Section 149(1)].
- Every listed company shall have one director elected by 'small shareholders'. In this behalf 'small shareholders' means a shareholder holding shares of nominal value of not more than twenty thousand rupees or such other sum as may be prescribed [Section 151].
- Any person who fails to get elected as a director in the general meeting can no longer be appointed as an additional director by the board of directors [Section 161].
- Prohibitions and restrictions regarding political contributions by a company has been done away. A company, other than a Government company and a company which has been in existence for less than three financial years, may contribute any amount directly or indirectly to any political party by passing a resolution at a Board meeting. [Section 182]
- The appointment of following whole time key managerial personnel for every listed company and every other company having a paid-up share capital of ₹5 crore or more shall be mandatory: (i) Managing director or chief executive officer or manager and in their absence a whole-time director, (ii) Company secretary, and (iii) Chief financial officer.

Further, an individual cannot be appointed or reappointed as the chairman of the company, as well as the managing director or chief executive officer of the company at the same time except where the articles provide otherwise or the company does not carry multiple businesses [Section 203].

- Secretarial audit (a compliance audit by an independent company secretary) has been made mandatory for every listed company and other specified companies effective from the financial year 2013–14 onwards. Certain 'Secretarial Standards' issued by the Institute of Company Secretaries of India (ICSI) shall be mandatory [Section 204].
- Provision made for investigation into the affairs of companies by Serious Fraud Investigation Office by the Central Government (SFIO) [Section 211].
- Existing restrictions on the merger or amalgamation of an Indian company with a foreign company in specific jurisdictions removed; facilitating cross-border corporate flexibility [Section 234].
- Provision made to obtain the status of a 'dormant company' which means an inactive company that doesn't trade and has no accounting transactions [Section 455].

Company: Concept and Origin

The term 'company' is derived from the Latin words '*com*', meaning with or together and '*pains*', meaning bread. Originally, it referred to a group of persons who would take their meals together. In common parlance, however, a company refers to an assemblage of people who have come together for some specific purpose; economic, or otherwise; and who have incorporated themselves into a distinct legal entity in the form of a corporation for that purpose. Companies are a useful device to do business, especially when the business has grown bigger than can be effectively managed by a few people, and also requires added financial support.

Company: Definition and Characteristics

Company: An artificial person created by law, having a separate entity, with a perpetual succession, and the members having limited liability.

The Companies Act, 2013 does not define a company in terms of its characteristic features. Section 2(20) merely reads, 'a company means a company formed and registered under this Act or under any previous company law'. Thus, the above section does not identify any describing feature of a company. However, to understand the nature of a company, the following definitions may prove of some help.

> *A company is an association of many persons who contribute money or monies worth to a common stock and employ in some trade or business and who share the profit and loss arising therefrom. The common stock so contributed is denoted in money and is the capital of the company. The persons who contribute to it or whom it pertains to are members. The proportion of capital to which each member is entitled is his share. The shares are always transferable albeit the right to transfer is often more or less restricted.*
>
> Lord Justice Lindley

> *A corporation is an artificial being, invisible, intangible, and existing only in contemplation of the law. Being a mere creation of law, it possesses only the properties, which the Charter of its creation confers upon it, either expressly or as incidental to its very existence.*
>
> Chief Justice Marshall

> *A company is an artificial person created by law, having a separate entity, with a perpetual succession and common seal.*
>
> Prof. Haney

The above definitions bring out the following distinct features of a company, which together make it a unique association and explicate its nature.

1. Independent legal entity
2. Limited liability
3. Everlasting existence
4. Separate property
5. Flexibility of investment
6. Capacity to sue and being sued
7. Separation of ownership and management
8. Proportionate representation
9. Right to own property

Independent legal entity After being incorporated under the Act, a company becomes an independent legal entity, with an existence separate from its members. It has its own identity (name), its assets and liabilities are separate and distinct from those of its members. It is capable of owning a property, incurring debt, having a bank account, employing people, entering into contracts, and suing and being sued separately.

Limited liability Limited liability is a concept whereby a person's financial liability is limited to a fixed sum, most commonly the value of a person's investment in a company or partnership with limited liability. A shareholder in a limited company is not personally liable for any of the debts of the company other than for the value of his investment in that company. In other words, a shareholder is liable to pay only the unpaid money due on the shares held by him when called upon to pay and nothing more, even if liabilities of the company far exceed its assets. By contrast, sole proprietors and partners in general partnerships are each liable for all the debts of the business due to unlimited liability.

Although a shareholder's liability for the company's actions is limited, the shareholder may still be liable for its own acts. For example, the directors of small companies (who are frequently also shareholders) are often required to give personal guarantees of the company's debts to those lending to the company. They will then be liable for those debts in the event that the company cannot pay, although the other shareholders will not be so liable. This is known as co-signing.

Everlasting existence A company does not die or cease to exist unless it is deliberately wound up or the objective for which it was formed has been accomplished. Membership of a company may keep on changing from time to time but that does not impair the life of the company. Death or insolvency of members does not have an effect on the subsistence of a company.

Separate property Since a company is a distinct legal entity, the company's property is its own. A shareholder cannot claim to be the owner of the company's property during the existence of the company. The Supreme Court of India has held that a shareholder is not the part-owner of the company or its property; he is only given certain rights by law, for example, to vote or attend meetings, or to receive dividends.

Flexibility of investment Shares in a company are freely transferable. When a shareholder transfers his shares to another person, the transferee steps into the shoes of the transferor and acquires all the rights of the transferor in respect of those shares. However, private companies can restrict the right of their members to transfer shares.

Capacity to sue and being sued A company can sue or be sued in its own name as distinct from its members. Similarly, a company has every right to enter into contractual obligations with other parties. However, the Supreme Court of India has held in the case of *State Trading Corporation of India vs. CTO* that a company cannot have the status of a citizen under the Constitution of India.

Separation of ownership and management A company is administered and managed by the Board of directors. The shareholders are simply the holders of the shares in the company and need not necessarily be the managers of the company.

Proportionate representation Proportional representation implies 'one share – one vote', i.e., if a person has 10 shares, he will have 10 votes in the company. This is in direct contrast to the voting principle of a co-operative society where the 'one member – one vote' principle applies, i.e., irrespective of the number of shares held; one member can have only one vote.

Right to own property Company is a distinct legal entity and can own, transfer, and manage a property in its own way. The company's property is its personal. A member cannot claim to be the owner of the company's property not only during the existence of the company, but in the event of its being wound-up too.

Company Distinguished from Ordinary Partnership Firm

A company differs from an ordinary partnership firm in several material respects, discussed as follows:

1. An ordinary or conventional partnership firm is governed by The Indian Partnership Act, 1932, whereas a company is governed by The Companies Act, 2013.
2. A partnership is sum total of persons who have come together to share the profits of the business carried on by all or any of them acting for all. It is not a distinct legal entity. Registration is not obligatory in case of partnership; it comes into

being on the basis of agreement, oral or written. Conversely, a company represents a group of persons who have associated together for the attainment of a specific goal, business, or otherwise. It enjoys a separate legal existence independent of its members after being registered (compulsorily) under the law.

3. Liability of the partners of a firm is unlimited. Whereas, the liability of shareholders of a limited company is limited to the extent of unpaid shares or the unpaid amount guaranteed by them.
4. Property of the firm belongs to the partners and they are collectively entitled to it. But in case of a company, the property belongs to the company and not to its members or shareholders.
5. A partner cannot transfer his interest in the partnership firm without the consent of all other partners. Whereas in case of a company, shares may be transferred freely without the permission of other members, unless contrary provisions exist in the articles, that usually happens in case of a private company.
6. In an ordinary partnership, the number of members must not exceed 10 in case of a banking business and 20 in other businesses. A public company may have as many members as it desires subject to a minimum of seven members. A private company cannot have more than 200 members.
7. There must be at least two members to form a partnership firm. The minimum number of members necessary for a public limited company is seven and for a private limited company is two.
8. In case of a partnership, consent of all the partners is required for any decision. In case of a company, decision of the majority members or shareholders prevails.
9. On the death of any partner, the partnership is dissolved unless there is a provision to the contrary. Conversely, on the death of a shareholder the company's existence does not get terminated.

Limited Liability Partnership Firm vs. Joint Stock Company

A joint stock company also differs from a limited liability partnership (LLP) firm in that the affairs of a company are regulated by the statute (i.e. Companies Act, 2013) whereas for an LLP it would be by an agreement (LLP Agreement) among the partners. The management-ownership divide inherent in a company is not there in an LLP. An LLP will have more flexibility as compared to a company and will be subjected to lesser compliance requirements as compared to latter. Moreover, incorporating an LLP firm is cost effective compared to a joint stock company, as the minimum statutory fee for incorporation of a company is ₹6000 whereas that of an LLP is ₹800. Also, a joint stock company is required to be incorporated with a minimum paid up capital of ₹5 lakh (for a public limited company) and ₹1 lakh, (for a private limited company) whereas there is no such minimum specified limit in case of an LLP. Also, unlike companies, compliances such as holding of statutory meetings, quarterly board meetings and similar compliances are not required for LLPs.

Kinds of Companies

Companies may be classified into the following categories:

1. Private and public companies
2. Limited and unlimited companies
3. One person company
4. Small company
5. Section 8 company
6. Parent and subsidiary companies
7. Government company
8. Foreign company
9. Dormant company

Private and Public Companies

On the basis of their defining characteristics, companies may be classified as private company and public company, as discussed below.

> **Private company:** A company, which by its articles restricts the transferability of its shares and prevents the public at large from subscribing to them.

Private company

'Private company' means a company which by its articles,

1. restricts the right to transfer its shares;
2. except in case of 'One Person Company', limits the number of its members to two hundred; and
3. prohibits any invitation to the public to subscribe for any securities of the company.

However, for the purpose of clause (ii), where two or more persons hold one or more shares in a company jointly, they shall be treated as a single member. Moreover, persons who are in the employment of the company; and persons who had been formerly in the employment of the company were members of the company while in that employment and have continued to be members after the employment ceased, shall not be included in the number of members [Section 2(68)].

If a private company contravenes any of the aforesaid provisions, it ceases to be a private company and thereby loses all the exemptions and privileges, which it otherwise is entitled to.

Public company

Public company: A company whose shares are traded freely on a recognized stock exchange....

'Public company' means a company which is not a private company.

However, a private company, which is a subsidiary of a public company, shall be deemed to be a public company [Section 2(71)].

Thus, a public company is one which:

1. does not restrict the right of its members to transfer their shares;
2. does not put a ceiling as to maximum number of its member i.e. it can have unlimited number of members; and
3. invites public to subscribe for its securities through IPO/FPO and is usually listed on a recognised stock exchange.

Nevertheless, a private company, which happens to be a subsidiary of a public company, shall also be treated as a public company.

Privileges and exemptions of a private limited company

A private limited company as against a public limited one enjoys the following privileges and exemptions:

1. Minimum number of members in respect of a private limited company is two as against seven in case of a public limited company [Section 2(68) & (71)].
2. Minimum number of directors is only two in respect of a private limited company whereas three in case of a public one [Section 149].
3. Private limited companies, now can issue equity shares with differential voting rights without fulfilling the requirement of track record of distributable profits for last three years, provisions in the articles, ordinary resolutions, etc. [Rule 4 of Companies (Share Capital and Debentures) Rules, 2014].
4. Ordinary resolution instead of a special one is enough for a private limited company for offering shares to its employees under the ESOP scheme at the time of allotment of shares [Section 62(1)(b)].
5. A private limited company (fulfilling the exemption criteria) can advance loan to its director and any person in whom directors are interested [Section 185(2)].
6. Private limited companies can enter into a contract with related parties in which directors are interested [Section 188].
7. Overall maximum managerial remuneration and managerial remuneration in case of absence or inadequacy of profits related restrictions do not apply in respect of a private limited company [Section 197(1)].

Conversion of a private limited company into a public limited company and vice-versa

A private limited company can be converted into a public limited one and vice-versa through alteration of articles of the company-in-question provided such alteration is approved by the Tribunal. In this behalf, the Companies Act, 2013 provides as under:

Subject to the provisions of this Act and the conditions contained in its memorandum, if any, a company may, by a special resolution, alter its articles including alterations having the effect of conversion of:

1. a private company into a public company; or
2. a public company into a private company.

However, when a company being a private company alters its articles in such a manner that they no longer include the restrictions and limitations which are required to be included in the articles of a private company under this Act, the company shall, as from the date of such alteration, cease to be a private company.

Any alteration having the effect of conversion of a public company into a private company shall not be valid unless it is approved by the Central Government by passing an order on an application made in the prescribed form and manner. [Section 14(*1*)].

Every alteration of the articles under this section and a copy of the order of the Central Government approving the alteration as per sub-section (*1*) shall be filed with the Registrar, together with a printed copy of the altered articles, within a period of fifteen days in such manner as may be prescribed, who shall register the same [Section 14(2)].

Limited and Unlimited Companies

A company may be limited or unlimited.

Limited company: A company wherein the liability of its members is limited either by share capital or guarantee.

Limited company

A limited company (either private or public) is one wherein the liability of its members is limited. A limited company may further be sub-classified as below.

A company limited by shares This is the most common form of a company used for business ventures. Specifically, a limited company is a 'company in which the liability of each shareholder or member is limited to the amount individually invested'. Shareholders have no financial liability in case of fully paid-up shares.

A company limited by guarantee Commonly used where companies are formed for non-commercial purposes, such as clubs or charities. The members undertake to contribute to the assets of the company a certain amount of money if the company goes into liquidation, but otherwise they have no economic rights in relation to the company. This type of company is common in England.

A company limited by guarantee with a share capital A company limited by guarantee with a share capital, a hybrid entity, usually used where the company is formed for non-commercial purposes, but the activities of the company are partly funded by investors who expect a return.

Unlimited company

The liability of members of an unlimited company is unrestricted. Therefore, their liability is similar to that of the partners of a conventional partnership firm. The Companies Act, 2013 does not prohibit the formation of an unlimited company and, particularly, a private unlimited company.

Unlimited company: A private company wherein the liability of its members are unrestricted.

Amway India Enterprise Private Limited, Blue Yacht Consultancy Private Limited, Geetanjali Woollens Private Limited, Bangalore Clinical Research Private Limited are some of the examples of private unlimited companies duly incorporated under the Companies Act.

Section 8 Companies

Not all companies have objectives of making profits by carrying out trade and commerce. Many companies primarily have charitable and non-profit objectives. Such entities are referred to as a Section 8 Company because they get license under Section 8 of The Companies Act, 2013. These companies dedicate all their incomes and profits towards the furtherance of their objectives.

The Companies Act, 2013 defines a Section 8 company as one whose objectives is to promote fields of commerce, art, science, research, education, sports, charity, social welfare, protection of environment, or other similar objectives. These companies apply their profits towards the furtherance of their cause and do not pay any dividend to their members. These companies erstwhile known as Section 25 companies under the Companies Act, 1956 with more or less the same provisions. The new Act has, however, prescribed more objectives that Section 8 companies can have. Well-known examples of Section 8 companies include Federation of Indian Chambers of Commerce and Industry (FICCI) and Confederation of Indian Industries (CII). The objective of these companies is facilitating the growth of trade and commerce and India.

The Central Government may grant a license to a person or an association of persons proposed to be registered under this Act as a 'limited company' if the following conditions are fulfilled:

1. The company is formed for the promotion of commerce, art, science, sports, education, research, social welfare, religion, charity, protection of the environment or any other such object;

2. It intends to apply its profits, if any, or other income in promoting its above objects; and
3. It intends to prohibit the payment of any dividend to its members. However, only a private company and not a public one can be formed with unlimited liability.

The applicants bear the responsibility to prove to the satisfaction of the Central Government that the proposed company is to be formed for the charitable objects. A limited company as discussed above.

Such companies shall be entitled to remove the word(s) 'Limited' or 'Private Limited' against their names and shall enjoy all the privileges and be subjected to all the obligations of limited companies.

A firm may be a member of the company registered under this Section [Section 8(1)].

However, a company registered under the above-mentioned Section shall not alter the provisions of its memorandum or articles except with the previous approval of the Central Government. Moreover, such company may convert itself into a company of any other kind only after complying with such conditions as may be prescribed [Section 8(4)].

Any other kind of limited company may be granted license by the Central Government to be registered under Section 8(1) if it fulfills the conditions laid down under clauses (a), (b), and (c), as mentioned above [Section 8(5)].

The Central Government may revoke the license granted to a company under Section 8(1), if the company contravenes any of the requirements or conditions of the Section or its affairs are conducted fraudulently or in a manner prejudicial to public interest. However, the company in question will be given a reasonable opportunity of being heard before passing of such order of revocation [Section 8(6)]. The 2013 Act thus provides for more stringent provisions for companies incorporated with charitable objects.

Small Company

Small company: A company (other than public company) whose paid up capital does not exceed ₹50 lakh and turnover as per last profit and loss account does not exceed ₹2 crore.

The concept of 'small company' has been introduced for the first time by the Companies Act, 2013. The Act identifies and classifies some companies as small companies based on their capital and turnover position for the purpose of providing certain privileges and exemptions to these companies.

'Small company' means a company, other than a public company,—

1. paid-up share capital of which does not exceeds fifty lakh rupees; and
2. turnover of which as per its profit and loss account for the immediately preceding financial year does not exceeds two crore rupees.

However, the above ceiling of turnover does not apply to –

(a) a holding or subsidiary company of a small company;
(b) a company registered under Section 8; or
(c) a company or body corporate by any special Act [Section 2 (85)].

Thus, only a private company can be classified as a 'small company'. And for qualifying as a small company, it is enough if either the capital does not exceed fifty lakh rupees and turnover as per its last year's profit and loss account does not exceed two crore rupees. Moreover, a company may be classified as a small company in a particular year but may become ineligible in the next year and may become eligible yet again in the subsequent year. Thus, the benefits and exemptions which are available during a particular year may stand withdrawn in the next year and become available again in the subsequent year.

One Person Company

One person company: A company formed with only one person (a natural person who is an Indian citizen and a resident of India) as its member.

One Person Company (OPC) is a new concept introduced by the Companies Act, 2013. As the name suggests, an OPC can be formed with only one person (a natural person who is an Indian citizen and a resident of India) as its member.

For the first time, the Act has allowed individuals to incorporate a company as an OPC – a new vehicle for individuals for carrying on business with limited liability. This is expected to have a significant effect on the way individuals and family owned businesses operate. The memorandum of such an OPC is required to indicate the name of the person who shall become member in the event of death or incapacity of the sole member. It is also required to specifically mention the word 'One Person Company' below the name wherever it is used [Section 2(62)].

Parent and Subsidiary Companies

A company shall be deemed to be a subsidiary of another company if:

1. That other company controls the composition of its Board of directors, or
2. That other company holds more than half of its equity share capital in face value
3. Where the first mentioned company is a subsidiary company of any company, which in turn is a subsidiary of that other company. For example, if company *B* is subsidiary of company *A*, and company *C* is subsidiary of company *B*, therefore, company *C* is also a subsidiary of company *A*.

The control of the composition of the Board of directors of the company means that the parent company has the power, at its discretion, to appoint or remove all or majority of directors of the subsidiary company without the consent or concurrence of any other person.

Government Company

Government company: Any company in which minimum 51 per cent of the paid-up share capital is held by the Central and/or State Government.

'Government Company' means any company in which not less than 51 per cent of the paid-up share capital is held by

1. the Central Government; or
2. any State Government or Governments; or
3. partly by the Central Government and partly by one or more State Governments.

A subsidiary of a Government company (i.e. which is otherwise a non-government company) shall also be treated as a Government company [Section 2(45)].

The following are some of the essential features of a government company:

1. It is formed under the provisions of the Indian Companies Act, 2013.
2. The total share capital or 51 per cent or more of the share capital is held by the Government.
3. It enjoys the status of a legal entity and therefore it can sue or be sued by others.
4. The finance of a government company is obtained from the government and from private shareholders.
5. The employees are governed by the rules prescribed for the company by the Board of directors.
6. It is not subject to budgeting, accounting, and audit rules applicable to a government department.
7. The directors are nominated by the government depending on participation of the private capital.

Foreign Company

Foreign company: A company which is incorporated under the laws of a different nation but conducts any of its business activities in India.

'Foreign Company' means any company or body corporate incorporated outside India which,

1. has a place of business in India by itself or through an agent, physically or through electronic mode; and
2. conducts any business activity in India in any other manner [Section 2(42)].

Thus, a 'foreign company' (in Indian context) is one which is incorporated under the laws of a different nation but conducts any of its business activities in India in whatever mode or manner.

Dormant Company

Dormant company: A company that does not trade and has no significant business transactions.

'Dormant company' status is a new phenomenon in the Companies Act, 2013 and is considered to be an excellent means of keeping assets in a company towards its future usage. As per Section 455, 'Where a company is formed and registered under this Act for a future project or to hold an asset or intellectual property and "has no significant accounting transaction", such a company or an inactive company may make an application to the Registrar in the prescribed manner for obtaining the status of a dormant company'.

Thus, a *'dormant company'* is one that doesn't trade and has no accounting transactions.

In this behalf, 'inactive company' means a company which, has not been carrying on any business or operation, or has not made any significant accounting transaction during The Last Two financial years, has not filed financial statements and annual returns during the last two financial years.

'Significant accounting transaction' means any transaction other than—

1. Payment of Fees by a company to the Registrar;
2. Payments made by it to fulfil the requirements of this Act or any other law;
3. Allotment of shares to fulfil the requirements of this Act; and
4. Payments for maintenance of its office and records [Explanation added to Section 455].

That is, above mentioned transactions have been excluded from 'significant accounting transactions'. If a company has made above mention transactions in last two year then also that company will fall under definition of inactive company.

A 'dormant company' may be either a public company or a private company or even a 'One Person Company'.

Process to get the status of 'dormant company' The Registrar on consideration of the application shall allow the status of a dormant company to the applicant and issue a certificate in such form as may be prescribed to that effect.

In case of a company which has not filed financial statements or annual returns for two financial years consecutively, the Registrar shall issue a notice to that company and enter the name of such company in the register maintained for dormant companies [Section 455(4)].

A dormant company shall have such minimum number of directors, file such documents and pay such annual fee as may be prescribed to the Registrar to retain its dormant status in the register and may become an active company on an application made in this behalf accompanied by such documents and fee as may be prescribed [Section 455(5)].

However, the Registrar shall strike off the name of a dormant company from the register of dormant companies, which has failed to comply with the requirements discussed above [Section 45(6)].

Advantage of 'dormant company' A dormant company offers exceptional advantage to the promoters who wish to hold an asset or intellectual property under the corporate shield for its usage at a later stage. For instant: if a promoter wants to buy lands now for its future project at a comparatively lesser price, he may do the same through dormant company so that he can use the land for its future project.

Lifting the Corporate Veil

Doctrine of corporate veil: A company has a separate personality from its members or shareholders.

The doctrine of 'corporate veil' implies that a company has a separate personality distinct from its members or shareholders. This signifies that the company has a life and existence of its own; can possess a property and deal with it the way it desires; and can sue and be sued in its personal capacity. Moreover, no shareholder can either individually or jointly claim any ownership rights in the assets of the company during its continuance of business or on its winding up. To facilitate all this, the Act has drawn a thick veil (curtain) between the company and those who have formed or run it. However, the separate personality of a company may create a range of problems due to some unexpected and sometimes unwelcome effects. In a number of circumstances, therefore, the courts have disregarded the Salomon principle as laid down by the House of Lords. Where the corporate personality is being used unjustly or as a sham device, the court will ignore the cloak (legal fiction) to reach the person(s) under it or reveal the true form and character of the concerned company. This is known as the corporate law concept of '*lifting or piercing the corporate veil*'. Under this doctrine, which is also known as 'disregarding the corporate entity', a stakeholder (shareholder or director) of a company is held liable for the debts or liabilities of the company despite the general principle that shareholders are immune from suits in contract or tort that otherwise would hold only the company liable. The rationale behind this is probably that the law will not allow the corporate form to be misused or used for the purposes which are not set out in the statute.

Formation of a Company: Introduction

Any business enterprise in which the capital is raised by the individual contributions of a group of shareholders is called a joint stock company. In accordance with Section 3 of the Companies Act, 2013, a company may be formed for any lawful purpose by (a) seven or more persons, where the company to be formed is to be a public company; or (b) two or more persons (but not more than 200), where the company to be formed is to be a private company; or (c) one person, where the company to be formed is to be 'One Person Company' that is to say, a private company, by subscribing their names to a memorandum and complying with the requirements of the Act in respect of registration. Bringing a company into existence, however, is not as straight and hassle-free as the creation of a sole proprietary or a conventional partnership firm. The reason being, a company is a legal entity which does not come into life on its own or through an agreement. Keeping in view the interest of potential stakeholders, the Act has laid down certain norms to be complied with by every company before it comes into existence. Accordingly, the formation of a joint stock company is full of legal and documentary compliance procedures. For the purpose of proper understanding, the whole process of formation of a joint stock company (in India) can be divided into two stages, namely,

1. Promotion
2. Incorporation
3. Commencement of business, etc.

Promotion

Promotion: The entire backing process by which a company is brought into life.

Promotion refers to the entire backing process by which a company is brought into life. It begins with the conceptualization of the birth of a company, and sets out the purpose for which it is to be formed. The persons who conceive the idea to form a company and initiate the process of formation of a company are called 'promoters'. The promoters enter into preliminary contracts with vendors and make arrangements for the preparation, advertisement, and the circulation of the prospectus, and arrangement of the necessary capital. However, a person who merely acts in his professional capacity on behalf of a promoter, say for example, a lawyer, a consultant, or a chartered accountant, etc. engaged for drawing up the agreement and other documents, or one who prepares the blueprints of the projected company on behalf of the promoters, and is paid in this behalf is not a promoter.

CORPORATE PERSONALITY: LANDMARK COURT CASE

Salomon vs. Salomon & Co. Ltd[2]

The corporate personality concept—*a company is an independent legal entity*—was firmly endorsed in *Salomon vs. Salomon & Co. Ltd*[2] by the House of Lords.

Aron Salomon, a sole proprietor decided to incorporate his boot manufacturing business as a limited company – Salomon & Co. Ltd. Apart from Mr. and Mrs. Salomon, their daughter and four sons were the only shareholders in the newly established company. Two elder sons became directors and Mr. Salomon himself was the managing director. Mr. Salomon owned 20,001 of the company's 20,007 shares of £1 each—the remaining six were shared individually between the other six shareholders. Mr. Salomon sold his business to the new corporation for almost £30,000, of which £10,000 was a debt to him, secured by a charge over the assets of the company. He was, thus, simultaneously the company's principal shareholder and its principal secured creditor. The company subsequently became insolvent following a depression in the industry as its assets were found to be worth £6000 and its debts amounted to £17,000 of which £ 10,000 were due to Mr. Salomon (secured by assets) and £7000 due to unsecured creditors. The unsecured creditors sued Mr. Salomon on the ground that he and his company were one and the same person and the company was a mere agent for him (Salomon), and, hence, they carry the preferential right as to repayment of their debts over Salomon.

The House of Lords held:

'The company is at law a different person altogether distinct from the shareholders and, though it may be true that after incorporation the business is precisely the same as it was before, and the same persons are managers, and the same hands received the profits, the company is not in law the agent of the shareholders or trustee for them. Nor are the shareholders, as members, liable in any shape or form, except to the extent and in the manner provided for by the Act.'

Accordingly, Mr. Salomon's claim—to be treated as a secured and preferential creditor—was held justified.

[2] 1897 (UK) AC 22

Promoter's Legal Position and Role

Promoters occupy a fiduciary position – *a position based on trust and confidence* – in the company. Accordingly, they have some basic duties towards the company, listed as follows:

1. They should not make any profits secretly at the expense of the company they promote. Secret profits are normally made by buying the assets as per the requirements of the company on their own behalf and then selling them to the company at a profit without making disclosure of same to the company or its members. Promoters may, however, make profits in their dealings with the company provided they disclose them to the company, for instance, promoters may transfer their own property to the company at a profit.
2. They should make full disclosure to the independent Board of directors, or in the prospectus of all material facts relating to the formation of the company including, of course, any profits made by them in transaction with the company.

Promoter's Remuneration

A promoter besides being reimbursed for preliminary expenses incurred by him in setting up and registering the company may be rewarded by the company for the efforts undertaken by him in forming the company in several ways under a valid contract. The common forms and modes of compensating a promoter in consideration of his services are as follows:

1. The company may pay him a lump sum amount for the services rendered. The articles of the company may provide for a fixed sum to be paid by the company to the promoters, although, such a provision has no contractual effect, and the promoters cannot sue to enforce it.
2. The promoter may make profits or earn commission on the transactions entered by him with the company after making full disclosure to an independent Board of directors or to the intended members.
3. The promoter may sell his own property to the company for cash or against fully paid shares in the company at an overvaluation after making full disclosures.
4. The promoter may be allotted fully or partly paid-up shares or debentures.

However, whatever be the remuneration or benefit paid to the promoter, it must be disclosed in the prospectus if it is paid within two years prior to the date of issue of prospectus.

Promoter's Liability

A promoter's role is pivotal towards the formation of the company. They, however, undoubtedly occupy a fiduciary position. In case of default by a promoter in fulfilling his duties, the company may rescind the contract, and if the former has made some secret profits on any related transaction, he may be compelled to account for it. If it is not possible to cancel the contract or where the promoter has already encashed the secret profits, the company can sue him for breach of trust. Damages up to the difference between the market value of the property and the contract price can be recovered from the promoter where he had sold his own property to the company.

The promoter shall be subject to civil as well as criminal liability for misstatement(s) or omission made in the prospectus, if any.

Civil liability for misstatement(s) in the prospectus

Where a person has subscribed for securities of a company, acting on any statement included, or the inclusion or omission of any matter, in the prospectus which is misleading and has sustained any loss or damage as a consequence thereof, company and every person who—

(a) is a director of the company at the time of the issue of the prospectus;
(b) has authorized himself to be named and is named in the prospectus as a director of the company, or has agreed to become such director, either immediately or after an interval of time;
(c) is a promoter of the company;
(d) has authorized the issue of the prospectus; and
(e) is an expert referred to in Section 26 (5), shall, besides punishment under Section 36, be liable to pay compensation to every person who has sustained such loss or damage.

Criminal liability for non-compliance of matters to be stated in the prospectus

Section 26 of the Act lays down matters to be stated in the prospectus. Non-compliance of the provision of this section may render a promoter punishable with imprisonment for a term which may extend to three years or with fine which shall not be less than fifty thousand rupees but which may extend to three lakh rupees, or both [Section 26].

Criminal liability for misstatement(s) in the prospectus

Where a prospectus issued, circulated or distributed includes any statement which is untrue or misleading, any person (including promoter, of course) who is found to be guilty of fraud (involving an amount of at least ten lakh rupees or one percent of the turnover of the company, whichever is lower) shall be criminally liable and punishable with imprisonment for a term which shall not be less than six months but which may extend to ten years and shall also be liable to fine which shall not be less than the amount involved in the fraud, but which may extend to three times the amount involved in the fraud. Moreover, if the fraud in question involves public interest, the term of imprisonment shall not be less than three years, unless the promoter proves either that the statement was immaterial or that he had reasonable ground to believe that the statement was true [Section 34 read with Section 447].

Incorporation

Incorporation: Giving legal form to an association of persons by registering it under the Companies Act; a procedure full of documentary formalities.

Incorporation or registration is the foremost obligation to be fulfilled to form any type of company under the Companies Act. That is, no company can come into existence without being formally registered under the Act. Incorporation of a company is a procedure full of documentary compliance formalities. That is, a company is incorporated by registering certain documents with the Registrar of Companies, and paying certain fees and stamp duty. Unless and until these formalities are duly complied with, a company does not have any legal recognition or existence of its own.

Documentation for Incorporation

For registration promoters have to file with the RoC, within whose jurisdiction the registered office of a company is proposed to be situated, the following documents and information:

1. The memorandum and articles of the proposed company duly signed by all the subscribers to the memorandum in such manner as may be prescribed;
2. A declaration in prescribed form by an advocate, a chartered accountant, a cost accountant, or a company secretary in practice, who is engaged in the formation of the company, and by a person named in the articles as a director, manager or secretary of the company, that all the requirements of this Act and the rules made thereunder in respect of registration and matters precedent or incidental thereto have been complied with;
3. An affidavit from each of the subscribers to the memorandum and from persons named as the first directors, if any, in the articles that he is not convicted of any offence in connection with the promotion, formation, or management of any company, or that he has not been found guilty of any fraud or misfeasance or of any breach of duty to any company under this Act or any previous company law during the preceding five years and that all the documents filed with the RoC for registration of the company contain information that is correct and complete and true to the best of his knowledge and belief;
4. The address for correspondence till its registered office is established;
5. The particulars of name, including surname or family name, residential address, nationality and such other particulars of every subscriber to the memorandum along with proof of identity as may be prescribed, and in the case of a subscriber being a company, such particulars as may be prescribed;
6. The particulars of the persons mentioned in the articles as first directors of the company, their names, including surnames or family names, the Director Identification Number (DIN), residential address, nationality and such other particulars including proof of identity as may be prescribed; and
7. The particulars of the interests of the persons mentioned in the articles as the first directors of the company in other forms or bodies corporate along with their consent to act as directors of the

company in such form and manner as may be prescribed [Section 7(1)].

Certificate of Incorporation and Corporate Identity Number

Certificate of incorporation: A document that evidences that the company bearing a specific name is a registered entity.

Certificate of incorporation is the most important document to bring a proposed company into existence. In accordance with Section 7(2), once all the required documents have been filed along with the registration fee, filing fee, stamp duty, as specified and they are found to be in order, the RoC will issue, under his seal and signature, the 'certificate of incorporation' of the company.

The certificate of incorporation is the conclusive documentary evidence that the requirements of the Companies Act have been complied with and the company bearing a specific name is duly registered.

On and from the date mentioned in the certificate of incorporation issued under sub-section (2), the Registrar shall allot to the company a corporate identity number, which shall be a distinct identity for the company and which shall also be included in the certificate [Section 7(3)].

Corporate identity number: A distinct identity for the company, included in the certificate of incorporation.

This certificate needs to be collected from the Registrar's office. After obtaining the certificate, the secretary of the company must send the notice of the registered address of the company, if it was not sent earlier, within 30 days of registration.

The company shall maintain and preserve at its registered office copies of all documents and information as originally filed under sub-section (1) till its dissolution under the Act [Section 7(4)].

Consequences of Incorporating a Company on the Basis of Fake Documentation

This certificate of incorporation is the birth document of the company and the proof of the existence of the company. Once this certificate is issued, a company cannot cease its existence unless it is dissolved by an order of the NCLT (National Company Law Tribunal) or otherwise. However, as per Section 7(7) of the Act, if a company has been incorporated by furnishing any false or incorrect information or representation or by suppressing any material fact or information in any of the documents or declaration filed or made for incorporating such company or by any fraudulent action, the Tribunal may, on an application made to it, on being satisfied that the situation so warrants,

1. pass such orders, as it may think fit, for regulation of the management of the company including changes, if any, in its memorandum and articles, in public interest or in the interest of the company and its members and creditors; or
2. direct that liability of the members shall be unlimited; or
3. direct removal of the name of the company from the register of companies; or
4. pass an order for the winding up of the company; or
5. pass such other orders as it may deem fit.

However, before any order is passed by the Tribunal under Section 7(7), mentioned above,

1. the company shall be given a reasonable opportunity of being heard in the matter; and
2. the Tribunal shall take into consideration the transactions entered into by the company, including the obligations, if any, contracted or payment of any liability.

Effect of Incorporation

From the date of incorporation mentioned in the certificate of incorporation, such subscribers to the memorandum and all other persons, as may, from time to time, become members of the company, shall be a body corporate by the name contained in the memorandum, capable of exercising all the functions of an incorporated company under the Act and having perpetual succession with power to acquire, hold and dispose of property, both movable and immovable, tangible and intangible, to contract and to sue and be sued, by the said name [Section 9].

Prospectus

After getting the company incorporated, promoters will raise finances. The public is invited to purchase shares and debentures of the company through an

Prospectus: A document containing detailed information about the company and an invitation to the public subscribing to the share capital and debentures.

advertisement. A document containing detailed information about the company and an invitation to the public subscribing to the share capital and debentures is issued. This document is called prospectus.

Commencement of Business, etc.

A company incorporated after the commencement of the Companies (Amendment) Act, 2019 and having a share capital shall not commence any business or exercise any borrowing powers unless—

(a) a declaration is filed (via e-form INC-20A) by a director within a period of one hundred and eighty days of the date of incorporation of the company in such form and verified in such manner as may be prescribed, with the Registrar (RoC) that every subscriber to the memorandum has paid the value of the shares agreed to be taken by him on the date of making of such declaration; and

(b) The company has filed with the RoC a verification of its registered office as provided in sub-section (2) of section 12. [Section 10A(1)]

Penalty for non-compliance If any default is committed in complying with the requirements of the above section, the company shall be liable to a penalty of ₹50,000 and every officer who is in default shall be liable to a penalty of ₹1,000 for each day during which such default continues but not exceeding an amount of one lakh rupees. [Section 10A (2)]

Moreover, where no such declaration has been filed with the RoC within a period of 180 days of the date of incorporation of the company and the RoC has reasonable cause to believe that the company is not carrying on any business or operations, he may initiate action for the removal of the name of the company from the register of companies under Chapter XVIII. [Section 10A(3)]

Prospectus under the Statute

'Prospectus' means any document described or issued as a prospectus and includes a red herring prospectus referred to in section 32 or shelf prospectus referred to in section 31 or any notice, circular, advertisement or other document inviting offers from the public for the subscription or purchase of any securities of a body corporate [Section 2(70)].

Thus, when a company allots securities to the public based on an offer that has been made, then, any document through which such an offer is made is considered to be a prospectus and it has to fulfil all the requirements of a prospectus. Thus, the issue of prospectus is essential when the company wishes the public to subscribe for its shares or debentures.

Red Herring Prospectus

Red herring prospectus: A prospectus that enables a company to issue securities utilising the same document more than once, which will help cut costs and save time.

The expression 'red herring prospectus' means a prospectus which does not include complete particulars of the quantum or price of the securities included therein.

According to Section 32(1), a company proposing to make an offer of securities may issue a red herring prospectus prior to the issue of a prospectus.

A company proposing to issue a red herring prospectus shall file it with the Registrar at least three days prior to the opening of the subscription list and the offer [Section 32(2)].

A red herring prospectus shall carry the same obligations as are applicable to a prospectus and any variation between the red herring prospectus and a prospectus shall be highlighted as variations in the prospectus [Section 32(3)].

From the above discussion, it may be concluded that a red herring prospectus is a draft or preliminary prospectus circulated by a company with respect to the initial public offering. It generally contains the information of the operation of the company but does not include complete particulars of the quantum or price of the securities included therein.

Shelf Prospectus

Shelf prospectus: A single prospectus for multiple, undefined future offerings or issues.

The expression 'shelf prospectus' refers a prospectus in respect of which the securities or class of securities included therein are issued for subscription in one or more issues over a certain period without the issue of a further prospectus [Section 31].

Thus, 'shelf prospectus' is a type of public offering where certain issuers are allowed to offer and sell single or multiple securities to the public without a separate prospectus for each issue or security concerned. Instead, there is a single prospectus for multiple, undefined future offerings or issues.

Any class or classes of companies, as the Securities and Exchange Board of India may provide by regulations in this behalf, may file a shelf prospectus with the Registrar at the stage of the first offer of securities included therein which shall indicate a period not exceeding one year as the period of validity of such prospectus, which shall commence from the date of opening of the first offer of securities under that prospectus, and in respect of a second or subsequent offer of such securities issued during the period of validity of that prospectus, no further prospectus is required [Section 31(1)].

A company filing a shelf prospectus shall be required to file an information memorandum containing all material facts relating to new charges created, changes in the financial position of the company as have occurred between the first offer of securities or the previous offer of securities and the succeeding offer of securities and such other changes as may be prescribed, with the Registrar within the prescribed time, prior to the issue of a second or subsequent offer of securities under the shelf prospectus [Section 31(2)].

Thus, a shelf prospectus is a type of prospectus issued by companies making multiple issues of securities. Changes may take place in the financial position of the company after the shelf prospectus is filed. Hence, these changes should be intimated to the Registrar of Companies (RoC). For this purpose, an 'Information Memorandum' should be filed in Form PAS-2 with the RoC, the Securities and Exchange Board of India (Sebi) and the NSE or BSE. It should be filed on the second, third and fourth issue of securities made under the shelf prospectus within one month before the issue.

The advantage of a shelf prospectus is that a new prospectus need not be issued every time the company issues securities. A maximum of four issues of securities can be made using a shelf prospectus. Moreover, a shelf prospectus should be used within a maximum of one year and a shelf prospectus can be filed only by companies issuing non-convertible debt bonds.

Applicability of Self Prospectus

The following kinds of companies/institutions are eligible to issue a shelf prospectus:

1. Public Financial Institutions (PFIs) (PFIs are companies whose paid-up share capital is held by the Central Government to the extent of more than 51 per cent. Examples are the Life Insurance Corporation of India, Infrastructure Development Finance Company Limited, Industrial Credit and Investment Corporation of India Limited, Industrial Finance Corporation of India, and Industrial Development Bank of India.)
2. Public sector banks
3. Non-banking Finance Companies (NBFCs)
4. Listed companies.

Conditions to be fulfilled for issuing shelf prospectus. The following conditions should be adhered to by a company opting to issue a shelf prospectus:

1. The company's net-worth should be more than ₹500 crore.
2. The company should have had distributable profit during the preceding three years.
3. An arrangement should be made for dematerialization of securities. The arrangement must be made with a depository registered with the Sebi i.e. either with NSDL or CDSL. A merchant banker should be appointed for the issue. The merchant banker must be registered with the SEBI.
4. In case debentures are issued, a debenture trustee should be appointed.
5. Credit rating should be obtained. The securities issued should have a credit rating of AA or more (Credit ratings are accepted only from credit rating agencies registered with the SEBI).
6. The company's directors or promoters should not have been faced with any regulatory action.
7. The company should not have defaulted in repayment of deposits during the preceding three years.
8. The company should have honoured its listing agreement during the preceding three years.

Contents of the Prospectus

Every prospectus issued by or on behalf of a public company either with reference to its formation or subsequently, or by or on behalf of any person who is or has been engaged or interested in the formation of a public company, shall be dated and signed and shall state the following information:

1. names and addresses of the registered office of the company, company secretary, Chief Financial Officer, auditors, legal advisers, bankers, trustees, if any, underwriters and such other persons as may be prescribed;
2. dates of the opening and closing of the issue, and declaration about the issue and allotment of letters and refunds within the prescribed time;
3. a statement by the Board of Directors about the separate bank account where all monies received out of the issue are to be transferred and disclosure of details of all monies including utilised and unutilised monies out of the previous issue in the prescribed manner;
4. consent of the directors, auditors, bankers to the issue, expert's opinion, if any, and of such other persons, as may be prescribed;
5. the authority for the issue and the details of the resolution passed therefor;
6. procedure and time schedule for allotment and issue of securities;
7. capital structure of the company in the prescribed manner;
8. main objects of the public offer, terms of the present issue and such other particulars as may be prescribed;
9. main objects and the present business of the company and its location, the schedule of implementation of the project;
10. particulars relating to
    (a) management perception of risk factors specific to the project;
    (b) gestation period of the project;
    (c) extent of progress made in the project;
    (d) deadlines for completion of the project; and
    (e) any litigation or legal action pending or taken by a Government Department or a statutory body during the last five years immediately preceding the year of the issue of prospectus against the promoter of the company;
11. minimum subscription, amount payable by way of premium, issue of shares otherwise than on cash;
12. details of directors including their appointments and remuneration, and such particulars of the nature and extent of their interests in the company as may be prescribed; and
13. disclosures in such manner as may be prescribed about sources of promoter's contribution; set out the following reports for the purposes of the financial information, namely
    (a) reports by the auditors of the company with respect to its profits and losses and assets and liabilities and such other matters as may be prescribed;
    (b) reports relating to profits and losses for each of the five financial years immediately preceding the financial year of the issue of prospectus including such reports of its subsidiaries and in such manner as may be prescribed.

Through its prospectus, a company, therefore, tries to convince the public that it offers best opportunity for their investment. A prospectus in this behalf outlines broad terms and conditions on which the shares or debentures have been offered to the public. The issue of prospectus is essential when the company wishes the public to purchase its shares or debentures. A private company, therefore, is exempt from issuing or filing a prospectus.

Filing of Prospectus with the Registrar

A prospectus must be filed with the Registrar of Companies before it is issued to the public.

No prospectus shall be issued by or on behalf of a company or in relation to an intended company unless on or before the date of its publication it has been delivered to the Registrar for registration, a copy thereof signed by every person who is named therein as a director or proposed director of the company or by his duly authorised attorney [Section 26(4)].

To reinforce the above-mentioned provision, section 26(8) specifically provides that no prospectus shall be valid if it is issued more than ninety days after the date on which a copy thereof is delivered to the Registrar.

Consequences of Issuing an Irregular Prospectus

If a prospectus is issued in contravention of the provisions of this section, the company shall be punishable with fine which shall not be less than fifty thousand rupees but which may extend to three lakh rupees and every person who is knowingly a party to the issue of such prospectus shall be punishable with imprisonment for a term which may extend to three years or with fine which shall not be less than fifty thousand rupees but which may extend to three lakh rupees, or with both [Section 26(9)].

Procedure of Online Incorporation of a Company in India

Online incorporation or registration of a company is a compact 8-step process. If all the formalities are done correctly and the Registrar of Companies (RoC) does not have a heavy workload and the proposed company's name is not rejected in first attempt, the applicant may get its 'Certificate of Incorporation' in maximum 14 working days.

STEP I: Apply for Name Approval

A. Login on MCA Website

Applicant has to login into their account on MCA Website. Existing users can use earlier account whereas new users have to create a new account. After login user has to click on the icon "RUN" (Reserve Unique Name) in MCA Service. An online form shall open. Applicant has to fill the information online as this form can't be download.

Note* since 26th January, 2018 e-form INC-1 has been omitted from the Companies Act, 2013.

B. Details required to be mentioned in online form:

(i) Entity type (i.e. Part I, OPC, Section 8 etc.) (Refer the below table, taken from the MCA link: http://www.mca.gov.in/MinistryV2/runServicerFAQ.html)

Entity type	Suffix allowed	Example
New Company/ (Others/Part 1 co.	Limited/Private Limited	ABC Limited
DEF Private Limited		
Producer Company	Producer Company Limited	GHI Producer Company Limited
Unlimited Company	Unlimited	JKL Limited
Private Company (OPC)	(OPC) Private Limited	MNO (OPC) Private Limited
IFSC Company	(IFSC) Limited/ (IFSC) Private Limited/IFSC Limited/IFSC Private Limited	PQR (IFSC) Limited/PQR IFSC Limited
STU (IFSC) Private Limited/STU (IFSC) Private Limited		
Section 8 Company	Other than 'Limited/Private Limited/(OPC) Private Limited'	VWX Electoral Trust
Nidhi Company	Nidhi Limited	MNO Nidhi Limited

(ii) CIN (Corporate Identification Number). It has to be entered only when an existing company wishes to change its name and is using RUN to reserve a new name)

(iii) Proposed name (Auto Check Facility)

(iv) Comment (Mention Objects of the proposed Company and any other relevant information Like Trade Mark etc.)

(v) Choose File (Any attachment); explained below.

C. Choose File:

This option is available to upload the PDF documents. If the applicant wants to attach any file, can be uploaded at this option. It is mandatory to attach relevant documents and No Objection Certificates (NOCs) only when a name requires the approval of a Sectoral Regulator or NOC etc., if applicable, as per the Companies (Incorporation) Rules, 2014.

It should also be noted that only one file is allowed to be uploaded as an attachment and the size of the file should not exceed 6MB. In case of multiple attachments, all the documents can be scanned into a sin gle file not exceeding 6MB in size before uploading the same.

D. Submission of Form on MCA Website:
After completion of above steps user shall submit the Form on the MCA website.

E. Payment of Fees:
Applicant has to pay fees (₹1,000) immediately after submission of form. There is no option of pay later challan in RUN. After payment challan shall be generated.

F. Validity of Reserved Name:
Reserved name shall be valid for 20 days from the date of approval of Name and 60 days in case of allotment (change) of name for an existing company.
Note* Approval of Name through "RUN" is an optional way. Companies can also directly apply for the Name in the SPICe form. Moreover, there is no need to mention the name or number of proposed Directors in the RUN.

STEP II: Preparation of Documents for Incorporation of Company

After name approval, the applicant has to prepare the under-mentioned documents for incorporation of the company:

- INC-9 – Declaration by first Subscriber(s) and Director(s) on plain paper.
- DIR-2 – Declaration from first Directors along with Copy of Proof of Identity and residential address on plain paper.
- NOC from the owner of the property on plain paper.
- Proof of Office address (Conveyance/ Lease deed/ Rent Agreement etc. along with rent receipts);
- Copy of the utility bills, not older than 2 months.
- In case of subscribers/ Director does not have a DIN, it is mandatory to attach: Proof of identity and residential address of the subscribers
- All the Subscribers should have Digital Signature.

STEP III: Fill the necessary information in SPICe Form

Once all the above mentioned documents/information are ready, applicant has to fill the information in the e-form i.e. Simplified Proforma for Incorporating a Company electronically (SPICe) – INC-32.

Features of SPICe (INC-32) form:

- Details of 7 subscribers (Maximum). In case of more subscribers, physically signed MOA and AOA shall be attached in the Form.
- Details of 20 directors (Maximum).
- Maximum 3 directors are allowed for filing application of allotment of DIN while incorporating a company.
- Applicant can apply for the name of the company also in this form.
- By affixation of DSC of the subscriber on the INC-33 (eMoA) date of signing will appear automatically in the form.
- Applying for PAN/TAN will be compulsory for all fresh incorporation applications filed in the new version of the SPICe form.
- In case of companies incorporated, with effect from the 26th day of January, 2018, with a nominal capital of less than or equal to ₹10 lakh or in respect of companies not having a share capital whose number of members as stated in the articles of association does not exceed twenty, fee on INC-32 (SPICe) shall not be applicable. However, such companies will have to bear stamp duty at par with other companies, stamp duty being the State matter.

Note: Earlier if a Person wished to incorporate a company then it had to apply for the DIN, approval of the name availability, separate form for the first director, registered office address, PAN, TAN etc. But SPICe is a single window form for the Incorporation of a company. Accordingly, this form can be used for the following purposes:
Application of DIN (up to 3 Directors)
Application for Availability of Name
No need to file separate form for first Director (DIR-12)
No need to file separate form for address of registered office (INC-22)
No need to file separate form for PAN and TAN
No need to file separately for GSTIN, ESIC Registration etc.

Note: Incorporating a company through Simplified Proforma for Incorporating Company electronically (SPICe -INC-32), with eMoA (INC-33), eAOA (INC-34), is the default option and most companies are required to be incorporated through SPICe only.

Obtaining director identification number (DIN)

An individual, who is an existing director, or intends to be appointed as one, is required to have a unique identification number, called 'Director Identification Number' (DIN). Thus, DIN is a unique identification number for an existing director or a person intending to become the director of a company. Up to 3 individuals may apply for the DIN in respect of a proposed company. DIN is unique to an individual and can be obtained online. One can be director in more than one company but his DIN will remain identical in respect of all the companies, he/she is a director in. To apply for DIN, one needs a scanned copy of a pass- port-sized photograph, the PAN card (passport in case of foreign national), soft copy of driver's license/voter ID/ any latest utilities bill. Indian nationals would have to self-attest these documents. Foreign nationals residing in commonwealth countries would need them notarised by the Indian embassy. Those not in commonwealth nations would also need them apostilled. If the proposed company has more than 3 directors without DINs, the incumbents would need to provide their details and apply for DINs separately.

Process for obtaining DIN online

1. Login into MCA account (http://www.mca.gov. in)
2. Fill the e-form DIN-1 online
3. Attach scanned copy of passport size photograph
4. For proof of identity attach self-attested softcopy of Passport/Driving License/Voter ID/PAN Card/ Latest Utilities Bill etc. In case of foreign nationals/ NRI residing in common wealth nations, identity proof should necessarily be a passport copy duly notarised by Indian embassy. Those not in commonwealth nations would also need them apostilled
5. For address proof attach attested softcopy of Passport/Voter Card/Ration card/Driving license/ Utilities bill
6. Affix the 'Digital Signature'
7. Upload the e-form by clicking on eformupload in your login a/c
8. Upon uploading, pay the fees (₹100) via electronic mode (net banking/card etc.)
9. Upon successful upload and payment of fees, DIN will be issued, provided the details filled by practicing CA/CS/CWA) are not found to be duplicated. Otherwise provisional DIN will be issued which shall be confirmed in a day or two.

STEP IV: Preparation of Memorandum (MOA) and Articles (AOA) – Electronic or Physical

After proper filing of SPICe form, applicant has to download the e-form INC-33 (MOA) and INC-34 (AOA) form the MCA site. After downloading the forms, fill all the information in the forms as per requirement of Table A to J of Schedule I. After completely filing of the form affix DSC of all the subscribers and professional on subscriber sheet of the MOA and AOA.

(Make Sure Professional and Subscriber sign the form on the same date).

In case of incorporation of a company where any of the subscribers of the MOA/AOA is signing at a place outside India, physical form of MOA & AOA shall be attached in e-form INC 32 in the respective format as specified in Table A to J in Schedule I without filing form INC 33 and INC 34.

Obtaining digital signature certificate (DSC)

The Information Technology Act, 2000 provides for use of 'Digital Signatures' on the documents submitted in electronic form in order to ensure the security and authenticity of the documents filed electronically. This is secure and authentic way to submit a document electronically. As such, all filings done by the companies/LLPs under MCA21 e-Governance programme are required to be filed using Digital Signatures by the person authorised to sign the documents. Digital signature in this behalf implies an encrypted digital code appended to an electronic document to verify that it was created by a known source and has not been altered. Since incorporation is now done online, at least one of the proposed company's directors' signatures will be needed on all the electronic documents. For this, the projected director would need a Digital Signature Certificate (DSC), also known as Class-II Digital Signature Certificate, which can be procured online from any one of the seven DSCs issuing Certifying Authorities (CAs) appointed by the Ministry of Corporate Affairs (MCA), namely, Tata Consultancy Services (TCS), National Informatics Centre (NIC), IDRBT Certifying Authority, Safe Script CA Services, MTNL Trust Line, (n) Code Solutions, and eMudhra. Digital Signature Certificate (DSC) Applicants can directly approach Certifying Authorities (CAs) with original supporting documents, and self-attested copies will be sufficient in this case. DSCs can also be obtained, wherever offered by CA, using Aadhar eKYC based authentication, and supporting documents are not required in this case. The DSCs are typically issued with one or two year validity, renewable on expiry of the period of initial issue.

Documentation required for the purpose of DSC For issuance of DSC the following documentation needs to be done with RoC online:

1. Softcopy of completed Class-II Digital Signature Certificate Form.
2. Identity Proof: Self-attested scan copy of PAN card or, in case of foreign national, copy of passport.
3. Address Proof: Self-attested scan copy of Passport/Voter ID/Ration Card/Driving License/Utilities Bill/Aadhar Card. If the Utilities Bill (Electricity/Telephone) is submitted, it should be in the name of the Applicant and not older than 2 months from the filing of the form (12 months, in case of foreign national).

Common reasons for rejection of DSC The following minor mistakes can cause a delay in issuing DSC hence should be avoided:

1. **Abbreviating Names:** Directors' names should be given in full and not in abbreviated form regardless of what is mentioned in the ID/Address proof.
2. **Spelling Mistakes:** Errors in the name are completely unacceptable.
3. **Old bills:** Always provide the latest utilities bill. Also, it needs to be in the applicant's name.
4. **Prefixes:** Names should not be prefixed with Mr/Ms/Shri, etc.

Payment of Stamp Duty

Once the above documentation is done, stamp duty will need to be paid electronically. The stamp duty varies by location. In certain states, such as Punjab and Kerala, it is costlier than in others. One can refer the following webpage for determining the stamp duty payable online: http://www.gov.in/MCA21/efiling/eStamp_rate.pdf

STEP V: Fill details of PAN & TAN

It is mandatory to mention the details of PAN & TAN in the Incorporation Form INC-32. Link to find out of Area Code to file PAN & TAN are given in Help Kit of SPICE Form.

STEP VI: Fill details of GSTIN, IEC in AGILE

Company can apply for registration of Goods and Services Tax Identification Number (GSTIN), Employees' State Insurance Corporation (ESIC) Registration and Employees' Provident Fund Organisation (EPFO) registration through e-form AGILE (INC 35). However, if the applicant doesn't want to apply for the GSTIN, it can select no.

STEP VII: Submission of Required Documents on MCA Website

Once all the 4 forms (INC-32, 33, 34, and AGILE) are ready with the applicant, upload all four documents through Linked form on MCA website and make the payment in respect thereof.

STEP VIII: Certificate of Incorporation

The RoC shall verify the documents online. If any changes are required, the applicant will be notified about the same. If it is all clear, the applicant the 'Incorporation certificate' can be generated with the help of CIN, PAN & TAN. The MCA nowadays issues only digital certificates. One can print out the certificate, if wishes so.

Exercises

I. Objective-type Questions

1. Which of the following is not a characteristic feature of a joint stock company?
   (a) Artificial person (b) Separate property
   (c) Carry on a business for gain (d) Perpetual sucession

2. A company which intends to apply its profits, if any, or other income in promoting its objects; and intends to prohibit the payment of dividend to its members, is known as:
   (a) Charitable company
   (b) OPC
   (c) Section 8 company
   (d) Section 25 company

3. Which the following companies cannot be a 'small company'?
   (i) a holding company or a subsidiary company;
   (ii) a company registered under Section 8 (a charitable company)
   (iii) a company or body corporate governed by any special Act
   (iv) One person company (OPC)
   Answer Codes:
   (a) (i) and (iii) (b) (i), (ii) and (iii)
   (c) (i), (iii) and (iv) (d) (i), (ii) and (iv)

4. Which of the following is not a valid ground for lifting the corporate veil under judicial interpretations?
   (a) Protection of revenue
   (b) Prevention of fraud or improper conduct
   (c) Determination of the enemy character of the company
   (d) Ultra vires acts

5. A charitable company must fulfil which of the following conditions?
   (a) The company is formed for the promotion of commerce, art, science, sports, education, research, social welfare, religion, charity, protection of the environment or any other such object
   (b) It intends to apply its profits, if any, or other income in promoting its above objects
   (c) It intends to prohibit the payment of any dividend to its members
   (d) All of the above

6. Which of the following is not a characteristic feature of a private ltd. company?
   (a) It restricts the right to transfer its shares
   (b) It limits the number of its members to two hundred (except in case of 'OPC')
   (c) It prohibits any invitation to the public to subscribe for any securities of the company
   (d) It has a minimum paid up share capital of ₹1 lakh

7. Promoters of a joint stock company shall not be liable for:
   (a) Misstatement(s) in the prospectus
   (b) Non-compliance of matters to be stated in the prospectus
   (c) Compliance of matters to be stated in the prospectus
   (d) Commencement of business by the company without conforming to capital subscription requirements

8. When a company has been incorporated by furnishing any false or incorrect information or by suppressing any material fact or information in any of the documents, the Tribunal is empowered to:
   (a) Direct that liability of the members shall be unlimited; or
   (b) Direct removal of the name of the company from the register of companies.
   (c) Pass an order for the winding up of the company.
   (d) Exercise any of the above options

9. Towards the fulfilment of their fiduciary duty, the promoters
   (a) Should not make any profits secretly at the expense of the company
   (b) Should make full disclosure to the Board of directors of all material facts relating to the formation of the company including any profits made by them in transaction with the company.
   (c) Should make full disclosure in the prospectus of all material facts relating to the formation of the company including any profits made by them in transaction with the company.
   (d) All of the above

10. Which of the following statements truly describes the organisation of The Companies Act, 2013?
    (a) It contains 470 Sections, spread over 20 Chapters and there are seven schedules appended to it
    (b) It contains 470 Sections, spread over 29 Chapters and there are seven schedules appended to it
    (c) It contains 470 Sections, spread over 29 Chapters and there are eight schedules appended to it
    (d) It contains 470 Sections, spread over 29 Chapters and there are nine schedules appended to it

II. Review Questions

1. Define a company and discuss the characteristic features of a duly incorporated company.
2. Distinguish between a private company and a public company. State the exemptions and privileges available to a private company.
3. 'A joint stock company is an artificial person created by law, having a separate entity, and with a perpetual succession.' Distinguish between a company and a partnership.
4. Write short notes on the following:
   (a) Conversion of a public company into a private company
   (b) Conversion of a private company into a public company
   (c) Companies with Charitable Objects
   (d) Small company
5. Describe the stages involved in the formation of a proposed public company.
6. Discuss the role and legal status of promoters. Describe also liabilities of promoters.
7. Describe the documentary requirements for incorporation of a joint stock company. What is the consequence of obtaining the certificate of incorporation by furnishing wrong information or concealing the material facts?
8. Write short notes on the following:
   (a) Effect of incorporation
   (b) Promoter's remuneration
   (c) Red Herring Prospectus
   (d) Shelf Prospectus

Answers to Objective-type Questions

1. (c)	2. (c)	3. (b)	4. (d)	5. (d)
6. (d)	7. (d)	8. (d)	9. (d)	10. (b)

17 Chapter in Review

LEARNING OUTCOMES

LO 1 Company: meaning and defining characteristics

LO 2 Kinds of companies

LO 3 Lifting the corporate veil

LO 4 Formation of company

LO 5 Prospectus

LO 6 Online incorporation of company

KEY TERMS

Company: An artificial person created by law, having a separate entity, with a perpetual succession, and members having limited liability.

Private company: A company, which by its articles restricts the transferability of its shares and prevents the public at large from subscribing to them.

Public company: A company whose shares are traded freely on a recognized stock exchange.

Limited company: A private or public company wherein the liability of its members is limited either by share capital or guarantee.

Unlimited company: A private company wherein the liability of its members are unrestricted.

Small company: A company (other than public company) whose paid up capital does not exceed ₹50 lakh and turnover as per last profit and loss account does not exceed ₹2 crore.

One person company: A company formed with only one person (a natural person who is an Indian citizen and a resident of India) as its member.

Government company: Any company in which minimum 51 per cent of the paid-up share capital is held by the Central and/or State Government.

Foreign company: A company which is incorporated under the laws of a different nation but conducts any of its business activities in India.

Dormant company: A company that does not trade and has no significant business transactions.

LO 1 A company is a voluntary association of persons characterised by a separate legal identity independent of its members; limited liability; everlasting existence; separate property; flexibility of investment; capacity to sue and being sued; separation of ownership and management; proportionate representation; and right to own property.

LO 2 Companies can broadly be classified as public and private limited companies, one person company (OPC), small company (which is also a private company), parent and subsidiary companies, Government company dormant company, foreign company, and Section 8 company. A private limited company can be converted into a public company and vice-versa. Unlike a public company, a private limited company enjoys certain privileges.

LO 3 If a company's corporate veil creates some unexpected problems or is being used unjustly, the court may disregard the legal fiction that all companies are wholly separate from their shareholders.

LO 4 There are three broad stages involved in the formation of a joint stock company in India: Promotion, incorporation, and commencement of business. Promotion begins with the conceptualization of the birth of a company and the purpose for which it is to be created. Promoters raise funds to finance the company's initial needs. After the company is registered, it receives a 'certificate of incorporation' after which the company becomes a valid entity. Every company limited by shares needs to comply with capital subscription formalities before it commences any business or exercises its borrowing powers.

LO 5 For raising capital, a proposed public company needs to prepare and issue a prospectus. A prospectus must be duly filed with the Registrar before it is issued and must be issued in strict compliance of the statutory provisions in this behalf, failing which the company and every person who is party to the issue of the prospectus shall be punishable.

LO 6 To facilitate startups, Ministry of Corporate Affairs, Government of India, provides for online incorporation of a company, which implies obtaining

Section 8 company: A company incorporated under the Companies Act for not-for-profit activities.

Doctrine of corporate veil: A company has a separate personality from its members or shareholders.

Promotion: The entire backing process by which a company is brought into life.

Incorporation: Giving legal form to an association of persons by registering it under the Companies Act; a procedure full of documentary formalities.

Certificate of incorporation: A document that evidences that the company bearing a specific name is a registered entity.

Corporate identity number: A distinct identity for the company, included in the certificate of incorporation.

Prospectus: A document containing detailed information about the company and an invitation to the public subscribing to the share capital and debentures.

Red herring prospectus: Preliminary prospectus which is filled by the company with the RoC and Sebi, generally with respect to the IPOs, that contains the information of the operation of the company but does not include complete particulars of the quantum or price of the securities included therein.

Shelf prospectus: A single prospectus for multiple, undefined future offerings or issues of securities, which will help cut costs and save time.

Digital signature: An encrypted digital code appended to an electronic document to verify that it was created by a known source and has not been altered.

Director identification number (DIN): A unique identification number for an existing director or a person intending to become the director of a company.

"Certificate of Incorporation" through electronic mode. There are two options to incorporate a new company online:

Option 1: By filing Form INC-29–Integrated Incorporation Form

Option 2: Apply for the name of a company to be registered by filing Form INC-1. After name approval, depending upon the proposed company type, file the prescribed incorporation forms.

CHAPTER 18

Memorandum and Articles, Share Capital and Debentures, Membership

Learning Objectives

- LO 1 Memorandum of association
- LO 2 Doctrine of *ultra vires*
- LO 3 Articles of association
- LO 4 Doctrine of constructive notice
- LO 5 Doctrine of indoor management
- LO 6 Share capital and debentures
- LO 7 ESOP
- LO 8 Sweat equity shares
- LO 9 Right issue
- LO 10 Bonus shares
- LO 11 Buy-back of securities
- LO 12 Membership

The present chapter on company law discusses provisions of the Companies Act concerning memorandum and articles of association, membership, and the capital of a company.

Memorandum and Articles of Association

For the incorporation or registration of a company there are two important documents, required to be prepared and filed with the Registrar of Companies, namely:

1. Memorandum of Association; and
2. Article of Association

Memorandum of Association

Memorandum of association: A document that regulates a company's external activities.

The purpose and objectives of a company are to be determined precisely and in advance by the promoters. For this purpose, the promoters of the proposed company device a basic document, known as 'Memorandum of Association' of a company, often simply called the memorandum. It is a document that regulates a company's external activities, i.e., governs the relationship between the company and the outside world.

Defining memorandum

'Memorandum' means memorandum of association of a company as originally framed or as altered from time to time in pursuance of any previous company law or of this Act [Section 2(56)].

Memorandum is the most fundamental document to be filed by any proposed company. It sets out the constitution of the company and specifies its relationship with the outside world. The substance of the memorandum can be explained as follows:

1. It defines the scope and limitations of the proposed company.
2. It is necessary to file a memorandum of association to incorporate a new company.
3. It is considered as an unalterable charter of the company. It is difficult to change or amend the memorandum because it defines certain powers, the company cannot go beyond.
4. Memorandum becomes a public document as soon as the company gets registered. This is because it enables shareholders, creditors, and other stakeholders to know what kind of enterprise they are dealing with.
5. Memorandum forms the outer framework within which the company operates.

Section 4 requires that the memorandum of a company shall be in respective forms, specified in Tables *A*, *B*, *C*, *D*, and *E* of *Schedule I* to the Act, as may be applicable to the company. Table *A* is applicable in case of a company limited by shares; Table *B* is applicable in case of companies limited by guarantee and not having share capital; Table *C* is applicable to a company limited by guarantee and having a share capital, Table *D* is applicable in case of an unlimited company and not having share capital; and Table *E* is applicable in respect of an unlimited company and having share capital.

Contents of the memorandum

As per Section 4 of the Companies Act, 2013, the memorandum of a limited company (either by shares or guarantee) can be divided into six distinct clauses, which are as follows.

Name clause The name clause contains the name of the company, which is of considerable importance as it establishes a company's identity. The choice of a name for a joint stock company is subject to a number of restrictions. The company cannot have a name, which is identical with or resemble too nearly to the name of an existing company registered under this Act or any previous company law; or is undesirable in the opinion of the Central Government. Moreover, a company cannot use a name which is prohibited under the Names and Emblems (Prevention of Misuse) Act, 1950, or use a name reflective of connection to government or state patronage unless prior approval of the Central Government has been obtained for the use of such word or expression. A company can change its name by passing a special resolution at a general meeting or by any other means provided in the Articles. The name of a public company limited by shares or by guarantee must end with the word 'Limited' and that of a private limited company with the words 'Private Limited'.

However, a company registered under Section 8 is free from the obligation of suffixing its name with the word/words, 'Limited/Private Limited'.

Registered office clause The state in which the registered office of a company will be situated is mentioned in this clause. The registered office of the company is the official address of the company where the statutory books and records must normally be kept and which is capable of receiving and acknowledging all communications and notices as may be addressed to it. The communication regarding exact location must be furnished to the RoC within 30 days from the date of incorporation of the company [Section 12].

Similarly, notice of every change of the situation of its verified registered office shall be given to the RoC within thirty days of the change. Every company must affix or print its name and address of its registered office, and keep the same painted or affixed on the outside of every office or place at which its activities are carried on, in a conspicuous position and in legible letters. The name must be written in one of the local languages and in English.

Moreover, every company shall have its name engraved in legible characters on its seal, if any, and inter alia have it printed on cheques, promissory notes, bills of exchange, , business letters, billheads, all official publications. [Section 12(3)].

Objects clause This is the most important clause of a company. It defines the activities, which a company can carry on and those, it cannot. This clause must state

1. The objects to be pursued by the company on its incorporation; and
2. Matters which are necessary for the furtherance of the objects.

In case of companies other than trading corporations whose objects are not confined to one state, the states to whose territories the objects of the company extend must be specified.

Liability clause This contains the nature of the liability of the members; whether limited or unlimited. A declaration that the liability of the members is limited, in case the company is limited by shares or guarantee, must be given under this clause. The memorandum of a company limited by guarantee must also state the amount that each member undertakes to contribute to the assets of the company in the event of its being wound-up. The effect of this clause is that in case of a company limited by shares, no member can be called upon to pay more than the uncalled amount on his/her shares. If his/her shares are already fully paid up, the shareholder has no liability toward the company even if the company is suffering from over-debtness.

The rule of limited liability of members is, however, subject to the following exceptions:

1. If a member agrees in writing to be bound by the alteration of Memorandum or Articles requiring him/her to take more shares or increase his/her liability, he/she shall be liable up to the amount agreed to by him/her.
2. If every member agrees in writing to re-register the company as an unlimited company and the company is re-registered as such, such members will have unlimited liability.
3. If to the knowledge of a member, the number of shareholders has fallen below the legal minimum (seven in the case of a public limited company and two in case of a private limited company) and the company has carried on business for more than six months, while the number is so reduced, the members for the time being constituting the company would be personally liable for the debts of the company contracted during that time.

Capital clause This clause is applicable in the case of a company having a share capital, which states the amount of share capital with which the company is to be registered, division thereof into shares of a fixed amount and the number of shares which the subscribers to the memorandum agree to subscribe, which shall not be less than one share. A company cannot issue share capital greater than the maximum amount of share capital stated in this clause without altering the Memorandum.

Subscription clause This clause contains the number of shares each subscriber to the Memorandum undertakes to subscribe for; indicated against his name. In the case of One Person Company, it contains the name of the person who in the event of death of the subscriber shall become the member of the company.

Thus, memorandum is the life-giving document of the company. That is, it is the document which brings the company into existence. It is the charter or constitution of the company containing the fundamental conditions upon which the company is incorporated. It is the foundation deed on which the structure of the company is built.

Doctrine of *Ultra Vires*

Doctrine of *ultra vires*: An act which is beyond the powers of the company and, therefore, void.

The word *ultra* means beyond, and *vires* means the powers. The Latin term *ultra vires*, therefore, means to describe an act which is beyond the powers. Any transaction (or act), which is not set out in the object clause of the company's memorandum, and is not necessarily or reasonably incidental to the attainment of the object(s), is *ultra vires* the company, and therefore, void, i.e., of no legal effect and does not bind the company. No rights and liabilities on the part of the company arise out of such transaction or act and it is a nullity, i.e., unenforceable even if every member agrees to it.

Consequences of an *Ultra Vires* Act

As stated earlier since an *ultra vires* act is devoid of any legal effect. Accordingly:

- The company cannot sue any person for enforcement of any of its rights under an *ultra vires* act or transaction.
- The directors of the company may be held personally liable to outsiders for an *ultra vires* (of directors' powers) act.

Exceptions However, the doctrine of *ultra vires* does not apply in the following cases:

1. If an act is *ultra vires* of directors' powers but *intra vires* of company, may be ratified by the company.
2. If an act is *ultra vires* the articles of the company but it is *intra vires* of the memorandum, the articles can be altered to rectify the error.
3. Where a company acquires a property through an investment which is *ultra vires* then the third party has no right over such property, i.e., such property shall still be secured. The creditors just have a right to follow its money or property if it exists as it is, and obtain an injunction from the court restraining the company from parting with it provided the aggrieved (third) party intervenes before the identity of the property is lost.

Alteration of Memorandum

A company which is desirous of altering the provisions of its memorandum may do so by passing a special resolution in this behalf after complying with the procedure specified in Section 13 of the Companies Act, 2013 [Section 13(1)].

However, a company limited by share capital may, if so authorised by its articles, alter the capital clause of its memorandum in its general meeting (i.e., by way of passing just an 'ordinary resolution') to increase its authorised capital by such amount as it thinks expedient [Section 61(1)(a)].

Procedure for Altering the Memorandum

1. Prior approval of the Central Government in writing will be a must for any change in the name of a company which shall be subject to the provisions of subsections (2) and (3) of Section 4.

   However, no such approval shall be necessary where the only change in the name of the company is the deletion therefrom, or addition thereto, of the word 'Private', owing to the conversion of any one class of companies to another class in accordance with the provisions of this Act [Section 13(2)].
2. When any change in the name of a company is made under sub-section (2), the Registrar shall enter the new name in the register of companies in place of the old name and issue a fresh certificate of incorporation with the new name and the change in the name shall be complete and effective only on the issue of such a certificate [Section 13(3)].
3. Approval of the Central Government (against an application in this behalf) shall be mandatory for the alteration of the memorandum relating to the place of the registered office from one State to another [Section 13(4)].
4. The Central Government shall dispose of the application under Section 13(4) within a period of 60 days and before passing its order may satisfy itself that the alteration has the consent

of the creditors, debenture-holders and other stakeholders or that the sufficient provision has been made by the company either for the due discharge of all its debts and obligations or that adequate security has been provided for such discharge [Section 13(5)].

5. Save as provided in Section 64, a company shall, in relation to any alteration of its memorandum, file with the Registrar, (*a*) the special resolution passed by the company in this behalf; and (*b*) the approval of the Central Government under Section 13(2), if the alteration involves any change in the name of the company [Section 13(6)].
6. Where an alteration of the memorandum results in the transfer of the registered office of a company from one State to another, a certified copy of the order of the Central Government approving the alteration shall be filed by the company with the Registrar of each of the States within such time and in such manner as may be prescribed, who shall register the same, and the Registrar of the State where the registered office is being shifted to, shall issue a fresh certificate of incorporation indicating the alteration [Section 13(7)].
7. A company, which has raised from public through prospectus and still has any unutilised amount out of the so raised, shall not change its objects for which it raised the money through prospectus unless a special resolution is passed by the company and—
   (a) the details, as may be prescribed, in respect of such resolution shall also be published in the newspapers (one in English and one in vernacular language) which is in circulation at the place where the registered office of the company is situated and shall also be placed on the website of the company, if any, indicating therein the justification for such change;
   (b) the dissenting shareholders shall be given an opportunity to exit by the promoters and shareholders having control in accordance with regulations to be specified by the Securities and Exchange Board [Section 13(8)].
8. The Registrar shall register any alteration of the memorandum with respect to the objects of the company and certify the registration within a period of 30 days from the date of filing of the special resolution in accordance with clause (*a*) of sub-section (*6*) of this section [Section 13(9)].

Alteration of the Memorandum to Be Void

In the case of a company limited by guarantee and not having a share capital, any alteration of the memorandum giving any person otherwise than as a member a right to participate in the divisible profits of the company, shall be void [Section 13(11)].

Articles of Association

A company is an incorporated body so there ought to be some rules and regulations formed for the management of its (internal) affairs and conduct of its business as well as the relation between the members and the company. Moreover, for smooth running of a company's business the rights and duties of its members and the company are to be well defined. 'Articles of Association', known as articles of incorporation in the US and Canada, is a document that contains the purpose of the company as well as the duties and responsibilities of its members, defined and recorded clearly. This is why articles are essential. It is an important document which needs to be filed with the Registrar of Companies, part of documentation towards the incorporation of the company.

Articles of association: A document that outlines the responsibilities of the directors, the kind of business to be undertaken, and the means by which the shareholders exert control over the board of directors.

Defining Articles

'Articles' means the articles of association of a company as originally framed, or as altered from time to time in pursuance of any previous companies law or of this Act [Section 2(5)].

'Articles' basically is a document of contract between a shareholder and the company and among shareholders themselves that they shall abide by the official procedure of internal management of the company as specified in the document (articles). Articles contain the rules and regulations for the internal administration of the company hence govern the conduct of a company's business by specifying the rights and duties of its members and directors. In practical terms, articles outline the responsibilities of the directors, the kind of business to be undertaken, and the means by which the shareholders exert control over the board of directors.

Contents of Articles

The items usually covered by the articles of a company include:

1. Powers, duties, rights, and liabilities of directors
2. Powers, duties, rights, and liabilities of members
3. Rules for meetings of the company
4. Dividends and reserves
5. Borrowing powers of the company
6. Share warrants
7. Alteration of capital
8. Calls on shares
9. Transfer and transmission of shares
10. Forfeiture of shares
11. Surrender of shares
12. Voting powers of members
13. Accounts and audit
14. Winding-up, etc.

The articles must be printed, divided into paragraphs, and numbered consecutively and must be signed by each subscriber to the Memorandum who shall add their address, description, and occupation in presence of at least one witness who must attest the signatures and likewise add his address, description, and occupation. The Articles of Association of the company, when registered, bind the company and its members to the same extent as if it was signed by the company and by each member.

The provisions of the articles must not be in conflict with the provisions of the memorandum. In case such a conflict arises, the memorandum will prevail.

Model Form of Articles

Normally, every company drafts its own articles. However, a company may adopt any one of the model forms of articles, with or without modifications, specified in Tables *F*, G, *H*, *I*, and *J* of Schedule I to the Act, as applicable. For example, if a company limited by shares does not have its own articles, the model set of 91 articles given in Table *F* can be adopted. Similarly, Table *G* is applicable to the companies limited by guarantee and having a share capital, Table *H* gives model form of articles for a company limited by guarantee and not having share capital, and Table *I* is applicable to an unlimited company and having a share capital, whereas Table *J* shall be applicable to an unlimited company and not having share capital.

Alteration of Articles

A company can alter or amend any of the provisions of its articles subject to provisions of the Act and subject to the conditions contained in its memorandum. A company by special resolution at a general meeting of its shareholders can alter its articles provided the said resolution is passed *bona fide* for the benefit of the company.

In this behalf, the Companies Act, 2013, provides as under:

Subject to the provisions of this Act and the conditions contained in its memorandum, if any, a company may, by a special resolution, alter its articles including alterations having the effect of conversion of

1. a private company into a public company; or
2. a public company into a private company.

However, where a company being a private company alters its articles in such a manner that they no longer include the restrictions and limitations which are required to be included in the articles of a private company under this Act, the company shall, as from the date of such alteration, cease to be a private company.

Any alteration having the effect of conversion of a public company into a private company shall not be valid unless it is approved by the Central Government [Section 14(1)].

Thus, an alteration of articles can be effected by a 3/4th majority of the shareholders but can be challenged on the ground that the alteration was not in the interest of the company. Furthermore, such alteration should not have the effect of converting a public company into a private company and vice versa unless the same has been approved by the Central Government.

Moreover, the 2013 Act introduces the entrenchment provisions in respect of the articles of association of a company. An entrenchment provision enables a company to follow a more restrictive procedure than passing merely a special resolution for altering a specific clause of articles of association. However, a private company can include entrenchment provisions only if agreed by all its members or, in case of a public company, if a special resolution is passed [Section 5].

Doctrine of Constructive Notice

Both, the memorandum and the articles, after being registered with the RoC, assume the character of public documents hence are accessible by any member of the public by paying the requisite fees [Section 399].

> **Doctrine of constructive notice:** A legal fiction that attributes notice of something to a person or entity, even though actual notice did not exist; a presumption that operates in favour of the company against the outsider.

Therefore, notice about the contents of these principal documents is said to be within the knowledge of both members and non-members of the company. Such notice is a deemed notice in case of members and a constructive notice in case of non-members. Thus, every person dealing with the company is deemed to have knowledge of the contents of the memorandum and the articles of the company. An outsider dealing with the company is presumed to have read the contents of the registered documents of the company. The further presumption is that he has not only read the documents but has also understood them fully in proper sense. This is known as the doctrine or rule of constructive notice. Accordingly, maxim of constructive notice is a presumption operating in favour of the company against the outsider. It prevents the outsider from alleging that he did not know that the constitution of the company rendered a particular act or a particular delegation of authority *ultra vires*. Thus, the doctrine (of *ultra vires*) arises from the doctrine of constructive notice, i.e., it works only in conjunction with the latter.

Doctrine of Indoor Management

The doctrine of indoor management or internal management of company's affairs is an exception to the rule of constructive notice, described above, and imposes an important limitation on it. According to this doctrine, 'persons dealing with the company are entitled to presume that internal requirements prescribed in the memorandum and articles have been properly observed'. The principle of indoor management is one of justice, equity, and good conscience and has emerged out of the concept of agency. The doctrine is partly dictated by practical necessity—persons contracting with a company are not expected to spend their time checking that any required resolution has properly been passed, that meetings have been duly convened by directors whose appointments have been duly made. They can presume that all that is being done regularly and in keeping with the memorandum and articles in view. Thus, the doctrine of management operates in favour of stakeholders against the company should there be any violation of the memorandum and/or articles.

Implications of the Doctrine of Indoor Management: Recent Decisions

The Indian courts of law have been applying the doctrine of indoor management frequently and interpreting it according to the cases in hand. The objective being the same, i.e., to protect the third party transacting with the company in good faith and being unaware of the complex internal management of the company.

In *Monark Enterprises vs Kishan Tulpule and Ors*[1], the Company Law Board (now NCLT) held.

'That the validity of the impugned (doubtful) transaction was not affected even if no resolution for entering into it was actually passed by the board of the company as the company had entered into and adopted the transaction throughout and implemented it after receiving consideration thereof. The doctrine of indoor management protected the transferee and the transferor. There was nothing to show that the transferee was aware of the alleged infirmity in respect of the resolution.'

In *Kirlampudi Sugar Mills Ltd vs G. Venkata Rao*[2], the Madras High Court averred:

'It is pertinent to note that the making of entries or maintenance of account books by the company predominantly relate to indoor management or the internal management of the affairs of the company with which a creditor is not concerned and the creditor will not have any control over the maintenance of the accounts and hence on that ground a creditor of the company cannot be non-suited. The company will be in the custody of all the records and a third

[1] AIR 1992 (2) Bom CR 406
[2] AIR 2003 (2) ALT 550

party creditor cannot be expected to know about the several internal affairs relating to the indoor management of the company as such, and hence the respondent or plaintiff or third party creditor cannot be expected to produce such a relevant material which would be in the custody of the opposite party and, hence, in such a case, non-production of such records by the company should be taken serious note of and this was rightly done by the trial court.'

Exceptions to the doctrine of indoor management

The doctrine of indoor management is subject to the following exceptions.

Knowledge of irregularity If a person, dealing with a company, has actual or constructive notice of the irregularity as regards internal management, he cannot seek benefit under the doctrine. He may, in some cases, be himself a part of the internal procedure.

Negligence The protection under the doctrine is also not available when the circumstances surrounding the contract are so suspicious as to warrant inquiry, and the outsider dealing with the company does not make proper inquiry.

Forgery The doctrine does not apply where a person relies upon a document that turns out to be forged since nothing can validate forgery. A company can never be held bound for forgeries committed by its officers.

Acts outside the scope of apparent authority If an officer of a company enters into a contract with a third party and if the act of the officer is beyond the scope of his authority, the company is not bound. The plaintiff can sue the company only if the power to act has in fact been delegated to the officer with whom he had entered into the contract.

Thus, the doctrine of indoor management seeks to protect the interest of the shareholders who are in a minority, or who remain in dark about whether the working of the internal affairs of the company are being carried out in accordance with the memorandum and articles. It is important to note that the doctrine of constructive notice can be invoked by the company and hence does not operate against the latter. It operates against the person who has failed to inquire but does not function in his favour. But the doctrine of 'indoor management' can be invoked by the person dealing with the company and cannot be invoked by the company.

Share Capital and Debentures: Introduction

Share capital: The funds raised by the company by selling its stock to a number of persons for cash or other considerations.

Share capital, another term for capital of a company, represents the funds raised by a company by selling its stock to a number of persons (shareholders) for cash or other considerations. That is, the share capital in relation to a company limited by shares is the aggregate sum of money divided into a specified number of shares, each having a fixed value. In the strict sense, as used in accounting, the share capital comprises the nominal values of all the shares issued i.e., the sum of their par values, as printed on the share certificates. However, in common parlance, the share capital is the total of the aforementioned nominal equity that a company raises in exchange for issuing an ownership interest therein and the premium collected thereon, if any. Sometimes shares are allocated in exchange for non-cash consideration, e.g. in case of mergers and acquisitions. For instance, company *A* acquires company *B* for shares; here the share capital is increased to the par value of the new shares, and the merger reserve is increased to the balance of the price of the company. A company may not always depend upon the equity capital to cater to its financial needs; it has to resort to borrowings to raise funds. The usual means of borrowing, provided authorised by the memorandum or articles, include debts from banks or financial institutions, public deposits, and debentures or bonds. A debenture in this behalf is a medium to long-term debt instrument used by large companies to borrow money.

Shares

Share: A fractional part of the share capital of the company.

A share is a fractional part of the share capital of a company. It signifies the interest of its possessor (shareholder) in the company measured by a sum of money. According to Section 2(84), 'share' means a share in the share capital of a company and includes stock. Accordingly, for practical purposes, a share is a right to participate in the profits made by the company so long as the latter is a going concern and declares dividends and in the assets of the company in the event of its being wound up. Every share in a company having a share capital shall be distinguished by its distinctive number. However, this is not applicable in respect of shares held by a person whose name is entered as holder of beneficial interest in such shares in the records of a depository (Section 45). In India, a share has been regarded as 'goods' within the meaning of the Sale of Goods Act under Section 2(7), which clearly states, 'Goods means any kind of movable property other than actionable claims and money, and includes stock and shares.'

Kinds of Shares

In accordance with Section 43 of the Companies Act, 2013, the share capital of a company limited by shares shall be of two kinds, namely equity share capital and preference share capital.

Equity share capital

Equity share capital with reference to any company limited by shares means all the share capital which is not preference share capital. Equity shareholders are the virtual owners of a company. Equity shares may be sub-classified as:

1. with voting rights; or
2. with differential rights as regards payment of dividend, voting or otherwise in accordance with such rules as may be prescribed by the statute.

Shares with differential rights, however, cannot exceed 25 percent of the total issued share capital.

Preference share capital

Preference share capital with reference to any company limited by shares, means that part of the issued share capital of the company which carries or would carry a preferential right with respect to

1. Payment of dividend;
2. Repayment of capital, in case of winding up of the company.

Thus, unlike equity shareholders, preference shareholders enjoy the preferential or superior rights as regards payment of dividend as well as repayment of the paid up capital. Depending upon the rights conferred by these shares, following are the major types of preference shares:

1. Cumulative or non-cumulative preference shares;
2. Redeemable or Irredeemable preference shares;
3. Participating or non-participating preference shares; and
4. Convertible or non-convertible preference shares.

A brief accounts of these are as follows:

1. Cumulative or non-cumulative preference shares
When unpaid dividends on preference shares due to inadequate profits are treated as arrears and are carried forward to subsequent years, then such preference shares are known as cumulative preference shares. It means unpaid dividend on such shares is accumulated till it is paid off in full. Non-cumulative preference shares on the other hand are ones which are entitled to dividend at a fixed rate out of the profits of current year only. They do not carry the right to receive arrears of dividend. If a company fails to pay dividend in a particular year then that need not to be paid out of future profits.

2. Redeemable and non-redeemable preference shares As the term indicates, those preference shares, which can be redeemed or repaid after the expiration of a fixed period or after giving the prescribed notice as desired by the company, are known as redeemable preference shares. Terms of redemption are, however, announced at the time of issue of such shares. Non-redeemable preference shares, on the other hand, are those which cannot be redeemed during the life time of the company. The amount of such shares is paid at the time of liquidation of the company.

3. Participating and non-participating preference shares Those preference shares which have a right to participate in any surplus profit of the company along with equity shareholders, in addition to the fixed rate of their dividend, are called participating preference shares. Likewise, in case of winding up, if after paying back both, the preference and equity shareholders there is any surplus left, the participating shareholders are entitled to share the surplus. On the other hand, preference shares, which have no right to participate on the surplus profit or in any surplus on liquidation of the company, are called non-participating preference shares.

4. Convertible and non-convertible preference shares Those preference shares which can be converted into equity shares at the option of their holders after a fixed period according to the terms and conditions of their issue, are known as convertible preference shares. Contrarily, preference shares, which are not convertible into equity shares, are called non-convertible preference shares.

Certificate of Shares

Certificate of shares is an official document issued under the common seal of the company, specifying the number of shares held by any person. This document is the prima facie evidence of the title of the person to such shares.

Share Capital: Some Terminologies

Authorised Share Capital

Authorised share capital: The total share capital, a company is allowed to issue.

Also referred to as nominal capital or at times, as registered capital, authorised capital is the total of the share capital which a concerned company is allowed (authorised) to issue. It is stated in the memorandum of a company and indicates the upper boundary for the actually issued share capital.

Authorised Capital = Issued Capital + Unissued Capital

Issued Capital

Issued capital: Aggregate face value of the company's shares offered for subscription by the general public or by a private placement, in case of a private ltd. company.

Issued capital is the aggregate face (nominal) value of the company's shares offered for subscription by the general public or by a private placement, in case of a private limited company. This may be less or equal to the authorised capital. The issued capital can be subdivided in another way, examining whether it has been paid for by investors:

Subscribed Capital

It is the substantial portion of the issued capital, which has been subscribed for by all the investors including the public. This may be less than the issued share capital as there may be capital for which no applications have been received yet i.e. 'unsubscribed capital'.

Subscribed capital: Substantial portion of the issued capital, which has been subscribed for by all the investors including the public.

Called-up Capital

It is the total amount of issued capital for which the shareholders are required to pay. This may be less than the subscribed capital as the company may ask shareholders to pay by installments.

Paid-up Capital

Paid-up capital: The amount of share capital paid by the shareholders in aggregate.

It is the amount of share capital paid by the shareholders in aggregate that is with the application (known as application money) and/or subsequently by way of allotment money and call money. This may be less than the called up capital as payments may be outstanding i.e. 'calls-in-arrears'. The 'calls-in-arrears' is called the unpaid capital.

ESOP

Employee stock ownership plan (ESOP): An employee-owner scheme that provides a company's workforce with an ownership interest in the company.

ESOP (Employee Stock Ownership Plan) is an employee-owner scheme that provides a company's workforce with an ownership interest in the company. Under these plans, the employer gives certain stocks of the company to the employee for negligible or less costs which remain in the ESOP trust fund, until the options vests and the employee exercises them or the employee leaves or retires from the company or institution. These plans are aimed at improving the performance of the company and increasing the value of the shares by involving stock holders, who are also the employees, in the working of the company. The ESOPs help in minimizing problems related to incentives.

Sweat Equity Shares

Sweat equity shares are equity shares issued by a company to its directors or employees at a discount, or for consideration other than cash, for providing

Sweat equity shares: Equity shares issued by a company to its directors or employees at a discount, or for consideration other than cash, for providing their know-how or making available rights in the nature of IPRs or value addition to the company.

their know-how or making available rights in the nature of intellectual property rights (IPRs) or value additions to the company [Section 2(88)].

A company may issue sweat equity shares in respect of a class of shares already issued if these conditions are met:

1. The issue of such shares is authorised by a special resolution passed by the company in a general meeting;
2. The resolution specifies the number of shares, the current market price, consideration, if any, and the class/es of directors or employees to whom such equity shares are to be issued; and
3. Where the equity shares of the company are listed on a recognised stock exchange, the sweat equity shares are issued in accordance with the regulations made by the Securities and Exchange Board in this behalf and if they are not so listed, the sweat equity shares are issued in accordance with such rules as may be prescribed [Section 54(1)].

The rights, limitations, restrictions and provisions as are for the time being applicable to equity shares shall be applicable to the sweat equity shares and the holder of such shares shall rank *pari passu* (equal in all respects) with other equity shareholders [Section 54(2)].

Right Issue

Right issue: A preferential subscription right that entitles a company's existing security holders to buy additional securities directly from the company in proportion to their existing holdings, within a fixed time period.

A right issue is a preferential subscription right that entitles a company's existing security holders to buy additional securities directly from the company in proportion to their existing holdings, within a fixed time period. In a rights offering, the subscription price at which each security may be purchased in generally at a discount to the current market price. Rights are often transferable, allowing the holder to sell them on the open market. When a company proposes to increase the share capital by issue of equity, convertible debentures (fully or partly), convertible preference shares to its existing equity shareholders, then companies (including private limited companies) have to comply with the new procedures laid out under Section 62 of the Companies Act, 2013, given below:

1. Where at any time, a company having a share capital proposes to increase its subscribed capital by the issue of further shares; such shares shall be offered—
   (a) to person who at the date of the offer are holders of equity shares of the company in proportion to the paid-up shares capital on those shares, by sending a letter of offer subject to following conditions, namely:—
      (i) the offer shall be made by a notice specifying the number of shares offered and limiting a time not less than fifteen days and not exceeding thirty days from the date of the offer within which the offer, if not accepted shall be deemed to have been declined;
      (ii) unless the article of the company otherwise provide, the offer shall be deemed to include a right exercisable by the person concerned to renounce the shares offered to him or any of them in favour of any other person and the notice shall contain a statement of this right;
      (iii) after the expiry of the time specified in the notice or receipt of earlier intimation from the person to whom the notice is given that he declines to accept the shares offered, the Board of Directors may dispose of them in such manner which is not disadvantageous to the shareholders and the company;
   (b) to employees under a scheme of employees' stock option by a special resolution passed by the company and subject to such conditions as may be prescribed; or
   (c) to any persons, if it is authorised by a special resolution, either for cash or for a consideration other than cash, if the price of such shares is determined by the valuation report of a registered valuer.

2. The notice of letter of offer shall be dispatched through the registered post or speed post or an electronic mode or courier or any other mode having proof of delivery to all the existing shareholders at least three days before opening of the issue.
3. These conditions shall not apply to the increase of the subscribed capital of a company caused by the exercise of an option as a term attached to the debentures issued or loan raised by the company to convert such debentures or loan into share in the company. However, the terms of issue of such debentures or loans containing such an option to convert should have been approved before the issue of such debentures or raising of a loan by a special resolution passed by the company in general meeting.
4. Where any debentures have been issued, or a loan has been obtained from any Government by a company, and if that Government considers it necessary in the public interest so to do, it may, by order, direct that such debentures or loans or any part thereof shall be converted into shares in the company on such terms and conditions that appear to the Government to be reasonable in the circumstances of the case even if terms of the issue of such debentures or the raising of such loans do not include a term for providing for an option for such conversion.
5. In determining the terms and conditions of conversion, the Government shall have due regard to the financial position of the company, the terms of issue of debentures or loans, as the case may be, the rate of interest payable on such debentures or loans and such other matters as it may consider necessary.
6. Where the Government has directed that any debentures or loan or any part thereof shall be converted into shares in a company and where no appeal has been preferred to the Tribunal or where such appeal has been dismissed, the memorandum of such company shall, where such order has the effect of increasing the authorised share capital of the company, stand altered and the authorised share capital of such company shall stand increased by an amount equal to the amount of the value of shares which such debentures or loans or part thereof have been converted into.

Bonus Shares

Bonus shares are additional shares given to the current shareholders without any additional cost in proportion to their holdings. These are company's accumulated earnings which are not given out in lieu of dividends, but are converted into free shares.

Bonus shares: Additional shares given to current shareholders without any additional cost in proportion to their holdings.

A company may issue fully paid-up bonus shares to its members, in any manner whatsoever, out of

1. Its free reserves
2. The security premium account
3. The capital redemption reserve account.

However, bonus shares cannot be issued by capitalizing reserves created by revaluation of assets [Section 63(1)].

The following conditions must be satisfied before issuing bonus shares:

1. The bonus issue must be authorised by the articles of the company.
2. The bonus issue must be authorised by the shareholders in the general meeting on the recommendation of the Board of Directors of the company.
3. The company must not have defaulted in payment of interest or principal in respect of fixed deposits or any other debt securities issued by it.
4. The company must not have defaulted in respect of the payment of statutory dues of the employees, such as, contribution to provident fund, gratuity, bonus, etc.
5. The company must have made partly paid-up shares, if any outstanding on the date of allotment, fully paid-up [Section 63(2)].

The basic principle behind bonus shares is that the total number of shares increases with a constant ratio of number of shares held to the number of shares outstanding. For instance, if Investor *A* holds 200 shares of a company and a company declares a 4:1 bonus, that is, for every one share, he gets 4 shares for free. That is total 800 shares for free and his total holding will increase to 1000 shares.

Companies issue bonus shares to encourage retail participation and increase their equity base. When price per share of a company is high, it becomes difficult for new investors to buy shares of that particular company. An increase in the number of shares reduces the price per share. But the overall capital remains the same even if bonus shares are declared.

Furthermore, bonus shares cannot be issued in lieu of dividend [Section 63(3)].

Private Placement

Private placement: Way of raising capital not through a public offering, but through a private offering, mostly to a small number of chosen investors.

Private placement (or non-public offering) is a way of raising capital not through a public offering, but through a private placement offer-cum-application to a select group of persons. Investors involved in private placements are usually institutional investors viz. large banks, mutual funds, insurance companies and pension funds. PIPE (Private Investment in Public Equity) deals are one type of private placement. Private placement, thus, is the opposite of a public issue, in which securities are made available for sale in the open market.

The Companies Act, 2013 requires that certain specified conditions are complied with in order to make an offer or invitation of offer by way of private placement through the issue of a private placement offer letter.

Section 42 of the Act, which deals with the private placement, provides as under:

1. A private placement shall be made only to a select group of persons who have been identified by the Board of Directors, called "identified persons". Number of these "identified persons" shall not exceed fifty or such higher number as may be prescribed [excluding the qualified institutional buyers and employees of the company being offered securities under a scheme of employees stock option in terms of provisions of Section 62(1)(b)], in a financial year
2. A company making private placement shall issue private placement offer and application in such form and manner as may be prescribed to identified persons, whose names and addresses are recorded by the company in such manner as may be prescribed.

   However, private placement offer and application shall not carry any right of renunciation at the end of the company concerned.

   Explanation I.—"private placement" means any offer or invitation to subscribe or issue of securities to a select group of persons by a company (other than by way of public offer) through private placement offer-cum-application, which satisfies the conditions specified in this section.

   Explanation II.—"qualified institutional buyer" means the qualified institutional buyer as defined in the Securities and Exchange Board of India (Issue of Capital and Disclosure Requirements) Regulations, 2009, as amended from time to time, made under the Securities and Exchange Board of India Act, 1992.

   Explanation III.—If a company, listed or unlisted, makes an offer to allot or invites subscription, or allots, or enters into an agreement to allot, securities to more than the prescribed number of persons, whether the payment for the securities has been received or not or whether the company intends to list its securities or not on any recognised stock exchange in or outside India, the same shall be deemed to be an offer to the public and shall accordingly be governed by the relevant provisions of the Companies Act, 2013.
3. Every identified person willing to subscribe to the private placement issue shall apply in the private placement and application issued to such person along with subscription money paid either by cheque or demand draft or other banking channel and not by cash.

   However, that a company shall not utilise monies raised through private placement unless allotment is made and the return of allotment is duly filed with the Registrar.
4. No fresh offer or invitation under this section shall be made unless the allotments with respect to any offer or invitation made earlier have been completed or that offer or invitation has been withdrawn or abandoned by the company:

   *However, subject to the maximum number of "identified persons", a company may, at any time, make more than one issue of securities to such class of "identified persons" as may be prescribed.

5. A company making an offer or invitation under this section shall allot its securities within sixty days from the date of receipt of the application money for such securities and if the company is not able to allot the securities within that period, it shall repay the application money to the subscribers within fifteen days from the expiry of sixty days and if the company fails to repay the application money within the aforesaid period, it shall be liable to repay that money with interest at the rate of twelve per cent. per annum from the expiry of the sixtieth day:

   However, monies received on application under this section shall be kept in a separate bank account in a scheduled bank and shall not be utilised for any purpose other than—
   (a) for adjustment against allotment of securities; or
   (b) for the repayment of monies where the company is unable to allot securities.
6. No company issuing securities under this section shall release any public advertisements or utilise any media, marketing or distribution channels or agents to inform the public at large about such an issue.
7. A company making any allotment of securities under this section, shall file with the Registrar a return of allotment within fifteen days from the date of the allotment in such manner as may be prescribed, including a complete list of all allottees, with their full names, addresses, number of securities allotted and such other relevant information as may be prescribed
8. If a company defaults in filing the return of allotment within the period prescribed, the company, its promoters and directors shall be liable to a penalty for each default of one thousand rupees for each day during which such default continues but not exceeding twenty-five lakh rupees.
9. If a company makes an offer or accepts monies in contravention of this section, the company, its promoters and directors shall be liable for a penalty which may extend to the amount raised through the private placement or two crore rupees, whichever is lower, and the company shall also refund all monies with interest to subscribers within a period of thirty days of the order imposing the penalty.
10. Any private placement issue not made in compliance of the relevant provisions of Section 42 [Listed as (1) above] shall be deemed to be a public offer and all the provisions of this Act and the Securities Contracts (Regulation) Act, 1956 and the Securities and Exchange Board of India Act, 1992 shall be applicable.

Buy-back of Securities

Buy-back of securities refers to purchase by a company of its own shares or other specified securities (ESOP, etc.). Buy-back is a very important tool for companies who want to reduce their share capital. Buy-back can be made out by a company out of

Buy-back of securities: Reacquisition of its own shares or other specified securities by a company in order to reduce its share capital in the market.

1. its free reserves;
2. the securities premium account; or
3. the proceeds of the issue of any shares or other specified securities.

However, no buy-back of any kind of shares or other specified securities shall be made out of the proceeds of an earlier issue of the same kind of shares or same kind of other specified securities [Section 68(1)].

Advantages of Buy-back

1. It is an alternative mode of reduction in capital without requiring approval of the Court/NCLT.
2. It improves the earnings per share.
3. It improves return on the capital, return on net worth and to enhance the long-term shareholders value.
4. It provides an additional exit route to shareholders when shares are undervalued or thinly traded.
5. It enhances consolidation of stake in the company.
6. It prevents unwelcome takeover bids.

Rules Governing Buy-back

Different rules governing buy-back of securities may be summarized as under:

Preliminary conditions as regards buy-back In accordance with Section 68(2) for a buy-back to be legitimate and justifiable, the under-mentioned conditions must be fulfilled:

1. It must be authorized by its articles;
2. A special resolution must have been passed at a general meeting of the company authorizing the buy-back, but the same is not required when:
   (a) the buy-back is 10% or less of the total paid-up equity capital and free reserves of the company; and
   (b) such buy-back has been authorized by the Board by means of a resolution passed at its meeting;
3. The buy-back must be twenty-five per cent or less of the aggregate of the paid-up capital and free reserves of the company. However, in case of equity shares, the same shall be taken as 25% of the total paid up equity capital only;
4. Debt equity ratio should be 2:1

   Where: Debt is the aggregate of secured and unsecured debts owed by the company after buy-back; and

   Equity is the aggregate of the paid-up capital and its free reserves.
5. All the shares or other specified securities for buy-back are fully paid-up;
6. If shares or securities are listed, buy-back will be in accordance with the regulations made by the Securities and Exchange Board in this behalf;
7. The buy-back in respect of unlisted shares or other specified securities is in accordance with Share Capital and Debentures Rules, 2014; and
8. No offer of buy-back shall be made within a period of one year from the date of the closure of the preceding offer of buy-back, if any.

Solvency declaration A company shall, before making such buy-back, file with the Registrar and the Securities and Exchange Board, a declaration of solvency signed by at least two directors of the company, one of whom shall be the managing director, if any, in such form as may be prescribed and verified by an affidavit to the effect that the Board of Directors of the company have made a full inquiry into the affairs of the company as a result of which they have formed an opinion that it is capable of meeting its liabilities and will not be rendered insolvent within a period of one year from the date of declaration adopted by the Board [Section 68(6)].

However, the above declaration of solvency shall not be filed with the Sebi by a company whose shares are not listed on any recognised stock exchange.

Extinguishment of certificate A company shall extinguish and physically destroy the shares or securities so bought back within seven days of the last date of completion of buy-back [Section 68(7)].

No further issue till 6 months Where a company completes a buy-back of its shares or other specified securities, it shall not make a further issue of the same kind of shares or other securities including allotment of new shares or other specified securities within a period of six months except by way of:

1. a bonus issue or
2. in the discharge of subsisting obligations such as conversion of warrants, stock option schemes, sweat equity or conversion of preference shares or debentures into equity shares [Section 68(8)].

Register of buy-back to be maintained A company shall maintain a register of the shares or securities so bought, the consideration paid for the shares or securities bought back, the date of cancellation of shares or securities, the date of extinguishing and physically destroying the shares or securities. The register of shares or securities bought back shall be maintained at the registered office of the company and shall be kept in the custody of the secretary of the company or any other person authorized by the board in this behalf. The entries in the register shall be authenticated by the secretary of the company or by any other person authorized by the Board for the purpose [Section 68(9)].

Return of buy-back and a declaration A company shall, after the completion of the buy-back under this section, file with the Registrar and the Securities and Exchange Board a return relating to the buy-back within thirty days of such completion [Section 68(10)].

Punishment for any default If a company makes any default in complying with the provisions of this section, the company shall be punishable with fine which shall not be less than one lakh rupees but which may extend to three lakh rupees and every officer of the company who is in default shall be punishable with imprisonment for a term which may extend to three years or with fine which shall not be less than one lakh rupees but which may extend to three lakh rupees, or with both [Section 68(11)].

Restriction on buy-back No company shall directly or indirectly purchase its own shares or other specified securities—

1. through any subsidiary company including its own subsidiary companies;
2. through any investment company or group of investment companies; or
3. if a default, is made by the company, in the repayment of deposits accepted either before or after the commencement of this Act, interest payment thereon, redemption of debentures or preference shares or payment of dividend to any shareholder, or repayment of any term loan or interest payable thereon to any financial institution or banking company. Provided that the buy-back is not prohibited, if the default is remedied and a period of three years has lapsed after such default ceased to subsist [Section 70(1)].

No buy-back if No company shall, directly or indirectly, purchase its own shares or other specified securities in case such company has not complied with the provisions of:

1. **Section 92:** Annual Return
2. **Section 123:** Declaration and Payment of Dividend
3. **Section 127:** Failure to pay Dividend
4. **Section 129:** Failure to give True and Fair Statement [Section 70(2)]

Reduction of Share Capital

Subject to confirmation by the Tribunal on an application by the company, a company limited by shares or limited by guarantee and having a share capital may, by a special resolution, reduce the share capital in any manner, and in particular, may-

(a) extinguish or reduce the liability on any of its shares in respect of the share capital not paid-up; or

(b) either with or without extinguishing or reducing liability on any of its shares, -

(i) cancel any paid-up share capital which is lost or is unrepresented by available assets; or

(ii) pay off any paid-up share capital which is in excess of the wants of the company, alter its memorandum by reducing the amount of its share capital and of its shares accordingly [Section 66(1)]

However, no such reduction shall be made if the company is in arrears in the repayment of any deposits accepted by it, either before or after the commencement of this Act, or the interest payable thereon.

The Tribunal shall give notice of every application made to it under Section 66(1) to the Central Government, Registrar of Companies and to the Securities and Exchange Board, in the case of listed companies, and the creditors of the company and shall take into consideration the representations, if any, made to it by that Government, Registrar, the Securities and Exchange Board and the creditors within a period of three months from the date of receipt of the notice.

However, where no representation has been received from the Central Government, Registrar, the Securities and Exchange Board or the creditors within the said period, it shall be presumed that they have no objection to the reduction [Section 66(2)].

The Tribunal may, if it is satisfied that the debt or claim of every creditor of the company has been discharged or determined or has been secured or his consent is obtained, make an order confirming the reduction of share capital on such terms and conditions as it deems fit.

However, no application for reduction of share capital shall be sanctioned by the Tribunal unless the accounting treatment, proposed by the company for such reduction is in conformity with the accounting standards specified in section 133 or any other provision of this Act and a certificate to that effect by the company's auditor has been filed with the Tribunal [Section 66(3)].

The order of confirmation of the reduction of share capital by the Tribunal under sub-section (3) shall be published by the company in such manner as the Tribunal may direct [Section 66(4)].

If any officer of the company—

1. knowingly conceals the name of any creditor entitled to object to the reduction;
2. knowingly misrepresents the nature or amount of the debt or claim of any creditor; or

3. abets or is privy to any such concealment or misrepresentation as aforesaid, he shall be liable under Section 447 [Section 66(10)].

If a company fails to comply with the provisions of sub-section (4), it shall be punishable with fine which shall not be less than five lakh rupees but which may extend to twenty-five lakh rupees [Section 66(11)].

Debentures

Debenture: An instrument of credit executed by a company under its common seal acknowledging indebtedness to some person(s) to secure the sum advanced by the latter.

The term 'debenture' is derived from the Latin word *'debere'*, which translates to 'to borrow' in English. Since a company finds it hard to borrow large sums of money from a single lender, it opts to split the required funds into several units, each of being an even value and offered to public in terms of debentures. As per Section 2(30) of the Companies Act, 2013, 'Debenture includes debenture stock, bonds, and any other securities of a company whether constituting a charge on the assets of the company or not.' Accordingly, a debenture is a security issued by a company in whatever form it is offered. However, the following shall not be treated as debenture:

(i) The instruments referred to in Chapter III-D of the RBI Act, 1934; and

(ii) Such other instrument, as may be prescribed by the Central Government in consultation with the RBI, issued by a company.

Palmer described debenture as 'an instrument under seal evidencing a debt, the essence of it being the admission of indebtedness.' Thus, a debenture is an instrument of credit executed by a company under its common seal acknowledging indebtedness to some person or persons to secure the sum advanced. A public limited company is allowed to raise debt or loan through debentures after getting the certificate of commencement of business if permitted by its memorandum or articles. Like shares, they are issued to the public at par, at a premium or at a discount. Debentures are usually secured by the company by a fixed or floating charge against its fixed assets. Debentureholders are creditors of the company. They have no voting rights but their claims rank prior to preference shareholders and equity shareholders. Their exact rights depend upon the nature of debentures they hold.

Kinds of Debentures

Debentures can be of following types:

1. Redeemable and irredeemable debentures On the basis of redeemability, debentures may either be redeemable or irredeemable. Redeemable debentures are those which can be redeemed or paid back at the end of a specified period mentioned on the debentures or within a specified period at the option of the company by giving notice to the debenture holders or by installments as per the terms of issue. Conversely, irredeemable debentures are those which are repayable at any time by the company during its existence. No date of redemption is specified and the debenture holders cannot claim their redemption. However, they become due for redemption if the company fails to pay interest on such debentures or on winding up of the company. They are also called perpetual debentures.

2. Secured and unsecured debentures From the point of view of security, debentures may either be secured or unsecured. Secured or mortgaged debentures carry either a fixed charge on the particular asset of the company or floating charge on all the assets of the company. Unsecured debentures, on the other hand, have no such charge on the assets of the company. They are also known as ordinary or naked debentures.

3. Registered and bearer debentures Registered debentures are registered with the company. Name, address and particulars of holdings of every debenture holders are recorded on the debenture certificate and in the books of the company. At the time of transfer, a regular transfer deed duly stamped and properly executed is required. Interest is paid only to the registered debenture holders. Bearer debentures, on the other hand, are transferred by mere delivery without any notice to the company. The company keeps no record for such debentures. Debentures-coupons are attached with the debentures-certificate and interest can be claimed by the coupon-holder.

4. Convertible and non-convertible debentures Convertible debentures are those which can be converted by the holders of such debentures into equity shares or preference shares. Contrarily, non-convertible debentures cannot be converted into shares. A company can also issue partially convertible debentures under which only a part of the debenture amount can be converted into equity shares.

Membership in a Company

Member: One of the company's owners whose name has been entered on the register of members.

Membership (in context of a company) implies the state of being a member in joint stock company. A member is usually one of the company's owners whose name has been entered on the register of members. Shareholders who join a firm at its inception are called 'founder members'. Company members share a common purpose and unite in order to focus their various talents and organize their collectively available skills or resources to achieve specific, declared goals. The rules governing membership of a company are normally set out in the company's 'Articles'.

Definition of a Member

'Member', in relation to a company, means

1. The subscriber to the memorandum of the company, who shall be deemed to have agreed to become member of the company, and on its registration, shall be entered as member in its register of members;
2. Every other person who agrees in writing to become a member of the company and whose name is entered in the register of members of the company; and
3. Every person holding shares of the company and whose name is entered as a beneficial owner in the records of a depository [Section 2(55)].

Who Can Become a Member?

Subject to the provisions of memorandum and articles, any person who is competent to contract can become a member of a company. Thus, every person who has attained the age of majority; who is of sound mind; and who is not otherwise disqualified from contracting by any law to which he is subject is competent to acquire membership in company. The position of certain persons in this behalf can be discussed as under:

1. **Minor:** An agreement with a minor is void *ab initio*. Accordingly, a minor cannot acquire membership or become shareholder in a company in normal course. In case a company allots shares to a minor and thereby enters his name in the Register of members in ignorance of fact of minority, the company shall be at liberty to repudiate the allotment and remove his name from the register as soon as it becomes aware of his minor character. But if the company fails to do so, the minor does not incur any liability (during his minority) as held in *Fazulbhoy Jaffar vs the Credit Bank of India*[3]. A minor, however, can become member in respect of fully paid shares if he acquires the same by way of transfer or transmission and his name can be validly entered on the Register of members [*Devan Singh vs Minerva Films Ltd.*[4]]
2. **Foreigner:** The law of contract does not forbid a foreigner to enter into a contract. Thus, a foreigner can invest in shares in a company and thereby acquire membership therein. This is, however, subject to regulations of FEMA.
3. **Company:** A company being a juristic person with self-regulating existence can acquire membership of another company by investing in the latter's shares. However, to do so, a company must be duly authorised by its memorandum. Notwithstanding, a subsidiary company cannot hold shares in its holding company [Section 19].
4. **Cooperative Society:** A registered cooperative society being treated as a 'person' having separate legal entity distinct from its member can become member in a company by investing in its shares.
5. **Conventional Partnership Firm:** A conventional partnership firm does not enjoy separate legal existence from the partners and treated as an unincorporated body. Thus, it is not capable to acquire membership in a company by any mode as it cannot be registered as a member in the 'Register of members' of a company. Partners of a firm, however, free to purchase shares in a company, individually or jointly. However,

[3] AIR 1914 Bom. 128
[4] AIR 1956 Punj. 106

a partnership firm may become member of a 'company with charitable objects' [Section 8(3)].

6. **Limited Liability Partnership Firm:** An LLP firm being a body-corporate in the eyes of law can sue and be sued and therefore competent to enter into a contract. Accordingly an LLP firm can purchase shares of a company and thereby become its member.
7. **Trade Union:** Like an LLP, a registered trade union can also invest in the shares of a company and thereby acquire membership therein [Section 3 of Trade Unions Act, 1926].

Modes of Acquiring Membership in a Company

A person can acquire membership in a company through any one of the following modes.

1. **By Subscribing to the Memorandum:** The subscribers of the memorandum of a company are deemed to have agreed to become members of the company, and on its registration are entered as members in its register of members. Thus, the signatories to the memorandum become members of the company, simply by reason of their having signed the memorandum. Neither application form nor allotment of shares is necessary for becoming a member in this case. Even entry in the register is not necessary to confer upon them rights and liability of membership.
2. **By Agreeing to Become a Member:** Agreeing to become a member can happen in any of the following ways:
   (a) By making an application to the company for allotment of shares and adhering to the norms and statutory requirements in this behalf.
   (b) By executing an instrument of transfer as transferee.
   (c) By consenting to the transmission of shares of a deceased member in his/her name. Transmission is different from transfer. It is an involuntary transfer. It takes place by operation of law, to a person who is entitled under the law to succeed to the estate of the deceased or lunatic automatically and does not require an instrument of transfer.

   However, the above provision does not apply to the following:
   (i) a company not having a share capital;
   (ii) a private company; or
   (iii) a company which was a private company before becoming a public company.
3. **By Allotment:** Ordinarily a person becomes a member of the company by holding equity share capital of the company and on his name being entered as beneficial owner in the records of the depository [Section 2(55)].
4. **By Principle of Estoppel:** If a person's name is improperly placed on the register of members and he knows and assents to it, that is, agrees in writing to become member or attends company meetings or/and accepts dividend, he shall be deemed to be a member. Under the principle of estoppel if a person holds himself out being in a position of membership which is not true, he will then be estopped from denying that he is a member.

   It is important to note that such a person whose name has been wrongly entered in the Register of Members, does not become liable as a member unless either he agrees in writing to become a member of the company or he has in fact accepted the position and acted as a member. That is, a person cannot be deemed to have become a member by means of 'estoppel' simply because his name is entered wrongly in the 'Register'.
5. **Nominee in Case of OPC:** In case of 'One Person Company' the nominee whose name is mentioned in the memorandum becomes the member in the event of death of the one and the sole member of the company [Section 4(1)(f)].

Distinction Between Shareholder and Member

The term 'shareholder' imples a person who holds or owns the shares. A 'member', on the other hand, denotes a person whose name appears on the Register of Members. For all practical purposes, however, the words 'shareholder' and 'member' are used interchangeably because in the normal course a shareholder will also be a member and a member will also be a shareholder. But if looked at from a closer angle, we may come across a few exceptional cases where a shareholder may not necessarily be a member and a member may not necessarily be a shareholder.

For instance, companies limited by guarantee or unlimited companies having no share capital will have only members but no shareholders. Contrarily, a holder of a share warrant is a shareholder but not a member as his name is removed from the register of members immediately after the issue of such share warrant. Similarly, a transferee or the legal representative of the deceased may be a shareholder but he may not be member until he gets his name entered in the register of members. On the other hand, the transferor or the deceased person is a member so long as his name is on the register of members whereas he cannot be termed a shareholder.

Register of Members

Every company shall keep and maintain 'register of members' in such form and in such manner as may be prescribed, namely:

(a) register of members indicating separately for each class of equity and preference shares held by each member residing in or outside India;
(b) register of debenture-holders; and
(c) register of any other security holders [Section 88(1)]..

Every register of members maintained under sub-section (1) shall include an index of the names included therein [Section 88(2)].

Moreover, the register and index of beneficial owners maintained by a depository under Section 11 of the Depositories Act, 1996, shall be deemed to be the corresponding register and index for the purpose of this Act [Section 88(3)].

In this behalf, 'Companies (Management and Administration) Rules, 2014' (hereinafter referred as rules) provide as under.

1. Every company limited by shares shall, from the date of its registration, maintain a register of its members in Form No. MGT.1.
2. In the case of a company not having share capital, the register of members shall contain the following particulars, in respect of each member, namely

   (a) Personal detail, namely, (i) Name of the member; (ii) Address (registered office address in case the member is a body corporate); (iii) E-mail address; (iv) Permanent Account Number (PAN) or Corporate Identification Number (CIN); (v) Unique Identification Number, if any; (vi) Father's/Mother's/Spouse's name; (vii) Occupation; (viii) Status; (ix) Nationality; (x) Name of the guardian and the date of birth of the member in case member is a minor, and (xi) Name and address of the nominee;
   (b) Date of becoming member;
   (c) Date of cessation;
   (d) Amount of guarantee, if any;
   (e) Any other interest if any; and
   (f) Instructions, if any, given by the member with regard to sending of notices etc.

However, in the case of existing companies, registered under The Companies Act, 1956, above particulars shall be compiled within six months from the date of commencement of these rules.

Maintenance of Register of Members: Consequences of Non-compliance

If the name of any person is, without sufficient cause, entered in the register of members of a company, or after having been entered in the register, is, without sufficient cause, omitted there from, or if a default is made, or unnecessary delay takes place in entering in the register, the fact of any person having become or ceased to be a member, the person aggrieved, or any member of the company, or the company may appeal in such form as may be prescribed, to the Tribunal, or to a competent court outside India, specified by the Central Government by notification, in respect of foreign members or debenture holders residing outside India, for rectification of the register [Section 59(1)].

The Tribunal may, after hearing the parties to the appeal under sub-section (1) by order, either dismiss the appeal or direct that the transfer or transmission shall be registered by the company within a period of ten days of the receipt of the order or direct rectification of the records of the depository or the register and in the latter case, direct the company to pay damages, if any, sustained by the party aggrieved [Section 59(2)].

However, the above provisions shall not restrict the right of a holder of securities, to transfer such securities and any person acquiring such securities shall be entitled to voting rights unless the voting rights have been suspended by an order of the Tribunal [Section 59(3)].

Where the transfer of securities is in contravention of any of the provisions of the Securities Contracts (Regulation) Act, 1956, the Securities and Exchange Board of India Act, 1992 or this Act or any other law for the time being in force, the Tribunal may, on an application made by the depository, company, depository participant, the holder of the securities or the Securities and Exchange Board, direct any company or a depository to set right the contravention and rectify its register or records concerned [Section 59(4)].

If any default is made in complying with the order of the Tribunal under Section 59(4), the company shall be punishable with fine which shall not be less than one lakh rupees but which may extend to five lakh rupees and every officer of the company who is in default shall be punishable with imprisonment for a term which may extend to one year or with fine which shall not be less than one lakh rupees but which may extend to three lakh rupees, or with both [Section 59(5)].

Rights of Members

In return for investing in a company shareholders or members get a bundle of rights in the company which may vary according to the type of shares acquired. Most companies only have one class of shares (equity shares). Members(equity shareholders) of a company enjoy the following basic rights under the provisions of the Companies Act, 2013.

1. **Right to Obtain Copies of Basic Documents:** Members of a company have the right to obtain copies of 'Memorandum, 'Articles' etc. within seven days of the request and subject to the payment of prescribed fee [Section 17].
2. **Right to Transfer Shares:** Every member of a company shall have a right to transfer his shares subject to the provisions of the Act and the articles [Section 44].
3. **Right to Vote:** Every member of a company limited by shares shall have a right to vote on every resolution placed before the company [Section 47(1)(a)].

   However, his voting rights on a poll shall be in proportion to his share in the paid up equity share capital of the company [Section 47(1)(b)].

   Members can speak at the meeting, vote by show of hands or demand a poll. The Companies Act, 2013 gives right of postal voting for certain fundamental decisions.

   Moreover, a member is also entitled to obtain, on request, minutes of proceedings at general meetings as also to inspect the minute-books [Section 119].
4. **Right to Call Extraordinary Meeting:** Members of a company may also demand from the Board of directors to call extraordinary General Meeting (EGM) for discussing any emergent matter. However, the requisition for an EGM must be signed by such number of members who hold on the date of the requisition, not less than one-tenth of the paid up voting capital [Section 100(2)(a)].

   In case of a company not having a share capital, the requisition for the EGM must be signed by such number of members who hold on the date of the requisition, not less than one-tenth of the total voting power of all the members having on the said date a right to vote [Section 100(2)(b)].
5. **Right to Receive Notice of a General Meeting:** Members of a company are entitled to receive the notice (not less than 21 clear days' of the general meetings specifying the meeting place and time and the agenda of the meeting. They have the right to attend the general meeting in person or through proxy [Section 101].

   Moreover, any member may apply to the Company Law Board (CLB) to call an AGM if the company has defaulted in conducting an AGM.
6. **Right to Appoint Proxy:** Every member of a company (limited by shares) entitled to attend and vote at a meeting of the company shall be entitled to appoint another person as a proxy to attend and vote at the meeting on his behalf [Section 105].

   However, a proxy shall not have the right to speak at such meeting and shall not be entitled to vote except on a poll.

7. **Right to Dividend, Rights Shares and Bonus Shares:** In case of a company limited by shares, every member has a fundamental right to dividend, rights shares, and bonus shares, as the case may be. Members have the right to receive the dividend within 30 days of the declaration [Section 126 read with Section 124].
8. **Right to Obtain Copy of Financial Statements:** Members have a right to obtain copy of financial statements, including consolidated financial statements, audited report and every other document required by law to be annexed or attached to the financial statements, which are to be laid before a company in its general meeting [Section 136].
9. **Right to Appoint Auditor:** Members are entitled to appoint an individual or a firm as an auditor of their company at the first annual general meeting who will hold office from the conclusion of that meeting till the conclusion of its sixth annual general meeting and thereafter till the conclusion of every sixth meeting. Moreover, members will ratify his appointment at every AGM [Section 139(1)].
10. **Right to Appoint and Remove Directors:** Members have the right to appoint directors in general meeting [Section 152(2)]. They also have the right to remove a director, not being a director appointed by the Tribunal under Section 242, before the expiry of his term through passing an ordinary resolution [Section 169].
11. **Right to Inspect Registers:** Members have the right to inspect Register of Members, Register of Debenture-holders, Register of Charges, Register of Investments, Minute Books of general meetings, Proxies lodged for the general meeting, and all returns filed by the company [Section 171].
12. **Right Against Oppression and Mismanagement:** The Companies Act confers rights to members in matters of mismanagement or oppression. Not less than 100 members of the company or not less than one-tenth of the total number of its members, whichever is less, or any member or members holding not less than one-tenth of the issued share capital of the company can apply to the Tribunal for relief in cases of oppression etc [Section 241 read with Section 244].

Liability of Members

A member of a company is subject to certain obligations and liabilities under the Act and the articles, summarized as under:

1. Every member of a company (limited by shares) holding partly paid-up shares becomes liable as contributory to pay, if called upon to do so, towards the assets of the company, should the company goes into liquidation [Section 285(3)(d)].
2. If in the course of the winding up of a company, it appears that any business of the company has been carried on with intent to defraud creditors of the company or any other persons or for any fraudulent purpose, the Tribunal the persons who were knowingly parties to the carrying on of the business in the manner personally responsible, without any limitation of liability, for all or any of the debts or other liabilities of the company [Section 339(1)].
3. In case of a company limited by guarantee, in the event of its being wound up the member may be asked to contribute to the assets of the company such amount as he had undertaken (i.e. to the extent of his guarantee) [Section 285(3)(e)].
4. If it appears to the Tribunal in the course of a winding up (by the Tribunal) that a member of the company has been guilty of any offence in relation to the company, he may be liable to be prosecuted by the liquidator upon the direction to the latter by the Tribunal [Section 342(1)].

Termination of Membership

A person ceases to be a member of a company if his name is removed from the register of members for a valid reason, which often takes place in the following circumstances.

1. When he transfers all his shares to another person and the transfer is registered by the company;
2. When his shares are validly forfeited by the company for non-payment of calls;
3. When he surrenders all his shares to the company and the latter accepts the surrender;
4. When a member dies and his share legal nominee gets his name registered in the Register of members through the process of transmission;

5. When a he is adjudged insolvent and as a consequence either he disclaims all his shares or his shares are transferred to a third party by the Official Assignee who (third party) gets his name registered with the company;
6. When his shares being redeemable preference shares have been redeemed by the company;
7. When he rescinds the contract of membership on the ground of misrepresentation, fraud or a material mistake in the prospectus;
8. When the company purchases his shares under a buy-back scheme under Section 68;
9. In case a company winds up. However, in this case he will be still liable as a contributory and entitled to a share in the surplus, if any.
10. Besides the above cases, the membership in a company also stands terminated in event of being removal of a member by the Central Government. The Central Government may, after consultation with the Chief Justice of India, remove any Member, who—
    (a) has been adjudged an insolvent; or
    (b) has been convicted of an offence which, in the opinion of the Central Government, involves moral turpitude; or
    (c) has become physically or mentally incapable of acting as such President, the Chairperson, or Member; or
    (d) has acquired such financial or other interest as is likely to affect prejudicially his functions as such President, the Chairperson or Member; or
    (e) has so abused his position as to render his continuance in office prejudicial to the public interest:

However, a Member shall not be removed on any of the grounds specified in clauses (b) to (e) without giving him a reasonable opportunity of being heard [Section 417(1)].

Exercises

I. Objective-type Questions

1. Subscription clause is applicable in case of:
   (a) Every limited company
   (b) Every public limited company
   (c) OPC
   (d) Small company

2. Object clause contains:
   (a) Authorised share capital
   (b) Issued share capital
   (c) Subscribed share capital
   (d) All of the above

3. Match the items of List I with those in List II:

List I	List II
(a) Table *F*	(i) Companies limited by guarantee and having share capital
(b) Table *G*	(ii) Companies limited by shares
(c) Table *H*	(iii) Companies limited by guarantee and not having share capital
(d) Table *I*	(iv) Unlimited Company and having share capital
(e) Table *J*	(v) Unlimited company and not having share capital

Answer Codes:

	(a)	(b)	(c)	(d)	(e)
A	(i)	(ii)	(iii)	(iv)	(v)
B	(i)	(ii)	(iv)	(v)	(iii)
C	(ii)	(i)	(iii)	(v)	(iv)
D	(ii)	(i)	(iii)	(iv)	(v)

4. Which of the following statements is true?
   (a) Doctrine of constructive notice arises from the doctrine of *ultra vires*
   (b) Doctrine of constructive notice arises from the doctrine of indoor management
   (c) Doctrine of indoor management arises from the doctrine of constructive notice
   (d) Doctrine of *ultra vires* arises from the doctrine of constructive notice

5. Which of the following can be invoked by the company and hence does not operate against the latter?
   (a) Doctrine of constructive notice
   (b) Doctrine of indoor management
   (c) Doctrine of *ultra vires*
   (d) Both (A) and (B)

6. A company cannot issue bonus shares to its members out of—
   (a) Free reserves
   (b) The security premium account
   (c) The capital redemption reserve account
   (d) The revaluation reserve account

7. Preference shareholders enjoy the preferential or superior rights as regards:
   (a) Payment of dividend
   (b) Repayment of the paid up capital
   (c) Payment of dividend as well as repayment of the paid up capital
   (d) None of the above

8. Which of the following statements are true in respect of the share capital in relation to a company limited by shares?
   (i) It is the aggregate sum of money divided into a specified number of shares each having a fixed value.
   (ii) It comprises the nominal values of all the shares issued i.e., the sum of their par values, as printed on the share certificates.
   (iii) It is the total of the nominal equity that a company raises in exchange for issuing an ownership interest therein and the premium collected thereon, if any.

   Codes:
   (a) Statement (i) is true alone
   (b) Statements (i) and (ii) are true
   (c) Statements (ii) and (iii) are true
   (d) Statement (i), (ii) and (iii) are true

9. __________ debentures are also called perpetual debentures
   (a) Redeemable debentures
   (b) Irredeemable debentures
   (c) Registered debentures
   (d) Secured Debentures

10. Which of the following conditions must be satisfied by a company to issue sweat equity shares?
   (i) A company may issue sweat equity shares in respect of a class of shares already issued
   (ii) Such an issue is authorised by a special resolution passed by the company in a general meeting.
   (iii) Minimum one year has, at the date of such issue, elapsed since the company had commenced its business.
   (iv) Where the equity shares of the company are listed on a recognised stock exchange, the sweat equity shares are issued in accordance with the regulations made by the Securities and Exchange Board in this behalf

   Codes:
   (a) Statements (i) and (ii) alone are true
   (b) Statements (ii) and (iii) alone are true
   (c) Statements (i), (ii) and (iii) alone are true
   (d) All the statements are true

11. 'Member' in relation to a company means:
   (a) The subscriber to the memorandum of the company
   (b) Every other person who agrees in writing to become a member of the company and whose name is entered in the register of members of the company

(c) Every person holding shares of the company and whose name is entered as a beneficial owner in the records of a depository
(d) Any of the above

12. Who among the following cannot become member of a company?
(a) Company
(b) Registered Trade Union
(c) Partnership firm
(d) Minor in respect of fully paid shares

13. The requisition for Extraordinary General Meeting (EGM) must be signed by such number of members, who hold on the date of the requisition, not less than:
(a) Not less than such number of members who hold not less than one-tenth of paid up share capital or represent one-tenth of total voting power, as the case may be
(b) 20% of total paid up voting capital
(c) 25% of total paid up voting capital
(d) 50% of total paid up voting capital

14. To seek relief from oppression and mismanagement of a company what is the minimum number of members required for applying to Tribunal?
(a) Not less than 100 members of the company
(b) In the case of a company having a share capital, not less than one hundred members of the company or not less than one-tenth of the total number of its members, whichever is less, or any member or members holding not less than one-tenth of the issued share capital of the company, subject to the condition that the applicant or applicants has or have paid all calls and other sums due on his or their shares;
(c) In the case of a company not having a share capital, not less than one-fifth of the total number of its membes.
(d) Either (b) or (c) above , although the Tribunal may, on an application made to it in this behalf, waive all or any of the requirements specified therein so as to enable the members to apply under Section 241.

15. 'Proxy' has a right:
(a) To attend the general meeting
(b) To attend and vote at meeting through poll
(c) To attend, speak and vote at meeting through poll
(d) To attend and vote at meeting by show of hands or through poll

II. Review Questions

1. 'The memorandum of association is an unalterable charter of a company.' Comment. Also discuss contents of memorandum.
2. What do you mean by articles of association? Discuss the rules governing alteration of articles.
3. Explain the 'Doctrine of *ultra vires*'.
4. What is a prospectus? List out its contents.
5. Define share capital. Describe the different types of shares which can be issued by a public limited company.
6. Discuss the provisions of the Companies Act, 2013 as regards further issue of shares to existing shareholders.
7. Comment on the following:
(a) Bonus Issue
(b) Sweat Issue of Equity Shares

(c) ESOP
(d) Preliminary conditions as regards Buy-back
(e) Private placement
(f) Reduction of share capital by a company

8. Define 'members' as per the Companies Act? Who may become member of company? Differentiate between a member and a shareholder.

9. Describe the rights and liability of a member.

10. What are the different modes of acquiring membership in a company? Describe also the modes of termination of membership.

11. What is a Register of members? Describe its contents. Discuss also consequence of non-compliance as regards maintain the Register.

Answers to Objective-type Questions

1. (c)	2. (a)	3. (d)	4. (d)	5. (a)
6. (d)	7. (c)	8. (d)	9. (b)	10. (d)
11. (d)	12. (c)	13. (a)	14. (d)	15. (b)

18 Chapter in Review

LEARNING OUTCOMES

LO[1] Memorandum of association
LO[2] Doctrine of *ultra vires*
LO[3] Articles of association
LO[4] Doctrine of constructive notice
LO[5] Doctrine of indoor management
LO[6] Share capital and debentures
LO[7] ESOP
LO[8] Sweat equity shares
LO[9] Right issue
LO[10] Bonus shares
LO[11] Buy-back of securities
LO[12] Membership

KEY TERMS

Memorandum of association: A document that regulates a company's external activities.

Doctrine of *ultra vires*: An act which is beyond the powers of the company and, therefore, void.

Articles of association: A document that outlines the responsibilities of the directors, the kind of business to be undertaken, and the means by which the shareholders exert control over the board of directors.

Doctrine of constructive notice: A legal fiction that attributes notice of something to a person or entity, even though actual notice did not exist; a presumption that operates in favour of the company against the outsiders.

Doctrine of indoor management: A presumption on the part of the stakeholders that the internal requirements with regard to 'articles' and 'memorandum' have been duly complied with.

Share capital: The funds raised by the company by selling its stock to a number of persons for cash or other considerations.

LO[1] Memorandum of association acts as the charter of the company and sets out the (a) name clause, (b) objects clause, (c) registered office clause, (d) liability clause (e) capital clause, and (f) association clause.

LO[2] Any act beyond the scope of the memorandum and not reasonably incidental to the attainment of the object(s) is *ultra vires* the company and therefore unenforceable.

LO[3] On the other hand, articles contain the set of rules for the internal administration of the company. Articles may be altered subject to provisions of the Companies Act.

LO[4] Every person dealing with the company is deemed to have knowledge of the contents of the memorandum and the articles. This is known as 'doctrine of constructive notice' and protects the interest of the company and its functionaries.

LO[5] An exception to 'doctrine of constructive notice' is known as 'doctrine of indoor management' which seeks to safeguard the interest of the stakeholders if company's administration attempts to misuse the former to their vested advantages.

LO[6] The share capital in relation to a company (i.e. one limited by shares) is the nominal value of equity that a company raises in exchange for issuing an ownership interest therein and the premium collected thereon, if any. Sometimes shares are also issued in exchange for non-cash consideration, e.g. in case of mergers and acquisitions. The share capital of a company limited by shares may be composed of both equity or ordinary shares and preference shares. However, equity shareholders are the virtual owners of a company. Preference shareholders, on the other hand, carry a preferential right with respect to payment of dividend as well as repayment of the capital, in case of winding up of the company. Besides share capital, companies also raise the required funds partly through issue of debentures or bonds to have a balanced capital structure.

LO[7] An employee stock ownership plan (ESOP) is an employee-owner program that provides a company's workforce with an ownership interest in the company.

Share: A fractional part of the share capital of the company.

Authorised share capital: The total share capital, a company is allowed to issue.

Issued capital: Aggregate face value of the company's shares offered for subscription by the general public or by a private placement, in case of a private ltd. company.

Subscribed capital: Substantial portion of the issued capital, which has been subscribed for by all the investors including the public.

Paid-up capital: The amount of share capital paid by the shareholders in aggregate.

Employee stock ownership plan (ESOP): An employee-owner scheme that provides a company's workforce with an ownership interest in the company.

Sweat equity shares: Equity shares issued by a company to its directors or employees at a discount, or for consideration other than cash, for providing their know-how or making available rights in the nature of IPRs or value addition to the company.

Right issue: A preferential subscription right that entitles a company's existing security holders to buy additional securities directly from the company in proportion to their existing holdings, within a fixed time period.

Bonus shares: Additional shares given to current shareholders without any additional cost in proportion to their holdings.

Private placement: Way of raising capital not through a public offering, but through a private offering, mostly to a small number of chosen investors.

Buy-back of securities: Reacquisition of its own shares or other specified securities by a company in order to reduce its share capital in the market.

Debenture: An instrument of credit executed by a company under its common seal acknowledging indebtedness to some person(s) to secure the sum advanced by the latter.

Member: One of the company's owners whose name has been entered on the register of members.

LO8 Sweat equity shares means such equity shares as are issued by a company to its directors or employees at a discount or for consideration, other than cash, for providing their know-how or making available rights in the nature of intellectual property rights or value additions, by whatever name called.

LO9 A right issue is a preferential subscription right that entitles a company's existing security holders to buy additional securities directly from the company in proportion to their existing holdings, within a fixed time period. In a rights offering, the subscription price at which each security may be purchased in generally at a discount to the current market price. Rights are often transferable, allowing the holder to sell them on the open market.

LO10 Bonus shares are additional shares given to the current shareholders without any additional cost in proportion to their holdings. These are company's accumulated earnings which are not given out in lieu of dividends, but are converted into free shares.

LO11 Reacquisition by a company of its own shares or other specified securities (ESOP, etc.) in order to reduce the number of shares in the market.

LO12 Membership (in context of a company) implies the state of being a member in joint stock company. Therefore, a member is one who agrees to become a member of a company and whose name is entered on its register of members. Company members share a common purpose and unite in order to focus their various talents and organize their collectively available skills or resources to achieve specific, declared goals. The rules governing membership of a company are normally set out in the company's 'Articles'.

CHAPTER

19 Management, Meetings and Winding Up of Company

Learning Objectives

LO 1 Directors: appointment, qualifications, disqualifications
LO 2 Managing director
LO 3 Managerial remuneration
LO 4 Corporate governance
LO 5 Kinds of company meetings; Board meetings, meetings of members
LO 6 Resolutions; minutes
LO 7 Winding up of company; modes of winding up
LO 8 Compulsory winding up: commencement; consequences
LO 9 Voluntary winding up
LO 10 Dissolution of a company and further developments

Company Management: An Overview

Company being a separate legal personality should be operated at a distance from its members. To facilitate this, members or say shareholders elect and appoint their representatives who can be entrusted with the responsibility of running the company. These elected members, actually concerned in the operation of the company (on behalf of the owners), are known as directors. The directors of a company can do what the company can do itself, of course, subject to the restrictions imposed by the Companies Act and articles of the company. The directors so appointed constitute a 'Board' as they jointly oversee the activities of the company. If the 'Board of directors' wishes one person to be particularly accountable for day to day affairs of the company's business on their behalf, that person is generally appointed as the Managing Director or the whole-time Director. Such a Managing Director or whole-time Director, however, works under the overall supervision and control of the Board of directors. The Act though does not expressly define the term 'director'; it contains specific provisions regarding qualifications, appointment, powers, duties, remuneration, removal, and liabilities of directors.

Who Can Be a Director?

Directors: Individuals who perform the directing function irrespective of the label attached to them.

Directors are those who perform the directing function irrespective of the label attached to them. Except this obligation, there is no formal academic or professional qualification, or an upper age limit fixed by company law for electing or appointing a person as director. Section 2(34) merely provides that director means a director appointed to the Board of a company.

However, only individuals barring minors can be directors. Every company shall have a Board of Directors consisting of individuals as directors [Section 149(1)].

Thus, no corporate body, association, or firm can be appointed as directors of a company.

Every company shall have

1. a minimum number of three directors in the case of a public company, two directors in the case of a private company, and one director in the case of a One Person Company; and
2. a maximum of fifteen directors.

However, a company may appoint more than fifteen directors after passing a special resolution.

Moreover, such class or classes of companies as may be prescribed shall have at least one woman director [Section 149(1)].

Every company existing on or before the date of commencement of this Act shall within one year from such commencement comply with the requirements of the above provision [Section 149(2)].

Every company shall have at least one director who has stayed in India for a total period of not less than one hundred and eighty-two days during the financial year i.e. a resident director [Section 149(3)].

Every listed public company shall have at least one-third of the total number of directors as independent directors and the Central Government may prescribe the minimum number of independent directors in case of any class or classes of public companies [Section 149(4)].

Independent Director

Independent director: A director other than a managing director or a whole-time director or a nominee director.

An independent director in relation to a company, means a director other than a managing director or a whole-time director or a nominee director,

1. who, in the opinion of the Board, is a person of integrity and possesses relevant expertise and experience;
2. (a) who is or was not a promoter of the company or its holding, subsidiary or associate company;
   (b) who is not related to promoters or directors in the company, its holding, subsidiary or associate company;
3. who has or had no pecuniary relationship, other than remuneration as such director or having transaction not exceeding 10 per cent of his total income or such amount as may be prescribed, with the company, its holding, subsidiary or associate company, or their promoters, or directors,

during the two immediately preceding financial years or during the current financial year;

4. none of whose relatives—
   (i) is holding any security of or interest in the company, its holding, subsidiary or associate company during the two immediately preceding financial years or during the current financial year:

   Provided that the relative may hold security or interest in the company of face value not exceeding fifty lakh rupees or two per cent. of the paid-up capital of the company, its holding, subsidiary or associate company or such higher sum as may be prescribed;
   (ii) is indebted to the company, its holding, subsidiary or associate company or their promoters, or directors, in excess of such amount as may be prescribed during the two immediately preceding financial years or during the current financial year;
   (iii) has given a guarantee or provided any security in connection with the indebtedness of any third person to the company, its holding, subsidiary or associate company or their promoters, or directors of such holding company, for such amount as may be prescribed during the two immediately preceding financial years or during the current financial year; or
   (iv) has any other pecuniary transaction or relationship with the company, or its subsidiary, or its holding or associate company amounting to two per cent. or more of its gross turnover or total income singly or in combination with the transactions referred to in sub-clause (i), (ii) or (iii);
5. who, neither himself nor any of his relatives
   (a) holds or has held the position of a key managerial personnel or is or has been employee of the company or its holding, subsidiary or associate company in any of the three financial years immediately preceding the financial year in which he is proposed to be appointed;
   (b) is or has been an employee or proprietor or a partner, in any of the three financial years immediately preceding the financial year in which he is proposed to be appointed, of (*A*) a firm of auditors or company secretaries in practice or cost auditors of the company or its holding, subsidiary or associate company; or (*B*) any legal or consulting firm that has or had any transaction with the company, its holding, subsidiary or associate company amounting to ten per cent or more of the gross turnover of such firm;
   (c) holds together with his relatives two per cent or more of the total voting power of the company; or
   (d) is a Chief Executive or director, by whatever name called, of any nonprofit organisation that receives twenty-five per cent or more of its receipts from the company, any of its promoters, directors or its holding, subsidiary or associate company or that holds two per cent or more of the total voting power of the company; or
6. who possesses such other qualifications as may be prescribed [Section 149(6)].

Disqualification (for Appointment) of Directors

A person shall not be eligible for appointment as a director of a company, if:

1. He is of unsound mind and stands so declared by a competent court;
2. He is an undischarged insolvent;
3. He has applied to be adjudicated as an insolvent and his application is pending;
4. He has been convicted by a court of any offence whether involving moral turpitude or otherwise and sentenced in respect thereof to imprisonment for not less than six months and a period of five years has not elapsed from date of expiry of the sentence. However, if a person has been convicted by a court of any offence and sentenced in respect thereof to imprisonment for a period of seven years, he shall not be eligible to be appointed as director in any company.
5. An order disqualifying him for appointment as a director has been passed by a court or Tribunal and the order is in force;

6. He has not paid any calls in respect of any shares of the company held by him, whether alone or jointly with others, and six months have elapsed from the last day fixed for the payment of the call;
7. He has been convicted of the offence dealing with related party transactions under Section 188 at any time during the last preceding five years; or
8. He has not been allotted Director Identification Number under Section 154 [Section 164(1)].

Besides, no person, who is or has been a director of a company which

1. has not filed financial statements or annual returns for a continuous period of three financial years; or
2. has failed to repay the deposits accepted by it or pay interest thereon or to redeem any debentures on the due date or pay interest due thereon or pay any dividend declared and such failure to pay or redeem continues for one year or more, shall be eligible to be re-appointed as a director of that company or appointed in other company for a period of five years from the date on which the said company fails to do so [Section 164(2)].

Moreover, a private company may by its articles provide for any disqualifications for appointment as a director in addition to those provided under Section 164(1) and (2) [Section 164(3)].

Director Identification Number

Director Identification Number: A unique identification number allotted to a potential director of any company by the Central Government.

Director Identification Number is a unique identification number allotted to a potential director of any company by the Central Government i.e. Ministry of Corporate Affairs. The concept of a DIN was introduced for the first time with the insertion of Sections 266A to 266G of Companies (Amendment) Act, 2006. The main purpose of introducing DIN is to keep a rich and authentic database of the directors of incorporated companies. Many a times it is seen that a duly incorporated company vanished with its director(s) after raising capital from the public and the probing agencies find it hard to trace them. DIN in this behalf is the ultimate device to help probing agencies trace the absconding director(s) and thereby address the issue. Significance of DIN can be assessed by the fact that no person shall be appointed as a director of a company unless he has been allotted the DIN under Section 154 by the Central Government or any other number by the latter itself which shall be treated as DIN [Section 152(3) read with Sections 153 & 154]. DIN not only helps fixing the identity of a director but also relates his participation in other companies, past and present. DIN holder is required to inform the Central Government about any change in his particulars as and when such changes take place. This keeps the database of the directors live.

Procedure for Allotment of DIN

Every individual intending to be appointed as director of a company shall make an application for allotment of Director Identification Number to the Central Government in the prescribed form and manner and along with the prescribed fees [Section 153].

As per the revised procedure for DIN allotment, any individual intending to apply for DIN shall have to make an online application in e-Form DIN 1 and follow the procedure by logging on to http://www.mca.gov.in/MCA21/

The Central Government shall allot a Director Identification Number to an applicant within one month from the receipt of the application provided the particular furnished therein found in order [Section 154].

However, no individual, who has already been allotted a Director Identification Number under section 154, shall apply for, obtain or possess another Director Identification Number [Section 155].

Every existing director shall intimate his Director Identification Number to the company/companies wherein he is a director within one month of its receipt from the Central Government [Section 156].

Company to Inform DIN to the Registrar

Every company shall, within fifteen days of the receipt of intimation under Section 156, furnish the Director Identification Number of all its directors to the Registrar or any other officer or authority as may be specified by the Central Government with such fees as may be prescribed with such additional fees as may be prescribed within the time specified under Section 403 and every such intimation shall be furnished in such form and manner as may be prescribed [Section 157(1)].

If any company fails to furnish the Director Identification Number under sub-section (1), such company shall be liable to a penalty of twenty-five thousand rupees and in case of continuing failure, with a further penalty of one hundred rupees for each day after the first during which such failure continues, subject to a maximum of one lakh rupees, and every officer of the company who is in default shall be liable to a penalty of not less than twenty-five thousand rupees and in case of continuing failure, with a further penalty of one hundred rupees for each day after the first during which such failure continues, subject to a maximum of one lakh rupees [Section 157(2)].

Moreover, every person or company, while furnishing any return, information or particulars as are required to be furnished under this Act, shall mention the Director Identification Number in such return, information or particulars in case such return, information or particulars relate to the director or contain any reference of any director [Section 158].

Consequences of Contravention

If any individual or director of a company makes default in complying with any of the provisions of Section 152, Section 155 or Section 156, such individual or director of the company shall be liable to a penalty which may extend to fifty thousand rupees and where the default is a continuing one, with a further penalty which may extend to five hundred rupees for every day after the first during which such default continues [Section 159].

Appointment of Directors

Appointment of directors may be discussed under the following heads.

Appointment of First Directors

First directors: Directors who hold office from the date of incorporation of the company until the first AGM, wherein directors are duly appointed by the shareholders.

First directors imply those directors who hold office from the date of incorporation of the company until the first AGM, wherein directors are duly appointed by the shareholders. Generally, the names of the first directors of a new company are provided for in its articles. However, if the articles are silent on this count then the subscribers to the memorandum (who are individuals) shall be deemed to be the first directors of the company until the directors are duly appointed. In case of 'One Person Company' an individual being member shall be deemed to be its first director until the director or directors are duly appointed by the member [Section 152(1)].

Appointment of regular directors

Regular director: Every person proposed to be appointed as a director by the company in general meeting or otherwise, who is supposed to furnish his Director Identification Number (DIN) and a declaration that he is not disqualified to be appointed as a director.

The first directors appointed by the articles or otherwise shall act until the first annual general meeting (AGM). In the first AGM the shareholders shall elect and appoint the directors on a regular basis [Section 152(2)].

Every person proposed to be appointed as a director by the company in general meeting or otherwise, shall furnish his Director Identification Number (DIN) and a declaration that he is not disqualified to become a director [Section 152(4)].

In the case of a public company, unless the articles provide for retirement of all the directors at every AGM, at least two-thirds of the total number of directors (excluding independent directors) shall be liable to retire by rotation. Thus, only one-third of total number of directors shall be non-rotational or permanent directors. For example, consider a company X Ltd., which has 10 directors. In this case, seven directors become liable to retire by rotation. These seven directors, unless otherwise become incompetent to act as directors, shall once again be appointed at the general meeting. The remaining three directors shall also be appointed at the general meeting. Two directors shall retire from office at every AGM, out of the seven directors who are eligible to retire by rotation [Section 152(6)].

The directors to retire by rotation at every AGM shall be those who have been longest in office since their last appointment, but as between persons who became directors on the same day, those who are to retire shall, in default of and subject to any agreement among themselves, be determined by lot [Section 152(d)].

Note: The first AGM mentioned at the beginning of Section 256 is actually the first general meeting held after the appointment is made under Section 255, and does not refer to the first AGM of the company.

Re-appointment of retiring directors

When a director retires, he/she can be reappointed or another person can be appointed as a director. The shareholders in their general meeting can also resolve that the vacancy may not be filled. However, if the post of a retiring director is not filled at the general meeting, and the meeting does not even pass a resolution for not filling the vacancy, the general meeting will be adjourned till same day in the next week at the same time and place. If that day happens to be a national holiday, the meeting will be held next succeding. If even on that day, the vacancy is not filled, or a resolution not to fill the vacancy is passed, then the retiring director is deemed to be re-appointed. However, he will not be deemed to be re-appointed under any of the following conditions:

(i) A resolution for his re-appointment has been specifically lost;
(ii) The director expresses his inability to continue as a director;
(iii) He is not qualified for appointment;
(iv) A resolution is required for the appointment or re-appointment of that director; or
(v) Section 162 (appointment of directors to be voted individually) is not applicable to the case [Section 152(7)(b)].

Appointment by the Board of Directors

The Board of directors is empowered to appoint directors in the following four categories:

1. Additional director
2. Alternate director
3. Nominee director
4. Casual director

Additional director

Additional director: A director appointed by the Board over and above regular directors if the articles so authorise.

The articles of a company may confer on its Board of Directors the power to appoint any person, other than a person who fails to get appointed as a director in a general meeting, as an additional director at any time who shall hold office up to the date of the next annual general meeting or the last date on which the annual general meeting should have been held, whichever is earlier [Section 161(1)].

Accordingly, the Board either at the meeting of the Board or by passing a special resolution in a general meeting can appoint an additional director on the Board if so authorised by the articles. He will although enjoy the same powers and rights as other directors but shall hold office only up to the date of the next AGM. Since the additional directors shall hold office only till the date of the next AGM, if the AGM is adjourned for any reason, he shall vacate his or her office on the due date, notwithstanding the adjournment of AGM.

It is pertinent to highlight that, in order to discourage inappropriate practices, the 2013 Act states that any person who fails to get elected as a director in the general meeting can no longer be appointed as an additional director by the board of directors [Section 161(1)].

Alternate director

The Board of Directors of a company may, if so authorised by its articles or by a resolution passed by the company in general meeting, appoint a person, not being a person holding any alternate directorship for any other director in the company or holding directorship in the same company, to act as an alternate director for a director during his absence for a period of not less than three months from India.

However, no person shall be appointed as an alternate director for an independent director unless he is qualified to be appointed as an independent director under the provisions of this Act [Section 161(2)].

Furthermore, an alternate director shall not hold office for a period longer than that permissible to the director in whose place he has been appointed and shall vacate the office if and when the director in whose place he has been appointed returns to India.

Furthermore, if the term of office of the original director is determined (i.e. expires) before he so returns to India, any provision for the automatic

Alternate director: A director appointed by the Board in place of a regular director in his absence from his office for a period of three months or more.

re-appointment of retiring directors in default of another appointment shall apply to the original, and not to the alternate director [Section 161(2)].

Nominee director

Nominee director: A person who acts as a non-executive director on the Board of directors of the company on behalf of an institution, such as a bank, or a financial institution, or some regulating agency etc.

If the articles of a company so provide, the Board may appoint any person as a director nominated by any institution in pursuance of the provisions of any law for the time being in force or of any agreement or by the Central Government or the State Government by virtue of its shareholding in a Government company [Section 161(3)].

A nominee director is a person who acts as a non-executive director on the Board of directors of the company on behalf of an institution, such as a bank or a, financial institution, or a, regulating agency etc. The purpose of a nominee director is the same as the role of an independent director wherein he seeks to safeguard the interest of the institution concerned.

Casual director

Casual director: A director appointed by the Board to fill the vacancy resulting by the death, resignation, removal of a regular director before the expiry of his term.

If the office of any director appointed by the company in general meeting is vacated before his term of office expires in the normal course, the resulting casual vacancy may, in default of and subject to any regulations in the articles of the company, be filled by the Board of Directors at a meeting of the Board , which shall be subsequently approved by members in the immediate next general meeting [Section 161(4)].

Thus, a casual director is one, appointed by the Board of Directors, if the articles so authorise, to fill the vacancy resulting by the death, resignation, removal of a regular director before the expiry of his term. However, any person so appointed shall hold office only till the date up to which the director in whose place he is appointed would have held office if it had not been vacated.

Appointment by the Central Government

Where all the directors of a company vacate their offices under any of the disqualifications specified in Section 167(1), in the absence of the promoter; the Central Government shall appoint the required number of directors who shall hold office till the directors are appointed by the company in the general meeting [Section 167(3)].

Appointment by the Tribunal

The Tribunal, upon the receipt of an application from any member of a company or from the Central Government for relief from oppressions etc., may appoint such number of persons as directors, who may be required by the Tribunal to report to the Tribunal on such matters as the Tribunal may direct [Section 242(2)(k) read with Section 241].

Appointment by Proportional Representation

The Act enables minority shareholders to have their representation on the Board, otherwise deprived, due to maxim of a simple majority vote, by giving an option to companies to appoint directors through a system of proportional representation. The articles may provide for the appointment of not less than two-thirds of the total number of the directors of a company, according to the principle of proportional representation. The proportional representation may be exercised by a single transferable vote or by a system of cumulative voting or otherwise. Such appointments shall be made once in every three years and casual vacancies of such directors shall be as per the statutory provision given under Section 161(4) [Section 163].

Appointment of Small Shareholders' Director

The Companies Act, 2013 provides for appointment of a director elected by 'small shareholders' with a view to enable them protect their interest. In accordance with Section 151, a listed company may have one director elected by 'small shareholders' in such manner and with such terms and conditions as may be prescribed.

For the above purposes 'small shareholders' means a shareholder holding shares of nominal value of not more than twenty thousand rupees or such other sum as may be prescribed [Explanation added to Section 151].

As per Rule 7 of the Companies (Appointment and Qualification of Directors) Rules, 2014, a listed company may upon notice of not less than 1000 small shareholders or 1/10th of the total number of such shareholders, whichever is lower, have a small shareholders' director elected by the small shareholders.

Ceiling on Directorships

The Companies Act puts a ceiling on directorships. Accordingly, no person shall hold office as a director, including any alternate directorship, in more than twenty companies (exclusive of directorship in dormant companies) at the same time.

However, the maximum number of public companies in which a person can be appointed as a director is ten which includes directorships in private companies that are either holding or subsidiary of a public company [Section 165(1)].

Thus, a person can hold directorship in ten public companies and ten private companies, whether or not latter are holding or subsidiary companies of the former i.e. public companies.

However, the members of a company may, by special resolution, specify any lesser number of companies in which a director of the company may act as director [Section 165(2)].

If a person, who is already holding offices as director in more than the specified number of companies (i.e. 20) immediately before the commencement of the Companies Act, 2013, shall within a period of one year from such commencement

1. choose not more than the specified limit of those companies, as companies in which he wishes to continue to hold the office of director;
2. resign his office as a director in the other remaining companies; and
3. intimate the choice made by him under clause (*a*), to each of the companies in which he was holding the office of a director before such commencement and to the Registrar having jurisdiction in respect of each such company [Section 165(3)].

Penalty for Non-compliance

Any person who holds office or acts as a director of more than 20 companies in contravention of the foregoing provisions shall be punishable with fine which shall not be less than five thousand rupees but which may extend to twenty-five thousand rupees for every day after the first during which the contravention continues [Section 165(6)].

Managing Director or Whole-Time Director

Managing director/ whole-time director: A director responsible to oversee day to day affairs of a company's business on behalf of the Board and appointed as such by the latter.

If the Board wishes one person to be particularly accountable for day to day affairs of the company's business on their behalf, that person is generally appointed as the Managing Director or the Whole-Time Director. Thus, managing director or a whole-time director is one who responsible to oversee day to day affairs of a company's business on behalf of the Board and appointed as such by the latter. He, however, will exercise his powers subject to the superintendence, control, and direction of the Board of directors.

Rules Governing the Appointment of the Managing Director or Whole-Time Director or Manager

In regards of appointment, reappointment, tenure etc. of the managing director or whole-time director or manager, Section 196 provides as under:

1. No company shall appoint or employ at the same time a managing director and a manager.
2. No company shall appoint or re-appoint any person as its managing director, whole-time director or manager for a term exceeding five years at a time.

   However, no re-appointment shall be made earlier than one year before the expiry of his (original) term.

3. No company shall appoint or continue the employment of any person as the managing director, whole-time director or manager who
   (a) is below the age of twenty-one years or has attained the age of seventy years;
   However, appointment of a person who has attained the age of seventy years may be made by passing a special resolution in which case the explanatory statement annexed to the notice for such motion shall indicate the justification for appointing such person.
   Moreover, where no such special resolution is passed but votes cast in favour of the motion exceed the votes, if any, cast against the motion and the Central Government is satisfied, on an application made by the Board, that such appointment is most beneficial to the company, the appointment of the person who has attained the age of seventy years may be made.
   (b) is an undischarged insolvent or has at any time been adjudged as an insolvent;
   (c) has at any time suspended payment to his creditors or makes, or has at any time made, a composition with them; or
   (d) has at any time been convicted by a court of an offence and sentenced for a period of more than six months.

4. A managing director, whole-time director or manager shall be appointed and the terms and conditions of such appointment and remuneration payable be approved by the Board of Directors at a meeting which shall be subject to approval by a resolution at the next general meeting of the company and by the Central Government in case such appointment is at variance to the conditions specified in Part I of that Schedule.

However, a notice convening the Board or general meeting for considering such appointment shall include the terms and conditions of such appointment, remuneration payable and such other matters including interest of a director or directors in such appointments, if any.

Moreover, a return in the prescribed form shall be filed within sixty days of such appointment with the Registrar.

Managerial Remuneration

Managerial remuneration refers to the compensation payable to the managerial personnel of a company, who generally comprise a managing director, directors, and a statutory manager, if any. It is usually determined in accordance with the provisions outlined in the articles of the company or by a resolution (special resolution if the articles so require) passed by the company in a general meeting. The remuneration payable to any such director determined as per the said provisions is inclusive of the remuneration payable to such director for services rendered by him in any other capacity.

> **Managerial remuneration:** Compensation payable to the managerial personnel of a company.

Overall Maximum Managerial Remuneration

Section 197, which deals with overall maximum managerial remuneration and managerial remuneration in case of nil or inadequate profits, provides as under.

1. The total managerial remuneration payable by a public company to its directors, including the managing director, whole-time director and its manager in respect of any financial year shall not exceed 11 per cent of the net profits of that company for that financial year computed in the manner laid down in Section 198.
   However, the company in general meeting may, with the approval of the Central Government, authorise the payment of remuneration exceeding eleven per cent of the net profits of the company, subject to the provisions of Schedule V.
   Moreover, except with the approval of the company in general meeting by a special resolution,
   (a) the remuneration payable to any one managing director; or whole-time director or manager shall not exceed five per cent of the net profits of the company and if there is more than one such director, remuneration shall not exceed ten per cent of the net

profits to all such directors and manager taken together;

(b) the remuneration payable to directors who are neither managing directors nor whole-time directors shall not exceed,

 (i) one per cent of the net profits of the company, if there is a managing or whole-time director or manager;

 (ii) three per cent of the net profits in any other case.

2. The percentages aforesaid shall be exclusive of any fees payable to directors under sub-section (5)
3. If in any financial year, a company has no profits or its profits are inadequate, the company shall not pay to its directors, including any managing or whole-time director or manager, by way of remuneration any sum exclusive of any fees payable to directors.
4. The remuneration payable to the directors of a company, including any managing or whole-time director or manager, shall be determined, in accordance with and subject to the provisions of this section, either by the articles of the company, or by a resolution or, if the articles so require, by a special resolution, passed by the company in general meeting and the remuneration payable to a director determined aforesaid shall be inclusive of the remuneration payable to him for the services rendered by him in any other capacity.

 However, any remuneration for services rendered by any such director in other capacity shall not be included if

 (a) the services rendered are of a professional nature; and

 (b) in the opinion of the Nomination and Remuneration Committee, if the company is covered under sub-section (1) of section 178, or the Board of Directors in other cases, the director possesses the requisite qualification for the practice of the profession.

5. A director may receive remuneration by way of fees for attending meetings of the Board or Committee thereof or for any other purpose whatsoever as may be decided by the Board.

 However, the amount of such fees shall not exceed the amount as may be prescribed.

 Moreover, different fees for different classes of companies and fees in respect of an independent director may be such as may be prescribed.

6. A director or manager may be paid remuneration either by way of a monthly payment or at a specified percentage of the net profits of the company or partly by one way and partly by the other.
7. The net profits for the purposes of this section shall be computed in the manner referred to in Section 198.
8. If any director draws or receives, directly or indirectly, by way of remuneration any such sums in excess of the limit prescribed by this section or without approval required under this section, he shall refund such sums to the company, within two years or such lesser period as may be allowed by the company, and until such sum is refunded, hold it in trust for the company. However, the company is empowered to waive the recovery of the said sum by passing a special resolution within two years from the date the sum becomes refundable.

If any person makes any default in complying with the provisions of this section, he shall be liable to a penalty of one lakh rupees and where any default has been made by a company, the company shall be liable to a penalty of five lakh rupees. [Section 196(15)].

Vacation of Office by Directors

As per Section 167, the office of a director shall become vacant under any one of the following circumstances:

1. He incurs any of the disqualifications specified in section 164;
2. He absents himself from all the meetings of the Board of Directors held during a period of twelve months with or without seeking leave of absence of the Board;
3. He acts in contravention of the provisions of section 184 relating to entering into contracts or arrangements in which he is directly or indirectly interested;

4. He fails to disclose his interest in any contract or arrangement in which he is directly or indirectly interested, in contravention of the provisions of section 184;
5. He becomes disqualified by an order of a court or the Tribunal;
6. He is convicted by a court of any offence, whether involving moral turpitude or otherwise and sentenced in respect thereof to imprisonment for not less than six months.

   The office shall be vacated by the director in the above case even if he has filed an appeal against the order of such court;
7. He is removed in pursuance of the provisions of this Act;
8. He, having been appointed a director by virtue of his holding any office or other employment in the holding, subsidiary or associate company, ceases to hold such office or other employment in that company.

A private company, however, may, by its articles, provide any other ground for the vacation of the office of a director in addition to those specified above [Section 167(4)].

Penalty for Not Vacating Office Due to Disqualifications

If a person functions as a director after his office has become vacant on account of any of the disqualifications, specified in (a) to (h) above, he shall be punishable with imprisonment for a term which may extend to one year or fine which shall not be less than one lakh rupees but which may extend to five lakh rupees, or with both [Section 167(2)].

Removal of Directors

Removal of directors: Termination of directors from the office before the expiry of their term on certain grounds.

Removal of director implies termination of directors from the office before the expiry of their term on certain grounds. Removal or termination of directors can be discussed under the following two heads:

1. Removal by company
2. Removal by the Tribunal

Removal by company

Under Section 169, a company (i.e., the shareholders) may, by an ordinary resolution requiring a special notice, remove a director, not being a director appointed by the Tr from the Board before the expiration of his term of office. However, the director concerned shall be entitled to be heard before passing of the resolution of his removal by the company.

Removal by the tribunal

Where on an application filed by any member of the company or the Central Government before the Tribunal against oppression and mismanagement of a company's affairs (i.e. under Section 241), the Tribunal finds that the relief should be granted, it may pass an order for the removal of the managing director, manger, or any of the directors of the company [Section 242(2)(h)].

When the appointment of a director is so finished, he shall not be entitled to claim any damages or compensation from the company for the loss of office. Moreover, such a director cannot be appointed, except with the leave (prior consent) of the Tribunal, in any managerial capacity (i.e., manager, managing director or director) for a period of five years from the date of Tribunal's order terminating or setting aside his contract with the company [Section 243].

Director's Resignation

Director's resignation: Vacating office by a director voluntarily before the expiry of their term.

Resignation means giving up a job or a position by someone. As per Section 168(1), a director may resign from his office by giving a notice in writing to the company and the Board shall on receipt of such notice take note of the same and the company shall intimate the Registrar in such manner, within such time and in such form as may be prescribed and shall also place the fact of such resignation in the report of directors laid in the immediately following general meeting by the company.

However, a director may also forward a copy of his resignation along with detailed reasons for the resignation to the Registrar within thirty days of resignation in such manner as may be prescribed.

The resignation of a director shall take effect from the date on which the notice is received by the company or the date, if any, specified by the director in the notice, whichever is later [Section 168(2)].

Notwithstanding, the director who has resigned shall be liable even after his resignation for the offences which occurred during his tenure.

Duties of Directors

Since directors exercise control and management over the company and companies are run (in principle at least) for the benefit of the shareholders, the law recognises strict duties to be discharged by the directors in relation to the exercise of their powers. Section 166 provides:

1. A director of a company shall act in accordance with the articles of the company.
2. A director of a company shall act in good faith in order to promote the objects of the company for the benefit of its members as a whole, and in the best interests of the company, its employees, the shareholders, the community, and for the protection of the environment.
3. A director of a company shall exercise his duties with due and reasonable care, skill and diligence and shall exercise independent judgment.
4. A director of a company shall not involve in a situation in which he may have a direct or indirect interest that conflicts, or possibly may conflict, with the interest of the company.
5. A director of a company shall not achieve or attempt to achieve any undue gain or advantage either to himself or to his relatives, partners, or associates and if such director is found guilty of making any undue gain, he shall be liable to pay an amount equal to that gain to the company.
6. A director of a company shall not assign his office and any assignment so made shall be void.
7. If a director of the company contravenes the above provisions, such director shall be punishable with fine which shall not be less than one lakh rupees but which may extend to five lakh rupees.

Powers of the Board of Directors

Powers Board of Directors can be discussed under the two heads:

1. General powers, and
2. Powers to be exercised at Board meetings.

General Powers of the Board

The Board of directors of a company shall be entitled to exercise all such powers, and to do all such acts and things, as the company is authorised to exercise and do [Section 179(1)].

However, as per proviso attached to the abovementioned section, the Board shall not exercise any power which is to be exercised by the company in the general meeting or which shall be inconsistent, if exercised, with the regulations contained in that behalf in the Act, or in the memorandum or articles of the company.

That is, the directors are not empowered to take action on issues that are stipulated to be the purview of the general meeting of the company, or are counter to regulations contained in the Act, or the memorandum and articles of the company.

However, no regulation made by the company in general meeting shall invalidate any prior act of the Board which would have been valid if that regulation had not been made [Section 179(2)].

Powers to be Exercised at Board Meetings

The Board is the principal organ of a company. Empowers it to exercise the following powers on behalf of the company, but it can do so only by means of resolutions passed at meetings of the Board.

(a) To make calls on shareholders in respect of money unpaid on their shares;
(b) To authorise buy-back of securities under Section 68;
(c) To issue securities, including debentures, whether in or outside India;
(d) To borrow monies;
(e) To invest the funds of the company;
(f) To grant loans or give guarantee or provide security in respect of loans;
(g) To approve the financial statement and the Board's report;
(h) To diversify the business of the company;
(i) To approve amalgamation, merger or reconstruction; and

(j) To take over a company or acquire a controlling or substantial stake in another company [Section 179(3)].

However, the Board may, by a resolution passed at a meeting, delegate to any committee of directors, the managing director, the manager or any other principal officer of the company or in the case of a branch office of the company, the principal officer of the branch office, the powers specified in clauses (*d*) to (*f*) on such conditions as it may specify.

Moreover, the acceptance by a banking company in the ordinary course of its business of deposits of money from the public repayable on demand or otherwise and withdrawable by cheque, draft, order or otherwise, or the placing of monies on deposit by a banking company with another banking company on such conditions as the Board may prescribe, shall not be deemed to be a borrowing of monies or, as the case may be, a making of loans by a banking company within the meaning of this section.

Restrictions on Powers of Board

Directors derive their powers or rights mainly from provisions in the articles, as the Act provides little guidance as to which actions are within the director's powers. More than defining the powers and rights of directors as to what they are, the Act, on the whole, places more emphasis on imposing restrictions on such rights and powers. Section 180(1) provides that the Board of Directors of a company shall exercise the following powers only with the consent of the company by a special resolution, namely:

1. To sell, lease, or otherwise dispose of the whole, or substantially the whole (20% or more of the value of the undertaking as per the audited balance sheet of the preceding financial year) of the undertaking of the company, or where the company owns more than one undertaking of the whole, or substantially the whole of any such undertaking.
2. To invest, other than in trust securities, the amount of compensation received by it as a result of any merger or amalgamation;
3. To borrow money, where the money to be borrowed, together with the money already borrowed by the company will exceed the aggregate of its paid-up share capital, free reserves and securities premium, apart from temporary loans obtained from the company's bankers in the ordinary course of business.

   However, the acceptance by a banking company, in the ordinary course of its business, of deposits of money from the public, repayable on demand or otherwise, and withdrawable by cheque, draft, order or otherwise, shall not be deemed to be a borrowing of monies by the banking company within the meaning of this clause.

   Explanation: For the purposes of this clause, the expression 'temporary loans' means loans repayable on demand or within six months from the date of the loan such as short-term, cash credit arrangements, the discounting of bills and the issue of other short-term loans of a seasonal character, but does not include loans raised for the purpose of financial expenditure of a capital nature.
4. To remit, or give time for the repayment of, any debt due from a director.

Loans to Directors

As per Section 185(1), no company shall, directly or indirectly, advance any loan, including any loan represented by a book debt to, or give any guarantee or provide any security in connection with any loan taken by, -

(a) any director of company, or of a company which is its holding company or any partner or relative of any such director; or

(b) any firm in which any such director or relative is a partner.

However, a company may advance any loan including any loan represented by a book debt, or give any guarantee or provide any security in connection with any loan taken by any person in whom any of the director of the company is interested, subject to the condition that -

(a) a special resolution is passed by the company in general meeting; and

(b) the loans are utilised by the borrowing company for its principal business activities [Section 185(2)]

Explanation - For the purposes of the above section, the expression "any person in whom any of the director of the company is interested" means -

(a) any private company of which any such director is a director or member;

(b) any body corporate at a general meeting of which not less than twenty-five per cent of the total voting power may be exercised or controlled by any such director, or by two or more such directors together; or

(c) any body corporate, the Board of directors, managing director or manager, whereof is accustomed to act in accordance with the directions or instructions of the Board, or of any director or directors, of the lending company.

However, nothing contained in this sub-sections (1) and (2) shall apply to -

1. The giving of any loan to a managing or whole-time director
   (a) As a part of the conditions of service extended by the company to all its employees; or
   (b) Pursuant to any scheme approved by the members by a special resolution; or
2. a company which in the ordinary course of its business provides loans or gives guarantees or securities for the due repayment of any loan and in respect of such loans an interest is charged at a rate not less than the rate of prevailing yield of one year, three year, five year or ten year Government security closest to the tenor of the loan; or.
3. any loan made by a holding company to its wholly owned subsidiary company or any guarantee given or security provided by a holding company in respect of any loan made to its wholly owned subsidiary company; or
4. any guarantee given or security provided by a holding company in respect of loan made by any bank or financial institution to its subsidiary company.

Consequences of Contravention of the

If any loan is advanced or a guarantee or security is given or provided in contravention of the provisions of with but which may extend to twenty-five lakh rupees, and the director or the other person to whom any loan is advanced or guarantee or security is given or provided in connection with any loan taken by him or the other person, shall be punishable with imprisonment which may extend to six months or with fine which shall not be less than five lakh rupees but which may extend to twenty-five lakh rupees, or with both [Section 185(2)].

Corporate Governance

Corporate governance: A set of processes, customs, policies, laws, and institutions affecting the way a company is directed, administered, or controlled.

Corporate governance, the buzzword of corporate identity, is used in a variety of contexts. In relation to company's decision-making it implies a set of processes, customs, policies, laws, and institutions affecting the way a company is directed, administered or controlled. The report of the Sebi Committee on Corporate Governance defines it as the acceptance by management of the inalienable rights of shareholders as the true owners of the corporation, and of their own role as trustees on behalf of the shareholders. It is about commitment to values, about ethical business conduct and about making a distinction between personal and corporate funds in the management of a company. The above definition is drawn from the Gandhian principle of trusteeship and the Directive Principles of the Indian Constitution. Corporate governance is viewed as ethics and moral duty. It also includes the relationships among the many stakeholders involved and the goals for which the corporation is governed. Corporate governance as a matter of fact concerns all issues about the best way to run a company.

Parties to Corporate Governance

Parties involved in corporate governance include the Chief Executive Officer (CEO), the Board of directors, management, and shareholders and other stakeholders which include suppliers, employees, creditors, customers, and the community at large.

In corporations, the shareholders delegate decision rights to the manager to act in the company's best interests. This separation of ownership from control implies a loss of effective control by shareholders over managerial decisions. Partly as a result of this separation between the two parties, a system of corporate governance controls is implemented to assist in aligning the incentives of managers with those of shareholders.

A Board of directors often plays a key role in corporate governance. It is their responsibility to endorse the organization's strategy, develop directional policy, appoint and remunerate senior executives, and to ensure accountability of the organization to its owners and authorities.

The Company Secretary is a high ranking professional who is trained to uphold the highest standards of corporate governance, effective operations, compliance, and administration.

All parties to corporate governance have an interest, whether direct or indirect, in the effective performance of the organization. Directors, workers, and management receive salaries, benefits, and reputation, while shareholders receive capital return. Customers receive goods and services, suppliers receive compensation for their goods or services. In return these individuals provide value in the form of natural, human, social, and other forms of capital.

Principles of Corporate Governance

Commonly accepted principles of corporate governance include

Rights and equitable treatment of shareholders Organizations should respect the rights of shareholders and help shareholders to exercise those rights. They can help shareholders exercise their rights by effectively communicating information that is understandable and accessible and encouraging shareholders to participate in general meetings.

Interests of other stakeholders Organizations should recognise that they have legal and other obligations to all legitimate stakeholders.

Role and responsibilities of the board The Board needs a range of skills and understanding to be able to deal with various business issues and to have the ability to review and challenge management performance. It needs to be of sufficient size and have an appropriate level of commitment to fulfil its obligations. There are issues about the appropriate mix of executive and non-executive directors. The key roles of a chairperson and a CEO should not be held by the same person.

Integrity and ethical behaviour Ethical and responsible decision making is not only important for public relations, but it is also a necessary element in risk management and avoiding lawsuits. Organizations should develop a code of conduct for their directors and executives that promotes ethical and responsible decision making.

Disclosure and transparency Organizations should clarify and make the roles and responsibilities of the board and management publicly known to provide shareholders with a level of accountability. The disclosure of material matters concerning the organization should be timely and balanced to ensure that all investors have access to clear, factual information.

Issues Involving Corporate Governance

Keeping in view the wide spectrum of corporate governance, it is not possible to give a complete listing of the issues involved therein. However, for reference, the following pressing issues can be enumerated:

1. Internal controls and the independence of the entity's auditors
2. Oversight and management of risks
3. Oversight of the preparation of the entity's financial statements
4. Review of the compensation arrangements for the chief executive officer and other senior executives
5. The resources made available to directors in carrying out their duties
6. The way in which individuals are nominated to positions on the Board
7. Dividend policy.

Company Meetings: Introduction

A company is an association of several persons for some common object(s) in which decisions are made according to the view of the majority. Various issues have to be discussed and decided accordingly. These deliberations take place through various meetings which occur between the members and between the directors as well. Thus, meeting, in this regard, may be defined as an assemblage or gathering of some authorised persons for conducting some lawful business. For a meeting to take place there must be, obviously, at least two persons attending it. However, in certain exceptional circumstances, one member can constitute a valid meeting even if he does not hold proxies for other members. The Companies Act, 2013 contains various provisions governing company meetings. These regulations have to be observed and complied with while holding such meetings. Hence, the importance of meetings cannot be under-emphasized in case of companies.

Kinds of Company Meetings

Company meetings can be categorised into the three types – meetings of members, board meetings, and other meetings. Meetings of members are again classified into two types – general meetings and class meetings. General meetings are sub-divided into annual meetings and extraordinary meetings. Other meetings include class meetings, meetings of debenture holders and creditors.

Figure 19.1 contains a flowchart depicting the various types of company meetings.

Meetings of Members

These are the meetings where members/shareholders of the company meet to discuss various matters and take decisions by means of passing resolutions. Meetings of members may be classified as general meetings and class meetings.

General Meetings

General meetings may take any of the following forms as and when required under the provisions of the Act:

1. Annual General Meeting, and
2. Extraordinary General Meeting.

Annual general meeting

An annual general meeting (AGM) must be held each year by every company other than a One Person Company. AGM is an important platform by which the general body of shareholders finds an opening to exercise their power of control.

Annual general meeting: Meeting of shareholders, held once in a year statutorily.

Rules relating to an annual general meeting

Following are the rules governing annual general meetings:

1. A company shall hold its first AGM within 9 months from the date of closing of the first financial year. In such a case, it need not hold any AGM in the year of its incorporation [Section 96(1)].

Figure 19.1 Kinds of company meetings

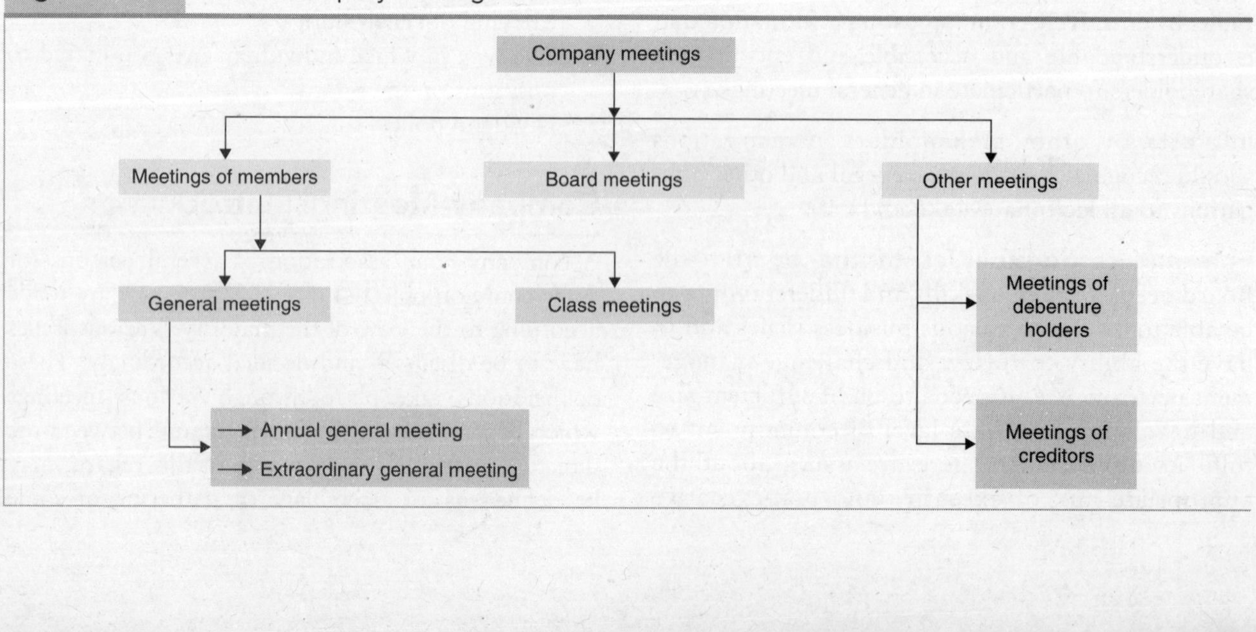

2. Not more than 15 months shall elapse between two AGMs of a company other than a One Person Company. However, every AGM (other than first AGM) shall be held within a period of six months from the date of closing of the first financial year [Section 96(1)].
3. In case there is some difficulty in holding any AGM (except the first one), the Registrar may, for any special reasons shown, grant an extension of time for holding the meeting by a period not exceeding three months [Section 96(1)].
4. Every annual general meeting shall be called during business hours, that is, between 9 a.m. and 6 p.m. on any day that is not a National Holiday and shall be held either at the registered office of the company or at some other place within the city, town or village in which the registered office of the company is situated [Section 96(2)].

   However, the Central Government may exempt any company from the provisions of this sub-section subject to such conditions as it may impose.
5. A notice of at least 21 clear days either in writing or through electronic mode shall be given to the members in the prescribed manner.

   However, a general meeting may be called after giving shorter notice, if consent, in writing or electronic mode, is accorded thereto-

   (i) in the case of an AGM, by not less than ninety-five per cent of the members entitled to vote thereat; and

   (ii) in the case of any other general meeting, by members of the company -

   (a) holding, if the company has share capital, majority in number of members entitled to vote and who represent not less than ninety-five per cent of such part of the paid-up share capital of the company as gives a right to vote at the meeting; or

   (b) having, if the company has no share capital, not less than ninety-five percent of the total voting power exercisable at that meeting [Section 101(1)].

   Every notice of a meeting shall specify the place, date, day and the hour of the meeting and shall contain a statement of the business to be transacted at such meeting [Section 101(2)].
6. The notice of the meeting shall be given to

   (a) Every member of the company, the legal representative of any deceased member or the assignee of an insolvent member;

   (b) The auditor or auditors of the company; and

   (c) Every director of the company [Section 101(3)].
7. Any member of a company entitled to attend and vote at a meeting of the company shall be entitled to appoint another person as a proxy to attend and vote at the meeting on his behalf. However, a proxy shall not have a right to speak at such meeting and shall not be entitled to vote except on a poll. A proxy form should be enclosed with the notice. The proxy form shall be signed by the appointer or his attorney duly authorised in writing [Section 101(1) & (5)].
8. Unless the articles of the company provide for a larger number,

   (a) in case of a public company,

   (i) five members personally present if the number of members as on the date of meeting is not more than one thousand;

   (ii) fifteen members personally present if the number of members as on the date of meeting is more than one thousand but up to five thousand;

   (iii) thirty members personally present if the number of members as on the date of the meeting exceeds five thousand shall be the quorum for a meeting of the company; and

   (b) in the case of a private company, two members personally present, shall be the quorum for a meeting of the company [Section 103(1)].

   Moreover, if the quorum is not present within half-an-hour from the time appointed for holding a meeting of the company

   (i) the meeting shall stand adjourned to the same day in the next week at the same time and place, or to such other date and such other time and place as the Board may determine; or

   (ii) the meeting, if called by requisitionists under section 100, shall stand cancelled.

   However, in case of an adjourned meeting or of a change of day, time or place of meeting under clause (*a*), the company shall give not less than three days notice to the members either individually or by publishing an advertisement in the newspapers (one in English and one in vernacular language) which is in circulation at the place where the registered office of the company is situated [Section 103(2)].

If at the adjourned meeting also, a quorum is not present within half-an-hour from the time appointed for holding meeting, the members present shall be the quorum [Section 103(3)].

9. Unless the articles of the company otherwise provide, the members personally present at the meeting shall elect one of themselves to be the Chairman thereof on a *show of hand* [Section 104].

Business to be transacted at an annual general meeting At every AGM, the following matters shall be transacted. Since such matters are transacted at every AGM, they are known as 'ordinary businesses'. All other matters and business to be transacted at the AGM are 'special businesses'.

The following matters constitute ordinary business at an AGM:

1. The consideration of financial statements and the reports of the Board of Directors and auditors;
2. The declaration of dividend
3. The appointment of directors in the place of those retiring
4. The appointment and fixing of the remuneration of the auditors [Section 102(2)].

In case any other business (special business) has to be transacted, a statement setting out the following material facts concerning each item of the special business to be transacted at a general meeting shall accompany the notice calling the meeting, namely:

1. the nature of concern or interest, financial or otherwise, if any, in respect of each items of
   (a) every director and the manager, if any;
   (b) every other key managerial personnel; and
   (c) relatives of the persons mentioned in sub-clauses (*a*) and (*b*);
2. any other information and facts that may enable members to understand the meaning, scope and implications of the items of business and to take decision thereon [Section 102(1)].

Consequences of not holding annual general meeting Default in holding an AGM may result in the following consequences:

1. Any member of the company may apply to the Tribunal which may in turn call, or direct the calling of the meeting, and give such ancillary or consequential directions as it thinks expedient. The NCLT may also direct that one member present in person or by proxy shall be deemed to constitute the meeting. A meeting held in pursuance of this order will be deemed to be an annual general meeting of the company [Section 97].
2. If any default is made in holding an AGM in accordance with Section 96/97/98 or in compliance with any directions of the Tribunal, as the case may be, the company and every officer of the company who is in default shall be punishable with fine which may extend to one lakh rupees and in the case of a continuing default, with a further fine which may extend to five thousand rupees for every day during which such default continues [Section 99].

Extraordinary general meeting

An extraordinary meeting is usually called by the Board of directors in emergencies, say, for taking up some urgent business that cannot be kept pending till the next AGM. Every business transacted at such a meeting is a special business. An explanatory statement of the special business must also accompany the notice calling the meeting. The notice should also give the nature and extent of the interest of the directors or manager in the special business, as also the extent of the shareholding interest in the company of every such person.

> **Extraordinary general meeting:** A meeting called by the Board of directors in emergent situation for taking up some urgent business that cannot be kept pending till the next AGM.

Who can call an extraordinary general meeting? An extraordinary general meeting may be called by:

1. **The Board on Requisitions:** The members of a company have the right to seek calling of an EGM by the Board. The Board of directors must call an extraordinary general meeting of the company if required to do so by the following number of members.

(a) in the case of a company having a share capital, such number of members who hold, on the date of the receipt of the requisition, not less than one-tenth of the paid-up share capital of the company as on that date carrying the right of voting;

(b) in the case of a company not having a share capital, such number of members who have, on the date of receipt of the requisition, not less than one-tenth of the total voting power of all the members having on the said date a right to vote [Section 100(2)].

2. **By the Requisitionists:** If the Board does not, within twenty-one days from the date of receipt of a valid requisition in regard to any matter, proceeds to call a meeting for the consideration of that matter on a day not later than forty-five days from the date of receipt of such requisition, the meeting may be called and held by the requisitionists themselves within a period of three months from the date of the requisition [Section 100(4)].

Class Meetings

Class meetings are meetings which are held by the holders of a particular class of shares (i.e., where the share capital of a company is divided into different classes of shares), e.g., preference shareholders. Such meetings are normally called when it is proposed to alter, vary or affect the rights of that particular class of shareholders. At such meetings, these members discuss the pros and cons of the proposal and resolve accordingly. Unless articles of the company otherwise provides, all provisions pertaining to calling of a general meeting and its conduct do apply to class meetings in the same way as they apply with respect to general meetings of the members. However, all resolutions in a class meeting are required to be passed as special resolutions.

Class meetings: Meetings held by the holders of a particular class of shares.

Meetings of the board

Meetings of the board refer to meetings of directors. The protection of investors is one of the primary themes of the Companies Act. The Act provides the shareholders a forum of self-protection. The forum is the general meeting of shareholders. Apart from this, having regard to the position and status envisaged for directors and the role that is assumed to them in the affairs of the company, it is also essential to hold meetings of the Board at regular intervals and to discuss in these meetings, all major concerns. This enables the directors to be in touch with the management of company affairs as often as they should be. Rules related to board meetings can be summarized as under.

1. Every company shall hold the first meeting of the Board of Directors within thirty days of the date of its incorporation and thereafter hold a minimum number of four meetings of its Board every year in such a manner that not more than one hundred and twenty days shall intervene between two consecutive meetings of the Board [Section 173(1)].

   However, the Central Government may, by notification, direct that the provisions of this sub-section shall not apply in relation to any class or description of companies or shall apply subject to such exceptions, modifications or conditions as may be specified in the notification.

2. The participation of directors in a meeting of the Board may be either in person or through video conferencing or other audio visual means, as may be prescribed, which are capable of recording and recognising the participation of the directors and of recording and storing the proceedings of such meetings along with date and time [Section 173(2)].

   Provided that the Central Government may, by notification, specify such matters which shall not be dealt within a meeting through video conferencing or other audio visual means.

3. A meeting of the Board shall be called by a minimum 'seven days' notice in writing to every director at his address registered with the company and such notice shall be sent by hand delivery or by post or by electronic means [Section 173(3)].

   However, a meeting of the Board may be called at shorter notice to transact urgent business subject to the condition that at least one independent director, if any, shall be present at the meeting:

   Furthermore, in case of absence of independent directors from such a meeting of the Board, decisions taken at such a meeting shall be circulated to all the directors and shall be final only on ratification thereof by at least one independent director, if any.

4. Every officer of the company whose duty is to give notice under this section and who fails to do so shall be liable to a penalty of twenty-five thousand rupees [Section 173(4)].
5. A One Person Company, a small company and a dormant company shall be deemed to have complied with the provisions of this section if at least one meeting of the Board of Directors has been conducted in each half of a calendar year and the gap between the two meetings is not less than ninety days [Section 173(5)].

   However, nothing contained in this sub-section and in section 174 shall apply to One Person Company in which there is only one director on its Board of Directors.
6. The quorum for a meeting of the Board of Directors of a company shall be one-third of its total strength or two directors, whichever is higher, and the participation of the directors by video conferencing or by other audio visual means shall also be counted for the purposes of quorum under this sub-section [Section 174(1)].
7. Where a meeting of the Board could not be held for the want of quorum, then, unless the articles of the company otherwise provide, the meeting shall automatically stand adjourned to the same day at the same time and place in the next week or if that day is a national holiday, till the next succeeding day, which is not a national holiday, at the same time and place [Section 174(4)].

Other Meetings

A company may provide through its articles for the meetings of other persons related to and interested in the affairs of the company, i.e., meetings of debenture holders and creditors of the company. The basic aim of the provision of these meetings is to ensure the protection of interest of debenture holders and creditors, as the case may be, in the affairs of the company. These meetings may be called by the company, either as a running concern or in the event of winding up to make certain arrangements with its debenture holders and creditors.

Voting by Show of Hands

The term 'vote' means an expression of a wish or opinion in a democratic and formal way for or against a proposal. Generally, preliminary matters are decided at a general meeting by a show of hands. If the majority of the persons raise their hands in favour of a particular resolution, then unless a poll is demanded under Section 109 or the voting is carried out electronically it is taken as passed [Section 107(1)].

A declaration by the Chairman of the meeting of the passing of a resolution or otherwise by show of hands under sub-section (1) and an entry to that effect in the books containing the minutes of the meeting of the company shall be conclusive evidence of the fact of passing of such resolution or otherwise [Section 107(2)].

Voting Through Electronic Means

The Central Government may prescribe the class or classes of companies and manner in which a member may exercise his rights to vote by the electronic means [Section 108].

Demand for poll

Voting by a show of hands operates on the principle of 'one member-one vote'. However, since the fundamental voting principle in a company is 'one share-one vote', if a poll is demanded, voting takes place accordingly.

Before or on declaration of the result of the voting on any resolution on a show of hands, a poll may be ordered to be taken by the Chairman of the meeting on his own motion, and shall be ordered to be taken by him on a demand made in that behalf,

1. in the case of a public company having a share capital, by the members present in person or by proxy where allowed, and having not less than one-tenth of the total voting power or holding shares on which an aggregate sum of not less than five lakh rupees or such higher amount as may be prescribed has been paid-up; and
2. in the case of any other company, by any member or members present in person or by proxy, where allowed, and having not less than one-tenth of the total voting power [Section 109(1)].

However, the demand for a poll may be withdrawn at any time by the persons who made the demand [Section 109(1)].

Postal ballot

A company

1. shall, in respect of such items of business as the Central Government may, by notification, declare to be transacted only by means of postal ballot; and
2. may, in respect of any item of business, other than ordinary business and any business in respect of which directors or auditors have a right to be heard at any meeting, transact by means of postal ballot, in such manner as may be prescribed, instead of transacting such business at a general meeting.
3. If a resolution is assented to by the requisite majority of the shareholders by means of postal ballot, it shall be deemed to have been duly passed at a general meeting convened in that behalf [Section 110].

Resolutions

Resolution: The formal decision of a meeting on any proposal placed before it.

A motion, with or without amendments is put to vote at a meeting. A motion when passed by requisite majority of votes by the shareholders becomes a company resolution. Thus, a resolution may be defined as the formal decision of a meeting on any proposal placed before it.

Kinds of Resolutions

Broadly speaking, there are three types of resolutions under The Companies Act, 2013: ordinary, special, and those requiring a special notice.

Ordinary resolution

Ordinary resolution: A resolution passed by a simple majority.

An ordinary resolution is one which is passed by a simple majority. As per Section 114(1), a resolution shall be an ordinary resolution if the notice required under this Act has been duly given and it is required to be passed by the votes cast, whether on a show of hands, or electronically or on a poll, as the case may be, in favour of the resolution, including the casting vote, if any, of the Chairman, by members who, being entitled so to do, vote in person, or where proxies are allowed, by proxy or by postal ballot, exceed the votes, if any, cast against the resolution by members, so entitled.

Special resolution

Special resolution: A resolution passed by at least three-fourths clear majority.

A special resolution is one which is passed by at least three-fourths clear majority, i.e., the number of votes cast in favour of the resolution is at least three times the number of votes cast against it, either by a show of hands or by a poll, in person or by proxy. As per Section 114(2), a resolution shall be a special resolution when

1. the intention to propose the resolution as a special resolution has been duly specified in the notice calling the general meeting or other intimation given to the members of the resolution;
2. the notice required under this Act has been duly given; and
3. the votes cast in favour of the resolution, whether on a show of hands, or electronically or on a poll, as the case may be, by members who, being entitled so to do, vote in person or by proxy or by postal ballot, are required to be not less than three times the number of the votes, if any, cast against the resolution by members so entitled.

Special resolutions are needed to decide on important matters of the company. Examples, where special resolutions are required are as follows:

1. To alter the object's clause of the memorandum;
2. To alter or change the name of the company with the approval of the Central Government
3. To alter the articles of the company; and
4. To change the name of the company by omitting the word 'Limited' or 'Private Limited'. The Central Government may allow a company with charitable objects to do so by a special resolution under Section 8 of the Companies Act, 2013.

Resolution requiring a special notice

Resolution requiring a special notice is a species of ordinary resolution. There are certain matters specified in the Act, which may be discussed at a general meeting for which a prior intention to move the resolution has to be given to the members. As per Section 115, where, by any provision of the Companies Act or in the articles of a company, a special notice is required of any resolution, notice of the intention to move such resolution shall be given to the company by such number of members holding not less than one percent of total voting power or holding shares on which such aggregate sum not exceeding five lakh rupees, as may be prescribed, has been paid-up and the company shall give its members a notice of the resolution in such manner as may be prescribed.

Such a prior intention in the form of a special notice enables the members to be prepared on the matter to be discussed and gives them time to indicate their views on the resolution.

In case a special notice of resolution is required by the Companies Act, by the articles of a company, the intention to propose such a resolution must be notified to the company at least 14 clear days before the meeting. 'Clear days' means that the day on which the notice is served or deemed to be served and the day of the meeting shall be excluded.

The following matters, in order to be taken up for discussion, require a special notice before the meeting:

1. To appoint an auditor other than a retiring auditor at an annual general meeting ;
2. To resolve at an annual general meeting that a retiring auditor shall not be reappointed;
3. To remove a director before the expiration of his period of office;
4. To appoint another director in place of a removed director; and
5. Where the articles provide for serving a special notice for a resolution, in respect of any specified matter.

A resolution requiring a special notice may be passed either as an ordinary resolution (with simple majority) or as a special resolution (with three-fourths majority).

Minutes

Minutes: Records of the proceedings of a meeting.

Every company must keep records of all the proceedings of a meeting, known as minutes. The minutes are a gist of the discussions at the meeting and the final decisions taken there at and act as evidence of the proceedings recorded therein. It normally includes only the resolutions actually passed. As per Section 118(1), every company causes minutes of the proceedings of every general meeting of any class of shareholders or creditors, and every resolution passed by postal ballot and every meeting of its Board of Directors or of every committee of the Board, to be prepared and signed in such manner as may be prescribed and kept within thirty days of the conclusion of every such meeting concerned, or passing of resolution by postal ballot in books kept for that purpose with their pages consecutively numbered.

The minutes of each meeting shall contain a fair and correct summary of the proceedings thereat. All appointments of officers made at any of the meetings must be included in the minutes of the meeting [Section 118(2) & (3)].

In the case of a meeting of the Board of directors or its Committee, the minutes must also state the names of directors present at the meeting, and the names of directors, if any, dissenting from, or not concurring with a resolution passed at the meeting [Section 118(4)].

The chairman may exclude from the minutes any matters which are defamatory, irrelevant or immaterial or which are detrimental to the interests of the company. The discretion of the Chairman with regard to the inclusion or exclusion of any matter is absolute and unfettered [Section 118(5) & (6)].

The minute books of the proceedings of general meetings must be kept at the registered office of the company. Every member will have a right to inspect, free of cost during business hours at the registered office of the company, the minute books. Furthermore, any member shall be entitled to be furnished, within seven days after he/she has made a request to the company, with a copy of any minutes on payment of Rupee one for every hundred words or fraction thereof.

If a person is found guilty of tampering with the minutes of the proceedings of meeting, he shall be punishable with imprisonment for a term which may extend to two years and with fine which shall not be less than twenty-five thousand rupees but which may extend to one lakh rupees [Section 118(4)].

Winding Up of a Company: Introduction

Winding up—a means by which a company is dissolved—is an unfortunate, but many times inevitable part of company management. A company either has to grow or it will decay and run out of business.

Some companies may flourish and grow, while some unfortunate ones may incur losses and may have to be closed down. Ironically, a company which is growing and making good profits may also land into trouble. Even blue-chip companies like Metal Box, GM Motors, and Guest Keen Williams, etc., have become sick. Conversely, a company like Reliance, which was nowhere on the industrial horizon about three decades ago, is now counted among the Fortune 500 companies in the world. On the other hand, a well-heeled MNC like the Lehman Brothers is facing possible closure after becoming bankrupt. Nonetheless, it does not mean that companies in financial difficulties alone are wound up. Legally, even a financially sound company can be wound up on the basis of numerous other grounds, though it is not usually done. Winding up or liquidation is not just a legal exercise to satisfy the debts of creditors, but also signifies the loss of brand value that the company enjoyed in its entire history.

Implication of Winding Up

Winding up: The means by which a company is dissolved.

Winding up is the process of bringing to an end the legal personality of a company as a corporate body. During this process the company ceases to carry on its usual business, the assets are realized, the proceeds are utilized in paying off the debts, and the surplus, if any, is distributed amongst contributories *pro rata*. Generally, 'winding up' is associated with sinking and loss making companies. To that extent, winding up is similar to insolvency proceedings in respect of an individual. However, even a solvent company can be wound up under certain compelling circumstances.

Modes of Winding Up

Compulsory winding up: Winding up by an order of the Tribunal.

The Insolvency and Bankruptcy Code, 2016 (hereinafter reffered to as 'the Code') has been notified with effect from November 15, 2016 and by virtue of Section 225 of the Code, the Companies Act, 2013 stands amended in accordance with Schedule XI of the Code. The aforesaid Schedule now Code defines the term 'winding up' by introducing a new section [Section 2(94A)] to the 2013 Act as "winding up under this Act or liquidation under the Insolvency and Bankruptcy Code, 2016'. Accordingly, certain winding up proceedings will now be goverened by the provisions of the 2013 Act whereas certain others under the Besides, other significant changes or amendments introduced by the Code include complete removal of provisions of 'voluntry winding up' and compulsory winding up on the ground of 'inability to pay debt' from the 2013 Act. These proceedings are now extend to deal with under the Code.

Therefore, winding up of a company can be studied under the following two modes:

1. Winding up by the Tribunal; or
2. Voluntarily winding up.

Winding up By the Tribunal

A company may, on a petition under Section 272, be wound up by the Tribunal in the following circuimstances:

(a) If the comapny has, by special resolution, resolved that the company be wound up by the Tribunal;

(b) If the company has acted against the interests of the sovereighty and integrity of India, the security of the State, friendly relations with foreign States, public order, decency or morality;

(c) If on an application made by the Registrar or any other person authorised by the Central Government by notification under this Act, the Tribunal is of the opinion that the affairs of the company have been conducted in a fraudulent and unlawful purpose or the persons concerned in the formation or management of its affairs have been guilty of fraud, misfeasance or misconduct in connection therewith and that it is proper that the company be wound up;

(d) If thecompany has made a default in filing with the Registrar its financial statements or annual returns for immediately preceding five consecutive financial years; or

(e) If the Tribunalis of the opinion that it is just and equitable that the company should be wound up [Section 271].

Process of Winding Up of a Company by the Tribunal

The process of winding up of a company can be studied under the following heads:

1. Petition for winding up
2. Exercise of powers by the Tribunal as regards petition
3. Directions for filing statement of affairs
4. Appointment of company liquidator
5. Removal and replacement of liquidator
6. Intimation to liquidator and Registrar
7. Custody of company's properties by the liquidator
8. Submission of report by Company Liquidator
9. Direction of Tribunal on report of Company Liquidator
10. Settlement of list of contributories and application of assets

Petition for winding up by the Tribunal

A petition to the Tribunal for winding up of a company, as per Section 272, can be made by any of the following.

1. Company itself;
2. Any contributory or contributories;
3. The company and any or all the, or contributories acting jointly;
4. The Registrar;
5. Any person authorised by the Central Government in that behalf; or
6. The Central Government or a State Government where the company has acted against the interests of the sovereignty and integrity of India, the security of the State, friendly relations with foreign States, public order, decency or morality.

Exercise of powers by the Tribunal

The Tribunal may, on receipt of a petition for winding up under Section 272 pass any of the following orders, namely:—

(a) dismiss it, with or without costs;
(b) make any interim order as it thinks fit;
(c) appoint a provisional liquidator of the company till the making of a winding up order;
(d) make an order for the winding up of the company with or without costs; or
(e) any other order as it thinks fit.

Provided that an order under this sub-section shall be made within ninety days from the date of presentation of the petition.

Provided further that before appointing a provisional liquidator under clause (c), the Tribunal shall give notice to the company and afford a reasonable opportunity to it to make its representations, if any, unless for special reasons to be recorded in writing, the Tribunal thinks fit to dispense with such notice.

Provided also that the Tribunal shall not refuse to make a winding up order on the ground only that the assets of the company have been mortgaged for an amount equal to or in excess of those assets, or that the company has no assets.

(2)Where a petition is presented on the ground that it is just and equitable that the company should be wound up, the Tribunal may refuse to make an order of winding up, if it is of the opinion that some other remedy is available to the petitioners and that they are acting unreasonably in seeking to have the company wound up instead of pursuing the other remedy [Section 273].

Directions for filing statement of affairs by the Tribunal to the company

(1) Where a petition for winding up is filed before the Tribunal by any person other than the

company, the Tribunal shall, if satisfied that a prima facie case for winding up of the company is made out, by an order direct the company to file its objections along with a statement of its affairs within thirty days of the order in such form and in such manner as may be prescribed.

Provided that the Tribunal may allow a further period of thirty days in a situation of contingency or special circumstances.

Provided further that the Tribunal may direct the petitioner to deposit such security for costs as it may consider reasonable as a precondition to issue directions to the company.

(2) A company, which fails to file the statement of affairs as referred to in sub-section (1), shall forfeit the right to oppose the petition and such directors and officers of the company as found responsible for such non-compliance, shall be liable for punishment under sub-section (4).

(3) The directors and other officers of the company, in respect of which an order for winding up is passed by the Tribunal under clause (d) of sub-section (1) of section 273, shall, within a period of thirty days of such order, submit, at the cost of the company, the books of account of the company completed and audited up to the date of the order, to such liquidator and in the manner specified by the Tribunal.

(4) If any director or officer of the company contravenes the provisions of this section, the director or the officer of the company who is in default shall be punishable with imprisonment for a term which may extend to six months or with fine which shall not be less than twenty-five thousand rupees but which may extend to five lakh rupees, or with both.

(5) The complaint may be filed in this behalf before the Special Court by Registrar, provisional liquidator, Company Liquidator or any person authorized by the Tribunal [Section 274].

Appointment of official liquidator

Official liquidator: Liquidator appointed by the Tribunal to conduct the winding up proceedings.

Proceedings of winding up are conducted by an official administrator, called 'liquidator' under the supervision of the Tribunal.

The rules governing the appointment of a liquidator are stated in Section 275 of The Companies Act, 2013, reproduced below:

1. For the purposes of winding up of a company by the Tribunal, the Tribunal at the time of the passing of the order of winding up shall appoint an Official Liquidator or a liquidator from the panel maintained under sub-section (2) as the Company Liquidator.
2. The provisional liquidator or the Company Liquidator, as the case may be, shall be appointed by the Tribunal from amongst the insolvency professionals registered under the Insolvency and Bankruptcy Code, 2016.
3. Where a provisional liquidator is appointed by the Tribunal, the Tribunal may limit and restrict his powers by the order appointing him or it or by a subsequent order, but otherwise he shall have the same powers as a liquidator.
4. The terms and conditions of appointment of a provisional liquidator or Company Liquidator and the fee payable to him or it shall be specified by the Tribunal on the basis of tasks required to be performed, experience, qualification of such liquidator and the size of the company.
5. Upon appointment as a provisional liquidator or Company Liquidator, as the case may be, such liquidator shall file a declaration within seven days from the date of appointment in the prescribed form disclosing conflict of interest or lack of independence in respect of his appointment, if any, with the Tribunal and such obligation shall continue throughout the term of his appointment.
6. While passing a winding up order, the Tribunal may appoint a provisional liquidator, if any, appointed under clause (*c*) of sub-section (1) of section 273, as the Company Liquidator for the conduct of the proceedings for the winding up of the company.

Removal and replacement of a liquidator

1. The Tribunal may, on a reasonable cause being shown and for reasons to be recorded in writing, remove the provisional liquidator or the Company Liquidator, as the case may

be, as liquidator of the company on any of the following grounds, namely:

(a) Misconduct;
(b) Fraud or misfeasance;
(c) Professional incompetence or failure to exercise due care and diligence in performance of the powers and functions;
(d) Inability to act as a provisional liquidator or as the case may be, Company Liquidator;
(e) Conflict of interest or lack of independence during the term of his appointment that would justify removal.

2. In the event of death, resignation or removal of the provisional liquidator or as the case may be, Company Liquidator, the Tribunal may transfer the work assigned to him or it to another Company Liquidator for reasons to be recorded in writing.
3. Where the Tribunal is of the opinion that any liquidator is responsible for causing any loss or damage to the company due to fraud or misfeasance or failure to exercise due care and diligence in the performance of his or its powers and functions, the Tribunal may recover or cause to be recovered such loss or damage from the liquidator and pass such other orders as it may think fit.
4. The Tribunal shall, before passing any order under this section, provide a reasonable opportunity of being heard to the provisional liquidator or, as the case may be, Company Liquidator [Section 276].

Intimation to Company Liquidator and Registrar

1. Where the Tribunal makes an order for appointment of provisional liquidator or for the winding up of a company, it shall, within a period not exceeding seven days from the date of passing of the order, cause intimation thereof to be sent to the Company Liquidator or provisional liquidator, as the case may be, and the Registrar.
2. On receipt of the copy of order of appointment of provisional liquidator or winding up order, the Registrar shall make an endorsement to that effect in his records relating to the company and notify in the Official Gazette that such an order has been made and in the case of a listed company, the Registrar shall intimate about such appointment or order, as the case may be, to the stock exchange or exchanges where the securities of the company are listed.
3. The winding up order shall be deemed to be a notice of discharge to the officers, employees and workmen of the company, except when the business of the company is continued.
4. Within three weeks from the date of passing of winding up order, the Company Liquidator shall make an application to the Tribunal for constitution of a winding up committee to assist and monitor the progress of liquidation proceedings by the Company Liquidator in carrying out the function as provided in sub-section (5) and such winding up committee shall comprise of the following persons, namely:—

   (i) Official Liquidator attached to the Tribunal;
   (ii) nominee of secured creditors; and
   (iii) a professional nominated by the Tribunal.

5. The Company Liquidator shall be the convener of the meetings of the winding up committee which shall assist and monitor the liquidation proceedings in following areas of liquidation functions, namely:—

   (i) taking over assets;
   (ii) examination of the statement of affairs;
   (iii) recovery of property, cash or any other assets of the company including benefits derived there from;
   (iv) review of audit reports and accounts of the company;
   (v) sale of assets;
   (vi) finalisation of list of creditors and contributories;
   (vii) compromise, abandonment and settlement of claims;
   (viii) payment of dividends, if any; and
   (ix) any other function, as the Tribunal may direct from time to time.

6. The Company Liquidator shall place before the Tribunal a report along with minutes of the meetings of the committee on monthly basis duly signed by the members present in the meeting for consideration till the final report for dissolution of the company is submitted before the Tribunal.

7. The Company Liquidator shall prepare the draft final report for consideration and approval of the winding up committee.
8. The final report so approved by the winding up committee shall be submitted by the Company Liquidator before the Tribunal for passing of a dissolution order in respect of the company.

Effect of winding up order - The order for the winding up of a company shall operate in favour of all the creditors and all contributories of the company as if it had been made out on the joint petition of creditors and contributories [Section 278].

Custody of company's properties

1. Where a winding up order has been made or where a provisional liquidator has been appointed, the Company Liquidator or the provisional liquidator, as the case may be, shall, on the order of the Tribunal, forthwith take into his or its custody or control all the property, effects and actionable claims to which the company is or appears to be entitled to and take such steps and measures, as may be necessary, to protect and preserve the properties of the company.
2. Notwithstanding anything contained in sub-section (1), all the property and effects of the company shall be deemed to be in the custody of the Tribunal from the date of the order for the winding up of the company.
3. On an application by the Company Liquidator or otherwise, the Tribunal may, at any time after the making of a winding up order, require any contributory for the time being on the list of contributories, and any trustee, receiver, banker, agent, officer or other employee of the company, to pay, deliver, surrender or transfer forthwith, or within such time as the Tribunal directs, to the Company Liquidator, any money, property or books and papers in his custody or under his control to which the company is or appears to be entitled [Section 283].

Submission of report by Company Liquidator

1. Where the Tribunal has made a winding up order or appointed a Company Liquidator, such liquidator shall, within sixty days from the order, submit to the Tribunal, a report containing the following particulars, namely:—
   (a) the nature and details of the assets of the company including their location and value, stating separately the cash balance in hand and in the bank, if any, and the negotiable securities, if any, held by the company:

   However, the valuation of the assets shall be obtained from registered valuers for this purpose;

   (b) amount of capital issued, subscribed and paid-up;
   (c) the existing and contingent liabilities of the company including names, addresses and occupations of its creditors, stating separately the amount of secured and unsecured debts, and in the case of secured debts, particulars of the securities given, whether by the company or an officer thereof, their value and the dates on which they were given;
   (d) the debts due to the company and the names, addresses and occupations of the persons from whom they are due and the amount likely to be realised on account thereof;
   (e) guarantees, if any, extended by the company;
   (f) list of contributories and dues, if any, payable by them and details of any unpaid call;
   (g) details of trademarks and intellectual properties, if any, owned by the company;
   (h) details of subsisting contracts, joint ventures and collaborations, if any;
   (i) details of holding and subsidiary companies, if any;
   (j) details of legal cases filed by or against the company; and
   (k) any other information which the Tribunal may direct or the Company Liquidator may consider necessary to include.
2. The Company Liquidator shall include in his report the manner in which the company was promoted or formed and whether in his opinion any fraud has been committed by any person in its promotion or formation or by any officer of the company in relation to the company since the formation thereof and any other matters

which, in his opinion, it is desirable to bring to the notice of the Tribunal.

3. The Company Liquidator shall also make a report on the viability of the business of the company or the steps which, in his opinion, are necessary for maximising the value of the assets of the company.
4. The Company Liquidator may also, if he thinks fit, make any further report or reports.
5. Any person describing himself in writing to be a creditor or a contributory of the company shall be entitled by himself or by his agent at all reasonable times to inspect the report submitted in accordance with this section and take copies thereof or extracts there from on payment of the prescribed fees [Section 281].

Directions of Tribunal on report of Company Liquidator

1. The Tribunal shall, on consideration of the report of the Company Liquidator, fix a time limit within which the entire proceedings shall be completed and the company be dissolved:

   However, the Tribunal may, if it is of the opinion, at any stage of the proceedings, or on examination of the reports submitted to it by the Company Liquidator and after hearing the Company Liquidator, creditors or contributories or any other interested person, that it will not be advantageous or economical to continue the proceedings, revise the time limit within which the entire proceedings shall be completed and the company be dissolved.

2. The Tribunal may, on examination of the reports submitted to it by the Company Liquidator and after hearing the Company Liquidator, creditors or contributories or any other interested person, order sale of the company as a going concern or its assets or part thereof:

   However, the Tribunal may, where it considers fit, appoint a sale committee comprising such creditors, promoters and officers of the company as the Tribunal may decide to assist the Company Liquidator in sale under this sub-section.

3. Where a report is received from the Company Liquidator or the Central Government or any person that a fraud has been committed in respect of the company, the Tribunal shall, without prejudice to the process of winding up, order for investigation under section 210, and on consideration of the report of such investigation it may pass order and give directions under sections 339 to 342 or direct the Company Liquidator to file a criminal complaint against persons who were involved in the commission of fraud.
4. The Tribunal may order for taking such steps and measures, as may be necessary, to protect, preserve or enhance the value of the assets of the company.
5. The Tribunal may pass such other order or give such other directions as it considers fit [Section 282].

Settlement of list of contributories and application of assets

1. As soon as may be after the passing of a winding up order by the Tribunal, the Tribunal shall settle a list of contributories, cause rectification of register of members in all cases where rectification is required in pursuance of this Act and shall cause the assets of the company to be applied for the discharge of its liability:

   However, where it appears to the Tribunal that it would not be necessary to make calls on or adjust the rights of contributories, it may dispense with the settlement of a list of contributories.

2. In settling the list of contributories, the Tribunal shall distinguish between those who are contributories in their own right and those who are contributories as being representatives of, or liable for the debts of, others.
3. While settling the list of contributories, the Tribunal shall include every person, who is or has been a member, who shall be liable to contribute to the assets of the company an amount sufficient for payment of the debts and liabilities and the costs, charges and expenses of winding up, and for the adjustment of the rights of the contributories among themselves, subject to the following conditions, namely:—

   (a) a person who has been a member shall not be liable to contribute if he has ceased to be a member for the preceding one year or more before the commencement of the winding up;

(b) a person who has been a member shall not be liable to contribute in respect of any debt or liability of the company contracted after he ceased to be a member;

(c) no person who has been a member shall be liable to contribute unless it appears to the Tribunal that the present members are unable to satisfy the contributions required to be made by them in pursuance of this Act;

(d) in the case of a company limited by shares, no contribution shall be required from any person, who is or has been a member exceeding the amount, if any, unpaid on the shares in respect of which he is liable as such member;

(e) in the case of a company limited by guarantee, no contribution shall be required from any person, who is or has been a member exceeding the amount undertaken to be contributed by him to the assets of the company in the event of its being wound up but if the company has a share capital, such member shall be liable to contribute to the extent of any sum unpaid on any shares held by him as if the company were a company limited by shares [Section 285].

Powers and Duties of Company Liquidator

Subject to the directions, if any, and overall control of the Tribunal, the Act besides imposing certain duties on the Company Liquidator, empowers latter to exercise number of powers in connection with winding up of a company by the Tribunal under Section 290(1). These powers and duties are as under:

(a) to carry on the business of the company so far as may be necessary for the beneficial winding up of the company;

(b) to do all acts and to execute, in the name and on behalf of the company, all deeds, receipts and other documents, and for that purpose, to use, when necessary, the company's seal;

(c) to sell the immovable and movable property and actionable claims of the company by public auction or private contract, with power to transfer such property to any person or body corporate, or to sell the same in parcels;

(d) to sell the whole of the undertaking of the company as a going concern;

(e) to raise any money required on the security of the assets of the company;

(f) to institute or defend any suit, prosecution or other legal proceeding, civil or criminal, in the name and on behalf of the company;

(g) to invite and settle claim of creditors, employees or any other claimant and distribute sale proceeds in accordance with priorities established under this Act;

(h) to inspect the records and returns of the company on the files of the Registrar or any other authority;

(i) to prove rank and claim in the insolvency of any contributory for any balance against his estate, and to receive dividends in the insolvency, in respect of that balance, as a separate debt due from the insolvent, and rateably with the other separate creditors;

(j) to draw, accept, make and endorse any negotiable instruments including cheque, bill of exchange, hundi or promissory note in the name and on behalf of the company, with the same effect with respect to the liability of the company as if such instruments had been drawn, accepted, made or endorsed by or on behalf of the company in the course of its business;

(k) to take out, in his official name, letters of administration to any deceased contributory, and to do in his official name any other act necessary for obtaining payment of any money due from a contributory or his estate which cannot be conveniently done in the name of the company, and in all such cases, the money due shall, for the purpose of enabling the Company Liquidator to take out the letters of administration or recover the money, be deemed to be due to the Company Liquidator himself;

(l) to obtain any professional assistance from any person or appoint any professional, in discharge of his duties, obligations and responsibilities and for protection of the assets of the company, appoint an agent to do any business which the Company Liquidator is unable to do himself;

(m) to take all such actions, steps, or to sign, execute and verify any paper, deed, document, application, petition, affidavit, bond or instrument as may be necessary,—

(i) for winding up of the company;
(ii) for distribution of assets;
(iii) in discharge of his duties and obligations and functions as Company Liquidator; and

(n) to apply to the Tribunal for such orders or directions as may be necessary for the winding up of the company.

Voluntary Winding Up

Voluntary winding up: Winding up of a company by the members in a predefined manner and subject to fufilment of certain conditions by the company.

Voluntary winding up process applies where the directors and shareholders decide to cease the affairs of their solvent limited company. Such type of winding up of a company can be initiated by the members of the company, if:

- If the company passes a special resolution in the General Meeting for its winding up.
- The company in general meeting passes a resolution requiring it to be wound up voluntarily as a result of the expiry of the period of its duration, if any, fixed by its articles or on the occurrence of any event in respect of which the articles provide that the company should be dissolved.

As the Code (The IBC, 2016) got the president assent on 28/05/2016 as per Section 255 and Schedule XI of the Code, the sections of voluntary winding up "Omitted" from Companies Act, 2013. The Insolvency and Bankruptcy Board of India (IBBI) has notified the IBBI (Voluntary Liquidation Process) Regulations, 2017. As a result of the same, with effect from 1st April, 2017 voluntary winding up shall be conducted under the Code. These Regulations shall apply to the voluntary liquidation of corporate persons under Chapter V of Part II of the Code.

Brief Highlights of IBBI Regulations, 2017:

- Insolvency Professionals shall act as liquidator.
- The corporate person shall from the liquidation commencement date cease to carry on its business except as far as required for the beneficial winding up of its business
- The liquidator shall endeavor to complete the liquidation process of the corporate person within twelve months from the liquidation commencement date.
- The liquidator shall preserve a physical or an electronic copy of the reports, registers and books of account referred to in Regulations 8 and 10 for at least eight years after the dissolution of the corporate person, either with himself or with an information utility.

Process of Voluntary Winding up

Voluntary winding up of a company is a comprehensive 10-step procedure, explained below:

Step 1 – Board Meeting

A Board meeting is to be convened by a majority of Directors for the following purposes:

1.1. To pass a resolution for proposal of Voluntary Liquidation of the company.

1.2. To prepare a declaration from majority of the directors of the company verified by an affidavit stating that—

(i) they have made a full inquiry into the affairs of the company and they have formed an opinion that either the company has no debt or that it will be able to pay its debts in full from the proceeds of assets to be sold in the voluntary liquidation; and
(ii) The company is not being liquidated to defraud any person [Section 59(3) (a) of the Code].

1.3. File the declaration with the RoC in e-form GNL-2

1.4. Attachment to Declaration:

(a) Audited financial statements and record of business operations of the company for the previous two years or for the period since its incorporation, whichever is later; and
(b) A report of the valuation of the assets of the company, if any, prepared by a registered valuer;

Step 2 – General Meeting

Within 4 weeks of passing of the above declaration, the company has to hold the meeting of its members for the following purposes:

2.1. To pass a special resolution for approving the proposal of voluntary liquidation of the company.

2.2. To appoint an insolvency professional to act as the liquidator. Resolution should contain the terms and conditions of the appointment of the insolvency professional, including the remuneration due to him.

2.3. To file the special resolution with the RoC in e-form MGT-14

Step 3 – Approval of Creditors if the Company Owes Debt

3.1. If the company owes any debt to any person, creditors representing two-thirds in value of the debt of the company shall approve the resolution passed above by the shareholders within seven days of passing of such special resolution.

3.2. Approval can be done by holding of meeting and thereby taking the consent of two-thirds of creditors in writing . The company will place the copy of resolutions before the creditors for their approval.

The voluntary liquidation of the company shall be deemed to have commenced from the date of passing of the resolution after approval from the creditors.

Step 4 – Public Announcement by the Liquidator

The liquidator shall make a public announcement in Form A of Schedule I within five days from his appointment (i.e. 5 days from the date of General Meeting).

4.1. The public announcement shall call upon stakeholders to submit their claims as on the liquidation commencement date; and provide the last date for submission of claim, which shall be thirty days from the liquidation commencement date.

4.2. The announcement shall be published-

(i) In one English and one regional language newspaper with wide circulation at the location of the registered office and principal office, if any, of the corporate person and any other location where in the opinion of the liquidator, the corporate person conducts material business operations;

(ii) On the website, if any, of the company; and

(iii) On the website, if any, designated by the Board for this purpose.

Step 5 – Proceedings By the Liquidator

5.1. The liquidator shall submit a 'Preliminary Report' to the company within 45 days from the liquidation commencement date, detailing as given below and preserve a physical as well as an electronic copy of the report for eight years after the dissolution of the company.

(a) The capital structure of the company

(b) The estimates of its assets and liabilities as on the liquidation commencement date based on the books of the company

(c) Whether he intends to make any further inquiry into any matter relating to the promotion, formation or failure of the Company or the conduct of the business thereof; and

(d) The proposed plan of action for carrying out the liquidation, including the timeline within which he proposes to carry it out and the estimated liquidation costs.

5.2. Maintenance of Registers and Books of Account:

5.2.1. The liquidator shall maintain the registers and books (as mentioned in regulation 10), as may be applicable, in relation to the voluntary liquidation of the company, and shall preserve them for a period of eight years after the dissolution of the corporate person.

5.2.2. Where the books of account of the corporate person are incomplete on the liquidation commencement date, the liquidator shall have them completed and brought up-to date, with all convenient speed.

5.2.3. The liquidator shall keep receipts for all payments made or expenses incurred by him

5.3. The liquidator may call for such other evidence or clarification as he deems fit from a Claimant for substantiating the whole or part of its claim.

5.3.2 Verification of claims:

5.3.2.1 The liquidator shall verify the claims submitted within thirty days from the last date for receipt of claims and may either admit or reject the claim, in whole or in part, as the case may be, as per Section 40 of the Code.

5.3.2.2. A creditor may appeal to the Adjudicating Authority against the decision of the liquidator as per Section 42 of the Code.

5.3.3. List of stakeholders:

5.3.3.1. The liquidator shall prepare the list of stakeholders within forty-five days from the last date for receipt of claims.

5.3.3.2. The liquidator shall prepare a list of stakeholders on the basis of proofs of claims submitted and accepted under these Regulations, with-

(a) the amounts of claim admitted, if applicable,
(b) the extent to which the debts or dues are secured or unsecured, if applicable,
(c) the details of the stakeholders, and
(d) The proofs admitted or rejected in part, and the proofs wholly rejected.

5.3.4. Payment of money into Bank Account:

5.3.4.1 The liquidator shall open a bank account in the name of the company followed by the words 'in voluntary liquidation', in a scheduled bank, for the receipt of all moneys due to the corporate person.

5.3.4.2. All payments out of the account by the liquidator above five thousand rupees shall be made by cheques drawn or online banking transactions against the bank account.

5.3.5. Distribution of proceeds:

5.3.5.1. The liquidator shall distribute the proceeds from realization within six months from the receipt of the amount to the stakeholders.

5.3.5.2. The liquidation costs shall be deducted before such distribution is made.

Step 6 – Completion of Liquidation Proceedings

6.1. The liquidator shall endeavour to wind up the affairs of the company within one year from the voluntary liquidation commencement date.

6.2. In the event of the voluntary liquidation continuing for more than one year, the liquidator shall.

6.2.1. call a meeting of the contributories of the corporate person within fifteen days from the end of the year in which he is appointed, and at the end of each succeeding year; and

6.2.2. Shall present a 'Status Report' indicating progress in liquidation, including-

(a) Settlement of list of stakeholders,
(b) Details of any property that remain to be sold and realized,
(c) Distribution made to the stakeholders, and
(d) Distribution of unsold property made to the stakeholders;
(e) Developments in any material litigation, by or against the corporate person; and
(f) Filing of, and developments in applications for avoidance of transactions in accordance with Chapter III of Part II of the Code.

6.2.3. The Status Report shall enclose an audited account of the voluntary liquidation showing the receipts and payments pertaining to liquidation since the liquidation commencement date.

Step 7 – Preparation of Final Report

On completion of the liquidation process, the liquidator shall prepare the 'Final Report' consisting of:

(a) An audited account of the voluntary liquidation, showing the receipts and payments pertaining to liquidation since the liquidation commencement date; and
(b) A statement demonstrating that-
    (i) The assets of the company has been disposed of;
    (ii) the debt of the company has been discharged to the satisfaction of the creditors; and
    (iii) No litigation is pending against the company or sufficient provision has been made to meet the obligations arising from any pending litigation.
(c) 7.1.3. sale statement in respect of all assets containing: i) the realized value; (ii) cost of realization, if any; (iii) the manner and mode of sale; (iv) an explanation for the shortfall, if the value realized is less than the value assigned by the registered valuer in the report of the valuation of assets (v) the person to whom the sale is made; and (vi) any other relevant details of the sale.

Step 8 - Submission Of Final Report/ Application With NCLT

8.1. The liquidator shall send the 'Final Report' by registered post at their registered address and by electronic means to:

(a) The contributories of the corporate person;
(b) The registrar; and
(c) The Insolvency and Bankruptcy Board of India.

8.2. Submission with NCLT:

Where the affairs of the company have been completely wound up, and its assets completely liquidated, the liquidator shall make an application to the NCLT in form NCLT-1 for the dissolution of such company.

Step 9 – Order By NCLT

The NCLT or Tribunal shall fix a date for the hearing of the petition. If the Tribunal satisfied with the application, it will pass an order that the corporate debtor shall be dissolved from the date of that order and the corporate debtor shall be dissolved accordingly.

Step 10 – Filing of Order With the RoC

The order of the Tribunal shall be filed with the Registrar by the company within a period of 14 days of the receipt of the copy of order, or such other time as may be fixed by the Tribunal.

Suspension of Process of Liquidation: If liquidator is of the opinion that the voluntary liquidation is being done to defraud a person, he shall make an application to the Adjudicatory Authority to suspend the process of voluntary liquidation. Where the liquidator is of the opinion that the corporate person will not be able to pay its debts in full from the proceeds of assets to be sold in the voluntary liquidation, he shall make an application to the Adjudicating Authority to suspend the process of voluntary liquidation.

Powers and duties of a company liquidator As per Section 314, the Company Liquidator shall:

order was made, within thirty days after the making of the order or such further time as the Tribunal may allow, to file a certified copy of the order with the Registrar who shall register the same, and if the Company Liquidator or the person fails so to do, the Company Liquidator or the person shall be punishable with fine which may extend to ten thousand rupees for every day during which the default continues [Section 356(2)].

Exercises

I. Objective-type Questions

1. Who among the following persons cannot be appointed as a director of any company?
   (a) an undischarged insolvent
   (b) a person found by a competent court to be of unsound mind
   (c) a person who has been convicted by a court of an offence involving moral turpitude and sentenced in respect thereof to imprisonment for not less than six months, and a period of five years has not elapsed from the date of the expiry of the sentence
   (d) All of the above

2. Who among the following is not a competent authority to remove a director from his office?
   (a) Shareholders (b) Board of Directors
   (c) Central Govt. (d) Tribunal

3. Which of the following duties is not a general duty of directors of a company?
   (a) Duty of good faith (b) Duty of care
   (c) Duty to attend Board meetings (d) Duty not to delegate

4. Annual general meeting (AGM) must be held by
   (a) Every company
   (b) Every public company
   (c) Every company other than a 'One Person Company'
   (d) Every company other than a 'One Person Company' and a 'Small Company'

5. When does the Board call an Extraordinary General Meeting?
   (a) Whenever directors think fit, by passing a resolution to that effect in the Board's meeting
   (b) On the requisition of members holding not less than one-tenth of the total voting rights on the matter of requisition
   (c) On the application of the Company Law Board
   (d) In all the above cases

6. The persons entitled to the notice of a class meeting are:
   (a) Every member of the company
   (b) Auditors of the company for the time being
   (c) Shareholders of the particular class only
   (d) Auditors (for the time being) and the shareholders of that particular class

7. A petition to the Tribunal for winding up of the company can be filed by:
   (a) Any contributory or contributories
   (b) Any person authorized by the Central Government in that behalf
   (c) The Registrar
   (d) Any of the above

8. Which of the following can be the solid reasons for passing the winding up order by the Tribunal?
   1. If the company has, by a special resolution, resolved that the company be wound up by the Tribunal.
   2. If the company has acted against the interests of the sovereignty and integrity of India, the security of the State, friendly relations with foreign States, public order, decency or morality.
   3. If the company has made a default in filing with the Registrar its financial statements or annual returns for immediately preceding five consecutive financial years.

   If the Tribunal is of the opinion that it is just and equitable that the company should be wound up.

   Answer Codes:
   (a) (1), (2), (3) and (5)
   (b) (1), (2), (3) and (4)
   (c) (1), (3), (4) and (5)
   (d) (1), (2), (3), (4) and (5)

9. A company is deemed to be unable to pay its debts if it fails to pay its creditor within three weeks of the demand a sum exceeding
   (a) ₹10,000
   (b) ₹25000
   (c) ₹50,000
   (d) ₹1,00,000

10. During the winding up process
    (i) The assets of the company are realized
    (ii) The surplus is paid back to the members *pro rata*
    (iii) The proceeds are utilized in paying off the debts and liabilities
    (iv) The company ceases to carry on its normal business.

    What is the correct sequence of above stages?
    (a) (i), (ii), (iii), (iv)
    (b) (i), (iii), (ii), (iv)
    (c) (iv), (i), (ii), (iii)
    (d) (iv), (i), (iii), (ii)

II. Review Questions

1. Who can be a 'Director'? Briefly discuss the modes of appointment of directors.

2. Can the directors of a company be appointed by the Board of directors? Elaborate.

3. Discuss the restrictions imposed in respect of director's powers.

4. Discuss briefly the provisions of The Companies Act, 2013 with regard to removal of a director from his/her office.

5. Comment on the following:
   (a) Alternate directors
   (b) Additional directors
   (c) Nominee director
   (d) Resignation by director
   (e) Appointment of directors by proportional representation
   (f) Independent directors

6. Discuss the rules governing to Board meetings.

7. Describe the relevance of an annual general meeting. Discuss the statutory provisions with respect to the notice of an annual general meeting as to the length, time, place, form and persons entitled thereto and the business, generally transacted.
8. Describe the essentials of a valid meeting.
9. Write explanatory notes on the following:
   (a) Quorum
   (b) Proxy
   (c) Motion
   (d) Minutes
   (e) Agenda
10. Define a resolution. Describe the purpose of ordinary and special resolutions, and resolutions requiring a special notice.
11. What do you mean by the winding up of a company? Briefly discuss whether is it possible to revive a dissolved company?
12. Describe the grounds for winding up by the Tribunal.
13. Discuss the consequences of a winding up order.
14. Describe the procedure of voluntary winding up of a company under the IBBI (Voluntary Liquidation Process) Regulations, 2017
15. Discuss the process of winding up of a company by the Tribunal.
16. Describe the powers and duties of a Company Liquidator appointed by the Tribunal.

Answers to Objective-type Questions

1. (d)	2. (b)	3. (c)	4. (c)	5. (d)
6. (d)	7. (d)	8. (d)	9. (d)	10. (d)

19 Chapter in Review

LEARNING OUTCOMES

LO 1 Directors: appointment, qualifications, disqualifications
LO 2 Managing director
LO 3 Managerial remuneration
LO 4 Corporate governance
LO 5 Kinds of company meetings; Board meetings, meetings of members
LO 6 Resolutions; minutes
LO 7 Winding up of company; modes of winding up
LO 8 Compulsory winding up: commencement; consequences
LO 9 Voluntary winding up
LO 10 Dissolution of a company and further developments

KEY TERMS

Directors: Individuals who perform the directing function irrespective of the label attached to them.

Independent director: A director other than a managing director or a whole-time director or a nominee director.

Director Identification Number: A unique identification number allotted to a potential director of any company by the Central Government.

First directors: Directors who hold office from the date of incorporation of the company until the first AGM, wherein directors are duly appointed by the shareholders.

Regular director: Every person proposed to be appointed as a director by the company in general meeting or otherwise, who is supposed to furnish his Director Identification Number (DIN) and a declaration that he is not disqualified to be appointed as a director.

Additional director: A director appointed by the Board over and above regular directors if the articles so authorise.

LO1 Directors are the elected representatives of shareholders, entrusted with the responsibility of running the company. A person shall not be eligible to become a director of a company incorporated under the Companies Act, 2013, if he/she suffers from any disqualifications outlined under the Act. When any fact arises during the tenure of office of a director which makes him/her ineligible to continue as a director, the Board may, upon being satisfied of that fact declare his/her office to be vacant.

LO2 The Board chooses one of its members to be the chair or chairperson of the Board of directors, traditionally called Managing Director. The managing director shall be appointed for an initial period not exceeding five years and shall be deemed to have been re-appointed unless the Board of directors passes a resolution to the contrary.

LO3 The directors may be paid out of the funds of the company such remuneration and allowances, including sitting fees for attending Board meetings, subject to provisions given in the Act.

LO4 Corporate governance concerns all issues about the best way to run a company.

LO5 Company meetings may be classified as: Meetings of Board of Directors, Meetings of members—Annual general meetings, and Extraordinary general meetings. Meetings of the Board refer to the meetings of directors. Every company must in each year hold in addition to any other meetings a general meeting as its Annual General Meeting (AGM). An AGM is an important means by which shareholders find an opportunity to exercise their power of control. All general meetings other than AGMs are called extraordinary general meetings.

LO6 A resolution is the formal decision of a meeting on any proposal put before it. There are broadly three types of resolutions under the Act: ordinary, special, and those requiring a special notice. Every company must keep details of all proceedings at the meetings in the form of minutes.

LO7 The winding up is the last stage in the life of a company, wherein its existence is dissolved and all its

Alternate director: A director appointed by the Board in place of a regular director in his absence from his office for a period of three months or more.

Nominee director: A person who acts as a non-executive director on the Board of directors of the company on behalf of an institution, such as a bank, or a financial institution, or some regulating agency etc.

Casual director: A director appointed by the Board to fill the vacancy resulting by the death, resignation, removal of a regular director before the expiry of his term.

Managing director/whole-time director: A director responsible to oversee day to day affairs of a company's business on behalf of the Board and appointed as such by the latter.

Managerial remuneration: Compensation payable to the managerial personnel of a company.

Removal of directors: Termination of directors from the office before the expiry of their term on certain grounds.

Director's resignation: Vacating office by a director voluntarily before the expiry of their term.

Corporate governance: A set of processes, customs, policies, laws, and institutions affecting the way a company is directed, administered, or controlled.

Annual general meeting: Meeting of shareholders, held once in a year statutorily.

Extraordinary general meeting: A meeting called by the Board of directors in emergent situation for taking up some urgent business that cannot be kept pending till the next AGM.

Class meetings: Meetings held by the holders of a particular class of shares.

Resolution: The formal decision of a meeting on any proposal placed before it.

Ordinary resolution: A resolution passed by a simple majority.

Special resolution: A resolution passed by at least three-fourths clear majority.

Minutes: Records of the proceedings of a meeting.

Winding up: The means by which a company is dissolved.

assets are used to satisfy the creditors and shareholders. A company can be wound up by the Tribunal or by the members of the company voluntarily. Since the enactment of The Insolvency and Bankruptcy Code, 2016 (Code) certain winding up proceedings, including related to appointment of company liquidator or liquidator, as the case may be, will now be governed by the provisions of the 2013 Act whereas certain others under the Code. Grounds for winding up by the Tribunal include a special resolution by the members; if the company has acted against the interests of the sovereignty and integrity of India, the security of the State, friendly relations with foreign States, public order, decency or morality; or any other ground which is just and equitable.

LO8 A petition for winding up by the Tribunal can be made by the company itself; any contributory or contributories; any combination of creditors, company or contributories acting jointly or separately; the Registrar of Companies; and any person authorised by the Central Government. A company may be wound up by the Tribunal (a) if the company has, by special resolution, resolved that the company be wound up by the Tribunal; (b) if the company has acted against the interests of the sovereignty and integrity of India, the security of the State, friendly relations with foreign States, public order, decency or morality; (c) if on an application made by the Registrar or any other person authorized by the Central Government by notification under this Act, the Tribunal is of the opinion that the affairs of the company have been conducted in a fraudulent manner or the company was formed for fraudulent and unlawful purpose or the persons concerned in the formation or management of its affairs have been guilty of fraud, misfeasance or misconduct in connection therewith and that it is proper that the company be wound up; (d) if the company has made a default in filing with the Registrar its financial statements or annual returns for immediately preceding five consecutive financial years; or (e) if the Tribunal is of the opinion that it is just and equitable that the company should be wound up.

LO9 Voluntary winding up process applies where the directors and shareholders decide to cease the affairs of their solvent limited company. Such type of winding up of a company can be initiated by the members of the company, if:

- The company passes a special resolution in the General Meeting for its winding up.

Compulsory winding up: Winding up by an order of the Tribunal.

Official liquidator: Also known as Company Liquidator, an insolvency professional registered under the Insolvency and Bankruptcy Code, 2016, appointed by the Tribunal to conduct the winding up proceedings under the overall directions of the latter.

Voluntary winding up: Winding up of a company by the members in a predefined manner and subject to fufilment of certain conditions by the company under the strict compliance of the relevant provisions of the Insolvency and Bankruptcy Code, 2016.

Liquidator: A person, duly appointed by the company in relation to voluntary winding up of a company, from amongst the insolvency professionals registered under the Insolvency and Bankruptcy Code, 2016. responsible for closing down the business of the company and utilising the sale proceeds to pay off its debts and adjusting the surplus, if any, among the shareholders.

- The company in general meeting passes a resolution requiring it to be wound up voluntarily as a result of the expiry of the period of its duration, if any, fixed by its articles or on the occurrence of any event in respect of which the articles provide that the company should be dissolved.

The Insolvency and Bankruptcy Board of India (IBBI) has notified the IBBI (Voluntary Liquidation Process) Regulations, 2017. As a result of the same, with effect from 1st April, 2017 voluntary winding up shall be conducted under the Insolvency and Bankruptcy Code, 2016.

LO10 A dissolved company may, however, be revived by the Tribunal under certain circumstances.

CHAPTER

20 Limited Liability Partnership

Learning Objectives

LO 1 What is limited liability partnership?

LO 2 Rationale behind introduction of LLP in India

LO 3 Structure of an LLP

LO 4 Procedure of formation of LLP in India

Limited Liability Partnership: An Introduction

Limited liability partnership: A partnership in which some or all the partners (depending on the agreement) have limited liabilities.

Limited Liability Partnership (LLP), a concept that is relatively new to India, is an alternative corporate business form in which, depending upon the agreement, some or all the partners enjoy limited liability. In LLP, one partner is not accountable for the acts (negligence or misconduct) of other partners. This unique characteristic of LLP sets it fundamentally apart from and advantageous to a conventional (unlimited liability) partnership. Since LLP contains elements of both 'a corporate structure' and 'a partnership firm structure', it may be called a hybrid between a company and a partnership which offers the dual benefits of limited liability of a company and the flexibility of a partnership. An LLP, however, is much closer to a private ltd. company.

Genesis and Foundation of LLP in India

The LLP structure exists in the countries like the UK, the US, various Gulf countries, Australia and Singapore. On the advice of experts who have studied LLP legislations in various countries, the Indian LLP Act, 2008, is broadly based on the UK LLP Act, 2000, and the Singapore LLP Act, 2005; which allow creation of LLP in a body corporate form, i.e., as a separate legal entity, separate from its partners/members.

The desirability of LLP form in India was expressed in the context of small enterprises by Bhat Committee (1972), Naik Committee (1992), Expert committee on 'Development of Small Sector Enterprises' headed by Sh. Abid Hussain in 1997 and the study group on 'Development of Small Sector Enterprises' (SSEs) headed by Dr. S.P. Gupta in 2001. The committees set up by the Ministry of Corporate Affairs, namely, Committee on Regulation of Private Companies and Partnerships headed by Sh. Naresh Chandra (2003), Committee on New Company Law (Dr. J.J. Irani Committee) (2005) also recommended for legislation on LLPs.

The Limited Liability Partnership (LLP) Bill was passed by the Rajya Sabha on 24 October, 2008 and by Lok Sabha on 12 December, 2008. The President gave assent to this Bill on 7 January, 2009, and thereby the Act (Limited Liability Partnership Act, 2008) came into effect from 1 April, 2009. The Act is divided into XIV chapters, spread over 81 sections, and has four schedules*. According to data from Ministry of Corporate Affairs, there are 11,616 LLPs registered in India by the end of October, 2015.

What is Limited Liability Partnership?

LLP is a new business vehicle that enables professional expertise and entrepreneurial initiative to combine and operate in flexible, innovative, and efficient manner. It is a hybrid between company and conventional partnership offering fundamentally:

1. the privilege of limited liability accorded to the partners of the LLP; and
2. the flexibility of internal control and management of firm's affairs through 'LLP Agreement', or in the absence of the Agreement, default provisions (Schedule I) covering the mutual rights and duties of LLP and its partners.

Salient Features of LLP

1. Distinct business model LLP is a form of business model which is organized and it operates on the basis of an agreement. It provides flexibility without imposing detailed legal and procedural requirements, enables professional or technical expertise and initiative to combine with financial risk taking capacity in an innovative and efficient manner. Every limited liability partnership shall use the words 'Limited Liability Partnership' or its acronym 'LLP' as the last words of its name.

2. Separate legal entity and perpetual succession LLP shall be a body corporate and a legal entity separate from its partners. It will have perpetual succession. The LLP is a separate legal entity, and is liable to the full extent of its assets but liability of the partners is limited to their agreed contribution in the LLP. The LLP can continue its existence irrespective of the changes in partners.

3. Ability to sue in its own name As a juristic legal person, an LLP can sue in its own name and can be sued by others. Partners are not liable to be sued for dues against the LLP. The LLP, however, is not relieved of the liability for its other obligations as a separate entity.

4. Liability of partners Limited Liability of Partners is the essential hallmark of an LLP which sets it fundamentally apart from a conventional partnership. Liability of one or more partners, depending upon the agreement, is limited to their agreed contribution in the LLP. Further, no partner would be liable on account of the independent or unauthorized actions of other partners; thus allowing individual partners to be shielded from joint liability created by another partner's wrongful business decisions or misconduct.

5. Control and influence LLP is capable of entering into contracts and holding property in its own name. Though Registrar of Companies (ROC) shall register an LLP and monitor its affairs, unlike corporate shareholders, its partners have the right to manage the business directly and independently. In contrast, corporate shareholders have to elect a board of directors under the provisions of corporate laws in force who in turn hire corporate officers who then have, as corporate individuals, the legal responsibility to manage the corporation in the corporation's best interest.

6. Mutual rights and duties of partners The mutual rights and duties of partners inter se and those of the LLP and its partners shall be governed by the agreement between the partners or between the LLP and the partners. This agreement would be known as 'LLP Agreement'. In the absence of the latter as to any matter, the mutual rights and liabilities of the partners shall be as provided for under Schedule I to the Act. Therefore, in case any LLP proposes to exclude provisions or requirements of Schedule I to the Act, it would have to enter into an LLP Agreement, specifically excluding applicability of any or all paragraphs of Schedule I.

7. Maintenance of accounts and filing of annual return must An LLP shall be under obligation to maintain annual accounts reflecting true and fair view of its state of affairs. Every LLP would be required to file annual return in 'Form 11' with the ROC within 60 days of closure of the financial year. The annual return will be available for public inspection on payment of prescribed fee to the Registrar (ROC). Since tax matters of all entities in India are addressed in the Income Tax Act, 1961, the taxation issues of an LLP shall be dealt with in accordance with the provisions in that Act.

8. Mode of winding up An LLP may be wound up either voluntarily (under The insolvency and Bankruptcy Code) or by the Tribunal (NCLT) established under The Companies Act, 2013.

Rationale Behind Introduction of LLP in India

LLP provides access to limited liability status which in turn encourages entrepreneurship and promotes business growth. It closes the gap in current framework by:

- Offering an alternative business vehicle to complement the traditional choices of business vehicles; and
- Providing flexibility and freedom to select the best business model that suits the needs and requirements of businesses on the basis of commercial criteria.

Moreover, LLP is more affordable vis-à-vis companies and offers more protection vis-à-vis sole proprietorship and conventional partnership.

For the above reasons, LLP is fast catching up as a strategic choice of business structure for many small businesses in India.

Structure of an LLP

> **LLP agreement:** Agreement determining the mutual rights, duties, and obligations of the partners in relation to each other and Limited Liability Partnership.

An LLP can be formed with a minimum of two partners who may be individuals or bodies corporate through their nominees. Besides, as per Section 7(1), every limited liability partnership shall have at least two designated partners who are individuals and at least one of them shall be a resident in India. In case of an LLP in which all the partners are bodies corporate or in which one or more partners are individuals and bodies corporate, at least two individuals who are partners of such LLP or nominees of such bodies corporate shall act as designated partners. There is no specific requirement to have any non-designated members and there is no specified limit of maximum number of partners in LLP. An LLP may be established such that all members are considered to be designated members. Designated members have the same rights and duties as any other member, but there are additional responsibilities such as signing accounts on behalf of the LLP, delivering accounts and annual returns to the Registrar of Companies, notifying the Registrar of changes to the LLP's members or registered office and acting on behalf of the LLP in the event of winding up, much in the way such duties and responsibilities fall on company directors.

In general terms, an LLP is governed by an 'Agreement'. Although there is no requirement to file any such governing document with Registrar of Companies; it is highly recommended that a formal agreement is established to ensure the business of the LLP has a proper framework for the resolution of disputes between members or for the provision of suitable exit strategies. The formal partnership agreement may also determine revenue split between members and varying responsibilities if appropriate.

The LLP must also have an official registered office. Unlike limited companies, there are no directors or company secretary, and of course, no shareholders. Every LLP shall have either the words 'Limited Liability Partnership' or its abbreviation 'LLP' as the last words of its name.

Procedure of Formation of Limited Liability Partnership in India

Incorporation is a simple process, tailored to provide an easy route to completion of the necessary formalities. Like formation of a joint stock company, LLP incorporations are now available online, i.e., electronically whereby the whole process can be completed within hours. The following steps are required to be undertaken for forming an LLP electronically in India:

Step I: Deciding the Partners and Designated Partners

An LLP can be incorporated with a minimum of at least two partners who may be individuals or bodies corporate through their nominees. Of the total number of partners, at least two shall be designated partners who are individuals, of which at least one must be 'Resident in India'. However, there is no specific requirement to have any non-designated partner and there is no maximum to the number of members allowed. An LLP may be established such that all members are considered to be designated partners.

A person 'Resident in India' means a person who has stayed in India for a period of not less than one hundred and eighty two days during the financial year immediately preceding the year in which the formation of LLP is sought.

'Designated partner' means a partner who is designated as such in the incorporation documents or who becomes a designated partner by and in accordance with the LLP Agreement.

Step II: Obtaining DPIN and Digital Signature

Designated partner identification number (DPIN)

Every designated partner must obtain a DPIN from the Central Government [Section 7(6)]. DPIN in this behalf is an eight digit numeric number allotted by the Central Government in order to identify a particular partner and can be obtained by making an online application in e-Form 7 to the Central Government and submitting the physical application along with necessary identity and address proof of the person applying with prescribed fees.

> **Designated partner:** A partner who is designated as such in the incorporation documents of an LLP or who becomes a designated partner by and in accordance with the LLP agreement.

Digital signature certificate The Information Technology Act, 2000, provides for use of digital signatures on the documents submitted in electronic form in order to ensure the security and authenticity of the documents filed electronically. As all the documents and forms required for incorporating an LLP in India to be filed electronically and under the signatures of Designated Partners, thus at least one Designated Partner has to obtain the digital signature certificates from government recognized Digital Signature Authority (DSA). The signatures shall also be required for signing and filing of all relevant forms and documents.

> **Designated Partner Identification Number (DPIN):** An eight digit numeric number allotted by the Central Government in order to identify a particular partner in respect of an LLP.

Step III: Choosing a Name for the LLP

The next step is to decide the name for the proposed LLP. The choice of name for an LLP follows the same rules as with limited companies. Anyone intending to incorporate an LLP has to evaluate the proposed name under the prescribed parameters and make an application in 'Form 1' (Application for reservation or change of name) for reservation of the desired name. The name of the LLP (to be incorporated) shall not be similar or identical with a company or LLP already registered in India and should not contain words prohibited under the Emblems and Names (Prevention of improper use) Act, 1950, or the ones which are undesirable in the opinion of the Central Government.

Step IV: Drafting of LLP Agreement

The next step is drafting of LLP Agreement governing the mutual rights and duties among the partners and among the LLP and its partners. As with any business partnership, it is vital that the partners draw up a suitable written agreement to determine issues such as control, division of revenue, and exit strategies.

The agreement inter alia should contain the following details:

1. Name of the proposed LLP
2. Names of the Partners and the Designated Partners
3. Form of contribution by each partner
4. Profit sharing ratio
5. Rights and duties of partners
6. Proposed business
7. Rules for governing the LLP

In case, no agreement is entered into, the rights and duties as prescribed under Schedule I to the LLP Act, 2008, shall be applicable to the proposed LLP. It is not necessary to have the LLP Agreement signed at the time of incorporation, as the details of the same needs to be filled in e-form 3 within 30 days of incorporation but in order to avoid any dispute between the partners as to the terms and conditions of the agreement after the formation of LLP, it is always beneficial to have the LLP Agreement drafted and executed before the incorporation of the LLP.

In case the agreement is executed outside India, then it must be notarized and consularized.

Step V: Filing of Incorporation Documents and Payment of Registration Fees

After drafting of LLP agreement, the next step is the filing of incorporation documents, consent of partners and their declaration electronically through prescribed e-forms with the Registrar of Companies for incorporation of the LLP and payment of prescribed fees based on the total monetary value of contribution of partners in the proposed LLP. A brief account of the relevant e-forms is given below:

Form 2: Incorporation document This is an informative document setting down the details of LLP, its partners including designated partners along with their share of contribution and consent for forming partnership to carry on a lawful business with profit motive along with declaration stating that all the requirements of Limited Liability Partnership Act, 2008, regarding incorporation of LLP in India have been duly complied with.

Form 3: Details of LLP agreement This form provides for the necessary information in respect to the LLP agreement entered between the partners.

Form 4: Consent of partners In this form, the consent of each partner to become a partner of an LLP along with their address and identity proof to be filed with the Registrar of Companies.

Forms 3 and 4 are required to be filed within 30 days of the incorporation.

Moreover, just like in case of formation of a joint stock company, the partners are required to subscribe their names along with signatures to the Subscription Sheet, which shall be witnessed by any chartered Accountant/Company Secretary/Advocate in practice.

In case the subscription sheet is executed outside India, then it must be notarized and consularized.

Step VI: Obtaining Certificate of Incorporation

After the ROC is satisfied that all the formalities with respect to the incorporation have been complied, he will issue a Certificate of Incorporation as to formation of the Limited Liability Partnership within maximum of 14 days from the date of filing of documents which shall be the conclusive evidence of formation of the LLP.

Source: adapted from www.mca.gov.in

LLP Versus Sole Proprietorship

An LLP is fundamentally a different personality from a sole proprietorship. The difference between the two can be discussed along the following points.

Legal Identity

Sole proprietorship in India is not an incorporated entity and therefore has no separate legal identity. In the eyes of the law and the public, the sole proprietor as the owner and his sole proprietorship business are one and the same. As a result, sole proprietor has absolute control over the business and its operations but he is personally responsible for all the debts and legal actions against the business. An LLP, on the other hand, has its own legal identity, separate from its members (partners) who own the entity and manage its affairs. This essentially implies that:

1. The entity (LLP) can incur and receive obligations and hold property in its own name, enter into contracts with its members, directors, employees, and with third parties.
2. The entity can sue and be sued in its own name.
3. The entity continues unchanged even if the identity of its participants changes.
4. The entity can enter into legal relationships with its members or directors.

The above privileges are not available with the sole proprietorship.

Extent of Liability

Since a sole proprietorship does not have a separate legal entity, the owner has unlimited liability. That is, creditors may sue you for debts incurred and can also obtain a decree to claim against his personal assets. Contrarily, since LLPs in India are setup as limited liability legal entities, their business obligations remain within the entity itself and thus shield their members or partners via the provision of limited liability. Essentially it means that the partners' exposure is limited to the amount they have invested in the entity and their personal assets are protected.

Perpetuity and Succession

As a sole proprietor, owner and his business are inseparable. The business has no perpetuity and comes to a standstill with the demise of its owner. LLPs, on the other hand, have a continued existence irrespective of the status of its partners. Partners' resignation or death does not normally affect the existence of the LLP.

Ease of Expansion

Central to the growth and expansion of any business is the capital. As a sole proprietor, it's quite difficult to raise funds externally through loans or investment in the business. Capital is limited to the owner's personal finances and the profits generated by the business. This makes business expansion difficult. While, generally, LLPs also face the difficulty of raising external capital, which is often limited to its partners' contributions, they can still take advantage of the ability to raise capital base by means of adding more partners.

Taxation

Sole proprietorships in India are not taxed at the business level but at the personal income level of the owners concerned. For sole proprietors, all business profits are considered as personal income of the owner and therefore taxed as part of the personal income as per the personal income tax slabs in force. Whereas, LLPs, in India, are treated as legal entities and therefore LLPs' profits are taxable as corporate profits.

Transfer of Ownership

Unlike, a sole proprietorship, an LLP cannot be sold as whole. Instead, each partner will have to individually transfer his interest in the firm.

Ongoing Maintenance

Sole proprietorships are the easiest and least expensive form of business to set up and maintain in India as there are no ongoing filing requirements or the annual renewal of the sole proprietorship. Ongoing maintenance of an LLP is little more complex than a sole proprietorship albeit less complex than a private limited company. In terms of annual compliance requirements, a LLP must submit an annual declaration of solvency or insolvency to authorities. There are no other documents to be filed.

Dissolution

Dissolving or terminating a sole proprietorship is easier than terminating an LLP. For an LLP, the procedure calls for issuing a notice of termination followed by a notice of cessation to the registration authorities (RoC). The termination process in case of LLP can take anywhere within 3 to 12 months, depending on the complexities involved.

LLP Versus Conventional Partnership

1. Conventional or traditional or say ordinary partnership is governed by the Partnership Act, 1932, while a limited liability partnership is exclusively governed by the Limited Liability Partnership Act, 2008.
2. Under ordinary partnership firm, every partner is liable, jointly with all the other partners and also severally, for all acts of the firm done while he is a partner. That is, liability of a partner is unlimited. Under LLP structure, on the other hand, liability of a partner is limited to his agreed contribution.
3. Unlike conventional partnership, in LLP no partner is liable for the independent acts of other partners. This unique characteristic of LLP shields individual partners from joint liability created by another partner's wrongful acts or misconduct. Mutual rights and duties of the partners within an LLP are governed by an agreement (LLP Agreement) between the partners or between the partners and the LLP as the case may be and in the absence of LLP Agreement by Schedule I whereas under ordinary partnership mutual rights and duties of partners are subject to agreement between the firm and the partners.
4. There shall not be any upper limit on number of partners in an LLP unlike an ordinary partnership firm where the maximum number of partners cannot exceed 20.

LLP Versus Joint Stock Company

A basic difference between an LLP and a joint stock company lies in that the affairs of a company are regulated by the statute (i.e. Companies Act, 2013) whereas for an LLP it would be by a contractual agreement between the partners. The management-ownership divide inherent in a company is not there in a limited liability partnership. LLP will have a flexible internal structure vis-à-vis a company and subject to lesser regulatory compliances such as holding quarterly Board meetings etc. as compared to latter. An LLP shall also be exempt from the applicability of dividend distribution tax and other levies such as minimum alternate tax or MAT.

Moreover, incorporating an LLP is cost effective compared to a joint stock company, as the minimum statutory fee for incorporation of a company is ₹6000, whereas that of LLP is ₹800. Also, a joint stock company is required to be incorporated with minimum paid up capital of ₹1 lakh, whereas there is no such minimum specified limit in case of LLP.

LLP: Gateway to Greater FDI

The LLP form of business organisation is sound in principle as it offers the twin benefit of limited liability and a flexible internal structure. LLPs have become the globally preferred vehicle of business to overcome tax issues and red tape that otherwise dog foreign investors. Multinationals registered as companies in India are lobbying the government to freely permit their conversion to limited liability partnerships (LLPs) ever since 'Department of Industrial Policy and Promotion (DIPP)' after consulting Reserve Bank of India and Department of Economic Affairs has announced a liberal policy on such entities. As part of the opening up announced very recently, foreign direct investment (FDI) through automatic route has been allowed in LLPs. The government has made the changes because it sees this as a gateway to greater investment from overseas. The new regulations allow 'downstream investments' in LLPs operating in India by their parents.

Any company with an annual turnover of more than ₹60 lakh in India can convert itself into an LLP. However, this process is burdened with complications as well as tax implications. The approval of Foreign Investment Board (FIPB) shall also be needed. For many existing companies that want to convert to an LLP, there is a capital gain tax exposure currently. Hence, the multinationals want government to allow them to convert freely without triggering capital gains tax, a major roadblock for existing companies to convert to LLP, among other things.

Source: Adapted from 'MNCs Lobby Govt. for Smooth LLP Conversion', *The Economic Times*, 16 November 2015, p. 15.

Exercises

I. Objective-type Questions

1. Which of the following statements are true in relation to an LLP?
   (i) Depending upon the agreement some or all partners have limited liability.
   (ii) There is no limit to the maximum number of partners.
   (iii) One partner is accountable for the acts of other partners.
   (iv) It is called a hybrid between a company and a partnership
   Answer Codes:
   (a) Statements (i), (ii) and (iii) are true
   (b) Statements (ii), (iii) and (iv) are true
   (c) Statements (i), (ii) and (iv) are true
   (d) Statements (i), (iii) and (iv) are true

2. Limited Liability Partnership Act, 2008, came into effect on:
   (a) 24 October, 2008 (b) 12 December, 2008
   (c) 7 January, 2009 (d) 1 April, 2009

3. The additional responsibilities of designated members include:
   (a) Signing accounts on behalf of the LLP
   (b) Delivering accounts and annual returns to the Registrar of Companies (ROC)
   (c) Notifying the ROC of changes to the LLP's members or registered office, if any and acting on behalf of the LLP in the event of winding up.
   (d) All of the above

4. The foremost step to form an LLP electronically is:
   (a) Obtaining DPIN and Digital Signature
   (b) Choosing a Name for the LLP
   (c) Drafting of LLP Agreement
   (d) Filing of Incorporation Documents and Payment of Registration Fees

5. Which is not true in respect of an LLP?
   (a) There must be at least two 'Designated Members' at all times
   (b) Designated members do not have the same rights and duties as any other member
   (c) There is no specific requirement to have any non-designated members
   (d) An LLP may be established such that all members are considered to be designated members

6. Which one of the following is an unincorporated organisation?
   (a) General/Unlimited Partnership Firm (b) Limited Liability Partnership Fir.
   (c) Private Ltd. Company (d) Public Ltd. Company

7. One of the major distinctions between a conventional (unlimited) partnership and LLP is:
   (a) In an LLP all the partners may not actively engage themselves in the function of the firm.
   (b) An LLP is a distinct business model.
   (c) In an LLP, one partner is not accountable for the acts (negligence or misconduct) of other partners.
   (d) An LLP offers the flexibility of internal control and management of firm's affairs through an 'Agreement'.

8. The mutual rights and duties of partners of an LLP shall be governed by
   (a) The LLP Act, 2008
   (b) The 'LLP Agreement'.
   (c) The Companies Act, 2013
   (d) The 'LLP Agreement' and in the absence of the latter as to any matter, the as per the Schedule I to the LLP Act

9. A *Limited Liability Partnership* may be wound up
   (a) Voluntarily
   (b) By the Tribunal to be established under The Companies Act, 2013
   (c) By the Registrar (ROC) if the firm fails to file annual return in the prescribed form with the ROC within 60 days of closer of the financial year
   (d) Either voluntarily or By the Tribunal to be established under The Companies Act, 2013

10. Besides any conventional partnership firm consisting of two or more partners engaged in a profit-making venture to become an LLP at its option; an LLP, in particular, can be formed with
   (a) A minimum of two partners who must be individuals
   (b) A minimum of two partners who must be resident individuals (ROI)
   (c) A minimum of two partners who must be resident individuals (ROI) or body corporate through their nominees.
   (d) A minimum of two partners who may be individuals or body corporate through their nominees.

II. Review Questions

1. What is Limited Liability Partnership? Discuss its structure.
2. Discuss the characteristic features of a limited liability partnership firm.
3. Discuss the essence of an LLP. Distinguish between an LLP and conventional partnership.
4. Comment on the following:
   (a) Rationale behind introduction of LLP in India
   (b) DPIN
   (c) LLP Versus Joint Stock Company
   (d) LLP Agreement
   (e) Designated Partner

Answers to Objective-type Questions

1. (c)	2. (d)	3. (d)	4. (a)	5. (b)
6. (a)	7. (c)	8. (d)	9. (d)	10. (d)

20 Chapter in Review

LEARNING OUTCOMES

LO 1 What is limited liability partnership?

LO 2 Rationale behind introduction of LLP in India

LO 3 Structure of an LLP

LO 4 Procedure of formation of LLP in India

KEY TERMS

Limited liability partnership: A partnership in which some or all the partners (depending on the agreement) have limited liabilities.

LLP agreement: Agreement determining the mutual rights, duties, and obligations of the partners in relation to each other and Limited Liability Partnership.

Designated partner: A partner who is designated as such in the incorporation documents of an LLP or who becomes a designated partner by and in accordance with the LLP agreement.

Designated Partner Identification Number (DPIN): An eight digit numeric number allotted by the Central Government in order to identify a particular partner in respect of an LLP.

LO1 The LLP is a body corporate and a legal entity separate from its members. It is considered to be a unique corporate business vehicle as it provides benefit of limited liability while allowing its members the flexibility of organizing its affairs internally. Minimum of two partners are required to form of an LLP but there is no any limit to the maximum number of partners. The LLP Act, 2008, also allows foreign nationals including foreign companies and LLPs to incorporate an LLP in India provided at least one designated partner of the 'to-be-incorporated LLP' is resident of India.

LO2 LLPs have become the globally-preferred vehicle of business to overcome tax issues and red tape that otherwise dog investors. Owing to flexibility in its structure and operation, it is proving useful for small and medium enterprises, in general, and for the enterprises in services sector, in particular.

LO3 The LLP is a formal structure that requires a written partnership agreement and usually comes with annual reporting requirements with the ROC as in case of a company. In any case, there must be at least two 'designated members' at all times, There is no specific requirement to have any non-designated members and there is no specified limit of maximum number of partners in LLP. As in a general partnership, all partners in an LLP can participate in the management of the partnership.

LO4 Incorporation of LLP firm is a simple 6-step process, available online, i.e., electronically whereby the whole process can be completed in 6 steps, namely, (i) deciding the partners and designated partners; (ii) obtaining DPIN and digital signature; (iii) choosing a name for the proposed LLP; (iv) drafting of LLP agreement; (v) filing of incorporation documents and payment of registration fee; and (vi) obtaining certificate of incorporation.

Part VI Other Business Legislations

CHAPTER 21 The Consumer Protection Act, 2019

Learning Objectives

LO 1 The Consumer Protection Act, 2019: An Overview
LO 2 The Act: salient features; aim and objectives
LO 3 Important Terms
LO 4 Rights of consumer; restrictive trade practice; unfair trade practice; service; trader
LO 5 Consumer Protection Councils
LO 6 Central Consumer Protection Authority
LO 7 Three-tier Grievance-redressal machinery
LO 8 Offences and penalties

Consumer protection is the practice of safeguarding buyers of goods and services in particular, and the public in general, against unfair practices, if any, prevailing in the market place. Consumer safeguard measures are often established by law of land. Such laws or regulations are primarily intended to prevent businesses from engaging in fraudulent or specified unfair or restrictive trade practices in order to gain an undue advantage over competitors or mislead consumers to serve their vested interests. Additionally, they can also provide additional protection for the general public which may be impacted by a product (or its production) even if they are not the direct purchasers or end-users of that product. For instance, certain government regulations require producers to disclose detailed information about their products—particularly in areas where public health or safety is an issue, such as with foods, drinks, chemicals, pharmaceutical drugs, or automobiles. Consumer protection, as a matter of fact, is linked to the idea of consumer rights and the formation of consumer organizations, which facilitate consumers make better choices in the marketplace and pursue complaints against businesses if dealt with unfairly. Consumer protection can also be asserted their rights via non-government organizations and individuals as consumer activism.[1]

The Consumer Protection Act, 2019: An Overview

The Consumer Protection Act, 2019[2] is an Act of the Parliament of India. It repeals and replaces the Consumer Protection Act, 1986. The Consumer Protection Bill, 2019 was introduced in the Lok Sabha on 8 July 2019 by the Minister of Consumer Affairs, Food and Public Distribution, Ram Vilas Paswan. It was passed by Lok Sabha on 30 July 2019 and later passed in Rajya Sabha on 6 August 2019. The bill received assent from President Ram Nath Kovind on 9 August, and was notified accordingly in the Gazette of India. The Act, however, has come into force with effect from 20 July 2020. The Act contains 107 sections which spread over VIII Chapters and extends to the whole of India.

The Consumer Protection Act, 2019, is another important milestone in the history of socio-economic legislations in India. It is one of the most progressive and comprehensive legislations enacted by the Parliament to safeguard interest of the consumers in the country. The Act attempts to give consumers complete protection from malpractices of manufacturers, producers, suppliers, wholesalers, retailers, and providers of various services and even celebrities at times who often indulge in misleading advertisements or endorsements of certain products at the cost of consumers' interests. The New Act fixes liability on endorsers taking cognizance of numerous instances wherein consumers have fallen prey to unfair trade practices in the recent past under the influence of celebrities acting as brand ambassadors. With this provision, now it becomes imperative for the endorser to take the onus and exercise due care and diligence to verify the veracity of the claims made in the advertisement to refute liability claims. The Act is designed to make available inexpensive and speedier justice to the consumer. Furthermore, in order to make the Consumer Protection Act more effective and purposeful, the new Act calls for establishment of a regulatory authority known as the Central Consumer Protection Authority (CCPA), with wide powers of enforcement. With the New Act in force, gone are the days, where the 'consumer was asked to beware'. A consumer is now the one who can assume to be treated like a King. Hence, it is important for consumer driven businesses (such as, retail, e-commerce erc.) to be mindful of the changes in the legal landscape and have robust policies dealing with consumer redressal in place. Consumer driven businesses must also strive to take extra precautions against unfair trade practices and unethical business practices in the larger interest of their businesses. The remedy provided to consumers under this Act will be through a three-tier quasi-judicial mechanism, comprising the District Commissions at the district level, State Commissions at the State level and the National Commission (located in Delhi) at the apex level like under previous legislation. In a nut shell, this Act was inevitable to resolve a large number of pending consumer complaints in consumer courts across the country.

[1] Adapted from Wikipedia

[2] This Act shall be referred to as CPA 2019 or just 'Act' at different places throughout the present chapter and references to sections in this chapter are to 'The Consumer Protection Act, 2019' unless otherwise specified.

Salient Features of the Act

The salient features of the Act are as follows:

1. The Act applies to all goods and services unless specifically exempted by the Central Government.
2. It covers all the sectors—private, public, and co-operative.
3. The provisions of the Act are chiefly compensatory in nature.
4. It seeks to confer upon the consumers the following six rights:
   (a) Right to safety,
   (b) Right to be informed,
   (c) Right to choose,
   (d) Right to be heard,
   (e) Right to seek redressal, and
   (f) Right to consumer awareness.
5. The Act also envisages establishment of Consumer Protection Councils at the central, state, and district levels, whose main objectives are to promote and protect the rights of consumers by rendering advice.
6. To provide a simple, speedy, and inexpensive redressal of consumer grievances, the Act envisages three-tier quasi-judicial machinery at the national, state, and district levels. These are—National Consumer Disputes Redressal Commission known as the National Commission, State Consumer Disputes Redressal Commissions (known as State Commissions) and the District Consumer Commissions.
7. Engagement of an advocate is not mandatory to file a complaint and pursue under the Consumer Protection Act, 2019.

Besides, the following additional features of the new legislation set it apart from the erstwhile Consumer Protection Act, 1986 and make is much more effectual in securing and protecting the interest of a consumer in the ever-dynamic contemporary commercial world.

1. **Wide Coverage of Transactions.** The new Act attempts to address the new set of challenges faced by consumers brought in by the digital age by broadening the definition of 'consumer'. The definition of 'consumer' has been expanded to include persons who buy goods or avail services through offline or online transactions, electronic means or by tele-shopping or direct selling or multi-level marketing. The new description now provides consumers with a remedy in case of marketing. Thus, seller at each level of multi-level marketing can be exposed to liability under CPA 2019, whereby a consumer's claim will not be restricted to only the manufacturer of the product but to all entities involved at various stages of production and marketing. Moreover, the previous Act did not specifically include e-commerce transactions, and this lacuna has been remedied by the new Act.
2. **Enhanced Pecuniary Jurisdiction of the Commissions.** The pecuniary jurisdiction of all three commissions have been raised under the new legislation. Accordingly, the District Commission can now entertain consumer complaints where the value of goods or services paid does not exceed ₹1,00,00,000 (Indian Rupees One Crore). The State Commission can entertain disputes where such value exceeds ₹1,00,00,000 (Indian Rupees One Crore) but does not exceed ₹10,00,00,000 (Indian Rupees Ten Crore). And the National Commission now can exercise jurisdiction where such value exceeds ₹10,00,00,000 (Indian Rupees Ten Crore). The increase in the pecuniary jurisdiction of all three commissions under CPA 2019 is an encouraging step as it should attract lesser number of claims in appellate commissions to an extent, thereby ensuring swifter disposal of cases.
3. **Ease of Filing Complaints.** The new Act offers flexibility to the consumers to file their complaints with the jurisdictional 'Consumer Commission', located at the place of residence or work of the consumer. This is unlike the erstwhile practice of filing it only at the place of purchase or where the seller or service provider has its registered official address. CPA 2019 also contains enabling provisions for consumers to file complaints electronically and for hearing and/or examining parties through video-conferencing. This is aimed at providing procedural ease and reducing inconvenience and harassment of the consumers.
4. **Establishment of Central Consumer Protection Authority.** CPA 2019 proposes the establishment

of a regulatory authority under Section 10(1), known as the Central Consumer Protection Authority (CCPA). CCPA will be equipped with extensive powers of enforcement to promote, protect, and enforce the rights of consumers by cracking down on unfair trade practices, and false and misleading advertisements that are detrimental to the interest of the public and consumers. The CCPA will have an investigative wing, headed by a Director-General, which may conduct inquiry or investigation into consumer law violations. The CCPA has been mandated to take *suo-moto* actions, recall products, order reimbursement of the price of goods or services, cancel licenses and file class action suits, if a consumer's complaint affects more than one individual.

5. **Product Liability and Penal Consequences.** There was no separate legislation governing 'product liability' in India, though it was addressed under the old legislation i.e., CPA 1986, if parties were included within the ambit of '*consumer*'. Insertion of "*Product Liability*" as a separate chapter in CPA 2019 and a new ground for filing a complaint has been one of the most significant additions to the New Act. Section 2(35) of CPA 2019 allows a person to make a claim of product liability against such manufacturer, seller or service provider for such defective products. Product liability means the responsibility of a product manufacturer or product seller, of any product or service, related to the product to compensate for any harm caused to a consumer by such defective product manufactured or sold or by deficiency in services relating to the product.

Who can be made liable:

The new Act has gone a step forward and defined a product manufacturer, product seller' and product service provider to provide clarity on who can be made liable for an action under Chapter VI of CPA 2019.

Ingredients to initiate product liability action:

1. Product manufacturer will be liable if product contains a manufacturing defect, or defective in design; or there is a deviation from manufacturing specifications; or does not conform to the express warranty; or fails to contain adequate instructions of correct usage to prevent any harm or any warning regarding improper or incorrect usage. Absence of negligence or fraud in making express warranty of a product cannot be pleaded as a defence.
2. Product seller who is not a product manufacturer may be held liable if (a) he has exercised substantial control over the designing, testing, manufacturing, packaging or labelling of a product that caused harm; or (b) he has altered or modified the product and such alteration or modification was the substantial factor in causing the harm; or (c) he has made an express warranty of a product independent of any express warranty made by a manufacturer and such product failed to conform to the express warranty made by the product seller which caused the harm; or (d) the product has been sold by him and the identity of product manufacturer of such product is not known, or if known, the service of notice or process or warrant cannot be effected on him or he is not subject to the law which is in force in India or the order, if any, passed or to be passed cannot be enforced against him; or (e) he failed to exercise reasonable care in assembling, inspecting or maintaining such product or he did not pass on the warnings or instructions of the product manufacturer regarding the dangers involved or proper usage of the product.
3. Product service provider may be liable if (a) the service provided was faulty or imperfect or deficient or inadequate in quality, nature or manner of performance which is required to be provided by or under any law for the time being in force, or pursuant to any contract or otherwise; or (b) there was an act of omission or commission or negligence or conscious withholding any information which caused harm; or (c) the service provider did not issue adequate instructions or warnings to prevent any harm; or (d) the service did not conform to express warranty or the terms and conditions of the contract.

CPA 2019 while defining a 'product' has specifically excluded human tissues, blood, blood products and organs from the definition of the product. CPA 2019 also lists down certain exceptions to "*product liability*" action, in circumstances where the products have been misused, or if the product being purchased by the employer for use at the workplace did not adhere to installation warnings or instructions, or if the nature of the product is such that the user should have known the associated dangers, etc.

6. New grounds to file complaints. While the provisions of CPA, 1986 prescribed six (6) major grounds to file complaints, CPA 2019 has increased the count to seven (7) and also substantially modified one of the existing grounds to file complaints as provided under Section 2(c)(i) of CPA 1986. The two key changes are:

1. *Introduction of Unfair Contracts.* In the previous legislation, a complaint could be filed only if *an unfair trade practice or a restrictive trade practice was adopted by any trader or service provider.* Now "*unfair contract*" has also been added which further broadens the ground to file complaints and allows consumers to challenge contracts which are unfair, unilateral and unreasonable. Unfair contract has been defined to include contracts between a manufacturer or trader or service provider on one hand, and a consumer on the other, having such terms which cause significant change in the rights of such consumer, including the following, namely:—

1. requiring manifestly excessive security deposits to be given by a consumer for the performance of contractual obligations; or
2. imposing any penalty on the consumer, for the breach of contract thereof which is wholly disproportionate to the loss occurred due to such breach to the other party to the contract; or
3. refusing to accept early repayment of debts on payment of applicable penalty; or entitling a party to the contract to terminate such contract unilaterally, without reasonable cause; or
4. permitting or has the effect of permitting one party to assign the contract to the detriment of the other party who is a consumer, without his consent; or
5. imposing on the consumer any unreasonable charge, obligation or condition which puts such consumer to disadvantage.

The above provisions would directly impact the financial institutions such as banks, as the apex court has already stated that the banks also get covered under the Act. This would specifically take into account contracts entered with banks, e-commerce platforms where parties are not left with any option but to agree to the standard terms to avail the services. With such a broad subjective definition, it remains to be seen how courts would interpret in case of online contracts.

2. *Expanding definition of "unfair trade practice"*. While CPA, 1986 had listed six (6) types of unfair trade practices, three (3) types of additional unfair trade practices have now been added to the list under the New Act, which are as follows:

1. failure or non-issuance of a bill or a cash memo;
2. refusal to take back or withdraw defective goods or withdrawal or discontinuance of deficient services or refusal to refund the consideration amount paid within the period as stipulated in the bill or cash memo or receipt or in the absence of such stipulation, refusal to withdraw defective goods or withdrawal or discontinuance of deficient services or refusal to refund the consideration amount paid within thirty (30) days; and
3. disclosure of consumer's personal information to any other person unless such disclosure is made in accordance with the provisions of any law for the time being in force or in public interest.

7. Massive Penalties for Misleading Advertisement. The CCPA (under CPA 2019) may impose a penalty of up to ₹10,00,000 (Indian Rupees Ten Lakhs) on a manufacturer or an endorser , for a false or misleading advertisement. The CCPA may also sentence them to imprisonment for up to two years for the same. In case of a subsequent offence, the fine may extend to ₹50,00,000 (Indian Rupees Fifty Lakhs) and imprisonment of up to 5 (five) years. The CCPA can also prohibit the endorser of a misleading advertisement from endorsing that particular product or service for a period of up to one year. For every subsequent offence, the period of prohibition may extend to three years. It is important to note that such penalty can be imposed on endorsers too; thereby bringing actors/actresses in the penalty net. However, the endorser would be exempted from any liability if s/he establishes that they exercised due care and diligence to verify the veracity of the claims before endorsing the same. Therefore, endorsers/actors/celebrities will also have to exercise a thorough due diligence/ research before signing up for any advertisements.

8. **Provision for Alternate Dispute Resolution.** Apart from the afore-mentioned changes, CPA 2019 provides for mediation as an Alternate Dispute Resolution (ADR) mechanism, making the process of dispute adjudication simpler and quicker. This will help with the speedier resolution of disputes and reduce pressure on consumer courts, who already have abundant cases pending before them. Mediation cells have been attached to all the three levels – National, State and District. Matters shall be referred to mediation cells if the parties' consent to it.

9. **Deletion of Healthcare from Definition of Services.** Lastly, the CPA 2019 does not explicitly specify 'healthcare' in the list of services enumerated in the definition of 'service' following stiff opposition from the medical fraternity which expressed apprehension that the CPA 2019 would be misused against them. However, it is pertinent to mention that the Government has reportedly stated that the 'Healthcare Amendment' will not spare healthcare services from the purview of the CPA 2019, in view of the order passed by the Supreme Court in case of Indian Medical Association Vs. V.P. Shantha[3], wherein it had read healthcare into the definition of services under the CPA 1986. The apex court of the country in the above case held that patients are consumers as long as they are making some form of payment for the medical service rendered. As a result, under the current consumer protection framework, a claim can be brought against doctors in case of deficiency of service.

Aim and Objectives of the Act

The Consumer Protection Act, 2019 was enacted primarily to promote and protect the rights of consumers in a further healthier way. The provisions of this statute are chiefly compensatory in nature, rather than being preventive or punitive. The Act attempts to provide simple, speedier, and inexpensive redressal to the consumers' grievances, and relief of a specific nature and award of compensation, wherever appropriate to the consumer. The new Act also seeks to widen its scope in addressing the consumer concerns.

[3] Refer Indian Medical Association Vs. V.P. Shantha and Anr under Landmark Judgments, pp

Major Concepts

Some of the important terms used in the Consumer Protection Act, 2019 are reproduced here.

Advertisement

"Advertisement" means any audio or visual publicity, representation, endorsement or pronouncement made by means of light, sound, smoke, gas, print, electronic media, internet or website and includes any notice, circular, label, wrapper, invoice or such other documents. [Section 2(1)].

Appropriate Laboratory

An appropriate laboratory means a laboratory or organisation-

1. recognised by the Central Government,
2. recognised by a State Government, subject to such guidelines as may be prescribed by the Central Government in this behalf, or
3. established by or under any law for the time-being in force, which is maintained, financed or aided by the Central Government, or a State Government, for carrying out analysis or test of any goods with a view to determining whether such goods suffer from any defect [Section 2(2)].

Central Authority

"Central Authority" means the Central Consumer Protection Authority established under Section 10 [Section 2(4)].

Complainant

"Complainant" means—

(i) a consumer; or
(ii) any voluntary consumer association registered under any law for the time being in force; or
(iii) the Central Government or any State Government; or
(iv) the Central Authority; or
(v) one or more consumers, where there are numerous consumers having the same interest; or

(vi) in case of death of a consumer, his legal heir or legal representative; or
(vii) in case of a consumer being a minor, his parent or legal guardian [Section 2(5)].

Complaint

"Complaint" means any allegation in writing, made by a complainant for obtaining any relief provided by or under this Act, that—

(i) an unfair contract or unfair trade practice or a restrictive trade practice has been adopted by any trader or service provider;
(ii) the goods bought by him or agreed to be bought by him suffer from one or more defects;
(iii) the services hired or availed of or agreed to be hired or availed of by him suffer from any deficiency;
(iv) a trader or a service provider, as the case may be, has charged for the goods or for the services mentioned in the complaint, a price in excess of the price—
  (a) fixed by or under any law for the time being in force; or
  (b) displayed on the goods or any package containing such goods; or
  (c) displayed on the price list exhibited by him by or under any law for the time being in force; or
  (d) agreed between the parties;
(v) the goods, which are hazardous to life and safety when used, are being offered for sale to the public—
  (a) in contravention of standards relating to safety of such goods as required to be complied with, by or under any law for the time being in force;
  (b) where the trader knows that the goods so offered are unsafe to the public;
(vi) the services which are hazardous or likely to be hazardous to life and safety of the public when used, are being offered by a person who provides any service and who knows it to be injurious to life and safety;
(vii) a claim for product liability action lies against the product manufacturer, product seller or product service provider, as the case may be [Section 2(6)].

Consumer

"Consumer" means any person who-

(i) buys any goods for a consideration which has been paid or promised or partly paid and partly promised, or under any system of deferred payment and includes any user of such goods other than the person who buys such goods for consideration paid or promised or partly paid or partly promised, or under any system of deferred payment, when such use is made with the approval of such person, but does not include a person who obtains such goods for resale or for any commercial purpose; or
(ii) hires or avails of any service for a consideration which has been paid or promised or partly paid and partly promised, or under any system of deferred payment and includes any beneficiary of such service other than the person who hires or avails of the services for consideration paid or promised, or partly paid and partly promised, or under any system of deferred payment, when such services are availed of with the approval of the first mentioned person, but does not include a person who avails of such service for any commercial purpose.

Explanation. —For the purposes of this clause, —

(a) the expression "commercial purpose" does not include use by a person of goods bought and used by him exclusively for the purpose of earning his livelihood, by means of self-employment;
(b) the expressions "buys any goods" and "hires or avails any services" includes offline or online transactions through electronic means or by teleshopping or direct selling or multi-level marketing [Section 2(7)].

Here, 'commercial purpose' does not include use of goods bought by a consumer and services availed by him exclusively for the purpose of earning his livelihood by means of self-employment.

The definition of 'consumer' given in the Act makes it clear that it includes not only the person who buys any goods or hires a service for consideration, but also any user of such goods or services, when such use is made with the approval of the buyer or hirer. This was necessary because the goods purchased or services hired by a buyer are also likely to be used by his family members, relatives, and friends. Under the general principles of the law of contract, however, such users of goods or service (beneficiaries) are not entitled to sue the supplier or trader of such goods on the ground of privity of contract. But, a person, who buys goods or hires service for any commercial purpose, other than for earning livelihood through self-employment, is not a consumer.

Consumer Dispute

"Consumer dispute" means a dispute where the person against whom a complaint has been made, denies or disputes the allegations contained in the complaint [Section 2(8)].

Defect (in Goods)

"Defect" means any fault, imperfection or shortcoming in the quality, quantity, potency, purity, or standard (of goods) which is required to be maintained by or under any law or under any contract, express or implied, or as is claimed by the trader in any manner whatsoever in relation to any goods or product and the expression "defective' shall be construed accordingly [Section 2(10)].

Deficiency (in Service)

(Almost equivalent to defect in goods) "Deficiency" means any fault, imperfection, shortcoming, or inadequacy in the quality, nature, and manner of performance (of a service) which is required to be maintained by or under any law, or has been undertaken to be performed by a person in pursuance of a contract or otherwise in relation to any service and includes-

> Deficiency (in service): Any fault, imperfection, shortcoming, or inadequacy in quality, nature, and manner of performance (of a service), required to be maintained under any law, or has been undertaken to be performed by a person in pursuance of a contract or otherwise.

(i) any act of negligence or omission or commission by such person which causes loss or injury to the consumer; and
(ii) deliberate withholding of relevant information by such person to the consumer [Section 2(11)].

Goods

'Goods' means every kind of movable property and includes "food" as defined under Section 3 of the Foods and Standards Act, 2006 [Section 2(21)].

Manufacturer

'Manufacturer' means a person who

1. makes or manufactures any goods or parts thereof; or
2. assembles parts thereof made or manufactured by others; or
3. puts or causes to be put his own mark on any goods made or manufactured by any other person [Section 2(24)].

Misleading Advertisement

"Misleading advertisement" in relation to any product or service, means an advertisement, which—falsely describes such product or service; or

(i) gives a false guarantee to, or is likely to mislead the consumers as to the nature, substance, quantity or quality of such product or service; or
(ii) conveys an express or implied representation which, if made by the manufacturer or seller or service provider thereof, would constitute an unfair trade practice; or
(iii) deliberately conceals important information [Section 2(28)].

Person

"Person" includes—

(i) an individual;
(ii) a firm whether registered or not;
(iii) a Hindu undivided family;
(iv) a co-operative society;
(v) an association of persons whether registered under the Societies Registration Act, 1860 or not;
(vi) any corporation, company or a body of individuals whether incorporated or not;
(vii) any artificial juridical person, not falling within any of the preceding sub-clauses [Section 2(31)].

Product

"Product" means any article or goods or substance or raw material or any extended cycle of such product, which may be in gaseous, liquid, or solid state possessing intrinsic value which is capable of delivery either as wholly assembled or as a component part and is produced for introduction to trade or commerce, but does not include human tissues, blood, blood products and organs[Section 2(33)].

Product Liability

"Product liability" means the responsibility of a product manufacturer or product seller, of any product or service, to compensate for any harm caused to a consumer by such defective product manufactured or sold or by deficiency in services relating thereto [Section 2(34)].

Restrictive Trade Practice

Restrictive trade practice: A business agreement, overt or implied one, between companies which controls prices or the areas in which goods are sold, preventing fair competition from other companies.

"Restrictive trade practice" means any trade practice which tends to bring about manipulation of price or its conditions of delivery or to affect flow of supplies in the market relating to goods or services in such a manner as to impose on the consumers unjustified costs or restrictions and shall include—

(i) delay beyond the period agreed to by a trader in supply of such goods or in providing the services which has led or is likely to lead to rise in the price;

(ii) any trade practice which requires a consumer to buy, hire or avail of any goods or, as the case may be, services as condition precedent for buying, hiring or availing of other goods or services [Section 2(41)].

Service

Service: The action of serving or assisting someone or the performance of work or job by one person for another.

'Service' means service of any description which is made available to potential users and includes, but not limited to, the provision of facilities in connection with banking, financing, insurance, transport, processing, supply of electrical or other energy, boarding or lodging or both, housing, construction, entertainment, amusement, or the purveying of news or other information but does not include the rendering of any service free of charge or under a contract of personal service [Section 2(42)].

Trader

'Trader', in relation to any goods, means a person who sells or distributes any goods for sale and includes the manufacturer thereof, and where such goods are sold or distributed in a packaged form, includes the packer thereof [Section 2(45)].

Trader: A person who sells or distributes any goods for sale and includes the manufacturer thereof.

Unfair Contract

"Unfair contract" means a contract between a manufacturer or trader or service provider on one hand, and a consumer on the other, having such terms which cause significant change in the rights of such consumer, including the following, namely: —

(i) requiring manifestly excessive security deposits to be given by a consumer for the performance of contractual obligations; or

(ii) imposing any penalty on the consumer, for the breach of contract thereof which is wholly disproportionate to the loss occurred due to such breach to the other party to the contract; or

(iii) refusing to accept early repayment of debts on payment of applicable penalty; or

(iv) entitling a party to the contract to terminate such contract unilaterally, without reasonable cause; or

(v) permitting or has the effect of permitting one party to assign the contract to the detriment of the other party who is a consumer, without his consent; or

(vi) imposing on the consumer any unreasonable charge, obligation or condition which puts such consumer to disadvantage [Section 2(46)].

Unfair Trade Practice

"Unfair trade practice" means a trade practice which, for the purpose of promoting the sale, use or supply of any goods or for the provision of any service, adopts any unfair method or unfair or deceptive practice including any of the following practices, namely:—

(i) making any statement, whether orally or in writing or by visible representation including by means of electronic record, which—

(a) falsely represents that the goods are of a particular standard, quality, quantity, grade, composition, style or model;

(b) falsely represents that the services are of a particular standard, quality or grade;

(c) falsely represents any re-built, second-hand, renovated, reconditioned or old goods as new goods;

(d) represents that the goods or services have sponsorship, approval, performance, characteristics, accessories, uses or benefits which such goods or services do not have;

(e) represents that the seller or the supplier has a sponsorship or approval or affiliation which such seller or supplier does not have;

(f) makes a false or misleading representation concerning the need for, or the usefulness of, any goods or services;

(g) gives to the public any warranty or guarantee of the performance, efficacy or length of life of a product or of any goods that is not based on an adequate or proper test thereof:

Provided that where a defence is raised to the effect that such warranty or guarantee is based on adequate or proper test, the burden of proof of such defence shall lie on the person raising such defence;

(h) makes to the public a representation in a form that purports to be-

(A) a warranty or guarantee of a product or of any goods or services; or

(B) a promise to replace, maintain or repair an article or any part thereof or to repeat or continue a service until it has achieved a specified result,

if such purported warranty or guarantee or promise is materially misleading or if there is no reasonable prospect that such warranty, guarantee or promise will be carried out;

(i) materially misleads the public concerning the price at which a product or like products or goods or services, have been or are, ordinarily sold or provided, and, for this purpose, a representation as to price shall be deemed to refer to the price at which the product or goods or services has or have been sold by sellers or provided by suppliers generally in the relevant market unless it is clearly specified to be the price at which the product has been sold or services have been provided by the person by whom or on whose behalf the representation is made;

(j) gives false or misleading facts disparaging the goods, services or trade of another person.

Explanation. — For the purposes of this sub-clause, a statement that is, —

(A) expressed on an article offered or displayed for sale, or on its wrapper or container; or

(B) expressed on anything attached to, inserted in, or accompanying, an article offered or displayed for sale, or on anything on which the article is mounted for display or sale; or

(C) contained in or on anything that is sold, sent, delivered, transmitted or in any other manner whatsoever made available to a member of the public,

shall be deemed to be a statement made to the public by, and only by, the person who had caused the statement to be so expressed, made or contained;

(ii) permitting the publication of any advertisement, whether in any newspaper or otherwise, including by way of electronic record, for the sale or supply at a bargain price of goods or services that are not intended to be offered for sale or supply at the bargain price, or for a period that is, and in quantities that are, reasonable, having regard to the nature of the market in which the business is carried on, the nature and size of business, and the nature of the advertisement.

Explanation — For the purpose of this sub-clause, "bargain price" means, —

(A) a price that is stated in any advertisement to be a bargain price, by reference to an ordinary price or otherwise; or

(B) a price that a person who reads, hears or sees the advertisement, would reasonably understand to be a bargain price having regard to the prices at which the product advertised or like products are ordinarily sold;

(iii) permitting—

(a) the offering of gifts, prizes or other items with the intention of not providing them as offered or creating impression that something is being given or offered free of charge when it is fully or partly covered by the amount charged, in the transaction as a whole;

(b) the conduct of any contest, lottery, game of chance or skill, for the purpose of promoting, directly or indirectly, the sale, use or supply of any product or any business interest, except such contest, lottery, game of chance or skill as may be prescribed;

(c) withholding from the participants of any scheme offering gifts, prizes or other items free of charge on its closure, the information about final results of the scheme.

Explanation. — For the purpose of this sub-clause, the participants of a scheme shall be deemed to have been informed of the final results of the scheme where such results are within a reasonable time published, prominently in the same newspaper in which the scheme was originally advertised;

(iv) permitting the sale or supply of goods intended to be used, or are of a kind likely to be used by consumers, knowing or having reason to believe that the goods do not comply with the standards prescribed by the competent authority relating to performance, composition, contents, design, constructions, finishing or packaging as are necessary to prevent or reduce the risk of injury to the person using the goods;

(v) permitting the hoarding or destruction of goods, or refusal to sell the goods or to make them available for sale or to provide any service, if such hoarding or destruction or refusal raises or tends to raise or is intended to raise, the cost of those or other similar goods or services;

(vi) manufacturing of spurious goods or offering such goods for sale or adopting deceptive practices in the provision of services;

(vii) not issuing bill or cash memo or receipt for the goods sold or services rendered in such manner as may be prescribed;

(viii) refusing, after selling goods or rendering services, to take back or withdraw defective goods or to withdraw or discontinue deficient services and to refund the consideration thereof, if paid, within the period stipulated in the bill or cash memo or receipt or in the absence of such stipulation, within a period of thirty days;

(ix) disclosing to other person any personal information given in confidence by the consumer unless such disclosure is made in accordance with the provisions of any law for the time being in force [Section 2(47)].

Rights of Consumer

Consumer interest is the focus of enlightened marketing mix. Business and consumerism both aim at the protection of consumer interest—business through self-regulation and consumerism through self-help. Consumerism invokes government assistance when business misbehaves and fails to fulfil its responsibilities. To facilitate this, the Act under Section 2(9) provides the following six rights of consumers:

1. **Right to Safety:** It is the right of the consumer to be protected against the marketing of goods and services by unscrupulous sellers, which are potentially hazardous to life and property. The goods purchased and services availed of should not only meet their immediate needs, but also fulfil long term interests.
2. **Right to be Informed:** This refers to the entitlement of the consumer to be informed about the quality, quantity, potency, purity, standard, and price of goods so as to protect the buyer against unfair trade practices. A consumer should insist on getting all the information about the product or service before making a choice or a decision. This will enable him/her to act wisely and responsibly, and also enable him to desist from falling prey to high pressure and misleading selling techniques.
3. **Right to Choose:** It is the right of the consumer to be assured, as far as possible, of access to a variety of goods and services at competitive price. In case of monopolies, it implies the right to be assurdof satisfactory quality and service at a fair and reasonable price.
4. **Right to be Heard:** This implies that consumer's interests will receive due consideration at appropriate fora. It also includes the consumer's liberty to be represented in various fora constituted for consumer welfare.

Figure 21.1 Organisational setup under the CPA

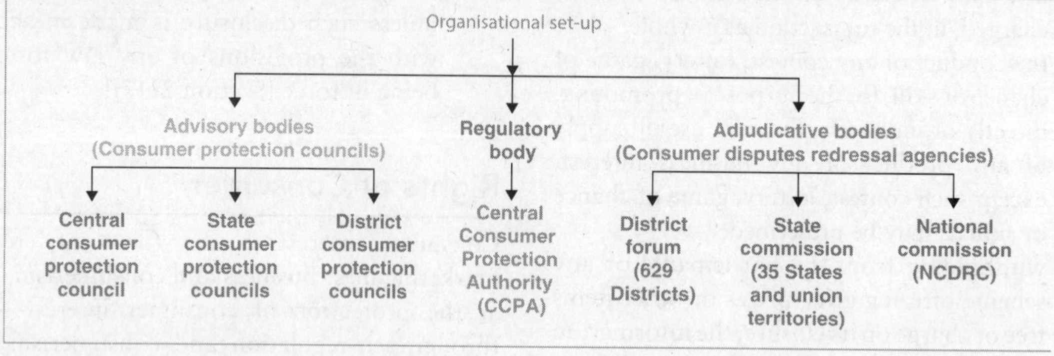

5. **Right to Seek Redressal of Grievances:** This refers to the privilege of the consumer to seek compensation against unfair trade practices or unscrupulous exploitation. It also includes the right to fair settlement of genuine grievances of the consumers. Consumers can also take the help of consumer organisations in seeking redressal of their grievances.
6. **Right to Consumer Awareness:** This refers to the entitlement of the consumer to acquire the knowledge and skill to be an informed buyer. Ignorance of consumers, particularly of rural folk, is the main cause of their exploitation. They should know their rights and must exercise them. Only then real consumer protection can be achieved.

Consumer Protection Councils

Besides the three-tier quasi-judicial machinery to settle consumers' grievances and complaints, the Act also provides for the setting up of Consumer Protection Councils at the Centre as well as State level for enforcement of consumer rights.

The Central Consumer Protection Council

Establishment

The Central Government may, by notification, establish with effect from such date as it may specify in such notification, a Central Consumer Protection Council to be known as the Central Council [Section 3(1)].

Composition

The Central Council shall be an advisory council and consist of the following members, namely,

1. the Minister in charge of the Department of Consumer Affairs in the Central Government, who shall be its Chairperson, and
2. such number of other official or non-official members representing such interests as may be prescribed [Section 3(2)].

Meetings of the Central Council

1. The Central Council shall meet as and when necessary, but at least one meeting of the council shall be held every year.
2. The Central Council shall meet at such time and place as the Chairman may think fit and shall observe such procedure in regard to the transaction of its business as may be prescribed [Section 4(2)].

Objects of the Central Council

The objects of the Central Council shall be to render advice on promotion and protection of the consumers' rights under this Act [Section 5]. This object will be achieved by exercising the following rights by the Central Council:

1. The right to be protected against the marketing of goods and services which are hazardous to life and property;
2. The right to be informed about the quality, quantity, potency, purity, standard, and price of goods

or services, as the case may be, so as to protect a small consumer against unfair trade practices;

3. The right to be assured, wherever possible, access to a variety of goods and services at competitive prices;
4. The right to be heard and to be assured that consumers' interests will receive due consideration at appropriate Commissions;
5. The right to seek redressal against unfair trade practices or restrictive trade practices or unscrupulous exploitation of consumers; and
6. The right to consumer education.

State Consumer Protection Councils

Establishment

The State Government may, by notification, establish with effect from such date as it may specify in such notification, a State Consumer Protection Council for such State to be known as the State Council [Section 6(1)].

Composition

The State Council shall be an advisory council and consist of the following members, namely

1. the Minister in-charge of Consumer Affairs in the State Government who shall be its Chairperson;
2. such number of other official or non-official members representing such interests as may be prescribed by the State Government;
3. such number of other official or non-official members, not exceeding ten, as may be nominated by the Central Government [Section 6(2)].

Meetings of the State Council

The State Council shall meet as and when necessary but not less than two meetings shall be held every year. Time and place of meeting shall be such as the Chairman may think fit and shall observe such procedure in regard to the transaction of its business as may be prescribed by the State Government [Section 6 (3)].

Objects of the State Council

The objects of every State Council shall be to render advice on promotion and protection of consumer rights under this Act within the State [Section 7].

District Consumer Protection Council

Establishment

The State Government shall, by notification, establish for every District with effect from such date as it may specify in such notification, a District Consumer Protection Council to be known as the District Council [Section 8(1)].

Composition

The District Council shall be an advisory council and consist of the following members, namely:—

(a) the Collector of the district (by whatever name called), who shall be the Chairperson; and

(b) such number of other official and non-official members representing such interests as may be prescribed.

Meetings of the District Council

The District Council shall meet at such time and place within the district as the Chairperson may think fit and shall observe such procedure in regard to the transaction of its business as may be prescribed [Section 8(3)].

The District Council shall meet at such time and place within the district as the Chairperson may think fit and shall observe such procedure in regard to the transaction of its business as may be prescribed [Section 8(4)].

Objects of the District Council

The objects of every District Council shall be to render advice on promotion and protection of consumer rights under the new Act within the district [Section 9].

Central Consumer Protection Authority

One of the major reforms brought in by CPA 2019 in the landscape of 'Consumer's Interest and Protection' is the establishment of the Central Consumer Protection Authority (CCPA) under Section 10(1) of the legislation, to be known as the 'Central Authority'.

The CCPA will be a national level regulator dealing with matters relating to violation of rights of consumers and unfair trade practices and false and misleading advertisements which are detrimental to the interest of public and consumer. The CCPA will have the powers to inquire or investigate into matters relating to violations of consumer rights or unfair trade practices *suo motu*, or on a complaint received, or on a direction from the central government.

CCPA will carry out the following functions, including: (i) inquiring into violations of consumer rights, investigating and launching prosecution at the appropriate forum; (ii) passing orders to recall goods or withdraw services that are hazardous, reimbursement of the price paid, and discontinuation of the unfair trade practices, as defined in the Bill; (iii) issuing directions to the concerned trader/manufacturer/endorser/advertiser/publisher to either discontinue a false or misleading advertisement, or modify it; (iv) imposing penalties, and; (v) issuing safety notices to consumers against unsafe goods and services.

The Central Authority shall consist of a Chief Commissioner and such number of other Commissioners as may be prescribed, to be appointed by the Central Government to exercise the powers and discharge the functions under this Act [Section 10(2)].

The headquarters of the Central Authority shall be at such place in the National Capital Region of Delhi, and it shall have regional and other offices in any other place in India as the Central Government may decide [Section 10(3)].

Investigation Wing

(1) The Central Authority shall have an Investigation Wing headed by a Director- General for the purpose of conducting inquiry or investigation under this Act as may be directed by the Central Authority.

(2) The Central Government may appoint a Director-General and such number of Additional Director-General, Director, Joint Director, Deputy Director and Assistant Director, from amongst persons who have experience in investigation and possess such qualifications, in such manner, as may be prescribed.

(3) Every Additional Director-General, Director, Joint Director, Deputy Director and Assistant Director shall exercise his powers, and discharge his functions, subject to the general control, supervision and direction of the Director-General.

(4) The Director-General may delegate all or any of his powers to the Additional Director-General or Director, Joint Director or Deputy Director or Assistant Director, as the case may be, while conducting inquiries or investigations under this Act.

(5) The inquiries or the investigations made by the Director- General shall be submitted to the Central Authority in such form, in such manner and within such time, as may be specified [Section 15].

Powers and Functions of Central Authority

(1) The Central Authority shall—
  - (a) protect, promote and enforce the rights of consumers as a class, and prevent violation of consumers rights under this Act;
  - (b) prevent unfair trade practices and ensure that no person engages himself in unfair trade practices;
  - (c) ensure that no false or misleading advertisement is made of any goods or services which contravenes the provisions of this Act or the rules or regulations made thereunder;
  - (c) ensure that no person takes part in the publication of any advertisement which is false or misleading.

(2) The Central Authority may, for any of the purposes aforesaid,—
  - (a) inquire or cause an inquiry or investigation to be made into violations of consumer rights or unfair trade practices, either *suo motu* or on a complaint received or on the directions from the Central Government;
  - (b) file complaints before the District Commission, the State Commission or the National Commission, as the case may be, under this Act;
  - (c) intervene in any proceedings before the District Commission or the State Commission or the National Commission, as the case may be, in respect of any allegation of violation of consumer rights or unfair trade practices;
  - (d) review the matters relating to, and the factors inhibiting enjoyment of, consumer rights, including safeguards provided for the protection of consumers under any other law for the time being in force and recommend appropriate remedial measures for their effective implementation;
  - (e) recommend adoption of international covenants and best international practices on consumer rights to ensure effective enforcement of consumer rights;

(f) undertake and promote research in the field of consumer rights;
(g) spread and promote awareness on consumer rights;
(h) encourage non-Governmental organizations and other institutions working in the field of consumer rights to co-operate and work with consumer protection agencies;
(i) mandate the use of unique and universal goods identifiers in such goods, as may be necessary, to prevent unfair trade practices and to protect consumers' interest;
(j) issue safety notices to alert consumers against dangerous or hazardous or unsafe goods or services;
(k) advise the Ministries and Departments of the Central and State Governments on consumer welfare measures; and
(l) issue necessary guidelines to prevent unfair trade practices and protect consumers' interest [Section 18].

Three-tier Grievance-redressal Machinery

In order to provide simple and speedy redressal of consumer grievances, the Consumer Protection Act, 2019 envisages a three-tier quasi-judicial machinery at the national, state and district levels as under:

1. National Consumer Disputes Redressal Commission or the 'National Commission' at the apex level. It is based in Delhi.
2. State Consumer Disputes Redressal Commissions or 'State Commissions'. These are based in state capitals.
3. District Consumer Disputes Redressal Commission or 'District Commission', established at the district level.

As on June 30, 2020, there are 35 State Commissions, one in each State or Union Territory and 629 district Commissions. The organisational setup established under the CPA is shown in Figure 21.1.

District Commission

Establishment

Section 28(1) of the new Act lays down that there shall be established for the purposes of this Act, a Consumer Disputes Redressal Commission, to be known as the 'District Commission', established by the State Government—in each district of the state—by notification. The State Government may, if it deems fit, establish more than one District Commission in a district.

> District Commission: Formally known as 'District Consumer Disputes Redressal Commission', first level dispute redressal agency established by the State Government in each district of the State, empowered to settle cases, where the value of compensation claimed is up to one crore rupees.

Composition

As envisaged in the law, the District Commission is a three-member bench, headed by a serving or retired district judge, or a person qualified to be one and two other members—one of whom is a woman—who are economics, law, commerce, or public affairs experts.

According to Section 28(2) of the Act, each District Commission shall consist of the following:

1. a President; and
2. not less than two and not more than such number members as may be prescribed, in consultation with the Central Government.

Term of office

Every member of the District Commission shall hold office for a term of five years or up to the age of 65 years, whichever is earlier. He shall not be eligible for re-appointment. However, a member may resign his/her office in writing under his/her hand addressed to the State Government.

Terms of engagement

The salary or honorarium and other allowances payable to, and the other terms and conditions of service of the members of the District Commission shall be such as may be prescribed by the State Government. However, the appointment of a member on whole-time basis shall be made by the State Government on the recommendations of the President of the State Commission taking into consideration such factors as may be prescribed including the work-load of the District Commission.

Jurisdiction of District Commission

The District Commission is empowered to settle cases, where the value of the goods or services paid as consideration does not exceed one crore rupees [Section 34(1)].

A complaint shall be instituted in a District Commission within the local limits of whose jurisdiction,-

(a) the opposite party or each of the opposite parties, where there are more than one, at the time of the institution of the complaint, ordinarily resides or carries on business or has a branch office or personally works for gain; or
(b) any of the opposite parties, where there are more than one, at the time of the institution of the complaint, actually and voluntarily resides, or carries on business or has a branch office, or personally works for gain, provided that in such case the permission of the District Commission is given; or
(c) the cause of action, wholly or in part, arises; or
(d) the complainant resides or personally works for gain [Section 34(2)]

The State Commission

Forming the middle tier of the redressal mechanism are the 'State Commissions, one in each state capital,

(a) to entertain-
   (i) complaints where the value of the goods or services paid as consideration, exceeds rupees one crore, but does not exceed rupees ten crore:

   Provided that where the Central Government deems it necessary so to do, it may prescribe such other value, as it deems fit;
   (ii) complaints against unfair contracts, where the value of goods or services paid as consideration does not exceed ten crore rupees;
   (iii) appeals against the orders of any District Commission within the State; and
(b) to call for the records and pass appropriate orders in any consumer dispute which is pending before or has been decided by any District Commission within the State, where it appears to the State Commission that such District Commission has exercised a jurisdiction not vested in it by law, or has failed to exercise a jurisdiction so vested or has acted in exercise of its jurisdiction illegally or with material irregularity [Section 47(1)].

State Commission: Formally known as 'State Consumer Disputes Redressal Commission', functions as middle tier of redressal mechanism, established by the State Government in the State concerned, empowered to settle cases, where the value of goods and services paid as consideration, exceeds rupees one crore, but does not exceed rupees ten crore.

Composition

Each State Commission shall consist of

(a) a President
(b) not less than four and not more than such number of members, as may be prescribed in consultation with the Central Government [Section 42(3)].

Salary and honorarium

The salary or honorarium and other allowances payable to, and the other terms and conditions of service of the President and members of the State Commission shall be such as may be prescribed by the State Government [Section 44].

Term of office

Every member of the State Commission shall hold office for a term of five years or up to the age of 67 years, whichever is earlier, and shall not be eligible for re-appointment.

Notwithstanding anything contained in sub-section (3), a person appointed as a President or as a member before the commencement of the Consumer Protection (Amendment) Act, 1993, shall continue to hold such office as President or member, as the case may be, till the completion of his term [Section 16(3)].

National Commission

At the apex of the redressal mechanism, the Central Government shall, by notification, establish a National Consumer Disputes Redressal Commission, to be known as the National Commission.

The National Commission shall ordinarily function at the National Capital Region and perform its functions at such other places as the Central Government may in consultation with the National Commission notify in the official budget [Section 53].

National Commission: Formally known as 'National Consumer Disputes Redressal Commission', functions at the apex level of redressal mechanism, established by the Central Government, empowered to settle cases, where the value of the goods or services paid as consideration exceeds rupees ten crore.

Composition

The National Commission shall consist of

(a) a President; and
(b) not less than four and not more than such number of members as may be prescribed [Section 54].

Compensation

The salary or honorarium and other allowances payable to and the other terms and conditions of service of the members of the National Commission shall be such as may be prescribed by the Central Government.

Term of office

President and members of the National Commission shall hold office for a term of five years from the date on which he/she enters his/her office and shall be eligible for re-appointment.

However, no President or members shall hold office as such after he has attained such age as specified in the rules made by the Central Government which shall not exceed, -

(a) in the case of the President, the age of seventy years;
(b) in the case of any other member, the age of seventy-seven years [Section 55(1)].

Jurisdiction

The National Commission shall have jurisdiction—

(a) to entertain—
   (i) complaints where the value of the goods or services paid as consideration exceeds rupees ten crore:

Provided that where the Central Government deems it necessary so to do, it may prescribe such other value, as it deems fit;

   (ii) complaints against unfair contracts, where the value of goods or services paid as consideration exceeds ten crore rupees;
   (iii) appeals against the orders of any State Commission;
   (iv) appeals against the orders of the Central Authority; and

(b) to call for the records and pass appropriate orders in any consumer dispute which is pending before or has been decided by any State Commission where it appears to the National Commission that such State Commission has exercised a jurisdiction not vested in it by law, or has failed to exercise a jurisdiction so vested, or has acted in the exercise of its jurisdiction illegally or with material irregularity.

(2) The jurisdiction, powers and authority of the National Commission may be exercised by Benches thereof and a Bench may be constituted by the President with one or more members as he may deem fit:

Provided that the senior-most member of the Bench shall preside over the Bench.

(3) Where the members of a Bench differ in opinion on any point, the points shall be decided according to the opinion of the majority, if there is a majority, but if the members are equally divided, they shall state the point or points on which they differ, and make a reference to the President who shall either hear the point or points himself or refer the case for hearing on such point or points by one or more of the other members and such point or points shall be decided according to the opinion of the majority of the members who have heard the case, including those who first heard it:

Provided that the President or the other member, as the case may be, shall give opinion on the point or points so referred within a period of two months from the date of such reference [Section 58].

Filing of a Complaint and the Procedure of Hearing

A complaint regarding a defect in any goods or deficiency in service, as the case may be, can be made in writing to the District Commission, either by the aggrieved consumer, or a consumer rights organisation on behalf of the consumers, or a group of aggrieved consumers or the Central or State Governments.

- A District Commission can take up complaints where the value of the goods or services paid as consideration does not exceed one crore rupees [Section 34(1)].
- Every State Commission is authorised to take up cases, where the value of goods and services paid as consideration, exceeds rupees one crore, but does not exceed rupees ten crore or the complaints against unfair contracts, where the value of goods or services paid as consideration does not exceed ten crore

rupees. State Commission shall also have the jurisdiction to entertain appeals against the orders of any District Commission within the State [Section 47(1)].

- The National Commission is authorised to entertain:
  - (i) complaints where the value of the goods or services paid as consideration exceeds rupees ten crore;
  - (ii) complaints against unfair contracts, where the value of goods or services paid as consideration exceeds ten crore rupees;
  - (iii) appeals against the orders of any State Commission; and
  - (iv) appeals against the orders of the Central Authority [Section 58(1)].

The respective Commissions, entitled to deal with the cases shall deal with them in the prescribed manner explained as follows.

Manner in Which a Complaint Can Be Made

A complaint, in relation to any goods sold or delivered or agreed to be sold or delivered or any service provided or agreed to be provided, may be filed with a District Commission by—

(a) the consumer,—

  (i) to whom such goods are sold or delivered or agreed to be sold or delivered or such service is provided or agreed to be provided; or

  (ii) who alleges unfair trade practice in respect of such goods or service;

(b) any recognised consumer association, whether the consumer to whom such goods are sold or delivered or agreed to be sold or delivered or such service is provided or agreed to be provided, or who alleges unfair trade practice in respect of such goods or service, is a member of such association or not;

(c) one or more consumers, where there are numerous consumers having the same interest, with the permission of the District Commission, on behalf of, or for the benefit of, all consumers so interested; or

(d) the Central Government, the Central Authority or the State Government, as the case may be:

Provided that the complaint under this sub-section may be filed electronically in such manner as may be prescribed [Section 35(1)].

(2) Every complaint filed under sub-section (*1*) shall be accompanied with such fee and payable in such manner, including electronic form, as may be prescribed [Section 35(2)].

Proceedings Before District Commission

(1) Every proceeding before the District Commission shall be conducted by the President of that Commission and at least one member thereof, sitting together.

(2) On receipt of a complaint made under Section 35, the District Commission may, by order, admit the complaint for being proceeded with or reject the same:

However, a complaint shall not be rejected under this section unless an opportunity of being heard has been given to the complainant:

Provided further that the admissibility of the complaint shall ordinarily be decided within twenty-one days from the date on which the complaint was filed.

(3) Where the District Commission does not decide the issue of admissibility of the complaint within the period so specified, it shall be deemed to have been admitted [Section 36].

Reference to Mediation

(1) At the first hearing of the complaint after its admission, or at any later stage, if it appears to the District Commission that there exist elements of a settlement which may be acceptable to the parties, except in such cases as may be prescribed, it may direct the parties to give in writing, within five days, consent to have their dispute settled by mediation in accordance with the provisions of Chapter V.

(2) Where the parties agree for settlement by mediation and give their consent in writing, the District Commission shall, within five days of receipt of such consent, refer the matter for mediation, and in such case, the provisions of Chapter V, relating to mediation, shall apply [Section 37].

Procedure on Admission of Complaint

(1) The District Commission shall, on admission of a complaint, or in respect of cases referred for mediation on failure of settlement by mediation, proceed with such complaint.

(2) Where the complaint relates to any goods, the District Commission shall, —

(a) refer a copy of the admitted complaint, within twenty-one days from the date of its admission to the opposite party mentioned in the complaint directing him to give his version of the case within a period of thirty days or such extended period not exceeding fifteen days as may be granted by it;

(b) if the opposite party on receipt of a complaint referred to him under clause (*a*) denies or disputes the allegations contained in the complaint, or omits or fails to take any action to represent his case within the time given by the District Commission, proceed to settle the consumer dispute in the manner specified in clauses (*c*) to (*g*);

(c) if the complaint alleges a defect in the goods which cannot be determined without proper analysis or test of the goods, obtain a sample of the goods from the complainant, seal it and authenticate it in the manner as may be prescribed and refer the sample so sealed to the appropriate laboratory along with a direction that such laboratory to make an analysis or test, whichever may be necessary, with a view to finding out whether such goods suffer from any defect alleged in the complaint or from any other defect and to report its findings thereon to the District Commission within a period of forty-five days of the receipt of the reference or within such extended period as may be granted by it;

(d) before any sample of the goods is referred to any appropriate laboratory under clause (*c*), require the complainant to deposit to the credit of the Commission such fees as may be specified, for payment to the appropriate laboratory for carrying out the necessary analysis or test in relation to the goods in question;

(e) remit the amount deposited to its credit under clause (*d*) to the appropriate laboratory to enable it to carry out the analysis or test mentioned in clause (*c*) and on receipt of the report from the appropriate laboratory, it shall forward a copy of the report along with such remarks as it may feel appropriate to the opposite party;

(f) if any of the parties disputes the correctness of the findings of the appropriate laboratory, or disputes the correctness of the methods of analysis or test adopted by the appropriate laboratory, require the opposite party or the complainant to submit in writing his objections with regard to the report made by the appropriate laboratory;

(g) give a reasonable opportunity to the complainant as well as the opposite party of being heard as to the correctness or otherwise of the report made by the appropriate laboratory and also as to the objection made in relation thereto under clause (*f*) and issue an appropriate order under section 39.

(3) The District Commission shall, if the complaint admitted by it under sub-section (2) of section 36 relates to goods in respect of which the procedure specified in sub-section (2) cannot be followed, or if the complaint relates to any services, —

(a) refer a copy of such complaint to the opposite party directing him to give his version of the case within a period of thirty days or such extended period not exceeding fifteen days as may be granted by the District Commission;

(b) if the opposite party, on receipt of a copy of the complaint, referred to him under clause (*a*) denies or disputes the allegations contained in the complaint, or omits or fails to take any action to represent his case within the time given by the District Commission, it shall proceed to settle the consumer dispute—

(i) *ex parte* on the basis of evidence brought to its notice by the complainant, where the opposite party omits or fails to take any action to represent his case within the time given by the Commission;

(ii) on the basis of evidence brought to its notice by the complainant and the opposite party, if the opposite party denies or disputes the allegations contained in the complaint, or

(c) decide the complaint on merits if the complainant fails to appear on the date of hearing.

(4) For the purposes of sub-sections (*2*) and (*3*), the District Commission may, by order, require an electronic service provider to provide such information, documents or records, as may be specified in that order.

(5) No proceedings complying with the procedure laid down in sub-sections (*1*) and (*2*) shall be called in question in any court on the ground that the principles of natural justice have not been complied with.

(6) Every complaint shall be heard by the District Commission on the basis of affidavit and documentary evidence placed on record:

Provided that where an application is made for hearing or for examination of parties in person or through video conferencing, the District Commission may, on sufficient cause being shown, and after recording its reasons in writing, allow the same.

(7) Every complaint shall be disposed of as expeditiously as possible and endeavour shall be made to decide the complaint within a period of three months from the date of receipt of notice by opposite party where the complaint does not require analysis or testing of commodities and within five months if it requires analysis or testing of commodities:

Provided that no adjournment shall ordinarily be granted by the District Commission unless sufficient cause is shown and the reasons for grant of adjournment have been recorded in writing by the Commission:

Provided further that the District Commission shall make such orders as to the costs occasioned by the adjournment as may be specified by regulations:

Provided also that in the event of a complaint being disposed of after the period so specified, the District Commission shall record in writing, the reasons for the same at the time of disposing of the said complaint.

(8) Where during the pendency of any proceeding before the District Commission, if it appears necessary, it may pass such interim order as is just and proper in the facts and circumstances of the case.

(9) For the purposes of this section, the District Commission shall have the same powers as are vested in a civil court under the Code of Civil Procedure, 1908 while trying a suit in respect of the following matters, namely: —

(a) the summoning and enforcing the attendance of any defendant or witness and examining the witness on oath;
(b) requiring the discovery and production of any document or other material object as evidence;
(c) receiving of evidence on affidavits;
(d) the requisitioning of the report of the concerned analysis or test from the appropriate laboratory or from any other relevant source;
(e) issuing of commissions for the examination of any witness, or document;
(f) any other matter which may be prescribed by the Central Government.

(10) Every proceeding before the District Commission shall be deemed to be a judicial proceeding within the meaning of Sections 193 and 228 of the Indian Penal Code, and the District Commission shall be deemed to be a criminal court for the purposes of section 195 and Chapter XXVI of the Code of Criminal Procedure, 1973.

(11) Where the complainant is a consumer referred to in sub-clause (*v*) of clause (*5*) of section 2, the provisions of Order I Rule 8 of the First Schedule to the Code of Civil Procedure, 1908 shall apply subject to the modification that every reference therein to a suit or decree shall be construed as a reference to a complaint or the order of the District Commission thereon.

(12) In the event of death of a complainant who is a consumer or of the opposite party against whom the complaint has been filed, the provisions of Order XXII of the First Schedule to the Code of Civil Procedure, 1908 shall apply subject to the modification that every reference therein to the plaintiff and the defendant shall be construed as reference to a complainant or the opposite party, as the case may be [Section 38].

Findings of the District Commission

Where the District Commission is satisfied that the goods complained against suffer from any of the defects specified in the complaint or that any of the allegations contained in the complaint about the services or any unfair trade practices, or claims for compensation under product liability are proved, it shall issue an order to the opposite party directing him to do one or more of the following, namely:-

(a) to remove the defect pointed out by the appropriate laboratory from the goods in question;
(b) to replace the goods with new goods of similar description which shall be free from any defect;
(c) to return to the complainant the price, or, as the case may be, the charges paid by the complainant along with such interest on such price or charges as may be decided;
(d) to pay such amount as may be awarded by it as compensation to the consumer for any loss or injury suffered by the consumer due to the negligence of the opposite party:

However, the District Commission shall have the power to grant punitive damages in such circumstances as it deems fit;

(e) to pay such amount as may be awarded by it as compensation in a product liability action under Chapter VI;
(f) to remove the defects in goods or deficiencies in the services in question;
(g) to discontinue the unfair trade practice or restrictive trade practice and not to repeat them;
(h) not to offer the hazardous or unsafe goods for sale;
(i) to withdraw the hazardous goods from being offered for sale;
(j) to cease manufacture of hazardous goods and to desist from offering services which are hazardous in nature;
(k) to pay such sum as may be determined by it, if it is of the opinion that loss or injury has been suffered by a large number of consumers who are not identifiable conveniently:

However, the minimum amount of sum so payable shall not be less than twenty-five per cent of the value of such defective goods sold or service provided, as the case may be, to such consumers;

(l) to issue corrective advertisement to neutralize the effect of misleading advertisement at the cost of the opposite party responsible for issuing such misleading advertisement;
(m) to provide for adequate costs to parties; and
(n) to cease and desist from issuing any misleading advertisement.

(2) Any amount obtained under sub-section (*1*) shall be credited to such fund and utilized in such manner as may be prescribed.

(3) In any proceeding conducted by the President and a member and if they differ on any point or points, they shall state the point or points on which they differ and refer the same to another member for hearing on such point or points and the opinion of the majority shall be the order of the District Commission:

Provided that the other member shall give his opinion on such point or points referred to him within a period of one month from the date of such reference.

(4) Every order made by the District Commission under sub-section (*1*) shall be signed by the President and the member who conducted the proceeding:

(5) Provided that where the order is made as per majority opinion under sub-section (*3*), such order shall also be signed by the other member [Section 39].

Review by District Commission

The District Commission shall have the power to review any of the order passed by it if there is an error apparent on the face of the record, either of its own motion or on an application made by any of the parties within thirty days of such order [Section 40].

Appeal against the order passed of District Commission

Any person aggrieved by an order made by the District Commission may prefer an appeal against such order to the State Commission on the grounds of facts or law within a period of forty-five days from the date of the order, in such form and manner, as may be prescribed:

Provided that the State Commission may entertain an appeal after the expiry of the said period of forty-five days, if it is satisfied that there was sufficient cause for not filing it within that period:

Provided further that no appeal by a person, who is required to pay any amount in terms of an order of the District Commission, shall be entertained by the State Commission unless the appellant has deposited fifty per cent. of that amount in the manner as may be prescribed:

Provided also that no appeal shall lie from any order passed under sub-section (*1*) of section 81 by the District Commission pursuant to a settlement by mediation under Section 80 [Section 41].

Power and Procedure Before State Commission

The provisions relating to complaints under Sections 35, 36, 37, 38 and 39 shall, with such modification as may be necessary, be applicable to the disposal of disputes by the State Commission [Section 49(1)].

Review by State Commission

The State Commission shall have the power to review any of the order passed by it if there is an error apparent on the face of the record, either of its own motion or on an application made by any of the parties within thirty days of such order [Section 50].

Appeal to National Commission

(1) Any person aggrieved by an order made by the State Commission in exercise of its powers conferred by sub-clause (*i*) or (*ii*) of clause (*a*) of sub-section (*1*) of section 47 may prefer an appeal against such order to the National Commission within a period of thirty days from the date of the order in such form and manner as may be prescribed.

However, the National Commission shall not entertain the appeal after the expiry of the said period of thirty days unless it is satisfied that there was sufficient cause for not filing it within that period:

Provided further that no appeal by a person, who is required to pay any amount in terms of an order of the State Commission, shall be entertained by the National Commission unless the appellant has deposited fifty per cent. of that amount in the manner as may be prescribed.

(2) An appeal shall lie to the National Commission from any order passed in appeal by any State Commission, if the National Commission is satisfied that the case involves a substantial question of law.

(3) In an appeal involving a question of law, the memorandum of appeal shall precisely state the substantial question of law involved in the appeal.

(4) Where the National Commission is satisfied that a substantial question of law is involved in any case, it shall formulate that question and hear the appeal on that question:

Provided that nothing in this sub-section shall be deemed to take away or abridge the power of the National Commission to hear, for reasons to be recorded in writing, the appeal on any other substantial question of law, if it is satisfied that the case involves such question of law.

(5) An appeal may lie to the National Commission under this section from an order passed *ex parte* by the State Commission [Section 51].

Hearing of an Appeal

An appeal filed before the State Commission or the National Commission, as the case may be, shall be heard as expeditiously as possible and every endeavour shall be made to dispose of the appeal within a period of ninety days from the date of its admission:

Provided that no adjournment shall ordinarily be granted by the State Commission or the National Commission, as the case may be, unless sufficient cause is shown and the reasons for grant of adjournment have been recorded in writing by such Commission:

Provided further that the State Commission or the National Commission, as the case may be, shall make such orders as to the costs occasioned by the adjournment, as may be specified by regulations:

Provided also that in the event of an appeal being disposed of after the period so specified, the State Commission or the National Commission, as the case may be, shall record in writing the reasons for the same at the time of disposing of the said appeal [Section 52].

Procedure Applicable to National Commission

The provisions relating to complaints under sections 35, 36, 37, 38 and 39 shall, with such modifications as may be considered necessary, be applicable to the disposal of complaints by the National Commission [Section 59].

Appeal against the order of National Commission

Any person, aggrieved by an order made by the National Commission in exercise of its powers, may prefer an appeal against such order to the Supreme Court within a period of 30 days from the date of the order:

Provided that Supreme Court may entertain an appeal after the expiry of the said period of 30 days if it is satisfied that there was sufficient cause for not filing it within that period [Section 67].

Provided further that no appeal by a person who is required to pay any amount in terms of an order of the National Commission shall be entertained by the Supreme Court unless that person has deposited fifty per cent. of that amount in the manner as may be prescribed [Section 67].

Finality of Order

Every order of a District Commission, State Commission, or the National Commission shall, if no appeal has been preferred against such order under the provisions of this Act, be final [Section 68].

Limitation Period

The District Commission, the State Commission or the National Commission shall not admit a complaint unless it is filed within two years from the date on which the cause of action has arisen. Notwithstanding, a complaint may be entertained after the above period, if the complainant satisfies the District Commission, the State Commission or the National Commission, as the case may be, that there was sufficient cause for not filing the complaint within such period [Section 60].

However, no such complaint shall be entertained unless the National Commission, the State Commission or the District Commission, as the case may be, records its reasons for condoning such delay [Proviso to Section 69].

Administrative Control

(1) The National Commission shall have the authority to lay down such adequate standards in consultation with the Central Government from time to time, for better protection of the interests of consumers and for that purpose, shall have administrative control over all the State Commissions in the following matters, namely:—

   (a) monitoring performance of the State Commissions in terms of their disposal by calling for periodical returns regarding the institution, disposal and pendency of cases;

   (b) investigating into any allegations against the President and members of a State Commission and submitting inquiry report to the State Government concerned along with copy endorsed to the Central Government for necessary action;

   (c) issuance of instructions regarding adoption of uniform procedure in the hearing of matters, prior service of copies of documents produced by one party to the opposite parties, furnishing of english translation of judgments written in any language, speedy grant of copies of documents;

   (d) overseeing the functioning of the State Commission or the District Commission either by way of inspection or by any other means, as the National Commission may like to order from time to time, to ensure that the objects and purposes of the Act are best served and the standards set by the National Commission are implemented without interfering with their quasi-judicial freedom.

(2) There shall be a monitoring cell to be constituted by the President of the National Commission to oversee the functioning of the State Commissions from the administrative point of view.

(3) The State Commission shall have administrative control over all the District Commissions within its jurisdiction in all matters referred to in sub-section (*1*).

(4) The National Commission and the State Commissions shall furnish to the Central Government periodically or as and when required, any information including the pendency of cases in such form and manner as may be prescribed.

(5) The State Commission shall furnish, periodically or as and when required to the State Government any information including pendency of cases in such form and manner as may be prescribed [Section 70].

Enforcement of Orders by the Commissions

Every order made by a District Commission, State Commission or the National Commission shall be enforced by it in the same manner as if it were a decree made by a Court in a suit before it and the provisions of Order XXI of the First Schedule to the Code of Civil Procedure, 1908 shall, as far as may be, applicable, subject to the modification that every reference therein to the decree shall be construed as reference to the order made under this Act [Section 71].

Penalty for Non-compliance of Order

(1) Whoever fails to comply with any order made by the District Commission or the State Commission or the National Commission, as the case may be, shall be punishable with imprisonment for a term which shall not be less than one month, but which may extend to three years, or with fine, which shall not be less than twenty-five thousand rupees, but which may extend to one lakh rupees, or with both.

(2) Notwithstanding anything contained in the Code of Criminal Procedure, 1973, the District Commission, the State Commission or the National Commission, as the case may be, shall have the power of a Judicial Magistrate of first class for the trial of offences under sub-section (*1*), and on conferment of such powers, the District Commission or the State Commission or the National Commission, as the case may be, shall be deemed to be a Judicial Magistrate of first class for the purposes of the Code of Criminal Procedure, 1973 [Section 72].

Appeal against Order Passed under Section 72

(1) Where an order is passed under Section 72, an appeal shall lie, both on facts and on law from—

- (a) the order made by the District Commission to the State Commission;
- (b) the order made by the State Commission to the National Commission; and
- (c) the order made by the National Commission to the Supreme Court.

(2) Except as provided in sub-section (*1*), no appeal shall lie before any court, from any order of a District Commission or a State Commission or the National Commission, as the case may be.

(3) Every appeal under this section shall be preferred within a period of thirty days from the date of order of a District Commission or a State Commission or the National Commission, as the case may be:

(4) Provided that the State Commission or the National Commission or the Supreme Court, as the case may be, may entertain an appeal after the expiry of the said period of thirty days, if it is satisfied that the appellant had sufficient cause for not preferring the appeal within the said period of thirty days [Section 73].

Offences and Penalties

The Consumer Protection Act , 2019 contains the following stringent provisions as regards offences and resulting penalties and other consequences to deter re-occurrence thereof: under Chapter VIII vide sections 88, 89, 90, 91, 92, and 93.

Penalty for non-compliance of direction of Central Authority

Whoever, fails to comply with any direction of the Central Authority under sections 20 and 21, shall be punished with imprisonment for a term which may extend to six months or with fine which may extend to twenty lakh rupees, or with both [Section 88].

Punishment for false or misleading advertisement

Any manufacturer or service provider who causes a false or misleading advertisement to be made which is prejudicial to the interest of consumers shall be punished with imprisonment for a term which may extend to two years and with fine which may extend to ten lakh rupees; and for every subsequent offence, be punished with imprisonment for a term which may extend to five years and with fine which may extend to fifty lakh rupees [Section 89].

Punishment for manufacturing for sale or storing, selling or distributing or importing products containing adulterant

(1) Whoever, by himself or by any other person on his behalf, manufactures for sale or stores or sells or distributes or imports any product containing an adulterant shall be punished, if such act—

(a) does not result in any injury to the consumer, with imprisonment for a term which may extend to six months and with fine which may extend to one lakh rupees;
(b) causing injury not amounting to grievous hurt to the consumer, with imprisonment for a term which may extend to one year and with fine which may extend to three lakh rupees;
(c) causing injury resulting in grievous hurt to the consumer, with imprisonment for a term which may extend to seven years and with fine which may extend to five lakh rupees; and
(d) results in the death of a consumer, with imprisonment for a term which shall not be less than seven years, but which may extend to imprisonment for life and with fine which shall not be less than ten lakh rupees.

(2) The offences under clauses (*c*) and (*d*) of sub-section (*1*) shall be cognizable and non-bailable.
(3) Notwithstanding the punishment under sub-section (*1*), the court may, in case of first conviction, suspend any licence issued to the person referred to in that sub-section, under any law for the time being in force, for a period up to two years, and in case of second or subsequent conviction, cancel the licence [Section 90].

Explanation.—For the purposes of this section,—

(a) "adulterant" means any material including extraneous matter which is employed or used for making a product unsafe;
(b) "grievous hurt" shall have the same meaning as assigned to it in section 320 of the Indian Penal Code.

Punishment for manufacturing for sale or for storing or selling or distributing or importing spurious goods

(1) Whoever, by himself or by any other person on his behalf, manufactures for sale or stores or sells or distributes or imports any spurious goods shall be punished, if such act—

(a) causing injury not amounting to grievous hurt to the consumer, with imprisonment for a term which may extend to one year and with fine which may extend to three lakh rupees;
(b) causing injury resulting in grievous hurt to the consumer, with imprisonment for a term which may extend to seven years and with fine which may extend to five lakh rupees;
(c) results in the death of a consumer, with imprisonment for a term which shall not be less than seven years, but may extend to imprisonment for life and with fine which shall not be less than ten lakh rupees.

(2) The offences under clauses (*b*) and (*c*) of sub-section (*1*) shall be cognizable and non-bailable.
(3) Notwithstanding the punishment under sub-section (*1*), the court may, in case of first conviction, suspend any licence issued to the person referred to in that sub-section, under any law for the time being in force, for a period up to two years, and in case of second or subsequent conviction, cancel the licence [Section 91].

Cognizance of offence by court

No cognizance shall be taken by a competent court of any offence under Sections 88 & 89 except on a complaint filed by the Central Authority or any officer authorised by it in this behalf [Section 92].

Penalty against vexatious search

The Director General or any other officer, exercising powers under section 22, who knows that there are no reasonable grounds for so doing, and yet—

(a) searches, or causes to be searched any premises; or
(b) seizes any record, register or other document or article,

shall, for every such offence, be punished with imprisonment for a term which may extend to one year, or with fine which may extend to ten thousand rupees or with both [Section 93].

Exercises

I. Objective-type Questions

1. Which of the following services shall not be covered under the Consumer Protection Act, 2019?
   (a) Professional services rendered by a Chartered Accountant engaged by a client
   (b) Medical procedures done by doctors at Escorts Heart Institute
   (c) Legal advice rendered by a practicing Supreme Court advocate
   (d) Legal advice rendered by a practicing Company Secretary

2. State which of the following is not a consumer for the purpose of goods?
   (a) One who buys any goods for a consideration for private use or consumption only
   (b) One who uses such goods with the approval of the buyer
   (c) One who buys goods for commercial purpose
   (d) One who buys some equipment for the purpose of self-employment

3. Who among the following can file a complaint under the Consumer Protection Act, 2019?
   (a) a consumer
   (b) the Central or the State Government
   (c) one or more consumers if there are many consumers having the common interest
   (d) Any of the above

4. The term 'manufacturer' means a person who
   (a) makes or manufacturers goods or parts thereof
   (b) assembles parts made or manufactured by others and claims the end product to be manufactured by himself
   (c) puts or causes to put his own mark on any goods made or manufactured by any other manufacturer and claims such goods to be made or manufactured by himself
   (d) All of the above

5. Which is not one of the salient features of the Consumer Protection Act, 2019?
   (a) The Act applies to all goods and services unless specifically exempted by the Central Government.
   (b) It covers only private sector.
   (c) The provisions of the Act are chiefly compensatory in nature.
   (d) Engagement of advocate is not mandatory to file and pursue a complaint under the Act.

6. Those complaints can be filed with the State Commission where the value of goods or services, paid as consideration is
   (a) Up to ₹50 lakh
   (b) Up to ₹1 crore
   (c) More than ₹1 crore but less than ₹10 crore
   (d) More than ₹1 crore

7. Which of the following right is not provided by the Consumer Protection Act, 2019 to the consumers?
   (a) Right to safety
   (b) Right to be informed
   (c) Right to seek redressal
   (d) Right to discipline

8. A complainant not satisfied with the order of the District Commission may prefer an appeal against the order before the State Commission within how much time from the date of passing the order by the district Commission:
   (a) 30 days
   (b) 45 days
   (c) 60 days
   (d) 90 days

9. Who among the following is not a consumer?
   (a) Insurance company
   (b) Licensee to run a PCO
   (c) Lottery ticket holder
   (d) All of the above

10. The time limit for filing a complaint before the District Commission, the State Commission, or the National Commission, as the case may be, is
    (a) One year from the date on which the cause of action arises
    (b) Two years from the date on which the cause of action arises
    (c) Three years from the date on which the cause of action arises
    (d) Five years from the date on which the cause of action arises

II. Review Questions

1. Describe the salient features of the Consumer Protection Act, 2019. Enumerate also the aim and objectives of the Act.
2. Explain 'unfair trade practice' under the Consumer Protection Act 2019.
3. Give the statutory definition of the following terms
   (a) Defect
   (b) Deficiency
   (c) Goods
   (d) Manufacturer
   (e) Person
   (f) Complaint
   (g) Complainant
4. Discuss briefly the composition, powers, and functions of the District Commission, State Commission, and National Commission.
5. What is a Central Consumer Protection Council? Discuss its objects.
6. Describe the administrative control to be exercised by the National Commission over all the State Commissions for the better protection of the interests of consumers
7. What are the provisions under the Consumer Protection Act, 2019 as regards establishment of Central Consumer Protection Authority (CCPA)?
8. Discuss the powers and functions of Central Consumer Protection Authority.
9. Give a summarised view of the Consumer Protection Act, 2019.
10. What is the role of 'Investigation Wing' of CCPA?

Answers to Objective-type Questions

1. (b)	2. (c)	3. (d)	4. (d)	5. (b)	6. (c)
7. (d)	8. (a)	9. (d)	10. (b)		

21 Chapter in Review

LEARNING OUTCOMES

LO 1 The Consumer Protection Act, 2019: An Overview

LO 2 The Act: salient features; aim and objectives

LO 3 Important Terms

LO 4 Rights of consumer; restrictive trade practice; unfair trade practice; service; trader

LO 5 Consumer Protection Councils

LO 6 Central Consumer Protection Authority

LO 7 Three-tier grievance-redressal machinery

LO 8 Offences and penalties

KEY TERMS

Central Consumer Protection Authority (CCPA): To be known as the Central Authority, CCPA will operate to regulate matters relating to violation of rights of consumers, unfair trade practices and false or misleading advertisements which are prejudicial to the interests of public and consumers and to promote, protect and enforce the rights of consumers as a class.

Deficiency (in service): Any fault, imperfection, shortcoming, or inadequacy in quality, nature, and manner of performance (of a service), required to be maintained under any law, or has been undertaken to be performed by a person in pursuance of a contract or otherwise.

District Commission: Formally known as 'District Consumer Disputes Redressal Commission', first level dispute redressal agency established by the State Government in each district of the State, empowered to settle cases, where the value of compensation claimed is up to one crore rupees.

National Commission: Formally known as 'National Consumer Disputes Redressal Commission', functions at the apex level of redressal mechanism, established by the Central Government, empowered to settle cases, where the value of the

LO 1 The Consumer Protection Act, 2019, which extends to the whole of India, is designed to make available cheap and quick remedy to a small consumer. It applies to all goods and services unless specifically exempted by the Central Government and covers all the sectors—private, public, and cooperative. The provisions of the Act are rather compensatory than preventive or punitive.

LO 2 Key features of the Consumer Protection Act, 2019 include: 1. Provision for the establishment of the Central Consumer Protection Authority (CCPA), which will protect, promote and enforce the rights of consumers firmly; 2. Ensuring fundamental rights of the consumers; 3. Prohibition and penalty for a misleading advertisement; and 4. Establishment of the Consumer Disputes Redressal Commissions (CDRCs) at the national, state and district levels to entertain complaints related to (a) overcharging or deceptive charging, (b) unfair or restrictive trade practices, (c) Sale of defective goods or services, and (d) sale of goods and services which may be hazardous to life.

The basic aim of the new Act is to save the rights of the consumers by establishing authorities for timely and effective administration and settlement of consumers' disputes.

LO 3 CPA, 2019 contains the statutory definition of all the key terms of the subject-matter of the Act.

LO 4 It seeks, *inter alia*, to promote and protect the rights of consumers such as—(a) right to safety, (b) right to be informed, (c) right to choose, (d) right to be heard, (e) right to seek redressal, and (f) right to consumer education.

LO 5 Consumer Protection Councils have been instituted with the task of enhancing consumer welfare and empowering consumers to make sure their rights are protected at Central, State as well as District level. Being advisory bodies, the object of these councils is to render advice on promotion and protection of the consumers' rights under this Act.

LO 6 Introduced in the new Act, CCPA aims to protect the rights of the consumer by cracking down on unfair trade practices, and false and misleading advertisements, which are prejudicial to the interests of the consumers in particular and public in general.

goods or services paid as consideration exceeds rupees ten crore.

Restrictive trade practice: A business agreement, overt or implied one, between companies which controls prices or the areas in which goods are sold, preventing fair competition from other companies.

Service: The action of serving or assisting someone or the performance of work or job by one person for another.

State Commission: Formally known as 'State Consumer Disputes Redressal Commission', functions as middle tier of redressal mechanism, established by the State Government in the State concerned, empowered to settle cases, where the value of goods and services paid as consideration, exceeds rupees one crore, but does not exceed rupees ten crore.

Trader: A person who sells or distributes any goods for sale and includes the manufacturer thereof.

LO[7] For simple, fast and inexpensive settlement of consumers' disputes and for matters connected therewith, the Act envisages three-tier quasi-judicial machinery comprising the (I) National Commission, (II) State Commission and (III) District Commissions; operating at national, state, and district levels respectively. Besides, to render advice on promotion and protection of the consumers' rights, the Act makes provision for the establishment of consumer protection councils at national, state as well as district level.

The CPA, 2019 has also introduced Central Consumer Protection Authority (CCPA) to protect the rights of the consumers by cracking down on unfair trade practices, and false and misleading advertisements that are detrimental to the interests of the public and consumers.

LO[8] Section 88 - Penalty for noncompliance of direction of the Central Authority: Imprisonment for a term which may extend to six months or with fine which may extend to twenty lakh rupees, or with both.

Section 89 - Punishment for false or misleading advertisement: Imprisonment for a term which may extend to two years and with fine which may extend to ten lakh rupees; and for every subsequent offence, be punished with imprisonment for a term which may extend to five years and with fine which may extend to fifty lakh rupees.

Section 90 - Punishment for manufacturing for sale or storing, selling or distributing or importing products containing adulterant: If such act (a) does not result in any injury to the consumer, imprisonment for a term which may extend to six months and with fine which may extend to one lakh rupees; (b) causes injury not amounting to grievous hurt to the consumer, imprisonment for a term which may extend to one year and with fine which may extend to three lakh rupees; (c) causes injury resulting in grievous hurt to the consumer, imprisonment for a term which may extend to seven years and with fine which may extend to five lakh rupees; and (d) results in the death of a consumer, imprisonment for a term which shall not be less than seven years, but which may extend to imprisonment for life and with fine which shall not be less than ten lakh rupees. Notwithstanding, the court may, in case of first conviction, suspend any licence issued to the person referred to in that sub-section, under any law for the time being in force, for a period up to two years, and in case of second or subsequent conviction, cancel the licence.

Section 91 - Punishment for manufacturing for sale or for storing or selling or distributing or importing spurious goods: (1) If such act (a) does not cause injury amounting to grievous hurt to the consumer, imprisonment for a term which may extend to one year and with fine which may extend to three lakh rupees; (b) causes injury resulting in grievous hurt to the consumer, imprisonment for a term which may extend to seven years and with fine which may extend to five lakh rupees; (c) results in the death of a consumer, imprisonment for a term which shall not be less than seven years, but may extend to imprisonment for life and with fine which shall not be less than ten lakh rupees. (2) The offences under clauses (b) and (c) of sub-section (1) shall be cognizable and non-bailable. (3) Notwithstanding the punishment under sub-section (1), the court may, in case of first conviction, suspend any licence issued to the person referred to in that sub-section, under any law for the time being in force, for a period up to two years, and in case of second or subsequent conviction, cancel the licence.

Section 92 - Cognizance of offence by the court of law: No cognizance shall be taken by a competent court of any offence under sections 88 and 89 except on a complaint filed by the Central Authority or any officer authorised by it in this behalf.

Section 93 - Penalty against vexatious search: The Director General or any other officer, exercising powers under Section 22, who knows that there are no reasonable grounds for so doing, and yet (a) searches, or causes to be searched any premises; or (b) seizes any record, register or other document or article, shall, for every such offence, be punished with imprisonment for a term which may extend to one year, or with fine which may extend to ten thousand rupees or with both.

CHAPTER

22 The Competition Act, 2002

Learning Objectives

LO[1] Role and origin of The Competition Act, 2002

LO[2] Aim and objectives of the Act

LO[3] Functions of Competition Commission of India (CCI)

The National Competition Policy was formulated by the Government of India with a view to achieve the highest sustainable levels of economic growth, entrepreneurship, employment, and standards of living for citizens; protect economic rights for just, equitable, inclusive, and sustainable economic and social development; promote economic democracy; and support good governance by restricting rent seeking practices. The Competition Act, 2002, as amended by the Competition (Amendment) Act, 2007 is an important legislation to promote the National Competition Policy. It was enacted by the Parliament in 2002 and extends to the whole of India except the State of Jammu and Kashmir—which is covered under a State-level-law. The Act provides, keeping in view the economic development of the country, for the establishment of a commission, known as the Competition Commission of India (CCI) or just Commission to promote and sustain an enabling competition culture through engagement and enforcement that would inspire the businesses to be fair, competitive, and innovative; enhance consumer welfare; and support economic growth. The Monopolies and Restrictive Trade (MRTP) Act, 1969, was repealed and the MRTP Commission stood dissolved henceforth.

Competition Commission: Aim and Objectives

The Commission aims to establish a robust competitive environment through:

- Proactive engagement with all stake holders, including consumers, industry, government, and international jurisdictions.
- Being a knowledge intensive organization with high competence levels.
- Professionalism, transparency, resolve, and wisdom in enforcements.

It seeks to:

1. Curb practices having an adverse effect on competition.
2. Promote and sustain competition in market.
3. Protect the interest of consumers and to ensure freedom of trade carried on other participants in markets in India, and for matters connected therewith or incidental thereto.

Important Provisions

Important provisions of the Act have been briefly explained below.

Prohibition of Anti-Competitive Agreements

1. No enterprise or association of enterprises or person or association of persons shall enter into any agreement in respect of production, supply, distribution, storage, acquisition or control of goods, or provision of services, which causes or is likely to cause an appreciable adverse effect on competition within India.
2. Any agreement entered into in contravention of the provisions contained in sub-section (1) shall be void.
3. Any agreement entered into between enterprises or associations of enterprises or persons or associations of persons or between any person and enterprise or practice carried on, or decision taken by, any association of enterprises or association of persons, including cartels, engaged in identical or similar trade of goods or provision of services, which
   (a) directly or indirectly determines purchase or sale prices;
   (b) limits or controls production, supply, markets, technical development, investment, or provision of services;
   (c) shares the market or source of production or provision of services by way of allocation of the geographical area of the market, or type of goods or services, or the number of customers in the market or any other similar way;
   (d) directly or indirectly results in bid rigging or collusive bidding, shall be presumed to have an appreciable adverse effect on competition.

   Explanation: For the purpose of this sub-section, 'bid rigging' refers to any agreement between enterprises or persons referred to in sub-section (3) engaged in identical or similar production or trading of goods or provision of services, which has the effect of eliminating or reducing competition for bids, or adversely affecting or manipulating the process for bidding

4. Any agreement amongst enterprises or persons at different stages or levels of the production chain in different markets, in respect of production, supply, distribution, storage, sale or price of, or trade in goods or provision of services, including
   (a) tie-in arrangement;
   (b) exclusive supply agreement;
   (c) exclusive distribution agreement;
   (d) refusal to deal;
   (e) resale price maintenance,

   shall be an agreement in contravention of sub-section (1) if such an agreement causes, or is likely to cause, an appreciable adverse effect on competition in India.

Explanation: For the purpose of this sub-section
   (a) 'Tie-in arrangement' includes any agreement requiring a purchaser of goods, as a condition of such purchase, to purchase some other goods;
   (b) 'Exclusive supply agreement' includes any agreement that restricts, in any manner, the purchaser in the course of his trade from acquiring or otherwise dealing in any goods other than those of the seller or any other person;
   (c) 'Exclusive Distribution Agreement' includes any agreement to limit, restrict or withhold the output or supply of any goods or allocate any area or market for the disposal or sale of the goods;
   (d) 'Refusal to Deal' includes any agreement which restricts, or is likely to restrict, by any method, the persons or classes of persons to whom goods are sold or from whom goods are bought;
   (e) 'Resale Price Maintenance' refers to any agreement to sell goods on the condition that the prices to be charged on the resale by the purchaser shall be the prices stipulated by the seller unless it is clearly stated that prices lower than those prices may be charged [Section 3].

Prohibition of Abuse of Dominant Position

1. No enterprise or group shall abuse its dominant position.
2. There shall be an abuse of dominant position, if an enterprise or a group
   (a) directly or indirectly imposes unfair or discriminatory
      (i) conditions in the purchase or sale of goods or service; or
      (ii) price in purchase or sale (including predatory price) of goods or service.
   (b) limits or restricts
      (i) production of goods or provision of services or market thereof; or
      (ii) technical or scientific development relating to goods or services to the prejudice of consumers; or
   (c) indulges in practice or practices resulting in denial of market access [in any manner]; or
   (d) subjects the conclusion of contracts to acceptance by other parties of supplementary obligations which, by their nature or according to commercial usage, have no connection with the subject of such contracts; or
   (e) uses its dominant position in one relevant market to enter into, or protect, another relevant market.

Dominant position: Ability to behave independently of its competitors, customers, suppliers and, ultimately, the final consumer.

Abuse of dominant position: Intentional anti-competitive acts by persons substantially in control of a market, that has had, is having, or is likely to have the effect of preventing or lessening competition.

Explanation: For the purpose of this Section, the expression
   (a) 'Dominant Position' refers to a position of strength enjoyed by an enterprise in the relevant market in India, which enables it to
      (i) operate independently of competitive forces prevailing in the relevant market; or
      (ii) affect its competitors or consumers or the relevant market in its favour.
   (b) 'Predatory Price' refers to the sale of goods or provision of services, at a price which is below the cost, as may be determined by

Combinations: Acquisition of one or more enterprises by one or more persons, or the merger or amalgamation of enterprises.

regulations, of production of the goods or provision of services, with a view to reduce competition or eliminate the competitors [Section 4].

Combinations Defined

Acquisition: Directly or indirectly, acquiring or agreeing to acquire (i) shares, voting rights, or assets of any enterprise; or (ii) control over the management or the assets of any enterprise.

The acquisition of one or more enterprises by one or more persons, or the merger or amalgamation of enterprises, shall be a combination of such enterprises and persons or enterprises, if

1. any acquisition where
   (a) the parties to the acquisition, being the acquirer and the enterprise, whose control, shares, voting rights, or assets have been acquired or are being acquired jointly have
      (i) in India, assets of the value of more than ₹1000 crore or turnover more than ₹3000 crore; or
      (ii) in India or outside India, in aggregate, assets of the value of more than US$ 500 million, including at least ₹500 crore in India, or turnover more than US$ 1500 million, including at least ₹1500 crore in India; or
   (b) the group, to which the enterprise whose control, shares, assets or voting rights have been acquired or are being acquired, would belong after the acquisition, jointly has or would jointly have,
      (i) in India, assets of the value of more than ₹4000 crore or turnover more than ₹12000 crore; or
      (ii) in India or outside India, in aggregate, assets of the value of more than US$ 2 billion including at least ₹500 crore in India, or turnover more than US$ 6 billion including at least ₹1500 crore in India; or
2. acquiring of control by a person over an enterprise when such a person already has direct or indirect control over another enterprise engaged in production, distribution or trading of a similar or identical or substitutable goods or provision of a similar or identical or substitutable service, if
   (a) the enterprise over which control has been acquired along with the enterprise over which the acquirer already has direct or indirect control jointly have
      (i) in India, assets of the value of more than ₹1000 crore or turnover more than ₹3000 crore; or
      (ii) in India or outside India, in aggregate, assets of the value of more than US$ 500 million, including at least ₹500 crore in India, or turnover million including at least ₹500 crore in India; or more than US$ 1500 million, including at least ₹1500 crore in India: or
   (b) the group, to which enterprise whose control has been acquired, or is being acquired, would belong after the acquisition, jointly has or would jointly have
3. in India, assets of the value of more than ₹4000 crore or turnover more than ₹12000 crore; or
4. in India or outside India, in aggregate, assets of the value of more than US$ 2 billion, including at least ₹500 crore in India, or turnover more than US$ 6 billion, including at least ₹1500 crore in India; or
5. any merger or amalgamation in which
   (a) the enterprise remaining after merger, or the enterprise created as a result of the amalgamation, as the case may be, has
6. in India, assets of the value of more than ₹100 crore or turnover more than ₹300 crore; or
7. in India or outside India, in aggregate, assets of the value of more than US$ 500 million, including at least ₹500 crore in India, or turnover more than US$ 1500 million, including at least ₹1500 crore in India; or
8. the group, to which the enterprise remaining after the merger or the enterprise created as a result of the amalgamation, would belong after the merger or the amalgamation, as the case may be, has, or would have
   (a) in India, assets of the value of more than ₹4000 crore or turnover more than ₹12,000 crore; or

(b) in India or outside India, in aggregate, assets of the value of more than US$ 2 billion, including at least ₹500 crore in India, or turnover more than US$ 6 billion, including at least ₹1500 crore in India;

Explanation: For the purpose of this Section

(a) 'Control' includes controlling the affairs or management by
   (i) one or more enterprises, either jointly or singly, over another enterprise or group;
   (ii) one or more groups, either jointly or singly, over another group or enterprise;

(b) 'Group' refers to two or more enterprises which, directly or indirectly, are in a position to
   (i) exercise 26% or more of the voting rights in the other enterprise; or
   (ii) appoint more than 50% of the members of the board of directors in the other enterprise; or
   (iii) control the management or affairs of the other enterprise;

(c) the value of assets shall be determined by taking the book value of the assets as shown in the audited books of account of the enterprise, in the financial year immediately preceding the financial year in which the date of proposed merger falls, as reduced by any depreciation [Section 5].

Regulation of Combinations

1. No person or enterprise shall enter into a combination which causes, or is likely to cause, an appreciable adverse effect on competition within the relevant market in India and such a combination shall be void.
2. Subject to the provisions contained in sub-section (1), any person or enterprise, who or which proposes to enter into a combination, shall give notice to the Commission, in the form as may be specified, and with the fee which may be determined by regulations, disclosing the details of the proposed combination, within 30 days of
   (a) approval of the proposal relating to the merger or amalgamation, referred to in clause (c) of Section 5, by the board of directors of the enterprises concerned with such a merger or amalgamation, as the case may be;
   (b) execution of any agreement or other document for acquisition referred to in clause (i) of Section 5 or acquiring of control referred to in clause (ii) of that Section.

2A. No combination shall come into effect until 210 days have passed from the day on which the notice has been given to the Commission under sub-section (2) or the Commission has passed orders under Section 31, whichever is earlier.

3. The Commission shall, after receipt of notice under sub-section (2), deal with such notice in accordance with the provisions contained in Sections 29, 30, and 31.
4. The provisions of this Section shall not apply to share subscription or financing facility or any acquisition by a public financial institution, foreign institutional investor, bank or venture capital fund, pursuant to any covenant of a loan agreement or investment agreement.
5. The public financial institution, foreign institutional investor, bank, or venture capital fund, referred to in sub-section (4), shall, within seven days from the date of the acquisition, file, in the form as may be specified by regulations, with the Commission, the details of the acquisition including the details of control, the circumstances for exercise of such control and the consequences of default arising out of such a loan agreement or investment agreement, as the case may be.

   Explanation: For the purpose of this Section, the expression
   (a) 'Foreign Institutional Investor' has the same meaning as assigned to it in clause (a) of the Explanation to Section 115AD of the Income-tax Act, 1961;
   (b) Venture Capital Fund has the same meaning as assigned to it in the Explanation to clause (23 FB) of Section 10 of the Income-tax Act, 1961 [Section 6].

Establishment

1. With effect from such date as the Central Government may, by notification, appoint, there shall be established, for the purposes of this Act,

a Commission to be called the 'Competition Commission of India'.

2. The Commission shall be a body corporate by the name aforesaid having perpetual succession and a common seal with power, subject to the provisions of this Act, to acquire, hold and dispose of property, both movable and immovable, and to contract, and shall, by the said name, sue or be sued.
3. The head office of the Commission shall be at such a place as the Central Government may decide from time to time.
4. The Commission may establish offices at other places in India [Section 7].

Composition

Trade: Any trade, business, industry, profession, or occupation relating to the production, supply, distribution, storage, or control of goods and includes the provision of any services.

1. The Commission shall consist of a Chairperson and not less than two and not more than six other Members to be appointed by the Central Government.
2. The Chairperson and every other Member shall be a person of ability, integrity and standing, and who has special knowledge of, and professional experience of not less than fifteen years in, international trade, economics, business, commerce, law, finance, accountancy, management, industry, public affairs or competition matters, including competition law and policy, which, in the opinion of the Central Government, may be useful to the Commission.
3. The Chairperson and other Members shall be whole-time Members [Section 8].

Selection Committee for Chairperson and Members of Commission

1. The Chairperson and other Members of the Commission shall be appointed by the Central Government from a panel of names recommended by a Selection Committee consisting of

   (a) the Chief Justice of India or his nominee — Chairperson;

   (b) the Secretary in the Ministry of Corporate Affairs — Member;

   (c) the Secretary in the Ministry of Law and Justice — Member;

   (d) two experts of repute who have special knowledge of, and professional experience in international trade, economics, commerce, law, finance, accountancy, management, industry, public affairs, or competition matters including competition law and policy — Members
2. The term of the Selection Committee and the manner of selection of the panel of names shall be such as may be prescribed [Section 9].

Term of Office of Chairperson and Other Members

1. The Chairperson and every other Member shall hold office for a term of five years from the date on which he enters upon his office and shall be eligible for re-appointment:

   However, the Chairperson or other Members shall not hold office after he/they has/have attained the age of 65 years.
2. A vacancy caused by the resignation or removal of the Chairperson or any other Member under Section 11 or by death or otherwise shall be filled by fresh appointment in accordance with the provisions of Sections 8 and 9.
3. The Chairperson and every other Member shall, before entering upon his office, make and subscribe to an oath of office and of secrecy in such form, manner and before such authority as may be prescribed.
4. In the event of the occurrence of a vacancy in the office of the Chairperson by reason of his death, resignation or otherwise, the senior-most Member shall act as the Chairperson until the date on which a new Chairperson, appointed in accordance with the provisions of this Act to fill such vacancy, enters upon his office.
5. When the Chairperson is unable to discharge his functions owing to absence, illness, or any other cause, the senior-most Member shall discharge the functions of the Chairperson until the date on which the Chairperson resumes the charge of his functions [Section 10].

Resignation, Removal, and Suspension of Chairperson and Other Members

1. The Chairperson or any other Member may, by notice in writing under his hand addressed to the Central Government, resign his office:

   Provided that the Chairperson or a Member shall, unless he is permitted by the Central Government to relinquish his office sooner, continue to hold office until the expiry of three months from the date of receipt of such notice or until a person duly appointed as his successor enters upon his office or until the expiry of his term of office, whichever is the earliest.

2. Notwithstanding anything contained in sub-section (1), the Central Government may, by order, remove the Chairperson or any other Member from his office if such a Chairperson or Member, as the case may be
   (a) is, or at any time has been, adjudged as insolvent; or
   (b) has engaged at any time, during his term of office, in any paid employment; or
   (c) has been convicted of an offence which, in the opinion of the Central Government, involves moral turpitude; or
   (d) has acquired such financial or other interest as is likely to affect prejudicially his functions as a Member; or
   (e) has so abused his position as to render his continuance in office prejudicial to the public interest; or
   (f) has become physically or mentally incapable of acting as a Member.

3. Notwithstanding anything contained in sub-section (2), no Member shall be removed from his office on the ground specified in clause (d) or clause (e) of that sub-section unless the Supreme Court, on a reference being made to it in this behalf by the Central Government, has, on an inquiry held by it in accordance with such procedure as may be prescribed in this behalf by the Supreme Court, reported that the Member ought on such ground or grounds to be removed [Section 11].

Restriction on Employment of Chairperson and Other Members in Certain Cases

The Chairperson and other Members shall not, for a period of two years from the date on which they cease to hold office, accept any employment in, or connected with the management or administration of, any enterprise which has been a party to a proceeding before the Commission under this Act.

However, nothing contained herein shall apply to any employment under the Central Government or a State Government or local authority or in any statutory authority or any corporation established by or under any Central, State or Provincial Act or a Government company [Section 12].

Administrative Powers of Chairperson

The Chairperson shall have the powers of general superintendence, direction, and control in respect of all administrative matters of the Commission.

However, the Chairperson may delegate such of his powers relating to administrative matters of the Commission, as he may think fit, to any other Member or officer of the Commission [Section 13].

Terms and Conditions of Service of Chairperson and Other Members

1. The salary, and the other terms and conditions of service of the Chairperson and other Members, including traveling expenses, house rent allowance and conveyance facilities, sumptuary allowance, and medical facilities shall be such as may be prescribed.

Service: Providing something of any description to potential users.

2. The salary, allowances and other terms and conditions of service of the Chairperson or a Member shall not be varied to his disadvantage after appointment [Section 14].

No act or proceeding of the Commission shall be invalid merely by reason of

1. any vacancy in, or any defect in the constitution of, the Commission; or

2. any defect in the appointment of a person acting as a Chairperson or as a Member; or
3. any irregularity in the procedure of the Commission not affecting the merits of the case [Section 15].

Appointment of Director General

1. The Central Government may, by notification, appoint a Director General for assisting the Commission in conducting an inquiry into the contravention of any of the provisions of this Act and for performing such other functions as are, or may be, provided by or under this Act.

   The number of other Additional, Joint, Deputy or Assistant Directors General or such officers or other employees in the office of Director General and the manner of appointment of such Additional, Joint, Deputy or Assistant Directors General, or such officers or other employees shall be such as may be prescribed.
2. Every Additional, Joint, Deputy and Assistant Directors General, or such officers or other employees shall exercise his powers, and discharge his functions, subject to the general control, supervision and direction of the Director General.
3. The salary, allowances, and other terms and conditions of service of the Director General and Additional, Joint, Deputy and Assistant Directors General, or such officers or other employees, shall be such as may be prescribed.
4. The Director General and Additional, Joint, Deputy and Assistant Directors General, or such officers or other employees shall be appointed from amongst persons of integrity and outstanding ability and who have experience in investigation, and knowledge of accountancy, management, business, public administration, international trade, law or economics, and other such qualifications as may be prescribed [Section 16].

Appointment of Secretary, Experts, Professionals, and Officers

1. The Commission may appoint a Secretary and such officers and other employees as it considers necessary for the efficient performance of its functions under this Act.
2. The salaries and allowances payable to and other terms and conditions of service of the Secretary and officers and other employees of the Commission and the number of such officers and other employees shall be such as may be prescribed.
3. The Commission may engage, in accordance with the procedure specified by regulations, such number of experts and professionals of integrity and outstanding ability, who have special knowledge of, and experience in, economics, law, business or such other disciplines related to competition, as it deems necessary to assist the Commission in the discharge of its functions under this Act [Section 17].

Duties of the Commission

It shall be the duty of the Commission to eliminate practices having an adverse effect on competition, promote and sustain competition, protect the interests of consumers and ensure freedom of trade carried on by other participants, in markets in India.

However, the Commission may, for the purpose of discharging its duties or performing its functions under this Act, enter into any memorandum or arrangement with the prior approval of the Central Government, with any agency of any foreign country [Section 18].

Inquiry into Certain Agreements and Dominant Position of Enterprise

1. The Commission may inquire into any alleged contravention of the provisions contained in subsection (1) of Section 3 or sub-section (1) of Section 4 either on its own motion or on
   (a) receipt of any information, in such a manner and accompanied by such a fee as may be determined by regulations, from any person, consumer or their association or trade association; or
   (b) a reference made to it by the Central Government or a State Government or a statutory authority.
2. Without prejudice to the provisions contained in sub-section (1), the powers and functions of the Commission shall include the powers and functions specified in sub-sections (3) to (7).

3. The Commission shall, while determining whether an agreement has an appreciable adverse effect on competition under Section 3, have due regard to all or any of the following factors, namely:
   (a) creation of barriers to new entrants in the market;
   (b) driving existing competitors out of the market;
   (c) foreclosure of competition by hindering entry into the market;
   (d) accrual of benefits to consumers;
   (e) improvements in production or distribution of goods or provision of services;
   (f) promotion of technical, scientific, and economic development by means of production or distribution of goods or provision of services.
4. The Commission shall, while inquiring whether an enterprise enjoys a dominant position or not under Section 4, have due regard to all or any of the following factors, namely:
   (a) market share of the enterprise;
   (b) size and resources of the enterprise;
   (c) size and importance of the competitors;
   (d) economic power of the enterprise including commercial advantages over competitors;
   (e) vertical integration of the enterprises or sale or service network of such enterprises;
   (f) dependence of consumers on the enterprise;
   (g) monopoly or dominant position whether acquired as a result of any statute or by virtue of being a Government company or a public sector undertaking or otherwise;
   (h) entry barriers including regulatory barriers, financial risk, high capital cost of entry, marketing entry barriers, technical entry barriers, economies of scale, high cost of substitutable goods or service for consumers;
   (i) countervailing buying power;
   (j) market structure and size of market;
   (k) social obligations and social costs;
   (l) relative advantage, by way of contribution to economic development, by the enterprise enjoying a dominant position having or likely to have an appreciable adverse effect on competition;
   (m) any other factor which the Commission may consider relevant for the inquiry.
5. For determining whether a market constitutes a 'relevant market' for the purposes of this Act, the Commission shall have due regard to the 'relevant geographic market' and 'relevant product market'.
6. The Commission shall, while determining the 'relevant geographic market', have due regard to all or any of the following factors, namely:
   (a) regulatory trade barriers;
   (b) local specification requirements;
   (c) national procurement policies;
   (d) adequate distribution facilities;
   (e) transport costs;
   (f) language;
   (g) consumer preferences;
   (h) need for secure or regular supplies or rapid after-sales services.
7. The Commission shall, while determining the 'relevant product market', have due regard to all or any of the following factors, namely:
   (a) physical characteristics or end-use of goods;
   (b) price of goods or service;
   (c) consumer preferences;
   (d) exclusion of in-house production;
   (e) existence of specialised producers;
   (f) classification of industrial products [Section 19].

> Relevant market: The market which may be determined by the Commission with reference to the relevant product market or the relevant geographic market, or with reference to both the markets.

> Relevant geographic market: A market comprising the area in which the conditions of competition for supply of goods or provision of services or demand of goods or services are distinctly homogenous and can be distinguished from the conditions prevailing in the neighbouring areas.

> Relevant product market: A market comprising all those products or services which are regarded as interchangeable or substitutable by the consumer, by reason of characteristics of the products or services, their prices, and intended use.

Inquiry into Combination by Commission

1. The Commission may, upon its own knowledge or information relating to acquisition referred

to in clause (a) of Section 5 or acquiring of control referred to in clause (b) of Section 5 or merger or amalgamation referred to in clause (c) of that Section, inquire into whether such a combination has caused, or is likely to cause, an appreciable adverse effect on competition in India.

However, the Commission shall not initiate any inquiry under this sub-section after the expiry of one year from the date on which such combination has taken effect.

2. The Commission shall, on receipt of a notice under sub-section (2) of Section 6, inquire whether a combination referred to in that notice or reference has caused or is likely to cause an appreciable adverse effect on competition in India.
3. Notwithstanding anything contained in Section 5, the Central Government shall, on the expiry of a period of two years from the date of commencement of this Act and thereafter every two years, in consultation with the Commission, by notification, enhance or reduce, on the basis of the wholesale price index or fluctuations in exchange rate of rupee or foreign currencies, the value of assets or the value of turnover.
4. For the purposes of determining whether a combination would affect, or is likely to have an appreciable adverse effect on, competition in the relevant market, the Commission shall have due regard to all or any of the following factors, namely:
   (a) actual and potential level of competition through imports in the market;
   (b) extent of barriers to entry into the market;
   (c) level of combination in the market;
   (d) degree of countervailing power in the market;
   (e) likelihood that the combination would result in the parties to the combination being able to significantly and sustainably increase prices or profit margins;
   (f) extent of effective competition likely to sustain in a market;
   (g) extent to which substitutes are available or are likely to be available in the market;
   (h) market share, in the relevant market, of the persons or enterprise in a combination, individually and as a combination;
   (i) likelihood that the combination would result in the removal of a vigorous and effective competitor or competitors in the market;
   (j) nature and extent of vertical integration in the market;
   (l) possibility of a failing business;
   (m) nature and extent of innovation;
   (n) relative advantage, by way of contribution to economic development, by any combination having or likely to have appreciable adverse effect on competition;
   (o) whether the benefits of the combination outweigh the adverse impact of the combination, if any [Section 20].

Reference by Statutory Authority

> Statutory authority: Any authority, board, corporation, council, institute, university, or any other body corporate, established by or under any Central, State, or Provincial Act for the purposes of regulating the production or supply of goods, or the provision of any services or markets there.

1. Where, in the course of a proceeding before any statutory authority, an issue is raised by any party that any decision which such a statutory authority has taken, or proposes to take, is, or would be, contrary to any of the provisions of this Act, then such a statutory authority may make a reference in respect of such an issue to the Commission:

   However, any statutory authority, may, suo motu, make such a reference to the Commission.
2. On receipt of a reference under sub-section (1), the Commission shall give its opinion, within 60 days of receipt of such a reference, to such statutory authority which shall consider the opinion of the Commission and thereafter, give its findings recording reasons thereof on the issues referred to in the said opinion [Section 21].

Reference by Commission

1. Where, in the course of a proceeding before the Commission, an issue is raised by any party that any decision which the Commission has taken during such proceeding or proposes to take, is or would be contrary to any provision of this Act whose implementation is entrusted to a statutory authority, the Commission may

make a reference in respect of such an issue to the statutory authority.

2. On receipt of a reference under sub-section (1), the statutory authority shall give its opinion within 60 days of the receipt of such reference, to the Commission which shall consider the opinion of the statutory authority, and thereafter give its findings recording reasons thereof on the issues referred to in the said opinion [Section 21A].

Meetings of Commission

1. The Commission shall meet at such times and places, and shall observe such rules and procedures in regard to the transaction of business at its meetings as may be provided by regulations.
2. If the Chairperson, for any reason, is unable to attend a meeting of the Commission, the senior-most Member present at the meeting, shall preside at the meeting.
3. All questions which come up before any meeting of the Commission shall be decided by a majority of the Members present and voting, and in the event of an equality of votes, the Chairperson or, in his absence, the Member presiding, shall have a second or/casting vote. However, the quorum for such a meeting shall be three Members [Section 22].

Procedure for Inquiry

1. On receipt of a reference from the Central Government or a State Government or a statutory authority or on its own knowledge or information received under Section 19, if the Commission is of the opinion that there exists a prima facie case, it shall direct the Director General to cause an investigation to be made into the matter.

   However, if the subject matter of information received is, in the opinion of the Commission, substantially the same as or has been covered by any previous information received, then the new information may be clubbed with the previous information.

2. Where, on receipt of a reference from the Central Government or a State Government or a statutory authority or information received under Section 19, the Commission is of the opinion that there exists no prima facie case, it shall close the matter forthwith and pass such orders as it deems fit and send a copy of its orders to the Central Government or the State Government or the statutory authority or the parties concerned, as the case may be.
3. The Director General shall, on receipt of direction under sub-section (1), submit a report on his findings within such period as may be specified by the Commission.
4. The Commission may forward a copy of the report referred to in sub-section (3) to the parties concerned.

   Notwithstanding, in case the investigation is caused to be made based on a reference received from the Central Government or the State Government or the statutory authority, the Commission shall forward a copy of the report referred to in sub-section (3) to the Central Government or the State Government or the statutory authority, as the case may be.

5. If the report of the Director General referred to in sub-section (3) recommends that there is no contravention of the provisions of this Act, the Commission shall invite objections or suggestions from the Central Government or the State Government or the statutory authority or the parties concerned, as the case may be, on such a report of the Director General.
6. If, after consideration of the objections and suggestions referred to in sub-section (5), if any, the Commission agrees with the recommendation of the Director General, it shall close the matter forthwith and pass such orders as it deems fit and communicate its orders to the Central Government or the State Government or the statutory authority or the parties concerned, as the case may be.
7. If, after consideration of the objections or suggestions referred to in sub-section (5), if any, the Commission is of the opinion that further investigation is called for, it may direct further investigation in the matter by the Director General or cause further inquiry to be made in the matter, or itself proceed with further inquiry in the matter, in accordance with the provisions of this Act.

8. If the report of the Director General referred to in sub-section (3) recommends that there is contravention of any of the provisions of this Act, and the Commission is of the opinion that further inquiry is called for, it shall inquire into such contravention in accordance with the provisions of this Act [Section 26].

Orders by Commission After Inquiry

Where, after inquiry, the Commission finds that any agreement referred to in Section 3 or action of an enterprise in a dominant position, is in contravention of Section 3 or Section 4, as the case may be, it may pass all or any of the following orders, namely:

1. direct any enterprise or association of enterprises or person or association of persons, as the case may be, involved in such agreement, or abuse of dominant position, to discontinue and not to re-enter such an agreement, or discontinue such abuse of dominant position, as the case may be;
2. impose such penalty as it may deem fit which shall be not more than ten per cent of the average of the turnover for the last three preceding financial years, upon each such person or enterprise which is party to such agreements or abuse:
3. [Omitted by Competition (Amendment) Act, 2007]
4. direct that the agreements shall stand modified to the extent and in the manner as may be specified in the order by the Commission;
5. direct the enterprises concerned to abide by such other orders as the Commission may pass and comply with the directions, including payment of costs, if any;
6. [Omitted by Competition (Amendment) Act, 2007]
7. pass other such orders or issue such directions as it may deem fit.

However, while passing orders under this Section, if the Commission finds that an enterprise in contravention to Section 3 or Section 4 of the Act is a member of a group as defined in clause (b) of the Explanation to Section 5 of the Act, and other members of such a group are also responsible for, or have contributed to, such a contravention, then it may pass orders, under this Section, against such members of the group [Section 27].

Division of Enterprise Enjoying Dominant Position

1. The Commission may, notwithstanding anything contained in any other law for the time being in force, by order in writing, direct the division of an enterprise enjoying dominant position to ensure that such an enterprise does not abuse its dominant position.
2. In particular, and without prejudice to the generality of the foregoing powers, the order referred to in sub-section (1) may provide for all or any of the following matters, namely:
   (a) the transfer or vesting of property, rights, liabilities, or obligations;
   (b) the adjustment of contracts either by discharge or reduction of any liability or obligation or otherwise;
   (c) the creation, allotment, surrender, or cancellation of any shares, stocks, or securities;
   (d) [Omitted by Competition (Amendment) Act, 2007]
   (e) the formation or winding up of an enterprise or the amendment of the memorandum of association or articles of association or any other instruments regulating the business of any enterprise;
   (f) the extent to which, and the circumstances in which, provisions of the order affecting an enterprise may be altered by the enterprise and the registration thereof;
   (g) any other matter which may be necessary to give effect to the division of the enterprise.
3. Notwithstanding anything contained in any other law for the time being in force, or in any contract or in any memorandum or articles of association, an officer of a company who ceases to hold office in consequence of the division of an enterprise shall not be entitled to claim any compensation for ceasing to hold office [Section 28].

Procedure for Investigation of Combination

1. Where the Commission is of the opinion that a combination is likely to cause, or has caused, an appreciable adverse effect on competition within the relevant market in India, it shall issue

a notice to show cause to the parties to combination calling upon them to respond within 30 days of the receipt of the notice as to why investigation in respect of such combination should not be conducted.

After receipt of the response of the parties to the combination under sub-section (1), the Commission may call for a report from the Director General and such report shall be submitted by the Director General within such time as the Commission may direct.

2. The Commission, if it is prima facie of the opinion that the combination has, or is likely to have, an appreciable adverse effect on competition, shall, within seven working days from the date of receipt of the response of the parties to the combination, or the receipt of the report from Director General called under sub-section (1A), whichever is later, direct the parties to the said combination to publish details of the combination within 10 working days of such direction, in such a manner as it thinks appropriate, for bringing the combination to the knowledge or information of the public and persons affected or likely to be affected by such combination.
3. The Commission may invite any person or member of the public affected or likely to be affected by the said combination, to file his written objections, if any, before the Commission within 15 working days from the date on which the details of the combination were published under sub-section (2).
4. The Commission may, within 15 working days from the expiry of the period specified in sub-section (3), call for such additional or other information as it may deem fit from the parties to the said combination.
5. The additional or other information called for by the Commission shall be furnished by the parties referred to in sub-section (4) within 15 days from the expiry of the period specified in sub-section (4).
6. After the receipt of all information and within a period of 45 working days from the expiry of the period specified in sub-section (5), the Commission shall proceed to deal with the case in accordance with the provisions contained in Section 31 [Section 29].

Orders of Commission on Certain Combinations

1. Where the Commission is of the opinion that a combination does not, or is not likely to, have an appreciable adverse effect on competition, it shall, by order, approve that combination including the combination in respect of which a notice has been given under sub-section (2) of Section 6.
2. Where the Commission is of the opinion that the combination has, or is likely to have, an appreciable adverse effect on competition, it shall direct that the combination shall not take effect.
3. Where the Commission is of the opinion that the combination has, or is likely to have, an appreciable adverse effect on competition, but such adverse effect can be eliminated by suitable modification to such combination; it may propose appropriate modification to the combination, to the parties to such combination.
4. The parties who accept the modification proposed by the Commission under sub-section (3) shall carry out such modification within the period specified by the Commission.
5. If the parties to the combination, who have accepted the modification under sub-section (4), fail to carry out the modification within the period specified by the Commission, such a combination shall be deemed to have an appreciable adverse effect on competition and the Commission shall deal with such a combination in accordance with the provisions of this Act.
6. If the parties to the combination do not accept the modification proposed by the Commission under sub-section (3), such parties may, within 30 working days of the modification proposed by the Commission, submit an amendment to the modification proposed by the Commission under that sub-section.
7. If the Commission agrees with the amendment submitted by the parties under sub-section (6), it shall, by order, approve the combination.
8. If the Commission does not accept the amendment submitted under sub-section (6), the parties shall be allowed a further period of 30 working days within which such parties

shall accept the modification proposed by the Commission under sub-section (3).

9. If the parties fail to accept the modification proposed by the Commission within 30 working days referred to in sub-section (6) or within a further period of 30 working days referred to in sub-section (8), the combination shall be deemed to have an appreciable adverse effect on competition and be dealt with in accordance with the provisions of this Act.
10. Where the Commission has directed under sub-section (2) that the combination shall not take effect, or the combination is deemed to have an appreciable adverse effect on competition under sub-section (9), then, without prejudice to any penalty which may be imposed or any prosecution which may be initiated under this Act, the Commission may order that
    (a) the acquisition referred to in clause (a) of Section 5; or
    (b) the acquiring of control referred to in clause (b) of Section 5; or
    (c) the merger or amalgamation referred to in clause (c) of Section 5, shall not be given effect to.

    Provided that the Commission may, if it considers appropriate, frame a scheme to implement its order under this sub-section.
11. If the Commission does not, on the expiry of a period of 210 days from the date of notice given to the Commission under sub-section (2) of Section 6, pass an order or issue direction in accordance with the provisions of sub-section (1) or sub-section (2) or sub-section (7), the combination shall be deemed to have been approved by the Commission.

    Explanation: For the purpose of determining the period of 210 days specified in this sub-section, the period of 30 working days specified in sub-section (6) and a further period of 30 working days specified in sub-section (8) shall be excluded.
12. Where any extension of time is sought by the parties to the combination, the period of 90 working days shall be reckoned after deducting the extended time granted at the request of the parties.
13. Where the Commission has ordered a combination to be void, the acquisition or acquiring of control or merger or amalgamation referred to in Section 5 shall be dealt with by the authorities under any other law for the time being in force, as if such acquisition or acquiring of control or merger or amalgamation had not taken place and the parties to the combination shall be dealt with accordingly.
14. Nothing contained in this Chapter shall affect any proceeding initiated or which may be initiated under any other law for the time being in force [Section 31].

Acts Taking Place Outside India But Having an Effect on Competition in India

The Commission shall, notwithstanding that

1. an agreement referred to in Section 3 has been entered into outside India; or
2. any party to such agreement is outside India; or
3. any enterprise abusing the dominant position is outside India; or
4. a combination has taken place outside India; or
5. any party to combination is outside India; or
6. any other matter or practice or action arising out of such agreement or dominant position or combination is outside India, have power to inquire in accordance with the provisions contained in Sections 19, 20, 26, 29, and 30 of the Act into such an agreement or abuse of dominant position or combination, if such an agreement, dominant position or combination has, or is likely to have, an appreciable adverse effect on competition in the relevant market in India, and pass such orders as it may deem fit in accordance with the provisions of this Act [Section 32].

Power to Issue Interim Orders

Where, during an inquiry, the Commission is satisfied that an act in contravention of sub-section (1) of Section 3 or sub-section (1) of Section 4 or Section 6 has been committed and continues to be committed, or that such an act is about to be committed, the Commission may, by order, temporarily restrain any party from carrying on such an act until the conclusion of the inquiry or until further orders, without giving notice to the party, where it deems it necessary [Section 33].

Appearance Before Commission

A person or an enterprise or the Director General may either appear in person or authorise one or more chartered accountants or company secretaries or cost accountants or legal practitioners or any of his or its officers to present his or its case before the Commission [Section 35].

Power of Commission to Regulate Its Own Procedure

1. In the discharge of its functions, the Commission shall be guided by the principles of natural justice and, subject to the other provisions of this Act and of any rules made by the Central Government, the Commission shall have the powers to regulate its own procedure.
2. The Commission shall have, for the purposes of discharging its functions under this Act, the same powers as are vested in a Civil Court under the Code of Civil Procedure, 1908 (5 of 1908) while trying a suit, in respect of the following matters, namely:
   (a) summoning and enforcing the attendance of any person and examining him on oath;
   (b) requiring the discovery and production of documents;
   (c) receiving evidence on affidavit;
   (d) issuing commissions for the examination of witnesses or documents;
   (e) requisitioning, subject to the provisions of Sections 123 and 124 of the Indian Evidence Act, 1872 (1 of 1872), any public record or document or copy of such record or document from any office.
3. The Commission may call upon such experts from the field of economics, commerce, accountancy, international trade, or from any other discipline as it deems necessary, to assist the Commission in the conduct of any inquiry by it.
4. The Commission may direct any person:
   (a) to produce before the Director General or the Secretary or an officer authorised by it, such books, or other documents in the custody or under the control of such a person so directed as may be specified or described in the direction, being documents relating to any trade, the examination of which may be required for the purposes of this Act;
   (b) to furnish to the Director General or the Secretary or any other officer authorised by it, as respects the trade, or such other information as may be in his possession in relation to the trade carried on by such a person as may be required for the purposes of this Act [Section 36].

Rectification of Orders

1. With a view to rectifying any mistake apparent from the record, the Commission may amend any order passed by it under the provisions of this Act.
2. Subject to the other provisions of this Act, the Commission may make
   (a) an amendment under sub-section (1) of its own motion;
   (b) an amendment for rectifying any such mistake which has been brought to its notice by any party to the order.

   Explanation: For the removal of doubts, it is hereby declared that the Commission shall not, while rectifying any mistake apparent from record, amend a substantive part of its order passed under the provisions of this Act [Section 38].

Execution of Orders of Commission Imposing Monetary Penalty

1. If a person fails to pay any monetary penalty imposed on him under this Act, the Commission shall proceed to recover the penalty in such manner as may be specified by the regulations.
2. In a case where the Commission is of the opinion that it would be expedient to recover the penalty imposed under this Act in accordance with the provisions of the Income-tax Act, 1961, it may make a reference to this effect to the concerned income-tax authority under that Act for the recovery of the penalty as tax due under the said Act.
3. Where a reference has been made by the Commission under sub-section (2) for the recovery of penalty, the person upon whom the penalty has been imposed shall be deemed to be the assessee in default under the Income Tax Act, 1961 and the provisions contained in Sections 221 to 227, 228A, 229, 231, and 232 of the said Act and the Second Schedule to that Act and any rules

made thereunder shall, in so far as may be, apply as if the said provisions were the provisions of this Act and referred to sums by way of penalty imposed under this Act instead of income-tax, and sums imposed by way of penalty, fine, and interest under the Income-tax Act, 1961 (43 of 1961) and to the Commission instead of the Assessing Officer.

Explanation: Any reference to sub-section (2) or sub-section (6) of Section 220 of the Income-tax Act, 1961, in the said provisions of that Act or the rules made thereunder, shall be construed as references to Sections 43 to 45 of this Act [Section 39].

Director General to Investigate Contravention

1. The Director General shall, when so directed by the Commission, assist the Commission in investigating any contravention of the provisions of this Act or any rules or regulations made thereunder.
2. The Director General shall have all the powers as are conferred upon the Commission under sub-section (2) of Section 36.
3. Without prejudice to the provisions of sub-section (2), Sections 240 and 240A of the Companies Act, 1956, so far as may be, shall apply to an investigation made by the Director General or any other person investigating under his authority, as they apply to an inspector appointed under that Act [Section 41].

Contravention of Orders of the Commission

1. The Commission may cause an inquiry to be made into compliance of its orders or directions made in exercise of its powers under the Act.
2. If any person, without reasonable cause, fails to comply with the orders or directions of the Commission issued under Sections 27, 28, 31, 32, 33, 42A, and 43A of the Act, he shall be punishable with a fine which may extend to rupees one lakh for each day during which such non-compliance occurs, subject to a maximum of rupees ten crore, as the Commission may determine.
3. If any person does not comply with the orders or directions issued, or fails to pay the fine imposed under sub-section (2), he shall, without prejudice to any proceeding under Section 39, be punishable with imprisonment for a term which may extend to three years, or with a fine which may extend to ₹25 crore, or with both, as the Chief Metropolitan Magistrate, Delhi, may deem fit.

   Provided that the Chief Metropolitan Magistrate, Delhi, shall not take cognizance of any offence under this Section save on a complaint filed by the Commission or any of its officers authorised by it [Section 42].

Compensation in Case of Contravention of Orders

Any person may make an application to the Appellate Tribunal for an order for the recovery of compensation from any enterprise for any loss or damage shown to have been suffered, by such a person as a result of the said enterprise violating directions issued by the Commission or contravening, without any reasonable ground, any decision or order of the Commission issued under Sections 27, 28, 31, 32, and 33 or any condition or restriction subject to which any approval, sanction, direction or exemption in relation to any matter has been accorded, given, made, or granted under this Act or delaying in carrying out such orders or directions of the Commission [Section 24A].

Penalty for Failure to Comply with Directions

If any person fails to comply, without reasonable cause, with a direction given by

1. the Commission under sub-sections (2) and (4) of Section 36; or
2. the Director General while exercising powers referred to in sub-section (2) of Section 41,

such person shall be punishable with fine which may extend to rupees one lakh for each day during which such failure continues subject to a maximum of rupees one crore, as may be determined by the Commission [Section 43].

Power to Impose Penalty for Non-furnishing of Information

If any person or enterprise fails to give notice to the Commission under sub-section (2) of Section 6, the Commission shall impose on such a person or enterprise a penalty which may extend to 1% of the total turnover or the assets, whichever is higher, of such a combination [Section 43A].

Penalty for Making False Statement or Omission to Furnish Information

If any person, being a party to a combination

1. makes a statement which is false in any material particular, or knowing it to be false; or
2. omits to state any material particular knowing it to be material,
   such a person shall be liable to a penalty which shall not be less than ₹50 lakh but which may extend to ₹1 crore, as may be determined by the Commission [Section 44].

Penalty for Offences in Relation to Furnishing of Information

1. Without prejudice to the provisions of Section 44, if a person, who furnishes or is required to furnish under this Act any particulars, documents or any information
   (a) makes any statement or furnishes any document which he knows or has reason to believe to be false in any material particular; or
   (b) omits to state any material fact knowing it to be material; or
   (c) willfully alters, suppresses, or destroys any document which is required to be furnished as aforesaid,
   such a person shall be punishable with a fine which may extend to rupees one crore as may be determined by the Commission.
2. Without prejudice to the provisions of sub-section (1), the Commission may also pass such other orders as it deems fit [Section 45].

Power to Impose Lesser Penalty

The Commission may, if it is satisfied that any producer, seller, distributor, trader, or service provider included in any cartel, which is alleged to have violated Section 3, has made a full and true disclosure in respect of the alleged violations and such disclosure is vital, impose upon such a producer, seller, distributor, trader, or service provider, a lesser penalty as it may deem fit, than leviable under this Act or the rules or the regulations.

> Cartel: An association of producers, sellers, distributors, traders, or service providers, who, by agreement amongst themselves, limit, control, or attempt to control the production, distribution, sale, or price of, or trade in goods or provision of services.

However, lesser penalty shall not be imposed by the Commission in cases where the report of investigation directed under Section 26 has been received before making such disclosure.

Provided further that lesser penalty shall be imposed by the Commission only in respect of a producer, seller, distributor, trader, or service provider included in the cartel, who has made the full, true, and vital disclosures under this Section and who continues to cooperate with the Commission till the completion of the proceedings before the Commission [Section 46].

Crediting Sums Realised by Way of Penalties to Consolidated Fund of India

All sums realised by way of penalties under this Act shall be credited to the Consolidated Fund of India [Section 47].

Contravention by Companies

1. Where a person committing contravention of any of the provisions of this Act, or of any rule, regulation, order made or direction issued thereunder is a company, every person who, at the time the contravention was committed, was in charge of, and was responsible to the company for the conduct of the business of the company, as well as the company, shall be deemed to be guilty of the contravention and shall be liable to be proceeded against and punished accordingly.

   Provided that nothing contained in this sub-section shall render any such person liable to any punishment if he proves that the contravention was committed without his knowledge or that he had exercised all due diligence to prevent the commission of such contravention.

2. Notwithstanding, where a contravention of any of the provisions of this Act or of any rule, regulation, order made or direction issued thereunder, has been committed by a company and it is proved that the contravention has taken place with the consent or connivance of, or is attributable to any neglect on the part of, any director, manager, secretary or other officer of the company, such a director, manager, secretary or other officer shall also be deemed to be guilty of that contravention and shall be liable to be proceeded against and punished accordingly [Section 48].

Grants by Central Government

The Central Government may, after due appropriation made by Parliament by law in this behalf, make to the Commission grants of such sums of money as the Government may think fit for being utilised for the purposes of this Act [Section 50].

Constitution of Competition Fund

1. There shall be constituted a fund, called the 'Competition Fund' or just 'Fund' and there shall be credited thereto
   (a) all Government grants received by the Commission;
   (b) [Omitted by Competition (Amendment) Act, 2007]
   (c) the fees received under this Act;
   (d) the interest accrued on the amounts referred to in Section 82 [clauses (a) and (c)].
2. The Fund shall be applied for meeting
   (a) the salaries and allowances payable to the Chairperson and other Members and the administrative expenses including the salaries, allowances, and pension payable to the Director General, Additional, Joint, Deputy or Assistant Directors General, the Registrar and officers, and other employees of the Commission;
   (b) the other expenses of the Commission in connection with the discharge of its functions and for the purposes of this Act.
3. The Fund shall be administered by a committee of such Members of the Commission as may be determined by the Chairperson.
4. The committee appointed under sub-section (3) shall spend monies out of the Fund for carrying out the objectives for which the Fund has been constituted [Section 51].

Accounts and Audit

1. The Commission shall maintain proper accounts and other relevant records and prepare an annual statement of accounts in such form as may be prescribed by the Central Government in consultation with the Comptroller and Auditor-General of India.
2. The accounts of the Commission shall be audited by the Comptroller and Auditor- General of India at such intervals as may be specified by him and any expenditure incurred in connection with such an audit shall be payable by the Commission to the Comptroller and Auditor-General of India.
3. The Comptroller and Auditor-General of India, and any other person appointed by him in connection with the audit of the accounts of the Commission, shall have the same rights, privileges and authority in connection with such an audit as the Comptroller and Auditor-General of India generally has, in connection with the audit of Government accounts and, in particular, shall have the right to demand the production of books, accounts, connected vouchers and other documents and papers, and to inspect any of the offices of the Commission.
4. The accounts of the Commission as certified by the Comptroller and Auditor-General of India or any other person appointed by him in this behalf, together with the audit report, shall be forwarded annually to the Central Government and that Government shall cause the same to be laid before each House of Parliament [Section 52].

Furnishing of Returns to the Central Government

1. The Commission shall furnish to the Central Government, at such time and in such form and manner as may be prescribed, or as the Central Government may direct, such returns and state-

ments and such particulars in regard to any proposed or existing measures for the promotion of competition advocacy, creating awareness, and imparting training about competition issues, as the Central Government may, from time to time, require.

2. The Commission shall prepare once in every year, in such form and at such time as may be prescribed, an annual report giving a true and full account of its activities during the previous year, and copies of the report shall be forwarded to the Central Government.
3. A copy of the report received under sub-section (2) shall be laid, as soon as possible after it is received, before each House of Parliament [Section 53].

Establishment of Appellate Tribunal

Appellate tribunal: Competition Appellate Tribunal, established under Section 53A(1).

1. The Central Government shall, by notification, establish an Appellate Tribunal to be known as Competition Appellate Tribunal
   - (a) to hear and dispose of appeals against any direction issued or decision made or order passed by the Commission under sub-sections (2) and (6) of Sections 26–28, Sections 31–33, Sections 38–39, Sections 43–43A, Sections 44–46 of the Act;
   - (b) to adjudicate on any claim for compensation that may arise from the findings of the Commission or the orders of the Appellate Tribunal in an appeal against any finding of the Commission or under Section 42A or under sub-section (2) of Section 53Q of this Act, and pass orders for the recovery of compensation under Section 53N of this Act.
2. The Headquarters of the Appellate Tribunal shall be at such a place as the Central Government may, by notification, specify [Section 53A].

Appeal to Appellate Tribunal

1. The Central Government or the State Government or a local authority or enterprise or any person, aggrieved by any direction, decision or order referred to in clause (a) of Section 53A may prefer an appeal to the Appellate Tribunal.
2. Every appeal under sub-section (1) shall be filed within a period of 60 days from the date on which a copy of the direction or decision or order made by the Commission is received by the Central Government or the State Government or a local authority or enterprise or any person referred to in that sub-section, and it shall be in such form and be accompanied by such fee as may be prescribed.

   However, the Appellate Tribunal may entertain an appeal after the expiry of the said period of 60 days if it is satisfied that there was sufficient cause for not filing it within that period.
3. On receipt of an appeal under sub-section (1), the Appellate Tribunal may, after giving the parties to the appeal an opportunity of being heard, pass such orders thereon as it thinks fit, confirming, modifying or setting aside the direction, decision or order appealed against.
4. The Appellate Tribunal shall send a copy of every order made by it to the Commission and the parties to the appeal.
5. The appeal filed before the Appellate Tribunal under sub-section (1) shall be dealt with by it as expeditiously as possible and endeavour shall be made by it to dispose of the appeal within six months from the date of receipt of the appeal [Section 53B].

Composition of Appellate Tribunal

The Appellate Tribunal shall consist of a Chairperson and not more than two other members to be appointed by the Central Government [Section 53C].

Qualifications for Chairperson and Members of Appellate Tribunal

1. The Chairperson of the Appellate Tribunal shall be a person, who is, or has been, a Judge of the Supreme Court or the Chief Justice of a High Court.
2. A member of the Appellate Tribunal shall be a person of ability, integrity, and standing, having special knowledge of, and professional experience of not less than 25 years in, competition matters including competition law and policy, international trade, economics, business, commerce, law, finance, accountancy, manage-

ment, industry, public affairs, administration, or in any other matter which, in the opinion of the Central Government, may be useful to the Appellate Tribunal [Section 53D].

Appointment of Appellate Tribunal

1. The Chairperson and members of the Appellate Tribunal shall be appointed by the Central Government from a panel of names recommended by a Selection Committee consisting of
   (a) the Chief Justice of India or his nominee … Chairperson;
   (b) the Secretary in the Ministry of Corporate Affairs … Member;
   (c) the Secretary in the Ministry of Law and Justice … Member.
2. The terms of the Selection Committee and the manner of selection of the panel of names shall be such as may be prescribed [Section 53E].

Term of Office of Chairperson and Members of Appellate Tribunal

The Chairperson or a member of the Appellate Tribunal shall hold office for a term of five years from the date on which he enters upon his office, and shall be eligible for re-appointment.

However, no Chairperson or other member of the Appellate Tribunal shall hold office after he has attained

1. in the case of the Chairperson, the age of 68 years;
2. in the case of any other member of the Appellate Tribunal, the age of 65 years [Section 53F].

Removal and Suspension of Chairperson and Members of Appellate Tribunal

1. The Central Government may, in consultation with the Chief Justice of India, remove from office the Chairperson or any other member of the Appellate Tribunal, who
   (a) has been adjudged an insolvent; or
   (b) has engaged at any time, during his terms of office, in any paid employment; or
   (c) has been convicted of an offence which, in the opinion of the Central Government, involves moral turpitude; or
   (d) has become physically or mentally incapable of acting as such Chairperson or other Member of the Appellate Tribunal; or
   (e) has acquired such financial or other interest as is likely to affect prejudicially his functions as such Chairperson or Member of the Appellate Tribunal; or
   (f) has so abused his position as to render his continuance in office prejudicial to the public interest.
2. Notwithstanding anything contained in sub-section (1), no Chairperson or a Member of the Appellate Tribunal shall be removed from his office on the ground specified in clause (e) or clause (f) of sub-section (1) except by an order made by the Central Government after an inquiry is made in this behalf by a Judge of the Supreme Court, in which such a Chairperson or member is informed of the charges against him and given a reasonable opportunity to be heard in respect of those charges [Section 53K].

Contravention of Orders of Appellate Tribunal

1. Without prejudice to the provisions of this Act, if any person contravenes, without any reasonable ground, any order of the Appellate Tribunal, he shall be liable for a penalty not exceeding ₹1 crore or imprisonment for a term up to three years or with both, as the Chief Metropolitan Magistrate, Delhi, may deem fit.

   Provided that the Chief Metropolitan Magistrate, Delhi, shall not take cognizance of any offence punishable under this sub-section, save on a complaint made by an officer authorised by the Appellate Tribunal.
2. Without prejudice to the provisions of this Act, any person may make an application to the Appellate Tribunal for an order for the recovery of compensation from any enterprise for any loss or damage shown to have been suffered by such a person as a result of the said enterprise contravening, without any reasonable ground, any order of the Appellate Tribunal or delaying carrying out such orders of the Appellate Tribunal [Section 53Q].

Right to Legal Representation

1. A person referring an appeal to the Appellate Tribunal may either appear in person or authorise one or more chartered accountants or company secretaries or cost accountants or legal practitioners or any of its officers to present his or its case before the Appellate Tribunal.
2. The Central Government or a State Government or a local authority or any enterprise referring an appeal to the Appellate Tribunal may authorise one or more chartered accountants or company secretaries or cost accountants or legal practitioners or any of its officers to act as presenting officers and every person so authorised may present the case with respect to any appeal before the Appellate Tribunal.
3. The Commission may authorise one or more chartered accountants or company secretaries or cost accountants or legal practitioners or any of its officers to act as presenting officers and every person so authorised may present the case with respect to any appeal before the Appellate Tribunal [Section 53S].

Appeal to Supreme Court

The Central Government or any State Government or the Commission or any statutory authority or any local authority or any enterprise or any person aggrieved by any decision or order of the Appellate Tribunal may file an appeal to the Supreme Court within 60 days from the date of communication of the decision or order of the Appellate Tribunal to them.

However, the Supreme Court may, if it is satisfied that the applicant was prevented by sufficient cause from filing the appeal within the said period, allow it to be filed after the expiry of the said period of 60 days [Section 53T].

Power to Punish for Contempt

The Appellate Tribunal shall have, and exercise, the same jurisdiction, powers and authority in respect of contempt of itself as a High Court has, and may exercise this purpose, the provisions of the Contempt of Courts Act, 1971 subject to modifications that,

1. the reference therein to a High Court shall be construed as including a reference to the Appellate Tribunal;
2. the references to the Advocate-General in Section 15 of the said Act shall be construed as a reference to such a Law Officer as the Central Government may, by notification, specify in this behalf [Section 53U].

Power to Exempt

The Central Government may, by notification, exempt from the application of this Act, or any provision thereof, and for such period as it may specify in such notification

1. any class of enterprise if such an exemption is necessary in the interest of security of the State or public interest;
2. any practice or agreement arising out of and in accordance with any obligation assumed by India under any treaty, agreement, or convention with any other country or countries;
3. any enterprise which performs a sovereign function on behalf of the Central Government or a State Government.

   However, in case an enterprise is engaged in any activity including the activity relatable to the sovereign functions of the Government, the Central Government may grant exemption only in respect of the activity relatable to the sovereign functions [Section 54].

Power of Central Government to Issue Directions

1. Without prejudice to the foregoing provisions of this Act, the Commission shall, in exercise of its powers or the performance of its functions under this Act, be bound by such directions on questions of policy, other than those relating to technical and administrative matters, as the Central Government may give in writing to it from time to time.

   However, the Commission shall, as far as practicable, be given an opportunity to express its views before any direction is given under this sub-section.
2. The decision of the Central Government whether a question is one of policy or not shall be final [Section 55].

Power of Central Government to Supersede Commission

1. If at any time the Central Government is of the opinion
   (a) that, on account of circumstances beyond the control of the Commission, it is unable to discharge the functions or perform the duties imposed on it by or under the provisions of this Act; or
   (b) that the Commission has persistently made default in complying with any direction given by the Central Government under this Act or in the discharge of the functions or performance of the duties imposed on it by or under the provisions of this Act and as a result of such default the financial position of the Commission or the administration of the Commission has suffered; or
   (c) that circumstances exist which render it necessary in the public interest so to do, the Central Government may, by notification and for reasons to be specified therein, supersede the Commission for such period, not exceeding six months, as may be specified in the notification.

   However, before issuing any such notification, the Central Government shall give a reasonable opportunity to the Commission to make representations against the proposed supersession and shall consider representations, if any, of the Commission.
2. Upon the publication of a notification under sub-section (1) superseding the Commission,
   (a) the Chairperson and other Members shall, from the date of supersession, vacate their offices;
   (b) all the powers, functions and duties which may, by or under the provisions of this Act, be exercised or discharged by or on behalf of the Commission shall, until the Commission is reconstituted under sub-section (3), be exercised and discharged by the Central Government or such authority as the Central Government may specify in this behalf;
   (c) all properties owned or controlled by the Commission shall, until the Commission is reconstituted under sub-section (3), vest in the Central Government.
3. On or before the expiration of the period of supersession specified in the notification issued under sub-section (1), the Central Government shall reconstitute the Commission by a fresh appointment of its Chairperson and other Members. In such cases, any person who had vacated his office under clause (a) of sub-section (2) shall not be deemed to be disqualified for re-appointment.
4. The Central Government shall cause a notification issued under sub-section (1) and a full report of any action taken under this Section and the circumstances leading to such action to be laid before each House of Parliament at the earliest [Section 56].

Restriction on Disclosure of Information

No information relating to any enterprise, being information which has been obtained by or on behalf of the Commission or the Appellate Tribunal for the purposes of this Act, shall, without the previous permission in writing of the enterprise, be disclosed otherwise than in compliance with or for the purposes of this Act or any other law for the time being in force [Section 57].

Chairperson, Members, Director General, Secretary, and Officers To Be Public Servants

The Chairperson and other Members and the Director General, Additional, Joint, Deputy or Assistant Directors General and Secretary and officers and other employees of the Commission and the Chairperson, Members, officers and other employees of the Appellate Tribunal shall be deemed, while acting or purporting to act in pursuance of any of the provisions of this Act, to be public servants within the meaning of Section 21 of the Indian Penal Code [Section 58].

Protection of Action Taken in Good Faith

No suit, prosecution or other legal proceedings shall lie against the Central Government or Commission or any officer of the Central Government or the Chairperson or any Member or the Director-

General, Additional, Joint, Deputy or Assistant Directors General or the Secretary or officers or other employees of the Commission or the Chairperson, Members, officers and other employees of the Appellate Tribunal for anything which is in good faith done or intended to be done under this Act or the rules or regulations made thereunder [Section 59].

Exercises

I. Objective-type Questions

1. Cartel includes an association of
   (a) producers
   (b) sellers/distributors
   (c) traders or service providers
   (d) All of the above

2. Goods refers to goods as defined in the Sale of Goods and includes
   (a) products manufactured, processed, or mined
   (b) debentures, stocks, and shares after allotment
   (c) in relation to goods supplied, distributed, or controlled in India, goods imported in India
   (d) All of the above

3. The order issued by the Competition Commission to direct the division of an enterprise enjoying dominant position may provide for
   (a) the transfer or vesting of property, rights, liabilities, or obligations
   (b) the adjustment of contracts either by discharge or reduction of any liability or obligation or otherwise
   (c) the creation, allotment, surrender, or cancellation of any shares, stocks, or securities
   (d) All of the above

4. Under the Competition Act, a person, for making a false statement, or omission to furnish material information, shall be punishable with a fine which shall not be
   (a) less than ₹1 lakh
   (b) less than ₹50 lakh
   (c) less than ₹50 lakh which may extend to rupees one crore
   (d) less than ₹1 crore rupees

5. Who, among the following, is empowered to supersede the Commission?
   (a) MRTP Commission
   (b) Central Government
   (c) President of India
   (d) Supreme Court

II. Review Questions

1. Define the following terms under the Competition Act:
   (a) Acquisition
   (b) Cartel
   (c) Enterprise
   (d) Relevant Market
   (e) Relevant Geographic Market

2. What are the provisions in The Competition Act governing
   (a) prohibition of certain agreements;
   (b) dominant position; and
   (c) regulations of combinations

3. Write a note on the establishment, composition, appointment and terms of the Chairperson and other Members of Competition Commission of India.
4. Describe briefly the duties, powers, and functions of the Competition Commission.
5. Discuss briefly the procedure for inquiry under Section 19 of the Competition Commission Act, 2002.
6. Describe the power of the Competition Commission concerning the division of an enterprise enjoying dominant position.
7. Express the penalty which can be imposed upon a person by the Competition Commission for
   (a) contravention of the orders of the Commission;
   (b) failure to comply with the directions of Commission and Director General and
   (c) making false statements, or omission to furnish material information.

Answers to Objective-type Questions

1. (d) **2.** (d) **3.** (d) **4.** (c) **5.** (b)

22 Chapter in Review

LEARNING OUTCOMES

LO 1 Role and origin of The Competition Act, 2002

LO 2 Aim and objectives of the Act

LO 3 Functions of Competition Commission of India (CCI)

KEY TERMS

Dominant position: Ability to behave independently of its competitors, customers, suppliers and, ultimately, the final consumer.

Abuse of dominant position: Intentional anti-competitive acts by persons substantially in control of a market, that has had, is having, or is likely to have the effect of preventing or lessening competition.

Combinations: Acquisition of one or more enterprises by one or more persons, or the merger or amalgamation of enterprises.

Acquisition: Directly or indirectly, acquiring or agreeing to acquire (i) shares, voting rights, or assets of any enterprise; or (ii) control over the management or the assets of any enterprise.

Appellate tribunal: Competition Appellate Tribunal, established under Section 53A(1).

Cartel: An association of producers, sellers, distributors, traders, or service providers, who, by agreement amongst themselves, limit, control, or attempt to control the production, distribution, sale, or price of, or trade in goods or provision of services.

Relevant market: The market which may be determined by the Commission with reference to the relevant product market or the relevant geographic market, or with reference to both the markets.

Relevant geographic market: A market comprising the area in which the conditions of competition for supply of goods or provision of services or demand of goods or services are distinctly homogenous and can be distinguished from the conditions prevailing in the neighbouring areas.

LO1 The Competition Act, 2002 governs Indian competition law. The Act is a replacement of the archaic MRTP Act, 1969, keeping in view the economic development of the country.

LO2 The Act aims at promoting economic efficiency of the nation using competition as one of the means of assisting the creation of market responsive to consumer preferences. The objectives of the Act are sought to be achieved through the Competition Commission of India (CCI), established by the Central Government. The CCI in turn seeks to check abuse of dominance by market players, promote and sustain healthy competition, protect the interests of consumers, and ensure freedom of trade in the markets and regulate combinations which cause or are likely to cause an appreciable adverse effect on competition within India.

LO3 To achieve its objectives, the fair trade regulator (CCI) endeavors to (i) make the markets work for the benefit and welfare of consumers, (ii) ensure fair and healthy competition in economic activities in the country for faster and inclusive growth and development of economy, (iii) implement competition policies with an aim to effectuate the most efficient utilization of economic resources, (iv) develop and nurture effective relations and interactions with sectoral regulators to ensure smooth alignment of sectoral regulatory laws in tandem with the competition law, and (v) effectively carry out competition advocacy and spread the information on benefits of competition among all stakeholders to establish and nurture competition culture in Indian economy.

Relevant product market: A market comprising all those products or services which are regarded as interchangeable or substitutable by the consumer, by reason of characteristics of the products or services, their prices, and intended use.

Service: Providing something of any description to potential users.

Statutory authority: Any authority, board, corporation, council, institute, university, or any other body corporate, established by or under any Central, State, or Provincial Act for the purposes of regulating the production or supply of goods, or the provision of any services or markets there.

Trade: Any trade, business, industry, profession, or occupation relating to the production, supply, distribution, storage, or control of goods and includes the provision of any services.

CHAPTER

23 The Securities and Exchange Board of India Act, 1992

Learning Objectives

- **LO 1** Sebi Act: What it is?
- **LO 2** Aim and objectives of the Act
- **LO 3** Role and functions of Sebi
- **LO 4** Powers of the Board

The Securities and Exchange Board of India Act, 1992 or in short Sebi Act provides for the establishment of a Board to protect the interests of investors in securities and to promote the development of, and to regulate, the securities market and for matters connected therewith or incidental thereto. It was enacted by Parliament and extends to the whole of India. Relatively a brief Act containing 35 sections, the legislation acts as a market regulator and governs all the Stock Exchanges and the Securities Transactions in India.

Sebi Act: Aim and Objectives

The Act aims at protecting the money of investors from frauds in stock markets by ensuring safe and transparent dealings in securities. To achieve this, it seeks to

1. promote the development of securities market;
2. regulate the functioning of the stock exchanges in India;
3. educate brokers and invesotors; and
4. reduce the unjust fluctuations in the market prices of shares by taking appropriate regulatory measures.

Major Concepts

Collective investment scheme: Any arrangement which satisfies the conditions specified in Section 11AA of the Sebi Act.

Some of the important terms used in the Sebi Act are briefly introduced below.

Board means the Securities and Exchange Board of India established under Section 3.

Chairman means the Chairman of the Board.

Collective investment scheme means any scheme or arrangement which satisfies the conditions specified in Section 11AA.

Existing securities and exchange board: The Securities and Exchange Board of India constituted under the Resolution of the Government of India No.1 dated 12 April 1988.

Existing Securities and Exchange Board means the Securities and Exchange Board of India constituted under the Resolution of the Government of India in the Department of Economic Affairs No.1 dated 12 April 1988.

Fund: Fund constituted under Section 14 of the Sebi Act.

Fund means the Fund constituted under Section 14.

Member: A member of the Board and includes the Chairman.

Member means a member of the Board and includes the Chairman.

Notification means a notification published in the Official Gazette.

Prescribed means prescribed by rules made under this Act.

Regulations: Regulations made by the Board under the Sebi Act.

Regulations mean the regulations made by the Board under this Act.

Reserve Bank means the Reserve Bank of India constituted under Section 3 of the Reserve Bank of India Act, 1934.

Securities has the meaning assigned to it in Section 2 of the Securities Contracts (Regulation) Act, 1956.

Important Provisions

Important provisions of the Act have been briefly explained below.

Establishment and Incorporation of Board

Securities: Instruments of investments which primarily include shares, stocks, bonds, debentures, debenture stocks, etc.

1. The Securities and Exchange Board of India (Sebi) or Board was constituted under the Sebi Act to administer its provisions. All the stock brokers, sub-brokers, share transfer agents, bankers to an issue, trustees of trust deed, registrars to an issue, merchant bankers, underwriters, portfolio managers, investment advisers and such other intermediary who may be associated with the Securities Markets are to register with the Board under the provisions of the Act, under Section 12 of the Sebi Act. The Board has the power to suspend or cancel such registration. The Board is bound by the directions vested by the Central Government from time to time on questions of policy and the Central Government reserves the right to supersede the Board.
2. The Board is a body corporate by the name aforesaid, having perpetual succession and a common seal, with power subject to the provisions of this Act, to acquire, hold and dispose of property, both movable and immovable, and to contract, and can, by the said name, sue or be sued.
3. The head office of the Board is at Mumbai.

4. The Board may establish offices at other places in India [Section 3].

Management of the Board

Chairman: Chairman of the Board.

1. The Board shall consist of the following:
   (a) A Chairman;
   (b) Two members from amongst the officials of the Ministry of the Central Government dealing with finance and administration of the Companies Act, 2013;
   (c) One member from amongst the officials of the RBI; and
   (d) Five other members of whom at least three shall be the whole-time members, to be appointed by the Central Government.
2. The general superintendence, direction and management of the affairs of the Board shall vest in a Board of members, which may exercise all powers and do all acts and things which may be exercised or done by the Board.
3. Save as otherwise determined by regulations, the Chairman shall also have powers of general superintendence and direction of the affairs of the Board and may also exercise all powers and do all acts and things which may be exercised or done by that Board.
4. The Chairman and members shall be appointed by the Central Government and the members referred to in clauses (b) and (c) of that sub-section shall be nominated by the Central Government and the Reserve Bank, respectively.
5. The Chairman and the other members shall be persons of ability, integrity, and standing who have shown capacity in dealing with problems relating to securities market or have special knowledge or experience of law, finance, economics, accountancy, administration, or in any other discipline which, in the opinion of the Central Government, shall be useful to the Board [Section 4].

Term of Office and Conditions of Service of Chairman and Members of Board

- The term of office and other conditions of service of the Chairman and the members referred to in clause (d) of sub-section (1) of Section 4 shall be such as may be prescribed.
- Notwithstanding anything contained in sub-section (1), the Central Government shall have the right to terminate the services of the Chairman or a member appointed under clause (d) of sub-section (1) of Section 4, at any time before the expiry of the period prescribed under sub-section (1), by giving him notice of not less than three months in writing or three months' salary and allowances in lieu thereof, and the Chairman or a member, as the case may be, shall also have the right to relinquish his office, at any time before the expiry of the period prescribed under sub-section (1), by giving to the Central Government notice of not less than three months in writing [Section 5].

Removal of Member from Office

The Central Government shall remove a member from office if he

1. is, or at any time has been, adjudicated as insolvent;
2. is of unsound mind and stands so declared by a competent court;
3. has been convicted of an offence which, in the opinion of the Central Government, involves a moral turpitude;
4. has, in the opinion of the Central Government, so abused his position as to render his continuation in office detrimental to the public interest [Section 6].

However, no member shall be removed under this clause unless he has been given a reasonable opportunity of being heard in the matter.

Meetings of Board

1. The Board shall meet at such times and places, and shall observe such rules of procedure in regard to the transaction of business at its meetings (including quorum at such meetings) as may be provided by regulations.
2. The Chairman or, if for any reason, he is unable to attend a meeting of the Board, any other member chosen by the members present from amongst themselves at the meeting shall preside at the meeting.
3. All questions which come up before any meeting of the Board shall be decided by a majority votes of the members present and voting, and, in the event of an equality of votes, the Chairman, or in his absence, the person presiding, shall have a second or casting vote [Section 7].

Member Not to Participate in Meetings in Certain Cases

Any member, who is a director of a company and who as such director has any direct or indirect pecuniary interest in any matter coming up for consideration at a meeting of the Board, shall, as soon as possible after relevant circumstances have come to his knowledge, disclose the nature of his interest at such meeting and such disclosure shall be recorded in the proceedings of the Board, and the member shall not take any part in any deliberation or decision of the Board with respect to that matter [Section 7].

Vacancies Not to Invalidate Proceedings of Board

No act or proceeding of the Board shall be invalid merely by reason of

1. any vacancy in, or any defect in the constitution of, the Board; or
2. any defect in the appointment of a person acting as a member of the Board; or
3. any irregularity in the procedure of the Board not affecting the merits of the case [Section 8].

Officers and Employees of Board

1. The Board may appoint such other officers and employees as it considers necessary for the efficient discharge of its functions under this Act.
2. The term and other conditions of service of officers and employees of the Board appointed under sub-section (1) shall be such as may be determined by regulations [Section 9].

Functions of Board

It shall be the duty of the Board to protect the interests of investors in securities and to promote the development of, and to regulate the securities market, by such measures as it thinks fit. To achieve this, the Board may provide for

1. regulating the business in stock exchanges and any other securities markets;
2. registering and regulating the working of stock brokers, sub-brokers, share transfer agents, bankers to an issue, trustees of trust deeds, registrars to an issue, merchant bankers, underwriters, portfolio managers, investment advisers and such other intermediaries who may be associated with securities markets in any manner;
   (a) registering and regulating the working of the depositories, participants, custodians of securities, foreign institutional investors, credit rating agencies, and such other intermediaries as the Board may, by notification, specify in this behalf;
3. registering and regulating the working of venture capital funds and collective investment schemes, including mutual funds;
4. promoting and regulating self-regulatory organizations;
5. prohibiting fraudulent and unfair trade practices relating to securities markets;
6. promoting investors' education and training of intermediaries of securities markets;
7. prohibiting insider trading in securities;
8. regulating substantial acquisition of shares and takeover of companies;
9. calling for information from, undertaking inspection, conducting inquiries and audits of the stock exchanges, mutual funds, other persons associated with the securities market, intermediaries and self-regulatory organizations in the securities market;
10. performing such functions and exercising such powers under the provisions of the Securities Contracts (Regulation) Act, 1956, as may be delegated to it by the Central Government;
11. levying fees or other charges for carrying out the purposes of this section;
12. conducting research for the above purposes; (la) calling from or furnishing to any such agencies, as may be specified by the Board, such information as may be considered necessary by it for the efficient discharge of its functions;
13. performing such other functions as may be prescribed [Section 11].

Board to Regulate or Prohibit Issue of Prospectus

1. Without prejudice to the provisions of the Companies Act, 2013, the Board may, for the protection of investors
   (a) specify, by regulations
      (i) the matters relating to issue of capital, transfer of securities, and other matters incidental thereto; and

(ii) the manner in which such matters shall be disclosed by the companies;

(b) by general or special orders

(i) prohibit any company from issuing prospectus, any offer document, or advertisement soliciting money from the public for the issue of securities;

(ii) specify the conditions subject to which the prospectus, such offer document or advertisement, if not prohibited, may be issued.

2. Without prejudice to the provisions of Section 21 of the Securities Contracts (Regulation) Act, 1956, the Board may specify the requirements for listing and transfer of securities and other matters incidental thereto [Section 11A].

Power to Issue Directions

If after making or causing to be made an enquiry, the Board is satisfied that it is necessary

1. in the interest of investors, or orderly development of securities market; or
2. to prevent the affairs of any intermediary or other persons referred to in Section 12 being conducted in a manner detrimental to the interest of investors or securities market; or
3. to secure the proper management of any such intermediary or person,

it may issue such directions

(a) to any person or class of persons referred to in Section 12, or associated with the securities market; or

(b) to any company in respect of matters specified in Section 11A, as may be appropriate in the interests of investors in securities and the securities market [Section 11B].

Power to Order Investigations

1. Where the Board has reasonable ground to believe that:

(a) the transactions in securities are being dealt with in a manner detrimental to the investors or the securities market; or

(b) any intermediary or any person associated with the securities market has violated any of the provisions of this Act or the rules or the regulations made or directions issued by the Board thereunder.

It may, at any time by order in writing, direct any person (hereafter in this section referred to as the Investigating Authority) specified in the order to investigate the affairs of such intermediary or persons associated with the securities market and to report thereon to the Board.

2. Without prejudice to the provisions of Sections 235 to 241 of the Companies Act, 1956, it shall be the duty of every manager, managing director, officer and other employee of the company, and every intermediary referred to in Section 12 or every person associated with the securities market to preserve and to produce to the Investigating Authority or any person authorised by it in this behalf, all the books, registers, other documents and record of, or relating to, the company or, as the case may be, of or relating to, the intermediary or such person, which are in their custody or power.
3. The Investigating Authority may require any intermediary or any person associated with securities market in any manner to furnish such information to, or produce such books, or registers, or other documents, or record before it or any person authorised by it in this behalf as it may consider necessary if the furnishing of such information or the production of such books, or registers, or other documents, or record is relevant or necessary for the purposes of its investigation.
4. The Investigating Authority may keep in its custody any books, registers, other documents and record produced under sub-Section (2) or sub-section (3) for six months and thereafter shall return the same to any intermediary or any person associated with securities market by whom or on whose behalf the books, registers, other documents, and record are produced:

Provided that the Investigating Authority may call for any book, register, other document, and record if they are needed again.

Provided further that if the person on whose behalf the books, registers, other documents, and record are produced requires certified copies of the books, registers, other documents, and record produced before the Investigating Authority, it shall give certified copies of such books, registers, other documents, and record to such person or on whose behalf the books, registers, other documents, and record were produced.

5. Any person, directed to make an investigation under sub-section (1), may examine on oath, any manager, managing director, officer and other employee of any intermediary or any person associated with securities market in any manner, in relation to the affairs of his business and may administer an oath accordingly and for that purpose may require any of those persons to appear before it personally.
6. If any person fails without reasonable cause or refuses
   (a) to produce to the Investigating Authority or any person authorised by it in this behalf any book, register, other document, and record which is his duty under sub-section (2) or sub-section (3) to produce; or
   (b) to furnish any information which is his duty under sub-section (3) to furnish; or
   (c) to appear before the Investigating Authority personally when required to do so under sub-section (5) or to answer any question which is put to him by the Investigating Authority in pursuance of that sub-section; or
   (d) to sign the notes of any examination referred to in sub-section (7), he shall be punishable with imprisonment for a term which may extend to one year, or with fine, which may extend to ₹1 crore, or with both, and also with a further fine which may extend to ₹5 lakh for every day after the first during which the failure or refusal continues.
7. Notes of any examination under sub-section (5) shall be taken down in writing and shall be read over to, or by, and signed by, the person examined, and may thereafter be used in evidence against him.
8. Where in the course of investigation, the Investigating Authority has reasonable ground to believe that the books, registers, other documents and record of, or relating to, any intermediary or any person associated with securities market in any manner, may be destroyed, mutilated, altered, falsified or secreted, the Investigating Authority may make an application to the Judicial Magistrate of the first class having jurisdiction for an order for the seizure of such books, registers, other documents, and record.
9. After considering the application and hearing the Investigating Authority, if necessary, the Magistrate may, by order, authorise the Investigating Authority
   (a) to enter, with such assistance, as may be required, the place or places where such books, registers, other documents and record are kept;
   (b) to search that place or those places in the manner specified in the order; and
   (c) to seize books, registers, other documents and record, it considers necessary for the purposes of the investigation:

   Provided that the Magistrate shall not authorise seizure of books, registers, other documents and record, of any listed public company or a public company (not being the intermediaries specified under Section 12) which intends to get its securities listed on any recognised stock exchange unless such company indulges in insider trading or market manipulation.
10. The Investigating Authority shall keep in its custody the books, registers, other documents and record seised under this section for such period not later than the conclusion of the investigation as it considers necessary and thereafter shall return the same to the company or the other body corporate, or, as the case may be, to the managing director or the manager or any other person, from whose custody or power they were seised and inform the Magistrate of such return:

    Provided that the Investigating Authority may, before returning such books, registers, other documents, and record as aforesaid, place identification marks on them or any part thereof.
11. Save as otherwise provided in this section, every search or seizure made under this section shall be carried out in accordance with the provisions of the Code of Criminal Procedure, 1973, relating to searches or seizures made under that Code [Section 11C].

Cease and Desist Order

If the Board finds, after causing an inquiry to be made, that any person has violated, or is likely to violate, any provisions of this Act, or any rules or regulations made thereunder, it may pass an order requiring such person to cease and desist from committing or causing such violation:

Provided that the Board shall not pass such order in respect of any listed public company or a public company (other than the intermediaries specified under Section 12) which intends to get its securities listed on any recognised stock exchange unless the Board has reasonable grounds to believe that such company has indulged in insider trading or market manipulation [Section 11D].

Registration of Stock Brokers, Share Transfer Agents

1. No stock broker, sub-broker, share transfer agent, banker to an issue, trustee of trust deed, registrar to an issue, merchant banker, underwriter, portfolio manager, investment adviser, and such other intermediary who may be associated with securities market shall buy, sell, or deal in securities except under, and in accordance with, the conditions of a certificate of registration obtained from the Board in accordance with the regulations made under this Act:

   However, a person buying or selling securities or otherwise dealing with the securities market as a stock broker, sub-broker, share transfer agent, banker to an issue, trustee of trust deed, registrar to an issue, merchant banker, underwriter, portfolio manager, investment adviser, and such other intermediary who may be associated with securities market immediately before the establishment of the Board for which no registration certificate was necessary prior to such establishment, may continue to do so for a period of three months from such establishment or, if he has made an application for such registration within the said period of three months, till the disposal of such application.

   Provided further that any certificate of registration, obtained immediately before the commencement of the Securities Laws (Amendment) Act, 1995, shall be deemed to have been obtained from the Board in accordance with the regulations providing for such registration.

   (a) No depository, participant, custodian of securities, foreign institutional investor, credit rating agency or any other intermediary associated with the securities market as the Board may by notification in this behalf specify, shall buy or sell or deal in securities except under and in accordance with the conditions of a certificate of registration obtained from the Board in accordance with the regulations made under this Act:

   Provided that a person buying or selling securities or otherwise dealing with the securities market as a depository, participant, custodian of securities, foreign institutional investor, or credit rating agency immediately before the commencement of the Securities Laws (Amendment) Act, 1995, for which no certificate of registration was required prior to such commencement, may continue to buy or sell securities or otherwise deal with the securities market until such time regulations are made under clause (d) of sub-section (2) of Section 30.

   (b) No person shall sponsor or cause to be sponsored or carry on or cause to be carried on any venture capital funds or collective investment schemes including mutual funds, unless he obtains a certificate of registration from the Board in accordance with the regulations:

   Provided that any person sponsoring or causing to be sponsored, carrying on or causing to be carried on any venture capital funds or collective investment schemes operating in the securities market immediately before the commencement of the Securities Laws (Amendment) Act, 1995, for which no certificate of registration was required prior to such commencement, may continue to operate till such time regulations are made under clause (d) of sub-section (2) of Section 30.

2. Every application for registration shall be in such manner and on payment of such fees as may be determined by regulations.
3. The Board may, by order, suspend or cancel a certificate of registration in such manner as may be determined by regulations.

However, no order under this sub-section shall be made unless the person concerned has been given a reasonable opportunity of being heard [Section 12].

Prohibition of Deceptive Devices, Insider Trading, and Substantial Acquisition of Securities

Deceptive devices: Any scheme, practice, or course of business which operates or would operate as a fraud or deceit upon any prospective investor.

Insider: Every director or any member of the staff of a company.

The Security regulator attempts to prohibit use of deceptive devices aimed at defrauding gullible investors Act. Besides, insider trading is a criminal offence under the Act. Insider trading, in this behalf, is the trading of a company's securities by individuals (directors or members of the staff of the issuer company) with access to confidential or non-public information about the company. Taking advantage of this privileged access is considered a breach of the individual's fiduciary duty and therefore is a criminal act under the Sebi Act. A company is required to report trading by corporate officers, directors, or other company members with significant access to privileged information to the Sebi or be publicly disclosed. From an economic public policy perspective, insider trading is viewed socially undesirable because it increases the cost of capital for securities traders and therefore depresses economic growth.

As per the Act, no person shall directly or indirectly

1. use or employ, in connection with the issue, purchase or sale of any securities listed or proposed to be listed on a recognised stock exchange, any manipulative or deceptive device or contrivance in contravention of the provisions of this Act or the rules or the regulations made thereunder;
2. employ any device, scheme or artifice to defraud in connection with issue or dealing in securities which are listed or proposed to be listed on a recognised stock exchange;
3. engage in any act, practice, course of business which operates or would operate as fraud or deceit upon any person, in connection with the issue, dealing in securities which are listed or proposed to be listed on a recognised stock exchange, in contravention of the provisions of this Act or the rules or the regulations made thereunder;
4. engage in insider trading;
5. deal in securities while in possession of material or non-public information or communicate such material or non-public information to any other person, in a manner which is in contravention of the provisions of this Act or the rules or the regulations made thereunder;
6. acquire control of any company or securities more than the percentage of equity share capital of a company whose securities are listed or proposed to be listed on a recognised stock exchange in contravention of the regulations made under this Act [Section 12A].

Insider trading: Trading in securities of a public company by individuals (directors and staff of the issuer company) with access to confidential or nonpublic information.

Finance, Accounts, and Audit

The provisions concerning finance, accounts, and audit of Sebi have been explained as under.

Grants by the Central Government

The Central Government may, after due appropriation made by Parliament by law in this behalf, make to the Board grants of such sums of money as that Government may think fit for being utilised for the purposes of this Act [Section 13].

Fund

1. There shall be constituted a Fund to be called the Securities and Exchange Board of India General Fund and there shall be credited thereto
   (a) all grants, fees, and charges received by the Board under this Act;
   (b) all sums received by the Board from such other sources as may be decided upon by the Central Government.
2. The Fund shall be applied for meeting
   (a) the salaries, allowances, and other remuneration of members, officers and other employees of the Board;

(b) the expenses of the Board in the discharge of its functions under Section 11;
(c) the expenses on objects and for purposes authorised by this Act [Section 14].

Accounts and Audit

1. The Board shall maintain proper accounts and other relevant records and prepare an annual statement of accounts in such form as may be prescribed by the Central Government in consultation with the Comptroller and Auditor General of India.
2. The accounts of the Board shall be audited by the Comptroller and Auditor General of India at such intervals as may be specified by him and any expenditure incurred in connection with such audit shall be payable by the Board to the Comptroller and Auditor General of India.
3. The Comptroller and Auditor General of India and any other person appointed by him in connection with the audit of the accounts of the Board shall have the same rights and privileges and authority in connection with such audit as the Comptroller and Auditor General generally has in connection with the audit of the Government accounts and, in particular, shall have the right to demand the production of books, accounts, connected vouchers, and other documents and papers and to inspect any of the offices of the Board.
4. The accounts of the Board as certified by the Comptroller and Auditor General of India or any other person appointed by him in this behalf together with the audit report thereon shall be forwarded annually to the Central Government and that Government shall cause the same to be laid before each House of Parliament [Section 15].

Penalties and Adjudication

A brief account of provisions for penalties and adjudication under the Act is given below.

Penalty for Failure to Furnish Information, Return

If any person, who is required under this Act or any rules or regulations made thereunder

1. to furnish any document, return or report to the Board, fails to furnish the same, he shall be liable to a penalty of ₹1 lakh for each day during which such failure continues or ₹1 crore, whichever is less;
2. to file any return or furnish any information, books or other documents within the time specified in the regulations, fails to file return or furnish the same within the time specified in the regulations, he shall be liable to a penalty of ₹1 lakh for each day during which such failure continues or ₹1 crore, whichever is less;
3. to maintain books of accounts or records, fails to maintain the same, he shall be liable to a penalty of ₹1 lakh for each day during which such failure continues or ₹1 crore, whichever is less [Section 15A].

Penalty for Failure by Any Person to Enter into Agreement with Clients

If any person, who is registered as an intermediary and is required under this Act or any rules or regulations made thereunder to enter into an agreement with his client, fails to enter into such agreement, he shall be liable to a penalty of ₹1 lakh for each day during which such failure continues or ₹1 crore, whichever is less [Section 15B].

Penalty for Failure to Redress Investors' Grievances

If any listed company or any person who is registered as an intermediary, after having been called upon by the Board in writing, to redress the grievances of investors, fails to redress such grievances within the time specified by the Board, such company or intermediary shall be liable to a penalty of ₹1 lakh for each day during which such failure continues or ₹1 crore, whichever is less [Section 15C].

Penalty for Certain Defaults in the Case of Mutual Funds

If any person, who is

1. required under this Act or any rules or regulations made thereunder to obtain a certificate of registration from the Board for sponsoring or carrying on any collective investment scheme, including mutual funds, sponsors or carries on any collec-

tive investment scheme, including mutual funds, without obtaining such certificate of registration, he shall be liable to a penalty of ₹1 lakh for each day during which he sponsors or carries on any such collective investment scheme including mutual funds, or ₹1 crore, whichever is less;
2. registered with the Board as a collective investment scheme, including mutual funds, for sponsoring or carrying on any investment scheme, fails to comply with the terms and conditions of certificate of registration, he shall be liable to a penalty of ₹1 lakh for each day during which such failure continues or ₹1 crore, whichever is less;
3. registered with the Board as a collective investment scheme, including mutual funds, fails to make an application for listing of its schemes as provided for in the regulations governing such listing, he shall be liable to a penalty of ₹1 lakh for each day during which such failure continues or ₹1 crore, whichever is less;
4. registered as a collective investment scheme including mutual funds fails to dispatch unit certificates of any scheme in the manner provided in the regulation governing such dispatch, he shall be liable to a penalty of ₹1 lakh for each day during which such failure continues or ₹1 crore, whichever is less;
5. registered as a collective investment scheme, including mutual funds, fails to refund the application monies paid by the investors within the period specified in the regulations, he shall be liable to pay a penalty of ₹1 lakh for each day during which such failure continues or ₹1 crore, whichever is less;
6. registered as a collective investment scheme, including mutual funds, fails to invest money collected by such collective investment schemes in the manner or within the period specified in the regulations, he shall be liable to a penalty of ₹1 lakh for each day during which such failure continues or ₹1 crore, whichever is less [Section 15D].

Penalty for Failure to Observe Regulations by Asset Management Company

Where any asset management company of a mutual fund registered under this Act, fails to comply with any of the regulations providing for restrictions on the activities of the asset management companies, such asset management company shall be liable to a penalty of ₹1 lakh for each day during which such failure continues or ₹1 crore, whichever is less [Section 15E].

Penalty for Failure in the Case of Stock Brokers

If any person, who is registered as a stock broker under this Act

1. fails to issue contract notes in the form and in the manner specified by the stock exchange of which such broker is a member, he shall be liable to a penalty not exceeding five times the amount for which the contract note was required to be issued by that broker;
2. fails to deliver any security or fails to make payment of the amount due to the investor in the manner within the period specified in the regulations, he shall be liable to a penalty of ₹1 lakh for each day during which such failure continues or ₹1 crore, whichever is less;
3. charges an amount of brokerage which is in excess of the brokerage specified in the regulations, he shall be liable to a penalty of ₹1 lakh or five times the amount of brokerage charged in excess of the specified brokerage, whichever is higher [Section 15F].

Penalty for Insider Trading

If any insider who

1. either on his own behalf or on behalf of any other person, deals in securities of a body corporate listed on any stock exchange on the basis of any unpublished price-sensitive information; or
2. communicates any unpublished price-sensitive information to any person, with or without his request for such information except as required in the ordinary course of business or under any law; or
3. counsels, or procures for any other person to deal in any securities of any body corporate on the basis of unpublished price-sensitive information,

shall be liable to a penalty of ₹25 crore or three times the amount of profits made out of insider trading, whichever is higher [Section 15G].

Penalty for Non-disclosure of Acquisition of Shares and Takeovers

If any person, who is required under this Act or any rules or regulations made thereunder, fails to

1. disclose the aggregate of his shareholding in the body corporate before he acquires any shares of that body corporate; or
2. make a public announcement to acquire shares at a minimum price; or
3. make a public offer by sending letter of offer to the shareholders of the concerned company; or
4. make a payment of consideration to the shareholders who sold their shares pursuant to letter of offer; he shall be liable to a penalty of ₹25 crore or three times the amount of profits made out of such failure, whichever is higher [Section 15H].

Penalty for Fraudulent and Unfair Trade Practices

If any person indulges in fraudulent and unfair trade practices relating to securities, he shall be liable to a penalty of ₹25 crore or three times the amount of profits made out of such practices, whichever is higher [Section 15HA].

Penalty for Contravention Where No Separate Penalty Has Been Provided

Whoever fails to comply with any provision of this Act, the rules or the regulations made or directions issued by the Board thereunder for which no separate penalty has been provided, shall be liable to a penalty which may extend to ₹1 crore [Section 15HB].

Power to Adjudicate

1. For the purpose of adjudging under Sections 15A, 15B, 15C, 15D, 15E, 15F, 15G, 15H, 15HA, and 15HB, the Board shall appoint any of its officers not below the rank of a Division Chief to be an adjudicating officer for holding an inquiry in the prescribed manner after giving any person concerned a reasonable opportunity of being heard for the purpose of imposing any penalty.
2. While holding an inquiry, the adjudicating officer shall have the power to summon and enforce the attendance of any person acquainted with the facts and circumstances of the case to give evidence or to produce any document which in the opinion of the adjudicating officer, may be useful for or relevant to the subject matter of the inquiry and if, on such inquiry, he is satisfied that the person has failed to comply with the provisions of any of the sections specified in sub-section (1), he may impose such penalty as he thinks fit in accordance with the provisions of any of those sections [Section 15I].

Factors to Be Taken into Account by the Adjudicating Officer

While adjudging quantum of penalty under Section 15I, the adjudicating officer shall have due regard to the following factors:

1. The amount of disproportionate gain or unfair advantage, wherever quantifiable, made as a result of the default.
2. The amount of loss caused to an investor or group of investors as a result of the default.
3. The repetitive nature of the default [Section 15J].

Crediting Sums Realised by Way of Penalties to Consolidated Fund of India

All sums realised by way of penalties under this Act shall be credited to the Consolidated Fund of India [Section 15JA].

Establishment, Jurisdiction, Authority, and Procedure of Appellate Tribunal

Establishment of Securities Appellate Tribunals

1. The Central Government shall, by notification, establish one or more Appellate Tribunals to be known as the Securities Appellate Tribunal to exercise the jurisdiction, powers and authority conferred on such Tribunal by or under this Act or any other law for the time being in force.

2. The Central Government shall also specify in the notification referred to in sub-section (1), the matters and places in relation to which the Securities Appellate Tribunal may exercise jurisdiction [Section 15K].

Composition of Securities Appellate Tribunal

A Securities Appellate Tribunal shall consist of a Presiding Officer and two other Members, to be appointed, by notification, by the Central Government.

However, the Securities Appellate Tribunal, consisting of one person only, established before the commencement of the Securities and Exchange Board of India (Amendment) Act, 2002, shall continue to exercise the jurisdiction, powers and authority conferred on it by or under this Act or any other law for the time being in force till two other members are appointed under this section [Section 15L].

Qualification for Appointment As Presiding Officer or Member of the Securities Appellate Tribunal

1. A person shall not be qualified for appointment as the Presiding Officer of a Securities Appellate Tribunal unless he is a sitting or retired Judge of the Supreme Court or a sitting or retired Chief Justice of a High Court.
2. A person shall not be qualified for appointment as Member of a Securities Appellate Tribunal unless he is a person of ability, integrity and standing who has shown capacity in dealing with problems relating to securities market and has qualification and experience of corporate law, securities laws, finance, economics, or accountancy:

   Provided that a member of the Board or any person holding a post at senior management level equivalent to Executive Director in the Board shall not be appointed as Presiding Officer or Member of a Securities Appellate Tribunal during his service or tenure as such with the Board or within two years from the date on which he ceases to hold office as such in the Board [Section 15M].

Tenure of Office of Presiding Officer and Other Members of Securities Appellate Tribunal

The Presiding Officer and every other Member of a Securities Appellate Tribunal shall hold office for a term of five years from the date on which he enters upon his office and shall be eligible for re-appointment:

However, no person shall hold office as the Presiding Officer/Member of the Securities Appellate Tribunal after he has attained the age of 68 years/62 years [Section 15M].

Salary and Allowances and Other Terms and Conditions of Service of Presiding Officers

The salary and allowances payable to and the other terms and conditions of service (including pension, gratuity and other retirement benefits) of the Presiding Officer and any other Member of a Securities Appellate Tribunal shall be such as may be prescribed:

Provided that neither the salary and allowances nor the other terms and conditions of service of the Presiding Officer and other Members of a Securities Appellate Tribunal shall be varied to their disadvantage after appointment [Section 15O].

Filling Up of Vacancies

If, for reason other than temporary absence, any vacancy occurs in the office of the Presiding Officer or any other Member, then the Central Government shall appoint another person in accordance with the provisions of this Act to fill the vacancy, and the proceedings may be continued before the Securities Appellate Tribunal from the stage at which the vacancy is filled [Section 15P].

Resignation and Removal

1. The Presiding Officer or any other Member of a Securities Appellate Tribunal may, by notice in writing under his hand addressed to the Central Government, resign his office:

   Provided that the Presiding Officer or any other Member shall, unless he is permitted by the Central Government to relinquish his office sooner, continue to hold office, until the expiry of three months from the date of receipt of such notice or until a person duly appointed as his successor enters upon his office or until the expiry of his term of office, whichever is the earliest.

2. The Presiding Officer or any other Member of a Securities Appellate Tribunal shall not be removed from his office except by an order by the Central Government on the ground of proved misbehaviour or incapacity after inquiry made by a Judge of the Supreme Court, in which the Presiding Officer or any other Member concerned has been informed of the charges against him and given a reasonable opportunity of being heard in respect of these charges.
3. The Central Government may, by rules, regulate the procedure for the investigation of misbehaviour or incapacity of the Presiding Officer or any other Member [Section 15Q].

Appeal to the Securities Appellate Tribunal

1. Save as provided in sub-section (2), any person aggrieved
   (a) by an order of the Board made, on and after the commencement of the Securities Laws (Second Amendment) Act, 1999, under this Act, or the rules or regulations made thereunder; or
   (b) by an order made by an adjudicating officer under this Act, may prefer an appeal to a Securities Appellate Tribunal having jurisdiction in the matter.
2. No appeal shall lie to the Securities Appellate Tribunal from an order made
   (a) by the Board on and after the commencement of the Securities Laws (Second Amendment) Act, 1999;
   (b) by an adjudicating officer, with the consent of the parties.
3. Every appeal under sub-section (1) shall be filed within a period of 45 days from the date on which a copy of the order made by the Board or the adjudicating officer, as the case may be, is received by him and it shall be in such form and be accompanied by such fee as may be prescribed:

   Provided that the Securities Appellate Tribunal may entertain an appeal after the expiry of the said period of 45 days if it is satisfied that there was sufficient cause for not filing it within that period.
4. On receipt of an appeal under sub-section (1), the Securities Appellate Tribunal may, after giving the parties to the appeal, an opportunity of being heard, pass such orders thereon as it thinks fit, confirming, modifying or setting aside the order appealed against.
5. The Securities Appellate Tribunal shall send a copy of every order made by it to the Board, the parties to the appeal and to the concerned Adjudicating Officer.
6. The appeal filed before the Securities Appellate Tribunal under sub-section (1) shall be dealt with by it as expeditiously as possible and endeavour shall be made by it to dispose of the appeal finally within six months from the date of receipt of the appeal [Section 15T].

Procedure and Powers of the Securities Appellate Tribunal

1. The Securities Appellate Tribunal shall not be bound by the procedure laid down by the Code of Civil Procedure, 1908, but shall be guided by the principles of natural justice and, subject to the other provisions of this Act and of any rules, the Securities Appellate Tribunal shall have powers to regulate their own procedure including the places at which they shall have their sittings.
2. The Securities Appellate Tribunal shall have, for the purposes of discharging their functions under this Act, the same powers as are vested in a civil court under the Code of Civil Procedure, 1908 (5 of 1908), while trying a suit [Section 15U].

Right to Legal Representation

The appellant may either appear in person or authorise one or more chartered accountants or company secretaries or cost accountants or legal practitioners or any of its officers to present his or its case before the Securities Appellate Tribunal [Section 15V].

Civil Court Not to Have Jurisdiction

No civil court shall have jurisdiction to entertain any suit or proceeding in respect of any matter which an Adjudicating Officer appointed under this Act or a Securities Appellate Tribunal constituted under this Act is empowered by or under this Act to determine and no injunction shall be granted by any court or other authority in respect of any action taken or to be taken in pursuance of any power conferred by or under this Act:

However, any person aggrieved by any decision or order of the Securities Appellate Tribunal may file an appeal to the Supreme Court within 60 days from the date of communication of the decision or order of the Securities Appellate Tribunal to him on any question of law arising out of such order:

Provided that the Supreme Court may, if it is satisfied that the applicant was prevented by sufficient cause from filing the appeal within the said period, allow it to be filed within a further period not exceeding 60 days [Section 15Y].

Miscellaneous Provisions

Power of Central Government to Issue Directions

1. Without prejudice to the foregoing provisions of this Act or the Depositories Act, 1996, the Board shall, in exercise of its powers or the performance of its functions under this Act, be bound by such directions on questions of policy as the Central Government may give in writing to it from time to time:

   Provided that the Board shall, as far as practicable, be given an opportunity to express its views before any direction is given under this sub-section.
2. The decision of the Central Government whether a question is one of policy or not shall be final [Section 16].

Power of Central Government to Supersede the Board

1. If at any time the Central Government is of opinion
   (a) that on account of grave emergency, the Board is unable to discharge the functions and duties imposed on it by or under the provisions of this Act; or
   (b) that the Board has persistently made default in complying with any direction issued by the Central Government under this Act or in the discharge of the functions and duties imposed on it by or under the provisions of this Act and as a result of such default the financial position of the Board or the administration of the Board has deteriorated; or
   (c) that circumstances exist which render it necessary in the public interest so to do, the Central Government may, by notification, supersede the Board for such period, not exceeding six months, as may be specified in the notification.
2. Upon the publication of a notification under sub-section (1) superseding the Board
   (a) all the members shall, as from the date of supersession, vacate their offices as such;
   (b) all the powers, functions, and duties which may, by or under the provisions of this Act, be exercised or discharged by or on behalf of the Board, shall until the Board is reconstituted under sub-section (3), be exercised and discharged by such person or persons as the Central Government may direct; and
   (c) all property owned or controlled by the Board shall, until the Board is reconstituted under sub-section (3), vest in the Central Government.
3. On the expiration of the period of supersession specified in the notification issued under sub-section (1), the Central Government may reconstitute the Board by a fresh appointment and in such case any person or persons who vacated their offices under clause (a) of sub-section (2), shall not be deemed disqualified for appointment:

   Provided that the Central Government may, at any time, before the expiration of the period of supersession, take action under this sub-section.
4. The Central Government shall cause a notification issued under sub-section (1) and a full report of any action taken under this section and the circumstances leading to such action to be laid before each House of Parliament at the earliest [Section 17].

Exercises

I. Objective-type Questions

1. Sebi, for the protection of investors, by general or special order, may
   (a) Specify the matters relating to issue of capital, transfer of securities, and other matters incidental thereto
   (b) Specify the manner in which such matters shall be disclosed by the companies
   (c) Prohibit any company from issuing prospectus, any offer document, or advertisement soliciting money from the public for the issue of securities
   (d) Provide for all of the above

2. The Board (Sebi) may direct the Investigating Authority to investigate the affairs of an intermediary or persons associated with the securities market and to report thereon to it, where the Board has reasonable ground to believe that
   (a) The transactions in securities are being dealt with in a manner detrimental to the investors or the securities market
   (b) Any intermediary or any person associated with the securities market has violated any of the provisions of this Act
   (c) In either of the above cases
   (d) In none of the above [(a) and (b)] cases

3. Securities and Exchange Board of India General Fund (Fund) shall be applied for meeting
   (a) The salaries, allowances, and other remuneration of members, officers, and other employees
   (b) The expenses of the Board in the discharge of its functions under Section 11
   (c) The expenses on objects and for purposes authorised by the Sebi Act
   (d) All of the above

4. If any person, who is required under Sebi Act or any rules or regulations made thereunder, to furnish any document, return or report to the Board, fails to furnish the same, he shall be liable to a penalty of
   (a) ₹1 lakh
   (b) ₹1 lakh for each day during which such failure continues or ₹1 crore, whichever is less
   (c) ₹1 lakh for each day during which such failure continues
   (d) ₹5000 for each day during which such failure continues or ₹1 crore, whichever is less

5. If any insider who, either on his own behalf or on behalf of any other person, deals in securities of a body corporate listed on any stock exchange on the basis of any unpublished price sensitive information, shall be liable to a penalty of
   (a) ₹25 crore or three times the amount of profits made out of insider trading, whichever is higher
   (b) ₹5 crore or three times the amount of profits made out of insider trading, whichever is higher
   (c) ₹1 crore or three times the amount of profits made out of insider trading, whichever is higher
   (d) ₹25 lakh or three times the amount of profits made out of insider trading, whichever is higher

II. Review Questions

1. Define and briefly explain the following terms under the Sebi Act:
   (i) Fund
   (ii) Board
   (iii) Notification
   (iv) Collective investment scheme

2. Discuss the powers and functions of Sebi Board.

3. Under what circumstances can Board exercise its power of investigation? What is the duty of company management towards investigation? Discuss also powers of Board in relation to investigation.

4. Briefly explain provisions made under Sebi Act concerning prohibition of manipulative and deceptive devices, insider trading, and substantial acquisition of securities or control.

5. What penalty can be imposed under Sebi Act on a person for the following under the Act or any rules or regulations made thereunder?
   (i) Failure to furnish information, return, etc.
   (ii) Failure to redress investors' grievances
   (iii) Failure to observe rules and regulations by an asset management company
   (iv) Insider trading

6. Who has the power to adjudicate a person under Sections 15A, 15 B, 15C, 15D, 15E, 15F, and 15G of Sebi Act? Discuss the factors to be taken into account by the adjudicating officer while adjudging quantum of penalty under Section 15I.

Answers to Objective-type Questions

1. (c) 2. (c) 3. (d) 4. (b) 5. (a)

23 Chapter in Review

LEARNING OUTCOMES

LO 1 Sebi Act: What it is?

LO 2 Aim and objectives of the Act

LO 3 Role and functions of Sebi

LO 4 Powers of the Board

KEY TERMS

Board: The Securities and Exchange Board of India established under Section 3 of the Sebi Act.

Chairman: Chairman of the Board.

Collective investment scheme: Any arrangement which satisfies the conditions specified in Section 11AA of the Sebi Act.

Existing securities and exchange board: The Securities and Exchange Board of India constituted under the Resolution of the Government of India No.1 dated 12 April 1988.

Fund: Fund constituted under Section 14 of the Sebi Act.

Member: A member of the Board and includes the Chairman.

Regulations: Regulations made by the Board under the Sebi Act.

Securities: Instruments of investments which primarily include shares, stocks, bonds, debentures, debenture stocks, etc.

Deceptive devices: Any scheme, practice, or course of business which operates or would operate as a fraud or deceit upon any prospective investor.

Insider: Every director or any member of the staff of a company.

Insider trading: Trading in securities of a public company by individuals (directors and staff of the issuer company) with access to confidential or nonpublic information.

LO 1 The Sebi Act, 1992 is an Indian legislation enacted by the Parliament of India which eventually paved the way of establishment of 'Securities and Exchange Board of India' (Sebi or say 'Board') for regulation and development of securities market in India.

LO 2 The market regulator or security watchdog (Sebi Act) seeks to protect the interests of investors in securities and to promote the development of, and regulate the securities market and for the matters connected therewith or incidental thereto.

LO 3 To achieve its objectives, the regulator (Sebi) may provide for (a) registering and regulating the working of stock brokers, bankers to an issue, underwriters, and other related parties; (b) registering and regulating the working of venture capital funds and collective investment schemes including mutual funds; (c) prohibiting fraudulent and unfair trade practices relating tosecurities markets; (d) promoting investors' education and training of intermediaries of securities markets; (e) prohibiting insider trading in securities; regulating substantial acquisition of shares and takeover of companies; and (f) performing such functions and exercising such powers under the provisions of the Securities Contracts (Regulation) Act, 1956, delegated to it by the Central Government from time to time.

LO 4 The Board (Sebi) is empowered to order for investigation where it has reasonable ground to believe that the transactions in securities are being dealt with in a manner detrimental to the investors' interest or the securities market.

CHAPTER

24 The Information Technology Act, 2000

Learning Objectives

LO 1 What is IT Act, 2000?

LO 2 Aim of the IT Act

LO 3 Issues that the IT Act addresses

LO 4 Documents or transactions unfazed by IT Act

In the contemporary digital era, electronic communication provides a cheaper, easy to operate and retrieve, and faster processing of transactions. The Information Technology (IT) Act, 2000, is an important legislation in this behalf that seeks to provide legal recognition for transactions carried out by means of electronic data interchange and other means of electronic communication, commonly referred to as 'electronic commerce' or E-Commerce. It involves use of alternatives to paper-based methods of communication and storage of information to facilitate electronic filing of documents, with the agencies concerned. IT Act allows unrestricted monitoring of all electronic communication, even for non-cognizable offences. This Act aims to provide the legal infrastructure for e-commerce in India. Though, India lacks a full fledged ICT framework for implementation of e-governance, yet IT Act *per se* is playing an important role to facilitate e-governance by giving legal recognition to and promoting online filing of income-tax returns, corporate returns etc. The Act extends to the whole of India and it also applies to any offence or contravention thereunder committed outside India by any person. The Government of India has brought major amendments to the Information Technology Act, 2000, in the form of the Information Technology Amendment Act, 2008. The new version of the IT Act has provided additional focus on information security. It has added several new sections on offences including cyber terrorism and data protection. Department of Electronics and Information Technology under the Ministry of Communication and Information Technology concerns itself with administration of the IT Act, 2000, and other IT-related laws.

IT Act: Aim and Objectives

The Information Technology Act, 2000, is an important law relating to Indian cyber laws. It aims at promoting E-Commerce and facilitating E-Governance. The Act strives to achieve the following objectives:

1. To give legal recognition to transactions done by electronic way or by use of the internet.
2. To grant legal recognition to digital signature for accepting any agreement via computer.
3. To provide facility of filling documents online.
4. To authorise any undertaking to store their data in electronic storage.
5. To prevent cyber crime by imposing high penalty for such crimes and protect privacy of internet users.
6. To give legal recognition for keeping books of account by bankers and other undertakings in electronic form.

Scope of the Act

The IT Act, 2000, which came into force with effect from October 17, 2000, extends to whole of India and applies to any offence or contravention committed within or outside India by any person irrespective of his nationality, provided such offence or contravention involves a computer, computer system and a network located in India.

The Act attempts to address the following issues:

1. Legal recognition of electronic documents or records
2. Legal recognition of digital signatures
3. Offences and contraventions
4. Justice dispensation systems for cybercrimes

As per Section 1(4), provisions of this Act shall not apply to the following documents or transactions:

1. Execution of a negotiable instrument (other than a cheque) as defined in Section 13 of the Negotiable Instruments Act, 1881.
2. Execution of a power-of-attorney as defined in Section 1A of the Powers-of-Attorney Act, 1882.
3. Creation of a trust as defined in Section 3 of the Indian Trusts Act, 1882.
4. Execution of a will as defined in clause (h) of Section 2 of the Indian Succession Act, 1925 including any other testamentary disposition by whatever name called.
5. Any contract for the sale or conveyance of immovable property or any interest in such property.
6. Any such class of documents or transactions as may be notified by the Central Government in the Official Gazette [Section 4].

The probable reason for disregarding the above documents and transactions from the application of the Act is that besides such documents or transactions are required to be authenticated by manual signatures the same require special attestation and/or registration formalities.

Major Concepts

Some of the important terms used in the Information Technology Act are briefly introduced below.

Access implies gaining entry into, instructing or communicating with the logical, arithmetical, or memory function resources of a computer, computer system, or computer network.

Addressee: A person who is intended by the originator to receive the electronic record but does not include any intermediary.

Addressee is a person who is intended by the originator to receive the electronic record but does not include any intermediary.

Adjudicating Officer means an adjudicating officer appointed under Section 46(1).

Affixing Digital signature means adoption of any methodology or procedure by a person for the purpose of authenticating an electronic record by means of digital signature.

Appropriate Government means any matter

1. Enumerated in List II of the Seventh Schedule to the Constitution;
2. Relating to any State law enacted under List III of the Seventh Schedule to the Constitution, the State Government, and in any other case, the Central Government.

Asymmetric Crypto System is a system of a secure key pair consisting of a private key for creating a digital signature and a public key to verify the digital signature.

Computer network: A set of computers connected together by (i) Internet or any other communication media; and (ii) terminals for the purpose of sharing information.

Certifying Authority is a person who has been granted a licence to issue a Digital Signature Certificate under Section 24.

Certification Practice Statement is a statement issued by a Certifying Authority to specify the practices that the Certifying Authority employs in issuing Digital Signature Certificates.

Computer refers to means any electronic magnetic, optical, or other high-speed data processing device or system which performs logical, arithmetic, and memory functions by manipulations of electronic, magnetic, or optical impulses, and includes all input, output, processing, storage, computer software, or communication facilities which are connected or related to the computer in a computer system or computer network.

Computer Network implies the interconnection of one or more computers through—

1. The use of satellite, microwave, terrestrial line or other communication media; and
2. Terminals or a complex consisting of two or more interconnected computers whether or not the interconnection is continuously maintained;

Computer Resource refers to a computer, computer system, computer network, data, computer data base or software.

Computer system refers to a device or collection of devices, including input and output support devices, and excluding calculators which are not programmable and capable of being used in conjunction with external files, which contain computer programmes, electronic instructions, input data and output data, that performs logic, arithmetic, data storage and retrieval, communication control and other functions.

Data: A representation of information, knowledge, facts, concepts, or instructions which is being prepared or has been prepared in a formalised manner.

Data implies a representation of information, knowledge, facts, concepts or instructions which is being prepared or has been prepared in a formalised manner, and is intended to be processed, is being processed, or has been processed in a computer system or computer network, and may be in any form (including computer printouts magnetic or optical storage media, punched cards, punched tapes) or stored internally in the memory of the computer.

Digital signature: The authentication of any electronic record by a subscriber by means of an electronic method or procedure in accordance with Section 3 of the IT Act.

Digital Signature refers to the authentication of any electronic record by a subscriber by means of an electronic method or procedure in accordance with Section 3.

Electronic Form with reference to information refers to any information generated, sent, received, or stored in media, magnetic, optical, computer memory, micro film, computer generated micro fiche or similar device.

Electronic gazette: Official gazette published in the electronic form.

Electronic Gazette refers to the Official Gazette published in the electronic form.

Electronic Record refers to any data, record or data generated, image or sound stored, received or sent in an electronic form or micro film or computer generated micro fiche.

Information includes data, text, images, sound, voice, codes, computer programs, software and databases or micro film or computer generated micro fiche.

Intermediary, with respect to any particular electronic message, is any person who, on behalf of another person, receives, stores, or transmits that message or provides any service with respect to that message.

Key Pair, in an asymmetric crypto system, implies a private key and its mathematically related public key, which are so related that the public key can verify a digital signature created by the private key.

Originator: A person who sends, generates, stores, or transmits any electronic message or causes any electronic message to be sent, generated, stored, or transmitted to any other person.

Originator refers to a person who sends, generates, stores, or transmits any electronic message or causes any electronic message to be sent, generated, stored, or transmitted to any other person, but does not include an intermediary.

Private key: The key of a key pair used to create a digital signature.

Private Key refers to the key of a key pair used to create a digital signature.

Public key: The key of a key pair used to verify a digital signature, which is listed in the Digital Signature Certificate.

Public Key refers to the key of a key pair used to verify a digital signature, which is listed in the Digital Signature Certificate.

Secure system: Computer hardware, software, and procedure that (i) is reasonably secure from unauthorised access and misuse; (ii) provides a reasonable level of reliability and correct operation, (iii) is reasonably suited to performing the intended functions, and (iv) adheres to generally accepted security procedures.

Secure System refers to computer hardware, software, and procedure that

1. is reasonably secure from unauthorised access and misuse;
2. provides a reasonable level of reliability and correct operation;
3. is reasonably suited to performing the intended functions; and
4. adheres to generally accepted security procedures;

Important Provisions

Important provisions of the Act have been briefly explained below.

Digital Signature: Authentication of Electronic Records

A digital signature is basically a way to ensure that an electronic record or document (e- mail, spreadsheet, text file, etc.) is authentic. The Act contains the following provisions in relation to digital signature:

1. Any subscriber may authenticate an electronic record by affixing his digital signature.
2. The authentication of the electronic record shall be effected by the use of the asymmetric crypto system and hash function which envelop and transform the initial electronic record into another electronic record.

   Explanation: For the purposes of this subsection, 'hash function' means an algorithm mapping or translation of one sequence of bits into another, generally smaller, set, known as 'hash result' such that an electronic record yields the same hash result every time the algorithm is executed with the same electronic record as its input, making it computationally infeasible—

(a) to derive or reconstruct the original electronic record from the hash result produced by the algorithm;

(b) that two electronic records can produce the same hash result using the algorithm.

3. Any person by the use of a public key of the subscriber can verify the electronic record.
4. The private key and the public key are unique to the subscriber and constitute a functioning key pair [Section 3].

Electronic Governance: Legal Recognition of Electronic Records

E-Governance: The public sector's use of information and communication technologies (ICT) with the aim of improving information and service delivery, encouraging citizen participation in the decision-making process and making government more accountable, transparent and effective.

E-Governance is the public sector's use of information and communication technologies (ICT) with the aim of improving information and service delivery, encouraging citizen participation in the decision-making process and making government more accountable, transparent and effective. The three main target groups that can be distinguished in governance concepts are government, citizens and businesses/interest groups. Generally four basic models of E-Governance are available—government-to-citizen (customer), government-to-employees, government-to-government and intergovernmental (government-to-business).

Where any law provides that information or any other matter shall be in writing or in the typewritten or printed form, then, notwithstanding anything contained in such a law, the requirement shall be deemed to have been satisfied if such information or matter is

1. rendered or made available in an electronic form; and
2. accessible so as to be usable for a subsequent reference [Section 4].

Electronic Governance: Legal Recognition of Digital Signatures

A Digital Signature is the electronic or digital equivalent of a physical signature. Just as a physical signature on a paper document establishes the origin of that document, a digital signature affixed to a digital document (soft copy) establishes the origin of that digital document. Digital signatures are considered much more secure and 'fool-proof' compared to physical signatures. While, physical signatures can be easily replicated or 'forged', the technology behind digital signatures makes it virtually impossible to forge them. More specifically, in India, the IT Act provides the legal sanctity for using digital signatures.

Where any law provides that information or any other matter shall be authenticated by affixing the signature or any document shall be signed or bear the signature of any person (then, notwithstanding anything contained in such a law, the requirement shall be deemed to have been satisfied, if such information or matter is authenticated by means of a digital signature affixed in such a manner as may be prescribed by the Central Government [Section 5].

Explanation: For the purposes of this section, 'signed', with its grammatical variations and cognate expressions, shall, with reference to a person, mean affixing his hand-written signature or any mark on any document, and the expression 'signature' shall be construed accordingly.

Use of Electronic Records and Digital Signatures in Government and Its Agencies

Because of the higher security associated with digital signatures and many advantages associated with storing documents electronically (as opposed to paper), governments in many countries, including India of-course, have passed laws and regulations encouraging (and in some cases mandating) the usage of digitally signed electronic documents rather than paper documents. In India, for instance, Income-tax returns, Corporate returns etc. are to be digitally signed and uploaded electronically.

1. Where any law provides for

   (a) the filing of any form application or any other document with any office, authority, body, or agency owned or controlled by the appropriate Government in a particular manner;

(b) the issue or grant of any licence, permit, sanction, or approval by whatever name called in a particular manner;
(c) the receipt or payment of money in a particular manner, then, notwithstanding anything contained in any other law for the time being in force, such a requirement shall be deemed to have been satisfied if such filing, issue, grant, receipt or payment, as the case may be, is effected by means of such electronic form as may be prescribed by the appropriate Government.

2. The appropriate Government may, for the purposes of sub-section (1), by rules, prescribe
   (a) the manner and format in which such electronic records shall be filed, created or issued;
   (b) the manner or method of payment of any fee or charges for filing, creation or issue of any electronic record under clause (a) [Section 6].

Retention of Electronic Records

1. Where any law provides that documents, records, or information shall be retained for any specific period, then, that requirement shall be deemed to have been satisfied if such documents, records, or information are retained in the electronic form, if
   (a) the information contained therein remains accessible so as to be usable for a subsequent reference;
   (b) the electronic record is retained in the format in which it was originally generated, sent, or received in a format which can be demonstrated to represent accurately the information originally generated, sent, or received;
   (c) the details which will facilitate the identification of the origin, destination, date and time of dispatch or receipt of such electronic record are available in the electronic record:

   However, this clause does not apply to any information which is automatically generated solely for the purpose of enabling an electronic record to be dispatched or received.
2. Nothing in this Section shall apply to any law that expressly provides for the retention of documents, records, or information in the form of electronic records [Section 7].

Publication of Rules and Regulations in the Electronic Gazette

Where any law provides that any rule, regulation, order, bye-law, notification or any other matter shall be published in the Official Gazette, then, such a requirement shall be deemed to have been satisfied if such a rule, regulation, order, bye-law, notification or any other matter is published in the Official Gazette or Electronic Gazette:

Provided that where any rule, regulation, order, bye-law, notification or any other matter is published in the Official Gazette or Electronic Gazette, the date of publication shall be deemed to be the date of the Gazette which was first published in any form.

A person has no right to insist on accepting document in eletronic form.

Nothing contained in Sections 6, 7 and 8 shall confer a right upon any person to insist that any Ministry or Department of the Central Government or the State Government or any authority or body established by or under any law or controlled or funded by the Central or State Government should accept, issue, create, retain, and preserve any document in the form of electronic records or effect any monetary transaction in the electronic form [Section 9].

Power to Make Rules by Central Government in Respect of Digital Signature

The Central Government may prescribe

1. the type of digital signature;
2. the manner and format in which the digital signature shall be affixed;
3. the manner or procedure which facilitates identification of the person affixing the digital signature;
4. control processes and procedures to ensure adequate integrity, security, and confidentiality of electronic records or payments; and
5. any other matter which is necessary to give legal effect to digital signatures [Section 10].

Attribution, Acknowledgment, and Despatch of Electronic Records

Attribution of Electronic Records

An electronic record shall be attributed to the originator

1. if it was sent by the originator himself;

Electronic records: Information captured through electronic means, and which may or may not have a paper record to back it up.

2. by a person who had the authority to act on behalf of the originator in respect of that electronic record; or
3. by an information system programmed by or on behalf of the originator to operate automatically [Section 11].

Acknowledgment of Receipt

1. Where the originator has not agreed with the addressee that the acknowledgment of the receipt of the electronic record be given in a particular form or by a particular method, an acknowledgment may be given by
   (a) any communication by the addressee, automated, or otherwise; or
   (b) any conduct of the addressee, sufficient to indicate to the originator that the electronic record has been received.
2. Where the originator has stipulated that the electronic record shall be binding only on receipt of an acknowledgment of such an electronic record by him, then, unless acknowledgment has been so received, the electronic record shall be deemed to have never been sent by the originator.
3. Where the originator has not stipulated that the electronic record shall be binding only on receipt of such acknowledgment, and the acknowledgment has not been received by the originator within the time specified or agreed or, if no time has been specified or agreed to within a reasonable time, then the originator may give notice to the addressee stating that no acknowledgment has been received by him, and specify a reasonable time by which the acknowledgment must be received by him, and if no acknowledgment is received within the aforesaid time limit, he may, after giving notice to the addressee, treat the electronic record as though it has never been sent [Section 12].

Time and Place of Dispatch and Receipt of Electronic Record

1. Unless otherwise agreed to between the originator and the addressee, the dispatch of an electronic record occurs when it enters a computer resource outside the control of the originator.
2. Unless otherwise agreed between the originator and the addressee, the time of receipt of an electronic record shall be determined as follows, namely:
   (a) if the addressee has designated a computer resource for the purpose of receiving electronic records,
      (i) receipt occurs at the time when the electronic record enters the designated computer resource; or
      (ii) if the electronic record is sent to a computer resource of the addressee that is not the designated computer resource, receipt occurs at the time when the electronic record is retrieved by the addressee;
   (b) if the addressee has not designated a computer resource along with specified timings, if any, receipt occurs when the electronic record enters the computer resource of the addressee.
3. Unless otherwise agreed to between the originator and the addressee, an electronic record is deemed to be dispatched at the place where the originator has his place of business, and is deemed to be received at the place where the addressee has his place of business.
4. The provisions of sub-section (2) shall apply notwithstanding that the place where the computer resource is located may be different from the place where the electronic record is deemed to have been received under sub-section (3).
5. For the purpose of this Section,
   (a) if the originator or the addressee has more than one place of business, the principal place of business shall be termed the place of business;
   (b) if the originator or the addressee does not have a place of business, his usual place of residence shall be deemed to be the place of business;
   (c) 'usual place of residence', in relation to a body corporate, refers to the place where it is registered [Section 13].

Secure Electronic Records and Secure Digital Signatures

Secure Electronic Record

Where any security procedure has been applied to an electronic record at a specific point of time, then such a record shall be deemed to be a secure electronic record from such a point of time to the time of verification [Section 14].

Secure Digital Signature

If, by application of a security procedure agreed to by the parties concerned, it can be verified that a digital signature, at the time it was affixed, was

1. unique to the subscriber affixing it;
2. capable of identifying such a subscriber;
3. created in a manner or using a means under the exclusive control of the subscriber and is linked to the electronic record to which it relates in such a manner that if the electronic record was altered the digital signature would be invalidated, then such a digital signature shall be deemed to be a secure digital signature [Section 15].

Security Procedure

The Central Government shall, for the purpose of this Act, prescribe the security procedure having regard to commercial circumstances prevailing at the time when the procedure was used, including

1. the nature of the transaction;
2. the level of sophistication of the parties with reference to their technological capacity;
3. the volume of similar transactions engaged in by other parties;
4. the availability of alternatives offered to but rejected by any party;
5. the cost of alternative procedures; and
6. the procedures in general use for similar types of transactions or communications [Section 16].

Regulation of Certifying Authorities: Appointment of Controller and Other Officers

1. The Central Government may, by notification in the Official Gazette, appoint a Controller of Certifying Authorities for the purposes of this Act, and may also, by the same or subsequent notification, appoint such a number of Deputy Controllers and Assistant Controllers as it deems fit.
2. The Controller shall discharge his functions under this Act subject to the general control and directions of the Central Government.
3. The Deputy Controllers and Assistant Controllers shall perform the functions assigned to them by the Controller under the general superintendence and control of the Controller.
4. The qualifications, experience, and terms and conditions of service of Controller, Deputy Controllers, and Assistant Controllers shall be such as may be prescribed by the Central Government.
5. The Head Office and Branch Office of the office of the Controller shall be at such places as the Central Government may specify, and these may be established at such places as the Central Government may think fit.
6. There shall be a seal of the Office of the Controller [Section 17].

Functions of the Controller

The Controller may perform all or any of the following functions, namely:

1. exercising supervision over the activities of the Certifying Authorities;
2. certifying public keys of the Certifying Authorities;
3. laying down the standards to be maintained by the Certifying Authorities;
4. specifying the qualifications and experience that which employees of the Certifying Authorities should possess;
5. specifying the conditions subject to which the Certifying Authorities shall conduct their business;
6. specifying the contents of written, printed or visual materials and advertisements that may be distributed or used in respect of a Digital Signature Certificate and the public key;
7. specifying the form and content of a Digital Signature Certificate and the key;
8. specifying the form and manner in which accounts shall be maintained by the Certifying Authorities;

9. specifying the terms and conditions subject to which auditors may be appointed and the remuneration to be paid to them;
10. facilitating the establishment of any electronic system by a Certifying Authority, either solely or jointly with other Certifying Authorities, and the regulation of such systems;
11. specifying the manner in which the Certifying Authorities shall conduct their dealings with the subscribers;
12. resolving any conflict of interest between the Certifying Authorities and the subscribers;
13. laying down the duties of the Certifying Authorities;
14. maintaining a data base containing the disclosure record of every Certifying Authority, containing such particulars as may be specified by regulations, which shall be accessible to the public [Section 18].

Recognition of Foreign Certifying Authorities

1. The Controller may, with the previous approval of the Central Government, and by notification in the Official Gazette, recognise any foreign Certifying Authority as a Certifying Authority for the purposes of this Act.
2. Where any Certifying Authority is recognised under sub-section (1), the Digital Signature Certificate issued by such Certifying Authority shall be valid for the purposes of this Act.
3. The Controller, if he is satisfied that any Certifying Authority has contravened any of the conditions and restrictions subject to which it was granted recognition under sub-section (1) may, for reasons to be recorded in writing, by notification in the Official Gazette, revoke such recognition [Section 19].

Controller to Act As Repository

1. The Controller shall be the repository of all Digital Signature Certificates issued under this Act.
2. The Controller shall
   (a) make use of hardware, software, and procedures that are secure of intrusion and misuse;
   (b) observe other such standards as may be prescribed by the Central Government, to ensure that the secrecy and security of the digital signatures is assured.
3. The Controller shall maintain a computerised data base of all public keys in such a manner that such a data base and the public keys are available to any member of the public [Section 20].

Licence to Issue Digital Signature Certificates

Having a 'Digital Signature Certificate' (DCS) is necessary to digitally sign a document. A DSC contains what is known as a 'key-pair' comprising a private key and a corresponding public key. The private key is to be maintained securely and confidentially (i.e. in private). The public key is shared with receivers of documents In India, the Government, via the 'Controller of Certifying Authorities' has authorized a set of entities to issue DSC. The process of obtaining a DSC essentially involves submission of paperwork that establishes applicant's identity to the issuer.

1. Any person may make an application, to the Controller, for a licence to issue Digital Signature Certificates.
2. No licence shall be issued under sub-section (1), unless the applicant fulfills such requirements with respect to qualification, expertise, manpower, financial resources, and other infrastructure facilities, which are necessary to issue Digital Signature Certificates as may be prescribed by the Central Government.
3. A licence granted under this Section shall
   (a) be valid for such period as may be prescribed by the Central Government;
   (b) not be transferable or heritable;
   (c) be subject to such terms and conditions as may be specified by the regulations [Section 21].

Application for Licence

1. Every application for issue of a licence shall be in such a form as may be prescribed by the Central Government.
2. Every application for issue of a licence shall be accompanied by
   (a) a certification practice statement;
   (b) a statement including the procedures with respect to the identification of the applicant;

(c) payment of such fees, not exceeding ₹25000 as may be prescribed by the Central Government;
(d) such other documents, as may be prescribed by the Central Government [Section 22].

Renewal of Licence

An application for renewal of a licence shall be

1. in the required form;
2. accompanied by such fees, not exceeding ₹5000, as may be prescribed by the Central Government and shall be made not less than 45 days before the date of expiry of the period of validity of the licence [Section 23].

Procedure for Grant or Rejection of Licence

The Controller may, on receipt of an application under sub-section (1) of Section 21, after considering the documents accompanying the application and such other factors, as he deems fit, grant the licence or reject the application.

However, no application can be rejected under this Section unless the applicant has been given a reasonable opportunity of presenting his case [Section 24].

Suspension of Licence

1. The Controller may, if he is satisfied after making such inquiries, as he thinks fit, that a Certifying Authority has,
   (a) made a statement in, or in relation to, the application for the issue or renewal of the licence, which is incorrect or false in material particulars;
   (b) failed to comply with the terms and conditions subject to which the licence was granted;
   (c) failed to maintain the standards specified under clause (b) of sub-section (2) of Section 20;
   (d) contravened any provisions of this Act, rule, regulation, or order made thereunder, revoke the licence:

   Provided that no licence shall be revoked unless the Certifying Authority has been given a reasonable opportunity of showing cause against the proposed revocation.
2. The Controller may, if he has reasonable cause to believe that there is any ground for revoking a licence under sub-section (1), by order, suspend such a licence pending the completion of any inquiry ordered by him.

   However, no licence can be suspended for a period exceeding ten days unless the Certifying Authority has been given a reasonable opportunity of showing cause against the proposed suspension.
3. No Certifying Authority whose licence has been suspended shall issue any Digital Signature Certificate during such suspension [Section 25].

Notice of Suspension or Revocation of Licence

1. Where the licence of the Certifying Authority is suspended or revoked, the Controller shall publish notice of such suspension or revocation, as the case may be, in the database maintained by him.
2. Where one or more repositories are specified, the Controller shall publish notices of such suspensions or revocations, as the case may be, in all such repositories:

   Provided that the data base containing the notice of such suspension or revocation, as the case may be, shall be made available through a web site which shall be accessible round the clock:

   Provided further that the Controller may, if he considers necessary, publicise the contents of database in such electronic or other media as he may consider appropriate [Section 26].

Power to Delegate

The Controller may, in writing, authorise the Deputy Controller, Assistant Controller, or any officer, to exercise any of the powers of the Controller under this Chapter [Section 27].

Power to Investigate Contraventions

1. The Controller, or any officer authorised by him in this behalf, shall take up for investigation any contravention of the provisions of this Act, rules or regulations made thereunder.

2. The Controller, or any officer authorised by him in this behalf, shall exercise powers like those which are conferred on Income-tax authorities under Chapter XIII of the Income-tax Act, 1961 and shall exercise such powers, subject to such limitations laid down under that Act [Section 28].

Access to Computers and Data

1. Without prejudice to the provisions of sub-section (1) of Section 69, the Controller, or any person authorised by him, shall, if he has reasonable cause to suspect that any contravention of the provisions of this Act, rules or regulations made thereunder has been committed, have access to any computer system, any apparatus, data or any other material connected with such system, for the purpose of searching or causing a search to be made for obtaining any information or data contained in or available to such computer system.
2. For the purposes of sub-section (1), the Controller or any person authorised by him, may, by order, direct any person in charge of, or otherwise concerned with the operation of, the computer system, data apparatus, or material, to provide him with such reasonable technical and other assistance as he may consider necessary [Section 29].

Certifying Authority to Follow Certain Procedures

Every Certifying Authority shall

1. make use of hardware, software and procedures that are secure from intrusion and misuse;
2. provide a reasonable level of reliability in its services which are reasonably suited to the performance of intended functions;
3. adhere to security procedures to ensure that the secrecy and privacy of the digital signatures are assured; and
4. observe such other standards as may be specified by regulations [Section 30].

Certifying Authority to Ensure Compliance of the Act

Every Certifying Authority shall ensure that every person employed or otherwise engaged by it complies, in the course of his employment or engagement, with the provisions of this Act, rules, regulations and orders made thereunder [Section 31].

Display of Licence

Every Certifying Authority shall display its licence at a conspicuous place of the premises in which it carries on its business [Section 32].

Surrender of Licence

1. Every Certifying Authority whose licence is suspended or revoked shall immediately after such suspension or revocation, surrender the licence to the Controller.
2. Where any Certifying Authority fails to surrender a licence under sub-section (1), the person in whose favour a licence is issued, shall be guilty of an offence and shall be punished with imprisonment which may extend up to six months or a fine which may extend up to ₹10,000 or both [Section 33].

Disclosure

1. Every Certifying Authority shall disclose in the manner specified by regulations
   (a) its Digital Signature Certificate which contains the public key corresponding to the private key used by that Certifying Authority to digitally sign another Digital Signature Certificate;
   (b) any certification practice statement relevant thereto;
   (c) notice of the revocation or suspension of its Certifying Authority certificate, if any; and
   (d) any other fact that materially and adversely affects either the reliability of a Digital Signature Certificate which that Authority has issued, or the Authority's ability to perform its services.
2. Where, in the opinion of the Certifying Authority, any event has occurred or any situation has arisen which may materially and adversely affect the integrity of its computer system or the conditions subject to which a Digital Signature Certificate was granted, then, the Certifying Authority shall
   (a) use reasonable efforts to notify any person who is likely to be affected by that occurrence; or

(b) act in accordance with the procedure specified in its certification practice statement to deal with such event or situation [Section 34].

Digital Signature Certificates

Electronic records: Information captured through electronic means, and which may or may not have a paper record to back it up.

Digital Signature Certificate (DSC) is a certificate, issued by a 'Certifying Authority', necessary for an undertaking to be able to digitally sign a document.

Certifying Authority to Issue Digital Signature Certificate

1. Any person may make an application to the Certifying Authority for the issue of a Digital Signature Certificate in such form as may be prescribed by the Central Government.
2. Every such application shall be accompanied by a fee not exceeding ₹25,000 as may be prescribed by the Central Government, to be paid to the Certifying Authority:

   However, while prescribing fees under sub-section (2) different fees may be prescribed for different classes of applicants.
3. Each such application shall be accompanied by a certification practice statement or, where there is no such statement, a statement containing such particulars as may be specified by regulations.
4. On receipt of an application under sub-section (1), the Certifying Authority may, after consideration of the certification, practice statement or any other statement under sub-section.
5. and after making such enquiries as it may deem fit, grant the Digital Signature Certificate or, for reasons to be recorded in writing, reject the application:

   Provided that no Digital Signature Certificate shall be granted unless the Certifying Authority is satisfied that
   (a) the applicant holds the private key corresponding to the public key to be listed in the Digital Signature Certificate;
   (b) the applicant holds a private key which is capable of creating a digital signature;
   (c) the public key to be listed in the certificate can be used to verify a digital signature affixed by the private key held by the applicant:

   However, no application shall be rejected unless the applicant has been given a reasonable opportunity of showing cause against the proposed rejection [Section 35].

Representations upon Issuance of Digital Signature Certificate

A Certifying Authority while issuing a Digital Signature Certificate shall certify that

1. it has complied with the provisions of this Act and the rules and regulations made thereunder;
2. it has published the Digital Signature Certificate or otherwise made it available to such a person relying on it and the subscriber has accepted it;
3. the subscriber holds the private key corresponding to the public key, listed in the Digital Signature Certificate;
4. the subscriber's public key and private key constitute a functioning key pair;
5. the information contained in the Digital Signature Certificate is accurate; and
6. it has no knowledge of any material fact, which, if it had been included in the Digital Signature Certificate, would adversely affect the reliability of the representations made in clauses (a) to (d) [Section 36].

Suspension of Digital Signature Certificate

1. Subject to the provisions of sub-section (2), the Certifying Authority which has issued a Digital Signature Certificate may suspend such a Digital Signature Certificate:
   (a) on receipt of a request to that effect from
      (i) the subscriber listed in the Digital Signature Certificate; or
      (ii) any person duly authorised to act on behalf of that subscriber,
   (b) if it is of opinion that the Digital Signature Certificate should be suspended in public interest

2. A Digital Signature Certificate shall not be suspended for a period exceeding 15 days unless the subscriber has been given an opportunity to be heard in the matter.
3. On suspension of a Digital Signature Certificate under this Section, the Certifying Authority shall communicate the same to the subscriber [Section 37].

Revocation of Digital Signature Certificate

1. A Certifying Authority may revoke a Digital Signature Certificate issued by it
   (a) where the subscriber, or any other person authorised by him, makes a request to that effect
   (b) upon the death of the subscriber
   (c) upon the dissolution of the firm or winding up of the company where the subscriber is a firm or a company.
2. Subject to the provisions of sub-section (3) and without prejudice to the provisions of sub-section (1), a Certifying Authority may revoke a Digital Signature Certificate which has been issued by it at any time, if it is of opinion that
   (a) a material fact represented in the Digital Signature Certificate is false or has been concealed;
   (b) a requirement for the issuance of the Digital Signature Certificate was not satisfied;
   (c) the Certifying Authority's private key or security system was compromised in a manner materially affecting the Digital Signature Certificate's reliability;
   (d) the subscriber has been declared insolvent or dead, or, where a subscriber is a firm or a company, has been dissolved, wound-up or otherwise ceased to exist
3. A Digital Signature Certificate shall not be revoked unless the subscriber has been given an opportunity to be heard in the matter.
4. On revocation of a Digital Signature Certificate under this Section, the Certifying Authority shall communicate the same to the subscriber [Section 38].

Notice of Suspension or Revocation

1. Where a Digital Signature Certificate is suspended or revoked under Section 37 or Section 38, the Certifying Authority shall publish a notice of such a suspension or revocation, as the case may be, in the repository specified in the Digital Signature Certificate for the publication of such a notice.
2. Where one or more repositories are specified, the Certifying Authority shall publish notices of such suspensions or revocations, as the case may be, in all such repositories [Section 39].

Duties of Subscribers

Generating Key Pair

Where any Digital Signature Certificate, the public key of which corresponds to the private key of that subscriber which is to be listed in the Digital Signature Certificate has been accepted by a subscriber, the subscriber shall generate the key pair by applying the security procedure [Section 40].

Acceptance of Digital Signature Certificate

1. A subscriber shall be deemed to have accepted a Digital Signature Certificate if he publishes or authorises the publication of a Digital Signature Certificate
   (a) to one or more persons
   (b) in a repository, or otherwise demonstrates his approval of the Digital Signature Certificate in any manner.
2. By accepting a Digital Signature Certificate, the subscriber certifies to all who reasonably rely on the information contained in the Digital Signature Certificate that
   (a) the subscriber holds the private key corresponding to the public key listed in the Digital Signature Certificate and is entitled to hold the same;
   (b) all representations made by the subscriber to the Certifying Authority and all material relevant to the information contained in the Digital Signature Certificate are true;
   (c) all information in the Digital Signature Certificate that is within the knowledge of the subscriber is true [Section 41].

Control of Private Key

1. Every subscriber shall exercise reasonable care to retain control of the private key corresponding

to the public key listed in his Digital Signature Certificate and take all steps to prevent its disclosure to a person not authorised to affix the digital signature of the subscriber.

2. If the private key corresponding to the public key listed in the Digital Signature Certificate has been compromised, the subscriber shall communicate this without any delay to the Certifying Authority in such manner as may be specified by the regulations.
   Explanation: For the removal of doubts, it is hereby declared that the subscriber shall be liable until he has informed the Certifying Authority that the private key has been compromised [Section 42].

Penalties and Adjudication

Penalty for Damage to Computer, Computer System

If any person, without the permission of the owner or any other person who is in-charge of a computer, computer system, or computer network,

1. accesses or secures access to such computer, computer system, or computer network;
2. downloads, copies or extracts any data, computer data base or information from such a computer, computer system or computer network, including information or data held or stored in any removable storage medium;
3. introduces, or causes to be introduced, any computer contaminant or computer virus into any computer, computer system, or computer network;
4. damages, or causes to be damaged, any computer, computer system or computer network, data, computer data base, or any other programme residing in such a computer, computer system or computer network;
5. disrupts, or causes disruption of, any computer, computer system or computer network;
6. denies access, or causes the denial of access, to any person authorised to access any computer, computer system or computer network by any means;
7. provides any assistance to any person to facilitate access to a computer, computer system, or computer network in contravention of the provisions of this Act, rules or regulations made thereunder;
8. charges the services availed of by a person to the account of another person by tampering with or manipulating any computer, computer system, or computer network, he shall be liable to pay damages by way of compensation not exceeding ₹1 crore to the person so affected.

Explanation: For the purpose of this Section,

1. **computer contaminant** means any set of computer instructions that are designed
   (a) to modify, destroy, record, transmit any data or programme residing within a computer, computer system or computer network; or
   (b) by any means usurp the normal operation of the computer, computer system, or computer network;
2. **computer data base** refers to a representation of information, knowledge, facts, concepts or instructions in text, image, audio, video that is prepared, or has been prepared, in a formalised manner, or has been produced by a computer, computer system or computer network, and is intended for use in a computer, computer system or computer network;
3. **computer virus** refers to any computer instruction, information, data, or programme that destroys, damages, degrades, or adversely affects the performance of a computer resource or attaches itself to another computer resource and operates when a programme, data, or instruction is executed, or some other event takes place in that computer resource;
4. **to damage** means to destroy, alter, delete, add, modify, or rearrange any computer resource by any means [Section 43].

Compensation for Failure to Protect Data

If a body corporate, possessing, dealing, or handling any sensitive personal data or information in a computer resource which it owns, controls, or operates is negligent in implementing and maintaining reasonable security practices and procedures and thereby causes wrongful gain to any person, such body corporate shall be liable to pay damages to the aggrieved party [Section 43A].

Penalty for Failure to Furnish Information Return

If any person who is required under this Act or any rules or regulations made thereunder to

1. furnish any document, return, or report to the Controller or the Certifying Authority, fails to furnish the same, he shall be liable to a penalty not exceeding ₹150,000 for each such failure;
2. file any return or furnish any information, books or other documents within the time specified in the regulations, fails to file return or furnish the same within the time specified in the regulations, he shall be liable to a penalty not exceeding ₹5000 for every day during which such failure continues;
3. maintain books of account or records, fails to maintain the same, he shall be liable to a penalty not exceeding ₹10,000 for every day during which the failure continues [Section 44].

Residuary Penalty

Whoever contravenes any rules or regulations made under this Act, for the contravention of which no penalty has been separately provided, shall be liable to pay a compensation not exceeding ₹25,000 to the person affected by such contravention [Section 45].

Power to Adjudicate

1. For the purpose of adjudging under this Chapter whether any person has committed a contravention of any of the provisions of this Act, or of any rule, regulation, direction or order made thereunder, the Central Government shall, subject to the provisions of sub-section (3), appoint an officer not below the rank of a Director to the Government of India, or an equivalent officer of a State Government, to be an adjudicating officer to hold an enquiry in the manner prescribed by the Central Government.
2. The adjudicating officer shall, after giving the person referred to in sub-section (1) reasonable opportunity for making a representation in the matter and if, on such inquiry, he is satisfied that the person has committed the contravention, impose such penalty or award such compensation as he thinks fit in accordance with the provisions of that Section.
3. No person shall be appointed as an adjudicating officer unless he possesses such experience in the field of Information Technology and legal or judicial experience as may be prescribed by the Central Government.
4. Where more than one adjudicating officers is appointed, the Central Government shall specify by order the matters and places with respect to which such officers shall exercise their jurisdiction.
5. Every adjudicating officer shall have the powers of a civil court which are conferred on the Cyber Appellate Tribunal under Section 58(2), and
   (a) all proceedings before it shall be deemed to be judicial proceedings within the meaning of Sections 193 and 228 of the Indian Penal Code;
   (b) shall be deemed to be a civil court for the purposes of Sections 345 and 346 of the Code of Criminal Procedure, 1973 [Section 46].

Factors to Be Taken into Account by the Adjudicating Officer

While adjudging the quantum of compensation under this Chapter, the adjudicating officer shall have due regard to the following factors, namely:

1. the amount of gain of unfair advantage, wherever quantifiable, made as a result of the default;
2. the amount of loss caused to any person as a result of the default;
3. the repetitive nature of the default [Section 47].

The Cyber Regulations Appellate Tribunal

Establishment of Cyber Appellate Tribunal

1. The Central Government shall, by notification, establish one or more appellate tribunals to be known as the Cyber Regulations Appellate Tribunal.
2. The Central Government shall also specify, in the notification referred to in sub-section (1),

the matters and places in relation to which the Cyber Appellate Tribunal may exercise jurisdiction [Section 48].

Composition of Cyber Appellate Tribunal

A Cyber Appellate Tribunal shall consist of one person only (hereafter referred to as the Residing Officer of the Cyber Appellate Tribunal) to be appointed, by notification, by the Central Government [Section 49].

Qualifications for Appointment As Presiding Officer of Cyber Appellate Tribunal

A person shall not qualify for appointment as the Presiding Officer of a Cyber Appellate Tribunal unless he

1. is, or has been, or is qualified to be, a Judge of a High Court; or
2. is or has been a member of the Indian Legal Service and is holding, or has held, a post in Grade I of that Service for at least three years [Section 50].

Term of Office

The Presiding Officer of a Cyber Appellate Tribunal shall hold office for a term of five years from the date on which he enters the office, or until he attains the age of 65 years, whichever is earlier [Section 51].

Salary, Allowances, and Other Terms and Conditions of Service of Presiding Officer

The salary and allowances payable to, and the other terms and conditions of service including pension, gratuity and other retirement benefits of the Presiding Officer of a Cyber Appellate Tribunal shall be such as may be prescribed:

Provided that neither the salary and allowances nor the other terms and conditions of service of the Presiding Officer shall be varied to his disadvantage after appointment [Section 52].

Filling Up of Vacancies

If, for reason other than temporary absence, any vacancy occurs in the office of the Presiding Officer of a Cyber Appellate Tribunal, the Central Government shall appoint another person in accordance with the provisions of this Act to fill the vacancy. The proceedings may be continued before the Cyber Appellate Tribunal from the stage at which the vacancy is filled [Section 53].

Resignation and Removal

1. The Presiding Officer of a Cyber Appellate Tribunal may, by notice in writing under his hand addressed to the Central Government, resign his office:

   Provided that the said Presiding Officer shall, unless he is permitted by the Central Government to relinquish his office sooner, continue to hold office until the expiry of three months from the date of receipt of such notice, or until a person duly appointed as his successor enters upon his office, or until the expiry of his term of office, whichever is the earliest.
2. The Presiding Officer of a Cyber Appellate Tribunal shall not be removed from office except by an order by the Central Government on the ground of proven misbehaviour or incapacity after an inquiry made by a Judge of the Supreme Court in which the Presiding Officer concerned has been informed of the charges against him and has been given reasonable opportunity to be heard in respect of these charges.
3. The Central Government may, by rules, regulate the procedure for the investigation of misbehaviour or incapacity of the Presiding Officer [Section 54].

Orders Constituting Appellate Tribunal To Be Final

No order of the Central Government appointing any person as the Presiding Officer of a Cyber Appellate Tribunal shall be called in question in any manner, and no act or proceeding before a Cyber Appellate Tribunal shall be called in question in any manner on the ground merely of any defect in the constitution of a Cyber Appellate Tribunal [Section 55].

Staff of the Cyber Appellate Tribunal

1. The Central Government shall provide the Cyber Appellate Tribunal with such officers and employees as that Government may think fit.

2. The officers and employees of the Cyber Appellate Tribunal shall discharge their functions under the general superintendence of the Presiding Officer.
3. The salaries, allowances and other conditions of service of the officers and employees or the Cyber Appellate Tribunal shall be such as may be prescribed by the Central Government [Section 56].

Appeal to Cyber Appellate Tribunal

1. Save as provided in sub-section (2), any person aggrieved by an order made by the Controller or an adjudicating officer under this Act may refer an appeal to a Cyber Appellate Tribunal having jurisdiction in the matter.
2. No appeal shall lie to the Cyber Appellate Tribunal from an order made by an adjudicating officer with the consent of the parties.
3. Every appeal under sub-section (1) shall be filed within a period of 25 days from the date on which a copy of the order made by the Controller or the adjudicating officer is received by the person aggrieved, and it shall be in such form and be accompanied by such fees as may be prescribed:

   Provided that the Cyber Appellate Tribunal may entertain an appeal after the expiry of the said period of 25 days if it is satisfied that there was sufficient cause for not filing it within that period.
4. On receipt of an appeal under sub-section (1), the Cyber Appellate Tribunal may, after giving the parties to the appeal an opportunity for being heard, pass such orders thereon as it thinks fit, confirming, modifying or setting aside the order appealed against.
5. The Cyber Appellate Tribunal shall send a copy of every order made by it to the parties to the appeal, and to the concerned Controller or adjudicating officer.
6. The appeal filed before the Cyber Appellate Tribunal under sub-section (1) shall be dealt with as expeditiously as possible and endeavour shall be made by the Tribunal to dispose of the appeal finally within six months from the date of receipt of the appeal [Section 57].

Procedure and Powers of the Cyber Appellate Tribunal

1. The Cyber Appellate Tribunal shall not be bound by the procedure laid down by the Code of Civil Procedure, 1908, but shall be guided by the principles of natural justice and, subject to the other provisions of this Act and of any rules, the Cyber Appellate Tribunal shall have powers to regulate its own procedure including the place at which it shall have its sittings.
2. The Cyber Appellate Tribunal shall have, for the purposes of discharging its functions under this Act, the same powers as are vested in a civil court under the Code of Civil Procedure, 1908, while trying a suit, in respect of the following matters, namely:
   (a) summoning and enforcing the attendance of any person and examining him on oath;
   (b) requiring the discovery and production of documents or other electronic records;
   (c) receiving evidence on affidavits;
   (d) issuing commissions for the examination of witnesses or documents;
   (e) reviewing its decisions;
   (f) dismissing an application for default or deciding it ex pane;
   (g) any other matter which may be prescribed.
3. Every proceeding before the Cyber Appellate Tribunal shall be deemed to be a judicial proceeding within the meaning of Sections 193 and 228, and for the purposes of Section 196 of the Indian Penal Code. The Cyber Appellate Tribunal shall be deemed to be a civil court for the purposes of Section 195 and Chapter XXVI of the Code of Criminal Procedure, 1973 [Section 58].

Right to Legal Representation

The appellant may either appear in person or authorise one or more legal practitioners or any of its officers to present his or its case before the Cyber Appellate Tribunal [Section 59].

Limitation

The provisions of the Limitation Act, 1963, shall, as far as may be, apply to an appeal made to the Cyber Appellate Tribunal [Section 60].

Civil Court Not to Have Jurisdiction

No court shall have jurisdiction to entertain any suit or proceeding in respect of any matter which an adjudicating officer appointed under this Act, or the Cyber Appellate Tribunal constituted under this Act, is empowered by or under this Act to determine, and no injunction shall be granted by any court or other authority in respect of any action taken, or to be taken, in pursuance of any power conferred by or under this Act [Section 61].

Appeal to High Court

Any person aggrieved by any decision or order of the Cyber Appellate Tribunal may file an appeal to the High Court within 60 days from the date of communication of the decision or order of the Cyber Appellate Tribunal on any question of fact or law arising out of such order.

However, the High Court may, if it is satisfied that the appellant was prevented by sufficient cause from filing the appeal within the said period, allow it to be filed within a further period not exceeding 60 days [Section 62].

Compounding of Contraventions

1. Any contravention under this Chapter may, either before or after the institution of adjudication proceedings, be compounded by the Controller or any other such officer as may be specially authorised by him in this behalf or by the adjudicating officer, as the case may be, subject to such conditions as the Controller or such other officer or the adjudicating officer may specify:

   Provided that such a sum shall not, in any case, exceed the maximum amount of the penalty which may be imposed under this Act for the contravention so compounded.
2. Nothing in sub-section (1) shall apply to a person who commits the same or similar contravention within a period of three years from the date on which the first contravention, committed by him, was compounded.

   Explanation: For the purposes of this sub-section, any second or subsequent contravention committed after the expiry of a period of three years from the date on which the contravention was previously compounded shall be deemed to be a first contravention.
3. Where any contravention has been compounded under sub-section (1), no proceeding or further proceeding, as the case may be, shall be taken against the person guilty of such contravention in respect of the contravention so compounded [Section 63].

Recovery of Penalty

A penalty imposed under this Act, if not paid, shall be recovered as an arrear of land revenue, and the licence or the Digital Signature Certificate, as the case may be, shall be suspended until the penalty is paid [Section 64].

Offences

Tampering with Computer Source Documents

Whoever knowingly or intentionally conceals, destroys or alters, or intentionally or knowingly causes another to conceal, destroy or alter, any computer source code used for a computer, computer programme, computer system or computer network, when the computer source code is required to be kept or maintained by law for the time being in force, shall be punishable with imprisonment up to three years, or with a fine which may extend up to ₹2 lakh, or with both.

Explanation: For the purposes of this section, 'computer source code' refers to the listing of programmes, computer commands, design and layout, and programme analysis of computer resource in any form [Section 65].

Hacking with Computer System

Hacking: Intentional access to a computer system without due authorization or exceeded authorized access.

If any person, dishonestly or fraudulently, does any act referred to in Section 43, he shall be punishable with imprisonment for a term which may extend to three years or with fine which may extend to five lakh rupees or with both [Section 66].

Note: In a related development, the Supreme Court on March 24, 2015 terming it unconstitutional struck down Section 66A of the IT Act which allowed arrests for posting offensive content on social media sites. The controversial provision made posting offensive material on social networking sites an offence punishable by up to three years in jail.

Punishment for Receiving Stolen Computer Resource or Communication Device

Whoever dishonestly received or retains any stolen computer resource of communication device knowing or having reason to believe the same to be stolen computer resource or communication device, shall be punished with imprisonment of either description for a term which may extend to three years or with fine which may extend to rupees one lakh or with both [Section 66B].

Punishment for Identity Theft

Whoever, fraudulently or dishonestly make use of the electronic signature, password or any unique identification feature of any other person, shall be punished with imprisonment of either description for a term which may extend to three years and shall also be liable to fine which may extend to rupees one lakh [Section 66B].

Punishment for Cheating by Personation by Using Computer Resource

Whoever, by means for any communication device or computer resource cheats by personating, shall be punished with imprisonment of either description for a term which may extend to three years and shall also be liable to fine which may extend to one lakh rupees [Section 66D].

Punishment for Violation of Privacy

Whoever, intentionally or knowingly captures, publishes or transmits the image of a private area of any person without his or her consent, under circumstances violating the privacy of that person, shall be punished with imprisonment which may extend to three years or with fine not exceeding two lakh rupees, or with both [Section 66E].

Punishment for Cyber Terrorism

1. Whoever,

   (a) With intent to threaten the unity, integrity, security of sovereignty of India or to strike terror in the people or any section of the people by—

      (i) denying or cause the denial of access to any person authorized to access computer resource; or

      (ii) attempting to penetrate or access a computer resource without authorization or exceeding authorized access; or

      (iii) introducing or causing to introduce any computer contaminant,

   and by means of such conduct causes or is likely to cause death or injuries to persons or damage to or destruction of property or disrupts or knowing that it is likely to cause damage or disruption of supplies or services essential to the life of the community or adversely affect the critical information infrastructure specified under Section 70; or

   (b) knowingly or intentionally penetrates or accesses a computer resource without authorization or exceeding authorized access, and by means of such conduct obtains access to information, data or computer database that is restricted; or any restricted information, data or computer database, with reasons to believe that such information, data or computer database so obtained may be used to cause or likely to cause injury to the interests of the sovereignty and integrity of India, the security of the State, friendly relations with foreign States, public order, decency or morality, or in relation to contempt of court, defamation or incitement to an offence, or to the advantage of any foreign nation, group of individuals, or otherwise, commits the offence of cyber terrorism.

2. Whoever commits or conspires to commit cyber terrorism shall be punishable with imprisonment which may extend to imprisonment for life [Section 66F].

> Cyber terrorism: Any premeditated, politically motivated attack against information, computer systems, computer programs, and data which results in violence against non-combatant targets by sub-national groups or clandestine agents.

Publishing of Information Which Is Obscene in Electronic Form

Whoever publishes or transmits or causes to be published in the electronic form any material which is lascivious or appeals to the prurient interest, or if its effect is such as to tend to deprave and corrupt persons who are likely, having regard to all relevant circumstances, to read, see or hear the matter contained or embodied in it, shall be punished on first conviction with imprisonment of either description for a term which may extend to five years and with fine which may extend to ₹1 lakh. In the event of a second or subsequent conviction, the punishment would be imprisonment of either description for a term which may extend to 10 years and also with fine which may extend to ₹2 lakh [Section 67].

Punishment for Publishing or Transmitting of Material Containing Sexually Explicit Act in Electronic Form

Whoever publishes or transmits or causes to be published or transmitted in the electronic form any material which contains sexually explicit act or conduct shall be punished on first conviction with imprisonment of either description for a term which may extend to five years and with fine which may extend to ten lakh rupees and in the event of second or subsequent conviction with imprisonment of either description for term which may extend to seven years and also with fine which may extend to ten lakh rupees [Section 67A].

Power of Controller to Give Directions

1. The Controller may, by order, direct a Certifying Authority or any employee of such Authority to take such measures or cease carrying on such activities as specified in the order, if those are necessary to ensure compliance with the provisions of this Act, rules or any regulations made thereunder.
2. Any person who fails to comply with any order under sub-section (1) shall be guilty of an offence and shall be liable on conviction to imprisonment for a term not exceeding three years or to a fine not exceeding ₹2 lakh, or to both [Section 68].

Government's Agency Power to Intercept Information

1. The Act empowers the Central/State Government's authorised agency to intercept, monitor or decrypt any information generated, transmitted, received, or stored in any computer resource if it is deemed fit in the interest of the sovereignty or integrity of India, defence of India, security of the State, friendly relations with foreign States or public order or for preventing incitement to the commission of any cognizable offence or for investigation of any offence.
2. The agency can also secure all the facilities and technical assistance from the subscriber or computer personnel to decrypt the information.
3. The subscriber or any person who fails to assist the agency shall be punishable with an imprisonment for a term which may extend to seven years [Section 69].

Protected System

1. The appropriate Government may, by notification in the Official Gazette, declare any computer, computer system, or computer network to be a protected system.
2. The appropriate Government may, by order in writing, authorise the persons who are authorised to access protected systems notified under sub-section (1).
3. Any person who secures access or attempts to secure access to a protected system in contravention of the provisions of this Section shall be punished with imprisonment of either description for a term which may extend to 10 years and shall also be liable to fine [Section 70].

Penalty for Misrepresentation

Whoever makes any misrepresentation to, or suppresses any material fact from, the Controller or the Certifying Authority for obtaining any licence or Digital Signature Certificate, as the case may be, shall be punished with imprisonment for a term which may extend to two years, or with fine which may extend to ₹1 lakh, or with both [Section 71].

Penalty for Breach of Confidentiality and Privacy

Save as otherwise provided in this Act or any other law for the time being in force, any person who, in pursuance of any of the powers conferred under this Act, rules or regulations made thereunder, has secured access to any electronic record, book, register, correspondence, information, document, or other material without the consent of the person concerned, discloses such electronic record, book, register, correspondence, information, document, or other material to any other person, shall be punished with imprisonment for a term which may extend to two years, or with fine which may extend to ₹1 lakh, or with both [Section 72].

Penalty for Publishing Digital Signature Certificate False in Certain Particulars

1. No person shall publish a Digital Signature Certificate or otherwise make it available to any other person with the knowledge that
   (a) the Certifying Authority listed in the certificate has not issued it; or
   (b) the subscriber listed in the certificate has not accepted it; or
   (c) the certificate has been revoked or suspended,
   unless such a publication is for the purpose of verifying a digital signature created prior to such suspension or revocation.
2. Any person who contravenes the provisions of sub-section (1) shall be punished with imprisonment for a term which may extend to two years, or with fine which may extend to ₹1 lakh, or with both [Section 73].

Publication for Fraudulent Purpose

Whoever knowingly creates, publishes, or otherwise makes available a Digital Signature Certificate for any fraudulent or unlawful purpose shall be punished with imprisonment for a term which may extend to two years, or with fine which may extend to ₹1 lakh, or with both [Section 74].

Act to Apply for Offence or Contravention Committed Outside India

1. Subject to the provisions of sub-section (2), the provisions of this Act shall apply also to any offence or contravention committed outside India by any person, irrespective of his nationality.
2. For the purposes of sub-section (1), this Act shall apply to an offence or contravention committed outside India by any person if the act or conduct constituting the offence or contravention involves a computer computer system, or computer network located in India [Section 75].

Confiscation

Any computer, computer system, floppies, compact disks, tape drives, or any other accessories related thereto, in respect of which any provision of this Act or rules, orders or regulations made thereunder has been or is being contravened, shall be liable to confiscation:

However, where it is established to the satisfaction of the court adjudicating the confiscation that the person in whose possession, power or control any such computer, computer system, floppies, compact disks, tape drives, or any other accessories relating thereto is/are found, is not responsible for the contravention of the provisions of this Act, rules, orders or regulations made thereunder, the court may, instead of making an order for the confiscation of such a computer, computer system, floppies, compact disks, tape drives, or any other accessories related thereto, make any other order authorised by this Act against the person contravening the provisions of this Act, rules, orders or regulations made thereunder, as it may think fit [Section 76].

Penalties or Confiscation Not to Interfere with Other Punishments

No penalty imposed or confiscation made under this Act shall prevent the imposition of any other punishment to which the person affected thereby is liable under any other law for the time being in force [Section 77].

Power to Investigate Offences

Notwithstanding anything contained in the Code of Criminal Procedure, 1973, a police officer not below the rank of Deputy Superintendent of Police shall investigate any offence under this Act [Section 78].

Network Service Providers Not To Be Liable in Certain Cases

For the removal of doubts, it is hereby declared that no person providing any service as a network service provider shall be liable under this Act, rules or regulations made thereunder for any third party information or data made available by him, if he proves that the offence or contravention was committed without his knowledge, or that he had exercised all due diligence to prevent the commission of such an offence or contravention.

Explanation: For the purposes of this Section,

- 'network service provider' means an intermediary;
- 'third party information' means any information dealt with by a network service provider in his capacity as an intermediary [Section 79].

Miscellaneous Provisions

Power of Police Officer and Other Officers to Enter, Search

1. Notwithstanding anything contained in the Code of Criminal Procedure, 1973, any police officer, not below the rank of a Deputy Superintendent of Police, or any other officer of the Central Government or a State Government authorised by the Central Government in this behalf, may enter any public place and search and arrest without warrant any person found therein who is reasonably suspected of having committed, or of committing, or of being about to commit, any offence under this Act.

   Explanation: For the purposes of this sub-section, the expression 'public place' includes any public conveyance, any hotel, any shop, or any other place intended for use by, or accessible to the public.
2. Where any person is arrested under sub-section (1) by an officer other than a police officer, such an officer shall, without unnecessary delay, take or send the person arrested before a magistrate having jurisdiction in the case, or before the officer-in-charge of a police station.
3. The provisions of the Code of Criminal Procedure, 1973 shall, subject to the provisions of this Section, apply, so far as may be, in relation to any entry, search or arrest, made under this Section [Section 80].

Act to Have Overriding Effect

The provisions of this Act shall have effect notwithstanding anything inconsistent therewith contained in any other law for the time being in force [Section 81].

Controller, Deputy Controller, and Assistant Controllers to Be Public Servants

The Presiding Officer and other officers and employees of a Cyber Appellate Tribunal, the Controller, the Deputy Controller, and the Assistant Controllers shall be deemed to be public servants within the meaning of Section 21 of the Indian Penal Code [Section 82].

Power to Give Directions

The Central Government may give directions to any State Government as to the carrying into execution in the State of any of the provisions of this Act or of any rule, regulation, or order made thereunder [Section 83].

Protection of Action Taken in Good Faith

No suit, prosecution or other legal proceeding shall lie against the Central Government, the State Government, the Controller or any person acting on behalf of him, the Presiding Officer, adjudicating officers, and the staff of the Cyber Appellate Tribunal, for anything which is done in good faith or is intended to be done in pursuance of this Act, or any rule, regulation or order made thereunder [Section 84].

Offences by Companies

1. Where a person committing a contravention of any of the provisions of this Act or of any rule, direction or order made thereunder is a company, every person who, at the time the contravention was committed, was in charge of, and was responsible to, the company for the conduct of business of the company as well as the company, shall be guilty of the contravention and shall be liable to be proceeded against and punished accordingly:

   However, nothing contained in this sub-section shall render any such person liable to punishment if he proves that the contravention took place without his knowledge, or that he exercised all due diligence to prevent such contravention.

2. Notwithstanding anything contained in sub-section (1), where a contravention of any of the provisions of this Act or of any rule, direction or order made thereunder has been committed by a company, and it is proved that the contravention has taken place with the consent or connivance of, or is attributable to any neglect on the part of, any director, manager, secretary, or other officer of the company, such a director, manager, secretary, or other officer shall also be deemed to be guilty of the contravention and shall be liable to be proceeded against and punished accordingly.

   Explanation: For the purposes of this section
   (a) 'company' means any corporate body and includes a firm or other association of individuals; and
   (b) 'director', in relation to a firm, refers to a partner in the firm [Section 85].

Removal of Difficulties

1. If any difficulty arises in giving effect to the provisions of this Act, the Central Government may, by order published in the Official Gazette, make such provisions not inconsistent with the provisions of this Act as appear to it to be necessary or expedient for removing the difficulty:

   Provided that no order shall be made under this Section after the expiry of a period of two years from the commencement of this Act
2. Every order made under this Section shall be laid, as soon as possible after it is made, before each House of Parliament [Section 86].

Constitution of Advisory Committee

1. The Central Government shall, as soon as possible after the commencement of this Act, constitute a Committee called the Cyber Regulations Advisory Committee.
2. The Cyber Regulations Advisory Committee shall consist of a Chairperson and such a number of other official and non-official members representing the interests principally affected or having special knowledge of the subject-matter, as the Central Government may deem fit.
3. The Cyber Regulations Advisory Committee shall advise
   (a) the Central Government either generally as regards any rules or for any other purpose connected with this Act;
   (b) the Controller in framing the regulations under this Act.
4. The non-official members of such Committee shall be paid such travelling and other allowances as the Central Government may fix [Section 88].

Special Provisions for Evidence Relating to Electronic Record

The contents of electronic records may be proved in accordance with the provisions of Section 65B [Section 65A].

Admissibility of Electronic Records

Any information contained in an electronic record which is printed on paper, stored, recorded or copied in optical or magnetic media produced by a computer (computer output) shall also be deemed to be a document, if the conditions mentioned in this Section are satisfied in relation to the information and the computer in question, and shall be admissible in any proceedings, without further proof or production of the original, as evidence of any contents of the original or of any fact stated therein of which direct evidence would be admissible [Section 65B].

Presumption As to Electronic Records and Digital Signatures

1. In any proceedings involving a secure electronic record, the Court shall presume, unless the contrary is proved, that the secure electronic record has not been altered since the specific point of time to which the secure status relates.
2. In any proceedings, involving a secure digital signature, the Court shall presume, unless the contrary is proved, that
   (a) the secure digital signature is affixed by subscriber with the intention of signing or approving the electronic record;
   (b) except in the case of a secure electronic record or a secure digital signature, nothing in this Section shall create any presumption

relating to the authenticity and integrity of the electronic record or any digital signature [Section 85B].

Presumption As to Digital Signature Certificates

The Court shall presume, unless the contrary is proved, that the information listed in a Digital Signature Certificate is correct, except for information specified as subscriber information which has not been verified, if the certificate was accepted by the subscriber [Section 85C].

Presumption As to Electronic Messages

After Section 88, the following section shall be inserted, namely:

The Court may presume that an electronic message forwarded by the originator through an electronic mail server to the addressee to whom the message purports to be addressed corresponds with the message as fed into his computer for transmission; but the Court shall not make any presumption as to the person by whom such message was sent.

Explanation: For the purpose of this Section, the expressions 'addressee' and 'originator' shall have the same meanings respectively assigned to them in clauses (b) and (za) of sub-section (1) of Section 2 of the Information Technology Act, 2000 [Section 85C].

Exercises

I. Objective-type Questions

1. 'Secure system' refers to computer hardware, software, and procedure that
   (a) is reasonably secure from unauthorised access and misuse, and adheres to generally accepted security procedure
   (b) provides a reasonable level of reliability and correct operation
   (c) is reasonably suited to performing the intended functions
   (d) complies with all of the above
2. 'Subscriber' refers to
   (a) a person in whose name the Digital Signature Certificate is issued
   (b) any person who, on behalf of another person, receives, stores, or transmits that message or provides any service with respect to that message
   (c) a person who has been granted a licence to issue a Digital Signature Certificate under Section 24
   (d) None of the above
3. A person shall be liable to pay damages by way of compensation to the person so affected if s/he without permission of the owner or any other person who is in charge of a computer, computer system, or computer network
   (a) accesses or secures access to such computer, computer system, or computer network
   (b) downloads, copies or extracts any data, computer data base, or information from such computer, computer system, or computer network including information or data held or stored in any removable storage medium
   (c) damages or causes to be damaged any computer, computer system, or computer network, data, computer data base or any other programmes residing in such a computer, computers system or computer network
   (d) commits any of the above acts

4. Who, among the following, is empowered to suspend or revoke the 'licence to issue Digital Signature Certificates' granted to a Certifying Authority?
   (a) Controller (b) Adjudicating officer
   (c) Cyber Appellate Tribunal (d) Central Government
5. If the Certifying Authority fails to furnish any document, return, or report to the Controller under Section 44, it shall be liable to a penalty
   (a) not exceeding ₹150,000 for each such failure
   (b) not exceeding ₹5000 for every day during which such failure continues
   (c) not exceeding ₹10,000 for every day during which such failure continues
   (d) not exceeding ₹25,000

II. Review Questions

1. Define the following terms under the Information Technology Act, 2000:
   (a) Addressee (b) Certifying Authority
   (c) Controller (d) Cyber Appellate Tribunal
   (e) Intermediary (f) Subscriber
   (g) Licence (h) Digital Signature
   (i) Secure System (j) Information
2. What is the Information Technology Act? Discuss its aim and objectives.
3. Describe the provisions of the IT Act as regards the following:
   (a) Legal recognition of electronic records
   (b) Authentication of electronic records
   (c) Retention of electronic records
   (d) Publication of rules, regulations etc., in the electronic Gazette
4. Who is a 'Controller'? Outline his functions and powers.
5. Describe the duties of subscribers. Discuss also the penalties and Adjudication under Section 43 of the IT Act, 2000 for (a) damage to a computer, computers system etc., and (b) failure to furnish information, return, etc.

Answers to Objective-type Questions

1. (d) 2. (d) 3. (d) 4. (d) 5. (d)

24 Chapter in Review

LEARNING OUTCOMES

LO1 What is IT Act, 2000?
LO2 Aim of the IT Act
LO3 Issues that the IT Act addresses
LO4 Documents or transactions unfazed by IT Act

LO1 The IT Act, 2000 provides for legal recognition to transactions, commercial or otherwise, carried out by means of electronic data interchange (EDI) and other means of electronic communication, commonly referred to as 'Electronic Commerce' or E-Commerce.

LO2 The Act aims to promote E-Commerce and facilitate E-Governance, nationally and internationally.

LO3 To attain its aim, the Act primarily addresses the following issues:

1. Legal recognition of electronic documents;
2. Legal recognition of digital signatures;
3. Offences and contraventions; and
4. Justice dispensation systems for cybercrimes.

LO4 The provisions of the Act do not apply to the following documents or transactions: (a) a negotiable instrument (other than a cheque), (b) a power-of-attorney, (c) a trust, (d) a will including any other testamentary disposition by whatever name called, (e) any contract for the sale or conveyance of immovable property or any interest in such property, and (f) any such class of documents or transactions as may be notified by the Central Government in the Official Gazette.

KEY TERMS

Addressee: A person who is intended by the originator to receive the electronic record but does not include any intermediary.

Computer network: A set of computers connected together by (i) Internet or any other communication media; and (ii) terminals for the purpose of sharing information.

Data: A representation of information, knowledge, facts, concepts, or instructions which is being prepared or has been prepared in a formalised manner.

Digital signature: The authentication of any electronic record by a subscriber by means of an electronic method or procedure in accordance with Section 3 of the IT Act.

Electronic form: Any information generated, sent, received, or stored in media, magnetic, optical, computer memory, micro film, computer generated micro fiche, or similar device.

Electronic gazette: Official gazette published in the electronic form.

Originator: A person who sends, generates, stores, or transmits any electronic message or causes any electronic message to be sent, generated, stored, or transmitted to any other person.

Private key: The key of a key pair used to create a digital signature.

Public key: The key of a key pair used to verify a digital signature, which is listed in the Digital Signature Certificate.

Secure system: Computer hardware, software, and procedure that (i) is reasonably secure from unauthorised access and misuse; (ii) provides a reasonable level of reliability and correct operation, (iii) is reasonably suited to performing the intended functions, and (iv) adheres to generally accepted security procedures.

E-Governance: The public sector's use of information and communication technologies (ICT) with the aim of improving information and service delivery, encouraging citizen participation in the decision-making process and making government more accountable, transparent and effective.

Electronic records: Information captured through electronic means, and which may or may not have a paper record to back it up.

Digital Signature Certificate (DSC): A certificate, issued by a 'Certifying Authority', necessary to have by an undertaking to digitally sign a document.

Hacking: Intentional access to a computer system without due authorization or exceeded authorized access.

Cyber terrorism: Any premeditated, politically motivated attack against information, computer systems, computer programs, and data which results in violence against non-combatant targets by sub-national groups or clandestine agents.

CHAPTER

25 The Right to Information Act, 2005

Learning Objectives

LO 1 What is RTI Act, 2005
LO 2 Applicability of the Act
LO 3 Mechanism of the Act
LO 4 Scope of the Act
LO 5 Important provisions of the Act

The Right to Information Act 2005 is a law enacted by the Parliament giving the citizens of India access to the records of the Public Authorities. Mr. Arvind Kejriwal, Ms. Aruna Rai, legendary political and social activist, founder of the Mazdoor Kisan Shakti Sangathan (MKSS) and the recipient of Ramon Magsaysay Award as well as Lal Bahadur Shastri National Award and Prof. Jean Dreze, acclaimed Belgium-born Indian development economist, have been instrumental in drafting the revolutionary legislation. The Act mandates timely response to citizens' (of India) requests for government information. In order to promote transparency and accountability in the working of every public authority and facilitate the citizens to secure information under the control of a public authority, the Act provides for the constitution of a Central Information Commission and State Information Commissions. The Act also requires every public authority to computerise its records for wide dissemination and to proactively publish certain categories of information so that the applicants need minimum recourse to request for the information formally. Information disclosure in India was hitherto restricted by the Official Secrets Act 1923 and various other special laws, which the new RTI Act now relaxes.

RTI Act: Aim and Objectives

The Act aims to provide for setting out the practical regime of right to information for citizens to secure access to information under the control of public authorities. It seeks to promote transparency and accountability in the working of every public authority.

Scope of the Act

The Right to Information Act covers the whole of India except Jammu and Kashmir, where J&K Right to Information Act, 2009 is in force. The Act is applicable to all constitutional authorities, including the executive, legislature, and judiciary; any institution or body established or constituted by an Act of Parliament or a State legislature. Bodies or authorities established or constituted by order or notification of appropriate government including bodies 'owned, controlled, or substantially financed' by government, or non-Government organizations 'substantially financed, directly or indirectly by funds' provided by the government are also covered in it. In a recent development, the Central Information Commission (CIC), setting a new benchmark in transparency in politics, held that political parties are also answerable to the people under the Right to Information Act as they seek to represent the people and to take decisions on their behalf. The Commission held six major parties, Congress, BJP, CPI-M, CPI, NCP, and BSP, fulfil the criteria of being public authorities under the Act. But ironically, they have so far resisted attempts to be listed as "public authorities" under RTI Act and thus be made liable to publicly disclose financial assets and provide with any such information as sought by the public for that matter. Notwithstanding, with the Supreme Court now asking all these six national parties why they should not be brought under the RTI, India is a step closer to making its political organisations accountable in their financial transactions.

> Appropriate government: Public authority, established, constituted, owned, controlled, or substantially financed by funds provided directly or indirectly by (i) the Central Government or the Union Territory administration or (ii) the State Government.

Private bodies are not within the Act's ambit directly. However, in a landmark decision of 30 Nov, 2006 (Sarbajit Roy versus DERC), CIC also reaffirmed that privatised public utility entities continue to be within the purview of the RTI Act.

The Act enables applicant citizens to (a) obtain copies of permissible governmental documents; (b) inspect permissible governmental documents; and (c) inspect permissible governmental works and also obtain samples.

Major Concepts

Some of the important terms used in the RTI Act are briefly introduced below.

Appropriate Government refers to a public authority which is established, constituted, owned, controlled or substantially financed by funds provided directly or indirectly

> Central public information officer (CPIO): Designated CPIO and includes a Central Assistant Public Information Officer designated as such under Section 5(2) of RTI Act.

1. by the Central Government or the Union Territory administration, the Central Government;
2. by the State Government, the State Government.

Chief Information Commissioner and Information Commissioner: Chief Information Commissioner (CIC) and Information Commissioner appointed under Section 12(3) of the RTI Act.

Central Information Commission (CIC) refers to the designated Central Information Commission constituted under Section 12(1).

Competent authority: (i) the Speaker in the case of the House of the People or the Legislative Assembly of a State or a UT having such Assembly and the Chairman in the case of the Council of States or Legislative Council of a State; (ii) CJI in the case of the Supreme Court; (iii) the Chief Justice of the High Court in the case of a High Court; (iv) the President or the Governor in the case of other authorities; (v) the Administrator appointed under Article 239 of the Constitution.

Central Public Information Officer (CPIC) refers to the designated Central Public Information Officer and includes a Central Assistant Public Information Officer designated as such under Section 5(2).

Chief Information Commissioner and Information Commissioner refer to the Chief Information Commissioner and Information Commissioner appointed under Section 12(3).

Competent authority means—

Information: Any material in any form, including records, documents, memos, e-mails, opinions, advices, press releases, circulars, orders, logbooks, contracts, reports, papers, samples, models, data material held in any electronic form, and information relating to any private body which can be accessed by a public authority under any other law.

1. the Speaker in the case of the House of the People or the Legislative Assembly of a State or a Union Territory having such Assembly and the Chairman in the case of the Council of States or Legislative Council of a State;
2. the Chief Justice of India in the case of the Supreme Court;
3. the Chief Justice of the High Court in the case of a High Court;
4. the President or the Governor in the case of other authorities established or constituted by or under the Constitution;
5. the Administrator appointed under Article 239 of the Constitution.

Information means any material in any form, including records, documents, memos, e-mails, opinions, advices press releases, circulars, orders, logbooks, contracts, reports, papers, samples, models, data material held in any electronic form, and information relating to any private body which can be accessed by a public authority under any other law for the time being in force.

Public authority: Any authority or body or institution of government established or constituted by/under (i) the Constitution, (ii) any other law made by Parliament, (iii) any other law made by State Legislature, (iv) notification issued or order made by the appropriate government, and includes any (a) body owned, controlled, or substantially financed and (b) NGO substantially financed, directly or indirectly by funds provided by the appropriate government.

Public Authority means any authority or body or institution of government established or constituted

1. by or under the Constitution;
2. by any other law made by Parliament;
3. by any other law made by State Legislature;
4. by notification issued or order made by the appropriate government, and includes any
   (a) body owned, controlled, or substantially financed; and
   (b) non-government organization substantially financed, directly or indirectly by funds provided by the appropriate government.

Record includes

1. any document, manuscript, and file;
2. any microfilm, microfiche, and facsimile copy of a document;
3. any reproduction of an image or images embodied in such microfilm (whether enlarged or not); and
4. any other material produced by a computer or any other device.

Right to information: Fundamental right of freedom of speech and expression.

Right to Information is associated with the fundamental right of freedom of speech and expression. It means the right to information accessible under this Act which is held by or under the control of any public authority and includes the right to—

1. inspection of work, documents, records;
2. takeg notes, extracts, or certified copies of documents or records;

3. taking certified samples of material;
4. obtaining information in the form of diskettes, floppies, tapes, video cassettes or in any other electronic mode, or through printouts where such information is stored in a computer or in any other device.

State Chief Information Commissioner and State Information Commissioner mean the State Chief Information Commissioner and the State Information Commissioner appointed under Section 15(3).

State Public Information Officer (SPIO) means the designated State Public Information Officer and includes a State Assistant Public Information Officer designated as such under Section 5(2).

Third party: A person other than the citizen (of India) seeking information and includes a public authority.

Third Party means a person other than the citisen making a request for information and includes a public authority.

Important Provisions

Important provisions of the Act have been briefly explained below.

Right to Information

Subject to the provisions of this Act, all citisens shall have the right to information [Section 3].

Obligations of Public Authorities

1. Every public authority shall
   (a) Maintain all its records duly catalogued and indexed in a manner and form which facilitates the right to information under this Act and ensure that all records that are appropriate to be computerised are, within a reasonable time and subject to availability of resources, computerised and connected through a network all over the country on different systems so that access to such records is facilitated;
   (b) Publish within 120 days from the enactment of this Act,
      (i) the particulars of its organization, functions, and duties;
      (ii) the powers and duties of its officers and employees;
      (iii) the procedure followed in the decision-making process, including channels of supervision and accountability;
      (iv) the norms set by it for the discharge of its functions;
      (v) the rules, regulations, instructions, manuals, and records, held by it or under its control or used by its employees for discharging its functions;
      (vi) a statement of the categories of documents that are held by it or under its control;
      (vi) the particulars of any arrangement that exists for consultation with, or representation by, the members of the public in relation to the formulation of its policy or implementation thereof;
      (vii) a statement of the boards, councils, committees and other bodies consisting of two or more persons constituted as its part or for the purpose of its advice, and as to whether meetings of those boards, councils, committees and other bodies are open to the public, or the minutes of such meetings are accessible for public;
      (viii) a directory of its officers and employees;
      (ix) the monthly remuneration received by each of its officers and employees, including the system of compensation as provided in its regulations;
      (x) the budget allocated to each of its agencies, indicating the particulars of all plans, proposed expenditures and reports on disbursements made;
      (xi) the manner of execution of subsidy programmes, including the amounts allocated and the details of beneficiaries of such programmes;
      (xii) particulars of recipients of concessions, permits, or authorizations granted by it;
      (xiii) details in respect of the information, available to or held by it, reduced in an electronic form;

(xiv) the particulars of facilities available to citisens for obtaining information, including the working hours of a library/reading room, if maintained for public use;

(xv) the names, designations and other particulars of the Public Information Officers;

(xvi) such other information as may be prescribed and thereafter update these publications every year.

(xvii) Publish all relevant facts while formulating important policies or announcing the decisions which affect the public;

(xviii) Provide reasons for its administrative or quasi-judicial decisions to affected persons.

2. It shall be a constant endeavour of every public authority to take steps in accordance with the requirements of clause (b) of sub-section (1) to provide as much information suo motu to the public at regular intervals through various means of communications, including the Internet, so that the public have minimum resort to the use of this Act to obtain information.
3. For the purposes of sub-section (1), every information shall be disseminated widely and in such a form and manner that is easily accessible to the public.
4. All materials shall be disseminated taking into consideration the cost effectiveness, local language, and the most effective method of communication in that local area. The information should be easily accessible, to the extent possible in electronic format with the Central/State Public Information Officer available free or at such cost of the medium or the print cost price as may be prescribed [Section 4].

   Explanation: For the purposes of sub-sections (3) and (4), 'disseminated' means making known or communicating the information to the public through notice boards, newspapers, public announcements, media broadcasts, the Internet, or any other means, including inspection of offices of any public authority.

Appointment of Central/State Public Information Officer

1. Every public authority shall, within 100 days of the enactment of this Act, designate as many officers as the Central/State Public Information Officers in all administrative units or offices under it as may be necessary to provide information to persons requesting for information under this Act.
2. Every public authority shall designate an officer, within 100 days of the enactment of this Act, at each sub-divisional level or other sub-district level as a Central/State Assistant Public Information Officer to receive the applications for information or appeals under this Act for forwarding the same forthwith to the Central/State Public Information Officer or senior officer specified under Section 19(1) or the Central/State Information Commission.

   However, where an application for information or appeal is given to a Central/State Assistant Public Information Officer, a period of five days shall be added in computing the period for response specified under Section 7(1).
3. Every Central/State Public Information Officer shall deal with requests from persons seeking information and render reasonable assistance to the persons seeking such information.
4. The Central/State Public Information Officer may seek the assistance of any other officer as he or she considers necessary, for the proper discharge of his or her duties.
5. Any officer, whose assistance has been sought under sub-section (4), shall render all assistance to the Central/State Public Information Officer seeking his or her assistance and for the purposes of any contravention of the provisions of this Act; such an officer shall be treated as a Central/State Public Information Officer [Section 5].

Procedure of Obtaining Desired Information

1. A person, who desires to obtain any information under this Act, shall make a request in writing or through electronic means in English or Hindi or in the official language of the area in which the

application is being made, with the prescribed fee to

(a) the Central/State Public Information Officer of the concerned public authority;

(b) the Central/State Assistant Public Information Officer specifying the particulars of the information sought by him or her [Section 6].

However, where such a request cannot be made in writing, the Central/State Public Information Officer shall render all reasonable assistance to the person making the request orally to reduce the same in writing.

2. An applicant making request for information is not under obligation to offer any explanation or reason to seek information.

Disposal of Request

Time limit The Act specifies time limits for replying to the request as under:

1. The Central/State Public Information Officer shall, as expediously as possible, and in any case within thirty days of the receipt of the request, provide the information on payment of prescribed fee, if any.
2. If the PIO transfers the request to another public authority (better concerned with the information requested), the time allowed to reply is 30 days, but computed from the day after it is received by the PIO of the transferee authority.
3. Information concerning allegations of violations of human rights by scheduled Security agencies (those listed in the Second Schedule to the Act) is to be provided within 45 days from the date of receipt of request but with the prior approval of the Central Information Commission.
4. If the information sought for concerns life or liberty of any person involved, the same shall be provided within 48 hours [Section 7].

Since the information is to be paid for, the reply of thę PIO is necessarily limited to either denying the request (in whole or part) and/or providing a computation of 'further fees'. The time between the reply of the PIO and the time taken to deposit the further fees for information is excluded from the time allowed.

If information is not provided within this period, it is deemed as refusal. Refusal with or without reason may be ground for appeal or complaint. Moreover, information not provided in the time prescribed is to be provided free of charge.

Fee applicable For Central Departments, as of there is a fee of ₹10 for filing the request, ₹2 per page of information and ₹5 for each hour of inspection after the first hour. If the applicant is a Below Poverty Line (BPL) Card holder, then no fee shall apply. Such BPL Card holders have to provide a copy of their BPL card along with their application to the Public Authority. States Government and High Courts, however, fix their own rules.

Rejection of request for information Where a request has been rejected, the Central/State Public Information Officer shall communicate to the person making the request

1. the reasons for such rejection;
2. the period within which an appeal against such rejection may be preferred; and
3. the particulars of the appellate authority.

Form in which information shall be provided Information shall ordinarily be provided in the form in which it is sought unless it would disproportionately divert the resources of the public authority or would be detrimental to the safety or preservation of the record in question [Section 7].

What is Not Open to Disclosure?

The following are exempt from disclosure under Section 8(1):

1. Information, disclosure of which would prejudicially affect the sovereignty and integrity of India, the security, strategic, scientific or economic interests of the State, relations with a foreign State, or lead to incitement of an offence.
2. Information which has been expressly forbidden to be published by any court of law or tribunal or the disclosure of which may constitute Contempt of Court.
3. Information, the disclosure of which would cause a breach of privilege of Parliament or the State Legislature.
4. Information, including commercial confidence, trade secrets, or intellectual property, the disclosure of which would harm the competitive position of a third party, unless the competent authority is satisfied that larger public interest warrants the disclosure of such information.

5. Information available to a person in his fiduciary relationship, unless the competent authority is satisfied that the larger public interest warrants the disclosure of such information.
6. Information received in confidence from a foreign Government.
7. Information, the disclosure of which would endanger the life or physical safety of any person, or identify the source of information or assistance given in confidence for law enforcement or security purposes.
8. Information which would impede the process of investigation or apprehension or prosecution of offenders.
9. Cabinet papers, including records of deliberations of the Council of Ministers, Secretaries, and other officers.
10. Information which relates to personal information, the disclosure of which has no relationship to any public activity or interest, or which would cause unwarranted invasion of the privacy of the individual.

    However, the information which cannot be denied to the Parliament or a State Legislature shall not be denied to any person by the above exemption.

A public authority may, however, allow access to information, which is exempt from disclosure otherwise under Section 8(1), if public interest in disclosure outweighs the harm to the protected interests [Section 8(2)].

Grounds for Rejection of a Request for Information

A Central/State Public Information Officer may reject a request for information where such a request for providing access would involve an infringement of copyright subsisting in a person other than the State [Section 9].

Partial Disclosure

1. Where a request for access to information is rejected on the ground that it is in relation to information which is exempt from disclosure, then access may be provided to those part(s) of the record which are not exempt from disclosure and which can reasonably be severed from parts containing exempt information to be provided.
2. Where access is granted to a part of the record under sub-section (1), the Central/State Public Information Officer shall give a notice to the applicant, informing—
   (a) that only part of the record requested, after severance of the record containing information which is exempt from disclosure, is being provided;
   (b) the reasons for the decision, including any findings on any material question of fact, referring to the material on which those findings were based;
   (c) the name and designation of the person giving the decision;
   (d) the details of the fees calculated by him or her and the amount of fee which the applicant is required to deposit; and
   (e) his or her rights with respect to review of the decision regarding non-disclosure of part of the information, the amount of fee charged or the form of access provided, including the particulars of the senior officer specified under sub-section (1) of Section 19 or the Central/State Information Commission time limit, process, and any other form of access [Section 10].

Central Information Commission

1. The Central Government shall, by notification in the Official Gazette, constitute a body to be known as the Central Information Commission to exercise the powers conferred on, and to perform the functions assigned to it, under this Act.
2. The Central Information Commission shall consist of—
   (a) the Chief Information Commissioner; and
   (b) such number of Central Information Commissioners, not exceeding ten, as may be deemed necessary.

> Central Information Commission: Set up under the RTI ACT is the authorised body, established in 2005 by the Government of India, to act upon complaints from those individuals who have not been able to submit information requests to a CPIO or State PIO due to either the officer not having been appointed, or because the respective Central APIO or State APIO refused to receive the application for information under the RTI Act.

3. The Chief Information Commissioner and Information Commissioners shall be appointed by the President of India on the recommendation of a committee consisting of
   (a) the Prime Minister, who shall be the Chairperson of the committee;
   (b) the Leader of Opposition in the Lok Sabha; and
   (c) a Union Cabinet Minister to be nominated by the Prime Minister.

   Explanation: For the purposes of removal of doubts, it is hereby declared that where the Leader of the Opposition in the House of the People (Lok Sabha) has not been recognised as such, the Leader of the single largest group in opposition of the Government in the House of the People shall be deemed to be the Leader of the Opposition.
4. The general superintendence, direction and management of the affairs of the Central Information Commission shall vest in the Chief Information Commissioner who shall be assisted by the Information Commissioners and may exercise all such powers and do all such acts and things which may be exercised or done by the Central Information Commission autonomously without being subjected to directions by any other authority under this Act.
5. The Chief Information Commissioner and Information Commissioners shall be persons of eminence in public life with wide knowledge and experience in law, science and technology, social service, management, journalism, mass media, or administration and governance.
6. The Chief Information Commissioner or an Information Commissioner shall not be a Member of Parliament/Legislature of any State or Union Territory or hold any other office of profit or be connected with any political party, or carry on any business or pursue any profession.
7. The headquarters of the Central Information Commission shall be at Delhi and the Central Information Commission may, with the previous approval of the Central Government, establish offices at other places in India [Section 12].

Term of Office of Chief Information Commissioner

- The Chief Information Commissioner shall hold office for a term of five years from the date on which he enters upon his office or till he attains the age of sixty-five years, whichever is earlier and shall not be eligible for reappointment.
- Every Information Commissioner shall hold office for a term of five years from the date on which he enters upon his office or till he attains the age of sixty-five years, whichever is earlier, and shall not be eligible for reappointment as an Information Commissioner [Section 13].

Notwithstanding, every Information Commissioner shall, on vacating his office, under this sub-section be eligible for appointment as the Chief Information Commissioner in the manner specified in Section 12(3).

It is important to note that where the Information Commissioner is appointed as the Chief Information Commissioner, his term of office shall not be more than five years in aggregate as the Information Commissioner and the Chief Information Commissioner [Section 13].

Removal/Suspension of Chief/Any Information Commissioner

1. Subject to the provisions of sub-section (3), the Chief Information Commissioner or any Information Commissioner shall be removed from office only by order of the President of India on the ground of proved misbehaviour or incapacity after the Supreme Court, on a reference made to it by the President, has, on inquiry, reported that the Chief Information Commissioner or any Information Commissioner ought, on such grounds, to be removed.
2. The President (of India) may suspend from office, and if deemed necessary, prohibit also from attending office during inquiry, the Chief Information Commissioner or Information Commissioner in respect of whom a reference has been made to the Supreme Court under sub-section (1) until the President has passed orders on receipt of the report of the Supreme Court on such reference.
3. The President may, by order, remove from office the Chief Information Commissioner or

any Information Commissioner, if that Chief Information Commissioner or Information Commissioner

(a) is adjudged an insolvent; or
(b) has been convicted of an offence which, in the opinion of the President, involves moral turpitude; or
(c) engages during his term of office in any paid employment outside the duties of his office; or
(d) is, in the opinion of the President, unfit to continue in office by reason of infirmity of mind or body; or
(e) has acquired such financial or other interest as is likely to affect prejudicially his functions as the Chief Information Commissioner or Information Commissioner.

4. If the Chief Information Commissioner or Information Commissioner, is in any way, concerned or interested in any contract or agreement made by or on behalf of the Government of India or participates in any way in the profit thereof or in any benefit or emolument arising thereof, otherwise than as a member and in common with the other members of an incorporated company, he shall, for the purposes of sub-section (1), be deemed to be guilty of misbehaviour [Section 14].

State Information Commission

State Information Commission: State level information commission, constituted by each State Government through a Gazette notification, consisting of one State Chief Information Commissioner (SCIC) and not more than 10 State Information Commissioners (SIC) to be appointed by the Governor concerned.

1. Every State Government shall, by notification in the Official Gazette, constitute a body to be known as the ... (Name of the State) Information Commission to exercise the powers conferred on, and to perform the functions assigned to, it under this Act.
2. The State Information Commission shall consist of
   (a) the State Chief Information Commissioner, and
   (b) such number of State Information Commissioners, not exceeding ten, as may be deemed necessary.
3. The State Chief Information Commissioner and the State Information Commissioners shall be appointed by the Governor on the recommendation of a committee consisting of
   (a) the Chief Minister, who shall be the Chairperson of the committee;
   (b) the Leader of the Opposition in the Legislative Assembly; and
   (c) a Cabinet Minister to be nominated by the Chief Minister.

   Explanation: For the purposes of removal of doubts, it is hereby declared that where the Leader of the Opposition in the Legislative Assembly has not been recognised as such, the Leader of the single largest group in opposition of the Government in the Legislative Assembly shall be deemed to be the Leader of the Opposition.
4. The general superintendence, direction and management of the affairs of the State Information Commission shall vest in the State Chief Information Commissioner who shall be assisted by the State Information Commissioners and may exercise all such powers and do all such acts and things which may be exercised or done by the State Information Commission autonomously without being subjected to directions by any other authority under this Act.
5. The State Chief Information Commissioner and the State Information Commissioners shall be persons of eminence in public life with wide knowledge and experience in law, science and technology, social service, management, journalism, mass media or administration and governance.
6. The State Chief Information Commissioner or a State Information Commissioner shall not be a Member of Parliament/Legislature of any State or Union Territory or hold any other office of profit or connected with any political party or carry on any business or pursue any profession.
7. The headquarters of the State Information Commission shall be at such a place in the State as the State Government may, by notifi-

cation in the Official Gazette, specify, and the State Information Commission may, with the previous approval of the State Government, establish offices at other places in the State [Section 15].

Term of Office of State Chief/Every State Information Commissioner

1. The State Chief Information Commissioner shall hold office for a term of five years from the date on which he enters upon his office or till he attains the age of sixty-five years, whichever is earlier, and shall not be eligible for reappointment.
2. Every State Information Commissioner shall hold office for a term of five years from the date on which he enters upon his office or till he attains the age of sixty-five years, whichever is earlier, and shall not be eligible for reappointment as such a State Information Commissioner.

   However, every State Information Commissioner shall, on vacating his office under this sub-section, be eligible for appointment as the State Chief Information Commissioner in the manner specified in sub-section (3) of section 15.

   Furthermore, where the State Information Commissioner is appointed as the State Chief Information Commissioner, his term of office shall not be more than five years in aggregate as the State Information Commissioner and the State Chief Information Commissioner.
3. The State Chief Information Commissioner or a State Information Commissioner, shall, before he enters upon his office, make and subscribe before the Governor or some other person appointed by the latter in that behalf, an oath or affirmation according to the form set out for the purpose in the First Schedule.
4. The State Chief Information Commissioner or a State Information Commissioner may, at any time, by writing under his hand addressed to the Governor, resign from his office.

   Besides, the State Chief Information Commissioner or a State Information Commissioner may be removed in the manner specified under Section 17 [Section 16].

Salaries and Allowances Payable to and Other Terms and Conditions of Service

1. The State Chief Information Commissioner shall be the same as that of an Election Commissioner;
2. The State Information Commissioner shall be the same as that of the Chief Secretary to the State Government [Section 16(5)].

   If the State Chief/State Information Commissioner, at the time of his appointment, is in receipt of a pension/retirement benefits, other than a disability or wound pension, in respect of any previous service under the Government of India or under the Government of a State, his salary in respect of the service as the State Chief/State Information Commissioner shall be reduced by the amount of that pension/retirement benefits.

Administrative/Staff Support to State Chief/State Information Commissioners

The State Government shall provide the State Chief Information Commissioner and the State Information Commissioners with such officers and employees as may be necessary for the efficient performance of their functions under this Act, and the salaries and allowances payable to and the terms and conditions of service of the officers and other employees appointed for the purpose of this Act shall be such as may be prescribed [Section 16(6)].

Removal/Suspension of State Chief Information Commissioner

1. The State Chief Information Commissioner or a State Information Commissioner shall be removed from his office only by order of the Governor on the ground of proved misbehaviour or incapacity, after the Supreme Court, on a reference made to it by the Governor, has, on inquiry, reported that the State Chief/State Information Commissioner ought on such ground be removed.
2. The Governor may suspend from office, and if deemed necessary, prohibit also from attending office during inquiry, the State Chief/State Information Commissioner in respect of whom a reference has been made to the Supreme Court

under sub-section (1) until the Governor has passed orders on receipt of the report of the Supreme Court on such a reference.

3. Notwithstanding anything contained in sub-section (1), the Governor may, by order, remove from office, the State Chief/State Information Commissioner if a State Chief/State Information Commissioner
   (a) is adjudged an insolvent; or
   (b) has been convicted of an offence which, in the opinion of the Governor, involves moral turpitude; or
   (c) engages during his term of office in any paid employment outside the duties of his office; or
   (d) is, in the opinion of the Governor, unfit to continue in office by reason of infirmity of mind or body; or
   (e) has acquired such financial or other interest as is likely to affect prejudicially his functions as the State Chief/State Information Commissioner.
4. If the State Chief/State Information Commissioner is, in any way, concerned or interested in any contract or agreement made by, or on behalf of, the Government of the State, or participates in any way in the profit thereof or in any benefit or emoluments arising thereof, otherwise than as a member and in common with the other members of an incorporated company, he shall, for the purposes of sub-section (1), be deemed to be guilty of misbehaviour [Section 17].

Role of Information Commissions

1. It shall be the duty of the Central Information Commission or State Information Commission to receive and inquire into a complaint from any person
   (a) who has been unable to submit a request to a Central/State Public Information Officer either by reason that no such officer has been appointed under this Act, or because the Central/State Assistant Public Information Officer has refused to accept his or her application for information or appeal under this Act for forwarding the same to the Central/State Public Information Officer or senior officer specified in Section 19(1) or the Central/State Information Commission;
   (b) who has been refused access to any information requested under this Act;
   (c) who has not been given a response to a request for information or access to information within the time limit specified under this Act;
   (d) who has been required to pay an amount of fee which he or she considers unreasonable;
   (e) who believes that he or she has been given incomplete, misleading or false information under this Act; and
   (f) in respect of any other matter relating to requesting or obtaining access to records under this Act.
2. Where the Central/State Information Commission is satisfied that there are reasonable grounds to inquire into the matter, it may initiate an inquiry in respect thereof.
3. The Central/State Information Commission shall, while inquiring into any matter under this Section, have the same powers as are vested in a civil court while trying a suit under the Code of Civil Procedure, 1908, in respect of certain matters, namely:
   (a) summoning and enforcing the attendance of persons and compelling them to give oral or written evidence on oath and to produce documents or things;
   (b) requiring the discovery and inspection of documents;
   (c) receiving evidence on affidavit;
   (d) requisitioning any public record or copies thereof from any court or office;
   (e) issuing summons for examination of witnesses or documents; and
   (f) any other matter which may be prescribed.
4. Notwithstanding anything inconsistent contained in any other Act of Parliament or State Legislature, the Central/State Information Commission may, during the inquiry of any complaint under this Act, examine any record to which this Act applies which is under the control of the public authority, and no such record may be withheld from it on any grounds [Section 18].

Remedies Available to Aggrieved Party

1. Any person who does not receive a decision within the specified time or is otherwise aggrieved by a decision of the Central/State Public Information Officer may, within 30 days from the expiry of such period or from the receipt of such a decision, file an appeal to an officer who is senior in rank to the Central/State Public Information Officer.

   However, such an officer may admit the appeal after the expiry of the period of 30 days if he or she is satisfied that the appellant was prevented by sufficient cause from filing the appeal in time.
2. Where an appeal is preferred against an order made by a Central/State Public Information Officer under Section 11 to disclose third party information, the appeal by the concerned third party shall be made within 30 days from the date of the order.
3. A second appeal against the decision under sub-section (1) shall lie within 90 days from the date on which the decision should have been made or was actually received, with the Central/State Information Commission:

   However, the Central/State Information Commission may admit the appeal after the expiry of the period of 90 days if it is satisfied that the appellant was prevented by sufficient cause from filing the appeal in time.
4. If the decision of the Central/State Public Information officer against which an appeal is preferred relates to information of a third party, the Central/State Information Commission shall give a reasonable opportunity of being heard to that third party.
5. In any appeal proceedings, the onus to prove that a denial of request was justified shall be on the Central/State Public Information Officer who denied the request.
6. An appeal under sub-section (1) or sub-section (2) shall be disposed of within 30 days of the receipt of the appeal or within such extended period not exceeding a total of 45 days from the date of filing thereof for reasons to be recorded in writing.
7. The decision of the Central/State Information Commission shall be binding.
8. In its decision, the Central/State Information Commission has the power to
   (a) require the public authority to take any such steps as may be necessary to secure compliance with the provisions of this Act, including—
      (i) by providing access to information, if so requested, in a particular form;
      (ii) by appointing a Central/State Public Information Officer;
      (iii) by publishing certain information or categories of information;
      (iv) by making necessary changes to its practices in relation to the maintenance, management, and destruction of records;
      (v) by enhancing the provision of training on the right to information for its officials;
      (vi) by providing it with an annual report in compliance with clause (b) of sub-section (1) of section 4;
   (b) require the public authority to compensate the complainant for any loss or other detriment suffered;
   (c) impose any of the penalties provided under this Act;
   (d) reject the application.
9. The Central/State Information Commission shall give notice of its decision, including any right of appeal, to the complainant and the public authority.
10. The Central/State Information Commission shall decide the appeal in accordance with such procedure as may be prescribed [Section 19].

Penalty for Non-compliance

When the Central/State Information Commission at the time of deciding any complaint or appeal is of the opinion that the Central/State Public Information Officer has, without any reasonable cause, refused to receive an application for information, not furnished information within the stipulated time or malafidely denied the request for information or knowingly given incorrect, incomplete or misleading information or destroyed information which was the subject of the request or obstructed in any manner in furnishing the information, the CIC can

1. impose a penalty of ₹250 for each day till application is received or information is furnished, subject to maximum of ₹25,000;
2. recommend for disciplinary action against the PIO in default under the service rules applicable to him [Section 20].

Miscellaneous Provisions

No suit, prosecution or other legal proceeding shall lie against any person for anything which is done in good faith or is intended to be done under this Act or any rule made thereunder [Section 21].

No court shall entertain any suit, application or other proceeding in respect of any order made under this Act and no such order shall be called in question otherwise than by way of an appeal under this Act [Section 23].

Exclusion of Certain Organisations

1. The Act shall not apply to the intelligence and security organizations specified in the Second Schedule, being organizations established by the Central Government, or any information furnished by such organizations to that Government:

   However, information pertaining to allegations of corruption and human rights violations shall not be excluded under this sub-section.

   Provided further that if the information sought is in respect of allegations of violation of human rights, the information shall only be provided after the approval of the Central Information Commission. Such information shall be provided within 45 days from the date of the receipt of request.
2. The Central Government may, by notification in the Official Gazette, amend the Schedule by including therein any other intelligence or security organization established by that Government or omitting any organization already specified therein and on the publication of such notification, such an organization shall be deemed to be included in/omitted from the Schedule.
3. Every notification issued under sub-section (2) shall be laid before each House of Parliament.
4. Nothing contained in this Act shall apply to such intelligence and security organizations being organizations established by the State Government, as that Government may, from time to time, by notification in the Official Gazette, specify.

   However, the information pertaining to the allegations of corruption and human rights violations shall not be excluded under this sub-section.
5. Every notification issued under sub-section (4) shall be laid before the State Legislature [Section 24].

Reporting Obligations of Central/State Information Commission

1. The Central/State Information Commission shall, as soon as practicable after the end of each year, prepare a report on the implementation of the provisions of this Act during that year and forward a copy thereof to the appropriate Government.
2. Each Ministry or Department shall, in relation to the public authorities within their jurisdiction, collect and provide such information to the Central/State Information Commission as is required to prepare the report under this Section and comply with the requirements concerning the furnishing of that information and keeping of records for the purposes of this Section.
3. Each report shall state, in respect of the year to which the report relates—
   (a) the number of requests made to each public authority;
   (b) the number of decisions where applicants were not entitled to access to the documents pursuant to the requests, the provisions of this Act under which these decisions were made and the number of times such provisions were invoked;
   (c) the number of appeals referred to the Central/State Information Commission for review, the nature of the appeals and the outcome of the appeals;
   (d) particulars of any disciplinary action taken against any officer in respect of the administration of this Act;

(e) the amount of charges collected by each public authority under this Act;
(f) any facts which indicate an effort by the public authorities to administer and implement the spirit and intention of this Act;
(g) recommendations for reform, including recommendations in respect of the particular public authorities, for the development, improvement, modernization, reform or amendment to this Act or other legislation or common law or any other matter relevant for operationalizing the right to access information.

4. The Central/State Government may, as soon as practicable after the end of each year, cause a copy of the report of the Central/State Information Commission referred to in sub-section (1) to be laid before each House of Parliament or before each House of the State Legislature, where there are two Houses, and where there is one House of the State Legislature before that House.
5. If it appears to the Central/State Information Commission that the practice of a public authority in relation to the exercise of its functions under this Act does not conform with the provisions or spirit of this Act, it may give to the authority a recommendation specifying the steps which ought, in its opinion, to be taken for promoting such conformity [Section 25].

Power to Make Rules to Carry Out the Provisions of the Act

1. The appropriate Government may, by notification in the Official Gazette, make rules to carry out the provisions of this Act.
2. In particular, and without prejudice to the generality of the foregoing power, such rules may provide for all or any of the following matters, namely:
(a) the cost of the medium or print cost price of the materials to be disseminated under sub-section (4) of Section 4;
(b) the fee payable under sub-section (1) of Section 6;
(c) the fee payable under sub-sections (1) and (5) of Section 7;
(d) the salaries and allowances payable to and the terms and conditions of service of the officers and other employees under sub-Section (6) of Section 13 and sub-section (6) of Section 16;
(e) the procedure to be adopted by the Central/State Information Commission in deciding the appeals under sub-section (10) of Section 19; and
(f) any other matter which is required to be, or may be, prescribed [Section 27].

The Second Schedule

Intelligence and Security Organisations Established by the Central Government

1. Intelligence Bureau
2. Research and Analysis Wing of the Cabinet Secretariat
3. Directorate of Revenue Intelligence
4. Central Economic Intelligence Bureau
5. Directorate of Enforcement
6. Narcotics Central Bureau
7. Aviation Research Centre
8. Special Frontier Force
9. Border Security Force
10. Central Reserve Police Force
11. Indo-Tibetan Border Police
12. Central Industrial Security Force
13. National Security Guards
14. Assam Rifles
15. Sashastra Seema Bal
16. Directorate General of Income Tax (Investigation)
17. National Technical Research Organisation
18. Financial Intelligence Unit, India
19. Special Protection Group
20. Defence Research and Development Organisation
21. Border Road Development Board
22. National Security Council Secretariat
23. Central Bureau of Investigation
24. National Investigation Agency
25. National Intelligence Grid

Exercises

I. Objective-type Questions

1. State whether each of the following statements is true or false:
   (i) Instead of written information, the applicant can request for personal examination of documents under the RTI Act.
   (ii) A good employee cannot seek information from his own department.
   (iii) Only citizens of India can seek information under the RTI Act.
   (iv) The PIO can reject a request for disclosure of information involving an infringement of copyright subsisting in a person other than the state.
   (v) A portion of information cannot be provided under the RTI Act.

2. Indicate the correct answer:
   (i) A person who desires to obtain any information under the Right to Information Act, shall make a request to
      (a) the Central Public Information Officer of the concerned authority
      (b) State Public Information Officer of the concerned public authority
      (c) the Central Assistant Public Information Officer or State Assistant Public Information Officer, as the case may be
      (d) Any of the above, as the case may be
   (ii) Record includes
      (a) any document, manuscript, and file
      (b) any microfilm, microfiche, and facsimile copy of a document
      (c) any reproduction of image or images embodied in such microfilm besides any other material produced by a computer or any other device
      (d) Any or all of the above
   (iii) 'Right to Information' means the right to information accessible under the RTI Act which is held by or under the control of any public authority and includes the right to
      (a) inspect work, documents, records
      (b) take notes, extracts or certified copies or documents or records, or obtain information in the soft form
      (c) take certified samples of material
      (d) All of the above
   (iv) Every public authority shall
      (a) maintain all its records duly catalogued and indexed in a manner and form which facilitates the right to information under the RTI Act
      (b) maintain all its records duly catalogued and indexed in a manner and form which facilitates the right to information under the RTI Act
      (c) publish within 120 days from the enactment of the RTI Act, all relevant facts/particulars/vital details concerning the authority
      (d) comply with all of the above
   (v) In its decision, the Central/State Information Commission has the power to
      (a) require the public authority to take any such steps as may be necessary to secure compliance with the provisions of the RTI Act
      (b) require the public authority to compensate the complainant for any loss or other detriment suffered
      (c) impose any of the penalties provided under this Act
      (d) reject the application besides resorting to above

II. Review Questions

1. Describe the obligations of public authorities as regards maintaining records and publishing information.
2. Enumerate the types of information which can be denied to any citisen by a public authority notwithstanding anything contained in the RTI Act.
3. Describe the duty of the Chief Information Commission/State Information Commission as regards receiving and inquiring into a complaint from any person.
4. Outline the powers vested in the Central Information Commission or State Information Commission, as the case may be, while inquiring into any matter under the RTI Act.
5. Describe the decision-related powers of the Chief Information Commission and the State Information Commission.

Answers to Objective-type Questions

1.	(i) True	(ii) False	(iii) True	(iv) True	(v) False
2.	(i) (d)	(ii) (d)	(iii) (d)	(iv) (d)	(v) (d)

25 Chapter in Review

LEARNING OUTCOMES

- **LO 1** What is RTI Act, 2005
- **LO 2** Applicability of the Act
- **LO 3** Mechanism of the Act
- **LO 4** Scope of the Act
- **LO 5** Important provisions of the Act

LO1 The RTI Act, 2005 is an Act of the Parliament of India that provides for setting out the practical regime of right to information for the citizens.

LO2 The Act applies to all the States and Union Territories of India except the State of Jammu and Kashmir, which has its own Act, called J&K Right to Information Act, 2009.

LO3 To promote transparency and accountability in the working of every public authority and facilitate the citizens (of India) to secure access to information under the control of public authorities, the Act provides for constitution of a Central Information Commission (CIC) and State Information Commissions.

LO4 The Act applies to all public authorities and also to NGOs, substantially financed by the Government. Private bodies, except privatised public utility companies, are not within the Act's ambit directly.

LO5 The Act enables applicant Indian citizens to (a) obtain copies of permissible governmental documents; (b) inspect permissible governmental documents; and (c) inspect permissible governmental works and obtain samples.

Besides, the Act requires every public authority to computerize their records for wide dissemination and to pro-actively publish certain categories of information so that the citizens need minimum recourse to request for information formally.

KEY TERMS

Appropriate government: Public authority, established, constituted, owned, controlled, or substantially financed by funds provided directly or indirectly by (i) by the Central Government or the Union Territory administration or (ii) the State Government.

Central public information officer (CPIO): Designated CPIO and includes a Central Assistant Public Information Officer designated as such under Section 5(2) of RTI Act.

Chief Information Commissioner and Information Commissioner: Chief Information Commissioner and Information Commissioner (CIC) appointed under Section 12(3) of the RTI Act.

Competent authority: (i) the Speaker in the case of the House of the People or the Legislative Assembly of a State or a UT having such Assembly and the Chairman in the case of the Council of States or Legislative Council of a State; (ii) CJI in the case of the Supreme Court; (iii) the Chief Justice of the High Court in the case of a High Court; (iv) the President or the Governor in the case of other authorities; (v) the Administrator appointed under Article 239 of the Constitution.

Information: Any material in any form, including records, documents, memos, e-mails, opinions, advices, press releases, circulars, orders, logbooks, contracts, reports, papers, samples, models, data material held in any electronic form, and information relating to any private body which can be accessed by a public authority under any other law.

Public authority: Any authority or body or institution of government established or constituted by/under (i) the Constitution, (ii) any other law made by Parliament, (iii) any other law made by State Legislature, (iv) notification issued or order made by the appropriate government, and includes any (a) body owned, controlled, or substantially financed and (b) NGO substantially financed, directly or indirectly by funds provided by the appropriate government.

Right to information: Fundamental right of freedom of speech and expression.

Third party: A person other than the citizen (of India) seeking information and includes a public authority.

Central Information Commission: Set up under the RTI ACT is the authorised body, established in 2005 by the Government of India, to act upon complaints from those individuals who have not been able to submit information requests to a CPIO or State PIO due to either the officer not having been appointed, or because the respective Central APIO or State APIO refused to receive the application for information under the RTI Act.

State Information Commission: State level information commission, constituted by each State Government through a Gazette notification, consisting of one State Chief Information Commissioner (SCIC) and not more than 10 State Information Commissioners (SIC) to be appointed by the Governor concerned.

CHAPTER

26 The Trade Unions Act, 1926

Learning Objectives

LO 1 Role of Trade Unions

LO 2 Aim and objectives of The Trade Unions Act, 1926

LO 3 Salient features of the Act

Trade unions are voluntary associations of workers pertaining to a particular trade, industry, or a company. They are formed to promote and protect the interest of their members by collective action. They are the most suitable organisations for balancing and improving the relations between the employer and the employees. They are formed not only to cater to the workers' economical, social, and political interests, but also for inculcating in them the sense of discipline and responsibility. Trade unions acquire an important place in the economic, political, and social setup of the country. The Trade Unions Act, 1926, is an important legislation to provide for the registration of trade unions and, in certain respects, to define the law relating to registered trade unions. The Act extends to the whole of India. It has been enacted in order to bring more transparency and to provide greater support to trade unionism in India. The legislation ensures their orderly growth, reduce their multiplicity, and promote internal democracy in the industrial organisations and the economy.

Major Concepts

Some of the important terms used in the Trade Unions Act are briefly introduced below.

Executive refers to the body, by whatever name called, to which the management of the affairs of a Trade Union is entrusted.

Office-bearer, in the case of a Trade Union, includes any member of the executive thereof, but does not include an auditor.

Prescribed means prescribed by regulations made under this Act.

Registered Office refers to that office of a Trade Union which is registered under this Act as the head office thereof.

Registered Trade Union refers to a Trade Union registered under this Act.

Registrar refers to

1. a Registrar of Trade Unions appointed by the appropriate Government under Section 3, and includes any Additional or Deputy Registrar of Trade Unions; and
2. in relation to any Trade Union, the Registrar appointed for the State in which the head or registered office, as the case may be, of the Trade Union is situated.

Trade Dispute refers to any dispute between the employers and workmen, or between workmen and workmen, or between employers and employers, which is connected with the employment or non-employment, or the terms of employment or the conditions of labour, of any person. 'Workmen' refers to all persons employed in trade or industry whether or not in the employment of the employer with whom the trade dispute arises.

> Trade dispute: Any dispute between the employers and workmen, or between workmen and workmen, or between employers and employers, which is connected with the employment or non-employment, or the terms of employment or the conditions of labour, of any person.

> Workmen: All persons employed in trade or industry whether or not in the employment of the employer with whom the trade dispute arises.

> Trade union: Any combination, whether temporary or permanent, formed primarily for the purpose of regulating the relations between workmen and employers, or between workmen and workmen, or between employers and employers, or for imposing restrictive conditions on the conduct of any trade or business, and includes any federation of two or more trade unions.

Trade Union refers to any combination, whether temporary or permanent, formed primarily for the purpose of regulating the relations between workmen and employers, or between workmen and workmen, or between employers and employers, or for imposing restrictive conditions on the conduct of any trade or business, and includes any federation of two or more Trade Unions: Provided that this Act shall not affect

1. any agreement between partners as to their own business;
2. any agreement between an employer and those employed by him as to such employment; or
3. any agreement in consideration of the sale of the goodwill of a business or of instruction in any profession, trade, or handicraft [Section 2].

Registration of Trade Unions

Registration of trade unions may be discussed as under:

Appointment of Registrars

The appropriate Government shall appoint a person to be the Registrar of Trade Unions for each State. The appropriate Government may appoint as many Additional and Deputy Registrars of Trade Unions as it thinks fit for the purpose of exercising and discharging, under the superintendence and direction of the Registrar, such powers and functions of the Registrar under this Act as it may, by order, specify, and define the local limits within which any such Additional or Deputy Registrar shall exercise and discharge the powers and functions so specified.

Where an Additional or Deputy Registrar exercises and discharges the powers and functions of a Registrar in an area within which the registered office of a Trade Union is situated, the Additional or Deputy Registrar shall be deemed to be the Registrar in relation to the Trade Union for the purposes of this Act [Section 3].

Mode of Registration

Any seven or more members of a Trade Union may, by subscribing their names to the rules of the Trade Union and by otherwise complying with the provisions of this Act with respect to registration, apply for registration of the Trade Union under this Act. Where an application has been made under sub-section (1) for the registration of a Trade Union, such an application shall not be deemed to have become invalid merely by reason of the fact that, at any time after the date of the application, but before the registration of the Trade Union, some of the applicants, but not exceeding half of the total number of persons who made the application, have ceased to be members of the Trade Union or have given notice in writing to the Registrar dissociating themselves from the application [Section 4].

Application for Registration

1. Every application for registration of a Trade Union shall be made to the Registrar, and shall be accompanied by a copy of the rules of the Trade Union and a statement of the following particulars:
   (a) the names, occupations, and addresses of the members making the application;
   (b) the name of the Trade Union and the address of its head office; and
   (c) the titles, names, ages, addresses, and occupations of the office-bearers of the Trade Union.
2. Where a Trade Union has been in existence for more than one year before the making of an application for its registration, there shall be delivered to the Registrar, together with the application, a general statement of the assets and liabilities of the Trade Union prepared in such a form and containing such particulars as may be prescribed [Section 5].

Provisions To Be Contained in the Rules of a Trade Union

A Trade Union shall not be entitled to registration under this Act, unless the executive thereof is constituted in accordance with the provisions of this Act, and the rules thereof provide for the following matters, namely:

1. the name of the Trade Union;
2. all the objectives for which the Trade Union has been established;
3. all the purposes for which the general funds of the Trade Union shall be applicable, all of which purposes shall be purposes to which such funds are lawfully applicable under this Act;
4. the maintenance of a list of the members of the Trade Union and adequate facilities for the inspection thereof by the office-bearers and members of the Trade Union;
5. the admission of ordinary members who shall be persons actually engaged or employed in an industry with which the Trade Union is connected, and also the admission of the number of honorary or temporary members as office-bearers required under Section 22 to form the executive of the Trade Union;
6. the payment of a subscription by members of the Trade Union which shall be not less than 25 paise per month per member;
7. the conditions under which any member shall be entitled to any benefit assured by the rules and under which any fine or forfeiture may be imposed on the members;
8. the manner in which the rules shall be amended, varied, or rescinded;
9. the manner in which the members of the executive and the other office-bearers of the Trade Union shall be appointed and removed;

10. the safe custody of the funds of the Trade Union, an annual audit, in such manner as may be prescribed, of the accounts thereof, and adequate facilities for the inspection of the account books by the office-bearers and members of the Trade Union; and
11. the manner in which the Trade Union may be dissolved [Section 6].

Power to Call for Further Particulars and to Require Alteration of Name

1. The Registrar may call for further information for the purpose of satisfying himself that any application complies with the provisions of Section 5, or that the Trade Union is entitled to registration under Section 6, and may refuse to register the Trade Union until such information is supplied.
2. If the name under which a Trade Union is proposed to be registered is identical to that by which any other existing Trade Union has been registered or, in the opinion of the Registrar, so nearly resembles such name as to be likely to deceive the public or the members of either Trade Union, the Registrar shall require the persons applying for registration to alter the name of the Trade Union stated in the application, and shall refuse to register the Union until such alteration has been made [Section 7].

Registration

The Registrar, on being satisfied that the Trade Union has complied with all the requirements of this Act in regard to registration, shall register the Trade Union by entering in a register, to be maintained in such form as may be prescribed, the particulars relating to the Trade Union contained in the statement accompanying the application for registration [Section 8].

Certificate of Registration

The Registrar, on registering a Trade Union under Section 8, shall issue a certificate of registration in the prescribed form which shall be conclusive evidence that the Trade Union has been duly registered under this Act [Section 9].

Cancellation of Registration

A certificate of registration of a Trade Union may be withdrawn or cancelled by the Registrar

1. on the application of the Trade Union to be verified in such manner as may be prescribed, or
2. if the Registrar is satisfied that the certificate has been obtained by fraud or mistake, or that the Trade Union has ceased to exist, or has wilfully and after notice from the Registrar contravened any provision of this Act, or allowed any rule to continue in force which is inconsistent with any such provision, or has rescinded any rule providing for any matter provision for which is required by Section 6:

   Provided that not less than two months' previous notice in writing specifying the ground on which it is proposed to withdraw or cancel the certificate shall be given by the Registrar to the Trade Union before the certificate is withdrawn or cancelled, otherwise than on the application of the Trade Union [Section 10].

Appeal

1. Any person aggrieved by any refusal of the Registrar to register a Trade Union or by the withdrawal or cancellation of a certificate of registration may, within such period as may be prescribed, appeal,
   (a) where the head office of the Trade Union is situated within the limits of a Presidency-town, to the High Court, or
   (b) where the head office is situated in any other area, to such a Court, not inferior to the Court of an additional or assistant Judge of a principal Civil Court of original jurisdiction, as the appropriate Government may appoint in this behalf for that area.
2. The appellate Court may dismiss the appeal, or pass an order directing the Registrar to register the Union and to issue a certificate of registration under the provisions of Section 9 or setting aside the order for withdrawal or cancellation of the certificate, as the case may be, and the Registrar shall comply with such an order.
3. For the purpose of an appeal under sub-section (1), an appellate Court shall, so far as may be possible, follow the same procedure and have the same powers as it follows and has when trying a suit under the Code of Civil Procedure, 1908, and may direct by whom the whole or any

part of the costs of the appeal shall be paid, and such costs shall be recovered as if they had been awarded in a suit under the said Code.

4. In the event of the dismissal of an appeal by any Court appointed under clause (b) of sub-section (1), the person aggrieved shall have a right of appeal to the High Court, and the High Court shall, for the purpose of such an appeal, have all the powers of an appellate Court under sub-sections (2) and (3), and the provisions of those sub-sections shall apply accordingly [Section 11].

Registered Office

All communications to the Trade Union may be addressed to its registered office. Notice of any change in the address of the head office shall be given within fourteen days of such change to the Registrar in writing, and the changed address shall be recorded in the register referred to in Section 8 [Section 12].

Incorporation of Registered Trade Unions

Every registered Trade Union shall be a body corporate by the name under which it is registered, and shall have perpetual succession and a common seal with power to acquire and hold both movable and immovable property and to contract, and shall by the said name sue and be sued [Section 13].

Certain Acts Not to Apply to Registered Trade Unions

The following Acts, namely:

1. The Societies Registration Act, 1860
2. The Co-operative Societies Act, 1912
3. The Companies Act, 1956

shall not apply to any registered Trade Union, and the registration of any such Trade Union under any such Act shall be void [Section 14].

Rights and Liabilities of Registered Trade Unions

Rights and liabilities of registered trade unions can be discussed as under:

Rights A registered trade union has the following rights at its disposal:

1. Recruit new members.
2. Ask employers about changes in wages and working conditions.
3. Initiate and participate in industrial action (strike etc.) to protect members' interest.
4. Apply the funds of the union for any lawful objects or purposes for the time being authorized under its constitution.
5. Participate in electing shop stewards and representatives.
6. Have union representation in a dispute with management.

Responsibilities A registered trade union is supposed to discharge the following responsibilities:

1. Not to put pressure on people to join the union.
2. Not to make unreasonable demand or threats from/to the management/employer.
3. Hold secret ballot, inform members, and take action peacefully.
4. Vote in elections.
5. Report problems to representatives and shop stewards.
6. Act within the law of land when initiating or taking part in an industrial action.

Besides, since trade unions are a part of society and as such have to take into consideration some important social responsibilities of trade unions which include:

1. Promoting and maintaining national integration by reducing the number of industrial disputes.
2. Incorporating a sense of corporate social responsibility in workers.
3. Achieving industrial peace.

Objects on Which General Funds May Be Spent

The general funds of a registered trade union shall not be spent on any other objects than the following:

1. the payment of salaries, allowances, and expenses to office-bearers of the Trade Union;
2. the payment of expenses for the administration of the Trade Union, including audit of the accounts of the general funds of the Trade Union;

3. the prosecution or defence of any legal proceeding to which the Trade Union or any member thereof is a party, when such prosecution or defence is undertaken for the purpose of securing or protecting any rights of the Trade Union as such, or any rights arising out of the relations of any member with his employer or with a person whom the member employs;
4. the conduct of trade disputes on behalf of the Trade Union or any member thereof;
5. the compensation to members for loss arising out of trade disputes;
6. allowances to members or their dependants on account of death, old age, sickness, accidents, or unemployment of such members;
7. the issue of, or the undertaking of liability under, policies of assurance on the lives of members, or under policies insuring members against sickness, accident, or unemployment;
8. the provision of educational, social, or religious benefits for members (including the payment of the expenses of funeral or religious ceremonies for deceased members) or for the dependants of members;
9. the upkeep of a periodical published mainly for the purpose of discussing questions affecting employers or workmen;
10. the payment, in furtherance of any of the objects on which the general funds of the Trade Union may be spent, of contributions to any cause intended to benefit workmen in general, provided that the expenditure in respect of such contributions in any financial year shall not at any time during that year be in excess of one-fourth of the combined total of the gross income which has up to that time accrued to the general funds of the Trade Union during that year and of the balance at the credit of those funds at the commencement of that year; and
11. subject to any conditions contained in the notification, any other object notified by the appropriate Government in the official Gazette [Section 15].

Constitution of a Separate Fund for Political Purposes

1. A registered Trade Union may constitute a separate fund, from contributions separately levied for or made to that fund, from which payments may be made, for the promotion of the civic and political interests of its members, in furtherance of any of the objects specified in sub-section (2).
2. The objects referred to in sub-section (1) are:
   (a) the payment of any expenses incurred, either directly or indirectly, by a candidate or prospective candidate for election as a member of any legislative body constituted under the Constitution or of any local authority, before, during, or after the election in connection with his candidature or election; or
   (b) the holding of any meeting or the distribution of any literature or documents in support of any such candidate or prospective candidate; or
   (c) the maintenance of any person who is a member of any legislative body constituted under the Constitution or of any local authority; or
   (d) the registration of electors or the election of a candidate for any legislative body constituted under the Constitution or for any local authority; or
   (e) the holding of political meetings of any kind, or the distribution of political literature or political documents of any kind.
3. In its application to the State of Jammu and Kashmir, references in sub-section (2) to any legislative body constituted under the Constitution shall be construed as including references to the Legislature of that State.
4. No member shall be compelled to contribute to the fund constituted under sub-section (1); and a member who does not contribute to the said fund shall not be excluded from any benefits of the Trade Union, or placed in any respect either directly or indirectly under any disability or at any disadvantage as compared with other members of the Trade Union (except in relation to the control or management of the said fund) by reason of his not contributing to the said fund; and contribution to the said fund shall not be made a condition for admission to the Trade Union [Section 16].

Criminal Conspiracy in Trade Disputes

An office-bearer or member of a registered Trade Union shall be liable to punishment under sub-section (2) of Section 120B of the Indian Penal Code, in respect of any agreement made between the members for the purpose of furthering any such object of the Trade Union as is specified in section 15, unless the agreement is an agreement to commit an offence [Section 17].

Immunity from Civil Suits in Certain Cases

1. No suit or other legal proceeding shall be maintainable in any Civil Court against any registered Trade Union or any office-bearer; or member thereof in respect of any act done in contemplation or furtherance of a trade dispute to which a member of the Trade Union is a party, solely on the ground that such an act induces some other person to break a contract of employment, or that it is in interference with the trade, business or employment of some other person or with the right of some other person to dispose of his capital or of his labour as he wills.
2. A registered Trade Union shall not be liable in any suit or other legal proceeding in any Civil Court in respect of any tortuous act done in contemplation or furtherance of a trade dispute by an agent of the Trade Union if it is proved that such person acted without the knowledge of, or contrary to express instructions given by, the executive of the Trade Union [Section 18].

Enforceability of Agreements

Notwithstanding anything contained in any other law for the time being in force, an agreement between the members of a registered Trade Union shall not be void or voidable merely by reason of the fact that any of the objects of the agreement are in restraint of trade: Provided that nothing in this Section shall enable any Civil Court to entertain any legal proceeding instituted for the express purpose of enforcing or recovering damages for the breach of any agreement concerning the conditions on which any members of a Trade Union shall or shall not sell their goods, transact business, work, employ, or be employed [Section 19].

Right to Inspect Books of Trade Union

The account books of a registered Trade Union and the list of members thereof shall be open to inspection by an office-bearer or a member of the Trade Union at such times as may be provided for in the rules of the Trade Union [Section 20].

Rights of Minors to Membership of Trade Unions

Any person who has attained the age of fifteen years may be a member of a registered Trade Union subject to any rules of the Trade Union to the contrary, and may, subject as aforesaid, enjoy all the rights of a member and execute all instruments and give all acquaintances necessary to be executed or given under the rules [Section 21].

Disqualifications of Office-bearers of Trade Unions

1. A person shall be disqualified for being chosen as, and for being, a member of the executive or any other office-bearer of a registered Trade Union if
   (a) he has not attained the age of eighteen years,
   (b) he has been convicted by a Court in India of any offence involving moral turpitude and sentenced to imprisonment, unless a period of five years has elapsed since his release.
2. Any member of the executive or other office-bearer of a registered Trade Union who, before the commencement of the Indian Trade Unions (Amendment) Act, 1964 has been convicted of any offence involving moral turpitude and sentenced to imprisonment, shall, on the date of such commencement, cease to be such a member or office-bearer unless a period of five years has elapsed since his release before that date.
3. In its application to the State of Jammu and Kashmir, the reference in sub-section (2) to the commencement of the Indian Trade Unions (Amendment) Act, 1964, shall be construed as reference to the commencement of this Act in the said State [Section 21A].

Proportion of Office-bearers To Be Connected With the Industry

Not less than one-half of the total number of the office-bearers of every registered Trade Union shall be persons actually engaged or employed in an industry with which the Trade Union is connected. However, the appropriate Government may, by special or general order, declare that the provisions of this section shall not apply to any Trade Union or class of Trade Unions specified in the order [Section 22].

Change of Name

Any registered Trade Union may, with the consent of not less than two-thirds of the total number of its members and subject to the provisions of Section 25, change its name [Section 23].

Amalgamation of Trade Unions

Amalgamation implies merging of two or more units or organisations into one to form one large unit or organisation. The Trade Unions Act does not restrict bona fide amalgamation of two or more registered trade unions to form one large trade union.

Amalgamation of trade unions: Merging of two or more registered trade unions to form one larger union.

Two or more registered Trade Unions may become amalgamated together as one Trade Union with or without dissolution or division of the funds of such Trade Unions or either or any of them, provided that the votes of at least one-half of the members of each or every such trade Union entitled to vote are recorded, and that at least sixty per cent of the votes recorded are in favour of the proposal [Section 24].

Notice of Change of Name or Amalgamation

1. Notice in writing of every change of name of every amalgamation, signed, in the case of a change of name, by the Secretary and by seven members of the Trade Union changing its name, and, in the case of an amalgamation, by the Secretary and by seven members of each and every Trade Union which is a party thereto, shall be sent to the Registrar, and where the head office of the amalgamated Trade Union is situated in a different State, to the Registrar of such a State.
2. If the proposed name is identical to that by which any other existing Trade Union has been registered or, in the opinion of the Registrar, so nearly resembles such a name as to be likely to deceive the public or the members of either Trade Union, the Registrar shall refuse to register the change of name.
3. Save as provided in sub-section (2), the Registrar shall, if he is satisfied that the provisions of this Act in respect of change of name have been complied with, register the change of name in the register referred to in Section 8, and the change of name shall have effect from the date of such registration.
4. The Registrar of the State in which the head office of the amalgamated Trade Union is situated shall, if he is satisfied that the provisions of this Act in respect of amalgamation have been complied with, and that the Trade Union formed thereby is entitled to registration under Section 6, register the Trade Union in the manner provided in Section 8, and the amalgamation shall have effect from the date of such registration [Section 25].

Effects of Change of Name and of Amalgamation

1. The change in the name of a registered Trade Union shall not affect any rights or obligations of the Trade Union or render defective any legal proceeding by or against the Trade Union, and any legal proceeding which might have been continued or commenced by or against it by its former name may be continued or commenced by or against it by its new name.
2. An amalgamation of two or more registered Trade Unions shall not prejudice any right of any of such Trade Unions or any right of a creditor of any of them [Section 26].

Dissolution of Trade Union

1. When a registered Trade Union is dissolved, notice of the dissolution signed by seven members and by the Secretary of the Trade Union shall, within fourteen days of the dissolution, be sent to the Registrar, and shall be registered by him if he is satisfied that the dissolution has been effected in accordance with the rules of the Trade Union, and the dissolution shall have effect from the date of such registration.
2. Where the dissolution of a registered Trade Union has been registered and the rules of the Trade Union do not provide for the distribution of funds of the Trade Union on dissolution, the Registrar shall divide the funds amongst the members in such a manner as may be prescribed [Section 27].

Returns of Trade Union

1. There shall be sent annually to the Registrar, on or before such date as may be prescribed, a general statement, audited in the prescribed manner, of all receipts and expenditure of every registered Trade Union during the year ending on the 31st day of December next preceding such prescribed date, and of the assets and liabilities of the Trade Union existing on the 31st day of December. The statement shall be prepared in such a form and shall comprise such particulars as may be prescribed.
2. Together with the general statement there shall be sent to the Registrar a statement showing all changes of office-bearers made by the Trade Union during the year to which the general statement refers, together with a copy of the rules of the Trade Union corrected up to the date of the dispatch thereof to the Registrar.
3. A copy of every alteration made in the rules of a registered Trade Union shall be sent to the Registrar within fifteen days of the making of the alteration.
4. For the purpose of examining the documents referred to in sub-sections (1), (2) and (3), the Registrar, or any officer authorised by him, by general or special order, may, at all reasonable times, inspect the certificate of registration, account books, registers, and other documents, relating to a Trade Union at its registered office, or may require their production at such a place as he may specify in this behalf, but no such place shall be at a distance of more than ten miles from the registered office of a Trade Union [Section 28].

Miscellaneous Provisions

Miscellaneous provisions of the Trade Unions Act can be discussed under the following heads:

Power to Make Regulations

1. The appropriate Government may make regulations for the purpose of carrying into effect the provisions of this Act.
2. In particular and without prejudice to the generality of the foregoing power, such regulations may provide for all or any of the following matters, namely:
   (a) the manner in which Trade Unions and the rules of Trade Unions shall be registered and the fees payable on registration;
   (b) the transfer of registration in the case of any registered Trade Union which has changed its head office from one State to another;
   (c) the manner in which, and the qualifications of persons by whom, the accounts of registered Trade Unions or of any class of such Unions shall be audited;
   (d) the conditions subject to which inspection of documents kept by Registrars shall be allowed, and the fees which shall be chargeable in respect of such inspections; and
   (e) any matter which is to be or may be prescribed [Section 29].

Publication of Regulations

1. The power to make regulations conferred by Section 29 is subject to the condition of the regulations being made after previous publication.
2. The date to be specified in accordance with clause (3) of Section 23 of the General Clauses Act, 1897 as that after which a draft of regulations proposed to be made will be taken into consideration shall not be less than three months from the date on which the draft of the proposed regulations was published for general information.
3. Regulations so made shall be published in the Official Gazette, and on such publication shall have effect as if enacted in this Act [Section 30].

Failure to Submit Returns

1. If default is made on the part of any registered Trade Union in giving any notice or sending any statement or other document as required by or under any provision of this Act, every office-bearer or other person bound by the rules of the Trade Union to give or send the same, or, if there is no such office-bearer or person every member of the executive of the Trade Union, shall be punishable with a fine which may extend to five rupees and, in the case of a continuing default, with an additional fine which may extend to five rupees for each week after the first during which

the default continues. However, the aggregate fine shall not exceed fifty rupees.

2. Any person who wilfully makes, or causes to be made, any false entry in, or any omission from, the general statement required by Section 28, or in or from any copy of rules or of alterations of rules sent to the Registrar under that Section, shall be punishable with a fine which may extend to five hundred rupees [Section 31].

Supplying False Information Regarding Trade Unions

Any person who, with intent to deceive, gives to any member of a registered Trade Union or to any person intending or applying to become a member of such Trade Union any document purporting to be a copy of the rules of the Trade Union or of any alterations to the same which he knows, or has reason to believe, is not a correct copy of such rules or alterations as are for the time being in force, or any person who, with the like intent, gives a copy of any rules of an unregistered Trade Union to any person on the pretence that such rules are the rules of a registered Trade Union, shall be punishable with a fine which may extend to two hundred rupees [Section 32].

Cognizance of Offences

1. No Court inferior to that of a Presidency Magistrate or a Magistrate of the First Class shall try any offence under this Act.
2. No Court shall take cognizance of any offence under this Act, unless complaint thereof has been made by, or with the previous sanction of, the Registrar or, in the case of an offence under Section 32, by the person to whom the copy was given, within six months of the date on which the offence is alleged to have been committed [Section 33].

Exercises

I. Objective-type Questions

1. 'Trade Union' refers to any combination, whether temporary or permanent, formed primarily for the purpose of regulating the relations between
   (a) workmen or employers
   (b) workmen and workmen
   (c) employers and employers
   (d) any of the above [(a), (b) and (c)]

2. The objects on which the general funds of a registered Trade Union cannot be spent:
   (a) the payment of salaries, allowances, and expenses to office-bearers of the Trade Union
   (b) the payment of expenses for the administration of the Trade Union, including audit of the accounts of the general funds of the Trade Union
   (c) the payment of any expenses incurred, either directly or indirectly, by a candidate or prospective candidate for election as a member of any legislative body constituted under the Constitution or any local authority
   (d) the compensation to members for loss arising out of trade disputes

3. Any two or more registered Trade Unions may become amalgamated together as one Trade Union provided that
   (a) At least two-thirds of the total number of members of each or every such Trade Union vote in favour of the proposal
   (b) At least one-half of the total numbers members of each or every such Trade Union vote in favour of the proposal
   (c) At least one-half of the total numbers members of each or every such Trade Union vote and that at least sixty percent of the votes recorded are in favour of the proposal
   (d) At least one-half of the total numbers members of each or every such Trade Union vote and that at least fifty one percent of the votes recorded are in favour of the proposal.

4. Where a registered Trade Union is dissolved,
   (a) notice of the dissolution signed by the seven members and by the Secretary of the Trade Union shall, within fourteen days of the dissolution, be sent to the Registrar
   (b) notice of the dissolution signed by the Secretary of the Trade Union shall, within fourteen days of the dissolution, be sent to the Registrar
   (c) notice of the dissolution signed by the seven members and by the Secretary of the Trade Union shall, within seven days of the dissolution, be sent to the Registrar
   (d) notice of the dissolution, signed by the seven members and by the Secretary of the Trade Union shall, within twenty one days of the dissolution, be sent to the Registrar.

5. If a registered Trade Union fails to submit its return to the Registrar, every office-bearer shall be punishable with a fine which may extend to
   (a) five rupees
   (b) five rupees and, in the case of a continuing default, with an additional fine which may extend to five rupees for each week after the first during which the default continues
   (c) five hundred rupees
   (d) five hundred rupees, and in the case of a continuing default, with an additional fine which may extend to five hundred rupees for each week after the first during which the default continue

II. Review Questions

1. Briefly describe the salient features of the Trade Unions Act, 1926.
2. Describe the procedure for registration of a Trade Union.
3. Enumerate the objects for which the general funds of a registered Trade Union can be spent.
4. Write a note on the amalgamation of Trade Unions.

Answers to Objective-type Questions

1. (d) 2. (c) 3. (c) 4. (a) 5. (b)

26 Chapter in Review

LEARNING OUTCOMES

LO 1 Role of Trade Unions

LO 2 Aim and objectives of The Trade Unions Act, 1926

LO 3 Salient features of the Act

KEY TERMS

Amalgamation of trade unions: Merging of two or more registered trade unions to form one larger union.

Trade dispute: Any dispute between the employers and workmen, or between workmen and workmen, or between employers and employers, which is connected with the employment or non-employment, or the terms of employment or the conditions of labour, of any person.

Workmen: All persons employed in trade or industry whether or not in the employment of the employer with whom the trade dispute arises.

Trade union: Any combination, whether temporary or permanent, formed primarily for the purpose of regulating the relations between workmen and employers, or between workmen and workmen, or between employers and employers, or for imposing restrictive conditions on the conduct of any trade or business, and includes any federation of two or more trade unions.

LO1 Trade unions—voluntary associations of workers—are formed to promote and protect the interest of their members by collective action. They are the most suitable organisations for balancing and improving the relations between the employer and the employees.

LO2 The Trade Unions Act, 1926, has been enacted in order to bring more transparency and to provide greater support to trade unionism in India. The Act ensures trade unions' orderly growth, reduce their multiplicity, and promote internal democracy in the industrial organisations and the economy.

LO3

1. No trade union (of workmen) shall be registered unless at least 10% or 100, whichever is less, subject to a minimum of 7 workmen engaged or employed in the establishment or industry with which it is connected are the members of such trade union on the date of making of application for registration.
2. A registered trade union shall at all times continue to fulfil the above requirement.
3. A provision for filing an appeal before the Industrial Tribunal/Labour Court in case of non-registration or for restoration of registration has been provided.
4. All office bearers of a registered trade union, except not more than one-third of the total number of office bearers or five, whichever is less, shall be persons actually engaged or employed in the establishment or industry with which the trade union is connected.
5. Minimum rate of subscription by members of the trade union is fixed at one rupee per annum for rural workers, three rupees per annum for workers in other unorganised sectors, and 12 rupees per annum in all other cases.
6. The employees who have been retired or have been retrenched shall not be construed as outsiders for the purpose of holding an office in the trade union concerned.
7. For the promotion of economical and political interest of its members, unions are authorised to set up separate political funds.

CHAPTER

27 The Factories Act, 1948

Learning Objectives

LO 1 Aim and objectives of The Factories Act, 1948

LO 2 Scope/applicability of the Act

LO 3 Enforcement agency of the legislation

LO 4 Compliance mechanism

LO 5 Maximum punishment for violation of the Act's provisions

The Factories Act, 1948, is a social legislation to consolidate and amend the law regulating labour in factories in India. It has been primarily enacted for the occupational safety, health, and welfare of workers at work places. It came into force on 1 April 1949 and extends to the whole of India. This legislation is enforced by technical officers i.e., Inspectors of factories and Deputy Chief Inspectors of factories who work under the control of the Chief Inspector of factories and the overall control of the Labour Commissioner, 'the State/Union Territory concerned'. All 'Labour Commissioners' in turn report to Chief Labour Commissioner, Government of India. Industries in which 10 or more workers are employed on any day of the preceding 12 months and are engaged in the manufacturing process being carried out with the aid of power, or 20 or more workers are employed in the manufacturing process being carried out without the aid of power, are covered under the provisions of this Act.

Salient Features of the Act

1. Approval of factory building plans before construction/extension, under the Delhi Factories Rules, 1950.
2. Grant of Licences under the Delhi Factories Rules, 1950, and to take action against factories running without obtaining Licence.
3. Renewal of Licences granted under the Delhi Factories Rules, 1950, by the Dy. Chief Inspectors of Factories.
4. Inspections of factories by District Inspectors of Factories, for investigation of complaints, serious/fatal accidents as well as suo moto inspections to check compliance of provisions of this Act relating to health, safety, welfare facilities, working hours, employment of young persons, and annual leave with wages, etc.

Major Concepts

Some of the important terms used in the Factories Act are briefly introduced below.

Adult: A person who has completed his 18th year of age.

Adult refers to a person who has completed his eighteenth year of age.

Adolescent: A person who has completed his 15th year of age but has not completed his 18th year.

Adolescent refers to a person who has completed his fifteenth year of age but has not completed his eighteenth year.

Calendar Year refers to the period of 12 months beginning with the first day of January in any year.

Child: A person who has not completed his 15th year of age.

Child refers to a person who has not completed his fifteenth year of age.

Competent Person A person or an institution recognised as such by the Chief Inspector for the purposes of carrying out tests, examinations and inspections required to be done in a factory under the provisions of this Act having regard to

1. the qualifications and experience of the person and facilities available at his disposal; or
2. the qualifications and experience of the persons employed in such an institution and the facilities available therein, with regard to the conduct of such tests, examinations and inspections, and more than one person or institution can be recognised as a competent person in relation to a factory.

Hazardous process: Any process or activity in relation to an industry involving risk or danger to somebody's health or safety or that resulting in pollution of the general environment.

Hazardous Process refers to any process or activity in relation to an industry specified in the First Schedule where, unless special care is taken, raw materials used therein or the intermediate or finished products, by-products, wastes or effluents thereof would

1. cause material impairment to the health of the persons engaged in or connected therewith, or
2. result in the pollution of the general environment.

Provided that the State Government may, by notification in the Official Gazette, amend the First Schedule by way of addition, omission or variation of any industry specified in the said Schedule.

Young person: A person who is either a child or an adolescent.

Young Person refers to a person who is either a child or an adolescent.

Prime Mover refers to any engine, motor, or other appliance which generates or otherwise provides power.

Transmission Machinery refers to any shaft, wheel, drum, pulley, system of pulleys, coupling, clutch, driving belt, or other appliance or device by which the motion of a prime mover is transmitted to or received by any machinery or appliance.

Machinery: Prime movers, transmission machinery, and all other appliances whereby power is generated, transformed, transmitted, or applied.

Machinery includes prime movers, transmission machinery, and all other appliances whereby power is generated, transformed, transmitted, or applied.

Manufacturing process: Any process for (i) making, altering, repairing, ornamenting, finishing, packing, oiling, washing, cleaning, breaking up, demolishing, or otherwise treating or adapting any article or substance with a view to its use, sale, transport, delivery or disposal, or (ii) pumping oil, water, sewage, or any other substance; or (iii) generating, transforming, or transmitting power; or (iv) composing types for printing, printing by letter press, lithography, photogravure or other similar process, or book binding; or (v) constructing, reconstructing, repairing, refitting, finishing, or breaking up ships or vessels; or (vi) preserving or storing any article in cold storage.

Manufacturing Process refers to any process for

1. making, altering, repairing, ornamenting, finishing, packing, oiling, washing, cleaning, breaking up, demolishing, or otherwise treating or adapting any article or substance with a view to its use, sale, transport, delivery or disposal, or
2. pumping oil, water, sewage, or any other substance; or
3. generating, transforming, or transmitting power; or
4. composing types for printing, printing by letter press, lithography, photogravure or other similar process, or book binding; or
5. constructing, reconstructing, repairing, refitting, finishing, or breaking up ships or vessels; or
6. preserving or storing any article in cold storage.

Worker: A person engaged in any manufacturing process, or in cleaning any part of the machinery or premises used for a manufacturing process, or in any other kind of work incidental to, or connected with, the manufacturing process, or the subject of the manufacturing process.

Worker refers to a person employed, directly or by or through any agency (including a contractor) with or without the knowledge of the principal employer, whether for remuneration or not, in any manufacturing process, or in cleaning any part of the machinery or premises used for a manufacturing process, or in any other kind of work incidental to, or connected with, the manufacturing process, or the subject of the manufacturing process, but does not include any member of the armed forces of the Union.

Factory: Any premises including the precincts thereof (i) where 10 or more workers are working, or were working on any day of the preceding 12 months, and in any part of which a manufacturing process is being carried on with the aid of power, or is ordinarily so carried on, or (ii) where 20 or more workers are working, or were working on any day of the preceding 12 months, and in any part of which a manufacturing process is being carried on without the aid of power, or is ordinarily so carried on.

Factory refers to any premises including the precincts thereof

1. where 10 or more workers are working, or were working on any day of the preceding 12 months, and in any part of which a manufacturing process is being carried on with the aid of power, or is ordinarily so carried on, or
2. where 20 or more workers are working, or were working on any day of the preceding 12 months, and in any part of which a manufacturing process is being carried on without the aid of power, or is ordinarily so carried on, but does not include a mine subject to the operation of the Mines Act, 1952 or a mobile unit belonging to the armed forces of the Union, a railway running shed or a hotel, restaurant or eating place.

Occupier of a factory: The person who has ultimate control over the affairs of the factory.

Occupier of a factory refers to the person who has ultimate control over the affairs of the factory.

Provided that

1. in the case of a firm or other association of individuals, any one of the individual partners or members thereof shall be deemed to be the occupier;
2. in the case of a company, any one of the directors shall be deemed to be the occupier;
3. in the case of a factory owned or controlled by the Central Government or any State Government, or any local authority, the person or persons appointed to manage the affairs of the factory by the Central Government, the State Government

or the local authority, as the case may be, shall be deemed to be the occupier.

However, in the case of a ship which is being repaired, or on which maintenance work is being carried out in a dry dock which is available for hire, the owner of the ship or his agent or master or other officer-in-charge of the ship or any person who contracts with such an owner, agent or master or other officer-in-charge to carry out the repair or maintenance work shall be deemed to be the occupier.

Important Provisions

Important provisions of the Act have been briefly explained below.

Power to Declare Different Departments To Be Separate Factories or Two or More Factories To Be a Single Factory

The State Government may, on its own or on an application made in this behalf by an occupier, direct, by an order in writing, and subject to such conditions as it may deem fit, that for all or any of the purposes of this Act, different departments or branches of a factory of the occupier specified in the application shall be treated as separate factories, or that two or more factories of the occupier specified in the application shall be treated as a single factory [Section 4].

Provided that no order under this Section shall be made by the State Government on its own motion unless an opportunity to beheard is given to the occupier.

Power to Exempt During Public Emergency

In any case of public emergency, the State Government may, by notification in the Official Gazette, exempt any factory or class or description of factories from all or any of the provisions of this Act, except Section 67 for such a period and subject to such conditions as it may think fit [Section 5].

However, no such notification shall be made for a period exceeding three months at a time.

Explanation: For the purpose of this Section, 'public emergency' refers to a grave emergency whereby the security of India or of any part of the territory thereof is threatened, whether by war or external aggression or internal disturbance.

Approval, Licensing, and Registration of Factories

1. The State Government may make rules
   (a) requiring, for the purposes of this Act, the submission of plans of any class or description of factories to the Chief Inspector or the State Government;
2. requiring the previous permission in writing of the State Government or the Chief Inspector to be obtained for the site on which the factory is to be situated and for the construction or extension of any factory or class or description of factories;
   (a) requiring, for the purpose of considering application for such permission, the submission of plans and specifications;
   (b) prescribing the nature of such plans and specifications and by whom they shall be certified;
   (c) requiring the registration and licensing of factories or any class or description of factories, and prescribing the fees payable for such registration and licensing and for the renewal of licences;
   (d) requiring that no licence shall be granted or renewed unless the notice specified in Section 7 has been given.
3. If, on an application for permission referred to in clause (aa)] of sub-section (1) accompanied by the plans and specifications required by the rules made under clause (b) of that sub-section, sent to the State Government or Chief Inspector by registered post, no order is communicated to the applicant within three months from the date on which it is so sent, the permission applied for in the said application shall be deemed to have been granted.
4. Where a State Government or a Chief Inspector refuses to grant permission to the site, construction or extension of a factory or to the registration and licensing of a factory, the applicant may, within 30 days of the date of such refusal, appeal to the Central Government if the decision

appealed was from the State Government, and to the State Government in any other case.

Notice by Occupier

1. The occupier shall, at least 15 days before he begins to occupy or use any premises as a factory, send to the Chief Inspector a written notice containing
   (a) the name and situation of the factory;
   (b) the name and address of the occupier;
      (i) the name and address of the owner of the premises or building (including the precincts thereof) referred to in Section 93;
   (c) the address to which communications relating to the factory may be sent;
   (d) the nature of the manufacturing process
      (i) carried on in the factory during the last 12 months in the case of factories in existence on the date of the commencement of this Act, and
      (ii) to be carried on in the factory during the next 12 months in the case of all factories;
   (e) the total rated horse power installed or to be installed in the factory, which shall not include the rated horse power of any separate stand-by plant;
   (f) the name of the manager of the factory (g) the number of workers likely to be employed in the factory;
   (g) the average number of workers per day employed during the last 12 months in the case of a factory in existence on the date of the commencement of this Act;
   (h) such other particulars as may be prescribed.
2. In respect of all establishments which come within the scope of the Act for the first time, the occupier shall send a written notice to the Chief Inspector containing the particulars specified in sub-section (1) within 30 days from the date of the commencement of this Act.
3. Before a factory engaged in a manufacturing process which is ordinarily carried on for less than 180 working days in the year resumes working, the occupier shall send a written notice to the Chief Inspector containing the particulars specified in sub-section (1) at least 30 days before the date of the commencement of work.
4. Whenever a new manager is appointed, the occupier shall send to the Inspector a written notice, and to the Chief Inspector a copy thereof, within seven days from the date on which such person takes charge.
5. During any period for which no person has been designated as manager of a factory or during which the person designated does not manage the factory, any person found acting as manager, or if no such person is found, the occupier himself, shall be deemed to be the manager of the factory for the purposes of this Act [Section 7].

The Inspecting Staff

The Inspecting Staff will look after the following functions:

General Duties of the Occupier

1. Every occupier shall ensure, so far as is reasonably practicable, the health, safety and welfare of all workers while they are at work in the factory.
2. Without prejudice to the generality of the provisions of sub-section (1), the matters to which such duty extends, shall include
   (a) the provision and maintenance of plants and systems of work in the factory that are safe and without risks to health;
   (b) the arrangements in the factory for ensuring safety and absence of risks to health in connection with the use, handling, storage, and transport of articles and substances;
   (c) the provision of such information, instruction, training, and supervision as are necessary to ensure the health and safety of all workers at work;
   (d) the maintenance of all places of work in the factory in a condition that is safe without risks to health and the provision and maintenance of such means of access to, and egress from, such places as are safe and without such risks;
   (e) the provision, maintenance, or monitoring of such a working environment in the factory for the workers that is safe, without risks to health and adequate as regards facilities and arrangements for their welfare at work.
3. Except in such cases as may be prescribed, every occupier shall prepare, and, as often as may be

appropriate, revise, a written statement of his general policy with respect to the health and safety of the workers at work and the organisation and arrangements for the time being in force for carrying out that policy, and bring the statement and any revision thereof to the notice of all the workers in such manner as may be prescribed [Section 7A].

General Duties of Manufacturers

1. Every person who designs, manufactures, imports or supplies any article for use in any factory shall
   (a) ensure, so far as is reasonably practicable, that the article is so designed and constructed as to be safe and without risks to the health of the workers when properly used;
   (b) carry out or arrange for the carrying out of such tests and examinations as may be considered necessary for the effective implementation of the provisions of clause (a);
   (c) take such steps as may be necessary to ensure that adequate information will be available
   (i) in connection with the use of the article in any factory;
   (ii) about the use for which it is designed and tested; and
   (iii) about any conditions necessary to ensure that the article, when put to such use, will be safe, and without risks to the health of the workers:

   Provided that where an article is designed or manufactured outside India, it shall be obligatory on the part of the importer to see
   - that the article conforms to the same standards as such an article manufactured in India, or
   - if the standards adopted in the country outside for the manufacture of such an article are above the standards adopted in India, that the article conforms to those standards.
2. Every person who undertakes to design or manufacture any article for use in any factory, may carry out or arrange for the carrying out of necessary research with a view of the discovery and, so far as is reasonably practicable, the elimination or minimization of any risks to the health or safety of the workers to which the design or article may give rise.
3. Nothing contained in sub-section (1) and (2) shall be construed to require a person to repeat the testing, examination or research which has been carried out otherwise than by him or at his instance in so far as it is reasonable for him to rely on the results thereof for the purposes of the said sub-sections.
4. Any duty imposed on any person by sub-section (1) and (2) shall extend only to things done in the course of business carried on by him and to matters within his control.
5. Where a person designs, manufactures, imports or supplies an article on the basis of a written undertaking by the user of such article to take the steps specified in such an undertaking to ensure, so far as is reasonably practicable, that the article will be safe and without risks to the health of the workers when properly used, the undertaking shall have the effect of relieving the person designing, manufacturing, importing or supplying the article from the duty imposed by clause (a) of sub-section (1) to such extent as is reasonable having regard to the term of the undertaking.
6. For the purpose of this Section, an article is not to be regarded as properly used if it is used without regard to any information or advice relating to its use which has been made available by the person who has designed, manufactured, imported or supplied the article.

   Explanation: For the purpose of this Section, 'article' shall include plant and machinery [Section 7B].

Inspectors

1. The State Government may, by notification in the Official Gazette, appoint such persons as possess the prescribed qualification to be Inspectors for the purposes of this Act and may assign to them such local limits as it may think fit.
2. The State Government may, by notification in the Official Gazette, appoint any person to be a Chief Inspector who shall, in addition to the powers conferred on a Chief Inspector under this Act, exercise the powers of an Inspector throughout the State.

   (2A) The State Government may, by notification in the Official Gazette, appoint as many Additional Chief Inspectors, Joint Chief Inspectors and Deputy Chief Inspectors, and as many other officers as it thinks fit, to assist the Chief Inspector and to exercise such of the powers of the Chief Inspector as may be specified in such a notification.

(2B) Every additional Chief Inspector, Joint Chief Inspector, Deputy Chief Inspector and every other officer appointed under sub-section (2A) shall, in addition to the powers of a Chief Inspector specified in the notification by which he is appointed, exercise the powers of an Inspector throughout the State.

3. No person shall be appointed under sub-section (1), subsection (2) sub-section (2A) or sub-section (5) or, having been so appointed, shall continue to hold office, who is, or becomes directly or indirectly, interested in a factory or in any process or business carried on therein or in any patent or machinery connected therewith.
4. Every District Magistrate shall be an Inspector for his District.
5. The State Government may also, by notification as aforesaid, appoint such public officers as it thinks fit to be additional Inspectors for all or any of the purposes of this Act, within such local limits as it may assign to them respectively.
6. In any area where there are more Inspectors than one, the State Government may, by notification as aforesaid, declare the powers which such Inspectors shall respectively exercise and the Inspector to whom the prescribed notices are to be sent.
7. Every Chief Inspector, Additional Chief Inspector, Joint Chief Inspector, Deputy Chief Inspector, Inspector and every other officer appointed under this Section shall be deemed to be a public servant within the meaning of the Indian Penal Code and shall be officially subordinate to such authority as the State Government may specify in this behalf [Section 8].

Powers of Inspectors

Subject to any rules made in this behalf, an Inspector may, within the local limits for which he is appointed,

1. enter, with such assistants, being persons in the service of the Government, or any local or other public authority, or with an expert as he thinks fit, any place which is used, or which he has reason to believe is used, as a factory;
2. make examination of the premises, plant, machinery, articles or substances;
3. inquire into any accident or dangerous occurrence, whether resulting in bodily injury, disability or not, and take on the spot or otherwise statements of any person which he may consider necessary for such inquiry;
4. require the production of any prescribed register or any other document relating to the factory;
5. seize, or take copies of, any register, record or other document or any portion thereof as he may consider necessary in respect of any offence under this Act, which he has reason to believe, has been committed;
6. direct the occupier that any premises or any part thereof, or anything lying therein, shall be left disturbed (whether generally or in particular respect) for so long as is necessary for the purpose of any examination under clause(b);
7. take measurements and photographs and make such recordings as he considers necessary for the purpose of any examination under clause (b), taking with him any necessary instrument or equipment;
8. in case of any article or substance found in any premises, being an article or substance which appears to him to have caused, or is likely to cause, danger to the health or safety of the workers, direct it to be dismantled or subject it to any process or test (but not so as to damage or destroy it unless the same is, in the circumstances necessary, for carrying out the purposes of this Act), and take possession of any such article or substance or a part thereof, and detain it for so long as is necessary for such examination;
   (a) exercise such other powers as may be prescribed.

   Provided that no person shall be compelled under this Section to answer any question or give any evidence tending to incriminate himself [Section 9].

Certifying Surgeons

1. The State Government may appoint qualified medical practitioners to be certifying surgeons for the purposes of this Act within such local limits or for such a factory or class or description of factories as it may assign to them respectively.
2. A certifying surgeon may, with the approval of the State Government, authorise any qualified medical practitioner to exercise any of his powers under this Act for such period as the certifying surgeon may specify and subject to such conditions as the State Government may think fit to impose. References in this Act to a certifying surgeon shall be deemed to include references to any qualified medical practitioner when so authorised.
3. No person shall be appointed to be, or authorised to exercise the powers of, a certifying surgeon, or having been so appointed or authorised, continue to exercise such powers, who is or becomes the occupier of a factory or is, or becomes directly or indirectly interested therein, or in any process or business carried on therein, or in any patent or machinery connected therewith, or is otherwise in the employ of the factory.

   However, the State Government may, by order in writing and subject to such conditions as may be specified in the order, exempt any person or class of persons from the provisions of this sub-section in respect of any factory or class or description of factories.
4. The certifying surgeon shall carry out such duties as may be prescribed in connection with
   (a) the examination and certification of young persons under this Act;
   (b) the examination of persons engaged in factories in such dangerous occupations or processes as may be prescribed;
   (c) the exercising of such medical supervision as may be prescribed for any factory or class or description of factories where
   (i) cases of illness have occurred which it is reasonable to believe are due to the nature of the manufacturing process carried on, or other conditions of work prevailing, therein;
   (ii) by reason of any change in the manufacturing process carried on or in the substances used therein or by reason of the adoption of any new manufacturing process or of any new substance for use in a manufacturing process, there is a likelihood of injury to the health of workers employed in that manufacturing process;
   (iii) young persons are, or are about to be, employed in any work which is likely to cause injury to their health.

   Explanation: In this section, 'qualified medical practitioner' refers to a person holding a qualification granted by an authority specified in the Schedule to the Indian Medical Degrees Act, 1916, or in the Schedules to the Indian Medical Council Act, 1933 [Section 10].

Health

Health implies the condition of a person's body or mind i.e. physical or mental state of a human being. As regards health, the Act contains the following provisions:

Cleanliness

1. Every factory shall be kept clean and free from effluvia arising from any drain, privy or other nuisance, and in particular
   (a) accumulation of dirt and refuse shall be removed daily by sweeping or by any other effective method from the floors and benches of workrooms and from staircases and passages, and disposed of in a suitable manner;
   (b) the floor of every workroom shall be cleaned at least once every week by washing, using disinfectant where necessary, or by some other effective method;
   (c) where a floor is liable to become wet in the course of any manufacturing process to such an extent as is capable of being drained, effective means of drainage shall be provided and maintained;
   (d) all inside walls and partitions, all ceilings or tops of rooms and all walls, sides and tops of passages and staircases shall

(i) where they are painted [other than with washable water-paint] or varnished, be repainted or re-varnished at least once every five years;

(ia) where they are painted with washable water paint, be repainted with at least one coat of such paint at least once every three years and washed at least once every six months;

(ii) where they are painted or varnished or where they have smooth impervious surfaces, be cleaned at least once every fourteen months by such method as may be prescribed;

(iii) in any other case, be kept whitewashed or colour washed, and the whitewashing or colour washing shall be carried out at least once every 14 months;

(iv) all doors and window frames and other wooden or metallic framework and shutters shall be kept painted or varnished, and the painting or varnishing shall be carried out at least once every five years;

(e) the dates on which the processes required by clause (d) are carried out shall be entered in the prescribed register.

2. If, in view of the nature of the operations carried on in a factory or class or description of factories or any part of a factory or class or description of factories, it is not possible for the occupier to comply with all or any of the provisions of sub-section (1), the State Government may by order exempt such a factory or class or description of factories [or part] from any of the provisions of that sub-section and specify alternative methods for keeping the factory in a clean state [Section 11].

Disposal of Wastes and Effluents

1. Effective arrangements shall be made in every factory for the treatment of wastes and effluents due to the manufacturing process carried out therein, so as to render them innocuous and for their disposal.
2. The State Government may make rules prescribing the arrangements to be made under sub-section (1) or requiring that the arrangements made in accordance with sub-section (1) shall be approved by such authority as may be prescribed [Section 12].

Ventilation and Temperature

1. Effective and suitable provision shall be made in every factory for securing and maintaining in every workroom
   (a) adequate ventilation by the circulation of fresh air, and
   (b) such a temperature as will secure to workers therein reasonable conditions of comfort and prevent injury to health; and, in particular,
      (i) walls and roofs shall be of such material and so designed that this temperature shall not be exceeded but kept as low as practicable;
      (ii) where the nature of the work carried on in the factory involves, or is likely to involve, the production of excessively high temperatures, such adequate measures as are practicable shall be taken to protect the workers there by separating the process which produces such temperatures from the workroom, by insulating the hot parts, or by other effective means.
2. The State Government may prescribe a standard of adequate ventilation and reasonable temperature for any factory or class or description of factories or parts thereof and direct that proper measuring instruments, at such places and in such positions as may be specified, shall be provided, and such records, as may be prescribed, shall be maintained.
3. If it appears to the Chief Inspector that excessively high temperatures in any factory can be reduced by the adoption of suitable measures, he may, without prejudice to the rules made under sub-section (2), serve on the occupier an order in writing specifying the measures which, in his opinion, should be adopted, and requiring them to be carried out before a specified date [Section 13].

Dust and Fumes

1. In every factory in which, by reason of the manufacturing process carried out, there is given off any dust or fume or other impurity of such a nature and to such an extent as is likely to be injurious or offensive to the workers employed therein, or any dust in substantial quantities, effective measures shall be taken to prevent its inhalation and accumulation in any workroom, and if any exhaust

appliance is necessary for this purpose, it shall be applied as near as possible to the point of origin of the dust, fume or other impurity, and such a point shall be enclosed so far as possible.

2. In any factory, no stationary internal combustion engine shall be operated unless the exhaust is conducted into the open air, and no other internal combustion engine shall be operated in any room unless effective measures have been taken to prevent such accumulation of fumes therefrom as are likely to be injurious to workers employed in the room [Section 14].

Artificial Humidification

1. In respect of all factories in which the humidity of the air is artificially increased, the State Government may make rules
   (a) prescribing standards of humidification;
   (b) regulating the methods used for artificially increasing the humidity of the air;
   (c) directing prescribed tests for determining the humidity of the air to be correctly carried out and recorded;
   (d) prescribing methods to be adopted for securing adequate ventilation and cooling of the air in the workrooms.
2. In any factory in which the humidity of the air is artificially increased, the water used for the purpose shall be taken from a public supply, or other source of drinking water, or shall be effectively purified before it is so used.
3. If it appears to an Inspector that the water used in a factory for increasing humidity which is required to be effectively purified under sub-section (2) is not effectively purified, he may serve on the manager of the factory an order in writing, specifying the measures which, in his opinion, should be adopted, and requiring them to be carried out before a specified date [Section 15].

Overcrowding

1. No room in any factory shall be overcrowded to an extent injurious to the health of the workers employed therein.
2. Without prejudice to the generality of sub-section (1), there shall be in every workroom of a factory in existence on the date of the commencement of this Act at least 9.9 cubic meters, and of a factory built after the commencement of this Act, at least 14.2 cubic meters of space for every worker employed therein, and for the purposes of this sub-section, no account shall be taken of any space which is more than 4.2 meters above the level of the floor of the room.
3. If the Chief Inspector by order in writing so requires, there shall be posted in each workroom of a factory a notice specifying the maximum number of workers who may, in compliance with the provisions of this Section, be employed in the room.
4. The Chief Inspector may, by order in writing, exempt, subject to such conditions, if any, as he may think fit to impose, any workroom from the provisions of this Section, if he is satisfied that compliance therewith in respect of the rooms is unnecessary in the interest of the health of the workers employed therein [Section 16].

Lighting

1. In every part of a factory where workers are working or passing there shall be provided and maintained sufficient and suitable lighting, natural or artificial, or both.
2. In every factory, all glazed windows and skylights used for lighting the workrooms shall be kept clean on both the inner and outer surfaces and, so far as compliance with the provisions of any rules made under sub-section (3) of Section 13 will allow, free from obstruction.
3. In every factory, effective provision shall, so far as is practicable, be made for the prevention of
   (a) glare, either directly from a source of light or by reflection from a smooth or polished surface;
   (b) the formation of shadows to such an extent as to cause eye-strain or the risk of accident to any worker.
4. The State Government may prescribe standards of sufficient and suitable lighting for factories or for any class of description of factories or for any manufacturing process [Section 17].

Drinking Water

1. In every factory, effective arrangements shall be made to provide and maintain at suitable points, conveniently situated for all workers employed therein, a sufficient supply of wholesome drinking water.
2. All such points shall be legibly marked 'drinking water' in a language understood by the majority of the workers employed in the factory, and no such point shall be situated within six meters of any washing place, urinal, latrine, spittoon, open drain carrying sullage or effluent, or any other source of contamination, unless a shorter distance is approved in writing by the Chief Inspector.
3. In every factory wherein more than 250 workers are ordinarily employed, provision shall be made for cooling drinking water during hot weather by effective means and for distribution thereof.
4. In respect of all factories or any class or description of factories, the State Government may make rules for securing compliance with the provisions of sub-sections (1), (2), and (3) and for the examination by prescribed authorities of the supply and distribution of drinking water in factories [Section 18].

Latrines and Urinals

1. In every factory
   (a) sufficient latrine and urinal accommodation of prescribed types shall be provided conveniently situated and accessible to workers at all times while they are at the factory;
   (b) separate enclosed accommodation shall be provided for male and female workers;
   (c) such accommodation shall be adequately lighted and ventilated, and no latrine or urinal shall, unless specially exempted in writing by the Chief Inspector, communicate with any workroom except through an intervening open space or ventilated passage;
   (d) all such accommodation shall be maintained in a clean and sanitary condition at all times;
   (e) sweepers shall be employed, whose primary duty it would be to keep the latrines, urinals, and washing places clean.
2. In every factory wherein more than 250 workers are ordinarily employed
   (a) all latrine and urinal accommodation shall be of prescribed sanitary types;
   (b) the floors and internal walls, up to a height of 90 continents of the latrines and urinals and the sanitary blocks, shall be laid in glazed tiles or otherwise finished to provided a smooth polished impervious surface;
   (c) without prejudice to the provisions of clauses (d) and (e) of sub-section (1), the floors, portions of the walls and blocks so laid or finished and the sanitary pans of latrines and urinals shall be thoroughly washed and cleaned at least once every seven days with suitable detergents or disinfectants, or with both.
3. The State Government may prescribe the number of latrines and urinals to be provided in any factory in proportion to the numbers of male and female workers ordinarily employed therein, and provide for such further matters in respect of sanitation in factories, including the obligation of workers in this regard, as it considers necessary in the interest of the health of the workers employed therein [Section 19].

Spittoons

1. In every factory there shall be provided a sufficient number of spittoons in convenient places and they shall be maintained in a clean and hygienic condition.
2. The State Government may make rules prescribing the type and the number of spittoons to be provided and their location in any factory and provide for such further matters relating to their maintenance in a clean and hygienic condition.
3. No person shall spit within the premises of a factory except in the spittoons provided for the purposes and a notice containing this provision and the penalty for its violation shall be prominently displayed at suitable places in the premises.
4. Whoever spits in contravention of sub-section (3) shall be punishable with fine not exceeding five rupees [Section 20].

Safety

Safety implies the state of being safe and protected danger or harm. The Act provides for the following safety measures:

Fencing of Machinery

1. In every factory the following, namely,
   (a) every moving part of a prime mover and every flywheel connected to a prime mover whether the prime mover or flywheel is in the engine house or not;
   (b) the headrace and tailrace of every water-wheel and water turbine;
   (c) any part of a stock-bar which projects beyond the head stock of a lathe; and
   (d) unless they are in such position or of such construction as to be safe to every person employed in the factory as they would be if they were securely fenced, the following, namely
      (i) every part of an electric generator, a motor or rotary converter;
      (ii) every part of transmission machinery; and
      (iii) every dangerous part of any other machinery shall be securely fenced by safeguards of substantial construction which shall be constantly maintained and kept in position while the parts of machinery they are fencing are in motion or in use.

   Provided that for the purpose of determining whether any part of machinery is in such position or is of such construction as to be safe as aforesaid, account shall not be taken of any occasion when
   - it is necessary to make an examination of any part of the machinery aforesaid while it is in motion or, as a result of such examination, to carry out lubrication or other adjusting operations while the machinery is in motion, being an examination or operation which is necessary to be carried out while that part of the machinery is in motion, or
   - in the case of any part of a transmission machinery used in such a process as may be prescribed (being a process of a continuous nature, the carrying on of which shall be, or is likely to be, substantially interfered with by the stoppage of that part of the machinery), it is necessary to make an examination of such part of the machinery while it is in motion or, as a result or such examination, to carry out any mounting or shipping of belts or lubrication or other adjusting operation while the machinery is in motion, and such examination or operation is made or carried out in accordance with the provisions of sub-section (1) of Section 22.
2. The State Government may by rules prescribe such further precautions as it may consider necessary in respect of any particular machinery or part thereof, or exempt, subject to such conditions as may be prescribed for securing the safety of the workers, any particular machinery or part thereof from the provisions of this section [Section 21].

Work on or Near Machinery in Motion

1. Where, in any factory, it becomes necessary to examine any part of machinery referred to in Section 21 while the machinery is in motion, or, as a result of such examination, to carry out
   (a) in a case referred to in clause (i) of the proviso to sub-section (1) of Section 21, lubrication or other adjusting operation; or
   (b) in a case referred to in clause (ii) of the proviso aforesaid, any mounting or shipping of belts or lubrication or other adjusting operation while the machinery is in motion, such an examination or operation shall be made or carried out only by a specially trained adult male worker wearing tight fitting clothing (which shall be supplied by the occupier) whose name has been recorded in the register prescribed in this behalf and who has been furnished with a certificate of his appointment, and, while he is so engaged,
      (i) such a worker shall not handle a belt at a moving pulley unless
         - the belt is not more than 15 centimeters in width;
         - the pulley is normally for the purpose of drive and not merely a fly-wheel or

balance wheel (in which case a belt is not permissible);
- the belt joint is either laced or flush with the belt;
- the belt, including the joint and the pulley rim, are in good repair;
- there is reasonable clearance between the pulley and any fixed plant or structure;
- secure foothold and, where necessary, secure handhold, are provided for the operator; and
- any ladder used for carrying out any examination or operation aforesaid is securely fixed or lashed or is firmly held by a second person;

(ii) without prejudice to any other provision of this Act relating to the fencing of machinery, every set screw, bolt and key on any revolving shaft, spindle, wheel or opinion, and all spur, worm, and other toothed or friction gearing in motion with which such worker would otherwise be liable to come into contact, shall be securely fenced to prevent such contact.

2. No woman or young person shall be allowed to clean, lubricate, or adjust any part of a prime mover or of any transmission machinery while the prime mover or transmission machinery is in motion, or to clean, lubricate, or adjust any part of any machine if the cleaning, lubrication, or adjustment thereof would expose the woman or young person to risk of injury from any moving part, either of that machine or of any adjacent machinery.
3. The State Government may, by notification in the Official Gazette, prohibit, in any specified factory or class or description of factories, the cleaning, lubricating, or adjusting by any person of specified parts of machinery when those parts are in motion [Section 22].

Employment of Young Persons on Dangerous Machines

1. No young person shall be required or allowed to work at any machine to which this Section applies, unless he has been fully instructed as to the dangers arising in connection with the machine and the precautions to be observed and
   (a) has received sufficient training in work at the machine, or
   (b) is under adequate supervision by a person who has a through knowledge and experience of the machine.
2. Sub-section (1) shall apply to such machines as may be prescribed by the State Government, being machines which, in its opinion, are of such a dangerous character that young person ought not to work at them unless the foregoing requirements are complied with [Section 23].

Striking Gear and Devices for Cutting off Power

1. In every factory
   (a) suitable striking gear or other efficient mechanical appliances shall be provided and maintained and used to move driving belts to and from fast and loose pulleys which form part of the transmission machinery, and such gear or appliances shall be so constructed, placed, and maintained as to prevent the belt from creeping back on to the fast pulley;
   (b) driving belts when not in use shall not be allowed to rest or ride upon shafting in motion.
2. In every factory, suitable devices for cutting off power in emergencies from running machinery shall be provided and maintained in every work-room.

   Provided that, in respect of factories in operation before the commencement of this Act, the provisions of this sub-section shall apply only to work-rooms in which electricity is used as power.
3. When a device, which can inadvertently shift from 'off' to 'on' position, is provided in a factory to cut off power, arrangements shall be provided for locking the device in a safe position to prevent accidental starting of the transmission machinery or other machines to which the device is fitted [Section 24].

Self-acting Machines

No traversing part of a self-acting machine in any factory and no material carried thereon shall, if the space over which it runs is a space over which any person is liable to pass, whether in the course of his employment or otherwise, be allowed to run on its outward or inward traverse within a distance of 45 centimeters from any fixed structure which is not a part of the machine [Section 25].

However, the Chief Inspector may permit the continued use of a machine installed before the commencement of this Act which does not comply with the requirements of this Section on such conditions for ensuring safety as he may think fit to impose.

Casing of New Machinery

1. In all machinery driven by power and installed in any factory after the commencement of this Act,
   (a) every set screw, bolt or key on any revolving shaft, spindle, wheel, or pinion shall be so sunk, encased or otherwise effectively guarded as to prevent danger;
   (b) all spur, worm, and other toothed or friction gearing which does not require frequent adjustment while in motion shall be completely encased, unless it is so situated as to be as safe as it would be if it were completely encased.
2. Whoever sells or lets on hire or, as agent of a seller or hirer, causes or procures to be sold or let on hire, for use in a factory any machinery driven by power which does not comply with the provisions of sub-section (1) or any rules made under sub-section (3), shall be punishable with imprisonment for a term which may extend to three months or with fine which may extend to ₹500 or with both.
3. The State Government may make rules specifying further safeguards to be provided in respect to any other dangerous part of any particular machine or class or description of machines [Section 26].

Prohibition of Employment of Eomen and Children Near Cotton-openers

No woman or child shall be employed in any part of a factory for pressing cotton in which a cotton-opener is at work. However, if the feed-end of a cotton-opener is in a room separated from the delivery end by a partition extending to the roof or to such height as the Inspector may in any particular case specify in writing, women and children may be employed on the side of the partition where the feed-end is situated [Section 27].

Hoists and Lifts

1. In every factory
   (a) every hoist and lift shall be
      (i) of good mechanical construction, sound material and adequate strength:
      (ii) properly maintained, and shall be thoroughly examined by a competent person at least once every six months, and a register shall be kept containing the prescribed particulars of every such examination;
   (b) every hoistway and liftway shall be sufficiently protected by an enclosure fitted with gates, and the hoist or lift and every such enclosure shall be so constructed as to prevent any person or thing from being trapped between any part of the hoist or lift and any fixed structure or moving part;
   (c) the maximum safe working load shall be plainly marked on every hoist or lift, and no load greater than such load shall be carried thereon;
   (d) the cage of every hoist or lift used for carrying persons shall be fitted with a gate on each side from which access is afforded to a landing;
   (e) every gate referred to in clause (b) or clause (d) shall be fitted with interlocking or other efficient devices to ensure that the gate cannot be opened except when the cage is at the landing and that the cage cannot be moved unless the gate is closed.
2. The following additional requirements shall apply to hoists and lifts used for carrying persons and installed or reconstructed in a factory after the commencement of this Act, namely
   (a) where the cage is supported by rope or chain, there shall be at least two ropes or chains separately connected with the cage and balance weight, and each rope or chain with its attachments shall be capable of carrying the whole weight of the cage together with its maximum load;
   (b) efficient devices shall be provided and maintained capable of supporting the cage together with its maximum load in the event of breakage of the ropes, chains, or attachments;
   (c) an efficient automatic device shall be provided and maintained to prevent the cage from over-running.

3. The Chief Inspector may permit the continued use of a hoist or lift installed in a factory before the commencement of this Act which does not fully comply with the provisions of sub-section (1) upon such conditions for ensuring safety as he may think fit to impose.
4. The State Government may, if, in respect of any class or description of hoist or lift, it is of the opinion that it would be unreasonable to enforce any requirement of sub-sections (1) and (2), by order direct that such requirement shall not apply to such a class or description of hoist or lift.

   Explanation: For the purpose of this Section, no lifting machine or appliance shall be deemed to be a hoist or lift unless it has a platform or cage, the direction or movement of which is restricted by a guide or guides [Section 28].

Lifting Machines, Chains, Ropes, and Lifting Tackles

1. In any factory, the following provisions shall be complied with in respect of every lifting machine (other than a hoist and lift) and every chain, rope, and lifting tackle for the purpose of raising or lowering persons, goods, or materials
   (a) all parts, including the working gear, whether fixed or movable, of every lifting machine and every chain, rope or lifting tackle shall be
      (i) of good construction, sound material and adequate strength, and free from defects;
      (ii) properly maintained; and
      (iii) thoroughly examined by a competent person at least once in every period of 12 months, or at such intervals as the Chief Inspector may specify in writing; and a register shall be kept containing the prescribed particulars of every such examination;
   (b) no lifting machine and no chain, rope or lifting tackle shall, except for the purpose of test, be loaded beyond the safe working load which shall be plainly marked thereon together with an identification mark and duly entered in the prescribed register; and where this is not practicable, a table showing the safe working loads of every kind and size of lifting machine or chain, rope or lifting tackle in use shall be displayed in prominent positions on the premises;
   (c) while any person is employed or working on or near the wheel track of a traveling crane in any place where he would be liable to be struck by the crane, effective measures shall be taken to ensure that the crane does not approach within six months of that place.
2. The State Government may make rules in respect of any lifting machine or any chain, rope or lifting tackle used in factories
   (a) prescribing further requirements to be complied with in addition to those set out in this Section;
   (b) providing for exemption from compliance with all or any of the requirements of this Section, where, in its opinion, such compliance is unnecessary or impracticable.
3. For the purposes of this Section, a lifting machine or a chain, rope, or lifting tackle, shall be deemed to have been thoroughly examined if a visual examination supplemented, if necessary, by other means and by the dismantling of parts of the gear, has been carried out as carefully as the conditions permit in order to arrive at a reliable conclusion as to the safety of the parts examined.

   Explanation: In this section
   (a) 'lifting machine' refers to a crane, crab, which teagle pulley block, gin wheel, transporter, or runway;
   (b) 'lifting tackle' refers to any chain sling, rope sling, hook, shackle, swivel, coupling, socket, clamp, tray, or similar appliance, whether fixed or movable, used in connection with the raising or lowering of persons, or loads by use of lifting machines [Section 29].

Revolving Machinery

1. In every factory in which the process of grinding is carried on, there shall be permanently affixed to, or placed near, each machine in use, a notice indicating the maximum safe working peripheral speed of every grindstone or abrasive wheel, the speed of the shaft or spindle upon which the

wheel is mounted, and the diameter of the pulley upon such a shaft or spindle necessary to secure such safe working peripheral speed.

2. The speeds indicated in notices under sub-section (1) shall not be exceeded.
3. Effective measures shall be taken in every factory to ensure that the safe working peripheral speed of every revolving vessel, cage, basket, flywheel, pulley, disc, or similar appliance driven by power is not exceeded [Section 30].

Pressure Plant

1. If, in any factory, any plant or machinery or any part thereof is operated at a pressure above atmospheric pressure, effective measures shall be taken to ensure that the safe working pressure of such a plant or machinery or part is not exceeded.
2. The State Government may make rules providing for the examination and testing of any plant or machinery referred to in sub-section (1) and prescribing such other safety measures in relation thereto as may in its opinion be necessary in any factory or class or description of factories.
3. The State Government may, by rules, exempt, subject to such conditions as may be specified therein, any part of any plant or machinery referred to in sub-section (1) from the provisions of this Section [Section 31].

Floors, Stairs, and Means of Access

In every factory

1. all floors, steps, stairs, passages and gangways shall be of sound construction and properly maintained and shall be kept free from obstructions and substances likely to cause persons to slip, and where it is necessary to ensure safety, steps, stairs, passages, and gangways shall be provided with substantial handrails;
2. there shall, so far as is reasonably practicable, be provided and maintained safe means of access to every place at which any person is at any time required to work;
3. when any person has to work at a height from where he is likely to fall, provision shall be made, so far as is reasonably practicable, by fencing or otherwise, to ensure the safety of the person so working [Section 32].

Pits, Sumps, and Openings in Floors

1. In every factory, every fixed vessel, sump, tank, pit or opening in the ground or in a floor which, by reason of its depth, situation, construction or contents, is or may be a source of danger, shall be either securely covered or securely fenced.
2. The State Government may, by order in writing, exempt, subject to such conditions as may be prescribed, any factory or class or description of factories in respect of any vessel, sump, tank, pit or opening from compliance with the provisions of this Section [Section 33].

Excessive Weights

1. No person shall be employed in any factory to lift, carry or move any load so heavy as to be likely to cause him injury.
2. The State Government may make rules prescribing the maximum weights which may be lifted, carried, or moved by adult men, adult women, adolescents, and children employed in factories or in any class or description of factories or in carrying on any specified process [Section 34].

Protection of Eyes

In respect of any such manufacturing process carried on in any factory as may be prescribed, which involves

1. risk of injury to the eyes from particles or fragments thrown off in the course of the process, or
2. risk to the eyes by reason of exposure to excessive light, the State Government may by rules require that effective screens or suitable goggles shall be provided for the protection of persons employed on, or in the immediate vicinity of, the process [Section 35].

Precautions Against Dangerous Fumes and Gases

1. No person shall be required or allowed to enter any chamber, tank, vat, pit, pipe, flue, or other confined space in any factory in which any gas,

fume, vapour, or dust is likely to be present to such an extent as to involve a risk to persons being overcome thereby, unless it is provided with a manhole of adequate size or other effective means of egress.

2. No person shall be required or allowed to enter any confined space as is referred to in subsection (1), until all practicable measures have been taken to remove any gas, fumes, vapour, or dust, which may be present so as to bring its level within the permissible limits and to prevent any ingress of such gas, fumes, vapour, or dust and unless
   (a) a certificate in writing has been given by a competent person, based on a test carried out by himself that the space is reasonably free from dangerous gas, fumes, vapour, or dust; or
   (b) such a person is wearing suitable breathing apparatus and a belt securely attached to a rope the free end of which is held by a person outside the confined space [Section 36].

Precautions Regarding the Use of Portable Electric Light

In any factory

1. no portable electric light or any other electric appliance of voltage exceeding 24 volts shall be permitted for use inside any chamber, tank, vat, pit, pipe, flue, or other confined space; unless adequate safety devices are provided and
2. if any inflammable gas, fume, or dust is likely to be present in such chamber, tank, vat, pit, pipe, flue, or other confined space, no lamp or light other than that of flame-proof construction shall be permitted to be used therein [Section 36A].

Explosive or Inflammable Dust and Gas

1. Where, in any factory, any manufacturing process produces dust, gas, fumes, or vapour of such character and to such extent as to be likely to explode on ignition, all practicable measures shall be taken to prevent any such a explosion by
   (a) effective enclosure of the plant or machinery used in the process;
   (b) removal or prevention of the accumulation of such dust, gas, fumes, or vapour;
   (c) exclusion or effective enclosure of all possible sources of ignition.
2. Where in any factory the plant or machinery used in a process such as is referred to in subsection (1) is not so constructed as to withstand the probable pressure which such an explosion as aforesaid would produce, all practicable measures shall be taken to restrict the spread and effects of the explosion by the provision in the plant or machinery of chokes, baffles, vents, or other effective appliances.
3. Where any part of the plant or machinery in a factory contains any explosive or inflammable gas or vapour under pressure greater than atmospheric pressure, that part shall not be opened except in accordance with the following provisions
   (a) before the fastening of any joint of any pipe connected with the part, or the fastening of the cover of any opening into the cover of any opening into the part is loosened, any flow of the gas or vapour into the part of any such pipe shall be effectively stopped by a stop-valve or other means;
   (b) before any such fastening as aforesaid is removed, all practicable measures shall be taken to reduce the pressure of the gas or vapour in the part of pipe to atmospheric pressure;
   (c) where any such fastening as aforesaid has been loosened or removed, effective measures shall be taken to prevent any explosive or inflammable gas or vapour from entering the part or pipe until the fastening has been secured, or, as the case may be, securely replaced.

   However, the provisions of this subsection shall not apply in the case of plant or machinery installed in the open air.
4. No plant, tank, or vessel which contains or has contained any explosive or inflammable substance shall be subjected in any factory to any welding, brazing, soldering, or cutting operation which involves the application of heat unless adequate measures have first been taken to remove such a substance and any fumes arising therefrom, or to render such a substance and fumes non-explosive or non-inflammable,

and no such substance shall be allowed to enter such plant, tank or vessel after any such operation until the metal has cooled sufficiently to prevent any risk of igniting the substance.

5. The State Government may, by rules, exempt, subject to such conditions as may be prescribed, any factory or class or description of factories from compliance with all or any of the provisions of this Section [Section 37].

Precautions in Case of Fire

1. In every factory, all practicable measures shall be taken to prevent outbreak of fire and its spread, both internally and externally, and to provide and maintain
   (a) safe means of escape for all persons in the event of a fire, and
   (b) the necessary equipment and facilities for extinguishing fire.
2. Effective measures shall be taken to ensure that in every factory all the workers are familiar with the means of escape in case of fire and have been adequately trained in the routine to be followed in such cases.
3. The State Government may make rules, in respect of any factory or class or description of factories, requiring the measures to be adopted to give effect to the provisions of sub-sections (1) and (2).
4. Notwithstanding anything contained in clause (a) of sub-section (1) or sub-section (2), if the Chief Inspector, having regard to the nature of the work carried on in any factory, the construction of such a factory, special risk to life or safety, or any other circumstances, is of the opinion that the measures provided in the factory, whether as prescribed or not, for the purposes of clause (a) of sub-section (1) or sub-section (2), are inadequate, he may, by order in writing, require that such additional measures as he may consider reasonable and necessary be provided in the factory before the date specified in the order [Section 38].

Power to Require Specifications of Defective Parts or Tests of Stability

If it appears to the Inspector that any building or part of a building or any part of the ways, machinery or plant in a factory is in such a condition that it may be dangerous to human life or safety, he may serve on the occupier or manager (or both) of the factory an order in writing requiring him before a specified date

1. to furnish such drawings, specifications, and other particulars as may be necessary to determine whether such building, ways, machinery, or plant can be used with safety, or
2. to carry out such tests in such manner as may be specified in the order, and to inform the Inspector of the results thereof [Section 39].

Safety of Buildings and Machinery

1. If it appears to the Inspector that any building or part of a building or any part of the ways, machinery or plant in a factory is in such a condition that it is dangerous to human life or safety, he may serve on the occupier or manager (or both) of the factory an order in writing specifying the measures which, in his opinion, should be adopted, and requiring them to be carried out before a specified date.
2. If it appears to the Inspector that the use of any building or part of a building or any part of the ways, machinery or plant in a factory involves imminent danger to human life or safety, he may serve on the occupier or manager (or both) of the factory an order in writing prohibiting its use until it has been properly repaired or altered [Section 40].

Maintenance of Buildings

If it appears to the Inspector that any building or part of a building in a factory is in such a state of disrepair as is likely to lead to conditions detrimental to the health and welfare of the workers, he may serve on the occupier or manager (or both) of the factory an order in writing specifying the measures which, in his opinion, should be taken, and requiring the same to be carried out before such date as is specified in the order [Section 40A].

Safety Officers

1. In every factory,
   (a) wherein one thousand or more workers are ordinarily employed, or

(b) wherein, in the opinion of the State Government, any manufacturing process or operation is carried on, which involves any risk of bodily injury, poisoning or disease, or any other hazard to health to the persons employed in the factory, the occupier shall, if so required by the State Government by notification in the Official Gazette, employ such number of Safety Officers as may be specified in that notification.

2. The duties, qualifications, and conditions of service of the Safety Officers shall be such as may be prescribed by the State Government [Section 40B].

Provisions Relating to Hazardous Processes

The Act provides the following provisions relating to hazardous processes:

Constitution of Site Appraisal Committees

1. The State Government may, for purposes of advising it to consider applications for grant of permission for the initial location of a factory involving a hazardous process, or for the expansion of any such factory, appoint a Site Appraisal Committee consisting of
   (a) the Chief Inspector of the State who shall be its Chairman;
   (b) a representative of the Central Board for the Prevention and Control of Water Pollution appointed by the Central Government under Section 3 of the Water (Prevention and Control of Pollution) Act, 1974;
   (c) a representative of the Central Board for the Prevention and Control of Air Pollution referred to in Section 3 of the Air (Prevention and Control of Pollution) Act, 1981;
   (d) a representative of the State Board appointed under Section 4 of the Water (Prevention and Control of Pollution) Act, 1974;
   (e) a representative of the State Board for the Prevention and Control of Air Pollution referred to in Section 5 of the Air (Prevention and Control of Pollution) Act, 1981;
   (f) a representative of the Department of Environment in the State;
   (g) a representative of the Meteorological Department of the Government of India;
   (h) an expert in the field of occupational health; and
   (i) a representative of the Town Planning Department of the State Government, and not more than five other members who may be co-opted by the State Government who shall be—
      (i) a scientist having specialised knowledge of the hazardous process which will be involved in the factory,
      (ii) a representative of the local authority within whose jurisdiction the factory is to be established, and
      (iii) not more than three other persons as deemed fit by the State Government.
2. The Site Appraisal Committee shall examine an application for the establishment of a factory involving hazardous process and make its recommendation to the State Government within a period of 90 days of the receipt of such applications in the prescribed form.
3. Where any process relates to a factory owned or controlled by the Central Government or to a corporation or a company owned or controlled by the Central Government, the State Government shall co-opt in the Site Appraisal Committee a representative nominated by the Central Government as a member of that Committee.
4. The Site Appraisal Committee shall have the power to call for any information from the person making an application for the establishment or expansion of a factory involving a hazardous process.
5. Where the State Government has granted approval to an application for the establishment or expansion of a factory involving a hazardous process, it shall not be necessary for the applicant to obtain a further approval from the Central Board or the State Board established under the Water (Prevention and Control of Pollution) Act, 1974 and the Air (Prevention and Control of Pollution) Act 1981 [Section 41A].

Compulsory Disclosure of Information by the Occupier

1. The occupier of every factory involving a hazardous process shall disclose, in the manner prescribed, all information regarding dangers, including health hazards and the measures to overcome such hazards arising from the exposure to or handling of the materials or substances in the manufacture, transportation, storage, and other processes, to the workers employed in the factory, the Chief Inspector, the local authority within whose jurisdiction the factory is situated and the general public in the vicinity.
2. The occupier shall, at the time of registering the factory involving a hazardous process, lay down a detailed policy with respect to the health and safety of the workers employed therein and intimate such policy to the Chief Inspector and the local authority and, thereafter, at such intervals as may be prescribed, inform the Chief Inspector and the local authority of any change made in the said policy.
3. The information furnished under sub-section (1) shall include accurate information as to the quantity, specifications and other characteristics of wastes and the manner of their disposal.
4. Every occupier shall, with the approval of the Chief Inspector, draw up an on-site emergency plan and detailed disaster control measures for his factory and make known to the workers employed therein and to the general public living in the vicinity of the factory the safety measures required to be taken in the event of an accident taking place.
5. Every occupier of a factory shall
   (a) if such factory engaged in a hazardous process on the commencement of the Factories (Amendment) Act, 1987, within a period of thirty days of such commencement; and
   (b) if such factory proposes to engage in a hazardous process at any time after such commencement, within a period of 30 days before the commencement of such process, inform the Chief Inspector of the nature and details of the process in such form and in such manner as may be prescribed.
6. Where any occupier of a factory contravenes the provisions of sub-section (5), the licence issued under Section 6 to such a factory shall, notwithstanding any penalty to which the occupier or factory shall be subjected to under the provisions of this Act, be liable for cancellation.
7. The occupier of a factory involving a hazardous process shall, with the previous approval of the Chief Inspector, lay down measures for the handling, usage, transportation, and storage of hazardous substances inside the factory premises and publicise them in the manner prescribed among the workers and the general public living in the vicinity [Section 41B].

Responsibility of Occupier for Hazardous Processes

Every occupier of a factory involving any hazardous process shall

1. maintain accurate and up-to-date health records or, as the case may be, medical records, of the workers in the factory who are exposed to any chemical, toxic, or any other harmful substances which are manufactured, stored, handled, or transported and such records shall be accessible to the workers subject to such conditions as may be prescribed;
2. appoint persons who possess qualifications and experience in handling hazardous substances and are competent to supervise such handling within the factory, and provide at the working place all the necessary facilities for protecting the workers in the manner prescribed.

   Provided that where any question arises as to the qualifications and experience of a person so appointed, the decision of the Chief Inspector shall be final;
3. provide for medical examination of every worker
   (a) before such worker is assigned to a job involving the handling of, or working with, a hazardous substance, and
   (b) while continuing in such a job, and after he has ceased to work in such job, at intervals not exceeding 12 months, in such manner as may be prescribed [Section 41C].

Power of Central Government to Appoint Inquiry Committee

1. The Central Government may, in the event of the occurrence of an extraordinary situation involving a factory engaged in a hazardous process, appoint an Inquiry Committee to inquire into the standards of health and safety observed in the factory with a view to finding out the causes of any failure or neglect in the adoption of any measures or standards prescribed for the health and safety of the workers employed in the factory or the general public affected or likely to be affected, due to such failure or neglect, and for the prevention and recurrence of such extraordinary situations in future in this factory or elsewhere.'
2. The Committee appointed under sub-section (1) shall consist of a Chairman and two other members and the terms of reference of the Committee and the tenure of office of its member shall be such as may be determined by the Central Government according to the requirements of the situation.
3. The recommendations of the Committee shall be advisory in nature [Section 41D].

Emergency Standards

1. Where the Central Government is satisfied that no standards of safety have been prescribed in respect of a hazardous process or class of hazardous processes, or where the standards so prescribed are inadequate, it may direct the Director-General of Factory Advice Service and Labour Institutes or any institution specialised in matters relating to standards of safety in hazardous processes, to lay down emergency standards for the enforcement of suitable standards in respect of such hazardous processes.
2. The emergency standards laid down under this sub-section shall, until they are incorporated in the rules made under this, be enforceable and have the same effect as if they had been incorporated in the rules made under this Act [Section 41E].

Permissible Limits of Exposure of Chemical and Toxic Substances

1. The maximum permissible threshold limits of exposure of chemical and toxic substances in manufacturing processes (whether hazardous or otherwise) in any factory shall be of the value indicated in the Second Schedule.
2. The Central Government may, at any time, for the purpose of giving effect to any scientific proof obtained from specialised institutions or experts in the field, by notification in the Official Gazette, make suitable changes in the said Schedule [Section 41F].

Workers' Participation in Safety Management

1. The occupier shall, in every factory where a hazardous process takes place, or where hazardous substances are used or handled, set up a Safety Committee consisting of an equal number of representatives of workers and management to promote cooperation between the workers and the management in maintaining proper safety and health at work and to review periodically the measures taken in that behalf:

   However, the State Government may, by order in writing and for reasons to be recorded, exempt the occupier of any factory or class of factories from setting up such a Committee.
2. The composition of the Safety Committee, the tenure of office of its members and their rights and duties shall be such as may be prescribed [Sectuib 41G].

Right of Workers to Warn About Imminent Danger

1. Where the workers employed in any factory engaged in a hazardous process have reasonable apprehension that there is a likelihood of imminent danger to their lives or health due to any accident, they may bring the same to the notice of the occupier, agent, manager, or any other person who is in charge of the factory or the process concerned directly or through their representatives in the Safety Committee and simultaneously bring the same to the notice of the Inspector.
2. It shall be the duty of the occupier, agent, manager, or the person in-charge of the factory or process to take immediate remedial action if

he is satisfied about the existence of such imminent danger and send a report forthwith of the action taken to the nearest Inspector.

3. If the occupier, agent, manager, or the person in charge referred to in sub-section (2) is not satisfied about the existence of any imminent danger as apprehended by the workers, he shall, nevertheless, refer the matter forthwith to the nearest Inspector whose decision on the question of the existence of such imminent danger shall be final [Section 41H].

Welfare Measures

Welfare measures: Various services, benefits and facilities offered to employees by the employers such as allowances, housing, transportation, medical insurance, and food etc.

Employee welfare is a term including various services, benefits and facilities offered to employees by the employers. The welfare measures need not be monetary but in any kind/forms. This includes items such as allowances, housing, transportation, medical insurance and food. Employee welfare also includes monitoring of working conditions, creation of industrial harmony through infrastructure for health, industrial relations and insurance against disease, accident and unemployment for the workers and their families. Through such generous benefits the employer makes life worth living for employees. As regards welfare measures for the workers the Act provides as under:

Washing Facilities

1. In every factory
   (a) adequate and suitable facilities for washing shall be provided and maintained for the use of the workers therein;
   (b) separate and adequately screened facilities shall be provided for the use of male and female workers;
   (c) such facilities shall be conveniently accessible and shall be kept clean.
2. The State Government may, in respect of any factory or class or description of factories or of any manufacturing process, prescribe standards of adequate, and suitable facilities for washing [Section 42].

Facilities for Storing and Drying Clothing

The State Government may, in respect of any factory or class or description of factories, make rules requiring the provision therein of suitable places for keeping clothing not worn during working hours and for the drying of wet clothing [Section 43].

Facilities for Sitting

1. In every factory, suitable arrangements for sitting shall be provided and maintained for all workers obliged to work in a standing position, in order that they may take advantage of any opportunities for rest which may occur in the course of their work.
2. If, in, the opinion of the Chief Inspector, the workers in any factory engaged in a particular manufacturing process or working in a particular room are able to do their work efficiently in a sitting position, he may, by order in writing, require the occupier of the factory to provide, before a specified date, such seating arrangements as may be practicable for all workers so engaged or working.
3. The State Government may, by notification in the Official Gazette, declare that the provisions of sub-section (1) shall not apply to any specified factory or class or description of factories or to any specified manufacturing process [Section 44].

First-aid Appliances

1. There shall, in every factory be provided and maintained so as to be readily accessible during all working hours, first-aid boxes or cupboards equipped with the prescribed contents, and the number of such boxes or cupboards to be provided and maintained shall not be less than one for every one hundred and fifty workers ordinarily employed at any one time in the factory.
2. Nothing except the prescribed contents shall be kept in a first-aid box or cupboard.
3. Each first-aid box or cupboard shall be kept in the charge of a separate responsible person who holds a certificate in first-aid treatment recognised by the State Government and who shall

always be readily available during the working hours of the factory.

4. In every factory where more than 500 workers are ordinarily employed, there shall be provided and maintained an ambulance room of the prescribed size, containing the prescribed equipment and in the charge of such medical and nursing staff as may be prescribed and those facilities shall always be made readily available during the working hours of the factory [Section 45].

Canteens

1. The State Government may make rules requiring that in any specified factory wherein more than 250 workers are ordinarily employed, a canteen or canteens shall be provided and maintained by the occupier for the use of the workers.
2. Without prejudice to the generality of the foregoing power, such rules may provide for
   (a) the date by which such canteen shall be provided;
   (b) the standards in respect of construction, accommodation, furniture, and other equipment of the canteen;
   (c) the foodstuffs to be served therein and the charges which may be made therefore these;
   (d) the constitution of a managing committee for the canteen and representation of the workers in the management of the canteen;
   (e) the items of expenditure in the running of the canteen which are not to be taken into account in fixing the cost of foodstuffs and which shall be borne by the employer;
   (f) the delegation to the Chief Inspector, subject to such conditions as may be prescribed, of the power to make rules under clause (c) [Section 46].

Shelters, Rest Rooms, and Lunch Rooms

1. In every factory wherein more than 150 workers are ordinarily employed, adequate and suitable shelters or rest rooms, and a suitable lunch room, with provision for drinking water, where workers can eat meals brought by them, shall be provided and maintained for the use of the workers.

   Provided that any canteen maintained in accordance with the provisions of Section 46 shall be regarded as part of the requirements of this sub-section.

   Provided further that where a lunch room exists, no worker shall eat any food in the work room.
2. The shelters or rest rooms or lunch rooms to be provided under sub-section (1) shall be sufficiently lighted and ventilated and shall be maintained in a cool and clean condition.
3. The State Government may
   (a) prescribe the standards in respect of construction, accommodation, furniture, and other equipment of shelters, rest rooms, and lunch rooms to be provided under this Section;
   (b) by notification in the Official Gazette, exempt any factory or class or description of factories from the requirements of this Section [Section 47].

Crèches

1. In every factory wherein more than 30 women workers are ordinarily employed there shall be provided and maintained a suitable room or rooms for the use of children under the age of six years of such women.
2. Such rooms shall provide adequate accommodation, shall be adequately lighted and ventilated, shall be maintained in a clean and sanitary condition and shall be under the charge of women trained in the care of children and infants.
3. The State Government may make rules
   (a) prescribing the location and the standards in respect of construction, accommodation, furniture, and other equipment of rooms to be provided under this Section;
   (b) requiring the provision in factories to which this Section applies of additional facilities for the care of children belonging to women workers, including suitable provision of facilities for washing and changing their clothing;
   (c) requiring the provision in any factory of free milk or refreshment or both for such children;
   (d) requiring that facilities shall be given in any factory for the mothers of such children to feed them at the necessary intervals [Section 48].

Welfare Officers

1. In every factory wherein five hundred or more workers are ordinarily employed, the occupier shall employ in the factory such number of welfare officers as may be prescribed.
2. The State Government may prescribe the duties, qualifications and conditions of service of officers employed under sub-section (1) [Section 49].

Power to Make Rules

The State Government may make rules

1. exempting, subject to compliance with such alternative arrangements for the welfare of workers as may be prescribed, any factory or class or description of factories from compliance with any of the provisions of this Chapter;
2. requiring in any factory or class or description of factories that representatives of the workers employed in the factory shall be associated with the management of the welfare arrangements of the workers [Section 50].

Working Hours of Adults

To protect the young persons from any short of employment related exploitation the Act provides as under:

Weekly Hours

No adult worker shall be required or allowed to work in a factory for more than 48 hours in any week [Section 51].

Weekly Holidays

1. No adult worker shall be required or allowed to work in a factory on the first day of the week (hereafter referred to as the said day), unless
   (a) he has or will have a holiday for a whole day on one of the three days immediately before or after the said day, and
   (b) the manager of the factory has, before the said day or the substituted day under clause (a), whichever is earlier,
      (i) delivered a notice at the office of the Inspector of his intention to require the worker to work on the said day and of the day which is to be substituted, and
      (ii) displayed a notice to that effect in the factory:

      Provided that no substitution shall be made which will result in any worker working for more than ten days consecutively without a holiday for a whole day.
2. Notices given under sub-section (1) may be cancelled by a notice delivered at the office of the Inspector and a notice displayed in the factory not later than the day before the said day or the holiday to be cancelled, whichever is earlier.
3. Where, in accordance with the provisions of sub-section (1), any worker works on the said day and has had a holiday on one of the three days immediately before it, that said day shall, for the purpose of calculating his weekly hours of work, be included in the preceding week [Section 52].

Compensatory Holidays

1. Where, as a result of the passing of an order or the making of a rule under the provisions of this Act exempting a factory or the workers therein from the provisions of Section 52, a worker is deprived of any of the weekly holidays for which provision is made in sub-section (1) of that Section, he shall be allowed, within the month in which the holidays were due to him or within the two months immediately following that month, compensatory holidays of equal number of the holidays so lost.
2. The State Government may prescribe the manner in which the holidays for which provision is made in sub-section (1) shall be allowed [Section 53].

Daily Hours

Subject to the provisions of Section 51, no adult worker shall be required or allowed to work in a factory for more than nine hours in any day:

Provided that, subject to the previous approval of the Chief Inspector, the daily maximum specified in this Section may be exceeded in order to facilitate the change of shifts [Section 54].

Intervals for Rest

1. The periods of work of adult workers in a factory each day shall be so fixed that no period shall exceed five hours and that no worker shall work for more than five hours before he has had an interval for rest of at least half an hour.

2. The State Government or, subject to the control of the State Government, the Chief Inspector, may, by written order and for the reasons specified therein, exempt any factory from the provisions of sub-section (1) so however that the total number of hours worked by a worker without an interval does not exceed six [Section 55].

Spread-over

The periods of work of an adult worker in a factory shall be so arranged that, inclusive of his intervals for rest under Section 55, they shall not spread over more than 10.5 hours in any day.

Provided that the Chief Inspector may, for reasons to be specified in writing, increase the spread-over up to twelve hours [Section 56].

Night Shifts

Where a worker in a factory works on a shift which extends beyond midnight

1. for the purpose of Sections 52 and 53, a holiday for a whole day shall mean in his case a period of 24 consecutive hours beginning when his shift ends;
2. the following day for him shall be deemed to be the period of 24 hours beginning when such a shift ends, and the hours he has worked after midnight shall be counted in the previous day [Section 57].

Prohibition of Overlapping Shifts

1. Work shall not be carried on in any factory by means of a system of shifts so arranged that more than one relay of workers is engaged in work of the same kind at the same time.
2. The State Government or subject to the control of the State Government, the Chief Inspector, may, by written order and for the reasons specified therein, exempt on such conditions as may be deemed expedient, any factory or class or description of factories or any department or section of a factory or any category or description of workers therein from the provisions of sub-section (1) [Section 58].

Extra Wages for Overtime

1. Where a worker works in a factory for more than nine hours in any day or for more than 48 hours in any week, he shall, in respect of overtime work, be entitled to wages at the rate of twice his ordinary rate of wages.
2. For the purposes of sub-section (1), the 'ordinary rate of wages' refers to the basic wages plus such allowances, including the cash equivalent of the advantage accruing through the concessional sale to workers of food grains and other articles, as the worker is for the time being entitled to, but does not include a bonus and wages for overtime work.
3. Where any workers in a factory are paid on a piece-rate basis, the time rate shall be deemed to be equivalent to the daily average of their full-time earnings for the days on which they actually worked on the same or identical job during the month immediately preceding the calendar month during which the overtime work was done, and such time rates shall be deemed to be the ordinary rates of wages of those workers.

   Provided that in the case of a worker who has not worked in the immediately preceding calendar month on the same or identical job, the time rate shall be deemed to be equivalent to the daily average of the earning of the worker for the days on which he actually worked in the week in which the overtime work was done.

   Explanation: For the purpose of this sub-section, in computing the earnings for the days on which the worker actually worked, such allowances, including the cash equivalent of the advantage accruing through the concessional sale to workers of food grains and other articles as the worker is for the time being entitled to, shall be included, but any bonus or wages for overtime work payable in relation to the period with reference to which the earnings are being computed shall be excluded.
4. The cash equivalent of the advantage accruing through the concessional sale to a worker of food grains and other articles shall be computed as often as may be prescribed on the basis of the maximum quantity of food grains and other articles admissible to a standard family.

Explanation 1: 'Standard family' refers to a family consisting of the worker, his or her spouse and two children below the age of 14 years requiring, in all, three adult consumption units.

Explanation 2: 'Adult consumption unit' refers to the consumption unit of a male above the age of fourteen years; and the consumption unit of a female above the age of 14 years; and that of a child below the age of fourteen years, and shall be calculated at the rates of .8 and .6 respectively of one adult consumption unit.

5. The State Government may make rules prescribing
   (a) the manner in which the cash equivalent of the advantage accruing through the concessional sale to a worker of food grains and other articles shall be computed; and
   (b) the registers that shall be maintained in a factory for the purpose of securing compliance with the provisions of this Section [Section 59].

Restriction on Double Employment

No adult worker shall be required or allowed to work in any factory on any day on which he has already been working in any other factory, save in such circumstances as may be prescribed [Section 60].

Notice of Periods of Work for Adults

1. There shall be displayed and correctly maintained in every factory in accordance with the provisions of sub-section (2) of Section 108, a notice of periods of work for adults, showing clearly for every day the periods during which adult workers may be required to work.
2. The periods shown in the notice required by sub-section (1) shall be fixed beforehand in accordance with the following provisions of this Section, and shall be such that workers working for those periods would not be working in contravention of any of the provisions of Sections, 51, 52, 54, 55, 56, and 58.
3. Where all the adult workers in a factory are required to work during the same periods, the manager of the factory shall fix those periods for such workers generally.
4. Where all the adult workers in a factory are not required to work during the same periods, the manager of the factory shall classify them into groups according to the nature of their work indicating the number of workers in each group.
5. For each group which is not required to work on a system of shifts, the manager of the factory shall fix the periods during which the group may be required to work.
6. Where any group is required to work on a system of shifts and the relays are not to be subject to predetermined periodical changes of shifts, the manager of the factory shall fix the periods during which each relay of the group may be required to work.
7. Where any group is to work on a system of shifts and the relays are to be subject to predetermined periodical changes of shifts, the manager of the factory shall draw up a scheme of shifts whereunder the periods during which any relay of the group may be required to work and the relay which will be working at any time of the day shall be known for any day.
8. The State Government may prescribe forms of the notice required by sub-section (1) and the manner in which it shall be maintained.
9. In the case of a factory beginning work after the commencement of this Act, a copy of the notice referred to in sub-section (1) shall be sent in duplicate to the Inspector before the day on which work is begun in the factory.
10. Any proposed change in the system of work in any factory which will necessitate a change in the notice referred to in sub-section (1) shall be notified to the Inspector in duplicate before the change is made, and except with the previous sanction of the Inspector, no such change shall be made until one week has elapsed since the last change [Section 61].

Register of Adult Workers

1. The manager of every factory shall maintain a register of adult workers, to be available to the Inspector at all times during working hours, or when any work is being carried on in the factory, showing
   (a) the name of each adult worker in the factory;
   (b) the nature of his work;
   (c) the group, if any, in which he is included;
   (d) where his group works on shifts, the relay to which he is allotted;

(e) such other particulars as may be prescribed.

Provided that, if the Inspector is of opinion that any muster roll or register maintained as part of the routine of a factory gives in respect of any or all the workers in the factory the particulars required under this Section, he may, by order in writing, direct that such a muster roll or register shall, to the corresponding extent, be maintained in place of, and be treated as, the register of adult workers in that factory.

(1A) No adult worker shall be required or allowed to work in any factory unless his name and other particulars have been entered in the register of adult workers.

2. The State Government may prescribe the form of the register of adult workers, the manner in which it shall be maintained and the period for which it shall be preserved [Section 62].

Hours of Work to Correspond with Notice Under Section 61 and Register Under Section 62

No adult worker shall be required or allowed to work in any factory otherwise than in accordance with the notice of periods of work for adults displayed in the factory and the entries made before-hand against his name in the register of adult workers of the factory [Section 63].

Power to Make Exempting Rules

1. The State Government may make rules defining the persons who hold positions of supervision or management or are employed in a confidential position in a factory, or empowering the Chief Inspector to declare any person, other than a person defined by such rules, as a person holding position of supervision or management or employed in a confidential position in a factory if, in the opinion of the Chief Inspector, such person holds such position or is so employed, and the provisions of this Chapter, other than the provisions of clause (b) of Section 66(1) shall not apply to any person so defined or declared.

   Provided that any person so defined or declared shall, where the ordinary rate of wages of such person does not exceed the wage limit specified in sub-section (6) of Section 1 of the Payment of Wages Act, 1936, as amended from time to time be entitled to extra wages in respect of overtime work under Section 59.

2. The State Government may make rules in respect of adult workers in factories providing for the exemption, to such extent and subject to such conditions as may be prescribed
   (a) of workers engaged on urgent repairs, from the provisions of Section 51, 52, 54, 55, and 56;
   (b) of workers engaged in work in the nature of preparatory or complementary work which must necessarily be carried on outside the limits laid down for the general working of the factory, from the provisions of Sections 51, 54, 55, and 56;
   (c) of workers engaged in work which is necessarily so intermittent that the intervals during which they do not work while on duty ordinarily amount to more than the intervals for rest required by or under Section 55, from the provisions of Sections 51, 54, 55, and 56;
   (d) of workers engaged in any work which for technical reasons must be carried on continuously from the provisions of Sections 51, 52, 54, 55, and 56;
   (e) of workers engaged in making or supplying articles of prime necessity which must be made or supplied every day, from the provisions of Section 51 and Section 52;
   (f) of workers engaged in a manufacturing process which cannot be carried on except during fixed seasons, from the provisions of Section 51, Section 52, and Section 54;
   (g) of workers engaged in a manufacturing process which cannot be carried on except at times dependent on the irregular action of natural forces, from the provisions of Sections 52 and 55;
   (h) of workers engaged in engine-rooms or boiler-houses or in attending to power-plant or transmission machinery, from the provisions of Section 51 and Section 52;

(i) of workers engaged in the printing of newspapers, who are held up on account of the breakdown of machinery, from the provisions of Sections 51, 54, and 56;
(j) of workers engaged in the loading or unloading of railway wagons or lorries or trucks, from the provisions of Section 51, 52, 54, 55, and 56;
(k) of workers engaged in any work, which is notified by the State Government in the Official Gazette as a work of national importance, from the provisions of Section 51, Section 52, Section 54, Section 55, and Section 56.

3. Rules made under sub-section (2) providing for any exemption may also provide for any consequential exemption from the provisions of Section 61 which the State Government may deem to be expedient, subject to such conditions as it may prescribe.
4. In making rules under this Section, the State Government shall not exceed, except in respect of exemption under clause (a) of sub-section (2), the following limits of work inclusive of over-time:
(a) the total number of hours of work in any day shall not exceed 10;
(b) the spread-over, inclusive of intervals for rest, shall not exceed 12 hours in any one day.

Provided that the State Government may, in respect of any or all of the categories of workers referred to in clause (d) of sub-section (2), make rules prescribing the circumstances in which, and the conditions subject to which, the restrictions imposed by clause (i) and clause (ii) shall not apply in order to enable a shift worker to work the whole or part of a subsequent shift in the absence of a worker who has failed to report for duty;

(c) the total number of hours of work in a week, including overtime, shall not exceed 60;
(d) the total number of hours of overtime shall not exceed 50 for any one quarter.

Explanation: 'Quarter' refers to a period of three consecutive months beginning on 1 January, 1 April, 1 July, or 1 October.

5. Rules made under this Section shall remain in force for not more than five years [Section 64].

Power to Make Exempting Orders

1. Where the State Government is satisfied that, owing to the nature of the work carried on or to other circumstances, it is unreasonable to require that the periods of work of any adult workers in any factory or class or description of factories should be fixed beforehand, it may, by written order, relax, or modify the provisions of Section 61 in respect of such workers therein, to such extent and in such manner as it may think fit, and subject to such conditions as it may deem expedient to ensure control over periods of work.
2. The State Government or, subject to the control of the State Government, the Chief Inspector, may by written order exempt, on such conditions as it or he may deem expedient, any or all of the adult workers in any factory or group or class or description of factories from any or all of the provisions of Sections 51, 52, 54, and 56 on the ground that the exemption is required to enable the factory or factories to deal with an exceptional press of work.
3. Any exemption granted under sub-section (2) shall be subject to the following conditions
(a) the total number of hours of work in any day shall not exceed twelve;
(b) the spread-over, inclusive of intervals for rest, shall not exceed 13 hours in any one day;
(c) the total number of hours of work in any week, including overtime, shall not exceed 60;
(d) no worker shall be allowed to work overtime for more than seven days at a stretch, and the total number of hours of overtime work in any quarter shall not exceed 75 [Section 65].

Further Restrictions on Employment of Women

1. The provisions of this Chapter shall, in their application to women in factories, be supplemented by the following further restrictions, namely
(a) no exemption from the provisions of Section 54 may be granted in respect of any woman;

(b) no woman shall be required or allowed to work in any factory except between the hours of 6 A.M. and 7 P.M.

Provided that the State Government may, by notification in the Official Gazette, in respect of any factory or group or class or description of factories, vary the limits laid down in clause (b), but so that no such variation shall authorise the employment of any woman between the hours of 10 P.M. and 5 A.M.;

(c) there shall be no change of shifts except after a weekly holiday or any other holiday.

2. The State Government may make rules providing for exemption from the restrictions set out in sub-section (1), to such extent and subject to such conditions as it may prescribe, of women working in fish-curing or fish-canning factories, where the employment of women beyond the hours specified in the said restrictions is necessary to prevent damage to, or deterioration in, any raw material.
3. The rules made under sub-section (2) shall remain in force for not more than three years at a time [Section 66].

Employment of Young Persons

To protect the young persons from any short of employment-related exploitation, the Act provides as under:

Prohibition of Employment of Young Children

No child who has not completed his fourteenth year shall be required or allowed to work in any factory [Section 67].

Non-adult Workers to Carry Tokens

A child who has completed his fourteenth year or an adolescent shall not be required or allowed to work in any factory unless

1. a certificate of fitness granted with reference to him under Section 69 is in the custody of the manager of the factory, and
2. such a child or adolescent carries, while at work, a token giving a reference to such certificate [Section 68].

Certificates of Fitness

1. A certifying surgeon shall, on the application of any young person or his parent or guardian accompanied by a document signed by the manager of a factory that such a person will be employed therein if certified to be fit for work in a factory, or on the application of the manager of the factory in which any young person wishes to work, examine such a person and ascertain his fitness for work in a factory.
2. The certifying surgeon, after examination, may grant to such young person, in the prescribed form, or may renew
   (a) a certificate of fitness to work in a factory as a child, if he is satisfied that the young person has completed his fourteenth year, that he has attained the prescribed physical standards and that he is fit for such work;
   (b) a certificate of fitness to work in a factory as an adult, if he is satisfied that the young person has completed his fifteenth year, and is fit for a full day's work in a factory.

   Provided that unless the certifying surgeon has personal knowledge of the place where the young person proposes to work and of the manufacturing process in which he will be employed, he shall not grant or renew a certificate under this sub-section until he has examined such a place.
3. A certificate of fitness granted or renewed under sub-section (2)
   (a) shall be valid only for a period of 12 months from the date thereof;
   (b) may be made subject to conditions in regard to the nature of the work in which the young person may be employed, or requiring re-examination of the young person before the expiry of the period of 12 months.
4. A certifying surgeon shall revoke any certificate granted or renewed under sub-section (2) if, in his opinion, the holder of it is no longer fit to work in the capacity stated therein in a factory.
5. Where a certifying surgeon refuses to grant or renew a certificate or a certificate of the kind requested, or revokes a certificate, he shall, if so requested by any person who could have applied

for the certificate or the renewal thereof, state his reasons in writing for so doing.

6. Where a certificate under this Section with reference to any young person is granted or renewed subject to such conditions as are referred to in clause (b) of sub-section (3), the young person shall not be required or allowed to work in any factory except in accordance with those conditions.
7. Any fee payable for a certificate under this Section shall be paid by the occupier and shall not be recoverable from the young person, his parents or guardian [Section 69].

Effect of Certificate of Fitness Granted to Adolescent

1. An adolescent who has been granted a certificate of fitness to work in a factory as an adult under clause (b) of sub-section (2) of Section 69, and who while at work in a factory carries a token giving reference to the certificate, shall be deemed to be an adult for all the purposes of Chapters VI and VIII:

(1A) No female adolescent or a male adolescent who has not attained the age of 17 years but who has been granted a certificate of fitness to work in a factory as an adult, shall be required or allowed to work in any factory except between 6 A.M. and 7 P.M.

Provided that the State Government may, by notification in the Official Gazette, in respect of any factory or group or class or description of factories

(a) vary the limits laid down in this sub-section so, however, that no such Section shall authorise the employment of any female adolescent between 10 P.M. and 5 A.M.;

(b) grant exemption from the provisions of this sub-section in the case of serious emergency where national interest is involved.

2. An adolescent who has not been granted a certificate of fitness to work in a factory as an adult under the aforesaid clause (b) shall, notwithstanding his age, be deemed to be a child for all the purposes of this Act [Section 70].

Working Hours for Children

1. No child shall be employed or permitted to work, in any factory
   (a) for more than four and a half hours in any day;
   (b) during the night.

   Explanation: For the purpose of this sub-section, 'night' shall mean a period of at least twelve consecutive hours which shall include the interval between 10 P.M. and 6 A.M.
2. The period of work of all children employed in a factory shall be limited to two shifts which shall not overlap or spread over more than five hours each; and each child shall be employed in only one of the relays which shall not, except with the previous permission in writing of the Chief Inspector, be changed more frequently than once in a period of 30 days.
3. The provisions of Section 52 shall apply also to child workers and no exemption from the provisions of that Section may be granted in respect of any child.
4. No child shall be required or allowed to work in any factory on any day on which he has already been working in another factory.
5. No female child shall be required or allowed to work in any factory except between 8 A.M. and 7 P.M [Section 71].

Notice of Periods of Work for Children

1. There shall be displayed and correctly maintained in every factory in which children are employed, in accordance with the provisions of sub-section (2) of Section 108 a notice of periods of work for children, showing clearly for every day the periods during which children may be required or allowed to work.
2. The periods shown in the notice required by sub-section (1) shall be fixed beforehand in accordance with the method laid down for adult workers in Section 61, and shall be such that children working for those periods would not be working in contravention of any of the provisions of Section 71.
3. The provisions of sub-sections (8), (9), and (10) of Section 61 shall apply also to the notice required by sub-section (1) of this Section [Section 72].

Register of Child Workers

1. The manager of every factory in which children are employed shall maintain a register of child workers, to be available to the Inspector at all times during working hours or when any work is being carried on in a factory, showing
   (a) the name of each child worker in the factory,
   (b) the nature of his work,
   (c) the group, if any, in which he is included,
   (d) where his group works on shifts, the relay to which he is allotted, and
   (e) the number of his certificate of fitness granted under Section 69.
   (1A) No child worker shall be required or allowed to work in any factory unless his name and other particulars have been entered in the register of child workers.
2. The State Government may prescribe the form of the register of child workers, the manner in which it shall be maintained, and the period for which it shall be preserved [Section 73].

Hours of Work to Correspond with Notice Under Section 72 and Register Under Section 73

No child shall be employed in any factory otherwise than in accordance with the notice of periods of work for children displayed in the factory and the entries made beforehand against his name in the register of child workers of the factory [Section 74].

Power to Require Medical Examination

Where an Inspector is of the opinion

- that any person working in a factory without a certificate of fitness is a young person, or
- that a young person working in a factory with a certificate of fitness is no longer fit to work in the capacity stated therein, he may serve on the manager of the factory a notice requiring that such a person or young person, as the case may be, shall be examined by a certifying surgeon, and this person or young person shall not, if the Inspector so directs, be employed, or permitted to work, in any factory until he has been so examined and has been granted a certificate of fitness or a fresh certificate of fitness, as the case may be, under Section 69, or has been certified by the certifying surgeon examining him not to be a young person [Section 75].

Power to Make Rules

The State Government may make rules

1. prescribing the forms of certificates of fitness to be granted under Section 69, providing for the grant of duplicates in the event of loss of the original certificates, and fixing the fees which may be charged for such certificates and renewals thereof and such duplicates;
2. prescribing the physical standards to be attained by children and adolescents working in factories;
3. regulating the procedure of certifying surgeons under this Chapter;
4. specifying other duties which certifying surgeons may be required to perform in connection with the employment of young persons factories, and fixing the fees which may be charged for such duties and the persons by whom they shall be payable [Section 76].

Annual Leave with Wages

1. Every worker who has worked for a period of 240 days or more in a factory during a calendar year shall be allowed, during the subsequent calendar year, leave with wages for a number of days calculated at the rate of
   (a) if an adult, one day for every 20 days of work performed by him during the previous calendar year;
   (b) if a child, one day for every 15 days of work performed by him during the previous calendar year.

   Explanation 1: For the purpose of this subsection
   (i) any days of lay off, by agreement or contract or as permissible under the standing orders;
   (ii) in the case of a female worker, maternity leave for any number of days not exceeding 12 weeks; and
   (iii) the leave earned in the year prior to that in which the leave is enjoyed; shall be deemed to be days on which the worker has worked in a factory for the purpose of computation

of the period of 240 days or more, but he shall not earn leave for these days.

Explanation 2: The leave admissible under this sub-section shall be exclusive of all holidays whether occurring during or at either end of the period of leave.

2. A worker whose service commences otherwise than on 1 January shall be entitled to leave with wages at the rate laid down in clause (i) or, as the case may be, clause (ii) of sub-section (1) if he has worked for two-thirds of the total number of days in the remainder of the calendar year.
3. If a worker is discharged or dismissed from service or quits his employment or is superannuated or dies while in service during the course of the calendar year, he or his heir or nominee, as the case may be, shall be entitled to wages in lieu of the quantum of leave to which he was entitled immediately before his discharge, dismissal, quitting of employment, superannuation, or death calculated at the rates specified in sub-section (1), even if he had not worked for the entire period specified in sub-section (1) or sub-section (2) making him eligible to avail of such leave, and such payment shall be made
   (a) where the worker is discharged or dismissed or quits employment, before the expiry of the second working day from the date of such discharge, dismissal, or quitting; and
   (b) where the worker is superannuated or dies while in service, before the expiry of two months from the date of such superannuation or death.
4. In calculating leave under this Section, fraction of leave of half a day or more shall be treated as one full day's leave, and fraction of less than half a day shall be omitted.
5. If a worker does not in any one calendar year take the whole of the leave allowed to him under sub-section (1) or sub-section (2), as the case may be, any leave not taken by him shall be added to the leave to be allowed to him in the succeeding calendar year.

   However, the total number of days of leave that may be carried forward to a succeeding year shall not exceed 30 in the case of an adult or 40 in the case of a child.

   Provided further that a worker who has applied for leave with wages but has not been given such leave in accordance with any scheme laid down in sub-sections (8) and (9) or in contravention of sub-section (10) shall be entitled to carry forward the leave refused without any limit.
6. A worker may at any time apply in writing to the manager of a factory not less than 15 days before the date on which he wishes his leave to begin, to take all the leave or any portion thereof allowable to him during the calendar year.

   Provided that the application shall be made not less than 30 days before the date on which the worker wishes his leave to begin, if he is employed in a public utility service as defined in clause (n) of Section 2 of the Industrial Disputes Act, 1947.

   Provided further that the number of times in which leave may be taken during any year shall not exceed three.
7. If a worker wants to avail of the leave with wages due to him to cover a period of illness, he shall be granted such leave even if the application for leave is not made within the time specified in sub-section (6); and in such a case, wages as admissible under Section 81 shall be paid not later than 15 days, or in the case of a public utility service not later than thirty days from the date of the application for leave.
8. For the purpose of ensuring the continuity of work, the occupier or manager of the factory, in agreement with the Works Committee of the factory constituted under Section 3 of the Industrial Disputes Act, 1947 or a similar Committee constituted under any other Act or if there is no such Works Committee or a similar Committee in the factory, in agreement with the representatives of the workers therein chosen in the prescribed manner, may lodge with the Chief Inspector a scheme in writing whereby the grant of leave allowable under this Section may be regulated.
9. A scheme lodged under sub-section (8) shall be displayed at some conspicuous and convenient places in the factory and shall be in force for a period of 12 months from the date on which it comes into force, and may thereafter be renewed with or without modification for a further period of 12 months at a time, by the manager in agreement with the Works Committee or a similar Committee, or as the case may be, in agreement with the representatives of the workers as specified in sub-section (8), and a notice of renewal shall be sent to the Chief Inspector before it is renewed.
10. An application for leave which does not contravene the provisions of sub-section (6) shall not

be refused, unless refusal is in accordance with the scheme for the time being in operation under sub-sections (8) and (9).

11. If the employment of a worker who is entitled to leave under sub-section (1) or sub-section (2), as the case may be, is terminated by the occupier before he has taken the entire leave to which he is entitled, or if having applied for and having not been granted such leave, the worker quits his employment before he has taken the leave, the occupier of the factory shall pay him the amount payable under Section 80 in respect of the leave not taken, and such payment shall be made, where the employment of the worker is terminated by the occupier, before the expiry of the second working day after such termination, and where a worker who quits his employment, on or before the next pay day.
12. The unavailed leave of a worker shall not be taken into consideration in computing the period of any notice required to be given before discharge or dismissal [Section 79].

Wages During Leave Period

1. For the leave allowed to him under Section 78 or Section 79, as the case may be, a worker shall be entitled to wages at a rate equal to the daily average of his total full time earnings for the days on which he actually worked during the month immediately preceding his leave, exclusive of any overtime and bonus but inclusive of dearness allowance and the cash equivalent of the advantage accruing through the concessional sale to the worker of food grains and other articles.

   Provided that in the case of a worker who has not worked on any day during the calendar month immediately preceding his leave, he shall be paid at a rate equal to the daily average of his total full time earnings for the days on which he actually worked during the last calendar month preceding his leave, in which he actually worked, exclusive of any overtime and bonus but inclusive of dearness allowance and the cash equivalent of the advantage accruing through the concessional sale to the workers of food rains and other articles.
2. The cash equivalent of the advantage accruing through the concessional sale to the worker of food rains and other articles shall be computed as often as may be prescribed, on the basis of the maximum quantity of food rains and other articles admissible to a standard family.

   Explanation 1: 'Standard family' refers to a family consisting of a worker, his or her spouse, and two children below the age of 14 years requiring in all three adult consumption units.

   Explanation 2: 'Adult consumption unit' refers to the consumption unit of a male above the age of 14 years. The consumption unit of a female above the age of 14 years and that of a child below the age of 14 years shall be calculated at the rates of .8 and .6 respectively of one adult consumption unit.
3. The State Government may make rules prescribing
   (a) the manner in which the cash equivalent of the advantage accruing through the concessional sale to a worker of food grains and other articles shall be computed; and
   (b) the registers that shall be maintained in a factory for the purpose of securing compliance with the provisions of this Section [Section 80].

Payment in Advance in Certain Cases

A worker who has been allowed leave for not less than four days, in the case of an adult, and five days, in the case of a child shall, before his leave begins, be paid the wages due for the period of the leave allowed [Section 81].

Mode of Recovery of Unpaid Wages

Any sum required to be paid by an employer, under this Chapter but not paid by him shall be recoverable as delayed wages under the provisions of the Payment of Wages Act 1936 [Section 82].

Power to Make Rules

The State Government may make rules directing managers of factories to keep registers containing such particulars as may be prescribed and requiring the registers to be made available for examination by Inspectors [Section 83].

Power to Exempt Factories

Where the State Government is satisfied that the leave rules applicable to workers in a factory provide benefits which in its opinion are not less favourable than those for which this Chapter makes provision it may, by written order, exempt the factory from all or any of the provisions of this Chapter subject to such conditions as may be specified in the order.

Explanation: For the purpose of this Section, in deciding whether the benefits which are provided for by any leave rules are less favourable than those for which this Chapter makes provision, or not, the totality of the benefits shall be taken into account [Section 84].

Special Provisions of the Factories Act

The Act also contains some 'Special Provisions', discussed below:

Power to Apply the Act to Certain Premises

1. The State Government may, by notification in the Official Gazette, declare that all or any of the provisions of this Act shall apply to any place wherein a manufacturing process is carried on with or without the aid of power or is so ordinarily carried on, notwithstanding that
   (a) the number of persons employed therein is less than 10, if working with the aid of power and less than 20 if working without the aid of power, or
   (b) the persons working therein are not employed by the owner thereof but are working with the permission of, or under agreement with, such owner.

   Provided that the manufacturing process is not being carried on by the owner only with the aid of his family.
2. After a place is so declared, it shall be deemed to be a factory for the purposes of this Act, and the owner shall be deemed to be the occupier, and any person working therein, a worker.
   Explanation: For the purpose of this Section, 'owner' shall include a lessee or mortgagee with possession of the premises [Section 85].

Power to Exempt Public Institutions

The State Government may exempt, subject to such conditions as it may consider necessary, any workshop or workplace where a manufacturing process is carried on and which is attached to a public institution maintained for the purposes of education, training, research or reformation, from all or any of the provisions of this Act.

Provided that no exemption shall be granted from the provisions relating to hours of work and holidays, unless the persons having the control of the institution submit, for the approval of the State Government, a scheme for the regulation of the hours of employment, intervals for meals, and holidays of the persons employed in or attending the institution or who are inmates of the institution, and the State Government is satisfied that the provisions of the scheme are not less favourable than the corresponding provisions of this Act [Section 86].

Dangerous Operations

Where the State Government is of the opinion that any manufacturing process or operation carried on in a factory exposes any persons employed in it to a serious risk of bodily injury, poisoning or disease, it may make rules applicable to any factory or class or description of factories in which the manufacturing process or operation is carried on

1. specifying the manufacturing process or operation and declaring it to be dangerous;
2. prohibiting or restricting the employment of women, adolescents or children in the manufacturing process or operation;
3. providing for the periodical medical examination of persons employed, or seeking to be employed, in the manufacturing process or operation, and prohibiting the employment of persons not certified as fit for such employment and requiring the payment by the occupier of the factory of fees for such medical examination;
4. providing for the protection of all persons employed in the manufacturing process or operation or in the vicinity of the places where it is carried on;
5. prohibiting, restricting, or controlling the use of any specified materials or processes in connec-

tion with the manufacturing process or operation;

6. requiring the provision of additional welfare amenities and sanitary facilities and the supply of protective equipment and clothing, and laying down the standards thereof, having regard to the dangerous nature of the manufacturing process or operation [Section 87].

Power to Prohibit Employment on Account of Serious Hazard

1. Where it appears to the Inspector that the conditions in a factory or part thereof are such that they may cause serious hazard by way of injury or death to the persons employed therein or to the general public in the vicinity, he may, by order in writing to the occupier of the factory, state the particulars in respect of which he considers the factory or part thereof to be the cause of such serious hazard, and prohibit such occupier from employing any person in the factory or any part thereof other than the minimum number of persons necessary to attend to the minimum tasks till the hazard is removed.
2. Any order issued by the Inspector under sub-section (1) shall have effect for a period of three days until extended by the Chief Inspector by a subsequent order.
3. Any person aggrieved by an order of the Inspector under sub-section (1), and the Chief Inspector under sub-section (2), shall have the right to appeal to the High Court.
4. Any person whose employment has been affected by an order issued under sub-section (1) shall be entitled to wages and other benefits and it shall be the duty of the occupier to provide alternative employment to him wherever possible and in the manner prescribed.
5. The provisions of sub-section (4) shall be without prejudice to the rights of the parties under the Industrial Disputes Act, 1947 [Section 87A].

Notice of Certain Accidents

1. Where in any factory an accident occurs which causes death, or which causes any bodily injury by reason of which the person injured is prevented from working for a period of 48 hours or more immediately following the accident, or which is of such nature as may be prescribed in this behalf, the manager of the factory shall send notice thereof to such authorities, and in such form and within such time, as may be prescribed.
2. Where a notice given under sub-section (1) relates to an accident causing death, the authority to whom the notice is sent shall make an inquiry into the occurrence within one month of the receipt of the notice or, if such authority is not the Inspector, cause the Inspector to make an inquiry within the said period.
3. The State Government may make rules for regulating the procedure at inquiries under this Section [Section 88].

Notice of Certain Dangerous Occurrences

Where in a factory any dangerous occurrence of such nature as may be prescribed occurs, whether causing any bodily injury or disability or not, the manager of the factory shall send notice thereof to such authorities, and in such form and within such time, as may be prescribed [Section 88A].

Notice of Certain Diseases

1. Where any worker in a factory contracts any disease specified in the Third Schedule, the manager of the factory shall send notice thereof to such authorities, and in such form and within such time, as may be prescribed.
2. If any medical practitioner attends on a person who is or has been employed in a factory, and who is or is believed by the medical practitioner to be, suffering from any disease specified in the third Schedule, the medical practitioner shall without delay send a report in writing to the office of the Chief Inspector stating
   (a) the name and full postal address of the patient,
   (b) the disease from which he believes the patient to be suffering, and
   (c) the name and address of the factory in which the patient is, or was last, employed.
3. Where the report under sub-section (2) is confirmed to the satisfaction of the Chief Inspector, by the certificate of a certifying

surgeon or otherwise, that the person is suffering from a disease specified in the Third Schedule, he shall pay to the medical practitioner such fee as may be prescribed, and the fee so paid shall be recoverable as an arrear of land-revenue from the occupier of the factory in which the person contracted the disease.

4. If any medical practitioner fails to comply with the provisions of sub-section (2), he shall be punishable with fine which may extend to ₹1000.
5. The Central Government may, by notification in the Official Gazette, add to or alter the Third Schedule and any such addition or alteration shall have effect as if it had been made by this Act [Section 89].

Power to Direct Enquiry into Cases of Accident or Disease

1. The State Government may, if it considers it expedient so to do, appoint a competent person to inquire into the causes of any accident occurring in a factory or into any case where a disease specified in the Third Schedule has been, or is suspected to have been, contracted in a factory, and may also appoint one or more persons possessing legal or special knowledge to act as assessors in such inquiry.
2. The person appointed to hold an inquiry under this section shall have all the powers of a Civil Court under the Code of Civil Procedure, 1908 (5 of 1908), for the purposes of enforcing the attendance of witnesses and compelling the production of documents and material objects, and may also, so far as may be necessary for the purposes of the inquiry, exercise any of the powers of an Inspector under this Act; and every person required by the person making the inquiry to furnish any information shall be deemed to be legally bound so to do within the meaning of Section 176 of the Indian Penal Code.
3. The person holding an inquiry under this Section shall make a report to the State Government stating the causes of the accident, or as the case may be, disease, and any attendant circumstances, and adding any observations which he or any of the assessors may think fit to make.
4. The State Government may, if it thinks fit, cause to be published any report made under this Section or any extracts therefrom.
5. The State Government may make rules for regulating the procedure at inquiries under this Section [Section 90].

Power to Take Samples

1. An Inspector may, at any time during the normal working hours of a factory, after informing the occupier or manager of the factory or other person for the time being purporting to be in charge of the factory, take, in the manner hereinafter provided, a sufficient sample of any substance used or intended to be used in the factory, such use being
   (a) in the belief of the Inspector in contravention of any of the provisions of this Act or the rules made thereunder, or
   (b) in the opinion of the Inspector likely to cause bodily injury to, or injury to the health or, workers in the factory.
2. Where the Inspector takes a sample under sub-section (1), he shall, in the presence of the person informed under that sub-section unless such person wilfully absents himself, divide the sample into three portions and effectively seal and suitably mark them, and shall permit this person to add his own seal and mark thereto.
3. The person informed as aforesaid shall, if the Inspector so requires, provide the appliances for dividing, sealing, and marking the sample taken under this Section.
4. The Inspector shall
   (a) forthwith give one portion of the sample to the person informed under sub-section (1);
   (b) forthwith send the second portion to a Government Analyst for analysis and report thereon;
   (c) retain the third portion for production to the Court before which proceedings, if any, are instituted in respect of the substance.
5. Any document purporting to be a report under the hand of any Government Analyst upon any substance submitted to him for analysis and report under this Section, may be used as evidence in any proceedings instituted in respect of the substance [Section 91].

Safety and Occupational Health Surveys

The Inspector, or the Director General of Factory Advice Service and Labour Institutes, or the Director General of Health Services, to the Government of India, or such other officer as may be authorised in this behalf by the State Government, or the Chief Inspector or the Director General of Factory Advice Service and Labour Institutes, or the Director General of Health Services may, at any time during the normal working hours of a factory, or at any other time as is found by him to be necessary, after giving notice in writing to the occupier or manager of the factory or any other person who for the time being purports to be in charge of the factory, undertake safety and occupational health surveys. The occupier or manager or other person shall afford all facilities for such a survey, including facilities for the examination and testing of plant and machinery and the collection of samples and other data relevant to the survey [Section 91A].

Penalties for Contraventions

The Act against violations of its any provisions provides for various penalties as under:

General Penalty for Offences

Save as is otherwise expressly provided in this Act and subject to the provisions of Section 93, if in, or in respect of, any factory there is any contravention of any of the provisions of this Act or of any rules made thereunder or of any order in writing given thereunder, the occupier and manager of the factory shall each be guilty of an offence and punishable with imprisonment for a term which may extend to two years or with fine which may extend to ₹1 lakh or with both, and if the contravention is continued after conviction, with a further fine which may extend to ₹1000 for each day on which the contravention is so continued.

Provided that where the above contravention has resulted in an accident causing death or serious bodily injury, the fine shall not be less than 25000 in the case of an accident causing death, and ₹5000 in the case of an accident causing serious bodily injury.

Explanation: In this Section and in Section 94 'serious bodily injury' refers to an injury which involves, or in all probability will involve, the permanent loss of the use of, or permanent injury to, any limb or the permanent loss of, or injury to, sight or hearing, or the fracture of any bone, but shall not include, the fracture of a bone or joint (not being a fracture of more than one bone or joint) of any phalanges of the hand or foot [Section 92].

Liability of Owner of Premises in Certain Circumstances

1. Where, in any premises, separate buildings are leased to different occupiers for use as separate factories, the owner of the premises shall be responsible for the provision and maintenance of common facilities and services, such as approach roads, drainage, water supply, lighting, and sanitation.
2. The Chief Inspector shall have, subject to the control of the State Government, power to issue orders to the owner of the premises in respect of the carrying out of the provisions of sub-section (1).
3. Where in any premises, independent or self-contained, floors or flats are leased to different occupiers for use as separate factories, the owner of the premises shall be liable as if he were the occupier or manager of a factory, for any contravention of the provisions of this Act in respect of
   (a) latrines, urinals, and washing facilities in so far as the maintenance of the common supply of water for these purposes is concerned;
   (b) fencing of machinery and plant belonging to the owner and not specifically entrusted to the custody or use of an occupier;
   (c) safe means of access to the floors or flats and maintenance and cleanliness of stair cases and common passages;
   (d) precautions in case of fire;
   (e) maintenance of hoists and lifts; and
   (f) maintenance of any other common facilities provided in the premises.
4. The Chief Inspector shall have, subject to the control of the State Government, power to issue orders to the owner of the premises in respect of the carrying out the provisions of sub-section (3).
5. The provisions of sub-section (3) relating to the liability of the owner shall apply where, in any premises, independent rooms with common latrines, urinals, and washing facilities are leased to different occupiers for use as separate factories.

6. The Chief Inspector shall have, subject to the control of the State Government, the power to issue orders to the owner of the premises referred to in sub-section (5) in respect of the carrying out of the provisions of Section 46 or Section 48.
7. Where, in any premises, portions of a room or a shed are leased to different occupiers for use as separate factories, the owner of the premises shall be liable for any contravention of the provisions of (i) Chapter III, except Sections 14 and 15; (ii) Chapter IV, except Sections 22, 23, 27, 34, 35, and 36; (iii) Section 42.
8. The Chief Inspector shall have, subject to the control of the State Government, power to issue orders to the owner of the premises in respect of the carrying out the provisions of sub-section (7).
9. In respect of sub-sections (5) and (7), while computing for the purposes of any of the provisions of this Act the total number of workers employed, the whole of the premises shall be deemed to be a single factory [Section 93].

Enhanced Penalty After Previous Conviction

1. If any person who has been convicted of any offence punishable under Section 92 is again guilty of an offence involving a contravention of the same provision, he shall be punishable on a subsequent conviction with imprisonment for a term which may extend to three years or with fine which shall not be less than ₹10,000 but which may extend to two lakh rupees or with both.

   Provided that the Court may, for any adequate and special reasons to be mentioned in the judgment, impose a fine of less than ₹10,000.

   Provided further that where contravention of any of the provisions of Chapter IV or any rule made thereunder or under Section 87 has resulted in an accident causing death or serious bodily injury, the fine shall not be less than ₹35,000 in the case of an accident causing death and ₹10,000 in the case of an accident causing serious bodily injury.
2. For the purposes of sub-section (1), no cognizance shall be taken of any conviction made more than two years before the commission of the offence for which the person is subsequently being convicted [Section 94].

Penalty for Obstructing Inspector

Whoever wilfully obstructs an Inspector in the exercise of any power conferred on him by or under this Act, or fails to produce on demand by an Inspector any registers or other documents in his custody kept in pursuance of this Act or of any rules made thereunder, or conceals or prevents any worker in a factory from appearing before, or being examined by, an Inspector, shall be punishable with imprisonment for a term which may extend to six months or with fine which may extend to ₹10,000 or with both [Section 95].

Penalty for Wrongfully Disclosing Results of Analysis

Whoever, except in so far as it may be necessary for the purposes of a prosecution for any offence punishable under this Act, publishes or discloses to any person the results of an analysis made under Section 91, shall be punishable with imprisonment for a term which may extend to six months or with fine which may extend to ₹10,000 or with both [Section 96].

Penalty for Contravention of the Provisions of Sections 41B, 41C, and 41H

1. Whoever fails to comply with, or contravenes, any of the provisions of Sections 41B, 41C or 41H or the rules made thereunder, shall, in respect of such failure or contravention, be punishable with imprisonment for a term which may extend to seven years and with fine which may extend to ₹2 lakh, and in case the failure or contravention continues, with additional fine which may extend to ₹5000 for every day during which such failure or contravention continues after the conviction for the first such failure or contravention.
2. If the failure or contravention referred to in sub-section (1) continues beyond a period of one year after the date of conviction, the offender shall be punishable with imprisonment for a term which may extend to 10 years [Section 96A].

Offences by Worker

1. Subject to the provisions of Section 111, if any worker employed in a factory contravenes any provision of this Act or any rules or orders made thereunder, imposing any duty or liability on workers, he shall be punishable with a fine which may extend to ₹500.
2. Where a worker is convicted of an offence punishable under sub-section (1), the occupier or manager of the factory shall not be deemed to be guilty of an offence in respect of that contravention, unless it is proved that he failed to take all reasonable measures for its prevention [Section 97].

Penalty for Using False Certificate of Fitness

Whoever knowingly uses or attempts to use, as a certificate of fitness granted to himself under Section 70, a certificate granted to another person under that Section, or who, having procured such a certificate, knowingly allows it to be used, or an attempt to use it to be made, by another person, shall be punishable with imprisonment for a term which may extend to two month or with fine which may extend to one thousand rupees or with both [Section 98].

Penalty for Permitting Double Employment of Child

If a child works in a factory on any day on which he has already been working in another factory, the parent or guardian of the child or the person having custody of or control over him or obtaining any direct benefit from his wages, shall be punishable with fine which may extend to ₹1000 unless it appears to the Court that the child so worked without the consent or connivance of such parent, guardian or person [Section 99].

Exemption of Occupier or Manager from Liability

Where the occupier or manager of a factory is charged with an offence punishable under this Act, he shall be entitled, upon complaint duly made by him and on giving to the prosecutor not less than three clear days' notice in writing of his intention so to do, to have any other person whom he charges as the actual offender brought before the Court at the time appointed for hearing the charge; and if, after the commission of the offence has been proved, the occupier or manager of the factory, as the case may be, proves to the satisfaction of the Court

1. that he has used due diligence to enforce the execution of this Act, and
2. that the said other person committed the offence in question without his knowledge, consent, or connivance that other person shall be convicted of the offence and shall be liable to the like punishment as if he were the occupier or manager of the factory, and the occupier or manager, as the case may be, shall be discharged from any liability under this Act in respect of such offence [Section 101].

Power of Court to Make Orders

1. Where the occupier or manager of a factory is convicted of an offence punishable under this Act, the Court may, in addition to awarding any punishment, by order in writing, require him, within a period specified in the order (which the Court may, if it thinks fit and on application in such behalf, from time to time extend) to take such measures as may be so specified for remedying the matters in respect of which the offence was committed.
2. Where an order is made under sub-section (1), the occupier or manager of the factory, as the case may be, shall not be liable under this Act in respect of the continuation of the offence during the period or extended period, if any, allowed by the Court, but if, on the expiry of such period or extended period, as the case may be, the order of the Court has not been fully complied with, the occupier or manager, as the case may be, shall be deemed to have committed a further offence, and may be sentenced by the Court to undergo imprisonment for a term which may extend to six months or to pay a fine which may extend to ₹100 for every day after such expiry on which the order has not been complied with, or both. Onus as to Age [Section 104].

   (a) When any act or omission would, if a person were under a certain age, be an offence punishable under this Act, and such aperson is, in the opinion of the Court prima facie, under such age, the burden shall be on the accused to prove that such a person is not under such age.

(b) A declaration in writing by a certifying surgeon relating to a worker that he has personally examined him and believes him to be under the age stated in such declaration shall, for the purposes of this Act and the rules made thereunder, be admissible as evidence of the age of that worker [Section 102].

Cognizance of Offences

1. No Court shall take cognizance of any offence under this Act except on complaint by, or with the previous sanction in writing of, an Inspector.
2. No Court below that of a Presidency Magistrate or of a Magistrate of the First Class shall try any offence punishable under this Act [Section 105].

Limitation of Prosecutions

No Court shall take cognizance of any offence punishable under this Act unless a complaint thereof made within three months of the date on which the alleged commission of the offence comes to the knowledge of an Inspector.

Provided that where the offence consists of disobeying a written order made by an Inspector, the complaint may be made within six months of the date on which the offence is alleged to have been committed.

Explanation: For the purpose of this Section

1. in the case of continuing offence, the period of limitation shall be computed with reference to every point of time during which the offence continues;
2. where, for the performance of any act, time is granted or extended on an application made by the occupier or manager of a factory, the period of limitation shall be computed from the date on which the time so granted or extended expired [Section 106].

Jurisdiction of Courts

For the purposes of conferring jurisdiction on any Court in relation to an offence under this Act or the rules made thereunder in connection with the operation of any plant, the place where the plant is for the time being situate shall be deemed to be the place where such offence has been committed [Section 106A].

Supplemental

The supplementary provisions of the Act can be summarised as under:

Appeals

1. The manager of a factory on whom an order in writing by an Inspector has been served under the provisions or this Act or the occupier of the factory may, within 30 days of the service of the order, appeal against it to the prescribed authority, and such authority may, subject to rules made in this behalf by the State Government, confirm, modify or reverse the order.
2. Subject to rules made in this behalf by the State Government (which may prescribe classes of appeals which shall not be heard with the aid of assessors), the appellate authority may, or if so required in the petition of appeal shall, hear the appeal with the aid of assessors, one of whom shall be appointed by the appellate authority and the other by such a body representing the industry concerned as may be prescribed.

   Provided that if no assessor is appointed by such a body before the time fixed for hearing the appeal, or if the assessor so appointed fails to attend the hearing at such time, the appellate authority may, unless satisfied that the failure to attend is due to sufficient cause, proceed to hear the appeal without the aid of this assessor or, if it thinks fit, without the aid of any assessor.
3. Subject to such rules as the State Government may make in this behalf and subject to such conditions of partial compliance or the adoption of temporary measures as the appellate authority may think fit to impose, the appellate authority may, if it thinks fit, suspend the order

appealed against pending the decision of the appeal [Section 107].

Display of Notices

1. In addition to the notices required to be displayed in any factory by or under this Act, there shall be displayed in every factory a notice containing such abstracts of this Act and of the rules made thereunder as may be prescribed and also the name and address of the Inspector and the certifying surgeon.
2. All notices required by or under this Act to be displayed in a factory shall be in English and in a language understood by the majority of the workers in the factory, and shall be displayed at some conspicuous and convenient place at or near the main entrance to the factory, and shall be maintained in a clean and legible condition.
3. The Chief Inspector may, by order in writing served on the manager of any factory, require that there shall be displayed in the factory any other notice or poster relating to the health, safety or welfare of the workers in the factory [Section 108].

Service of Notices

The State Government may make rules prescribing the manner of the service of orders under this Act on owners, occupiers, or managers of factories [Section 109].

Returns

The State Government may make rules requiring owners, occupiers, or mangers of factories to submit such returns, occasional, or periodical, as may in its opinion be required for the purposes of this Act [Section 110].

Obligations of Workers

1. No worker in a factory
   (a) shall wilfully interfere with or misuse any appliance, convenience, or other thing provided in a factory for the purposes of securing the health, safety, or welfare of the workers therein;
   (b) shall wilfully and without reasonable cause do anything likely to endanger himself or others; and
   (c) shall wilfully neglect to make use of any appliance or other thing provided in the factory for the purposes of securing the health of safety of the workers therein.
2. If any worker employed in a factory contravenes any of the provisions of this Section or of any rule or order made thereunder, he shall be punishable with imprisonment for a term which may extend to three months, or with fine which may extend to ₹100, or with both [Section 111].

Right of Workers

Every worker shall have the right to

1. obtain from the occupier, information relating to workers' health and safety at work,
2. get trained within the factory wherever possible, or, to get himself sponsored by the occupier for getting trained at a training centre or institute duly approved by the Chief Inspector, where training is imparted for workers' health and safety at work.
3. represent to the Inspector directly or through his representative in the matter of inadequate provision for protection of his health or safety in the factory [Section 111A].

Publication of Rules

1. All rules made under this Act shall be published in the Official Gazette, and shall be subject to the condition of previous publication; and the date to be specified under clause (3) of Section 23 of the General Clauses Act, 1897, shall be not less than 45 days from the date on which the draft of the proposed rules was published.
2. Every rule made by the State Government under this Act shall be laid, as soon as may be after it is made, before the State Legislature [Section 115].

Restriction on Disclosure of Information

1. Every Inspector shall treat as confidential the source of any complaint brought to his notice on the breach of any provision of this Act.

2. No inspector shall, which making an inspection under this Act, disclose to the occupier, manager or his representative that the inspection is made in pursuance of the receipt of complaint.

Provided that nothing in this sub-section shall apply to any case in which the person who has made the complaint has consented to disclose his name [Section 118A].

Exercises

I. Objective-type Questions

1. Appointment of a Welfare Officer under the Factories Act, 1948, is compulsory ________ employees are employed.
   (a) 50 (b) 500 (c) 1000 (d) 100
2. A Crèche is mandatory under the Factories Act where ________ workers are employed
   (a) 30 (b) 100 (c) 30 women (d) 250
3. A canteen for the use of the workers, providing subsidised food, is statutory under the Factories Act where ________ workers are employed.
   (a) 250 (b) 1000 (c) 100 (d) 150
4. Under the Factories Act, the appointment of a Safety Officer is mandatory where the number of employees exceeds ________
   (a) 1000 (b) 500 (c) 100 (d) 50
5. An adult worker under the Factories Act is eligible for leave with wages at 1 day for every ________ days worked during the preceding year.
   (a) 50 (b) 20 (c) 15 (d) 240
6. Under the Factories Act, no worker is permitted to work for more than ________ hours in a day.
   (a) 8 (b) 9 (c) 10 (d) 24
7. Under the Factories Act, white washing of the factory building should be carried out in every ________ months.
   (a) 12 (b) 24 (c) 26 (d) 14
8. Where a worker works in a factory for more than ________ hours in any day or for more than ________ hours in any week, he shall, in respect of overtime work, be entitled to wages at the rate of twice his ordinary rate of wages.
   (a) 8, 56 (b) 8, 48 (c) 9, 48 (d) 9, 54
9. Repainting or re-varnishing under the Factories Act is required to be carried out in every ________ years.
   (a) 5 (b) 10 (c) 3 (d) 1
10. Under the Factories Act, 'child' refers to a person who has not completed his ________ year of age.
   (a) fourteenth (b) fifteenth
   (c) eighteenth (d) sixteenth

II. Review Questions

1. Describe the following terms as defined under the Factories Act, 1948:
   (a) Adolescent; (b) Child;
   (c) Adult; (d) Manufacturing Process; and
   (e) Worker.

2. Discuss in brief the provisions of the Factories Act, 1948, relating to health, safety, and welfare.
3. Describe the provisions of the Factories Act relating to hazardous processes.
4. Describe the provision relating to welfare measures under the Factories Act.
5. Discuss the following in the context of the Factories Act, 1948:
   (a) Employment of young persons;
   (b) Annual leave with wages;
   (c) Dangerous operation; and
   (d) General penalty for offences.

Answers to Objective-type Questions

1. (d) 2. (d) 3. (d) 4. (d) 5. (a)
6. (b) 7. (d) 8. (c) 9. (a) 10. (b)

27 Chapter in Review

LEARNING OUTCOMES

LO 1 Aim and objectives of The Factories Act, 1948

LO 2 Scope/applicability of the Act

LO 3 Enforcement agency of the legislation

LO 4 Compliance mechanism

LO 5 Maximum punishment for violation of the Act's provisions

KEY TERMS

Adult: A person who has completed his 18th year of age.

Adolescent: A person who has completed his 15th year of age but has not completed his 18th year.

Child: A person who has not completed his 15th year of age.

Hazardous process: Any process or activity in relation to an industry involving risk or danger to somebody's health or safety or that resulting in pollution of the general environment.

Young person: A person who is either a child or an adolescent.

Machinery: Prime movers, transmission machinery, and all other appliances whereby power is generated, transformed, transmitted, or applied.

Manufacturing process: Any process for (i) making, altering, repairing, ornamenting, finishing, packing, oiling, washing, cleaning, breaking up, demolishing, or otherwise treating or adapting any article or substance with a view to its use, sale, transport, delivery or disposal, or (ii) pumping oil, water, sewage, or any other substance; or (iii) generating, transforming, or transmitting power; or (iv) composing types for printing, printing by letter press, lithography, photogravure or other similar process, or book binding; or (v) constructing, reconstructing, repairing, refitting, finishing, or breaking

LO1 The Factories Act, 1948, is a social legislation which has been enacted for the occupational safety, health, and welfare of workers at work places.

LO2 It applies to the industries in which 10 or more workers are employed on any day of the preceding 12 months and are engaged in manufacturing process being carried out with the aid of power, or 20 or more than 20 workers are employed in manufacturing process being carried out without the aid of power.

LO3 The enforcement of this legislation is carried out on district basis by the 'District Inspectors of Factories' for investigation of complaints; fatal accidents; and to check compliance of provisions of the Act relating to health, safety, welfare measures, working hours, employment of young persons, annual leave with wages, etc.

LO4 After inspection, 'Improvement Notices' are issued to the defaulting managements and ultimately legal action is initiated against them. The Inspectors of Factories file challans against the defaulters in the Courts of Metropolitan Magistrates. The work of the Inspectors is supervised by the 'Deputy Chief Inspector of Factories' on district basis.

LO5 This Act provides for a maximum punishment up to two years or a fine up to 1 lakh or both.

up ships or vessels; or (vi) preserving or storing any article in cold storage.

Worker: A person engaged in any manufacturing process, or in cleaning any part of the machinery or premises used for a manufacturing process, or in any other kind of work incidental to, or connected with, the manufacturing process, or the subject of the manufacturing process.

Factory: Any premises including the precincts thereof (i) where 10 or more workers are working, or were working on any day of the preceding 12 months, and in any part of which a manufacturing process is being carried on with the aid of power, or is ordinarily so carried on, or (ii) where 20 or more workers are working, or were working on any day of the preceding 12 months, and in any part of which a manufacturing process is being carried on without the aid of power, or is ordinarily so carried on.

Occupier of a factory: The person who has ultimate control over the affairs of the factory.

Welfare measures: Various services, benefits and facilities offered to employees by the employers such as allowances, housing, transportation, medical insurance, and food etc.

CHAPTER

28 The Securities Contracts (Regulation) Act, 1956

Learning Objectives

LO 1 The Securities Contracts (Regulation) Act, 1956

LO 2 Role of the Act

LO 3 Aim and objectives of the Act

LO 4 Registration from Sebi mandatory for dealing in securities

LO 5 Recognition to stock exchange by the Central Government

The Securities Contracts (Regulation) Act, 1956, is an important law to regulate the transactions in securities. It was enacted by the Parliament in 1956 and extends to the whole of India. The Act seeks to prevent unwanted transactions in securities by regulating the business of dealing therein and by providing for certain other matters connected therewith. This is the principal Act which governs the trading of securities in India. As per the provisions of the Act, the business of dealing in securities cannot be carried out without a registration from Sebi. Any Stock Exchange which is desirous of being recognised has to make an application under the Sebi Act. The recognition to the Exchange, however, shall be granted by the Central Government under the provisions of the Securities Contracts (Regulation) Act.

Major Concepts

Contract [under the Securities Contracts (Regulation) Act]: A deal for, or relating to, the purchase or sale of securities.

Some of the important terms used in the Securities Contracts Act are briefly introduced below.

Contract refers to a contract for, or relating to, the purchase or sale of securities.

Derivative includes

1. A security derived from a debt instrument, share, or loan, whether secured or unsecured, a risk instrument or contract for differences, or any other form of security;
2. A contract which derives its value from the prices, or index or prices, of underlying securities.

Derivative: (i) A security derived from a debt instrument, share, or loan, whether secured or unsecured, a risk instrument or contract for differences, or any other form of security; (ii) a contract which derives its value from the prices, or index or prices, of underlying securities.

Government Security refers to a security created and issued, whether before or after the commencement of this Act, by the Central Government or a State Government for the purpose of raising a public loan and having one of the forms specified in clause (2) of Section 2 of the Public Debt Act, 1944.

Member: A member of a recognised stock exchange.

Member refers to a member of a recognised stock exchange.

Option in securities: A contract for the purchase or sale of a right to buy or sell, or a right to buy and sell, securities in the future.

Option in Securities refers to a contract for the purchase or sale of a right to buy or sell, or a right to buy and sell, securities in the future, and includes a teji, a mandi, a teji mandi, a galli, a put, a call, or a put and call in securities.

Recognised Stock Exchange refers to a stock exchange which is, for the time being, recognised by the Central Government under Section 4.

Rules, with reference to the rules relating in general to the constitution and management of a stock exchange, include, in the case of a stock exchange which is an incorporated association, its memorandum and articles of association.

Securities Appellate Tribunal refers to a Securities Appellate Tribunal established under sub-section (1) of Section 15K of the Securities and Exchange Board of India (Sebi) Act, 1992.

Securities include

1. shares, scrips, stocks, bonds, debentures, debenture stocks, or other marketable securities of a like nature in or of any incorporated company or other body corporate;
   (a) derivatives;
   (b) units or any other instrument issued by any collective investment scheme to the investors in such schemes;
2. Government Securities;
   (a) any other such instruments as may be declared by the Central Government to be securities; and
3. rights or interests in securities.

Spot delivery contract: A contract which provides for actual delivery of securities and the payment of a price thereof either on the same day as the date of the contract or on the next day.

Spot Delivery Contract refers to a contract which provides for

- actual delivery of securities and the payment of a price thereof either on the same day as the date of the contract or on the next day, the actual period taken for the dispatch of the securities or the remittance of money thereof through the post being excluded from the computation of the period aforesaid if the parties to the contract do not reside in the same town or locality;

- transfer of the securities by the depository from the account of a beneficial owner to the account of another beneficial owner when such securities are dealt with by a depository.

Stock exchange: Body of individuals, whether incorporated or not, constituted for the purpose of assisting, regulating, or controlling the business of buying, selling, or dealing in securities.

Stock Exchange refers to any body of individuals, whether incorporated or not, constituted for the purpose of assisting, regulating, or controlling the business of buying, selling, or dealing in securities [Section 2].

Important Provisions

Important provisions of the Act have been briefly expiained below.

Application for Recognition of Stock Exchanges

1. Any stock exchange, which is desirous of being recognised for the purposes of this Act, may make an application in the prescribed manner to the Central Government.
2. Every application under sub-section (1) shall contain such particulars as may be prescribed, and shall be accompanied by a copy of the bye-laws of the stock exchange for the regulation and control of contracts and also a copy of the rules relating in general to the constitution of the stock exchange and in particular, to
   (a) the governing body of such a stock exchange, its constitution and powers of management and the manner in which its business is to be transacted;
   (b) the powers and duties of the office bearers of the stock exchange;
   (c) the admission into the stock exchange of various classes of members, the qualifications, for membership, and the exclusion, suspension, expulsion, and re-admission of members therefrom or thereinto;
   (d) the procedure for the registration of partnerships as members of the stock exchange in cases where the rules provide for such membership; and the nomination and appointment of authorised representatives and clerks [Section 3].

Grant of Recognition to Stock Exchanges

1. If the Central Government is satisfied, after making such inquiry as may be necessary in this behalf and after obtaining such further information, if any, as it may require:
   (a) that the rules and bye-laws of a stock exchange applying for registration are in conformity with such conditions as may be prescribed with a view to ensure fair dealing and to protect investors;
   (b) that the stock exchange is willing to comply with any other conditions (including conditions as to the number of members) which the Central Government, after consultation with the governing body of the stock exchange and having regard to the area served by the stock exchange and its standing and the nature of the securities dealt with by it, may impose for the purpose of carrying out the objects of this Act; and
   (c) that it would be in the interest of the trade and also in the public interest to grant recognition to the stock exchange; it may grant recognition to the stock exchange subject to the conditions imposed upon it as aforesaid and in such form as may be prescribed.
2. The conditions which the Central Government may prescribe under clause (a) of sub-section (1) for the grant of recognition to the stock exchanges may include, among other matters, conditions relating to
   (a) the qualifications for membership of stock exchanges;
   (b) the manner in which contracts shall be entered into and enforced as between members;
   (c) the representation of the Central Government on each of the stock exchanges by such number of persons, not exceeding three, as the Central Government may nominate in this behalf; and
   (d) the maintenance of the accounts of the members and their audit by chartered accountants, whenever such an audit is required by the Central Government.

3. Every grant of recognition to a stock exchange under this Section shall be published in the Gazette of India and also in the Official Gazette of the State in which the principal office as of the stock exchange is situated, and such recognition shall have effect from the date of its publication in the Gazette of India.
4. No rules of a recognised stock exchange relating to any of the matters specified in sub-section (2) of Section 3 shall be amended except with the approval of the Central Government [Section 4].

Withdrawal of Recognition

If the Central Government is of the opinion that the recognition granted to a stock exchange under the provisions of this Act should, in the interest of the trade, or in the public interest, be withdrawn, the Central Government may serve on the governing body of the stock exchange a written notice that the Central Government is considering the withdrawal of recognition for the reasons stated in the notice. After giving an opportunity to the governing body to be heard in the matter, the Central Government may withdraw, by notification in the Official Gazette, the recognition granted to the stock exchange.

Provided that no such withdrawal shall affect the validity of any contract entered into or made before the date of the notification, the Central Government may, after consultation with the stock exchange, make such provision as it deems fit in the notification of withdrawal or in any subsequent notification similarly published for the due performance of any contracts outstanding on that date [Section 5].

Power of Central Government to Call for Periodical Returns or Direct Inquiries To Be Made

1. Every recognised stock exchange shall furnish to the Sebi such periodical returns relating to its affairs as may be prescribed.
2. Every recognised stock exchange and every member thereof shall maintain and preserve for a period, not exceeding five years, such books of account, and other documents as the Central Government, after consultation with the stock exchange concerned, may prescribe in the interest of the trade or in the public interest. Such books of account, and other documents shall be subject to inspection at all reasonable times by the Sebi.
3. Without prejudice to the provisions contained in sub-sections (1) and (2), the Sebi, if it is satisfied that it is in the interest of the trade or in the public interest so to do, may, by order in writing
   (a) call upon a recognised stock exchange, or any member thereof, to furnish in writing such information or explanation relating to the stock exchange as the Sebi may require; or
   (b) appoint one or more persons to make an inquiry in the prescribed manner in relation to the affairs of any of the members of the stock exchange in relation to the stock exchange and submit a report of the result of such an inquiry to the Sebi.
4. Where an inquiry in relation to the affairs of a recognised stock exchange or the affairs of any of its members in relation to the stock exchange has been undertaken under sub-section (3)
   (a) every director, manager, secretary, or other officer of such stock exchange;
   (b) every member of such stock exchange;
   (c) if the member of the stock exchange is a firm, every partner, manager, secretary, or other officer of the firm; and
   (d) every other person or body of persons who has had dealings in the course of business with any of the persons mentioned in clauses (a), (b), and (c) whether directly or indirectly;

   shall be bound to produce before the authority making the inquiry all such books of account and other documents in his custody or power relating to or having a bearing on the subject-matter of such inquiry and also to furnish the authorities, within such time as may be specified, any such statement or information relating thereto as may be required of him [Section 6].

Annual Reports To Be Furnished to Central Government by Stock Exchanges

Every recognised stock exchange shall furnish the Central Government with a copy of the annual report, and such an annual report shall contain such particulars as may be prescribed [Section 7].

Power of Recognised Stock Exchange to Make Rules Restricting Voting Rights

1. A recognised stock exchange may make rules or amend any rules made by it to provide for all or any of the following matters, namely:
   (a) the restriction of voting rights to members only in respect of any matter placed before the stock exchange at any meeting;
   (b) the regulation of voting rights in respect of any matter placed before the stock exchange at any meeting, so that each member may be entitled to have one vote only, irrespective of his share of the paid-up equity capital of the stock exchange;
   (c) the restriction on the right of a member to appoint another person as his proxy to attend and vote at a meeting of the stock exchange; and
   (d) such incidental, consequential and supplementary matters as may be necessary to give effect to any of the matters specified in clauses (a), (b), and (c).
2. No rules of a recognised stock exchange made or amended in relation to any matter referred to in clauses (a) to (d) of sub-section (1) shall have effect until they have been approved by the Central Government and published by that Government in the Official Gazette and, in approving the rules so made or amended, the Central Government may make such modifications therein as it thinks fit, and on such publication, the rules as provided by the Central Government shall be deemed to have been validly made, notwithstanding anything to the contrary contained in the Companies Act, 1956 [Section 7A].

Power of the Central Government to Direct Rules To Be Made or to Make Rules

1. Where, after consultation with the governing bodies of stock exchanges generally or with the governing body of any stock exchange in particular, the Central Government is of the opinion that it is necessary or expedient to do so, it may, by order in writing, together with a statement of the reasons thereof, direct recognised stock exchanges generally or any recognised stock exchange in particular, as the case may be, to make any rules or to amend any rules already made in respect of all or any of the matters specified in sub-section (2) of Section 3 within a period of two months from the date of the order.
2. If any recognised stock exchange fails or neglects to comply with any order made under sub-section (1) within the period specified therein, the Central Government may make the rules for, or amend the rules made by, the recognised stock exchange, either in the form proposed in the order, or with such modifications thereof as may be agreed to between the stock exchange and the Central Government.
3. Where, in pursuance of this Section, any rules have been made or amended, the rules so made or amended shall be published in the Gazette of India and also in the Official Gazette or Gazettes of the State or States in which the principal office or offices of the recognised stock exchange or exchanges is or are situated, and, on the publication thereof in the Gazette of India, the rules so made or amended shall, notwithstanding anything to the contrary contained in the Companies Act, 1956, or in any other law for the time being in force, have effect as if they had been made or amended by the recognised stock exchange or stock exchanges, as the case may be [Section 8].

Power of Recognised Stock Exchange to Make Bye-laws

1. Any recognised stock exchange may, subject to the previous approval of the Sebi, make bye-laws for the regulation and control of contracts.
2. In particular, and without prejudice to the generality of the foregoing power, such bye-laws may provide for:
   (a) the opening and closing of markets and the regulation of the hours of trade;
   (b) a clearing house for the periodical settlement of contracts and differences thereunder, the delivery of and payment for securities, the passing on of delivery orders and the regulation and maintenance of such a clearing house;

(c) the submission to the Sebi by the clearing house as soon as may be after each periodical settlement of all or any of the following particulars as the Sebi may, from time to time require, namely:

(i) the total number of each category of security carried over from one settlement period to another.

(ii) the total number of each category of security, contracts in respect of which have been squared up during the course of each settlement period.

(iii) the total number of each category of security actually delivered at each clearing;

(d) the publication by the clearing house of all or any of the particulars submitted to the Sebi under clause (c) subject to the directions, if any, issued by the Sebi in this behalf;

(e) the regulation or prohibition of blank transfers;

(f) the number and classes of contracts in respect of which settlements shall be made or differences paid through the clearing house;

(g) the regulation, or prohibition of badlas or carry-over facilities;

(h) the fixing, altering or postponing of days for settlements;

(i) the determination and declaration of market rates, including the opening, closing, highest, and lowest rates for securities;

(j) the terms, conditions, and incidents of contracts, including the prescription of margin requirements, if any, and conditions relating to them, to, and the forms of contracts in writing;

(k) the regulation of the entering into, making, performance, rescission, and termination, of contracts, including contracts between members or between a member and his constituent, or between a member and a person who is not a member, and the consequences of default or insolvency on the part of a seller or buyer or intermediary, the consequences of a breach or omission by a seller or buyer, and the responsibility of members who are not parties to such contracts;

(l) the regulation of taravani business including the placing of limitations thereon;

(m) the listing of securities on the stock exchange, the inclusion of any security for the purpose of dealings and the suspension or withdrawal of any such securities, and the suspension or prohibition of trading in any specified securities;

(n) the method and procedure for the settlement of claims or disputes, including settlement by arbitration;

(o) the levy and recovery of fees, fines, and penalties;

(p) the regulation of the course of business between parties to contracts in any capacity;

(q) the fixing of a scale of brokerage and other charges;

(r) the emergencies in trade which may arise, whether as a result of pool or syndicated operations or cornering or otherwise, and the exercise of powers in such emergencies including the power to fix maximum and minimum prices for securities;

(s) the regulation of dealings by members for their own account;

(t) the separation of the functions of jobbers and brokers;

(u) the limitations on the volume of trade done by any individual member in exceptional circumstances;

(v) the obligation of members to supply such information or explanation and to produce such documents relating to the business as the governing body may require.

3. The bye-laws made under this Section may:

(a) specify the bye-laws, the contravention of which shall make a contract entered into otherwise than in accordance with the bye-laws void under sub-section (1) of Section 14;

(b) provide that the contravention of any of the bye-laws shall render the member concerned liable to one or more of the following punishments, namely:

(i) fine,

(ii) expulsion from membership,

(iii) suspension from membership for a specified period,

(iv) any other penalty of a like nature not involving the payment of money.

4. Any bye-laws made under this Section shall be subject to such conditions in regard to previous publication as may be prescribed, and, when approved by the Sebi, shall be published in the Gazette of India and also in the Official Gazette of the State in which the principal office of the recognised stock exchange is situated, and shall have effect from the date of its publication in the Gazette of India: Provided the Sebi is satisfied in any case that in the interest of the trade or in the public interest any bye-laws should be made immediately, it may, by order in writing specifying the reasons thereof, dispense with the condition of previous publication [Section 9].

Power of Sebi to Make or Amend Bye-laws of Recognised Stock Exchanges

1. Sebi may, either on a request in writing received by it in this behalf from the governing body of a recognised stock exchange or on its own motion, if it is satisfied after consultation with the governing body of the stock exchange that it is necessary or expedient so to do and after recording its reasons for so doing, make bye-laws, for all or any of the matters specified in Sction 9 or amend any bye-laws made by such stock exchange under that Section.
2. Where, in pursuance of this Section any bye-laws have been made or amended, the bye-laws so made or amended shall be published in the Gazette of India and also in the Official Gazette of the State in which the principal office of the recognised stock exchange is situated, and on the publication thereof in the Gazette of India, the bye-laws so made or amended shall have effect as if they had been made or amended by the recognised stock exchange concerned.
3. Notwithstanding anything contained in this Section, where the governing body of a recognised stock exchange objects to any bye-laws made or amended under this Section by the Sebi on its own motion, it may, within [two months] 25 of the publication thereof in the Gazette of India under sub-section (2), apply to the Sebi for revision thereof. The Sebi may, after giving an opportunity to the governing body of the stock exchange to be heard in the matter, revise the bye-laws so made or amended, and where any bye-laws so made or amended are revised as a result of any action taken under this sub-section, the bye-laws so revised shall be published and shall become effective as provided in sub-section (2).
4. The making or the amendment or revision of any bye-laws under this Section shall in all cases be subject to the condition of the previous publication:

   Provided that if the Sebi is satisfied in any case that, in the interest of the trade or in the public interest, any bye-laws should be made, amended or revised immediately, it may, by order in writing specifying the reasons for this, dispense with the condition of previous publication [Section 10].

Power of Central Government to Supersede Governing Body of a Recognised Stock Exchange

1. Without prejudice to any other powers vested in the Central Government under this Act, where the Central Government is of the opinion that the governing body of any recognised stock exchange should be superseded, then, notwithstanding anything contained in any other law for the time being in force, the Central Government may serve on the governing body a written notice that the Central Government is considering the supersession of the governing body for the reasons specified in the notice. After giving an opportunity to the governing body to be heard in the matter, it may, by notification in the Official Gazette, declare the governing body of such a stock exchange to be superseded, and may appoint any person or persons to exercise and perform all the powers and duties of the governing body, and, where more persons than one are appointed, may appoint one of such persons to be the chairman and another to be the vice-chairman thereof.
2. On the publication of a notification in the Official Gazette under sub-section (1), the following consequences shall ensue, namely:
   (a) the members of the governing body which has been superseded shall, as from the date of the notification of supersession, cease to hold office as such members;

(b) the person or persons appointed under sub-section (1) may exercise and perform all the powers and duties of the governing body which has been superseded;

(c) all such property of the recognised stock exchange as the person or persons appointed under sub-section (1) may, by order in writing, specify in this behalf as being necessary for the purpose of enabling him or them to carry on the business of the stock exchange, shall vest in such person or persons.

3. Notwithstanding anything to the contrary contained in any law or the rules or bye-laws of the recognised stock exchange the governing body of which is superseded under sub-section (1), the person or persons appointed under that sub-section shall hold office for such period a may be specified in the notification published under that sub-section and, the Central Government may from time to time, by like notification, vary such period.

4. The Central Government may, at any time before the determination of the period of office of any person or persons appointed under this Section, call upon the recognised stock exchange to reconstitute the governing body in accordance with its rules; and, on such re-constitution, all the property of the recognised stock exchange which has vested in, or was in the possession of, the person or persons appointed under sub-section (1), shall re-vest, as the case may be, in the governing body so re-constituted [Section 11].

Provided that until a governing body is so re-constituted, the person or persons appointed under sub-section (1), shall continue to exercise and perform their powers and duties.

Power to Suspend Business of Recognised Stock Exchanges

If, in the opinion of the Central Government, an emergency has arisen, and, for the purpose of meeting the emergency, the Central Government considers it expedient so to do, it may, by notification in the Official Gazette, for reasons to be set out therein, direct a recognised stock exchange to suspend its business for a period not exceeding seven days and subject to such conditions as may be specified in the notification, and if, in the opinion of the Central Government, the interest of the trade or the public interest requires that the period should be extended, it may, by like notification, extend the said period from time to time [Section 12].

Provided that where the period of suspension is to be extended beyond the first period, no notification extending the period of suspension shall be issued unless the governing body of the recognised stock exchange has been given an opportunity to be heard in the matter.

Contracts and Options in Securities

As regards contracts and options in securities, the Act provides as under:

Contracts in Notified Areas Illegal in Certain Circumstances

If the Central Government is satisfied, having regard to the nature or the volume of transactions in securities in any State or area, that it is necessary to do so, it may, by notification in the Official Gazette, declare this Section to apply to such State or area, and thereupon every contract in such State or area which is entered into after the date of the notification otherwise than between members of a recognised stock exchange in such State or area or through or with such members shall be illegal [Section 13].

Additional Trading Floor

A stock exchange may establish an additional trading floor with the prior approval of the Sebi in accordance with the terms and conditions stipulated by the said Board.

Explanation: For the purpose of this Section, 'additional trading floor' means a trading ring or trading facility offered by a recognised stock exchange outside its area of operation to enable the investors to buy and sell securities through such a trading floor under the regulatory framework of the stock exchange [Section 13A].

Contracts in Notified Areas To Be Void in Certain Circumstances

1. Any contract entered into in any State or area specified in the notification under Section 13, which is

in contravention of any of the bye-laws specified in that behalf under clause (a) of sub-section (3) of Section 9, shall be void:

(a) as respects the rights of any member of the recognised stock exchange who has entered into such contract in contravention of any such bye-laws, and also

(b) as respects the rights of any other person who has knowingly participated in the transaction entailing such contravention.

2. Nothing in sub-section (1) shall be construed to affect the right of any person other than a member of the recognised stock exchange to enforce any such contract, or to recover any sum under or in respect of such a contract, if such a person had no knowledge that the transaction was in contravention of any of the bye-laws specified in clause (a) of sub-section (3) of Section 9 [Section 14].

Members May Not Act As Principals in Certain Circumstances

No member of a recognised stock exchange shall, in respect of any securities, enter into any contract as a principal with any person other than a member of a recognised stock exchange, unless he has secured the consent or authority of this person and discloses in the note, memorandum or agreement of sale or purchase, that he is acting as a principal:

Provided that where the member has secured the consent or authority of such a person other than in writing, he shall secure written confirmation from this person of such consent or authority within three days from the date of the contract.

Provided further that no such written consent or authority of such a person shall be necessary for closing out any outstanding contract entered into by this person in accordance with the bye-laws, if the member discloses in the note, memorandum or agreement of sale or purchase in respect of such closing out that he is acting as a principal [Section 15].

Power to Prohibit Contracts in Certain Cases

1. If the Central Government is of the opinion that it is necessary to prevent undesirable speculation in specified securities in any State or area, it may, by notification in the Official Gazette, declare that no person in the State or area specified in the notification shall, save with the permission of the Central Government, enter into any contract for the sale or purchase of any security specified in the notification except to the extent and in the manner, if any, specified therein.
2. All contracts in contravention of the provisions of sub-section (1) entered into after the date of the notification issued thereunder shall be illegal [Section 16].

Licensing of Dealers in Securities in Certain Cases

1. Subject to the provision of sub-section (3) and to the other provisions contained in this Act, no person shall carry on or purport to carry on, whether on his own behalf or on behalf of any other person, the business of dealing in securities in any State or area to which Section 13 has not been declared to apply, and to which the Central Government may, by notification in the Official Gazette declare this section to apply, except under the authority of a licence granted by the Sebi.
2. No notification under sub-section (1) shall be issued with respect to any State or area unless the Central Government is satisfied, with regard to the manner in which securities are being dealt with in such State or area, that it is desirable or expedient in the interest of the trade or in the public interest that such dealings should be regulated by a system of licensing.
3. The restrictions imposed by sub-section (1) in relation to dealings in securities shall not apply to the doing of anything by or on behalf of a member of any recognised stock exchange [Section 17].

Exclusion of Spot Delivery Contracts from Sections 13, 14, 15, and 17

1. Nothing contained in Sections 13, 14, 15, and 17 shall apply to spot delivery contracts.
2. Notwithstanding anything contained in sub-section (1), if the Central Government is of opinion that, in the interest of the trade or in the public interest, it is expedient to regulate and control the business of dealing in spot delivery contracts also in any State or area (whether Section 13 has been

declared to apply to that State or area or not), it may, by notification in the Official Gazette, declare that the provisions of Section 17 shall also apply to such a State or area in respect of spot delivery contracts generally or in respect of spot delivery contract for the sale or purchase of such securities as may be specified in the notification, and may also specify the manner in which, and the extent to which, the provision of that Section shall so apply.

Notwithstanding anything contained in any other law for the time being in force, contracts are

(a) traded on a recognised stock exchange;
(b) settled in the clearing house of the recognised stock exchange, in accordance with the rules and bye-laws of such a stock exchange [Section 18A].

Stock Exchanges Other Than Recognised Stock Exchanges Prohibited

1. No person shall, except with the permission of the Central Government, organise or assist in organising or be a member of any stock exchange (other than a recognised stock exchange) for the purpose of assisting in, entering into or performing any contracts in securities.
2. This Section shall come into force in any State or area on such date as the Central Government may, by notification in the Official Gazette, appoint [Section 19].

Listing of Securities

The Act has framed the following rules for listing of securities:

Conditions for Listing

Where securities are listed on the application of any person in any recognised stock exchange, such a person shall comply with the conditions of the listing agreement with that stock exchange [Section 21].

Right of Appeal Against Refusal of Stock Exchanges to List Securities of Public Companies

Where a recognised stock exchange acting in pursuance of any power given to it by its bye-laws refuses to list the securities of any public company or collective investment scheme, the company or scheme shall be entitled to be furnished with reasons for such refusal,

1. within 15 days from the date on which the reasons for such refusal are furnished to it, or
2. where the stock exchange has omitted or failed to dispose of, within the time specified in sub-section (1) of Section 73 of the Companies Act, 1956 (hereafter in this Section referred to as the 'specified time'), the application for permission for the shares or debentures to be dealt with on the stock exchange, within 15 days from the date of expiry of the specified time or within such further period, not exceeding one month, as the Central Government may, on sufficient cause being shown, allow, appeal to the Central Government against such refusal, omission or failure, as the case may be, and thereupon the Central Government may, after giving the Stock Exchange an opportunity of being heard
   (a) vary or set aside the decision of the stock exchange; or
   (b) where the stock exchange has omitted or failed to dispose of the application within the specified time, grant or refuse the permission, and where the Central Government sets aside the decision of the recognised stock exchange or grants the permission, the stock exchange shall act in conformity with the orders of the Central Government.

   Provided that no appeal shall be preferred against refusal, omission or failure, as the case may be, under this Section on and after the commencement of the Securities Laws (Second Amendment) Act, 1999 [Section 22].

Right of Appeal to Securities Appellate Tribunal Against Refusal of Stock Exchange to List Securities of Public Companies

1. Where a recognised stock exchange, acting in pursuance of any power given to it by its bye-laws, refuses to list the securities of any public company, the company shall be entitled to be furnished with reasons for such refusal, and may
   (a) within 15 days from the date on which the reasons for such refusal are furnished to it, or

(b) where the stock exchange has omitted or failed to dispose of, within the time specified in sub-section (1A) of Section 73 of the Companies Act, 1956 (hereafter in this Section referred to as the 'specified time'), the application for permission for the shares or debentures to be dealt with on the stock exchange, within 15 days from the date of expiry of the specified time or within such further period, not exceeding one month, as the Securities Appellate Tribunal may, on sufficient cause being shown, allow, appeal to the Securities Appellate Tribunal having jurisdiction in the matter against such refusal, omission or failure, as the case may be, and thereupon the Securities Appellate Tribunal may, after giving the stock exchange, an opportunity of being heard
   (i) vary or set aside the decision of the stock exchange; or
   (ii) where the stock exchange has omitted or failed to dispose of the application within the specified time, grant or refuse the permission, and where the Securities Appellate Tribunal sets aside the decision of the recognised stock exchange or grants the permission, the stock exchange shall act in conformity with the orders of the Securities Appellate Tribunal.
2. Every appeal under sub-section (1) shall be in such form and be accompanied by such fees as may be prescribed.
3. The Securities Appellate Tribunal shall send a copy of every order made by it to the Board and parties to the appeal.
4. The appeal filed before the Securities Appellate Tribunal under sub-section (1) shall be dealt with by it as expeditiously as possible and endeavour shall be made by it to dispose of the appeal finally within six months from the date of receipt of the appeal [Section 22A].

Procedure and Powers of Securities Appellate Tribunal

1. The Securities Appellate Tribunal shall not be guided by the principles of natural justice and, subject to the other provisions of this Act and of any rules, the Securities Appellate Tribunal shall have powers to regulate its own procedure including the places at which it shall have its sittings.
2. The Securities Appellate Tribunal shall have, for the purpose of discharging its functions under this Act, the same powers as are vested in a civil court under the Code of Civil Procedure, 1908, while trying a suit, in respect of the following matters, namely:
   (a) summoning and enforcing the attendance of any person and examining him on oath;
   (b) requiring the discovery and production of documents;
   (c) receiving evidence on affidavits;
   (d) issuing commissions for the examination of witnesses or documents;
   (e) reviewing its decisions;
   (f) dismissing an application for default or deciding it ex-parte;
   (g) setting aside any order of dismissal of any application for default or any order passed by it ex-parte; and
   (h) any other matter which may be prescribed.
3. Every proceeding before the Securities Appellate Tribunal shall be deemed to be a judicial proceeding, within the meaning of Sections 193 and 228, and for the purposes of Section 196 of the Indian Penal Code. The Securities Appellate Tribunal shall be deemed to be a civil court for all the purposes of Section 195 and Chapter XXVI of the Code of Criminal Procedure, 1973 [Section 22B].

Right to Legal Representations

The appellant may either appear in person or authorise one or more chartered accountants or company secretaries or cost accountants or legal practitioners or any of its officers or present his or its case before the Securities Appellate Tribunal [Section 22C].

Limitation

The provisions of the Limitation Act, 1963 shall, as far as may be, apply to an appeal made to a Securities Appellate Tribunal [Section 22D].

Civil Court Not to Have Jurisdiction

No civil court shall have jurisdiction to entertain any suit or proceeding in respect of any matter which a Securities Appellate Tribunal is empowered by or under this Act to determine and no injunction shall be granted by any court or other authority in respect of any action taken or to be taken in pursuance of any power conferred by or under this Act [Section 22E].

Appeal to High Court

Any person aggrieved by any decision or order of the Securities Appellate Tribunal may file an appeal to the High Court within 60 days from the date of communication of the decision or order of the Securities Appellate Tribunal on any question of fact or law arising out of such an order.

Provided that the High Court may, if it is satisfied that the appellant was prevented by sufficient cause from filing the appeal within the said period, allow it to be filed within a further period not exceeding 60 days [Section 22F].

Penalties and Procedures

Penalties

1. Any person who
   (a) without reasonable excuse (the burden of proving which shall be on him) fails to comply with any requisition made under sub-section (4) of Section 6; or
   (b) enters into any contract in contravention of any of the provisions contained in Section 13 or Section 16; or
   (c) contravenes the provisions contained in Section 17 or Section 19; or
   (d) enters into any contract or derivative in contravention of Section 18 A or the rules made under Section 30.
   (e) owns or keeps a place other than a recognised stock exchange which is used for the purpose of entering into or performing any contracts in contravention of any of the provisions of this Act and knowingly permits such place to be used for such purposes; or
   (f) manages, controls, or assists in keeping any place other than a recognised stock exchange which is used for the purpose of entering into or performing any contracts in contravention of any of the provisions of this Act or at which contracts are recorded or adjusted or rights or liabilities arising out of contracts are adjusted, regulated or enforced in any manner whatsoever; or
   (g) not being a member of a recognised stock exchange or his agent authorised as such under the rules or bye-laws of such a stock exchange or not being a dealer in securities licenced under Section 17; or
   (h) not being a member of a recognised stock exchange or his agent authorised as such under the rules or bye-laws of such stock exchange or not being a dealer in securities licenced under Section 17, canvasses, advertises, or touts in any manner either for himself or on behalf of any other person for any business connected with contracts in contravention of any of the provisions of this Act; or
   (i) joins, gathers or assists in gathering at any place other than the place of business specified in the bye-laws of a recognised stock exchange, any person or persons for making bids or offers or for entering into or performing any contracts in contravention of any of the provisions of this Act; shall, on conviction, be punishable with imprisonment for a term which may extend to one year, or with fine, or with both.
2. Any person who enters into any contract in contravention of the provisions contained in Section 15 [or who fails to comply with the provisions of Section 21 or with the orders of the Central Government under Section 22 or with the orders of the Securities Appellate Tribunal] shall, on conviction, be punishable with fine which may extend to one thousand rupees [Section 23].

Offences by Companies

1. Where an offence has been committed by a company, every person who, at the time when the offence was committed, was in charge of, and was responsible to, the company for the conduct of the business of the company, as well as the company, shall be deemed to be guilty of the offence, and shall be liable to be proceeded against and punished accordingly.

   Provided that nothing contained in this sub-section shall render any such person liable to any punishment provided in this Act, if he proves that the offence was committed without his knowledge or that he exercised all due diligence to prevent the commission of such offence.

2. Notwithstanding anything contained in sub-section (1), where an offence under this Act has been committed by a company and it is proved that the offence has been committed with the consent or connivance of, or is attributable to any gross negligence on the part of any director, manager, secretary, or other officer of the company, such director, manager, secretary, or other officer of the company, shall also be deemed to be guilty of that offence and shall be liable to be proceeded against and punished accordingly [Section 24].

Certain Offences to be Cognisable

Notwithstanding anything contained in the Code of Criminal Procedure, 1898, any offence punishable under Section 23(1) shall be deemed to be a cognisable offence within the meaning of that Code [Section 25].

Jurisdiction to Try Offences Under This Act

No court inferior to that of a presidency magistrate or a magistrate of the first class shall take cognisance of or try any offence punishable under this Act [Section 26].

Miscellaneous Provisions

Miscellaneous provisions of the Act can be summarised as under:

Title to Dividends

1. It shall be lawful for the holder of any security whose name appears on the books of the company issuing the said security to receive and retain any dividend declared by the company in respect thereof for any year, notwithstanding that the said security has already been transferred by him for consideration, unless the transferee who claims the dividend from the transferor has lodged the security and all other documents relating to the transfer which may be required by the company with the company for being registered in his name within 15 days of the date on which the dividend became due.

Explanation: The period specified in this Section shall be extended

(a) in case of death of the transferee, by the actual period taken by his legal representative to establish his claim to the dividend;
(b) in case of loss of the transfer deed by theft or any other cause beyond the control of the transferee, by the actual period taken for the replacement thereof; and
(c) in case of delay in the lodging of any security and other documents relating to the transfer due to causes connected with the post, by the actual period of the delay.

2. Nothing contained in sub-section (1) shall affect
(a) the right of a company to pay any dividend which has become due to any person whose name is for the time being registered in the books of the company as the holder of the security in respect of which the dividend has become due; or
(b) the right of the transferee of any security to enforce against the transferor or any other person his rights, if any, in relation to the transfer in any case where the company has refused to register the transfer of the security in the name of the transferee [Section 27].

Right to Receive Income from Collective Investment Scheme

1. It shall be lawful for the holder of any securities, being units or other instruments issued by collective investment scheme, whose name appears on the books of the collective investment scheme issuing the said security to receive and retain any income in respect of units or other instruments issued by the collective investment scheme declared by the collective investment scheme in respect thereof for any year notwithstanding that the said security, being units or other instruments issued by collective investment scheme, has already been transferred by him for consideration, unless the transferee who claims the income in respect of units or other instruments issued by collective investment scheme from the transfer or has lodged the security and all other

documents relating to the transfer which may be required by the collective investment scheme with the collective investment scheme for being registered in his name within 15 days of the date on which the income in respect of units or other instruments issued by the collective investment scheme became due.

Explanation: The period specified in this Section shall be extended

(a) in the case of death of the transferee, by the actual period taken by his legal representative to establish his claim to the income in respect of units or other instrument issued by collective investment scheme;

(b) in the case of loss of the transfer deed by theft or any other cause beyond the control of the transferee, by the actual period taken for the replacement thereof; and

(c) in the case of delay in the lodging of any security, units or other instruments issued by the collective investment scheme, and other documents relating to the transfer due to causes connected with the post, by the actual period of the delay.

2. Nothing contained in sub-section (1) shall affect

(a) the right of a collective investment scheme to pay any income from units or other instruments issued by the collective investment scheme which has become due to any person whose name is, for the time being, registered in the books of the collective investment scheme as the holder of the security being units or other instruments issued by the collective investment scheme in respect of which the income in respect of units or other instruments issued by the collective scheme has become due; or

(b) the right of transferee of any security, being units or other instruments issued by the collective investment scheme, to enforce against the transferor or any other person his rights, if any, in relation to the transfer in any case where the company has refused to register the transfer of the security being units or other instruments issued by collective investment scheme in the name of the transferee [Section 27A].

Act Not to Apply in Certain Cases

1. The provisions of this Act shall not apply to

(a) the Government, the Reserve Bank of India, any local authority or any corporation set up by a special law or any person who has effected any transaction with or through the agency of any such authority as is referred to in this clause;

(b) any convertible bond or share warrant or any option or right in relation thereto, in so far as it entitles the person in whose favour any of the foregoing has been issued to obtain at his option from the company or other body corporate, issuing the same or from any of its shareholders or duly appointed agents, shares of the company or other body corporate, whether by conversion of the bond or warrant or otherwise, on the basis of the price agreed upon when the same was issued.

2. Without prejudice to the provisions contained in sub-section (1), if the Central Government is satisfied that, in the interests of trade and commerce or the economic development of the country, it is necessary or expedient to do so, it may, by notification in the Official Gazette, specify any class of contracts as contracts to which this Act or any provision contained therein shall not apply, and also the conditions, limitations, or restrictions, if any, subject to which it shall not so apply [Section 28].

Protection of Action Taken in Good Faith

No suit, prosecution or other legal proceeding whatsoever shall lie in any court against the governing body or any member, office bearer or servant of any recognised stock exchange or against any person or persons appointed under sub-section (1) of Section 11 for anything which is done in good faith or intended to be done in pursuance of this Act or of any rules or bye-laws made thereunder [Section 29].

Power to Delegate

The Central Government may, by order published in the Official Gazette, direct that the powers (except the power under Section 30) exercisable by such conditions, if any, as may be specified in the order, be exercisable also by the Sebi or the Reserve Bank of India constituted under Section 3 of the Reserve Bank of India Act, 1934 [Section 29A].

Power to Make Rules

1. The Central Government may, by notification in the Official Gazette, make rules for the purpose of carrying into effect the objects of this Act.
2. In particular, and without prejudice to the generality of the foregoing power, such rules may provide for,
   (a) the manner in which applications may be made, the particulars which they should contain and the levy of a fee in respect of such applications;
   (b) the manner in which any inquiry for the purpose of recognising any stock exchange may be made, the conditions which may be imposed for the grant of such recognition, including conditions as to the admission of members if the stock exchange concerned is to be the only recognised stock exchange in the area; and the form in which such recognition shall be granted;
   (c) the particulars which should be contained in the periodical returns and annual reports to be furnished to the Central Government;
   (d) the documents which should be maintained and preserved under Section 6 and the periods for which they should be preserved;
   (e) the manner in which any inquiry by the governing body of a stock exchange shall be made under Section 6;
   (f) the manner in which the bye-laws to be made or amended under this Act shall before being so made or amended be published for criticism;
   (g) the manner in which applications may be made by dealers in securities for licences under Section 17, the fee payable in respect thereof and the period of such licences, the conditions subject to which licences may be granted, including conditions relating to the forms which may be used in making contracts, the documents to be maintained by licenced dealers and the furnishing of periodical information to such authority as may be specified and the revocation of licences for breach of conditions;
   (h) the requirements which shall be complied with
      (i) by public companies for the purpose of getting their securities listed on any stock exchange;
      (ii) by collective investment scheme for the purpose of getting their units listed on any stock exchange.
      (iii) The form in which an appeal may be filed before the Securities Appellate Tribunal under Section 22A and the fees payable in respect of such an appeal.
   (i) any other matter which is to be or may be prescribed.
3. Any rules made under this Section shall, as soon as may be, after their publication in the Official Gazette, be laid before both Houses of Parliament [Section 30].

Exercises

I. Objective-type Questions

1. 'Derivative' includes
   (a) a security derived from a debt instrument, share, loan, whether secured or unsecured
   (b) risk instrument or contract for differences or any other form of security
   (c) a contract which derives its value from the prices, or index or prices, of underlying securities
   (d) all of the above

2. 'Option in securities' means a contract for the purchase or sale of
   (a) right to buy or sell
   (b) right to buy and sell

(c) securities in future
(d) All of the above, besides including a teji, a mandi, a teji mandi, a galli, a put, a call, or a put and call in securities

3. 'Securities' include
(a) shares, scrips, stocks, bonds, debentures, debenture stock, or other marketable securities of a like nature in or of any incorporated company or other body corporate
(b) Government securities
(c) rights or interests in securities
(d) all of the above

4. 'Spot delivery contract' means a contract which provides for
(a) actual delivery of securities
(b) actual delivery of securities and the payment of a price for them either on the same day as the date of the contract or on the next day
(c) transfer of the securities by the depository from the account of a beneficial owner to the account of another beneficial owner when such securities are dealt with by a depository
(d) All of the above

5. A recognised stock exchange may make rules or amend any rules made by it to provide for
(a) the restriction of voting rights to members only in respect of any matter placed before the stock exchange at any meeting
(b) the regulation of voting rights in respect of any matter placed before the stock exchange at any meeting so that each member may be entitled to have one vote only, irrespective of his share of the paid-up equity capital of the stock exchange
(c) the restriction on the right of a member to appoint another person as his proxy to attend and vote at a meeting of the stock exchange
(d) any or all of the above besides such incidental, consequential and supplementary matters as may be necessary to give effect to any of the matters specified in clauses

II. Review Questions

1. Define the following terms under the Securities Contracts (Regulation) ACT, 1956:
(a) Contract
(b) Derivative
(c) Option in securities
(d) Securities

2. Describe the powers of the Central Government
(i) to call for periodical returns or direct inquiries to be made by a recognised stock exchange
(ii) to supersede governing body of a recognised stock exchange.

3. Discuss the powers of a recognised stock exchange to make rules restricting voting rights etc. and to make bye-laws.

4. Write a note on the listing of securities in any recognised stock exchange explaining the procedure and powers Securities Appellate Tribunal in this behalf.

5. Discuss briefly the penalties payable by a person who fails to comply with any provisions contained in Sections, 6, 17, 18A, or rules made under Section 30. Explain also the scenario in case the offence under the Securities Contracts (Regulation) Act has been committed by a company.

Answers to Objective-type Questions

1. (d) 2. (d) 3. (d) 4. (d) 5. (d)

28 Chapter in Review

LEARNING OUTCOMES

LO 1 The Securities Contracts (Regulation) Act, 1956

LO 2 Role of the Act

LO 3 Aim and objectives of the Act

LO 4 Registration from Sebi mandatory for dealing in securities

LO 5 Recognition to stock exchange by the Central Government

KEY TERMS

Contract [under the Securities Contracts (Regulation) Act]: A deal for, or relating to, the purchase or sale of securities.

Derivative: (i) A security derived from a debt instrument, share, or loan, whether secured or unsecured, a risk instrument or contract for differences, or any other form of security; (ii) a contract which derives its value from the prices, or index or prices, of underlying securities.

Member: A member of a recognised stock exchange.

Option in securities: A contract for the purchase or sale of a right to buy or sell, or a right to buy and sell, securities in the future.

Spot delivery contract: A contract which provides for actual delivery of securities and the payment of a price thereof either on the same day as the date of the contract or on the next day.

Stock exchange: Body of individuals, whether incorporated or not, constituted for the purpose of assisting, regulating, or controlling the business of buying, selling, or dealing in securities.

LO 1 The principal Act that governs the trading of securities in India. The Act provides for direct and indirect control of virtually all aspects of security trading and the running of stock exchanges. It aims to regulate transactions in securities.

LO 2 The legislation gives Central Government regulatory jurisdiction over (a) stock exchanges through a process of recognition and continued supervision; (b) contracts in securities; and (c) listing of securities on stock exchanges.

LO 3 The Act seeks to prevent undesirable transactions in securities by regulating the business of dealing therein and by providing for certain other matters connected therewith. As a condition of recognition, a stock exchange complies with conditions prescribed by the Central Government.

LO 4 By virtue of the provisions of the Act, the business of dealing in securities cannot be carried out without a registration from Sebi. Any stock exchange which is desirous of being recognised has to make an application under the Sebi Act.

LO 5 The Central Government grants recognition to a stock exchange under the Securities Contracts (Regulation) Act.

CHAPTER

29 The Depositories Act, 1996

Learning Objectives

LO 1 Important provisions of The Depositories Act, 1996

LO 2 Rights and obligations of depositories, participants, issuers, and beneficial owners

LO 3 Power of the Board (Sebi) to call for information and enquiry

LO 4 Penalty for offences under the Act by companies

The Depositories Act, 1996, is an important legislation to provide for the regulation of depositories, which facilitate the holding of securities in dematerialised (electronic) form. It was enacted by the Parliament in 1996 and extends to the whole of India. This legislation seeks to promote efficiency in settlement systems and curb the menace of fake, forged, and stolen securities. The Act paved the way for the establishment of NSDL (National Securities Depository Limited), the first depository in India. NSE joined hands with the leading financial institutions to establish NSDL. CDSL (Central Depository Securities Limited), the second depository in the country, was promoted by BSE jointly with leading banks such as SBI, Bank of India, Bank of Baroda, HDFC Bank, Standard Chartered Bank, Union Bank of India, and Centurion Banks. It started its operations in 1999. In the depository system, the transfer of ownership of securities is done through simple account transfers. The investor who is known as beneficial owner (BO) has to open a demat account through any DP for dematerialisation of his holdings and transferring securities. This seems more or less similar to holding funds in bank accounts. This method does away with all the risks and hassles normally associated with paperwork. The cost of transacting in a depository environment is considerably lower as compared to transacting in certificates.

Major Concepts

Some of the important terms used in the Depositories Act are briefly introduced below.

Beneficial owner: An investor whose name is recorded with a depository.

Beneficial Owner refers to an investor whose name is recorded as such with a depository.

Board means the Securities and Exchange Board of India established under Section 3 of the Sebi Act, 1992.

Bye-laws mean bye-laws made by a depository under Section 26.

Company Law Board means the Board of Company Law Administration constituted under Section 10 E of the Companies Act, 1956.

Depository means a company formed and registered under the Companies Act, 1956, and which has been granted a certificate of registration under Section 12(1A) of the Sebi Act, 1992.

Depository: An organisation which holds securities of investors in electronic form at their request through a registered 'DP' and which has been granted a certificate of registration under the Sebi Act.

Depository Participant (DP) refers to an agent of the depository who offers depository services to investors. As per Sebi guidelines, financial institutions, banks, stockbrokers, etc., are eligible to act as DPs.

Depository participant (DP): An agent of the depository who offers depository services to investors.

Issuer refers to any person making an issue of securities.

Issuer: Any person making an issue of securities.

Record includes the records maintained in the form of books or stored in a computer or in such other form as may be determined by regulations.

Registered Owner refers to a depository whose name is entered as such in the register of the issuer.

Registered owner: A depository whose name is entered as such in the register of the issuer.

Regulations mean the regulations made by the Board.

Security means such security as may be specified by the Board.

Service means any service connected with recording of allotment of securities or transfer of ownership of securities in the record of a depository.

Important Provisions

Important provisions of the Act have been briefly explained below.

Certificate of Commencement of Business by Depositories

1. No depository shall act as a depository unless it obtains a certificate of commencement of business from the Board.
2. A certificate granted under sub-section (1) shall be in such form as may be specified by the regulations.

3. The Board shall not grant a certificate under sub-section (1) unless it is satisfied that the depository has adequate systems and safeguards to prevent manipulation of records and transactions provided that no certificate shall be refused under this section unless the depository concerned has been given a reasonable opportunity of being heard [Section 3].

Rights and Obligations of Depositories, Participants, Issuers, and Beneficial Owners

Rights and obligations of depositories, participants, issuers and beneficial owners can be discussed under the following heads:

Agreement Between Depository and Participant

1. A depository shall enter into an agreement with one or more participants as its agent(s).
2. Every agreement under sub-section (1) shall be in such form as specified by the bye laws [Section 4].

Services of Depository

Any person, through a participant, may enter into an agreement, in such form as specified by the bye-laws, with any depository for availing its services [Section 5].

Surrender of Certificate of Security

1. Any person who has entered into an agreement under Section 5 shall surrender the certificate of security, for which he seeks to avail the services of a depository, to the issuer in such manner as may be specified by the regulations.
2. The issuer, on receipt of the certificate of security under sub-section (1), shall cancel the certificate of security and substitute in its records the name of the depository as a registered owner in respect of that security and inform the depository accordingly.
3. A depository shall, on receipt of information under sub-section (2), enter the name of the person referred to in sub-section (1) in its records, as the beneficial owner [Section 6].

Registration of Transfer of Securities with Depository

1. Every depository shall, on receipt of intimation from a participant, register the transfer of security in the name of the transferee.
2. If a beneficial owner or a transferee of any security seeks to have custody of such security the depository shall inform the issuer accordingly [Section 7].

Options to Receive Security Certificate or Hold Securities with Depository

1. Every person subscribing to securities offered by an issuer shall have the option either to receive the security certificates or hold securities with a depository.
2. Where a person opts to hold a security with a depository, the issuer shall intimate to such a depository the details of allotment of the security, and, on receipt of such information, the depository shall enter in its records the name of the allottee as the beneficial owner of that security [Section 8].

Securities in Depositories To Be in Fungible Form

1. All securities held by a depository shall be dematerialised and shall be in a fungible form i.e., returnable or negotiable in paper form.
2. Nothing contained in Sections 153, 153A, 153B, 187B, 187C, and 372 of the Companies Act, 1956, shall apply to a depository in respect of securities held by it on behalf of the beneficial owners [Section 9].

Rights of Depositories and Beneficial Owner

1. Notwithstanding anything contained in any other law for the time being in force, a depository shall be deemed to be the registered owner for the purposes of effecting transfer of ownership of security on behalf of a beneficial owner.
2. Save as otherwise provided in sub-section (1), the depository as a registered owner shall not have any voting rights or any other rights in respect of securities held by it.

3. The beneficial owner shall be entitled to all the rights and benefits and be subjected to all the liabilities in respect of his/her securities held by a depository [Section 10].

Register of Beneficial Owner

Every depository shall maintain a register and an index of beneficial owners in the manner provided in Section 150, Section 151 and Section 152 of the Companies Act, 1956 [Section 11].

Pledge or Hypothecation of Securities Held in a Depository

1. Subject to such regulations and bye-laws, as may be made in this behalf, a beneficial owner may, with the previous approval of the depository, create a pledge or hypothecation in respect of a security owned by him/her through a depository.
2. Every beneficial owner shall give intimation of any such pledge or hypothecation to the depository and such a depository shall thereupon make entries in its records accordingly.
3. Any entry in the records of a depository under sub-section (2) shall be evidence of a pledge or hypothecation [Section 12].

Furnishing of Information and Records by Depository and Issuer

1. Every depository shall furnish to the issuer information about the transfer of securities in the name of beneficial owners at such intervals and in such a manner as may be specified by the bye-laws.
2. Every issuer shall make available to the depository copies of the relevant records in respect of securities held by such a depository [Section 13].

Option to Opt Out in Respect of Any Security

1. If a beneficial owner seeks to opt out of a depository in respect of any security he/she shall inform the depository accordingly.
2. The depository shall, on receipt of intimation under sub-section (1), make appropriate entries in its records and shall inform the issuer.
3. Every issuer shall, within 30 days of the receipt of intimation from the depository and on fulfilment of such conditions and on payment of such fees as may be specified by the regulations, issue the certificate of securities to the Beneficial Owner or the transferee, as the case may be [Section 14].

The Bankers' Books Evidence Act to Apply to Depositories

The Banker's Books Evidence Act, 1891, shall apply in relation to a depository as if it were a bank as defined in Section 2 of that Act [Section 15].

Depositories to Indemnify Loss in Certain Cases

1. Without prejudice to the provisions of any other law for the time being in force, any loss caused to the Beneficial Owner due to the negligence of the depository or the participant, the depository shall indemnify such a Beneficial Owner.
2. Where the loss due to the negligence of the participant under sub-section (1) is indemnified by the depository, the depository shall have the right to recover the same from the participant [Section 16].

Rights and Obligations of Depositories

1. Subject to the provisions of this Act, the rights and obligations of the depositories, participants, and the issuers whose securities are dealt with by a depository shall be specified by the regulations.
2. The eligibility criteria for admission of securities into the depository shall be specified by the regulations [Section 17].

Enquiry and Inspection

Power of the Board to Call for Information and Enquiry

1. The Board, on being satisfied that it is necessary in the public interest or in the interest of investors to do so, may, by order in writing
   (a) call upon any issuer, depository, participant, or beneficial owner to furnish in writing such information relating to the securities held in a depository, as it may require; or

(b) authorise any person to make an enquiry or inspection in relation to the affairs of the issuer, beneficial owner, depository, or participant, who shall submit a report of such enquiry or inspection to it within such period as may be specified in the order.

2. Every director, manager, partner, secretary, officer or employee of the depository, or issuer or the participant or beneficial owner shall, on demand, produce before the person making the enquiry or inspection, all information or such records and other documents in his/her custody having a bearing on the subject matter of such enquiry or inspection [Section 18].

Power of Board to Give Directions in Certain Cases

Save as provided in this Act, if after making, or causing to be made, an enquiry or inspection, the Board is satisfied that it is necessary

1. in the interest of investors, or orderly development of securities market; or
2. to prevent the affairs of any depository or partic ipant being conducted in the manner detrimental to the interests of investors or securities market, it may issue such directions:
   (a) to any depository or participant or any person associated with the securities market; or
   (b) to any issuer, as may be appropriate in the interest of investors or the securities market [Section 19].

Penalty for Offences

Whoever contravenes or attempts to contravene or abets the contravention of the provisions of this Act or any regulations or bye-laws made thereunder shall be punishable with imprisonment for a term which may extend to five years, or with fine, or with both [Section 20].

Offences by Companies

1. Where an offence under this Act has been committed by a company, every person who at the time the offence was committed was in charge of, and was responsible to, the company for the conduct of the business of the company, as well as the company, shall be deemed to be guilty of the offence and shall be liable to be proceeded against and punished accordingly:

   Provided that nothing contained in this subsection shall render any such person liable to any punishment provided in this Act, if he proves that the offence was committed without his knowledge or that he had exercised all due diligence to prevent the commission of such an offence.

2. Notwithstanding anything contained in subsection (1), where an offence under this Act has been committed by a company and it is proved that the offence has been committed with the consent or connivance of, or is attributable to any neglect on the part of, any director, manager, secretary or other officer of the company, such a director, manager, secretary or other officer shall also be deemed to be guilty of the offence and shall be liable to be proceeded against and punished accordingly [Section 21].

   Explanation: For the purposes of this section,
   (a) Company means any body or corporate and includes a firm or other association of individuals; and
   (b) Director, in relation to a firm, means a partner in the firm.

Miscellaneous

Cognizance of Offences by Courts

1. No court shall take cognizance of any offence punishable under this Act or any regulations or bye-laws made there under, save on a complaint made by the Board.
2. No court inferior to that of a Metropolitan Magistrate or a Judicial Magistrate of the First Class shall try any offence punishable under this Act [Section 22].

Appeals

1. Any person aggrieved by an order of the Board made under this Act, or the regulations made there under, may prefer an appeal to the Central Government within such time as may be prescribed.
2. No appeal shall be admitted if it is preferred after the expiry of the period prescribed therefore.

However, an appeal may be admitted after the expiry of the period prescribed if the appellant satisfies the Central Government that he had sufficient cause for not preferring the appeal within the prescribed period.

3. Every appeal made under this Section shall be made in such form and shall be accompanied by a copy of the order appealed against and by such fees as may be prescribed.
4. The procedure for disposing of an appeal shall be such as may be prescribed.

However, before disposing of an appeal, the appellant shall be given a reasonable opportunity to be heard [Section 23].

Power of Central Government to Make Rules

1. The Central Government may, by notification in the Official Gazette, make rules for carrying out the provisions of this Act.
2. In particular, and without prejudice to the generality of the foregoing power, such rules may provide for all or any of the following matters, namely:
   (a) the time within which an appeal may be preferred under sub-section (1) of Section 23;
   (b) the form in which an appeal may be preferred, under sub-section (3) of Section 23 and the fees payable in respect of such appeal;
   (c) the procedure for disposing of an appeal under sub-section (4) of Section 23 [Section 24].

Power of Board to Make Regulations

1. Without prejudice to the provisions contained in Section 30 of the Securities and Exchange Board of India Act, 1992 (15 of 1992), the Board may, by notification in the Official Gazette, make regulations consistent with the provisions of this Act and the rules made thereunder to carry out the purposes of this Act.
2. In particular, and without prejudice to the generality of the foregoing power, such regulations may provide for:
   (a) the form in which record is to be maintained under clause (i) of sub-section (1) of Section 2;
   (b) the form in which the certificate of commencement of business shall be issued under sub-section (2) of Section 3;
   (c) the manner in which the certificate of security shall be surrendered under sub-section (1) of Section 6;
   (d) the manner of creating a pledge or hypothecation in respect of security owned by a beneficial owner under sub-section (1) of Section 12;
   (e) the conditions and the fees payable with respect to the issue of certificate of securities under sub-section (3) of Section 14;
   (f) the rights and obligations of the depositories, participants and the issuers under sub-section (1) of Section 17;
   (g) the eligibility criteria for admission of securities in the depository under sub-section (2) of Section 17 [Section 25].

Power of Depositories to Make Bye-laws

1. A depository shall, with the previous approval of the Board, make bye-laws consistent with the provisions of this Act and the regulations.
2. In particular, and without prejudice to the generality of the foregoing power, such bye-laws shall provide for:
   (a) the eligibility criteria for admission and removal of securities in the depository;
   (b) the conditions subject to which the securities shall be dealt with;
   (c) the eligibility criteria for admission of any person as a participant;
   (d) the manner and procedure for dematerialization of securities;
   (e) the procedure for transactions within the depository;
   (f) the manner in which securities shall be dealt with or withdrawn from a depository;
   (g) the procedure for ensuring safeguards to protect the interests of participants and beneficial owners;
   (h) the conditions of admission into and withdrawal from a participant by a beneficial owner;
   (i) the procedure for conveying information to the participants and beneficial owners on dividend declaration, shareholder meetings and other matters of interest to the beneficial owners;

(j) the manner of distribution of dividends, interest and monetary benefits received from the company among beneficial owners;
(k) the manner of creating pledge or hypothecation in respect of securities held with a depository;
(l) oversea rights and obligations among the depository, issuer, participants and beneficial owners;
(m) the manner and the periodicity of furnishing information to the Board, issuer, and other persons;
(n) the procedure for resolving disputes involving depository, issuer, company, or a beneficial owner;
(o) the procedure for proceeding against the participant committing breach of the regulations and provisions for suspension and expulsion of participants from the depository and cancellation of agreements entered with the depository;
(p) the internal control standards including the procedure for auditing, reviewing and monitoring.

3. Where the Board considers it expedient so to do, it may, by order in writing, direct a depository to make any bye-laws or to amend or revoke any bye-laws already made within such period as it may specify in this behalf.
4. If the depository fails or neglects to comply with such an order within the specified period, the Board may make the bye-laws or amend or revoke the bye-laws made either in the form specified in the order or with such modifications thereof, as the Board thinks fit [Section 26].

Removal of Difficulties

1. If any difficulty arises in giving effect to the provisions of this Act, the Central Government may, by order published in the Official Gazette, make such provisions not inconsistent with the provisions of this Act as appear to it to be necessary or expedient for removing the difficulty:

   However, no order shall be made under this Section after the expiry of a period of two years from the commencement of this Act.
2. Every order made under this Section shall be laid, as soon as possible after it is made, before each House of Parliament [Section 29].
3. Though the depository system has effectively eliminated paper-based certificates which were prone to be fake, forged, and counterfeit resulting in bad deliveries, yet a lot needs to be done to make the markets efficient and investor friendly.

Exercises

I. Objective-type Questions

1. Beneficial owner means
   (a) a person whose name is recorded as such with a depository
   (b) any person making an issue of securities
   (c) a person registered as such under sub-section 1A of Section 12 of the Sebi Act
   (d) a company formed and registered under the Companies Act, 1956 and which has been granted a certificate of registration under the Sebi Act

2. Rules made by the Central Government for carrying out the provisions of the Depositories Act may provide for
   (a) the time within which an appeal may be preferred under sub-section (1) of Section 23
   (b) the form in which an appeal may be preferred, under sub-section (3) of Section 23 and the fees payable in respect of such an appeal
   (c) the procedure for disposing of an appeal under sub-section (4) of Section 23
   (d) for all or any of the above matters

3. Regulations made by the Board may provide for
   (a) the form in which record is to be maintained
   (b) the rights and obligations of the depositories, participants, and the issuers
   (c) the manner in which the certificate of security shall be surrendered
   (d) all of the above
4. Bye-laws made by the depositories shall provide for
   (a) the eligibility criteria for admission and removal of securities in the depository
   (b) the eligibility criteria for admission of any person as a participant
   (c) the manner and procedure for dematerialization of securities
   (d) all of the above
5. Who is a registered owner?
   (a) a depository whose name is entered as such in the register of the issuer
   (b) any person making an issue of the securities
   (c) a person whose name is recorded as such with a depository
   (d) all of the above

II. Review Questions

1. Define the following terms under the Depositories Act, 1996:
   (a) Beneficial owner (b) Board
   (c) Participant (d) Issuer
   (e) Depository (f) Registered owner
2. Under what circumstances can the Board issue directions to any depository, participant, issuer?
3. Explain the power of the Central Government to make rules for carrying out the provisions of the Depositories Act. Outline the matters that these rules may provide for, in particular.
4. Comment on the 'power of the Board to make regulations'.
5. 'The bye-laws made by the depositories shall provide for certain matters'. Enumerate these matters.

Answers to Objective-type Questions

1. (a) 2. (d) 3. (d) 4. (d) 5. (a)

29 Chapter in Review

LEARNING OUTCOMES

LO[1] Important provisions of The Depositories Act, 1996

LO[2] Rights and obligations of depositories, participants, issuers, and beneficial owners

LO[3] Power of the Board (Sebi) to call for information and enquiry

LO[4] Penalty for offences under the Act by companies

KEY TERMS

Beneficial owner: An investor whose name is recorded with a depository.

Depository: An organisation which holds securities of investors in electronic form at their request through a registered 'DP' and which has been granted a certificate of registration under the Sebi Act.

Depository participant (DP): An agent of the depository who offers depository services to investors.

Issuer: Any person making an issue of securities.

Registered owner: A depository whose name is entered as such in the register of the issuer.

LO[1] The introduction of depository system has brought a revolutionary change in the way the capital market operates. The Depositories Act, 1996 in this behalf is an important legislation. Towards the capital market reforms, the Act provides for the regulation of the depositories in securities. It paved the way for the establishment of two depositories—NSDL and CDSL, respectively, with the objective of enhancing efficiency in settlement systems and also to reduce the peril of fake, forged, and stolen securities. In the depository system, securities are held in depository accounts (in dematerialised form), more or less similar to holding funds in bank accounts. The transfer of ownership of securities is done through simple account transfers. This process provides convenient, dependable, and secure depository services at affordable cost to all market participants.

LO[2] The Beneficial Owner and the Depository Participant (DP) shall be bound by the provisions of the Depositories Act, 1996, SEBI (Depositories and Participants) Regulations, 1996, Rules and Regulations of Securities and Exchange Board of India (SEBI), Circulars/Notifications/Guidelines issued thereunder, Bye-laws and Business Rules/Operating Instructions issued by the Depositories and relevant notifications of Government Authorities as may be in force from time to time. The DP shall open/activate demat account of a Beneficial Owner in the Depository system only after receipt of complete account opening form, KYC and supporting documents as specified by SEBI from time to time.

LO[3] The Board, in the public interest or in the interest of investors, may, by order in writing (a) call upon any issuer, depository, participant, or beneficial owner to furnish in writing such information relating to the securities held in a depository, as it may require; or (b) authorise any person to make an enquiry or inspection in relation to the affairs of the issuer, beneficial owner, depository, or participant, who shall submit a report of such enquiry or inspection to it within specified time period.

LO[4] Whoever contravenes or attempts to contravene or abets the contravention of the provisions of the Act or any regulations or bye-laws made thereunder shall be punishable with imprisonment for a term which may extend to five years, or with fine, or with both.

CHAPTER

30 The Foreign Exchange Management Act, 1999

Learning Objectives

LO 1 The Foreign Exchange Management Act (FEMA), 1999

LO 2 Scope of the Act

LO 3 Aim and objectives of the Act

LO 4 Important provisions of FEMA

Capital account transaction: A transaction which alters the assets or liabilities, including contingent liabilities, outside India of persons resident in India or assets or liabilities in India of persons resident outside India, and includes transactions referred to in Section 6(3) of FEMA.

Currency: All currency notes, postal notes, postal orders, money orders, cheques, drafts, traveler's cheques, letters of credit, bills of exchange and promissory notes, credit cards, or such other similar instruments, as may be notified by RBI.

The Foreign Exchange Management Act, 1999 (FEMA) is a law to consolidate and amend the law relating to foreign exchange, introduced as a replacement of earlier law, 'The Foreign Exchange Regulation Act, 1973 (FERA). Unlike other laws where everything is permitted unless specifically prohibited, under the erstwhile Foreign Exchange Regulation Act (FERA), 1973, everything was prohibited unless specifically permitted. Hence, the tenor and the tone of the Act was very drastic. Under FERA, a person was presumed guilty unless he proved himself innocent, whereas under other laws, a person is presumed innocent unless he is proven guilty. The deals in Foreign Exchange were to be 'managed' instead of 'regulated'. The switch to FEMA was done with the objective of facilitating external trade and payments and for promoting the orderly development and maintenance of foreign exchange market in India.

FEMA that extends to whole of India has enabled a new foreign exchange management regime consistent with the emerging framework of the World Trade Organisation (WTO). It serves to make transactions for external trade (exports and imports) easier. Transactions involving current account for external trade no longer require RBI's permission.

Major Concepts

Currency notes: Means and includes cash in the form of coins and bank notes.

Some of the important terms used in the FEMA are briefly introduced below.

Adjudicating Authority means an officer authorised by the Central Government for holding an inquiry and imposing any penalty against a person alleged to have committed contravention of any provision of FEMA under Section 16(1) [Section 2(a)].

Appellate Tribunal means the Appellate Tribunal for Foreign Exchange established under Section 18.

Current account transaction: A transaction other than a capital account transaction and includes (i) payments due in connection with foreign trade, other current business, services, and short-term banking and credit facilities in the ordinary course of business; (ii) payments due as interest on loans and as net income from investments; (iii) remittances for living expenses of parents, spouse, and children residing abroad; and (iv) expenses in connection with foreign travel, education, and medical care of parents, spouse and children.

Authorised Person means an authorised dealer, money changer, off-shore banking unit or any other person for the time being authorised under Section 10(1) to deal in foreign exchange or foreign securities [Section 2(c)].

Bench means a Bench of the Appellate Tribunal.

Capital Account Transaction means a transaction which alters the assets or liabilities, including contingent liabilities, outside India of persons resident in India or assets or liabilities in India of persons resident outside India, and includes transactions referred to in Section 6(3).

Chairperson means the Chairperson of the Appellate Tribunal [Section 2(f)].

Chartered Accountant shall have the meaning assigned to it in clause (b) of Section 2(1) of the Chartered Accounts Act, 1949.

Export: (i) Taking out of India to a place outside India any goods and (ii) provision of services from India to any person outside India.

Currency includes all currency notes, postal notes, postal orders, money orders, cheques, drafts, traveller's cheques, letters of credit, bills of exchange and promissory notes, credit cards, or such other similar instruments, as may be notified by the Reserve Bank.

Foreign currency: Any currency other than Indian currency.

Currency Notes means and includes cash in the form of coins and bank notes.

Current Account Transaction means a transaction other than a capital account transaction and includes

1. payments due in connection with foreign trade, other current business, services, and short-term banking and credit facilities in the ordinary course of business;

2. payments due as interest on loans and as net income from investments;
3. remittances for living expenses of parents, spouse, and children residing abroad; and
4. expenses in connection with foreign travel, education, and medical care of parents, spouse and children [Section 2(j)].

Director of Enforcement means the Director of Enforcement appointed under Section 36(1) [Section 2(k)].

Export means

1. the taking out of India to a place outside India any goods and
2. provision of services from India to any person outside India.

Foreign Currency means any currency other than Indian currency [Section 2(m)].

Foreign exchange: Foreign currency and includes (i) deposits, credits, and balances payable in any foreign currency; (ii) drafts, traveler's cheques, letters of credit, or bills of exchange, expressed or drawn in Indian currency but payable in any foreign currency; and (iii) drafts, traveler's cheques, letters of credit, or bills of exchange drawn by banks, institutions or persons outside India, but payable in Indian currency.

Foreign Exchange means foreign currency and includes

1. deposits, credits, and balances payable in any foreign currency;
2. drafts, traveller's cheques, letters of credit, or bills of exchange, expressed or drawn in Indian currency but payable in any foreign currency; and
3. drafts, traveller's cheques, letters of credit, or bills of exchange drawn by banks, institutions or persons outside India, but payable in Indian currency [Section 2(n)].

Foreign security means any security, in the form of shares, stocks, bonds, debentures, or any other instrument denominated or expressed in foreign currency and includes securities expressed in foreign currency, but where redemption or any form of return such as interest or dividends is payable in Indian currency [Section 2(o)].

Foreign security: Any security, in the form of shares, stocks, bonds, debentures, or any other instrument denominated or expressed in foreign currency and includes securities expressed in foreign currency, but where redemption or any form of return such as interest or dividends is payable in Indian currency.

Import means bringing into India any goods or services [Section 2(p)].

Import: Bringing into India any goods or services.

Indian Currency means currency which is expressed or drawn in Indian rupees but does not include special bank notes and special one rupee notes issued under Section 28A of the Reserve Bank of India Act, 1934 [Section 2(q)].

Indian currency: Currency which is expressed or drawn in Indian rupees but does not include special bank notes and special one rupee notes issued under Section 28A of the RBI Act.

Person includes

1. an individual/a Hindu undivided family/a company/a firm;
2. an association of persons or a body of individuals, whether incorporated or not;
3. every artificial juridical person, not falling within any of the preceding sub-clauses; and
4. any agency, office, or branch owned or controlled by such person [Section 2(u)].

Person Resident in India means

1. a person residing in India for 182 days or more during the preceding financial year but does not include
   (a) a person who has gone out of India or who stays outside India, in either case
      (i) for or on taking up employment outside India, or
      (ii) for carrying on outside India a business or vocation outside India, or
      (iii) for any other purpose, in such circumstances as would indicate his intention to stay outside India for an uncertain period;
   (b) a person who has come to or stays in India, in either case, otherwise than
      (i) for or on taking up employment in India, or
      (ii) for carrying on in India a business or vocation in India, or
      (iii) for any other purpose, in such circumstances as would indicate his intention to stay in India for an uncertain period,
2. any person or body corporate registered or incorporated in India,
3. an office, branch or agency in India owned or controlled by a person resident outside India,
4. an office, branch or agency outside India owned or controlled by a person resident in India [Section 2(v)].

Person Resident Outside India means a person who is not resident in India [Section 2(w)].

Repatriate to India means bringing into India the realised foreign exchange and

- the selling of such foreign exchange to an authorised person in India in exchange for rupees, or
- the holding of realised amount in an account with an authorised person in India to the extent notified by the Reserve Bank, and includes use of the realised amount for discharge of a debt or liability denominated in foreign exchange and the expression 'repatriation' shall be construed accordingly [Section 2(y)].

ate to India: Bringing dia the realised foreign ge and the selling of reign exchange to an sed person in India in ge for rupees, or the ; of realised amount in ount with an authorised in India to the extent d by RBI, and includes he realised amount harge of a debt or denominated in foreign ge and the expression ation shall be construed ngly.

Security means shares, stocks, bonds and debentures, Government securities as defined in the Public Debt Act, 1944, savings certificates to which the Government Savings Certificates Act, 1959 (46 of 1959) applies, deposit receipts in respect of deposits of securities, and units of the Unit Trust of India established under Section 3(1) of the Unit Trust of India Act, 1963 or of any mutual fund and includes certificates of title to securities, but does not include bills of exchange or promissory notes other than Government promissory notes or any other instruments which may be notified by the Reserve Bank as security for the purposes of this Act.

Transfer: Sale, purchase, exchange, mortgage, pledge, gift, loan, or any other form of transfer of right, title, possession, or lien.

Transfer includes sale, purchase, exchange, mortgage, pledge, gift, loan, or any other form of transfer of right, title, possession, or lien [Section 2(ze)].

Important Provisions

Important provisions of the Act have been briefly explained below.

Dealing in Foreign Exchange, Etc.

No person shall

1. deal in or transfer any foreign exchange or foreign security to any person not being an authorised person;
2. make any payment to or for the credit of any person resident outside India in any manner;
3. receive otherwise through an authorised person, any payment by order or on behalf of any person resident outside India in any manner; and
4. enter into any financial transaction in India as consideration for or in association with acquisition or creation or transfer of a right to acquire, any asset outside India by any person [Section 3].

Holding of Foreign Exchange

Save as otherwise provided in this Act, no person resident in India shall acquire, hold, own, possess or transfer any foreign exchange, foreign security or any immovable property situated outside India [Section 4].

Current Account Transactions

Any person may sell or draw foreign exchange to or from an authorised person if such sale or drawal is a current account transaction: Provided that the Central Government may, in public interest and in consultation with the Reserve Bank, impose such reasonable restrictions for current account transactions as may be prescribed [Section 5].

Capital Account Transactions

1. Subject to the provisions of sub-section (2), any person may sell or draw foreign exchange to or from an authorised person for a capital account transaction.
2. The Reserve Bank may, in consultation with the Central Government, specify
   (a) any class or classes of capital account transactions which are permissible;
   (b) the limit up to which foreign exchange shall be admissible for such transactions: Provided that the Reserve Bank shall not impose any restriction on the drawal of foreign exchange for payments due on account of amortisation of loans or for depreciation of direct investments in the ordinary courts of business.
3. Without prejudice to the generality of the provisions of sub-section (2), the Reserve Bank may,

by regulations, prohibit, restrict or regulate the following:

(a) transfer or issue of any foreign security by a person resident in India;
(b) transfer or issue of any security by a person resident outside India;
(c) transfer or issue of any security or foreign security by any branch, office or agency in India of a person resident outside India;
(d) any borrowing or lending in rupees in whatever form or by whatever name called;
(e) any borrowing or lending in rupees in whatever form or by whatever name called between a person resident in India and a person resident outside India;
(f) deposits between persons resident in India and persons resident outside India;
(g) export, import, or holding of currency or currency notes;
(h) transfer of immovable property outside India, other than a lease not exceeding five years, by a person resident in India;
(i) acquisition or transfer of immovable property in India, other than a lease not exceeding five years, by a person resident outside India;
(j) giving of a guarantee or surety in respect of any debt, obligation, or other liability incurred
    (i) by a person resident in India and owed to a person resident outside India; or
    (ii) by a person resident outside India.

4. A person resident in India may hold, own, transfer or invest in foreign currency, foreign security, or any immovable property situated outside India if such currency, security or property was acquired, held or owned by such person when he was resident outside India or inherited from a person who was resident outside India.
5. A person resident outside India may hold, own, transfer or invest in Indian currency, security or any immovable property situated in India if such currency, security or property was acquired, held or owned by such person when he was resident in India or inherited from a person who was resident in India.
6. Without prejudice to the provisions of this Section, the Reserve Bank may, by regulation, prohibit, restrict, or regulate establishment in India of a branch, office or other place of business by a person resident outside India, for carrying on any activity relating to such branch, office or other place of business [Section 6].

Export of Goods and Services

1. Every exporter of goods shall
   (a) furnish to the Reserve Bank or to such other authority a declaration in such form and in such manner as may be specified, containing true and correct material particulars, including the amount representing the full export value or, if the full export value of the goods is not ascertainable at the time of export, the value which the exporter, having regard to the prevailing market conditions, expects to receive on the sale of the goods in a market outside India;
   (b) furnish to the Reserve Bank such other information as may be required by the Reserve Bank for the purpose of ensuring the realisation of the export proceeds by such exporter.
2. The Reserve Bank may, for the purpose of ensuring that the full export value of the goods or such reduced value of the goods as the Bank determines, having regard to the prevailing market conditions, is received without any delay, direct any exporter to comply with such requirements as it deems fit.
3. Every exporter of services shall furnish to the Reserve Bank or to such other authorities a declaration in such form and in such manner as may be specified, containing the true and correct material particulars in relation to payment for such services [Section 7].

Realisation and Repatriation of Foreign Exchange

Where any amount of foreign exchange is due or has accrued to any person resident in India, such a person shall take all reasonable steps to realise and repatriate to India such foreign exchange within such period and in such a manner as may be specified by the Reserve Bank [Section 8].

Exemption from Realisation and Repatriation in Certain Cases

The provisions of Sections 4 and 8 shall not apply to the following:

1. Possession of foreign currency or foreign coins by any person up to such limit as the Reserve Bank may specify.
2. Foreign currency account held or operated by such person or class of persons and the limit up to which the Reserve Bank may specify.
3. Foreign exchange acquired or received before the 8 July 1947, or any income arising or accruing thereon which is held outside India by any person in pursuance of a general or special permission granted by the Reserve Bank.
4. Foreign exchange held by a person resident in India up to such limit as the Reserve Bank may specify, if such foreign exchange was acquired by way of gift or inheritance from a person referred to in clause (c), including any income arising therefrom.
5. Foreign exchange acquired from employment, business, trade, vocation, services, honorarium, gifts, inheritance, or any other legitimate means up to such limit as the Reserve Bank may specify.
6. Such other receipts in foreign exchange as the Reserve Bank may specify [Section 9].

Authorised Person

1. The Reserve Bank may, on an application made to it in this behalf, authorise any person to be known as authorised person to deal in foreign exchange or in foreign securities, as an authorised dealer, money changer or off-shore banking unit or in any other manner as it deems fit.
2. An authorisation under this Section shall be in writing and shall be subject to the conditions laid down therein.
3. An authorisation granted under sub-section (1) may be revoked by the Reserve Bank at any time if the Reserve Bank is satisfied that
   (a) it is in the public interest so to do; or
   (b) the authorised person has failed to comply with the condition subject to which the authorisation was granted or has contravened any of the provisions of the Act or any rule, regulation, notification, direction, or order made thereunder:

   Provided that no such authorisation shall be revoked on any ground referred to in clause (b) unless the authorised person has been given a reasonable opportunity of making a representation in the matter.
4. An authorised person shall, in all his dealings in foreign exchange or foreign security, comply with such general or special directions or orders as the Reserve Bank may, from time to time, think fit to give, and, except with the previous permission of the Reserve Bank, an authorised person shall not engage in any transaction involving any foreign exchange or foreign security which is not in conformity with the terms of his authorisation under this Section.
5. An authorised person shall, before undertaking any transaction in foreign exchange on behalf of any person, require that person to make such declaration and to give such information as will reasonably satisfy him that the transaction will not involve and is not designed for the purpose of any contravention or evasion of the provisions of this Act or of any rule, regulation, notification, direction or order made thereunder, and where the said person refuses to comply with any such requirement or make only unsatisfactory compliance therewith, the authorised person shall refuse in writing to undertake the transaction and shall, if he has reason to believe that any such contravention or evasion as aforesaid is contemplated by the person, report the matter to the Reserve Bank.
6. Any person, other than an authorised person, who has acquired or purchased foreign exchange for any purpose mentioned in the declaration made by him to authorised person under sub-section (5) does not use it for such purpose or does not surrender it to authorised person within the specified period or uses the foreign exchange so acquired or purchased for any other purpose for which purchase or acquisition or foreign exchange is not permissible under the provisions of the Act or the rules or regulations or direction or order made thereunder shall be deemed to have committed contravention of the provisions of the Act for the purpose of this Section [Section 10].

Reserve Bank's Powers to Issue Directions to Authorised Person

1. The Reserve Bank may, for the purpose of securing compliance with the provisions of this Act and of

any rules, regulations, notifications, or directions made thereunder, give to the authorised persons any direction in regard to making of payment or the doing or desist from doing any act relating to foreign exchange or foreign security.

2. The Reserve Bank may, for the purpose of ensuring the compliance with the provisions of this Act or of any rule, regulation, notification, direction or order made thereunder, direct any authorised person to furnish such information, in such manner, as it deems fit.
3. Where any authorised person contravenes any direction given by the Reserve Bank under this Act or fails to file any return as directed by the Reserve Bank, the Reserve Bank may, after giving reasonable opportunity of being heard, impose on the authorised person a penalty which may extend to ₹10,000 and in the case of continuing contravention with an additional penalty which may extend to ₹2000 for every day during which such contravention continues [Section 11].

Power of Reserve Bank to Inspect Authorised Person

1. The Reserve Bank may, at any time, cause an inspection to be made, by any officer of the Bank specially authorised in writing by the Reserve Bank in this behalf, of the business of any authorised person as may appear to it to be necessary or expedient for the purpose of
   (a) verifying the correctness of any statement, information or particulars furnished to the Bank;
   (b) obtaining any information or particulars which such authorised person has failed to furnish on being called upon to do so;
   (c) securing compliance with the provisions of this Act or of any rules, regulations, directions or orders made thereunder.
2. It shall be the duty of every authorised person, and where such person is a company or a firm, every director, partner or other officer of such company or firm, as the case may be, to produce to any officer making an inspection under sub-section (1), such books, accounts, and other documents in his custody or power and to furnish any statement or information relating to the affairs of such person, company, or firm as the said officer may require within such time and in such manner as the said officer may direct [Section 12].

Contravention of Provisions and Penalties

For contravention of any of its provisions, the Act provides for the following penalties:

Penalties

1. If any person contravenes any provision of this Act, or contravenes any rule, regulation, notification, direction, or order issued in exercise of the powers under this Act, or contravenes any condition subject to which an authorisation is issued by the Reserve Bank, he shall, upon adjudication, be liable to a penalty up to thrice the sum involved in such contravention where such amount is quantifiable, or up to ₹2 lakh where the amount is not quantifiable, and where such contravention is a continuing one, further penalty which may extend to ₹5000 for every day after the first day during which the contravention continues.
2. Any Adjudicating Authority adjudging any contravention under sub-section (1), may, if he thinks fit, in addition to any penalty which he may impose for such contravention direct that any currency, security, or any other money or property in respect of which the contravention has taken place, shall be confiscated to the Central Government and further direct that the foreign exchange holdings, if any, of the persons committing the contraventions or any part thereof, shall be brought back into India or shall be retained outside India in accordance with the directions made in this behalf [Section 13].

   Explanation: For the purposes of this sub-section, 'property' in respect of which contravention has taken place, shall include
   (a) deposits in a bank, where the said property is converted into such deposits;
   (b) Indian currency, where the said property is converted into that currency; and
   (c) any other property which has resulted out of the conversion of that property.

Enforcement of the Orders of Adjudicating Authority

1. Subject to the provisions of sub-section (2) of Section 19, if any person fails to make full payment of the penalty imposed on him under Section 13 within a period of 90 days from the date on which the notice for payment of such penalty is served on him, he shall be liable to civil imprisonment under this Section.
2. No order for the arrest and detention in civil prison of a defaulter shall be made unless the Adjudication Authority has issued and served a notice upon the defaulter calling upon him to appear before him on the date specified in the notice and to show cause why he should not be committed to the civil prison, and unless the Adjudicating Authority, for reasons in writing, is satisfied
   (a) that the defaulter, with the object or effect of obstructing the recovery of penalty, has after the issue of notice by the Adjudicating Authority, dishonestly transferred, concealed, or removed any part of his property, or
   (b) that the defaulter has, or has had since the issuing of notice by the Adjudicating Authority, the means to pay the arrears or some substantial part thereof and refuses or neglects or has refused or neglected to pay the same.
3. Notwithstanding anything contained in sub-section (1), a warrant for the arrest of the defaulter may be issued by the Adjudicating Authority if the Adjudicating Authority is satisfied, by affidavit or otherwise, that with the object or effect of delaying the execution of the certificate the defaulter is likely to abscond or leave the local limits of the jurisdiction of the Adjudicating Authority.
4. Where appearance is not made pursuant to a notice issued and served under sub-section (1), the Adjudicating Authority may issue a warrant for the arrest of the defaulter.
5. A warrant of arrest issued by the Adjudicating Authority under sub-section (3) or sub-section (4) may also be executed by any other Adjudicating Authority within whose jurisdiction the defaulter may for the time being be found.
6. Every person arrested in pursuance of a warrant of arrest under this Section shall be brought before the Adjudicating Authority issuing the warrant as soon as practicable and in any event within 24 hours of his arrest (exclusive of the time required for the journey):

   Provided that, if the defaulter pays the amount entered in the warrant of arrest as due and the costs of the arrest to the officer arresting him, such officer shall at once release him.

   Explanation: For the purposes of this sub-section, where the defaulter is a Hindu undivided family, the karta (head) thereof shall be deemed to be the defaulter.
7. When a defaulter appears before the Adjudicating Authority pursuant to a notice to show cause or is brought before the Adjudicating Authority under this Section, the Adjudicating Authority shall give the defaulter an opportunity showing cause why he should not be committed to the civil prison.
8. Pending the conclusion of the inquiry, the Adjudicating Authority may, in his discretion, order the defaulter to be detained in the custody of such officer as the Adjudicating Authority may think fit or release him on his furnishing the security to the satisfaction of the Adjudicating Authority for his appearance as and when required.
9. Upon the conclusion of the inquiry, the Adjudicating Authority may make an order for the detention of the defaulter in the civil prison and shall in that event cause him to be arrested if he is not already under arrest:

   Provide that in order to give a defaulter an opportunity of satisfying the arrears, the Adjudicating Authority may, before making the order of detention, leave the defaulter in the custody of the officer arresting him or of any other officer for a specified period not exceeding 15 days, or release him on his furnishing security to the satisfaction of the Adjudicating Authority for his appearance at the expiration of the specified period if the arrears are not satisfied.
10. When the Adjudicating Authority does not make an order of detention under sub-section (9), he shall, if the defaulter is under arrest, direct his release.
11. Every person detained in the civil prison in execution of the certificate may be so detained
   (a) where the certificate is for a demand of an amount exceeding ₹1 crore, up to three years, and

(b) in any other case, up to six months:

Provided that he shall be released from such detention on the amount mentioned in the warrant for his detention being paid to the officer-in-charge of the civil prison.

12. A defaulter released from detention under this Section shall not, merely by reason of his release, be discharged from his liability for the arrears, but he shall not be liable to be arrested under the certificate in execution of which he was detained in the civil prison.
13. A detention order may be executed at any place in India in the manner provided for the execution of warrant of arrest under the Code of Criminal Procedure, 1973 (2 of 1974) [Section 14].

Power to Compound Contravention

- Any contravention under Section 13 may, on an application made by the person committing such contravention, be compounded within 180 days from the date of receipt of application by the Director of Enforcement or such other officers of the Directorate of Enforcement and officers of the Reserve Bank as may be authorised in this behalf by the Central Government in such manner as may be prescribed.
- Where a contravention has been compounded under sub-section (1), no proceeding or further proceeding, as the case may be, shall be initiated or continued, as the case may be, against the person committing such contravention under that Section, in respect of the contravention so compounded [Section 15].

Appointment of Adjudicating Authority

1. For the purpose of adjudication under Section 13, the Central Government may, by an order published in the Official Gazette, appoint as many officers of the Central Government as it may think fit, as the Adjudicating Authorities for holding an inquiry in the manner prescribed after giving the person alleged to have committed contravention under Section 13, against whom a complaint has been made, a reasonable opportunity of being heard for the purpose of imposing any penalty.

   However, where the Adjudicating Authority is of opinion that the said person is likely to abscond or is likely to evade in any manner, the payment of penalty, if levied, it may direct the said person to furnish a bond or guarantee for such amount and subject to such conditions as it may deem fit.
2. The Central Government shall, while appointing the Adjudicating Authorities, also specify in the order published in the Official Gazette, their respective jurisdictions.
3. No Adjudicating Authority shall hold an enquiry except upon a complaint in writing made by any officer authorised by a general or special order by the Central Government.
4. The said person may appear either in person or take the assistance of a legal practitioner or a chartered accountant of his choice for presenting his case before the Adjudicating Authority.
5. Every Adjudicating Authority shall have the same powers of a civil court which are conferred on the Appellate Tribunal under Section 28(2) and
   (a) all proceedings before it shall be deemed to be judicial proceedings within the meaning of Sections 193 and 228 of the Indian Penal Code;
   (b) shall be deemed to be a civil court for the purposes of Sections 345 and 346 of the Code of Criminal Procedure, 1973.
6. Every Adjudicating Authority shall deal with the complaint under sub-section (2) as expeditiously as possible and endeavour shall be made to dispose of the complaint finally within one year from the date of receipt of the complaint:

   However, where the complaint cannot be disposed of within the said period, the Adjudicating Authority shall record periodically the reasons in writing for not disposing of the complaint within the said period [Section 16].

Appeal to Special Director (Appeals)

1. The Central Government shall, by notification, appoint one or more Special Directors (Appeals) to hear appeals against the orders of the Adjudicating Authorities under this Section and shall also specify in the said notification the matter and places in relation to which the Special Director (Appeals) may exercise jurisdiction.

2. Any person aggrieved by an order made by the Adjudicating Authority, being an Assistant Director or Enforcement or a Deputy Director of Enforcement, may prefer an appeal to the Special Director (Appeals).
3. Every appeal under sub-section (1) shall be filed within 45 days from the date on which the copy of the order made by the Adjudicating Authority is received by the aggrieved person and it shall be in such form, verified in such manner and be accompanied by such fee as may be prescribed:

   Provided that the Special Director (Appeals) may entertain an appeal after the expiry of the said period of 45 days, if he is satisfied that there was sufficient cause for not filing it within that period.
4. On receipt of an appeal under sub-section (1), the Special Director (Appeals) may after giving the parties to the appeal an opportunity of being heard, pass such order thereon as he thinks fit, confirming, modifying or setting aside the order appealed against.
5. The Special Director (Appeals) shall send a copy of every order made by him to the parties to appeal and to the concerned Adjudicating Authority.
6. The Special Director (Appeals) shall have the same powers of a civil court which are conferred on the Appellate Tribunal under Section 28(2) and
   (a) all proceedings before him shall be deemed to be judicial proceedings within the meaning of Sections 193 and 228 of the Indian Penal Code;
   (b) shall be deemed to be a civil court for the purposes of Sections 345 and 346 of the Code of Criminal Procedure, 1973 [Section 17].

Appellate Tribunal

The Central Government shall, by notification, establish an Appellate Tribunal to be known as the Appellate Tribunal for Foreign Exchange to hear appeals against the orders of the Adjudicating Authorities and the Special Director (Appeals) under this Act [Section 18].

Appeal to Appellate Tribunal

1. Save as provided in sub-section (2), the Central Government or any person aggrieved by an order made by an Adjudicating Authority, other than those referred to in sub-section (1) of Section 17, or the Special Director (Appeals), may prefer an appeal to the Appellate Tribunal:

   Provided that any person appealing against the order of the Adjudicating Authority or the Special Director (Appeals) levying any penalty, shall while filing the appeal, deposit the amount of such penalty with such authority as may be notified by the Central Government:

   Provided further that where in any particular case, the Appellate Tribunal is of the opinion that the deposit of such penalty would cause undue hardship to such person, the Appellate Tribunal may dispense with such deposit subject to such conditions as it may deem fit to impose so as to safeguard the realisation of penalty.
2. Every appeal under sub-section (1) shall be filed within a period of 45 days from the date on which a copy of the order made by the Adjudicating Authority or the Special Director (Appeals) is received by the aggrieved person or by the Central Government and it shall be in such form, verified in such manner and be accompanied by such fee as may be prescribed:

   Provided that the Appellate Tribunal may entertain an appeal after the expiry of the said period of 45 days if it is satisfied that there was sufficient cause for not filing it within that period.
3. On receipt of an appeal under sub-section (1), the Appellate Tribunal may, after giving the parties to the appeal an opportunity of being heard, pass such orders thereon as it thinks fit, confirming, modifying or setting aside the order appealed against.
4. The Appellate Tribunal shall send a copy of every order made by it to the parties to the appeal and to the concerned Adjudicating Authority or the Special Director (Appeals), as the case may be.
5. The appeal filed before the Appellate Tribunal under sub-section (1) shall be dealt with by it as expeditiously as possible and endeavour shall be made by it to dispose of the appeal finally within 180 days from the date of receipt of the appeal:

   Provided that where any appeal could not be disposed of within the said period of 180 days, the Appellate Tribunal shall record its reasons in writing for not disposing off the appeal within the said period [Section 19].

The Appellate Tribunal may, for the purpose of examining the legality, propriety or correctness of any order made by the Adjudicating Authority under Section 16 in relation to any proceeding, on its own motion or otherwise, call for the records of such proceedings and make such order in the case as it thinks fit.

Composition of Appellate Tribunal

1. The Appellate Tribunal shall consist of a Chairperson and such number of Members as the Central Government may deem fit.
2. Subject to the provisions of this Act
   (a) the jurisdiction of the Appellate Tribunal may be exercised by Benches thereof;
   (b) a Bench may be constituted by the Chairperson with one or more Members as the Chairperson may deem fit;
   (c) the Benches of the Appellate Tribunal shall ordinarily sit at New Delhi and at such other places as the Central Government may, in consultation with the Chairperson, notify;
   (d) the Central Government shall notify the areas in relation to which each Bench of the Appellate Tribunal may exercise jurisdiction.
3. Notwithstanding anything contained in subsection (2), the Chairperson may transfer a Member from one Bench to another Bench.
4. If at any stage of the hearing of any case or matter it appears to the Chairperson or a Member that the case or matter is of such a nature that it ought to be heard by a Bench consisting of two Members, the case or matter may be transferred by the Chairperson or, as the case may be, referred to him for transfer, to such Bench as the Chairperson may deem fit [Section 20].

Qualifications for Appointment of Chairperson, Member, and Special Director (Appeals)

1. A person shall not be qualified for appointment as the Chairperson or a Member unless he
   (a) in the case of Chairperson, is or has been, or is qualified to be, a Judge of a High Court; and
   (b) in the case of a Member, is or has been, or is qualified to be, a District Judge.
2. A person shall not be qualified for appointment as a Special Director (Appeals) unless he
   (a) has been a member of the Indian Legal Service and has held a post in Grade I of that Service; or
   (b) has been a member of the Indian Revenue Service and has held a post equivalent to a Joint Secretary to the Government of India [Section 21].

Terms of Office

The Chairperson and every other Member shall hold office as such for a term of five years from the date on which he enters upon his office.

However, no Chairperson or other Member shall hold office as such after he has attained

- in the case of the Chairperson, the age of 65 years;
- in the case of any other Member, the age of 62 years [Section 22].

Terms and Conditions of Service

The salary and allowances payable to and the other terms and conditions of service of the Chairperson, other Members, and the Special Director (Appeals) shall be such as may be prescribed [Section 23].

However, neither the salary and allowances nor the other terms and conditions of service of the Chairperson or a Member shall be varied to his disadvantage after appointment.

Vacancies

If, for reason other than temporary absence, any vacancy occurs in the office of the Chairperson or a Member, the Central Government shall appoint another person in accordance with the provisions of this Act to fill the vacancy and the proceedings may be continued before the Appellate Tribunal from the stage at which the vacancy is filled [Section 24].

Resignation and Removal

1. The Chairperson or a Member may, by notice in writing by his hand addressed to the Central Government, resign his office:

   Provided that the Chairperson or a Member shall, unless he is permitted by the Central Government to relinquish his office sooner, continue to hold office until the expiry of three months from the date of receipt of such notice or until a person duly appointed as his successor enters upon his office or until the expiry of term of office, whichever is the earliest.

2. The Chairperson or a Member shall not be removed from his office except by an order by the Central Government on the ground of proved misbehaviour or incapacity after an inquiry made by such person as the President may appoint for this purpose in which the Chairperson or a Member concerned has been informed of the charges against him and given a reasonable opportunity of being heard in respect of such charges [Section 25].

Miscellaneous Provisions

Miscellaneous provisions of the Act can be summarised as under:

Directorate of Enforcement

1. The Central Government shall establish a Directorate of Enforcement with a Director and such other officers or class of officers as it thinks fit, and they shall be called officers of Enforcement, for the purposes of this Act.
2. Without prejudice to the provisions of sub-section (1), the Central Government may authorise the Director of Enforcement or an Additional Director of Enforcement or a Special Director of Enforcement or a Deputy Director of Enforcement to appoint officers of Enforcement below the rank of an Assistant Director of Enforcement.
3. Subject to such conditions and limitations as the Central Government may impose, an officer of Enforcement may exercise the powers and discharge the duties conferred or imposed on him under this Act [Section 36].

Empowering Other Officers

- The Central Government may, by order and subject to such conditions and limitations as it thinks fit to impose, authorise any officer of customs or any central excise officer or any police officer or any other officer of the Central Government or a State Government to exercise such of the powers and discharge such of the duties of the Director of Enforcement or any other officer of Enforcement under this Act as may be stated in the order.
- The officers referred to in sub-section (1) shall exercise the like powers which are conferred on the income tax authorities under the Income Tax Act, 1961, subject to such conditions and limitations as the Central Government may impose [Section 38].

Power to Make Rules

1. The Central Government may, by notification, make rules to carry out the provisions of this Act.
2. Without prejudice to the generality of the foregoing power, such rules may provide for
   (a) the imposition of reasonable restrictions on current account transactions under Section 5;
   (b) the manner in which the contravention may be compounded under sub-section (1) of Section 15;
   (c) the manner of holding an inquiry by the Adjudicating Authority under sub-section (1) of Section 16;
   (d) the form of appeal and fee for filing such appeal under Sections 17 and 19;
   (e) the salary and allowances payable to and the other terms and conditions of service of the Chairperson and other Members of the Appellate Tribunal and the Special Director (Appeals) under Section 23;
   (f) the salaries and allowances and other conditions of service of the officers and employees of the Appellate Tribunal and the office of the Special Director (Appeals) under sub-section (3) of Section 27;
   (g) the additional matters in respect of which the Appellate Tribunal and the Special Director (Appeals) may exercise the powers of a civil court under Section 28;
   (h) the authority or person and the manner in which any document may be authenticated under Section 39; and
   (i) any other matter which is required to be, or may be, prescribed [Section 46].

Power to Make Regulations

1. The Reserve Bank may, by notification, make regulations to carry out the provisions of this Act

and the rules made thereunder. Such regulations may provide for

(a) the permissible classes of capital account transactions, the limits of admissibility of foreign exchange for such transactions, and the prohibition, restriction or regulation of certain capital account transactions under Section 6;
(b) the manner and the from in which the declaration is to be furnished under clause (a) of sub-section (1) of Section 7;
(c) the period within which and the manner of repatriation of foreign exchange under Section 8;
(d) the limit up to which any person may possess foreign currency or foreign coins under clause (a) of Section 9;
(e) the class of persons and the limit up to which foreign currency account may be held or operated under clause (b) of Section 9;
(f) the limit up to which foreign exchange acquired may be exempted under clause (d) of Section 9;
(g) the limit up to which foreign exchange acquired may be retained under clause (e) of Section 9;
(h) any other matter which is required to be, or may be specified [Section 47].

Exercises

I. Objective-type Questions

1. Foreign exchange means foreign currency and includes
   (a) deposits, credits, and balances payable in any foreign currency,
   (b) drafts, traveller's cheques, letters of credit, or bills of exchange, expressed or drawn in Indian currency but payable in any foreign currency,
   (c) drafts, traveller's cheques, letters of credit, or bills of exchange drawn by banks, institutions or persons outside India, but payable in Indian currency
   (d) All of the above

2. Person includes
   (a) an individual/a Hindu undivided family/a company/a firm
   (b) an association of persons or a body of individuals
   (c) every artificial juridical person, not falling within any of the preceding sub-clauses, or any agency, office or branch owned or controlled by such person
   (d) All of the above

3. If any person contravenes any provision of FEMA, he shall, upon adjudication, be liable to a penalty
   (a) up to thrice the sum involved in such contravention
   (b) up to thrice the sum involved in such contravention or ₹2 lakh whichever is higher
   (c) up to thrice the sum involved in such contravention where such amount is quantifiable, or up to ₹2 lakh where the amount is not quantifiable
   (d) Besides above (c) where such contravention is a continuing one, further penalty which may extend to ₹5000 for every day after the first day during which the contravention continues.

4. 'Property' in respect of which contravention is said to have taken place, shall include
   (a) deposits in a bank, where the said property is converted into such deposits
   (b) Indian currency, where the said property is converted into that currency
   (c) any other property which has resulted out of the conversion of that property
   (d) All of the above

5. A person shall not be qualified for appointment as the Chairperson of Appellate Tribunal unless s/he
   (a) has been or is qualified to be a Judge of a High Court
   (b) has been or is qualified to be a District Judge

(c) has been a member of the Indian Legal Service and has held a post in Grade I of that Service
(d) has been a member of the Indian Revenue Service and has held a post equivalent to a Joint Secretary to the Government of India

II. Review Questions

1. Define the following terms under FEMA:
   (a) Authorised person
   (b) Capital account transaction
   (c) Currency
   (d) Foreign exchange
   (e) Repatriate to India
   (f) Security

2. Discuss in brief FEMA provisions governing the following:
   (a) Holding of foreign exchange
   (b) Capital account transactions
   (c) Export of goods and services
   (d) Authorised dealer

3. Discuss the penalty which can be imposed under FEMA if a person contravenes any provision of this Act, or contravenes any rule, regulation, notification, direction issued in exercise of the powers under this Act.

4. Who is 'Special Director'? Describe his role.

5. Describe the composition of Appellate Tribunal. Discuss the qualifications for appointment of Chairperson, Member of Appellate Tribunal and for Special Director (Appeal). Outline also their terms of office.

6. Discuss the procedure to be followed by Appellate Tribunal to hear appeal against the orders of the Adjudicating Authorities and the Special director (Appeals) under this Act.

Answers to Objective-type Questions

1. (d) 2. (d) 3. (d) 4. (d) 5. (a)

30 Chapter in Review

LEARNING OUTCOMES

LO1 The Foreign Exchange Management Act (FEMA), 1999

LO2 Scope of the Act

LO3 Aim and objectives of the Act

LO4 Important provisions of FEMA

KEY TERMS

Capital account transaction: A transaction which alters the assets or liabilities, including contingent liabilities, outside India of persons resident in India or assets or liabilities in India of persons resident outside India, and includes transactions referred to in Section 6(3) of FEMA.

Currency: All currency notes, postal notes, postal orders, money orders, cheques, drafts, traveler's cheques, letters of credit, bills of exchange and promissory notes, credit cards, or such other similar instruments, as may be notified by RBI.

Currency notes: Means and includes cash in the form of coins and bank notes.

Current account transaction: A transaction other than a capital account transaction and includes (i) payments due in connection with foreign trade, other current business, services, and short-term banking and credit facilities in the ordinary course of business; (ii) payments due as interest on loans and as net income from investments; (iii) remittances for living expenses of parents, spouse, and children residing abroad; and (iv) expenses in connection with foreign travel, education, and medical care of parents, spouse and children.

Export: (i) Taking out of India to a place outside India any goods and (ii) provision of services from India to any person outside India.

Foreign currency: Any currency other than Indian currency.

Foreign exchange: Foreign currency and includes (i) deposits, credits, and balances payable in any foreign currency; (ii) drafts, traveler's cheques, letters of credit, or bills of exchange, expressed or drawn in

LO1 FEMA is the replacement of the Foreign Exchange Regulation Act (FERA), 1973, since the latter had become incompatible with the pro-liberalisation policies of the Government of India.

LO2 The Act extends to the whole of India.

LO3 The Act aims at facilitating external trade and payments by promoting the orderly development and maintenance of foreign exchange market in India.

LO4

1. This legislation seeks to make offences related to foreign exchange civil ones.
2. Regulates foreign exchange market, the Act imposes restrictions on people living in India who carry out transactions in foreign exchange, foreign security, or who own or hold immovable property abroad.
3. It restricts the transactions involving foreign exchange or foreign security and payments from outside the country to India—the transactions should be made only through an authorised person.
4. The RBI is empowered by this Act to subject the capital account transactions to a number of restrictions.
5. People living in India will be permitted to carry out transactions in foreign exchange, foreign security, or to own or hold immovable property abroad if the currency, security, or property was owned or acquired when he/she was living outside India, or when it was inherited by him/her from someone living outside India.
6. Exporters are required to furnish their export details to RBI. To ensure that the transactions are carried out properly, RBI may ask the exporters to comply with its necessary requirements.

Indian currency but payable in any foreign currency; and (iii) drafts, traveler's cheques, letters of credit, or bills of exchange drawn by banks, institutions or persons outside India, but payable in Indian currency.

Foreign security: Any security, in the form of shares, stocks, bonds, debentures, or any other instrument denominated or expressed in foreign currency and includes securities expressed in foreign currency, but where redemption or any form of return such as interest or dividends is payable in Indian currency.

Import: Bringing into India any goods or services.

Indian currency: Currency which is expressed or drawn in Indian rupees but does not include special bank notes and special one rupee notes issued under Section 28A of the RBI Act.

Repatriate to India: Bringing into India the realised foreign exchange and the selling of such foreign exchange to an authorised person in India in exchange for rupees, or the holding of realised amount in an account with an authorised person in India to the extent notified by RBI, and includes use of the realised amount for discharge of a debt or liability denominated in foreign exchange and the expression repatriation shall be construed accordingly.

Transfer: Sale, purchase, exchange, mortgage, pledge, gift, loan, or any other form of transfer of right, title, possession, or lien.

CHAPTER

31 Environmental Law

Learning Objectives

LO 1 What is Environmental Law?

LO 2 Aim and subject matter of 'Environmental Legislations'

LO 3 Consequence of violation of the provisions of environmental legislations

LO 4 Role and significance of NGT vis-à-vis environmental protection

The fight for a clean environment continues in a climate of increasing urgency. Constitution of India imposes a duty on every citizen to protect and improve the natural environment, including forests, lakes, rivers, and wildlife. Even before India's independence in 1947, several environment legislations existed. However, the real impetus for bringing about a well-developed framework came only after the UN Conference on the Human Environment (Stockholm, 1972). Under the influence of this declaration, the National Council for Environmental Policy and Planning, within the Department of Science and Technology, was set up in 1972. This Council later evolved into a full-fledged Ministry of Environment and Forests (MoEF) in 1985, which today is the apex administrative body in the country for ensuring environmental protection. The Environment Protection Act (EPA), 1986, came into force soon after the infamous Bhopal Gas Tragedy. It is considered an umbrella legislation as it fills many gaps in the existing laws. It empowers the Central Government to establish authorities equipped with the directive of preventing environmental pollution in all its forms and to tackle specific environmental problems that are peculiar to different parts of the nation. Thereafter, a number of laws came into existence. The emergence of increased public consciousness about the protection of environment has become an international issue. People around the globe observe the World Environment Day (on 5 June), the Earth Day (on 22 April), and the World Water Day (on 22 March), every year, to demonstrate their concern for clean air, clean water, and sustainable energy resources. In India, under the judicial system of the country, National Green Tribunal (NGT) Act, 2010 enables creation of a special tribunal (NGT) to handle the swift disposal of environment related issues and cases.

Sustainable development: Development that meets the needs of the present without compromising the ability of future generations to meet their own needs.

Environment vs Environmental Law

'Environment' includes water, air, and land and the inter-relationship which exists among and between water, air, and land, and human beings, other living creatures, plants, micro-organisms, and property. Whereas 'environmental law' is a complex body of statutes, common law, treaties, conventions, regulations, and policies which, broadly, operate to regulate the interaction of humanity and the natural environment for the purpose of reducing the adverse impact of human activities.

Environment: Conditions that affect the behaviour and development of somebody or something.

Natural environment: Conditions or surroundings comprising water, air, land, human being, other living creatures, plants, microorganisms, and properties and for matters connected there with.

Environmental laws: Network of treaties, statutes, regulations and common and customary laws addressing the effects of human activity on the natural environment.

This can be divided into the following two major subjects:

1. Pollution control and remediation;
2. Resource conservation and management.

Following is a list of the environmental legislations that arose in part due to ineffective solution of environmental problems and issues at common law:

- General
- Forest and wildlife
- Water
- Air

General (Environment Protection) Legislations

A brief account of general (environment protection) legislations is given as under:

The Environment (Protection) Act (EPA), 1986

Environment (protection) Act (EPA): Legislation that seeks to provide for the protection and improvement of the natural environment.

The Environment (Protection) Act (EPA) was enacted in 1986. It extends to the whole of India, including the State of Jammu and Kashmir. EPA is said to be an 'umbrella' legislation passed to provide a framework for the Central Government towards the coordination of activities of various Central and State agencies under previous legislations, such as Water Act, Air Act, etc.

The Act seeks to provide for the protection and improvement of the environment that includes water, air, land, human being, other living creatures, plants, micro-organisms, and properties and for matters connected there with. It empowers the Central Government to initiate measures to protect and improve environmental quality, control, and reduce pollution from all sources, and prohibit or restrict the setting and/or operation of any industrial facility on environmental grounds. The Act was amended in 1991.

Measures to protect environment

The Act empowers the Central Government to make such rules as it deems necessary for protecting and improving the quality of the environment and preventing, controlling, and abating environmental pollution. Such rules may provide for all or any of the following matters:

1. The standards of quality of air, water, or soil for various areas and purposes
2. The maximum allowable limits of concentration of various environmental pollutants (including noise) for different areas
3. The procedures and safeguards for the handling of hazardous substances
4. The prohibition and restrictions on the handling of hazardous substances in different areas
5. The prohibition and restriction on the location of industries and carrying on process and operations in different areas
6. The procedures and safeguards for the prevention of accidents which may cause environmental pollution and for providing remedial measures for such accidents

Penalty for non-compliance

The owner or occupier of a company, factory, or an institution who fails to comply with or contravenes any of the provisions of this Act shall be punishable with imprisonment for a term which may extend to five years or with fine which may extend to one lakh rupees, or with both. And in case the failure or contravention continues, the owner/occupier shall be punishable with additional fine which may extend to five thousand rupees for every day during which such failure or contravention continues after the conviction for the first such failure or contravention. If the failure or contravention continues beyond a period of one year after the date of conviction, the offender shall be punishable with imprisonment for a term which may extend to seven years.

Moreover, the CPCB or State boards have the power to close or cancel or deny the authorisation to run the company/factory/institution, whichever is causing pollution.

The Environment (Protection) Rules, 1986

The Environment (Protection) Rules notified by Ministry of Environment and Forests (MoEF) lay down procedures for setting standards of emission or discharge of environmental pollutants. The responsible body for implementing these rules and seeking compliance thereof is the Central Pollution Control Board of India. It is a statutory organization body established in 1974 under Water (Prevention and Control of Pollution) Act, 1974. The Board provides technical services to MoEF as regards provisions of the Environment (Protection) Act, 1986.

The Environment (Protection) Rules: Rules notified by MoEF which lay down procedures for setting standards of emission or discharge of environmental pollutants.

The Hazardous Wastes (Management and Handling) Rules, 1989

The Hazardous Wastes (Management and Handling) Rules aim to control the generation, collection, treatment, import, storage, and handling of hazardous waste. Accordingly, before hazardous waste is delivered at the hazardous waste site, the occupier or operator of a facility shall ensure that the hazardous waste is packaged in a manner suitable for storage and transport and the labelling and packaging shall be easily visible and be able to withstand physical conditions and climate factors. Moreover, packaging, labeling, and transport of hazardous wastes shall be in accordance with the provisions of the rules issued by the Central Government under the Motor Vehicles Act, 1988, and other guidelines issued from time to time.

Hazardous waste: Waste that is dangerous or potentially harmful to the health of human beings and other living things or the environment.

The Manufacture, Storage, and Import of Hazardous Chemical Rules, 1989

The Manufacture, Storage, and Import of Hazardous Chemical Rules framed under the Environment

(Protection) Act, 1986, by the Government of India apply to workplaces in which hazardous chemicals are manufactured or stored. These rules define the terms used in this context, and set up an authority to inspect, once a year, the industrial activity connected with hazardous chemicals and isolated storage facilities.

The Manufacture, Use, Import, Export, and Storage of Hazardous Micro-organisms/Genetically Engineered Organisms, or Cells Rules, 1989

The Manufacture, Use, Import, Export, and Storage of Hazardous Micro-organisms/Genetically Engineered Organisms or Cells Rules were framed by the Central Government in the exercise of the powers conferred by Sections 6, 8, and 25 of the Environment (Protection) Act, 1986. These rules were introduced with a view to protect the environment, nature, and health in connection with the application of gene technology and microorganisms.

The Public Liability Insurance Act, 1991

With the growth of hazardous industries, risks from accidents, processes, and operations, not only to the persons employed in such undertakings but also to the public who may be in vicinity, have increased. The people who are affected by accidents in the hazardous installations are, very often, economically weaker sections and suffer great hardships because of delayed relief and compensation. While the workers and employees of hazardous installations are protected under separate laws, members of the public are not assured of any relief except through long legal process. To ameliorate the sufferings of members of the public due to accidents which take place in hazardous installations it was found essential to provide for mandatory Public Liability Insurance. To achieve this objective, the Public Liability Insurance Bill was introduced in the Parliament. The Public Liability Insurance Act, 1991, is in consonance with the spirit of principle of the Rio Declaration, in as much as it aims at providing for public liability insurance for the purpose of providing immediate relief to the persons affected by accident occurring while handling any hazardous substance or matters connected therewith or incidental thereto.

The National Environmental Tribunal Act, 1995

In 1995, the Central Government established the National Environment Tribunal (through the National Environment Tribunal Act, 1995) to provide for strict liability for damage arising out of accidents caused from the handling of hazardous substances. This Act aims to award compensation for damages to persons, property, and the environment arising from any activity involving hazardous substances.

The National Environment Appellate Authority Act, 1997

The National Environment Appellate Authority Act has been created to hear appeals with respect to restrictions of areas in which classes of industries, etc., are carried out or prescribed subject to certain safeguards under the EPA.

The Biomedical Waste (Management and Handling) Rules, 1998

The Biomedical Waste (Management and Handling) Rules is a legal binding on the healthcare institutions to streamline the process of proper handling of hospital waste such as segregation, disposal, collection, and treatment. With a view to control the indiscriminate disposal of hospital waste/biomedical waste, MoEF has issued a notification on Biomedical Waste Management under the Environment (Protection) Act. Govt. of NCT of Delhi in its notification dated 6th July, 1999, has authorised Delhi Pollution Control Committee (DPCC) for the purpose of granting authorisation for collection, reception, storage, treatment, and disposal of biomedical waste to implement the Biomedical Waste Management Rules, 1998. These rules will apply to hospitals, nursing homes, veterinary hospitals, animal houses, pathological labs, and blood banks, generating hospital wastes except such occupier of clinics, dispensaries, pathological labs, blood banks providing treatment/service to less than one thousand patients per month.

The Environment (Siting for Industrial Projects) Rules, 1999

The Environment (Siting for Industrial Projects) Rules, 1999, framed by the Central Government in exercise of the powers conferred by the Environment (Protection) Act lay down detailed provisions relating to areas to be avoided for siting of industries, precautionary measures to be taken for site selecting, and also the aspects of environmental protection which should have been incorporated during the implementation of the industrial development projects.

The Municipal Solid Wastes (Management and Handling) Rules, 2000

The Municipal Solid Wastes (Management and Handling) Rules, 2000, apply to every municipal authority responsible for the collection, segregation, storage, transportation, processing, and disposal of municipal solid wastes which consists of household waste, construction and demolition debris, sanitation residue, and waste from streets. This garbage is generated mainly from residential and commercial complexes. Under these rules, it is obligatory on the part of all the municipal authorities to arrange for collection, segregation, transportation, and suitable disposal of municipal wastes of the municipal towns/cities.

The Ozone Depleting Substances (Regulation and Control) Rules, 2000

The Ozone Depleting Substances (Regulation and Control) Rules have been laid down for the regulation of production and consumption of ozone depleting substances. India signed the Montreal Protocol along with its London Amendment in 1992 and also ratified the Copenhagen, Montreal, and Beijing Amendments in 2003 mindful of the precautionary measures needed for the protection of the ozone layer, otherwise its modifications would result into the amount of solar ultraviolet radiation having biological effect that reaches the earth surface and potential consequences for human health, for organisms, ecosystems, and material. Government of India as a party to the protocol continues its action, measures, and adoption of necessary regulations with the sole objective of protection of ozone layer.

The Batteries (Management and Handling) Rules, 2001

The Batteries (Management and Handling) Rules, 2001, shall apply to every manufacturer, importer, re-conditioner, assembler, dealer, auctioneer, consumer, and bulk consumer involved in the manufacture, processing, sale, purchase, and use of batteries or components so as to regulate and ensure the environmentally safe disposal of used batteries.

The Noise Pollution (Regulation and Control, Amendment) Rules, 2002

The Noise Pollution (Regulation and Control) (Amendment) Rules lay down such terms and conditions as are necessary to reduce noise pollution and permit use of loud speakers or public address systems during night hours (between 10:00 pm to 12:00 midnight) on or during any cultural or religious festive occasion. These rules apply to diesel generator (DG) sets as well. Accordingly, the maximum permissible sound pressure level for new DG sets with rated capacity up to 1000 KVA, manufactured on or after 1st July, 2003, shall be 75 decibel at 1 metre from the enclosure surface. Moreover, towards the compliance of these rules, the DG sets should be provided with integral acoustic enclosure at the manufacturing stage itself.

Pollution: The action or process of making land, water, air, etc., dirty and unsafe or unsuitable to use.

The Biological Diversity Act, 2002

The Biological Diversity Act, 2002, is an act to provide for the conservation of biological diversity, sustainable use of its components, and fair and equitable sharing of the benefits arising out of the use of biological resources and knowledge associated with it.

Forest and Wildlife Protection Legislations

Forest and wildlife protection legislations have been briefly introduced below.

Indian Forest Act 1927 and Amendment 1984

Indian Forest Act 1927 and Amendment 1984 are one of the many surviving colonial statutes. This Act was enacted by the Indian Parliament in view of rapid deforestation and the resulting environmental degradation. It was enacted to 'consolidate the law related to forest, the transit of forest produce, and the duty chargeable against timber and other forest produce'. It defines what a forest offence is, what are the acts prohibited inside a reserved forest, and what are the penalties that can be imposed on the violation of the provisions of the Act? It also defines the procedure to be followed for declaring an area to be a reserved forest, a protected forest, or a village forest.

Wildlife Protection Act 1972, Rules 1973, and Amendment 1991

Wildlife Protection Act 1972, Rules 1973, and Amendment 1991 provide for the protection of birds and animals and for all matters that are connected to it whether it be their habitat or the waterhole or the forests that sustain them. The Act empowers the Central and State governments to declare any area a wildlife sanctuary, national park, or closed area. There is a blanket ban on carrying out any industrial activity inside these protected areas. It provides for authorities to administer and to implement the Act; regulate the hunting of wild animals; protect specified plants, sanctuaries, national parks, and closed areas; restrict trade or commerce in wild animals or animal articles; and miscellaneous matters. The Act prohibits hunting of animals except with permission of authorised officer when an animal has become dangerous to human life or property or is disabled or diseased beyond recovery.

Forest (Conservation) Act 1980 and Rules 1981

Forest (Conservation) Act 1980 and Rules 1981 were enacted by the Parliament to check further deforestation and conserve forests and to provide for matters connected therewith or ancillary or incidental thereto. It strictly restricts and regulates the de-reservation of forests or use of forest land for non-forest purposes without the prior approval of Central Government. The Act also lays down the pre-requisites for the diversion of forest land for non-forest purposes.

Water Pollution Protection Legislations

Following is the brief account of water pollution protection legislations.

The Easement Act, 1882

An easement is a right which the owner or occupier of certain land possesses, as such, for the beneficial enjoyment of that land, to do and continue to do something, or to prevent and continue to prevent something being done, in or upon or in respect of certain other land not his own. Accordingly, the Easement Act allows private rights to use a resource that is groundwater by viewing it as an attachment to the land. It also states that all surface water belongs to the state and is a state property.

The Indian Fisheries Act, 1897

Fishing in India is a major industry in its coastal states, employing over 14 million people. India is a major exporter of fish in the world. In 2010, the country exported over 700,000 metric tons of fish to some 90 countries generating revenue of over $1.9 billion. Marine and freshwater catch fishing combined with aquaculture fish farming is a rapidly growing industry in India. In 2010, India was the sixth largest producer of marine and freshwater capture fisheries, and the second largest aquaculture farmed fish producer in the world. To protect and promote this benevolent industry, several key laws and regulations are relevant at the central level. These include the British-era Indian Fisheries Act (1897), which penalizes the killing of fish by poisoning water and by using dynamite or other explosive substance in any way whether coastal or inland.

The Inland Stream Vessel Act, 1917

The Inland Stream Vessel Act, 1917, provides a mandatory rule of the fresh water for the use of the passengers.

The River Boards Act, 1956

The River Boards Act, 1956, enables the states to enroll the Central Government in setting up an Advisory River Board to resolve issues in inter-state cooperation. The Act provides for the establishment of River Boards for the regulation and development of inter-State rivers and river valleys.

The Water (Prevention and Control of Pollution) Act, 1974

The Water (Prevention and Control of Pollution) Act, 1974, establishes an institutional structure for preventing and abating water pollution. It establishes standards for water quality and effluent. Polluting industries must seek permission to discharge waste into effluent bodies. The CPCB (Central Pollution Control Board) was constituted under this Act.

Air Pollution Protection Legislations

A brief account of major air pollution protection legislations is given below.

The Factories Act, 1948

The Factories Act, 1948, was the first to express concern for the working environment of the workers. It is an Act to consolidate and amend the law regulating labour in factories. While ensuring the safety and health of the workers, the Act contributes to environmental protection. The Act contains a comprehensive list of 29 categories of industries involving hazardous processes, which are defined as a process or activity where unless special care is taken, raw materials used therein or the intermediate or the finished products, by-products, wastes or effluents would:

1. Cause material impairment to the health of the persons engaged
2. Result in the pollution of the general environment

The amendment of 1987 has sharpened its environmental focus and expanded its application to hazardous processes. The amendment requires the following compulsory disclosure of information by the occupier of every factory involving a hazardous process:

1. The occupier of every factory involving a hazardous process shall disclose in the manner prescribed all information regarding dangers, including health hazards and the measures to overcome such hazards arising from the exposure to or handling of the materials or substances in the manufacture, transportation, storage, and other processes to the workers employed in the factory, the Chief Inspector, the local authority within whose jurisdiction the factory is situated, and the general public in the vicinity.
2. The occupier shall, at the time of registering the factory involving a hazardous process, lay down a detailed policy with respect to the health and safety of the workers employed therein and intimate such policy to the Chief Inspector and the local authority and, thereafter, at such intervals as may be prescribed, inform the Chief Inspector and the local authority of any change made in the said policy.
3. The information furnished under sub-section (1) shall include accurate information as to the quantity, specifications, and other characteristics of wastes and the manner of their disposal.
4. Every occupier shall, with the approval of the Chief Inspector, draw up an onsite emergency plan and detailed disaster control measures for his factory and make known to the workers employed therein and to the general public living in the vicinity of the factory the safety measures required to be taken in the event of an accident taking place.
5. Every occupier of a factory shall
   (a) if such a factory is engaged in a hazardous process on the commencement of the Factories (Amendment) Act, 1987, within a period of 30 days of such commencement; and
   (b) if such factory proposes to engage in a hazardous process at any time after such commencement, within a period of 30 days before the commencement of such process, inform the Chief Inspector of the nature and details of the process in such form and in such manner as may be prescribed.
6. Where any occupier of a factory contravenes the provisions of sub-section (5), the license issued under Section 6 to such factory shall, notwithstanding any penalty to which the occupier or factory shall be subjected to under the provisions of this Act, be liable for cancellation.
7. The occupier of a factory involving a hazardous process shall, with the previous approval of the Chief Inspector, lay down measures for the handling, usage, transportation, and storage of

hazardous substances inside the factory premises and the disposal of such substances outside the factory premises and publicise them in the manner prescribed among the workers and the general public living in the vicinity.

The Air (Prevention and Control of Pollution) Act, 1981

The Air (Prevention and Control of Pollution) Act, 1981, provides for the control and abatement of air pollution. It entrusts the power of enforcing this act to the CPCB. The Act is very innovative in its approach. It empowers the State board to lay down the standards for emission of air pollutants into the atmosphere from industrial plants, automobiles, or from any other source having in view the standards laid down by the Central board.

If an industry is already in operation, it should have applied for consent to the board within a period of three months from the date the area is declared as air pollution control area under Section 19 of the Act. The salient features of the Act are as follows:

1. The Central board is to advise the Central Government on matters of air pollution, specify desirable air quality standards, coordinate activities of the State boards, train persons engaged in air pollution control, discriminate information and data relating to the Air Act, etc. The State boards are empowered with similar powers within their respective states.
2. The Act empowers the State board to establish laboratories and appoint Government analysts for analyzing samples of air or emission for the purpose of implementing the Act.
3. The Act also empowers the State Government to declare any area within the state as an air pollution control area after consulting the State boards. In such areas, the Act prohibits operation of any industrial plant without prior permission from the Government; besides, the Act also prohibits the use of certain fuels, materials, or appliances that may cause air pollution in the air pollution control area.
4. The Act empowers boards to issue direction including closure, prohibition, or regulation of any industry, operation, or process and for stopping and control of water or power supply and other sources.

The Air (Prevention and Control of Pollution) Rules, 1982

The Air (Prevention and Control of Pollution) Rules, 1982, define the procedures of the meetings of the Central Pollution Control Boards and the powers entrusted to them.

The Atomic Energy Act, 1982

The Atomic Energy Act, 1982, deals with the radioactive waste. The Act provides for the development, control, and use of atomic energy for the welfare of the people of India and for other peaceful purposes and for the matters connected therewith. The purpose of the Atomic Energy Act (AEA) is to assure the proper management of source, special nuclear material, and byproduct material. The AEA and the statutes that amended it delegate the control of nuclear energy primarily to the Department of Energy (DOE), the Nuclear Regulatory Commission (NRC), and the Environmental Protection Agency (EPA). DOE authority extends to the following:

1. Source material—(i) uranium, thorium, or any other material that is determined by the NRC pursuant to the provisions of Section 61 of the AEA to be a source material; or (ii) ores containing one or more of the foregoing materials, in such concentration as the NRC may by regulation determine from time to time.
2. Special nuclear material—(i) plutonium, uranium enriched in the isotope 233 or the isotope 235, and any other material that the NRC, pursuant to the provisions of Section 51 of the AEA, determines to be special nuclear material, but does not include source material; or (ii) any material artificially enriched by any of the foregoing, but does not include source material.
3. Byproduct material—(i) any radioactive material (except special nuclear material) yielded in or made radioactive by exposure to radiation incident to the process of producing or utilizing special nuclear material, and (ii) the tailings or wastes produced by the extraction or concentra-

tion of uranium or thorium from any ore processed primarily for its source material content.

The Air (Prevention and Control of Pollution) Amendment Act, 1987

The Air (Prevention and Control of Pollution) Amendment Act, 1987, empowers the Central and State Pollution Control Boards (SPCBs) to meet with grave emergencies of air pollution.

Role of National Green Tribunal in Protecting Environment

National Green Tribunal (NGT): A special tribunal for the expeditious disposal of the cases pertaining to environmental issues.

National Green Tribunal (NGT or say just the Tribunal in this behalf) is the creation of National Green Tribunal Act, 2010 (of the Parliament of India) for the expeditious disposal of the cases pertaining to environmental issues. The Tribunal aims at ensuring the citizens of India the right to a healthy environment as a fundamental right.

The Tribunal has original jurisdiction on matters of 'substantial damage to environment due to specific activity' (such as pollution). However, no specific method is defined in Law for determining 'substantial' damage to environment, property, or public health. The powers of tribunal related to an award are equivalent to civil court and tribunal may transmit any order/award to civil court having local jurisdiction. However, the tribunal does not follow civil law. It, rather follows principles of natural justice. The NGT Act specifies that an application for an issue or dispute related to environment can be filed with the Tribunal in a prescribed manner within six months only when first time dispute arose. However, the Tribunal may further grant 60 days grace period after the six months are over if it is satisfied that appellant was prevented by sufficient cause from filing the application.

Besides, Tribunal is also competent to hear cases for several Acts such as Forest (Conservation) Act, Biological Diversity Act, Environment (Protection) Act, Water & Air (Prevention & control of Pollution) Acts, etc. and also have appellate jurisdiction related to above Acts after establishment of Tribunal within a period of 30 days of award or order received by aggrieved party. The NGT Act says that decision taken by majority of members shall be binding and every order of Tribunal shall be final. Any person aggrieved by an award, decision, or order of the Tribunal may appeal to the Supreme Court within 90 days of commencement of award, but Supreme Court can entertain appeal even after 90 days if appellant satisfied SC by giving sufficient reasons.

Some of the notable orders of the Tribunal include 'Yamuna Conservation Zone', 'Coal Blocks in Chhattisgarh Forests', and 'Ban on decade old Diesel vehicles in NCR'.

Exercises

I. Objective-type Questions

1. Environmental legislation is designed:
   (a) To control or eliminate pollution
   (b) To control and eliminate environmental damage
   (c) To regulate the quantity of pollutants produced or prohibit their production
   (d) To take care of all of the above

2. The protection of environment is the responsibility of
   (a) The Central government
   (b) The State governments
   (c) The local/municipal authorities
   (d) All of the above

3. Which of the following provides a mandatory rule of the fresh water for the use of the passengers?
   (a) The Water (Prevention and Control of Pollution) Act, 1974
   (b) Indian Ports Act, 1908

(c) The Indian Stream Vessel Act, 1917
(d) The Indian Fisheries Act, 1897

4. The following Act, passed in 1986, is said to be an 'umbrella' legislation passed to provide a framework for the Central Government towards the coordination of activities of various Central and State agencies under previous legislations such as Water Act, Air Act, etc.
(a) Conservation Act
(b) Environment Protection Act (EPA)
(c) Umbrella Act
(d) Forest Act

5. In view of the rapid deforestation and the resulting environmental degradations our Parliament enacted the __________ Act in 1927.
(a) Deforestation Act
(b) Biodiversity Act
(c) Wildlife Act
(d) Forest Act

6. The World Environment Day is observed on
(a) 5 June
(b) 2 June
(c) 5 January
(d) 5 December

7. The Earth Day is observed on
(a) 22 May
(b) 22 April
(c) 20 July
(d) 20 March

8. The Act which deals with radioactive waste is
(a) EPA
(b) The Biological Diversity Act
(c) The Atomic Energy Act
(d) The Air (Prevention and Control of Pollution) Act

9. Which of the following provides for the maximum permissible level of emission or discharge of pollutants from industries?
(a) The Factories Act, 1948
(b) The Environmental (Protection) Rules, 1986
(c) Hazardous Wastes (Management and Handling) Rules, 1989
(d) Bio-medical Waste (Management and Handling) Rules, 1998

II. Review Questions

1. Discuss the objectives and significance of environmental legislation in force.
2. Describe briefly environmental laws that exclusively deal with air and water.
3. 'EPA is an umbrella legislation passed to provide a framework for the Central Government towards coordination of activities of various Central and State agencies under previous laws.' Comment.
4. Describe the legislations in force that seek to provide protection to wildlife and forests.
5. Enumerate the general environmental regulations in force in India and discuss their subject-matters.

Answers to Objective-type Questions

1. (d)	2. (d)	3. (c)	4. (b)	5. (a)
6. (a)	7. (b)	8. (c)	9. (d)	

31 Chapter in Review

LEARNING OUTCOMES

LO 1 What is Environmental Law?

LO 2 Aim and subject matter of 'Environmental Legislations'

LO 3 Consequence of violation of the provisions of environmental legislations

LO 4 Role and significance of NGT vis-à-vis environmental protection

KEY TERMS

Environment: Conditions that affect the behaviour and development of somebody or something.

Natural environment: Conditions or surroundings comprising water, air, land, human being, other living creatures, plants, microorganisms, and properties and for matters connected there with.

Environmental laws: Network of treaties, statutes, regulations and common and customary laws addressing the effects of human activity on the natural environment.

Sustainable development: Development that meets the needs of the present without compromising the ability of future generations to meet their own needs.

Environment (Protection) Act (EPA): Legislation that seeks to provide for the protection and improvement of the natural environment.

The Environment (Protection) Rules: Rules notified by MoEF which lay down procedures for setting standards of emission or discharge of environmental pollutants.

Hazardous waste: Waste that is dangerous or potentially harmful to the health of human beings and other living things or the environment.

Pollution: The action or process of making land, water, air, etc., dirty and unsafe or unsuitable to use.

National Green Tribunal (NGT): A special tribunal for the expeditious disposal of the cases pertaining to environmental issues.

LO1 'Environmental Law' is a collective term describing international treaties, statutes, regulations, and common law or national legislation, designed to (a) control or eliminate pollution, (b) control and eliminate environmental damage, and (c) regulate the quantity of pollutants produced or prohibit their production.

LO2 All the environmental legislations aim at addressing the environmental problems by monitoring activities to ensure compliance and regulating conduct thereof. Also, these legislations attempt to (a) address the harms to the environment, (b) deal with discharge of harmful substances in the air, (c) deal with discharge of harmful substances in the water, and (d) address the cleanup of past pollution.

LO3 Violation of the provisions of the environmental legislations warrant penalty, including imprisonment. However, Directors and other officers of a company can avoid responsibility for environmental damage should they exercise due diligence which requires personal monitoring of premises after issuing directives and follow up initiatives relating to hazardous products and processes.

LO4 National Green Tribunal Act, 2010, an Act of the Parliament of India, enables creation of a special tribunal, the National Green Tribunal (NGT) for the expeditious disposal of the cases pertaining to environmental issues. At judicial level, NGT assures the citizens of India the right to a healthy environment as a fundamental right.

CHAPTER

32 Intellectual Property Rights

Learning Objectives

LO 1 Subject matter of intellectual property
LO 2 Aim and objectives of intellectual property laws
LO 3 Intellectual Property Rights
LO 4 Patents
LO 5 Copyrights
LO 6 Design
LO 7 Trademark
LO 8 Trade dress
LO 9 Trade secrets
LO 10 Contemporary issues in intellectual property rights

'Intellectual Property Rights', a buzzword in the contemporary business world, refers to moral and legal claims or entitlements over intellectual property (IP). IP, in turn, implies the ownership of an idea, design etc. by the person who came up with it. Intellectual property issues are gaining importance since globalization of the economy. Many products that used to be traded as low-technology goods or commodities now contain a higher proportion of invention and design in their value. Films, music recordings, books, computer software, on-line services, clothing, food, plants, biotechnology products, and many others are bought and sold because of the information, creativity, and identity they contain—not usually because of the plastic, metal, cloth, paper, or other material used to make them.

Intellectual property rights: Moral and legal claims or entitlements over intellectual property.

With the liberalization of the Indian economy, it is increasingly believed that adequate protection of intellectual property is a necessary element in encouraging foreign investment. Moreover, in other newly liberalised and rapidly expanding markets, like China, counterfeiting and piracy of branded goods is an issue in India. The types of counterfeit goods run the gamut from software, electronics, and clothing to pharmaceuticals and cosmetics. While counterfeits clearly do harm to brand equity, some may also pose a risk to consumers, such as counterfeit pharmaceuticals. Intellectual property laws—the Trademarks Act of 1999 and the Copyright Act of 1957—empower authorities to take action to prevent infringement, including counterfeit goods.

Subject Matter of Intellectual Property

IP is the creation of human intellect. It encompasses ideas, knowledge, invention, innovation, creativity, and research, all being the product of human mind and is similar to any property, whether movable or immovable, wherein the proprietor or the owner may exclusively use his property at will and has the right to prevent others from using it but with his permission. The rights relating to intellectual property are known as 'Intellectual Property Rights'.

Intellectual property: Ownership of an idea, design etc. by the person who came up with it.

IP is divided into two broad categories: Industrial property, which includes inventions (patents), trademarks, industrial designs, and geographic indications of source; and Copyright, which includes literary and artistic works such as novels, poems, plays, films, musical works, and artistic works such as drawings, paintings, photographs, and sculptures, and architectural designs. Rights related to copyright include those of performing artists in their performances, producers of phonograms in their recordings, and those of broadcasters in their radio and television programs. The innovations and creative expressions of indigenous and local communities are also IP, yet because they are 'traditional' they may not be fully protected by existing IP systems. Access to, and equitable benefit-sharing in, genetic resources also raise IP questions.

Rationale Behind Intellectual Property Protection

Most of the IP laws (with the exception of trademarks law) aim to promote progress. By exchanging limited exclusive rights for disclosure of inventions and creative works, society and the patentee/copyright owner mutually benefit, and an incentive is created for inventors and authors to create and disclose their work. Keeping in view the above aim, IP laws for time being in force seek to achieve the following objectives.

Financial Incentive

These exclusive rights allow owners of intellectual property to benefit from the property they have created, providing a financial incentive for the creation of an investment in intellectual property, and in case of patents, pay associated research and development costs. Some commentators, such as David Levine and Michele Boldrin, dispute this justification.

Economic Growth

The World Intellectual Property Organisation (WIPO) treaty and several related international agreements are premised on the notion that the protection of intellectual property rights is essential to maintaining economic growth. The WIPO Intellectual Property Handbook gives two reasons for intellectual property laws. One is to give statutory expression to the moral and economic rights of creators in their creations and the rights of the public in access to those creations. The second is to promote, as a deliberate act of government policy, creativity and the dissemination and application of its results and to encourage fair trading which would contribute to economic and social development.

The Anti-Counterfeiting Trade Agreement (ACTA) states that 'effective enforcement of intellectual property rights is critical to sustaining economic growth across all industries and globally'.

Economists estimate that two-thirds of the value of large businesses in the US can be traced to intangible assets. 'IP-intensive industries' are estimated to generate 72 per cent more value added (price minus material cost) per employee than 'non-IP-intensive industries'.

A joint research project of the WIPO and the United Nations University measuring the impact of IP systems on six Asian countries found 'a positive correlation between the strengthening of the IP system and subsequent economic growth.'

Protection of Moral and Material Interests

Article 27 of the Universal Declaration of Human Rights clearly states that everyone has the right to the protection of the moral and material interests resulting from any scientific, literary, or artistic production of which he is the author. Although the relationship between intellectual property and human rights is a complex one, there are moral arguments for intellectual property.

The arguments that justify intellectual property fall into three major categories. Personality theorists believe that intellectual property is an extension of an individual. Utilitarian believe that intellectual property stimulates social progress and pushes people to further innovation. Lockeans[1] argue that intellectual property is justified based on deservedness and hard work.

Various moral justifications for private property can be used to argue in favour of the morality of intellectual property, such as the following:

Natural rights/Justice argument This argument is based on Locke's idea that a person has a natural right over the labour and/or products which are produced by his/her body. Appropriating these products is viewed as unjust. Although Locke had never explicitly stated that natural right applied to products of the mind, it is possible to apply his argument to intellectual property rights, in which it would be unjust for people to misuse another's ideas.

Utilitarian–pragmatic argument According to this rationale, a society that protects private property is more effective and prosperous than societies that do not. Innovation and invention in the 19th century America has been said to be attributed to the development of the patent system. By providing innovators with 'durable and tangible return on their investment of time, labor, and other resources', intellectual property rights seek to maximise social utility. The presumption is that they promote public welfare by encouraging the 'creation, production, and distribution of intellectual works'.

Utilitarian argument Utilitarians argue that without intellectual property, there would be a lack of incentive to produce new ideas. Systems of protection such as intellectual property optimise social utility.

'Personality' argument This argument is based on a quote from Hegel, 'Every man has the right to turn his will upon a thing or make the thing an object of his will, that is to say, to set aside the mere thing and recreate it as his own'. European intellectual property law is shaped by this notion that ideas are an 'extension of oneself and of one's personality'. Personality theorists argue that by being a creator of something, one is inherently at risk and vulnerable for having their ideas and designs stolen and/or altered. Intellectual property protects these moral claims that have to do with personality.

International Dimension of Intellectual Property

International dimension of Intellectual Property may be studied through the following international treaties governing intellectual property rights in global context.

Paris Convention for the Protection of Industrial Property

The Paris Convention for the Protection of Industrial Property, signed in Paris, France, on 20 March 1883, was one of the first intellectual property treaties. It

1

established a Union for the protection of industrial property. It addresses patents, trademarks, unfair competition whether or not implicating marks, and the related industrial property of industrial designs, utility models, geographical indications, trade names, possibly trade secrets within the context of unfair competition, but not copyright. The Convention is still in force as of 2014 and is administered by the World Intellectual Property Organization (WIPO), based in Geneva, Switzerland.

Contracting Members

The Convention was initially (i.e. in 1883) signed by 11 countries, namely: Belgium, Brazil, France, Guatemala, Italy, the Netherlands, Portugal, El Salvador, Serbia, Spain and Switzerland. As of September 2014, the Convention has 176 contracting member countries including India of course, which makes it one of the most widely adopted treaties worldwide. Notably, Taiwan and Burma are not parties to the Convention. However, according to Article 27 of its Patent Act, Taiwan recognizes priority claims from contracting members.

Substantive Provisions of the Convention

The substantive provisions of the Convention fall into three main categories: national treatment, priority right and common rules.

National treatment

According to Articles 2 and 3 of this treaty, juristic and natural persons who are either national of or domiciled in a state party to the Convention shall, as regards the protection of industrial property, enjoy in all the other countries of the Union, the advantages that their respective laws grant to nationals. That is, when an applicant files an application for a patent or a trademark in a foreign country member of the Union, the application receives the same treatment as if it came from a national of this foreign country.

Priority right

The 'Convention priority right', also called 'Paris Convention priority right' or 'Union priority right', provides that an applicant from one contracting State shall be able to use its first filing date (in one of the contracting State) as the effective filing date in another contracting State, provided that the applicant files a subsequent application within 6 months (for industrial designs and trademarks) or 12 months (for patents and utility models) from the first filing.

Common rules

The convention besides invoking common rules concerning trademarks, and unfair competition among the member countries, provides for the following substantive rules protecting patents and patentees:

1. The principle of independence of patents A patent application in one country of the Union is examined and granted or denied independent of applications for patents for the same or related inventions filed in other countries within and without the Union.

2. Right of the inventor to be mentioned The inventor has the right to be named as such in the patent.

3. Patentability not effected by restrictions on the product A patent shall not be refused or invalidated because the product patented or obtained by means of a patented process is subject to restrictions on its sale or importation under the domestic law.

4. Importation of patented products or products made from patented processes Importation into a member country of products for which a patent has been granted in that country manufactured in another member country cannot result in forfeiture of patent rights in the country of importation.

5. Failure to work and compulsory licenses Member countries are allowed to enact protectionist legislative measures granting compulsory licenses in order to prevent abuses that might result from the exclusive rights conferred by a patent for invention.

6. Grace period for maintenance fees Holding patents in member states shall be entitled to a grace period of at least six months to pay prescribed maintenance fees, and allows member states to provide for the restoration of patents that have lapsed by reason of non-payment of maintenance fees.

Berne Convention for the Protection of Literary and Artistic Works

The Berne Convention for the Protection of Literary and Artistic Works, usually known as the Berne

Convention, is an international agreement governing copyright, which was first accepted in Berne, Switzerland, in 1886. The Berne Convention followed in the footsteps of the Paris Convention for the Protection of Industrial Property of 1883, which in the same way had created a framework for international integration of the other types of intellectual property: patents, trademarks and industrial designs except the copyright.

Like the Paris Convention, the Berne Convention set up two bureaus to handle administrative tasks. In 1893 these two small bureaus merged and became the United International Bureau for the Protection of Intellectual Property (BIRPI), situated in Berne. In 1960, BIRPI moved to Geneva, to be closer to the United Nations and other international organizations in that city. In 1967 it became the World Intellectual Property Organization (WIPO), and in 1974 became an organization within the United Nations. As of September 2014, there are 168 nations including India that are parties to the Berne Convention. This includes 167 UN member states.

The Berne Convention states that all works except photographic and cinematographic shall be copyrighted for at least 50 years after the author's death, but parties are free to provide longer terms, as the European Union did with the 1993 Directive on harmonizing the term of copyright protection. For photography, the Berne Convention sets a minimum term of 25 years from the year the photograph was created, and for cinematography the minimum is 50 years after first showing, or 50 years after creation if it hasn't been shown within 50 years after the creation. Countries under the older revisions of the treaty may choose to provide their own protection terms, and certain types of works (such as phonorecords and motion pictures) may be provided shorter terms.

Patent Cooperation Treaty

The Patent Cooperation Treaty (PCT) is an international patent law treaty, concluded in 1970. It provides a unified procedure for filing patent applications to protect inventions in each of its contracting states. A patent application filed under the PCT is called an international application, or PCT application.

A single filing of a PCT application is made with a Receiving Office (RO) in one language. It then results in a search performed by an International Searching Authority (ISA), accompanied by a written opinion regarding the patentability of the invention, which is the subject of the application. Finally, the relevant national or regional authorities administer matters related to the examination of application (if provided by national law) and issuance of patent.

A PCT application does not itself result in the grant of a patent, since there is no such thing as an 'international patent', and the grant of patent is a prerogative of each national or regional authority. In other words, a PCT application, which establishes a filing date in all contracting states, must be followed up with the step of entering into national or regional phases to proceed towards grant of one or more patents. The PCT procedure essentially leads to a standard national or regional patent application, which may be granted or rejected according to applicable law, in each jurisdiction in which a patent is desired.

The contracting states, the states which are parties to the PCT, constitute the International Patent Cooperation Union. A majority of the world's countries are parties to the PCT, including all of the major industrialized countries (with a few exceptions, including Argentina, and Taiwan). India being a signatory to WTO is a member of PCT. As of 12 July 2013, there were 148 contracting states to the PCT. Saudi Arabia became the 147th contracting state on 3 May 2013 and Iran the 148th contracting state on 4 July 2013.

The International Union for the Protection of New Varieties of Plants (UPOV)

As early as 1930, the United States of America introduced a special form of exclusive right called a plant patent, which was, however, available only for asexually reproduced varieties. Subsequently a group of European States came together in 1961 to establish the International Convention for the Protection of New Varieties of Plants (the Convention), which was revised in 1972, 1978 and 1991. The Convention also establishes the International Union for the Protection of New Varieties of Plants which is known as UPOV (the name 'UPOV' is an acronym derived from the French translation of these words). The Convention as revised in 1991 is called 'the 1991 Act.' The Convention potentially protects all plant varieties irrespective of their mode of reproduction or of the technology used in their development.

UPOV is an independent, international, intergovernmental organization, with an international legal personality. Its headquarters are in Geneva, and it employs its own staff. As of June 10, 2014, *UPOV* has 72 *members* including India. UPOV cooperates very closely in administrative matters with the World Intellectual Property Organization (WIPO), a specialized agency of the United Nations. The Secretary-General of UPOV is the Director General of WIPO, the UPOV headquarters is in the same building as WIPO, and UPOV receives a range of support services from WIPO.

WCT and WPPT

The Berne Convention for the Protection of Literary and Artistic Works, after its adoption in 1886, was revised quite regularly, approximately every 20 years, until revisions which took place in Stockholm in 1967 and in Paris in 1971. The revision conferences were convened, in general, in order to find responses to new technological developments, such as sound recording technology, photography, radio, cinematography and television. In the 1970s and 1980s, a number of important new technological developments took place, namely: reprography, video technology, compact cassette systems facilitating 'home taping,' satellite broadcasting, cable television, the increase of the importance of computer programs, computer storage of works and electronic databases, etc. After the adoption of the TRIPS Agreement under the auspices of GATT, the preparatory work of new copyright and related rights norms in the WIPO committees was intensified to deal with problems not addressed by the TRIPS Agreement. Finally, in 1996 the WIPO Diplomatic Conference on Certain Copyright and Related Rights Questions adopted two treaties – the WIPO Copyright Treaty (WCT) and the WIPO Performances and Phonograms Treaty (WPPT).

WCT provides additional protections for copyright for deemed necessary due to advances in information technology since the formation of previous copyright treaties before it. It ensures that computer programs are protected as literary works, and that the arrangement and selection of material in databases is protected. It provides authors of works with control over their rental and which they may not have under the Berne Convention alone. It also prohibits unauthorized modification of rights management information contained in works. As of December 2014, the treaty has been ratified by 93 states. India is also a proud member of the treaty.

WPPT on the other hand supplements the Berne Convention for the Protection of Literary and Artistic Works (Berne Convention) and the International Convention for the Protection of Performers, Producers of Phonograms and Broadcasting Organizations (Rome Convention). Like WCT, WPPT was created to address changes in digital technology and communications, particularly the distribution of digitally protected works over the Internet. The WPPT IS implemented in the U.S. as the Digital Millennium Copyright Act (DMCA). Besides India, the WPPT was adopted by a consensus of 100 member states of the European Union (EU) in Geneva, Switzerland on December 20, 1996.

Categories of Intellectual Property Rights

In order to develop a proper understanding, all the IPRs can be classified under the following two broad areas:

1. One area of IPRs can be characterised as the protection of distinctive signs, in particular, trademarks (which distinguish the goods or services of one undertaking from those of other undertakings) and geographical indications (which identify a good as originating in a place where a given characteristic of the good is essentially attributable to its geographical origin).
2. Other types of IPRs are related to protection of industrial property to stimulate innovation, design, and creation of technology. This category includes inventions (protected by patents), industrial designs, and trade secrets, which are of value.

Accordingly, common types of intellectual property rights include the following:

- Patents
- Copyright
- Industrial design rights
- Trademarks
- Trade dress, and
- 'Trade Secrets'

Patents

Patent: An exclusive right granted by a sovereign state (Central Government) to an inventor for a limited period of time in exchange of detailed public disclosure of an invention.

Patents, as a matter of fact, form the heart of intellectual property. The term 'patent' has originated from the Latin word patere, which means 'to lay open', i.e., to make available for public inspection. In modern usage, a patent grants an inventor or their assignee exclusive or say monopoly right to make, use, sell, and import an invention for a limited period of time, in exchange for the public disclosure of the invention. An invention in this behalf is a new, useful, and non-obvious solution to a specific technological problem, which may be a product or a process. Some other types of intellectual property rights are also called patents in some jurisdictions: industrial design rights are called design patents in the US, plant breeders' rights are sometimes called plant patents, and utility models are sometimes called petty patents or innovation patents.

A patent is an exclusionary right as it provides its inventor with the right to exclude others from making, using, selling, offering for sale, or importing the patented invention for the term of the patent, which is usually 20 years from the filing date. Like any other property right, it may be sold, licensed, mortgaged, assigned or transferred, given away, or simply abandoned.

The Patents Act, 1970

In India, The Patents Act, 1970, deals with the patenting of inventions. An invention relating to a product or a process that is new, non-obvious, i.e., inventive, and has industrial application can be patented in India provided it does not fall into the category of non-patentable under the (Indian) Patents Act. A patent application can be filed with the office of Controller of Patents, which is headquartered in Kolkata with sittings at Delhi, Chennai, and Mumbai, either alone or jointly, by true and first inventor or his assignee. The application is referred by the Controller to the Examiner upon a formal request by the Applicant to check whether the invention is non-obvious and useful and also if the invention has already been claimed by some other person. After the First Examination Report is issued, the Applicant is given an opportunity by the patent office to meet the objections raised in the report. The Applicant has to comply with the requirements within 12 months from the issuance of the First Examination Report. If the requirements of the first examination report are not complied with within the stipulated time, then the application is treated to have been abandoned by the applicant. After the removal of objections and compliance of requirements, the Controller publishes the application in the official gazette to give an opportunity to public to register their pre-grant opposition under Section 25(1), against the grant of patent, if any. After successful removal of objections, if any, a patent is granted and notified in the Patent Office Journal. Now the patent holder (patentee) is free to use, sell, assign, or license his right in patent. However, a post-grant opposition under Section 25(2) can be filed by any person interested within 12 months from the date of publication of grant.

What is not patentable in India?

By merely fulfilling the basic patentability requirements, i.e., the invention should be novel, inventive, and capable of industrial application, one cannot get patent for all the inventions in India even though they meet all the above criteria. In broad-spectrum, inventions which are contrary to public order or morality or likely to cause serious intolerance to human, animal, or plant life or health or to the environment are categorically prohibited under the (Indian) Patents Act. Sections (3) and (4) of the Act have extensive list of areas which are not patentable in India. A recap of such areas is given below:

1. An invention which is frivolous or which claims anything obvious or contrary to the well established natural law. An invention, the primary or intended use of which would be contrary to law or morality or injurious to public health.

2. A discovery, scientific theory, or mathematical method.
3. A mere discovery of any new property or new use for a known substance or of the mere use of a known process, machine, or apparatus unless such known process results in a new product or employs at least one new reactant.
4. A substance obtained by a mere admixture resulting only in the aggregation of the properties of the components thereof or a process for producing such substance.
5. A mere arrangement or re-arrangement or duplication of a known device each functioning independently of the other in its own way.
6. A method or process of testing applicable during the process of manufacture for rendering the machine, apparatus, or other equipment more efficient for the improvement or restoration of the existing machine, apparatus, or other equipment or for the improvement or control of manufacturer.
7. A method of agriculture or horticulture.
8. A method or process for the medicinal, surgical, curative, prophylactic, or other treatment of human beings or any process for a similar treatment of animals or plants to render them free of disease or to increase their economic value or that of their products.
9. An invention relating to atomic energy falling under the Atomic Energy Act, 1962.

Patent monopoly and doctrine of exhaustion

A patent is granted for an invention that is new, inventive, and is capable of industrial applications. The patent holder is able to exploit and control the use of patented matter since a patent gives its owner the right to exclude third party, not having his consent, from making, using, offering for sale, selling, or importing the patented invention during the term of the patent. The underlying principle behind providing these exclusive rights is to 'promote the progress of science and useful arts' by providing inventors the incentive to invest in researching and developing innovative technology. However, as a measure of natural law of justice doctrine of exhaustion operates which dictates that the patent owner's exclusive rights be limited in scope. Accordingly, upon receiving compensation, patentee's voluntary introduction of a patented good into commerce without restriction prevents him from exercising his right to exclude others from using or reselling that good.

The doctrine was first recognised by the United States Supreme Court in 1873 in Adams vs. Burke. In that case, the patentee authorised a licensee to make, use, and sell patented coffin lids only within a ten-mile radius in Boston. A customer of the licensee bought the coffin lids within the ten-mile radius, but later resold the lids outside the ten-mile radius. The patentee sued the customer, but the Supreme Court found no infringement. In 2008 also, the United States Supreme Court issued its unanimous decision in Quanta Computer, Inc. vs. LG Electronics, Inc. and held, the patent law cannot be used to control the subsequent use or disposition of a product 'that substantially embodies a patent' once the product has been sold with authority of the patent owner. 'The authorised sale of an article that substantially embodies a patent exhausts the patent holder's rights and prevents the patent holder from invoking the patent law to control post sale use of the article'.

Incremental innovation, generic drugs, and patent protection

Courts in India are empowered to disallow patent guard to a patent holder in the interest of masses if the patent holder fails to fulfill the stipulated measure or tends to exploit the patent. Very recently, the Supreme Court (of India) upheld the Intellectual Property Appellate Board's (IPAB) decision to deny patent protection to Novartis, the Swiss multinational pharmaceutical company in respect of its anti-blood cancer drug, branded as Glivec, saying it is an example of 'incremental innovation' under Section 3(d) of the Indian Patents Act and thus not liable for protection. The court clearly said that the company failed to satisfy the criteria stipulated in the Act such as research data clarifying the increased 'therapeutic efficacy' of the innovation. The ruling ends Novartis' attempts to secure a patent for the drug and strikes a balance between patents and affordability. Patients would have otherwise been forced to pay ₹1.20 lakh for a month's dosage if the court case had gone in favour of Novartis. Generic variants of Glivec, comparable in dosage, strength, and intended use, offered by Cipla Ltd., an Indian Pharmaceutical Major, cost just ₹8,000 per month. Novartis' earlier challenge to the constitutionality and TRIPs compatibility of Indian patent law was rebuffed by the Madras High Court in 2007 and no appeal was pursued. The judgment on Glivec is a blow for a patent regime with a higher threshold of inventiveness. Just prior to this, Roche Ltd., a Swiss Global healthcare company, was stripped off its patent for Peginterferon, a powerful antiviral drug treatment for chronic hepatitis *B* and *C* in February, 2013, by IPAB, good eight years after it was granted. Previously, the multinational patentee (Roche) had been denied injunction by Delhi High Court on the ground that it sold a more expensive drug than the infringing generic manufacturer. The rulings on Glivec and Peginterferon marked a crucial conclusion to a saga that has been several decades in the making. Here it is pertinent to mention that IPAB is authorised to hear and adjudicate upon appeals from most of the decisions, orders, or directions made by the Patent Controller as well as all pending appeals from the Indian High Courts under the Patents Act. The IPAB has its headquarters at Chennai and has sittings at Mumbai, Delhi, Kolkata, and Ahmadabad.

The Indian patent law, which albeit has come under severe criticism (owing to above Supreme Court ruling) from the US and UK based Pharma MNCs, has become a mode of sorts for developing and under-developed countries who are trying to frame stringent norms that would keep bad patents at bay. Taking a cue from India, the Philippines adopted a law similar to Section 3(d) [of Indian Patents Act, 1970]—that denies patents on incremental innovations and was pivotal in the Novartis judgment while formulating its patent law. Uganda, which will introduce its patent bill in 2016, has partially adopted India's Section 3(d) in it. Moreover, IP Australia, a government-appointed body that looks into the issue of patent laws in Australia, released a draft report last week that raised concerns against the indiscriminate grant of patents to minor innovations; it further called for an independent body to vet new approvals. Similarly, several South Asian countries have amended their patent laws to include compulsory license provisions to allow the entry of generic drugs in case of an emergency, unusual circumstances, or public interest. For example, in October 2012, Indonesia issued compulsory licenses on seven HIV/AIDS drugs and a hepatitis *B* medicine manufactured by Merck & Co, GSK, Bristol-Myers Squibb, Abbott, and Gilead.

National policy on IPR by government-constituted think-tank

The Commerce and Industry Ministry has most recently constituted a six-member 'Think-Tank' to draft the National Intellectual Property Rights (IPR) policy. This policy moots the concept of 'innovation patents' or 'petty patents' which is being seen as the latest development in the IP Protection system in India and seems to give a ray of hope to the architects of small inventions against all sorts of commercial misuse of their innovations. The panel, being chaired by retired Justice Ms. Prabha Sridevan, will identify areas in IPRs where study needs to be conducted and furnish recommendations in this regard to the Ministry of Commerce and Industry. The expert group, set up by Department of Industrial Policy and Promotion (DIPP), will also advise the government on best practices to be followed in trademark offices, patent offices and other government offices dealing with IPRs to create an efficient and transparent system of functioning in the said offices. Embracing an idea from the US, China, Japan, Australia, Germany and others, who protect Utility Models, several experts have argued for some form of IP protection for what is commonly known as 'Jugaad Innovation' that takes place across sectors in India. Probably taking a cue from them the above panel on IPRs has proposed exclusive protection for small inventions through a new law on utility models to boost B2B, industry-academia ties.

Also known as 'petty patents' and 'innovation patents', this form of intellectual property grants exclusive rights to the owner to prevent others from commercially using protected innovation for a limited period of time. Requirements will be less stringent than for patents and terms of protection offered to them are also typically shorter (average 7–10 years), though rules vary across nations. They are popular with Micro, Small and Medium Enterprises (MSMEs), being easier to obtain and cheaper to maintain. MSMEs account for about 45% of the manufacturing sector's output, thereby contributing considerably towards the nation's GDP, but according to the 'Think-Tank', their potential IP assets are recognized only in a limited, often informal manner. India has a large number of inventions that may not satisfy the criteria of patentability, but are novel, utilitarian and inventive. The current framework leaves out a large number of inventors from protecting their products through IPRs, particularly those from the MSMEs and informal sectors.

Other major reforms recommended by the above 'Think-Tank' include having a specialized patent bench in the high courts of Bombay, Calcutta, Delhi and Madras for speedy disposal of patent-related cases, creation of a body in the government to coordinate IP related matters with ministries.

Copyright

Copyright: Exclusive right of the creator of an original work to his creation (work). It gives the creator of an original work exclusive right to it, usually for a limited time.

A copyright gives the creator of an original work exclusive right to it, usually for a limited time. The rights of authors of literary and artistic works (such as books and other writings, musical compositions, paintings, sculpture, computer programs, and films) are protected by copyright. In addition, protection is granted to related or neighbouring rights like the rights of performers (e.g., actors, singers, and musicians), producers of phonograms (sound recordings), and broadcasting organizations. Copyright may apply to a wide range of creative, intellectual, or artistic forms, or 'works'. Copyright does not cover ideas and information themselves, only the form or manner in which they are expressed.

India's copyright law, laid down in the Indian Copyright Act, 1957, as amended by Copyright (Amendment) Act, 1999, fully reflects the Berne Convention on copyrights, to which India is a party. Additionally, India is party to the Geneva Convention for the Protection of Producers of Phonograms and to the Universal Copyright Convention. India is also an active member of WIPO, Geneva, and UNESCO.

The copyright law has been amended periodically to keep pace with changing requirements. The recent amendment to the copyright law, which came into force in May 1995, has ushered in comprehensive changes and brought the copyright law in line with the developments in satellite broadcasting, computer software, and digital technology. The amended law has made provisions for the first time to protect performer's rights as envisaged in the Rome Convention.

Several measures have been adopted to strengthen and streamline the enforcement of copyrights. These include the setting up of a Copyright Enforcement Advisory Council, training programs for enforcement officers, and setting up special policy cells to deal with cases relating to infringement of copyrights.

Industrial Design Rights

An industrial design right protects the visual design of objects that are not purely utilitarian or functional in nature (and are not themselves copyrightable) but have some aesthetic or ornamental value. For example, while the design of a piece of luggage is purely functional (a useful article) hence not copyrightable, the addition of certain ornamental, artistic elements to the design may make those parts of that luggage 'artistic' and thus copyrightable. An industrial design or say just design consists of the creation of a shape, configuration, or composition of pattern or color, or combination of pattern and color in three-dimensional form containing artistic value. The designs in India are governed by the Designs Act, 2000 which has replaced the Design Act, 2011. The essential purpose of design law it to promote and protect the registered designs. It is also intended to promote innovative (design) activity in the field of industries. The Designs Act of 2000 inter alia includes not only trademarks alone but also the 'artistic works'. Therefore the definition of design under the new Act is an improved one and more comprehensive. A design to be registrable must be new or original. 'Original', in relation to a design, means originating from the author of such design and includes the cases which though old in themselves yet are new in their application. It should not previously be published in India or anywhere in the world. It should be significantly distinguishable from known designs or combination of known designs and should not comprise or contain scandalous or obscene matter. It should also be not contrary to public order or morality.

On the design being registered, the Controller General of Patents, Designs and Trade Marks (CGPDTM) grants a certificate of registration to the proprietor. When a design is registered, the registered proprietor of the design shall have copyright in the design during ten years from the date of registration. Provision for the extension of the period of the copyright for another 5 years is also provided under the new Act. Copyright under the Act means the exclusive right to apply a design to any article in any class in which the design is registered. The Designs Act, 2000 uses the term piracy of registered designs instead of term infringement in relation to violation of a registered design and provides for harsh disciplinary actions against the offenders.

Trademarks

Trademark: A recognizable sign, design, or expression which identifies products or services of a particular source from those of others.

A trademark (or trade mark) is a recognizable sign, design or expression which identifies products or services of a particular source from those of others. As per Section 2(m) of Trademark Act, a mark can include a device, brand, heading, label, ticket, name, signature, word, letter, numeral, shape of goods, packaging, or combination of colours, or any such combinations. Trademarks are used to claim exclusive properties of products or services. They serve to identify a particular business as the source of goods or services. A trademark may be located on a package, a label, a voucher, or on the product itself. Trademarks can be owned, but also licensed. Licenses can be bought from trademark owners and brokers. It should be noted here that one may confuse between trademarks and brands. However, whereas trademarks have purely legal implications, branding focuses exclusively on aspects of marketing.

The Government of India provides protection to trademarks statutorily under the Trademark Act, 1999, and also under the common law remedy of passing off. Statutory protection of trademark is administered by the Controller General of Patents, Designs, and Trademarks, a government agency which reports to the Department of Industrial Policy and Promotion (DIPP), under the Ministry of Commerce and Industry. The law of trademark deals with the mechanism of registration, protection of trademark, and prevention of fraudulent trademark. The law also provides for the rights acquired by registration of trademark, modes of transfer, and assignment of the rights, nature of infringements, penalties for such infringement, and remedies available to the owner in case of such infringement.

Trademark registration gives exclusive proprietary rights to the mark's owner. Applications for registration of trademarks are to be filed in the prescribed manner. Any person claiming to be the proprietor of a trademark used or proposed to be used by him, who is desirous of registering it, shall apply in writing to the Registrar in the prescribed manner for the registration of his trade mark. The application inter alia shall

1. Explain with sufficient precision, a description by words, of the trademark if necessary, to determine the right of the application;
2. Be able to depict the graphical representation of the trademark;
3. Be considered as a three-dimensional trademark only if the application contains a statement to that effect;
4. Be considered as a trademark consisting of a combination of colours only if the application contains a statement to that effect.

Applications are examined to ensure compliance with the law and to ensure they do not conflict with marks that are already registered or pending. Details and exhaustive explanation for adoption of the mark by the applicant must appear to be reasonably justified and convincing. Accepted applications are advertised in the Trade Marks Journal and opposition may be filed within three-month time from the date of publication in the Journal; a one-month extension for filing opposition can be obtained within the three-month period. Registration is good for 10 years, renewable every 10 years. However, a trademark that has not been used for five years or more from the date of registration can be cancelled for non-use.

Trademark owners alleging infringement of their registered mark by another mark can file suit, seeking an injunction, damages, and an order for delivery-up of the infringing labels and marks for destruction. Unregistered trademarks well known in India or internationally may be protected against misuse in a passing off action.

Trade Dress

Trade dress: Visual appearance of a product or its packaging that signify the source of the product to consumers.

Trade dress is a legal term of art that generally refers to characteristics of the visual appearance of a product or its packaging (or even the design of a building) that signify the source of the product to consumers. A product's trade dress—its distinctive appearance, color, design, shape, packaging, and even its aroma—is a crucial component of its brand equity. India's Trademarks Act of 1999 specifically included elements of trade dress, for both products and packaging, within its definition of trademark.

Courts in India have consistently reinforced trade dress protection. One of the most cited cases is Colgate Palmolive Co. vs. Anchor Health and Beauty Care Pvt. Ltd. in the Delhi High Court. The plaintiff disputed the use by the other company of a distinctive red and white pattern in a precise proportion, together with the style of lettering on dentifrice packaging. Colgate argued it has used the red and white pattern since 1951, where the defendant started using its design in 1996. The court ruled for the plaintiff, indicating that the infringement on Colgate's well-established and distinctive color scheme could cause both confusion in the marketplace and dilution of Colgate's brand. In another case, Kangaro Industries Ltd. vs. Evershine STY, the Delhi High Court issued an injunction to stop the defendant's use of a distinctive design and color combination featuring the image of a frog. Kangaro, a well-known office equipment and stationery brand, was found to have prior rights to this distinctive trade dress. Other similar cases have upheld the trade dress rights of other well-known brands, including Cadbury Gems and its distinctive 'pillow' packaging.

Trade Secrets

A fifth type of intellectual property, in addition to patents, trademarks (including trade dress), industrial design rights, and copyrights, is trade secrets. Broadly speaking, any confidential business information which provides an enterprise a competitive edge may be considered a trade secret. It may be a formula, practice, business process, design, device, pattern, or compilation of information which is not generally known or reasonably ascertainable, by which a business can obtain an economic advantage over competitors or customers. The unauthorised use of such information by persons other than the holder is regarded as an unfair practice and a violation of the trade secret. In the US, trade secret law is primarily handled at the state level under the Uniform Trade Secrets Act, which most states have adopted, and a federal law, the Economic Espionage Act of 1996, which makes the theft or misappropriation of a trade secret a federal crime.

Trade secret: Any confidential business information that provides an enterprise with a competitive advantage.

In India, the protection of trade secrets is Common Law based. However, Section 27 of the Indian Contract Act provides some sort of limited remedy; it bars any person from disclosing any information which he acquires as a result of a contract. Courts can protect trade secrets by enjoining misappropriation, ordering parties that have misappropriated a trade secret to take steps to maintain its secrecy, as well as ordering payment of a royalty to the owner. Courts can also award damages, court costs, and reasonable attorneys' fees. This protection is, however, very limited because a trade secret holder is only protected from unauthorised disclosure and use which is referred to as misappropriation. If a trade secret holder fails to maintain secrecy or if the information is independently discovered, becomes released, or otherwise becomes generally known, protection as a trade secret is lost. Trade secrets do not expire so protection continues until discovery of loss.

Protection of trade secrets is very important and one of the most challenging tasks for the Indian government as this will enhance the foreign investment in India giving a boost to the Indian economy. Foreign investors have to be assured of the protection of their trade secrets, so that they can do business with our country. A proper policy for trade secret protection will further enhance the security in our own industry. Almost all the countries in the world have a policy for the protection of trade secrets and India also being a signatory to the TRIPs is under an obligation to amend its laws or create a new law in order to safeguard the trade secrets of various businesses. So a proper policy for the protection of trade secrets in India is the need of the hour in order to provide a sense of security among the foreign investors and the local businessmen regarding their trade secrets which will further boost the Indian economy.

Enforcement of IPRs

Intellectual property rights have to be enforceable. Or, more precisely, the TRIPs Agreement says that governments have to provide effective procedures for enforcement. However, the question of discussing enforcement routinely in the TRIPs Council has sometimes been controversial.

Some developed countries considered counterfeiting and piracy to be a serious problem and wanted to discuss it; developing countries resisted, fearing that this would target them and be used to argue for new standards more stringent than those in TRIPs.

Recently (in 2011) the discussion has focused on an Anti-Counterfeiting Trade Agreement (ACTA) negotiated by a group of countries. The ACTA countries said that the opposition to undertaking work on enforcement in the WTO was one reason why they negotiated the agreement outside the WTO.

A number of developing countries said they were concerned about the possibility that access to medicines could be impeded, that pressure would increase on countries to protect intellectual property to a higher standard than required in the WTO (the ACTA countries said they would not), and about the implications for the WTO system of discussing an agreement negotiated outside the WTO.

Emerging Issues in Intellectual Property

Intellectual property plays an important role in an increasingly broad spectrum, ranging from the Internet to healthcare to nearly all aspects of science and technology and literature and arts. Understanding the role of intellectual property in these areas—many of them still emerging—often requires significant new research and study. In an effort to promote informed discussion of the intellectual property issues involved in these fields, WIPO regularly produces various explanatory publications on current issues of interest.

Briefly, following are some of the issues, recently discussed in the TRIPs Council and brought out by WIPO.

TRIPs and Public Health

No conflict The 2001 Doha Declaration on TRIPs and Public Health was a political statement affirming that intellectual property protection and public health objectives do not contradict each other: 'We agree that the TRIPs Agreement does not and should not prevent members from taking measures to protect public health'. It gave governments the confidence to use the flexibilities available in the TRIPs Agreement, e.g., compulsory licensing and parallel imports.

Rule-change needed: The 'paragraph 6 system' One issue needed a change in the rules. The declaration's paragraph 6 dealt with TRIPs Article 31(f), which limited the amount nations could export under a compulsory license to countries needing the medicines. A 'waiver' agreed in 2003, and a pending amendment agreed in 2005, allow generic medicines to be made under compulsory licenses exclusively for export to countries that cannot produce the medicines themselves.

WHO-WIPO-WTO cooperation An important result of the 2001 declaration has been closer work between the World Health Organization, World Intellectual Property Organization, and WTO. This has focused both on access to medicines and incentives for research and development so that new medical technologies become available. Ensuring poorer patients are able to access medicines and other health products involves proper (rational) use of the products, affordable prices, properly designed health systems, suitable financing, and careful selection strategies for procuring the products.

TRIPs, Biodiversity, Traditional Knowledge, Plants, and Life Forms

In the TRIPs Council, these topics are usually discussed—a 'triplet' of related issues. They come under the Doha Development Agenda although members disagree on whether they are negotiations. These issues are also discussed in separate consultations chaired by the Director-General or a deputy.

Animals and plants TRIPs Article 27.3(b) deals with patentability or non-patentability of plant and animal inventions, and the protection of plant varieties. It has been under review in the TRIPs Council for several years. The Doha Declaration added:

TRIPs and CBD The relationship between the TRIPs Agreement and the UN Convention on Biological Diversity.

Traditional knowledge The protection of traditional knowledge and folklore.

The TRIPs Council's review of the three is guided by the TRIPs Agreement's objective (i.e., innovation and technology transfer for social and economic benefits) and principles (i.e., health and other social and economic objectives, and the abuse of rights), and must take development fully into account.

Technology Transfer to Least-developed Countries

Intellectual property protection should contribute to technical innovation and the transfer of technology. Producers and users both should benefit; so should economies and societies at large. Developing and least developed countries, in particular, see technology transfer as part of the bargain in which they have agreed to protect intellectual property rights. The TRIPs Agreement includes a number of provisions on this. For instance, it says one of the purposes of protecting intellectual property is to promote innovation and technology transfer, and it requires developed countries' governments to provide incentives for their companies and institutions to transfer technology to least-developed countries.

Geographical Indications

Geographical indications are place names (in some countries also words associated with a place) used to identify the origin and quality, reputation or other characteristics of products (for example, 'Champagne', 'Tequila', or 'Roquefort').

Geographical indications: Place names used to identify the origin and quality, reputation, or other characteristics of products.

The TRIPs Agreement handles this in three articles.

Standard Article 22 defines geographical indications and sets a standard level of protection. All have to be protected in order to avoid misleading the public and to prevent unfair competition.

Higher Article 23 applies only to protection for wines and spirits and says that subject to a number of exceptions their names have to be protected against incorrect use even where this would not mislead the public.

Exceptions Article 24 implies, for example, that a term does not have to be protected in a country if it has become generic or has already been protected as a trademark in that country.

Two issues are debated in the TRIPs Council under the Doha mandate: negotiations to create a multilateral geographical indication register for wines and spirits; and discussions on extending the higher level of protection beyond wines and spirits.

'Non-violation' Complaints

WTO agreements allow countries to bring cases against each other if one feels that another government's action or a specific situation has deprived it of an expected benefit, even if no agreement has been violated. However, opinions differ among WTO members on whether non-violation cases are feasible in intellectual property. The TRIPs Agreement contains a temporary restraint on bringing non-violation complaints. This has been extended several times, more recently from one Ministerial Conference to the next.

Exercises

I. Objective-type Questions

1. Which IPR Act deals with protection of computer software in India?
   (a) Patents Act, 1970
   (b) Copyright Act, 1970
   (c) Trademarks Act, 1999
   (d) The Designs Act, 2000
2. Negotiations about intellectual property rights are most important to:
   (a) India
   (b) Russia
   (c) China
   (d) The United States
3. The objective(s) of intellectual property law is/are
   (a) financial incentive
   (b) economic growth
   (c) protection of moral and material interests
   (d) all of the above
4. Locke's idea that 'a person has a natural right over the labour and/or products which are produced by his/her body' is justified by which of the following arguments?
   (a) Utilitarian–pragmatic argument
   (b) Justice argument
   (c) Personality argument
   (d) Utilitarian argument
5. What is the term of a patent?
   (a) 10 years
   (b) 20 years
   (c) 25 years
   (d) Unlimited
6. What does 'utilitarian' indicate in context of copyrights?
   (a) Novelty
   (b) Functional
   (c) Not useful
   (d) Obsolete
7. Infringement in relation to copyright implies:
   (a) breach
   (b) honour
   (c) credit
   (d) nobility
8. The owner of a patent can grant license:
   (a) to registered companies only
   (b) to individuals only
   (c) to anyone
   (d) to anyone but only after taking permission from the Controller General of Patents, Designs, and Trademarks
9. A patent application was filed in February 2000. The patent was granted in September 2011. In 2012, the inventor wants to file for some improvements in the invention. The patent on improvement would be valid until:
   (a) 2032
   (b) 2020
   (c) 2031
   (d) none of the above
10. When can an opposition to the grant of a patent be filed in India?
    (a) Anytime after the publication of the article but before the grant of patent
    (b) Anytime after the grant of the patent
    (c) Within one year after publication of the grant of the patent
    (d) Both (a) and (c)

II. Review Questions

1. What does property refer to in legal sense?
2. What is the relation of copyright to protection of industrial design?

3. Describe the aim and objectives of intellectual property laws for time being in force.
4. What is not patentable in India? Describe the procedure for grant of patents in India.
5. Enumerate the seven types of intellectual properties recognised by TRIPs Agreement. ,
6. Give a brief overview of intellectual property laws in India.
7. 'A patent to be granted protection under Indian patent law, the patent in question should be worthy of patent protection'. Do you agree? Elaborate in the light of leading recent rulings of the Supreme Court and the High Courts of India.
8. Write an explanatory note on 'incremental innovation, generic medicines, and patent protection'.

Answers to Objective-type Questions

1. (b) 2. (d) 3. (d) 4. (b) 5. (b)
6. (b) 7. (a) 8. (c) 9. (b) 10. (d)

32 Chapter in Review

LEARNING OUTCOMES

LO[1] Subject matter of intellectual property

LO[2] Aim and objectives of intellectual property laws

LO[3] Intellectual Property Rights

LO[4] Patents

LO[5] Copyrights

LO[6] Design

LO[7] Trademark

LO[8] Trade dress

LO[9] Trade secrets

LO[10] Contemporary issues in intellectual property rights

KEY TERMS

Intellectual property rights: Moral and legal claims or entitlements over intellectual property.

Intellectual property: Ownership of an idea, design etc. by the person who came up with it.

Patent: An exclusive right granted by a sovereign state (Central Government) to an inventor for a limited period of time in exchange of detailed public disclosure of an invention.

Copyright: Exclusive right of the creator of an original work to his creation (work). It gives the creator of an original work exclusive right to it, usually for a limited time.

Trademark: A recognizable sign, design, or expression which identifies products or services of a particular source from those of others.

Trade dress: Visual appearance of a product or its packaging that signify the source of the product to consumers.

Trade secret: Any confidential business information that provides an enterprise with a competitive advantage.

LO[1] The rights relating to intellectual property (IP) are known as 'intellectual property rights'. IP refers to the ownership of an idea, design etc. by the person who came up with it. IP is divided into two categories: Industrial property, which includes inventions (patents), trademarks, industrial designs, and geographic indications of source; and copyright, which includes literary and artistic works such as novels, poems, plays, films, musical works, and artistic works—drawings, paintings, sculptures, and architectural designs.

LO[2] The stated objectives of most intellectual property laws is to promote progress and offer an incentive for inventors and authors to create and disclose their work.

LO[3] The rights relating to intellectual property (IP) are known as 'intellectual property rights and imply moral and legal claims over intellectual property.

LO[4] A patent grants an inventor or its assignee exclusive or monopoly right to make, sell, use, and import an invention for a limited period of time, in exchange for public disclosure of the invention.

LO[5] A copyright gives the creator of an original work exclusive right to it, usually for a limited period of time. Copyright may apply to a wide range of creative, intellectual, or artistic forms, or 'works'.

LO[6] A design constitutes the ornamental or aesthetic aspect of an article. A design may consist of three-dimensional features, such as the shape or surface of an article, or of two-dimensional features, such as patterns, lines or colour.

LO[7] A trademark is a recognizable sign, design, or expression which identifies products or services of a particular source from those of others.

LO[8] Trade dress is a legal term of art that generally refers to characteristics of visual appearance of a product or its packaging that signify the source of the product to consumers.

LO[9] A trade secret may comprise any confidential business information which provides an enterprise a competitive edge. Trade secrets may include formulae,

Geographical indications: Place names used to identify the origin and quality, reputation, or other characteristics of products.

practices, business processes, designs, devices, patterns, and compilations of information which is not generally known, by which a business can obtain economic advantage over competitors or customers.

LO[10] Some of the contemporary issues in intellectual property, recently discussed in the TRIPs Council and brought out by WIPO, include TRIPs and public health; TRIPs, biodiversity, traditional knowledge, plants and life forms; technology transfer to least-developed countries; geographical indications; 'non-violation' complaints; and above all enforcement of intellectual property rights.

CHAPTER

33 The Goods and Services Tax Act, 2017

Learning Objectives

LO 1 Major events that led to introduction of GST

LO 2 GST: Subject-matter and objective

LO 3 Taxes subsumed into GST

LO 4 Working of Dual GST Model

LO 5 Recent amendments in Goods and Services Tax

On 27 March 2017, the then Union Finance Minister Arun Jaitley introduced the much-awaited one-nation, one-tax regime—'The Central Goods and Services Tax' (GST). It was estimated that rolling out of the GST can add up to 2 per cent to India's economic growth. GST in India is a comprehensive, multi-stage, and destination-based tax that will be levied on every value addition.

Rolled out on July 1, 2017, GST is being viewed as the largest indirect-tax reform in independent India as it brings most of the indirect taxes under one roof, which adds transparency besides simplifying the existing (indirect) tax regime.

Major Events that Led to the Introduction of GST

GST has been introduced in the country after a 13-year long journey since it was first discussed in the report of the Kelkar Task Force on indirect taxes. A brief chronology outlining the major milestones on the proposal for introduction of GST in India is as follows:

1. In 2003, the Kelkar Task Force on indirect taxes had suggested a comprehensive Goods and Services Tax (GST) based on the VAT principle.
2. A proposal to introduce a national-level Goods and Services Tax (GST) by 1 April 2010 was first mooted in the budget speech for the financial year 2006–07.
3. Since the proposal involved reform/restructuring of not only indirect taxes levied by the centre but also the states, the responsibility of preparing a design and road map for the implementation of GST was assigned to the Empowered Committee of State Finance Ministers (EC).
4. Based on inputs from the Government of India and States, the EC released its First Discussion Paper on Goods and Services Tax in India in November 2009.
5. In order to take the GST-related work further, a joint working group consisting of officers from central as well as state governments was constituted in September 2009.
6. In order to amend the Constitution to enable introduction of GST, the Constitution (115th Amendment) Bill was introduced in the Lok Sabha in March 2011. As per the prescribed procedure, the Bill was referred to the Standing Committee on Finance of the Parliament for examination and report.
7. Meanwhile, in pursuance of the decision taken in a meeting between the Union Finance Minister and the Empowered Committee of State Finance Ministers on 8 November 2012, a 'Committee on GST Design', consisting of the officials of the Government of India, State Governments, and the Empowered Committee was constituted.
8. This committee had a detailed discussion on GST design including the Constitution (115th) Amendment Bill and submitted its report in January 2013. Based on this Report, the EC recommended certain changes in the Constitution Amendment Bill in their meeting at Bhubaneswar in January 2013.
9. The Empowered Committee in the Bhubaneswar meeting also decided to constitute three committees of officers to discuss and report on various aspects of GST, as follows:
   (a) Committee on Place of Supply Rules and Revenue Neutral Rates;
   (b) Committee on dual control, threshold, and exemptions; and
   (c) Committee on IGST and GST on imports.
10. The Parliamentary Standing Committee submitted its report in August 2013 to the Lok Sabha. The recommendations of the Empowered Committee and the recommendations of the Parliamentary Standing Committee were examined in the ministry in consultation with the Legislative Department. Most of the recommendations made by the Empowered Committee and the Parliamentary Standing Committee were accepted and the draft amendment bill was suitably revised.
11. The final draft Constitutional Amendment Bill incorporating the above-stated changes was sent to the Empowered Committee for consideration in September 2013.
12. The EC once again made certain recommendations on the Bill after its meeting in Shillong in November 2013. Certain recommendations of the Empowered Committee were incorporated

in the draft Constitution (115th Amendment) Bill. The revised draft was sent for consideration of the Empowered Committee in March 2014.

13. The 115th Constitutional (Amendment) Bill, 2011, for the introduction of GST, was placed in the Lok Sabha in March 2011 and lapsed with the dissolution of the 15th Lok Sabha.
14. In June 2014, the draft Constitution Amendment Bill was sent to the Empowered Committee after approval of the new Government.
15. Based on a broad consensus reached with the Empowered Committee on the contours of the bill, the cabinet on 17 December 2014 approved the proposal for introduction of a bill in the Parliament for amending the Constitution of India to facilitate the introduction of Goods and Services Tax (GST) in the country. The bill was introduced in the Lok Sabha on 19 December 2014 and was passed by the Lok Sabha on 6 May 2015. It was then referred to the Select Committee of Rajya Sabha, which submitted its report on 22 July 2015.

What is GST?

The Goods and Services Tax (GST) is a uniform indirect tax levied on goods and services across the country. Its basic features can be summarized as under:

1. GST was introduced in India on 1 July 2017 and applicable throughout India, which replaces multiple cascading taxes levied by the central and state governments.
2. It is a comprehensive, multi-staged, and destination-based tax. Comprehensive, because it has subsumed almost all the indirect taxes except a few state taxes; multi-staged, as the GST is imposed at every step in the production process, but is meant to be refunded to all parties in the various stages of production other than the final consumer; and destination-based tax, as it is collected from point of consumption and not point of origin unlike previous taxes.
3. GST is governed by a GST Council and its Chairman is the Finance Minister of India.
4. GST is levied on all transactions such as sale, transfer, purchase, barter, lease, or import of goods and/or services.
5. Under GST, goods and services have been classified into four categories to be taxed @ 0%, 5%, 12%, 18%, and 28%, respectively. However, petrol and petroleum products (i.e., petroleum crude, high-speed diesel, motor spirit/petrol, natural gas, aviation turbine fuel), electricity, and alcoholic drinks for human consumption (i.e., not for commercial use) are not taxed under GST and instead taxed separately by the individual state governments.
6. There is a special rate of 0.25% on rough precious and semi-precious stones and 3% on gold. In addition, a cess of 22% or other rates on top of 28% GST applies on few items, such as aerated drinks, luxury cars, and tobacco products.
7. Some products have been exempted by the government and remain untaxed under GST, such as dairy products, products of milling industries, fresh vegetables and fruits, meat products, and other groceries and necessities.

GST has been proposed to replace a slew of indirect taxes with a unified tax and, therefore, sets to dramatically reshape the country's 2 trillion dollar economy.

Objective of GST

Many developed nations impose tax on manufacturing, sale, and consumption using a single, comprehensive tax regime. The main objective of GST is to eliminate excessive taxation. Central and state agencies often calculate taxes based not on the original cost of the product but over and above the several layers of tax already levied on the product. This negatively affects the gross domestic product (GDP) of a nation. It is also expected to disincentivise tax evasion, lower the tax rates, and make business operations easier. Pre-GST, the statutory tax rate for most goods was about 26.5%. Post-GST, most goods are expected to be in the 18% tax range.

Benefits of GST

GST offers various benefits to various interest groups, summarized as under:

1. **For trade and industry**
   (a) *Easy compliance* A robust and comprehensive IT system would be the foundation of

the GST regime in India. Therefore, all taxpayer services such as registrations, returns, payments, etc., would be available to the taxpayers online, which would make compliance easy and transparent.

(b) **Uniformity of tax rates and structures** GST will ensure that indirect tax rates and structures are common across the country; thereby, increasing certainty and ease of doing business. In other words, GST would make doing business in the country tax-neutral, irrespective of the choice of place of doing business.

(c) **Removal of cascading** A system of seamless tax credits throughout the value chain and across boundaries of states would ensure that there is minimal cascading of taxes. This would reduce hidden costs of doing business.

(d) **Improved competitiveness** Reduction in transaction costs of doing business would eventually lead to an improved state of competitiveness for the trade and industry.

(e) **Gain to manufacturers and exporters** The subsuming of major Central and State taxes in GST, complete and comprehensive set-off of input goods and services, and phasing out of Central Sales Tax (CST) would reduce the cost of locally manufactured goods and services. This will increase the competitiveness of Indian goods and services in the international market and give boost to Indian exports. The uniformity in tax rates and procedures across the country will also go a long way in reducing the compliance cost.

2. **For Central and State Governments**

(a) ***Simple and easy to administer*** Multiple indirect taxes at the central and state levels are being replaced by GST. Backed with a robust end-to-end IT system, GST would be simpler and easier to administer than all other indirect taxes of the Centre and State levied so far.

(b) **Better controls on leakage** GST will result in better tax compliance because of a robust IT infrastructure. Due to seamless transfer of input tax credit from one stage to another in the chain of value addition, there is an in-built mechanism in the design of GST that would incentivize tax compliance by traders.

(c) **Higher revenue efficiency** GST is expected to decrease the cost of collection of tax revenues of the Government and will, therefore, lead to higher revenue efficiency.

3. **For the consumer**

(a) ***Single and transparent tax proportionate to the value of goods and services*** Due to multiple indirect taxes being levied by the centre and state, with incomplete or no input tax credits available at the progressive stages of value addition, the cost of most goods and services in the country today is laden with many hidden taxes. Under GST, there would be only one tax from the manufacturer to the consumer, leading to transparency of taxes paid to the final consumer.

(b) **Relief in overall tax burden** Because of efficiency gains and prevention of leakages, the overall tax burden on most commodities will come down, which will benefit consumers.

Taxes Subsumed into GST at the Centre and State Level

The single GST replaces several former taxes and levies, which include: central excise duty, services tax, additional customs duty, surcharges, state-level value-added tax, and Octroi (entry tax). Other levies which were applicable on inter-state transportation of goods have also been done away with in GST regime. India adopted a Dual GST model, meaning that taxation is administered by both the Union and State Governments. Transactions made within a single state are levied with Central GST (CGST) by the Central Government and State GST (SGST) by the government of that state. For inter-state transactions and imported goods or services, an Integrated GST (IGST) is levied by the Central Government. GST is a consumption-based tax; therefore, taxes are paid to the state where the goods or services are consumed and not the state in which they were produced. IGST complicates tax collection for state governments by disabling them from collecting the tax owed to them directly from the central government. Under the previous system, a state would only have to deal with a single government in order to collect tax revenue.

GST Council

GST Council is the governing body of GST having 34 members, out of which 2 members are from the Centre and 32 members are from the 29 States and 3 Union Territories with legislation. The council contains the following members: (a) Union Finance Minister (as chairperson) (b) Union Minister of States in charge of revenue or finance (as member) (c) the ministers of states in charge of finance or taxation or other ministers as nominated by each state government (as member).

GST Council is an apex member committee to modify, reconcile or to procure any law or regulation based on the context of goods and services tax in India. The council at present is headed by the union finance minister Ms. Nirmala Sitharaman assisted with the finance minister of all the states of India. The GST council is responsible for any revision or enactment of rule or any rate changes of the goods and services in India.

Implementation Mechanism of GST in India

Keeping in mind the federal structure of India, there will be two components of GST – Central GST (CGST) and State GST (SGST). Both Centre and States will simultaneously levy GST across the value chain. Tax will be levied on every supply of goods and services. Centre would levy and collect Central Goods and Services Tax (CGST), and States would levy and collect the State Goods and Services Tax (SGST) on all transactions within the state. The input tax credit of CGST would be available for discharging the CGST liability on the output at each stage. Similarly, the credit of SGST paid on inputs would be allowed for paying the SGST on output. No cross utilization of credit would be permitted.

For the implementation of GST in the country, the Central and State Governments have jointly registered Goods and Services Tax Network (GSTN) as a not-for-profit, Non-Government Company to provide shared IT infrastructure and services to Central and State Governments, tax payers, and other stakeholders. The key objectives of GSTN are to provide a standard and uniform interface to the taxpayers and shared infrastructure and services to Central and State/UT governments.

GSTN is working on developing a state-of-the-art comprehensive IT infrastructure including the common GST portal providing front-end services of registration, returns, and payments to all taxpayers, as well as the backend IT modules for certain states that include processing of returns, registrations, audits, assessments, appeals, etc. All states, accounting authorities, RBI, and banks, are also preparing their IT infrastructure for the administration of GST.

There would no manual filing of returns. All taxes can also be paid online. All mismatched returns would be auto-generated, and there would be no need for manual interventions. Most returns would be self-assessed.

How does GST Work?

A nationwide tax reform cannot function without strict guidelines and provisions. The GST Council has devised a fool-proof method of implementing this new tax regime by dividing it into three categories. Let our experts explain this to you in detail.

When GST is implemented, there will be 3 kinds of applicable Goods and Services Tax: CGST, SGST, and IGST.

CGST where the revenue will be collected by the central government

SGST where the revenue will be collected by the state governments for intra-state sales

IGST where the revenue will be collected by the central government for inter-state sales

In most cases, the tax structure under the new regime will be as follows:

Transaction	New Regime	Old Regime	Comments
Sale within the state	CGST + SGST	VAT + central excise/ service tax	Revenue will now be shared between the Centre and the State
Sale to another state	IGST	Central Sales Tax + excise/service tax	There will only be one type of tax (central) now in case of inter-state sales.

Figure 1 GST within State

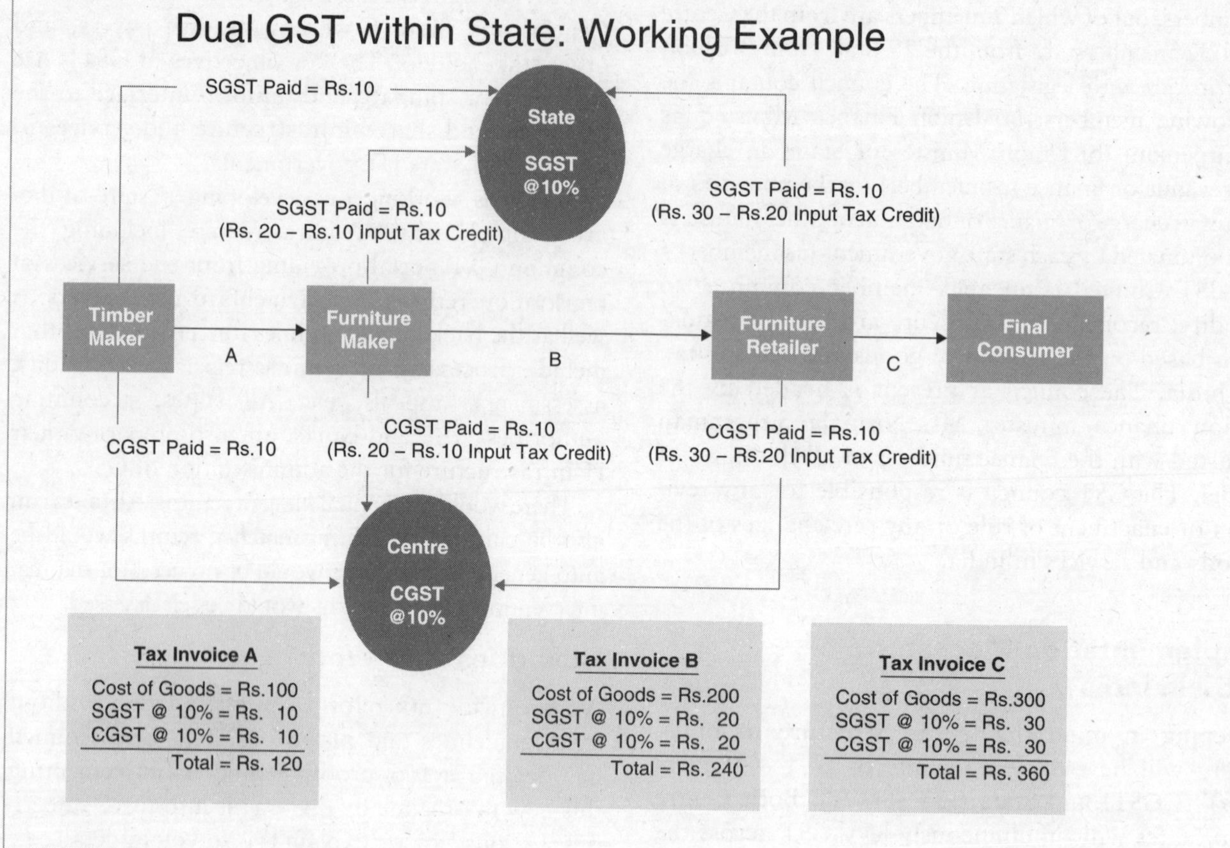

Example

A dealer in Maharashtra sold goods to a consumer in Maharashtra worth ₹10,000. The GST rate is 18% comprising CGST rate of 9% and SGST rate of 9%. In such cases, the dealer collects ₹1800 and of this amount, ₹900 will go to the central government and ₹900 will go to the Maharashtra government.

Now, let us assume the dealer in Maharashtra had sold goods to a dealer in Gujarat worth ₹10,000. The GST rate is 18%, comprising of CGST rate of 9% and SGST rate of 9%. In such case the dealer has to charge ₹1800 as IGST. This IGST will go to the Centre. There will no longer be any need to pay CGST and SGST.

Working of Dual GST Model

The CGST and the SGST would be levied simultaneously on every transaction of supply of goods and services except on exempted goods and services, goods which are outside the purview of GST and the transactions which are below the prescribed threshold limits. Further, both would be levied on the same price or value unlike State VAT, which is levied on the value of the goods inclusive of Central Excise.

A diagrammatic representation of the working of the Dual GST model within a state is shown in Figure 1.

Cross Utilization of Credits between Goods and Services under GST

Cross utilization of credit of CGST between goods and services would be allowed. Similarly, the facility of cross utilization of credit will be available in case of SGST. However, the cross utilization of CGST and SGST would not be allowed except in the case

Figure 2

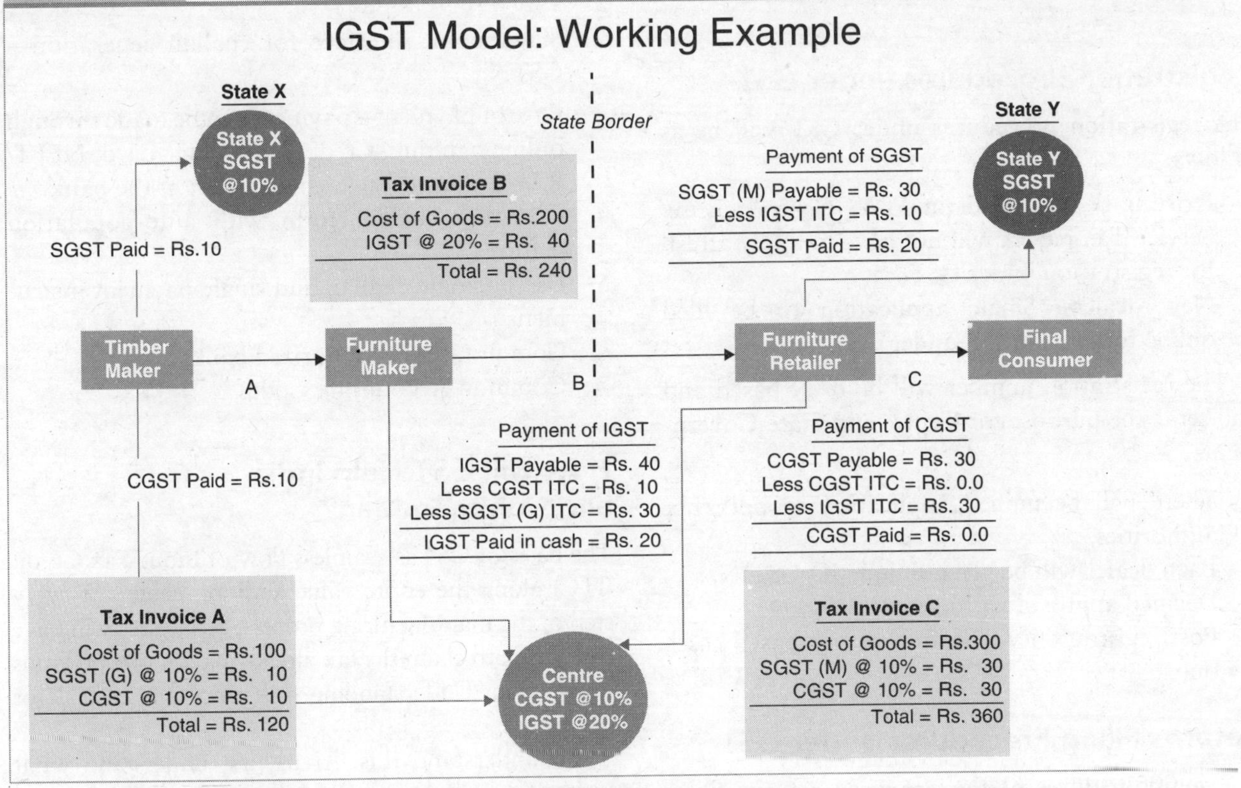

of inter-state supply of goods and services under the IGST model which is explained in the answer to the next question.

Inter-State Transactions of Goods and Services to be Taxed under GST in terms of IGST

In case of inter-state transactions, the Centre would levy and collect the Integrated Goods and Services Tax (IGST) on all inter-state supplies of goods and services under Article 269A (1) of the Constitution. The IGST would roughly be equal to CGST plus SGST. The IGST mechanism has been designed to ensure seamless flow of input tax credit from one state to another. The inter-state seller would pay IGST on the sale of goods to the Central Government after adjusting credit of IGST, CGST, and SGST on the purchases (in that order). The exporting state will transfer to the Centre the credit of SGST used in payment of IGST. The importing dealer will claim credit of IGST while discharging his output tax liability (both CGST and SGST) in own state. The Centre will transfer to the importing state the credit of IGST used in payment of SGST. Since GST is a destination-based tax, all SGST on the final product will ordinarily accrue to the consuming state.

A diagrammatic representation of the working of the IGST model for inter-state transactions is shown in Figure 2, and there would be no need for manual interventions. Most returns would be self-assessed.

How will Imports be Taxed under GST?

The additional duty of excise or CVD and the special additional duty or SAD presently being levied on imports will be subsumed under GST. As per explanation to clause (1) of Article 269A of the Constitution, IGST will be levied on all imports into the territory of India. Unlike in the present regime, the states in which imported goods are consumed will now gain their share from this IGST paid on imported goods.

Registration Procedures under GST

The registration procedures under GST will be as follows:

1. **Existing dealers** Existing VAT/Central excise/Service Tax payers will not have to apply afresh for registration under GST.
2. **New dealers** Single application to be filed online for registration under GST.

The registration number will be PAN based and will serve the purpose for Centre and State Governments.

- There will be unified application to both tax authorities.
- Each dealer will be given unique ID GSTIN.
- Deemed approval within three days.
- Post registration verification in risk-based cases only.

Returns Filing Procedures under GST

The major features of the proposed returns filing procedures under GST are as follows:

1. Common return would serve the purpose of both Centre and State Governments.
2. There are eight forms provided for in the GST business processes for filing for returns. Most of the average tax payers would be using only four forms for filing their returns. These are return for supplies, return for purchases, monthly returns, and annual return.
3. Small taxpayers who have opted composition scheme shall have to file return on quarterly basis.
4. Filing of returns shall be completely online. All taxes can also be paid online.

Unlike the existing return processes, GST requires to be filed every month by businessmen, which will make it easier once the 'hands on' processes are set.

Payment Procedures for GST

The major features of the payments procedures under GST are as follows:

1. Electronic payment process—no generation of paper at any stage
2. Single-point interface for challan generation—GSTN
3. Ease of payment – payment can be made through online banking, Credit Card/Debit Card, NEFT/RTGS, and through cheque/cash at the bank.
4. Common challan form with auto-population features
5. Use of single challan and single payment instrument
6. Common set of authorized banks
7. Common Accounting Codes

How will GST Help India and Common Man?

The basis of GST is seamless flow of Input Tax Credit (ITC) along the entire value addition chain. At every step of the manufacturing process, businesses will have the option to claim the tax already paid in the previous transaction. Understanding this process is crucial for businesses.

To understand this, let us first understand what Input Tax Credit is. It is the credit an individual receives for the tax paid on the inputs used in manufacturing the product. So, if there is a 10% tax that the individual must submit to the government, he can subtract the amount he has paid in taxes at the time of purchase and submit the balance amount to the government.

Let us understand this with a hypothetical numerical example, as follows:

- Say, a shirt manufacturer pays ₹100 to buy raw materials. If the rate of taxes is set at 10%, and there is no profit or loss involved, then he has to pay ₹10 as tax. So, the final cost of the shirt now becomes ₹(100 + 10 =) 110.
- At the next stage, the wholesaler buys the shirt from the manufacturer at ₹110 and adds a label to it. When he is adding label, he is adding value. Therefore, the cost increases by say ₹40. On top of this, he has to pay a 10% tax, and the final cost, therefore, becomes ₹(110 + 40 =) 150 + 10% tax = ₹165.
- Now, the retailer pays ₹165 to buy the shirt from the wholesaler because the tax liability

had passed on to him. He has to package the shirt, and when he does that, he is adding value again. This time, let us say, his value add is ₹30. Now when he sells the shirt, he adds this value (plus the VAT he has to pay the government) to the final cost. So, the cost of the shirt becomes ₹214.5. Let us see a breakup for this:

Cost = ₹165 + value add = ₹30 + 10% tax = ₹195 + ₹19.5 = ₹214.5

So, the customer pays ₹214.5 for a shirt, the cost price of which was basically only ₹170 (₹110 + ₹40 + ₹30). Along the way the tax liability was passed on at every stage of transaction and the final liability comes to rest with the customer. This is called the **Cascading Effect of Taxes** where a tax is paid on tax and the value of the item keeps increasing every time this happens.

Action	Cost	10% Tax	Total
Buys raw material @ 100	100	10	110
Manufactures @ 40	150	15	165
Adds value @ 30	195	19.5	214.5
Total	170	44.5	214.5

In the case of GST, there is a way to claim credit for tax paid in acquiring input. What happens in this case is that the individual who has paid a tax already can claim credit for this tax when he submits his taxes.

In our example, when the wholesaler buys from the manufacturer, he pays a 10% tax on his cost price because the liability has been passed on to him. Then he adds value of ₹40 on his cost price of ₹100 and this brings up his cost to ₹140. Now he has to pay 10% of this price to the government as tax. But he has already paid one tax to the manufacturer. So, this time what he does is, instead of paying ₹(10% of 140 =) 14 to the government as tax, he subtracts the amount he has paid already. So, he deducts the ₹10 he paid on his purchase from his new liability of ₹14, and pays only ₹4 to the government. So ₹10 becomes his input credit.

When he pays ₹4 to the government, he can pass on its liability to the retailer. So, the retailer pays ₹(140 + 14 =) 154 to him to buy the shirt. At the next stage, the retailer adds value of ₹30 to his cost price and has to pay a 10% tax on it to the government. When he adds value, his price becomes ₹170. Now, if he had to pay 10% tax on it, he would pass on the liability to the customer. But he already has input credit because he has paid ₹14 to the wholesaler as the latter's tax. Now he reduces ₹14 from his tax liability of ₹(10% of 170 =) 17 and has to pay only ₹3 to the government. And, therefore, he can now sell the shirt for ₹(140 + 30 + 17) 187 to the customer.

Action	Cost	10% Tax	Actual Liability	Total
Buys raw material	100	10	10	110
Manufactures @ 40	140	14	4	154
Adds value @ 30	170	17	3	187
Total	170		17	187

In the end, every time an individual was able to claim input tax credit, the sale price for him reduced and the cost price for the person buying his product reduced because of a lower tax liability. The final value of the shirt also, therefore, reduced from ₹214.5 to ₹187; thus reducing the tax burden on the final customer.

So, essentially, GST is going to have a two-pronged benefit. One, it will reduce the cascading effect of taxes and, second, by allowing input tax credit, it will reduce the burden of taxes and, hopefully, prices.

GST Helpline

Gstseva.com is a free GST tax website for *GST* updates, GST news, GST information, GST helpline, GST happening, GST advisory, GST solutions, and lots of GST stuff of goods and services. Software development company KDK Softwares has launched a national toll-free helpline service for resolving GST-related queries. The toll-free helpline number (1800 103 9271) will be available in six languages – English, Hindi, Gujarati, Marathi, Kannada, and Malayalam.

Goods and Services Tax is being viewed as India's biggest indirect tax reform. Its significance and success can be judged from the fact that the collections from customs duty and IGST from imports post implementation of GST has almost doubled to ₹30,000 crore in July 2017. The revenue collected includes those on account of customs duty, Integrated-GST (IGST) from imports, Countervailing Duty (CVD), special addition duty (SAD), and cess collection on imported items. Positive outcomes of the GST includes the trucks' travel time in inter-state movement, which dropped by 20%, because of disbanding of interstate check posts.

Recent Amendments in the Goods and Services Tax

Since July 1, 2017 to date there have been innumerable material changes and amendments in the GST Law brought out by various Circulars issued time-to-time. As per the notification issued by 'Indian Trade Portal, Department of Commerce, Ministry of Commerce and Industry, Government of India' Some material changes have been made in the GST, applicable from April 1, 2019, which include but not limited to the following:

1. **Threshold limit to take registration increased to ₹40 lakh**

   As per Section 23 of the CGST Act, every person is required to obtain the GST registration if his turnover from supply of goods or services exceeds ₹20 lakh. This threshold limit has been increased to ₹40 lakh only if the supplier is engaged in the exclusive supply of goods. Therefore, any person who is engaged in supply of goods and his total turnover in the current financial year does not exceed ₹40 lakh, is not required to take registration under GST. This exemption from GST registration is subject to various conditions, inter alia, he is not making any Inter-state supply, he is not a non-resident taxable person, etc. This has been made applicable by Notification No. 10/2019-IT dated 07.03.2019. This notification came into force from April 1, 2019.

2. **Registration required without a threshold limit Under the Reverse Charge Mechanism (RCM)**

   Generally, the supplier of goods or services is liable to pay GST. However, in specified cases like imports and other notified supplies, the liability may be cast on the recipient under the reverse charge mechanism. Reverse Charge means the liability to pay tax is on the recipient of supply of goods or services instead of the supplier of such goods or services in respect of notified categories of supply. There are two type of reverse charge scenarios provided in law. First is dependent on the nature of supply and/or nature of supplier. This scenario is covered by Section 9 (3) of the CGST/SGST (UTGST) Act and Section 5 (3) of the IGST Act. Second scenario is covered by Section 9 (4) of the CGST/SGST (UTGST) Act and Section 5 (4) of the IGST Act where taxable supplies by any unregistered person to a registered person is covered. As per the provisions of Section 9(3) of CGST / SGST (UTGST) Act, 2017 /Section 5(3)of IGST Act, 2017, the Government may, on the recommendations of the Council, by notification, specify categories of supply of goods or services or both, the tax on which shall be paid on reverse 86 GST FLYERS charge basis by the recipient of such goods or services or both and all the provisions of this Act shall apply to such recipient as if he is the person liable for paying the tax in relation to the supply of such goods or services or both. Similarly, Section 9(4) of CGST / SGST (UTGST) Act, 2017 / Section 5(4) of IGST Act, 2017 provides that the tax in respect of the supply of taxable goods or services or both by a supplier, who is not registered, to a registered person shall be paid by such person on reverse charge basis as the recipient and all the provisions of this Act shall apply to such recipient as if he is the person liable for paying the tax in relation to the supply of such goods or services or both. Accordingly, wherever a registered person procures supplies from an unregistered supplier, he need to pay GST on reverse charge basis. However, supplies where the aggregate value of such supplies of goods or service or both received by a registered person from any or all the unregistered suppliers is less than five thousand rupees in a day are exempted. (Notification 8/2017-Central Tax (Rate) dated 28.06.2017). However, vide notification no.38/2017-Central Tax (Rate) dated 13.10.2017, (corresponding IGST notification no.32/2017-Integrated Tax

(Rate) dated 13.10.2017) all categories of registered persons are exempted from the provisions of reverse charge under 9(4) of CGST / SGST (UTGST) Act, 2017 / section 5(4) of IGST Act, 2017, till 31.03.2018. This exemption is available only till 31.03.2018. The provisions of section 9(4) of the CGST Act, 2017, will not be applicable to supplies made to a TDS deductor in terms of notification no.9/2017-Central Tax (Rate) dated 28.06.2017. Thus, Government entities 87 who are TDS Deductors under Section 51 of CGST Act, 2015, need not pay GST under reverse charge in case of procurements from unregistered suppliers.

Section 24(1) of CGST Act specified the persons requiring registration without a threshold limit of ₹20/10 lakh. However, Section 24(1) of CGST is not applicable to persons who are not liable for registration under Section 23 of Act. However, if he is liable under reverse charge, registration under GST will be required.

Section 24 of the CGST Act is independent of Section 23 of the CGST Act. Hence, a person dealing only in exempted products is not required to be registered under GST, *if he is not liable under reverse charge.*

In case the person is liable under reverse charge, he needs to take GST registration even if engaged in exempted supplies.

2. **Threshold Limit for composition scheme increased to ₹1.5 crore**

The existing threshold limit on gross turnover in previous financial year to avail of the composition scheme has been increased from ₹1 to 1. 5 Crore. In respect of special category States (North-Eastern States), the threshold limit has been increased from ₹50 lakh to ₹75 lakh. Consequently, the taxable persons can substantially reduce their compliance burden as they would be required to file GST returns on quarterly basis instead of monthly basis. This benefit has been extended vide Notification No. 14/2019 – Central Tax dated March 7, 2019 and this notification shall come into force from April 1, 2019.

3. **New Scheme available @ 6% to Intra-State Suppliers of Goods or Service**

Wherein an Intra-state supplier can now pay GST at the rate of 6% (3% for Central and 3% for respective State) on first supplies of goods or services for ₹50 lakh. With effect from April 1, 2019 the benefit of this scheme can be availed. This scheme shall be available only if the aggregate turnover of supplier does not exceed ₹50 lakh during the previous financial year. This has been made effective vide Notification No. 02/2019 – Central Tax (Rate) dated March 7, 2019.

The benefit of this scheme shall not be available to service providers who are rendering services in multiple States or through e-commerce websites.

4. **Due dates for filing of GSTR-1 and GSTR-3B and other GSTR announced**

4.1 **12th June 2020 datewise as under:**

40th GST Council meeting concluded with major announcements made for MSMEs as under:

(i) GSTR-3B late fee waiver for prior period July 2017-January 2020 for taxpayers with a Nil liability. A maximum cap in late fee of ₹500 has been fixed per pending returns for the rest of them, provided it is filed between 1st July 2020 and 30th September 2020.

(ii) Interest Relief and Late fee waiver for taxpayers with aggregate turnover of up to ₹5 crore as under:

(a) Tax payments for February, March and April 2020: Interest will be applicable at a reduced rate of 9% p.a. instead of 18% p.a., if return is filed after 6th July 2020 but before 30th September 2020.

(b) Tax payments for May, June and July 2020: Late fee and interest charge will be waived off if return is filed by the staggered dates of September 2020 (due dates yet to be announced).

(iii) Period for seeking revocation of cancelled GST registrations allowed till 30th September 2020 for all those registrations which were cancelled till 12th June 2020.

4.2 **30th July 2020**

(i) A new refined format of e-invoice has been notified by CBIC adding 20 new fields and removing 13 fields. Certain fields have undergone changes in character length as well.

(ii) e-invoicing system shall apply to those taxpayers with annual turnover exceeding ₹500 crore instead of existing ₹100 crore.

(iii) Special Economic Zones (SEZs) units shall also be exempted from issuing e-invoices.

4.3 **13th July 2020**

The due date to file GSTR-4 (Annual Return) has been extended to 31st August 2020 from 15th July 2020.

4.4 **1st July 2020**

Taxpayers can now file a Nil GSTR-1 via SMS.

4.5 A further extension granted for filing annual returns (GSTR-9) and reconciliation statement (GSTR-9C) for FY 2018-19 until 30th September 2020.

4.6 Companies can file GSTR-3B using EVC option until 30th June 2020

5. **Option to opt for Composition Scheme**

The time limit to opt into the composition scheme for the FY 2020-21 in form CMP-02 has been extended up to 30th June 2020. It applies for both taxpayers registered under section 10 of the CGST Act as well as the taxpayers opting for the scheme notified via CGST (Rate) notification no. 2/2019 dated 7th March 2019.

6. **Last chance to avail Input Tax Credit relating to F.Y. 2018-19**

A registered person shall not be entitled to take input tax credit in respect of any invoice or debit note for supply of goods or services or both after the due date of furnishing of the return under section 39 for the month of September following the end of financial year to which such invoice or invoice relating to such debit note pertains or furnishing of the relevant annual return, whichever is earlier.

As per the aforesaid provision, the time limit for taking input tax credit for the financial year 2018-19 is up to the filing of return (GSTR-3B) for the month of September 2019. The due date of filing of GSTR-3B for the month of September 2019 is 20th of October 2019.

The registered person can avail input tax credit of GST paid from July, 2017 to March, 2018, latest by the due date of furnishing the return for the month of March, 2019 i.e., by April 20, 2019. Legal wording can also be referred to removal of difficulty order no. 2/2018 dated 31.12.2018.

7. **Availing benefit of reduced GST rates by real estate developers or builders**

The GST Council in its 33rd and 34th meetings had recommended the GST rate of 1% in case of affordable houses and 5% in other cases, without input tax credit. The promoters shall be given a one-time option to continue to pay tax at the old rates (i.e., @ 8% or 12% with ITC) on ongoing projects (if construction and actual booking have started before 01-04-2019) which have not been completed by March 31, 2019. The option shall be exercised once within a prescribed time frame and where the option is not exercised within the prescribed time limit, new rates shall apply.

8. **Benefits related to Specific Industry**

Specific Industry comprises the following:

(a) Money changer (Forex Dealer); or

(b) Air travel agent; or

(c) Dealer of second hand (imported) goods opting for 'Margin Scheme'; or

It is suggested that the above mentioned eligible registered persons intended to determine the value of their supplies as per the valuation rules. They can exercise the option at the beginning of the Financial Year that is on or before April 1, 2019.

Besides, taxpayer engaged in Life insurance business have been given the option to determine the value of such supply as per rule 32 of the CGST Rules, 2017.

10. **Availing Input tax credit by Banks, Financial Institutions or NBFCs**

Banks or financial institution or NBFCs have been given an option to avail 50% of the eligible Input tax credit on inputs, capital goods and input services. This option to be exercised at the beginning of the F.Y. that is on or before April 1, 2019, as the option once exercised cannot be withdrawn during the remaining part of the financial year.

11. **Aadhar authentication/physical verification of the place of business for GST registration ***

Where an applicant, other than a person notified under sub-section 6D of Section 25 of Central Goods and Services Tax (CGST) Act, 2017 opts for authentication of Aadhaar number, he shall, while submitting the application under sub-rule (4), with effect from 21st August, 2020, undergo authentication of Aadhaar number and the date of submission of the application in such cases shall be the date of authentication of the Aadhaar number, or fifteen days from the submission of the application in Part B of FORM GST REG-01 under sub-rule (4), whichever is earlier.

However, where a person, other than a person notified under sub-section 6D of Section 25, fails to undergo authentication of Aadhaar number as specified in sub-rule (4A) of rule 8 or does not opt for authentication of Aadhaar number, the registration shall be granted only after physical verification of the place of business in the presence of the said person, in the manner provided under rule 25.

Provided further that the proper officer may, for reasons to be recorded in writing and with the approval of an officer not below the rank of Joint Commissioner, in lieu of the physical verification of the place of business, carry out the verification of such documents as he may deem fit.

*CBIC (Central Board of Indirect Taxes and Customs) Notification No. 62/2020 – Central Tax, 20 August, 2020

12. **GST Acts amended from time to time and applicable from the date of enactment**

Amendments made to all Central Acts (CGST, IGST, UTGST, and GST Compensation to States) with reference to amendments brought in by The Finance Bill, 2018 dated 28.03.2018, Central Goods and Services Tax (Amendment) Act, 2018 dated 29.08.2018, The Finance (No.2) Act, 2019 dated 01.08.2019, The Finance Act, 2020 dated 27.03.2020 and The Taxation and Other Laws (Relaxation of Certain Provisions) Ordinance, 2020 [No.2 of 2020] dated 31.03.2020, Integrated Goods and Services Tax (Amendment) Act, 2018 dated 29.08.2018 and Union Territory Goods and Services Tax (Amendment) Act, 2018 dated 29.08.2018.

Some of the major changes/amendments in respect of above are summarised below:

(a) Manner of utilization of ITC has been amended by inserting Section 49A in the CGST Act. Now the credit of IGST needs to be utilized first in full for the payment of IGST, CGST, SGST and UTGST respectively.

(b) Section 9(4) relating to reverse charge applicability on purchases made by registered person from unregistered person is replaced and now it applies to specific class.

(c) Now only e-commerce operators who are required to collect tax at source under Section 52 of the CGST Act, 2017 are mandatorily required to obtain GST registration.

(d) Composition dealers as per Section 10 of CGST Act, 2017 are allowed to supply services to the extent of 10% of the turnover in the preceding financial year or ₹5 lakh, whichever is higher.

(e) Multiple GST registrations within the same state for each place of business have been allowed. The concept of business vertical is done away with.

(f) Issue of consolidated debit/credit note is allowed in respect of multiple invoices issued in a financial year rather than single debit/credit note in respect of each invoice.

(g) The receipt of payment in Indian rupees which is permitted by the Reserve Bank of India for services exported out of India, will be covered in the definition of 'Export of Services' as per the IGST Act, 2017.

(h) The CBIC has notified that taxpayers can claim input tax credit in the GSTR-3B return from February 2020 to August 2020, without applying the rule of capping provisional ITC claims at 10% of the eligible ITC as per GSTR-2A. While filing the GSTR-3B of September 2020, the taxpayers must cumulatively adjust ITC as per the above rule from February 2020.

Some of the important deadlines that extend to 31st August 2020

Many GST compliance deadlines will be ended to 31st August, 2020, owing to Covid-19 crisis summarised below:

1. **GSTR-4 (2019-20):** GSTR-4 is a form to be filed annually by composition dealer. 31st August, 2020 is the last date for filing of **GSTR-4 for financial year 2019-20** as per the Notification No. 59/2020 dated 13 July, 2020.
2. **ITC 04:** ITC-04 is related to job worker and submitted by the principal every quarter. It is furnished on or before 25th day of the month succeeding the quarter. Last date of ITC 04 of the 4th quarter of 2019-20 and first quarter of 2020-21 is 31st August, 2020 as per the Notification No. 55/2020 dated 27 June, 2020.
   Details of the following to be furnished in ITC-04
   - Goods sent to job worker
   - Goods received back from the job worker or sent out from business place of job-work.
3. **GSTR-5:** GSTR-5 is to be submitted by Non-Resident taxable person. The due date of submission of GSTR-5 will be as under:
   - Within 20 days after the end of a calendar month, or
   - Within 7 days after the last day of validity period of registration.

   Whichever occurs earlier.

   As per Notification No. 55/2020 dated 27.06.2020, due date for GSTR-5 for the month of March 2020 to July 2020 is extended to 31st August, 2020.
4. **GSTR-5A:** GSTR-5A is submitted by the OIDAR (Online Information Database Access and Retrieval) services providers. GSTR-5A is furnished on or before within 20 days after the end of the month. As per Notification No. 55/2020 dated 27.06.2020, due date for GSTR-5A for the month of March 2020 to July 2020 is extended to 31st August, 2020.
5. **GSTR-6:** GSTR-6 is filed by input service distributors (ISD). It is filed within 13 days from the end of the month. As per Notification No. 55/2020 dated 27.06.2020, due date for GSTR-6 for the month of March 2020 to July 2020 is extended to 31st August, 2020. The details of invoices on which credit has been received and details of tax invoices issued by ISD to be furnished in the GSTR-6.
6. **GSTR-7:** GSTR-7 is to be filed by TDS deductor. It is furnished within 10 days after the end of the month in which tax has been deducted at source. As per Notification No. 55/2020 dated 27.06.2020, due date for GSTR-7 for the month of March 2020 to July 2020 is extended to 31st August, 2020.
7. **GSTR-8:** GSTR-8 is submitted by E-commerce operator who collects tax at source under the section 52. It is furnished within 10 days after the end of the month in which collection of tax at source is made. As per Notification No. 55/2020 dated 27.06.2020, due date for GSTR-8 for the month of March 2020 to July 2020 is extended to 31st August, 2020.
8. **Letter of Undertaking (LUT):** Due date for filing of LUT for the financial year 2020-21 is extended to 31st August, 2020 as per Notification No. 55/2020 dated 27.06.2020. Letter of Undertaking (LUT) is a document that exporters can file in respect of export of goods or services without having to pay taxes. Any registered person can furnish LUT in form GST RFD 11 and export goods without the payment of integrated tax.

Exercises

I. Objective-type Questions

1. GST was implemented in India with effect from:
   (a) 1st January 2016
   (b) 1st April 2016
   (c) 1st July, 2016
   (d) 1st July 2017
2. India has chosen the dual GST model of which of the following countries?
   (a) Canada
   (b) China
   (c) Japan
   (d) USA
3. Which of the following items is not taxed separately by the State Government concerned i.e., still comes under GST Net?
   (a) Electricity
   (b) Petrol and petroleum products
   (c) Alcoholic drinks for human consumption
   (d) Gold
4. Which of the following goods attracts minimum GST?
   (a) Rough precious and semi-precious stones
   (b) Gold jewellery
   (c) Silver
   (d) Electricity
5. The country with highest GST rate in the world is:
   (a) Brazil
   (b) Canada
   (c) China
   (d) India
6. The maximum rate for SGST/UTGST is?
   (a) 28
   (b) 14
   (c) 20
   (d) 30
7. Which code is used to classify goods and services under GST?
   (a) HSN Code
   (b) SAC/HSN Code
   (c) GST Code
   (d) SAC Code
8. What does "I" in IGST stand for?
   (a) Internal
   (b) Integrated
   (c) Internal
   (d) Intra
9. ____________ is the first state in India to pass GST Bill in India?
   (a) Assam
   (b) Bihar
   (c) Gujarat
   (d) Telangana
10. How many types of GST India has?
    (a) 2
    (b) 3
    (c) 4
    (d) 5

II. Review Questions

1. What is GST? What is GST's impact? How does GST work?
2. What are the underlying benefits of GST?
3. Enumerate the taxes subsumed into GST at the Centre and State level?
4. How well GST is helping India and common man?
5. Describe the 'Registration' and 'Returns Filing' Procedures under GST.

6. Outline the important recent developments that took place in GST regime.
7. Give the working example of IGST Model
8. Summarise the major events that led to the Introduction of GST in India.

Answers to Objective-type Questions

1. (d) 2. (a) 3. (d) 4. (b) 5. (d)
6. (c) 7. (b) 8. (b) 9. (a) 10. (b)

33 Chapter in Review

LEARNING OUTCOMES

LO1 Major events that led to introduction of GST

LO2 GST: Subject-matter and objective

LO3 Taxes subsumed into GST

LO4 Working of Dual GST Model

LO5 Recent amendments in Goods and Services Tax

KEY TERMS

Aggregate turnover: Total value of all taxable supplies, exempt supplies, exports of goods and/or services, and interstate supplies of a person having the same PAN, computed on the pan-India basis excluding taxes. However, the value of inward supplies on which taxation is based on reverse-charge mechanism shall not be included.

Application Service Providers (ASPs): GST Suvidha Providers (GSPs) but are more wholesome than GSPs. The support provided by ASPs will address most taxpayer compliance difficulties as they work as a liaison between the taxpayers and the GSPs.

Appropriate government: The Central Government for IGST, UTGST and CGST, and the State Government for SGST.

ARN: Abbreviation for 'Application Reference Number; which is created at the time of submitting enrolment application that is signed using EVC or DSC over the GSTN Portal. Under ARN, a unique number is provided for doing any transaction at GST System Portal.

CGST: The tax levied under the Central Goods and Services Tax Act, 2016.

Composite supply: A supply consisting of two or more goods and/or services, which are naturally bundled and provided together, one being a principal supply.

Credit note: A document issued by a taxable person in relation to the tax invoice exceeding the taxable value and/or tax payable in respect of supply, or where the goods supplied are returned by the recipient, or where the services supplied are found to be deficient.

LO1 Major events that led to introduction of GST can be summarized as under:

1. Goods and Services Tax (GST) was first discussed in the report of the 'Kelkar Task Force on Indirect Taxes', way back in 2003.
2. A proposal to introduce a National level GST by April 1, 2010 was first mooted in the Budget Speech for the financial year 2006-07.
3. Since the proposal involved reform/restructuring of not only indirect taxes levied by the Centre but also the States, the responsibility of preparing a Design and Road Map for the implementation of GST was assigned to the Empowered Committee of State Finance Ministers (EC).
4. The Parliamentary Standing Committee submitted its Report in August, 2013 to the Lok Sabha. The recommendations of the Empowered Committee and the Parliamentary Standing Committee were examined by the Ministry of Finance in consultation with the Legislative Department.
5. Based on a broad consensus reached with the Empowered Committee on the contours of the Bill, the Cabinet on 17.12.2014 approved the proposal for introduction of a Bill in the Parliament for amending the Constitution of India to facilitate the introduction of GST in the country.
6. Lok Sabha and Rajya Sabha have unanimously passed the 122nd Constitutional Amendment Bill in August, 2016 which later got the assent of the President and the much-awaited 'Goods and Services Tax' was finally rolled out with effect from July 1, 2017.

LO2 GST is a comprehensive indirect tax levied on manufacture, sale and consumption of goods as well as services at the national level which has subsumed all indirect taxes levied on goods and services by the states and the Centre. Primary objective of GST is to eliminate the double taxation i.e., cascading effects of taxes on production and distribution cost of goods and services.

LO3 In India, a dual GST model is in force whereby a Central Goods and Services Tax (CGST) and a State Goods and Services Tax (SGST) is levied on the taxable value of every transaction of supply of goods and services.

Debit note: A document issued by a taxable person relating to the taxable value and/or tax charged as per the tax invoice when found to be less than the taxable value and/or tax payable in respect of such supply.

Goods: All types of movable property, including actionable claim, growing crops, grass, and things attached to the land that are agreed to be severed before supply or under a contract of supply. But excludes securities and money.

Goods and Services Tax Network (GSTN): A non-profit, public-private partnership company. Its main purpose is to provide IT infrastructure and services to Central and State Governments, taxpayers, and other stakeholders to facilitate the implementation of GST.

GSTIN: Acronym for Goods and Services Tax Identification Number, a unique 15-digit alphanumeric code allotted to every taxpayer registered; mandatory for businesses with annual turnover exceeding ₹40 lakh.

GSP: Abbreviation for 'GST Suvidha Provider', GSP are Third-party applications that assist the taxable person in accessing the GST portal in an enriched manner by being more user-friendly and customer-centred. GSP, in fact, was introduced by GSTN to redistribute its work in multiple channels to stop hanging process of the servers on the last moment of return submission date. GSP will integrate with the Common Portal.

Harmonized System Nomenclature (HSN) Code: A numeral used to classify goods for taxation purposes provided by the World Customs Organization.

IGST: Integrated Goods and Services Tax levied under IGST Act, 2017.

Input service distributor: An office of the supplier of goods and/or services that receives tax invoices issued under section 31 toward the receipt of input services and issues a prescribed document for distributing the credit of CGST, SGST, UTGST and/or IGST paid for the said services.

Input tax: In relation to a registered person, the central tax, state tax, integrated tax or Union territory tax charged on any supply of goods or services or both made to him. However, it does not include the tax paid under the composition levy.

LO4 New changes/amendments in the GST, applicable from April 1, 2019, include but not limited to the following:

1. Threshold limit to take registration has been increased to ₹40 lakh.
2. Threshold Limit for composition scheme has been increased to ₹1.5 crore.
3. New Scheme is now available @ 6% to Intra-State Suppliers of Goods or Service.
4. Due dates for filing of GSTR-1 and GSTR-3B have been announced.
5. Option to opt for 'Composition Scheme'.
6. GST is to be paid quarterly and return is to be filed annually.

Intrastate supply of goods: The supply of goods during intrastate trade or commerce regarding subsection (1) of Section 8 of IGST Act, 2017.

Output tax: The CGST/SGST on taxable supply of goods and/or services made by a taxable person or by his agent. It excludes tax payable on a reverse-charge basis.

Reverse charge: The tax liability on the recipient of the supply of goods and/or services instead of the supplier of such goods and/or services.

Services: Anything other than goods, money and securities but includes activities relating to the use of money or its conversion by cash or by any other mode, from one form, currency or denomination, to another form, currency or denomination for which a separate consideration is charged.

SGST: The State Goods and Services Tax Act, 2017. State tax means the tax imposed under SGST Act, 2017.

UIN: Abbreviation for Unique Identity Number, UIN is an ID used to identify specialized agencies who are non-taxable on Indian soil. These agencies can be bodies of United Nations, consulates, foreign embassies or organizations that are exempted either by the UN or by our government(s).

Zero-rated supply: Supply of any goods and/or services including export of goods and/or services or supply of goods and/or services to a SEZ developer or a SEZ unit.

Appendix A: Example Cases

Kuber Dhana

Mr. Rajesh Sharma, an employee, had signed a bond of two years with Kuber Dhana, a finance company, at the time of his placement. After seven months, he submitted his resignation as he had decided to switch his job and join a competitor of his current firm. However, Kuber Dhana refused to accept his resignation and instead suggested him to avail 'Garden Leave[1]' that was also included in his contract of employment. This way Kuber Dhana was successful in resolving the issue and to hold back Mr. Rajesh Sharma from joining any of its competitors. While proceeding on the said leave, he was told that the contract of his employment still remained valid. However, a few days before the expiration of the aforesaid leave period, Kuber Dhana sent a notice to Mr. Rajesh Sharma asking him to resume his duties; else it would be considered as a violation of terms of his contract of employment.

Mr. Rajesh Sharma, without paying any heed to the notice, took up employment with a close competitor of Kuber Dhana. On the same day, the counsellor of Kuber Dhana wrote to Mr. Rajesh Sharma that his failure to re-join his office was a breach and abrogation of his employment contract. I in the contract, it was also mentioned that the employee would need to pay an amount equal to 40% of his average salary for the remaining period of his contract if he/she wished to leave. Accordingly, Kuber Dhana claimed ₹402,300 from Rajesh and filed a writ petition in a court of law against him to recover the said amount.

Mr. Rajesh Sharma, pleaded that his employment relationship stood terminated when he had proceeded on 'Garden Leave' and therefore he committed no breach by joining some other firm; coincidently a rival firm of Kuber Dhana. The Court held that despite the termination of the employment relationship, the contract vis-a-vis its terms and conditions still stood valid, and, therefore, Kuber Dhana had the legal right to claim the damages from Rajesh.

On an appeal filed by Rajesh against the verdict, the full bench of the Court of Appeal maintained that the employer has a right to direct the employee to return to job on the basis of the terms of contract of employment signed between them. The Court upheld that the conduct of the employee in declining to return to work was a breach of terms of the employment, and on this ground his appeal was rejected. Mr. Rajesh Sharma, thereby, was ordered to pay Kuber Dhana ₹402,300 as damages.

Questions:

1. According to you, was Mr. Rajesh Sharma right in resigning and joining the competitor? What should have been his approach to safeguard his interest?
2. How should the company Kuber Dhana have approached when Mr. Rajesh Sharma had submitted his resignation?
3. What should the employee consider while signing a contract along with a bond restriction?

[1] 'Garden Leave' or 'Gardening Leave' describes the practice where an employee leaving a job, having resigned or otherwise had their employment terminated, is instructed to stay away from work during the notice period, while still remaining on the payroll. This practice is often used to prevent employees from taking with them up-to-date (and perhaps sensitive) information when they leave their current employer; especially when they are leaving to join a competitor.

Kumar Enterprises Ltd

Kumar Enterprises Ltd deals in office stationery. The firm takes part in tenders in various government organizations and has a huge non-government customer base as well. The firm is owned by Mr. Kumar and his wife. The firm has recently agreed to deliver a large consignment of stationeries to M/s Rupali & Sons.

The final quotation given by Mr. Kumar included the rate for each individual item his firm sells, delivery terms, and validity of the contract. Ms. Rupali, MD of the firm, awarded Mr. Kumar the contract after accepting the quotation, after around 45 days.

Mr. Kumar, on his part, acknowledged the order and delivered the required stationery within the stipulated time, as mentioned in the quotation. However, the rates stated in the invoice were higher than the ones mentioned in the quotation. Ms. Rupali, furious about the discrepancy, wrote a strong mail to Kumar Enterprises demanding a proper explanation for the said mismatch in the rates.

Mr. Kumar reverted quoting that the recent increase in the wholesale rates compelled him to increase the rates. He, however, admitted that he should have sought consent from M/s Rupali & Sons before raising the invoice. The mail could do little in quelling Ms. Rupali's displeasure and she wrote back stating that she would have thought twice before awarding Kumar the contract had she known that the rates were going to rise. She accused Mr. Kumar of following unethical business practice.

Mr. Kumar wrote back referring to a clause mentioned in his original quotation that the rates were valid only for a month and were subject to change without prior notification to the customer. Ms. Rupali, on the contrary, felt that she had been duped in a very subtle way and she could not do much about it given that Kumar had a firm legal footing.

After having thought about the problem for quite a few days, Ms. Rupali came up with an idea. She wrote to Mr. Kumar requesting him to come to her office for an amicable settlement of the issue. Mr. Kumar responded in affirmative and reached her office on the designated date. Ms. Rupali attempted to re-negotiate the terms of the contract and stressed on the fact that since the rates were substantially higher than what was originally quoted, she would take more time before she could clear the dues. She also asked Mr. Kumar to send her a backdated quotation on mail so that it would match the rates mentioned in the invoice. At the end of the meeting, she asked Mr. Kumar to mail her the salient points discussed in the meeting.

Mr. Kumar did as Ms. Rupali had asked him to. But to his utter dismay, he received a legal notice some days later. The notice accused him of fraudulent business practices and of sending backdated quotations to parties with the intent to cheat them. Moreover, it said that the order stands cancelled owing to supply of material of sub-standard quality and Mr. Kumar should arrange to take back the delivery of the stationery at his own expense.

Mr. Kumar was too shocked to think. He approached his lawyer who advised him to fight the case in a court of law.

Questions:

1. Where all do you think Mr. Kumar has gone wrong in the whole incident?
2. Is Ms. Rupali right in the way she has responded? Moral grounds notwithstanding, is she likely to get full support of the law?
3. Do you think that Mr. Kumar has no option but to take back the goods supplied to M/s Rupali & Sons?
4. Suppose you are the lawyer Mr. Kumar has sought advice from in the matter, what would you advise him to do and why? Cite provisions from the law of Contract and Sale of Goods Act to justify your advice.

Mamta Toys

Mamta was the owner of a store which dealt in imported electronic toys. She had started the business in 1986 by renting a shop located in the upscale Connaught Place market. Her business kept on flourishing day by day as she had started advertising through the Internet as well as other electronic media. By 2003, the business reached to such a great height of success that she thought of taking help and support from her family. In the month of November 2003, she had put forth this proposal before her family. After a series of discussions within the family, it was decided that Mamta would likely take retirement in a couple of years and her 17-year old daughter Alya would help her run the business hence forth. In return, Alya would be entitled a monthly stipend of ₹5,000. It was decided (orally) that Mamta would deposit the amount in a recurring deposit (RD) bank account in her own name and handover the total amount to Alya once she retired. However, when Mamta retired at the end of the year 2015, she decided to donate the total deposited amount to a local charitable dispensary and handed over the store jointly to her daughter and son, Jignesh, who had returned to India after completing his BBA from abroad. It was also resolved that both, the sister and the brother, would run the business jointly and share the income thereof equally.

Although Mamta, being the sole owner of the shop, had the exclusive right to give anything in charity as per her will and wish, but still this seemed in contradiction with her words and promise to Alya to allow her a fixed incentive for helping her in running the business. As per the law of contract, an employee can take refuge in law if the employer breaches the terms of the contract of their employment. One can understand that in this entire incident, Mamta had involved her daughter in order to take help from her, and, in return, had promised to pay the latter a sum of ₹5,000 per month; and now in violation of her promise, she wished to donate to charity the amount so accumulated in the RD account. Alya's friends suggested her to deal with this issue in the context of law of breach of contract. They convinced Alya that the act of her mother retracting on her promise is tantamount to breach of contract made with Alya. They also informed her that an employee has got exclusive right to approach the court of law, should the employer not fulfil the promise made with the former. Even though charity is a good deed, but with this decision of Mamta, she has deprived her daughter Alya from her right to compensation for the work she had performed in running the business.

Questions:

1. Where do you think Mamta has gone wrong in the entire incident?
2. What advice would you have given to Alya keeping in mind her relationship with her mother?
3. Can a case be filed against Mamta for a breach of contract?
4. How do you think Alya should handle this situation?
5. Was the advice extended to Alya by her friends to approach the court of law genuine?
6. Suppose you are Alya's lawyer and Alya comes to you to seek your advice. What would you advise her and why? Which provision of law would you cite from the Contract Act to support your advice?

RDM Finance Ltd

Mr. Sunil Gupta was the General Manager of RDM International Finance Ltd, a leading finance company based in Delhi. One day, Mr. Gupta got a phone call from Mr. R. Aggarwal, Rohit Suri, and Ankit Kaul that they were the directors of Aggarwal Marbles Ltd., and would like to meet him personally for raising some loan for their business. They fixed an appointment with Mr. Gupta for their meeting. During the meeting, they told Mr. Gupta that their company Aggarwal Marbles Ltd was doing good business and asked if his company could provide a loan of ₹60 lakh to their company. They also ensured that the loan would be repaid with interest within 6 months. After the meeting, the directors of Aggarwal Marbles continued to visit Mr. Gupta's office for pursuing the request for granting of the loan. Relying on their persuasion, Mr. Gupta's company granted them the loan of ₹60 lakh by means of cheques drawn on Corporation Bank, New Delhi, unaware of the unfair intention of these persons.

When the loan repayment became due, Mr. R. Aggarwal issued two cheques to the finance company for repayment of the loan, for ₹60 lakh towards the payment of the principal sum and ₹86,625 towards the payment of interest, both the instruments drawn on Punjab National Bank.

When these cheques were deposited with the bank for clearance, they were returned dishonoured for 'insufficient funds' in the drawer's account. The finance company contacted Aggarwal Marbles Ltd several times by phone and by writing letters and asked them to pay the amount but they failed to pay the money. After some days, the directors of Aggarwal Marbles started avoiding Mr. Gupta's calls.

Upset with all these failed attempts, Mr. Gupta wrote a final letter to Aggarwal Marbles Ltd telling its directors that he would file a case against them in the consumer court if they further failed to make the payment. Finally, the debtors came to his office and requested to grant them six more months for the repayment of the loan amount. They pleaded that due to some mishap, they had suffered some financial losses. They issued two fresh cheques towards the payment of their loan, drawn against Nainital Bank Ltd.

Again, when these cheques were sent to the bank for clearance, they were returned dishonoured due to insufficient balance. Furious, Mr. Gupta approached the police alleging that the above-mentioned acts of the accused persons were fraudulent and committed with the common intention to cheat his firm. On the basis of his complaint, the police registered an FIR against the three persons named in the complaint.

Questions:

1. Before straightaway filing FIR with the police, what action Mr. Gupta should have initiated against Aggarwal Marbles for bouncing of their cheques for insufficiency of funds in their bank account, as per the provisions of Negotiable Instruments Act?
2. Do you think Mr. Gupta would be able to recover his money just through the FIR route?
3. Do you think Mr. Gupta should have been more cautious while granting loan to the company?
4. Do you think Mr. Gupta should have kept some security against the loan amount granted to Aggarwal Marbles?
5. Do you think the directors of Aggarwal Marbles genuinely have the financial crisis as they have stated? What are your views on the matter?

Software Assurance Koncept (SAK) Ltd

Software Assurance Koncept (SAK) Ltd, a global IT company, spreading across various nations, keeps on hunting for people with IT skills. This hiring process becomes more crucial when the firm needs people for some or the other niche skills such as ARIBA, DRUPAL, etc. As more people are hired for onshore projects, this company offers lucrative promotions and perks. One of the loyal employees of SAK Ltd., named Ramesh, who has worked in the company for more than five years, was looking forward to his promotion from the position of Assistant Manager to the post of Manager.

Ramesh was having the skill set and competency to qualify for this promotion. For instance, he was certified in JAVA, ORACLE, and SAS. Apart from these technical skills, he was certified in Project Management, Software Estimations, Six Sigma Green Belt, and his project team was selected as the best team in the company.

The promotion was due in the month of March 2014, and the employee had to go through a series of assessments. These assessments included an online written test for judging aspiring candidates' technical skills, personality, language, etc., followed by two rounds of close interaction with the senior management. However, due to company's promotion policies and some other internal constraints, only one-tenths of the total workforce was eligible for promotion.

Looking at this scenario, Ramesh was very anxious about his promotion, and approached Mr. Joshi, the HR Manager, to get more clarity on this. As the HR manager was friendly with Ramesh, he revealed verbally that he (Ramesh) is on the top of the list of candidates to be promoted, and, therefore, he should not worry about this anymore. Filled with joy, he started wondering about his next position. Ramesh even shared his delight with his close friends in his office. Everyone was happy about his promotion as he was well behaved in the company and deserved the promotion owing to his commitment and skills.

Ramesh went through the series of steps for promotion and was asked to wait for a few days for the result to be displayed. In May 2014, the final list of promoted candidates was displayed on the company's website. But, to his utter dismay, Ramesh could not find his name on the list. Highly disappointed, Ramesh went to his boss to seek an explanation. His boss, Mr. Radha Krishnan, told him (Ramesh) that there were other employees senior to him in the ranking who were promoted. Ramesh argued that he was eligible for promotion as per the company's policy, and mere seniority in terms of number of years of service rendered by someone should not matter. Besides, according to him, he did very well in the test too. He submitted to his boss that if not promoted, he will sue the company.

Ramesh also discussed this with the HR Manager, as the latter had shown him his name appearing at the top of the promotion list of the candidates. The HR Manager explained that the said merit list was simply based on the marks obtained by the candidates in the written test, but the promotion policy takes into account several other factors as well. Still not convinced with the clarifications tendered to him, Ramesh went on to file a lawsuit against his company for not promoting him.

Questions:

1. Is Ramesh right in filing a case against SAK Ltd? Explain.
2. Do you think that the denial of promotion to Ramesh by SAK Ltd is a breach of terms of contract of employment? If yes, explain.
3. What are the chances of Ramesh winning or losing the case against the company and why?
4. Can Ramesh file a case against his boss personally also? Elucidate.

Stellarways Agency

An agency, Stellarways, arranged for Mr. Sanjeev Singh to be placed in a pharmaceutical company, AbChem Limited, in Indore for a contractual term of 12 months to provide consultancy related to maternity drugs. Similar to other agencies, Stellarways had advertised the opening along with all the eligibility conditions. Responding to the advertisement, Mr. Singh had approached the agency with his resume for the job. Stellarways took his preliminary interview and prepared him to face the final interview with AbChem Limited. To the agency, Sanjeev appeared as fulfilling all the eligibility criteria laid out by the pharmaceutical company.

Mr. Singh attended the final interview and got selected. He was offered the role of a consultant and was given the joining date. When he was offered this role, Stellarways prepared the contract between themselves and AbChem Limited. They also prepared a 'Consultancy Agreement' between AbChem Limited and Mr. Singh. In both the documents, it was mentioned that the pharmaceutical company can end the contract if and when the company deemed fit considering that the services of the consultant were no more required. This was stated as 'early termination clause' in the contract. This was also an indication that both the parties can part their ways if and when they wish so. The agreement was mutually signed by Mr. Singh and the company, and the latter resumed his job.

Mr. Singh was performing his role very well and everything was going smooth. However, around 6 months later, there was some restructuring in the pharmaceutical company related to the manufacturing of drugs and pharmaceuticals and also marketing of the products. As a result, Mr. Singh's consultancy was no longer needed by the pharmaceutical company. The company gave notice to Stellarways and Stellarways, in turn, informed Mr. Singh about termination of his job.

Although Mr. Singh received formal and proper notice period along with an ex-gratia payment, he was not happy that his job was terminated before the completion of the contract period of 1 year. He approached the court of law, putting an allegation on Stellarways that he was kept in dark about the pharmaceutical company's policy as regards termination of service before the completion of the contract period. Mr. Singh claimed that he should be compensated by the company for the remaining period of his service of six months, which was approximately ₹4.2 lakh.

The court summoned Stellarways to inquire about the various facets of the claim, along with notifying them the risks and financial loss the agency might face if found guilty. The agency drafted a sturdy defence to counter the claim. The agency also wrote to Mr. Singh explaining how his claim was not valid and would be rejected by the court. Upon going through these details, Mr. Singh reluctantly agreed to withdraw his petition. To an extent, he was convinced that everything done by the Company as well as the Agency was fool proof and he might not gain anything by pleading his petition in the court of law and would rather be a loser.

Questions:

1. Do you think Mr. Singh should have pleaded his petition in the court instead of withdrawing it?
2. What do you suggest Mr. Singh should have done at the time of signing the contract to protect his interests?
3. How was Stellarways agency responsible for this situation of Mr. Sanjeev Singh?
4. Was AbChem Limited correct in ending the contract before time? Explain.
5. What should a candidate look for in a job contract?

Appendix B: Landmark Judgements

Angoori Devi & Ors vs Dalbir Singh & Another[1]

Parties Involved

1. Angoori Devi – Buyer of Dalbir Singh's land – Appellant/Defendant No. 1
2. Santish – Co-buyer of Dalbir Singh's land – Appellant/ Defendant No. 2
3. Randhir Singh, maternal uncle of Dalbir Singh, and Ranbir Singh, son-in-law of Randhir Singh
4. Haryana Gramin Bank – Respondent No. 2/ Defendant No. 3
5. Dalbir Singh – Plaintiff/Respondent No. 1

Legislations Cited/Referred

The Indian Contract Act, 1872 – Sections 7, 10, 13, and 14

Facts in Brief

1. The present appeal (i.e., RSA – Regular Second Appeal) arises from the judgement and decree passed by Civil Judge, Jind, and against the judgement and decree passed by Additional District Judge, Jind, vide which suit for declaration and permanent injunction preferred by Dalbir Singh, son of Ajit Singh (insane and feeble-minded person) through his maternal uncle Mahavir Singh as guardian appointed by the Court.
2. Plaintiff/respondent No. 1 (Dalbir Singh) through his maternal uncle/guardian (Mahavir Singh) had sought declaration to the effect that the sale deed dated 25 Feb 2008 and subsequent mutation sanctioned on the basis of the said sale deed are illegal, null, and void and are not binding on his rights.
3. Respondent No. 1/plaintiff, a person of sub-normal mind residing under the custody of his maternal uncle Mahavir Singh, is the owner in possession of sum total land.
4. On 8 March 2008, it came to the knowledge of Respondent No. 1/plaintiff that his land has been transferred in the name of appellants by *misrepresentation and fraud* by executing a sale deed which is illegal and liable to be set aside. It was alleged by Respondent No. 1/plaintiff that on 2 Feb 2008, his maternal uncle Randhir Singh along with his son-in-law came to his village and took him along on the pretext of medical check-up.
5. It was claimed in the writ petition, filed in the sessions court against the above transaction, that Respondent No. 1/plaintiff was not competent to execute and register the sale deed being sub-normal mind person.
6. As per the stand of the appellants/defendants No. 1 and 2, they had purchased the land vide sale deed dated 25 Feb 2008 by paying the consideration amount of ₹18 lakh and, thereafter, mutation was sanctioned.
7. It has been denied by the appellants/defendants No. 1 and 2 that Respondent No. 1/plaintiff is of insane mind and he had sold this property after the death of his parents by his free and sweet will.
8. After executing the sale deed, the suit property stands mortgaged by the appellants/defendants No. 1 and 2 with Haryana Gramin Bank, Jind, as the appellants/ defendants No. 1 and 2 had applied for a tractor loan of ₹3.00 lakh and Kisan Credit Card of ₹1,50,000/- and had, thus, mortgaged the land vide mortgage deed and mutation has been sanctioned in favour of the bank.

Discussion in Brief

1. On the pleadings of the parties, the following issues were framed by the Trial Court:
   (a) Whether the impugned sale deed and consequent mutation alleged to have been executed by plaintiff in favour of defendants pertaining to the suit

[1] RSA No. 1076 of 2019, PHHC

land is illegal, null, and void, result of fraud, misrepresentation, undue influence, or coercion; and is liable to be set aside and not binding on the rights of plaintiff ?

(b) If issue No. 1 is proved, whether the plaintiff is entitled for the relief of permanent injunction as prayed for?

(c) Whether the suit of the plaintiff is not maintainable?

(d) Whether the suit is bad for want of proper court fees?

(e) Whether the suit has been filed by Mahavir Singh, who is the real beneficiary of the suit, and if so to what extent?

(f) Relief sought by the parties?

2. The following ad ditional issues were framed subsequently by the Trial Court:

(a) Whether defendants No. 1 and 2 have taken the possession of suit land illegally and forcibly and during the pendency of the suit ?

(b) Whether the plaintiff is entitled for possession of the suit land ?

(c) Whether defendant No. 3 is a bona fide mortgagee and has acted upon in good faith by advancing the loan to the defendants No. 1 and 2 by mortgaging the land in dispute as a collateral security of the due payment of loan availed by defendants No. 1 and 2?

3. After taking into consideration the evidence on record, the Trial Court vide judgement and decree dated 23 Oct 2010 decreed the suit of respondent No. 1/plaintiff.

4. The appeal filed by the appellants/defendants No. 1 and 2 against the said judgement and decree was dismissed by the first Appellate Court vide judgement and decree dated 17 Sep 2018. Hence, the present appeal by the appellants/defendants No. 1 and 2.

5. Learned counsel for the appellants has argued that the sale deed was executed after the appellants/defendants No. 1 and 2 paid the valuable consideration of ₹18 lakh to Respondent No. 1/plaintiff in the presence of the attesting witnesses, which was duly scribed at the instance of Dalbir Singh. It has been further argued that the sale deed being a registered document carries presumption of genuineness.

6. Per contra, learned counsel for Respondent No. 1/plaintiff – caveator – has argued that it has been established on record that Respondent No. 1/plaintiff is a special person who lost his mother when he was a child and his father deserted him, and the present suit had been filed through Mahavir Singh, who is the maternal uncle of Dalbir Singh and legal guardian. No consideration amount was paid to Dalbir Singh while alienating his land in favour of appellants/defendants No. 1 and 2. It has been argued that Respondent No. 1/plaintiff is suffering from severe sub-normality of mind and is unable to formulate or rationalise consequences of his own and, *thus, the sale deed dated 25 Feb 2008 is outcome of misrepresentation, coercion, and fraud*, which has been committed by the appellants/defendants No. 1 and 2 in collusion with Randhir Singh, maternal uncle of Dalbir Singh, and his son-in-law Ranbir Singh.

7. It is a case where it has been established on record that Respondent No.1/plaintiff Dalbir Singh falls under the definition of the term 'idiocy'. The term 'idiocy' has been explained by Professor Modi's *Medical Jurisprudence and Toxicology*, 19 ed, p 388, as follows:

Idiocy – This is a congenital condition due to defective development of the mental faculties. All grades of this condition exist from the helpless life of a mere vegetable organism of one which can be compared with the life of young children, as far as mental development is concerned. An idiot is wanting in memory and will power is devoid of emotion who has to initiative of any kind, is unable to fix attention of any subject and is unable to guard himself against common physical danger. He is usually quite, gentle and timid.

9. The counsel of Dalbir Singh contended that the said sale deed is an act of non-free mind, non-consent, under the influence of fraud and misrepresentation. Respondent No.1/plaintiff Dalbir Singh had not stepped into the school premises at any stage nor had he an exposure to the outside world and is an illiterate, unmarried, issueless, and hapless man of the age of 29 years. He lost his mother when he was a child and his father deserted him. The person like him always remain under the influence of his relatives, either under maternal uncles or paternal uncles.

10. Dalbir Singh's counsel further argued that it has come on record that his maternal uncle Randhir Singh and Ranbir Singh (son-in-law of Randhir Singh) took him on the pretext of his medical check-up and got executed the sale deed in question. It has also come on record that Randhir Singh and Ranbir Singh had suffered a disclosure statement before the police in a criminal case – both of them had received consideration amount of ₹10,70,000/- from Angoori Devi and Santosh, appellants/ defendants No. 1 and 2, which they had divided among themselves, out of

the sale consideration of ₹18.00 lakh as cost of sale deed. Thus, it is a clear case where Respondent No.1/ plaintiff Dalbir Singh was never handed over the sale consideration.

11. Counsel for Respondent No. 1/plaintiff – caveator – finally submitted before Punjab and Haryana High Court as under:

To draw conclusion regarding the fate of the sale deed, it will be relevant to discuss Sections 7, 10, 13, and 14 of the Indian Contract Act, 1872, which read as under:

Section 7. Acceptance must be absolute – In order to convert a proposal into a promise the acceptance must:

(1) be absolute and unqualified;

(2) be expressed in some usual and reasonable manner, unless the proposal prescribes the manner in which it is to be accepted. If the proposal prescribes a manner in which it is to be accepted, and the acceptance is not made in such manner, the proposer may, within a reasonable time after the acceptance is communicated to him, insist that his proposal shall be accepted in the prescribed manner, and not otherwise; but, if he fails to do so, he accepts the acceptance.

Section 10. What agreements are contracts – All agreements are contracts if they are made by the free consent of parties competent to contract, for a lawful consideration and with a lawful object, and are not hereby expressly declared to be void. Nothing herein contained shall affect any law in force in (1) [India], and not hereby expressly repealed, by which any contract is required to be made in writing or (2) in the presence of witnesses, or any law relating to the registration of documents.

Section 13. 'Consent' defined – Two or more persons are said to 7 of 9 consent when they agree upon the same thing in the same sense.

Section 14. 'Free consent' defined – Consent is said to be free when it is not caused by:

(1) coercion, as defined in Section 15, or (2) undue influence, as defined in Section 16, or (3) fraud, as defined in Section 17, or (4) misrepresentation, as defined in Section 18, or (5) mistake, subject to the provisions of Sections 20, 21, and 22. Consent is said to be so caused when it would not have been given but for the existence of such coercion, undue influence, fraud, misrepresentation, or mistake.

Judgement

The High Court of Haryana and Punjab, after going through the above Sections, held, it is crystal clear that by law a valid contract is always entered into by free consent of the parties competent to contract for lawful consideration and with lawful objective and not expressly declared to be void. Meaning thereby, the consent of the parties must be free and for execution of the instrument, i.e., sale deed, voluntary deposition is essence of such a deed.

In the present case, Respondent No.1/plaintiff Dalbir Singh who had remained under the influence of persons so as to be unable to formulate any independent decision of his own and unable to formulate the rational consequences of his own act. The other factor which has also come to the mind of this Court that after execution of the sale deed dated 25 Feb 2008, the appellants/defendants No. 1 and 2 mortgaged the suit land in favour of defendant No. 3 – bank, vide mortgage deed dated 3 April 2008 for obtaining the tractor loan. It has also come on record that the defendant No. 3 had filed a recovery suit of the outstanding amount against the appellants/defendants No. 1 and 2. This fact also clearly shows that immediately after execution of the sale deed, the appellants rushed to the bank for obtaining a loan on the property which had been allegedly purchased from Respondent No. 1/ plaintiff Dalbir Singh who is a person of 'idiocy' and had never been handed over the consideration amount by the appellants.

It is clear that if any of the contracting party does not have the capacity, then the said contract is void. The unsoundness of mind is one of the circumstances which renders the contract void. From the logical outcome of the Privy Council decision in Mohori Bibi vs Dharmodas Ghose (1930) 30 Cal 539 case of a minor's incompetency, it naturally follows that a lunatic's contract must always be void under the Indian law. The Indian law regarding the contractual capacity of mentally disordered persons clearly provides that where a person, imbalanced in mind, executes a sale deed, the transferee cannot acquire any right, title, or interest. Held, ultimately, the judgements passed by the lower courts are well reasoned and are affirmed. No substantial question of law arises in this case which would warrant interference by this Court. Hence, the appeal stands dismissed.

Aradhna Fabrics Pvt. Ltd vs United India Insurance Co. Ltd[1]

Parties Involved

1. Aradhna Fabrics Pvt. Ltd – Insured – Complainant
2. United India Insurance Co. Ltd – Sole opposite party

Legislations Cited/Referred

The Consumer Protection Act, 1986
The Indian Contract Act – Sections 14, 15, 16, 17, 18, 20, 21, and 22

Facts in Brief

1. The complainant company obtained four policies from the opposite party United India Insurance Co. Ltd, thereby insuring its building, plant, machinery, and accessories, furniture, fixtures, and fittings as well as the stock of yarn/fabric/cloth, kept at its factory premises at 144, Industrial Area A, Ludhiana.
2. On the intervening night of 29-30 April 2007, a fire broke out in the factory premises of the complainant causing immense damage to the building, plant, and machinery as well as the stock kept in the factory. Upon the information of fire having been given to the said insurance company, S. Soni & Co. were appointed as the surveyors and loss assessors. A claim of ₹6.68 crore along with ₹1.60 lakh towards out of pocket expenses was lodged with the insurance company by the complainant. The surveyors submitted a report dated 8 Dec 2007, assessing the loss at ₹5,23,34,842.88/- on reinstatement basis and ₹3,70,30,083.83/- on depreciation basis. On receipt of the aforesaid report, the insurance company made part payment of ₹3 crore to the complainant. The surveyors submitted a final report dated 22 Oct 2008, assessing the loss to the complainant at ₹5,00,88,091/-.
3. Being aggrieved from the failure to make the balance payment, the complainant approached The National Consumers Disputes Redressal Commission (NCDRC or, say, Commission) on 24 Sep 2009, seeking the following reliefs:
   - Direct the opposite party to pay the entire claim amount of ₹6.68 crore as per claim form, i.e., as per policies, and also the increase in labour and material expenses, which is expected @ 15% to 20% up to the time of filing the complaint to reinstate the building/machineries, etc., and grant special punitive damages; and
   - Pay interest @ 15% after three months from the date of the loss up to the date of payment and special costs.

Discussion in Brief

1. The complaint has been resisted by the insurance company on the ground that after making part payment of ₹3 crore to the complainant, in early 2008, they made payment of ₹2,00,46,882/- to the complainant vide cheque dated 15 Oct 2009, and the said payment was duly accepted by the complainant in settlement of its claim.
2. In view of the stand taken by the insurance company in the reply filed by it, NCDRC heard the learned counsel for the parties on the question as to whether having accepted a sum of ₹2,00,46,882/- in addition to the interim payment of ₹3 crore from the opposite party, the complainant was estopped from claiming any amount and the complaint is liable to be dismissed or not.
3. It has been contended by the learned counsel for the complainant that since they were not receiving any further payment from the insurance company, they were left with no other option but to accept the offer made by the insurance company. This was also his

[1] NCDRC Case No. 151 of 2009

contention that the payment of ₹2,00,46,882/- was accepted by the complainant under protest and on having been pressurised by the insurance company and while being in financial hardships.

4. The learned counsel for the opposite party, on the other hand, contended that there was no compulsion on the complainant to accept the aforesaid amount, particularly when an interim payment of ₹3 crore had already been received by it from the insurance company and, in fact, the complainant had voluntarily accepted the aforesaid payment of ₹2,00,46,882/- in full and final settlement of its claim. It was also pointed out by the learned counsel for the insurance company that the amount paid to the complainant was not an arbitrary amount but was exactly the amount recommended by the surveyors vide their report dated 22 Oct 2008.
5. The defendant put forth the defence of *accord and satisfaction* on the basis of a full and final discharge voucher issued by the plaintiff whereas the plaintiff alleged that it was obtained by fraud/coercion/undue influence and, therefore, not valid. It would consider the evidence as to whether there was any fraud, coercion, or undue influence. If it found that there was none, it will accept the voucher as being in discharge of the contract and reject the claim without examining the claim on merits. The arbitration agreement can thus be invoked to refer the disputes to arbitration.
6. On the contrary, if it is found that the discharge voucher had been obtained by fraud/undue influence/coercion, it will ignore the same, examine whether the plaintiff had made out the claim on merit and decide the matter accordingly. The position will be the same even when there is a provision for arbitration.
7. The legal proposition, which emerges from some referred decisions, viz., United India Insurance Co. Ltd vs Ajmer Singh Cotton & General Mills & Ors (1999), National Insurance Co. Ltd vs Nipha Exports (P) Ltd, National Insurance Co. Ltd vs Sethia Shoes (2007), and New India Assurance Co. Ltd vs Genus Power Infrastructure Ltd, 2015, AIR SCW 67, is that although issue of a discharge voucher accepting a particular amount in full and final settlement of its claim is not conclusive when there are allegations of fraud, undue influence, etc., mere bald allegations are not sufficient in this regard and such allegations cannot be accepted by the court, unless the insured places material before the concerned Court/Forum which would substantiate the plea of fraud, undue influence, etc., taken by him and establish that the discharge voucher executed by him was not voluntary and was in fact a product of exercise of fraud, undue influence, coercion, misrepresentation, etc., on the part of the insurer.
8. The onus will be upon the insured to substantiate the plea of fraud, undue influence, etc., taken by him. As observed in National Insurance Co. vs Boghara Polyfab Pvt. Ltd (2009), if it is found that there was no fraud, coercion, undue influence, etc. the court/forum concerned has to accept the voucher as being in discharge of the contract and reject the claim without examining it on merit. If, however, it is found that the discharge voucher was obtained by use of fraud, undue influence, coercion, etc., it has to be ignored and the claim needs to be examined and decided on merit.
9. In the present case, the complainant was already before this Commission when the discharge voucher came to be executed and submitted by it to the insurance company. Interim payment of ₹3 crore had already been made to the complainant before it approached this Commission. If the insurance company offered a sum of ₹2,00,46,882/- to it and the said offer was not acceptable to the complainant, nothing prevented it from filing an application before this Commission for a direction to the insurance company to make payment of the aforesaid amount of ₹2,00,46,882/- without prejudice to the rights and contentions of the parties. Had such a course been adopted by the complainant, which was duly represented by a counsel; it would have been possible for this Commission to pass such an order and thereafter adjudicate the claim on merit. That, however, was not done and the complainant had not given any explanation for not adopting the aforesaid course of action. The inevitable inference, therefore, would be that the complainant voluntarily entered into a settlement with the insurance company accepting the amount of ₹2,00,46,882/- in full and final settlement of its claim.
10. Free consent is defined in Section 14 of the Indian Contract Act, which reads as under:
Consent is said to be free when it is not caused by: (1) coercion, as defined in Section 15 or (2) undue influence, as defined in Section 16, or (3) fraud, as defined in Section 17, or (4) misrepresentation, as defined in Section18, or (5) mistake, subject to the provisions of Sections 20, 21 and 22. Consent is said to be so caused when it would not have been given but for the existence of such coercion, undue influence, fraud, misrepresentation, or mistake."

Judgement

The Commission observed that the consent given by a person would be deemed to be a free consent and would be binding upon the parties to the contract unless it can be shown that it was obtained by exercise of coercion, undue influence, fraud, misrepresentation, or mistake as defined in the stated relevant Sections.

The Commission held, in the case before it, that there was no such relationship between the complainant and the opposite party that the opposite party can be said to be in a position to dominate the will of the complainant company and use that position to obtain an undue influence over the complainant company. There is no allegation of concealment of any material fact by the insurance company from the complainant with a view to obtain the consent of the complainant company to the aforesaid settlement. Section 17 of the Act is therefore not applicable. There is no allegation of any misrepresentation within the meaning of Section 18 of the Contract Act and, therefore, the aforesaid section also does not apply.

No case of coercion is made out by the complainant company since there is no allegation of committing, or threatening to commit, any act forbidden by the Indian Penal Code or unlawful detaining, or threatening to detain, any property, to the prejudice of the complainant, with intention of causing the complainant to enter into any settlement

For the reasons stated hereinabove, considering the settlement between the parties being true and fair, the complaint does not survive anymore and is accordingly dismissed. No order as costs.

Belaire Owners Association vs DLF Ltd[1]

Parties Involved

1. Belaire Owners Association – Association formed by the apartment allottees of a building complex, Belaire, situated in DLF City, Phase V, Gurgaon, being constructed by Opponent Party 1 (DLF Ltd) – Informant/Complainant
2. DLF Ltd – India's topmost realty major – Opponent Party 1
3. Haryana Urban Development Authority (HUDA) – Opponent Party 2
4. Department of Town and Country Planning (DTCP), Haryana – Opponent Party 3

Legislation Cited/Referred

1. The Competition Act, 2002 – Sections 2, 4, 19 (7), and 27
2. The Consumer Protection Act, 1986 – Section 2(o) and Section 2(u)
3. MRTP Act – Section 2(r)
5. The Companies Act, 1956 – Section 62
6. Delhi Development Act

Facts in Brief

1. OP-1 announced a Group Housing Complex, named as the Belaire consisting of 5 multi-storied residential buildings to be constructed on the land earmarked in Zone 8, Phase V, DLF City, Gurgaon, Haryana.
2. As per the advertisement of OP-1, each of the five multi-storied buildings was to consist of 19 floors and the total number of apartments to be built therein was to be 368 and the construction was to be completed within a period of 36 months.
3. However, in place of 19 floors with 368 apartments, which was the basis of the apartment allottees booking their respective apartments, now 29 floors have been constructed.
4. Consequently, not only the areas and facilities originally earmarked for the apartment allottees are substantially compressed but also the project has been abnormally delayed.
5. The fall-out of the delay is that hundreds of apartment allottees have to bear huge financial losses, as while on one hand, their hard-earned money is blocked, and on the other hand, they have to wait indefinitely for occupation of their respective apartments.

Discussion in Brief

1. The informant in the case (Belaire Owners Association) has alleged unfair conditions meted out by DLF Ltd.
2. It has been alleged that by abusing its dominant position, DLF Ltd (OP-1) has imposed arbitrary, unfair, and unreasonable conditions on the apartment allottees of the housing complex, Belaire, being constructed by it.
3. The aggrieved flat owners of Belaire housing complex in Gurgaon, Haryana, had complained that DLF had inordinately delayed the project and inserted one-sided contract clauses on apartment buyers. For instance, the allotees who failed to pay instalments on time were to cough up 15-18 per cent interest, whereas the builder would only have to shell out compensation at the rate of ₹5/sq. ft a month for delay beyond three years.
4. Buyers complained that they also had no exit option except when DLF failed to deliver possession within the agreed time.
5. According to one such complaint, DLF had promised to complete its residential project in Gurgaon, namely Belaire, in 2009, but buyers are yet to get possession.

[1] LNIND 2011 CCI 62

In addition, DLF has increased the number of floors in the apartment complex from the original figure given to buyers. This led to the number of apartments in Belaire increasing to 564 from 384.

6. Further, the money would be refunded without interest and that too only after DLF resold all the 564 apartments.
7. The Commission has concluded that DLF Ltd is in contravention of Section 4(2)(a)(i) by imposing unfair conditions on the sale of its services to consumers.
8. A company violates Section 4(2)(a) of the Competition Act when it directly or indirectly imposes unfair or discriminatory conditions or prices with respect to the purchase or sale of goods or services.

Judgement

Competition watchdog – Competition Commission of India (CCI) – imposed a penalty of ₹630 crore on DLF for "grossly abusing' its dominant market position.

CCI's hefty penalty amounts to seven per cent of the company's average annual turnover over the past three years. It is the highest such penalty imposed by CCI so far, observed by legal experts.

The Commission also directed DLF to modify 'unfair conditions' within three months. Adopting a harsh tone, the CCI said "....the brutal disregard to consumer right that has been displayed in its action of cancelling allotments and forfeiting deposits and...keeping buyers in the dark about the eventual shape, size, location, etc., of the apartment cannot be termed as fair."

Appeal against CCI Order by DLF Ltd

DLF Ltd filed an appeal against the CCI order in the Supreme Court but to no avail. The apex court directed the appellant (DLF Ltd) to deposit ₹630 crore fine slapped on it by the CCI for allegedly resorting to unfair business practices.

The apex court said the total amount will be deposited within three months with its registry pending the outcome of the appeal filed by DLF against the order of Competition Appellate Tribunal's upholding the penalty of ₹630 crore imposed by the CCI.

"We direct the appellant (DLF) to deposit the amount of ₹630 crore in this court," a bench comprising Justices Ranjana Prakash Desai and N.V. Ramana said in its interim order. The bench said that so far as the interest on the amount was concerned it has to be determined as per the 9 Nov 2011 order of the CCI that was fixed at 9 per cent.

It also directed DLF to file a fresh undertaking that in the event of dismissal of the appeal, it will pay such amount as directed by the court. DLF pleaded that it should be granted at least six months' time to deposit the amount. However, the bench said it was inclined to grant three months' time only.

Further, the bench directed that out of ₹630 crore, the real estate major has to deposit ₹50 crore in three weeks and the Registry (CCI) will be at liberty to invest it in any of the nationalised banks.

Hukmi Chand vs Jaipur Ice & Oil Mills Co. & Ors[1]

Parties Involved

1. Hukmi Chand – Appellant
2. Kalicharan – Defendant No. 1
3. Hukmichand – Defendant No. 2
4. Ramniranjan Lal – Defendant No. 3
5. Genia Bai – Defendant No. 4
6. Rajgopal, minor son of Kalicharan – Defendant No. 5
7. Jaipur Ice & Oil Mills Co. – Plaintiff

Facts of the Case

1. This is a defendant's Special Appeal under Section 18 of the Rajasthan High Court Ordinance against the judgement of the learned single Judge dated 9 Dec 1969, and arises out of a suit for injunction.
2. The Jaipur Ice & Oil Mills Co., hereinafter referred to as the Company, was ordinarily composed of six partners, viz., Kishanlal, Mahadeo Prasad, Satya Narayan, Kalicharan, Bishambhar Dass, and Jeewan Prasad, and a partnership deed was executed on 28 Feb 1947.
3. The firm had acquired a plot of land measuring 260' x 325' at Bani Park. Jaipur, on a part of which the factory had been constructed, and a residential house on a piece of this land measuring 325' x 88' with its own money. It started manufacturing ice, oil, and soap in Bani Park, Jaipur.
4. Two of its partners, Bishambar Dass and Jiwan Prasad, left the firm on 27 April 1949, and the rest of the four partners, above named, continued the partnership business up to 31 March 1958, on which date the firm was dissolved under a dissolution deed.
5. At the time of dissolution of the firm under the dissolution deed dated 31 March 1958, Kalicharan retired from the partnership and was paid ₹26,454.00 as a share of the capital invested by him, and over and above that he was also paid ₹11,001/- as his share of the price of the goodwill of the firm.
6. At the time of dissolution of the firm, it was agreed between Kalicharan (Defendant No. 1), the retired partner, on the one hand, and Kishanlal, Mahadeo Prasad, and Satya Narain, on the other, vide Clause 12 of the dissolution deed, that the aforesaid land measuring 325' x 83' and the house standing thereon would be the exclusive property of Kalicharan with full rights of sale and mortgage, and that Kalicharan would get a boundary wall constructed or have a wire fencing on this piece of land, open a separate door towards the road side, but would not have any entrance or exit towards the factory compound. It was also agreed that Kalicharan would not carry out the same kind of business, i.e., ice factory, on the land in his possession.
7. Kalicharan subsequently sold a piece of land measuring 88' x 162' out of 325' x 88', which was exclusively left to him under the deal to his father Ram Niranjan Lal for a consideration of ₹3168/- by a registered sale deed, dated 12 January 1959.
8. Thereafter, by deed dated 11 February 1959, Ramniranjan Lal entered into partnership with Smt. Genia Bai, wife of Kalicharan and Hukum Chand, son of Kalicharan, for carrying out business of ice and also admitted Rajgopal Kanodia, minor son of Kalicharan, to the benefits of partnership. They also applied for a licence to put up an ice factory on the aforesaid land measuring 88' x 162' in their possession and started making further preparations in the direction of establishing an ice factory.
9. The Company subsequently filed a suit through its partner Mahadeo Prasad on 29 November 1961 in the Court of Munsiff (East), Jaipur City, against Kalicharan, Hukmichand, Ramniranjan Lal, Genia Bai, and Rajgopal, minor son of Kalicharan, for issuing a permanent injunction restraining the

[1] LNIND 1980 RAJ 37

defendants from putting up an ice factory on the disputed land and prohibiting them to do any business of manufacturing of ice.

Discussion in Brief

1. Kalicharan and Hukmichand filed separate written statements and a number of pleas, but the suit was decreed by the Trial Court by passing an injunction order against the defendants and the appeal of the defendants was also dismissed. By the time, Hukmichand filed a second appeal before this court and it was heard by a learned single Judge; the only point which survived was as to the effect of Clauses 12 and 13 of the dissolution deed, which contained restrictive covenant; a covenant (or say an agreement or understanding) imposing a restriction on the use of land so that the value and enjoyment of adjoining land will be preserved.
2. The conclusions arrived at by the Trial Court were that Clause 13 of the dissolution deed did not impose unreasonable restraint of trade on the defendant Kalicharan and his transferees, and, consequently, the defendants were bound by the restrictive covenant and were not entitled to put up an ice factory on the land in question in pursuance of that restraint clause. This finding was affirmed in appeal by the learned Senior Civil Judge (2), Jaipur City. The learned single Judge has also affirmed that finding and has held that restrictive covenant contained in Clause 13 of the dissolution deed, in his opinion, is reasonable regard being had to the nature of the business and further that this restrictive covenant is binding on the transferees of Kalicharan, viz., Ramniranjan Lal and others.
3. The learned Advocate for the appellant has submitted that looking to the nature of the business, the restrictive covenant contained in Clause 13 of the dissolution deed is not reasonable, in as much as Kalicharan (Defendant No. 1) has been restrained from exercising a lawful trade without any regard to time and, therefore, is void. He further contends that the restrictive covenant at any rate is not a covenant running with the land, and, therefore, it is not binding on the transferees of Kalicharan (Defendant No. 1), viz., defendants 2 to 5, including the appellant.
4. The Court observed that it will first like to deal, as to whether the covenant in restraint of trade, contained in Clause 13 of the dissolution deed is reasonable or not. It will be useful to reproduce Clauses 12 and 13 of the dissolution deed as under:

Clause 12 – That the 1st party (Kalicharan) has constructed a residential bungalow on a piece of land measuring 325' x 88' (sketch attached herewith) out of the factory land, from his own capital and it has been mutually agreed by the parties that the land aforesaid and the bungalow in question shall be the sole property of the 1st party and he has full rights to sell or mortgage. The 1st party shall get a boundary wall constructed or fencing by wire, having a separate door towards the road side. No entrance or exit would be made through the factory compound and if made shall be treated as trespass.

Clause 13 – That the 1st party shall not carry out the same kind of business, i.e., ice factory, within the area of the land as per above Clause No. 12 in his possession.

5. The Court said that before we construe the above clauses of dissolution deed and express ourselves as to whether this agreement in restraint of trade is reasonable or not, we would like to deal with the law codified in Section 27 of the Indian Contract Act, 1872, and Sections 36, 54, and 55, respectively, of the Indian Partnership Act, 1932, reproduced as under:

Section 27 of the Contract Act – *Agreement in restraint of trade void – Every agreement by which any one is restrained from exercising a lawful profession, trade, or business of any kind is to that extent void.*

Exception 1 – One who sells the goodwill of a business may agree with the buyer to refrain from carrying out a similar business, within specified local limits, so long as the buyer, or any person deriving title to the goodwill from him, carries out a like business therein; provided that such limits appear to the Court reasonable, regard being had to the nature of the business.

Section 36 of Partnership Act – *(1) An outgoing partner may carry on a business competing with that of the firm and he may advertise such business, but subject to contract to the contrary, he may not*

(a) use the firm name,

(b) represent himself as carrying on the business of the firm, or

(c) solicit the custom of persons who were dealing with the firm before he ceased to be a partner.

(2) A partner may make an agreement with his partners that on ceasing to be a partner he will not carry on any business similar to that of the firm within a specified period or within specified local limits; and notwithstanding anything contained in Section 27 of the Indian Contract Act, 1872, such agreement shall be valid if the restrictions imposed are reasonable.

Section 36 of Partnership Act – *Partners may, upon or in anticipation of the dissolution of the firm, make an agreement that some or all of them will not carry out a business similar to that of the firm within a specified period or within specified local limits; and notwithstanding anything contained in Section 27 of the Indian Contract Act, 1872, such agreement shall be valid if the restrictions imposed are reasonable.*

Section 55 of the Partnership Act – *(1) In settling the accounts of a firm after dissolution, the goodwill shall, subject to contract between the partners, be included in the assets, and it may be sold either separately or along with other property of the firm.*

(2) Where the goodwill of a firm is sold after dissolution, a partner may carry out a business competing with that of the buyer and he may advertise such business, but subject to agreement between him and the buyer, he may not

(a) use the firm name,

(b) represent himself as carrying out the business of the firm, or

(c) solicit the custom of persons who were dealing with the firm before its dissolution.

(3) Any partner may, upon the sale of the goodwill of a firm, make an agreement with the buyer that such partner will not carry on business within specified local limits, and, not withstanding anything contained in Section 27 of the Indian Contract Act, 1872, such agreement shall be valid if the restrictions imposed are reasonable.

Judgement

The Court, on the basis of the perusal of Clauses 12 and 13 of the 'Dissolution Deed' in the light of Section 27 of the Indian Contract Act, 1872, and Sections 36, 54, and 55, respectively, of the Indian Partnership Act, 1932, opined that the doctrine in restraint of trade is capable of applying where the restraint also relates to a particular piece of property. Defendant No. 1 Kalicharan had voluntarily entered into an agreement containing Clause 13 of the dissolution deed that he would not carry out the same kind of business, i.e., an ice factory, within the area of land measuring 325' x 88'. He had done so after taking ₹11,001/- as his share in the goodwill. He or his assignees, who had purchased a part of this land calling notice of the covenant contained in Clause 13, cannot be permitted to use the land in a manner inconsistent with the contract entered into by Kalicharan with the plaintiffs while separating from the partnership business. Therefore, the defendants (2 to 5) who are none else but close relations of Kalicharan (Defendant No. 1) are also bound by Clause 13 of the dissolution deed. Hence, it can hardly be disputed that if a covenant in restraint of trade is valid, i.e., the conditions imposed are reasonable, a breach of it can be restrained by injunction.

In view of what has been discussed and stated above, we (the Court) are of the opinion that this special appeal has no force and we hereby dismiss it with costs.

Interlink Services Pvt. Ltd vs S. P. Bangera[1]

Legislation Cited/Referred

Section 151 of Civil Procedure Code , Article 10, Article 7, Section 31 of the Indian Contract Act , Section 42 of the Specific Relief Act, 1963 , Civil Procedure Code

Facts of the Case

1. The plaintiff, Interlink Services Pvt. Ltd., is a private limited company and carries on work *inter alia* as Agents and Consultants for various manufacturers for promoting their products and sale services.
2. SIDEL-SA a company incorporated and registered in France, who manufacturers various types of machines including Blow Moulding machines and equipment had entered into a contract of agency dated July 28, 1994 with the plaintiff, made effective from 1. 3. 1994.
3. One Husky Injection Moulding System SA of Luxembourg (for short Husky) which is also manufacturer of injection moulding systems for preforms etc. had also entered into another contract of agency with the plaintiff, dated July 1, 1994.
4. The terms of both the agencies were in identical terms and the agency (Interlink Services Pvt. Ltd.) was for a period of 2 years, renewable automatically for similar periods unless written notice of cancellation is given by either party before six months from the expiry of the contract period.
5. The defendant, Mr. S P Bangera, is a plastic technologist, who has established his own independent consultancy firm operating in the name of M/s. High Tech Consultants rendering technical services to the plastic industry in India.
6. For carrying out the work of agency for various clients including Sidel and Husky, Plaintiff had a subsidiary unit known as Petequip.
7. After these aforesaid two agency contracts were taken, the plaintiff (Interlink Services Pvt. Ltd.) and the defendant (S P Bangera), a consultant, agreed to work on certain terms under a contract entered into dated 30th July, 1994 for a period of one year commencing with effect from 01-08-1994 on commission basis to be paid by Petequip to the defendant at the rates and terms as specified in this agreement.
8. Meanwhile Peterquip had also entered into a contract of agency business with the defendant independently.
9. Owing to some misunderstanding and disputes arouse subsequently between the plaintiff and the defendant, the former filed petition suit against the latter in the high court of Delhi for decree for permanent injunction restraining defendant directly or indirectly from dealing with or entering into any *contract*, agreement or understanding with any of the principals of the plaintiff (i.e. Sidel as well Husky) contrary to agreement even if it was already granted interim injunction ex-parte.

Brief Discussion

1. After about a year's working of the two agencies, there were some comments made by Sidel and Husky as well as by the defendant to the plaintiff about the unsatisfactory working of existing arrangement and a request was made to suitably modify the same on the terms which would be acceptable to all the parties.

[1] LNIND, 1997, Delhi 26

2. In pursuance of these comments certain discussions took place between the defendant and plaintiff and the proposed Understanding/arrangement arrived at between them was reduced into writing in the form of a letter, signed by all these three persons. This letter was also sent to both Sidel and Husky.
3. A notice of cancellation of agency was given by Sidel to the plaintiff which the latter alleged that was not valid as it was not of 6 months duration as the agreement of agency could be terminated by 6 months prior to expiry.
4. IT is thus alleged that there was subsisting contract between the plaintiff and Sidel and yet the defendant informed the plaintiff vide letter dated 16. 7. 1996 that he was entering into a direct contract of agency with sidel and would work directly with them which is in complete breach of trust and in violation of the agreement.
5. Plaintiff has accordingly filed the present suit for a decree for permanent injunction restraining defendant directly or indirectly from dealing with or entering into any contract, agreement or understanding with any of the principals of the plaintiff including Sidel and Husky contrary to the agreement dated 28. 7. 1995 for a period of 3 years commencing from 1. 8. 1996. The plaintiff in this behalf was initially granted interim injunction restraining the defendant from acting on behalf of the plaintiff or dealing or entering into *contract* with his principals, Sidel and Husky, directly.
6. Defendant contested the claim of the plaintiff and *inter alia* pleaded that the agreement dated 30. 7. 1994 between the plaintiff and defendant was for a period of one year from 1. 8. 1994. However, it was later on modified on 14. 7. 1995 on changed terms and was made valid for the period of one year from April 1, 1995. This agreement came to an end on 31. 3. 1996 and since 1. 4. 1996 there has been no contract or subsisting agreement between the plaintiff and the defendant. The arrangement as contained in the letter dated 28. 7. 1995 between the plaintiff and defendant was not a binding or enforceable and valid contract and at the most it was a contingent contract as defined under *section 31 of the* Contract *Act* and as the terms and conditions as mentioned in this contract had not been complied with or fulfilled, it is a void and unenforceable contract in view of sections 32 and 33 of the Contract Act in as much as the arrangements contemplated in letter dated 28. 7. 1995 were neither implemented nor accepted by Sidel or Husky and they terminated the agency agreements of the plaintiff; Sidel w. e. f. 1. 8. 96 and Husky w. e. f. 1. 7. 1996 and there was no subsisting agency agreement between the plaintiff and Husky or Sidel thereafter. The mutual agreement between plaintiff and defendant having come to an end on 31. 3. 1996 there was no new or subsisting agreement to work together. It is also alleged that the plaintiff has concealed material fact about termination of its agency by Husky. Suit is also not maintainable under section 41 (e), 41 (h), 41 (i) of the , *Specific Relief Act* . The suit and the application for interim injunction are thus liable to be dismissed and the ex-parte injunction granted is also liable to be vacated.

Judgement

Taking into account defendant's arguments the Court held as under:

1. Section 42 of the Specific Relief Act, 1963 prescribes that notwithstanding anything contained in clause (e) of Section 41, where a contract comprises an affirmative agreement to do certain act coupled with negative agreement, express or implied, not to do a certain act, the circumstance that the Court is unable to compel specific performance of the affirmative agreement shall not preclude it from granting an injunction to perform the negative agreement and this is subject to proviso that the plaintiff has not failed to perform the contract so far it is binding on him.
2. Injunction can be granted in a contract which cannot be specifically performed where the contract between the parties contains affirmative terms and negative covenants.
3. There is no positive subsisting contract between the parties and as such the question of issuing permanent injunction for enforcement of negative covenant would not arise.
4. The ex-parte injunction granted is also stands vacated.

Larsen and Toubro Ltd vs Shree Ahuja Properties & Realtors Pvt. Ltd & Punjab National Bank[1]

Legal Principles Involved/ Legislations Cited/Referred

1. Section 10 of The Commercial Courts, Commercial Division and Commercial Appellate Division of High Courts Act, 2015
2. The Arbitration and Conciliation Act, 1996
3. The Companies Act, 1956
4. The Banking Regulations Act, 1949,
5. The Indian Contract Act, 1872 [Sections 124, 125, 126, 127 & 128]

Facts of the Case

The above petition was filed by Larsen and Toubro Ltd. (L & T) under The Arbitration and Conciliation Act, 1996 against one Shree Ahuja Properties & Realtors Pvt. Ltd. (Respondent No.1) and Punjab National Bank (Respondent No. 2). The petitioner-appellant claims that a sum of Rs.115,80,88,257/- as on 30th September, 2016, is due and payable by Respondent No.1. In the light of the denials by the respondent, these disputes and differences have been projected and sought to be brought within the purview of the arbitration agreement. The petitioner learnt that the first respondent has approached its banker (Respondent No. 2) and invoked (i.e. encashed) the performance guarantee by means of misinterpretation of facts and fraud. L & T, a multinational company, registered under the provisions of the Companies Act, 1956, is the largest Engineering Company and, *inter-alia*, engaged in the business of construction, engineering, power development, power equipment manufacturing and related activities. The first respondent is a private limited company registered under the same Companies Act and, *inter-alia*, carrying on business of real estate development. The second respondent is a Nationalized Bank, carrying on banking business in terms of the Banking Regulations Act, 1949.

Brief Discussion

L & T (petitioner) participated in a tender, floated by Shree Ahuja Properties & Realtors Pvt. Ltd., the first respondent, in or about November, 2009, expressing its desire of constructing a world class residential complex at Prabhadevi, Mumbai and the contract was awarded to them. The contract involved execution of work such as procurement and construction of building and other facilities. The scope of the work was set out in the agreement. After mutual discussions, eventually a letter of acceptance was issued and a regular contract drawn up dated 2nd March, 2010. Then, the salient features of this contract are set out. In the Arbitration Petition itself it is stated that by inserting a clause in the contract a performance guarantee for a sum of ₹10 crore was issued on behalf of the petitioner by the second respondent – Punjab National Bank. The bank undertakes keep the first respondent indemnified to the extent of the sum of ₹10 crore from and against all losses and damages that may be caused or suffered by the first respondent for any default or defaults on the part of the contractor in performance of the contract or carrying out any works under the contract or otherwise in the observance and performance of any of the terms and conditions relating thereto.

[1] LNIND 2017 BOM 144

The petitioner (L & T) and the first respondent had a dispute arising out of alleged non-payment of the petitioner's dues in respect of the works carried out. The works were carried out as per the revised scope of work and activities mutually agreed between the petitioner and the first respondent in the year 2013. The petitioner claims that it is entitled to receive compensation for costs and additional expenses incurred due to the delay caused by the first respondent. The petitioner was prevented from completing the balance work within the agreed and extended period as set out in the contract agreement and supplementary agreement. The petitioner, therefore, states that it is not permissible for the first respondent to invoke this bank guarantee for it has served its purpose and stands lapsed. The works have been completed, the possession of four units has been handed over to the end users, the occupation certificate received has also been handed in. Therefore, there is no occasion for invoking this performance agreement. The petitioner challenges the said invocation by alleging that the performance guarantee's purpose has been fully satisfied and served. All rights and obligations thereunder have come to an end and stood extinguished. It is, therefore, liable to be discharged and returned. The petitioner alleges that from the conduct of the first respondent, it is apparent that they have an ulterior motive of not making payment causing wrongful loss to the petitioners, yet proceeding to encash this performance guarantee. It is in these circumstances that the petitioners have claimed the following relief:

"That pending the commencement and hearing and final disposal of the proposed Arbitration proceedings, and the making and implementation of the Award therein, the Respondent No.1 and persons claiming through them be directed to furnish security for an amount of ₹115,80,88,257/- (Rupees One Hundred Fifteen Crore Eighty Lakh Eighty Eight Thousand Two Hundred Fifty Seven only being the outstanding amount due and payable by the Respondent No.1 to the Petitioner as per particulars of claim annexed as Exhibit 'T to the Petition either by way of unconditional Bank Guarantee in favour of the Petitioner or depositing the said amount in this Hon'ble Court."

Judgement

In the written submissions, the first respondent denied all the contentions and allegations in the petition. It was specifically contended that the performance guarantee was not a bank guarantee per se, but in the form of a contract of indemnity and, therefore, the well settled legal principles pertaining to encashment of a bank guarantee would not apply, is entirely erroneous and incorrect. The first respondent has justified the invocation of this performance guarantee by contending that there is no pleading and proof of any fraud and special equities. It is in these circumstances that in the absence of governing principles which would enable seeking an injunction and restraint against encashment of such a guarantee, it can be invoked. There is no substance in the appellant's petition and it ought to be dismissed. It is upon such pleadings that the learned Judge considered the respondent's request and, though initially granted an ad-interim injunction, has subsequently vacated it by the impugned order. In the circumstances, L & T has not made out a case for any reliefs as sought or otherwise, and the above Petition is dismissed.

Maniyan Nadar & Ors vs Harikumar & Ors[1]

Parties Involved

Maniyan Nadar: - Appellant - Buyer of minor's property
Harikumar: – Quondam minor - Defendant No. 1
Another Buyer of minor's property – Defendant No. 2
Sister and de facto guardian of minor-in-question – Defendant No. 3

Legislation Cited/Referred

Hindu Minority and Guardianship Act, 1956 – Sections 8 and 11
Indian Contract Act – Section 11 and 65
Specific Relief Act – Sections 33

Facts in Brief

1. A civil suit for declaration that sale deed executed by the 3rd defendant, sister of the quondam minor plaintiff, in favour of defendants 1 and 2 is void and also to allow the plaintiff to recover possession of the plaint schedule property from defendants 1 and
2. The suit was decreed i.e. Plaintiff's (Harikumar's) suit for recovery and declaration that sale deed executed by his sister (Defendant no. 3) during his minority was void was allowed by Trial Court and upheld by Lower Appellate Court.
3. Against the judgment and decree, the defendants 1 and 2 (i.e. Maniyan Nadar, buyer of quondam minor's property and another co-buyer) preferred an appeal before the District Court, Thiruvananthapuram - Whether concurrent findings of Lower Courts could be interfered.
4. Additional District Judge (of Thiruvananthapuram District Court) after a detailed consideration, dismissed the appeal confirming the judgment and decree of the trial court.
5. Against that judgment and decree, defendants 1 and 2 filed an appeal in the Kerala High Court.

Discussion

1. Common substantial questions of law arising in the appeals, observed by the Court, are the following:
   i Is a minor, who repudiates an alienation of his property by a defacto guardian, always bound to restore the benefits derived by him?
   ii Is the minor under all circumstances liable to compensate the purchaser of property, either personally or out of his assets, in the event he succeeds in establishing that the alienation is void?
   iii What is the liability of the defacto guardian who represented the minor in the document of alienation?
   iv Is the purchaser entitled to claim title to a property purchased in the name of the minor by utilizing the sale consideration provided by the former?
2. Shri K.B. Pradeep, counsel of the appellants, contested that the erstwhile minor plaintiff cannot be allowed to unjustly enrich himself by recovering the property sold for valid consideration during his minority and also by allowing him to retain another property, purchased in his name during minority by utilizing the sale consideration. Shri K. B. Pradeep further contended that it is not only inequitable, but also in contravention of the provisions in the Indian Contract Act.
3. In reply to the above argument counsel for the plaintiff submitted that the minor at no point of time, staked any claim over the property in question. According to the plaintiff, he is not interested in any property transferred by his sister to his name by utilizing the sale consideration mentioned in the sale deed. It is also contended that sister was actually acting against his interest at the time when the sale deed was executed.
4. Section 8 of the Act 1956 deals with the powers of a natural guardian of Hindu minor. According to Section 6 of the Act 1956, in the case of a Hindu minor, who is a boy or an unmarried girl, the father

[1] LNIND 2015 KER 8437

and after him, the mother shall be the natural guardians and they can act subject to the restrictions mentioned in the Section.

5. At any rate, 3rd defendant sister cannot be treated as natural guardian of the plaintiff. Section 8 of the Act 1956 has no application to the facts of this case. Section 11 of the Act 1956 says that after commencement of the Act, no person shall be entitled to dispose of or deal with the property of a Hindu minor merely on the ground of his or her being the defacto guardian of the minor.

6. According to Shri K. B. Pradeep, Sections 64 and 65 of the Contract Act command the plaintiff to disgorge the benefits derived out of the transaction. Section 64 of the Contract Act deals with the consequences of rescission of a voidable contract. Transaction executed by a defacto guardian of a Hindu minor, that too without any sanction from a court, is void *abinitio*. That proposition is now well settled. Therefore, Section 64 of the Contract Act *per se* has no application.

7. Section 65 of the Contract Act reads as follows: *Obligation of person who has received advantage under void agreement, or contract that becomes void – When an agreement is discovered to be void, or when a contract becomes void, any person who has received any advantage under such agreement or contract is bound to restore it, or to make compensation for it to the person from whom he received it.*

8. The relevant question is whether the plaintiff, in the admitted facts and circumstances of this case, is bound to restitute the benefits derived by him on account of the said transaction. The precedents on the question of minor's responsibility to restitute the benefits derived from a transaction which was later found to be void are not uniform. It is most relevant to remember that the precedents on any question of law should be applied with utmost regard to the facts and circumstances in each case.

9. The law stated in Section 65 of the Contract Act is one touching the principle of restitution. The Section visualizes two contingencies. First one, after a benefit has been received by one party, the agreement is discovered to be void later. Second one, the contract becomes void by subsequent happenings. The Section is intended to prevent unjust enrichment.

10. Learned Judges considered the question and summarized the law as follows:

A contract entered into with a minor is a nullity for want of legal competency. Except otherwise provided by statute, it is not enforceable and it does not give rise to any rights or liabilities.

It follows from this legal position that a person, who parted with his goods can trace them into the hands of the quondam minor and recover them back in specie, for he has not lost his title to them. But he cannot seek to recover their price or damages for, if allowed, he would be indirectly asking for the enforcement of the contract and to recover damages for the breach. Nor can a person who lends money to such a minor, recover it. If allowed to do so, the Court would be enforcing a contract of loan.

11. It was also observed that by applying the principle of equity, the court could refuse relief to a quondam minor, if he seeks relief on the basis of a void contract and if he derived any benefit by a fraudulent representation. That principle is also not applicable to this case, as there is no contention raised by defendants 1 and 2 that the minor reaped the benefits by extending a fraudulent representation.

Judgement

Held, minor who repudiated alienation of his property by defacto guardian was not bound to restore benefits if purchaser was aware of his minority and minor was not guilty of any fraud, misrepresentation etc. In absence of fraud or misrepresentation, purchaser could not claim any relief against minor either personal or against his property. Defacto guardian was liable personally for dealing with Hindu minor's property in contravention of Section 11 of Hindu Minority and Guardianship Act, 1956 depending on terms in document. In declaration of document of title void, property shown as security would not automatically get transferred to purchaser. Only remedy of Defendant nos. 1 & 2 was to proceed against defacto guardian i.e. Defendant no.3 subject to terms of sale deed and sanction of law. Concurrent findings recorded by Lower Courts were upheld by the Kerala High Court —No merit in appeal—Appeal Dismissed.

Microsoft Corporation vs Kiran[1]

Parties Involved

Microsoft Corporation – Plaintiff

Kiran – Defendant

Legislations Cited/Referred

Copyright Act, 1957- Sections 7, 14, 17, 40 and 115(4) respectively

Facts of the Case

1. The plaintiff, Microsoft Corporation, is a company organized and existing under the laws of the State of Washington, USA. The plaintiff has its marketing subsidiary, Microsoft Corporation India Private Limited, located in New Delhi. The plaintiff is stated to be one of the world's widely known companies and is also the largest software publisher in the world.
2. The computer software of the plaintiff including various operating systems such as Microsoft Windows 2000 and Windows XP 2002 and application software such as Microsoft Office have acquired great fame and renown throughout the world.
3. It is stated that the software developed and marketed by the plaintiff is "computer programme" within the meaning of Section 2 (ffc) of the Copyright Act, 1957 (herein after referred to as the said Act) and included in the definition of a literary work as per Section 2(o) of the said Act. As per Section 2 (ffc), "computer programme" means a set of instructions expressed in words, codes, schemes or in any other form, including a machine readable medium, capable of causing a computer to perform a particular task or achieve a particular result.
4. The plaintiff's computer programmes are "works" that were first published in the USA and are also registered in the USA. These programmes have been created by the employees of the plaintiff, for the plaintiff.
5. Both, the computer programme, as well as the supplementary User Instructions and Manuals, are 'original literary works' as contemplated under Section 2(o) and Section 13(1)(a) of the Copyright Act, 1957.
6. The plaintiff is the owner of the said copyrights. The rights of authors of member countries of the Berne and Universal Copyright Conventions are protected under Indian Copyright law.
7. Since both, India and the USA, are signatories to both the Universal Copyright Convention as well as the Berne Convention, Plaintiff's works are protected in India under Section 40 of the Copyright Act, 1957 read with the International Copyright Order, 1999.
8. The case of the plaintiff is that the plaintiff being the owner of the copyright in the aforesaid literary works within the meaning of Section 17 of the Copyright Act, 1957 is entitled to all exclusive rights flowing from such ownership as set out in Section 14 of the Copyright Act.
9. The plaintiff has instituted a suit for permanent injunction restraining the infringement of copyrights, trademarks, passing off, rendition of accounts, damages, etc. against the defendants.

Brief Discussion

1. The plaintiff said to have suffered incalculable damage to its intellectual property rights and business on account of various forms of copyright piracy. A brief description of common methods of copyright infringement employed in relation to computer software is described in its plaint reproduced below:
   (a) Reproducing the plaintiff s software and the packaging of that software, so that purchasers are deliberately misled into believing that the product they are buying is genuine software.
   (b) Reproducing or "burning" the plaintiff s software onto a blank CD, where no attempt is made to represent that the copy is genuine.

[1] LNIND 2007 DEL 1023

(c) Reproducing a number of the plaintiff s programme on a single CD-ROM, known as a "compilation" CD.

2. It is stated that there is another form of piracy that is assuming great significance in the information age is that of Internet piracy. Internet piracy occurs when software is downloaded from the Internet or distributed via the Internet without the permission of the copyright owner. Common Internet sites used for this infringing activity include online classified advertisements, Auction Houses, newsgroups, personal web sites and Bulletin Board Service (BBS) sites.
3. It is stated that defendant no. 2 of which defendant no. 1 is stated to be the Manager, is indulging in this illegal activity of counterfeiting and piracy. It is the case of the plaintiff that in September 2002, the plaintiff received the information that the defendants are infringing the plaintiff s copyright, trademarks and other intellectual property rights by carrying on business of unauthorised hard disk loading i.e. preloading various software of the plaintiff company onto hard disk of the computer that were being assembled and sold by them.
4. In order to ascertain if the defendants were indeed involved in such infringing activity, an independent investigator was sent to the outlet of the defendants to place an order for a computer with defendants. The decoy investigator was given the delivery of the computer which is stated to be loaded with the un-licenced software of the plaintiff company.
5. Subsequently, a 'Technical Expert' inspected the computer purchased from the defendant who opined that the plaintiff s programmes contained in the hard disk of the computer are unlicensed and/or pirated versions of the plaintiff s software.
6. On a comparison of the software being sold by the defendants, and software originating from the plaintiff, it was found that the software supplied by the defendants were pirated versions of original plaintiff s computer programmes. The following were the discrepancies in the software, supplied by the defendants, observed by the expert:
   (a) The software supplied by the defendants does not have the accompanying User s Manual and was not shrink wrapped;
   (b) The software supplied by the defendants does not have Software Licence Agreement as in the case of the Plaintiff s software; and
   (c) The software supplied by the defendants does not have the order number which is always present on the software of the plaintiff.
7. Accordingly the plaintiff addressed a letter to the defendants informing that by their action they had infringed the intellectual property rights that vest in the plaintiff. Through the said letter, the defendants were called upon for a settlement meeting and cautioned that a failure on their part to attend the meeting would leave the plaintiff with no choice but to resort to suitable legal action to protect their rights.
8. However, the defendants did not pay any heed to this call of the plaintiff and, therefore, the plaintiff has filed the present suit.

Judgement

Delhi High Court in the present case held, Plaintiff had ownership of copyright in software and hardware products including in computer programme and had exclusive right to exploit it for commercial gain Plaintiff also had the exclusive right to use its registered trademark Defendants attempted to counterfeit products of Plaintiff and pass off its goods as that of Plaintiff Defendants had no right to use trade mark and trade name owned by Plaintiff in respect of same goods. Acts of defendants caused loss to Plaintiff and also led to inferior goods being sold to public who were deceived by counterfeit products sold by the defendants. Permanent injunction issued against defendants. A decree of damages was also passed in favour of the plaintiff and against the defendants for a sum of ₹5 lakh due to deliberate and calculated infringement of copyright and trademark of Plaintiff. Accordingly, the suit decreed in favour of Plaintiff with costs.

Ram Bishwas vs UP State Mineral Development Corporation, District Officer 1997[1]

Parties Involved

Ram Bishwas – Petitioner

U.P. State Mineral Development Corporation Ltd. (for short the corporation) – Respondent No. 1

U.P. Govt. – Respondent No. 2

District Officer of the Corporation – Respondent No. 3

Legislations Cited/Referred

The Indian Contract ACT, 1872 – Sections 11 and 23

Facts of the Case

1. A 'Public Notice', dated 16-1-1995, was issued by Uttar Pradesh State Mineral Development Corporation Ltd. under Chapter VI of U. P. Minor Minerals (Concession) Rules, 1963, inviting bids from the eligible parties for grant of mining permit subject to fulfilment of the terms and conditions of the bid and the permit.
2. In pursuance of the above notice petitioner Ram Bishwash and others including respondent No. 3 applied for grant of mining permits in respect of sand/morum.
3. They offered their bids. The bid of respondent No. 3 was found highest as such it was accepted and a mining permit was granted to him.
4. It is this grant of permit in the name of respondent No. 3 that has been challenged by means of this petition on the ground that the respondent No. 3 being an employee of the corporation; was legally incapable of entering into any business contract during the course of his employment.

Brief Discussion

1. The writ petition was listed before the aforesaid Division Bench of this Court. Having heard learned Counsel for the parties and having considered the facts and circumstances of the case one Hon'ble Member of the Division Bench arrived at the opinion that the permit in question deserves to be quashed and the other Hon'ble member opined that there is no cause to quash the permit in question. Both the Hon'ble Judges recorded their respective opinion separately. Thus, under the order of Hon'ble Chief Justice of High Court of Judicature at Allahabad referred to above, aforesaid writ petition was listed before this Bench.
2. Learned Counsel for the parties perused the record and opinions recorded by respective Hon'ble Judges forming the Division Bench.
3. The root question involved in this petition is as to whether an employee of the Corporation is capable of entering into any business contract during the course of his employment in the Corporation?
4. Learned Counsel for the petitioner contended that the respondent No. 3 being an employee of the Corporation is dis qualified during the course of this employment for entering into any business contract by virtue of Rule 89 of the U. P. State Mineral Development Corporation Ltd. Employee Service Rules, 1978 (for short the Rules) which expressly prohibits the employee of the Corporation from engaging directly or indirectly in any trade or business or under taking any employment and as such the contract in question is clearly hit by Section 11 of the Contract Act .
5. Learned Counsel further con tended that the Court regards the business contracts entered into by the employees during the course of their employment as immoral and opposed to public policy and, therefore, the contract in question is void ab initio under Section 23 of the Indian Contracts Act.
6. Counsel for the respondent No. 3 contended that the contract in question may be in violation of Rule 89 of the Rules and for violation of Rule 89, the respondent No. 3 may be held able for departmental action

[1] LNIND ALL 263 (Equivalent: 1997 2 AWC 1231 All)

but it would not render the contract itself null and void. He further con tended that Rule 89 of the Rules having no force of law cannot render the contract illegal or opposed to public policy.

7. In the instant case the position admitted to the parties is that the respondent No. 3 is an employee of the Corporation and he entered into the contract in question during the course of his employment. The Corporation is a U. P. Government undertaking and thus is an instrumentality of the State. The Corporation has framed its Rules for regulation the service conditions and conduct of its employees. Relevant Rule 89 Reads as under:"no employee shall, except with the previous sanction of the Corporation, engage directly or indirectly in any trade or business or undertake any employment:

   Provided that any employee may, without such sanction undertake honorary work of a social or charitable nature or occasional work or a literary artistic or scientific character, subject to the condition that his official duties don't thereby suffer and that he informs his Head of the Department and when he is himself the Head of the Department, the Corporation, within one month of his undertaking such a work; but he shall not undertake, or shall continue such work if so directed, by the Corporation.

8. A bare perusal of this provision makes it crystal clear that no employee of the Corporation can engage himself in any trade or business, directly or indirectly, except with previous sanction of the Corporation, so long he is subject to these Rules or in other words so long he is subject to these Rules or in other words so long he is in the employment of the Corporation. The case of the respondent No. 3 is not that he has obtained previous sanction of the Corporation for entering into the contract in question.

9. Section 11 of Indian Contract Act, which deals with the competency of the parties to a contract reads as under:

   "Who are competent to contract Every person is competent to contract who is of the age of majority according to the law to which he is subject and who is of sound mind and is not disqualified from contracting by any law to which he is subject. "

   For the purposes of this case the phrase 'not disqualified from contracting law to which he is subject' is relevant. Disqualification from contract ing by any law to which a contracting party is subject is one of the incapacities which renders an agreement unenforceable by law.

10. The case was also examined as to whether the contract in question is in conformity with the provisions of *Section 23 of Indian Contract Act* which reads as under:

    "What considerations and objects are lawful and what not - The consideration or object of an agreement is lawful, unless-

    it is forbidden by law; or

    is of such nature that, if permitted, it would defeat the provisions of any law; or

    is fraudulent; or

    involves or implies injury to the person or property of another; or

    the court regards it as immoral, or op posed to public policy."

11. The principle of public policy states *Ex dolo malo non oritur actio* i. e. no Court will lend its aid to a man who founds his cause of action upon an immoral or an illegal Act.

Judgement

Held, business contracts entered into by employees during course of their employment as **immoral and opposed to public policy** as Respondent No. 3 did not obtain previous sanction of Corporation for entering into contract in question.

Rule 89 of the U. P. Minor Minerals (Concession) Rules, 1963, disqualified Respondent No. 3 from entering into contract in question as on date of contract in question he was employee of Corporation.

Respondent no. 3 had no capacity to enter into contract in question within meaning of Section 11 of the Act — One of terms and conditions of this contract was that Respondent No. 3 should not enter into any other trade business, except with previous sanction of Corporation, which was never obtained by the latter. The Court opined that contract in question was null and void as hit by Sections 11 and 23 of the Act and permit granted to Respondent No. 3 was liable to be quashed henceforth.

Taj Mahal Hotel vs United India Insurance Co. Ltd & Ors[1]

Basic Principles of Law/Legislation and Its Relevant Sections Applied

Indian *Contract* Act, 1872, Contracts of Bailment - Sections 148, 149, 151 and 152

Parties Involved

1. Taj Mahal Hotel – Appellant
2. United India Insurance Company – Respondent/ Complainant No. 1
3. Car owner – Respondent No. 2
4. Insurer of Taj Mahal Hotel for issuing nonindustrial risk insurance/liability policy to the latter – Respondent No. 3

Facts of the Case

1. On the night of 1 August 1998, respondent No. 2 (complainant No. 2) visited the Taj Mahal Hotel in his Maruti Zen car, which was insured with United India Insurance (respondent No. 1/complainant No. 1). Upon reaching the hotel, respondent No. 2 handed over his car and its keys to the hotel valet for parking, and then went inside the hotel.
2. The parking tag handed over to him read *inter alia:* "*Important Condition:* This vehicle is being parked at the request of the guest at his own risk and responsibility in or outside the Hotel premises. In the event of any loss, theft or damage, the management shall not be held responsible for the same and the guest shall have no claim whatsoever against the management."
3. When respondent No. 2 came out of the hotel at about 1am, he was informed that his vehicle had been driven away by another person.
4. Upon enquiry with the security officer, he found that three young boys had come to the hotel in their separate car, parked it, and gone inside the hotel. After some time, they came out and asked the valet to bring their car to the porch. During this process, one of the boys, one Deepak, picked up the keys of the car of Respondent No. 2 from the desk, went to the car parking, and stole the Maruti Zen car. Though the security guard tried to stop him, he sped away. A complaint was lodged with the police, but the car remained untraced.
5. Thereupon, a complaint was lodged with the police, but the car remained untraced. The insurance company settled the claim raised by the car owner in respect of the stolen car for ₹280,000 . Thereafter, Respondent No. 2 executed a power of attorney (POA) and a letter of subrogation in favour of respondent No. 1.

Brief Discussion

1. After respondent No. 2 executed a power of attorney (POA) and a letter of subrogation in favour of respondent No. 1which they both then approached the State Consumer Commission by filing a complaint against the hotel seeking payment of the value of the car and compensation for deficiency in service.
2. The State Consumer Commission dismissed the complaint on the ground that an insurance company acting as a subrogate cannot qualify as a consumer.
3. Respondent No. 1 filed an appeal before the National Consumer Commission, which remanded the complaint back to the State Consumer Commission, observing that the car insurance company had *locus standi*to file the complaint.
4. The State Consumer Commission allowed the complaint and directed the hotel to pay the insurance company a sum of ₹280,000 (the value of the car) with interest at 12% per annum and ₹50,000 as litigation costs.

[1] LNIND 2019 SC 907

5. In addition, it directed payment of ₹100,000 to respondent No. 2 for inconvenience and harassment faced by him. An appeal against this order was dismissed by the National Consumer Commission. In addition, it was held that the liability of a hotel cannot be precluded by a printed notice on the parking tag disclaiming liability. An appeal was then filed by the hotel before the Supreme Court.

Judgement

The Supreme Court held that the consumer complaint is maintainable as it was filed by the insurer as a subrogate along with the original owner as a co-complainant. The court further held that a hotel owner cannot contract out of liability for its negligence, or that of its staff, in respect of a vehicle of its guest in any circumstance. Even where there is a general or specific exemption clause, there remains a *prima facie* burden of proof on the hotel to explain that any loss or damage caused to the vehicles parked was not on account of its negligence, or want of care per sections 151 and 152 of the Contract Act. Thus, liability should be affixed on the Appellant-hotel due to want of the requisite care towards the car bailed to it. The court accordingly dismissed the appeal filed by hotel.